CHILD DEVELOPMENT

A THEMATIC APPROACH

THIRD EDITION

CHILD DEVELOPMENT

A THEMATIC APPROACH

Danuta Bukatko
College of the Holy Cross

Marvin W. Daehler
University of Massachusetts, Amherst

Houghton Mifflin Company   Boston   New York

To Don and Nicholas
D. B.

To June, and to Curtis, Joshua, and Renée
M. W. D.

Sponsoring editor: David C. Lee
Senior associate editor: Jane Knetzger
Senior project editor: Carol Newman
Senior production/design coordinator: Jennifer Waddell
Senior manufacturing coordinator: Marie Barnes
Marketing manager: Pamela Laskey

Cover design: Harold Burch Design, New York City.
Cover image: William Whitehurst, NYC.

Printed in the U.S.A.

Library of Congress Catalog Card Number: 97-72451

ISBN: 0-395-86827-0

2 3 4 5 6 7 8 9-QH-01 00 99 98

BRIEF CONTENTS

CONTENTS

4 THE PRENATAL PERIOD AND BIRTH   99

5 PHYSICAL GROWTH AND MOTOR SKILLS   143

6 BASIC LEARNING AND PERCEPTION   180

10 INTELLIGENCE 322

11 EMOTION 352

12 SELF AND VALUES 388

GENDER 430

THE FAMILY 461

PEERS 496

16 SCHOOL AND MEDIA 529

FEATURES

As we undertook this revision, we continued to hold the same vision we had when we wrote the previous two editions. Specifically, we wanted to capture for students the excitement of studying child development, a field that has continued to yield a provocative and fascinating array of information about the individual in his or her most formative years. Yet, the same explosion of information that has allowed us to understand and marvel at the complexities of development has created a dilemma for us as teachers and, we suspect, for many instructors. How do we help students sift through the enormous number of developmental findings so that they carry away from the course the most important ideas? Furthermore, how do we give to students a meaningful sense of the child as a whole being, given that so many developmental researchers focus on specialized aspects of development?

A THEMATIC APPROACH

To meet these goals, we have continued to hold to our commitment of providing a comprehensive, topically organized, up-to-date picture of development from conception to adolescence. Most important, we draw students' attention to the themes that replay themselves throughout the course of development, those fundamental issues that resurface continually and that provide coherence to the seemingly disparate research findings. The themes, we believe, can serve as frameworks to help students remember the multitude of facts about child development. They can also serve as organizing ideas for lectures or for the questions instructors pose on examinations or other assignments. We highlight the following six themes throughout our discussion of child development:

- What roles do nature and nurture play in development?
- How does the sociocultural context influence development?
- How does the child play an active role in development?
- Is development continuous or discontinuous?
- How prominent are individual differences in development?
- How do the various domains of development interact?

Additionally, by drawing out these themes, we hope to stimulate readers to think about the *process* of development, or *why* development proceeds as it does. We believe that when students engage in this sort of reflection, they will become more adept critical thinkers. We also believe that they are more likely to appreciate the ramifications of theory and research for applied issues such as parenting practices, education, and social policy for children, which are ultimately concerns for us all.

ORGANIZATIONAL CHANGES AND UPDATED COVERAGE

We have made two noteworthy changes in the organization of the third edition. First, Chapters 1 and 2 have been reversed to introduce the themes and theoretical underpinnings of development earlier (now Chapter 1) and to provide a context in which discussion of methodological issues could be carried out (now Chapter 2). Second, much of Vygotsky's theory has been consolidated and presented in Chapter 8.

In updating this edition, we have included over six hundred new references, but we have also tried to balance coverage of contemporary research with the retention of important classic studies. Information on a number of key topics has been added, among them the following:

- The distinction between shared and nonshared environment and evidence that nonshared environment has a substantial impact on development (Chapter 3)
- The more positive course of development for infants born with AIDS (Chapter 4)
- Increasing evidence for the important role of nutrition on development (Chapter 5)
- Face perception in children (Chapter 6)
- Neuropsychological findings on language development (Chapter 7)
- Autobiographical memory (Chapter 9)
- The relationship between brain development and memory (Chapter 9)
- The development of scientific reasoning (Chapter 9)
- The development of emotion regulation (Chapter 11)
- Expanded treatment of childhood temperament (Chapter 11)
- Further evidence for the emergence of conscience at an early age (Chapter 12)
- Additional research based on relational theories of gender development (Chapter 13)
- Expanded information on parenting in ethnically diverse families (Chapter 14)
- Factors that contribute to success in school by African American and Asian American children (Chapter 16)

Our efforts to include research on multicultural topics have been greatly facilitated by the increasing attention developmental researchers have paid to issues of diversity and cross-cultural topics in journals and books. Approximately ten percent of our new research citations describe children from different ethnic or social class backgrounds.

NEW FEATURES

We have developed two new features that are intended to sharpen two goals that we had in previous editions: (1) demonstrating the applied usefulness of research findings in developmental psychology and (2) drawing a link between knowledge about normative developmental processes and development that takes less typical pathways.

Research Applied to Parenting/Education   Beginning with Chapter 3, we have identified some of the implications of research that extend beyond the laboratory. In doing so, our goal is to help students think about questions and concerns that typically affect parents and teachers in their interactions with children. This feature addresses such topics as the steps parents might take to reduce the risk of sudden infant death syndrome and the strategies teachers might follow to promote gender equity in the classroom. Each topic covered in this feature is introduced with a continuation of the chapter-opening vignette and is followed by a set of points which, based on our current knowledge, leads to positive consequences for children and their development. These points, of course, should not be considered the final word on the subject, but they will help readers to understand how research has led to practical benefits for children, parents, and teachers. For a complete list of topics covered in this feature, see p. xiii.

Atypical Development   Rather than include a separate chapter focused on developmental problems, we have chosen to include within most chapters a feature concerned with atypical development. In doing so, we hope to emphasize that the same processes that help to explain normal development also can help us understand development that is different from the norm. We believe that the reverse is also true—that understanding atypical development can illuminate the factors that guide more typical child development. Thus, we consider such topics as attention-deficit hyperactivity disorder, antisocial behavior, and language impairment. A complete list of topics appears on p. xiii.

RETAINED FEATURES

In keeping with our overall goals and objectives, we have retained several features from previous editions of this book.

Key Themes in Development   Within each chapter, some or all of the six developmental themes identified above serve to organize and provide coherence for the material. We see these themes as pedagogical tools designed to help students discern the importance and interrelatedness of various facts, and as vehicles for instructors to encourage critical analysis among students. The themes are highlighted for students in several ways.

1. The themes most immediately relevant to a chapter are listed at its start.
2. Indicators in the margins of the chapter point to discussions of each key theme.
3. Each chapter closes with a brief synopsis of how the key themes are illustrated in the domain explored by the chapter.

Students and instructors may, of course, find additional instances of the six themes we have identified. They may also locate new and additional themes. We encourage this process in keeping with our desire to set in motion a search on the part of readers for integration and coherence in the vast material that constitutes the scientific study of child development.

Chronology Charts   From our own experience as teachers who have adopted a topical approach to child development, we know that students often get so immersed in the information on a given topic that they lose sense of the child's achievements over time. Consequently, in most chapters, we include one or two Chronology Charts that summarize the child's specific developmental attainments at various ages. One of the points we emphasize in this text is that there are individual differences in the rates, and sometimes the paths, of development. Therefore, we caution students that these figures are meant only to give a picture of the overall trajectory of development, a loose outline of the sequence of events we expect to see in many children. Nonetheless, we believe that these guidelines will give students a sense of the patterns and typical timing of important events in the child's life, and that they will serve as another organizing device for the material presented in each chapter. For comparative and review purposes, students can locate all the Chronology Charts by consulting the list on p. xiv.

Controversies: Thinking It Over   Important questions about development often do not have clear-cut answers. In the real world, however, decisions must frequently be made about children and their families in the face of conflicting research findings or theoretical beliefs. Should children serve as eyewitnesses in courts of law? Should students be academically tracked in school? A special feature found in each chapter considers questions like these to help students critically assess the opposing positions that experts take and to appreciate some of the applied implications of developmental theory and research. Approximately one-third of these controversies are new to this edition. The controversies can serve as the foundation for debate and extended discussion in the classroom. In keeping with this objective, we have framed the Controversies in open-ended ways, concluding with questions designed to stimulate critical thinking among students. A full list appears on p. xiv.

Study Aids   The chapter outlines, chapter recaps, and marginal and end-of-text glossaries all serve to underscore important themes, terms, and concepts. We hope that students will actively utilize these aids to reinforce what they have learned in the chapter body. In addition, we employ several strategies to make the material in this text more accessible to students: vignettes to open the chapter (a number of these are new), the new "Research Applied to Parenting/Education" feature, the liberal use of examples throughout the text, and an extensive program of illustrations accompanied by instructive captions.

ORGANIZATION AND COVERAGE

We begin the text with two chapters that set the stage for the balance of the book. Chapter 1 introduces the six developmental themes, followed by the major theories of development. We also discuss how various theorists have taken explicit or implicit positions on the six themes. Chapter 2 considers the historical and scientific roots of developmental psychology and the research methodologies the field typically employs today.

The next three chapters deal primarily with the biological underpinnings and physical changes that characterize child development. Chapter 3 explains the mechanisms of heredity and evaluates the role of genetics in the expression of many human traits and behaviors. Chapter 4 sketches the major features of prenatal development and focuses on how environmental factors such as teratogens can modify the genetic blueprint for physical and behavioral development. Chapter 5 outlines the major features of physical and motor skill development and includes a special section on brain growth and differentiation.

The next group of chapters focuses on the development of the child's various mental capacities. Chapter 6 reviews the literature on both children's learning and the development of perception, including the most recent findings on early intermodal perception as well as perceptual development in older children. Chapter 7 describes language development, highlighting the contemporary research on infant language and the social context of language acquisition. Chapter 8 features Piaget's and Vygotsky's theories of cognitive development as well as recent research spurred by their ideas. Chapter 9 continues the discussion of cognitive development from the information-processing perspective. Chapter 10 provides students with a picture of traditional models of intelligence along with more recent views, such as Sternberg's triarchic theory and Gardner's theory of multiple intelligence.

The child's growing social and emotional achievements constitute the focus of the next group of chapters. We devote Chapter 11 to a treatment of emotional development. Chapter 12 covers two other rapidly expanding areas of interest: social cognition and moral development. The latter is discussed under the broader framework of the concept of values. Chapter 13 covers the most recent ideas on gender development, including substantial treatment of gender schema theory.

In the final portion of the text, we consider the most important external forces that shape the path of child development—the family, peers, and the schools and media. Chapter 14 adopts a family systems approach to emphasize how various family members continually influence one another. A separate chapter entirely dedicated to the influence of peers, Chapter 15, covers the expanding research on this topic. Chapter 16 considers the special influence of schools on child development, along with another powerful aspect of contemporary culture—television.

ANCILLARIES

Several ancillary materials accompany this text to enhance the teaching and learning experience. For this edition, we played an active role in the revision process.

Test Bank   The Test Bank was prepared by Laura L. Mitchell of the University of Massachusetts/Amherst with the assistance of Marvin Daehler. Laura brings a fresh perspective to creating the test items, most of which are new and revised. The Test Bank includes nearly two thousand multiple-choice items. Each question is accompanied by a key that provides the learning objective, text page on which the answer can be found, type of question (Fact, Concept, or Application), and correct answer. Since we are committed to the idea that students should be encouraged to engage in critical thinking about child development, we have retained a set of essay questions for each chapter and a concluding set of essay questions that might constitute part of a cumulative final examination in the course.

Computerized Test Bank   All test items are available on disk in PC or Macintosh formats. The test generation software allows instructors to edit questions as well as integrate their own test items.

Instructor's Resource Manual   The Instructor's Manual has been revised by Danuta Bukatko. It contains a complete set of chapter outlines and learning objectives, as well as lecture topics, classroom exercises, demonstrations, and handouts. Approximately half of the topics for lecture and classroom discussion are new. An added feature is a list of useful Internet sites that instructors and students may consult to obtain the latest information on different topics in child development.

Study Guide   The Study Guide, originally prepared by Carolyn Greco-Vigorito of St. John's University and Michael Vigorito of Seton Hall University, has been revised for this third edition by Marvin Daehler. The Study Guide contains the same set of learning objectives that appear in the Instructor's Resource Manual and the Test Bank. In addition, each chapter of the Study Guide includes a key terms section and a self-quiz consisting of thirty multiple-choice questions. An answer key tells students not only which response is correct but why each of the other choices is incorrect.

Transparencies   A set of color transparencies also accompanies the text. Some of the transparencies duplicate figures from the text, while others serve to supplement the text's illustration program.

Multimedia Policy   For information on the variety of videos and multimedia products available to adopters, contact your Houghton Mifflin representative.

Psychology Web Site   For access to useful and innovative teaching and learning resources that support this book, visit Houghton Mifflin's Psychology web site by pointing to the Houghton Mifflin homepage at http://www.hmco.com and going to the College Division's Psychology page.

ACKNOWLEDGMENTS

Our students at Holy Cross and the University of Massachusetts continue to serve as the primary inspiration for our work on this text. Each time we teach the child development course, we see their enthusiasm and appreciation for what we teach, but we also find that we learn from them how to communicate our messages about developmental processes more effectively.

We also appreciate the insightful comments and criticisms provided by the reviewers for this text. Their classroom experiences have provided a broader perspective than our own, and we believe our book becomes stronger because of their valued input. We would like to express our thanks to the following individuals who served in this capacity:

Jeffrey T. Coldren, Youngstown State University

S. A. Fenwick, Augustana College

Gary H. Frankie, University of Guelph

Brenda O. Gilbert, Southern Illinois University at Carbondale

Michele Hoffnung, Quinnipiac College

Gary D. Levy, University of Wyoming

Janice H. Kennedy, Georgia Southern University

David R. Pederson, University of Western Ontario

Lizette Peterson, University of Missouri at Columbia

John C. Reibsamen, Triton College

Donna J. Tyler Thompson, Midland College

Mary J. Zembar, Wittenburg University

In addition, we would like to express our gratitude to colleagues at our respective institutions for reading and commenting on various chapters or just plain sharing ideas that were helpful in our revision. At Holy Cross, Ogretta McNeil was especially important in maintaining our sensitivity to multicultural issues in child development. At the University of Massachusetts, Daniel Anderson, Carole Beal, Neal Berthier, Richard Bogartz, Rachel Clifton, Gary Marcus, and Nancy Myers have provided a wealth of information and stimulating ideas in formal seminars and informal hallway conversations. Just as these faculty colleagues have offered insightful perspectives, so too have a spirited company of former and present graduate students at the university who have carried out research on a number of aspects of development. Their number is too great to identify individually, so they must be thanked collectively. They will, however, surely be aware of our admiration for their efforts to enhance our knowledge of development. Among them, Zhe Chen, Karen Yanowitz, and Laura L. Mitchell deserve special mention because, in addition to their individual contributions, they have often had to accommodate their schedules and endeavors to the demands imposed by this work.

As with previous editions, several individuals at Houghton Mifflin have demonstrated their talent, dedication, and professionalism. David Lee, who became our sponsoring editor with this edition, has shown exceptional enthusiasm and support for this project. Carol Newman, who oversaw production, kept the process humming along on schedule. For her conscientious work, we are grateful. Ann Schroeder and Jessyca Broekman did an outstanding job of capturing visually the concepts we were trying to convey with words. Joanne Tinsley provided a fresh and insightful perspective in her work as developmental editor. Finally, as we have in the past, we owe great thanks to Jane Knetzger, senior associate editor, whose patience we surely tried with regard to the schedule. Jane's ability to prod us to think about how to best achieve our goals and vision for this text has been central in the course that this revision process has taken.

Finally, we would like to thank our families for their support during the revision of this text. Nick's own growth has sustained the idea that child development is a marvel to watch, and his day-to-day experiences have on occasion been the source of inspiration for various segments that appear in this book. Don learned to accept with good will and supportiveness the increasing demands that the book schedule made on him. Special thanks to June, who continued to accept the demands that such a project entails, and also thanks to Curtis, Joshua, and Renée, who have now joined the ranks of young adulthood. The progress and success they demonstrate in their chosen professions bear witness to the value and rewards of understanding the extraordinary spectacle that is the focus of this book: children and their development.

Danuta Bukatko

Marvin W. Daehler

CHILD DEVELOPMENT

A THEMATIC APPROACH

1 THEMES AND THEORIES

ight from the start Robert was a handful. A restless infant who slept poorly and cried constantly, he grew into an extremely active toddler who threw frequent temper tantrums. As he continued through preschool, Robert's behavior became an even greater problem. By the time he entered kindergarten, he displayed serious difficulties in participating in group activities and minding teachers. Robert's parents had always refused to use physical punishment to discipline their son, but now found themselves facing a painful question: had they, in the words of an old saying, "spared the rod and spoiled the child"?

hen we think about how to understand children and their development, common sense seems like the logical place to start. The caregivers responsible for your upbringing may have had little opportunity to steep themselves in the latest professional advice on rearing children. Instead, your caregivers very likely relied on their own prior experience and the advice of relatives and friends to decide what was best for you. Even if not actively involved in child rearing, you also have preconceptions based on your childhood—perhaps further influenced by personal observations, study, or work with children—about how children grow and "what's best" for them. These kinds of experiences make up the common sense and parenting wisdom by which generations of caregivers have reared children, and they are frequently shared across cultures. In fact, Robert's parents may have considered spanking their son had they known that the Ovambo of southwest Africa say, "A cranky child has not been spanked," and that at one time Japanese parents were advised to "bring up your beloved child with a stick."

Yet at times common sense and prevailing cultural practices provide few decisive answers concerning children. And some child-rearing practices may promote unexpected and possibly undesirable outcomes. For example, is physical punishment of children a good thing? Caregivers in many societies often believe spanking, hitting, and even whipping the child are the best ways to prevent unacceptable behaviors such as aggression. But is this the most desirable response to the dilemma Robert's parents faced? Perhaps not. Researchers, for example, have found that children whose parents typically resort to physical punishment often initiate more aggressive acts toward others than children whose parents rely on alternative methods of disciplining inappropriate conduct (Bandura & Walters, 1959; Dodge, Pettit, & Bates, 1994). Moreover, this outcome has been observed in children in Native American (McCord, 1977) and British working-class homes (Farrington, 1991) as well as in families in the United States, Australia, Finland, Poland, and Israel (Eron, Huesmann, & Zelli, 1991). In other words, under some circumstances, physical punishment appears to encourage rather than discourage aggressive actions and may escalate into increasingly coercive interactions between parent and child. In Robert's case, an attentional deficit or some other disorder may underlie his hyperactive behavior, another reason spanking may be ineffective in helping him to control that behavior. This is precisely the point where the need for scientific study of children and their development enters.

WHAT IS DEVELOPMENT?

Development, as we will use the term, means all the physical and psychological changes a human being undergoes in a lifetime, from the moment of conception until death. The study of human development is, above all, the study of change. And at no other time of life does change take place at such a rapid pace as in childhood and adolescence. From the very moment of birth, changes in body and behaviors are swift and impressive. Even in a few short months, the newborn who looks so helpless (we will see that the true state of affairs is otherwise) comes to control his own body, to locomote, and to master simple tasks such as self-feeding. In the years that follow, the

development Physical and psychological changes in the individual over a lifetime.

child learns to understand and speak a language, displays more and more complex thinking abilities, shows a distinct personality, and develops a social network along with the skills necessary to interact with other people. The range and complexity of every young person's achievements in the first two decades of life can only be called extraordinary.

One of the goals of this book is to give you an overview of the most significant changes in behavior and thinking processes that occur in this time span. Accordingly, much of the material you will encounter in the pages that follow describe the growing child's accomplishments in many domains of development. We will begin by observing the formation of basic physical and mental capabilities in children; we will then examine the social and emotional skills children develop as they reach out to form relationships with their family members, peers, and others. In these chapters, we will also discuss more thoroughly, for example, the issue of aggressive behavior and what research suggests about how Robert's parents might address this problem. Thus, our second important goal is to help you appreciate just why children develop in the specific ways they do. That is, we will also try to explain developmental outcomes in children. How do the genetic blueprints inherited from parents shape the growing child? What is the role of the environment—the people, objects, and events the child interacts with or experiences? How does the society or culture in which the child lives influence development? Does the child play a passive or an active role in this process? Do the changes that take place occur gradually or suddenly? Do all children follow the same developmental pathways at the same ages, and if not, what factors explain individual differences in development? And how do the many facets of development influence one another? As you may imagine, the answers to these questions are neither simple nor always obvious.

Developmental psychology is the discipline concerned with the scientific study of changes in human behaviors and mental activities as they occur over a lifetime. *Developmental psychologists* rely on the general principles of scientific research to collect information about growth and change in children. This approach has its limitations: researchers have not necessarily studied every important aspect of child development, and sometimes research does not point to clear, unambiguous answers about the nature of development. Indeed, psychologists often disagree on the conclusions they draw from a given set of data. Nonetheless, scientific fact-finding has the advantage of being verifiable and is also more objective and systematic than personal interpretations of children's behavior. As you read about development in the chapters that follow, the controversies as well as the unequivocal conclusions, we hope you will use them to sharpen your own skills of critical analysis.

An essential ingredient of the scientific process is the construction of a **theory,** a set of ideas or propositions that helps to organize or explain observable phenomena. As one researcher has stated, "The basic aim of science is theory" (Kerlinger, 1964). Does this claim surprise you? For many students, theories seem far less interesting than the vast assortment of intellectual, linguistic, social, physical, and other behaviors and capabilities that show changes with time. However, by describing children's accomplishments in a systematic, integrated way, theories organize or make sense of the enormous amount of information researchers have gleaned. Theories of development also help to *explain* our observations. Is your neighbor's little boy shy because he inherited this trait, or did his social experiences encourage him to become this way? Did your niece's mathematical skills develop from her experience with her home computer, or does she just have a natural flair for numbers? Was Robert's behavior influenced by the difficult circumstances that accompanied his upbringing or by the way his caregivers responded to his outbursts, or did he have difficulty controlling his behavior because of some biological factor? Psychologists are interested in understanding the factors that contribute to the emergence of behavioral skills and capacities, and their theories are ways of articulating ideas about what causes various behaviors to develop in individual children.

A good theory goes beyond description and explanation, however. It leads to *predictions* about behavior, predictions that are clear and easily tested. If shyness is the

developmental psychology
Systematic and scientific study of changes in human behaviors and mental activities over time.

theory   Set of ideas or propositions that helps to organize or explain observable phenomena.

result of the child's social experiences, for example, the withdrawn four-year-old should profit from a training program that teaches social skills. If, on the other hand, shyness is a stable, unchangeable personality trait, even extensive training in sociability may have very little impact. Being able to explain and predict behavior is not only gratifying, it is essential for translating ideas into applications—creating meaningful programs and ways to assist parents, teachers, and others who work to enhance and promote the development of children. For example, when a theory proposes that adults are an important source of imitative learning and that parents who display aggressive behavior provide a model for responding to a frustrating situation, we can begin to understand why common proverbs such as "spare the rod and spoil the child" sometimes need to be reevaluated.

In this chapter, our discussion focuses on several broad theories and perspectives that have influenced explanations of children's behavior and promoted developmental research. No one theory is sufficient to provide a full explanation of all behavior. Some theories strive to make sense of intellectual and cognitive development; others focus on social, emotional, personality, or some other aspect of development. Theories also vary in the extent to which they present formalized, testable ideas. Thus, some are more useful than others in providing explanations for behavior that can be rigorously evaluated. And they often disagree in their answers to the fundamental questions of development. In fact, before we examine specific theories, let us consider a cluster of basic questions that all theories of development must address.

SIX MAJOR THEMES IN DEVELOPMENTAL PSYCHOLOGY

As you read about different aspects of child development—language acquisition, peer relationships, motor skills, emergence of self-worth, and many others—you will find that certain questions about development surface again and again. We call these questions the *themes in development*. You also will notice that various theories provide different answers to these questions. Good theories, grounded in careful research, help us to think about and understand these major themes. But what are these key questions?

What Roles Do Nature and Nurture Play in Development?

We have all heard expressions such as "He inherited a good set of genes" or "She had a great upbringing" to explain some trait or behavior. These explanations offer two very different answers to a basic question of child development, one that has fueled controversy among theorists since the beginnings of psychology and continues to rage even today. Dubbed the **nature-nurture debate,** the dispute centers on whether the child's development is the result of genetic endowment or environmental influences.

Do children typically crawl at nine months and walk at twelve months of age as part of some inborn unfolding program or because they have learned these motor responses? Do they readily acquire language because their environment demands it or because they are genetically predisposed to do so? Are boys more aggressive than girls because of cultural conditioning or biological factors? Is the child's intelligence an inherited capacity or the result of environmental stimulation (or lack thereof)? Researchers want to do more than describe the course of the child's accomplishments; they also want to identify the factors influencing their achievements. In some areas, such as the development of intelligence and the emergence of gender roles, the debate over nature versus nurture has become particularly heated.

Why all the sound and fury about such a question? One reason is that the answer has major implications for children's developmental outcomes, for parenting practices, for the organization of schooling, and for how we apply theory. If, for example,

nature-nurture debate Ongoing theoretical controversy over whether development is the result of the child's genetic endowment or the kinds of experiences the child has had.

experiments support the theory that intelligence is guided largely by heredity, providing children with rich learning experiences may have minimal impact on their eventual levels of intellectual skill. If, on the other hand, research and theory more convincingly show that intellectual development is shaped primarily by environmental events, it becomes vital to provide children with the kinds of experiences that will optimize their intellectual growth. Such theories also are likely to have an impact on public policy by affecting how funds are allocated to social and educational programs.

Psychologists now recognize that both nature and nurture are essential to all aspects of behavior and that these two forces together help to mold what the child becomes. Thus, the controversy has shifted away from a concern with identifying *which* of these two factors is critical in any given situation. Instead, the question is *how*, specifically, each contributes to development. The problem for researchers is to determine the manner in which heredity and environment *interact* to fashion the behaviors we see in children and eventually in adults. As will soon be apparent, developmental theories have taken very different positions on this question.

How Does the Sociocultural Context Influence Development?

Development is influenced by more than just the immediate environment of the family. Children grow up within a larger social community, the *sociocultural context*. The sociocultural context includes unique customs, values, and beliefs about the proper way to rear children and the ultimate goals for their development. Think back to your family and the cultural standards and values that determined how you were reared. Were you allowed to be assertive and to speak your mind, or were you expected to be compliant toward adults and never challenge them? Were you encouraged to fend for yourself, or were caregivers, relatives, and even cultural institutions such as the school, church, or some other agency expected to assist with your needs throughout childhood, adolescence, and perhaps even into your early adult years? How was your development affected by your family's economic status and educational attainments? By your gender and ethnic identity?

The values and resources of the sociocultural circumstances in which a child lives have a major impact on physical, social, emotional, cognitive, and other aspects of

Children grow up in many different cultures and social settings. This Chinese-American family, sharing dinner, may have adopted some customs and values from American culture, yet probably maintains many traditions and practices brought with them from China. Various sociocultural contexts provide the backdrop in which specific parenting practices are carried out. Researchers must consider these different kinds of experiences to fully understand development.

development. These sociocultural factors affect everything from the kinds of child-rearing practices parents engage in to the level of health care and education children receive; they affect children's physical well-being, social standing, sense of self-esteem, "personality," and emotional expressiveness as well. As you explore the various domains of development, you will come to appreciate that many developmental outcomes that appear to be the result of inborn dispositions or the immediate environment are, in fact, heavily influenced by the sociocultural context. And, as with the nature-nurture debate, the precise relationship of sociocultural context to various areas of development has generated much heated discussion among theorists.

How Does the Child Play an Active Role in Development?

When children learn to speak, have they passively recorded the language they heard in their environment and reproduced it as if they were playing back a tape recording? Or are they more actively engaged in acquiring the sounds, grammar, and meanings of words and putting them together in new ways? Do children exhibit masculine and feminine gender stereotypes simply by imitating the behaviors of men and women around them? Or do they somehow construct mental interpretations of "male" and "female" activities that in turn drive their own behavior? Do parents set the emotional tone for interactions with their young infants? Or do infants take the initiative in determining whether playing or bathing will be stressful or happy events? In other words, do infants and children somehow regulate and determine their own development?

Most researchers today believe that children take an active role in their own growth and development. That active role may be evident at two different levels. The first begins with certain attributes and qualities that children possess and exhibit, such as curiosity about and eagerness to engage in the physical and social world surrounding them. By virtue of being a male or a female, being placid or active, being helpful or refusing to cooperate, and by eventually taking an interest in such things as dinosaurs, music, or sports, children elicit reactions from others. Thus, children are not simply passive recipients of surrounding influences, blank slates on which the environment writes; their own capacities and efforts to become immersed in, to get "mixed up" with, their physical and social world often modify the kinds of things that happen to them and can affect their development in profound ways.

A second, perhaps more fundamental way in which children may contribute to their own development is through actively constructing and organizing ways of thinking, feeling, communicating, and so forth that assist them in making sense of their world. Children may formulate these conceptualizations to help them respond to and understand the rich array of physical and social events that comprise their experience. As you will soon see, questions about how children directly influence their own development are theoretically controversial as well.

Is Development Continuous or Discontinuous?

Does the way in which children think at age seven or eight change radically after they reach adolescence? Does the two-year-old enter a "terrible twos" phase in personality development, marked by a refusal to cooperate and frequent shouts of "no!" not found at other ages? What is the best way to explain the differences so immediately apparent when we compare the problem-solving competencies of the one-year-old, four-year-old, nine-year-old, and sixteen-year-old?

Everyone agrees that children's behaviors and abilities change, sometimes in dramatic ways. However, there is much less consensus on how best to explain these changes. On the one hand, development can be viewed as a *continuous* process in which new attainments in thinking, language, and social behavior are characterized by gradual, steady, small *quantitative* advances. For example, substantial progress in reasoning or problem solving may stem from the ability to remember more and more pieces of information. Or, as neural coordination and muscle strength gradually increase, the infant may advance from crawling to walking—a progression that,

Development as a Continuous Versus a Discontinuous Process

Children display many changes in their abilities and behaviors throughout development. However, theorists disagree on how best to describe these changes. According to some, the best way to explain development is in terms of the gradual acquisition of structures and processes underlying growth. Others believe development undergoes a series of stagelike transformations during which underlying processes and structures exhibit rapid reorganization followed by a period of relative stability.

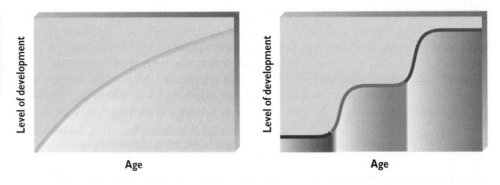

by anyone's account, has substantial consequences for both child and caregiver. Thus, even though at two given points in time the child's ability to think or locomote may look very different, the transformation may arise from continuous, quantitative improvements in the speed, efficiency, or strength with which mental or physical processes are carried out rather than from a dramatic reorganization of some underlying capacity.

Alternatively, some theories explain development in terms of the child's progress through a series of **stages,** or periods when innovative developmental accomplishments abruptly surface, presumably because some fundamental reorganization in thinking or other capacities underlying behavior has taken place. In this view, development undergoes rapid transitions as one stage ends and a new one begins, followed by relatively stable periods during which the child's behaviors and abilities change very little (see Figure 1.1). Abrupt or rapid changes reflect *qualitative* advances in how children perceive, think, feel, or behave. These distinct periods in their lives are marked by dramatic reorganization. From this perspective, children establish distinctive ways of thinking, for instance, during the early school years and move to another level of thinking in adolescence. Or a child may indeed pass through a unique phase of personality development in toddlerhood dubbed the "terrible twos."

A related issue concerns the importance of specific kinds of experiences at particular points in a child's growth. For example, if an infant does not establish a secure, positive emotional relationship with her caregiver in the first year of life, will her ability to initiate positive relationships with others suffer in the future? If a child has not been exposed to a second language by the beginning of adolescence, will he ever be able to achieve native fluency and pronunciation in the new language? Some theories propose that there are **sensitive** or *critical periods* when the child is highly vulnerable or responsive to specific kinds of environmental events. Thus, the absence of some particular experience during a sensitive time may lead to behavioral difficulties. For example, some experts believe that the failure to form a strong emotional bond with a caregiver in infancy is linked to serious emotional problems later in childhood. Experience with specific events during a sensitive period could be the basis for new achievements or serious disruptions in development.

Evidence to support continuity, discontinuity, or sensitive periods in human development is difficult to obtain. Few, if any, aspects of human growth appear to mimic the dramatic transformations found in the life cycle of an insect as it changes from egg to larva, to pupa, and finally to adult, periods in which a stable physical organization is followed by rapid reorganization and emergence of a new period in the life cycle. Yet over a period of months and years, children do become quite different. Whether these changes are best understood as quantitative or qualitative advances and the degree to which they are dependent on highly specific experiences are points of frequent disagreement among theories of development.

How Prominent Are Individual Differences in Development?

Psychologists are very much interested in understanding the changes common to all children as they grow from infant to adult. Thus, we often refer to the "average" or

stage Developmental period during which the organization of thought and behavior is qualitatively different from that of an earlier or later period.

sensitive period Brief period during which specific kinds of experiences have significant positive or negative consequences for development and behavior. Also called *critical period.*

"typical" child as if every baby, six-year-old, or adolescent should be capable of engaging in some specific level of physical, mental, or social activity. But does every child proceed along the same path in his or her development?

Parents of two or more children frequently comment on how unique each child is. One child may have learned to speak before reaching one year of age, another not until eighteen months. One may have shown an interest in music, another in athletics. Perhaps one child repeatedly challenged the parent's authority, while another cheerfully complied with parental demands and requests.

Biological and experiential differences certainly contribute to wide variations in behavior and competency displayed by children, even those born to and reared by the same set of parents. Although human growth must go forward within certain constraints, we must also come to appreciate that development may proceed along many paths and at quite different rates from one individual to another. Theories differ as to how and to what extent the diversity found in children's development can be explained by general or individual principles of development.

How Do the Various Domains of Development Interact?

Many times the child's development in one domain will have a direct bearing on her attainments in other domains. Consider just one example: how a child's physical growth might influence her social and emotional development. A child who has become taller than her peers may experience very different interactions with adults and peers than a child who is small for his age. The taller child might be given more responsibilities by a teacher or be asked by peers to lead the group more frequently. These opportunities may instill a sense of worth and offer occasions to practice social skills less frequently available to the smaller child. As these social skills are exercised and become more refined and advanced, the taller child may receive still more opportunities that promote social and even cognitive development.

Few theories have considered the interaction among domains of development in depth; nevertheless, this is a vital aspect of the complicated dynamics underlying development. Our ultimate aim is to understand the child as a whole individual, not just as someone who undergoes, for example, physical, perceptual, emotional, cognitive, or social development. To do so, we must keep in mind that no single component of development unfolds in isolation from the rest.

Where do you stand on each of these themes? Do you think development is influenced primarily by nature or nurture? Do you believe a society's trends, values, and resources greatly affect an individual's development? To what extent are you convinced that children actively determine their own futures? Would you describe changes throughout infancy and childhood in terms of continuous or discontinuous processes? How would you explain the diversity you observe in children's development? How important are advances or difficulties in one domain for a child's development in other domains? These are not easy questions to answer. And you will soon see that different theoretical approaches often propose conflicting answers to these questions. Moreover, the themes, summarized in Figure 1.2, will continue to have an important influence on our discussion of developmental psychology. Beginning with Chapter 3 we will point them out at the start, and throughout each chapter as another way to help you consider your answers to these questions. Now let's take a closer look at several important theories contributing to our understanding of development.

LEARNING THEORY APPROACHES

Learning theorists study how principles of learning cause the individual to change and develop. **Learning,** the relatively permanent change in behavior that results from experience, undoubtedly contributes to why the infant smiles as her mother approaches, the three-year-old says a polite "thank you" upon receiving his grandmother's present, the five-year-old displays newfound skill in tying her shoes, and the

learning Relatively permanent change in behavior as a result of such experiences as exploration, observation, and practice.

FIGURE 1.2

Six Major Themes in Developmental Psychology

The study of children and their development must address a number of questions, or what are identified here as themes in development. Answers to these issues are often influenced by the theoretical orientations that guide research. Throughout this chapter and the chapters that follow, we will repeatedly consider these themes and the ways developmental psychologists attempt to answer these questions. Charts, like the one here, will appear in every chapter dealing with particular areas of development.

KEY THEMES IN DEVELOPMENT

NATURE/NURTURE
What roles do nature and nurture play in development?

CONTINUITY/ DISCONTINUITY
Is development continuous or discontinuous?

SOCIOCULTURAL INFLUENCE
How does the sociocultural context influence development?

INDIVIDUAL DIFFERENCES
How prominent are individual differences in development?

CHILD'S ACTIVE ROLE
How does the child play an active role in the process of development?

INTERACTION AMONG DOMAINS
How do the various domains of development interact?

adolescent expresses a clear preference about the most fashionable item of clothing to wear.

In the extreme, some learning theorists believe, as John B. Watson did, that learning mechanisms can be exploited to create virtually any type of person:

> *Give me a dozen healthy infants, well-formed, and my own specified world to bring them up in and I'll guarantee to take any one at random and train him to become any type of specialist I might select—doctor, lawyer, artist, merchant-chief, and yes, even beggar-man and thief, regardless of his talents, penchants, tendencies, abilities, vocations, and race of his ancestors. (Watson, 1930, p. 104)*

Although present-day supporters of learning seldom take such a radical position on the modifiability of human potential, they are in agreement that basic principles of learning can have a powerful influence on development (Bijou, 1989; Gewirtz & Peláez-Nogueras, 1992; Schlinger, 1992).

Behavior Analysis

Behavior analysis is a theoretical account of development that relies on several basic principles of learning, particularly *classical* and *operant* conditioning, to explain developmental changes in behavior. Behavior analysis sprang from the radical learning position introduced by John B. Watson and was extended in more recent years by B. F. Skinner (1953, 1974) and others. Nearly a century ago, the Russian physiologist Ivan Pavlov observed that dogs would often begin to salivate at the sound of a bell or some other arbitrary stimulus. Pavlov already knew that food innately triggers the release of saliva, a natural, physiologically based reaction to the food. But here was evidence that previously neutral stimuli could also come to have this effect. Pavlov recognized the powerful implications of this observation; responses appearing to be reflexive or automatic physical responses, such as salivation, could in fact occur in situations other than those that innately elicit them. This type of learning is called **classical conditioning**. In classical conditioning, a neutral stimulus begins to elicit a response after being repeatedly paired with another stimulus that already elicits that response. We learn certain behaviors and emotions as a result of classical conditioning. For example, children and adults may become anxious upon entering a dental office because of its association with previous painful treatments performed by the dentist.

behavior analysis Learning theory perspective that explains the development of behavior according to the principles of classical and operant conditioning.

classical conditioning Type of learning in which a neutral stimulus repeatedly paired with another stimulus that elicits a reflexive response eventually begins to elicit the reflexlike response by itself.

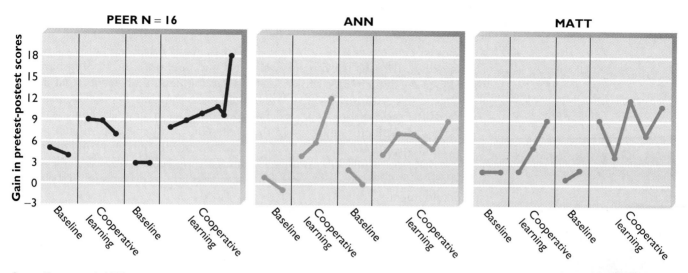

Source: Dugan et al., 1995.

FIGURE 1.3

Enhancing Children's Learning Through Applied Behavioral Analysis

When groups of nine- and ten-year-olds were systematically reinforced for displaying social skills such as sharing ideas, praising the efforts of others, and helping peers to master social studies material during cooperative study periods, they showed greater learning than when taught by a more traditional teacher-led lecture and discussion (baseline). The benefits of learning using such a procedure even extended to two children, Ann and Matt, who were autistic and identified as far less socially responsive than their peers. The results suggest that inclusive classrooms that implement behavioral techniques to enhance social interactions and encourage cooperative learning can lead to benefits for a wide range of children.

To understand a second basic principle of learning, consider two babies who smile as their caregivers approach. With one baby, the caregiver stops, says "Hi, baby!", and briefly rocks the cradle. With the other baby, the caregiver walks on past, preoccupied. Or consider two fifth graders, one who receives an enthusiastic response from teacher and peers on her book report, the other whose report is acknowledged with only a polite thank-you from the teacher. Which baby is more likely to repeat his smiling response when the caregiver nears again? Which fifth grader is more likely to work hard on the next book report? If you reasoned in both cases that the first is more likely than the second because the behavior was followed by a stimulus event (attention or approval) that often increases the frequency of a behavior, you know something about the principle of operant conditioning. **Operant conditioning** (also called *instrumental conditioning*) refers to the process by which the frequency of various behaviors changes depending on whether their performance is followed by rewarding or desired outcomes. Behavior analysts have used this principle to account for the emergence of such straightforward behaviors as the one-year-old's waving good-bye to far more sophisticated skills involving memory, language, social interaction, and complex problem solving.

Operant and classical conditioning have been shown to have enormous potential to change behavior. *Behavior modification,* sometimes called *applied behavior analysis,* involves the systematic application of operant conditioning to modify human activity. In one example, Erin Dugan and her colleagues (Dugan et al., 1995) investigated whether nine- and ten-year-olds would benefit from systematic reinforcement involving cooperative learning. Instead of asking the children to master topics in social studies via a traditional teacher-led presentation and discussion of the information, each group of three or four students working together was reinforced via a sticker chart when members displayed group-oriented social skills such as sharing ideas, offering praise to one another, and demonstrating other appropriate levels of encouragement and help with respect to cooperatively learning the relevant materials. Not only did these kinds of behaviors increase substantially during the periods of cooperative learning, but so did the actual learning by the students. Figure 1.3 demonstrates the significant gain in performance on test materials following each week of cooperative learning compared to baseline periods during which traditional teacher-led lecture and discussion were implemented. Of special interest in this study were two children identified as autistic and generally lacking proficient social skills. Nevertheless, these two children also benefited academically when students were reinforced for assisting one another in learning the material cooperatively.

Operant and classical conditioning have become powerful means by which teachers, therapists, and caregivers bring about changes in behavior ranging from the

operant conditioning Type of learning in which the pattern and frequency of behaviors that are learned depend on whether the behaviors produce rewarding or desired outcomes. Also called *instrumental conditioning*.

elimination of temper tantrums or thumb sucking to encouraging healthy diets and safe driving habits. Even some of its detractors have suggested that behavior analysis may have done more to benefit human welfare than any other psychological theory (Hebb, 1980). For this reason alone, classical and operant conditioning have appealed to many in their efforts to understand development. Yet behavior analysis has drawn extensive criticism. Its critics, including some learning theorists, remain unconvinced that a behavior can be understood without taking into account the child's feelings and reasons for engaging in that behavior. In other words, mental, emotional, and motivational factors also play a prominent role in how a child interprets and responds to stimulation. Among various learning perspectives, social learning theory attempts to incorporate some of these factors into its explanation of behavior and development.

Social Learning Theory

Social learning theory emphasizes the importance of learning through observation and imitation of the behaviors displayed by others. Social learning theorists start with the assumption that whether an adult will be friendly, outgoing, confident, and honest rather than shy and perhaps hostile and untrustworthy largely depends on the child-rearing practices parents and caregivers use to socialize him as a child. Although operant and classical conditioning play a substantial role in these child-rearing practices, social learning theorists underscore **observational learning,** the acquisition of behaviors from listening to and watching other people, as a particularly important means of learning new behaviors. The two-year-old who stands before a mirror pretending to shave in imitation of his father is displaying observational learning. Similarly, you may have witnessed the embarrassment of a parent whose three-year-old has uttered a profanity, a behavior probably acquired by the same process.

According to Albert Bandura, psychology's best-known spokesperson for social learning, a society could never effectively convey complex language, social and moral customs, or other achievements to its younger members if each behavior had to be learned solely through operant and classical conditioning. Bandura (1965) notes that significant learning occurs, often completely without error, through the act of watching and imitating another person, a *model*. For example, girls in one region of Guatemala learn to weave simply by watching an expert, an approach to learning new skills common to the fields, homes, and shops of communities all over the world. Social learning theorists propose that many kinds of complex social activities, including the acquisition of gender roles, aggression, prosocial responses (such as willingness to assist others), resistance to temptation, and other facets of moral development, are learned primarily through observing others (Bandura & Walters, 1963).

In accounting for the acquisition of complex behaviors, Bandura has often referred to cognitive processes within his theory, now known as *social cognitive theory*. Bandura (1989) has identified four sets of cognitive processes he believes are especially important in observational learning. Attentional processes determine what information will be acquired from models, and memory processes convert these observations into stored mental representations. Production processes then transform these mental representations into matching behaviors, and motivational processes define which behaviors are likely to be performed. As each of these processes becomes more sophisticated, observational and other forms of learning become increasingly refined and proficient, and the child becomes more effective in regulating his or her own behavior (Grusec, 1992).

Learning Theory and Themes in Development

As our discussions of behavior analysis and social cognitive theory suggest, not all learning theorists share the same views about the prime determinants of develop-

social learning theory
Theoretical approach emphasizing the importance of learning through observation and imitation of behaviors modeled by others.

observational learning
Learning that takes place by simply observing another person's behavior.

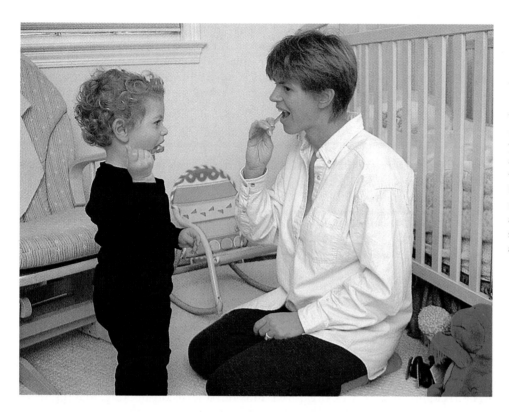

Social learning theory emphasizes the important role that observation of another person's behavior plays in learning. This mother is modeling one common activity for her two-year-old—learning how to brush teeth. Although this young child still may not have all the details of brushing his teeth quite right, observational learning provides an important mechanism by which she and others acquire many socially desirable customs and behaviors.

ment. What stance do behavior analysts and social cognitive theorists take on the six major developmental themes we introduced at the beginning of this chapter?

■ *Nature/Nurture*   Behavior analysts believe that although biological and genetic factors may limit the kinds of responses that can be performed and help to define which events are reinforcing or punishing, it is the environment that controls behavior. For behaviorists, each child's activity reflects an accumulated history of events associated with reinforcement or punishment, accidentally or intentionally delivered by the environment. In social cognitive theory, biological and other internal factors along with the environment are believed to play a mutual, interactive role in contributing to development (Bandura, 1989).

■ *Sociocultural Influence*   Behaviorists believe that although societies differ in the behaviors viewed as desirable or unacceptable, the mechanisms of learning are universal for individuals in all cultures. Rewards and punishments delivered in the immediate environment are the key to understanding development. Social learning theorists have given sociocultural context more emphasis than behaviorists have by pointing out, for example, that advances in communication technology such as television expand the opportunity for children and adults to acquire many novel skills and patterns of behavior through observational learning.

■ *Child's Active Role*   In keeping with their strong emphasis on environmental stimulation, behaviorists believe the child plays a passive role in development. Skinner claimed that "a person does not act upon the world, the world acts upon him" (1971, p. 211). According to Skinner, psychologists should abolish references to unobservable mental or cognitive constructs such as motives, goals, needs, or thoughts in their explanations of behavior. Bandura's social cognitive theory differs from behavior analysis by embracing mental and motivational constructs and processes for interpreting and understanding others as well as the self. Social cognitive theory therefore confers a much more active status on the child than does behavior analysis. Whereas behavior analysts see children adjusting and reacting to their environment, social cognitive theorists see them as encoding and processing observations and selecting whether and when to perform modeled behaviors on the basis of cognitive skills and motivational factors.

■ *Continuity/Discontinuity*   Both behavior analysts and social learning theorists consider development to be continuous rather than stagelike, with relatively smooth transitions and without dramatic qualitative changes. Any departure from this pattern would stem from abrupt shifts in environmental circumstances, such as what might take place when the child enters school or the adolescent enters the work environment.

■ *Individual Differences*   The general principles of classical and operant conditioning and observational learning apply to all individuals. Individual differences arise primarily from the unique kinds of experiences each person receives, for example, the specific models she or he is exposed to or the particular behaviors rewarded by others in the environment.

■ *Interaction Among Domains*   Finally, whereas behavior analysts explain development in all domains in terms of the basic principles of learning, social cognitive theorists stress that learning is linked to the child's physical, cognitive, and social development. Thus, this latter perspective acknowledges the interaction among different domains of development by recognizing that what the child learns is a consequence of what he or she feels, believes, and thinks.

COGNITIVE-DEVELOPMENTAL APPROACHES

According to **cognitive-developmental theory,** behavior reflects the emergence of various cognitive *structures,* organized units or patterns of thinking, that influence how the child interprets experience. Cognitive-developmental theories tend to share the fundamental assumption that normal children display common mental, emotional, and social capabilities despite widely varying experiences (Horowitz, 1987a). Most three- and four-year-olds around the world, for example, believe that a gallon of water, when poured from one container to another of a different shape, changes in amount or quantity, an error children rarely make once they reach seven or eight years of age. Cognitive-developmental theorists explain this profound change in reasoning in terms of children acquiring new ways of understanding their world.

The most extensive and best-known cognitive-developmental theory was put forward by Jean Piaget. His vigorous defense of physical and mental *action* as the basis for cognitive development and his belief that intellectual capacities undergo *qualitative* reorganization at different stages of development have had a monumental impact, not only on developmental psychologists but on educators and other professionals working with children as well. More than a decade after Piaget's death in 1980, Piagetian insights continue to be disseminated through the writings of his many students and collaborators (Beilin, 1989, 1992; Beilin & Pufall, 1992) and his numerous contributions continue to be appreciated (Flavell, 1996). The few pages we devote here to Piaget's theory will touch on only his core ideas and concepts. His keen observations and theoretical contributions, however, will be discussed in the chapters that follow.

Piaget's Theory

Piaget's vision of human development was based on two overriding assumptions about intelligence: (1) it is a form of biological adaptation, and (2) it becomes organized as the individual interacts with the external world (Piaget, 1971). Thus, for Piaget, thinking exhibits two inborn qualities. The first is **adaptation,** a tendency to adjust or become more attuned to the conditions imposed by the environment. The second is **organization,** a tendency for intellectual structures and processes to become more systematic and coherent. Just as arms, eyes, lungs, heart, and other physical structures assemble and take shape to carry out biological functions, so do mental structures array themselves in ever more powerful patterns to support more complex thought. These changes, however, depend on the opportunity to look and

cognitive-developmental theory   Theoretical orientation, most frequently associated with Piaget, emphasizing the active construction of psychological structures to interpret experience.

adaptation   In Piagetian theory, the inborn tendency to adjust or become more attuned to conditions imposed by the environment; takes place through assimilation and accommodation.

organization   In Piagetian theory, the inborn tendency for structures and processes to become more systematic and coherent.

touch, handle and play with, and construct and order the rich assortment of experiences stemming from the environment. From the abundant encounters provided in commonplace physical and social experiences, the child confronts unexpected and puzzling outcomes that ultimately lead to reorganizations in thought.

Schemes　The basic mental structure in Piaget's theory is a **scheme,** a coordinated and systematic pattern of action or way of reasoning. A scheme is a kind of template for acting or thinking applied to similar classes of objects or situations. The infant who sucks at her mother's breast, at her favorite pacifier, and at her thumb is exercising a scheme of sucking. The toddler who stacks blocks, pots and pans, and then shoe boxes is exercising a scheme of stacking. The six-year-old who realizes that his eight matchbox cars can be stored in an equal number of boxes regardless of how they are scattered about the floor is also exercising a scheme, this time one concerned with number. Each of these schemes is a kind of intelligence, a way of knowing and structuring reality.

　The infant's schemes are limited to patterns of action applied to objects: sucking, grasping, shaking, and so forth. The older child's schemes will often involve mental processes and be far more complex as he or she reasons about such things as classes of objects, number, or spatial relations, and, by adolescence, the meaning of life and the origins of the universe. At all levels of development, individuals apply schemes as a means of interacting with the environment. For Piaget, earlier schemes set the stage for constructing new and more sophisticated schemes. From simple reflexes such as grasping and sucking emerge schemes for holding or hugging or hitting. And from these actions children construct new schemes—for categorizing objects, for relating to family and friends, and so forth.

Assimilation and Accommodation　Piaget believed that schemes change through two complementary processes. The first, **assimilation,** refers to the process of interpreting an experience in terms of current ways of understanding things. The second, **accommodation,** refers to the modifications in behavior and thinking that take place when the old ways of understanding, the old schemes, no longer fit. To illustrate these two processes, Piaget used the biological analogy of ingesting and digesting food. To take in nutrients for physical growth, the child must first ingest food. The way the child chews it, how enzymes react to it, and the speed and manner in which the muscles of the stomach contract to move food along the digestive tract are examples of accommodating to the particular form or type of food the child has eaten. Once food has been broken down into easily digestible components, the body can assimilate the nutrients using the physical structures available.

　Consider another example: the toddler who has begun to walk. He freely moves about the floor of his home, but when approaching the steps leading to either the bedroom upstairs or the basement below, he pauses, says "Stairs," and turns away. He does the same thing when coming across sets of stairs while visiting his grandmother's or neighbor's house. He recognizes, in other words, perhaps after repeatedly hearing his parents say, "Stop! You'll fall down!" and maybe even experiencing a fall on some steps, that stairs are forbidden and *assimilates* other instances of staircases within this scheme or knowledge of "things that can cause me to fall."

　One early winter day, when the temperature has dropped below freezing, this same toddler and his father go for a walk outdoors. Following some distance behind, the father suddenly shouts, "Stop! You'll fall down!" The toddler appears puzzled, looks around as if searching for something, and utters, "Stairs." His father, sensing his son's confusion, points to the ice that has formed on the sidewalk and adds, "There aren't any stairs here, but you can fall down on ice, too." Through this new encounter, the child comes to *accommodate* his understanding of "things that cause me to fall" to include not just stairs but also ice and, eventually, perhaps a slippery rug or toys left lying about on the floor. So, too, when the baby first begins to drink from a cup instead of feeding from her mother's breast, she must accommodate to this new experience: shape her lips and mouth in new ways to take in the milk. In a

Jean Piaget's keen observations and insights concerning the behavior of children laid the groundwork for his theory of cognitive development. Piaget's ideas about how thinking develops have influenced psychologists, educators, and many others in their attempts to understand children.

scheme　In Piagetian theory, the mental structure underlying a coordinated and systematic pattern of behaviors or thinking applied across similar objects or situations.

assimilation　In Piagetian theory, a component of adaptation; process of interpreting an experience in terms of current ways (schemes) of understanding things.

accommodation　In Piagetian theory, a component of adaptation; process of modification in thinking (schemes) that takes place when old ways of understanding something no longer fit.

similar manner throughout development, the child's intellectual capacities become reshaped and reorganized as the child attempts to adjust—that is, accommodate—to new experiences.

For Piaget, assimilation and accommodation are complementary aspects of all psychological activity, processes engaged in a constant tug of war in the never-ending goal of acquiring understanding. We attempt to assimilate experience within our current schemes or levels of intellectual knowledge. At the same time, however, our schemes are continually pressured to change, to accommodate, since we regularly confront new experiences that fail to fit our understanding. Just as the toddler needs to recognize the many circumstances that may contribute to his falling down, so must he, and other children, establish increasingly mature schemes for thinking about other aspects of the surrounding world.

Fortunately, adaptation in the form of newer and more complex schemes is the result of this continuous dynamic. The outcome of increased adaptation is a greater balance, a more effective fitting together of the many pieces of knowledge that make up the child's understanding. The process by which assimilation and accommodation bring about more organized and powerful schemes for thinking is called **equilibration**. Each new experience can cause imbalance, which can be corrected only by modification of the child's schemes. In trying to make sense of his or her world, the child develops more adaptive ways of thinking.

The Piagetian Stages   During some periods of development, schemes may undergo substantial modification and reorganization. The more effective levels of knowledge that emerge from these restructurings are the basis for different stages in Piaget's theory of development. Piaget proposed that development proceeds through four stages: *sensorimotor, preoperational, concrete,* and *formal.* Table 1.1 briefly identifies these stages. Each higher stage is defined by the appearance of a qualitatively different level of thinking, an increasingly sophisticated form of knowledge through which the child displays greater intellectual balance for responding to the environment. However, each new stage does not suddenly appear full-blown; it arises from the integration and incorporation of earlier ways of thinking.

Piaget's wide range of observations, his frequently surprising findings about what infants and children can and cannot do, and his challenging theoretical explanations and assumptions have sparked a wealth of research on cognitive, social, and moral development. Many researchers applaud his innovative conceptualizations concerning development but disagree with Piaget's specific interpretations for them. For example, Piaget vigorously embraced the notion of children as active participants in their own development, a viewpoint that others have widely adopted (Siegler & Ellis, 1996). However, the central concept of qualitative differences in thinking between children and adults, and particularly of stagelike transformations, has been far less favorably received (Brainerd, 1978b; Carey, 1985a; Thelen & Smith, 1994). Researchers also suggest that Piaget overestimated the ages at which certain kinds of thinking are displayed and have argued that infants and children can use symbols or can reason logically far earlier than he theorized (for example, Flavell, Miller, & Miller, 1993; Gelman & Gallistel, 1978; Mandler, 1992). We will consider Piaget's position and the many pieces of evidence that support or challenge his theory more fully in Chapter 8.

Piaget's Theory and Themes in Development

How does Piaget's theory address the six major themes of development?

■ *Nature/Nurture*   Piaget theorized that a number of biologically based factors contribute to cognitive development. Among them is maturation, the gradual unfolding over time of genetic programs for development. Another factor is the child's inherent tendency to act, physically or mentally, on the environment. As a result of those actions, schemes become modified and changed. Still another factor is equili-

equilibration   In Piagetian theory, an innate self-regulatory process that, through accommodation and assimilation, results in more organized and powerful schemes for adapting to the environment.

TABLE 1.1	Piaget's Stages of Cognitive Development	
Stage	**Emerging Cognitive Structure (Schemes)**	**Typical Achievements and Behaviors**
Sensorimotor (birth until 1½–2 years)	Sensory and motor actions, initially reflexes, quickly differentiate by means of accommodation and coordinate to form adaptive ways of acting on the environment.	Infants suck, grasp, look, reach, and so forth, responses that become organized into complex activities such as hand-eye coordination and are applied to the environment to solve problems such as reaching for and manipulating objects. Practical knowledge of space and the consequences of physical actions is acquired. Object permanence and rudimentary symbols, although still closely tied to sensorimotor events, emerge.
Preoperational (1½–7 years)	Symbols stand for or represent objects and events, but communication and thought remain relatively inflexible, heavily influenced by physical appearance and the child's own perspective.	Children begin to acquire language and mental imagery, to understand drawings and to display pretend play. They may have difficulty understanding that another person sees, feels, or thinks differently from themselves. Thinking appears unidimensional, focused on a single perceptual aspect. Reasoning about categories, relations, space, time, and causality is inconsistent.
Concrete Operational (7–11 years)	Cognitive operations permit logical reasoning about objects, events, and relationships. Thought, however, remains limited to concrete objects and events.	Children are no longer fooled by appearance. They recognize that some things do not affect quantity and other characteristics of objects and can reason effectively about classes of objects and their relationships.
Formal Operational (11 years and above)	Operations can be performed on operations. Thought becomes abstract, and all possible outcomes can be considered.	Adolescents are able not only to imagine but to reason about hypothetical outcomes. Abstract issues (for example, religion, morality, alternative lifestyles) can be considered and systematically evaluated. Adolescents are able to think about their own thinking.

bration, the self-regulatory process of achieving a more adaptive balance in physically responding to and mentally understanding objects, events, and the relationships among them. Nevertheless, for Piaget development is clearly the product of the interaction of these factors with experience. Piaget emphasized the interaction between nature and nurture in his cognitive-developmental theory.

■ *Sociocultural Influence* For Piaget, children develop in much the same way in all cultures around the world, in part because of their similar biological makeups and the common physical world to which all humans must adapt and in part due to the common threads that exist within their social environments. Social experience in the form of cultural or educational opportunities, however, could affect the speed and ultimate level of progress in cognitive development.

■ *Child's Active Role* In Piaget's theory, knowledge is far more than simply a mirror of the physical or social world. Instead, knowledge is *constructed,* that is, created and formed by the continuous revision and reorganization of intellectual structures in conjunction with experience. Piaget's constructivist model depicts a mind actively engaged in knowing and understanding its environment. Thinking is active. That activity leads to increasingly effective ways of thinking. Children, then, are highly active participants in determining what they learn and how they understand reality.

■ *Continuity/Discontinuity* Although recognizing continuous changes, Piaget's theory focuses on describing and understanding the ways schemes undergo reorganization and change to form distinctive discontinuous stages in development. In his later writings and conversations, Piaget began to downplay the importance of stages (Piaget, 1971; Vuyk, 1981). He believed that an overemphasis on stages had led to too much concern with describing periods of intellectual stability or equilibrium when, in fact, cognition is always undergoing development. Cognitive development, he eventually concluded, is more like a spiral in which change constantly occurs, although sometimes at faster rates than at others (Beilin, 1989).

■ *Individual Differences*   Piaget placed very little emphasis on individual differences in development. His goal was to identify the principles that applied to cognitive and other aspects of development in all children. Individual differences, where they arise, could stem from variations in biological and/or experiential factors, but were not a primary focus of his theory.

■ *Interaction Among Domains*   Piaget's theory has implications for many other domains of development. For example, his ideas about cognitive development have been used to explain changes in communication, moral thinking, and aspects of *social cognition* such as how children understand the thoughts, intentions, feelings, and views of others. Nevertheless, Piaget has been criticized for paying relatively little attention to how social and emotional domains influence cognitive development.

INFORMATION-PROCESSING APPROACHES

Computer information processing as a metaphor for human thinking has generated so many models and theories that it is difficult to single out any one approach as a prototype. However, many contemporary research programs in developmental psychology are based on assumptions associated with this perspective. One common thread underlying **information-processing** points of view is the notion that humans, like computers, have a *limited capacity* for operating with information. As development proceeds, changes in cognitive structures and the implementation of more sophisticated strategies, for example, help older children to process information more fully and effectively.

Why have information-processing ideas become so popular in psychology? One reason is disenchantment with learning, Piagetian, and other perspectives for explaining behavior. For instance, although learning theories attempt to identify which kinds of human behaviors are acquired, they have offered fewer insights into what kind of mind we possess to be able to do those things. Piaget's cognitive-developmental theory addresses this latter issue, but his explanations have been difficult to translate into ideas about how the mind actually functions.

Contributing to the surge in interest in information processing has been the popularity of the computer as an alternative, albeit limited, model of symbol manipulation. Humans operate with symbols (information). So do computers. To carry out these manipulations, computers have physical structures (hardware) that follow nonphysical, conceptual programs (software) to function. What analogues to the computer's physical structures and programs might exist in the human mind? The human mind can be said to possess cognitive structures—for example, a short- and long-term memory and an executive system—and processes such as strategies, rules, and plans that influence attention, decision making, remembering, and so forth. What sets an information-processing theory apart from most other theories is its detailed effort to explain exactly how the child comes to identify the letters of the alphabet, remember the tables of multiplication, recall the main ideas of a story, give a classmate directions to his or her home, decide whether it is safe to cross the street, or recognize that a friend has become angry—abilities that are influenced by sensing, perceiving, representing, storing, retrieving, and manipulating information.

Figure 1.4 shows a highly simplified information-processing model. This model identifies several cognitive structures through which information may flow as it is registered, manipulated, and stored. In addition, the model suggests ways in which

information processing
Theoretical approach that views humans as having a limited ability to process information, much like computers.

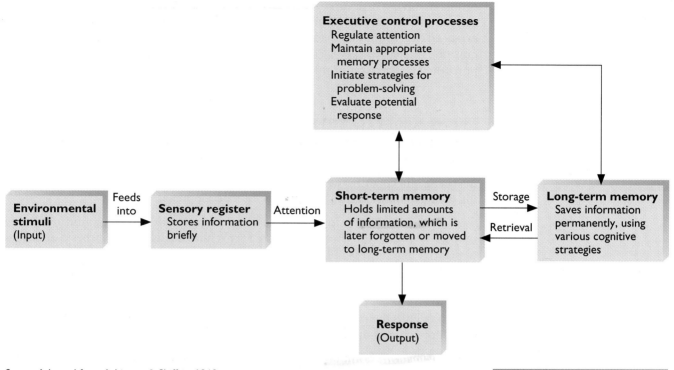

Source: Adapted from Atkinson & Shiffrin, 1968.

FIGURE 1.4

A Schematic Model of Human Information Processing

This highly simplified model includes several cognitive structures and processes many information-processing theorists believe to be important in cognitive development. As the arrows indicate, information often flows in several directions between various structures. The goal of information-processing models is to identify those structures and processes at work when a child responds to his or her environment.

cognitive processes operate on this information. Executive control processes, for instance, may regulate attention, initiate strategies for solving problems, and evaluate potential response output.

Information-processing models often rely on measures such as time to complete a task, kinds of responses, or errors in performing a task to evaluate what is involved in reasoning, problem solving, or some other activity. Consider the six-year-old who successfully completes a few simple addition problems. The question, from an information-processing perspective, might be: How did she do this task? She may have had lots of practice with this activity, having learned the answer to each particular problem by rote over many months of exposure. Or she may carry out some kind of strategy that permits her to consistently arrive at the correct answer. For example, she could start with the first number of the addition problem and then add one unit the number of times indicated by the second number. Thus, for the problem 3 + 5, she may begin at 3 and add 1 to it the necessary five times to arrive at the correct answer.

How could we tell whether she was engaging in the first procedure, primarily retrieving information from long-term rote memory, or the second, utilizing a rule to determine the answer? One clue could come from the length of time it takes to solve various addition problems. If she is using the first technique, she can be expected to solve each problem given to her in about the same length of time. If she uses the second technique, however, she will likely take much longer to answer those problems when the second number is very large and requires more addition.

As this example illustrates, information-processing theorists often attempt to describe the rules and procedures the child follows in completing a task as a convenient way to summarize how knowledge and thinking develop. For example, in preparing for a quiz on the capitals of European countries, a twelve-year-old might elect to rehearse the name of each city and country over and over, visualize the city's name on a geographic map of Europe, or link it as the capital of a particular country in some other way. These strategies are processing activities that could facilitate remembering the necessary material, and information-processing perspectives would attempt to pinpoint which is actually being used. Advances in memory, concept formation, and problem-solving tasks are often theorized to result from changes in the kinds of rules, strategies, or procedures children employ. Moreover, this perspective has been extended to account for development in many other domains, including language acquisition, social skills, even personality development. We will consider information-processing perspectives more fully in a number of the chapters that follow.

Information-Processing Approaches and Themes in Development

Because of the wide variety of information-processing models theorized to account for changes in cognitive development, we can draw only broad conclusions concerning their positions on the various themes in development.

■ **Nature/Nurture**   In contrast to most other theories, information-processing models have said little about the nature versus nurture debate. Some basic capacities to perceive and process information are assumed to be present at or before birth, and the system may be attuned to respond in certain ways, for example, to language and other kinds of information. The environment has an obvious impact on development since it provides input for processing by the mind. The implicit assumption in most models is that basic cognitive structures and processes interact with experience to produce changes in the system.

■ **Sociocultural Influence**   As in the case of learning theory, the sociocultural context of development has largely been ignored by information-processing theorists. This is probably because researchers have typically focused on identifying how the mind operates on specific problems rather than on how the mind is affected by the kinds of problems a culture presents to it.

■ **Child's Active Role**   The limitations of the computer as a metaphor for human information processing are most evident when we consider the child's active contributions to development. Whereas computers are generally perceived as passive machines that must be programmed, few information-processing theorists accept this view of the mind. While we do, of course, react to the environment, we also initiate and construct strategies and procedures that assist in processing information more effectively. From this perspective, children take an increasingly active role in controlling their own learning and development.

■ **Continuity/Discontinuity**   In most information-processing models, cognitive development is theorized to undergo quantitative rather than qualitative changes. For example, children retain increasing numbers of items in both short-term and long-term memory and interpret information and apply various strategies more efficiently and effectively with development. Similarly, the acquisition of new strategies for storing and retrieving information, new rules for problem solving, and new ways of thinking about and processing information are interpreted as shifts in ability that come about because of relatively small, continuous improvements in the capacity to process information. Some information-processing theories, however, include qualitative changes as well.

■ **Individual Differences**   Most information-processing theories pay little heed to individual differences in development. However, their potential to explain such differences in terms of variations in rules, strategies, and other procedures for processing information is considerable.

■ **Interaction Among Domains**   A notable limitation of many information-processing models is their failure to consider emotional, motivational, and other domains of behavior. How social factors such as instructions, modeling, and the cultural context of learning lead to developmental changes in processing information is also rarely spelled out (Klahr, 1989). However, an increasing number of information-processing approaches have been formulated to explain other domains of development. For example, some researchers now interpret the formation of peer relationships in terms of changes in information-processing capacities. Thus, this type of model has begun to provide fruitful ways to document and explain age-related differences in many domains, including language, social, and personality development, as well as in cognitive development.

PSYCHOSOCIAL APPROACHES

For the most part, the theoretical models we have examined so far have been concerned with learning and cognitive development. With *psychosocial* models, we shift to a substantially greater focus on emotional growth and personality. At one time, Sigmund Freud's theory of personality was extremely influential in explaining emotional and personality development. However, many generations of researchers have reinterpreted and expanded on Freud's ideas. Among these researchers is Erik Erikson, who, along with Freud, theorized that personality development progresses through stages. During each stage, the child must resolve conflicts between needs or feelings and external obstacles. The satisfactory resolution of these conflicts leads to a healthy personality and a productive lifestyle. Because of Freud's significant influence on Erikson's thinking, we begin by briefly summarizing important features of Freud's developmental theory.

Freud's Psychosexual Theory of Development

Freud proposed in his **psychosexual theory of development** that many aspects of the individual's personality originate in an early and broad form of childhood sexuality. The fuel powering human behavior, according to Freud, is a set of biological instincts that make demands on the mind. The psychological tension induced by these instincts, called *libido* or *libidinal energy,* gradually builds and requires eventual discharge. Under many circumstances, this energy is reduced as rapidly as possible. Sometimes, however, tensions such as those associated with hunger or pain in infants cannot be discharged immediately. From these delays, mental structures and behavioral responses eventually become organized to achieve more satisfactory ways of reducing tension. These acts might include such behaviors as calling out to the caregiver as a signal to be fed or eventually learning to feed oneself, responses that reduce libidinal urges by effective, rational, and socially acceptable means.

The locus of tension and the optimal way to reduce needs change with age. Freud identified five stages of psychosexual development, periods during which libidinal energy is usually associated with a specific area of the body. He called these stages the **oral stage,** the **anal stage,** the **phallic stage,** and, after a period of **latency** during middle childhood, the **genital stage.** Table 1.2 summarizes major characteristics of these stages.

Freud believed that the individual's progression through these stages is greatly influenced by maturation. Within this perspective, personality is organized by how effectively libidinal energy is reduced by activities associated with the dominant region of the body emphasized at each stage. However, the environment also plays a critical role in this normal progression. Lack of opportunity to have needs sufficiently met or to express them adequately during a critical period is predicted to have negative consequences for how the child relates to others and for feelings of self-worth. The infant whose sucking needs are not gratified, for example, becomes *fixated,* that is, preoccupied with actions associated with the mouth for the rest of his or her life.

Freud's theory of psychosexual development has been criticized extensively by later schools of psychology and by anthropologists and others who argue that his views are culture bound. In particular, it was noted early on that the sources of conflict that affect social and personality development differ among societies, especially where family composition and locus of authority depart from the pattern of strong

psychosexual theory of development Freud's theory that an individual's personality originates in early forms of childhood sexuality and that gratification of this sexuality changes throughout various stages of development.

oral stage In Freudian theory, the first psychosexual stage, between birth and about one year of age, during which libidinal energy is focused on the mouth.

anal stage In Freudian theory, the second psychosexual stage, between about one and three years of age, during which libidinal energy is focused on control of defecation.

phallic stage In Freudian theory, the third psychosexual stage, between about three and five years of age, when libidinal energy focuses on the genitals and resolution of unconscious conflict leads to the formation of the superego.

latency In Freudian theory, a period from about six to eleven years of age when libidinal energy is suppressed and energies are focused on intellectual, athletic, and social achievements appropriate to the adult years.

genital stage In Freudian theory, the final psychosexual stage, beginning with adolescence, in which sexual energy is directed toward peers of the opposite sex.

TABLE 1.2	Freud's Stages of Psychosexual Development

Stage	Focus	Consequences for Personality
Oral (birth to 12 months)	Libidinal energy centered on the mouth. Gratification through sucking, chewing, eating, and biting.	Inadequate opportunity to suck may lead to fixations in the form of thumb sucking or other oral activity such as preoccupation with food, eating, or other forms of taking things in (for example, wealth or power). Also possibility of "biting" (sarcastic) personality.
Anal (1–3 years)	Libidinal energy centered on the anal region. Gratification through controlling and expelling fecal waste through the anal sphincters.	If toilet-training demands are too lax, fixations may occur in the form of being messy, disorderly, wasteful, or excessively demonstrative. Strict toilet training may result in possessive, retentive (frugal and stingy) personality and excessive concern with cleanliness and orderliness.
Phallic (3–5 years)	Libidinal energy centered on genitals. Gratification possible through masturbation but more likely through expressions of desire for opposite-sex parent.	Beginning rivalry with members of the same sex. Fixations appear as inordinate ties to opposite-sex parent or difficulty in achieving appropriate relationships with members of same and opposite sex.
Latency (5 years to adolescence)	Libidinal energy is submerged (latent) and not exhibited through any specific body region.	Because libidinal energy is submerged, there are relatively few important long-term consequences. Much of the energy is channeled into emotionally safe areas, such as intellectual, athletic, and social achievements.
Genital (adolescence and beyond)	Libidinal energy centered on mature forms of genital stimulation. Gratification directed toward reproductive functions.	Complete independence from parents becomes possible. A balance between love and work marks normal psychosexual development.

parental influence found in traditional Western societies of Freud's time (Malinowski, 1927). The major theory to address these criticisms has been offered by Erik Erikson.

Erikson's Psychosocial Theory

Despite the fact that he never received a formal degree after high school, his contributions to psychology earned Erik Erikson prestigious clinical and academic positions as well as the admiration of many. In his classic work *Childhood and Society* (1950), Erikson built on Freud's developmental theory to chart eight stages of development, as summarized in Table 1.3. The first five stages match Freud's psychosexual model in their time of appearance. The last three describe additional stages of personality development during adulthood.

In his description of these eight stages, Erikson modified Freudian theory in two significant ways. First, he moved away from an accent on biological and sexual sources of tension to an emphasis on the psychological needs to be successfully negotiated at each stage of development. During the first stage (comparable to Freud's oral stage), for example, Erikson theorized that *incorporation* or taking in is the primary mode for acting adaptively toward the world. In Erikson's view, this mode of activity extends beyond the mouth and includes other senses, such as looking and hearing, and motor systems, such as reaching and grasping, systems designed to expand the infant's resources for absorbing and responding to reality. Each subsequent stage identified another important mode for adapting to the environment.

Erikson's second major modification to Freud's theory was to assign society a more critical role in shaping and forming reality for the child. Communities create

TABLE 1.3	Erikson's Stages of Psychosocial Development	
Stage	**Adaptive Mode**	**Significant Events and Outcomes**
Basic Trust Versus Mistrust (birth to 1 year)	Incorporation—to take in (and give in return)	Babies must find consistency, predictability, and reliability in their caregivers' behaviors. Out of these experiences babies learn to trust the world and themselves or to gain a sense of hope.
Autonomy Versus Shame and Doubt (1–3 years)	Control—to hold on and to let go	The child begins to explore, to make messes, to say "no!", to make choices. From these opportunities the child comes to understand what is socially acceptable or unacceptable without losing the feeling of being able to manage or the sense of will.
Initiative Versus Guilt (3–6 years)	Intrusion—to go after	The child begins to make plans, set goals, and persist in both physical and social exchanges. Even though frustration is inevitable, the child's goal is to remain enthusiastic and bold and to gain a sense of purpose.
Industry Versus Inferiority (6 years to puberty)	Construction—to build things and relationships	The child acquires and extends skills to the wider culture, performs "work" in the sense of education or support of the family. Failure and feelings of inadequacy occur, but the child must be able to feel competent and achieve a sense of skill.
Identity Versus Identity Confusion (puberty to adulthood)	Integration—to be oneself (or not be oneself)	The adolescent attempts to bring together experiences to discover his or her identity and place in society. This trying out of many roles should lead to an answer to the question "Who am I?" or a sense of fidelity to self.
Intimacy Versus Isolation (young adulthood)	Solidarity—to lose and find oneself in another	The young adult who has achieved a sense of identity is no longer self-absorbed and can now share himself or herself with another. Inability to do so contributes to feelings of isolation and self-absorption and the absence of a sense of love.
Generativity Versus Stagnation (middle adulthood)	Productivity—to make and to take care of	The adult not only produces things and ideas through work but also creates and cares for the next generation. Lack of productive endeavors leads to boredom, stagnation, and the absence of a sense of caring.
Integrity Versus Despair (old age)	Acceptance—to be (by having been) and to face not being	The older adult reviews his or her life and reevaluates its worth. Acceptance of that life, even though all goals have not been achieved, and of death contributes to a sense of wisdom.

their own demands and set their own criteria for socializing the child. In one society an infant may be permitted to breast-feed whenever hungry over a period of several years, whereas infants in another society may be nursed or bottle-fed on a meticulously arranged schedule and weaned within the first year of life. In another example, the timing and severity of toilet training, as well as the means by which caregivers initiate it, may differ vastly from one society to another. Cultures differ in the requirements imposed on the child, yet each child must adapt to his own culture's regulations. Thus, Erikson's **psychosocial theory of development** highlights the child's composite need to initiate adaptive modes of functioning while meeting the variety of demands framed by the society in which she lives.

As in Freudian stages, maturation plays an important role in the movement from one to another of the eight Eriksonian stages. Similarly, Erikson theorized that the individual confronts a specific crisis as society imposes new demands in each stage. The resolution of each crisis may or may not be successful, but triumphs at earlier stages lay the groundwork for the negotiation of later stages. Moreover, each society

psychosocial theory of development Erikson's theory that personality develops through eight stages of adaptive functioning to meet the demands framed by society.

Erik Erikson outlined eight stages of personality development. His psychosocial theory emphasized that at each stage, individuals must successfully adapt to new forms of demands placed upon them by society. He also stressed that cultures frequently differ in how they help individuals to negotiate these demands.

has evolved ways to help individuals meet their needs. Caregiving practices, educational programs, social organizations, occupational training, and moral and ethical support are examples of cultural systems established to foster healthy, productive psychosocial development.

Perhaps the common theme underlying the various features of Erikson's theory is the search for **identity,** or the acceptance of both self and one's society. At each stage, this search is manifested in a specific way. The needs to develop a feeling of trust for a caregiver, acquire a sense of autonomy, initiate exchanges with the world, and learn and become competent in school and other settings are examples of how the infant and child discovers who and what she or he is and will become. During adolescence, the individual confronts the issue of identity directly. But the answer to "Who am I?" is elaborated and made clearer as the individual progresses through each psychosocial stage.

In summary, Erikson redirected Freud's somewhat pessimistic views of personality development away from the need to restrain and control desires toward a consideration of the practices society uses to encourage and promote healthy social and personality development. Erikson, however, painted development with a broad brush, and consequently his theory is frequently criticized for its vagueness. Still, just as Piaget's insights highlighted meaningful issues in cognitive development, so did Erikson—regardless of the precision of his specific formulations—have a flair for targeting crucial issues in social and personality development.

Psychosocial Theory and Themes in Development

Our discussion of Erikson's theory has already focused on a number of themes in development, but let's consider them once more.

■ *Nature/Nurture*   A biological contribution to behavior, extended from Freud's theory, is evident in Erikson's positions as well. Yet psychosocial theory must be considered interactionist, given the momentous role the presence and absence of appropriate socializing experiences play in resolving conflicts that arise at every stage.

■ *Sociocultural Influence*   The broader sociocultural context in which caregivers encourage children to master, explore, and engage in their physical and social environment, especially during the early years of life, plays a critical role in Erikson's theory of development. For Erikson, the sociocultural context is a key factor in understanding an individual's personality and social relationships.

■ *Child's Active Role*   In Erikson's theory, the emphasis on establishing an identity for self within society suggests an active role for the child in development. Each stage, in fact, identifies a particular task or way to effectively adapt to sustain a healthy personality.

■ *Continuity/Discontinuity*   In Erikson's eight stages in personality development, the successful negotiation of earlier stages lays the groundwork for continued psychological growth. The individual unable to work through a crisis at one time, however, may still effectively resolve it at a later stage. From this perspective, Erikson's theory views each stage not as a critical period but as a major time during which to reconcile important individual and social needs.

■ *Individual Differences*   The psychosocial stages are common to every individual in every culture. However, the success with which each stage is negotiated can vary dramatically from one individual to another and from one society to another. Although not specifically focused on individual differences in development, Erikson's theory offers many insights into how and why these differences might come about.

■ *Interaction Among Domains*   Although not spelled out in detail, Erikson links social, emotional, and cognitive development together in the individual's efforts to achieve identity. For example, a sense of trust emerges from taking in through the

identity   In Eriksonian psychosocial theory, the acceptance of both self and society, a concept that must be achieved at every stage but is especially important during adolescence.

senses as well as the motor system; a sense of industry reflects intellectual competence as well as the ability to interact effectively with others; and discovering one's identity requires the integration of all of one's psychological skills and competencies.

CONTEXTUAL APPROACHES

Psychologists have long recognized that children live in vastly different circumstances and that these differences can have a dramatic influence on development. For example, even the immediate family in which the child lives is subject to enormous variation: some children grow up in households with a single parent, others with two parents, and still others with grandparents and maybe even aunts and uncles; children in foster care, on the other hand, may be shuffled frequently from one family to another. In addition, siblings within the same family may receive quite different experiences as a function of being the eldest or youngest or being singled out for certain kinds of treatment and expectations by family members. Number of siblings, economic resources, space and privacy, independence, and emotional atmosphere are among the vast assortment of factors that vary in the immediate surroundings of children.

Differences in the contexts of development extend far beyond a child's immediate family, however. Physical surroundings, access to schools, job opportunities, technological innovations, natural disasters, political systems, and war, as well as the cultural dictates of the community, influence the way children are reared. Some of these circumstances will be more supportive of development than others. Apart from the physical and sociocultural contexts in which each child lives is still another factor: the innate and species-specific predispositions, the context that equips the child to learn and develop.

Developmental theories usually focus on immediate experience, defined narrowly in terms of contemporary circumstances and recent events, and how it affects development. Yet culture, the historical legacy of earlier generations of a given social group, as well as the evolutionary pressures that have shaped humans to exist in their natural environment, are also major factors affecting growth. Put another way, the transformation from infant to child to adult takes place via a complex, multidirectional system of influences (Gottlieb, 1991). Contextual models, sometimes called *systems views*, are concerned with understanding this broad range of biological, physical, and sociocultural settings and how they affect development. Let's first examine contextual theories that address the sociocultural contributions to a child's development.

Contextual approaches to development give recognition to the dramatic impact that broad uncontrollable factors can have on children's lives. These children at a feeding center in Somalia receive food under the watchful eye of Italian U.N. troops and Somali police. Wars and famines are examples of major events that affect children in many different regions of the world. Researchers are beginning to recognize that they need to consider these types of experiences if they are to fully understand development.

Ecological Systems Theory

The most extensive description of the context in which development proceeds has been put forth in the **ecological systems theory** proposed by Urie Bronfenbrenner (1986, 1989). Ecological theories in general stress the need to understand development in terms of the everyday environment in which children are reared, a concern that is seldom the focus of many other theories. For example, Bronfenbrenner claims that "much of contemporary developmental psychology is the science of the strange behavior of children in strange situations with strange adults for the briefest possible periods of time" (Bronfenbrenner, 1977, p. 513). Development, Bronfenbrenner believes, must be studied not only in the home but also in the schools, neighborhoods, and communities where it takes place.

One of Bronfenbrenner's major theoretical contributions has come from his comprehensive portrait of the environment—the ecological forces and systems that exist at several different but interrelated levels. These levels can be conceptualized as a series of concentric rings, as shown in Figure 1.5. At the center is the child's biological and psychological makeup, including her cognitive capacities and socioemotional and motivational propensities (for example, temperament and personality) for responding to and acting on the environment. These characteristics and traits have evolved to make humans unique from other organisms, and they are also potential sources of individual differences among children.

Settings with the most immediate and direct impact on an individual's biological and psychological qualities comprise the **microsystem**. These settings include the home and members of the household, social and educational circumstances (including classmates, teachers, and classroom resources), and neighborhoods (including physical layout, friends, and acquaintances). The microsystem comprises the "activities, roles, and interpersonal relations experienced by the developing person" (Bronfenbrenner, 1993, p. 15) as that individual interacts in increasingly complex ways with the physical and social events that are the immediate environment.

The **mesosystem** includes the many interrelationships among the various settings within the microsystem. For example, opportunities and expectations within the family, such as access to books and learning to read or an emphasis on acquiring basic academic and socialization skills, may critically influence the child's experiences and success in another microsystem, the school. As another example, a child who spends different parts of each year with divorced parents living in separate neighborhoods may undergo frequent moves between the two homes. In addition to affecting relationships within the family, this arrangement may have repercussions for the range and kinds of friendships the child can establish with peers.

Social, economic, political, religious, and other settings in which the child is not personally involved but that directly bear on those who interact with the child can also influence development. These wider contexts make up the **exosystem**. In many countries today, for example, the child seldom is part of either parent's work environment. Nevertheless, the parent who encounters a difficult problem at work may bring frustrations home and express them through angry exchanges with members of the family. Urban renewal planned at city hall may have dramatic consequences for children and their interactions with peers, hopefully for the better, but perhaps not always with that effect. Skirmishes between rival villages or countries may bring poverty if the family breadwinner is killed in fighting. Thus, contexts removed from the child's immediate environment can still have a powerful impact on development.

The broadest context, embracing all others, is the **macrosystem**. The macrosystem includes the major historical events (for example, famines or wars) and the spiritual and religious values, legal and political practices, and ceremonies and customs shared by a cultural group. Natural disasters and wars can disrupt and devastate conventional microsystems such as schools and neighborhoods as well as individual families. Cultural beliefs about child rearing, the role of schools and family in education, the importance of maintaining kinship affiliations, tolerance for different lifestyles, and the ethical and moral conventions of a society affect the child both directly (through the socialization practices of the caregivers) and indirectly (through

ecological systems theory Bronfenbrenner's theory that development is influenced by experiences arising from broader social and cultural systems as well as a child's immediate surroundings.

microsystem In Bronfenbrenner's ecological systems theory, the immediate environment provided in such settings as the home, school, workplace, and neighborhood.

mesosystem In Bronfenbrenner's ecological systems theory, the environment provided by the interrelationships among the various settings of the microsystem.

exosystem In Bronfenbrenner's ecological systems theory, environmental settings that indirectly affect the child by influencing the various microsystems forming the child's immediate environment.

macrosystem In Bronfenbrenner's ecological systems theory, major historical events and the broad values, practices, and customs promoted by a culture.

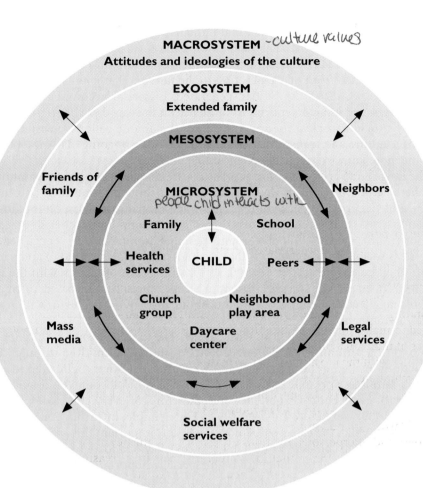

MACROSYSTEM *—culture values*
Attitudes and ideologies of the culture

EXOSYSTEM
Extended family

MESOSYSTEM

Friends of family

MICROSYSTEM
people child interacts with

Neighbors

Family   School

Health services   CHILD   Peers

Church group   Neighborhood play area

Mass media

Daycare center

Legal services

Social welfare services

FIGURE 1.5

Bronfenbrenner's Ecological Model

At the core of Bronfenbrenner's ecological model is the child's biological and psychological makeup, based on individual genetic and developmental history. This makeup continues to be affected and modified by the child's immediate physical and social environment (*microsystem*) as well as interactions among the systems within this environment (*mesosystem*). Other broader social, political, and economic conditions (*exosystem*) influence the structure and availability of microsystems and the manner in which they affect the child. Finally, social, political, and economic conditions are themselves influenced by the general beliefs and attitudes (*macrosystem*) shared by members of the society.

Source: Adapted from Garabino, 1982.

the cultural norms and strictures defining acceptable and desirable behavior). The macrosystem represents the accumulated insights of previous generations of caregivers, an evolving wisdom that continues to be added to and transformed by succeeding generations. This historical context too has far-reaching consequences for each individual's psychological development.

Bronfenbrenner's ecological systems theory underscores the many levels of a child's surroundings that influence development. Specific settings within the microsystem have direct consequences for behavior but are often governed and regulated by larger settings and contexts. Researchers frequently use labels to stand for these larger units (for example, socioeconomic class, ethnic group, or region such as rural and urban). But such labels, Bronfenbrenner argues, fail to give adequate weight to the belief systems, resources, lifestyles, and cultural values that underlie and critically influence and guide development. To simply state that ethnic differences exist, for example, does not help to identify the reverberating elements of the broader cultural belief systems in which these differences are embedded, nor does it acknowledge the interactive, multidimensional nature of the various levels of these systems.

Vygotsky's Sociohistorical Theory

Bronfenbrenner's ecological systems theory highlights the many different contexts in which development proceeds. Lev Vygotsky's sociohistorical theory blends these different levels into one overarching concept: culture. What is culture? It is, of course, the many facets of the environment that humans have created and continue to produce, including physical artifacts such as tools and furnishings. But even more important, culture includes language and the practices, values, and beliefs accumulated and communicated from one generation to the next via that language system. Culture, in other words, is the human-generated, historical accumulation of one's surroundings, and it has an enormous influence on the way that children are reared. Vygotsky's **sociohistorical theory** emphasizes the unique collective wisdom compiled by a culture and transmitted to the child through ongoing, daily interactions with the more knowledgeable members of that culture.

The range and variety of cultural practices are immense. In some communities, members emphasize skill in weaving; in others, fishing and hunting; and in still others, athletic prowess. Some cultures encourage allegiance and respect for kin such as grandparents or other elders; others do not. Some communities cherish peace and harmony; others prize competition and perhaps domination. A central tenet of Vygotsky's sociohistorical theory is that as children become exposed to and participate in their community, they begin to internalize and adopt, often with the guidance of a skilled partner such as a parent or teacher, the culturally based, often more mature and effective methods of thinking about and solving problems with respect to the environment.

Infants, of course, are not born with culture. The tools and ways of thinking that are a part of a community, however, can be transferred to children through social interactions involving the guidance and observations of others better versed in the society's resources and style of thinking. Thus, the cultural context is an indispensable part of every child's experience and, therefore, of every child's development (Wertsch, 1989; Wertsch & Tulviste, 1992). For example, in sitting down with and reading to the child, the caregiver demonstrates how important this activity is so that eventually the child comes to value it in her own behavior and as part of her own culture. Vygotsky believed that language is an especially important tool in this dialogue because it too is internalized by the child to affect thinking and problem solving. We will have more opportunity to discuss Vygotsky's ideas in later chapters. As you will see, his views have become especially important in considering the larger context in which development takes place.

One quality that permeates both ecological systems theory and sociohistorical views of development is the seamless alloy that embodies development as the child is affected by and, in turn, actively influences, his or her surroundings (Sameroff, 1987). Development is dynamic, a never-ending *transaction* involving continuing, reciprocal exchanges: people and settings transform the child, who in turn affects the people and settings surrounding him, which further reshape the child in an endless progression.

Consider the baby born with low birth weight. Such an infant often displays a sharp, shrill cry and has difficulty nursing. Because of these factors and the baby's fragile appearance, a mother who might otherwise feel confident may become anxious and uncertain about her caregiving abilities. Her apprehensions may translate into inconsistent behaviors to which the baby, in turn, responds with irregular patterns of feeding and sleeping. These difficulties further reduce the mother's confidence in her abilities and enjoyment of her baby, leading to fewer social interactions and less positive stimulation for the infant. As a consequence, achievements in other areas of development, such as language acquisition, may be delayed. But what factor, precisely, caused the delay? To answer this question, we might point to the child's low birth weight or the mother's avoidance of her infant, but these explanations still fall far short of capturing the many complex elements that contributed to the mother's behaviors and the child's development (Sameroff, 1987).

The teenage years offer many other good examples. The adolescent caught shoplifting at the urging of a friend may initiate parental perceptions of him that further elevates conflict between them. The girl unable to resist her boyfriend's urgings to engage in sexual activity may set in motion a course of events that dramatically alters her role from that of a student with many friends and freedoms to

sociohistorical theory
Vygotsky's developmental theory emphasizing the importance of cultural tools, symbols, and ways of thinking that the child acquires from more knowledgeable members of the community.

Lev Vygotsky's sociohistorical theory emphasizes that the cultural experiences to which children are exposed become an indispensable part of their development. This Maya Indian father in Guatemala is teaching his young child how to make bricks. In doing so, the parent is transmitting important information to his offspring. By becoming aware of how communities transmit knowledge to their younger members, we can begin to appreciate how culture influences attitudes, beliefs, and values as well as cognitive development.

that of mother with many responsibilities and little time to herself. The contexts for her own development have changed dramatically. Can we reasonably single out one critical factor to explain her current situation? Perhaps in some sense yes, but many factors, both immediate and historical, have generated an intricate web of events leading to this outcome; to isolate any single cause does injustice to the complexity of human development.

The importance of these complex transactions becomes especially apparent when psychologists apply interventions that attempt to modify the course of development. The mother who has avoided her low-birth-weight infant because of a widening gulf of anxious reactions brought about by disappointments and unhappy exchanges will need more than simply to be told to start talking to her child to encourage his language development. She may need to gain a greater understanding of the typical problems such babies face, receive support and reinforcement for her efforts to initiate confident caregiving skills, and acquire richer insights into how development is affected by experiences, only some of which she can control.

Ethological Theory

Development is influenced by yet one more broad context: the biological history and constraints that have been a part of human evolution. In the nineteenth century, Darwin and other biologists concluded that adaptive traits—those that improved the likelihood of survival and thus ensured a greater number of offspring for further reproduction—were more likely to be found in succeeding generations of a species. Darwin hypothesized that through *evolution,* the descent of living species from earlier species of animals, humans inherited biological traits and capacities that improved their rate of survival. **Ethology** is the discipline specifically concerned with understanding how adaptive behaviors evolved and what functions they still serve for the continuation of the species.

Ethological theory surfaced in the 1930s when European zoologists such as Konrad Lorenz (1963/1966) and Niko Tinbergen (1951) investigated aggressive actions and the courtship and mating rituals of species such as the mallard duck and stickleback fish. Their observations led to explanations that took into account the *mutual* interchange between the inherited, biological bases of behavior and the environment

ethology Theoretical orientation and discipline concerned with the evolutionary origins of behavior and its adaptive and survival value in animals, including humans.

Konrad Lorenz, an ethologist, is being followed by young geese who have imprinted to him. Imprinting in young animals typically occurs to other members of the same species who, under normal circumstances, are present shortly after hatching or the birth of an animal. One question posed by ethologists is whether human infants also show some form of imprinting.

in which that behavior was exhibited (Hinde, 1989). Consider, for example, the kinds of questions Robert Hinde (1965), another well-known ethologist, wanted to answer. How is hormone production in female canaries influenced by temperature and length of daylight? How does this hormone production interact with responsivity to male courtship displays and the initiation of nest building? Questions such as these, concerned with behaviors that arise from the interaction between biological and environmental factors, are typical in research on animals in their natural habitats and are also relevant to the complex behaviors of human beings.

Ethological studies propose answers to questions such as the following: Why do babies cry or smile? Why might the ten-year-old fight or be friendly? Ethologists point out the adaptive value of such activities for the individual in the specific environment in which he or she is growing up.

Ethological theory proposes that human infants, as well as the offspring of other species of animals, begin life with a set of innate, *species-specific* behaviors common to all members. In human babies, these include reflexes such as sucking and grasping and may also include more complex activities such as babbling, smiling, and orienting to interesting sensory events—behaviors exhibited by normal infants around the world. These species-specific behaviors help infants meet their needs either directly, as in the case of sucking as a means of ingesting food, or indirectly, as in the case of smiling, a behavior that attracts caregivers and encourages them to provide support.

Besides innate behaviors, the young of many species are predisposed to certain kinds of learning that are not easily reversed and promote their continued survival, learning that may occur only during limited sensitive periods in development. One of the best-known examples is found in various species of birds, including geese. Usually, shortly after hatching, the gosling begins to follow and prefer being near a particular stimulus. Normally, that stimulus will be another goose, its mother. In acquiring this behavior, the gosling not only learns about its species more generally but also increases the likelihood of being fed and protected. This form of learning that takes place during a brief interval early in life and is difficult to modify once established is known as **imprinting**.

Do other animals show imprinting? Mammals such as horses and sheep do. What about human infants? John Bowlby's (1969) theory of attachment suggests that they do, at least to some degree. Bowlby noted that the crying, babbling, and smiling behaviors of young infants signal needs and elicit supportive and protective responses from adults. These behaviors, along with following and talking in older infants, become organized and integrated with social and emotional reactions of caregivers to form the basis for attachment, a mutual system of physical, social, and emotional stimulation and support between caregiver and young. We will discuss attachment more fully in Chapter 11, but ethological principles are evident in a related controversial issue that we introduce here: bonding of caregiver to infant.

imprinting   Form of learning, difficult to reverse, during a sensitive period in development in which an organism tends to stay near a particular stimulus.

Does it matter whether infants and their caregivers are together during the first few hours and days after birth? It does for some species of animals, but what about for humans? In 1976, Marshall Klaus and John Kennell reported that

CONTROVERSY: THINKING IT OVER

How Important Is Bonding?

the events occurring in the first days following the delivery of a baby are extremely important for establishing a long-term positive relationship between caregiver and infant. One group of mothers experienced the typical sequence of events observed in most hospitals in the United States at that time, a brief glance or two at the baby after delivery followed by regularly scheduled twenty-to-thirty-minute visits for feeding every three to four hours during the day. A second group of mothers were encouraged to cuddle and engage in skin-to-skin contact with their babies for an hour immediately after birth and to interact with them several additional hours each day during the hospital stay. Observations of these two groups of mothers while in the hospital, a month later, and even after one and two years indicated that mothers permitted the extra interactions cuddled, looked at, soothed, and nurtured their babies more than mothers given the usual hospital routine. Furthermore, infants who were cuddled immediately after birth were reported to perform better on various tests of physical and mental development (Klaus & Kennell, 1976, 1982).

From these findings Klaus and Kennell concluded that shortly after giving birth, human mothers enter a sensitive period during which they establish a strong emotional bond with their infants. This bond may come about because hormones present during the birth process lead the mother to be especially receptive to forming an early attachment. Alternatively, the intense emotional and anxiety-ridden experiences accompanying the delivery process are suddenly replaced and reinterpreted as positive feelings as the mother has the opportunity to focus on her responsive baby. Whatever the reason for this finding, it had an immense impact on hospital practices throughout the nation, leading many doctors and experts in child care to encourage early and frequent interactions between mothers (and even fathers) and their newborns.

But is this early experience critical? Diane Eyer (1993, 1994) has recently claimed that it is not. There is time, she said, not just during the first few days after birth but throughout the first year of life and even beyond, to develop a close and loving relationship with a baby or young child and to initiate the kind of caregiving and support that will establish a healthy relationship for both parent and child. Others have also challenged the findings reported by Klaus and Kennell, unable to replicate differences in interactions for mothers who do and do not have the opportunity to establish an early bond (Chess & Thomas, 1986; Goldberg, 1983; Svejda, Campos, & Emde, 1980). Furthermore, when cultures that encourage mothers to have early contact with their babies or fathers to be involved with the birth process are compared with cultures that do not promote these activities, few differences emerge in the extent to which nurturance or affection for infants is expressed (Lozoff, 1983).

Have the substantial efforts of doctors and hospitals to augment parent-infant contact shortly after birth been helpful to parenting? Or have these ventures yielded relatively few benefits and fostered needless anxiety for those who have not had this opportunity? Could the enormous investment in early and frequent contact between caregiver and baby help to produce other positive outcomes that researchers have yet to clearly document? If so, what might such benefits be? What are some of the ethical implications of research designed to help answer these questions?

The importance of bonding continues to be disputed. Regardless of their position, everyone agrees that parents *should* have the opportunity to participate in the birth and caregiving process to whatever extent is possible and comfortable for them. But should greater efforts be made to ensure that all parents establish a constructive relationship with their offspring as soon after birth as possible? Or do other routes exist for instituting positive and supportive relationships so that mothers and fathers need not fear that their newborns will be permanently harmed by the lack of opportunity to bond?

Contextual Approaches and Themes in Development

Contextual models generally agree on many of the themes in development, and where differences exist, they are most often found in ethological theories.

■ *Nature/Nurture* Most contextual theories emphasize nurture. Except for ethological theories, the biological contributions to development receive little attention. For ethologists, however, behaviors are closely linked to nature because they have helped, or continue to help, humans survive. Thus, the biological context is every bit as important as other contexts for development. Yet even in ethological theories, the interaction between nature and nurture is considered paramount.

■ *Sociocultural Influence*   Perhaps more than any other theoretical orientation, contextual theories are concerned with the ways broad sociocultural patterns affect development. Contextual theories attempt to find evidence for how the larger social systems and settings in which children are reared affect their behavior and shape their minds.

■ *Child's Active Role*   Contextual models, even those having an ethological focus, tend to view the child as being actively engaged with the environment. In calling for their caregivers, exploring and playing, and seeking out playmates, infants and children elicit reactions from the adults and peers around them. Contextual models emphasize that characteristics of the child trigger and alter environmental events, and these changes further influence development. Both individual and environment change in highly interdependent ways, and the relationship between the two is *bidirectional,* each influencing the other (Bell, 1968).

■ *Continuity/Discontinuity*   Contextual models place little emphasis on qualitative changes in development. Instead, such models describe the continuous ebb and flow of interactions that transpire throughout development to produce incremental change. Most contextual theorists emphasize how the child's unique circumstances promote gradual advances in thought and behavior. However, ethologists often emphasize that particular periods in development are critical for establishing certain competencies. For example, infancy is considered a crucial time for forming emotional ties with caregivers.

■ *Individual Differences*   Aside from ethological theories, contextual perspectives focus less on highlighting universal experiences that promote development and more on the unique configuration of circumstances that foster cognitive, linguistic, social, and personality development. Given the immense number of factors potentially affecting the child, individual differences are often an important aspect to be explained by such theories.

■ *Interaction Among Domains*   Not surprisingly, most contextual models are typically concerned with the entire fabric of human growth and claim substantial interactions among cognitive, linguistic, social, and other domains. Ethological theorists especially focus on the interrelationship between biological and other aspects of development.

WHAT DEVELOPS?

All theories of development, of course, are ultimately concerned with the simple question "What develops?" As you have seen in this chapter, the answers differ. For learning theorists, what develops is a set of responses. For Piaget, it is a set of cognitive structures. For information-processing enthusiasts, it is mental structures and strategies for responding. For psychosocial theorists, it is identity. For most contextual theorists, it is a pattern of mutually supportive individual and cultural relationships. For ethologists, it is adaptive behaviors.

Theories, by giving us models for observing and interpreting behavior, have had an enormous influence on the way we view children and their development. Why so many different theories? The reason is that each brings an important perspective to our understanding of development. Some remind us of the importance of emotions, others of cognitive structures. Some keep us honest about the role of our biological nature; others perform the same service for the culture in which we are born and reared. Various theories enrich and broaden our understanding of development. We will frequently draw on their contributions for interpreting the many behaviors of children. We hope you will, too.

At the beginning of this chapter, we asked you to note your position on each of six major themes of development. As we have introduced developmental theories, we have also discussed their positions on these themes. Table 1.4 summarizes these positions for the major theories introduced in this chapter. As you read further in this

| TABLE 1.4 | The Main Developmental Theories and Where They Stand on the Six Themes in Development |

Theme	Learning Theories	Piagetian Theory	Information-Processing Models	Psychosocial Theory	Contextual Theories Sociocultural	Ethological
What roles do nature and nurture play in development?	Environment is more important than heredity.	Maturation sets limits on how rapidly development proceeds, but experience is necessary for the formation of cognitive structures. Interaction between nature and nurture.	Of relatively minor concern. Structures and processes presumably have an inherent basis, but experience is likely to be important for their effective operation.	Erikson stressed an interactional position that emphasizes the socialization demands of the society in which a child is reared along with a biological contribution borrowed from Freud's theory.	A major emphasis is the environmental factors that interact with biological structures.	Behavior is biologically based, but the environment elicits and influences these biologically based patterns.
How does the sociocultural context influence development?	Sociocultural factors are likely to determine which behaviors are reinforced, punished, or available from models, but this level of context is not stressed since the principles of learning are considered to be universal.	Piaget believed the cognitive structures underlying thought are universal. Sociocultural context might affect the rapidity or final level of thinking, but sociocultural differences are not stressed.	Of relatively minor concern. However, the rules, strategies, and procedures acquired to perform tasks may differ from one culture to another.	Erikson incorporated sociocultural context as a major component of his theory.	A critical determinant of behavior. Culture contains the historical knowledge that has permitted former and current members of the group to interact successfully with the environment.	Not emphasized. Ethological principles of development are presumed to apply in all cultures.
How does the child play an active role in development?	The child is not active in behavior analysis, but more actively engages the environment to determine what is learned in social cognitive theory.	Knowledge is based on underlying cognitive structures constructed by the child.	The child determines what information is processed and the rules, strategies, and procedures initiated to perform tasks.	The child is actively in search of an identity.	The child plays a central role in determining what kind of environment is established, how it changes, and how it further affects behavior. The influences of the child and the environment are bidirectional.	The child is biologically equipped to interact with the environment and actively contributes to developmental outcomes.
Is development continuous or discontinuous?	Continuous. Development is cumulative, consisting of the acquisition of a greater and greater number of learned responses.	Stagelike. Four qualitatively different stages emerge, each involving a reorganization of cognitive structures that permits more effective adaptation to the demands of the world.	Usually continuous. Development consists of the acquisition of more effective structures and processes for performing tasks.	Stagelike, although the individual may return to earlier stages to work through unresolved conflicts.	Continuous. Development involves transactions between the individual and the environment.	Continuous, although there are certain times when particular issues must be resolved.
How prominent are individual differences in development?	Individual differences are not emphasized; the laws of learning are universal. However, variations in experience can be a major source of individual differences.	Individual differences are not a primary focus of Piaget's theory.	Little emphasis is placed on individual differences; however, variations in structures, strategies, and other processes could help to explain individual differences in behavior.	Psychosocial stages are universal, however, individuals may proceed through and resolve each need in quite different ways.	Stresses the unique configuration of events that contribute to individual differences in explaining behavior.	Not emphasized.
How do the various domains of development interact?	Learning proceeds on many different fronts and is highly situational.	In Piaget's theory, stagelike advances in cognition have implications not only for thinking and problem solving but also for moral and social development, since many achievements in these domains depend on cognitive skills.	Development is usually considered to be domain specific. However, recent efforts have been made to understand social and emotional relationships in terms of information-processing models.	Failure to progress through psychosocial stages may disrupt progress in many different domains besides personality development.	Because of the strong mutual interdependence between individual and environment, all aspects of development are closely interrelated.	Social and psychological aspects of development are intimately linked to biological aspects, and all domains of development are linked together by their common contribution to adaptation.

book, you may find yourself revising your own stand on the six themes. We trace their presence throughout the remainder of this book with marginal cues placed beside important research and discussion that bear on each theme. Beginning with Chapter 3, we also open each chapter with a list of the most relevant themes discussed in it and conclude by summarizing how the themes have applied to the developmental domain under discussion.

CHAPTER RECAP

SUMMARY OF TOPICS

Developmental psychology has two main goals: to describe changes in behavior and mental processes that occur over time and to understand the reasons development occurs in the way that it does. To meet these goals more effectively, several developmental *theories* have been formulated to explain and predict behavior. These theories vary in their answers to several important questions concerning development.

■ SIX MAJOR THEMES IN DEVELOPMENTAL PSYCHOLOGY

Six recurring issues that every developmental theory must address are:

  ■ What roles do nature and nurture play in development?
  ■ How does the sociocultural context influence development?
  ■ How does the child play an active role in development?
  ■ Is development continuous or discontinuous?
  ■ How prominent are individual differences in development?
  ■ How do the various domains of development interact?

The various theories examined in this chapter differ in their answers to these questions and how completely they address these recurrent themes.

■ LEARNING THEORY APPROACHES

Learning theories, especially *behavior analysis,* emphasize the critical role of the environment, and especially *operant* and *classical conditioning,* for bringing about behavioral change. Even complex behaviors are the product of basic principles of learning. Social learning theories, particularly *social cognitive theory* as outlined by Bandura, add *observational learning* as an important mechanism by which behavior is continuously modified and changed.

■ COGNITIVE-DEVELOPMENTAL APPROACHES

Piaget's *cognitive-developmental theory* focuses on the child's construction of *schemes* or patterns of thought as development progresses through a series of qualitatively different stages. Through *assimilation* and *accommodation* a child's schemes, or

intellectual structures, actively adapt to the demands of the environment and become more organized, rational, and logical. Cognitive structures not only determine the way the child interprets and understands the world but also influence social and moral development.

■ INFORMATION-PROCESSING APPROACHES

Information-processing models use the computer as a metaphor to describe the cognitive structures and processes available to children in their efforts to comprehend, reason about, and respond to information. Perceptual, memory, and other structures as well as attentional, storage, retrieval, and other processes are posited to explain behavior.

■ PSYCHOSOCIAL APPROACHES

Psychosocial theory focuses on personality development. Freud's *psychosexual theory of development,* the predecessor to Erikson's psychosocial theory, posits that development proceeds maturationally through several stages in which specific body systems become especially effective in reducing libidinal energy. Failure to successfully negotiate these stages results in personality disturbances. Erikson's *psychosocial theory of development* emphasizes the sociocultural context in which behavioral needs are met. Development proceeds through a series of crises involving an individual's *identity.* Individuals who manage to resolve these crises become people who can successfully contribute to society.

■ CONTEXTUAL APPROACHES

Contextual models view human development from a broader framework. *Ecological systems theory* looks beyond the immediate context of an individual interacting with family, peers, and friends to the broader sociocultural contexts of his or her society. Vygotsky's *sociohistorical theory* views culture as the historical legacy of a community and emphasizes that development results from social interactions in which this heritage is transferred to and becomes part of an individual's way of thinking. *Ethological theory* pays special attention to the biological heritage each individual brings into the world. This heritage includes a history of species-specific behaviors that have been found to be adaptive throughout evolution.

2 STUDYING CHILD DEVELOPMENT

W hen five months old, the noted evolutionary theorist Charles Darwin wrote of his infant son, Doddy, in 1840,

> . . . associated ideas arising independently of any instruction became fixed in his mind; thus as soon as his hat and cloak were put on, he was very cross if he was not immediately taken out of doors. When exactly seven months old, he made the great step of associating his nurse with her name, so that if I called it out he would look round for her. . . . when a few days under nine months, he associated his own name with his image in the looking-glass, and when called by name would turn toward the glass even when at some distance from it. When a few days over nine months, he learnt spontaneously that a hand or other object causing a shadow to fall on the wall in front of him was to be looked for behind. (Darwin, 1877, p. 290)

I n just such informal records of their own offspring, Darwin and other nineteenth-century European scientists were taking the first steps toward the systematic observation of the child that would burgeon in the next century into a flourishing multidisciplinary field. The only surprise is that human development became a focus of serious study comparatively late in the history of science, for few fields offer a subject—the developing human being—that undergoes such dramatic transformations over time. Despite its relatively short history, however, developmental psychology has grown into a thriving modern-day enterprise conducted by individuals who are firmly committed to the idea that theories and hypotheses, like those described in Chapter 1, should be thoroughly and systematically tested using sound principles of science.

Research conducted around the world, especially in the last three decades, has yielded many important insights about the process of human development and the theories that describe it. Needless to say, a substantial number of these discoveries also have practical implications for our interactions with children, and we will see many examples as we look at the various environments inhabited by children. For example, newborn nurseries for premature infants now contain rocking chairs so that parents and nurses can rock and stimulate babies previously confined to isolettes. Bilingual education programs capitalize on the ease with which young children master the complexities of language. Many day care centers teach prosocial behaviors to young children. Research, in other words, can make a real difference in the lives of children.

Because research plays a central role in providing us with information about the process of development, we devote this chapter to a discussion of the methods typically used by developmental psychologists, along with the strengths and weaknesses of each approach. We hope that by alerting you to important issues in methodology, you will be better equipped to think critically about the findings of the numerous studies you will encounter in subsequent chapters.

THE SCIENTIFIC STUDY OF THE CHILD: HISTORICAL PERSPECTIVES

The field of developmental psychology has grown at an astonishing rate since Darwin recorded his observations of his baby boy. Each year hundreds of books and articles about children's growth are published for professionals interested in specific theoretical issues and for parents or teachers who wish to bring a more informed perspective to the challenging enterprises of child rearing and education. Scientists and laypersons, however, have not always had such a focused and conscious desire to understand the process of child development. In fact, societal attitudes toward childhood *as a concept* have shifted considerably over the last several centuries, a phenomenon that has paved the way for the contemporary emphasis on children as the subjects of scientific study.

The Concept of Childhood

Contemporary society views childhood as a separate, distinct, and unique period in the span of human life: during this special time children are to be protected, nurtured, loved, and for the most part kept free of adult responsibilities and obligations. Child labor laws try to ensure that children are not abused in the work world, and the institution of public education signals our society's willingness to devote significant resources to their academic training. But childhood was not always viewed in this way. As we look back through time, we see that prevailing beliefs about human nature and the social order shaped attitudes about the nature of childhood and hence the treatment and rearing of children (Borstelmann, 1983).

KEY THEME
Sociocultural Influence

Children in Medieval and Renaissance Times   From the Middle Ages through premodern times, European society's attitudes toward children differed strikingly from our contemporary society's. Though their basic needs to be fed and clothed were tended to, children were not coddled or protected in the same way infants in our society are. As soon as they were physically able, usually at age seven or so, children were incorporated into the adult world of work; they harvested grain, learned craft skills, and otherwise contributed to the local economy. In medieval times, Western European children did not have special clothes, toys, or games. Once they were old enough to shed swaddling clothes, they wore adult fashions and pursued adult pastimes such as archery, chess, and even gambling (Ariès, 1962).

In certain respects, however, premodern European society regarded children as vulnerable, fragile, and unable to assume the full responsibilities of adulthood. Medical writings alluded to the special illnesses of young children, and laws prohibited

In premodern Europe, children often dressed like adults and participated in many adult activities. At the same time, though, children were seen as fragile and in need of protection.

marriages of children under age twelve (Kroll, 1977). Religious movements of this era proclaimed the innocence of children and urged that they be educated. Children's souls, as well as adults', must be saved, said clerics, and they held that parents were morally responsible for their children's spiritual well-being. Parents recognized that children were also a financial responsibility and helped them to set up their own households as they approached adulthood and marriage (Pollock, 1983; Shahar, 1990). Thus, even though medieval children were incorporated quickly into the adult world, they were recognized both as different from adults and as possessing special needs.

A noticeable shift in attitudes toward children occurred in Europe during the sixteenth century. In 1545, English physician and lawyer Thomas Phayre published the first book on pediatrics. In addition, the advent of the printing press during this century made possible the wide distribution of other manuals on the care of infants and children. The first grammar schools were established and educated upper-class boys in economics and politics. Upper-class girls attended convent schools or received private instruction intended to cultivate modesty and obedience as well as other skills thought to be useful in their future roles as wives and mothers (Shahar, 1990).

Probably one of the most significant social changes occurred as a result of the transition from agrarian to trade-based economies in the sixteenth and seventeenth centuries and the subsequent growth of industrialization in the eighteenth century. As people relocated from farms to towns and as the production of goods shifted outside the home, the primary role of the family in Western society changed from ensuring economic survival to the nurturing of children (Hareven, 1985). Closeness and emotional attachment increasingly became the hallmarks of parent-child relations.

The Age of Enlightenment   The impact of these sweeping social changes was consolidated by the writings of several key thinkers who shaped the popular understanding of childhood. In the seventeenth and eighteenth centuries, two philosophers proposed important but distinctly different ideas about the nature and education of children. In his famous treatise *An Essay Concerning Human Understanding,* published in 1690, the British philosopher John Locke (1632–1704) described his views on the acquisition of human knowledge. Virtually no information is inborn, according to Locke. The newborn's mind is a *tabula rasa,* literally a "blank slate," on which perceptual experiences are imprinted. Locke's philosophy of **empiricism,** the idea that environmental experiences shape the individual, foreshadowed the modern-day psychological school of behaviorism. Locke believed that rewards and punishments from others, imitation, and the associations the child forms between stimuli are key elements in the formation of the mind.

In a second work, *Some Thoughts Concerning Education* (1693), Locke expounded further on his philosophy of training children:

> *The great mistake I have observed in people's breeding their children . . . is that the mind has not been made obedient to discipline and pliant to reason when it was most tender, most easy to be bowed. . . . He that is not used to submit his will to the reason of others when he is young, will scarce hearken to submit to his own reason when he is of an age to make use of it.*

But Locke also contends that

> *If the mind be curbed and humbled too much in children, if their spirits be abased and broken by too strict a hand over them, they will lose all vigour and industry and are in a worse state than the former.*

These statements convey Locke's belief that early experiences and proper training are important, but child rearing and education should proceed through the use of reason rather than harsh discipline. In his view, parents must find a balance between being overly indulgent and overly restrictive as they manage their child's behavior. As we will see, many of these same themes resound in contemporary research on

KEY THEME
Nature/Nurture

empiricism   Theory that environmental experiences shape the individual; more specifically, that all knowledge is derived from sensory experiences.

good parenting and represent a contrast to the strict discipline characteristic of Western society before the eighteenth century.

The second influential philosopher of the Enlightenment was Jean Jacques Rousseau (1712–1778), a French thinker who embraced the ideal of the child as a "noble savage." According to Rousseau, children are born with a propensity to act on impulses, but not necessarily with the aim of wrongdoing. They require the gentle guidance of adult authority to bring their natural instincts and tendencies in line with the social order. In *Émile* (1762), Rousseau set forth these beliefs about child rearing:

> *Never command him to do anything whatever, not the least thing in the world. Never allow him even to imagine that you assume to have any authority over him. Let him know merely that he is weak and that you are strong; that by virtue of his condition and your own he is necessarily at your mercy.*
>
> *. . . Do not give your scholar any sort of verbal lesson, for he is to be taught only by experience. Inflict on him no species of punishment, for he does not know what it is to be in fault.*

Rousseau emphasized the dynamic relationship between the curious and energetic child and the demands of his or her social environment as represented by adults. A major aspect of the process of development, Rousseau believed, is the resolution of conflicts between the individual tendencies of the child and the needs of the larger society; adults should not stifle the child's natural development and spirit through domination. Contemporary theories that acknowledge the active role of the child in the process of development have distinct roots in Rousseau's writings.

Rousseau also advanced some radical ideas about education. Children, he held, should not be forced to learn by rote the vast amounts of information that adults perceive as important. Instead, teachers should capitalize on the natural curiosity of children and allow them to discover on their own the myriad facts and phenomena that make up the world. Rousseau's ideas on the nature of education would be incorporated in the twentieth-century writings of Jean Piaget.

Both Locke and Rousseau emphasized the notion of the child as a developing, as opposed to a static, being. Both challenged the supposition that children are merely passive subjects of adult authority, and both advanced the idea that children should be treated with reason and respect. Having been elevated by the efforts of these worthy thinkers to an object of intellectual interest, the child was now ready to become the subject of scientific study.

KEY THEME
Nature/Nurture

KEY THEME
Child's Active Role

The Origins of Developmental Psychology

By the mid- to late-1800s, scholars in the natural sciences, especially biology, saw in the study of children an opportunity to support their emerging theories about the origins of human beings and their behaviors. Charles Darwin, for example, hypothesized that the similarities between the behaviors of humans and those of other species were the result of common evolutionary ancestors. Similarly, Wilhelm Preyer, another biologist, was initially interested in the physiology of embryological development but soon extended his investigations to behavioral development after birth.

Although these early attempts to study childhood scientifically were not explicitly conducted for the purpose of understanding child behavior and were often methodologically flawed, they paved the way for the systematic psychological study of the child that emerged by the end of that century. In the United States and Europe, key researchers who participated in the birth of psychology as an academic discipline began to show an interest in studying children specifically and applied the general methods of scientific observation to this end. By the beginning of the twentieth century, developmental psychology was established as a legitimate area of psychological inquiry.

The Baby Biographers: Charles Darwin and Wilhelm Preyer   The excerpt from Charles Darwin's 1840 notes at the beginning of the chapter marks one of the first records of the close scrutiny of a child for the purpose of scientific understanding. Eager to uncover important clues about the origins of the human species, Darwin undertook to record in great detail his infant son's behaviors during the first three years of life. Darwin documented the presence of early reflexes, such as sucking, as well as the emergence of voluntary motor movements, language, and emotions such as fear, anger, and affection. When he saw similarities, he linked the behaviors of the young child to other species, such as when, for example, he concluded that the infant's comprehension of simple words was not unlike the ability of "lower animals" to understand words spoken by humans (Darwin, 1877).

In 1882, the German biologist Wilhelm Preyer published *The Mind of the Child*, a work that described in great detail the development of his son Axel during his first three years of life. Preyer wrote meticulously of his son's sensory development, motor accomplishments, language production, and memory, even noting indications of an emerging concept of self. Although Preyer followed in the footsteps of several previous "baby biographers," including Darwin, he was the first to insist that observations of children be conducted systematically and scientifically. Accordingly, Preyer advocated that observations be taken unobtrusively and recorded immediately, that they be repeated several times each day, and that whenever possible the recordings of more than one observer be compared.

One major problem with the observations conducted by several of the baby biographers was the subjective nature of the interpretations they sometimes made about children's observable behaviors. How do we know, for example, that a given facial expression made by an infant actually signifies "sympathy," a notation Darwin made in his records about his son? The very fact that he was recording his own child's behavior introduces still another dimension of observer bias; parents typically are not the most objective observers of their own child's behavior. Moreover, not all of the baby biographers made their observations at regular intervals. Sometimes they made entries in their "diaries" on a daily basis; other times weeks would go by before an entry was made. Nonetheless, by advocating the application of scientific techniques to the study of children, the baby biographers, and Preyer in particular, set in motion the beginnings of the child development movement in the United States.

G. Stanley Hall: The Founder of Modern Child Psychology   The psychologist perhaps most responsible for launching the new discipline of child study in the United States was G. Stanley Hall, who, in 1878, became the first American to obtain a Ph.D. in psychology. Hall is also known for founding the first psychological journal in the United States in 1887 and, in 1891, the first journal of developmental psychology, *Pedagogical Seminary* (now called the *Journal of Genetic Psychology*). In addition, he founded and served as the first president of the American Psychological Association.

As the first American to study in Europe with the pioneer psychologist Wilhelm Wundt, G. Stanley Hall returned to the United States in 1880 with an interest in studying the "content of children's minds." Adopting the questionnaire method he had learned about in Germany, he had teachers ask about two hundred kindergarten-age children questions such as "Have you ever seen a cow?" or "What are bricks made of?" The percentage of children who gave particular answers was tabulated, and comparisons were made between the responses of boys and girls, city children and country children, and children of different ethnic backgrounds (Hall, 1891). For the first time, researchers were collecting data to compare groups of children, in contrast to previous approaches that had emphasized the detailed examination of individual children. By transplanting the questionnaire method from Europe to the United States, Hall introduced a new method by which researchers interested in children could approach their studies.

Alfred Binet and the Study of Individual Differences   The French psychologist Alfred Binet is known primarily as the developer of the first formal assessment scale

G. Stanley Hall is considered to be the founder of modern child psychology.

of intelligence. Binet was a pioneer in the study of **individual differences,** those unique characteristics that distinguish one person from others in the larger group. Although the trend in the United States at that time was to study the psychological characteristics or behaviors groups of people shared, Binet's work underscored the importance of identifying varying patterns of abilities.

Binet's original interest lay in the general features of children's thinking, including memory and reasoning about numbers. His studies of children's thinking were to provide the basis for more formal tests of children's mental abilities. In response to a request from the Ministry of Public Instruction in Paris for a tool to screen for students with learning problems, Binet and another colleague, Théodore Simon, developed a series of tasks to systematically measure motor skills, vocabulary, problem solving, and a wide range of other higher-order thought processes (Binet & Simon, 1905). This instrument could identify patterns in mental capabilities that were unique to each child.

The idea of mental testing caught on very quickly in the United States, especially among clinicians, school psychologists, and other professionals concerned with the practical side of dealing with children. For the first time, it was legitimate, even important, to consider variation in mental abilities from person to person.

James Mark Baldwin: Developmental Theorist   Much early developmental psychology emphasized the construction of methodologies for studying children and collecting data about their behavior. James Mark Baldwin, like his contemporaries, joined in by observing movement patterns, handedness, and color vision in infants (Cairns, 1992). Considered the founder of academic psychology in Canada (Hoff, 1992), Baldwin established a laboratory devoted to the systematic study of development at the University of Toronto. Soon, however, his interests shifted away from gathering empirical data. He became one of the most important developmental theorists of the early twentieth century.

One of Baldwin's most important propositions was that development is a dynamic and hierarchical process such that "Every genetic change ushers in a real advance, a progression on the part of nature to a higher mode of reality" (Baldwin, 1930, p. 86). Baldwin applied these ideas to the domain of cognitive development by suggesting that mental advances occur in a stagelike sequence in which the earliest thought is prelogical but gives way to logical, and eventually hyperlogical or formal reasoning. Many modern-day psychologists see a link between Baldwin's ideas and those of Piaget.

Baldwin is also recognized for his unique ideas about social development and the formation of personality. Instead of characterizing the child as a passive recipient of the behaviors and beliefs endorsed by the larger society, he described the child's emerging self as a product of continual reciprocal interactions between the child and others. Children imitate those around them, and in turn others are affected by the child's behaviors. The proposition that development results from a mutual dynamic between the child and others took a long time to catch on among psychologists, but this idea, so popular today—and one of the themes of development we emphasize throughout this text—is actually almost a century old (Cairns & Ornstein, 1979).

By the start of the 1900s, the foundations of developmental psychology as a scientifically based discipline were firmly laid out. Psychologists were well poised to begin the study of differences among groups of children, individual differences among children, and the hypotheses generated by emerging theories of development.

The Growth of Developmental Psychology in the Twentieth Century

From the beginning of this century to the mid-1940s, psychologists interested in development concentrated their efforts on gathering descriptive information about children. At what ages do most children achieve the milestones of motor development such as sitting, crawling, and walking? When do children develop emotions such as fear and anger? What are children's beliefs about punishment, friendship, and

KEY THEME
Individual Differences

KEY THEME
Continuity/Discontinuity

KEY THEME
Child's Active Role

individual differences   Unique characteristics that distinguish a person from other members of a larger group.

During the early twentieth century, many psychologists established the norms of development, the ages at which most children are able to accomplish tasks such as climbing stairs and walking.

morality? It was during this era of intensive fact gathering that many *norms* of development—that is, the ages at which most children are able to accomplish a given developmental task—were established. For example, Arnold Gesell established the norms of motor development for the first five years of life, guidelines that are still useful to psychologists, pediatricians, and other professionals who work with children in diagnosing developmental problems or delays (Gesell & Thompson, 1934, 1938).

Over the years, questions about norms gave way to research on the variables that might be related to specific aspects of development or even cause it to occur in the way it does. For example, is maturation or experience responsible for the sequence of motor behaviors most children seem to display? Does the predictable sequence of language development occur because of biological influences or learning? What factors lead to the emergence of emotional ties children form with caregivers? Researchers today continue to ask questions of these sorts, recognizing more and more the complexities of the influences on child development.

The first half of the twentieth century saw the founding of many major institutes or research centers that attracted bright young scholars who dedicated their lives to the scientific study of children. A further sign of the professionalization of the discipline was the formation of the Society for Research in Child Development (SRCD) in 1933 for scientists who wished to share their growing knowledge of child behavior and development. Today the membership of this society numbers about five thousand (SRCD, 1996) and includes developmental researchers working in settings such as colleges, universities, research institutes, and hospitals.

Scholars now approach child development from an assortment of disciplines, including anthropology, sociology, education, medicine, biology, and several subareas of psychology (for example, neuropsychology, comparative psychology, and clinical psychology), as well as the specialized area of developmental psychology. Each discipline has its own biases, as defined by the questions each asks about development and the methodological approaches it employs to answer those questions. Nonetheless, our pooled knowledge now gives us a better understanding of development than we might expect from a field that officially began only a century ago.

RESEARCH METHODS IN DEVELOPMENTAL PSYCHOLOGY

Like their colleagues in all the sciences, researchers in child development seek to gather data that are objective, measurable, and capable of being replicated in controlled studies by other researchers. Their studies, in other words, are based on the **scientific method.** Frequently they initiate research to evaluate the predictions of a specific theory (for example, is cognitive development stagelike, as Piaget suggests?). The scientific method dictates that theories must be revised or elaborated as new observations confirm or refute them. The process of scientific fact-finding involves a constant cycle of theorizing, empirical testing of the resulting hypotheses, and revision (or even outright rejection) of theories as the new data come in. Alternatively, the investigators may formulate a research question to determine an application of theory to a real-world situation (for example, can early intervention programs for preschoolers boost IQ scores?). Regardless of the motivation, the general principles of good science are as important to research in child development as they are to any other research arena. Although many of the methods child development researchers use are the very same techniques psychologists routinely employ in other specialized areas, some methodological approaches are particularly useful in studying changes in behavior or mental processes that occur over time.

Measuring Attributes and Behaviors

scientific method   Use of objective, measurable, and repeatable techniques to gather information.

variable   Factor having no fixed or constant value in a given situation.

All researchers are interested in identifying relationships among **variables,** those factors in a given situation that have no fixed or constant value. In child development studies, the variables are individual attributes, experiences, or behaviors that differ from one time to the next or from one person to another. Ultimately, researchers are interested in determining the causal relationships among variables; that is, they wish to identify those variables directly responsible for the occurrence of other variables. Does watching television cause children to behave aggressively? Do withdrawn children have academic problems once they enroll in school? Does the way a parent interacts with a toddler raise or lower the child's later intelligence? In posing each of these questions, researchers are hypothesizing that some attribute or experience of the child is causally related to another attribute or behavior.

The first problem the researcher faces is that of **operationally defining,** or specifying in measurable terms, the variables under study. Take the case of aggression. This term can be defined as parental ratings of a child's physical hostility, the child's own reports of his or her level of violent behavior, or the number of hits and kicks recorded by an observer of the child's behavior. The key point is that variables must be defined in terms of precise measurement procedures that other researchers can use if they wish to repeat the study.

The measurement of variables must also be valid and reliable. **Validity** refers to how well an assessment procedure actually measures the variable under study. Parental reports of physical violence, for example, or even the child's own self-reports may not be the best indicators of aggression. Parents may not want a researcher to know about their child's misbehavior, or they may lack complete knowledge of how their child behaves outside the home. Children's own reports may not be very accurate because the children may wish to present themselves to adults in a certain way. If a trained observer records the number of hits or kicks the child displays during a school day, the resulting measurement of aggression is likely to be valid.

Reliability is the degree to which the same results will be obtained consistently if the measure is administered repeatedly or if several observers are viewing the same behavior episodes. In the first case, suppose a child takes an intelligence test one time, then two weeks later takes the test again. If the test has high *test-retest reliability,* she should obtain similar scores on the two testing occasions. In the second case, two or more observers viewing a child's behavior should agree about what they are seeing (for example, did the child smile in the presence of a stranger?); if they do agree, the test has high *inter-rater reliability.* Both types of reliability are calculated mathematically and are usually reported by researchers in their published reports of experiments; both are very important factors in good scientific research. Measurements of behavior that fluctuate dramatically from one observation time to another or from one observer to another are virtually useless as data.

Methods of Collecting Data

What is the best way for researchers in developmental psychology to gather information about children? Should they simply watch children as they go about their routines in natural settings? Should children be brought into the researcher's laboratory to be observed? Should the researcher ask the child questions about the topic under study? Each approach offers advantages and disadvantages, and the choice of research tactic will often depend on the nature of the investigator's questions. If we are interested in exploring children's spontaneous tendencies to behave aggressively as they play (for example, do boys play more aggressively than girls?), we will probably find a *naturalistic approach* most appropriate. If we want to see whether children's behavior is influenced by the presence of an aggressive model, we might use a *structured observation* to systematically expose some children to this manipulation in a laboratory setting. If we want to examine how children understand aggression, its antecedents, and its consequences, we might adopt another strategy, such as a *structured interview* or a *questionnaire.* Sometimes researchers combine two or more of these data collection methods within a study or series of studies.

Naturalistic Observation Researchers have no better way to see how children really behave than to observe them in natural settings: in their homes, playgrounds,

operational definition
Specification of variables in terms of measurable properties.

validity Degree to which an assessment procedure actually measures the variable under consideration.

reliability Degree to which a measure will yield the same results if administered repeatedly.

In naturalistic observations, researchers observe and record children's behaviors in real-life settings such as play-grounds, schools, or homes.

schools, and other places that are part of their everyday lives. After all, the ultimate goal of developmental psychology is to describe and explain changes in behavior that actually occur. **Naturalistic observations** do not involve the manipulation of vari-ables; researchers simply observe and record behaviors of interest from the natural series of events that unfold in a real-world setting.

A study by Theodore Wachs and his colleagues (Wachs et al., 1993), for example, used naturalistic observations to assess the relationship between specific caregiver behaviors and the competence of toddlers as they matured from eighteen to thirty months of age. The study was conducted in Egypt. Twice a month, researchers ob-served children and their caregivers in their homes for a period of thirty minutes, noting such behaviors as how frequently caregivers vocalized to the children and the amount of physical contact between caregiver and child. Several observations were made of toddler behavior as well, including ratings of the child's alertness, the num-ber of vocalizations the child made, and the amount of time the child spent actively playing with objects. The results showed that, as in Western families, the more vocal stimulation the caregiver provided, the more alert, vocal, and actively involved with the environment was the child.

The methodology of this study had many positive features. First, Wachs and his co-researchers operationally defined the variables of interest by clearly specifying which behaviors should be recorded. For example, the amount of physical contact the caregiver gave to the child was defined as "the number of times during the obser-vation the child is picked up, held, or carried by an adult or older child" (p. 602). Second, these researchers were aware that caregivers and children might react to the presence of a stranger by behaving in untypical or "unnatural" ways. To reduce such **participant reactivity,** a preliminary observation was conducted when the children were seventeen months of age to acclimate the family to the presence of observers in the home. Finally, to minimize the effects of **observer bias,** the possibility that the researcher would interpret ongoing events to be consistent with his or her prior hypotheses, two independent observers (one of whom was unfamiliar with the pur-poses of the study) coded caregiver and child behaviors to ensure reliability of the findings.

An important advantage of naturalistic observations is that researchers can see the events and behaviors that precede the target behaviors they are recording; they can also note the consequences of those same target behaviors. In this way, they may be able to discern important relationships in sequences of events. Moreover, naturalistic observations give researchers powerful insights into which variables are important to

naturalistic observation
Study in which observations of naturally occurring behavior are made in real-life settings.

participant reactivity
Tendency of individuals who know they are under observation to alter natural behavior.

observer bias   Tendency of researchers to interpret ongoing events as being consistent with their research hypotheses.

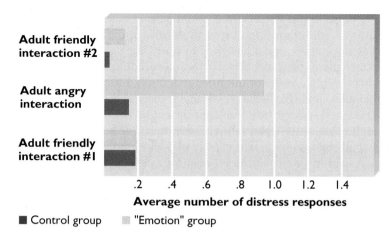

.2 .4 .6 .8 1.0 1.2 1.4
Average number of distress responses

■ Control group   ▨ "Emotion" group

Source: Adapted from Cummings, Iannotti, & Zahn-Waxler, 1985.

FIGURE 2.1

A Structured Observation

What happens when two-year-old children observe two adults having a friendly interaction, followed by an angry exchange, then by another friendly interaction? The graph shows the average number of distress responses (expressions of anxiety, crying, and so forth) displayed by children who witnessed this sequence of events compared to those of a control group that saw a series of three neutral exchanges. This structured observation showed that exposure to adult anger heightened children's distress.

study in the first place, insights they may not derive solely by observing children in the laboratory. Often the trends or phenomena identified in such preliminary studies become the focus of more intensive, controlled laboratory experiments. And, as we mentioned earlier, naturalistic observations have the distinct advantage of examining real-life behaviors as opposed to behaviors that may emerge only in response to some contrived laboratory manipulation.

Some cautions regarding this method are in order, however. First, a wide range of variables may influence the behaviors under observation, and it is not always clear which ones have the most impact. What causes young children to be alert, vocal, and involved with their environment? Is it the responsiveness of the caregiver? Or does some other factor, such as the child's general health status, play a larger role? Cause-and-effect relationships, furthermore, cannot be deduced. Do vocal caregivers cause toddlers to be alert, or do alert toddlers elicit verbalizations from their caregivers? Answering questions such as these requires the systematic manipulation of variables, a tactic that is part of other research approaches.

Structured Observation   Researchers cannot always depend on a child to display behaviors of scientific interest to them during observation. Researchers who observe a child in the home, school, or other natural setting may simply not be present when vocalization, sharing, aggression, or other behaviors they wish to study occur. Therefore, developmental psychologists may choose to observe behaviors in a more structured setting, usually the laboratory, where they devise situations to elicit those behaviors of interest to them. **Structured observations** are the record of specific behaviors the child displays in a situation the experimenter constructs. Structured observations, like naturalistic observations, are a way to collect data by looking at and recording the child's behaviors, but this form of looking takes place under highly controlled conditions.

A study of the effects of adult emotions on the emotions of two-year-olds illustrates how such structured observations are frequently conducted (Cummings, Iannotti, & Zahn-Waxler, 1985). Pairs of children were brought to a laboratory playroom along with their mothers. While the children played, two adults entered the room and engaged first in a friendly, pleasant interaction, then in an angry exchange, and finally in a friendly, conciliatory manner. The children's emotional reactions (particularly bodily or facial expressions of anxiety and vocalizations such as crying) during the different phases of the experimental session were recorded by several trained observers. In addition, a control group of children witnessed the adults in a series of three neutral communications. The results, shown in Figure 2.1, indicated that exposure to the adults' angry exchanges generated significant distress among two-year-olds compared to their reactions in the presence of the friendly exchanges and compared to the control group.

structured observation Study in which behaviors are recorded as they occur within a situation constructed by the experimenter, usually in the laboratory.

Although these researchers could have attempted to conduct their study of reactions to adult emotions through naturalistic observation in children's homes or preschools, they might have had to wait a long time for the appropriate interactions to take place spontaneously. Furthermore, adults in natural settings display emotions with varying degrees of intensity, making it difficult for the experimenters to ensure that all of their participants witnessed exactly the same emotional states. By doing a structured observation, the experimenters could control the precise nature of the adult emotional displays the children saw. The adult actors were carefully trained so that all children witnessed exactly the same emotional scenes in the same order.

A liability of structured observations, especially if they are conducted in the laboratory, is that children may not react in the same ways in the research room that they do in "real life." Being in a strange environment with unfamiliar experimenters or other participants in the study may make children behave in ways that are not typical. For example, children may show heightened distress at adult anger when they are in an unfamiliar environment. One solution to this problem is to confirm the results of laboratory studies by conducting similar studies in children's natural environments.

Structured observations can focus on a variety of types of behaviors. Like many structured observations, the study by Cummings and colleagues focused on children's overt actions, in this case their facial displays and physical activities. Researchers often record other behaviors, such as the number of errors children make in a problem-solving task, the kinds of memory strategies they display, or the amount of time they take to learn a specified task. When structured observations are conducted in the laboratory, it is also possible for researchers to obtain *physiological measures,* the shifts in heart rate, brain wave activity, or respiration rate that can indicate the child's reaction to changes in stimuli. This technique is especially useful in examining the behavior of infants, because the range of overt responses very young children usually display is more limited than that of older children.

The Interview and the Questionnaire　Sometimes the best way to glean information about what children know or how they behave is not simply to observe them but to ask them directly. Researchers have found that talking with children about their conceptions of friendships, gender roles, problem-solving skills—in fact, almost anything in the child's world—has yielded a wealth of material for analysis.

Many investigators use the technique of **structured interviews,** studies in which each participant is asked the same sequence of questions. For example, the goal of a recent study conducted by Mary Levitt and her colleagues (Levitt, Guacci-Franco, & Levitt, 1993) was to explore the sources of social support for seven-, ten-, and fourteen-year-old children from different ethnic backgrounds. More than three hundred African American, Anglo American, and Hispanic American children were interviewed individually about the people most important in their lives. Each child was questioned by an interviewer of the same cultural background as the child to maximize the child's comfort with the session and the accuracy of his or her responses. Examples of the standard questions employed in this study include "Are there people who make you feel better when something bothers you or you are not sure about something?" and "Are there people who like to be with you and do fun things with you?" The results showed that for all children, regardless of ethnic background, the family was an important source of social support. Moreover, members of the extended family (such as grandparents, aunts, or uncles) played an increasing role during middle childhood, while peers assumed a significant support role during adolescence.

Another "asking" technique researchers use with children is to obtain written responses to a standard set of items in a **questionnaire.** Because questionnaires can be administered to large numbers of children at the same time, researchers can use this method to obtain a large set of data very quickly. Questionnaires can also be scored quickly, particularly if the items ask participants to pick from a set of multiple-choice items or to rate items on a numerical scale. Children, however, may have difficulty understanding the items and may not be able to answer accurately without guidance

structured interview　Standardized set of questions administered orally to participants.

questionnaire　Set of standardized questions administered to participants in written form.

from an adult. Under those conditions, oral interviews with individual children may provide more reliable and valid information about how children think and feel.

Researchers who use interviews and questionnaires to collect data from children must be careful, though. Sometimes young respondents, like their adult counterparts, will try to present themselves in the most favorable light or answer questions as they think the researcher expects them to. In the study of children's sources of social support, for example, participants may have said they talked with their parents when they had problems because they knew this was the expected response. To prompt participants to answer as honestly as possible, researchers try not to react positively or negatively as the participant responds and also try to explain the importance of answering truthfully before the start of the interview or questionnaire.

Another way to collect data by interview is the **clinical method,** a flexible, open-ended technique in which the investigator may modify the questions in reaction to the child's response. A notable example was Jean Piaget's use of the clinical method to explore age-related changes in children's thinking capabilities. Consider the following segment, in which Piaget (1929) questions a six-year-old boy about the sun:

Piaget: How did the sun begin?
Child: It was when life began.
Piaget: Has there always been a sun?
Child: No.
Piaget: How did it begin?
Child: Because it knew that life had begun.
Piaget: What is it made of?
Child: Of fire . . .
Piaget: Where did the fire come from?
Child: From the sky.
Piaget: How was the fire made in the sky?
Child: It was lighted with a match. (p. 258)

Note how Piaget follows the child's line of thinking with each question he asks. The format of the interview changes with an older boy, age nine years:

Piaget: How did the sun start?
Child: With heat.
Piaget: What heat?
Child: From the fire.
Piaget: Where is the fire?
Child: In heaven.
Piaget: How did it start?
Child: God lit it with wood and coal.
Piaget: Where did he get the wood and coal?
Child: He made it. (p. 265)

Piaget gained some enormous insights into the thinking processes of children by using the probing, interactive questions typical of the clinical method. Having the flexibility to follow the child's train of thought rather than sticking to a rigid protocol of predetermined questions allows the researcher to gather fresh insights. The weakness of this approach, however, lies precisely in this flexibility. Because the questions asked of different participants are likely to vary, systematic comparisons of their answers are difficult to make. Moreover, the researcher may be tied to a theoretical orientation that biases the formulation of questions and the interpretation of answers. Nonetheless, the clinical method can be a valuable research tool, particularly in exploring the way children think and reason.

The Meta-analytic Study Sometimes researchers do not actually collect empirical data themselves but instead make a statistical analysis of a body of previously published research on a specific topic that allows them to draw some general conclusions. Instead of looking or asking, they "crunch" data; that is, they combine the

clinical method Flexible, open-ended interview method in which questions are modified in reaction to the child's responses.

results of numerous studies to assess whether the central variable common to all has an important effect. This technique, called **meta-analysis**, is particularly useful when the results of studies in the same area are inconsistent or in conflict with one another.

A good example of meta-analysis is a study conducted by Janet Hyde and her colleagues to assess the existence of sex differences in children's mathematical skills (Hyde, Fennema, & Lamon, 1990). Many researchers have concluded that boys perform better than girls on tests of mathematical skill, particularly after age twelve or thirteen (Halpern, 1986; Maccoby & Jacklin, 1974). Such observations have spawned numerous debates about the origins of this sex difference. Is mathematical skill biologically given, or is it learned through experiences in the environment? The answer to this question has important educational implications for male and female students. Hyde and her colleagues collected one hundred studies conducted from 1967 through 1987 that examined the question of sex differences in mathematics performance. (This body of studies represented the participation of more than 3 million participants!) For each study, a statistical measure representing *effect size* was computed, a mathematical way of expressing the size of the difference in male and female scores. Hyde and her colleagues (1990) found that the average difference between males and females across all studies was small, leading the researchers to conclude that sex differences in mathematical ability are not large enough to be of great scientific significance.

Conducting a meta-analysis requires the careful transcription of hundreds of statistical figures, a powerful computer, and a good deal of computational skill. Because the researcher taking this approach did not design the original studies, she or he cannot always be sure the central variables have been defined in identical ways across studies. Moreover, studies that do not present their data in the form necessary for analysis may have to be eliminated from the pool; potentially valuable information may thus be lost. Despite these difficulties, the meta-analytic approach allows researchers to draw conclusions based on a large corpus of research, not just individual studies, and thereby to profit from an accumulated body of knowledge. This technique has recently become increasingly popular in developmental research and has provoked the reevaluation of more than one traditional notion about children.

From our discussion it should be clear that there is no one right way to study children. Researchers must consider their overall goals and their available resources as they make decisions about how to construct a research study. Table 2.1 summarizes the advantages and disadvantages of the four general types of data collection just described.

Research Designs

Besides formulating their hypotheses, identifying the variables, and choosing a method of gathering information about children, investigators must select the research design they will use as part of their study. The *research design* is the overall conceptual approach that defines whether the variables will be manipulated, how many children will be studied, and the precise sequence of events as the study proceeds. Research designs may be fairly complex, and an investigator might choose more than one design for each part of a large study. Generally, however, researchers select from one of three study types: the correlational, the experimental, and the single-case design.

The Correlational Design   Studies in which the researcher looks for systematic relationships among variables use the correlational design and are called **correlational studies**. Instead of manipulating the variables, in this design the investigator obtains measures of two or more characteristics of the participants and sees whether changes in one variable are accompanied by changes in the other. Some variables show a **positive correlation**; that is, as the values of one variable change, scores on the other variable change in the same direction. For example, if a positive correlation exists be-

meta-analysis Statistical examination of a body of research studies to assess the effect of the common central variable.

correlational study Study that assesses whether changes in one variable are accompanied by systematic changes in another variable.

positive correlation Relationship in which changes in one variable are accompanied by systematic changes in another variable in the same direction.

Approach	Description	Advantages	Disadvantages
Naturalistic Observations	Observations of behaviors as they occur in children's real-life environments.	Can note antecedents and consequences of behaviors; see real-life behaviors.	Possibility of participant reactivity and observer bias; less control over variables; cause-and-effect relationships difficult to establish.
Structured Observations	Observations of behaviors in situations constructed by the experimenter.	More control over conditions that elicit behaviors.	Children may not react as they would in real life.
Interviews and Questionnaires	Asking children (or parents) about what they know or how they behave.	Quick way to assess children's knowledge or reports of their behaviors.	Children may not always respond truthfully or accurately; systematic comparisons of responses may be difficult; theoretical orientation of researcher may bias questions and interpretations of answers.
Meta-analytic Studies	Statistical analysis of other researchers' findings to look for the size of a variable's effects.	Pools a large body of research findings to sort out conflicting findings; no participants are observed.	Requires careful mathematical computation; variables may not have been defined identically across all studies.

TABLE 2.1

Advantages and Disadvantages of Information-Gathering Approaches

tween children's television viewing and their aggression, as the number of hours of TV viewing increases, the number of aggressive acts committed increases as well. A **negative correlation** indicates that as scores on one variable change, scores on the other variable change in the opposite direction. Thus, using our example, a negative relationship exists if aggression decreases as TV viewing increases.

The statistic used to describe the strength of a relationship between two variables is called the **correlation coefficient,** or *r*. Correlation coefficients may range from +1.00 (perfectly positively correlated) to −1.00 (perfectly negatively correlated). As the correlation coefficient approaches 0.00 (which signifies no relationship), the relationship between the two variables becomes weaker. A rule of thumb is that correlations of .70 or higher usually signify strong relationships, whereas those below .20 represent weak relationships. In most cases, values falling in between indicate a moderate relationship between two variables.

We can use a portion of a study conducted by Carol MacKinnon-Lewis and her colleagues (MacKinnon-Lewis et al., 1994) to illustrate the key features of correlational research. One objective of these investigators was to see if relationships existed between boys' aggressive behaviors and several family variables, such as the number of negative life events the child experienced. The latter included experiences such as a parent leaving home or a divorce between parents. The investigators found a statistically significant correlation of $r = .40$ between the number of negative life events reported by boys and the number of fights they started with peers. Thus, the more stress the boys experienced within the family, the more fights they initiated in school. In contrast, the number of negative life events experienced by boys correlated $r = .04$ with the mothers' tendency to judge their sons as having hostile intentions in interactions with others, suggesting no relationship between these two variables.

Because researchers do not actively manipulate the variables in correlational studies, they must be cautious about making statements about cause and effect when strong relationships are found. In the above study, for example, do negative life events cause boys to be aggressive? Or does their aggression contribute to stress and negative events within the family? Still another possibility is that some third factor not measured by the researchers influences both variables. Perhaps, for example, the child's father is aggressive and that factor influences both the son's aggression and the number of negative life events in the family.

negative correlation Relationship in which changes in one variable are accompanied by systematic changes in another variable in the opposite direction.

correlation coefficient (r) Statistical measure, ranging from +1.00 to −1.00, that summarizes the strength and direction of the relationship between two variables; does not provide information about causation.

Despite these limitations on interpretation, correlational studies are often a useful first step in exploring which variables might be causally related to one another. In addition, in many instances experimenters are unable to manipulate the variables that are the suspected causes of certain behavior. In the above study, for example, it would be impossible to systematically vary the number of negative life events experienced by boys. In such cases, correlational studies represent the only approach available to understanding the influences on child development.

The Experimental Design   The **experimental design** involves the manipulation of one or more **independent variables**—the variables that are manipulated or controlled by the investigator, often because they are the suspected cause of a behavior—to observe the effects on the **dependent variable**, the suspected outcome. One major goal of this type of study is to control for as many as possible of the factors that can influence the outcome, aside from the independent variables. Experimental studies are frequently conducted in laboratory situations, where it is possible to ensure that all participants are exposed to the same environmental conditions and the same task instructions. In addition, **random assignment** of participants to different treatment groups (in which one group is usually a *control group* that receives no treatment) helps to avoid any systematic variation aside from that precipitated by the independent variables. As a consequence, one distinct advantage of the experimental study design is that cause-and-effect relationships among variables can be identified.

To illustrate the experimental design, consider the following question: Are different sweet substances—sucrose, fructose, glucose, and lactose—equally effective in reducing crying in newborn infants? Elliott Blass and Barbara Smith (1992) investigated this question in an experimental study involving one- to three-day-old infants. During the prestimulation phase, each infant rested in a bassinet for five minutes. In the next five-minute phase, each infant received one of five solutions in its mouth: sucrose, fructose, glucose, lactose, or water. The assignment of a particular solution to each infant was randomly determined. Finally, infants were observed for an additional five minutes, the poststimulation phase. During all the observation phases, the amount of infant crying was recorded. Thus, the independent variable was the type of solution infants received and the dependent variable was the percentage of time infants cried.

In this experiment, many other factors that could affect infant crying were controlled. For example, the nursery temperature was held at seventy-five degrees, all infants had their diapers changed right before the experimental session began, and all infants were tested in a bassinet. When other variables are controlled, the researcher can be more confident that the independent variable is causing changes in the dependent variable.

All infants, regardless of experimental condition, spent between 45 and 55 percent of the time crying prior to receiving a solution in the mouth. Figure 2.2 shows the percentage of time infants spent crying in the stimulation phase of the experiment. The graph shows that fructose and sucrose produced the least amount of crying, while lactose and glucose were less effective in soothing infants. Similar results were found for the poststimulation phase. Can other hypotheses account for these findings? Because babies were randomly assigned to experimental conditions, it is not likely that the happiest babies were in the fructose and sucrose groups. And because all infants experienced the same experimental procedures except for the type of solution, it is difficult to argue for other explanations of these data.

The experimental approach has been the traditional design choice for many developmental psychologists because of the "clean" answers it provides about the causes of developmental phenomena. Yet it has also been criticized for providing a narrow portrait of child development. Development in the real world is likely to be caused by many variables; few changes are likely to be the result of a single or even a few independent variables. In that sense, experimental studies typically fail to capture the complexities of age-related changes. Moreover, we have already mentioned that children may not react normally when they are brought into the laboratory setting, where most experiments are conducted. Children may "clam up" because they are shy

---

experimental design   Research method in which one or more independent variables are manipulated to determine the effect on other, dependent variables.

independent variable   Variable manipulated by the experimenter; the suspected cause.

dependent variable   Behavior that is measured; suspected effect of an experimental manipulation.

random assignment   Use of principles of chance to assign participants to treatment and control groups; avoids systematic bias.

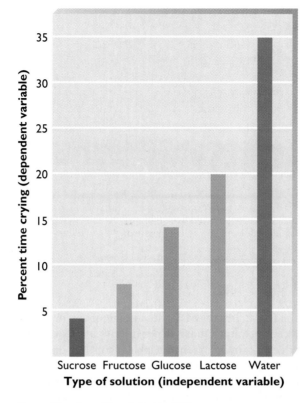

Source: Data from Blass & Smith, 1992.

FIGURE 2.2

An Experimental Study

In this example of an experimental design, newborn infants were observed for five minutes as they lay in a bassinet (prestimulation) and then received one of four sweet solutions or water for five minutes (stimulation). Finally, they were observed for another five minutes (poststimulation). The percentage of time crying was recorded in each phase. In this experiment, the type of solution given to the infants was the independent variable and the percentage of time they spent crying was the dependent variable. The graph shows what happened during the stimulation phase. Sucrose and fructose resulted in a substantial decrease in crying compared to the other solutions.

about being in unfamiliar surroundings with strangers and mechanical equipment. Or they may rush through the experimental task just to get it over with.

In recognition of these problems, many researchers have tried to achieve a more homelike feeling in their laboratories, with comfortable couches, chairs, tables, and rugs instead of sterile, bare-walled rooms filled with equipment. Another tactic has been to conduct **field experiments,** in which the experimental manipulations are actually carried out in a natural setting, such as the child's home or school. In one such field experiment, Grover Whitehurst and his colleagues (Whitehurst et al., 1994) randomly assigned children attending their preschools to one of three experimental conditions to see if the type of reading experiences they had influenced their language skills. For six weeks, a ten-minute period was allocated each day to one of the following conditions: (1) school reading, where the teacher read a book and concurrently asked children numerous questions about the story and promoted discussion; (2) school plus home reading, where teachers read to children in the same special manner as above, but parents were also trained to read to children at home using an active discussion approach; and (3) control, where children engaged in ten minutes of teacher-supervised play. The groups were formed such that no more than five children participated in each at any single time. The results, displayed in Figure 2.3, showed that at the end of six weeks, children in both reading groups scored significantly higher on a test of vocabulary compared with the control group and that the school plus home reading group scored higher than the school reading group. In the follow-up phase six months later, both reading groups continued to show advantages over the control group in language skills. Because the only known variation in children's experiences was systematically introduced by the researchers in their manipulation of the independent variable (the type of reading group children were exposed to), changes in behavior could be attributed to type of reading program. In addition, the natural setting of this field experiment minimized the problems associated with bringing children into the artificial surroundings of a laboratory.

In some instances, it is not possible for the researcher to randomly assign participants to treatment groups because of logistical or ethical difficulties. In these cases,

field experiment Experiment conducted in a "natural," real-world setting such as the child's home or school.

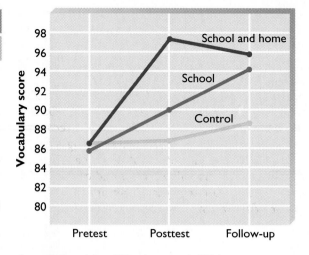

FIGURE 2.3

A Field Experiment

The data from Whitehurst et al.'s (1994) field study show that children who had special reading experiences at school and at school plus home received higher scores on a test of vocabulary on a posttest (six weeks after the program began) and a follow-up (six months later) compared to the control group. A field experiment employs many of the features of an experiment, but is conducted in a natural setting.

Source: Adapted from Whitehurst et al., 1994.

the researcher may take advantage of the natural separation of participants into different groups. **Quasi-experiments** are studies in which researchers investigate the effects of independent variables that they do not manipulate themselves but occur as a result of children's natural experiences. Suppose a researcher wanted to explore the effects of day care centers of varying quality on children's social competence. It would be unethical to assign children randomly to high- and low-quality centers. Yet in everyday life, children do attend centers that differ in the overall quality of experience provided. Deborah Vandell and her colleagues (Vandell, Henderson, & Wilson, 1988) observed the free play of four-year-olds who attended good- and poor-quality day care centers. Good-quality centers were defined as those with better-trained teachers, better adult-child ratios, smaller classes, and more materials than poor-quality centers. When children from the two types of centers were compared on a range of social behaviors, Vandell and her colleagues noted that children from the better centers were rated as more socially competent, happier, and capable of more friendly interactions with their peers than children from the poorer centers.

Because the researchers did not randomly assign participants to each group, we must be careful in how we interpret the results of this and other quasi-experimental studies. The children who attended poor- and good-quality centers may have consistently differed in ways that better account for their differences in social behavior than simply the nature of the day care center they attended. Families with children in poor-quality centers may have had more limited financial resources and may have been under more stress than those who sent their children to better centers. Vandell and her colleagues accounted for this possibility by statistically controlling for parental social class. However, other aspects of the home or family (for example, family interaction styles), rather than qualities of the day care experience, may in fact have caused differences in children's social behavior and general emotional disposition. Although these types of methodological problems often accompany quasi-experimental studies, they do offer researchers a way to address important questions about the complex influences on child development, questions that often have powerful real-world implications.

The Single-Case Design Some notable discoveries about developmental processes have come from the in-depth examination of a single child or just a few children. At times, psychologists make an intensive description of an individual child, much as the baby biographers did. Freud and Piaget both relied heavily on such **case studies** of individuals to formulate their broad theories of personality and cognitive development, respectively. In other instances, researchers introduce experimental treatments to one or a few children and note any changes in their behavior over time. Frequently the purpose of these **single-case designs** is to evaluate a clinical treatment

quasi-experiment Study in which the assignment of participants to experimental groups is determined by their natural experiences.

case study In-depth description of psychological characteristics and behaviors of an individual.

single-case design Study that follows only one or a few participants over a period of time.

for a problem behavior or an educational program designed to increase or decrease specific activities in the child.

Suppose we wish to evaluate the effectiveness of a treatment for stuttering in children. One team of researchers selected four boys, ages ten to eleven years, who had difficulties with stuttering (Gagnon & Ladouceur, 1992). Their first step was to record the percentage of stuttered syllables each boy spoke during the baseline period, prior to the start of the treatment. Next, the treatment was begun. During two one-hour sessions per week, each boy received instruction on how to recognize stuttering and how to regulate breathing during stuttering. Special speaking exercises and parent information sessions were also introduced. Finally, the participants' speech was assessed at one month and six months following the end of treatment. Figure 2.4 shows the decline in percentage of stuttered syllables among the children from baseline through follow-up periods. Was the treatment effective? The facts

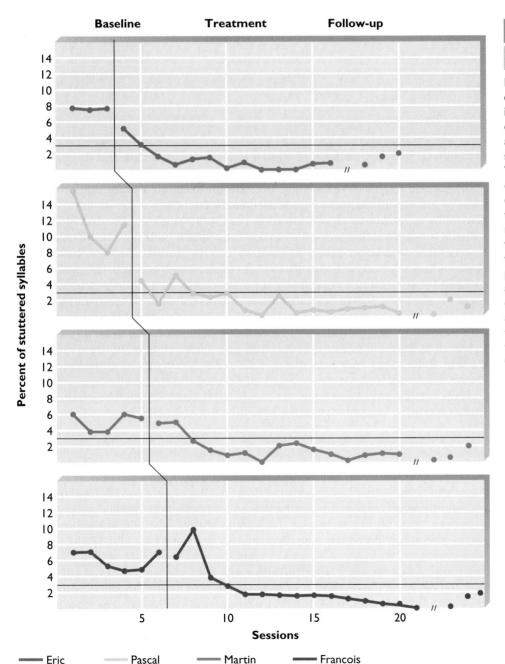

FIGURE 2.4

A Single-Case Design

In this example of a single-case design, four boys with stuttering problems were observed during a baseline period. Next, a program to treat their speech problems was begun. The graph shows that the percentage of stuttered syllables declined dramatically following the onset of treatment and remained low during the follow-up period. Because the four children showed similar patterns of behavior change, and because the behavior change was maintained long after the treatment ended, the researchers concluded that their treatment was effective.

Source: Gagnon & Ladouceur, 1992.

Design	Description	Strengths	Weaknesses
Correlational Design	Researcher sees if changes in one variable are accompanied by systematic changes in another variable.	Useful when conditions do not permit the manipulation of variables.	Cannot determine cause-and-effect relationships.
Experimental Design	Researcher manipulates one or more independent variables to observe the effects on the dependent variable(s).	Can isolate cause-and-effect relationships.	May not yield information about real-life behaviors.
Field Experiment	Experiment conducted in real-life, naturalistic settings.	Can isolate cause-and-effect relationships; behaviors are observed in natural settings.	Less control over treatment conditions.
Quasi-experiment	Assignment of participants to groups is determined by their natural experiences.	Takes advantage of natural separation of children into groups.	Factors other than independent variables may be causing results.
Single-Case Design	In-depth observation of one or a few children over a period of time.	Does not require large pool of participants.	Ability to generalize to the larger population may be limited.

TABLE 2.2

Strengths and Weaknesses of Research Designs

that all four participants showed similar declines in stuttering and the stuttering remained low during follow-up several months later suggest that it was.

Single-case designs do not require large groups of children or the random assignment of participants to groups. Each participant essentially serves as his or her own control by experiencing all conditions in the experiment over a period of time. As with any study involving only one or a few individuals, however, researchers' ability to generalize to a larger group of children may be limited. Perhaps the child or children they selected for the study were particularly responsive to the treatment, a treatment that might not work as well for other children. In addition, the researcher must be aware of any other circumstances concurrent with the treatment that may have actually produced the behavior changes. For example, did the children in the stuttering study mature neurologically, and did that maturation cause the reduction in speech problems? The fact that the treatment started at different times for each of the four children and was immediately followed by a decrease in stuttering suggests that the treatment and not some other factor caused the changes.

Table 2.2 presents an overview of the strengths and weaknesses of single-case studies and other research designs we have briefly examined here.

Strategies for Assessing Developmental Change

The developmental researcher faces a problem unique to this field: how to record the changes in behavior that occur over time. The investigator has two choices: to observe individual children repeatedly over time or to select children of different ages to participate in one study at a given time. Each approach has its strengths and limitations, and each has contributed substantially to our understanding of child development.

The Longitudinal Study   **Longitudinal studies** assess the same sample of participants repeatedly at various points in time, usually over a span of years. This approach has the longest historical tradition in developmental psychology. The early baby biographies were in essence longitudinal observations, and several major longitudinal projects initiated in the early 1900s continued for decades. One of the most famous is Lewis Terman's study of intellectually gifted children, begun in 1921 (Terman, 1925; Terman & Oden, 1959).

longitudinal study   Research in which the same participants are repeatedly tested over a period of time, usually years.

Terman identified 952 children ages two to fourteen years who had scored 140 or above on a standardized test of intelligence. He was interested in answering several questions about these exceptionally bright children. Would they become extraordinarily successful later in life? Did they possess any specific cluster of common personality traits? Did they adapt well socially? The sample was followed until most participants reached sixty years of age, and a wealth of information was collected over this long span of time. One finding was that many individuals in this sample had highly successful careers in science, academics, business, and other professions. In addition, contrary to many popular stereotypes, high intelligence was associated with greater physical and mental health and adaptive social functioning later in life.

Longitudinal research is costly and requires a substantial research effort. Participants followed over a period of years often move or become unavailable for other reasons; just keeping track of them requires constant and careful recordkeeping. In addition, one might raise questions about the characteristics of the people who remain in the study: perhaps they are less mobile, or perhaps those who agree to participate in a thirty-year study have unique qualities that can affect the interpretation of the project's results (for example, they may be less energetic or be more curious

Longitudinal studies assess the same individuals over a span of years, sometimes ranging from infancy through adolescence. This strategy for assessing developmental change allows researchers to identify the stability of many human characteristics.

about themselves and more introspective). Another difficulty lies in the fact that participants who are tested repeatedly often get better at the tests, not because of any changes in their abilities but because the tests become more familiar over time. Participants who take a test of spatial skill again and again may improve due to practice with the test and not as a result of any developmental change in their abilities. If the researcher attempts to avert this outcome by designing a different version of the same test, the problem then becomes whether the two tests are similar enough!

One of the biggest methodological drawbacks of longitudinal research is the possibility of an **age-history confound**. Suppose a researcher began a twenty-year longitudinal study in 1970 and found that individuals' gender-role beliefs became less stereotyped as the years progressed; that is, participants were less likely to believe that females are dependent, passive, and emotional and males are independent, aggressive, and logical. Are these shifts in attitude associated with development? Or did some historical factor, such as the "women's movement," bring about the changes in beliefs? Because participants age as cultural and historical events occur, it is often difficult to decide which factor affects the results of a longitudinal study. Moreover, consider a twenty-year longitudinal study begun in the 1940s versus a similar study begun in the 1990s. Many of the factors that are likely to influence children's development today—television, day care, and computers, to name a few—probably would not have been included in studies begun five decades ago.

Despite all these difficulties, the longitudinal approach has distinct advantages no other research tactic offers; in fact, certain research questions in child development can *only* be answered longitudinally. If a researcher is interested in identifying the *stability* of human characteristics—that is, how likely it is that early attributes will be maintained later in development—the longitudinal approach is the method of choice. Only by observing the same person over time can we answer such questions as "Do passive infants become shy adults?" or "Do early experiences with peers affect the child's ability to form friendships in adolescence?" For researchers interested in understanding the process of development and the factors that precede and follow specific developmental phenomena, particularly with respect to individual differences, the longitudinal strategy remains a powerful one.

The Cross-Sectional Study   Possibly the most widely used strategy for studying developmental differences is the **cross-sectional study,** in which children of varying ages are examined at the same point in time. Cross-sectional studies take less time to complete and are usually more economical than longitudinal studies.

A good example of cross-sectional research is the investigation of children's responses to repeated questions about a past event conducted by William Cassel and his colleagues (Cassel, Roebers, & Bjorkland, 1996). Children from kindergarten, second, and fourth grades, as well as adults, watched a video of two children fighting over a bicycle. One week later, participants were asked to recall what they saw. In one portion of the experiment, they were also asked two increasingly misleading questions about the videotaped episode. Figure 2.5 shows the results: kindergartners gave significantly more incorrect responses to the misleading questions compared to the other age groups.

The cross-sectional approach allowed the researchers to make a rapid assessment of the children's performance without waiting for them to grow several years older. They were, however, unable to draw conclusions about individual children and about how characteristics observable at one age might be related to characteristics at another age. Would the children who were most resistant to misleading suggestions also resist those suggestions years later? The cross-sectional approach does not provide answers to these kinds of questions. Most cross-sectional studies involve pooling the scores of individual participants such that the average performance of an entire group of children of a specified age is reported; the average scores of two or more groups of children are then compared. The result is that information about individuals is not the focus of data analysis in this type of study.

age-history confound   In longitudinal studies, the co-occurrence of historical factors with changes in age; affects the ability to interpret results.

cross-sectional study   Study in which individuals of different ages are examined at the same point in time.

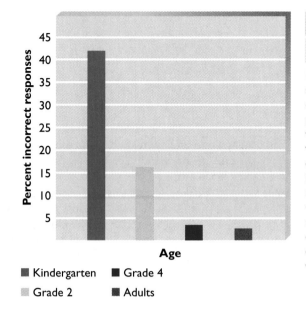

FIGURE 2.5

A Cross-Sectional Study

In this example of a cross-sectional study, children of different ages were asked progressively misleading questions about a video clip they watched. Kindergarten children made significantly more incorrect responses to such repeated misleading questions. Cross-sectional studies allow researchers to examine age differences in performance quickly and efficiently.

■ Kindergarten ■ Grade 4
□ Grade 2   ■ Adults

Source: Data from Cassel, Roebers, & Bjorkland, 1996.

Another difficulty with cross-sectional designs is that cohort effects may interfere with our ability to draw clear conclusions. **Cohort effects** are all the characteristics shared by children growing up in a specific social and historical context. For example, many of today's five-year-olds have had extensive peer experience through their enrollment in day care and other preschool programs, whereas many fifteen-year-olds probably have not. A researcher comparing the two groups might mistakenly conclude that younger children are more sociable than older children, but the differential exposure to agemates early in life—that is, the cohort effect—may be responsible for the findings rather than changes in sociability with age. Cross-sectional studies are a quick means of providing descriptions of age changes in all sorts of behaviors. Where they sometimes fall short is in helping us to understand the processes underlying those age-related changes.

The Sequential Study   One way to combine the advantages of both the longitudinal and cross-sectional approaches is the **sequential study,** in which groups of children of different ages are followed repeatedly but for only a few years. For example, a research group wanted to study age changes in patterns of television viewing of the educational program "Sesame Street" (Pinon, Huston, & Wright, 1989). Two groups of children—a group of three-year-olds and a group of five-year-olds—were followed for a period of two years. During specified weeks within this two-year period, families kept diaries of the children's television viewing. At the same time, the researchers wanted to examine the relationship between a number of family characteristics, such as parental education and maternal employment, and children's tendency to watch "Sesame Street."

Fig. 2.6 shows that children's viewing of "Sesame Street" peaked at about age three-and-a-half or four and then declined. These researchers also found that age-related events in the children's lives were associated with the declines after age four. For example, as children entered preschools or kindergartens, they tended to watch less television. Similarly, as mothers returned to work and sent their children to child care, children's viewing decreased. The benefit of the sequential design was that it allowed information about a four-year age span to be obtained in two years. Information about the stability of television viewing for individual children was available, just as it would have been in a longitudinal study. At the same time, the researchers halved the amount of time it took to find out about children's viewing tendencies

cohort effects Characteristics shared by individuals growing up in a given sociohistorical context that can influence developmental outcomes.

sequential study Study that examines groups of children of different ages over a period of time; usually shorter than a longitudinal study.

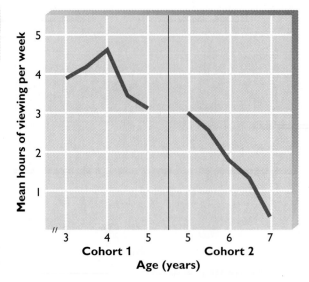

Source: Adapted from Pinon, Huston, & Wright, 1989.

FIGURE 2.6

A Sequential Study

Age differences in behavior patterns over time can be assessed with sequential studies. In one such study, television viewing of "Sesame Street" by two age groups, a group of three-year-olds (Cohort 1) and a group of five-year-olds (Cohort 2), was recorded over a period of two years, thus giving information about ages three through seven. As the graph shows, children's interest in this show peaked around age four, then declined over the next several years. The sequential approach combines the advantages of the longitudinal and cross-sectional approaches.

from ages three through seven. Although most developmental researchers still prefer to conduct cross-sectional studies because of their expediency, the sequential study provides a convenient way to reap the advantages of both cross-sectional and longitudinal approaches to studying developmental change.

Table 2.3 summarizes the relative benefits of each of the research strategies for assessing developmental change.

Cross-Cultural Studies of Development

Some of the most fundamental questions about the nature of development concern the universality of the various features of psychological growth. Do all children learn language in the same way, regardless of the specific language they acquire? Does children's thinking develop in a universal sequence? Are certain emotions common to all children regardless of attitudes about the appropriateness of crying, smiling, or feeling angry in the larger social group in which they live?

TABLE 2.3	Strategies for Assessing Developmental Change		
Approach	**Description**	**Advantages**	**Disadvantages**
Longitudinal Study	Repeated testing of the same group of children over an extended period of time.	Can examine the stability of characteristics.	Requires a significant investment of time and resources; problems with participant attrition; can have age-history confound.
Cross-Sectional Study	Comparison of children of different ages at the same point in time.	Requires less time; less costly than longitudinal study.	Cannot study individual patterns of development or the stability of traits; subject to cohort effects.
Sequential Study	Observation of children of two or more different ages over a shorter period of time than in longitudinal studies.	Combines the advantages of both longitudinal and cross-sectional approaches; can obtain information about stability of traits in a short period of time.	Has same problems as longitudinal studies, but to a lesser degree.

These Indian school girls are on a field trip to an archaeological site. Do the emotions they express in the context of learning and exploring resemble those of children from other cultures?

If psychological development does display universal features, this circumstance has far-reaching implications. It could imply, for a start, that a child's behavior is largely shaped by biological factors and, more specifically, by the genes that govern the unfolding of some human behaviors. Variations in aspects of psychological development across cultures, on the other hand, imply that the differences in the child's experiences weigh heavily in bringing about those behaviors. **Cross-cultural studies,** which compare children from different cultural groups on one or more behaviors or pattern of abilities, can be extremely useful in answering questions such as these.

Take, for example, a reported finding about infants' linguistic behaviors. Among young infants in the United States, it has been found that females vocalize more than males under age one year (Lewis, 1969; Lewis & Freedle, 1973). Particularly because this sex difference appears so early in life, it might be tempting to conclude that females are biologically predisposed toward strong verbal skills. Yet a study of Greek infants has demonstrated that male infants show greater vocal responsiveness to their mothers than females do (Roe et al., 1985). This one finding alone casts doubt on a biological explanation of sex differences in vocalization.

Cross-cultural studies can present unique challenges to the researcher. If children from two cultural backgrounds are being compared, the researcher must make sure the tasks are well understood and have equivalent forms despite differences in language or the kinds of activities the children are used to doing. For example, children in some cultures may never have seen a photograph or a two-dimensional drawing. Asking these children to categorize objects in pictorial form may place them at an unfair disadvantage if they are to be compared with children who have extensive experience with two-dimensional representations. Moreover, if the researcher is an outsider to the cultural group being observed, he or she may provoke atypical reactions from the individuals under study. Parent-child interactions, peer play, and many other behaviors may not occur as they would in the natural course of events because of the presence of an outside observer. Cross-cultural researchers must thus pay special attention to the possibility of participant reactivity.

These problems aside, cross-cultural studies can provide important insights into almost all aspects of child development. For this reason, we will draw on available cross-cultural work as we discuss each aspect of the growth of children.

cross-cultural study   Study that compares individuals in different cultural contexts.

ETHICAL ISSUES IN DEVELOPMENTAL RESEARCH

All psychologists are bound by professional ethics to treat the participants under study humanely and fairly. In general, researchers try to minimize the risk of any physical or emotional harm that might come to participants from taking part in research and to maximize the benefits that will accrue from the findings of their work. The American Psychological Association has drawn up the following specific guidelines for the use of human participants. First, participants must give **informed consent** before participating in a research project; that is, they must be told the purposes of the study and informed of any potential risks to their well-being, and then they must formally agree to participate. Second, participants have the right to decline to participate or to stop participation, even in the middle of the experiment. Third, if participants cannot be told the true purpose of the experiment (sometimes knowing the experimenter's objective will influence how participants behave), they must be debriefed at the conclusion of the study. When participants are **debriefed,** they are told the true objective of the study and the reasons for any deception on the part of the experimenter. Finally, data collected from participants must be kept confidential. To ensure that experimenters comply with these guidelines, most research institutions have review boards that evaluate any potential risks to participants and the researchers' compliance with ethical practice.

The same ethical guidelines apply to using children as participants in research, but frequently the implementation of these guidelines becomes a difficult matter. Who provides informed consent in the case of an infant or a young toddler, for example? (The parents do.) Is it proper to deceive children about the purposes of a study if they cannot understand the debriefing? (In general, it is a good idea to avoid any kind of deception with children, such as telling them you are interested in how quickly they learn a game when you are really interested in whether they will be altruistic with their play partner.) Are some subjects of study taboo, such as asking children about their concepts of death, suicide, or other frightening topics that might affect them emotionally? (Such studies, if conducted, must be planned very carefully and conducted only by trained professionals.) What about cases in which treatments are suspected to have beneficial outcomes for children? Can the control group properly have the treatment withheld? For example, if we suspect that children's participation in an early intervention preschool program will have real benefits for them, should children in the control group be kept out of it? (One solution to this thorny problem is to offer the control group the beneficial treatment as soon as possible after the conclusion of the study, although this is not always a satisfactory compromise. The control group still has to wait for a beneficial treatment or intervention.)

Many researchers assume that children's vulnerability to risk as they participate in psychological experiments decreases as they grow older. Because infants and young children have more limited cognitive skills and emotional coping strategies, they are viewed as less able to protect themselves and their rights during participation in research. This assumption certainly has some logical basis. Some types of research, however, may actually pose a greater threat to older children. As Ross Thompson (1990) has pointed out, older children are developing a self-concept and a more elaborate understanding of the ways others evaluate them. Older children may thus be more susceptible to psychological harm than younger children when the researcher compares their performance with that of others or when they think teachers or parents may learn about their performance. In addition, older children may be more sensitive to research results that reflect negatively on their families or sociocultural groups. These situations require awareness on the part of the researcher of the subtle ways children can be adversely affected by the research enterprise.

Table 2.4 sets forth the ethical guidelines on using children as participants in research established by the Society for Research in Child Development (1996). Probably the overriding guiding principle is that children should not be subjected to any physical or mental harm and should be treated with all possible respect. In fact, be-

informed consent Participant's formal acknowledgment that he or she understands the purposes, procedures, and risks of a study and agrees to participate in it.

debriefing Providing research participants with a statement of the true goals of a study after initially deceiving them about its purposes.

TABLE 2.4	Ethical Guidelines in Conducting Research with Children

■ *Nonharmful procedures:* The investigator may not use any procedures that could impose physical or psychological harm on the child. In addition, the investigator should use the least stressful research operation whenever possible. If the investigator is in doubt about the possible harmful effects of the research, he or she should consult with others. If the child will be unavoidably exposed to stress in research that might provide some diagnostic or therapeutic benefits to the child, the study should be reviewed by an institutional review board.

■ *Informed consent:* The investigator should inform the child of all features of the research that might affect his or her willingness to participate and should answer all questions in a way the child can comprehend. The child has the right to discontinue participation at any time.

■ *Parental consent:* Informed consent should be obtained in writing from the child's parents or from other adults who have responsibility for the child. The adult has the right to know all features of the research that might affect the child's willingness to participate and can refuse consent.

■ *Deception:* If the research necessitates concealment or deception about the nature of the study, the investigator should make sure the child understands the reasons for the deception after the study is concluded.

■ *Confidentiality:* All information about participants in research must be kept confidential.

■ *Jeopardy:* If, during research, the investigator learns of information concerning a jeopardy to the child's well-being, the investigator must discuss the information with the parents or guardians and experts to arrange for assistance to the child.

■ *Informing participants:* The investigator should clarify any misconceptions that may have arisen on the part of the child during the study. The investigator should also report general findings to participants in terms they can understand.

Source: Adapted from the ethical standards set by the Society for Research in Child Development, 1996.

cause children are frequently unable to voice their concerns and have less power than adults do, developmental researchers must be especially sensitive to their comfort and well-being.

Researchers often study issues that are sensitive but can have important consequences for the well-being of children. For example, a researcher might be interested in finding out the factors that predict the emergence of eating disorders in adolescents or the consequences of parental drug abuse for the child. Both studies would probably involve a longitudinal method in

CONTROVERSY: THINKING IT OVER

Should Researchers Reveal Information They Learn About Participants in Their Studies?

which participants are followed over a period of months or even years. Celia Fisher (1994) points out, though, that research that can be very illuminating about the nature of childhood problems often raises difficult ethical dilemmas. Suppose the researcher discovers a particular child has a serious eating disorder or that a young child has ingested harmful illegal drugs kept by parents in the home. Ethical guidelines state that researchers who discover that a child is at risk must take steps to make sure the child obtains appropriate assistance. However, as a consequence, the child may drop out of the study to receive some form of treatment or intervention. If that happens for several of the children, the opportunity to complete the research project could be lost, along with the potential benefits of the results of the research project for a larger group of children.

What are the ethical obligations of the researcher in such situations? Should the concerns about the welfare of individual children override any potential benefits of the research for children in general? Moreover, what should be done about the issue of confidentiality in cases like these? Should the identities of children with serious problems be revealed to parents, school personnel, or others responsible for their well-being? Does the age of the child matter in such decisions? That is, should these decisions be handled differently for adolescents than for younger children?

CHAPTER RECAP

SUMMARY OF TOPICS

Like other scientists, developmental psychologists are concerned with using sound methodologies to glean information about children. Research is used to test theories, but also to gather information that can have significant applications for children.

■ THE SCIENTIFIC STUDY OF THE CHILD: HISTORICAL PERSPECTIVES

Attitudes toward children have changed in society over the centuries. During medieval times, children were quickly incorporated into the adult world, although their vulnerability was also recognized. Philosophers such as John Locke and Jean Jacques Rousseau contributed to a growing interest in the nature of childhood during the seventeenth and eighteenth centuries. The systematic study of children began with the baby biographers of the nineteenth century, who made extensive observations of individual children. At the beginning of the twentieth century, G. Stanley Hall introduced the questionnaire method for studying large groups of children and Alfred Binet led the movement to study *individual differences* in children's behavior and abilities. Theorists such as James Mark Baldwin formulated hypotheses about the nature of the child. Much of the early empirical work in developmental psychology focused on establishing norms of behavior. Today research in developmental psychology is guided by a rich array of theoretical, empirical, and applied questions.

■ RESEARCH METHODS IN DEVELOPMENTAL PSYCHOLOGY

Researchers can choose from a number of specific techniques for gathering data about children. *Naturalistic observations* involve the systematic recording of behaviors as they occur in children's everyday environments. *Structured observations,* usu-

ally conducted in the laboratory, allow the experimenter more control over the situations that accompany children's behaviors. Researchers can employ *interviews* or *questionnaires* if they are interested in children's own reports of what they know or how they behave. Finally, *meta-analytic studies* permit investigators to analyze the results of a large body of published research to draw general conclusions about behavior.

Three basic research designs are employed in psychological research. In the *correlational design,* the investigator attempts to see whether changes in one variable are accompanied by systematic changes in another variable. However, correlations between variables do not prove cause-and-effect relationships. In the *experimental design,* the researcher manipulates one or more independent variables to see if they have an effect on the dependent variable. In the *single-case design,* the researcher intensively studies one or a few individuals over a period of time. Each of these designs offers advantages and disadvantages, with the researcher's choice dictated by the specific questions to be answered as well as the types of resources available.

There are three strategies for assessing developmental change. *Longitudinal studies* test the same participants repeatedly over an extended period of time. *Cross-sectional studies* examine participants of different ages at the same time. *Sequential studies* examine children of two or more ages over a period of time, usually shorter than that used in longitudinal studies. *Cross-cultural studies* have a special place in developmental psychology because they often address questions of the universality of human behaviors.

■ ETHICAL ISSUES IN DEVELOPMENTAL RESEARCH

One last important consideration for the researcher is the ethical dimension of conducting studies with children. Children, like all human participants, must be treated with fairness and dignity and must be protected from harm.

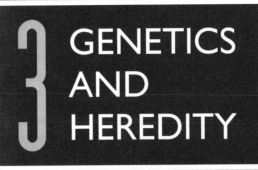

3 GENETICS AND HEREDITY

NATURE/NURTURE
What roles do nature and nurture play in development?

CHILD'S ACTIVE ROLE
How does the child play an active role in the effects of heredity on development?

INDIVIDUAL DIFFERENCES
How prominent are individual differences in development?

" He was shy. He's always been shy, ever since he was a baby. I remember those first weeks at the day care center, how Jeremy clung to me, clutched my hand, even grabbed my leg whenever I started to walk toward a group of children. The teacher said he would get over being so timid. But when I came to visit, Jeremy would be off to the side watching what everyone else was doing; he was hardly ever in the center of a group. Every time I saw him like that, it reminded me of myself in grade school. The other kids talked with each other, shared things so easily, always seemed so popular. I guess Jeremy just takes after me. No matter how I try to encourage him, he hangs back from the rest of the group just like I did."

Jeremy's mother paused. "Cindy is so different. She is usually the center of attention, never bashful with a stranger. Her teachers often comment about Cindy's enthusiasm in class. She's one of the first to raise her hand, answer a question, volunteer to lead the group in some kind of activity. She has all of her father's warmth and charm. It comes so naturally to the two of them!"

Parents often describe their children in ways such as this, but what precisely are the mechanisms by which we "take after" our parents? Can we inherit aspects of personality such as being shy or outgoing? Though we may readily grant the contribution of nature to eye color, gender, height, and many other physical traits, heredity's role in whether we are complacent or quick tempered, prone to alcoholism, likely to suffer depression, bright and quick-witted, reserved or sociable continues to provoke controversy. Yet, as Sandra Scarr, a leading researcher in behavioral genetics, has stated, "Parents of two or more children know perfectly well that their children are different for reasons that have nothing to do with their training regimens" (1987, p. 227).

In Chapter 1, we noted how theories often differ concerning the roles of nature and nurture in various domains of development. The disagreements persist today. In this chapter, we more closely examine hereditary contributions to development. Major advances in our understanding of the basic biological units of inheritance and their effects on behavior help us to better appreciate the mutual, interactive relationship between nature and nurture. Experiences mold, modify, and enhance biological predispositions, and in a similar manner, genetic endowment influences, perhaps even actively promotes, selection and preference for certain kinds of environments. Our goal is to understand just how such complex interactions evolve.

We will begin with a brief overview of the principles of heredity. The blueprint for human development is replicated in nearly every cell of our body. This blueprint includes genetic instructions that distinguish us from other species of plants and animals. Regardless of the language we speak, the work we do, the color of our skin, or how friendly we are, we share a genetic underpinning that makes us distinctly human. But this biological inheritance also contributes to our individuality. All of us, with the exception of identical twins, begin with a set of genetic instructions that, when combined with various experiences, ensures that each of us is unique, different from everyone else, even though we belong to the same species. Imagine the monotony of a world populated by only one kind of person! Biologists emphasize that genetic diversity is important for another reason: it helps to ensure the survival of our species.

In this chapter, we also examine several examples of hereditary anomalies and diseases that pose problems for development. As researchers have come to learn more about the ways in which genetic variation occurs, we have begun to design environments to help minimize the restrictions individuals may inherit. We consider too how genetic counseling assists parents in deciding whether to have children.

Most psychological development, of course, cannot be linked to simple genetic instructions. Intelligence, temperament, and personality, along with several kinds of mental conditions, are the outcome of complex interactions between genetic and environmental events. In the final section of this chapter, we consider research involving identical and fraternal twins, siblings, adopted children, and other family relationships to help us understand the complex tapestry genetic and environmental factors weave for cognitive, social-emotional, and personality development. In the past, researchers often attempted to determine how much nature and nurture, respectively, contribute to development. But understanding how these factors influence each other ultimately will yield far greater insights concerning behavior and the process of human development (Plomin & McClearn, 1993; Wachs, 1992).

PRINCIPLES OF HEREDITARY TRANSMISSION

Whether we have freckles, blonde hair, or a certain type of personality can be influenced by genetic factors, but none of these characteristics is bestowed on us at conception any more directly than our ultimate height is. We must make a distinction, then, between what is supplied as our genetic makeup and the kinds of individuals we eventually become. That difference serves as the basis for distinguishing between **genotype,** a person's constant, inherited genetic endowment, and **phenotype,** an individual's observable, measurable features, characteristics, and behaviors. A given phenotype is the product of complex interactions involving the genotype and the many events that comprise an individual's *experience.*

Modern theories of the genotype can be traced to a series of experiments reported in 1866 by Gregor Mendel, an Austrian monk. From his observations of the characteristics of generations of peas, Mendel theorized that hereditary characteristics are determined by pairs of particles called *factors* (later termed **genes,** the specialized sequences of molecules that form the genotype). He also proposed that the information provided by the two members of a pair of genes is not always identical. These different forms of a gene are today known as **alleles.** The terms *gene* and *allele* are often used interchangeably, but an allele refers to the specific variation (and sometimes many possible variations exist) a particular gene can take. Since differences may exist between the allelic forms of the gene pair, the information carried by one member of the pair can dominate or mask the information carried by the other member. Or the information may interact so that the phenotype reflects the combined influence of both alleles.

Mendel also outlined the basic principle by which genes are transferred from one generation to another. He concluded that offspring randomly receive one member of every pair of genes from the mother and one from the father. This is possible because the parents' **gametes,** or sex cells (egg and sperm), carry only one member of each pair of genes. Thus, when egg and sperm combine during fertilization, a new pair of

KEY THEME
Nature/Nurture

genotype Total genetic endowment inherited by an individual.

phenotype Observable and measurable characteristics and traits of an individual; a product of the interaction of the genotype with the environment.

gene Large segment of nucleotides within a chromosome that codes for the production of proteins and enzymes. These proteins and enzymes underlie traits and characteristics inherited from one generation to the next.

allele Alternate form of a specific gene; provides a genetic basis for many individual differences.

gametes Sperm cells in males, egg cells in females, normally containing only twenty-three chromosomes.

genes, one inherited from each parent, is reestablished in the offspring. That individual, in turn, may transmit either member of this new pair to subsequent children. In this way, a given genotype can be passed on from one generation to the next.

At about the same time Mendel's research was published, biologists discovered **chromosomes,** long, threadlike structures in the nucleus of nearly every cell in the body. In the early 1900s, several researchers independently hypothesized that genes are located on chromosomes. Yet another major breakthrough occurred in 1953 when James Watson and Francis Crick deciphered the structure of chromosomes and, in so doing, proposed a powerfully elegant way by which genes are duplicated during cell division. By 1956, researchers had documented the existence of forty-six chromosomes in normal human body cells. Research being conducted in the present decade is well on the way to mapping the entire **human genome,** the set of genes and sequencing of complex molecules that make up the genetic information contained in all forty-six chromosomes (Guyer & Collins, 1993).

The Building Blocks of Heredity

How could hereditary factors play a part in Jeremy's shyness and Cindy's friendliness, or in a child's remarkable mathematical ability or yet another's mental retardation? To understand the genotype and its effects on appearance, behavior, personality, or intellectual ability, we must consider genetic mechanisms at many different levels.

To begin with, every living organism is composed of cells—in the case of mature humans, trillions of cells. As Figure 3.1 indicates, within the nucleus of nearly all cells are the chromosomes that carry genetic information critical to their functioning. Genes, regions within the strands of chromosomes, determine the production of enzymes and specific proteins in the cell. The genes, in turn, are made up of various arrangements of four different chemical building blocks called **nucleotides** that contain one of four nitrogen-based molecules (*adenine, thymine, cytosine,* or *guanine*). The nucleotides link together in one of only two kinds of pairings to form the rungs of a remarkably long, spiral, ladderlike structure called **DNA** or **deoxyribonucleic acid** (see Figure 3.1). An average of about a thousand nucleotide pairs make up each gene, although some genes have substantially more pairings (National Research Council, 1988). Specific genes differ from one another in number and sequence of nucleotide pairings and in their location on the chemical spiral staircases, or chains of DNA that we call the chromosomes.

Just as Mendel had theorized, hereditary attributes are influenced by pairs of genes or, more specifically, the two allelic forms of the pair. One member of the pair is located on a chromosome inherited from the mother, the other on a chromosome inherited from the father. These two chromosomes are called *homologous* (similar). Human beings have twenty-three homologous pairs, or a total of forty-six chromosomes.

Figure 3.2 shows a **karyotype** or photomicrograph of these twenty-three pairs. They are numbered from 1 to 22 in the case of the **autosomes,** those pairs of homologous chromosomes that are distinguished from the remaining two chromosomes, which genetically determine sex. The two members of this twenty-third pair in females, called **X chromosomes,** are relatively large and similar in size and shape. But for males, the two members of this pair are quite different. The normal male has one X chromosome and one much smaller **Y chromosome,** a chain of DNA believed to carry far less genetic information. Nevertheless, the Y chromosome has a major function in promoting the development of the male *gonads* (testes) and, consequently, in helping to determine whether an individual will become male rather than female.

Cell Division and Chromosome Duplication

Each child begins life as a single cell created when a sperm cell, normally containing twenty-three chromosomes, from the father unites with an ovum (egg), normally containing an additional twenty-three chromosomes, from the mother. This fertilized egg cell is called a **zygote.** The developmental processes started by this union are

---

chromosomes Threadlike structures of DNA, located in the nucleus of cells, that form a collection of genes. A human body cell normally contains forty-six chromosomes.

human genome Entire inventory of nucleotide base pairs comprising the genes and chromosomes of humans.

nucleotide Repeating basic building block of DNA consisting of nitrogen-based molecules of adenine, thymine, cytosine, and guanine.

deoxyribonucleic acid (DNA) Long, spiral staircase–like sequence of molecules created by nucleotides identified with the blueprint for genetic inheritance.

karyotype Pictorial representation of an individual's chromosomes.

autosomes Twenty-two pairs of homologous chromosomes. The two members of each pair are similar in size, shape, and genetic function. The two sex chromosomes are excluded from this class.

X chromosome Larger of the two sex chromosomes associated with genetic determination of sex. Normally females have two X chromosomes and males only one.

Y chromosome Smaller of the two sex chromosomes associated with genetic determination of sex. Normally males have one Y chromosome and females none.

zygote Fertilized egg cell.

FIGURE 3.1   The Building Blocks of Heredity

Hereditary contributions to development can be observed at many levels. This figure depicts five major levels. Nearly every cell in the human body carries the genetic blueprint for development in the chromosomes. Specific regions on each chromosome, the genes, regulate protein and enzyme production and can be further examined in terms of the nucleotides, chemical molecules that are the building blocks for the genes. Each of these different levels of the individual's biological makeup can offer insights into the mechanisms by which the genotype affects the phenotype, the observable expression of traits and behaviors.

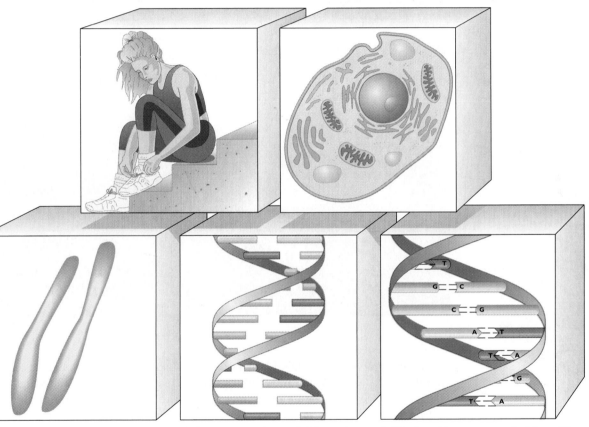

1. The **human body** has about 10 trillion cells. Proteins determine the structure and function of each cell.

2. Most **cells** contain a nucleus. Located within the nucleus are 46 chromosomes which carry the instructions that permit the cell to manufacture various proteins and enzymes.

3. A **chromosome** is a long thin strand of DNA organized as a coiled double helix. A full set of 46 chromosomes contains about 100,000 genes.

4. A **gene** is made up of thousands of nucleotide pairs. Each gene typically has enough information to specify the production of a particular protein.

5. **Nucleotides**, composed of four different kinds of chemical building blocks—adenine (A), thymine (T), cytosine (C), and guanine (G)—are the smallest genetic unit and are paired in specific combinations. A project is now under way to map and sequence the estimated 3 billion pairs of nucleotides that make up the total complement of genes and chromosomes.

Source: Adapted from Isensee, 1986.

more fully described in Chapter 4. Remarkably, however, nearly every one of the millions of different cells in the newborn, whether specialized for bone or skin, heart or brain, or in some other way, contains the same genetic blueprint established in the initial zygote.

How does this extraordinary duplication of DNA from one cell to another and from one generation to the next take place? The division process for most cells is called **mitosis**. During mitosis, genetic material in the nucleus is reproduced such

mitosis Process of cell division that takes place in most cells of the human body and results in a full complement of identical material in the forty-six chromosomes in each cell.

FIGURE 3.2

Chromosomes in the Normal Human Male

This karotype depicts the twenty-two homologous pairs of autosomes and the two sex chromosomes in the normal human male. In females, the twenty-third pair of chromosomes consists of an XX pair instead of an XY pair.

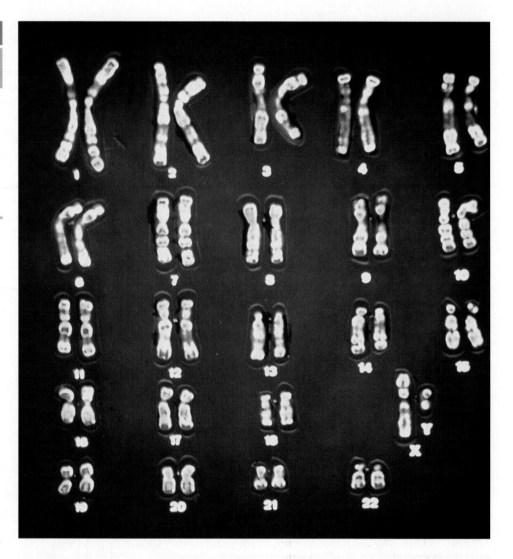

meiosis   Process of cell division that forms the gametes; normally results in twenty-three chromosomes in each human egg and sperm cell rather than the full complement of forty-six chromosomes.

that a full complement of DNA becomes available to each new cell. Before cell division occurs, the chemical bonds linking the nucleotides that form the rungs of the DNA ladder weaken. The joined pairs of nucleotides separate as though they were being unzipped from each other. While this process is taking place, additional nucleotides are manufactured in the cell to become attached to the separated nucleotides. Because each nucleotide can combine with only one other type, the two newly formed strands of DNA are rebuilt exactly as in their original sequence. These two copies of DNA eventually separate completely so that one becomes a member of each of the two new daughter cells, as depicted in Figure 3.3.

The process of cell division associated with the gametes (the sex cells) is called **meiosis**. Meiosis, which results in twenty-three chromosomes in the egg and sperm cells, actually involves *two* successive generations of cell divisions. In the first stage, each of the forty-six chromosomes begins to replicate. However, before the identical replicas split apart, the cell divides and each daughter cell receives only one chromosome from each of the twenty-three pairs, as pictured in Figure 3.4. In the second stage, the replicas of the twenty-three chromosomes split apart and the cell divides once more, each cell again receiving one of the replicas. Thus, from these two successive divisions, four cells are produced, each with twenty-three chromosomes. Figure 3.4 illustrates the process of meiosis for sperm cells.

Random segregation of the twenty-three homologous chromosome pairs in the first stage of meiosis yields more than 8 million possible combinations of gametes with one or more different sets of chromosomes. Along with an equivalent number of possible unique arrangements from a mate, mother and father together have a

FIGURE 3.3	The Process of Mitosis

The process of mitotic cell division generates nearly all the cells of the body except the gametes. During mitosis, each chromosome replicates to form two chromosomes with identical genetic blueprints. As the cell divides, one member of each identical pair becomes a member of each daughter cell. In this manner, complete genetic endowment is replicated in nearly every cell of the body.

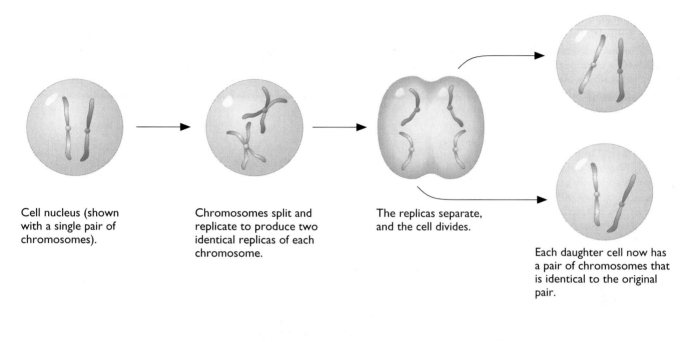

Cell nucleus (shown with a single pair of chromosomes).

Chromosomes split and replicate to produce two identical replicas of each chromosome.

The replicas separate, and the cell divides.

Each daughter cell now has a pair of chromosomes that is identical to the original pair.

FIGURE 3.4	The Process of Meiosis for Sperm Cells

As meiosis begins (a), DNA replicates as in mitotic cell division. However, before the replicated arms split apart, one member of each pair of homologous chromosomes moves to become part of each first-generation daughter cell (b). Once the first generation of daughter cells is established, DNA replicas split as part of the second meiotic division (c). Thus, one replica of one member of the pair of homologous chromosomes is contributed to each second-generation daughter cell (d). From these two successive divisions, four cells, each with twenty-three chromosomes, are produced.

Cell with 46 chromosomes (only one pair of homologous chromosomes is shown here). Each member of the pair has begun to replicate similar to mitotic cell division.

First meiotic cell division begins but does not proceed as in mitosis. Instead of the replicated chromosome splitting apart, one member of each homologous pair becomes a part of the first-generation daughter cell.

The second meiotic division proceeds after the first is completed; now the replicated chromosome acquired in the first-generation daughter cell splits apart.

Each of the four gametes produced by the two-step process now has acquired one member of the pair of homologous chromosomes.

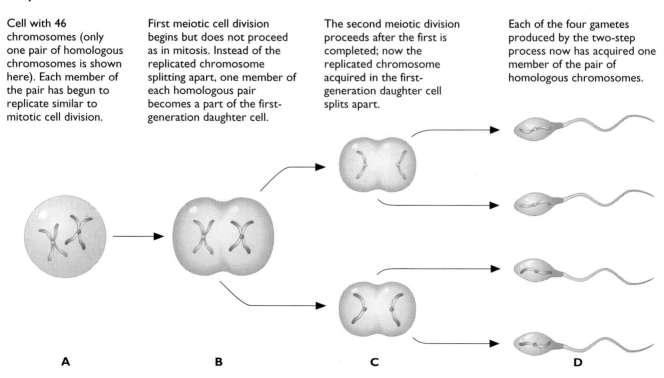

A   B   C   D

Crossing Over: The Exchange of Genetic Material Between Chromosomes

In the process known as cross-ing over, genetic material is ex-changed between homologous pairs of chromosomes during the first stage of meiotic cell division. (a) Initially, autosomes that have begun DNA replica-tion align with each other. (b) Genetic material between homologous chromosomes is exchanged. (c) One member of each homologous pair of chro-mosomes randomly segregates or relocates to two different regions of the parent cell, and the first generation of cell divi-sion in meiosis takes place.

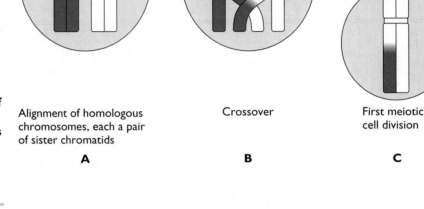

Alignment of homologous chromosomes, each a pair of sister chromatids

A

Crossover

B

First meiotic cell division

C

KEY THEME
Individual Differences

KEY THEME
Nature/Nurture

crossing over   Process during the first stage of meiosis when genetic material is exchanged between autosomes.

homozygous   Genotype in which two alleles of a gene are identical, thus having the same effects on a trait.

heterozygous   Genotype in which two alleles of a gene are different. The effects on a trait will depend on how the two alleles interact.

dominant allele   Allele whose characteristics are reflected in the phenotype even when part of a heterozygous genotype. Its genetic characteristics tend to mask the characteristics of other alleles.

gene pool of about 64 trillion different combinations from which their offspring may derive. But the potential for genetic variability is actually far greater because of the phenomenon known as **crossing over,** a key part of the first stage of meiosis. Before homologous chromosome pairs separate in the first cell division, they mysteriously align, and segments of DNA transfer, or cross over, from one member to the other member of the pair (Guyer & Collins, 1993), as shown in Figure 3.5. As a result of the genetic variability ensured by crossing over, it is virtually impossible for two individ-uals to have the same genetic makeup, even siblings, unless the two are identical twins.

Gene Expression

We have briefly described key structures of inheritance—nucleotides, genes, and chromosomes—and the way these are replicated in cells of the body, including gametes. But how does the genotype affect the phenotype? That is, how does the un-derlying genetic blueprint promote the appearance of blue eyes, baldness, and dark skin or such complex traits as shyness, schizophrenia, and intelligent problem solv-ing? The answer begins with the alleles, the alternative forms a particular gene may take. The presence of different allelic forms of a gene, then, form the hereditary foun-dation for individual differences such as whether hair will be curly or straight or eyes will be blue, brown, or hazel.

We have already learned that each of us typically inherits two genes that code for a particular enzyme or protein in the cell, one from our mother and the other from our father. These may be identical—that is, have the same allelic form—or they may differ. When both have the same allelic form, a person's genotype is said to be **homozygous** for whatever characteristic that gene affects. For example, three differ-ent alleles exist for the gene that governs blood type: A, B, and O. When both inher-ited alleles are A, both B, or both O, a person has a homozygous genotype for blood type. But if an individual inherits two different alleles of the gene for blood type, let's say A and B, that person's genotype is **heterozygous;** he or she has Type AB blood.

The consequences of a homozygous genotype are usually straightforward: the child's phenotype will be influenced by whatever characteristics are specified by that particular allelic form. But the effects of a heterozygous genotype depend on how the alleles influence each other. When a child's phenotype shows the effects of only one of the two allelic forms, the one whose characteristics are observed is considered to be **dominant;** the allelic form whose influence is not evident in the phenotype is con-

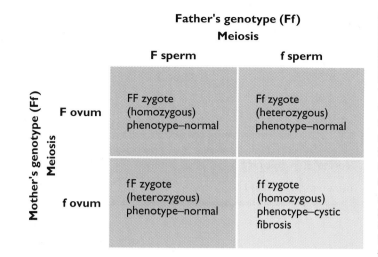

Father's genotype (Ff)
Meiosis

	F sperm	f sperm
F ovum	FF zygote (homozygous) phenotype–normal	Ff zygote (heterozygous) phenotype–normal
f ovum	fF zygote (heterozygous) phenotype–normal	ff zygote (homozygous) phenotype–cystic fibrosis

Mother's genotype (Ff) Meiosis

FIGURE 3.6

The Pattern of Inheritance for Cystic Fibrosis

The inheritance of cystic fibrosis is one of many traits and diseases that are influenced by a single pair of genes. In this figure, F symbolizes a normal allele and f represents the allele for cystic fibrosis. When parents with a heterozygous genotype for this disease have children, their offspring may inherit a homozygous genotype with normal alleles (FF), a heterozygous genotype with one normal and one abnormal allele (Ff or fF), or a homozygous genotype with two abnormal alleles (ff). Because the normal allele dominates, children with a heterozygous genotype will not exhibit cystic fibrosis. When both alleles carry genetic information for the disease, however, cystic fibrosis will occur.

KEY THEME
Individual Differences

sidered to be **recessive**. For example, a person who inherits both an A and an O allele for blood type will still be classified as having Type A; the allele for Type A is dominant and the allele for Type O recessive.

Cystic fibrosis, a leading cause of childhood death among Caucasian children, provides another example of a dominant-recessive relationship between alleles. The vast majority of Caucasian children inherit a gene pair that does not include the allelic form that codes for cystic fibrosis; they have a homozygous genotype that contributes to a normal phenotype. About one in twenty-five people of Caucasian ancestry, however, has a heterozygous genotype in which one gene is normal and the other abnormal in that it carries the genetic information that results in cystic fibrosis. The normal allele is *dominant.* Thus, someone who is heterozygous for this condition can lead an ordinary, productive life. But a child of a mother and father, each of whom has a heterozygous genotype, may inherit two normal alleles, inherit both a normal and an abnormal allele, or inherit two abnormal alleles for cystic fibrosis (see Figure 3.6). In the latter homozygous condition, the two recessive abnormal alleles are no longer masked by a normal gene; this child (about 1 in every 2,500 Caucasian children) will suffer from cystic fibrosis. Medical researchers today are actively investigating the potential for *gene therapy,* the replacement of the gene that codes for cystic fibrosis by a normal gene, to reduce and even eliminate the devastating consequences of this inherited disorder (Welsh & Smith, 1995).

For other genes, the child's phenotype will reflect the influence of both allelic forms when they differ, either in some blended or intermediate form or in some unblended form in which elements or characteristics of both allelic forms are evident. When the characteristics of both alleles are observed in some unblended form, the alleles exhibit **codominance**. For example, a child with Type AB blood has inherited a gene for Type A blood from one parent and another gene for Type B blood from the other parent.

Table 3.1 shows a number of traits and characteristics of individuals affected by single genes exhibiting dominant-recessive patterns. But we must be cautious when drawing inferences about these dominant-recessive relationships. Many traits are **polygenic,** that is, determined by several genes, each located, perhaps, on different sets of chromosomes and with effects of varying size. No single gene may be necessary or sufficient for a particular trait. For example, even eye color, although largely governed by the dominant-recessive relationship between allelic forms of a single gene, as suggested in Table 3.1, is affected by other genes as well.

Gene Functioning and Regulation of Development

How do genes influence the development of a phenotype? Although exceptions exist, genetic information is typically conveyed from the DNA in the cell's nucleus to the organic and inorganic substances in other parts of the cell. This process is performed

recessive allele Allele whose characteristics do not tend to be expressed when part of a heterozygous genotype. Its genetic characteristics tend to be masked by other alleles.

codominance Condition in which individual, unblended characteristics of two alleles are reflected in the phenotype.

polygenic Phenotypic characteristic influenced by two or more genes.

	Dominant Traits	Recessive Traits
TABLE 3.1 Alleles of Genes That Display a Dominant and Recessive Pattern of Phenotypic Expression	Brown eyes	Gray, green, blue, hazel eyes
	Curly hair	Straight hair
	Normal hair	Baldness
	Dark hair	Light or blond hair
	Nonred hair (blond, brunette)	Red hair
	Normal skin coloring	Albinism (lack of pigment)
	Immunity to poison ivy	Susceptibility to poison ivy
	Normal skin	Xeroderma pigmentosum (heavy freckling and skin cancers)
	Thick lips	Thin lips
	Roman nose	Straight nose
	Earlobe free	Earlobe attached
	Cheek dimples	No dimples
	Extra, fused, or short digits	Normal digits
	Second toe longer than big toe	Big toe longer than second toe
	Double-jointedness	Normal joints
	Normal color vision	Red-green colorblindness
	Farsightedness	Normal vision
	Normal vision	Congenital eye cataracts
	Retinoblastoma (cancer of the eye)	Normal eye development
	Normal hearing	Congenital deafness
	Type A blood	Type O blood
	Type B Blood	Type O blood
	Rh-positive blood	Rh-negative blood
	Normal blood clotting	Hemophilia
	Normal metabolism	Phenylketonuria
	Normal blood cells	Sickle cell anemia
	Familial hypercholesterolemia (error of fat metabolism)	Normal cholesterol level at birth
	Wilms tumor (cancer of the kidney)	Normal kidney
	Huntington's disease	Normal brain and body maturation
	Normal respiratory and gastrointestinal functioning	Cystic fibrosis
	Normal neural and physical development	Tay-Sachs disease

by *ribonucleic acid,* or *RNA,* a molecule somewhat similar to DNA. RNA copies segments of the nucleotide sequences making up genes (Guyer & Collins, 1993). The message carried by the RNA initiates a series of biochemical processes that eventually produce complex enzymes or proteins to give the cell its unique ability to function. Enzymes act as catalysts, promoting additional biochemical reactions; their presence and timing are fundamental to the development and operation of all organs and systems of the human body. Thus, our appearance and our behavior are, in part, the end result of an extensive chain of biochemical processes started by the instructions initiated in the genotype.

The information conveyed by different allelic forms of a gene may cause one or more biochemical events in the chain to be modified, or disrupted (Holton, 1995). Such a disruption occurs, for example, in **phenylketonuria (PKU),** a genetic condition in which *phenylalanine,* an amino acid in milk and high-protein foods such as meat, cannot be metabolized normally. As a result, phenylalanine and other metabolic products accumulate in the blood, and the nervous system becomes deprived of needed nutrients. The eventual consequences are often convulsions, severe mental retardation, hyperactivity, and other behavioral problems. Remember, however, that a phenotype is the product of the interaction between genotype and environment. In the case of PKU, intervention in the form of reducing phenylalanine in the diet can help prevent severe mental retardation. Here, then, is an excellent example illustrating that genes do not have all the information built into them to cause particular developmental outcomes; environmental factors interact with the genotype to yield a specific phenotype.

Many mysteries remain concerning how genes influence development. For example, humans are believed to have about 100,000 *structural genes* that code for the production of different kinds of enzymes and other proteins governing the physiological functions of a cell. Yet structural genes account for only a very small percentage of the approximately 3 billion base-pairs estimated to be in the human genome (Green, Cox, & Myers, 1995; Hagerman, 1996). Some of the remaining DNA consists of another type of gene, called *regulator genes,* that start and stop the functioning of structural genes (Plomin, 1987). Regulator genes appear to be responsive to environmental signals, factors within and outside the cell itself, to determine when structural genes become activated. Vast networks of structural, regulator, and probably other kinds of genes interact, both with themselves and with their environment, to affect development.

Complex human activity is affected by many genes. How these genes influence the wide range of behaviors of interest to psychologists remains largely unknown. Nonetheless, we can identify the consequences of several specific gene mutations as well as chromosomal disturbances that have serious repercussions for development. We will now examine some of these gene and chromosomal abnormalities to further illustrate the contribution of the genotype to human development. Keep in mind that fortunately these more serious abnormalities affect a relatively small number of individuals. However, the momentous consequences for those individuals will often reverberate to affect the family and many others within a community.

GENE AND CHROMOSOMAL ABNORMALITIES

Changes in the structure of genes, or **mutations,** introduce genetic diversity among individuals. Mutations occur relatively often. Nearly half of all human conceptions have been estimated to have some kind of genetic or chromosomal error (Plomin, DeFries, & McClearn, 1990). Most of these mutations are lost through spontaneous abortion very soon after conception. A small number will have little impact on development, but others can have enduring, often negative consequences for an individual's behavior and quality of life. Even if the mutation does not have an immediate effect, it may be passed on from one generation to the next, a major way different alleles of a gene are established in populations. Still other disorders can be linked to disturbances involving the larger structural units of inheritance, the chromosomes.

Nearly 8 percent of individuals below age twenty-five have a disorder that can be linked to genetic factors (Baird et al., 1988). More than four thousand different disorders associated with specific genes, some inherited and others occurring as mutations, have been identified in humans (McKusick, 1994). Many more will likely be discovered as the human genome is mapped more completely.

KEY THEME
Nature/Nurture

KEY THEME
Individual Differences

phenylketonuria (PKU) Recessive genetic disorder in which phenylalanine, an amino acid, fails to be metabolized. Unless dietary changes are made to reduce intake of phenylalanine, severe mental retardation occurs.

mutation Sudden change in molecular structure of a gene; may occur spontaneously or be caused by an environmental event such as radiation.

Gene Disorders

An estimated 100,000 infants are born each year in the United States alone with some kind of disorder caused by a single dominant or recessive gene. For about twenty thousand of these babies, the problem is serious (Knowles, 1985). Table 3.2 lists a few of the more serious gene disorders. In most cases, the effects are evident at birth (*congenital*), but the consequences of some are not observed until childhood or even late adulthood. We will discuss several dominant and recessive disorders to illustrate their effects on development and the interventions and treatments available for them.

Disorder	Estimated Frequency (live births in U.S.)	Phenotype, Prognosis, and Prenatal Detection
Autosomal Dominant Disorders		
Huntington's Disease	1 in 10,000–12,000	See text. Gene located on chromosome 4. Prenatal detection possible.
Marfan Syndrome	1 in 10,000–20,000	Tall, lean, long limbed, with gaunt face (some believe Abraham Lincoln had syndrome). Frequent eye problems. Cardiac failure in young adulthood common. Suicide second most common cause of death. Associated with increased paternal age. Gene located on chromosome 15. Prenatal detection possible.
Neurofibromatosis (von Recklinghausen's disease)	1 in 3,500	Symptoms range from a few pale brown spots on skin to severe tumors affecting peripheral nervous system and visibly distorting appearance. Minimal intellectual deficits in about 40% of cases. Gene for major form located on chromosome 17. Gene for other form located on chromosome 22. Prenatal detection possible.
Williams Syndrome	1 in 25,000	Mental retardation, including delayed motor and language acquisition. However, individuals eventually acquire surprisingly well-developed language abilities; difficulty in processing the wholes of a spatial array, although able to process local detail.
Autosomal Recessive Disorders		
Albinism	1 in 10,000–20,000. Several forms; frequency differs among various populations. Most common form occurs in about 1 in 15,000 African Americans, 1 in 40,000 Caucasians, but much more frequently among some Native American tribes (1 in 200 among Hopi and Navajo, 1 in 132 among San Blas Indians of Panama).	Affected individuals lack pigment *melanin*. Extreme sensitivity to sunlight and visual problems. Prenatal detection possible.
Congenital Hypothyroidism	1 in 3,000 of European origin.	Dwarfism, severe mental deficiency. Treatment with thyroid hormones successful but must be continued throughout life. Many countries currently screen newborns for disease.
Cystic Fibrosis	Most common genetic disease in Caucasian populations in U.S., especially those of Northern European descent, affecting about 1 in 2,500. One in 25 Americans is carrier. Less common among African American and Asian American populations.	Respiratory tract becomes clogged with mucus; lungs likely to become infected. Death often in young adulthood, but individuals may have children. Prognosis for females poorer than for males. Therapy helps delay effects. Gene located on chromosome 7. Prenatal detection possible. Some countries regularly screen newborns for disease.

Disorder	Estimated Frequency (live births in U.S.)	Phenotype, Prognosis, and Prenatal Detection
Galactosemia	1 in 60,000	Mental retardation, cataracts, cirrhosis of the liver caused by accumulation of galactose in body tissues because of absence of enzyme to convert this sugar to glucose. Those heterozygous for this condition have half the normal enzyme activity, but this is enough for normal development. Galactose-free diet only treatment. Prenatal detection possible. Some countries currently screen newborns for defect.
Gaucher Disease	1 in 600 Ashkenazic Jews. Other, rarer forms found in all populations.	Enlarged spleen contributing to pain, cardiac failure, and failure to thrive. Frequent bone fractures, bruising, and bleeding. Gene located on chromosome 1. Prenatal detection possible.
Phenylketonuria	1 in 10,000–12,000. Somewhat higher rate of incidence in Caucasian and Asian than in African American populations.	See text. Gene located on chromosome 12. Prenatal detection possible.
Sickle Cell Anemia	1 in 450 African Americans. Also frequently found in malaria-prone regions of world.	See text. Gene located on chromosome 11. Prenatal detection possible.
Tay-Sachs Disease	1 in 3,000 Ashkenazic Jews. Very rare in other populations. 1 in 30 Ashkenazic Jews are carriers; in other populations, 1 in 300 are carriers.	Signs of mental retardation, blindness, deafness, and paralysis begin 1 to 6 months after birth. Death normally occurs by 3 or 4 years of age. Prenatal detection possible.
Thalassemia (Cooley's anemia)	1 in 800–2,500 in populations of Greek and Italian descent. Much less frequent in other populations.	Severe anemia beginning within 2 to 3 months of birth, stunted growth, increased susceptibility to infections. Death usually occurs in 20s or 30s. Gene located on chromosome 11. Prenatal detection possible.
Sex-Linked Disorders		
Colorblindness (red-green)	About 1 in 100 males of Caucasian descent see no red or green. About 1 in 15 males of Caucasian descent experience some decrease in sensitivity to red or green colors.	Those who are completely red-green colorblind lack either green-sensitive or red-sensitive pigment for distinguishing these colors and see them as yellow. Those who show lesser sensitivity to red or green perceive reds as reddish browns, bright greens as tan, and olive greens as brown.
Duchenne Muscular Dystrophy	1 in 7,000 males. Most common of many different forms of muscular dystrophy. Several forms, including Duchenne, are X linked.	Progressive muscle weakness and muscle fiber loss. Mental retardation in about ⅓ of cases. Few ever live long enough to reproduce. Responsible gene located on short arm of X chromosome; appears to be massive in number of nucleotide pairs. Prenatal detection possible.
Fragile X Syndrome	1 in 1250 males; 1 in 2,000 females.	See text. Prenatal detection possible.
Hemophilia	1 in 10,000 Caucasian male births for the most common form.	Failure of blood to clot. Several different forms; not all are sex linked. Queen Victoria of England was carrier for the most common form. Potential for bleeding to death, but administration of clot-inducing drugs and blood transfusions reduces hazard. At risk for exposure to blood-transmitted diseases such as AIDS. Prenatal detection possible.

TABLE 3.2   Some Inherited Gene Disorders

Sources: Adapted from Beaudet et al., 1995; Buchanan 1993; Committee on Genetics, 1996; Scriver et al., 1995; Wang & Bellugi, 1993.

Huntington's Disease: A Dilemma for Genetic Counseling   About twenty-five thousand Americans have **Huntington's disease,** and many more are at risk for developing it as they enter their adult years. The symptoms often appear slowly but relentlessly increase in severity over a period of fifteen to twenty years. These symptoms usually include personality changes, depression, a gradual loss of motor control and memory, and other mental impairments caused by massive cell death in the brain.

Since Huntington's disease is caused by a dominant gene on chromosome 4, each child of an affected parent has a 50 percent chance of acquiring it. The disease continues to be transmitted from one generation to the next because its onset is usually delayed until an individual is about forty years of age. By this time, before its symptoms begin to appear, a carrier may have children.

Recent progress in molecular genetics now permits testing of individuals to determine whether they have inherited Huntington's disease. Unfortunately, however, it cannot be cured or treated at the present time. Thus, the decision to carry out such screening presents an enormous conflict for those who have a family history of the disease; the test results can provide a potentially devastating glimpse into their future, and affected individuals run the risk of being unable to obtain various forms of insurance. *Genetic counselors,* professionals who advise parents about whether their children may or may not inherit a genetic defect, also face the ethical dilemma of whether to encourage prospective parents to have the test, since its results are important for determining whether offspring are at risk (Grady, 1987). Screening can be conducted prenatally to determine whether the fetus has inherited Huntington's disease as well.

Sickle Cell Anemia: A Disorder Arising Out of Adaptive Circumstances   **Sickle cell anemia** is a genetic disorder whose incidence is extremely high in many regions of West Africa and around the Mediterranean basin. Sickle cell anemia is also found in about 1 out of every 450 African Americans (Buchanan, 1993) and in high numbers of Greek Americans and others whose ancestors came from regions where malaria commonly occurs. The defect, inherited as a recessive gene on chromosome 11, introduces a change in a single amino acid in hemoglobin, the molecule that permits the red blood cells to carry oxygen. As a result, red blood cells become crescent shaped rather than round.

Sickle-shaped cells are ineffective in transporting oxygen; they also survive for a much shorter duration than normal red blood cells, and the bone marrow has difficulty replacing them. The consequence is often anemia, jaundice, low resistance to infection, susceptibility to stroke as well as severe pain, and damage to various organs when the distorted cells block small blood vessels. During the elementary school years, children with sickle cell anemia appear quite similar to peers who do not have the disorder in terms of emotional well-being, viewing themselves no differently in terms of social satisfaction, competencies, and feelings of depression. However, children with sickle cell anemia, especially girls, tend to be somewhat less popular in the classroom and boys somewhat less aggressive, perhaps because of their more limited energy and slower physical development (Noll et al., 1996).

More than 2 million, or about one in every twelve, African Americans are carriers of the sickle cell gene. These individuals, who possess a heterozygous genotype, have the **sickle cell trait**. They manufacture a relatively small proportion of cells with abnormal hemoglobin. Few of these individuals show symptoms of sickle cell anemia; most live normal lives. But insufficient oxygen, which may occur in high-altitude regions, when flying in unpressurized airplane cabins, or after strenuous exercise, can trigger sickling of red blood cells in those who have the trait. Nevertheless, carriers of the sickle cell gene are more resistant to malaria than are individuals who have normal hemoglobin. This adaptive feature probably accounts for the high incidence and persistence of the trait in populations where malaria is present.

Phenylketonuria: An Environmentally Modifiable Genetic Disorder   Phenylketonuria (PKU), a recessive metabolic disorder affecting about one in every eleven

Huntington's disease   Dominant genetic disorder characterized by involuntary movements of the limbs, mental deterioration, and premature death.

sickle cell anemia   Genetic blood disorder common in regions of Africa and other areas where malaria is found and among descendants of these regions. Abnormal blood cells carry insufficient oxygen.

sickle cell trait   Symptoms shown by those possessing a heterozygous genotype for sickle cell anemia.

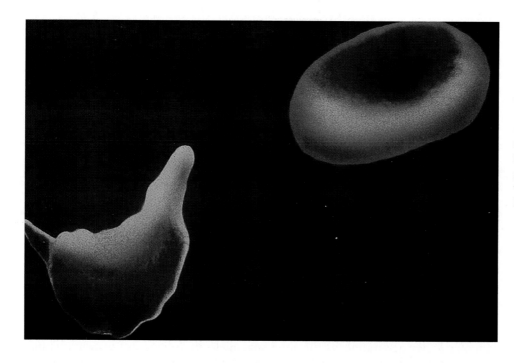

Individuals who suffer from sickle cell anemia, a genetically inherited disorder, have a large proportion of crescent-shaped red blood cells like the one shown at the bottom left. A normal red blood cell (upper right) is round and doughnut-shaped. Sickle-shaped cells are ineffective in transporting oxygen and may cause damage to various organs and pain by blocking small blood vessels.

thousand newborns, is caused by the mutation of a gene on chromosome 12. As indicated earlier, it provides a good illustration of how genes can interact with the environment to foster a particular phenotype or capacity. Treatment to reduce the effects of this debilitating genetic disorder consists of changing the child's environment, in this case, diet.

An infant with PKU appears normal at birth. However, retardation sets in soon thereafter and becomes severe by four years of age if the condition is untreated. Fortunately, screening performed shortly after birth (required in hospitals in nearly all areas of the United States and many other countries) can detect elevated levels of phenylalanine. An infant identified as having PKU can then be placed on a diet low in phenylalanine to prevent its more serious effects. Experts agree the diet must be started relatively early, within the first few months after birth, and continued at least through adolescence to ensure nearly normal mental development (Legido et al., 1993). However, concerns exist about how accurately PKU can be detected within twenty-four hours of birth, the time frame in which increasing numbers of newborns are now released from the hospital (Sinai et al., 1995).

Even though the more serious consequences of this genetic disorder can be prevented, a completely normal prognosis for these children remains problematic. The diet is difficult to maintain; it requires a careful balance between excessive phenylalanine to prevent neural damage and sufficient nutrients. Blood tests may be needed as often as twice a month to keep metabolite concentrations within an acceptable range, a regimen for which child, parents, and testing centers may be ill prepared. Even under optimal conditions, children with PKU may show some growth and intellectual deficiencies, particularly in the area of planning and problem solving (Diamond, 1993; Ris et al., 1994). The bland and unappetizing diet can be a source of conflict between child and caregiver as well, creating management problems within households attempting to lead relatively normal lives (Scriver & Clow, 1988).

Individuals with PKU who successfully reach adulthood may still need to be concerned about their diets. For example, children born to mothers with PKU often suffer congenital heart defects and mental retardation (Walters, 1995). Elevated levels of phenylalanine in the mother's blood appear to cause serious damage to fetal development. If a mother returns to a low-phenylalanine diet before or early in her pregnancy, the risks can be reduced substantially (Platt et al., 1992). Although dietary modifications are helpful, it remains unclear whether this intervention completely eliminates the negative consequences of PKU.

KEY THEME
Nature/Nurture

KEY THEME
Child's Active Role

Sex-Linked Disorders   Relatively few genes are known to exist on the Y chromosome, but the X chromosome carries many. This imbalance has substantial implications for a number of disorders said to be sex linked because the gene associated with them is carried on the X chromosome. Hemophilia, red-green colorblindness, and Duchenne muscular dystrophy (see Table 3.2) have nothing to do with differentiation of sex but are sex linked because they are fostered by genes on the X chromosome. As a consequence, these disorders are found much more frequently in males than in females.

As with genes for autosomes, those that are sex linked often have a dominant-recessive relationship. Thus, females, who inherit two genes for sex-linked traits, one on each X chromosome, are much less likely to display the deleterious effects associated with an abnormal recessive gene than are males, who, if they inherit the damaging allele, have no second, normal allele to mask its effects. Hemophilia, a condition in which blood does not clot normally, is a good example since it is nearly always associated with a defective gene on the X chromosome. Because the allele for hemophilia is recessive, daughters who inherit it typically do not exhibit hemophilia; the condition is averted by an ordinary gene on the second X chromosome that promotes normal blood clotting. A female can, however, serve as a carrier. If she possesses a heterozygous genotype for hemophilia, the X chromosome with the abnormal allele has a fifty-fifty chance of being transmitted to either her son or her daughter. When a son inherits the abnormal allele, he will exhibit hemophilia because the Y chromosome does not contain genetic information to counter the allele's effects. If a daughter inherits the abnormal allele, she will be a carrier who may then transmit it to her sons and daughters, as has occurred in several interrelated royal families of Europe.

Fragile X Syndrome: A Sex-Linked Disorder and Major Contributor to Mental Retardation   Geneticists have identified a structural anomaly that consists of a pinched or constricted site near the end of the long arm of the X chromosome in some individuals (see Figure 3.7). This anomaly, termed **fragile X syndrome,** may be the most frequently inherited source of mental retardation (Hagerman, 1996; Nussbaum & Ledbetter, 1995). Males with fragile X syndrome commonly have a long, narrow face, large or prominent ears, and large testes. Cardiac defects and relaxed ligaments (permitting, for example, hyperextension of finger joints) are also frequent components of the disorder. Behavioral attributes include poor eye contact and limited responsiveness to many forms of external stimulation as well as hand flapping, hand biting, and other unusual mannerisms such as mimicry. Mental retardation seems to become increasingly severe with development (Hagerman, 1996). Females who possess a heterozygous genotype often show some reduction in intelligence and, to a much lesser extent, some of the physical characteristics of the disorder. Many of these women display a normal range of intelligence, although, as with other sex-linked gene disorders, they are carriers for the syndrome.

An unusual feature of this disorder is that its severity seems to increase from one generation to the next, a phenomenon termed *anticipation*. This progression begins when one set of three nucleotides, which repeats about thirty times in the normal gene on the X chromosome, for some reason expands to fifty to two hundred repetitions. Once this expansion occurs, the gene seems to become unstable for subsequent offspring so that additional copies of the three nucleotides are spewed out, as though the replication process has difficulty turning off (Hagerman, 1996; Oostra & Halley, 1995; Turk, 1995). The inheritance of this unchecked expansion is accompanied by a spectrum of learning difficulties ranging from mild to severe mental retardation. Thus, the size of the abnormal segment of the gene, along with the severity of the disorder, appears to increase as it is passed from a grandfather, where the initial amplification may occur (even if he shows no evidence of the disorder), to a daughter (who may be minimally affected since she has an additional X chromosome to compensate for the disorder), to a grandson (who now displays full-blown fragile X syndrome).

The phenomenon of anticipation is found in several other inherited disorders, in-

fragile X syndrome   Disorder associated with a pinched region of the X chromosome; a leading genetic cause of mental retardation in males.

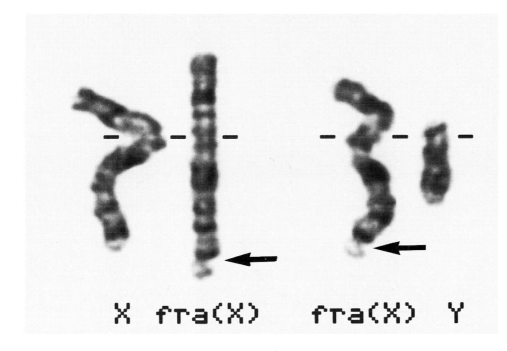

X fra(X)   fra(X) Y

FIGURE 3.7

Chromosome Illustrating
Fragile X Syndrome

**Fragile X syndrome is one of
the most frequently occurring
genetic causes of mental retardation. This photomicrograph
illustrates the pinched or
constricted portion of the
X chromosome in an affected
male and one of the pair of
X chromosomes in a heterozygous female.**

cluding one we have already discussed, Huntington's disease. Here too researchers
have demonstrated an expansion of a set of three nucleotides, this time on chromosome 4, that seems to be responsible for increasingly earlier onset of the disorder
over succeeding generations (Simonoff, Bolton, & Rutter, 1996).

Chromosome Disorders

Mutations in specific genes are only one of several sources of variation in the human
genome. Occasionally whole sections of a chromosome are deleted or duplicated, or
an extra chromosome is transmitted to daughter cells during cell division. When this
happens, normal development is often disrupted. Approximately half of all conceptions that result in spontaneous abortion are believed to include such chromosomal
abnormalities (Jacobs & Hassold, 1995). Moreover, human embryonic growth virtually never proceeds when a complete pair of autosomes is missing or when an extra
pair of autosomes is inherited. **Trisomy,** the inheritance of an extra chromosome,
also very often results in the loss of the zygote or miscarriage in early pregnancy
(Jacobs & Hassold, 1995). However, three copies of chromosomes 13, 18, and 21 may
be observed in surviving human newborns. Of these, trisomy 21, or Down syndrome, occurs most frequently.

Trisomy 21 (Down Syndrome)   Trisomy 21, one of the most common genetic
causes of mental retardation, arises in about one out of every one thousand live
births (Scriver et al., 1995). Physically observable features associated with trisomy 21
include an epicanthal fold that gives an almond shape to the eye, flattened facial features, poor muscle tone, short stature, and short, broad hands, including an unusual
crease of the palm. About 40 percent of infants with Down syndrome have congenital heart defects. Cataracts or other visual impairments are also common, as are deficiencies in the immune system that create high susceptibility to infection and
leukemia. Physical development is slowed compared to normal children, as is intellectual development. However, mental retardation becomes most apparent as the
child approaches school age; she or he often shows limited advances on more demanding cognitive tasks (Epstein, 1995).

   Approximately 95 percent of babies born with Down syndrome have an extra
twenty-first chromosome. Nearly 90 percent of these errors originate in egg cells, and

trisomy   Condition in which an
extra chromosome is present.

FIGURE 3.8

Relationship Between
Maternal Age and the
Incidence of Down
Syndrome

The incidence of Down syndrome increases dramatically
as a function of the mother's
age. One in every 1,500 babies
born to a mother age twenty-
one has Down syndrome. For
forty-nine-year-old mothers,
the incidence is much higher:
one in every ten babies has
Down syndrome. Two explanations, the "older egg" and the
"relaxed selection" hypotheses, have been offered to
account for these findings.

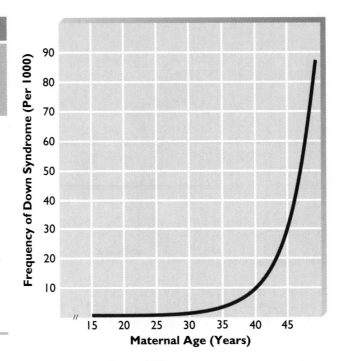

Source: Data from Epstein, 1989.

the remainder arise from errors during the production of sperm cells (Jacobs & Hassold, 1995). A small percentage of infants with Down syndrome have a segment of
chromosome 21, perhaps as little as its bottom third, shifted to another chromosome
(Epstein, 1995). Another small percentage display a mosaic genotype, that is, have
chromosomal deviations in only a portion of their body cells. The severity of Down
syndrome in these latter individuals seems to be related to the proportion of cells exhibiting trisomy.

The probability of giving birth to an infant with trisomy 21 increases with the age
of the mother, as is true for most other forms of trisomy (see Figure 3.8). Although
mothers over thirty-five years of age give birth to only about 16 percent of all babies,
they bear more than half of the infants with Down syndrome. The father's age shows
virtually no relationship to the incidence of Down syndrome (Epstein, 1995). To
explain these findings, experts have often proposed an "older egg" hypothesis.
According to this view, the ova, which begin the first phases in meiosis even before
the mother's own birth, change with age, either from the passage of time or perhaps
because of increased exposure to potentially hazardous biological and environmental conditions. These older egg cells, released during ovulation in the later childbearing years, are then more susceptible to chromosomal errors while undergoing the
final steps of meiosis. Other researchers have proposed a "relaxed selection" hypothesis to account for the increased frequency of Down syndrome in older mothers. Since
a large proportion of conceptions involving trisomy 21 do not proceed normally,
according to the relaxed selection view, older mothers are less likely than younger
mothers to spontaneously abort a zygote with trisomy 21. At the present time,
however, no consistent explanation exists to account for these maternal age effects
(Epstein, 1995; Jacobs & Hassold, 1995).

Thanks to better medical and physical care, the majority of individuals born with
Down syndrome now live more than thirty years and many beyond fifty years (Patterson, 1987). Although in the past the cognitive abilities of individuals with Down
syndrome were considered to be quite low, many learn and show considerable proficiency in reading and writing. But we still have much to discover about the disorder.
For example, individuals with trisomy 21 who survive beyond age thirty frequently
develop the abnormal brain cells and show some of the same behavioral symptoms

KEY THEME
Individual Differences

The young boy being observed by a peer as he paints in this classroom has trisomy 21, or Down syndrome, a leading cause of mental retardation. When given the opportunity to learn in an enriching environment such as this one, children born with trisomy 21 may acquire basic academic abilities as well as engage in normal childhood activities.

found in adults who acquire Alzheimer's disease (Epstein, 1995). Alzheimer's disease is characterized by memory and speech disturbances, personality changes, and increasing loss of intellectual functioning, typically in individuals between fifty and seventy-five years of age, although the symptoms may begin much earlier. At least one form of Alzheimer's disease is thought to be inherited, and, not surprisingly, the responsible gene appears to be located on chromosome 21.

Structural Aberrations of Chromosomes   Other changes in chromosomes, including deletions, duplications, and relocations of parts of DNA, also occur. As with a chromosomal trisomy, the consequences are usually so severe that the pregnancy ends soon after conception. But this is not always the case. For example, the deletion of a small segment of the fifth chromosome is responsible for *cri du chat* or *cat-cry syndrome,* in which infants exhibit a cry similar to a cat's (hence its name), severe mental retardation, microcephaly (very small head size), short stature, and other congenital anomalies. Mental retardation and severe physical deformations often accompany structural aberrations observed in other chromosomes as well.

Sex Chromosome Abnormalities   As we have already noted, males normally have an X and a Y sex chromosome and females have two X chromosomes. However, variations in the number of sex chromosomes can occur in humans. For example, an individual may inherit only a single X (XO), an extra chromosome (XXX, XXY, XYY), and, on rare occasions, even pairs of extra chromosomes (for example, XXXX, XXYY, XXXY). Table 3.3 describes the consequences of several of these variations in more detail.

When an extra Y chromosome was first identified in some adults, a few researchers contended that it was closely linked to an assortment of abnormal and socially unacceptable behaviors. For example, in the 1960s several published reports claimed the XYY pattern existed surprisingly often in retarded and hard-to-manage, highly aggressive inmates in penal institutions; the extra Y chromosome was believed to be the basis of their antisocial behaviors. Despite a number of methodological problems with this research, the view that XYY males are more aggressive than other males was widely disseminated by the media. The extra Y chromosome was even

TABLE 3.3	Examples of Observed Sex Chromosome Abnormalities	
Disorder	**Estimated Frequency (live births in U.S.)**	**Phenotype and Prognosis**
XO (Turner syndrome)	1 in 1,200–2,500 females (more than 90% are spontaneously aborted); 80% of cases involve the absence of the paternal X chromosome.	*Characteristics.* Short stature, usually normal psychomotor development, but limited development of secondary sexual characteristics. Failure to menstruate and sterility due to underdeveloped ovaries. Webbed, short neck. Near-average range of intelligence but serious deficiencies in spatial ability and directional sense. *Prognosis.* Increased stature and sexual development, including menstruation, but not fertility, can be induced through administration of estrogen and other hormones. In vitro fertilization permits carrying of child when adult.
XXX (Triple-X syndrome or "superfemale")	1 in 500–1,200 females; 90% have received two copies of maternal X chromosome.	*Characteristics.* Not generally distinguishable. Some evidence of delay in speech and language development, lack of coordination, poor academic performance, and immature behavior. Sexual development usually normal. *Prognosis.* Many are essentially normal, but substantial proportion have language, cognitive, and social-emotional problems.
XXY (Klinefelter syndrome)	1 in 500–1,000 males (increased risk among older mothers); 50% received two maternal chromosomes, 50% two paternal sex chromosomes.	*Characteristics.* Tend to be tall, beardless, with feminine body contour, high-pitched voice. Some evidence for poor auditory short-term memory and difficulty with reading. Testes underdeveloped, individuals sterile. *Prognosis.* Many with normal IQ, but about 20% may have occasional mild to moderate retardation.
XYY ("supermale")	1 in 700–1,000 males	*Characteristics.* Above-average height, near-average range of intelligence. *Prognosis.* Most lead normal lives and have offspring with a normal number of chromosomes. Higher proportion than normal incarcerated, but crimes no more violent than those of XY men.

Sources: Adapted from Beaudet et al., 1995; Bender, Linden, & Robinson, 1987; Jacobs & Hassold, 1995; Knowles, 1985; Plomin, DeFries, & McClearn, 1990.

used in courts of law to argue for leniency for criminals who inherited this chromosomal pattern. Today we know the extra Y chromosome is linked to above-average height and sometimes lowered intelligence. This physical and intellectual combination may account for the slightly elevated percentage of XYY men in prison compared to normal XY males. In fact, children with sex chromosome anomalies display a wide range of phenotypic expressions; large proportions of individuals who inherit an additional sex chromosome or receive a single X chromosome lead ordinary lives.

The wide variation in phenotypes associated with sex chromosome anomalies may be due to experiential factors. Bruce Bender and his colleagues at the University of Colorado School of Medicine studied forty-six children with variations in number of sex chromosomes such as those described in Table 3.3 (Bender, Linden, & Robinson, 1987). These children, born between 1964 and 1974, were identified by screening forty thousand consecutive births in the Denver area. Those with sex chromosome abnormalities were more likely to have neuromotor, psychosocial, language, and school problems than siblings who had a normal XX or XY complement. But

KEY THEME
Nature/Nurture

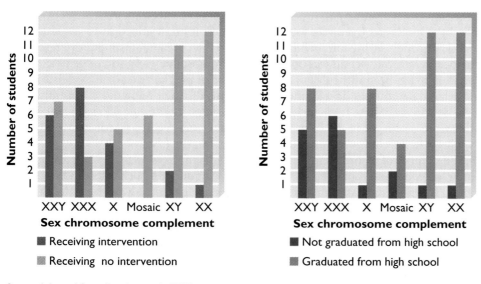

Source: Adapted from Bender et al., 1995.

FIGURE 3.9

Need for Educational Intervention Among Adolescents with Sex Chromosome Abnormalities and Their Siblings

Adolescents who inherit an extra sex chromosome (X or Y) or only one X chromosome (Turner's syndrome) often need more assistance in high school and may be somewhat less likely to graduate than their siblings who have a normal complement of sex chromosomes (XY or XX). Academic progress among high schoolers with a mosaic pattern of normal and abnormal sex chromosomes appears similar to that of their siblings. A closer inspection of the circumstances in which adolescents are reared also reveals that those with sex chromosome abnormalities who are more successful academically live in families that provide more stable and supportive environments. Thus, individuals with sex chromosome deviations may be more susceptible to disruptions or stress than their siblings.

this was true for school and psychosocial problems only if children were growing up in a family where they experienced severe stress, such as exposure to drug abuse or considerable illness, lack of effective parenting by caregivers, or poverty. In the absence of such tensions, children with sex chromosome abnormalities showed no greater evidence of school or psychosocial problems than their siblings, although they did continue to show more neuromotor and language impairment.

More recently, Bender and his colleagues followed the progress of thirty-nine of these children as they moved through adolescence (Bender et al., 1995). As Figure 3.9 shows, more of these students, compared to their siblings with a normal complement of sex chromosomes, needed special education assistance in high school and were less likely to graduate. This was especially true for girls with an extra X chromosome. These groups also exhibited somewhat more depression in psychiatric interviews and lower overall functioning and adaptation to adolescence. Even so, children with a mosaic pattern of abnormal sex chromosomes showed just as much progress in school as their siblings did. And, as in their earlier studies, the researchers note that the presence of a stable and supportive family environment seemed to contribute to more positive development in adolescents with sex chromosome abnormalities, particularly those with XXY and X complements. These findings, then, further suggest that children and adolescents with sex chromosome abnormalities may be more vulnerable to disruptions in the caregiving environment than children with a normal complement of sex chromosomes.

GENETIC COUNSELING

Advances in detecting gene and chromosomal defects as well as in understanding the biochemical and metabolic consequences of various inherited disorders have led to a rapidly expanding medical and guidance specialty called **genetic counseling**. Obtaining family histories to summarize the occurrence of various diseases among ancestors and relatives is usually the first step. If warranted, parental **genetic screening** may be carried out. From the results of various tests, genetic counselors can provide prospective parents with estimates of the likelihood of bearing a child with a specific disorder. For example, screening can be completed for Tay-Sachs disease in Ashkenazic Jews, sickle cell trait among descendants of regions where malaria is prevalent, thalassemia for individuals of Mediterranean ancestry, and other disorders for which the family history indicates that one or both parents might be carriers.

For many conditions, genetic counselors are able to go beyond providing estimates. Through a variety of prenatal tests, they can determine if a particular fetus has

genetic counseling Medical and counseling specialty concerned with determining and communicating the likelihood that prospective parents will give birth to a baby with a genetic disorder.

genetic screening Systematic search using a variety of tests to detect individuals at developmental risk due to genetic anomalies.

a chromosomal abnormality or one of many other kinds of genetic defects. There may be a number of reasons to carry out such tests in addition to evidence for genetic disorders in the family history. For example, prenatal testing is often recommended if a previous child was born with a chromosomal variation or genetic disorder, if there has been difficulty in completing prior pregnancies, or if evidence exists for delayed or unusual development in the fetus during pregnancy (Committee on Genetics, 1994). These tests, including *amniocentesis, chorionic villus sampling,* and others, are discussed in detail in Chapter 4. They often can provide answers about whether specific conditions are present or absent in the fetus.

The number of disorders for which prenatal diagnosis is possible is increasing at a remarkable rate and today stands at well over two hundred. Such tests can be accompanied by enormous apprehension as prospective parents await the outcomes. In fact, some expectant women almost feel coerced into using these technological advances to learn more about their pregnancies (Henifin, 1993; Wertz & Fletcher, 1993). Yet a physician who fails to at least offer prenatal diagnosis in circumstances where it can be informative runs legal risks for incompetent obstetric practice.

Prospective parents have choices regarding whether or not to have such tests performed. In many cases they would like to know about possible problems, if for no other reason than to effectively prepare for and address them even before birth. In fact, a substantial number of expectant women who learn that the fetus carries some abnormality still elect to continue the pregnancy, especially if the problem is less severe and possibilities exist for prenatal or postnatal therapy (Pride et al., 1993). As screening procedures become more widespread, prospective parents should also seek out and be provided with counseling resources to deal with the potentially worrisome psychological effects of learning that one is a carrier for a genetic disease or that a baby may be born with some disorder.

Other issues are associated with prenatal testing that prospective parents as well as experts need to consider. Who will have access to the results? For example, might insurance companies or other health organizations drop coverage if they become aware of test results that indicate expensive medical treatment in the future? Is it legitimate to conduct such tests solely to determine sex? For example, might some parents choose to terminate a pregnancy solely on the basis of the sex of the fetus, a practice that already may be followed to some extent in some regions of the world? Moreover, should not all groups have the choice to undergo such tests? For example, women of African American and Hispanic identity, at least in some areas of the United States, are far less likely to take part in some forms of prenatal testing than Caucasian or Asian women (Kuppermann, Gates, & Washington, 1996). But the extent to which cultural differences in preference and attitude about such tests, socioeconomic factors, or knowledge of the tests' availability contribute to these differences is unknown.

R ecent advances in the field of reproductive technology have revolutionized our understanding of human conception and childbearing. They have also dramatically affected traditional notions about what it means to be a parent.

CONTROVERSY: THINKING IT OVER

When Is a Parent a Parent?

Couples at risk for bearing children with a genetic disease or women who report difficulty in bearing a child, estimated at about 5 million in the United States alone (Collins, 1995), now can explore many options in addition to adoption in their efforts to become parents. Each new alternative brings hope to many couples but raises a tangle of ethical and legal issues as well.

If a male carries a genetic disorder or is infertile, couples may elect *artificial insemination by donor.* In this procedure, a donor, usually anonymous and presumably selected because of his similarity to a prospective father in physical and other characteristics, contributes sperm that are then artificially provided to the mother when ovulation occurs. Unfortunately, practitioners of artificial insemination, apart from fertility clinics, are not always licensed, nor are they required to receive special training. Thus, the degree of safety and even the frequency of this practice are unknown (Guinan, 1995). In addition, whereas adopted children are often informed of their status, children born via artificial insemination are seldom aware that their legal and biological fathers are not the same person. Even if told, however, these individuals typically would be unable to obtain further information, since doctors who draw on sperm banks are not required to keep records linking donors and recipients (Guinan, 1995). In fact, in one widely publicized case in New Jersey, one doctor, the operator of the fertility clinic, eventually was identified as the donor in numerous conceptions, unbeknown to the many families that sought his services.

If a female is the carrier of a genetic disease or is infertile, options include *surrogate motherhood* and *in vitro fertilization*. Surrogate motherhood has sometimes been termed the "renting" of another woman's womb, but this concept can be misleading since, in many cases, the surrogate mother often donates an egg for prenatal development as well as her womb. The surrogate is thus the biological mother as well as the bearer of the child who has been conceived by artificial insemination using the prospective father's sperm (Henifin, 1993). With in vitro fertilization, eggs are removed from a woman's ovaries, fertilized in a laboratory dish with the prospective father's sperm, and transferred to another woman's uterus. In this situation, the biological and social mothers may be one and the same except during the gestational period, when the surrogate mother's womb is used. Alternatively, a woman who cannot conceive normally might undergo in vitro fertilization and carry her own or another woman's fertilized egg during her pregnancy.

Legal, medical, and social controversy swirl around both surrogate motherhood and in vitro fertilization (Collins, 1995; Henifin, 1993). Legal debates center on who is the rightful father or mother. In one highly publicized case in the United States involving Baby M, a woman was impregnated by artificial insemination by a man whose wife was afflicted with multiple sclerosis. At birth, this biological and gestational mother was to surrender the child to the genetic father and his wife for adoption. After delivery, however, she refused to relinquish custody of the child. Who should be the legal parent? In the Baby M case, the court ruled against the surrogate mother. In another recent case in California, the court ruled that a baby conceived from a woman's egg and her husband's sperm via in vitro fertilization and carried to term by a surrogate should be reared by the genetic couple rather than the gestational mother (Henifin, 1993). However, the debate surrounding these and similar cases continues as judicial systems try to resolve who is the legal parent: the genetic, the gestational, or the caregiving or social mother.

Other controversies focus on the costly medical procedures and complicated ethical and social issues associated with in vitro fertilization and surrogate motherhood. For example, in the United States, in vitro fertilization typically costs $8,000 to $10,000 for the medical procedures alone. When this figure is multiplied over several undertakings (because fewer than 20 percent of all attempts result in a live birth), the expense is more likely to be in the range of $40,000 to $70,000 (Neumann, Gharib, & Weinstein, 1994). Should medical insurance be mandated to pay the high costs associated with these attempts, as it already is in a few states (Collins, 1995)? Will these new technologies also lead to increased pressures to use genetic engineering to ensure only healthy offspring?

The desire to have their own children is a powerful motive for most couples. New advances in reproductive technology will help many to reach that goal. Yet these advances have spawned dilemmas that many nations have not fully resolved. Despite uncertainties, many children who are born to parents by means of these new technologies grow up with few emotional, behavioral, or other problems. Susan Golombok and her colleagues (Golombok et al., 1995) studied eighty-six children conceived

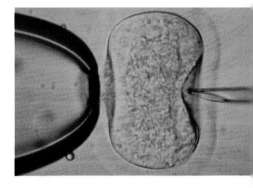

In vitro fertilization is one of several reproductive technologies that can assist men and women with fertility problems in their attempts to have healthy offspring. In this procedure, an egg cell is surgically removed from the woman's ovary to permit it to be fertilized by a sperm cell. After cell division begins, the zygote is inserted in the woman's uterus where it can implant and continue to grow. Prior to its insertion in the uterus, individual cells also can be tested to determine whether the zygote carries a hereditary defect.

by donor insemination or in vitro fertilization between four and eight years of age in the United Kingdom—nearly half of the children estimated to be conceived in this manner within that age range in that country—and found them to be similar to naturally conceived children in feelings toward their mothers and fathers, perceived competence, social acceptance, and other measures. In other words, their emotions, behavior, and relationships with parents were no different than those of other children.

DEVELOPMENTAL AND BEHAVIORAL GENETICS

As our previous discussion indicates, chromosomal errors and particular genes can have drastic, often devastating effects on physical, intellectual, and social development. Yet similarities observed among relatives—the quick tempers of two brothers; the wry sense of humor in a mother and daughter; the musical talent of a grandfather and his grandchildren; and, as we saw at the beginning of the chaper, Jeremy's shy, reserved personality, so reminiscent of his mother's own childhood—are not likely to have been influenced by a single, isolated gene. Might these attributes and behaviors reflect a hereditary contribution involving many genes? Or are these phenotypic resemblances the result of experiences shared by kin?

Many attributes and behaviors are undoubtedly influenced by polygenic relationships. Researchers engaged in **behavior genetics** are concerned with learning to what extent the diversity of human traits, abilities, and behaviors is influenced by combinations of genes versus experience. This focus on assessing the hereditary and experiential bases of individual differences distinguishes behavior geneticists from ethologists, who attempt to understand the adaptive value of behaviors such as attachment and aggression that have evolved biologically and are universally shared by members of the same species.

The Methods of Behavioral Geneticists

When working with subjects such as the fruit fly or mouse, behavior geneticists often use *selective breeding* experiments to learn whether certain phenotypic expressions can be increased or decreased in offspring. In this procedure, members of a species that display a specific attribute are bred to each other, usually over many generations. If the attribute is inherited, subsequent generations of offspring can be expected to display it more and more frequently or strongly. For example, after thirty generations of selective breeding in which mice displaying a high level of activity were bred only to each other, as were mice showing only a low level of activity, researchers observed no overlap in terms of the amount of activity displayed by the two groups (DeFries, Gervais, & Thomas, 1978). Those bred for high activity were thirty times more active; they would run the equivalent of a football field during two three-minute test periods compared to the low-activity mice, which would not even run the equivalent of a first down (Plomin, 1986).

Selective breeding in various species of animals has revealed genetic contributions to many different attributes, including aggressiveness, emotionality, maze learning, and sex drive (Plomin, DeFries, & McClearn, 1990). But selective breeding, of course, cannot be used to examine human behavior. Instead, behavior geneticists gain information about hereditary and environmental influences on human behavior by examining resemblances among family members. These studies investigate similarities among *identical* and *fraternal twins,* siblings, and other members of families who are genetically different from one another to varying degrees.

Identical, or *monozygotic, twins* come from the same zygote: a single egg fertilized by a single sperm. A cell division takes place early in development that creates two separate embryos from this zygote, and the twins are genetically identical.

behavior genetics Study of how characteristics and behaviors of individuals, such as intelligence and personality, are influenced by the interaction between genotype and experience.

identical twins Two individuals who originate from a single zygote (one egg fertilized by one sperm), which early in cell division separates to form two separate cell masses. Also called *monozygotic twins.*

Fraternal, or *dizygotic, twins* come from two different zygotes, each created from a separate egg and separate sperm. Although sharing the womb at the same time, fraternal twins are no more genetically similar than siblings born at different times, each averaging about half of their genes in common.

If identical twins resemble each other more than fraternal twins in intelligence or shyness, one *potential* explanation for this similarity is their common genotype. The degree of resemblance is usually estimated from one of two statistical measures: concordance rate or correlation coefficient. The **concordance rate** is the percentage of pairs of twins in which both members have a specific attribute when one twin is identified as having it. Concordance rate is used when measuring characteristics that are either present or absent, such as schizophrenia or depression. If both members of every twin pair have a particular trait, the concordance rate will be 100 percent. If only one member of every pair of twins has some particular trait and the other does not, the concordance rate will be 0 percent.

When attributes vary on a continuous scale such that they can be measured in terms of amount or degree, resemblances are estimated from a *correlation coefficient*. This statistic helps to determine whether variables such as intelligence or shyness, which may be quantified from lower to higher, are more similar for identical than for fraternal twins or more similar among siblings than among unrelated children.

Identical twins may resemble one another more than fraternal twins because identical twins share the same genotype. However, another explanation for any greater resemblance may be that identical twins share more similar experiences. Although some behavior geneticists do not believe the similarity of twins' experiences represents a major problem in twin research (Plomin, DeFries, & McClearn, 1990), one way to reduce its effects is to study biologically related family members who have been adopted or reared apart from one another. If an attribute is greatly influenced by genetic factors, children should still resemble their biological siblings, parents, or other family members more than their adoptive relatives. On the other hand, if the environment is the primary determinant of an attribute, separated children can be expected to resemble their adoptive parents or other adopted siblings more closely than their biological parents or siblings.

Adoption studies pose many challenges for evaluating hereditary and environmental influences because children are often placed in homes similar to those of their biological parents. As a consequence, the contributions of family environment and heredity to an attribute become extremely difficult to tease apart. In addition, information on the biological family may not be readily available in the case of adoption. Because of these kinds of difficulties, major family resemblance projects investigating genotype-environment interactions often combine family, twin, and adoption methods. The Colorado Adoption Project, for example, has been conducting longitudinal research on resemblances between (1) parents and their natural children, (2) adoptive parents and their adopted children, and (3) parents and their biological children who have been adopted into other homes for nearly twenty years (Loehlin, Horn, & Willerman, 1990; Plomin, 1996). Another project, the Minnesota Study of Twins Reared Apart, has assessed a variety of psychological and physiological characteristics exhibited by identical and fraternal twins reared together or twins reared apart and having virtually no contact with each other prior to adulthood (Bouchard et al., 1990; Hur & Bouchard, 1995). These and other longitudinal studies have provided us with valuable information on the genetic and experiential contributions to family resemblance. But before we describe some of the conclusions from these studies, we need to consider the potential relationships that exist between heredity and experience more carefully.

These identical twins have already anticipated a question that they probably are asked often. Because their genetic makeup is the same, identical or monozygotic twins typically look very much alike and display very similar traits and behaviors. Twin studies provide important information about the contributions of heredity and environment to development.

Conceptualizing the Interaction Between Genotype and Environment

Is behavior completely determined by the genes? Is it influenced only by experience? Neither of these extreme positions, of course, is voiced very often today. Instead, how

fraternal twins Siblings who share the same womb at the same time but originate from two different eggs fertilized by two different sperm cells. Also called *dizygotic twins*.

concordance rate Percentage of pairs of twins in which both members have a specific trait identified in one twin.

KEY THEME
Nature/Nurture

KEY THEME
Individual Differences

KEY THEME
Nature/Nurture

a genotype influences development may depend to a great extent on the environment. Similarly, how an environment affects behavior often depends on the genotype. These conditional relationships are the basis for complex *interactions* between genotype and environment; the influence of one on the other is not constant across individuals or, probably, even during different periods of development (Plomin, Owen, & McGuffin, 1994).

Consider the repercussions of inheriting the gene that expresses phenylketonuria (PKU), discussed earlier in this chapter. For individuals with this genotype, near-normal intellectual development depends on an environment in which protein—more specifically, phenylalanine—is minimized, especially during the formative years. In contrast, intellectual development for someone without PKU is largely unaffected, or may possibly even be improved, by the presence of substantial protein in the diet.

Does the concept of interaction between a single-gene condition and the environment extend to polygenic factors? Most certainly, yes. For example, some children appear to succeed in chronically impoverished, stressful rearing conditions or in otherwise dysfunctional families containing profound caregiving deficits; many other children are highly vulnerable to such conditions. Resilient children display extraordinary personal and intellectual achievements or are socially far above the norm compared to other children reared in harsh contexts (Garmezy, 1993; Rutter, 1990). A unique array of family, community, and other experiential factors, including a positive temperament, self-reliance, and good coping skills, as well as nurturant caregiving, may promote these competencies (Werner, 1995). Many of these successful children very likely inherited a combination of genetic qualities that empower them to rise above the environmental circumstances so debilitating to other children.

Range of Reaction   The interactive relationship between genotype and environment can be conceptualized in terms of the concept of **range of reaction,** the notion that, depending on environmental conditions and genotype, a phenotype may be expressed over a broad range (Turkheimer, Goldsmith, & Gottesman, 1995). Figure 3.10 illustrates this concept for intellectual performance. Consider a child with Down syndrome (represented, for example, by Child C in Figure 3.10). Transferring this child from an unstimulating institutional setting (a restricted environment) and engaging him in supportive learning activities (more enriched environments) very likely will help him to achieve a much higher level of cognitive functioning (Feuerstein, Rand, & Rynders, 1988). The performances of children with other genotypes (as represented by Child A and Child B in Figure 3.10) can be enormously affected too, depending on whether they are reared in deprived or stimulating conditions.

We need to be cautious, however, in thinking about the concept of range of reaction. It reflects only what we presently know about the way genotypes are expressed in environments familiar to us (Gottlieb, 1995). For example, some day, when events concerning how trisomy 21 affects enzymes and proteins essential to neural events are more fully understood, an environment may be fashioned that promotes far higher levels of intelligent behavior in children with Down syndrome. New advances in knowledge of biological processes and the other, much broader complex of multidirectional influences that we call environment may help to drastically modify the way a genotype is expressed in specific behavior (Bronfenbrenner & Ceci, 1994).

Canalization   The principle of **canalization,** or a kind of "channeling" of development, suggests yet another way to think about genotype-environment relationships. This principle helps to shed light on the emergence of behaviors common to all members of a species as well as individual differences. As originally proposed, a highly canalized attribute is one influenced primarily by the genotype; experiential factors can have an impact on the course of development, but only under extreme conditions (Waddington, 1971). Imagine an emerging capacity such as water flowing through terrain in which channels of varying depth have been cut. The channels help

range of reaction   Range of phenotypic differences possible as a result of different environments interacting with a specific genotype.

canalization   Concept that the development of some attributes is governed primarily by the genotype and only extreme environmental conditions will alter the phenotypic pattern for these attributes.

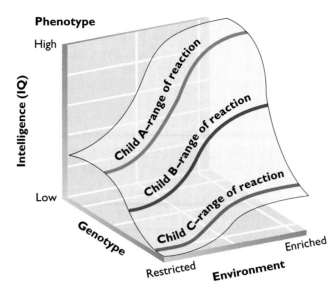

Source: Adapted from Turkheimer, Goldsmith, & Gottesman, 1995.

FIGURE 3.10

The Concept of Range of Reaction for Intellectual Performance

As the product of the interaction between genotype and the environment, the phenotype for any attribute shows a broad range of reaction. For example, the intelligence score of any child, even one who is born with the potential for high intellectual ability, is likely to be limited when the environment is severely restricted. An enriched environment will benefit all children, although perhaps those with greater intellectual potential (Child A or B) more than a child with less intellectual potential (Child C).

to steer the flow in one of several possible directions. However, the channels are so deeply cut by the genotype for some phenotypes that only extreme environmental pressures can change their course.

Various aspects of early motor development tend to emerge on a fairly regular basis during infancy. Presumably the genotype has carved a relatively deep course for their appearance. However, as you will learn in Chapter 5, the emergence of early motor skills is not completely protected from disturbances in experience. Other aspects of early development, including the onset of babbling and smiling at interesting events, which are important components of social responsivity, may also be highly canalized.

Gilbert Gottlieb (1991) has extended these ideas about canalization, proposing that the channeling process may come about not only through the genotype but also from early experiential influences. Thus, exposure to certain types of critical stimulation may steer development just as hereditary information can. As an example, Gottlieb cites research on mallard ducklings. If prevented from hearing their own vocalizations and instead exposed to a chicken's call early in development, the ducklings later show a preference for the chicken's call rather than for sounds produced by members of their own species.

Conceptualizing the Correlation Between Genotype and Environment

KEY THEME
Nature/Nurture

Although behavioral geneticists attempt to determine what portion of various traits such as activity level, sociability, or intelligence derives from the genes and what portion comes from the environment, the task is laden with difficulties. Not only do genotype and environment interact, they are also linked or *correlated* with each other in several complex ways (Plomin, DeFries, & Loehlin, 1977; Scarr, 1992; Scarr & McCartney, 1983).

Passive Links One correlation between genotype and experience arises from the tendency for parents to establish a child-rearing environment in harmony with their own interests and preferences. Assume, for example, that sociability has some genetic basis. Sociable parents may transmit this orientation to their children either through their genes, through the social environment created in their home, or through both mechanisms. This kind of correlation between genotype and environment is labeled as *passive,* since it has been created for the child by the parents. Jeremy and Cindy might have been influenced by this passive correlation. Jeremy's mother stayed home until Jeremy was three years of age. Thus, while Jeremy was young, his mother, who was shy, had the opportunity to structure her household and interactions in ways that met her needs, and Jeremy had considerable opportunity to experience the kind of environment his mother preferred. But soon after Cindy was born, her mother returned to work. Cindy spent much of her infancy and toddler years with a day care provider who was far more outgoing and sociable. Because for these two siblings both genotype and early environment may have differed, we cannot easily separate their contributions to later social development.

In most families, the correlation between the genetic and environmental components of child rearing is likely to be positive; that is, the environment will contain features that support and complement the child's genetic potential. But a negative correlation is also possible, such as when a highly active child is adopted into a sedentary family or when parents elect to rear their children in ways that depart from their own backgrounds and genetic propensities. A parent who feels he or she was too shy during childhood and, as a consequence, missed out on many social activities may actively initiate play groups and other projects designed to promote sociability in a child.

Evocative Links   Another type of correlation between genotype and environment, termed *evocative* or *reactive,* occurs when aspects of the environment, particularly other people, support or encourage behaviors that may have a genetic component; that is, other people's behavior almost seems to be in response to or evoked by the child's genotype. For example, an active preschooler is likely to prompt teachers to provide large-muscle toys to dissipate some of her energy. A ten-year-old's propensity for reading may encourage a teacher to offer additional academic exercises for learning. A sociable child is more likely to attract the attention of peers than a shy or passive child. Jeremy's preference for standing on the sidelines led to a tendency for others in the preschool to ignore him; Cindy's gregariousness helped to ensure that she was often called on in her group. Thus, attributes that have a biological basis are likely to evoke patterns of behavior from others that complement the child's genetic tendencies.

KEY THEME
Child's Active Role

Active, Niche-Picking Links   In yet another type of correlation between genotype and environment, termed *active,* the child may be attracted by and eagerly seek out experiences more compatible with his or her genotype. Bright children may prefer to exercise their intellect and to play with peers who are also bright. The athletic child may find little pleasure in practicing the piano but spend countless hours skateboarding and playing basketball. Jeremy preferred to play by himself, Cindy to play with others. Any genetic basis for these traits and activities can, in turn, influence the kind of environment a child attempts to create and experience. Sandra Scarr and Kathleen McCartney (1983) described this kind of linkage as **niche picking** to emphasize that children and adults selectively construct and engage environments responsive to their genetic orientations.

Scarr and McCartney (1983; Scarr, 1992) believe the impacts of passive, evocative, and active correlations between genotype and environment change with development. The experiences infants receive are often determined for them by their caregivers. Thus, initial correlations between genotype and environment are likely to be more greatly influenced by passive factors. As children gain greater independence and control of their environment, however, others around them are likely to notice and support their individual differences, and niche picking becomes an increasingly important factor as children choose their own interests and activities.

An important implication of these changing relationships is that children within the same family may become less similar to one another as they grow older and become freer of the common environment their parents provide. Older siblings can select niches befitting their individual genotypes more easily than can younger chil-

niche picking   Tendency to actively select an environment compatible with a genotype.

Niche picking, the tendency of a child to seek out and become attracted to activities that are compatible with his genotype, may be an important aspect of the interaction between nature and nurture. This child, proud to display his gymnastic skills on the parallel bars, may have demonstrated athleticism at an early age. As a way of finding his own niche among peers and in society, he may continue to work hard at improving his gymnastic routine.

dren. When Sandra Scarr and Richard Weinberg (1977) studied adopted children, they obtained support for this prediction. During early and middle childhood, adopted but biologically unrelated children showed similarities in intelligence, personality, and other traits. Perhaps these resemblances came about both as a result of adoption procedures that encouraged the placement of children in homes somewhat like their biological homes and from the common family environment shared by adopted children. As adopted siblings neared the end of adolescence, however, they no longer exhibited similarities in intelligence, personality, or other traits; the passive influence of the common environment established by the adoptive parents had become supplanted by active niche picking.

The notion of niche picking provides us with an even more startling prediction. When identical twins are reared apart, they may, with increasing age, actually come to resemble each other more, and perhaps as much as, identical twins reared together! This greater correspondence would emerge as others react to their similar behaviors and as opportunities arise for the twins to make more choices. In the Minnesota Study of Twins Reared Apart, pairs of identical twins, separated as infants and having no interactions with each other until well into adulthood, revealed remarkable similarities not only in gait, posture, gestures, and habits such as straightening eyeglasses but also in storytelling skill, spontaneous giggling, phobic tendencies, hobbies, and interests, resemblances rarely observed between fraternal twins reared apart and usually not considered to have a strong genetic basis (Bouchard, 1984; Bouchard et al., 1990; Lykken et al., 1992). Furthermore, identical twins reared apart showed as high a correlation on many intellectual tasks and personality variables as those reared together. These results suggest that niche picking can be a powerful means of maintaining behaviors initiated by the genotype.

Hereditary and Environmental Influences on Behavior

Research findings involving studies of family resemblances, adopted children, and identical and fraternal twins reared together and apart can be, and often are, interpreted in many different ways precisely because of the complex interactions and relationships genotype and environment share in shaping behavior. These interpretations can sometimes have powerful implications for intervention and social policy (Baumrind, 1993; Jackson, 1993; Scarr, 1992, 1993). Should families or communities,

KEY THEME
Nature/Nurture

for example, expend resources for educational and mental health efforts if a substantial biological basis for behavior exists? Or does this kind of question, concerned with *how much* heredity contributes to variations in the human phenotype, fail to recognize that educational and social opportunities are essential even where genetic contributions are considerable?

Consider the following: about 90 percent of the variability in height among individuals reared in a typical community is believed to be a consequence of genetic factors. However, even though height is strongly influenced by the genotype, its average increase among young adult males in Japan since the end of World War II has been about three-and-a-half inches (Angoff, 1988). Clearly changes in the environment have had a profound impact on a characteristic that receives a significant contribution from the genes. As Stephen Ceci (1990) has pointed out, environmental factors can surely be expected to have an impact on other characteristics as well.

Robert Plomin (1994, 1996) emphasizes one other interesting point about the work that often has revealed a substantial genetic contribution to various kinds of behaviors. Environmental influences frequently account for *more* of the variability in human behavior than does the genotype. Moreover, research in behavioral genetics has begun to provide intriguing insights into *how* environmental factors affect development. Let's examine some of the findings more closely.

Intelligence   In Chapter 10 we discuss limitations in using the intelligence quotient (IQ) as the primary symbol of intellectual ability. Unfortunately, most studies have relied on IQ to measure the contributions of genotype and environment to intelligence, and many of these studies suffer from methodological problems as well. Nevertheless, a consistent pattern has emerged concerning the important role *both* environmental and genetic factors play in intellectual development (Scarr, 1992). For example, Table 3.4 summarizes correlations on IQ test scores among pairs of late adolescents and adults who share different genetic relationships with one another. Environmental contributions are revealed by findings that individuals reared together show somewhat higher correlations for intelligence scores than those with the same genetic relationship reared apart. Nevertheless, the impact of the genotype on intelligence is also evident. The correlations for IQ increase as the similarity in genotypes rises.

We can make sense of several additional findings by considering Scarr and McCartney's (1983; Scarr, 1992) analysis of developmental relationships between

TABLE 3.4	Relationship	Correlation	Number of Pairs
IQ and Degrees of Relatedness: Similarities of Genetically Related and Unrelated Individuals Who Live Together and Apart	**Genetically identical**		
	Identical twins together	.86	1,300
	Identical twins apart	.76	137
	Same person tested twice	.87	456
	Genetically related by half of the genes		
	Fraternal twins together	.55	8,600
	Biological sisters and brothers	.47	35,000
	Parents and children together	.40	4,400
	Parents and children apart	.31	345
	Genetically unrelated		
	Adopted children together	.00	200
	Unrelated persons apart	.00	15,000

Source: Adapted from Plomin & DeFries (1980).
Note: Based on data from Scarr & Weinberg (1978) and Teasdale & Owen (1985) on older adolescents who are comparable in age to other samples in this table. Younger adopted children resemble one another to a greater degree, with correlations around .24, according to samples of eight hundred pairs.

genetic and environmental correlations. For example, IQ scores for younger adopted children reared together are positively correlated (about .24) rather than unrelated as Table 3.4 indicates for older individuals. Moreover, intelligence has been found to be highly correlated in infancy and early childhood for *both* identical and fraternal twins and, with increasing age, to become *even greater* for identical twins but decline to the level reported in Table 3.4 for fraternal twins (Fischbein, 1981; Wilson, 1978, 1983, 1986). These kinds of findings probably reflect the impact of passive links (the similar rearing environment created by the parents) on intelligence early in childhood and more opportunity for niche picking later in development.

Identical twins, however, do not always become more similar as they grow older. As twins who have been reared together become older, fraternal, and to some extent identical, twins become more dissimilar on many aspects of intelligence tests (McCartney, Harris, & Bernieri, 1990). Perhaps they actively attempt to establish a *unique* niche in the family and community, efforts that may also be encouraged by parents of the twins (Schachter, 1982).

How significant is heredity for intellectual development? Assessments of **heritability,** the proportion of variability in the phenotype that can be accounted for by genetic influences, are estimated to be about 50 percent among white American and European middle-class children, the population studied most thoroughly (Neisser et al., 1996). This proportion increases somewhat into adulthood. However, a classic investigation by Marie Skodak and Harold Skeels (1949) illustrates the substantial impact experience can have even if intellectual development has a high hereditary basis. One hundred children born to mentally retarded mothers, most of whom were from low socioeconomic backgrounds, were adopted before six months of age into homes that were economically and educationally well above average. These children displayed above-average intelligence throughout childhood and adolescence and substantially higher IQs than their biological parents, an outcome reflecting the contribution of environmental factors. Despite their high levels, however, the children's IQs were still substantially correlated with those of their biological mothers, indicating a hereditary contribution to these scores as well.

IQ can undergo impressive boosts in some kinds of environments; nevertheless, measures of intelligence for adopted children continue to be highly correlated with those for their biological parents, indicating a genetic contribution (Loehlin, Willerman, & Horn, 1988; Turkheimer, 1991). Moreover, certain cognitive abilities, such as memory for where an object has been hidden, categorization, and word comprehension, in addition to overall IQ, are significantly influenced by hereditary as well as environmental factors in young children (Emde et al., 1992).

Temperament and Personality   Many personality traits also reflect genetic influences, although their heritability appears to be somewhat less than for intelligence (Loehlin, 1992; Plomin, 1994). However, **temperament,** an early-appearing constellation of personality traits, has been of particular interest in terms of possible genetic influences (Buss & Plomin, 1984; Rothbart & Derryberry, 1981; Thomas & Chess, 1977). Arnold Buss and Robert Plomin identified three broad qualities frequently describing the temperaments of infants and very young children. One of these is *sociability,* the tendency to be shy or inhibited and somewhat fearful of new experiences versus outgoing and uninhibited, qualities that are likely precursors to introversion and extroversion, respectively, in older children and adults. Another trait is *emotionality,* the ease with which an individual becomes distressed, upset, or angry and the intensity with which these emotions are expressed. The third trait is *activity,* as evidenced by the tempo and vigor with which behaviors are performed.

Selective breeding studies with various species of animals indicate that sociability, emotionality, and activity level have a hereditary component; family resemblance and adoption studies in humans lead to the same conclusion. For example, identical twins consistently show higher correlations for sociability (typically between .40 and .60 on various measures) than fraternal twins (typically between .10 and .30) (Emde et al., 1992; Matheny, 1989; Robinson et al., 1992). Perhaps inherited differences in physiological reactivity underlie these variations in social responsiveness (Kagan,

KEY THEME
Child's Active Role

KEY THEME
Individual Differences

heritability Proportion of variability in the phenotype that is estimated to be accounted for by genetic influences.

temperament Stable, early-appearing constellation of individual personality attributes believed to have a hereditary basis; includes sociability, emotionality, and activity level.

Snidman, & Arcus, 1992; Kagan, 1994). Young children who remain aloof and are reluctant to play with novel toys, such as Jeremy, display increased heart rate and muscle tension in unfamiliar situations compared to children who are more outgoing and spontaneous, such as Cindy.

Studies comparing infant twins on emotionality and activity also reveal higher correlations for identical twins than for fraternal twins (Plomin, 1987). Consistent racial and ethnic differences have been reported as well and have been attributed to genetic differences in temperament. When Daniel Freedman (1979) compared Caucasian and Chinese American newborns, he found Caucasian babies were more irritable and harder to comfort than Chinese American infants. More recently, research with four-month-olds from Boston, Dublin, and Beijing indicated that American infants were more active and fretful than those in Dublin, who in turn were more reactive than those in China (Kagan et al., 1994).

Does the environment also play some important role in temperament and other personality differences? Studies comparing the personalities of unrelated children in the same household report that the correlations are fairly low and often approach zero, especially in later childhood and adolescence (Plomin & Daniels, 1987). Behavioral geneticists have uncovered some other surprising findings. *Shared environment,* the kinds of experiences children in a home or community bear in common and are assumed to foster similarity, appears to be less influential than psychologists often claim (Bouchard, 1994; Plomin, 1995). In contrast, *nonshared environment,* the experiences unique to individual children as they interact with parents, peers, and others, can play a powerful role in development, one that tends to make children in the family *different* rather than similar (Plomin, 1996).

How can this be? Parents typically report that they treat their children in similar ways. Adolescent siblings, however, often argue that is not the case! Observations of how parents interact with their offspring seem to provide plenty of ammunition supporting the adolescents; siblings often are exposed to different experiences (Hetherington, Reiss, & Plomin, 1994).

"Y ou always liked Jeremy more than me!" shouted Cindy to her mother as she reluctantly, and angrily, began to pick up her toys. Her mother, stung by the charge, couldn't shake her uneasiness over Cindy's outburst as she went to prepare dinner.

RESEARCH APPLIED TO PARENTING

Treating Siblings the Same or Differently

"Maybe because he was shy, it just seemed simpler to take care of Jeremy" she speculated to herself. "Cindy and her friends were always more boisterous and likely to get into mischief. Have I treated Jeremy and Cindy differently even though I thought I was rearing them the same way? Cindy just seemed to need more disciplining."

KEY THEME
Individual Differences

Should parents be encouraged to treat their children differently or in a similar manner? The answer to such a question is far from clear, but it is helpful to point out several things that research indicates parents might consider in confronting this matter.

1. *Expect siblings to kindle different reactions from others.* Because all children, with the exception of identical twins, are born with different genotypes, they are likely to evoke distinctive kinds of responses from family members, teachers, peers, and others. These responses can, in turn, serve to magnify existing differences in a child's behavior. Recognizing that genetic differences contribute to temperament and personality can help parents to appreciate individual differences when more than one child is part of the family.

2. *Assume siblings will actively search out ways to be different from one another.* Children may actively seek out environments and experiences that complement their

Parents with more than one child often want to treat each of them equally, but need to fine-tune their parenting efforts to the needs and age-appropriate activities of individual children. Fine motor skills demonstrated by the older sibling may permit her to color or carry out other activities that are beyond the capacity of the younger sibling who, as shown here, has found her own way to keep busy. By providing individual support and avoiding "favoritism," parents seem to help siblings learn to appreciate each other's abilities.

strengths, that is, they will engage in niche picking to set themselves apart from others within the family. Such efforts may even be observed in identical twins, children with the same genotype, as one twin takes on a more active role in leadership, becomes more studious, or engages in more social interactions than the other. Whether it stems from biology or experience, the opportunity to find one's niche within the family, as well as the larger community, seems to be an important aspect of development for all children.

KEY THEME
Child's Active Role

3. *Anticipate that siblings will experience family events in different ways and will need to be treated differently in some circumstances.* Siblings within the family—by virtue of their birth order, spacing, and unique events such as an illness, the death of a grandparent, or a move to a new neighborhood—will necessarily receive unique experiences because of their specific developmental status. In fact, distinct socialization practices for children of different ages may be the norm since treatment by caregivers could otherwise be developmentally inappropriate. For example, younger children typically need more nurturance and care, whereas older children may have a need for greater independence and greater responsibility. Most caregivers do report that they treat their children differently (Dunn & McGuire, 1994). These differences are already noticed by children as young as 5 years of age. Moreover, if given the choice, younger children would prefer being the oldest child in the family; that is, in the eyes of younger children, an older child seems to have higher status (McHale, et al., 1995).

KEY THEME
Individual Differences

4. *Treat siblings impartially when possible and appropriate.* Impartial treatment of siblings by parents, to the extent that it is appropriate, is associated with less conflict between siblings and between children and their parents (Brody & Stoneman, 1994; McHale, et al., 1995). In other words, parents who are able to maintain a balance between socialization practices that are equitable within the limits of age-appropriate differences, have children who can interact effectively and in constructive ways with others, including their siblings. These findings lead to the conclusion that differences in parenting arising from the individual needs of children can have positive consequences, but only as long as these differences do not reflect a form of parental "favoritism."

TABLE 3.5		Identical Twins	Fraternal Twins
The Genetic Basis of Selected Behavioral and Personality Disorders: Twin Data	**Twin Concordances**		
	Conduct disorder	.85	.70
	Manic-depression	.65	.20
	Autism	.65	.10
	Unipolar depression	.45	.20
	Alcoholism—males	.40	.20
	Schizophrenia	.40	.10
	Alcoholism—females	.30	.25

Evidence for the genetic basis of behavioral and personality disorders is often supported by studies of twins. For these disorders, the likelihood that both members of a pair will display the disorder, if exhibited by one, is greater when the pair are identical twins rather than fraternal twins. However, environmental factors may contribute to high concordance rates for both identical and fraternal twins, as is likely for conduct disorders.

Source: Data from Plomin, 1994.

KEY THEME
Nature/Nurture

Behavioral and Personality Disorders   Table 3.5 summarizes the concordance rate for identical and fraternal twins for a variety of behavioral and personality disorders. None of these findings indicates 100 percent concordance even in identical twins, despite the identity of their genetic makeup. Thus, environmental factors play an important role in the manifestation of each of these problems. In fact, concordance measures for *conduct disorders* (fighting and aggressive behavior, failure to accept parental discipline) in both identical and fraternal twins are relatively high, suggesting that environmental factors contribute substantially to their appearance in both groups.

Alcoholism, despite frequent efforts to link it to a single gene, also tends to show only a modest genetic component. On the other hand, *schizophrenia,* a form of psychopathology that includes disturbances in thoughts and emotions such as delusions and hallucinations, does appear to show some genetic contribution. As the biological relationship to someone diagnosed as having schizophrenia increases, an individual's risk for the same diagnosis rises. When one twin has schizophrenia, the other twin is about three times more likely to display schizophrenia if identical than if fraternal. Adoption studies provide further confirmation for a role of the genotype; schizophrenia is far more prevalent among adopted children who are the biological offspring of a schizophrenic parent than those of a nonschizophrenic parent (Gottesman & Shields, 1982). At the present time, no single gene seems to be responsible for the findings; instead, polygenic contributions are more likely.

The genetic contribution to *manic depression,* a disorder characterized by rapid and wide mood swings between feverish activity and withdrawn, depressed behaviors, appears to be substantial. Family studies reveal that children of a manic-depressive parent are at far greater risk for displaying the illness than children without such a parent. Research on adoptees provides further evidence that genotype plays a role; the risk for adopted children whose biological parents have the illness is about three times greater than for adopted children whose biological parents do not have it (Knowles, 1985).

Recent work on *autism* (more fully described in Chapter 8), a disorder that historically was assumed to be largely the consequence of improper caregiving, also reveals an ample hereditary contribution (Rutter et al., 1993).

Other Characteristics   A host of other characteristics, including empathy, reading disabilities, sexual orientation, susceptibility to various illnesses such as heart disease and cancer, and even a propensity to watch television, have been identified as having a genetic linkage (LeVay & Hamer, 1994; Plomin et al., 1990; Plomin, Owen, & McGuffin, 1994; Zahn-Waxler, Robinson, & Emde, 1991). In addition, how individuals perceive their family environments also appears to be influenced by the genotype (Hur & Bouchard, 1995; Plomin et al., 1994). Remember, however, that the genotype codes for proteins and enzymes that, in the context of a cellular environment, support patterns of neural, hormonal, and brain activity. These in turn sustain the development of traits and behaviors in individuals. Thus, identifying a genetic component in this multifaceted array of systems and settings provides knowledge about only one of many levels of influence. Understanding how the genotype along with the environment creates that influence remains a critical goal for unlocking the complex theme of nature and nurture in development.

CHAPTER RECAP

SUMMARY OF DEVELOPMENTAL THEMES

NATURE/NURTURE   What roles do nature and nurture play in development?

The phenotype, the observable behaviors and characteristics of an individual, is the product of a complex interaction between genotype and environment. Environment includes biological contexts, such as the foods we eat, but more frequently we consider the interaction between nature and nurture in terms of how experiences provided by caregivers and others affect behavior and development. The relationship between genotype and environment is further complicated by passive, reactive, and niche-picking correlations. As a consequence, experiential factors are tightly interwoven with genotype to produce the range and variety of behaviors and characteristics an individual displays. Both genotype and environment are indispensable to development.

CHILD'S ACTIVE ROLE   How does the child play an active role in the effects of heredity on development?

Researchers recognize the child's active efforts to seek out environments that support and maintain behavioral orientations

and preferences that are influenced by hereditary factors. As the child achieves greater control over the environment, he or she has increasing opportunities to find a niche. In other words, behaviors, activities, and skills the child displays are not only a consequence of imposed social and physical experiences but also reflect the selective efforts of the child to discover environments that are interesting, challenging, and supportive. Inherited and environmentally imposed influences may be met with eager support or active resistance to determine each child's unique life history.

INDIVIDUAL DIFFERENCES   How prominent are individual differences in development?

Individual differences are pervasive in intellectual, temperamental, and a host of other cognitive, social, and emotional aspects of development. Hereditary and environmental factors determine these differences. Alleles of genes contribute to the wide range of physical, cognitive, emotional, and social adaptations displayed by individuals. These individual differences are not solely produced by genes; they are also the product of a rich medley of physical, social, and cultural contexts in which each individual matures. A distinctive combination of genes and experiences promotes the abundant diversity we observe in human abilities and behavior.

SUMMARY OF TOPICS

■ PRINCIPLES OF HEREDITARY TRANSMISSION

The structures and principles of heredity must be examined at several levels, including (1) the individual, (2) the cells making up the body of that individual, (3) the chromosomes located within the nucleus of those cells, (4) the genes comprising segments of each chromosome, and (5) the nucleotide pairs that form the biochemical building blocks for the genes. A central unit of hereditary information is the *gene*. Genes are segments of the twenty-three pairs of *chromosomes* that are made up of *deoxyribonucleic acid,* or *DNA*.

Variants of pairs of genes, or *alleles,* interact with one another in *dominant-recessive* and other ways to establish different patterns of inheritance for particular traits or characteris-

tics. *Mitosis* is the process of cell division by which the chromosomes are duplicated in body cells. The *gametes,* or sex cells, are formed by *meiosis,* a process of cell division in which one member of each pair of chromosomes is randomly selected for each sperm or egg cell. This random process, combined with *crossing over,* ensures that every individual, with the exception of identical twins, has a unique hereditary blueprint.

Hereditary contributions to development begin at conception, when the twenty-three chromosomes in a sperm cell unite with the twenty-three chromosomes in the egg. Males and females differ in the composition of the twenty-third pair of chromosomes. In females, both members of the pair are *X chromosomes*. In males, one is an X and the other is a *Y chromosome*. Gene disorders associated with this twenty-third pair of chromosomes are said to be *sex linked*.

■ GENE AND CHROMOSOMAL ABNORMALITIES AND GENETIC COUNSELING

A number of inherited abnormalities associated with chromosomes and alleles can lead to severe disruptions in physical and behavioral development. *Genetic counseling* provides prospective parents with information on the likelihood of having children affected by birth defects and may suggest a variety of tests to determine whether an individual is a carrier of the disorder or whether the fetus is affected by it. New advances can assist those who are unable to have children or may be concerned about the inheritance of disorders in their offspring.

■ DEVELOPMENTAL AND BEHAVIORAL GENETICS

A *genotype* constitutes hereditary information and interacts with the environment to determine the *phenotype,* that is, measurable characteristics, traits, or behaviors. The genotype may establish a range of possible outcomes for development; however, its relative contribution to a particular phenotype may dif-fer from one individual to the next as a function of environmental conditions. Understanding hereditary contributions is made even more difficult by correlations between genotype and environment. For example, caregivers with specific genotypes are likely to provide supportive environments, that is, a *passive* correlation; parents, peers, and others are likely to *react* in ways that accommodate genetic inclinations; and active *niche picking* takes place whereby children attempt to find or create environments that support their individual genetic propensities.

Identifying to what degree and how genotype and environment contribute to development remains a major goal of *behavior genetics*. Most human attributes, whether simple physical traits or complex capacities, are polygenic, that is, influenced by several genes. Behavior geneticists conduct studies of family members, including identical and fraternal twins, siblings, and adopted children, to demonstrate that both the genotype and the environment make important contributions to intelligence, temperament, personality characteristics, mental illness, and many other aspects of human behavior.

4 THE PRENATAL PERIOD AND BIRTH

NATURE/NURTURE
What roles do nature and nurture play in prenatal development and birth?

CONTINUITY/DISCONTINUITY
Is development before and after birth continuous or discontinuous?

SOCIOCULTURAL INFLUENCE
How does the sociocultural context influence prenatal development and birth?

INDIVIDUAL DIFFERENCES
How prominent are individual differences in prenatal development and the newborn?

t was a rough meeting. Her boss had not been enthusiastic about the new marketing plans. Carmen knew her ideas were a gamble too. Back in the calm of her own office, Carmen's thoughts drifted to a more carefree time as a child in her small village in the Caribbean.

Then she felt it: the first unmistakable twitching, the fluttery motion of a tiny elbow. Or was it a leg?

Although Carmen and her husband were thrilled by the news of her pregnancy, the first four months had been difficult. Morning sickness, Carmen's hectic schedule, and her mother's serious illness had left little time to enjoy the remarkable changes leading up to this first stirring. Carmen had seen the ultrasound picture just a few weeks earlier. But it was this extraordinary movement within her womb that made it finally seem so real. She was going to have a baby! Yet concern gnawed at the borders of Carmen's exhilaration. She savored a glass of wine with dinner each evening; had she drunk too much? She quit smoking as soon as she had learned the news; had it been soon enough? And what about the pressures of this job?

ost women experience both pride and apprehension when they learn they are pregnant. Those feelings are often influenced by a multitude of social and cultural views and ideas about pregnancy. Although societies differ enormously in their specific beliefs, anthropologists report that expectant women around the world are often urged to avoid certain activities and carry out various rituals for the sake of their unborn. In Western civilizations, admonitions about pregnancy exist as well; obstetricians may advise a pregnant woman to stop smoking, avoid alcohol, and let someone else clean the cat's litterbox. Did Carmen, then, have good reason to be concerned about her pregnancy?

Fortunately, the mysteries surrounding this remarkable time are beginning to be unraveled. Our discussion of prenatal development will open with a brief description of the amazing sequence of events taking place between conception and birth. At no other time does growth progress so rapidly or do so many physical changes occur in a matter of weeks, days, and even hours. Some cultures, such as the Chinese, tacitly acknowledge these dramatic happenings by granting the baby a year of life when born. As we will soon learn, in the typical nine months of confinement to the womb, the fetus has indeed undergone an epic journey.

Although fetal growth proceeds in a highly protected environment, we are also discovering the ways drugs, diseases, and other external factors affect prenatal development. We will summarize our current understanding of these influences as well. We will then consider the birth process and take a first quick look at the newborn's states and characteristics.

THE STAGES OF PRENATAL DEVELOPMENT

Three major overlapping periods define the life of a human organism. **Prenatal development** is launched from the moment of conception and continues to the beginning of labor. All but the first few days of this period are spent within the confines of the womb. The **perinatal period** dawns about the seventh month of pregnancy and extends until twenty-eight days after birth. This phase is associated with the impending birth, the social and physical setting for delivery, and the baby's first adjustments to his or her new world. Among the events included in the perinatal period are the medical and obstetrical practices associated with delivery and the preparations and care provided by parents and others to assist in the transition from the womb to life outside. **Postnatal development** begins after birth. The child's environment now includes the broader physical and social world afforded by caregivers and others responsible for the infant's continued growth.

Prenatal development is further divided into three stages. The first, the **germinal period,** also known as the **period of the zygote,** encompasses the first ten to fourteen days following conception. Cell division and migration of the newly fertilized egg, culminating with its implantation in the uterine wall, characterize the germinal period. The second stage, the **embryonic period,** continues from about two to eight weeks after conception. The formation of structures and organs associated with the nervous, circulatory, respiratory, and other systems mark the embryonic period. The final stage, the **fetal period,** lasts from about eight weeks after conception to birth. This period is distinguished by substantial physical growth, and organs and systems are refined in preparation for functioning outside the womb. This entire process begins the moment sperm and egg fuse.

Fertilization

Even before her own birth, Carmen, like most other human females, had formed approximately 5 million primitive egg cells in her ovaries. Their numbers, however, declined with development; by puberty perhaps only thirty thousand remained. Of this abundant supply, about four hundred will mature and be released over time for potential fertilization during the childbearing years (Samuels & Samuels, 1986). In contrast, male sperm production begins only at puberty, when an incredible 100 million sperm (about a thousand per second) may be formed daily.

The opportunity for human conception begins about the fourteenth day after the start of the menstrual period. At this time, a capsulelike *follicle* housing a primitive egg cell in one of the ovaries begins to mature. As it matures and changes position, the follicle eventually ruptures and discharges its valuable contents from the ovary. The expelled egg cell, or *ovum,* is carried into the Fallopian tube. This organ serves as a conduit for the egg, which is moved toward the uterus at the leisurely rate of about one-sixteenth inch per hour. The Fallopian tube also provides a receptive environment for fertilization if sperm are present (Abel, 1989). In the absence of this event, the unfertilized ovum survives only about twenty-four hours.

Sperm reach the Fallopian tube by maneuvering from the vagina through the cervix and the uterus. Sperm can migrate several inches an hour with the assistance of their tail-like appendages. Fewer than one hundred may negotiate the six- or more hour trip into the Fallopian tube, but these typically survive about forty-eight hours and sometimes even longer.

If an ovum is present, sperm seem attracted to it (Roberts, 1991). The egg also prepares for fertilization in the presence of sperm. Cells initially surrounding the ovum loosen their protective grip, permitting the egg to be penetrated (Nilsson, 1990). As soon as one sperm cell breaks through the egg's protective linings, enzymes rapidly transform its outer membrane to prevent others from invading. Genetic material from egg and sperm quickly mix to establish a normal complement of forty-six chromosomes. The egg, the body's largest cell, barely visible to the naked eye,

KEY THEME
Continuity/Discontinuity

prenatal development   Period in development from conception to the onset of labor.

perinatal period   Period beginning about the seventh month of pregnancy and continuing until about four weeks after birth.

postnatal development   Period in development following birth.

germinal period   Period lasting about ten to fourteen days following conception before the fertilized egg becomes implanted in the uterine wall. Also called *period of the zygote.*

embryonic period   Period of prenatal development during which major biological organs and systems form. Begins about the tenth to fourteenth day after conception and ends about the eighth week after conception.

fetal period   Period of prenatal development, from about the eighth week after conception to birth, marked by rapid growth and preparation of body systems for functioning in the postnatal environment.

Human development begins with the penetration of the egg by a single sperm as shown here (egg and sperm are magnified greatly). Although the egg is the body's largest cell and the sperm its smallest, each contributes twenty-three chromosomes to form the hereditary basis for the development of a new living entity.

weighs about 100,000 times more than the sperm, the body's smallest cell. Despite the enormous difference in size, both contribute equivalent amounts of genetic material for the new entity that is formed.

The Germinal Period

After fertilization, the zygote continues to migrate down the Fallopian tube (see Figure 4.1). Within twenty-four to thirty hours after conception, the single cell divides into two cells, the first of a series of mitotic divisions called *cleavages*. At roughly twelve-hour intervals these cells divide again to form four, then eight, then sixteen cells. During the cleavages, the zygote remains about the same size; thus, individual cells become smaller and smaller.

After three days, about the time the zygote is ready to enter the uterus, it has become a solid sphere of sixteen cells called a *morula*. Each cell is alike in its capacity to generate a separate identical organism; each contains and has access to the master genetic blueprint. By the fourth day after conception, however, the cells begin to segregate to carry out specific functions. One group forms a spherical outer cellular layer that eventually becomes various membranes providing nutritive support for the embryo (Moore, 1989). A second, inner group of cells organizes into a mass that will develop into the embryo (Cross, Werb, & Fisher, 1994). This differentiated group of cells is now called a *blastocyst*.

About the sixth day after conception, the blastocyst begins the process of attaching to the uterine wall to tap a critical new supply of nutriments. By about the tenth to fourteenth day after conception, the implantation process is completed. In preparing for this event, the blastocyst began secreting hormones and other substances to inhibit menstruation, or the shedding of the uterine lining, and to keep the woman's immune system from rejecting the foreign object. One of these hormones eventually becomes detectable in the woman's urine as a marker in pregnancy tests.

The Embryonic Period

The embryonic period, which begins with the implantation of the blastocyst and continues until about the eighth week after conception, is marked by the rapid

FIGURE 4.1   Fertilization and the Germinal Period

During the early development of the human embryo, an egg cell is released from a maturing follicle within the ovary and fertilization takes place in the Fallopian tube, transforming the egg cell or ovum into a zygote. Cleavage and multiplication of cells proceed as the zygote migrates toward the uterus. Differentiation of the zygote begins within the uterus, becoming a solid sixteen-cell sphere known as the *morula*, then a differentiated set of cells known as the *blastocyst*, which prepares for implantation in the uterine wall. Once implanted, it taps a vital source of nutriments to sustain further development. (The numbers indicate days following fertilization.)

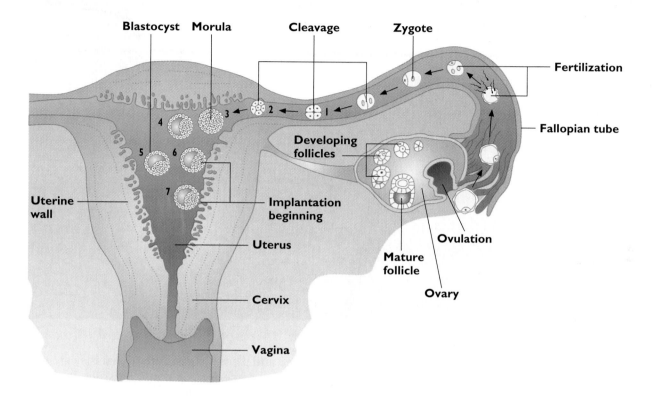

differentiation of cells to form most of the organs and systems within the body. Differentiation is achieved by the migration and production of specialized cells having distinctive functions.

Formation of Body Organs and Systems   The first step in the formation of various body organs and systems involves the migration of unspecialized embryonic cells to establish a three-layered embryo (Abel, 1989). The three layers serve as the foundation for all tissues and organs in the body. The *endoderm,* or inner layer, will give rise to many of the linings of internal organs such as lungs, the gastrointestinal tract, the liver, the pancreas, the bladder, and some glands. The *mesoderm,* or middle layer, eventually develops into skeleton and muscles, the urogenital system, the lymph and cardiovascular systems, and other connective tissues. The *ectoderm,* or outer layer, will form skin, hair, and nails, but its earliest derivatives will be the central nervous system and nerves.

How, by simply migrating to a layered configuration, do undifferentiated cells come to establish a highly distinctive set of organs and systems? Understanding this process remains one of the most important unresolved issues in prenatal development (Barinaga, 1994). However, the immediate environment appears to play a major role. Although at first unspecialized, each cell's potential or fate becomes constrained by its association with neighboring tissues. In other words, cells are induced by their surroundings to take on certain forms and functions. For example, if cells

KEY THEME
Nature/Nurture

This view of the embryo, approximately six weeks following conception, reveals the fluid-filled amniotic sac that provides the buoyant, liquid environment surrounding it. The small, dark circular spot in the head region is the retina of the eye since the eyelid has yet to develop and cover it.

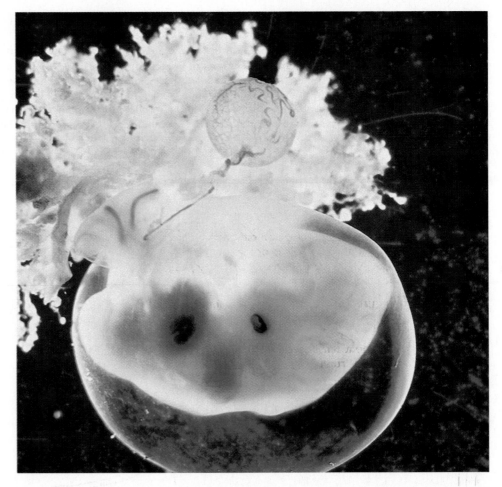

from the ectodermal layer are removed and placed in a culture so that they grow in isolation from other cell layers, they form epidermal, or skinlike, tissues. If placed with a layer of mesodermal cells, however, a nervous system will emerge. The mechanisms inducing such differentiation remain unknown, but biochemical substances are likely to be involved in this critical influence of the immediate environment on cellular growth (Abel, 1989).

Because the embryonic period is the major time for development of organs and systems, many possibilities for disruption exist. We will consider some examples later when we discuss the influence of environmental factors on the embryo. Under normal conditions, however, the sequence of primary changes in prenatal development proceeds in a fairly regular pattern. Table 4.1 summarizes several of these changes.

Early Brain and Nervous System Development About the fifteenth day after conception, a small group of cells at one end of the ectoderm starts to grow rapidly. The growth creates a reference point for the cephalo (head) and the caudal (tail) regions of the embryo and helps to distinguish left from right side. The cells induce the development of the *neural* tube, which in turn initiates the formation of the spinal cord, nerves, and eventually the brain.

Rapid changes in the neural tube begin about the fourth week. At first, the neural tube is open at both ends. The tube begins closing in the brain region and, a few days later, in the caudal region. Its failure to knit shut at either end can have drastic consequences for development. In *anencephaly,* a condition in which the cephalic region of the neural tube does not close, the cerebral hemispheres fail to develop and most of the cortex is missing at birth. Newborns with such a condition survive only a short time.

Spina bifida is a condition that arises when the caudal region of the neural tube fails to close. The resulting cleft in the vertebral column permits spinal nerves to

3 Weeks*

Precursors to vertebrae begin to organize.

Blood vessels form and connect to precursor of umbilical cord.

Blood vessels and tubes establish primitive, one-chambered heart that starts to beat by 21st day.

Major segments of brain begin to differentiate.

Embryo grows to about 2 millimeters in length (about 1/10 inch).

4 Weeks

Disc-shaped embryo forms more cylindrical appearance as it folds on cephalo and caudal ends and on right and left side.

Thickening stripe of tissue develops on either side of trunk to begin chest and stomach muscle production. Swelling occurs near upper end of stripe to form arm buds by about day 26. Two days later similar swellings begin at caudal end of stripe to form early buds for lower limbs.

Rudimentary liver, gall bladder, stomach, intestines, pancreas, thyroid, and lungs created.

Nerves begin to form.

Embryo grows to about 6 millimeters (about 1/4 inch) and appears to have tail-like cartilage curving under rump.

5 Weeks

Basic mouth and esophagus develop.

Elbow, wrist regions, and paddle-shaped plate with ridges for future fingers take shape.

Heart differentiates into upper and lower regions.

Embryo grows rapidly, about 1 millimeter a day (.04 inches), but is still less than 1/2 inch in length.

6–7 Weeks

Upper lip, jaws, teeth, eyelids, nostrils, tip of nose, and tongue are formed as head size becomes dominant.

Embryo possesses short, webbed fingers, and foot plate has also begun to differentiate.

Heart divides into four chambers.

Many muscles differentiate and take final shape.

Neurons form rapidly.

Tail-like cartilage regresses.

Embryo begins to show reflexive responses to touch, first around facial region.

8–12 Weeks

Fetus appears to have widely separated eyes and ears set lower in head than they eventually will be.

Eyelids fuse shut about 9th week.

Fingernails, toenails, and hair follicles form.

Fetus begins to show differentiation of external reproductive organs (if male about 9th week, if female several weeks later).

Bones start to grow.

Startle and sucking responses first appear. Fetus displays hiccups and flexes arms and legs.

TABLE 4.1

Chronology of Important Events During Prenatal Development

This table describes the sequence of prenatal development based on the findings of research. Individual differences exist in the exact ages at which embryo and fetus display the various developmental achievements outlined here.

TABLE 4.1 (cont.)

Chronology of Important Events During Prenatal Development

13–16 Weeks

Fingerprints and footprints established.

Spinal cord begins to form.

If female, large numbers of primitive egg cells are created.

Other reflexes, including swallowing and sucking, emerge.

Eyelids have closed.

Fetus sprouts soft, downlike hair at end of this period.

17–20 Weeks

Fetus becomes covered by cheeselike, fatty material secreted by oil glands that probably protects the skin constantly bathed in amniotic fluid.

Eyebrows and hair visible.

Fetal heartbeat can be heard through woman's abdomen.

Fetus displays stable pattern of sleep and wakefulness and often assumes a favorite position.

21–25 Weeks

Skin appears wrinkled and has a pink to reddish cast caused by blood in capillaries, which are highly visible through translucent skin.

Eyes fully formed and may be opened and closed.

Fetus can see and hear and produce crying sounds if born prematurely.

26–29 Weeks

Fat deposits accumulate beneath surface of skin to give fetus a much less wrinkled appearance.

Downy hair may disappear or may remain and be present at birth.

Hair may begin to grow on head.

Lungs are sufficiently developed to permit breathing of air should birth occur.

Nerve cell formation completed, and brain begins to take on wrinkled and fissured appearance.

30–38 Weeks

Fat continues to accumulate, giving full-term newborn chubby appearance and helping to insulate baby from varying temperatures once born.

Fetus adds about half its total weight.

Skin color turns from red to pink to white to bluish pink for all babies, regardless of racial makeup.

*From conception.

grow outside the protective vertebrae. In more serious cases, the infant may be paralyzed and lack sensation in the legs. Surgery often must be performed after birth to keep the condition from getting worse, but lost capacities cannot be restored, and malformations in brain development and impaired intellectual development may accompany spina bifida (Abel, 1989; Wills, 1993).

The frequency of both neural tube defects, now about six in every ten thousand births, has declined sharply over the last twenty years in the United States, especially for anencephaly, where the pregnancy is often not carried to term (Limb & Holmes, 1994). A better understanding of nutritional needs early in pregnancy, particularly of folic acid and other components of the vitamin B complex, also appears to be an important explanation for the decline (Yen et al., 1992).

The second month after conception is marked by continued rapid development of the head and brain. Nerve cells show an explosive increase in number, with as many as 100,000 neurons generated every minute (Nilsson, 1990). Neurons also undergo extensive migration once the neural tube closes and soon make contact with one another. The head greatly enlarges relative to the rest of the embryo to account for about half of total body length. Nevertheless, the embryo is still tiny; it is less than one-and-a-half inches long and weighs only about half an ounce. However, nearly all organs are established by this time, and the embryo is recognizably human.

One of the most striking milestones is reached about the fifth week after conception, when the nervous system begins to function. Now irregular and faint brain wave activity can be recorded. Soon, if the head or upper body is touched, the embryo exhibits reflex movements. In a few more weeks muscles may flex, but it will still be some time before the woman is able to feel any movement.

The Fetal Period

The change from embryo to fetus is signaled by the emergence of bone tissue at about the eighth week after conception. Organ differentiation continues, particularly in the reproductive system and the brain. However, the fetal period is best known for growth in size and the genesis of processes that assist organs and systems in functioning. One positive consequence is that the fetus becomes much less susceptible to potentially damaging environmental factors.

During the third month after conception, the fetus increases to about three-and-a-half inches in length and about one-and-a-half ounces in weight. Its movements become more pronounced. At nine weeks, the fetus opens and closes its lips, wrinkles its forehead, raises and lowers its eyebrows, and turns its head. By the end of twelve weeks, the behaviors have become more coordinated. The fetus can, for example, display sucking and the basic motions of breathing and swallowing. Fingers will bend if the arm is touched, and the thumb can be opposed to fingers, an indication that peripheral muscles and nerves are functioning in increasingly sophisticated ways (Samuels & Samuels, 1986).

The Second Trimester   By the end of the third month, the fetus has completed the first of three trimesters of prenatal development. In the second trimester, the fetus's body grows more rapidly than at any other time. By the end of the fourth month, the fetus is about eight to ten inches long, although it still weighs only about six ounces. During the sixth month, the fetus rapidly starts to gain weight, expanding to about one-and-a-half pounds and reaching a length of about fourteen inches.

By the middle of the second trimester, fetal movements such as those Carmen felt, known as *quickening,* are unmistakable to the woman. The fetus stretches and squirms as well. Near the end of this trimester, brain wave patterns begin to look like those observed in the newborn. Should birth occur at this time, there is a small chance of survival if specialized medical facilities are available. Although a baby born at this stage can breathe regularly for a number of hours, the surfaces of air sacs in the lungs tend to stick together, interfering with the transfer of oxygen and carbon dioxide, unless production of substances that prevent the problem has begun.

The Third Trimester   The final months add finishing touches to the astonishing progression in prenatal development. The cerebral hemispheres, the regions of the brain most heavily involved in complex mental processing, grow rapidly, folding and developing fissures to give them a wrinkled appearance. Myelin, which helps to insulate and speed the transmission of neuronal impulses, begins to form and surround some nerve fibers. Brain wave patterns indicating different stages of sleep and wakefulness can also be observed. The sense organs are developed sufficiently to enable

By about eighteen weeks after conception, the fetus engages in movements, identified as *quickening,* which are often felt by a woman. Some of these actions may bring the thumb into the mouth, as shown here, which will result in sucking. In fact, when born, some infants have callouses on their thumbs from engaging in this fetal practice.

the fetus to smell and taste as well as to hear, see, and feel and even learn, as we will see in Chapter 6. The fetus continues to gain weight rapidly (nearly half a pound per week), although growth slows in the weeks just preceding birth. Control of body temperature and rhythmic respiratory activity remain problematic if birth occurs at the beginning of the third trimester. Nevertheless, **viability,** or the ability of the fetus to survive outside the womb, dramatically improves over the course of these three months.

The onset of birth to a woman between ages nineteen and thirty-four can be expected when the fetus reaches a gestational age of about 277 days. However, as any parent knows, variability in the duration of preparing for this long-anticipated event is the norm. The average gestational period appears to be a few days shorter for Japanese and Black babies compared to Caucasian babies, for infants born to mothers younger than nineteen or older than thirty-four years, and for second and later children compared to firstborns (Mittendorf et al., 1990, 1993). **Gestational age,** commonly employed in the medical profession to gauge prenatal growth, is derived from the date of onset of the woman's last menstrual period before conception. This method of calculation makes the embryo or fetus about fifteen days older than when age is determined from the date of conception (Reece et al., 1995).

Prenatal Diagnosis

We saw in Chapter 3 how genetic counselors use prenatal diagnostic procedures to assist couples at risk for having children with a genetic disease. These procedures can detect several hundred defects, including many that are environmentally induced as well as those with a hereditary basis. For example, some tests carried out on an expectant woman's blood in the second trimester of pregnancy (such as the alpha fetoprotein test and triple screen test) may signal the possibility of neural tube defects or other problems. These tests, however, provide only an indication of increased risk, and other diagnostic tests must be carried out to confirm or disconfirm the sus-

viability   Ability of the baby to survive outside the mother's womb.

gestational age   Age of fetus derived from onset of mother's last menstrual period.

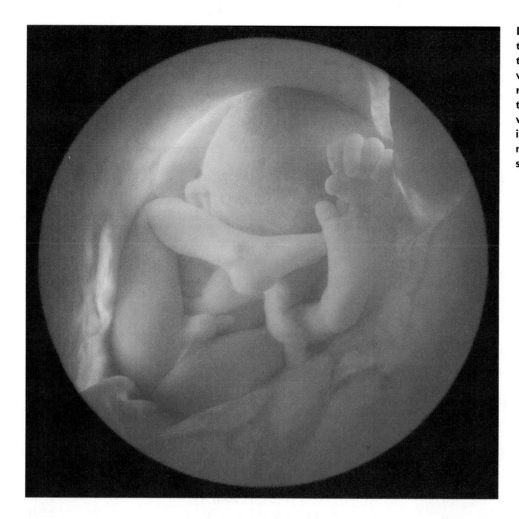

In the last few weeks of the third trimester of pregnancy, the fetus continues to gain weight and grow at a fairly rapid pace. As a consequence, the confining quarters of the womb become crowded, forcing the fetus to curl up in a more ball-like configuration as shown here.

pected problem. Fetal blood sampling, the withdrawal of blood directly from the fetus while in utero, can assist in detecting several anomalies as well (Ghidini et al., 1993). Perhaps the best-known procedures for prenatal diagnosis are amniocentesis, chorionic villus sampling, and ultrasonography.

Amniocentesis   In **amniocentesis,** a small amount of amniotic fluid is withdrawn through a syringe inserted in the woman's abdominal wall (see Figure 4.2). Fetal cells collected by this procedure are tested for biochemical composition and chromosomal makeup. Amniocentesis is usually performed during the fourteenth to sixteenth week after conception; analyses performed on the cells often require several additional weeks for completion. The risks from amniocentesis are small, but the possibility of infection and spontaneous abortion may increase. The safety and effectiveness of the procedure performed at earlier times (eleven to fourteen weeks after conception) are still being explored (Shulman et al., 1994).

Chorionic Villus Sampling   In **chorionic villus sampling,** a biopsy or small sample of hairlike projections (*villi*) is taken from the chorion, the outer wall of the membrane in which the embryo develops. This test permits chromosomal and biochemical analyses as early as the fifth week of prenatal development, although the procedure is usually performed between eight and twelve weeks after conception. Information gained at this earlier time in pregnancy can considerably reduce uncertainty and anxiety about the possibility of defects (Caccia et al., 1991). However, the procedure is somewhat more difficult to perform than amniocentesis and has been linked to a slightly increased risk of miscarriage and limb malformations (Hsieh et al., 1995; Report of NICHHD Workshop, 1993).

amniocentesis   Method of sampling the fluid surrounding the developing fetus by insertion of a needle. Used to diagnose fetal genetic and developmental disorders.

chorionic villus sampling Method of sampling fetal chorionic cells. Used to diagnose embryonic genetic and developmental disorders.

FIGURE 4.2   The Process of Amniocentesis

In this prenatal screening procedure, a needle is inserted into the amniotic fluid sur-rounding the fetus. A small amount of fluid is withdrawn, and cells shed by the fetus are separated from the fluid by centrifuge. The cells are cultured and submitted to various biochemical and other tests to determine whether chromosomal, genetic, or other developmental defects exist.

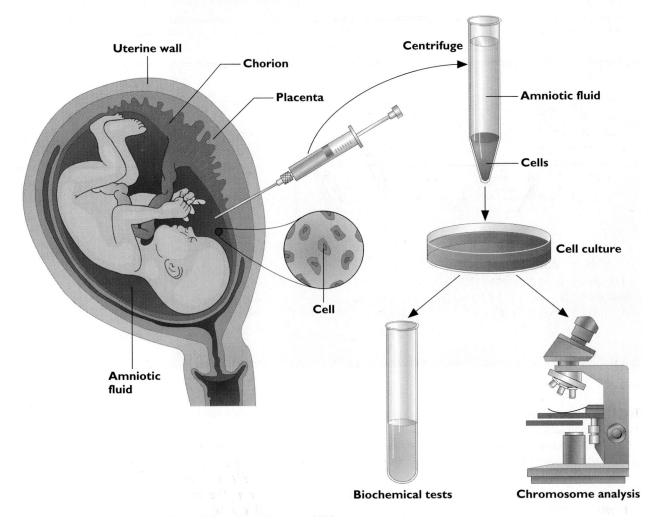

Source: Adapted from Knowles, 1985.

Amniocentesis and chorionic villus sampling are typically performed only when there is an increased risk of impaired fetal development. Women who are older than thirty-five, have experienced frequent miscarriages, have other children or relatives with genetic defects, or for whom maternal blood samples or ultrasonography raise concerns may be offered these tests.

Ultrasonography   **Ultrasonography,** often called *ultrasound,* is now used routinely in many countries to help determine whether fetal growth is proceeding normally. Sound waves, reflecting at different rates from tissues of varying density, are repre-sented on video monitors and even printed to form a picture of the fetus. The picture can reveal such problems as microcephaly (small head size), cardiac mal-formations, cleft lip and palate, and neural tube and other physical disabilities. Ultra-sonography is also widely used to assist in carrying out prenatal diagnostic tests, to verify the age of the fetus (interpretation of maternal and fetal blood tests are often highly dependent on an accurate assessment of age), and to monitor lifesaving oper-ations that may on rare occasions be performed on the fetus within the womb (Har-

ultrasonography   Method of using sound wave reflections to obtain a representation of the developing fetus. Used to estimate gestational age and detect fetal physical abnormalities.

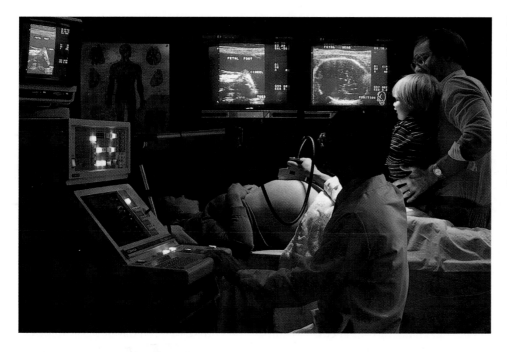

Newer technologies have enriched our understanding of the development of the fetus and have helped to improve the well-being of women during pregnancy. One of these advances, ultrasound, provides a visual glimpse of the fetus. The images can help this young child as well as the parents to understand what is happening during prental development.

rison, 1996). Although not universally recommended in the United States because of lingering concerns about its safety (Newnham et al., 1993), ultrasonography has become a common and popular tool for informing specialists as well as prospective parents such as Carmen about the course of prenatal development.

ENVIRONMENTAL FACTORS INFLUENCING PRENATAL DEVELOPMENT

The union of ovum and sperm, the migration of the zygote to the uterus, the differentiation of organs and systems within the embryo, and the growth of the fetus are among the most complex processes known to exist. We can readily imagine that a host of events must occur, and at the right times, for prenatal development to proceed normally. We have already learned, for example, how individual cells are altered by their environmental context to establish three layers of cells that form the different systems of the body. But what about other types of influences? What kinds of environmental support do embryo and fetus receive in their liquid, somewhat buoyant surroundings, and how well protected are they from intrusions that can disrupt their development?

Support Within the Womb

The embryo and fetus are sustained by a number of major structures, including the placenta, the umbilical cord, and the amniotic sac. The **placenta,** formed by cells from both the blastocyst and the uterine lining, produces essential hormones for the fetus. Just as important, it serves as the exchange site at which oxygen and nutrients are absorbed from the woman's circulatory system and carbon dioxide and waste products are excreted from the embryo's circulatory system (Cross, Werb, & Fisher, 1994). The transfer takes place via a network of intermingling blood-rich capillaries originating in the woman's and the fetus's circulatory systems. Blood cells are too large to cross the membranes separating the two systems, but smaller molecules of oxygen, carbon dioxide, nutrients, and hormones can traverse the barrier. So can some chemicals, drugs, and diseases that interfere with fetal development, as we will see shortly.

placenta Support organ formed by cells from both blastocyst and uterine lining; serves as exchange site for oxygen, nutrients, and waste products.

The **umbilical cord** is the conduit to and from the placenta for the blood of the fetus. It contains two arteries and a vein embedded in a gelatinlike substance with the approximate consistency of a firm rubber hose. The pressure from the circulating blood helps to prevent the cord from kinking or knotting.

The fetus lives in the womb surrounded by the fluid-filled **amniotic sac**. Amniotic fluid helps to stabilize temperature, insulates the fetus from bumps and shocks, and contains substances necessary for the development of the lungs. The fluid is constantly recirculated and renewed as the fetus ingests nutrients and urinates. Cells from fetal membranes are part of amniotic fluid and can be examined by amniocentesis, the prenatal screening procedure described earlier.

Principles of Teratology

KEY THEME
Nature/Nurture

Most fetuses negotiate the average thirty-eight-week period from conception to birth as healthy, vigorous newborns. Yet, as we saw in Chapter 3, genetic factors can modify normal progress. So too can environmental factors. The study of birth disabilities and behavioral problems that arise from environmental influences during the prenatal period is called *teratology*. Environmental agents that cause such disruptions are known as **teratogens**.

The fact that external agents can upset the course of prenatal development in humans was first appreciated in 1941 when McAllister Gregg, an ophthalmologist, confirmed that rubella, commonly called German measles, caused visual anomalies in the fetus. During this same decade, many infants born to women exposed to the atomic bomb were reported to have birth defects. This finding, along with studies involving animals, implicated radiation as a teratogen (Warkany & Schraffenberger, 1947). Yet the import of these early observations was not fully understood until researchers documented that women who had taken a presumably harmless anti-nausea drug called *thalidomide* frequently bore infants with severe arm and leg malformations (McBride, 1961).

The thalidomide tragedy made it absolutely clear that human embryos could be harmed seriously by environmental agents without adversely affecting the woman or others during postnatal development (Wilson, 1977). To accept this notion, specialists had to abandon a fundamental misconception about the relationship between a woman and her fetus. Many experts argued that a placental barrier filters out virtually all harmful agents, providing the embryo with a highly insulated, sheltered world. But we now recognize that the embryo may be susceptible to virtually any substance if exposure to it is sufficiently concentrated (Samuels & Samuels, 1986).

KEY THEME
Individual Differences

A number of broad generalizations have emerged from research on teratogens since the 1960s (Abel, 1989; Vorhees, 1986; Wilson, 1977). These principles help to explain the sometimes bewildering array of adverse consequences that specific drugs, diseases, and other agents can have on development.

■ *The Principle of Susceptibility: Individuals within species as well as species themselves show major differences in susceptibility to different teratogens* Thalidomide provides a good example of this principle. Scientists knew that extremely large amounts of the drug caused abnormal fetal development in rats (Cohen, 1966). However, the doses given to pregnant women in Europe and Canada, where thalidomide was administered to reduce morning sickness and anxiety, were considerably smaller. For reasons unknown, the embryos of humans and other primates are far more sensitive to small amounts of thalidomide than are the embryos of other species. More than seven thousand babies were born without limbs or with limb defects and intellectual retardation before the species difference was recognized. The genotype of an individual woman and her fetus may also affect susceptibility. Some fetuses were exposed to thalidomide between the third and eighth week after conception, the interval during which it usually causes anomalies, yet at birth these babies showed no ill effects from the drug (Kajii, Kida, & Takahashi, 1973).

umbilical cord Conduit of blood vessels through which oxygen, nutrients, and waste products are transported between placenta and embryo.

amniotic sac Fluid-filled, transparent protective membrane surrounding the fetus.

teratogen Any environmental agent that can cause deviations in prenatal development. Consequences may range from behavioral problems to death.

FIGURE 4.3 | Sensitive Periods in Prenatal Development

During prenatal development, organs and systems undergo periods in which they are more or less sensitive to teratogenic influences, enviromental agents that can cause deviations in development. The potential for major structural defects (dark-colored sections) is usually greatest during the embryonic period, when many organs are forming. However, many regions of the body, including the central nervous system, continue to have some susceptibility to teratogens (light-colored sections) during the fetal period.

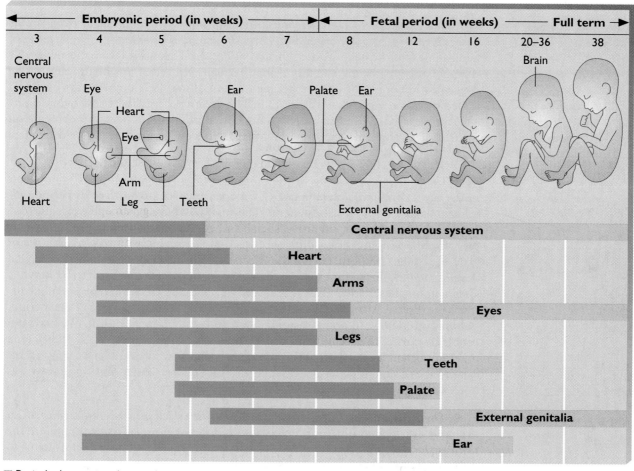

■ Period when major abnormality occurs ■ Period when minor defect or abnormality occurs

Source: Adapted from Moore, 1989.

■ *The Principle of Critical or Sensitive Periods: The extent to which a teratogen affects the fetus depends on the stage of development during which exposure occurs* Many human organs and systems are most sensitive to toxic agents during the third to eighth week after conception, when they are still being formed. Figure 4.3 illustrates the periods during which specific organs of the body show the greatest susceptibility. It also shows that vulnerability to teratogens exists throughout much of prenatal development. In fact, the brain continues to undergo substantial neural differentiation, migration, and growth during the second and third trimesters of pregnancy as well as the weeks and months after birth. As a consequence, exposure to teratogens throughout prenatal development may have especially important behavioral consequences.

■ *The Principle of Access: The accessibility of a given teratogen to a fetus or an embryo influences the extent of its damage* Many factors determine when and to

KEY THEME
Continuity/Discontinuity

KEY THEME
Sociocultural Influence

what extent an embryo or a fetus is exposed to a teratogen. Cultural and social practices may prevent or encourage a pregnant woman to use drugs, be inoculated for certain diseases, or frequent locations that expose her to chemicals and other toxins. For example, use of cocaine may be socially approved in one segment of a culture and avoided in another. Even when a teratogen is present, it must still gain access to the uterine environment. How a woman has been exposed to the agent, the way she metabolizes it, and how it is transported to the womb influence whether a teratogen reaches a sufficient threshold to have some effect.

■ *The Principle of Dose-Response Relationships: The amount of exposure or dosage level of a given teratogen influences the extent of its damage*   The severity of teratogenic effects often is related to level of dosage. The more a woman smokes, for example, the greater the likelihood that her baby will be of low birth weight. The concentration of a toxic agent reaching the fetus, however, cannot always be determined from the woman's exposure to it. The severity of an illness a woman experiences, for example, from rubella, does not always predict the effect of the disease on the fetus. Her physical condition and other factors determine how much of the teratogen reaches the fetus.

■ *The Principle of Teratogenic Response: Teratogens do not show the same effects uniformly on prenatal development*   Teratogens may cause death or disrupt development of specific organs and systems. They may also have behavioral consequences, impairing sensorimotor, cognitive, social, and emotional development. The principles of species and individual differences, as well as timing, duration, and intensity of exposure to the teratogen, govern the effect a specific teratogen will have on prenatal development. Rubella, for example, may cause visual, auditory, cardiac, or nervous system anomalies, depending on the week of pregnancy in which the woman contracts the disease. Alcohol can cause congenital defects during the embryonic period, but may interfere with prenatal weight gain and contribute to postnatal behavioral problems during the second and third trimesters of pregnancy (Abel, 1989). One other important implication of this principle is that very different teratogenic agents can produce a similar pattern of disabilities. Thus, efforts to pinpoint why a baby was born with a given anomaly are not always successful.

■ *The Principle of Interference with Specific Mechanisms: Teratogens affect prenatal development by interfering with biochemical processes that regulate the differentiation, migration, or other basic functions of cells*   This principle helps to differentiate folk beliefs from scientific explanations of fetal anomalies. Looking at a frightening visual stimulus, for example, has no direct consequence for the fetus. However, hormonal imbalances induced by chronic levels of stress may have an impact on development. A teratogen such as alcohol may have physical, behavioral, and other repercussions because it interferes with normal fetal metabolism, including neural cell growth and migration.

■ *The Principle of Developmental Delay and "Sleeper Effects": Some teratogens may delay development temporarily with no long-term negative consequences; others may cause developmental problems only late in development*   Although some teratogenic effects can be observed at birth and are permanent and irreversible, others may be nullified, especially when a supportive caregiving environment is provided. However, the effects of teratogens on development are probably substantially underestimated because many produce "sleeper effects." These are consequences that go unnoticed at birth but seed problems that become apparent in childhood and even later. A well-known example of a sleeper effect involves women treated with *diethylstilbestrol (DES),* a hormone administered from the 1940s through the 1960s to prevent miscarriages. When children of the treated women reached adulthood, females showed a high rate of genital tract cancers and males displayed a high incidence of abnormalities of the testes.

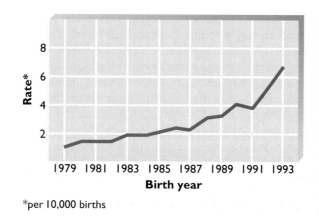

*per 10,000 births

Source: Data from Centers for Disease Control, 1995.

FIGURE 4.4

Reported Rate of Fetal Alcohol Syndrome in the United States, 1979–1993

The rate of reported cases of fetal alcohol syndrome in the United States appears to be on the rise, especially in recent years. This change may reflect a true increase in the frequency of fetal alcohol syndrome or a greater awareness on the part of doctors about the syndrome. Regardless of the reason for the increase, the cause of the disorder is preventable and the increase suggests that more intervention efforts are needed to alert women to the dangers of consuming large amounts of alcohol during pregnancy.

Drugs as Teratogens

Now that we have considered general principles involving teratogens, we can examine the effects specific environmental agents have on the embryo or fetus. A number of substances expectant women may use, either as medicine or as mood-altering devices, frequently become part of the intrauterine world.

Alcohol   Carmen expressed concern about a daily glass of wine with her evening meal. Did she have reason to be worried? Perhaps. She may want to reconsider this practice. Because alcohol readily crosses the placenta, its concentration in the fetus is likely to be similar to that in the woman (Abel, 1981). Thus, every time Carmen took a drink, she provided her fetus with a proportionate amount of alcohol. Moreover, because it lacks some enzymes to effectively degrade alcohol, the fetus may be exposed to it for a longer period of time (Reece et al., 1995).

Alcohol consumption by pregnant women continues, sometimes at far higher levels than Carmen's, in many cultures. From 9 to 11 percent of pregnant American women are considered heavy or problem drinkers (Abel, 1982). *Heavy drinking* usually refers to consumption of two or more 12-ounce glasses of beer, two or more 2½-ounce glasses of wine, or two or more ⅝-ounce glasses of distilled spirits a day, or ten to fourteen drinks during one week. As many as 300,000 infants born each year in the United States may be exposed to this amount of alcohol on a regular basis. The numbers may be substantially greater in some Western European nations (such as France and Italy) and other countries (U.S. Department of Health, Education, and Welfare, 1978).

Widespread recognition of the dangers of alcohol emerged in the early 1970s when a constellation of deficits, including prenatal and postnatal growth retardation, microcephaly, abnormal facial features, mental retardation, and behavioral problems such as hyperactivity and poor motor coordination, were observed in babies born of alcoholic women (Jones & Smith, 1973); these deficits were grouped under the rubric of **fetal alcohol syndrome (FAS)**. As Figure 4.4 indicates, nearly seven in every ten thousand newborns display FAS, a rate that has grown more than sixfold since data were first collected in 1979 (Centers for Disease Control, 1995). Hopefully, one reason for this increase is better reporting rather than increased consumption. Nevertheless, alcohol is probably the single most frequent cause of mental retardation in industrialized countries (Reece et al., 1995).

Women who drink heavily throughout pregnancy are far more likely to bear infants diagnosed with FAS than women who drink moderately or infrequently or who discontinue heavy drinking early in pregnancy (Autti-Rämö et al., 1992; Weiner & Morse, 1988). Binge drinking, even infrequently, appears to be especially hazardous because it exposes the fetus to highly concentrated alcohol levels (Chasnoff, 1986;

KEY THEME
Sociocultural Influence

fetal alcohol syndrome (FAS) Cluster of fetal abnormalities stemming from mother's consumption of alcohol; includes growth retardation, defects in facial features, and intellectual retardation.

This young Swedish girl, displaying features often associated with fetal alcohol syndrome, was born to a mother who was alcoholic. Physical characteristics, including microcephaly (small head size), eyes widely set apart, and flat thin upper lip are often accompanied by delayed physical growth and mental retardation.

Streissguth et al., 1994). Heavy drinkers are also more likely than moderate or light drinkers to give birth to infants with *fetal alcohol effects (FAE)*, which is considered to be a milder form of fetal alcohol syndrome. Manifestations of FAE include less severe mental and growth retardation and more subtle behavioral problems, including hyperactivity, learning and language disabilities, shortened attention span, sleep disturbances, and poor socialization and communication skills. These problems extend into early childhood and beyond (Autti-Rämö et al., 1992).

How does alcohol produce such effects? One way is by directly modifying cell functioning, including cell differentiation, migration, and growth. Examination of infants with fetal alcohol syndrome who died shortly after birth reveals structural changes in the brain caused by delays and errors in the way neurons migrate to form the cortex, or outer layer, of the brain (Clarren et al., 1978). The metabolism of alcohol also requires substantial amounts of oxygen. Less oxygen may be available to the fetus for the growth and functioning of neural and other cells (Abel, 1982).

What about the effects of lesser amounts of alcohol, perhaps as little as the single drink a day Carmen enjoys? Even this amount, some researchers report, is linked to an increase in spontaneous abortions and to reduced alertness, less vigorous body activity, more tremors, and slower learning in newborns compared to babies of women who do not drink (Jacobson & Jacobson, 1996; Mills et al., 1984; Streissguth et al., 1994). Recent work by Anne Streissguth and her colleagues shows that prenatal exposure to moderate amounts of alcohol contributes to measurable deficits in attention and school performance, small declines in IQ, and more frequent behavioral problems in children and adolescents (Streissguth et al., 1994; Bookstein et al., 1996). Findings such as these have led the American Academy of Pediatrics to recommend complete abstinence during pregnancy because no "safe dose for alcohol has been established" (American Academy of Pediatrics, 1993).

Cigarette Smoking   About 15 percent of women in the United States smoke during pregnancy, although this percentage has been declining in recent years (Kendrick & Merritt, 1996). The percentage is substantially higher among Caucasian (18 percent) and African American women (12 percent) than among Hispanic women (5 percent). It may also be far higher in other countries where less effort has been directed at publicizing the negative health consequences of smoking. Was Carmen's decision to quit smoking during her pregnancy a good one?

No evidence exists to indicate that smoking during pregnancy causes major congenital defects. However, nicotine and some other of the more than twenty-five hundred chemicals found in tobacco smoke (American College of Obstetricians, 1994) do have serious consequences for fetal and infant mortality, birth weight, and possibly postnatal development. The most consistent finding from studies of babies born to smokers compared to nonsmokers is their smaller size (Cliver et al., 1995; Nordentoft et al., 1996; Sprauve, 1996). The more and the longer a woman smokes during pregnancy, the lower her baby's average weight at birth, even when equated for length of gestation (because babies of women who smoke are also likely to be born a few days early). Babies of women who use tobacco weigh about two hundred grams (about seven ounces) less than other babies. Spontaneous abortions, stillbirths, and neonatal deaths also increase in pregnant women who smoke (Streissguth et al., 1994).

As with alcohol consumption, a reduction in oxygen may account for the effects. Smoking increases carbon monoxide, which displaces oxygen, in the red blood cells of both woman and fetus. Nicotine also reduces blood flow to the placenta. Moreover, a fetus's heart rate goes up when a woman smokes, a reaction that may be designed to maintain adequate oxygen (Samuels & Samuels, 1986). Babies of women who use tobacco also have larger placentas and more frequent placental abnormalities than babies of the same weight born to nonsmoking women (Meyer & Tonascia, 1977; Weinberger & Weiss, 1988).

The behavioral and long-term consequences of prenatal exposure to smoke are less well understood and are often confounded by postnatal exposure to smoke and

KEY THEME
Individual Differences

other factors. Some researchers have found that infants born to smokers display poorer learning (Martin et al., 1977), a higher-pitched cry (Nugent et al., 1996), and reduced visual alertness (Landesman-Dwyer, Keller, & Streissguth, 1978), but infant tests of development have not uncovered a consistent pattern of deficits (Eskenazi, 1984). In Great Britain, older children of women who smoked during pregnancy lagged several months behind children of nonsmokers on general ability, reading, and mathematics tests (Butler & Goldstein, 1973). The findings, though, could stem from possible postnatal differences in exposure to smoke, among many other factors. Recent research in the United States (Weitzman, Gortmaker, & Sobol, 1992) and New Zealand (Fergusson, Horwood, & Lynskey, 1993) reveals a small but significant increase in behavioral problems in four-to-twelve-year-olds born to women who smoked during pregnancy. Again, additional factors could account for these differences, although in the New Zealand study the increase appeared to be limited to smoking during pregnancy and not to exposure to parental smoking after pregnancy. Still, other researchers have failed to find evidence of poorer performance on cognitive, academic, or other tasks for children exposed to smoke prenatally (Lefkowitz, 1981; Streissguth et al., 1994). Even though the long-term behavioral consequences remain controversial, Carmen's decision to stop smoking seems to make sense.

Prescription and Over-the-Counter Drugs   Legal drugs in addition to alcohol and tobacco can be hazardous for fetal development. Some are known teratogens (see Table 4.2), but knowledge of the effects of many remains perilously limited. Aspirin, for example, has been demonstrated to impair behavioral competence in the offspring of lower animals. One well-controlled study found that aspirin may also be associated with lower IQ in early childhood (Streissguth et al., 1984). Certainly large doses of aspirin, but also alternative pain relievers such as acetaminophen, may increase risk to the fetus (Reece et al., 1995).

Caffeine too has been implicated in birth defects in animals, although studies have failed to reveal any consistent link in humans. Heavy coffee consumers (more than three cups a day) deliver babies of lower birth weight than those who drink less or no coffee (Narod, de Sanjosé, & Victora, 1991). Caffeine also may have behavioral consequences for the fetus. Lawrence Devoe and his colleagues (1993) used ultrasound to record biweekly two-hour observations of fetal activity during the final ten weeks of pregnancy in ten heavy caffeine consumers (>500 milligrams, or five cups, daily) and ten low caffeine consumers (<200 milligrams, or two cups, daily). Fetuses exhibited considerably more arousal (defined by irregular heart rate and breathing activity, frequent body movements, and rapid eye movements) when exposed to the higher amounts of caffeine. The more highly aroused infants may have consumed more energy, a factor that could contribute to their lower birth weight. However, the long-term implications of this difference in activity remain unknown.

KEY THEME
Individual Differences

Perhaps an even greater concern is the number of prescription and over-the-counter drugs consumed during pregnancy. Most expectant women use at least one medication, and the average is more than three (Buitendijk & Bracken, 1991). Little is known about the effects of many of these products, and even less is known about the interactive consequences when multiple drugs are used. For these reasons expectant women are often advised to take *no* drugs during pregnancy, including over-the-counter remedies, or to take them only under the close supervision of their physicians.

Illegal Drugs   The effects of illegal drugs such as marijuana, heroin, and cocaine on prenatal development are even more difficult to untangle than the effects of prescription and over-the-counter medications. Drug users are rarely certain of the contents or concentrations of the drugs they consume. Wide variation in frequency of use, the possibility of interactions from exposure to multiple drugs, poor nutritional status, inadequate or no prenatal care, and potential psychological and physiological differences both before and after taking such drugs compound the problem of isolating their teratogenic effects. The lifestyles of many illegal-drug users can be described as

TABLE 4.2	Prescription and Other Frequently Used Drugs and Their Effects on Prenatal Development

Drug	Description and Known or Suspected Effects
Alcohol	See text.
Amniopterin	Anticancer agent. Facial defects and a number of other congenital malformations as well as mental retardation.
Amphetamines	Stimulants for the central nervous system, some types frequently used for weight control. Readily cross placental barrier. Fetal intrauterine growth retardation often reported, but may be a result of accompanying malnutrition or multiple-drug use (Rodgers & Lee, 1988). Increased amounts and duration of exposure prenatally found to be correlated with aggressive behavior in 8-year-olds (Billing et al., 1994).
Antibiotics (strepto-mycin, tetracycline)	Streptomycin associated with hearing loss. Tetracycline associated with staining of baby's teeth if exposure occurs during second or third trimester.
Aspirin	Possibility of increased bleeding in both mother and infant. See text for other complications that can arise.
Barbiturates (pento-barbital, phenobarbital, secobarbital)	Sedatives and anxiety reducers. Considerable evidence of neurobiological and behavioral complications in rats. Readily cross human placenta; concentrations in fetus may be greater than in woman. Newborns may show withdrawal symptoms (Brown & Fishman, 1984). No consistent evidence of long-term effects in humans.
Benzodiazepines (chlor-diazepoxide, diazepam)	Tranquilizers. Not shown to have teratogenic effects (Rogers & Lee, 1988). Newborns may display withdrawal symptoms (Eskenazi, 1984).
Caffeine	See text.
Hydantoins	Treatment for epilepsy. Produce *fetal hydantoin syndrome,* including heart defects, cleft lip or palate, decreased head size, and mental retardation. Controversy continues over whether effects are entirely caused by drug or by conditions associated with the mother, including her epilepsy (Eskenazi, 1984).
Lithium	Treatment for manic depression. Crosses placenta freely. Known to be teratogenic in premammalian animals. Strong suggestive evidence of increased cardiovascular defects in human infants. Behavioral effects unknown. Administration at time of delivery markedly reduces infant responsivity (Kerns & Davis, 1986).
Retinoids	Antiacne medicine. Effects similar to large amounts of vitamin A.
Sex Hormones (androgens, estrogens, progestins)	Contained in birth control pills, fertility drugs, and other drugs to prevent miscarriages. Continued use of birth control pills during pregnancy associated with heart and circulatory disorders. Behavioral and personality implications suspected. Masculinization of female embryo from exposure to high doses of androgens or progestins.
Thalidomide	Reduces morning sickness and anxiety. Deformities of the limbs, depending on time of exposure, often accompanied by mental retardation (Gouin-Decarie, 1969).
Tobacco	See text.
Tricyclics (imipramine, desimipramine)	Antidepressants. Some tricyclics cross the placenta. Studies with rats reveal developmental and behavioral disturbances. Studies with humans reveal no consistent findings (Kerns & Davis, 1986).
Vitamins	Large amounts of vitamin A known to cause major birth defects. Excessive amounts of other vitamins may also cause prenatal malformations (Reece et al., 1995).

Note: This listing is not meant to be exhaustive, and other drugs may have teratogenic effects. No drug should be taken during pregnancy without consultation with a qualified physician.

essentially chaotic (Chasnoff, 1992). At least 10 percent of expectant women in the United States are estimated to be drug abusers; some 375,000 infants are born to them each year (National Association for Perinatal Addiction Research and Education, 1988; Sprauve, 1996).

Research with animals has shown that the psychoactive ingredients associated with marijuana cross the placenta and are stored in the amniotic fluid (Harbison & Mantilla-Plata, 1972). They may also be transferred postnatally through the mother's milk (Dalterio & Bartke, 1979). Still, efforts to determine the effects of marijuana on the human fetus and postnatal development reveal few consistent findings (Zuckerman & Bresnahan, 1991). As with tobacco, fetal weight and size appear to be reduced. Length of gestation may also be shorter for heavy marijuana users, a finding consistent with giving marijuana to speed labor, a practice carried out at one time in Europe.

The cries of newborns exposed to marijuana tend to be higher pitched and more variable than the cries of infants not so exposed (Lester & Dreher, 1989). This kind of cry has sometimes signaled neurophysiological disturbances in infants exposed to other risks. Visual problems, lower scores on memory and verbal tasks, and more restless sleep patterns in early childhood also are reported with prenatal exposure to marijuana (Dahl et al., 1995; Fried, 1986; Fried & Watkinson, 1990). However, social and economic differences in the backgrounds of the children could account for these findings. In fact, in some cultures, such as Jamaica, marijuana use correlates positively with neonatal test performance (Dreher, Nugent, & Hudgins, 1994).

KEY THEME
Individual Differences

KEY THEME
Sociocultural Influence

The effects of heroin and morphine became a public concern as early as the late 1800s when doctors reported withdrawal symptoms in newborns whose mothers used these substances (Zagon & McLaughlin, 1984). By the early 1900s, heroin and morphine were known to be transmitted through the placenta as well as through the mother's milk. Today an estimated nine thousand infants born in the United States each year are exposed to heroin or *methadone,* a pharmacologically similar product (Sprauve, 1996). Often given under regulated conditions as a heroin substitute, methadone's effects on fetal development are just as powerful as heroin's.

Although congenital defects have not been positively linked to heroin and methadone, stillbirths and infant deaths are more frequent and lower birth weight is common (American College of Obstetricians and Gynecologists, 1994). About 60 to 70 percent of infants born to heroin- and methadone-addicted women also undergo withdrawal symptoms such as diarrhea, sweating, a distinctive high-pitched cry, tremors, and irritability (Sprauve, 1996).

Developmental difficulties continue to be observed in infants and children exposed to heroin and methadone. However, these may be largely a consequence of poor nutrition, limited care from caregivers, or additional factors that often complicate their postnatal experiences. Methadone programs that offer high-quality prenatal care, emphasize adequate nutrition, and furnish other kinds of support to the addict can reduce, and perhaps eliminate, many of the negative effects (Rodgers & Lee, 1988). Three-to-six-year-olds in Israel who showed no neurological deficits after being exposed to heroin prenatally but continued to be reared by their mothers, or whose fathers rather than mothers were addicted to heroin, displayed cognitive deficits and behavioral problems similar to those of children reared in environmentally deprived conditions where drugs were not involved. On the other hand, children who were exposed to heroin prenatally but were adopted into families of middle or high socioeconomic status showed far fewer cognitive and behavioral problems and no more difficulties than unexposed children in families of similar professional and educational status (Ornoy et al., 1996). These findings suggest that caregiving can play a powerful role in lessening the negative impact of prenatal exposure to heroin in children, at least for those who do not experience neurological damage.

More than 150,000 infants delivered each year in the United States, perhaps nearly one-third of babies in some metropolitan areas, are estimated to be born to mothers who used cocaine during pregnancy (Gomby & Shiono, 1991; Ostrea et al., 1992). Cocaine in its many forms—including *crack,* an especially potent and addictive form—readily crosses into the placenta. Once it reaches the fetus, it stays longer than in adults because the immature organs of the fetus have difficulty breaking down the substance. Cocaine can also continue to influence the baby after birth through the mother's milk.

Early reports alleged that cocaine causes serious, permanent damage to fetus and infant. Indeed, prematurity, low birth weight, and small head size have been documented widely in such infants (Hawley, 1994; Zuckerman & Frank, 1994). However, seizures and strokes, respiratory difficulties, and kidney and genital malformations, noted in a troubling proportion of cocaine-exposed offspring, remain unproven consequences (Chasnoff, 1992).

KEY THEME
Individual Differences

Behaviorally, cocaine-exposed newborns are often portrayed as being easily overstimulated, having difficulty shifting from states of sleep to alertness and back again, and being socially unresponsive and easily irritated. These patterns, which may reflect evidence of withdrawal, are not consistently observed (Woods et al., 1993; Zuckerman & Bresnahan, 1991), but older infants do display slower learning, attentional and early information-processing deficits, and more limited emotional expression (Alessandri et al., 1993; Mayes et al., 1995). When they become older, children exposed prenatally to cocaine may show delays in language acquisition, attentional problems, intellectual deficits, and difficulty regulating their own behavior (Chasnoff, 1992; Azuma & Chasnoff, 1993). However, whether these outcomes are a result of prenatal exposure to cocaine or often-accompanied lower birth weight, exposure to other drugs, or the quality of the home environment and other factors remains difficult to sort out (Hawley, 1994; Zuckerman & Frank, 1994). The prognosis for children subjected to cocaine in utero improves markedly when interventions are undertaken to reduce or eliminate these other risk factors (Chasnoff, 1992). Thus, cocaine, along with many other drugs we have discussed, seems to create potential, but not always inevitable, obstacles to development; much can be done to improve the developmental outlook for many drug-exposed children.

Because prenatal development is so closely tied to the intrauterine environment, little research has been conducted on the father's abuse of drugs or other teratogens and their effects on the fetus. Studies with lower animals, and some with humans, suggest that the sperm of men who consume alcohol or use cocaine or other drugs may carry toxic substances that can disrupt normal prenatal development (Yazigi, Odem, & Polakoski, 1991). However, the woman is regularly assigned far greater responsibility for prenatal events, as the following controversy reveals.

In the last decade, perhaps as many as two hundred American women in twenty-four states have been prosecuted on charges of child abuse and neglect, delivery of drugs to a minor, or assault with a deadly weapon for allegedly harming their fetuses through exposure to potentially

CONTROVERSY:
THINKING IT OVER

Should a Drug-Abusing Expectant Woman Be Charged with Child Abuse?

dangerous drugs (Lieb & Sterk-Elifson, 1995). Consider, for example, the circumstances surrounding the prosecution of Jennifer Johnson. Both a son, born in 1987, and a daughter, born in 1989, tested positive for exposure to cocaine. In 1991 Johnson was convicted in Florida of delivering drugs to her children at birth via the umbilical cord. Although that conviction has since been overturned by the Florida supreme court, the issues surrounding this and similar cases deeply divide law enforcement and social service agencies in the United States and other Western European countries (Peak & Del Papa, 1993).

What are an expectant woman's moral and legal responsibilities to the fetus? Should a concerned society make every effort to deter the use of a drug that may be dangerous to the fetus, including, if necessary, the threat of criminal charges, to ensure that every newborn begins life as healthy as possible? Some say yes. A number of U.S. states have implemented laws permitting a newborn to be removed from a parent on the grounds of child abuse or neglect as a result of drug exposure during pregnancy. After all, anyone found to provide such illegal substances to a child would certainly expect to face criminal charges. Is the situation that much different in the case of a pregnant woman and her fetus?

Others believe the situation is vastly different and further claim that criminal charges are counterproductive (Beckett, 1995; Farr, 1995). Drug laws, they argue, have proven ineffective in helping large numbers of abusers change their behavior. A woman using drugs is not likely to gain control over this activity during pregnancy, especially because there are both a severe shortage of treatment programs to help deal with addiction during pregnancy and limited support services to assist with other aspects of pregnancy. If legislation were in place that specifically targeted pregnant drug users, prospective mothers, out of fear of being prosecuted, might actually be driven away from the care and treatment needed for both themselves and their fetuses.

The ethical and legal controversies certainly extend well beyond these arguments. For example, should laws designed to protect and benefit children also be generalized to the fetus? Or is the relationship between a woman and her fetus qualitatively different, one that requires other important considerations, including the right of privacy? Further, does enough evidence exist to convincingly demonstrate that a particular drug causes problems for the newborn? Or are poor nutrition and a host of other social and economic factors that often accompany drug use, and over which the woman may have little control, the primary culprits in impaired fetal development? Some contend that expectant women who use drugs do not set out to *make* trouble; rather, they are people who are *in* trouble (Gusfield, 1981).

KEY THEME
Sociocultural Influence

The costs of drug abuse both to the individuals involved and to society as a whole are considerable. Is recourse to the judicial system a desirable and effective means of helping the newborn? Or might such laws constitute a smokescreen that obscures and diverts resources from newborns' needs? If laws devoted to fetal protection are established, should they also extend to situations involving legal drugs such as alcohol and tobacco, where research, particularly in the case of alcohol, convincingly demonstrates teratogenic effects (Streissguth et al., 1994)? Could even Carmen be convicted for drinking her daily glass of wine? Should litigation be one means of trying to resolve this difficult issue?

Diseases as Teratogens

Two to 8 percent of babies born to American women are exposed to one or more diseases or other forms of illness during pregnancy (Saltzman & Jordan, 1988). Fortunately, most babies are unaffected, but some diseases have physical and behavioral consequences for the fetus (see Table 4.3). The effects may occur even when the woman is completely unaware of illness.

Rubella Before widespread vaccination, the last outbreak of rubella (German measles) in the United States in 1964 caused congenital defects in an estimated twenty thousand infants (Andiman & Horstmann, 1984). Very few problems associated with this disease have been reported in this country since then. Unfortunately, however, rubella continues to be a major cause of fetal malformations and death worldwide because vaccination programs are limited in many less developed countries.

KEY THEME
Sociocultural Influence

The most common problems associated with rubella include growth retardation, cataracts, hearing impairment, heart defects, and mental retardation. Virtually any organ may be affected, depending on when the disease is contracted during prenatal

TABLE 4.3	Diseases and Other Conditions That May Affect Prenatal Development
Sexually Transmitted Diseases	
Acquired Immunodeficiency Syndrome (AIDS)	See text.
Chlamydia	Nearly always transmitted to infant during delivery via infected birth canal. Estimated 100,000 (of 155,000 exposed in the United States) become infected. Often causes eye infection in infant and some increased risk of pneumonia. Other adverse effects suspected (McGregor & French, 1991).
Gonorrhea	If acquired prenatally, may cause premature birth (Reece et al., 1995). Most frequently contracted during delivery through infected birth canal and may then attack eyes. In the United States and many other countries, silver nitrate eye drops are administered to all newborns to prevent blindness.
Hepatitis B	Associated with premature birth, low birth weight, increased neonatal death, and liver disorders (Pass, 1987). Most frequently contracted during delivery through birth canal or postnatally.
Herpes Simplex	Of its two forms, only one is transmitted primarily through sexual activity. Both forms, however, can be transmitted to the fetus, causing severe damage to the central nervous system (Pass, 1987). Most infections occur during delivery through birth canal containing active herpes lesions. Even when treated, the majority of infants will die or suffer central nervous system damage (Nahmias, Keyserling, & Kernick, 1983). If known to carry the virus, women may need to be tested frequently during pregnancy to determine if the disease is in its active, contagious state because symptoms may not be present even when active. If the disease is active, cesarean delivery is used to avoid infecting the baby.
Syphilis	Damage to fetus does not begin until about 18 weeks after conception. May then cause death, mental retardation, and other congenital defects (Reece et al., 1995). Infected newborns may not show signs of disease until early childhood.
Other Diseases and Maternal Conditions	
Cholera	Increased risk of stillbirth.
Cytomegalovirus	See text.
Diabetes	Risk of congenital malformations and death to fetus two to three times higher than for babies born to nondiabetic women (Coustan & Felig, 1988). Excessive size at birth also common. Effects are likely to be a consequence of metabolic disturbances rather than of insulin. Rapid advances in care have helped reduce risks substantially for diabetic women.
Hypertension (chronic)	Probability of miscarriage or infant death increased.
Influenza	Some forms linked to increased heart and central nervous system abnormalities as well as spontaneous abortions (Reece et al., 1995)
Mumps	Increased risk of spontaneous abortion and stillbirth.
Pregnancy-Induced Hypertension	5%–10% of expectant women experience significant increase in blood pressure, often accompanied by *edema* (swelling of face and extremities as a result of water retention), rapid weight gain, and protein in urine during later months of pregnancy. Condition is also known as *pre-eclampsia* (or *eclampsia,* if severe) and *toxemia.* Under severe conditions, woman may suffer seizures and coma. The fetus is at increased risk for death, brain damage, and lower birth weight. Adequate protein consumption helps minimize problems. Drugs used to treat high blood pressure may be just as hazardous to fetus as the condition itself.

TABLE 4.3 (cont.)	Diseases and Other Conditions That May Affect Prenatal Development
Other Diseases and Maternal Conditions	
Rh Incompatibility	Blood containing a certain protein is Rh positive, Rh negative if it lacks that protein. Hereditary factors determine which type the individual possesses. If fetus's blood is Rh positive, it can cause formation of antibodies in blood of woman who is Rh negative. These antibodies can cross placental barrier to destroy red blood cells of fetus. May result in miscarriage or stillbirth, jaundice, anemia, heart defects, and mental retardation. Likelihood of birth defects increases with succeeding pregnancies because antibodies are usually not present until after birth of first Rh-positive child. A vaccine (Rhogam) can be administered to the mother within 3 days after childbirth, miscarriage, or abortion to prevent antibody formation.
Rubella	See text.
Smallpox	Increased risk of spontaneous abortion and stillbirth.
Toxoplasmosis	See text.
Varicellazoster (chicken pox)	Skin and muscle defects, intrauterine growth retardation, limb reduction.

development (Andiman & Horstmann, 1984). Up to 50 percent of infants born to women with rubella during the first month of pregnancy will have congenital abnormalities. This figure declines to 22 percent, 6 percent, and fewer than 1 percent during the second, third, and fourth months, respectively (Reece et al., 1995).

Toxoplasmosis Toxoplasmosis is caused by a parasite found in many mammals and birds. Twenty to 40 percent of adults in various regions of the United States and Great Britain have been exposed to it (Feldman, 1982; Peckham & Logan, 1993). However, the disease occurs more frequently in tropical regions. An unusual aspect of the parasite is that part of its life cycle can be completed only in cats. Humans occasionally contract the disease by touching cat feces containing the parasite or, even more frequently, by eating raw or partially infected cooked meat, especially pork and lamb. Children and adults are often unaware of their exposure, because the infection may have no symptoms or cause only a minor fever or rash.

About 3 percent of women who contract toxoplasmosis during pregnancy will have an infected baby (MacLeod & Lee, 1988). Infections early in pregnancy can have devastating consequences; fortunately, risk of transmission to the fetus at this time is lowest. Growth retardation, jaundice, accumulation of fluid in the brain, and visual and central nervous system damage are the most frequent teratogenic outcomes. Some infants show no symptoms at birth; only later may mental retardation, neuromuscular abnormalities, impaired vision, and other eye problems become apparent (MacLeod & Lee, 1988).

Cytomegalovirus Cytomegalovirus (CMV), which causes swelling of the salivary glands and mononucleosis-like symptoms in adults, is the single most frequent infection found in newborns today, affecting one to two of every one hundred babies. As many as 10 percent of infected infants can be expected to sustain some congenital damage (Demmler, 1991). CMV and other members of the herpes virus family share the property of latency; after contracting the disease, an individual may show no symptoms for many years, only to have it recur at any time. No effective treatment exists.

CMV is most frequently reported in Asia and Africa and among lower socioeconomic groups, in which up to 85 percent of the population may be infected. Yet 45 to 55 percent of middle- and high-income groups in Europe and the United States are

KEY THEME
Sociocultural Influence

infected as well (Hagay et al., 1996). Transmission occurs through sexual contact, through blood transfusions, and via other body fluids. CMV can be passed easily from child to child as children play together, for example, in day care centers or between a child and an adult through physical contact. Fortunately, the consequences of contracting the virus in early childhood are far less devastating than when contracted at birth or during early infancy.

Babies are most frequently exposed to CMV during birth or early thereafter, when the disease is active in the mother. But infection can occur within the womb or through breast feeding (Adler, 1992; Stagno & Cloud, 1994). Among infants who acquire the disease prenatally, growth retardation, jaundice, skin disorders, and small head size are common consequences. About one-third of infants showing these characteristics at birth will die in early infancy; a large percentage of those who survive will be mentally retarded. About half of infants sustaining congenital damage from CMV show no symptoms at birth, but many will subsequently display progressive loss of hearing or other, subtler defects, including minimal brain dysfunction, visual or dental abnormalities, or motor and neural problems (Andiman & Horstmann, 1984; Pass, 1987; Saltzman & Jordan, 1988).

Sexually Transmitted and Other Diseases   Several diseases identified as teratogenic are transmitted primarily through sexual contact, or the infection and its symptoms are usually concentrated in the genitourinary tract (see Table 4.3). Syphilis and certain strains of herpes simplex, for example, are virtually always contracted from infected sexual partners. On the other hand, some diseases, such as acquired immunodeficiency syndrome (AIDS) and hepatitis B, can be acquired through exposure to infected blood as well.

Sexually transmitted diseases (STDs) can interfere with reproduction in a number of ways. They may compromise the woman's health (AIDS, gonorrhea, hepatitis B, herpes simplex, syphilis), scar or disturb reproductive organs so that conception and normal pregnancy cannot proceed (chlamydia, gonorrhea), directly infect the fetus (AIDS, herpes simplex, syphilis), and interfere with healthy postnatal development (AIDS, hepatitis B, herpes simplex, syphilis) (Lee, 1988). In recent years, their frequency has risen rapidly in populations around the world. None, however, has had as dramatic an impact as AIDS.

Of the estimated 12,000 children with human immunodeficiency virus type 1 (HIV) in the United States living in 1994 and the more than 1½ million children identified with the disease worldwide, most were infected prenatally or during birth (Gwinn & Wortley, 1996). About 25 percent of the approximately 6,500 infants in the United States born in 1994 to HIV-positive women were infected and could be expected to eventually acquire AIDS. Fortunately, since 1995, new medical treatments have reduced the transmission rate considerably (see Figure 4.5).

About half of the infants infected with HIV at birth begin to show symptoms of AIDS by about five years of age. Although some infants show rapid deterioration in early childhood, the average length of survival today is somewhat greater than nine years (Barnhart et al., 1996). Early researchers frequently reported visual, motor, cognitive, language, and social impairments by the time HIV-infected children reached school age. Yet about two-thirds of children reaching nine years of age still show normal school achievement, suggesting that the course of the disease may be less devastating for cognitive and other aspects of development than originally thought (Tardieu et al., 1995).

Environmental Hazards as Teratogens

Radiation was one of the earliest confirmed teratogens, and it can cause genetic mutation as well. Radiation's effects include spontaneous abortion, small head size, and other defects associated with the skeleton, genitals, and sensory organs. Even low doses of radiation have been linked to increased risks of cancer and neural damage; pregnant women are urged to avoid unnecessary x-rays and other circumstances where exposure might occur.

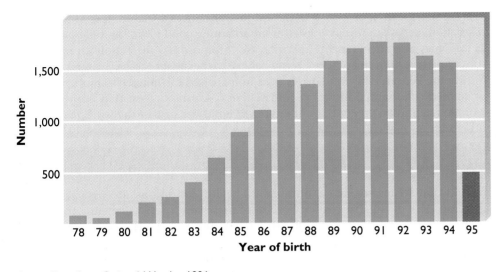

FIGURE 4.5

Number of Infants Infected with HIV, 1978–1995

The number of infants infected with HIV, the precursor to AIDS, increased dramatically between 1978 and the early 1990s. However, new drugs, particularly zidovudine, when provided to pregnant women known to be infected with HIV, have been found to reduce the likelihood of transmission of the infection by about two-thirds. Although figures are not yet available since zidovudine began to be regularly prescribed, the consequences of its administration can be seen in the expected dramatic decline of infants reported to be infected with HIV beginning in 1995.

Source: Data from Gwinn & Wortley, 1996.

Chemicals and other elements in the environment pose another significant source of potential risks. Known teratogens include lead, mercury, and polychlorinated biphenyls (a synthetic hydrocarbon once used in transformers, hydraulic fluids, and other industrial equipment), as well as many elements found in paints, dyes and coloring agents, solvents, oven cleaners, pesticides, herbicides, food additives, artificial sweeteners, and cosmetic products (cf. Needleman & Bellinger, 1994). Careless handling and disposal of such elements and their excessive production and use—they pervade the foods we eat and the air we breathe—are one problem. In addition, many women of childbearing age are exposed to hazardous substances in the workplace (see Table 4.4). Even concerns about video terminals have been voiced, but no evidence now exists to indicate that they are harmful to the fetus (Bentur & Koren, 1991).

With increasing awareness of the negative effects of certain chemicals and other environmental elements have come new and complex social and legal issues pertaining to women in the workplace. Some companies have barred women in their child-

Occupation	Hazardous Substances	TABLE 4.4
Cleaning personnel	Soaps, detergents, solvents	Occupational Hazards for Women of Childbearing Age
Electronic assemblers	Lead, tin, antimony, trichloroethylene, methyl chloride, resins	
Hairdressers and cosmetologists	Hair-spray resins, aerosol propellants, solvents, dyes	
Health personnel	Anesthetic gases, x-rays, laboratory chemicals	
Painters	Lead, titanium, toluene	
Photographic processors	Caustics, bromides, iodides, silver nitrate	
Plastic workers	Formaldehyde, vinyl chloride	
Printing personnel	Ink mists, methanol, carbon tetrachloride, lead, solvents, trichloroethylene	
Textile and garment workers	Formaldehyde, dyes, asbestos, solvents, flame retardants	
Transportation personnel	Carbon monoxide, lead	

Source: Adapted from Samuels & Bennett, 1983.

bearing years from jobs involving hazardous substances to reduce risk. But do these restrictions serve to prevent women from obtaining good jobs? Some elements, such as lead, may also affect fertility and increase chromosomal aberrations in men (Bentur & Koren, 1991). In addition, some believe that exposure to hazardous chemicals during the Persian Gulf war has resulted in increased birth defects among offspring of soldiers who served in that region. These concerns suggest that both men and women need to be vigilant about environmental hazards in the workplace and in other settings that could affect their offspring.

Women's Conditions and Prenatal Development

In addition to teratogens, a number of health conditions are associated with increased risk during pregnancy. Several of these conditions (diabetes, pregnancy-induced and chronic hypertension, Rh incompatibility) and their consequences for the fetus are summarized in Table 4.3. Additional factors influencing the prenatal environment include the age of the woman, her nutritional status, and her emotional state.

KEY THEME
Sociocultural Influence

Age   The number of older mothers is on the rise in the United States as women postpone pregnancy to establish careers or for other reasons. Is pregnancy riskier in older women? As we saw in Chapter 3, the likelihood of having a child with Down syndrome increases markedly during the later childbearing years. Some studies also report increased prematurity and mortality and greater difficulty during labor, especially for older women having their first child (Reece et al., 1995). The findings are likely due, in large part, to increased health-related problems (hypertension, diabetes, and others) that can accompany increased age. Healthy women older than thirty-five routinely deliver healthy infants just as do women between twenty and thirty-five years of age.

Teenagers, on the other hand, may be at considerably greater risk for delivering less healthy babies (McAnarney, 1987). Lack of adequate prenatal care is one reason; pregnant teenagers in the United States, particularly those who are very young and unmarried, often do not seek medical services. Another reason pregnancy at these early ages poses more problems is the complicated nutritional needs of adolescents; many teenagers are still growing themselves. The teenage pregnancy rate in the

Teenage mothers give birth to as many as 500,000 babies in the United States each year. Many of them will be unmarried teens who have received little or even no prenatal care, factors that increase the risk for delivering less healthy babies.

United States is substantially higher than in other industrialized nations, double and even triple those of most Western European nations. In any given year, about one in twenty teenagers is likely to bear a child; over 70 percent of the approximately 500,000 births to teenagers each year will be to unmarried teens (Children's Defense Fund, 1996).

Nutrition   What foods are needed for the health of the woman and her fetus? The seemingly obvious but important answer is a well-balanced diet. Physical and neural growth of the fetus can be severely impaired when a woman fails to maintain a balanced diet or to gain sufficient weight. Extreme malnutrition during prenatal development can be especially detrimental. During World War II, famines occurred in parts of Holland and in Leningrad in the former Soviet Union. When the malnutrition occurred during the first few months of pregnancy, death, premature birth, and nervous system defects were especially frequent. When famine occurred later in prenatal development, retardation in fetal growth and low birth weights were more likely (Antonov, 1947). Although not everyone agrees about the guidelines, women of normal weight for their height are typically advised to gain about twenty-five to thirty-five pounds during pregnancy. Those underweight for their height are encouraged to gain even more and those overweight to gain a bit less (Abrams, 1996; Johnson & Yancey, 1996).

Diets must be sufficient not only in number of calories but also with respect to adequate protein, vitamins, and other nutrients. In fact, intake of many nutrients should be increased during pregnancy, as Table 4.5 indicates. Fortunately, unless deficiencies are so severe that malformations and deficits in neuron formation cannot be overcome, many cognitive problems associated with prenatal undernutrition and the lowered birth weight that often accompanies it may still be reversed when adequate nourishment and stimulation are provided following birth (Pollit, 1996; Zeskind & Ramey, 1981).

Stress   Cultural beliefs about potentially harmful consequences of frightening or stressful events on fetal development are pervasive, and many societies encourage a calm atmosphere for pregnant women (Samuels & Samuels, 1986). In studies in which researchers have carefully measured anxiety, the existence of family conflict, the frequency of positive and negative life events, and the availability of physical and

KEY THEME
Sociocultural Influence

TABLE 4.5

Nutritional Need Differences Between Nonpregnant and Pregnant Women 24 Years of Age

Nutrient	Nonpregnant	Pregnant	Percent Increase	Dietary Sources
Folic acid	180 mcg	400 mcg	+ 122	Leafy vegetables, liver
Vitamin D	5 µg	10 µg	+ 100	Fortified dairy products
Iron	15 mg	30 mg	+ 100	Meats, eggs, grains
Calcium	800 mg	1200 mg	+ 50	Dairy products
Phosphorus	800 mg	1200 mg	+ 50	Meats
Pyridoxine	1.6 mg	2.2 mg	+ 38	Meats, liver, enriched grains
Thiamin	1.1 mg	1.5 mg	+ 36	Enriched grains, pork
Zinc	12 mg	15 mg	+ 25	Meats, seafood, eggs
Riboflavin	1.3 mg	1.6 mg	+ 23	Meats, liver, enriched grains
Protein	50 g	60 g	+ 20	Meats, fish, poultry, dairy
Iodine	150 mcg	175 mcg	+ 17	Iodized salt, seafood
Vitamin C	60 mg	70 mg	+ 17	Citrus fruits, tomatoes
Energy	2200 kcal	2500 kcal	+ 14	Proteins, fats, carbohydrates
Magnesium	280 mg	320 mg	+ 14	Seafood, legumes, grains
Niacin	15 mg	17 mg	+ 13	Meats, nuts, legumes
Vitamin B-12	2.0 mcg	2.2 mcg	+ 10	Animal proteins
Vitamin A	800 µg	800 µg	0	Dark green, yellow, or orange fruits and vegetables, liver

Source: Reece et al., 1995.

social support for the woman before and during pregnancy, stress has been linked to greater complications during both pregnancy and birth. The most frequently reported consequences associated with anxiety appear to be longer labor, the need for more anesthesia during delivery, and more birthing complications. High stress during pregnancy seems to contribute to more frequent preterm births and infants with lower birth weight (Wadhwa et al., 1993). In addition, fatigue associated with long hours at work, especially work that involves prolonged standing, seems to increase preterm births (Luke et al., 1995).

Research with animals indicates that when the female is under stress, blood flow is diverted from the womb. Hormones that can interfere with normal growth are also released. Stress also may indirectly affect prenatal development by leading a woman to increase smoking, consume more alcohol, or engage in other activities known to have negative effects on the fetus (McAnarney & Stevens-Simon, 1990).

The social support a pregnant woman receives from family and friends is an important factor that can lessen the consequences of stress during pregnancy. Among women who experience a variety of life changes before and during pregnancy, those with strong social and personal support—for example, those who can obtain a ride to work, get help when sick, or borrow needed money—have far fewer complications than women without such resources (Norbeck & Tilden, 1983). In fact, women who receive as little as twenty minutes of psychosocial support that addresses their concerns and offers encouragement during regular prenatal visits have babies who weigh more than the babies of women who do not receive this support (Rothberg & Lits, 1991). How well a family functions during stressful times may be a more important predictor of complications during and after pregnancy than how many stressful events are actually experienced (Smilkstein et al., 1984).

Carmen expressed concern about the considerable pressure of her work and worried about her mother's illness. However, Carmen had a supportive husband and other family members with whom she could share her apprehensions during pregnancy. She, like many other women, was unable to completely eliminate stress in her life. Pregnant women must juggle work, family, and many other obligations. Because Carmen established opportunities to relax and her family provided emotional and social support to help her manage her stress, she was minimizing potentially negative outcomes. Efforts couples initiate to reduce stress or respond to it in adaptive ways can be effective preventive medicine both during pregnancy and after (Samuels & Samuels, 1986).

A Final Note on Environment and Prenatal Development

After learning about the many teratogens and other factors that can affect prenatal development, we may be surprised that babies manage to be born healthy at all. But they do so every day. We should wonder, rather, at the rich complexity of prenatal development and appreciate more deeply that it proceeds normally so much of the time. Ninety to 95 percent of babies born in the United States are healthy and fully prepared to adapt to their new environment. Knowledge of teratogens allows prospective parents as well as others in the community to maximize the chances that all infants will be equipped to enter the world with as many resources as possible.

BIRTH AND THE PERINATAL ENVIRONMENT

Carmen's husband wasn't thrilled. "Why do I need to go to childbirth classes?" he asked. "You're the one delivering the baby! It will probably be some boring lecture anyway. Besides, I don't have time." Carmen's frantic work schedule blunted her enthusiasm as well. The doctor had given her all these pamphlets on various classes, options to deliver at the hospital or a birthing center, and breathing and other exercises she should practice. She recalled her mother's words about Carmen's birth in another country thirty years before: "The midwife and several friends came to my home. It was kind of like a party. No hospital, no doctor, no big deal." Carmen muttered under her breath, "Why couldn't it be as simple now?" Her husband's voice brought her back to the issue at hand. "Hey, this really looks interesting. A weekend retreat, including childbirth classes with other expectant couples at this neat hotel!"

Societies vary enormously in the techniques and rituals that accompany the transition from fetus to newborn. Some interpret pregnancy and birth as natural and healthy, others, as an illness requiring medical care and attention (Newton, 1955). The !Kung, a hunting-and-gathering people living in the Kalahari Desert of Africa, build no huts or facilities for birthing. They view birth as part of the natural order of events, requiring no special intervention (Shostak, 1981). In contrast, pregnancy and childbirth in the United States and many other countries throughout much of the twentieth century has been regarded more as an illness to be managed by professionally trained medical personnel (Dye, 1986). In 1900 fewer than 5 percent of babies were born in hospitals in the United States (Wertz & Wertz, 1977). Today about 99 percent of all babies in the United States are born in hospitals (Declercq, 1993).

KEY THEME
Sociocultural Influence

Preparing for Childbirth

With the shift in many countries during the first half of the twentieth century from childbirth at home to childbirth in the hospital came an increase in the use of medication during delivery. In fact, putting the expectant mother to sleep during childbirth was a common practice and was often accompanied by the extensive use of other drugs to reduce discomfort. Concerns about the impact of these medications during labor, along with reports of unmedicated but seemingly pain-free delivery by women in other cultures, prodded professionals and expectant parents alike to reconsider how best to prepare for the birth of a baby. After observing one woman who reported a pain-free delivery, Grantley Dick-Read, a medical practitioner in Great Britain, concluded that difficult childbirth was fostered largely by the tension and anxiety in which Western civilization cloaked the event. Dick-Read (1959) proposed that women be taught methods of physical relaxation, given information about the process of childbirth, and encouraged to cultivate a cooperative relationship with their doctors to foster a more natural childbirth experience. Others, including Fernand Lamaze (1970), adopted similar ideas, adding procedures to divert thoughts from pain and encouraging breathing activities to support the labor process.

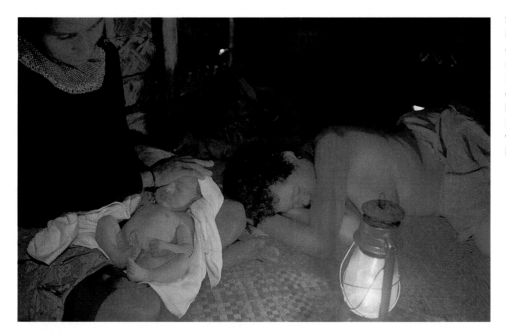

Societies differ enormously in their approach to the birth of a baby. In the United States, most births occur in hospitals. In contrast, more than four of every five births in the Trobriand Islands, part of Papua New Guinea, take place in villages where a midwife is in charge.

In recent years, **prepared** (or **natural**) **childbirth,** procedures practiced during pregnancy and childbirth and designed to minimize pain and reduce the need for medication during delivery, has become a popular alternative for prospective mothers. Women who attend classes and adhere to the recommendations of Lamaze and other childbirth education programs (including the National Childbirth Trust in the United Kingdom) generally require fewer and lower amounts of drugs during delivery than women who have not participated in prepared childbirth. Women who attend childbirth classes may experience no less pain, but relaxation techniques and an additional element frequently promoted in these programs—the assistance of a coach or trainer, often the father—seem to help counter the discomfort.

Nurturing and Caring During Labor

*I*n the foggy haze between sleep and alertness, the 5:00 a.m. nudge seemed a bit more insistent than usual to Carmen's husband. Indeed, it was: Carmen was in labor. She and her husband started timing the contractions as they prepared to set off for the hospital. They had returned from their weekend retreat several weeks earlier eagerly anticipating the birth of their first child. As they expected, natural childbirth was discussed, but so were other options to increase comfort, ranging from massage to hypnosis to more traditional medication. They toured the birthing center at the hospital, asked questions, and learned much from other prospective parents, who seemed to be just as nervous about parenting as they were. The queries other couples raised didn't seem silly; Carmen hoped the questions she and her husband asked weren't either. They also were shown how Carmen's husband could assist during labor and that a midwife, rather than a physician, could be assigned to manage the delivery. To Carmen's relief, her husband warmed to his upcoming role like a duck to water. And Carmen felt a midwife would provide exactly the kind of support she wanted when the big day finally arrived.

KEY THEME
Nature/Nurture

In addition to exhilaration, most women delivering a baby go through a lot of hard work and some perhaps considerable discomfort. It can be a very anxious time. Human birth differs from that of other species of mammals in that it typically requires some form of assistance (Rosenberg, 1992; Trevathen, 1988). In many cultures, the help comes from friends and relatives or from midwives, just as it did in the United States many decades ago (Wertz & Wertz, 1977). With the relocation of childbirth to hospitals, however, women became isolated from family and friends, and a more private and impersonal procedure emerged. Perhaps with that change something very important was lost. Research has helped to identify this loss and has led to alternatives in birthing practices that may benefit both men and women as they become new parents.

1. *Include the partner or some other trusted companion in preparing for and during childbirth.* Studies carried out in Guatemala and, more recently, in the United States demonstrate that a supportive companion during delivery is helpful to women (Kennell et al., 1991; Klaus & Kennell, 1982). In the Guatemalan studies, first-time mothers were assigned a *doula,* an experienced companion who stayed with the mother, encouraged her, and provided information about what was happening during labor. Women given these personal attendants spent far shorter times in labor, required drugs or forceps less frequently, and delivered babies who showed less fetal distress and difficulty breathing than women who received only routine nursing care. Today fathers or other partners are actively encouraged to take on some of these functions. Indeed, in one study in Australia, women gave their husbands/partners very high marks for their help, their encouragement, and providing a sense of well-being. Nearly 90 percent of women indicated that the presence of their husbands/partners during labor was essential (Cunningham, 1993). In fact, additional attendants improved the woman's satisfaction with each attendant even more.

prepared childbirth Procedures practiced during pregnancy and childbirth designed to minimize pain and reduce the need for medication during delivery. Also called *natural childbirth.*

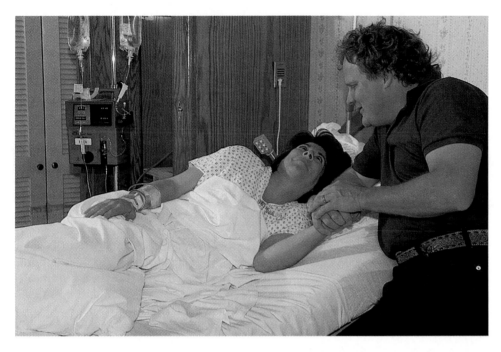

Today, fathers, and sometimes other friends and family members, are encouraged to furnish social and emotional support to women who are about to deliver a baby. When such support is provided by trusted companions, labor is shorter, fewer drugs are required, and babies are born showing less distress.

2. *Consider what type of practitioner might be most beneficial during childbirth.* Of course, fathers or other partners who assist in labor are not likely to be experts in the process. Midwives, nurses, or others far more experienced in childbirth, whose additional primary function is to provide personal assistance while managing labor, have received positive evaluations as well. Compared to physicians, midwives who oversee birthing report a lower rate of deliveries undergoing cesarean births or other surgical procedures and less use of medication by the mother (Butler et al., 1993; Sakala, 1993). This is the case even though midwives frequently assist women who face elevated risks. Whereas about 5 percent of births in the United States are now accompanied by midwives, this figure is nearly 75 percent in many European countries (Alan Guttmacher Institute, 1993).

3. *Explore the different alternatives available to assist in delivering a baby.* The positive outcomes achieved by midwives appear to stem from an attitude that inspires women to not just deliver babies but also draw on their own inner resources as well as their support networks for giving birth. For example, midwives are likely to suggest greater flexibility in positioning and moving about during labor, perhaps even soaking in a tub. Standing, squatting, or sitting in special chairs, or even hanging from a bar, are increasingly being offered as alternatives to the traditional recumbent position for delivery. These choices can increase a woman's comfort through the natural benefits of gravity and thus reduce stress for both mother and baby.

As we will repeatedly discover in later chapters, a supportive environment promotes development in children of all ages. Research on the availability of attendants and midwives in childbirth as well as alternative positions for delivering a baby indicate a similar positive return, not only to the newborn but to the men and women taking on the new responsibility of parenting.

Alternative Birth Settings The perception of traditional hospital settings as impersonal and regimented, coupled with a desire to make delivery more relaxing and natural, has led to other revolutionary changes in childbirth practices. Birthing centers within hospitals have become less institutional and more homelike in terms of furnishings and the inclusion of family members and friends. They also often provide

KEY THEME
Sociocultural Influence

a single room in which labor, delivery, and postpartum care occur under the supervision of the same nursing staff. Home delivery and freestanding birthing centers (FSBCs) have become further options. These alternatives, staffed primarily by midwives, seem to offer women a greater sense of comfort and support, further separate the experience of pregnancy from the concept of illness, and permit women to have greater control over what happens to both them and their babies (Eakins, 1984; Sakala, 1993).

Alternative birthing environments, however, raise the issue of safety. Virtually all of the more than one hundred FSBCs licensed in the United States require women at risk for complications to use traditional medical facilities and have arrangements with nearby hospitals if emergencies arise (Bergman, 1994). Many more birthing centers have been created within hospitals so that medical facilities are close by. But for home deliveries, back-up services are often less readily available, especially when that choice is made solely for economic reasons or is unplanned. The safety of planned home births with licensed midwives in attendance matches that for hospital births (Mathews & Sadak, 1991), but the mortality rate increases nearly twentyfold when home deliveries are unintended. Still, in the Netherlands, where about one-third of all births are attended by midwives in the home, cities that have the highest percentage of home births compared to hospital births actually report fewer numbers of problems during delivery (Hafner-Eaton & Pearce, 1994).

Labor and Delivery

When labor begins, the wet, warm, and supportive world within the uterus undergoes a rapid transformation, and the fetus must adjust to an earthshaking series of events. During normal birth, the fetus begins to be subjected to increasingly stronger pressure. Because the birth canal is somewhat smaller than the size of the head, pressure—as great as thirty pounds of force—will probably cause the head to become somewhat elongated and misshapen (Trevathen, 1987). This is possible because the cerebral plates are not yet knitted together, allowing them to slide up and over one another. At times the fetus may experience brief disruptions in oxygen as the flow of blood in the umbilical cord is temporarily obstructed. And then the infant emerges head first into a strange, new world, one drier, possibly colder, and often much brighter and noisier. Within minutes the new arrival must begin to take in oxygen. The baby must also soon learn to coordinate sucking, swallowing, and breathing to obtain sufficient nutrients.

Labor is a complicated, interactive process involving the fetus, the woman, and the placenta. What brings its onset? The answer remains largely unknown, although the pituitary gland of the fetus may play a significant role (Trevathen, 1987). The first of the three traditional stages of labor (see Figure 4.6) begins with brief, mild contractions perhaps ten to fifteen minutes apart. These contractions become increasingly frequent and serve to alter the shape of the cervix, preparing it for the fetus's descent and entry into the narrow birth canal. Near the end of the first stage, which on average lasts about eleven hours for firstborns and about seven hours for later-borns, dilation of the cervix proceeds rapidly to allow passage through the birth canal. The second stage consists of the continued descent and birth of the fetus. This stage usually requires a little less than an hour in firstborns and about twenty minutes in later-borns. In the third stage, which lasts about fifteen minutes, the placenta is expelled. These durations are, however, averages; enormous variation exists from one woman to another.

Medication During Childbirth   In Western societies, births are often accompanied by some form of medication. Anesthesia blocks the transmission of pain, analgesics lessen feelings of discomfort, and sedatives help the woman to relax. All of these drugs readily pass through the placenta and enter the fetus's circulatory system. Critics of the routine use of drugs point out that babies whose mothers receive high doses during labor are less attentive and responsive to caregivers, are more irritable, and gain weight more slowly than babies exposed to small amounts or no drugs at

KEY THEME
Continuity/Discontinuity

FIGURE 4.6	The Three Stages of Childbirth

In the first stage of labor the cervix, the neck of the uterus, dilates and thins to open a passage through the birth canal. The amniotic fluid, if not already lost, helps by exerting firm, even pressure on the cervix. When the pressure becomes too great, the sac containing the amniotic fluid will rupture, a process known as "breaking the water." The head of the fetus will soon enter the birth canal, and the second stage of labor begins. During the second stage of labor, each contraction continues to push the fetus farther along the approximately four inches of the birth canal. During a normal delivery, the head emerges first (known as *crowning*), much as though pushing through the neck of a tight turtleneck sweater. Once the head has emerged, shoulders twist around in the birth canal and the head turns sideways to permit delivery of the rest of the body. In the final stage of labor, the placenta is delivered.

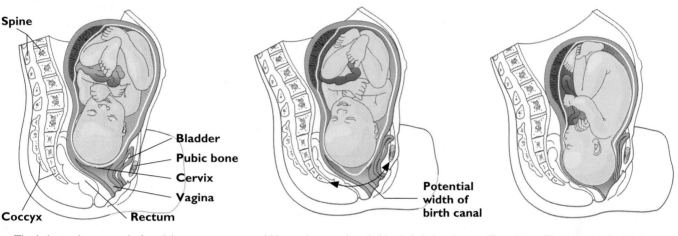

The baby in the uterus before labor

Water about to break (the baby's head now rests inside the cervix)

Transition: The baby in the birth canal

STAGE 1

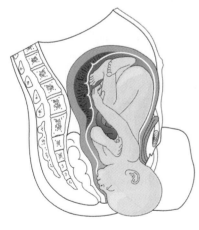

The baby about to be born

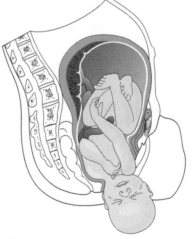

The head rotates sideways after it emerges

STAGE 2

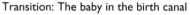
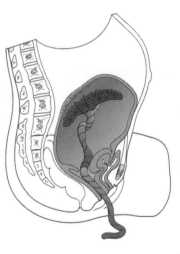

The delivery of the placenta

STAGE 3

all (Brazelton, Nugent, & Lester, 1987). Moreover, some behavioral differences may persist well beyond infancy. Heavy use of drugs during labor has been associated, for example, with an increased incidence of learning disorders among school-age children (Brackbill, McManus, & Woodward, 1985).

Developmental differences between babies born to medicated and nonmedicated women, however, are not consistent. Some experts believe the negative effects of exposure to drugs at birth have been markedly overstated and occur only when medications are used excessively (Kraemer et al., 1985). Thus, women need not experience unreasonable pain or feel guilty if drugs are administered. Efforts to make the birth process gentler, such as by reducing illumination and noise or delivering the

Labor and delivery are accompanied by strong emotions. The discomforts associated with labor very likely are mixed with tears of joy, as this mother seems to be demonstrating when seeing her newborn baby for the first time.

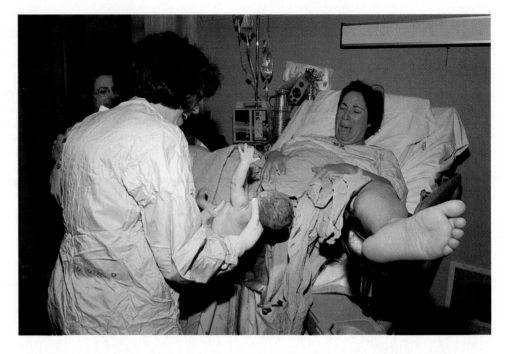

KEY THEME
Individual Differences

KEY THEME
Sociocultural Influence

baby under water, have also been proposed (Daniels, 1989; LeBoyer, 1975). The advantages of these practices for either women or infants have not been documented, although, as we have already seen, providing a network of social support does help.

Cesarean Birth   A *cesarean birth* is the delivery of a baby through a surgical incision in the woman's abdomen and uterus. Cesarean births are recommended when labor fails to progress normally, when the baby's head is very large, or when birth is *breech* (foot or rump first) rather than head first. Concerns about stress on the fetus that might lead to increased risk of brain damage, vaginal infections that might be transmitted to the baby, and expensive malpractice suits (should things go awry during vaginal delivery) have led to more than a fivefold increase in the frequency of cesarean sections in the past thirty years in the United States. Today about 22 percent of deliveries in the United States are cesarean rather than vaginal (Guyer et al., 1995), a rate that is far higher than in all other countries except Brazil and Puerto Rico (Centers for Disease Control, 1993).

Women who undergo cesarean section face an increased risk of infection and a longer hospital stay than women who give birth vaginally. Moreover, cesarean babies are likely to be exposed to greater maternal medication. Other concerns center on the different experiences both mother and infant receive under such circumstances. For example, when cesarean babies are delivered before labor begins, they do not have a misshapen head and appear perfectly healthy. However, they have substantially lower levels of two stress hormones, adrenaline and noradrenaline, known to facilitate respiration by helping to keep the lungs open and clear. The hormones also enhance cell metabolism, circulation of the blood to the brain, and activity level, factors that help the infant make the transition to his or her new environment and to become responsive to caregivers. Thus, cesarean babies generally tend to have more trouble breathing, are less active, sleep more, and cry less than other babies (Trevathen, 1987).

Birth Trauma   The increase in the frequency of cesarean sections in the United States has come about partly because of concerns about birth trauma, or injuries sustained at birth. A potentially serious consequence is *anoxia,* or deprivation of oxygen. Anoxia can result from damage to or lengthy compression of the umbilical cord or head during birth. It also may result from failure of the baby to begin regular breathing after birth. If oxygen deprivation lasts more than a few minutes, severe damage to the central nervous system, including cerebral palsy, can result.

Fortunately, brief periods of anoxia have few long-lasting effects. Furthermore, an adequate postnatal caregiving environment can help to counter potentially negative outcomes for infants experiencing periods of anoxia (Sameroff & Chandler, 1975). Concerns about anoxia and other birth traumas, however, have led to the rapidly expanded use of **fetal monitoring devices** during labor. Most of these devices record fetal heartbeat to determine whether the fetus is undergoing stress during delivery. However, some experts question whether the devices are more beneficial than the ordinary stethoscope for making medical decisions in all but high-risk pregnancies (Shy et al., 1990). Moreover, others argue that reliance on some medically sophisticated equipment promotes a cascading series of interventions that only exacerbate the difficulty of delivery. In fact, by focusing on a supportive context to reduce anxiety, less birth trauma will occur than that the technology was designed to prevent (Hafner-Eaton & Pearce, 1994; Sakala, 1993).

Low Birth Weight

As infant and childhood diseases have come under greater control in recent decades, the treatment and prevention of low-birth-weight infants (those weighing less than twenty-five hundred grams, or five-and-a-half pounds) has gained increased attention. Mortality rate rapidly declines as birth weight increases to normal levels. The United States has a higher proportion of infants born with low birth weight than many other developed countries, a major reason its infant mortality rate is also higher (see Figure 4.7).

Babies with low birth weight fall into two groups: those born preterm (less than thirty-five weeks conceptual age) whose development has generally proceeded normally but has been cut short by early delivery and those born near their expected arrival date and are *small for gestational age (SGA)*. Thus, low-birth-weight infants comprise a heterogeneous group, perhaps needing separate types of medical treatment and intervention and facing different developmental outcomes. Congenital anomalies are somewhat more frequent in SGA infants, for example, whereas respiratory distress is more likely among infants who are born preterm (Starfield et al., 1982).

Caring for Infants with Low Birth Weight   In general, infants born with low birth weight face many obstacles. The frequency of cerebral palsy, seizure disorders, and other neurological problems increases, especially for infants of very low (less than fifteen hundred grams) or extremely low birth weight (less than one thousand grams, or about two-and-a-quarter pounds). For these infants, the first major task is to maintain physiological stability. Another critical task is to achieve regular cycles of activity involving sleep and wakefulness, patterns that infants of normal birth weight routinely display within a few weeks of birth. Low-birth-weight infants have trouble falling asleep, awakening, maintaining alertness, and settling into regular and efficient feeding schedules (Barnard, 1987).

Respiratory difficulties, hyperactivity, greater frequency of illness, and disruption of parental caregiving and family functioning are common problems for these infants as well (Blackman, 1991). For example, at one time parents were either excluded completely from neonatal intensive care units (NICUs), the specialized medical facilities designed to care for low-birth-weight infants, or cautioned to handle these babies as little as possible. Are low-birth-weight infants too fragile to receive stimulation beyond that necessarily imposed by medical treatment?

Concern that low-birth-weight infants may not receive adequate stimulation began to surface as evidence emerged showing its benefits for social and intellectual development in infants of normal birth weight (Ramey, Bryant, & Suarez, 1987; Thoman, 1993). But what kind of experience should it be? Should caregivers offer *compensatory stimulation,* attempting to duplicate what the baby would have gained if still in the womb? Examples might include oscillating devices or waterbeds to simulate movements the fetus experiences prenatally; muffled recordings of a human

KEY THEME
Individual Differences

KEY THEME
Sociocultural Influence

KEY THEME
Nature/Nurture

fetal monitoring device
Medical device used to monitor fetal heartbeat during delivery.

FIGURE 4.7

Infant Mortality in Selected
Developed Countries

**The infant mortality rate
(deaths before one year of age
per thousand live births) is a
measure that provides an indication of the overall health of a
nation. A number of countries
have a lower infant mortality
rate than the United States.**

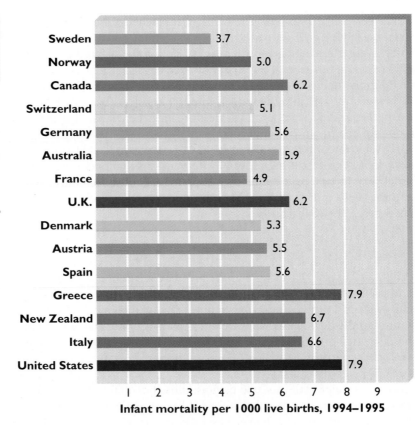

Source: Data from United Nations Statistical Office, 1996.

KEY THEME
Individual Differences

---

voice, a heartbeat, or other sounds to match those usually heard in the womb; and
opportunities for nonnutritive sucking, an activity in which the fetus occasionally
engages (Thoman, 1993). Or, since low-birth-weight babies must react to gravity,
organize respiratory and digestive functions, and process stimulation much as all
infants do, should caregiving be *enriching*, that is, approximate the visual and auditory stimulation, handling, and social contact a typical newborn might receive?

Benefits from both compensatory and enriching stimulation have sometimes been
reported: more rapid weight gain, shorter hospital stays, fewer medical and eating
problems, more regular breathing and heart rate, improvements in sensorimotor development, more stable and longer periods in quiet states, and smoother transitions
from one state to another (Gorski, 1991; Thoman, 1993). However, not all low-birth-
weight babies are helped. Perhaps an appropriate level of stimulation for a low-birth-
weight baby at one point in development is ineffective, or even overstimulating, at
another. Thus, there is an ongoing need to explore and identify those experiences
that complement and promote development in these children (Thoman, 1993).
Questions also remain about whether those who benefit are able to maintain the
gains. Perhaps children are exposed to social and rearing conditions upon leaving the
hospital that are far more important determinants of their subsequent development.

Promoting Development in Low-Birth-Weight Children   In general, low-birth-
weight infants lag behind other children in development. A higher proportion, especially those with extremely low birth weights, display visuomotor and language
deficits, learning disabilities, behavior problems, and fewer social skills, and suffer
more peer rejection as children (Lukeman & Melvin, 1993; McCormick, Workman-
Daniels, & Brooks-Gunn, 1996). The problems are likely to culminate in poorer
school achievement and the need for more special education intervention (Klebanov,
Brooks-Gunn, & McCormick, 1994; Pharoah et al., 1993). Fortunately, many low-
birth-weight children still do surprisingly well. An analysis of data from more than
eighty studies conducted in North America, Europe, Australia, and New Zealand

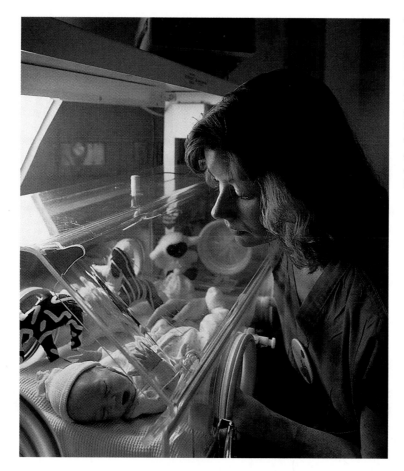

This infant, although born prematurely, has the opportunity to explore a rich array of brightly colored toys in his new environment. He also receives frequent handling by caregivers. Questions, however, remain about how much and what kinds of stimulation are optimal for the development of children born with low birth weight.

concluded that only small differences in intellectual and developmental capabilities exist among low-birth-weight compared to normal-weight children (Aylward et al., 1989).

As we have begun to see in other examples of children with special needs, one very important factor contributing to positive developmental outcomes appears to be the support and encouragement of parents in their efforts to care for low-birth-weight infants. Providing parents with opportunities to engage in suitable caregiving in the hospital setting, instructing them to recognize the specific needs of their infant and what behaviors to expect, and extending the emotional support of professional staff and other parents are types of assistance that have proven beneficial to low-birth-weight children (Achenbach et al., 1993; McCormick et al., 1993; Ramey et al., 1992). For example, Jeanne Brooks-Gunn and her colleagues (1993) found that low-birth-weight children in families who participated in educational day care programs, received regular home visits, and joined in frequent parent group meetings were able to maintain higher levels of performance on cognitive tests than children in families for whom these resources were unavailable (see Figure 4.8). Even simply permitting the mother to observe the administration of a standard infant test or providing her with weekly reports on the infant's activities increases sensitivity to and involvement with her infant, which in turn fosters her baby's development (Szajnberg et al., 1987; Widmayer & Field, 1981; Worobey & Belsky, 1982).

KEY THEME
Nature/Nurture

Additional Issues Concerning Low Birth Weight Attempts to reduce complications associated with low birth weight have proceeded on two fronts. Improved medical care in NICUs (called *special care baby units* in the United Kingdom) and supportive caregiving have permitted more low-birth-weight, especially extremely low-birth-weight, infants to survive and develop normally. A second major assault on the problem has been in the form of prevention. Researchers have catalogued a long list of demographic, medical, and behavioral factors associated with low birth weight, for

FIGURE 4.8

Low-Birth-Weight Children's Cognitive Development as a Function of Intervention

In a large-scale study investigating the effects of providing home visits and educational child care for low-birth-weight infants and their families, Brooks-Gunn and her colleagues (1993) found that performance on measures of intellectual development was substantially better for those who received the intervention than for those who did not. Although some decline in scores occurred even for the group receiving intervention, it was far less than for those who did not receive the intervention. Both groups performed similarly at the youngest age (twelve months), perhaps because tests measuring cognitive skills often are not very sensitive to differences at that age.

KEY THEME
Sociocultural Influence

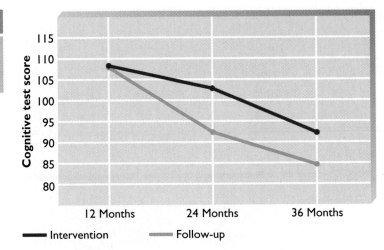

Source: Brooks-Gunn et al., 1993.

example, inadequate prenatal care and nutrition, heavy smoking, and drug use. Many of these factors are preventable. Thus, educational programs targeted to pregnant women at high risk, including teenagers, have become increasingly important. These programs can be successful in reducing the incidence of low birth weight, especially when offered consistently and early in the course of pregnancy (Fangman et al., 1994; Seitz & Apfel, 1994). Indeed, future progress in addressing the problems that accompany low birth weight is likely to be more closely tied to improved and more widespread programs of prevention than to new medical advances.

THE NEWBORN

Even parents of a healthy infant may be in for a surprise when they see their baby for the first time. Unless delivered by cesarean section, the baby is likely to have a flattened nose and a large, distorted head, resulting when the bones of the skull override one another during passage through the narrow birth canal. The skin of all babies, regardless of racial background, is a pale pinkish color and often is covered by an oily, cheeselike substance (the vernix caseosa) that protects against infection. Sex organs are swollen due to high levels of sex hormones.

If the parents are startled, though, just imagine what kind of adjustment the baby must make! The new environment introduces others who actively relate to the baby. If the child is wanted, she or he will be cuddled and talked to, fussed over, and rocked by one, maybe two, perhaps many people. If unwanted, the child may rarely experience such events. The newborn, in other words, enters a social environment that can be supportive and responsive, or barren and uninviting, or some level in between. Needs such as nutrition, formerly met by the placenta and various structures in the womb, now depend on social interaction for their gratification. Mothers, fathers, grandparents, siblings, and others become the major resource for physical and psychological growth.

An infant's most immediate need after emerging from the womb is to breathe. Pressure on the chest during delivery probably helps to clear the baby's fluid-filled lungs, but the shock of cool air, perhaps accompanied by jiggling, a slap, or some other less than gentle activity by a birth attendant, makes the first breath more like a gasp, quickly followed by a reflexive cry. The umbilical cord may continue to pulse for several minutes after birth, and in most societies the cord is not cut until after it ceases to do so (Trevathen, 1987). In the United States, however, the cord is usually cut immediately, a practice that has come under criticism because the placenta continues to provide an oxygen-rich source of blood for a short time after delivery (Desmond, Rudolph, & Phitaksphraiwan, 1963).

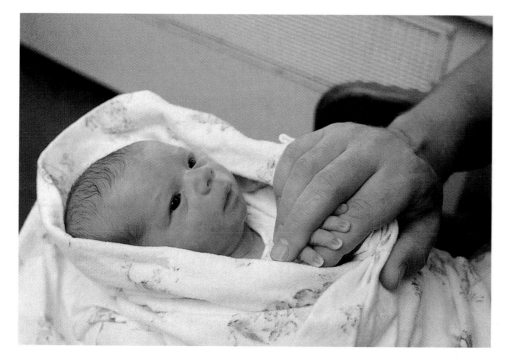

This two-day-old baby, holding her father's hand, has entered a world where new forms of physical and social stimulation can be experienced. Although newborns and young infants spend much of their time sleeping, this infant is engaged in alert inactivity, a time in which she may be learning much about her environment.

The second major task the baby must accomplish upon entering the world is to regulate body temperature. Babies lose body heat about four times more rapidly than adults because of their lower fat reserve and relatively large body surface (Bruck, 1962). As a consequence, newborns, although they can effectively maintain their temperature when held close to a caregiver's body, are often quickly placed under heaters (Hill & Shronk, 1979).

Assessing Newborns

Newborns typically weigh five-and-a-half to ten pounds and measure eighteen to twenty-two inches in length. Many measures for evaluating their health have become available in recent years, but one routinely administered is the *Apgar Scale* (Apgar, 1953). Typically assessed at both one and five minutes after birth, the Apgar measures five vital signs: heart rate, respiratory effort, muscle tone, reflex responsivity, and color. Each vital sign is scored 0, 1, or 2 based on the criteria described in Table 4.6. In the United States, 90 percent of infants receive a total score of 7 or better; those who score less than 4 are considered to be at risk.

KEY THEME
Individual Differences

	Ratings				
Vital Sign	*0*	*1*	*2*		**TABLE 4.6**
					The Apgar Scoring System
Heart Rate	Absent	Slow (below 100)	Over 100		
Respiratory effort	Absent	Slow, irregular	Good, crying		**The Apgar Scale is used at and shortly after birth to diagnose the physical condition of a newborn. The ratings for each vital sign are added for a total score ranging from 0 to 10. An infant who scores less than 4 is considered to be at risk.**
Muscle tone	Flaccid	Some flexion of extremities	Active motion		
Reflex responsivity	No response	Grimace	Vigorous cry		
Color	Blue, pale	Body pink, extremities blue	Completely pink		

Source: Adapted from Apgar, 1953.

A more extensive measure, developed by T. Berry Brazelton (1973) and given several days after birth, is the *Neonatal Behavioral Assessment Scale (NBAS)*. The NBAS evaluates the baby's behavior on a variety of dimensions, such as ability to interact with the tester, responsiveness to objects in the environment, reflex motor capacities, and ability to control behavioral state. Typical questions include: Does the baby watch while the examiner moves her head back and forth and side to side and calls out to her in a high-pitched voice? Does the baby cuddle or resist being held? Does the baby remove a cloth placed over his face, grasp a forefinger placed in his hand, attempt to hold his head upright while in a sitting position, and become quiet within a reasonable time after being fussy?

Newborn performance on the NBAS has been used to assess neurological condition and can indicate whether certain prenatal or perinatal conditions, as well as intervention programs, have had an effect (Korner, 1987; Tronick, 1987). An NBAS score can also predict later developmental outcomes. Babies who score poorly on the scale continue to be somewhat less responsive to caregivers in the first few months after birth (Vaughn et al., 1980). In general, however, the predictive validity of the NBAS (along with other infant tests) for long-term development is only modest at best (Brazelton, Nugent, & Lester, 1987). Nevertheless, parents who observe while examiners give the NBAS or who are trained to give it themselves seem to become more responsive to and effective in interactions with their infants (Worobey, 1985).

Newborn States

Babies sleep. They sleep a lot. But newborns and young infants display a wide variety of states: regular and irregular sleep, drowsiness, alert inactivity, alert activity, and crying. Crying or distress usually begins with whimpering but swiftly shifts to full-scale cries, often accompanied by thrashing of arms and legs. During alert activity the infant also exhibits vigorous, diffuse motor activity, but such exertions are not accompanied by signs of distress. During alert inactivity the baby is relatively quiet, at least in terms of motor activity, but actively engages in visual scanning of the environment. In this state, the baby appears to be most responsive to sensory stimulation and may be learning a great deal.

Although individual differences are great, newborns average sixteen to seventeen hours of sleep a day. Sleep and wake cycles are extremely short, and babies are easily disrupted by external stimulation. As the weeks pass, infants gradually sleep less but for longer periods; by about three to five weeks of age, a pattern begins to emerge in which the longest sleep periods take place at night (Thompson, 1982). But naps during the day continue to be a regular occurrence through the preschool years. In fact, in some cultures, such naps are never eliminated.

The development of sleep patterns differs substantially across various cultures. In the United States, parents eagerly look forward to having their infants adopt a routine that matches their own. A significant milestone is reached when the baby of three or four months finally sleeps through the night. In some cultures, such as the Kipsigi of rural Kenya, however, infants are permitted more flexibility and will not sleep through the night until much older (Super & Harkness, 1982).

Like adults, infants display two distinct sleep states. During active or *REM (rapid-eye-movement)* sleep, eye movements and muscle jerks are frequent and breathing and heart rate are irregular. During quiet sleep (*NREM*), eye and muscle movements are few and physiological activity is more regular. The proportion of time spent in the two states, however, shifts dramatically with development, from about eight in sixteen hours in REM sleep as a newborn to about two in seven hours of sleep as an adult.

Active or REM sleep has been linked to dreaming, but it is not clear whether young infants dream. Even if they do, why do they spend so much time in REM sleep? REM sleep is believed to be important for normal brain activity (Roffwarg, Muzio, & Dement, 1966). *Autostimulation theory* proposes that REM sleep provides

KEY THEME
Individual Differences

KEY THEME
Sociocultural Influence

powerful stimulation to the central nervous system, which in adults is interpreted as sensory and motor activity associated with dreaming. According to this theory, stimulation during REM sleep compensates for the relatively brief number of hours each day the infant is awake. Infants kept awake for relatively lengthy periods of time show reduced amounts of REM sleep, and premature infants, whose wakeful periods are even shorter, show more REM sleep than full-term babies (Halpern, MacLean, & Baumeister, 1995). If autostimulation theory is correct, it is a further demonstration of how important stimulation is for development, even at those times when a large amount of sleep is essential as well.

CHAPTER RECAP

SUMMARY OF DEVELOPMENTAL THEMES

NATURE/NURTURE What roles do nature and nurture play in prenatal development and birth?

Prenatal development is the product of complex interactions involving genetic instructions inherited from parents (see Chapter 3) and the expectant woman's physical and emotional conditions, as well as exposure to drugs, diseases, hazardous chemicals, and medications before and during pregnancy and during labor. We have seen, for example, that differentiation of organs and systems in the embryo typically obeys principles established by biochemical and physiological processes. Yet these processes do not operate in a vacuum. Teratogens and various intrauterine conditions can radically alter the normal developmental path. Thus, events in the life of the woman may change the immediate environment within her womb, with drastic consequences for the fetus. The reactions, attitudes, and availability of the newborn's caregivers and the stimulation they provide are other major sources of potential influence on the baby's development.

SOCIOCULTURAL INFLUENCE How does the sociocultural context influence prenatal development and birth?

The immediate internal environment of the fetus and the perinatal environment provided for the newborn can be influenced dramatically by the larger social, economic, and cultural settings in which pregnancy and birth take place. The woman's actions during pregnancy are often modified or regulated by a network of expectations, advice, and resources within the culture in which she lives. An expectant woman in one community, for example, may have access to medical and other kinds of care that provide a more or less healthy environment for the fetus than a woman in another community. Industry or governing units may legislate controls on chemical pollution in one country and ignore them in another. Scientific and technological advances in prenatal testing, birthing practices, and newborn care may be available in one region of the world but not another; even when available, however, not all parents may have the economic resources or desire to use them.

CONTINUOUS/DISCONTINUOUS Is development before and after birth continuous or discontinuous?

When the zygote attaches to the uterine wall and taps a new source of nourishment, its course of development changes dramatically. Once the various organs and systems are formed and become less susceptible to environmental disruptions, the fetus achieves a vastly different status. The process of birth itself is a major transition. Such spectacular changes fit with discontinuous or stagelike descriptions of development. So do the marked shifts in vulnerability to teratogens observed during prenatal development. Underlying the progressions, however, are biochemical and physiological processes governing cell proliferation, differentiation, and the emergence and functioning of biological systems that can be seen as continuous. Many dramatic changes are essentially the product of modest accumulative modifications in the multifaceted, complex environment that promotes development.

INDIVIDUAL DIFFERENCES How prominent are individual differences in prenatal development and the newborn?

Newborns everywhere undergo many common gestational experiences; however, individual differences already have begun to surface. Many differences arise because, contrary to once widely held beliefs, the fetus is not immune to the influences of the larger world. Because of exposure to teratogens and other maternal conditions, babies will differ in their physical and behavioral qualities and their ability to cope with and adapt to their new environment. Greater knowledge of and sensitivity to those differences by caregivers, whether exhibited by a newborn with special needs such as one with low birth weight or by an infant who falls within the typical range for newborns, can help to ensure success for the continued development of every child.

SUMMARY OF TOPICS

■ THE STAGES OF PRENATAL DEVELOPMENT

Prenatal development is the period that extends from conception to birth. During this time, a newly fertilized ovum is transformed from a single-celled *zygote* into the complex, active organism that is the newborn. During the *germinal period,* about the first ten to fourteen days after conception, the zygote migrates from the Fallopian tube to the uterus, becomes multicelled, and implants itself in the uterine wall to gain access to a new source of nutrients directly from the woman.

The *embryonic period* begins after implantation and continues until about the eighth week after conception. This period is marked by development of the *placenta* and other supportive structures within the uterine environment and by the differentiation of cells into tissues that form the major organs and systems of the embryo. Many vital organs, including the brain, begin forming at this time. The embryo is susceptible to a variety of *teratogens,* environmental agents that can disrupt development and interfere with later behavior.

The *fetal period,* beginning in about the eighth week after conception and lasting until birth, is marked by continued growth and refinement of organs and systems. Neurons continue to form and migrate during this period. Brain activity, sensory reactions, and movement are more easily detected.

■ ENVIRONMENTAL FACTORS INFLUENCING PRENATAL DEVELOPMENT

Many drugs, diseases, chemicals, and other agents can cross the placental barrier and induce fetal death, produce congenital malformations, and contribute to other negative outcomes in development. The effects of exposure to a specific teratogen depend on many factors, such as the genetic susceptibility of the woman and her fetus, stage of fetal development, and means of access and level of exposure of the teratogen to the fetus. Teratogens can have different consequences, ranging from transient delays to irreversible defects to outcomes apparent only much later in development. Conditions of the woman, including how much stress she experiences, the availability of social and emotional support, and her nutritional and health status, can also influence fetal development.

■ BIRTH AND THE PERINATAL ENVIRONMENT

The practices and procedures surrounding the birth and initial care of a baby are part of the *perinatal period* of development. Cultures differ enormously in their methods of managing childbirth. Differences include where the baby is born, who is present at birth, and how much and what kinds of medication are made available to the woman during labor. Concerns about isolated and restrictive surroundings, as well as an overreliance on medication in traditional hospital settings, have led to a variety of methods to prepare for and deliver children.

As infant and childhood diseases have come under increasing control, researchers have directed attention to the prevention and treatment of low-birth-weight infants. Despite the immediate obstacles facing both low-birth-weight and small-for-gestational-age babies, many become normal children and adults. Compensatory and enrichment programs increase early weight gains and other aspects of early development.

■ THE NEWBORN

The brief but climactic beginnings taking place prenatally and perinatally set the stage for the long course of *postnatal development.* Tests such as the Apgar and Neonatal Behavioral Assessment scales provide some indication of the baby's physiological state and ability to interact with caregivers and respond to stimulation. Newborns and infants display a number of states. A relatively large proportion of their time is engaged in REM sleep, a state that may provide them with stimulation even when asleep.

5 PHYSICAL GROWTH AND MOTOR SKILLS

KEY THEMES IN PHYSICAL GROWTH AND MOTOR SKILLS

NATURE/NURTURE
What roles do nature and nurture play in physical growth and motor skill development?

SOCIOCULTURAL INFLUENCE
How does the sociocultural context influence physical growth and motor skill development?

CHILD'S ACTIVE ROLE
How does the child play an active role in the process of physical growth and motor skill development?

CONTINUITY/DISCONTINUITY
Are physical growth and motor skill development continuous or discontinuous?

INDIVIDUAL DIFFERENCES
How prominent are individual differences in physical growth and motor skill development?

INTERACTION AMONG DOMAINS
How do physical growth and motor skill development interact with other domains of development?

She stared intently at the thirteen-year-old who had just finished. Danielle couldn't believe what she had just seen. How could any girl her own age do that? Danielle's words expressed admiration and awe, but her voice was tinged with envy as she confided to her best friend, "We've been in gymnastics ever since we were five. If we tried that, we'd probably break our necks!"

Even as a toddler, Danielle seemed captivated by leaping and tumbling. Her parents took great pride in their daughter's graceful athleticism and precocious motor skills. Danielle enrolled in ballet and gymnastics at an early age. Both activities had been fun. As Danielle became older and more skilled, however, she especially seemed to thrive on the competition that permeated the gymnastics meets. She liked being good at what she did; she preferred being the best. However, she couldn't imagine anyone at her age with the dexterity and endurance to carry out that kind of routine. Through the applause, her friend had no difficulty hearing Danielle mutter, "I'll bet I can do that. I don't care if I do break my neck."

Physical growth and advances in motor skills are among the most readily apparent signs of development as it progresses from infancy through childhood and into adolescence. Few children become Olympic gymnasts, but virtually all acquire a sophisticated set of motor skills and physical abilities. The transformation is accompanied by less obvious, but no less revolutionary, neurological changes in the brain.

Growth of the body and brain and the development of physical skills significantly influence, and in turn are influenced by, social, emotional, and cognitive aspects of development. Consider how newfound motor coordinations may, for example, dramatically awaken cognition. The six-month-old who begins to reach for and grasp objects acquires a fresh and powerful means of gaining information and, at the same time, a new way to control and influence her environment. So, too, the child who just learned to ride his bike opens up broader vistas to explore and, at the same time, must learn to avoid new dangers that may accompany this feat.

The reactions of others to changing stature and accomplishments can arouse a child's pride and promote renewed efforts, or they can lead to discouragement and apprehension. For example, when children begin to crawl, they may confront new barriers and repeated choruses of "no, don't do that." How these freshly imposed limits, inspired by burgeoning physical capacities, are faced and resolved can affect many other aspects of solving problems or building relationships with others. Or consider the toddler who insists on dressing himself but still lacks the fine motor skills needed to button and unbutton. Will his frustrations overtax his mother's patience as she tries to get him to day care and herself to work on time? His need for increasing autonomy and his efforts to master new motor skills are two facets of the same developmental impulse, but they may crash headlong into other agendas his mother must balance as part of her daily routine.

Danielle, who is physically poised and skilled, displays confidence in the demands of learning a new and difficult gymnastic routine. That self-assurance could very easily extend to her social interactions and to her academic challenges. The child who fails to display certain competencies or lacks physical attributes valued in a society—for example, is shorter, less coordinated, or otherwise physically distinctive—may receive strikingly different treatment compared to the child who is tall, strong, or athletic.

How do body, brain, and motor skills develop? Are they determined only by genetic factors, or do parenting, cultural, or other environmental events influence their course? How important are appearance, early maturity, and physical prowess to achievements in other domains of development? In this chapter we explore these kinds of questions by examining the distinctive ways in which the child's body, brain, and motor skills develop. Let's begin by considering physical growth.

BODY GROWTH AND DEVELOPMENT

The mysterious ability to grow never ceases to amaze most observers. For parent and child alike, the ever-higher pencil marks on the bathroom wall give eloquent testimony to this process. A long-absent aunt who cries, "My, how you've grown!" may summon a grin from the wary seven-year-old or a blush from the self-conscious thirteen-year-old. She is, however, confirming for both children the social importance of this sign of increasing maturity.

We tend to use the words *grow* and *develop* interchangeably in describing the physical transformations of childhood, but they do not refer to the same processes. Strictly speaking, *growth* is the increase in size of the body or its organs, whereas *development* refers not only to changes in size but also to the orderly patterns, such as growth spurts, and the more complicated levels of functioning associated with physical and other changes.

Norms of Growth

By recording information about the size and weight of large numbers of children from diverse populations, we can determine whether a particular child's individual growth falls within the range expected for his or her chronological age and ethnic background. These **norms,** quantitative measures that provide typical values and variations in height and weight for children, have become an essential reference for attempting to answer questions about how biological and experiential factors influence growth.

Length and Height The most rapid increase in body length, as we saw in Chapter 4, occurs during the fourth month of prenatal development, when the fetus grows about 1.5 millimeters a day (Sinclair, 1985). Babies continue to grow rapidly, albeit at a somewhat slower rate, during the remaining prenatal weeks and also postnatally, especially during the first six months. In fact, if growth rate during the first six months after birth were sustained, the average ten-year-old would be about one hundred feet tall (McCall, 1979). One rule of thumb is that girls reach approximately half their adult height at about one-and-one-half years of age and boys at about two years of age (Krogman, 1972).

norms Measures of average values and variations in some aspect of development, such as physical size and motor skill development, in relation to age.

Variation in height is just one of the many ways that children of the same age differ in their physical development. These individual differences are most pronounced as children approach adolescence. Perhaps the ability of these children to play the clarinet is as varied as their height and clothes.

KEY THEME
Individual Differences

Throughout infancy and childhood boys and girls grow at similar rates, although individual children, of course, may differ enormously. For example, sudden growth spurts of one-quarter to one-half inch occasionally occur literally overnight in infants and toddlers (Lampl, Veldhuis, & Johnson, 1992). Over a longer span of time, growth rate generally follows a slow and steady pace throughout much of childhood. At about ten or eleven years of age, however, many girls begin an adolescent growth spurt, a period when growth occurs at nearly double the rate in childhood. Because the growth spurt usually does not start in boys until about two years later, girls may tower over their male peers for a brief period in early adolescence. Figure 5.1 illustrates the growth typically observed in many populations of children during their first eighteen years.

Weight   In contrast to that of height, the maximum rate of increase in weight takes place shortly after birth. In their first few days, newborns typically lose excess body fluids and shed 5 to 10 percent of their birth weight. They then usually make rapid weight gains, normally doubling their birth weight in about five months and nearly tripling it by the end of the first year (Pinyerd, 1992). If the gains for the first six months were sustained, the average ten-year-old would weigh in at about 240,000 tons (McCall, 1979). Weight gains are smallest during childhood between ages two and three and gradually increase until just before adolescence. During the adolescent growth spurt, however, a girl can expect to put on thirty-five pounds and a boy forty-five pounds.

Patterns in Body Growth

Specific organs and systems of the body often develop at rates different from that for the body as a whole. The most dramatic example probably is head size. Two months after conception, the head constitutes nearly 50 percent of total body length. By birth, however, head size represents only about 25 percent, and by adulthood only about 12 to 13 percent of total body length, as Figure 5.2 shows. The central nervous system, along with the head, shows an early and extremely rapid increase in weight. By five or six years of age, the child has reached 90 percent of the adult level for brain and head size.

Other organs, for example, the muscles and the respiratory and digestive systems, follow the pattern of overall general weight change: substantial gains during the first two years; a slower, more stable increase throughout childhood; and a rapid increase

FIGURE 5.1 Growth in Height and Weight over the First Eighteen Years

Height and, to a lesser extent, weight rapidly increase in the first two years following birth. Changes in height and weight continue at a fairly modest rate throughout childhood, followed by a brief, more rapid upturn sometime during the preadolescent or adolescent years. However, there is a wide range in height and weight among children, especially during the adolescent years. For example, this figure shows the heights and weights of boys and girls between the 0.4 to 99.6 percentile, derived from studies carried out in the United Kingdom during the past decade.

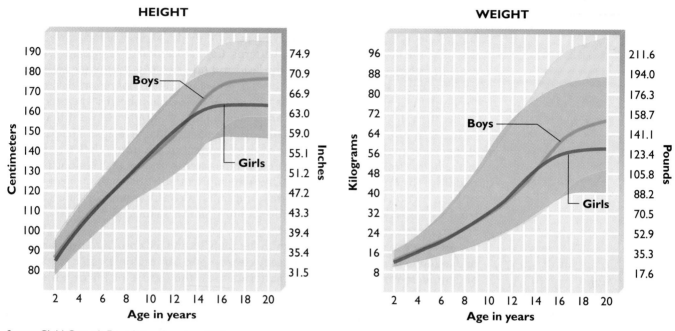

Source: Child Growth Foundation, London, 1996.

FIGURE 5.2 Changes in Body Proportions During Prenatal and Postnatal Growth

The size of the human head in proportion to the rest of the body shows striking changes over the course of prenatal to adult development. Two months after conception, the head comprises about half of the entire length of the body. By adulthood, the head makes up only about 12 to 13 percent of total body length. The head's tendency to grow more rapidly than regions of the body near the "tail" demonstrates the pattern of cephalocaudal development.

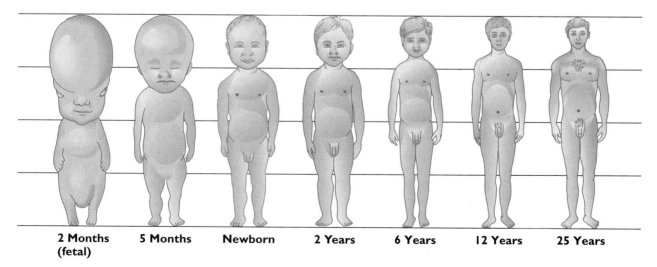

Source: Adapted from Robbins et al., 1928.

during adolescence. However, the reproductive system, not surprisingly, follows a strikingly different pattern: only during adolescence do organs associated with reproduction begin to mature and rapidly approach their adult size. The patterns mirror the functional importance of various systems of the body at specific points in development. The brain's relatively early maturity makes possible neural involvement in many aspects of early behavior acquisition and development. Similarly, the increase in the weight of the reproductive organs during adolescence is an important component in the emergence of adult sexual maturity.

Directionality of Growth   The varying growth trends we observe for many parts of the body often follow two common patterns. **Cephalocaudal development** (*cephalocaudal* combines the Greek words for *head* and *tail*) describes the tendency for systems and parts of the body near the head to grow faster than those more distant from the head. In Chapter 4, we noted that the end of the neural tube near the head closes earlier than the lower end of the spinal column and that upper limbs differentiate earlier than lower limbs, as predicted by the cephalocaudal principle. The pattern is also evident in the more rapid rate of development of the head relative to the rest of the body. **Proximodistal development** refers to the finding that regions near the middle of the body also tend to differentiate more rapidly than regions near the periphery. A good example is the ability of infants to control body parts nearer their trunks, such as their upper arms and legs, much sooner than areas more distant, such as their fingers and toes.

Not all physical changes conform to the cephalocaudal or proximodistal principle of development. During the adolescent growth spurt, for example, some parts of the body undergo rapid growth in a pattern almost the reverse of the proximodistal principle. We are all familiar with the teenager who seems to be all hands and feet. Hands and feet are in fact among the first body parts to show a dramatic change during this period; they are followed by arms and legs and, last of all, the trunk (Tanner, 1978). An adolescent, in other words, is likely to outgrow his shoes first, then his trousers, and finally his jacket.

KEY THEME
Individual Differences

Individual and Group Differences   Children show substantial deviations from the norm in their rates of physical growth and development. Individual variations in size are already noticeable at birth; for example, boys tend to be slightly longer and heavier than girls at this time (Copper et al., 1993). Individual differences in growth continue throughout infancy and childhood, often becoming especially evident during the adolescent years, when children are likely to show enormous variation in the timing, speed, and duration of the adolescent growth spurt. In the United States, the onset of rapid adolescent growth typically occurs between ages ten and fourteen for girls and between ages twelve and sixteen for boys (Sinclair, 1985). A girl who once towered over her childhood girlfriends may suddenly find at age thirteen that she is looking up to them, temporarily at least. A boy whose athletic skills were unremarkable may find himself the starting center for the junior high basketball team if he undergoes an early adolescent growth spurt.

KEY THEME
Sociocultural Influence

Variability in growth occurs among ethnic and cultural groups as well. For example, although individual differences account for much of the variability in size, American infants of African heritage tend to weigh slightly less than American infants of European heritage at birth, even when social class, gestational age, and other factors known to affect birth weight are equated (Goldenberg et al., 1991). Variability in height among ethnically and culturally diverse populations is further exhibited throughout childhood. Figure 5.3 illustrates the average height of eight-year-old girls from a number of regions of the world.

cephalocaudal development
Pattern in which organs, systems, and motor movements near the head tend to develop earlier than those near the feet.

proximodistal development
Pattern in which organs and systems of the body near the middle tend to develop earlier than those near the periphery.

Determinants of Body Growth and Development

What are the roles of nature and nurture in human physical growth? On the one hand, the contributions of nature, or heredity, are suggested by research indicating signifi-

| FIGURE 5.3 | Ethnic and Cultural Differences in Growth |

Ethnic and cultural differences in growth are strikingly apparent in this graph of the average height of eight-year-old girls from selected regions of the world. Girls in northern and Eastern Europe are nearly a half-foot taller, on average, than girls of this age in India; similar results have been found for boys. These variations may reflect both hereditary and environmental conditions.

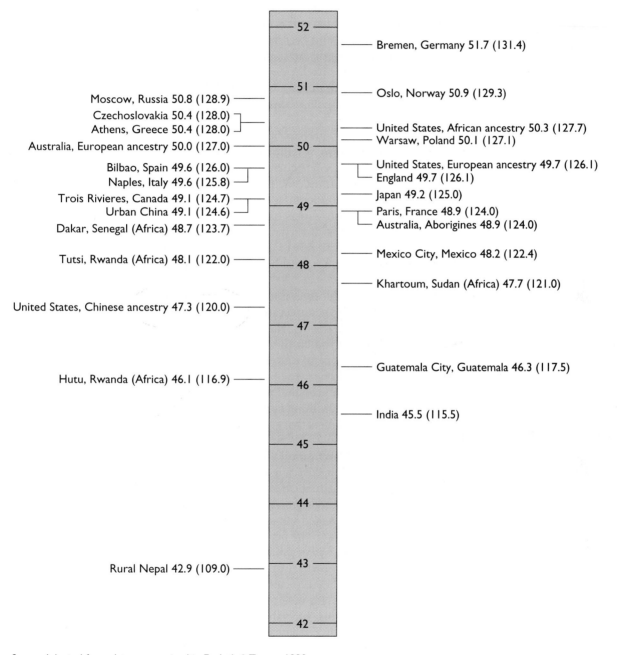

Source: Adapted from data summarized in Eveleth & Tanner, 1990.
Note: Height in centimeters is in parentheses.

cant biological influences on physical development as well as correlations among related family and cultural members in mature size and in the onset and pattern of physical changes. On the other hand, nurture, or environment—including diet, disease, and social and emotional circumstances—has a bearing on physical growth as well. But just how do biology and environment affect physical development?

KEY THEME
Nature/Nurture

Hypothalamus

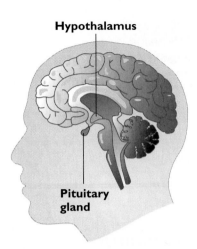

Pituitary gland

FIGURE 5.4

Two Important Organs of the Brain That Affect Growth and Physical Development

The hypothalamus and the pituitary gland, located near each other at the base of the brain, are two organs believed to play a central role in the regulation of growth. The hypothalamus may be the locus for a growth center that compares actual height with a genetically determined template for height. Hormones released by the hypothalamus stimulate the release of other hormones by the pituitary gland that promote growth.

catch-up growth Increase in growth rate after some factor, such as illness or poor nutrition, has disrupted the expected, normal growth rate.

lagging-down growth Decrease in growth rate after some factor, such as a congenital or hormonal disorder, has accelerated the expected, normal growth rate.

hormones Chemicals produced by various glands that are secreted directly into the bloodstream and can therefore circulate to influence cells in other locations of the body.

Genetic Factors A person's height is likely to be closely related to that of his or her mother and father. A late-maturing adolescent often shares late maturity with other family members (Rallison, 1986). What is true for the family in miniature is also true for larger human populations that are genetically related. The Lese of Zaire, for example, are much taller as a group than their nearby neighbors the Efe, the pygmies of the Ituri rain forest. Even body proportions differ among groups. For example, although many individual differences and much overlap occur among people of different ethnic backgrounds, leg and arm lengths tend to be relatively greater in individuals of African descent, and even more so in Australian aborigines, than in other ethnic groups when length of the torso is equated (Eveleth & Tanner, 1990). Such similarities and differences implicate genetic factors in physical development. But genes do not control growth *directly*. Genes regulate physical development by means of neural and hormonal activity in different organs and body systems.

Neural Control Many researchers believe the brain includes a growth center, a genetically established program or template that monitors and compares expected and actual rates and levels of growth for the individual (Sinclair, 1985). The claim has been supported by observations of **catch-up growth,** an increase in growth rate that often occurs if some environmental factor interferes with normal increases in height during infancy or childhood. Illness or malnutrition, for example, may disrupt physical growth. However, if the duration and severity are limited and do not occur at some critical time, the child's rate of growth often accelerates once she or he recovers. The acceleration continues until height "catches up" to the level expected had no disruption occurred.

The presence of a growth center is also suggested by the converse finding: **lagging-down growth** (Prader, 1978). Some rare congenital and hormonal disorders produce unusually rapid growth. If the disorder is corrected, growth halts or slows until actual and projected height match the trajectory established before the disruption. Where might this neural control center be located? Researchers theorize that the *hypothalamus,* a small region near the base of the brain (see Figure 5.4), orchestrates the genetic instructions for growth. Special cells in the hypothalamus may compare actual with genetically programmed growth and may direct other cells in the hypothalamus to produce hormones that stimulate growth.

Hormonal Influences **Hormones,** chemicals produced by various glands that are secreted directly into the bloodstream and can therefore circulate to influence cells in other locations of the body, furnish another key mechanism for converting genetic instructions into physical development. For example, hormones produced by cells in the hypothalamus, the suspected site of the growth center, trigger or inhibit production of still other hormones in the nearby *pituitary gland* (see Figure 5.4), including one known as *human growth hormone (HGH).* Infants with insufficient HGH may be nearly normal in size at birth, but their growth slows dramatically over the ensuing months and years; they typically reach an adult height of only about four to four-and-a-half feet. HGH, however, only indirectly promotes growth. It spurs the production of *somatomedins,* specialized hormones manufactured by many other cells in the body that directly regulate cell division for growth (Underwood, 1991).

The hypothalamus and pituitary gland produce still other hormones important for physical changes, including those that occur during puberty. However, variations in amounts of many hormones, as long as they fall within a reasonable range, do not account for individual differences in height. Individual differences seem to depend on the sensitivity of cells to the hormones (Tanner, 1978). For example, the pygmy Efe produce normal quantities of HGH but seem unable to use it to produce one kind of somatomedin important for growth to heights typical of other groups (Merimee, Zapf, & Froesch, 1981).

Nutrition and Health For a large proportion of the world's children, adequate nutrition and exposure to diseases may be the primary determinants of whether physical growth proceeds normally or even at all. We pointed out some consequences of malnutrition for fetal development in Chapter 4. As the phenomenon of catch-up growth indicates, illness and nutritional deprivation can affect postnatal growth as well. Data gathered during much of the first half of the twentieth century from one city in Germany revealed that the average height of children at various ages increased gradually over the years, a trend reported in most Western societies. However, during World Wars I and II, when food was far more limited in that city, the pattern of gradual increments in average height leveled off and even showed a decline for some age groups (Howe & Schiller, 1952). In 1984, a severe, three-month-long drought struck Kenya while researchers were engaged in a study of malnutrition in that region (McDonald et al. 1994). Food intake was cut sharply. The normal rate of weight gain among elementary school children was halved, and the mothers of the children lost weight during the interval.

Research carried out in Bogota, Colombia, reveals that dietary supplements designed to improve nutrition positively affect children's physical growth and development. All family members in one group in which infants were at risk for malnutrition were given additional food to enrich their diets. The supplements were begun when the woman was in her third trimester of pregnancy and were continued until the target child reached three years of age. At the end of the period, children who received the protein-rich supplement were on average more than an inch taller and nearly one-and-a-half pounds heavier than children in families that did not receive the supplement. The targeted children continued to be larger at age six, three years after the supplements were discontinued (Super, Herrara, & Mora, 1990).

Severe protein-energy malnutrition can have a devastating effect on growth. Infants with *marasmus* fail to grow because they lack sufficient calories. Consequences include eventual loss in weight; wrinkly, aged-looking skin; an abdomen that is often shrunken; and a hollow appearance to the body. Another prevalent form of protein-energy malnutrition is *kwashiorkor*, or failure to develop because the diet either contains an inadequate balance of protein or includes potentially harmful toxins (Hendrickse, 1991; Jellife & Jellife, 1992). Kwashiorkor typically appears in one-to-three-year old children who have been weaned, usually because of the arrival of a newborn sibling, and whose subsequent sources of protein are inadequate or contaminated.

KEY THEME
Nature/Nurture

KEY THEME
Individual Differences

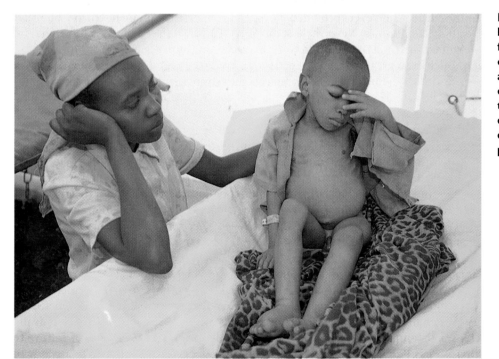

In many countries, large numbers of young children suffer from *kwashiorkor*. This young child, living in a refugee camp at Bakauu, Rwanda, displays the distended, bloated stomach so typical of this nutritional disorder because his diet either does not include sufficient protein or it contains toxins.

KEY THEME
Child's Active Role

KEY THEME
Interaction Among Domains

The symptoms of kwashiorkor—lethargic behavior and an apathetic look, wrinkled skin, a distended stomach, and a thin, wispy, reddish-orange cast to the hair—have been depicted repeatedly in all their horror by the world media. Kwashiorkor leads not only to disruption in growth of the body but also to deterioration of the brain. Although some of the damage can be quickly reversed when adequate nutrition is reinstated early (Gunston et al., 1992), long-term cognitive deficits and poorer school-related performance may persist due to impaired attention and memory (Galler et al., 1990). Studies of the effects of supplementary feeding during the first few years of life provided for nutritionally deprived families in Colombia, Guatemala, Jamaica, Taiwan, and Indonesia indicate that both motor and mental development are enhanced (Pollit, 1994). Benefits to intellectual development extend into adolescence even when the supplementary diet is discontinued in the preschool years (Pollitt et al., 1993).

As Figure 5.5 suggests, malnutrition operates at many levels to produce negative consequences for development. For example, cognitive deficits may stem from lessened motivation or curiosity and an inability to respond to or engage the environment (Brown & Pollitt, 1996; Ricciuti, 1993). To illustrate, during the relatively brief drought in Kenya, schoolchildren became less attentive in class and less active on the playground (McDonald et al., 1994). To counter the disruption in motivation, attention, and activity level that can accompany malnutrition, some projects have been designed to encourage mothers to become more competent and effective teachers and caregivers for their young children. In one study in Jamaica, two groups of hospitalized, severely malnourished one-year-olds, along with a third group of children of the same age hospitalized for other reasons, were followed into adolescence (Grantham-McGregor et al., 1994). During their hospitalization and for three years thereafter, one group of the nutritionally deprived children were given extra play opportunities and mothers were taught how to positively influence their children's development. This group showed substantially higher performance on developmental and intelligence tests throughout the fourteen-year period compared to the group not receiving the intervention. However, their scores continued to fall below those of the children who had been hospitalized for reasons other than malnutrition.

Teaching and supporting parents to enrich caregiver-child interactions may benefit more than cognition. Consider once more the findings of the study of infants at risk in Colombia. In one group, researchers included twice-weekly home visits to stimulate learning and development until the target child was three years of age. The home visitor, however, provided no specific instructions on nutrition or other health-related topics. Nevertheless, this intervention resulted in gains in height and weight by the time the children were six years old (Super, Herrara, & Mora, 1990). Although even greater growth benefits occurred when food supplements were combined with the home visits, the findings demonstrate that programs to improve emotional and social support within the family can augment both physical and mental development.

Deficiencies in specific nutritional elements—for example, vitamins A, B complexes, D, and K, as well as iron and calcium—are also linked to growth disorders affecting hundreds of thousands of children throughout the world (Hansen, 1990). Some of these disorders, especially iron-deficiency anemia, spawn lower performance on intelligence and other kinds of psychological tests. Although the problem is often assumed to be limited to low-income countries, iron-deficiency anemia is the largest nutritional concern in the United States, affecting perhaps as many as 20 percent of some ethnic groups (Pollitt, 1994).

Social-Emotional Factors   How important are social-emotional factors in physical growth? Some of the cross-cultural research suggests that caregiving practices can have important consequences. Early studies of institutionalized children (Spitz, 1946b) painted vivid images of massive disruption in physical growth, or even death, if a warm, consistent caregiver was unavailable to the infant. A label of **failure to thrive** was attached to these children. Today this label is often applied to any boy or girl below the third percentile in weight or height compared to other children of the

failure to thrive   Label applied to any child whose growth in height or weight is below the third percentile for children of the same age.

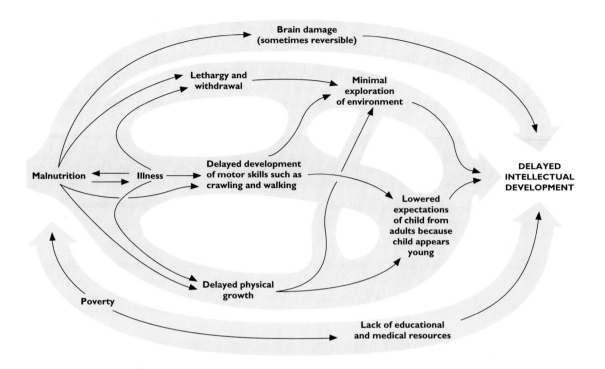

FIGURE 5.5

The Many Routes by which Malnutrition Affects Development

Nutritional deprivation can influence development at many different levels. More frequent and severe illness, delayed growth, and slower motor skill development are among the more visible consequences. Lower intellectual development is often an outcome as well. Malnutrition can damage the brain directly. However, limited capacity to engage the environment and other repercussions from the kinds of experiences a malnourished child receives may take a further toll on intellectual development. The context in which it often persists, such as poverty and the lack of essential resources, must also be factored into a consideration of how nutritional deprivation affects development.

same age. Some children fall into this classification simply because they have inherited short stature, are normally slow in growth, or were small from the start; others qualify due to disease or some other medical cause.

When no specific genetic, biological, or medical basis can be identified for growth retardation, the condition is labeled *nonorganic failure-to-thrive syndrome*. For some reason, these children are not taking in or processing sufficient nutrients to maintain normal growth despite the availability of adequate nutritional resources. Why might this be the case? Research has not yet uncovered the answer. However, characteristics associated with both parent and child may be involved. These infants and young children with the syndrome tend to be more passive and apathetic and display less facial expressivity than other infants and children (Abramson, 1991; Maggioni & Lifschitz, 1995). They may also be fussier about what they eat, despite the best efforts of parents to encourage food intake. These responses, in turn, can contribute to feelings of incompetence in the parents (Bithoney et al., 1995).

Although the problem may be worsened by characteristics of the infant or child, parental behavior can further complicate the situation. For example, mothers of failure-to-thrive infants are often reported to display less pleasure, positive affect, and support in their communications (Drotar, 1991; Liggon et al., 1992). They also interfere or act more arbitrarily while interacting with their infants, even during feeding, than other mothers (Boddy & Skuse, 1994). Concerned about their children becoming overweight or about allergic reactions, still other parents restrict the amounts of food offered or overemphasize some foods at the expense of others (e.g., fruit juices but not milk), resulting in an inadequately balanced diet (McCann et al., 1994; Roesler, Barry, & Bock, 1994).

Secular Trends   Increased knowledge of nutrition and the ability to treat disease have yielded dramatic changes in patterns of growth in many societies in recent generations. These generational changes are termed **secular trends**. As any young woman who has ever tried on her grandmother's wedding dress knows, children today grow faster and become taller as adults than did previous generations in most regions of the world. Between 1880 and 1950, the average height of Western European and American children increased by nearly four inches. A slower increase or even stability in size has been found since the 1960s. Similar findings have been re-

secular trend Consistent pattern of change over generations.

ported for other cultures, although at different times. For example, in Japan the most substantial changes in height took place between 1950 and 1970 (Tanner, 1978). Improved nutrition, better medical care, and the abolition of child labor account not only for secular trends in greater height across generations but also for the larger size of children from professional, highly educated, and urban families compared to children of poorer families and those in rural populations (Tanner, 1978).

The Social-Emotional Consequences of Body Growth

Our attempts to understand physical growth and the factors that influence it help us in thinking about additional kinds of questions related to this domain of development. For example, is physical size important to the way others interact with a child, and, if so, does it affect other aspects of development?

Height   Many societies share a mystique about tallness, the notion that height directly correlates with such traits as competence and leadership. Some individuals have argued that height dramatically bears on the work people do, their success, the social lives they lead, their attractiveness to others, and their self-esteem and sense of worth (Gillis, 1982). Research has shown that height does affect impressions of a child's abilities. Mothers of young children of the same age, for example, perceive taller boys as more competent (able to get along better with others, less likely to cry when frustrated, and so forth). They treat smaller boys as younger and in a more overprotective manner (Eisenberg et al., 1984; Rotnem, 1986; Sandberg, Brook, & Campos, 1994). The same is true of children judged on the basis of maturity of facial features (Zebrowitz, Kendall-Tackett, & Fafel, 1991). Moreover, boys believe it is important to be tall and muscular (Cobb, 1954); those substantially shorter than the average height for their age report extensive teasing from their peers; greater dissatisfaction with their skills, especially in athletic endeavors; and increasing unhappiness as they approach adolescence (Finch, 1978).

Surprisingly, lower self-esteem among children of short stature has not been consistently reported (Rieser, 1992; Sandberg et al., 1994). Nevertheless, older boys especially often yearn to be tall and athletic in appearance. Until recently, little could be done to alter the course of a child's rate of growth or eventual height. Today, however, human growth hormone can be produced synthetically. For children whose lack of growth stems from insufficient HGH, the breakthrough represents an enormously positive step toward promoting growth. However, an increasing number of children who are genetically short or whose delay in growth is a normal part of their pattern of maturation are also being given HGH to speed up growth or increase their height.

Should such treatments, which tend to be motivated by perceptions and expectations about the benefits of being tall rather than by a medical condition, be encouraged? Neither the effectiveness nor the potential for negative side effects of such supplemental hormones is fully understood (Allen, 1996; Drug and Therapeutics Committee, 1995). Attempting to alter normal physical development to conform to a cultural stereotype is a drastic action that raises many ethical issues. The argument that such treatment forestalls negative social and emotional consequences is often countered with the charge that the stereotype, not the child, is what needs to be modified.

Obesity   Common criteria for obesity include weight 20 percent greater than that considered ideal for a person's height, age, and sex or some other measure of body fat (such as skin-fold thickness) above the eightieth percentile for the child's reference group (Epstein & Wing, 1987). Being overweight has strong social-emotional consequences in most cultures. American and other industrialized societies tend to view obesity negatively, although in earlier eras it carried positive connotations of substance and prosperity and still does in many developing countries (Sobal & Stunkard, 1989). For example, adolescent females in some societies are encouraged to increase their body fat in preparation for marriage (Brown & Konner, 1987).

In Western cultures, children as young as six, when describing drawings or photographs of people who are chubby or thin, are likely to label obese figures as "lazy," "cheater," or "liar," although they seldom apply such terms to their overweight friends (Kirkpatrick & Sanders, 1978; Lawson, 1980). Moreover, overweight ten- and eleven-year-olds experience more negative interactions involving peers than do other children (Baum & Foreham, 1984).

Genetic factors may predispose some children to obesity. Adopted children show a closer relationship to the weights of their biological parents than to those of their adoptive parents; and identical twins, whether reared together or apart, tend to gain similar levels of weight (Stunkard et al., 1990). Overweight parents often have obese children, although this relationship may reflect either hereditary or environmental influences because parents serve as models for their children's eating and exercise habits. A heavy infant is about twice as likely as an infant of normal weight to be obese later in life, but the longer a child continues to be overweight, the more likely it is that he or she will remain obese as an adult (Epstein, Wing, & Valoski, 1985).

KEY THEME
Nature/Nurture

Controlling weight is complicated by the tendency of obese children to be more sensitive to external food-related cues and less responsive to internal hunger cues compared to their normal-weight peers (Ballard et al., 1980; Costanzo & Woody, 1979). Overweight preschoolers appear to regulate calorie intake less effectively, perhaps because their mothers, who may be very concerned about their own weight, assume greater control over their children's food intake (Johnson & Birch, 1994). Obese children also tend to be less accurate in reporting just how much they do eat (Maffeis et al., 1994). These findings suggest that a constellation of child and family variables contribute to obesity.

Recent health surveys reveal, at least in the United States, a worrisome increase in obesity in African American, European American, and Native American children in recent decades (Byers, 1992; Gortmaker et al., 1987; Troiano et al., 1995). What are the reasons for this secular trend? Researchers have advanced various hypotheses. For example, compared to a generation ago, children spend more time in sedentary activities such as watching television (Gortmaker et al., 1987). More limited physical activity has been accompanied by dietary shifts from fresh fruits and vegetables to calorie-laden snack and convenience foods. Whatever the reason, this is an instance in which our culture, while attaching a negative label to a physical condition on the one hand, may actively promote it on the other. We will have more to say about the impact of this conflict later in this chapter in our discussion of dieting and eating disorders.

THE BRAIN AND NERVOUS SYSTEM

Now that we have a picture of body growth and development, we can begin to examine other important physiological and physical changes that accompany increasing maturity. In particular, we focus first on changes in the brain and nervous system. Information about the central nervous system, for example, can begin to shed light on the growth of motor skills and other aspects of physical growth and also on development in cognitive, social, and other domains.

The Developing Brain

Even before birth, brain growth is rapid, as Figure 5.6 shows. The weight of the brain swiftly increases, from about 4 percent of its adult weight at five months after conception to about 25 percent at birth and about 80 percent of its adult weight by four years of age (Spreen et al., 1984). Much of that growth takes place in the *cerebral cortex,* the region of the brain most closely identified with mental processing and complex human behavior.

Compared to other areas of the brain, the cerebral cortex is relatively late in its development. The *brainstem* and *midbrain,* which are involved in basic reflexes and sensory processing as well as such essential biological functions as digestion, elimination, and respiration, are fairly well established at birth. Within the cerebral cortex, regions associated with motor and sensory functions tend to be among the first to mature. Even within these areas a cephalocaudal and proximodistal pattern of

FIGURE 5.6

The Developing Human Brain

During prenatal development, the human brain shows dramatic increases in size and the cerebral cortex takes on a convoluted pattern to increase surface area. During the last trimester of prenatal development, the brain takes on an adultlike shape, and by birth most of the neurons have formed. The brain's weight increases most dramatically from about the fifth prenatal month until the infant is about two-and-a-half years of age. The drawings have been made to a common scale; however, the first five have been enlarged to a common size to show details.

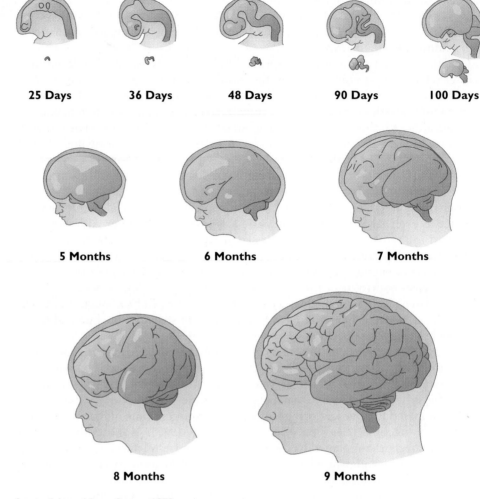

25 Days   36 Days   48 Days   90 Days   100 Days

5 Months   6 Months   7 Months

8 Months   9 Months

Source: Adapted from Cowan, 1979.

neuron   Nerve cell within the central nervous system that is electrochemically designed to transmit messages between cells.

myelin   Sheath of fatty cells that insulates and speeds neural impulses by about tenfold.

glial cells   Brain cells that provide the material from which myelin is created, nourish neurons, and provide a scaffolding for neuron migration.

growth is evident: neural development accompanying the control of the head and upper body progresses more quickly than neural development associated with the lower trunk or legs.

With development, **neurons,** cells that carry electrochemical messages as neural impulses, *proliferate,* that is, increase in number. Neurons also *migrate*—move to various regions of the brain—and *differentiate*—increase in size, complexity, and functioning. One notable aspect of differentiation is the increased number and kinds of *synapses,* the space-filled junctures associated with the branches or dendrites of the neuron that permit it to communicate with other neurons. Parts of many neurons also become surrounded by **myelin,** a sheath of fatty material that serves to insulate and speed neural impulses by about tenfold. An estimated ten times more **glial cells** (from the Greek word for *glue*) than neurons also form within the brain (Blinkov & Glezer, 1968). Glial cells provide the material from which myelin develops, facilitate the transfer of nutrients to neurons, and establish a scaffolding for neuron migration (Tanner, 1978).

Neuron Proliferation   The production of new nerve cells is known as *neuron proliferation.* Neuron production in humans begins near the end of the first month of prenatal development, shortly after the neural tube closes, and much of it, at least in the cerebral cortex, is completed before birth (Casaer, 1993; Huttenlocher, 1994). Thus, at a very early age, a finite but very large number—certainly well over 100 billion—of young neurons form (Shatz, 1992).

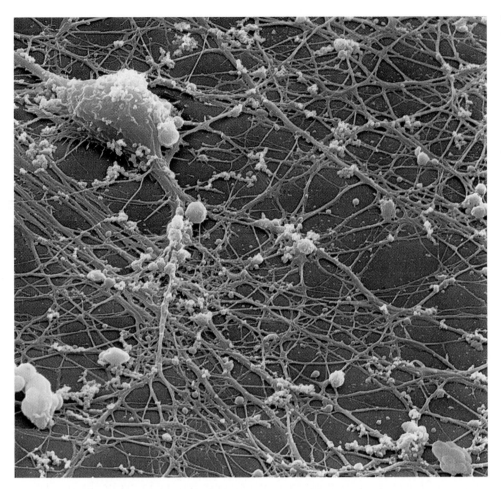

This color-enhanced photo, taken with a scanning electron microscope, shows a neuron. Neurons carry the electro-chemical messages that are the basis for behavior. Even before birth, massive numbers of neu-rons are manufactured and migrate to various regions of the brain where they begin to establish connections with other neurons.

Neuron Migration   Shortly after their formation, neurons move from the neural tube, where they were produced, to other locations within the brain. How do neu-rons know where to migrate and when to stop migrating? Both neurochemical and mechanical information probably play a role. Young neurons attach to and maneu-ver along the surfaces of fibers of glial cells radiating to the region of their destina-tion, detaching at programmed locations. Both the production and migration of large numbers of neurons in the cortex occur in waves, especially during the seventh and eleventh weeks of gestational age (Spreen et al., 1984). Neurons may migrate a great distance, passing through levels of older neurons that already have reached their final destination. The consequence for some regions of the brain is an *inside-out pattern* of development in which layers of nerve cells nearer the outer surface are younger than layers deeper in the cortex (Rakic, 1981). Some teratogens, including mercury and alcohol, are known to interfere with the onset and path of neuron mi-gration. In fact, developmental defects ranging from mental retardation to behav-ioral disorders, including some forms of schizophrenia and dyslexia, have been linked to interference in the migratory patterns of nerve cells (Nowakowski, 1987).

KEY THEME
Continuity/Discontinuity

KEY THEME
Nature/Nurture

Neuron Differentiation   Whereas neuron proliferation and migration take place prenatally for the most part, neuron differentiation—the process of enlarging, form-ing synapses with other neurons, and beginning to function—flourishes postnatally. Perhaps it continues even into adulthood. Neural differentiation, along with the growth of glial cells and other supportive tissues, including myelin, contributes to the substantial postnatal increase in the size of the brain.

Some aspects of neuron differentiation proceed without external stimulation. Ex-perience, however, plays a major role in the selection, maintenance, and strengthen-ing of connections among many neurons (Shatz, 1992). Work investigating the

KEY THEME
Nature/Nurture

effects of vision on brain development in cats illustrates the complex relationship (Hubel & Wiesel, 1979). By the time a kitten's eyes open, neurons in the visual receptor areas of the cerebral cortex have already established some connections and can respond, for example, to sensory information from either eye or to visual patterns with a broad range of characteristics. But the neurons become far more selective and tuned to particular kinds of sensory information as the kitten experiences specific forms of visual stimulation. Some neurons may, for example, begin to respond to information arising from one or the other eye only and to transitions in dark-light patterns in the visual field that are vertical or horizontal or at some other spatial orientation.

Without stimulation and the opportunity to function, neurons are unlikely to establish or maintain many connections with other neurons; their synaptic density will be substantially reduced. For example, in the visual cortex the total number of synapses rises meteorically in the first few months after birth; but then the connections show a substantial decline, presumably because some dendrites fail to make contact with other neurons. These dramatic changes can be seen in Figure 5.7. Neurons may even die if no synapses are formed with other neurons. In fact, one theory holds that massive cell death, perhaps as great as 50 to 75 percent of neurons, occurs during normal development in the brains of some animals and in some regions of the human brain, although probably not in the cerebral cortex (Huttenlocher, 1994). Here again we see the complex interaction between biological and environmental events in development. The typical infant is genetically equipped with the capacity for neurons to generate many synaptic connections, perhaps far more than a person will ever need. That surplus provides the opportunity for a rich variety of experiences to affect development; it also means that if damage or destruction occurs to some synapses early in life, others may replace them.

Plasticity in Brain Development

Because of the unspecialized nature of young neurons, the immature brain displays **plasticity,** or the ability, within limits, of alternate regions of the cerebral cortex to take on specialized sensory, linguistic, and other information-processing requirements (Kolb, 1989). Infants or children who suffer damage to regions of the cerebral cortex that process speech, for example, are often able to recover, because neurons in other parts of the cortex take on this function. On the other hand, the prognosis for recovery of language in adults after an accident or a stroke is often much poorer, because the remaining neurons in various regions of the brain have become dedicated to processing certain kinds of experiences (Lenneberg, 1967).

William Greenough and his colleagues contend that neurons in human and other mammalian brains exhibit two different kinds of plasticity (Greenough, Black, & Wallace, 1987). Some neurons are sensitive to *experience-expectant information*. As a result of a long evolutionary process, these neurons begin to grow and differentiate rapidly about the time they can be expected to receive the kinds of stimulation important to their functioning. In many mammals, for example, parts of the visual cortex involved in depth or pattern perception develop quite rapidly shortly before and after the eyes open or, in the case of humans, shortly before and after birth. Research with lower animals indicates that visual deprivation during these periods—being reared in the dark or without patterned light, for example—results in the permanent loss of some kinds of depth and pattern vision, losses that do not occur when equivalent lengths of deprivation occur during other periods (Movshon & Van Sluyters, 1981).

Other neurons are sensitive to *experience-dependent information*. Many kinds of events cannot be expected to occur at predicted times during development. Each person learns different and unique things, even into old age. The distinctive perceptual features forming the image of a neighbor or the attributes defining the concept of democracy are unique representations registered within an individual's neural system. This type of learning, which is assumed to be linked to neuron differentiation, can occur at any time in development. Here, then, is a form of plasticity that extends

KEY THEME
Continuity/Discontinuity

plasticity　Capacity of immature systems, including regions of the brain and the individual neurons within those regions, to take on different functions as a result of experience.

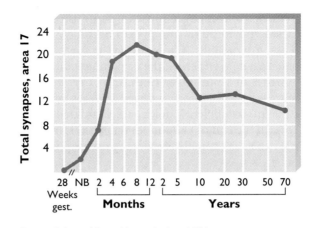

Source: Adapted from Huttenlocher, 1994.

FIGURE 5.7

Estimated Number of Synapses for Neurons in the Human Visual Cortex as a Function of Age

Differentiation of the neurons in the human visual cortex proceeds rapidly shortly after birth and reaches a peak before the end of the first year. The number of synapses ($\times 10^{11}$), connections of dendrites to other neurons, then declines to about half of the original peak number over the lifespan. The rapid increment is associated with visual stimulation after birth and accompanies significant improvements in visual abilities before a year of age, as we will see in Chapter 6. The number of synapses reflects an initial overproduction; those that become functional are then likely to be maintained over the remaining years. Other regions of the cortex may show a similar pattern of rapid increase and then decline in number of synapses, although perhaps at different periods in development.

beyond sensitive periods of development and implicates neural differentiation as a critical aspect of brain functioning throughout a person's lifetime.

Brain Lateralization

One of the brain's most obvious physical characteristics is its two mirrorlike structures, a *left* and *right* hemisphere. By and large, sensory information and motor responses on the left side of the body in humans are processed by the right hemisphere and those on the right side of the body are processed by the left hemisphere. In addition, in most adults the left hemisphere is especially involved in language functioning, whereas the right hemisphere is more typically engaged in processing spatial, emotional, or other nonverbal information (Michel, 1988; Saxby & Bryden, 1985). But these differences are by no means absolute. For example, speech is controlled primarily by the left hemisphere in about 95 percent of right-handed adults but only in about 70 percent of left-handed adults (Kinsbourne & Hiscock, 1983). Furthermore, in all individuals the right hemisphere can comprehend and initiate speech, although it may be more limited in its capacity to do so.

Does hemispheric specialization exist already at birth, or does the brain show progressive **lateralization,** the process by which one hemisphere comes to dominate the other in terms of a particular function? Based on research on left-hemisphere damage in children, Eric Lenneberg (1967) proposed that at least until age two, both hemispheres are capable of carrying out language functions equally well and that lateralization increases only gradually until adolescence. Other researchers, however, suggest lateralization begins much earlier (Kinsbourne & Hiscock, 1983), perhaps as a consequence of exposure to fetal testosterone (Geschwind & Galaburda, 1987; McManus & Bryden, 1991). For example, most infants lie with the head oriented to the right rather than to the left, an orientation that later predicts hand preference (Michel, 1988), and even before three months of age most babies more actively use and hold objects longer in the right hand than in the left (Hawn & Harris, 1983). They also turn to stimulation coming from the right side more frequently (Siqueland & Lipsitt, 1966). Furthermore, infants are able to better identify changes in speech sounds heard in their right ear and to detect shifts in the timbre of musical notes better in their left ear (Best, Hoffman, & Glanville, 1982). However, the evidence of early hemispheric differences does not preclude the possibility that at later ages either hemisphere is capable of taking over the other's functions if necessary.

MOTOR SKILL DEVELOPMENT

With development, cartilage is transformed into bone and bones elongate and increase in number to become scaffolding to support the body in new physical orientations. As the central nervous system matures, neural commands begin to coordinate

lateralization Process by which one hemisphere of the brain comes to dominate the other, for example, processing of language in the left hemisphere or of spatial information in the right hemisphere.

thickened and enlarged muscles, permitting more powerful and refined motor activities. Cephalocaudal and proximodistal principles are evident in the emergence of many motor skills. These principles are augmented by two other complementary patterns: *differentiation,* the enrichment of global and relatively diffuse actions with more refined and skilled ones, and *integration,* the increasingly coordinated actions of muscles and sensory systems. Throughout infancy and childhood, motor skills become more efficient, coordinated, and deliberate or automatic as the task requires. Toward the end of childhood, many skills become highly specialized talents: youngsters such as Danielle are already accomplished athletes; others her age are concert musicians.

KEY THEME
Interaction Among Domains

Motor skill development was a prominent feature of study early in the history of developmental psychology. More recently, enormous interest in this topic has resurfaced. If, as Piaget suggested, sensorimotor activity serves as the prototype and first stage in the construction of knowledge, the acquisition, coordination, and integration of basic motor skills can provide important insights into early cognitive and perceptual development as well (Benson, 1988; Bushnell & Boudreau, 1993).

TABLE 5.1	Typical Reflexes Observed in Newborns and Infants

Many of the reflexes the newborn displays can also be elicited during the later weeks of fetal development (Gundy, 1987). Considerable variability exists among infants in the ways many reflexes are displayed and the ages at which they can be elicited (Touwen, 1974). The presence or absence of any single reflex provides only one among many indicators of healthy or atypical development.

Name of Reflex	Testing Procedure	Response	Developmental Course	Significance
Primitive Reflexes				
Palmar or Hand Grasp	Place finger in hand.	Hand grasps object.	Birth to about 4 months.	Absence may signal neurological defects; persistence could interfere with voluntary grasping.
Rooting	Stroke corner of mouth lightly.	Head and tongue move toward stimulus.	Birth to about 5 months.	Mouth is brought to stimulus to permit sucking.
Sucking	Place finger in mouth or on lips.	Sucking begins.	Birth to about 6 months.	Ensures intake of potential nutrients.
Moro	(1) Sit child up, allow head to drop about 20 degrees backward, or (2) make a loud noise, or (3) lower baby rapidly.	Baby extends arms outward, hands open; then brings hands to midline, hands clenched, spine straightened.	Birth to about 5–7 months.	Absence may signal neurological defects; persistence could interfere with acquisition of sitting.
Plantar or Foot Grasp	Place pressure on ball of foot.	Toes curl as if grasping.	Birth to about 9 months.	Absence may signal spinal cord defect.
Babinski	Stroke bottom of foot.	Toes fan and then curl.	Birth to about 1 year.	Absence may signal neurological defects.
Asymmetric Tonic Neck Reflex	Place baby on back, arms and legs extended, and rotate head 90 degrees.	Arm on face side extends, arm on back side of head flexes.	About 1 month to 4 months.	Absence may signal neurological defects; persistence could prevent rolling over, coordination.

TABLE 5.1	Typical Reflexes Observed in Newborns and Infants *(continued)*			
Name of Reflex	**Testing Procedure**	**Response**	**Developmental Course**	**Significance**
Postural Reflexes				
Stepping	Hold baby under arms, upright, leaning forward.	Makes walklike stepping movements.	Birth to about 3 months.	Absence may signal neurological defects.
Labyrinthine	(1) Place baby on back.	Extends arms and legs.	Birth to about 4 months.	Absence may signal neurological defects.
	(2) Place baby on stomach.	Flexes arms and legs.		
Swimming	Place baby in water.	Holds breath involuntarily; arms and legs move as if trying to swim.	Birth to about 4–6 months.	Absence may signal neurological defects.
Placing	Hold baby under arms, upright, top of foot touching bottom edge of table.	Lifts foot and places on top of table.	Birth through 12 months.	Absence may signal neurological defects.
Landau Reaction	Place baby on stomach, hold under chest.	Lifts head, eventually other parts of body, above chest.	Head at 2 months, other parts of body later.	Absence may signal neurological defects; inadequate muscle tone for motor development.
Body Righting	Rotate hips or shoulder.	Rotates remainder of body.	4 months to more than 12 months.	Absence may signal neurological defects; difficulty in gaining postural control and walking.

The First Actions: Reflexes

At first glance, newborns seem helpless and incompetent. Babies eat, sleep, and cry; their diapers always seem to need changing. Yet a more careful look reveals that infants enter their new world with surprisingly adept sensory abilities, along with **reflexes,** involuntary reactions to touch, light, sound, and other kinds of stimulation, some of which are exhibited even prenatally.

Reflexes are among the building blocks that soon give rise to voluntary movements and the acquisition of developmental milestones or significant achievements in motor skills. Along with breathing and swallowing, *primitive reflexes* such as rooting and sucking (see Table 5.1) provide nourishment for survival of the infant. Among our evolutionary ancestors, other reflexes, such as the Moro and palmar reflexes, helped to protect newborns from danger. *Postural reflexes,* such as stepping, swimming, and body righting (which are surprisingly similar to later voluntary movements), appear to be designed to maintain a specific orientation to the environment. If primitive or postural reflexes are absent, are too strong or too weak, display unequal strength when normally elicited from either side of the body, or continue to

reflex Involuntary movement in response to touch, light, sound, or other form of stimulation; controlled by subcortical neural mechanisms.

Among the reflexes that babies display is the swimming reflex. When young infants are placed in water, breathing is suspended, and they engage in swim-like movements with their arms and legs.

be exhibited beyond certain ages, a pediatrician may begin to suspect cerebral palsy or some other neurological impairment and developmental difficulties for the baby (Blasco, 1994).

*D*anielle's parents faithfully attended Danielle's gymnastics meets and were ardent supporters of her efforts. Danielle wasn't always pleased by the watchful presence they exhibited toward her, their only daughter. But she was beginning to more fully understand it. When Danielle was four, her parents introduced her to a baby brother. Danielle remembered how proud she had been to hold him and to "help her mother." But all that changed a few months later. On that tragic morning, she had been awakened by the frantic voices of her parents and strangers—emergency medical technicians, she learned later—in her baby brother's room. She suspected something terrible had happened, and it had: her brother had died. She was frightened then and for a long time thereafter. Her fears subsided only gradually as her parents picked up the pieces of their lives. They still kept her brother's picture on their bedroom dresser, and Danielle looked at it often. As the only child now, she frequently wondered what it would have been like to grow up with a little brother.

RESEARCH APPLIED TO PARENTING

Helping to Reduce Sudden Infant Death Syndrome

To survive in the postnatal environment, the infant must synchronize rooting and sucking with swallowing and breathing. In fact, the inability to coordinate these reflexes often makes nursing difficult for premature infants (Rosenblith & Sims-Knight, 1985). But organizing and controlling breathing can be a problem for a small number of older infants as well. The abrupt, unexplained death of a baby or toddler who stops breathing during sleep is known as **sudden infant death syndrome (SIDS)**. The deaths are particularly tragic because they occur with no identifiable warnings.

sudden infant death syndrome (SIDS) Sudden, unexplained death of an infant or a toddler as a result of cessation of breathing during sleep.

SIDS, once known as *crib death*, has in the past claimed the lives of between one and two of every thousand live births in the United States. Much higher rates have been reported in some other countries. The frequency of SIDS peaks two or three months after birth. Thus, the highest incidence occurs at a time when basic automatic respiratory reflexes governed by the brainstem begin to be supplemented by voluntary, cortex-regulated breathing essential for vocalization and the emergence of speech.

Although no specific cause has been identified, SIDS is associated with a number of variables, including the colder months of the year, economically depressed neighborhoods, having a cold, being a male, being a later-born or a member of a multiple birth, and low birth weight. Parents may have little control over some of these factors, but research is showing that they can take steps to reduce the risk of SIDS:

1. *"Back to Sleep."* Up until the past decade, parents were often advised to place their babies in a prone position (on their stomachs) when ready for sleep. However, research conducted around the world (Australia, Britain, New Zealand, the Netherlands, Norway, Sweden, and many other countries, including the United States) reveals that when parents stop this practice, the incidence of SIDS declines (Willinger, Hoffman, & Hartford, 1994). Thus, pediatricians have initiated a "back to sleep" campaign that encourages parents to place infants who are healthy on their backs or sides to sleep. This single change has been estimated to reduce the incidence of SIDS as much as 50 percent in recent years in some nations, including the United States.

KEY THEME
Sociocultural Influence

2. *Eliminate exposure to cigarette smoke and other drugs.* Numerous studies have confirmed that a mother's smoking or use of other drugs during pregnancy is associated with a greater likelihood of SIDS. However, recent research further shows that exposure even to passive smoke after birth (from mother, father, or other live-in adults) increases the risk as well (Klonoff-Cohen et al., 1995).

3. *Provide firm bedding and good ventilation.* The incidence of SIDS in Australia and New Zealand had been among the highest in the world (Orenstein, 1992). In these countries, less firm bedding (use of wool or of bark from the ti tree) appears to have contributed to the risk of SIDS, especially for infants sleeping prone, perhaps because of a tendency for this softer bedding to trap carbon dioxide (Kemp, Nelson, & Thach, 1994). Adequate ventilation helps to disperse carbon dioxide as well.

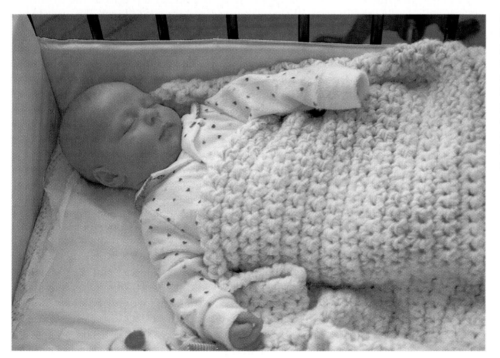

Placing infants on their backs in preparation for sleep appears to have reduced the frequency of sudden infant death syndrome (SIDS). The decline in SIDS associated with this practice is reported in many countries, including the United States, where pediatricians have recently launched a "back to sleep" campaign.

4. *Breast feed, if possible, and follow immunization schedules.*   Statistically, breast-fed babies are at lower risk for SIDS, at least if a mother does not smoke (Klonoff-Cohen et al., 1995). This benefit could stem from properties of breast milk that help to protect infants from certain illnesses that may affect respiratory ability. Some types of immunizations may have a similar benefit.

Unfortunately, SIDS remains one of the most frequent causes of death in infants less than a year of age. But until a better understanding of its cause is found, parents can implement practices that seem to reduce the risk. James McKenna and his colleagues (McKenna et al., 1990) have voiced concerns about yet one other practice that may be related to SIDS: infants sleeping in a room apart from their mothers. In co-sleeping arrangements, mothers and infants synchronize sleep, breathing, and arousal patterns. McKenna and his colleagues suggest that the synchrony could help arouse infants from *apnea,* irregular patterns or temporary cessations in breathing. Historically, and in many cultures yet today, co-sleeping for mothers and infants is the norm. For example, Mayan mothers view putting very young children in a separate room at night as almost equivalent to child neglect (Morrelli et al., 1992). However, American mothers typically justify such a practice, especially after the baby is a few months old, as a way to encourage self-reliance and independence. Decisions about sleeping arrangements are deeply ingrained in cultural beliefs concerning the values of closeness and interdependence and of privacy and self-reliance. But whether the recent tendency in some cultures to favor separate sleeping arrangements for mother and infant also has a bearing on SIDS remains to be proven.

KEY THEME
Sociocultural Influence

Motor Milestones

In addition to reflexes, babies exhibit **rhythmical stereotypies,** repeated sequences of motions performed with no apparent goal (Thelen, 1996). Rubbing one foot against the other, rocking back and forth, bouncing up and down, swaying side to side, striking or banging objects, mouthing and tonguing activities, and shaking and nodding the head are just a few of the movements produced to exercise bones, joints, and muscles. Although probably not governed by deliberate, directed efforts, stereotypies, along with some early reflexes, appear to be the bits and pieces of the primitive melody of behavior that eventually are recruited and integrated into organized voluntary motor skills and activities (Thelen, 1996).

Directed voluntary actions begin during their first year as infants gradually gain neuromotor control of their heads, arms, and legs. Some of these actions—grasping, crawling, and walking, for example—are motor milestones: once mastered, new worlds open up to the infant. Moreover, they lead caregivers to respond to the infant in different ways: childproofing the home to prevent accidents, supporting greater independence, expecting more mature behavior. Most gains in infant movement illustrate progress in (1) *postural control,* the ability to maintain an upright orientation to the environment; (2) *locomotion,* the ability to maneuver through space; and (3) *manual control,* the ability to manipulate objects (Keogh & Sugden, 1985).

KEY THEME
Child's Active Role

Postural Control   Keeping the head upright and stable at about two to three months of age represents one of the first milestones in infant motor development. As the Chronology on the next page indicates, this achievement is followed by mastery of other significant postural skills, such as maintaining an upright sitting position, moving to a standing position, and standing without assistance. The milestones, built on various postural reflexes among other things, often reflect a cephalocaudal progression. Head control, for example, precedes control of the trunk, and command of the legs is the last to develop. The integration of postural skills is also important. For example, the ability to keep the head upright while sitting or while standing on a stable surface is one thing; the ability to do this when being carried about or during

rhythmical stereotypies   Repeated sequences of movements, such as leg kicking, hand waving, or head banging, that have no apparent goal.

CHRONOLOGY
Motor Skill Development

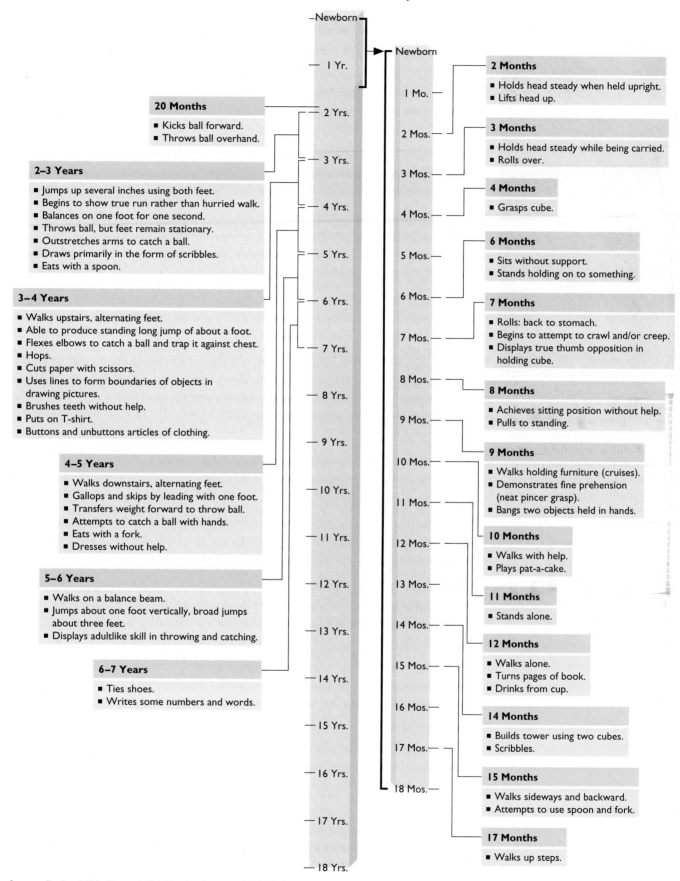

Newborn

1 Yr.

20 Months
- Kicks ball forward.
- Throws ball overhand.

2–3 Years
- Jumps up several inches using both feet.
- Begins to show true run rather than hurried walk.
- Balances on one foot for one second.
- Throws ball, but feet remain stationary.
- Outstretches arms to catch a ball.
- Draws primarily in the form of scribbles.
- Eats with a spoon.

3–4 Years
- Walks upstairs, alternating feet.
- Able to produce standing long jump of about a foot.
- Flexes elbows to catch a ball and trap it against chest.
- Hops.
- Cuts paper with scissors.
- Uses lines to form boundaries of objects in drawing pictures.
- Brushes teeth without help.
- Puts on T-shirt.
- Buttons and unbuttons articles of clothing.

4–5 Years
- Walks downstairs, alternating feet.
- Gallops and skips by leading with one foot.
- Transfers weight forward to throw ball.
- Attempts to catch a ball with hands.
- Eats with a fork.
- Dresses without help.

5–6 Years
- Walks on a balance beam.
- Jumps about one foot vertically, broad jumps about three feet.
- Displays adultlike skill in throwing and catching.

6–7 Years
- Ties shoes.
- Writes some numbers and words.

2 Yrs. / 3 Yrs. / 4 Yrs. / 5 Yrs. / 6 Yrs. / 7 Yrs. / 8 Yrs. / 9 Yrs. / 10 Yrs. / 11 Yrs. / 12 Yrs. / 13 Yrs. / 14 Yrs. / 15 Yrs. / 16 Yrs. / 17 Yrs. / 18 Yrs.

Newborn

1 Mo.

2 Months
- Holds head steady when held upright.
- Lifts head up.

3 Months
- Holds head steady while being carried.
- Rolls over.

4 Months
- Grasps cube.

6 Months
- Sits without support.
- Stands holding on to something.

7 Months
- Rolls: back to stomach.
- Begins to attempt to crawl and/or creep.
- Displays true thumb opposition in holding cube.

8 Months
- Achieves sitting position without help.
- Pulls to standing.

9 Months
- Walks holding furniture (cruises).
- Demonstrates fine prehension (neat pincer grasp).
- Bangs two objects held in hands.

10 Months
- Walks with help.
- Plays pat-a-cake.

11 Months
- Stands alone.

12 Months
- Walks alone.
- Turns pages of book.
- Drinks from cup.

14 Months
- Builds tower using two cubes.
- Scribbles.

15 Months
- Walks sideways and backward.
- Attempts to use spoon and fork.

17 Months
- Walks up steps.

Sources: Bayley, 1993; Cratty, 1986; Frankenburg et al., 1992; Gallahue, 1989; Newborg, Stock, & Wnek, 1984; Robertson, 1984; Winner, 1986.
This chart describes the sequence of motor skill development based on the findings of research and indicates the age at which approximately half of the infants or children tested in the United States begin to demonstrate the skill. Children often show individual differences in the exact ages at which they display the various developmental achievements outlined here.

Once a baby can stand, he or she will often cruise or move about by stepping side to side while holding onto furniture or objects. It is one of the many milestones infants achieve in their diligent attempts to gain independent locomotion.

KEY THEME
Child's Active Role

self-movement requires integration of far more information to retain motor control (Keogh & Sugden, 1985).

Locomotion   Achievements in the ability to move about the environment are also summarized in the Chronology. One early milestone in locomotion is the capacity to roll over. Then comes success at initiating forward motion, a skill marked by considerable variation (Freedland & Bertenthal, 1994). Some infants use arms to pull and legs to push, others use only arms or legs, and still others scoot forward while sitting. *Crawling,* locomotion with stomach touching the floor, may soon give way to *creeping,* locomotion on hands and knees—and then again it may not. The varieties of forward motion invented by babies often generate lively discussions among caregivers.

Once babies are able to pull themselves upright, they often *cruise,* that is, move by holding onto furniture or other objects while stepping sideways. Forward walking while holding onto someone's hand typically follows. By about twelve months of age, half of American babies and infants in many other countries walk alone, a skill that continues to be refined throughout infancy and early childhood.

Prewalking and walking skills likely depend on the growth of higher brain centers, but even before independent walking many of the components of this ability are evident. For example, when babies six months of age are placed on a treadmill and held so they do not have to support their full weight, they display alternating stepping similar to that involved in walking (Thelen & Ulrich, 1991). Even six-week-olds produce surprisingly coordinated leg movements when lying on their backs (Thelen, Skala, & Kelso, 1987). These findings illustrate how the environment—in this case, gravity—and task constraints can be important factors affecting the infant's capacity to display various milestones.

Manual Control   In the weeks that follow birth, infants make enormous progress in reaching. Newborns display *prereaching* in their attempts to contact objects that catch their attention, but their efforts are neither accurate nor coordinated with grasping (Bushnell, 1985). Still, movements show speeding up, slowing down, and changes in direction just as in later, more accurate reaches (Hofsten & Rönnqvist, 1993). Directed reaching, which infants tackle in vastly different ways, begins at about three months of age (Thelen et al., 1993). By about five to six months, infants display mature, *ballistic* reaches, more rapidly and accurately retrieving an object in the visual field. In learning to gain mastery over these reaches, infants engage in a series of submovements, not always perfectly executed but often quickly corrected to meet the goal of obtaining the target (Berthier, 1996). Although the ability to see their own hands is not necessary in these reaches, babies eventually do appear to make use of such visual cues to help them retrieve an object (Ashmead et al., 1993; Clifton et al., 1993; Robin, Berthier, & Clifton, 1996).

When first attempting to reach, very young infants typically keep their hands closed in fistlike fashion. By about four months of age, infants awkwardly pick up an object by grasping it with the palm of the hand. Over the next few months, they shift from using the inner palm to using opposing thumb and fingertips, a progression that culminates in a *neat pincer grasp* at about nine months of age (Connolly & Elliott, 1972). This development, in turn, sets the stage for the elegant manual control required to hold, inspect, and manipulate, skills that help the baby learn about and control objects (Karniol, 1989).

Another important component of motor skill is increased coordination between the two hands. Very young infants often attempt to grasp objects with both hands, but once babies gain greater postural control, such as being able to sit by themselves, one-handed reaches become far more frequent (Rochat, 1992). In addition, infants who can sit by themselves are more likely to integrate leaning forward with reaching than infants who have not yet achieved this milestone (Rochat & Goubet, 1995). Increased coordination is further reflected in the appearance of complementary hand orientations, such as holding a toy dump truck in one hand while using the other hand to fill it with sand. This *functional asymmetry* emerges at about five to six months of age but becomes especially refined as the child enters the second year and begins to display self-help and advanced motor tasks requiring sophisticated use of both arms and hands.

Motor Skills in the Preschool and Later-Childhood Years

Many fundamental motor skills the child acquires in the first two years of life continue to be modified and refined in the preschool and elementary school years. For example, children show increasingly effective body and eye-hand or eye-foot *coordination,* evident in their greater ability to hop and skip or, perhaps, kick, dribble, and catch a ball. With increasing age, children also demonstrate better *balance,* reflected in the ability to walk greater distances on a beam or stand on one foot for a longer period of time; increased *speed,* shown by running short distances more rapidly; improved *agility,* revealed, for example, in the ability to shift directions quickly while running; and greater *power,* shown by jumping higher or longer distances or throwing a ball farther and faster than at younger ages. The Chronology on page 165 summarizes major accomplishments for some of these abilities during early childhood.

In general, activities that exercise large muscles attract the interest of toddlers and preschoolers. These activities include pulling and pushing things, stacking and nesting large objects, and, eventually, riding toys such as kiddie cars and tricycles. As preschoolers begin to organize and display more interest in energetic games and athletic activities—jumping, hopping, running, balancing, and catching or throwing a ball—feats that emphasize speed, strength, and efficiency of performance become frequent ingredients of their everyday schedule. When first attempting to execute these skills, young children often fail to prepare or follow through on their actions, and the speed or force needed to complete them in a mature way is absent. Any parent who has tried to avoid a three-year-old's fastball fired at point-blank range will have a healthy appreciation for developmental changes that lead to performing actions with reasonable force. Before finally demonstrating mastery of a skill, children may have difficulty synchronizing all of the complex movements.

Some motor exercises foster greater competence in self-help skills (such as dressing and grooming), assembling items (such as stacking and puzzle construction), and sophisticated dexterity (such as writing and drawing). Older preschoolers supplement their large-muscle and athletic exercises with coloring and drawing, cutting and sculpting, and other activities that demand small-muscle coordination, a longer attention span, and more sophisticated planning and organization.

Motor skills during middle childhood become more efficient and better controlled, involve more complex and coordinated movements, and are exhibited more quickly and in a wider variety of contexts and circumstances (Keogh & Sugden, 1985). With the exception of balance, boys tend to slightly outperform girls on many gross motor tasks (Gallahue, 1989) by the time they enter elementary school. However, differences between boys and girls may become especially large for some activities as children enter the adolescent years, as Figure 5.8 indicates for running speed and the distance a youngster can throw a ball.

KEY THEME
Continuity/Discontinuity

Fine motor coordination improves dramatically during the school years as well. This is perhaps no more apparent than in the progress children display in drawing and writing. At age six or seven, children may be limited to printing relatively large, uppercase letters of the alphabet using motions involving the entire arm. Yet in a few years, this will be supplanted by cursive writing of normal size, which demands more sophisticated wrist and finger movements. In addition, model construction or needlework, mastering the complex finger sequencing needed to play musical instruments, and more detailed drawings confirm that motor skills are undergoing significant developmental advances.

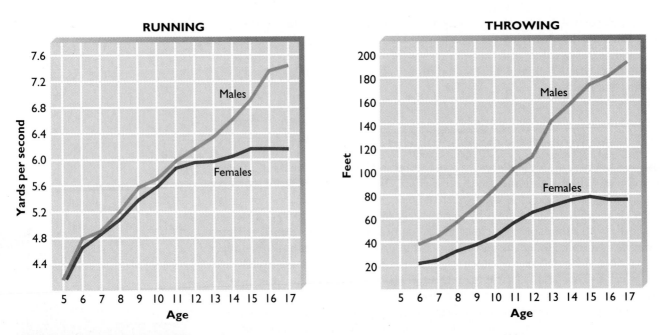

Source: Gallahue, 1989, adapted from Haubenstricker & Seefeldt, 1986.

FIGURE 5.8

Running Speed and Throwing Distance for Boys and Girls at Different Ages

Boys tend to outperform girls on many motor skill tasks during the elementary school years, as indicated by these data on speed of running and distance throwing a ball, summarized from a number of studies carried out since 1960. The differences between girls and boys often increase substantially as children enter adolescence.

KEY THEME
Nature/Nurture

As children grow older, the range of differences in individual abilities often increases (J. Clark, 1988). The effect may, of course, stem from practice, because some children focus on acquiring particular skills relevant to their social and cultural milieus. The acquisition of expertise or specialized motor skills in sports, dance, crafts, hobbies, playing musical instruments, and, in some cultures, trade- or work-related endeavors permits older children to engage their environment with increasing competence, become more effective members of their society, and gain greater social status among peers and adults.

Determinants of Motor Development

To what extent do the emergence, refinement, and integration of motor skills depend on genetic or maturational factors? Or are the dramatic changes the consequence of practice, cultural, or other experiential factors? Many pioneers in developmental psychology advocated a strong maturational theory to explain the orderly acquisition of motor skills. But changes in motor skills, just as changes in other domains of development, are better understood as the unique confluence of biological and experiential factors.

Biological Contributions   One of the strongest arguments in support of a genetic or maturational basis for the development of motor skills is the tendency of these skills to be displayed at predictable times and in similar ways in normal children. Although individual differences exist, greater concordance in sitting and walking is found for identical than for fraternal twins and greater similarity in gross motor activities such as running, jumping, and throwing in children who are more closely related biologically (Malina, 1980). Even intellectually and physically disabled babies attain major milestones in an orderly manner, although at a later age than other children. For example, blind children who show substantial delays in acquiring postural, locomotion, and manual coordination skills eventually acquire these skills nonetheless (Tröster & Brambring, 1993). Children with Down syndrome also exhibit the usual order of achievements, although they need more time, particularly when health complications such as heart disease are present (Zausmer & Shea, 1984). Perhaps, then, infants and children are *genetically preadapted* to exhibit righting and balancing reflexes, bone and muscle growth, and a maturing central nervous system designed to interact effectively over time with the physical and social environment (Kopp, 1979).

Experiential Contributions   Could experiential variables also play a role in motor development? With respect to the acquisition of expert motor skill, the answer is most certainly yes. However, it may be true for attaining fundamental developmental milestones as well. Lack of opportunity to engage in physical activity seriously interferes with reaching developmental milestones, as research on children reared in institutions reveals. For example, in an orphanage in Teheran, Iran, Wayne Dennis (1960) found that babies who spent most of their first year lying in cribs and receiving few other forms of stimulation typically did not walk before age three or four. Although in blind children reaching for objects, crawling, and walking may be substantially delayed, when special programs encourage blind infants to acquire self-initiated movement, they do so at ages more comparable to their sighted peers' (Fraiberg, 1977).

Before these observations were made, several investigators in the 1930s conducted studies with sets of twins to test the role of experience in motor skill development. Typically, one twin received extensive training in, say, handling blocks, climbing stairs, or roller skating; the other twin did not (Gesell & Thompson, 1934; Hilgard, 1932; McGraw, 1935). However, when given a chance to acquire the skills, the untrained twin often rapidly achieved the same level of accomplishment the trained twin did. In another early study, Wayne and Marsena Dennis investigated childrearing practices among the Hopi Indians (Dennis & Dennis, 1940). Some Hopi Indian mothers practiced the tribal tradition of tightly swaddling their babies in a cradleboard; the mother would strap the board to her back for all but about an hour a day during her waking hours for the first six to twelve months of her child's life. These Hopi babies had little opportunity to practice sitting up, crawling, and walking. Other Hopi mothers reared infants without swaddling. The researchers found that swaddling had little bearing on when infants initiated walking, an observation reconfirmed in a more recent study of the effects of Hopi rearing customs (Harriman & Lukosius, 1982).

What can we conclude from these investigations? Perhaps that the normal range of daily activities in which infants and children are engaged, or, in the case of infants reared on cradleboards, the experience gained in strengthening their postural orientation, appears to be sufficient to promote normal locomotor development (Rosenblith & Sims-Knight, 1985). But consider other, more recent findings. Philip Zelazo and his colleagues (Zelazo, 1983) asked: Do infants from one to seven weeks of age, given a few minutes of daily practice with the placing and stepping reflexes, retain them and begin walking earlier than infants who receive no special training or whose legs are passively moved back and forth? Zelazo found they did. He concluded that experiences that prevent the loss of certain reflexes provide a foundation for early walking. Moreover, practice in stepping or sitting helps infants acquire these skills as well (Zelazo et al., 1993). Thus, activities that maintain or encourage various components of complex motor skills can influence their development.

Esther Thelen (Thelen & Smith, 1994; Thelen & Ulrich, 1991) has applied a far broader perspective to such findings. She has argued that all complex motor skills require the assembling and reassembling of multiple processes involving, among other things, motivation, elements of the nervous system that regulate posture and balance, increased bone and muscle strength, and changes in body proportions. The assemblages are further constrained by the biodynamics of the human body as well as the situational context. However, when the right improvisation of components matches the context, infants display surprising mastery of motor skills or advance to new levels of competence. Neither biological nor experiential factors alone are responsible. Instead, motor development is a dynamic system; its multiple components become "tuned" into sequences of more effective, self-organized actions over time (Lockman & Thelen, 1993).

In the Navajo culture babies are often swaddled for most of the day. Wayne Dennis' research with Hopi infants who were also cared for in this way suggests that this baby, despite the lack of opportunity to practice sitting up, crawling, and standing alone, will begin to walk about the same time as an infant who has not been swaddled.

KEY THEME
Sociocultural Influence

Cross-Cultural Differences

Given the multiple processes involved, it should not be surprising to learn that ethnic and cultural differences in motor development exist as well (Werner, 1972). At birth and throughout their first year, African American babies, as well as infants among the Wolof of Senegal, Gusii of Kenya, Yoruba of Nigeria, Bantu of South Africa, and Ganda of Uganda, typically outperform Caucasian infants on a variety of motor skills (Lester & Brazelton, 1982; Werner, 1972). African American children also run faster, throw farther, and have greater skill in balancing than American children of the same age of Caucasian backgrounds (Bonds, 1969; Huntsinger, 1959). Yet the factors contributing to these differences are not easy to untangle.

Charles Super (1976) spent three years testing all sixty-four children born from 1972 to 1975 in a fairly prosperous rural community in a high-altitude region of Kenya. His monthly tests revealed that the babies were able to sit, stand, and walk about a month earlier than babies in the United States. Parents in the Kenyan community made extensive efforts to teach certain skills. For example, they provided special props to encourage the infant to sit or held the baby's hands in structured activities involving walking. In fact, their language, as in some other regions of East Africa, contained distinctive words to denote the specialized training. The more caregivers promoted specific motor skills, the earlier their children tended to display them. For example, 93 percent of one group of caregivers said they taught their babies to crawl, and babies in this group began crawling at about five-and-a-half months of age. In contrast, only 13 percent of the caregivers in a nearby group expressed support for teaching their infants to crawl, and these babies did not crawl until about eight months of age. Caregivers in some of the communities also believed it was important to teach babies to walk and carried out exercises to encourage them to do so. Their infants continued to exhibit the stepping reflex until walking began, a finding that confirms Zelazo's hypothesis about the contribution of training in attaining this developmental milestone.

Many factors could contribute to the cultural differences, but one finding strongly implicates childrearing efforts. Advanced motor development in this part of Kenya was limited to sitting, standing, and walking, skills considered culturally important. Other milestones not taught or valued, such as head control or the ability to roll over, were acquired later than when American infants attained them. A similar observation comes from Jamaica. Some mothers in that country perform special stretching and massaging exercises to encourage their infants to sit and walk alone (Hopkins & Westra, 1990). Children of these mothers sit by themselves and walk earlier than other children.

We cannot be certain whether training focused on particular skills or more general experiences are responsible for cultural differences. Children in East Africa, for example, spend more time in an upright position, seated on a caregiver's lap or riding on her back, than children in the United States (Super, 1976). The activities may strengthen trunk and leg muscles to aid the earlier appearance of sitting, standing, and walking. However, gains achieved from training in one of two particular skills, such as stepping or sitting, do not appear to generalize to the other (Zelazo et al., 1993).

Now consider the children of the Ache of Eastern Paraguay, who are significantly delayed in acquiring a host of motor skills. For example, walking is delayed until twenty-one to twenty-three months of age (Kaplan & Dove, 1987). This small band, which engages in hunting and gathering, does not encourage the acquisition of motor skills in infants. When families migrate to the forests, the women closely supervise their children younger than three years, preventing them from venturing more than a yard or so into the uncleared vegetation and spending 80 to 100 percent of their time in physical contact with them (Kaplan & Dove, 1987). For the Ache, keeping infants close by may be crucial for their continued survival, but gives little opportunity for infants to practice motor skills. Because the Ache have been relatively isolated and the total population at times quite small, genetic factors cannot be ruled out as contributing to the delay, but cultural concerns and efforts to either promote or discourage the acquisition of motor skills appear to have a significant effect on their development.

PHYSICAL MATURITY

Having learned about the major advances in physical size, brain, and motor skill development during infancy and childhood, we can now turn to the many changes that accompany the transition to adulthood. The growth spurt of early adolescence is only one of numerous indicators of approaching physical maturity. Accompanying the growth spurt are important changes in the body that reflect sexual maturity. We briefly consider these progressions and the psychological issues a young person may confront during the passage from late childhood to early adulthood.

Defining Maturity

Because rate of growth and final level of growth vary so greatly among individuals and for different parts of the body, researchers have turned to other criteria to define physical maturity. One reliable indicator is **skeletal maturity,** the extent to which *ossification,* the chemical transformation of cartilage into bony tissue, has been completed. The change begins prenatally about the eighth week after conception, when cartilage in the ribs and in the center of the long bones of the arms and legs is transformed. The process continues into late adolescence or early adulthood, when bones in the wrist and ankle are finally completely formed. Degree of ossification is measured by x-rays of the sizes, shapes, and positions of bones, particularly those in the hand and forearm. Although skeletal maturity has become the standard for defining the end of physical growth, other, more visible markers of approaching maturity appear just before and during the adolescent years. These important markers comprise a series of events associated with **puberty,** the developmental milestone reached when a young person gains the ability to reproduce.

During puberty, the *primary sexual organs*—testes and penis in males; vagina, uterus, and ovaries in females—enlarge and become capable of functioning. *Secondary sexual characteristics* that distinguish men from women, such as facial hair or breasts, also mature. Puberty is accompanied by other changes that catapult adolescents from a childlike to an adultlike appearance. Boys take on a more muscular and angular look as shoulders widen and the fat tissue of childhood is replaced with muscle. Girls' hips broaden, a change especially adaptive to bearing children. Girls also tend to retain a higher proportion of fat to muscle tissue and assume a more rounded appearance overall than boys.

Like the growth spurt, the timing of each of the many events associated with puberty differs enormously from one young person to another. Within each individual, moreover, the various signs of puberty emerge at different times (Brooks-Gunn & Reiter, 1990). As a rule, however, this cluster of characteristics tends to appear somewhat earlier in girls than in boys. Figure 5.9 identifies several phenomena associated with sexual maturity and the average age at which they take place for boys and girls.

Typically, enlargement of the testes in boys begins at about eleven-and-a-half years of age; pubic hair starts to appear about six months afterward; and growth of the penis, deepening of the voice, and a rapid increase in height six months after that. The first spontaneous ejaculation of semen normally follows about a year after the penis begins to enlarge. Further markers, such as the growth of facial and body hair, occur even later. In some boys, however, the indicators of increased sexual maturity unfold at much younger or older chronological ages. The growth of the testes, for example, may begin as early as nine-and-a-half years of age and be nearly complete by age thirteen-and-a-half for some boys, whereas such growth is just beginning for others.

The onset of various signs of approaching sexual maturity in girls is every bit as variable as that for boys. Breast development and rapid growth typically begin in the

KEY THEME
Continuity/Discontinuity

KEY THEME
Individual Differences

skeletal maturity Extent to which cartilage has ossified to form bone; provides the most accurate estimate of how much additional growth will take place in the individual.

puberty Developmental period during which a sequence of physical changes takes place that transforms the person from an immature individual to one capable of reproduction.

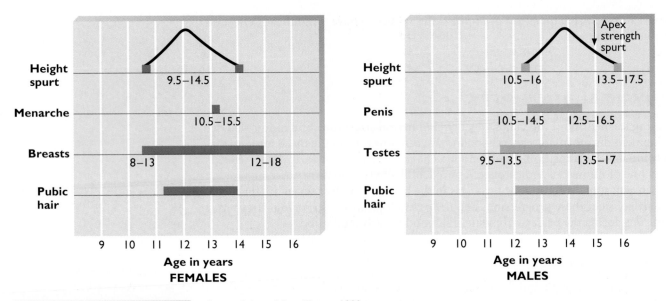

Source: Adapted from Tanner, 1990.

FIGURE 5.9

Normal Range of Ages in the Development of Sex Characteristics in Males and Females

The various changes accompanying puberty have a typical age of onset and cessation for males and females, but the specific times vary within as well as among individuals. The peaking lines connecting onset and cessation of the time line for height spurt reflect changes in the rate of increase in height over the duration of the growth spurt. The numbers under the time lines mark the earlier and later ages when these transitions take place for many children. Note especially the age differences for girls and boys.

tenth year, the appearance of pubic hair by age eleven, and underarm hair about the thirteenth year. In the United States, **menarche,** the first menstrual period, typically occurs before the twelfth and thirteenth birthday (Cauffman & Steinberg, 1996) and after peak height increments. However, as with other indicators of puberty, its initial appearance varies considerably from one girl to the next. In the United States, the events associated with puberty take place somewhat earlier in African American girls than in Caucasian American girls (Morrison et al., 1994). Menarche is usually considered the indicator of sexual maturity in females, although it is not synonymous with reproductive ability. *Ovulation,* the release of an egg cell during menstruation, may not occur for another twelve to eighteen months after menarche.

What triggers these remarkable changes? As with the growth spurt, the brain, including the hypothalamus and pituitary gland, and various hormones are centrally involved. In girls the hypothalamus may monitor metabolic cues associated with body size or the ratio of fat to muscle, because weight appears to be a good predictor of onset of menarche and because extremely high levels of exercise and poor nutrition can delay its occurrence (Frisch, 1983; Moffitt et al., 1992). Pituitary secretions stimulate the *adrenal glands,* located just above the kidneys, to increase the manufacture of a hormone important for the growth spurt and the emergence of underarm and pubic hair in girls. Still other *gonadotropic* (gonad-seeking) hormones released by the pituitary gland stimulate the production of estrogen and progesterone by the ovaries and regulate the menstrual cycle. Estrogen promotes the development of the breasts, uterus, and vagina as well as the broadening of the pelvis. Even parenting relationships, such as greater stress in the family, which can affect hormonal balances, may accelerate development (Graber, Brooks-Gunn, & Warren, 1995).

Gonadotropic hormones also contribute to the production of sperm and elevate the production of testosterone by the testes in boys. For boys testosterone promotes further growth in height, an increase in size of the penis and testes, and the appearance of secondary sexual characteristics such as pubic and facial hair.

KEY THEME
Individual Differences

Early Versus Late Maturity

Today adult height in most industrialized societies is typically reached by about age seventeen; a century ago, it often was not achieved until about age twenty-three (Rallison, 1986). Changes in the age of menarche reveal a similar trend toward increasingly early occurrences over recent generations (see Figure 5.10). The secular changes stem from improved socioeconomic conditions, including more adequate nutrition. However, individual differences in development continue to be evident during the

menarche   First occurrence of menstruation.

adolescent years. Do these often temporary differences affect socioemotional development? The answer appears to be yes, but let's first consider how young people feel about the changes accompanying puberty.

Most teenagers express concerns about the physical changes that attend puberty. Research on how adolescents view these events has focused primarily on girls and their reactions to menarche (Greif & Ulman, 1982). Girls who are unprepared for menarche, either due to lack of information or because of its early onset, perceive the event more negatively than other girls, whose reactions are often a mixture of positive and negative feelings (Koff & Rierdan, 1995; Ruble & Brooks-Gunn, 1982).

Today, thanks to earlier and more complete education, girls' reactions to menarche seem to be less negative than in previous generations, at least in developed countries (Brooks-Gunn, 1984). Greater communication within the family, including emotional support and assurance that menstruation is normal and healthy, correlates with a more positive attitude (Brooks-Gunn & Ruble, 1980; Koff & Rierdan, 1995). However, girls are initially reluctant to discuss their first menstruation with friends (Brooks-Gunn et al., 1986). Parents may also display considerable uneasiness or embarrassment about discussing such events. This is especially true of fathers, who rarely participate in such discussions; their daughters, in turn, usually do not desire their participation (Koff & Rierdan, 1995; Paikoff & Brooks-Gunn, 1991). Moreover, conflict, particularly between mother and daughter, tends to increase at this time, a factor that could contribute to ambivalent emotional reactions to this new sign of maturity (Holmbeck & Hill, 1991; Steinberg, 1988).

The limited research conducted with boys suggests that they are often uninformed, surprised, and confused about their first spontaneous nocturnal emission of sperm (Stein & Reiser, 1994). For many boys, sex education classes often either fail to explain what they need to know or are provided too late to prepare them. Their feelings about the event are mixed, and they seldom talk about it with others (Gaddis & Brooks-Gunn, 1985; Stein & Reiser, 1994). Despite conflicting reactions to this particular event, in American culture—and probably in most others—early maturity seems to have positive aspects for boys (Alsaker, 1992; Peterson, 1988). Compared to early maturers, late-maturing boys report more negative feelings about themselves, feel more rejected, express stronger dependency and affiliative needs, and are more rebellious toward their parents (Mussen & Jones, 1957). Although late maturers want

KEY THEME

Interaction Among Domains

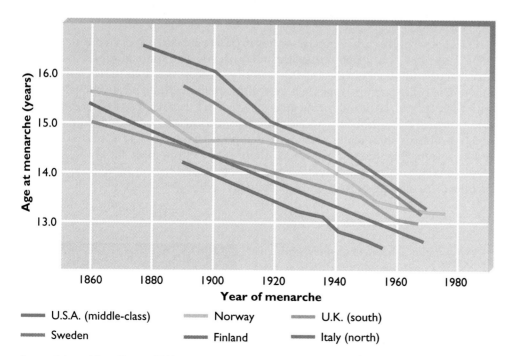

FIGURE 5.10

Secular Trends in the Age of Menarche

Evidence exists for a secular trend in the decrease in age of the onset of menarche from 1845 through 1960. Although most of the data were obtained by questioning adolescents and young adults, some, especially those from earlier generations, depended on the memories of older individuals.

Source: Adapted from Tanner, 1990.

to be well liked and accepted, their efforts to obtain social approval often translate into attention-getting, compensatory, and childish behaviors disruptive to success with peers and adults (Mussen & Jones, 1958). The differences continue to be observed even into adulthood (Jones, 1965).

What are girls' reactions to early and late maturity? Here the picture differs somewhat (Alsaker, 1992; Greif & Ulman, 1982; Simmons, Blyth, & McKinney, 1983). Early maturity may enhance status and prestige for girls just as for boys, but it can also be embarrassing; decrease their popularity, at least among agemates; and lead to greater social pressure and expectations from older friends, parents, and other adults to conform to more mature behavior patterns (Brooks-Gunn, 1989). The findings of one study of Swedish girls beginning when they were ten years of age reveal some negative social consequences of early maturity (Magnusson, Stattin, & Allen, 1986). Girls who reached menarche early were more likely than late-maturing girls to engage in a variety of norm-breaking activities, such as staying out late, cheating on exams, pilfering, or using alcohol. This was especially true for the girls who matured first; they preferred older and more mature friends who may have inspired their greater independence from socially approved conventions of behavior.

Indeed, among those maturing early but reporting no older friends, the frequency of norm-breaking activities was about the same as for girls who matured later. As they grew older, early maturers with and without older friends began to look more alike in their frequency of many norm-breaking activities, and late maturers began to engage in such activities as use of alcohol as often as early maturers. Still, a few unacceptable behaviors, such as the use of drugs, remained higher throughout adolescence among early-maturing than among late-maturing girls.

KEY THEME
Sociocultural Influence

How young adolescents feel about pubertal changes and evaluate their own status in relation to their peers may help to explain the findings on early and late maturity. Consider the cultural ideals of beauty and maturity that exist in most Western societies. Slenderness and long legs are considered desirable traits in women. Although initially taller than their peers during the growth spurt, early-maturing girls have less opportunity to grow tall and often end up somewhat shorter, heavier, and more robust than their later-maturing peers (Faust, 1983). The physical outcomes deviate from the ideal portrayed in the media; not surprisingly, early-maturing girls are therefore less satisfied with their weight and appearance than late-maturing girls (Koff & Rierdan, 1991). In contrast, early-maturing boys more quickly assume the rugged, muscular physique stereotypically portrayed in American society as ideal for men and are more pleased by their weight and appearance than late-maturing boys (Peterson, 1988).

Girls who mature early and boys who mature late are also out of step with most of their classmates. Young people usually prefer friends who share interests, and interests change with increasing maturity. Late-maturing boys may find that their peers move on to other pursuits, making it more difficult to maintain positive relationships with their friends. Early-maturing girls may redirect friendships to older peers. But this desire can be a problem, because it may contribute to increased behavior and school problems and greater personal unhappiness caused by pressures to conform to older peers (Magnusson, Stattin, & Allen, 1986; Simmons et al., 1987). In other words, biological, immediate social, and broader cultural factors combine to help define the consequences of early and late maturity.

Danielle worked extremely hard over the next few months. She soon perfected the move that she so coveted and continued to make advances in her gymnastic accomplishments. But Danielle also was becoming concerned about her best friend's participation in the sport. Just like Danielle, her pal and confidant was eager to be an expert gymnast. Unlike Danielle's parents, however, her friend's parents were

ATYPICAL DEVELOPMENT

Dieting and Eating Disorders

much taller and heavier, and her friend was growing more and more like them. What troubled Danielle were the frequent comments her friend shared about trying to lose weight, dieting, and staying small.

In the United States many young people, especially women, are dissatisfied with their weight. In fact, more than 40 percent of high school women report they are dieting (Centers for Disease Control, 1991), and as many as 75 percent indicate they have attempted to lose up to five or more pounds through dieting at some time (Emmons, 1996). Similar percentages of girls have been found to be dieting in Australia and probably in many other Western countries as well (Paxton et al., 1991). Concern about weight seems especially prevalent among Caucasian and Hispanic youth and a bit less so among young African American women. Repeated messages from fashion magazines, and perhaps from family and peers (that occasionally escalate to the level of teasing), stress the importance of slenderness for beauty and success and undoubtedly place enormous pressure even on preteenagers to control weight (Levine, Smolak, & Hayden, 1994). As women in general have gotten heavier over the past decades, many continue to seek an ideal appearance similar to Miss Universe.

The large number of girls who attempt to diet has become an almost normative, although troubling, aspect of growing up in many cultures. However, a substantial number of teenagers, especially girls, including many who are not obese, go to great and even life-threatening lengths to reduce their weight. Anorexia nervosa and bulimia nervosa are two self-initiated forms of such extreme weight control efforts. *Anorexia nervosa* is a kind of self-imposed starvation. Individuals with anorexia appear to be obsessed with avoiding appearing too heavy and as a consequence become dangerously thin. As weight loss becomes severe, muscle tissue degenerates, bone marrow changes, menstrual periods are disrupted in girls, and cardiac stress and arrhythmia can occur. *Bulimia nervosa* is an eating disorder in which the individual often engages in recurrent bouts of binge eating, sometimes consuming enormous quantities of high-calorie, easily digested food. For many, binge eating alternates with self-induced vomiting. These actions may also be accompanied by use of laxatives or diuretics to help control weight. Although they share with anorexic individuals an intense concern about their bodies, individuals suffering from bulimia often fall within a normal weight range for their age and height.

A substantial increase in these disorders has been reported since the 1970s (Bryant-Waugh & Lask, 1995). They are most frequently found among Caucasian, middle-to-upper-income young women (Harris, 1991), but appear to be increasing

KEY THEME
Child's Active Role

KEY THEME
Sociocultural Influence

Concerns about attractiveness, physical size, and especially weight, become especially common among girls during adolescence. Repeated messages in fashion magazines and on television often portray unrealistic body shape and weight-control efforts.

in males and some cultural groups that have begun to adopt Western values (Hsu, 1990; Smith & Krejci, 1991). Their frequency may also be greater in certain groups, such as athletes and dancers, who are especially concerned about physical appearance (Phelps & Bajorek, 1991; Taub & Blinde, 1992). Eating disorders may begin as part of the larger spectrum of anxieties adolescents and young adults experience about physical changes during puberty, and a genetic link may well exist, especially for anorexia nervosa. However, cultural ideals of physical attractiveness, insecurities about family and friends, the hormonal and other physiological changes that are occurring, and concerns about puberty may all play a role. Sociocultural, psychological, and biological factors appear to interact so that, not surprisingly, the treatments most effective for dealing with such disorders have not been easy to identify (Hsu, 1996). Individuals experiencing eating disorders should be strongly encouraged to seek professional help.

Adolescent Sexual Behavior

Few changes accompanying puberty are as contentious in many families as the increased sexuality that attends physical maturity. Anthropological research indicates that the majority of cultures are likely to permit or at least tolerate some sexual activity during the teen years. But Western societies have generally been more restrictive in its expression (Schlegel & Barry, 1991). Nevertheless, large numbers of teenagers in the United States are engaging in sexual relations, and at young ages (see Figure 5.11). Similar levels are often reported in other Western nations (Newcomer & Baldwin, 1992).

What factors seem to play a role in whether a teenager will engage in sexual intercourse? Teenagers who perceive their parents as permissive about discipline and rules are more likely than other teenagers to initiate sexual relationships. But those who see their parents as extremely strict in these matters are more sexually active than teenagers who view their parents as moderately restrictive (Miller et al., 1986). Sexually active older siblings, absence of the father in the home, difficulty in school, early dating activity, friends who engage in sexual behavior, absence of religious practices and beliefs, and participation in other problem and risk-taking behaviors all correlate with early sexual behavior (Bingham & Crockett, 1996; Harvey & Spigner, 1995; Santelli & Beilenson, 1992). However, a fairly substantial proportion of these individuals, especially females and those with a stronger religious orientation, report that they wish they had delayed this activity (de Gaston, Jensen, & Weed, 1995).

Aside from the moral and ethical issues adolescent sexual behavior raises are other

KEY THEME
Interaction Among Domains

KEY THEME
Child's Active Role

KEY THEME
Individual Differences

FIGURE 5.11

Percentage of Women in the United States Ages 15 to 18 Reporting Premarital Sexual Intercourse, 1970–1988

The percentage of women indicating they engaged in premarital sexual intercourse continued to rise during the 1970s and 1980s. However, more recent surveys reveal that these percentages have reached a plateau and have remained fairly stable since 1988 through the most recent year in which data are available (1993). The percentages would be higher if plotted for males. The data indicate that a large number of adolescents are engaging in sexual activity prior to marriage despite concerns in this country about the appropriateness of such behavior for young people.

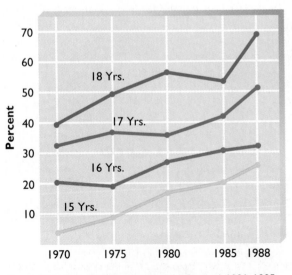

Source: Data from Centers for Disease Control, 1991, 1995.

important health and social consequences. Among the most frequent concerns are sexually transmitted diseases, teenage pregnancy, and the tendency of teenage parents to drop out of school. Compared to twenty-five years ago, a far lower proportion of teenagers in the United States, if they do become pregnant, now marry (Glazer, 1993). This trend, along with increased sexual activity and inconsistent contraceptive use, resulted in pregnancy for approximately 20 percent of unmarried American women of European heritage age eighteen years or younger and 40 percent of African heritage during the 1980s (Furstenberg, Brooks-Gunn, & Chase-Lansdale, 1989), a rate that has remained fairly stable into the 1990s. Nearly half the pregnancies terminate before the birth of a baby, but well over 300,000 babies are born every year to single teenage women in the United States. Only about half of these women will finish high school. Moreover, their children will often have difficulty when they begin school (Brooks-Gunn & Furstenberg, 1986). The long-term negative consequences of becoming a single parent at such a young age are just some of the reasons adolescent sexual behavior is of so much concern, not only to the families of teenagers but to the professionals who work with them as well.

Because of the risks associated with sexual activity, such as pregnancy and contracting AIDS or other sexually transmitted diseases, many individuals working with elementary, junior high, and high school students in the United States, England (Editor, 1994), and other countries

CONTROVERSY: THINKING IT OVER

Should Sex Education Be Part of the School Curriculum?

have argued that young people need to be better educated about their sexuality. Nearly everyone agrees that instruction about sex should begin in the home at a young age, taught by parents. But beyond that consensus, much less accord exists about sex education.

Parents generally wish to see instruction about sexuality provided in the school; polls conducted on the issue seem to reveal a preference for such instruction. For example, it is not unusual to find that about 80 percent of adults in the United States believe sex education is appropriate, and, when given the opportunity, only a small proportion of parents ask to have their children excused from sex education classes (Fine, 1988). In fact, sex education is either required or recommended in nearly all states today and in many other countries where formal education is offered (Kirby et al., 1994).

What, then, is this controversy over sex education all about? The answer is what the curriculum should be. From the perspective of some people, the emphasis should be on encouraging young people to abstain from sexual relationships until they are married or, at the least, until they are mature enough to effectively handle the complexities and consequences of interpersonal relationships. To promote anything other than abstinence sends a mixed message that communicates a double standard: "Avoid sexual relationships, but in case you can't, here is what you should know."

From the perspective of others, however, sex education in the schools should not be presented within the context of moral or prescriptive lessons but instead should provide clear information and access to resources that will help young people be comfortable with their emerging sexuality. Perhaps a somewhat tempered perspective is that while young people should be encouraged to postpone sexual involvement, many teenagers, and sometimes even children who are just approaching the teenage years, already engage in sexual activity, are unlikely to change their behavior, and therefore need to learn to engage in it responsibly and safely. Moreover, young people should be given practice in recognizing situations that could lead to sexual activity and learn how to modify and comfortably resist those situations if they prefer not to participate.

Tests of the effectiveness of various sex education curricula have yielded mixed results (Kirby et al., 1994). Although knowledge of sexuality typically increases, young people do not consistently report they are involved in less sexual activity or engage in it more responsibly or safely; nor has the incidence of teenage pregnancy always been found to decline even in programs that emphasize complete abstinence. On the other hand, no evidence exists to indicate that sex education programs increase sexual activity (Berne & Huberman, 1995), another fear that is occasionally expressed.

Why might these efforts have had limited effect? Is it that such programs need to be offered at earlier ages because many young people do not participate in sex education classes until they are already sexually active (Santelli & Beilenson, 1992)? Or is it that the curricula typically provided on this topic have been uninteresting and ineffective, presenting extensive information about the biology of reproduction but little about the social skills needed to respond to the many pressures young people face to engage in sexual relationships? Would the outcome differ if programs were more comprehensive, supplemented by multifaceted efforts of parents, youth and religious leaders, other community resources, and the mass media? Have programs stressing abstinence, which for the most part have only recently gained widespread adoption, not been in schools long enough to prove themselves? Or are these latter programs too biased and narrow in their focus, often emphasizing fear instead of knowledge, extolling a simplistic solution to a complex problem that can have life-and-death consequences for young people today?

CHAPTER RECAP

SUMMARY OF DEVELOPMENTAL THEMES

NATURE/NURTURE   What roles do nature and nurture play in physical growth and motor skill development?

Physical growth, brain development, and the acquisition of motor skills are the product of complex systems influenced by both biology and experience. Biological processes, both genetic and hormonal, augment growth, the proliferation and migration of neurons, and events associated with the development of motor skills. At the same time, the transformation from relatively immature infant to increasingly competent child and adolescent is affected by experience and the many different forms of influence caregivers provide. Important stimulation ranges from providing adequate emotional, social, and nutritional support for physical growth to practice and training in encouraging the acquisition of motor skills and talents.

SOCIOCULTURAL INFLUENCE   How does the sociocultural context influence physical growth and motor skill development?

Physical growth and motor skill development are embedded within settings, resources, and beliefs promoted by the society in which the child lives. For example, the extent to which a culture encourages specific skills, from the acquisition of motor milestones to skilled athletic ability, or values a particular physical attribute, such as being slender, affects the efforts of children to display these qualities. Knowledge of nutrition, views about physical appearance, and the availability of leisure time, as well as educational practices, have produced changing secular trends for many aspects of development, including growth in height, onset of menarche, and the prevalence of obesity.

CHILD'S ACTIVE ROLE   How does the child play an active role in the process of physical growth and motor skill development?

Babies seem to be intrinsically motivated to exercise rudimentary motor skills. Once a child attains locomotion or other skills, she or he provokes new reactions from caregivers that may include being denied access to cupboards and light sockets or being prevented from pouncing on the usually patient family dog. New physical competencies may also be exercised to improve their speed, accuracy, and efficiency. From these efforts can emerge expertise that fuels further progress in athletic, artistic, and other endeavors. Rapid growth or early maturity may affect not only the child's interests but also the expectations and reactions of others. Excessive concerns about weight, for example, and the emergence of sexual maturity may influence the kinds of interactions in which the child or adolescent engages both within and outside the home, interactions that can have dramatic consequences for future development.

CONTINUITY/DISCONTINUITY   Are physical growth and motor skill development continuous or discontinuous?

Physical growth, brain development, and the acquisition of motor skills show spurts at certain times in development. The patterns often give rise to conceptions of stagelike development. But even dramatic changes such as those exhibited in attaining motor milestones in infancy or during the pubertal changes of adolescence are grounded in processes undergoing continuous transformations. Small, incremental changes in the relative strength of muscles or production of hormones, for example, may initiate substantive dynamic reorganizations in complex systems of behavior. Physical and skill changes observed in children may bring about dramatic reactions from others that are interpreted as stagelike in growth and motor skill development.

INDIVIDUAL DIFFERENCES   How prominent are individual differences in physical growth and motor skill development?

Individual differences are a hallmark of physical growth and motor skill development. Variations may arise from biological or experiential factors that can limit or augment development. The differences can significantly influence the child and the reactions of others, as early or late maturity or precocious or delayed skill acquisition demonstrates. Individual differences are pervasive and readily apparent, and an important aspect of behavior to be appreciated as well as explained.

INTERACTION AMONG DOMAINS   How do physical growth and motor skill development interact with other domains of development?

A child's physical size and weight, as well as improvements in the execution and coordination of motor skills, have dramatic influences on the responses and expectations of caregivers, peers, and others and, in turn, on how the child feels about his or her body and abilities. For example, once capable of walking, the child has a greater ability to initiate independence, which may lead parents to grant more freedoms and at the same time demand more responsibilities. Similarly, the young adolescent's status with peers is often influenced by signs of his or her physically maturing body and other aspects of physical stature, coordination, and skill. These qualities are evaluated by others and influence the child's evaluation of self.

SUMMARY OF TOPICS

■ BODY GROWTH AND DEVELOPMENT

Norms reveal a common pattern of rapid height and weight gain in the months before and after birth, much slower but regular increases in size beginning at about two years of age, and a final growth spurt before or during early adolescence. Growth is also marked by considerable variation among individuals and cultural groups and for specific systems of the body.

Cephalocaudal and *proximodistal* principles apply to many patterns of physical growth. Biological factors help to regulate physical development. Cells in the hypothalamus may determine whether growth is proceeding according to genetic instructions. Many hormones interact in complex ways to influence growth as well. Nutrition, disease, and even social-emotional experiences further affect physical development.

Improved nutrition and prevention of disease have yielded secular increases in final height over the last several centuries in many regions of the world. Yet malnutrition and inadequate, neglectful, or abusive caregiving can result in severe stunting of growth. Insufficient rates of growth and obesity have significant consequences for the child's social interactions with others and appear to be major concerns for children and their families.

■ THE BRAIN AND NERVOUS SYSTEM

Brain growth proceeds rapidly during fetal and early postnatal development. Much of *neuron* proliferation and migration to various locations in the brain occurs before birth; however, differentiation of neurons continues throughout development. Differentiation may proceed at critical or sensitive times for experience-expectant information but occurs throughout development for experience-dependent information. *Glial cell* formation, *myelination,* and the operation and organization of nervous system networks also begin prenatally and continue to develop after birth. Infants display behaviors suggestive of hemispheric specialization, or *lateralization,* at birth, but both hemispheres may have equal potential for higher-order processing of information.

■ MOTOR SKILL DEVELOPMENT

Infants display *reflexes* and spend considerable time producing *stereotypies* that may serve as building blocks underlying complex voluntary behavior. Postural, locomotor, and manual control undergo regular patterns of differentiation and integration. Throughout infancy and childhood, motor skills become more efficient and quick.

Failure to integrate higher-order voluntary and lower-order brain reflex mechanisms that control breathing is hypothesized as one cause of *sudden infant death syndrome (SIDS).* Genetic preadaptation may assist in initiating the emergence of milestone motor skills, but research indicates that experience is equally important for their acquisition. Many processes influenced by both biological and environmental factors contribute to individual and cross-cultural differences in the appearance of early motor skills and later skill acquisition.

■ PHYSICAL MATURITY

Maturity is defined not by size but by ossification of bone material. Many signs of approaching sexual maturity, including the adolescent growth spurt, begin earlier in girls than in boys. Boys in Western societies seem to benefit from early maturity, but the effects for girls are less clear. The different consequences may stem from the reactions and pressures of peers and perceived cultural values regarding body size and shape. Eating disorders and new patterns of sexual behavior appear to be major concerns for adolescents and their families.

6 BASIC LEARNING AND PERCEPTION

KEY THEMES IN BASIC LEARNING AND PERCEPTION

NATURE/NURTURE
What roles do nature and nurture play in learning and perceptual development?

SOCIOCULTURAL INFLUENCE
How does the sociocultural context influence learning and perceptual development?

CHILD'S ACTIVE ROLE
How does the child play an active role in learning and perceptual development?

INDIVIDUAL DIFFERENCES
How prominent are individual differences in learning and perceptual development?

INTERACTION AMONG DOMAINS
How do learning and perceptual development interact with development in other domains?

The apartment had suddenly grown terribly quiet. The three other babies and their mothers who had been helping to celebrate Chad's first birthday had departed. Only Tanya, Chad's mother, remained with him as the light faded at the end of the day. Picking up the torn gift wrappings, Tanya reflected on the events of the past year. She thought back to her first glimpse of Chad. She had counted his toes and fingers to make sure all were there. She had wondered aloud, as she first held him, "What do you see? Can you hear me? What are you thinking?" Tanya had vowed to be a good mother, to help Chad learn. As she began to vacuum the cake crumbs from the floor, she wasn't sure she was keeping her promise. She couldn't afford the colorful playland that had beckoned to him at the toy store. She never seemed to have enough money now that Chad's father had moved out. Was it fair for Chad not to have things that delighted him and from which he could learn so much? Chad also sometimes challenged her, and she became angry with him. What was he learning from these kinds of exchanges?

What can a newborn learn or hear, or see or feel? Only twenty-five or thirty years ago obstetricians and pediatricians, and even some psychologists, might have answered, "Very little and perhaps nothing at all" (Haith, 1990). But a far different answer has emerged in recent years. Newborns have already begun to engage in the lifelong process of learning. Their visual abilities are already providing enormous amounts of information from which to learn. If newborns can see, can they also hear—for example, a mother's lullaby? Can they identify the subtle smells of their mothers' bodies, feel the prick of a nurse's pin or the pain of circumcision? If the answer to these questions is yes, they also have the potential to learn a great deal about their world beginning in infancy. What had Chad been learning? Being reared in the angular world of city skyscrapers, might he, for example, see and learn about things far differently than a child growing up in a tropical rain forest? How important were these early experiences for his development?

These are precisely the kinds of questions psychologists have often asked. Why? Because learning and perception are fundamental processes by which children come to understand and respond to their world. Perception, the interpretation of sensory information from visual, auditory, and other sensory receptors, is the vehicle by which one gleans information about the world. Learning, a means of acquiring new skills and behaviors from experience, is an extremely important form of adaptation. Through learning children avoid dangers, achieve satisfactions, and become contributing members of the families, communities, and cultures in which they live. We

181

begin this chapter by discussing basic processes in learning; then we consider sensory and perceptual development in infants and children. These basic processes serve as the foundation for the more complex aspects of learning and intellectual and social development examined in the chapters that follow.

KEY THEME
Nature/Nurture

BASIC LEARNING PROCESSES IN INFANCY AND CHILDHOOD

Learning permits adaptation to the environment. The wide variety of learning infants and children display helps them to respond to the demands of their physical and social environments and to achieve goals and solve problems. Children learn, for example, that a stove can be hot, that hitting a sibling will make their parents angry, and that a symbol of a male on a door signals the right (or wrong) one to enter. From watching other children present a class project, they learn how to make their own assignments more interesting or more effective for their classmates. What are the basic forms of learning? How early do these important capacities appear in infants and young children? How important are they throughout development? Consider first what is perhaps one of the simplest forms of learning: *habituation.*

Habituation

The gradual decline in the intensity, frequency, or duration of a response to the repetitious occurrence of a stimulus is known as **habituation.** Even newborns display habituation. For example, they may show less arousal—that is, reductions in heart rate or fewer searching eye movements—as they are repeatedly patted on the arm or hear the same bell ringing over and over. Habituation is thus a simple, adaptive form of learning: learning to ignore things that offer little new information and that, in a sense, have become boring.

Once babies have habituated to an event, they often display a renewed response to a change in the stimulus. For example, if touched on the leg instead of the arm or exposed to a sound other than the ringing of a bell, they may become aroused once again. The return of a response is an example of **recovery from habituation** (sometimes called **dishabituation**) and suggests that the baby perceives the new stimulus as different from the old one.

Low-birth-weight, brain-damaged, and younger babies tend to habituate less rapidly than older, more mature infants (Krafchuk, Tronick, & Clifton, 1983; Rovee-Collier, 1987). In fact, as we will see in Chapter 10, an infant's rapid habituation and recovery from habituation to new stimuli is associated with greater intelligence and cognitive capacities in later childhood. Thus, although it is a simple form of learning, habituation may nonetheless be an important process in intellectual development.

Classical Conditioning

As we learned in Chapter 1, in *classical conditioning* a neutral event paired with a stimulus that triggers an inborn response can come to elicit a response similar to the one triggered by the original stimulus. Consider a nipple placed in a newborn's mouth; it tends to elicit sucking. The nipple is an **unconditioned stimulus (UCS);** the sucking response it elicits is an **unconditioned response (UCR).** After a series of trials in which a neutral stimulus—say, a distinctive odor—is paired with the nipple (the UCS), the odor may also begin to elicit sucking even when the nipple is not present. The odor has become a **conditioned stimulus (CS),** and the sucking response it initiates a **conditioned response (CR).** Table 6.1 summarizes the sequence of steps in classical conditioning for this and other typical examples.

Infants display classical conditioning within hours after birth. Elliot Blass and his colleagues (Blass, Ganchrow, & Steiner, 1984) demonstrated this by pairing a tactile stimulus, stroking of the newborn's forehead (CS), with the delivery of a sugar solu-

habituation Gradual decline in intensity, frequency, or duration of a response over repeated or lengthy occurrences of the same stimulus.

recovery from habituation Reinstatement of the intensity, frequency, or duration of a response to a stimulus that has changed. Also called *dishabituation.*

dishabituation See *recovery from habituation.*

unconditioned stimulus (UCS) Stimulus that, without prior training, elicits a reflexlike response (unconditioned response).

unconditioned response (UCR) Response that is automatically elicited by the unconditioned stimulus (UCS).

conditioned stimulus (CS) Neutral stimulus that begins to elicit a response similar to the unconditioned stimulus (UCS) with which it has been paired.

conditioned response (CR) Learned response that is exhibited to a previously neutral stimulus (CS) as a result of pairing the CS with an unconditioned stimulus (UCS).

TABLE 6.1	Examples of Classical Conditioning

Classical conditioning is learning in which a neutral cue (conditioned stimulus), through its association with a cue (unconditioned stimulus) that naturally elicits a reflexlike response (unconditioned response), comes to elicit the same response (conditioned response).

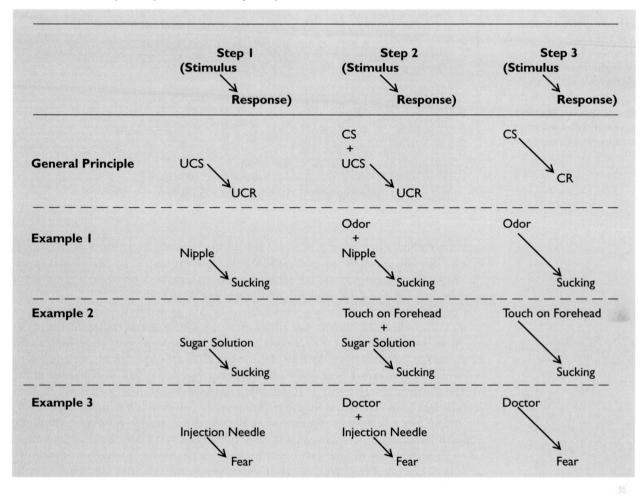

tion to the mouth (UCS) that elicited sucking (UCR). Newborns learned to orient and initiate sucking (CR) with stroking of the forehead (CS) alone. But other types of classical conditioning are difficult for infants to learn. For example, researchers have not been able to successfully condition infants younger than three or four weeks to respond to aversive stimuli, such as foot withdrawal at loud noises or a painful prick. Perhaps the youngest infants lack the motor and neural abilities needed to escape noxious events; they must depend on caregivers for protection until they acquire simple locomotor skills for avoiding aversive stimuli (Rovee-Collier, 1987). However, other important associations, particularly those surrounding feeding activity, can be acquired through classical conditioning shortly after birth.

Operant Conditioning

In *operant* (or *instrumental*) *conditioning,* the frequency of spontaneous, sometimes novel behaviors changes as a result of positive and negative consequences. Put another way, behaviors tend to increase when followed by rewards (**positive reinforcement**) or the removal of aversive events (**negative reinforcement**) and to decrease when followed by the loss of rewards (**negative punishment**) or an aversive outcome (**positive punishment**). The term *positive* in this context indicates that when a behavior occurs, it causes a stimulus event that either increases the rate of the response (reinforcement) or decreases it (punishment). The term *negative* in this context indi-

positive reinforcement
Occurrence of a stimulus that strengthens a response when it follows that response. Also known as a *reward.*

negative reinforcement
Withdrawal of an aversive stimulus that, upon its removal, serves to strengthen a preceding response.

negative punishment
Withdrawal or loss of a desired stimulus or reward that, upon its removal, weakens or decreases the frequency of a behavior.

positive punishment An aversive stimulus that, when occurring following a response, serves to decrease the frequency of the response.

FIGURE 6.1

Positive and Negative
Reinforcement and
Punishment

**Reinforcement leads to an
increase in the rate of responding; punishment leads to a
decrease in the rate of responding.** *Positive* **refers to
the presentation of a stimulus
following a response;** *negative*
**refers to the withdrawal of a
stimulus following a response.**

Rate of response

	Increases	**Decreases**
Response leads stimulus to be Delivered	**Positive reinforcement** (Increases behavior by delivering a desired stimulus) Example: Infant says, "cookie" → Mother gives praise	**Positive punishment** (Decreases behavior by delivering an aversive stimulus) Example: Toddler throws toys → Father yells, "Stop it"
Response leads stimulus to be Withdrawn	**Negative reinforcement** (Increases behavior by removing an aversive stimulus) Example: Child cleans messy room → Parent stops "nagging"	**Negative punishment** (Decreases behavior by removing a desired stimulus) Example: Teenager out past curfew → Parent grounds teenager

cates that when a behavior occurs, it leads to the removal of a stimulus and its removal either increases the rate of the response (reinforcement) or decreases it (punishment). Figure 6.1 summarizes these relationships and provides examples of
positive and negative reinforcement and punishment.

Operant conditioning can also be observed in infants within the first few hours of
birth. For example, newborns will either increase or decrease pressure during sucking when the availability of milk, a positive reinforcer, is contingent on an increase or
a decrease in pressure (Sameroff, 1972). As with classical conditioning, operant conditioning seems to work best with behaviors important to infants, such as searching
for (head turning, mouthing) and obtaining food (sucking) or other stimuli that are
comforting. Even premature infants weighing only two or three pounds show learning through conditioning; in a two-week period, they came to more quickly touch
and maintain longer contact with a toy bear that exhibited a breathing pattern similar to their own rate of respiration compared to a bear that showed no respiratory
activity (Thoman & Ingersoll, 1993). In other words, the bear that displayed breathing proved to be a reinforcing source of stimulation and infants learned to find and
make contact with it. Full-term babies only a few weeks of age can acquire complex
chains of behavior, such as making two head turns in one direction and two in the
other, through operant conditioning (Papoušek, 1967).

Sensory stimuli seem to be especially powerful reinforcers for infants. Babies will
work hard, modifying the frequency or rate of vocalizing, smiling, and other behaviors under their control, to see and hear things (Lipsitt, 1982). These kinds of sensory stimulation, of course, typically occur in the presence of parents, grandparents,
neighbors, and siblings who, as major sources of reinforcers, encourage the baby to
become responsive to them.

A s the last rays of sun disappeared,
Tanya shifted her focus to preparing
Chad for bed. After putting on his pa-
jamas and playing with him a few more minutes, she rocked him and sang a lullaby before
giving him a final hug and kiss. But just as
she was about to lay him in his crib, Chad
started to cry. Tanya tried to ignore his sobs,

**RESEARCH APPLIED TO
PARENTING**

**Reducing Sleep
Disturbances Through
Changes in Learned
Behavior**

but as they intensified to screams, she knew Chad, still wound up from the party, would
not go to sleep right away this night. Indeed, he had been doing the same thing for the

last several weeks. Why would this evening be any different? Tanya picked him up, played with him a bit longer, and then lay down with him in her own bed until he finally fell asleep. She moved Chad to his own crib later that evening.

Even more distressing for Tanya, however, were Chad's frequent awakenings. Usually, two or three times each night, he would cry so hard that she would have to go through the same bedtime routine until he fell asleep again. Tanya was having difficulty getting the sleep that she desperately needed, and it was beginning to take a toll on her relationship with Chad.

Surveys of parents reveal that somewhere between 10 and 40 percent of infants and young children have difficulty going to sleep or returning to sleep after awakening in the middle of the night (Blampied & France, 1993; Johnson, 1991). Most of these difficulties do not stem from serious developmental problems, but they can become a major challenge for parents as they try to obtain sufficient rest for themselves.

Principles of classical and operant learning can account for most sleep difficulties; they can also provide answers to eliminating the problem. For example, for a variety of reasons such as illness, teething, or some other discomfort, an older infant or a young child may become upset and have considerable difficulty falling asleep. Under such circumstances, parents often—and in such cases, quite appropriately—pick up, rock, or otherwise soothe the child until she or he falls asleep. However, such activities are usually powerful reinforcers that can strengthen fussing, crying, or other attention-getting behaviors. Thus, long after the initial distress has been resolved, a child may still display sleep difficulties at bedtime or after awakening in the middle of the night. The principles of learning suggest a number of steps to take to address this issue (Adair et al., 1992; Blampied & France, 1993; Ferber, 1985):

1. *Provide positive routines in preparation for bedtime.*   Older infants and young children need to learn to associate certain cues with preparing themselves for sleep. These should include regular, quiet activities such as reading or gentle rocking about the same time each evening to reduce arousal level and increase expectations—that is, set the stage—for sleep onset.

2. *Arrange for falling asleep in the child's own crib or bed.*   Children need to associate certain rooms and other spatial cues with falling asleep. Otherwise, particularly if they awaken in the middle of the night, those cues are not available to help them return to sleep.

Establishing bedtime routines can help young children prepare for sleep. Quiet activities such as looking at and reading a book together with a parent as well as the availability of a comforting toy such as a doll should help this toddler make the transition from wakefulness to sleep.

3. *Offer comforting resources to substitute for parental attention.* A favorite toy, blanket, or other item may help young children soothe themselves in preparing for sleep. Once such items become associated with falling to sleep, they can also be important cues for subsequently promoting sleep if the child awakens later in the night.

4. *Reduce and eventually eliminate parental cues for falling asleep.* Parental attention can be a highly positive reinforcer that interferes with falling asleep. Sleep difficulties often arise when parents rock, hold, or otherwise engage their children in trying to get them back to sleep; the parents' presence and falling asleep become a learned association (Ferber, 1985).

Infants less than four to six months of age should not be expected to adopt a sleep schedule. Parents need to follow their young infant's lead, feeding and providing other care and assistance even when tired themselves. However, older infants and young children may need to learn the skill of falling asleep. If soothing and rocking seem to be effective, parents can feel more confident that hunger, pain, or some other problem is not the reason for failing to fall asleep. In considering learning principles and sleep problems, Richard Ferber and others suggest that when an older infant or a young child has difficulty, parents implement a progressive *delayed-responding technique* to reduce the association between caregiver presence and falling asleep. If a young child starts to cry after being put to bed, wait five minutes. Then check to see that she or he is all right and does not need to be fed, changed, or provided with other care; but limit the visit to two or three minutes and to reassuring behaviors other than picking up, feeding, and so forth. Leave while the child is still awake to promote cues for falling asleep without the parent's presence. If crying continues, wait for ten minutes before returning and follow the same procedure. If crying still continues, wait for fifteen minutes and continue checking at that interval until the child falls asleep. On subsequent days, start with a ten-minute, then a fifteen-minute, then a twenty-minute interval before beginning to check.

By sticking to such a schedule, a child fairly rapidly learns that it is time to sleep and that those positive reinforcements from parenting will be available at another time. Of course, an illness or a significant change in the child's life can upset a child so that sleep disturbances return for awhile. But once the immediate problem is addressed, parents may need to reimplement the steps that encourage sleep both for their child and themselves.

Classical and operant conditioning are often called on to explain the acquisition of many other behaviors throughout infancy and childhood. Through repeated associations of events and from positive outcomes, including the reinforcing actions of caregivers or "instructors," children become more skilled and proficient in a rich variety of endeavors. Consider the six-year-old learning to write the letters of the alphabet. At first, of course, neither the sizes nor the shapes of the letters are skillfully reproduced, but the teacher may express enormous satisfaction with these early efforts. With practice and as the child's ability improves, the teacher begins to expect far more legible symbols before granting praise to the student. Precisely these kinds of contingencies are central to *applied behavior analysis,* described in Chapter 1. Indeed, both parents and teachers encourage a rich variety of functional skills and educational achievements through the use of such procedures (Alberto & Troutman, 1995).

It is difficult to imagine, however, that habituation, classical conditioning, and the systematic implementation of reinforcers and punishment are the basis for mastering all the vital tasks of childhood. One element that seems to be missing from this discussion so far is children's active role in observing and interpreting events that occur in their surroundings. As we saw in Chapter 1, social learning theorists have considered observational learning an important means by which children acquire many

KEY THEME

Child's Active Role

complex social and cognitive skills (Bandura, 1977b). Individuals often learn behaviors important to the community by observing the activities of others, who in turn provide further guidance. Imitation has become an increasingly important element in explaining learning throughout development.

Imitation

When does imitation become possible? How important is this ability in the learning of infants and children? Andrew Meltzoff and M. Keith Moore (1983, 1992, 1994) argue that even newborns and very young infants imitate a variety of responses, including tongue protrusion, mouth opening, and possibly even facial expressions portraying such emotions as happiness, sadness, and surprise (Field et al., 1982). Although some investigators have been unable to replicate these results, many others, including the authors of one study involving infants from Nepal (see Figure 6.2), report amazing imitative competence in neonates (Reissland, 1988).

Even more controversial is what the imitative behaviors mean. Piaget (1962), for example, claimed infants younger than eight to twelve months could imitate someone else's behavior, but only when able to see themselves making these responses. Because babies cannot view their own faces, imitative facial gestures would be impossible, according to Piaget, until after about a year of age, when symbolic capacities emerge. From this perspective, then, facial gestures are stereotyped, rigid responses triggered by or tethered, so to speak, to limited forms of stimulation. For example, perhaps tongue protrusion by a model arouses the infant, which in turn promotes a sucking response that naturally invokes tongue protrusion from the infant (Karmiloff-Smith, 1995). If this is the case, infants could be responding to just a few types of stimuli and producing a kind of reflexive motor activity that is not really a form of imitation (Anisfeld, 1996).

Meltzoff and Moore (1989, 1992, 1994) counter that very young infants imitate a variety of responses, modify their imitations to increasingly match the modeled behavior over time, and exhibit their imitations primarily to other people and not to inanimate objects. These arguments contradict the view that such behaviors are simply a fixed pattern of reflexive actions. They propose instead that infants imitate in order to continue interacting with others. In fact, babies as young as six weeks will imitate behaviors of a model up to twenty-four hours later. The infant produces these imitative actions, according to Meltzoff and Moore, to help determine whether the model is the same person seen earlier, that is, as a way to help to identify and communicate with the model. If this interpretation is correct, imitation has an important social-communicative function and signals one of the earliest games babies play to learn about others in their surroundings.

FIGURE 6.2

Facial Imitation in Newborns

Within an hour after birth, babies in Nepal showed different responses when an experimenter used pursed versus widened lip movements. On the left, the baby broadens his lips in response to widened lips by the model. On the right, the baby exposes his tongue in response to pursed lips by the model. The findings support the highly controversial position that even newborns are capable of imitating facial gestures.

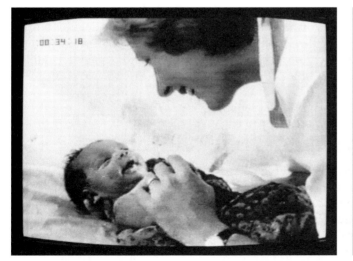
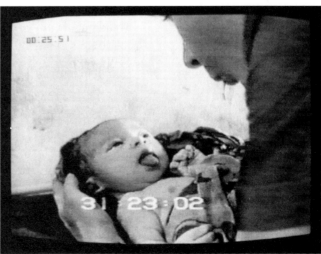

Between six and twelve months of age, infants display far more frequent and precise imitations, matching a wide range of modeled behaviors (Kaye & Marcus, 1981). Piaget and others (McCall, Parke, & Kavanaugh, 1977) believed that **deferred imitation,** the ability to imitate well after some activity has been demonstrated, is not possible until about eighteen to twenty-four months of age. Piaget believed deferred imitation, along with pretend play and the emergence of language, marks an important transition from one stage of thinking to the next and provides one of the first major pieces of evidence for symbolic capacities (see Chapter 8). However, as we have already seen, Meltzoff and Moore claim infants as young as six weeks can reproduce a model's behavior a day after seeing it.

Deferred imitation involving actions associated with objects also can be observed far earlier than Piaget claimed. For example, six-month-olds will remove a mitten from a puppet's hand, shake it, and try to put it back on the puppet after observing this sequence of actions performed by a model twenty-four hours earlier (Barr, Dowden, & Hayne, 1996). Moreover, toddlers as young as fourteen months who see a peer pulling, pushing, poking, and inserting toys in the laboratory or at a day care center will reproduce the behaviors in their own homes as much as two days later when given the same toys (Hanna & Meltzoff, 1993). The capacity for deferred imitation, then, appears to exist much sooner than previously assumed. In fact, the results accord well with research on memory (discussed in Chapter 9) showing that infants younger than one year can recognize stimuli hours and even days later.

The observances of imitation at very young ages are important from a social learning perspective, providing clear and compelling evidence that infants, as well as older children, learn many new behaviors by observing others. For example, by about age two, children readily imitate actions performed on objects by a model. And when that happens, it can promote continued play with the objects by both the model who initiates and the observer who imitates the action, leading to an escalation of social and imitative games among children (Eckerman & Stein, 1990). To illustrate, when a toddler squeezed a horn and another person imitated that action, the toddler was more likely to repeat the behavior a number of times than when some other action followed the response initiated by the toddler. Mothers also report that two-year-olds increasingly imitate responsible behaviors such as chores and self-care (pretending to cook, brushing teeth) rather than affective or attention-getting actions such as laughing, sighing, shouting, or pounding (Kuczynski, Zahn-Waxler, & Radke-Yarrow, 1987). Thus, observational learning, along with the parent's direct application of reinforcers and punishments, undoubtedly plays a powerful role in the socialization of young children.

Knowing how to address a revered elder, care for a flock of sheep, read and solve complex mathematics problems, and navigate from one location to another within the city, over mountainous terrain, or between widely dispersed islands are just a few of the many complex skills children acquire that involve various facets of learning. Because learning is exhibited within the confines of a rich context of additional social and cognitive processes, its importance will continue to be evident in our discussion of many other aspects of development. Our examination of some of these other processes begins with a consideration of the sensory and perceptual abilities that help to make learning possible.

SENSORY AND PERCEPTUAL CAPACITIES

Although habituation, classical and operant conditioning, and observational learning contribute to mastering new behaviors and enriching each individual's skills and competencies, these forms of learning are influenced and driven by still other basic processes, including sensation and perception. Tanya's queries about whether Chad could see or hear as she first held her son are the kinds of questions many parents pose to their newborns even as they seem to provide their own answers by vocaliz-

KEY THEME
Interaction Among Domains

deferred imitation   Ability to imitate a model's behavior hours, days, and even weeks after observation.

ing, making funny facial expressions, touching, caressing, and rocking the baby. Still, the uncertainty remains: what do infants sense and perceive?

More than a century ago, William James (1890) theorized that for the newborn the world must consist of a "big blooming buzzing confusion." This view was built on the notion that the infant has to learn the pattern of features associated with a particular perceptual stimulus. Only by repeated experiences associated with distinct sensations could the infant come to appreciate the human face, for example, or a particular sequence of sounds as an organized, perceptually important event.

Is this theory valid today? Some researchers think not. James and Eleanor Gibson and many of their students have offered a strikingly different view of the early perceptual capacities of infants (Pick, 1992). For them, babies come into the world well equipped to respond to important aspects of stimuli to which they are exposed. They already have organized perceptual systems that permit them to adaptively react to sensory stimulation. Of course, experience affords ever greater opportunity to learn which properties of sensory events are stable and important and which can be ignored.

To clarify these different positions, we often distinguish between **sensation,** the registration of a basic unit of information such as a visual feature or an aspect of sound by a sensory receptor or the brain, and **perception,** the process of organizing and interpreting sensations. Perception occurs when the infant recognizes his mother's face by sight or interprets a sequence of sounds as a familiar lullaby. Sensations are the building blocks; perception is the order and meaning imposed on those basic elements.

Today most developmental psychologists think the sensory world of the neonate is less chaotic and more organized than James suggested. As we consider evidence supporting this view, we can make two broad observations about research on sensory and perceptual development. First, vision has been studied far more thoroughly than any other sensory domain. To some extent, this bias reflects the widespread belief that sight provides the major source of information for humans. Visual development, however, has also been easier to study than development of hearing, smell, and other senses. Second, knowledge of sensory and perceptual development in newborns and young infants has expanded far more rapidly than knowledge of their development in older infants and children (Aslin & Smith, 1988). The disparity reflects the efforts of researchers to uncover the earliest appearance of sensory and perceptual capacities and the finding that many important changes in these domains occur in the first few months after birth.

Methods of Measuring Infant Sensory and Perceptual Capacities

How can we possibly know what babies see, hear, or smell when they are unable to tell us about it in words? Researchers have devised ingenious techniques, some quite simple, to help answer this question. Most techniques are based on measures of **attention,** that is, alertness or arousal focused on a specific aspect of the environment. For example, when infants display attentional differences, looking longer at one thing than at another, they are communicating that they can perceive differences between them. A closer look at several types of studies will illustrate this point.

Preferential Behaviors In 1958 Robert Fantz placed babies on their backs in an enclosed, criblike chamber. Through a peephole, he and his colleagues observed how long the babies gazed at different visual stimuli inserted in the top of the brightly illuminated chamber. Observers were able to determine where the infants were looking because the reflection of the stimulus could be seen on the *cornea,* the outer surface of the babies' eyes, as they looked at the objects. Using this method, Fantz (1961) found that infants attended to some things longer than others. For example, babies one to six months old looked at disks decorated with bull's eyes, stripes, newsprint, or facelike figures far longer than solid-colored circles (see Figure 6.3).

KEY THEME
Nature/Nurture

sensation Basic information in the external world that is processed by the sensory receptors.

perception Process of organizing and interpreting sensory information.

attention State of alertness or arousal that allows the individual to focus on a selected aspect of the environment.

FIGURE 6.3

Preferential Looking

When Robert Fantz showed infants two to three months of age the different visual stimuli shown here, he found that the babies preferred to look at those that illustrated some pattern (for example, a facelike figure, newsprint, or a bull's eye) over those that consisted of a single solid color. This example of the preferential looking procedure was an important early demonstration that infants have the capacity to discriminate different visual stimuli. Note that the strongest preference was exhibited for the facelike stimulus.

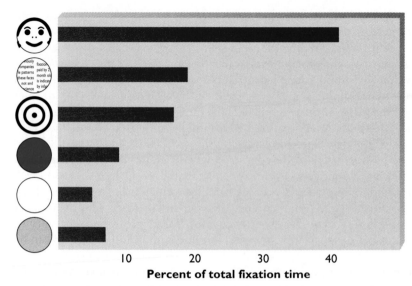

Percent of total fixation time

Source: Adapted from Fantz, 1961.

The simple methodology encouraged many researchers to study the visual capacities of infants by observing their *preferential looking,* the tendency to look at some things more than others. The procedure has some limitations, however. What can we conclude, for example, when the infant looks at both members of a pair of stimuli for the same amount of time? Is the infant unable to discriminate the two, or does she prefer to look at one just as much as the other? Nor can we be certain what features the baby is processing when gazing at a stimulus.

Despite the limitations, babies often show preferences in what they attend to, and this simple procedure has proven enormously useful in assessing their visual capacities. In fact, by using special photographic techniques involving infrared lights and appropriate film, researchers can pinpoint specific regions and aspects of a figure at which the baby looks and how she or he visually inspects a stimulus. Such procedures have revealed, for example, which features of a human face infants are most likely to attend, as Figure 6.4 shows.

FIGURE 6.4

Visual Scanning

Using specialized techniques, researchers can often pinpoint the specific features in a visual stimulus at which infants are looking. Here the typical patterns of scanning these facelike stimuli by a one- and two-month-old have been recorded. Note how the younger infant's gaze tends to be directed to the outer or external regions of the facial stimulus, that is, hair and chin. The older infant's gaze is more frequently directed to inner features such as the eyes and mouth.

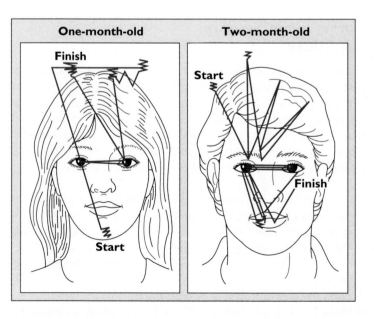

Source: Adapted from Salapatek, 1975.

Habituation   In another technique that capitalizes on the infant's tendency to prefer looking at some things more than others, babies are shown the same stimulus for relatively lengthy periods or in a series of trials. *Habituation* of attention, the simple form of learning described earlier, is the typical outcome. A change in the stimulus, however, may elicit *recovery from habituation*, or, if the habituated stimulus is paired with one that is dissimilar, the infant may show a preference for the new one, both indicators that the child has perceived a difference.

To illustrate the use of a habituation procedure, consider the work of Janet Frick and John Colombo (1996). They were interested in whether infants perceived the whole of a figure as being the same when some of its features were removed. They were also interested in whether individual differences in this ability may already exist by four months of age. To answer these questions, they presented infants with an array of either concentric squares or diamonds such as those shown in Figure 6.5. Infants were shown either the square or the diamond array until they had accumulated a predetermined amount of time looking at it or until they no longer paid much attention to it. Then the infants were presented with the figure displayed in two orientations, one the same as originally viewed during the habituation period and the other rotated forty-five degrees, but this time with the corners missing. Would the infants continue to recognize the figure even with the corners missing? If they did, they could be expected to look longer at the figure whose orientation had changed, since it would be more novel than the stimulus whose orientation had not

| FIGURE 6.5 | Perceiving the Whole Figure |

Using a habituation procedure, Janet Frick and John Colombo showed that some infants as young as four months recognize the whole of a figure even when some segments are missing. Infants were habituated to the square or diamond-shaped array. They were then shown the array in the same orientation (familiar) and rotated 45° (novel) on test trials, but with the corners missing. Only infants who attended to the visual information with brief glances during the familiarization period demonstrated a preference for the stimulus whose orientation had changed when the corners were missing, presumably because they were able to process the information fairly rapidly. Other infants, whose attention to the figure during the familiarization period occurred in relatively prolonged gazes, showed no preference for the novel orientation when the corners were no longer present, perhaps because they could not process the information in the visual array as rapidly. These findings illustrate the use of a habituation procedure to test infant perceptual capacities and indicate that individual differences in processing information may already have important consequences for what four-month-olds perceive.

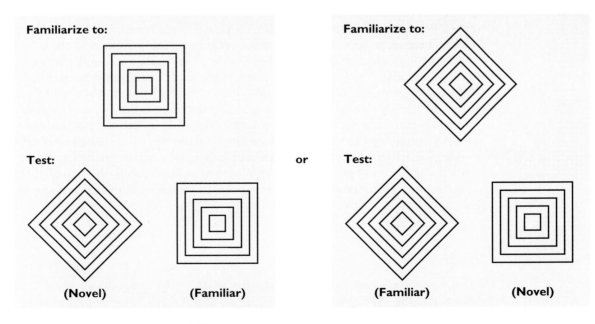

Source: Adapted from Frick & Colombo, 1996.

changed and because previous research had shown that infants could recognize a change in the orientations of figures when the corners were not removed (Cornell, 1975; Schwartz & Day, 1979).

However, Frick and Colombo found that when corners were deleted, only some infants looked longer at the stimulus in its novel orientation, whereas others did not. Why did these two groups of infants differ? The answer may be related to their speed of processing the visual information. Babies who appeared to recognize the change in the orientation of the figure, that is looked longer at the figure in its novel orientation even when the corners were missing, had attended to the figure during the habituation phase in relatively brief attentional bursts; they seemed to process the figure in short, rapid glances to it. However, infants who did not prefer the novel orientation of the figure on test trials attended to the stimulus during the habituation phase in one or two prolonged gazes, perhaps because it took them longer to process the information in the visual array. These two groups of infants showed a similar pattern of attending—either brief, frequent looks or longer, prolonged gazes—when viewing other visual arrays, suggesting a stable individual difference in attention. The perception of the array in terms of its more global orientation (as a diamond or a square) seemed to depend on this individual difference in processing the information. As we will see in Chapter 10 when we discuss intellectual development, individual differences in habituation or speed of processing information seem to predict later cognitive abilities as well.

Habituation and recovery from habituation can be used to assess other sensory abilities in infants. For example, babies often turn their heads away from unpleasant odors. Yet just as adults frequently report that they no longer notice a lingering unpleasant smell, infants also habituate to repeated presentations of the same odor. However, a baby who starts turning his head away again when a slightly different odor is presented demonstrates that he can distinguish the old and new smells.

Operant Conditioning   More complex forms of learning, such as operant conditioning, can be used to further test an infant's ability to discriminate sensory cues. To receive milk and other tangible rewards such as interesting visual and auditory patterns, babies will learn to suck faster or slower, turn their heads, look, and perform other behaviors that indicate discrimination of sensory stimuli.

Operant conditioning procedures figure prominently in research on auditory perception. One procedure popularized by Peter Eimas and his colleagues (1971) has proven especially informative. Babies are given a special nipple designed to record their rate of sucking. A baby who sucks energetically or at a rapid rate may be rewarded by hearing some pleasant sound, for example, the consonant-vowel pairing *pa*. After hearing *pa* repeatedly, the rate of sucking typically declines as the infant habituates to the stimulus. What will the baby do when a different sound, such as *ba*, is introduced? Infants as young as one month begin to suck at a high rate again in order to keep hearing *ba*. They can discriminate the new consonant-vowel pair from *pa*; they are already able to distinguish some important sounds that occur in language.

In addition to behavioral methods—preferential looking, habituation, and operant conditioning—procedures using physiological responses such as heart rate or the neurological activity of the brain and even of individual neurons can be recorded to clarify the sensory and perceptual abilities of infants. Fortunately, the results of the various methods often complement one another in providing information about infant sensory and perceptual capacities.

Vision

Because newborns have limited motor skills, we are often tempted to assume their sensory systems—their eyes, ears, noses, mouths, and skin—must be passive receptors awaiting stimulation. But Eleanor J. Gibson and James J. Gibson convincingly argue that perceiving is an active "process of *obtaining* information about the world"

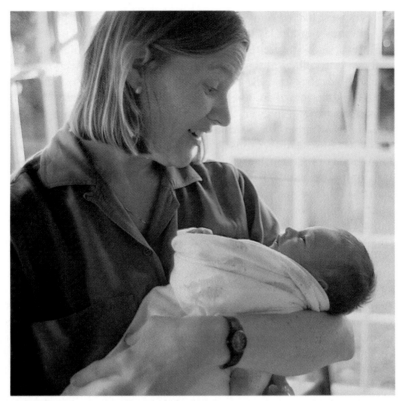

This newborn must perform a variety of visuomotor responses including focusing her eyes on the features of her mother's face if she is to make sense out of this new source of information. Visuomotor skills rapidly improve during the first few months of life, one factor that permits a baby to soon recognize her caregiver's face.

(J. J. Gibson, 1966). "We don't simply see, we look" (E. J. Gibson, 1988, p. 5). The Gibsons' emphasis on the active nature of vision applies to all sensory domains at every developmental level; even neonates mobilize sensory receptors to respond to stimulation flowing from their bustling environment.

Visuomotor Skills   The eye includes a lens designed to refract, or bend, light. As a result, visual images are focused onto the *retina,* the part of the back of the eye that houses the sensory receptors for light. The lens of the human eye is variable; small, involuntary muscles change its shape so that images of objects viewed at different distances are brought into focus, a process called **visual accommodation**. When the lens works effectively, the eye can see things clearly.

Newborns display limited visual accommodation, but the process improves rapidly to nearly adultlike levels by about three months of age (Aslin, 1987a). Poorer accommodative ability, along with the relatively small size of the eye, tends to cause images to be projected behind rather than on the retina in very young infants (Banks, 1980). In addition, the *pupillary reflex,* which controls the amount of light entering the eye, is sluggish during the first few months after birth, further reducing the ability to focus (Aslin, 1987a). As a result, infants are unable to see small details of stimuli. However, they discriminate best those patterns and objects about eight to twenty inches away, the typical distance of a caregiver's face when holding or feeding the baby.

Eye movements are another essential part of looking. **Saccades,** rapid shifts or movements of the eye to inspect an object or to look at something in the periphery of the visual field, are produced within hours of birth (Lewis, Maurer, & Kay, 1978). At first, the saccades are initiated slowly and cover only small distances; neonates must launch a sequence of them to "catch up" to a peripheral target (Aslin, 1993). Saccades typically become more accurate, however, during the first three to four months and continue to improve in accuracy throughout childhood (Fioravanti et al., 1995).

Humans exhibit another pattern of eye movements, **smooth visual pursuit,** which consists of maintaining fixation on a slowly moving target almost as though

visual accommodation
Visuomotor process by which small involuntary muscles change the shape of the lens of the eye so that images of objects seen at different distances are brought into focus on the retina.

saccade   Rapid eye movement to inspect an object or view a stimulus in the periphery of the visual field.

smooth visual pursuit   Consistent, unbroken tracking by the eyes that serves to maintain focus on a moving visual target.

the eyes were locked onto it. Newborns display only brief periods of smooth pursuit (Kremenitzer et al., 1979), and its execution continues to improve through eight months of age (Shupert & Fuchs, 1988). Nevertheless, infants readily turn their eyes and heads to follow, and prefer looking at, a moving object over a static visual array (Nelson & Horowitz, 1987).

In looking toward an object, both eyes normally move together in the same direction. Sometimes, however, the eyes must rotate in opposite directions, turning toward each other as, for example, when a person tries to see a fly that has landed on his or her nose. This response, called **vergence,** occurs when fixations shift between far and near objects; otherwise, we would see double images. Vergence occurs irregularly in infants younger than two months, especially when objects are not static and move to different depths (Hainline & Riddell, 1995; Thorn et al., 1994). For example, young babies' eyes may fail to rotate far enough toward each other to converge on a visual target. The development of some mechanisms for perceiving depth depend on this coordination. If vergence is not readily demonstrated during the first few years of life, a condition called "lazy eye" or *amblyopia* may develop, and the child may begin to suffer a permanent loss in depth perception (Banks, Aslin, & Letson, 1975).

Acuity and Color Perception   How well are young infants able to see despite their immature visuomotor skills? The question concerns **visual acuity,** the ability to discriminate *contours,* that is, transitions in dark-light shading that signal borders and edges of elements in a visual array.

One common test of visual acuity, the *Snellen test,* is based on identifying letters or other symbols on a chart twenty feet away. Babies, of course, cannot name letters, so other procedures are used to test their visual acuity. Several methods have been devised, but one that has proven reasonably good relies on preferential looking. As an array of, say, black and white stripes appears more frequently (the stripes become narrower), the pattern becomes more difficult to see, and the stimulus eventually appears gray. Infants unable to detect the stripes quickly lose interest, preferring to attend instead to a pattern they can still detect. By pairing stimuli with different frequencies of stripes and observing preferential looking, researchers can gauge the visual acuity of infants.

Two key findings emerge from the many investigations of visual acuity in infants. First, even newborns detect contours, although their acuity is much poorer than that of children or adults. In fact, under some conditions acuity is estimated to improve more than forty-five-fold from birth to adulthood. Second, acuity improves rapidly during the first six months after birth and continues to improve at a slower rate for several years thereafter (Adoh & Woodhouse, 1994). The improvement, especially during early infancy, is owed to enhanced visuomotor skills and neural pathways for vision, changes in the shape and physical characteristics of the eye, and, especially, greater efficiency in the functioning of visual receptors in the retina (Banks & Shannon, 1993).

Can babies also see colors? Once again the answer is yes, at least after a few months of age. The retina contains two major types of receptor cells: *rods,* which are sensitive only to the intensity of light (functioning already at birth), and *cones,* which are sensitive to the different wavelengths of light. The cones contribute to color perception. Although very young infants may not see a full range of hues, color vision for several hues is possible by three months and perhaps even earlier for some colors, such as red (Adams, Courage, & Mercer, 1994).

In summary, basic visuomotor skills and sensory capacities are available to infants. Very early on, babies look at and see a richly patterned and probably colorful array of events. Their vision is not as keen as it soon will become, but even newborns are not blind. At first vision is limited to the more glaring and distinctive features, but these are more than adequate for perception, that is, for interpreting and giving meaning to the visual environment that is an integral part of the infant's new sensory world.

vergence   Ability of the eyes to rotate in opposite directions to fixate on objects at different distances; improves rapidly during first few months after birth.

visual acuity   Ability to make fine discriminations among elements in a visual array by detecting contours, transitions in light patterns that signal borders and edges.

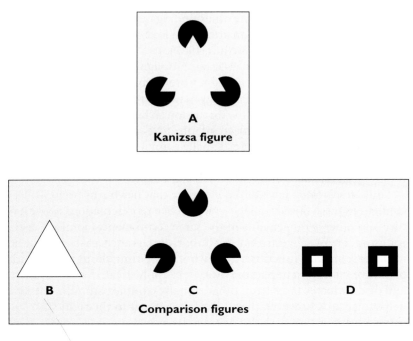

Kanizsa figure

B

Comparison figures

C

D

Source: Adapted from Treiber & Wilcox, 1980.

FIGURE 6.6

Infants' Subjective Perception of Form

Infants as well as adults perceive the subjective triangular figure (A) even though no contour is present to define it. After becoming habituated to the Kanizsa figure, babies are shown other figures, including a standard triangle formed by visible contours (B), the indented circular figures rotated to eliminate the subjective triangle (C), or a completely different array of stimuli (D). Infants show the least recovery from habituation to the traditional triangle (B), suggesting that they perceived the triangular shape produced by the Kanizsa figure.

KEY THEME
Nature/Nurture

KEY THEME
Child's Active Role

Perception of Pattern and Form   Few questions fascinate psychologists more than when and how infants recognize patterns and other configurations of visual arrays. Are babies born with the ability to perceive wholes and units? Some researchers think so. Others have argued the more traditional view, that this capacity is acquired only through extensive visual experience; infants become aware of or construct perceptions of integrated, holistic, and meaningful visual figures through repeated opportunities to process contours, angles, shading, and other primary sensory features.

As we have already learned, neonates detect contours of stimuli as well as their motions (Haith, 1980; Karmel & Maisel, 1975). At two to three months of age, they begin to perceive much more. Now infants inspect and analyze the components of complex stimuli, scanning a greater variety of their features (Bronson, 1994). A good example of this developmental change is exhibited by the **externality effect:** infants younger than about two months typically focus on a few of the outer contours of a complex stimulus and explore the internal features less systematically. Older infants tend to scan its internal features as well (Maurer, 1983; Salapatek, 1975). We saw an illustration of the externality effect in the discussion of preferential looking. Babies younger than two months tend to fixate on external contours of the face such as hair or the chin line; older infants much more frequently inspect internal features such as the eyes or mouth. Very young infants do attend to the smaller internal elements when these show movement or are made brighter, but their attention is usually affected by the presence of an outer contour (Bushnell, Gerry, & Burt, 1983). On the other hand, older infants carry out a much more deliberate, organized visual search, exploring the entire pattern or array (Bronson, 1994).

Other experiments provide further evidence that babies perceive entire forms and patterns at least within a few months after birth. One especially convincing illustration involves subjective, or gradient-free, contours. Look at the Kanizsa figure shown in Figure 6.6. You should see a highly visible white triangle standing above three black, disklike figures at each of its corners. But closer inspection will reveal that the brain subjectively assumes the triangular form; no contour is present to mark its edges. Infants, perhaps when as young as one or two months and certainly by three to four months, perceive the subjective figures too, a powerful demonstration that perception of a triangular array, not of isolated features, is taking place (Ghim, 1990;

externality effect   Tendency for infants younger than two months to focus on the external features of a complex stimulus and explore the internal features less systematically.

Treiber & Wilcox, 1980). Many other findings confirm that attention to the configuration of a pattern begins soon after birth and continues to improve throughout infancy (Dodwell, Humphrey, & Muir, 1987).

Some perceptual patterns are especially significant to the infant. Recall the findings shown in Figure 6.3, that babies prefer looking at facelike stimuli over some other kinds of visual patterns. Do even newborns recognize faces, perhaps the faces of their caregivers? Based on the discussion so far, it should not be surprising to learn that by about two months of age infants do assign great importance to the face, attending to it more than to other, equally complex arrays. But an even earlier, perhaps innate preference also makes evolutionary sense, because faces are a vital source of information for social and emotional relationships.

Some researchers have found evidence that newborns prefer, at least for moving configurations, a facelike image—two eyelike representations above a mouthlike feature—to other arrangements of the same components (Johnson et al., 1991). Mark Johnson (1992) suggests that this inborn preference arises from a fairly primitive visual system that functions in newborns. Within about two months of age, this primitive system is supplanted by a more sophisticated visual system that explores and discriminates faces from other, equally complex stimuli. The primitive system helps to ensure, however, that the infant gets off to the right start by preferring an extremely important perceptual array: the face.

When does a baby discriminate his or her mother's face from that of another person's? Perhaps within days after birth (Bushnell, Sai, & Mullen, 1989). However, as you might guess, this recognition is based on outer elements, such as hairline or head contours, rather than on a full appreciation of a mother's facial features (Pascalis et al., 1995). The conclusion is that infants are attracted to and identify significant aspects of the human face early in their development and make rapid strides in perceiving and recognizing this important social stimulus.

Perception of Objects   The visual environment is really made up of objects and their surfaces. How does a baby perceive a rattle apart from the table on which it lies or the family dog as distinct from the floor on which it sits? James J. Gibson (1979) argued that the dynamic flow of visual information created by movement of objects or of a person's eyes, head, or body, called **kinetic cues,** provides infants with abundant information for distinguishing one object from another.

A series of experiments carried out by Philip Kellman, Elizabeth Spelke, and their colleagues supports Gibson's position regarding the importance of kinematic information for perceiving objects, even in infants as young as three months of age (Kellman, 1993, 1996; Kellman & Spelke, 1983). Babies viewed a rod, the midsection of which was hidden by a rectangular block; only the ends of the rod were visible (see Figure 6.7). How do infants interpret this perceptual array? Do they respond as though there were a single complete rod located behind the block or as though there were two short rods protruding above and below the block with the space in between covered by the block? To find out, the babies were habituated to the rod and block.

As Figure 6.7 shows, in some conditions the rod and block were moved in various ways during habituation. The results revealed that infants interpreted the rod as complete, not broken, as long as its two protruding ends appeared to move together and independently of the block during habituation trials, even if the visible ends were of quite different shapes. However, if neither the rod nor the block moved, rod and block shifted together in the same direction, or only the occluding block moved during habituation trials, the infants did not "fill in" the unseen portion of the rod; they treated the stimulus as two short rods separated by an intervening space.

Is the perception of a coherent object innate? Might even newborns interpret the rod as being complete in such situations? Alan Slater and his colleagues think the answer is no (Slater et al., 1996). Under movement conditions in which older infants treated the separated segments as novel, newborns treated the complete rod as novel. Newborns did not fill in or make perceptual inferences about the occluded segment of the stimulus.

kinetic cue   Perceptual information provided by movement of eyes, head, or body or of objects in the environment; important source of information for depth perception, even for infants.

| FIGURE 6.7 | Inference of Unity and Coherence |

Under some conditions, four-month-olds respond as if they perceived an occluded rod as a single complete figure. Infants are habituated to one of the seven familiarization displays shown here and are then presented with the test displays. After viewing conditions A, B, and C, infants respond to the complete rod in the test display as novel, indicating they perceived the rod in A, B, and C as being broken. When shown conditions D, E, F, or G, however, infants appear to perceive the rod as a connected whole, showing less attention to the complete rod than to the broken rod in the test display. The results indicate that young infants are able to infer unity and coherence for objects. Recent research suggests newborns do not make these perceptual inferences.

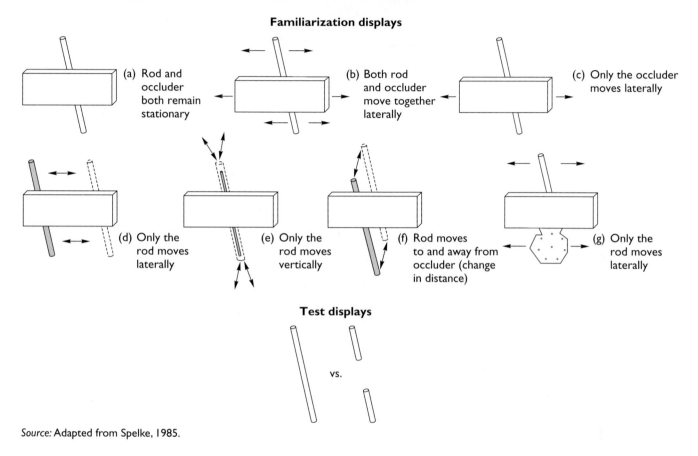

Familiarization displays

(a) Rod and occluder both remain stationary

(b) Both rod and occluder move together laterally

(c) Only the occluder moves laterally

(d) Only the rod moves laterally

(e) Only the rod moves vertically

(f) Rod moves to and away from occluder (change in distance)

(g) Only the rod moves laterally

Test displays

vs.

Source: Adapted from Spelke, 1985.

The importance of kinetic cues, and motion in general, to early infant perceptual development is demonstrated in yet another phenomenon known as *biological motion*. Bennett Bertenthal and his colleagues (Bertenthal, 1993; Proffitt & Bertenthal, 1990) carried out a series of studies in which infants were shown lights moving as though attached to the head and major joints of a person walking. Adults who observe the pattern readily interpret the light movement as though it were someone walking. In other conditions, the pattern of lights was inverted or an equivalent amount of motion was shown, but the lights were scrambled so that the motion did not simulate the appearance of a person walking. Using attentional and habituation measures, these experiments demonstrated that by the time infants have reached three to five months of age, the "walker" has taken on special meaning to them compared to other patterns of light motion. For Bertenthal and his associates, these and other, similar kinds of findings indicate that infants come equipped with perceptual processes and constraints that readily permit them to extract and organize kinetic information into meaningful patterns.

Depth Perception In addition to seeing to the left and right and above and below, we note the depth or distance of objects. Yet visual images are recorded on the retina in two dimensions. When and how do we acquire the ability to perceive depth? One

FIGURE 6.8

The Visual Cliff

In the visual cliff, a setting used to test depth perception, a baby is placed on a plank, and a caregiver attempts to coax the child to cross to either side. Infants are much less likely to crawl on the glass support when the textured surface appears far below them than when it appears immediately beneath the glass.

source of information is *binocular vision.* Sensory information differs slightly for each eye. The ability to fuse the two distinct images to perceive a single object is called **stereopsis,** a capacity that improves markedly during the first four months after birth. Stereopsis provides clues to depth as effectively for six-month-olds as for adults (Fox et al., 1980; Held, Birch, & Gwiazda, 1980).

Still other sources of information about depth and distance are available to infants. A classic series of studies involving the **visual cliff** suggests that kinetic cues are among them. The visual cliff consists of a large sheet of glass bisected by a relatively narrow plank. A patterned surface is placed immediately under the glass on one side, but much farther below it on the other (see Figure 6.8). Richard Walk (1968) found that an infant placed on the plank and old enough to crawl can usually be coaxed to cross the shallow side but is much less likely to crawl over the deep side. In one study, Walk put a patch on one eye of each young subject to eliminate binocular cues to depth. Infants were still far more reluctant to crawl over the deep side, perhaps because the cues provided by their own heads and body movements signaled depth.

Even babies too young to crawl can identify the shallow and deep sides of the visual cliff. When placed face down on the glass surface, two-to-three-month-olds respond differently to the two sides of the cliff; they become quieter, are less fussy, and show a greater decrease in heart rate on the deep side than on the shallow side (Campos, Langer, & Krowitz, 1970). Such reactions suggest that infants have not yet associated anxiety or fear with depth and find the visual information provided by the deep side more interesting than the shallow side. In fact, depth cues may already influence attention at birth because newborns prefer looking at three-dimensional objects to looking at two-dimensional figures (Slater, Rose, & Morison, 1984).

stereopsis   Ability to perceive a single image of an object even though perceptual input is binocular and differs slightly for each eye; significant source of cues for depth perception.

visual cliff   Experimental apparatus used to test depth perception in which the surface on one side of a glass-covered table is made to appear far below the surface on the other side.

Sudden expansion or contraction of an image provides yet another kind of cue to an object's location. Infants older than three weeks produce avoidancelike behaviors, such as blinking and backward head movements, in reaction to rapidly expanding shadows that suggest an impending collision. However, they do not respond this way to rapidly shrinking shadows if the expansion suggests that the object will miss or if it suggests a three-dimensional space or opening such as a doorway (Ball & Tronick, 1971; Náñez & Yonas, 1994). Younger infants fail to exhibit these different reactions, either because they have not learned what the visual cues might mean or because they are too immature to respond to them.

Finally, other cues, collectively described as *pictorial* because they can be perceived in photos or two-dimensional arrays, signal depth. Pictorial cues include relative size (near objects appear larger), shadows, interposition of surfaces (one surface hides another), and linear perspective (lines converging toward a horizon). Infants begin to use many of the cues to identify nearer configurations by about five to seven months of age (Granrud et al., 1984; Yonas & Owsley, 1987). Thus, infants respond very early on to an abundant array of cues signaling depth and the three-dimensionality of objects.

In summary, when does the infant begin to see patterns, objects, and depth? The answer is at least within the first two to four months (Ghim & Eimas, 1988), as indicated in the Chronology of visual abilities summarized for infancy on page 200. Newborns are attracted to and detect features of their visual environment. Their capacity to process larger, more organized, and meaningful patterns emerges soon thereafter as visuomotor processes mature and are modified by experience. Based on infants' early ability to construct and recognize coherent, integrated perceptual arrays, researchers conclude that the infant's visual world is far less of a "blooming buzzing confusion" than William James suspected.

Audition

Just as opinion once held that newborns are blind, so did it assert that newborns are deaf (Spears & Hohle, 1967). However, the fetus is listening well before birth. Sound affects not only brain wave patterns and the heart rate of the fetus during its last few weeks in utero (Aslin, 1987b) but also activity level as revealed by ultrasound scans (Kisilevsky & Muir, 1991). In fact, responses to low-frequency sounds, the kind that are produced in human speech, are evident in the fetus as early as nineteen weeks gestational age. Sensitivity to a wide range of sounds at lower and lower intensities increases dramatically during the remainder of the prenatal period (Hepper & Shahidullah, 1994).

Persuasive evidence that fetuses hear also comes from several studies indicating that newborns prefer to listen to the sounds they heard before birth. Anthony De-Casper and Melanie Spence (1986) asked expectant women to read aloud a passage from Dr. Seuss's *The Cat in the Hat*. Women read the passage twice a day during the last six weeks of pregnancy; their fetuses were exposed to the story for a total of about three-and-a-half hours before birth. Two or three days after birth, the babies listened to either the same passage or a new story while outfitted with a special pacifier that recorded rate of sucking. Depending on rate of sucking, the recording of the story would turn on or off. When newborns heard *The Cat in the Hat,* they modified their rate of sucking to listen to it but did not do so for the new story. Some kind of learning about the Dr. Seuss story apparently took place prenatally.

What precisely does the fetus hear, and what is it learning from these exposures? We are not really sure. As newborns, infants prefer to listen to their mothers' voice rather than the voice of a stranger (DeCasper & Fifer, 1980), so they have already discovered something about the characteristics of their mothers' speech. They seem to be especially responsive to lower-frequency sounds, demonstrating a clear preference for the mother's voice over an unfamiliar voice when it contains such acoustic cues (Spence & Freeman, 1996). In contrast, newborns do not discriminate whispers produced by their mothers from whispers produced by an unfamiliar voice. However,

KEY THEME
Nature/Nurture

CHRONOLOGY
Visual Development

Newborn

Newborn

- Shows minimal accommodation; limited, sluggish saccades; incomplete vergence.
- Detects contours, but acuity and contrast sensitivity remain relatively poor.
- Prefers attending to highly visible contours, angles, features in motion, and three-dimensional over two-dimensional stimuli.
- Exhibits externality effect.

1–3 Months

- Shows accommodation; near normal adultlike vergence.
- Smooth visual pursuit emerges.
- Discriminates cues to depth.
- Responds to rapidly expanding visual images.
- Explores internal as well as external features of stimuli.
- Recognizes shape of simple figures and more detailed patterns and objects.
- Prefers attending to increasingly complex patterns, including those with facelike organization.
- Detects basic colors.

4–8 Months

- Exhibits stereopsis.
- Saccadic eye movements become larger more rapid, and accurate.
- Shows adultlike smooth visual pursuit.
- Acuity and contrast sensitivity approach normal.
- Displays fear of depth on visual cliff.
- Discriminates many pictorial (two-dimensional) cues to depth.
- Distinguishes symmetrical from asymmetrical patterns.
- Processes "subjective" contours.
- Perceives occluded objects as wholes.
- Becomes responsive to "biological motion."

Newborn
1 Yr.
2 Yrs.
3 Yrs.
4 Yrs.
5 Yrs.
6 Yrs.
7 Yrs.
8 Yrs.
9 Yrs.
10 Yrs.
11 Yrs.
12 Yrs.
13 Yrs.
14 Yrs.
15 Yrs.
16 Yrs.
17 Yrs.
18 Yrs.

Newborn
1 Mo.
2 Mos.
3 Mos.
4 Mos.
5 Mos.
6 Mos.
7 Mos.
8 Mos.
9 Mos.
10 Mos.
11 Mos.
12 Mos.
13 Mos.
14 Mos.
15 Mos.
16 Mos.
17 Mos.
18 Mos.

This chart describes the sequence of visual development in infancy based on the findings of research. Children often show individual differences in the exact ages at which they display the various developmental achievements outlined here.

the fetus has learned more about sound than just the mother's voice. After expectant women in France repeatedly recited a rhyme from the thirty-third to thirty-seventh week of their gestation period, changes in fetal heart rate in response to the rhyme revealed that the fetus differentiated that rhyme from another, novel rhyme even when recited by someone else (DeCasper et al., 1994).

The fetus may hear a great deal of things from its auditory environment. The findings have led to the publicizing of "sensory curricula" for the fetus, such as patterned sounds or complex auditory or vibroacoustic events (for example, heartbeat or drumbeat sounds), delivered to the fetus through a belt worn by the expectant woman. Or perhaps caregivers play certain kinds of music or engage in other repetitious exercises during pregnancy in an effort to stimulate the unborn's auditory receptors and nervous system. But with such practices have come concerns that some sounds may be so intense that they actually damage delicate sensory organs that are just beginning to function.

Hearing Little research exists on exactly how well babies hear in the first few months after birth. Nevertheless, six-month-olds detect high-frequency sounds nearly as well as preschoolers, who in turn are able to hear such sounds better than adults (Schneider et al., 1986). Furthermore, by this age babies are able to distinguish two different high-frequency sounds much as adults do (Olsho, 1984). Although the ability to detect low-frequency sounds appears earliest prenatally and markedly improves during the first two years after birth, it probably reaches its peak somewhere around ten years of age (Trehub et al., 1988).

Can infants determine the direction and distance from which a sound is coming? Shortly after birth babies display **sound localization,** the ability to locate a sound in space, by turning their heads or eyes in the direction of the sound. This early ability, which may be reflexive, declines during the first two months and then reemerges at about four months of age in the form of a more deliberate search for sound (Field et al., 1980). Locating the precise position from which a sound originates markedly improves throughout infancy and into early childhood (Ashmead, Clifton, & Perris, 1987; Morrongiello, 1988; Morrongiello, Fenwick, & Chance, 1990). By six to eight months of age, infants also begin to appreciate the distance from which a sound emanates. At this age, babies exposed to a sound in the dark produced by an object beyond their reach are less likely to attempt to retrieve the object than an object producing a sound within their reach (Clifton, Perris, & Bullinger, 1991).

Perception of Sound Patterns Are babies able to perceive patterns in sound? Can they distinguish music from noise? Might they even have a preference for some kinds of music? Two- and three-month-olds do recognize changes in intervals between brief bursts of sound (Demany, McKenzie, & Vurpillot, 1977). Between six months and a year of age, they also begin to distinguish more complex rhythms and patterns of sounds (Clarkson, 1996; Morrongiello, 1984). For example, at eight months of age babies recognize changes in short (six-note) melodies, including a transposition in key and the shift of a single note in a sequence to either a higher or a lower frequency (Trehub, Bull, & Thorpe, 1984; Trehub, Thorpe, & Morrongiello, 1985). In fact, four-and-a-half- to six-month-olds can boast of some budding capacities as music critics! Carol Krumhansl and Peter Jusczyk (1990) chose short passages of Mozart minuets and introduced brief pauses at locations judged by adults to be either natural or awkward places for a musical phrase to end. Babies preferred looking at a loudspeaker that played only natural versions to those that played unnatural versions of the Mozart selections. Babies are indeed sensitive to rhythmic and melodic contour (Trehub, 1987), and the ability to detect satisfying musical phrasings may be important not only for appreciating music but also for the phrasing and sound rhythms that commonly underlie speech.

Speech Research on infants' hearing abilities has often been conducted to answer one question: how soon do babies perceive human speech? The ability to interpret speech sounds as meaningful elements of language probably begins in the second six

sound localization Ability to determine a sound's point of origin.

months of life. That developmental story is discussed in Chapter 7. However, can even younger infants discriminate speech sounds?

The smallest unit of sound that affects the meaning of a word, called a **phoneme,** consist of bursts of acoustic energy produced at several different frequencies. Phonemes are surprisingly complicated stimuli, and a difference of less than one-fiftieth of a second in the onset or transition of a frequency of sound is enough for adults to discriminate the distinctive phonemes /p/, /b/, and /t/ in the sounds *pa, ba,* and *ta.* (Linguists use slashes to identify the phonemes of a language.) Are infants able to hear the differences? Indeed they are. In fact, before six months of age babies distinguish all the important sounds in any of the hundreds of languages spoken around the world (Werker & Desjardins, 1995).

How are infants able to detect the subtle differences? Two answers with very different implications for language development have been proposed. One possibility is that babies are born with a "speech module," an innate capacity to detect and process the subtle and complicated sounds that make up human language (Fodor, 1983). The complexity of language acquisition, according to this view, requires a specialized ability because the cognitive skills of infants and young children are so limited. Another view is that phoneme discrimination hinges on general auditory capacities, capacities not limited to processing speech sounds or even necessarily unique to humans but capacities that infants are able to exploit quite early in development.

What evidence exists for either of these positions? Two research findings lend support to the view that speech perception involves special language-oriented mechanisms. The first comes from the extremely complex relationship between the acoustic properties of phonemes and their perception. For example, the /b/ phoneme in the words *beak* and *book* are quite different acoustically, although people treat the sounds as equivalent. Researchers argue that the absence of a simple set of rules for signaling the phoneme /b/ in the two words makes the presence of a special mechanism for speech perception highly likely (Kuhl, 1987).

A second finding is based on **categorical perception,** the classification of sounds as the same even when they differ on some continuous physical dimension, except when on opposite sides of a critical juncture. For example, the English consonants /b/ and /p/ in the sounds *ba* and *pa* differ only in voice onset time (VOT), the period during which the vocal chords begin to vibrate relative to the release of air by the vocal apparatus. Small changes in VOT are not heard as more or less like *ba* or *pa.* Instead, English speakers hear only *ba* as long as VOT continues to fall on one side of the categorical boundary and only *pa* when it falls on the other side. But if the difference in VOT crosses a critical point, the phoneme boundary, the two sounds are readily distinguishable. Infants as young as one month already demonstrate categorical perception for many different speech sounds (Aslin, 1987b; Kuhl, 1987).

However, researchers remain uncertain about whether babies are born with a special sensory mode for speech because categorical perception can be observed with some sounds other than those found in speech. Monkeys, even chinchillas, also distinguish speech sounds categorically (Kuhl & Miller, 1978; Kuhl & Padden, 1983), a finding that further argues against a specialized innate ability to process phonemes in humans.

Regardless of what accounts for phoneme perception, infants also lose some competencies when the sounds are not a part of their auditory environment. For instance, younger infants appear to be more sensitive than older infants to phonemes found in languages other than their own. In one study, six-to-eight-month-olds reared in an English-speaking environment could readily discriminate among phonemes used in Hindi, whereas eleven-to-thirteen-month-olds had more difficulty with this task (Werker & Lalonde, 1988). This finding has been observed for other phonemes in languages that infants do not hear in their speech environment (Best et al., 1995: Werker & Desjardins, 1995). Adults can regain the lost discriminations only with considerable practice or under highly restricted listening conditions (Werker, 1989). Thus, it does not appear that we completely lose the capacity to make these discriminations. Instead, toward the end of the first year of exposure to speech, our auditory and, perhaps, our cognitive functioning undergo a reorganization that

phoneme   Smallest unit of sound that changes the meanings of words.

categorical perception   Inability to distinguish among sounds that vary on some basic physical dimension except when those sounds lie at opposite sides of a critical juncture point on that dimension.

limits our sensitivity to the sounds not utilized in the language we hear (Lalonde & Werker, 1995).

As with vision, psychologists have often been surprised at the many competencies infants display with respect to sound. The Chronology on page 204 summarizes some of the early abilities displayed in this domain.

The loss of information from any sensory modality can have important consequences for cognitive and social-emotional development. Fortunately, births of blind infants in Western countries are now fairly rare, and infants born with

ATYPICAL DEVELOPMENT

Detecting Hearing Loss in Infants

other visual defects such as cataracts can often be quickly identified so that interventions can be provided early to correct the problem. However, deafness and other hearing disabilities still strike an estimated one to two in every one thousand infants born in the United States (Parving, 1994). Many of these children will not be identified until they are two or three years old.

New techniques can indicate the possibility of hearing loss and are often administered to newborns at risk, for example, those born to families with a history of hearing impairment or those exposed to cytomegalovirus and other diseases or drugs that are known to affect hearing. Yet because auditory screening at birth is not universal and would not detect hearing loss that occurs postnatally, such procedures identify only about half of the infants who have hearing impairments (Eilers & Berlin, 1995).

KEY THEME
Individual Differences

Rebecca Eilers and D. Kimbrough Oller (1994) recently identified one behavioral difference that markedly distinguishes normally hearing and deaf or profoundly hearing-impaired children: *canonical babbling*. Even deaf children produce vocalizations, but canonical babbling refers to utterances such as "mamama, babi, adah, nana," sequenced expressions that sound very much as though the baby is trying to talk, or what we often think of as babbling. Normally hearing infants virtually always produce such sequences before eleven months of age, whereas infants with severe hearing difficulties do not. Thus, normal infants who fail to produce canonical babbling by this age should be tested for hearing loss using appropriate audiologic measures. Early detection of impaired hearing will permit correction or assistance from hearing aids and other devices or the implementation of special education programs involving sign language or other language training that can offset many developmental problems stemming from the absence of this important sensory channel.

Smell, Taste, and the Cutaneous Senses

Developmental researchers have given far less attention to smell, taste, and the *cutaneous senses*—the receptor systems of the skin responsible for perceiving touch, pressure, pain, and temperature—than to vision or hearing. These senses also function shortly after birth and furnish crucial adaptive and survival cues for the baby. Smell, for example, may be critical for determining what is edible and may also be involved in early attachment to the caregiver.

Smell Facial expressions, changes in rate of respiration, and approach-avoidance activities involving head turning are just a few of the responses indicating that newborns detect odors. The typical procedure consists of a series of trials in which a researcher holds a stimulus-saturated cotton swab just beneath the baby's nose for a few seconds. Do babies turn up their noses at the unpleasant smell of rotten eggs?

CHRONOLOGY
Auditory Development

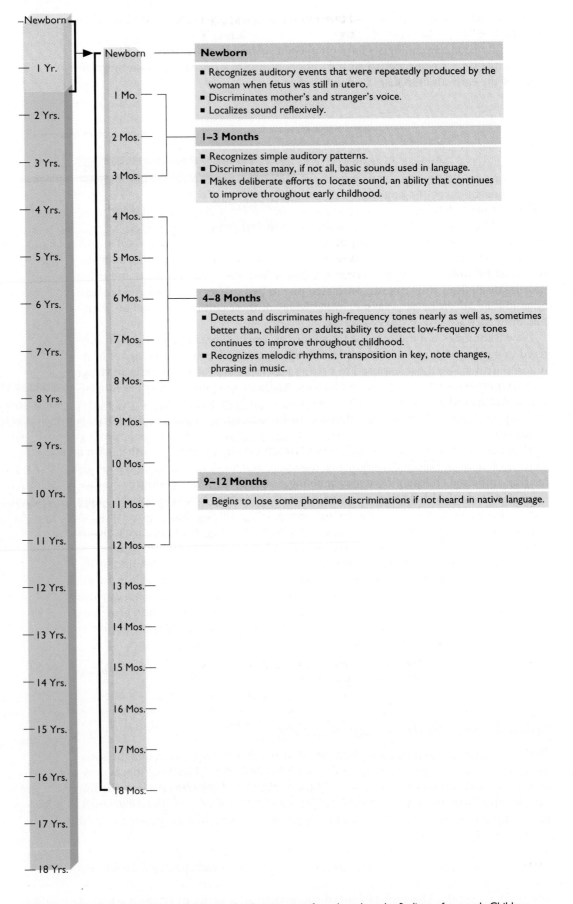

Newborn

- Recognizes auditory events that were repeatedly produced by the woman when fetus was still in utero.
- Discriminates mother's and stranger's voice.
- Localizes sound reflexively.

1–3 Months

- Recognizes simple auditory patterns.
- Discriminates many, if not all, basic sounds used in language.
- Makes deliberate efforts to locate sound, an ability that continues to improve throughout early childhood.

4–8 Months

- Detects and discriminates high-frequency tones nearly as well as, sometimes better than, children or adults; ability to detect low-frequency tones continues to improve throughout childhood.
- Recognizes melodic rhythms, transposition in key, note changes, phrasing in music.

9–12 Months

- Begins to lose some phoneme discriminations if not heard in native language.

This chart describes the sequence of auditory development in infancy based on the findings of research. Children often show individual differences in the exact ages at which they display the various developmental achievements outlined here.

Can they detect the food-related smells of fish, butter, banana, or vanilla? They most certainly can (Engen, Lipsitt, & Kaye, 1963; Rieser, Yonas, & Wikner, 1976; Steiner, 1979). Moreover, newborns become increasingly sensitive to these and other smells during the first few days of life (Lipsitt, Engen, & Kaye, 1963; Self, Horowitz, & Paden, 1972).

Parent-infant recognition occurs by odor among many species of animals. Can human infants identify their caregivers this way as well? Aidan MacFarlane (1975) offered two breast pads to newborns, one worn by the infant's mother and the other unused. Two-to-four-day-olds oriented toward both pads about the same length of time, but by five days of age infants turned their heads longer in the direction of the pad the mother had used. By six days of age, infants also preferred a pad obtained from their own mothers to one from an unfamiliar mother.

What cues are babies detecting, a mother's milk or odors from her body? Perhaps both. A series of experiments conducted by Richard Porter and his colleagues (Cernoch & Porter, 1985; Makin & Porter, 1989; Porter et al., 1992) showed that two-week-olds are attracted to a breast pad worn by a nursing mother, regardless of whether the mother is familiar. However, nursing (but not bottle-fed) two-week-olds also recognize the unique odor of their mothers' bodies, orienting more to a breast or underarm pad worn by their own mothers than to one worn by someone else. The findings suggest that after the close and frequent contact involved in nursing, neonates become familiar with and able to discriminate their caregivers from others on the basis of odor.

To test the familiarity hypothesis, René Balogh and Richard Porter (1986) taped a substance releasing either a cherry or ginger fragrance inside the bassinets of some newborns. The substance remained for about twenty-three hours, and babies were tested with the odors within forty-eight hours of birth. Girls, but not boys, demonstrated a clear preference for the familiar stimulus, results consistent with the hypothesis that early exposure to an odor can lead to its preference. Sex differences in this and other studies with infants indicate that girls are more sensitive to odors than boys (Fernandez & Bahrick, 1994), a finding also reported in tests of olfactory capacities of children and adults (Doty et al., 1984; Makin & Porter, 1989).

Can mothers also identify their infants on the basis of odor? Indeed, within the first few days of birth and after brief contact, not only mothers but also fathers, grandmothers, and aunts can recognize newborn kin by their smell alone. In other words, humans may inherit some family olfactory signature about which they are sensitive or learn very quickly (Porter, Balogh, & Makin, 1988).

KEY THEME
Nature/Nurture

Taste   Receptors for the basic tastes of sweet, sour, salty, and bitter, located mostly on the tongue, develop well before birth; the fetus may already taste as it swallows amniotic fluid. Facial expressions and rate of sucking reveal that newborns can discriminate among tastes (see Figure 6.9). Sweet stimuli, for example, elicit a relaxed facial expression resembling a smile; sour stimuli produce lip pursing or a puckered expression; and bitter stimuli elicit mouth opening as though expressing disgust (Steiner, 1979).

Innate preferences for some tastes may help infants to meet nutritional needs and protect them from harmful or dangerous substances. Preferences can, however, be modified by experience. For example, babies fed sweeter fluids in the first few months after birth ingest more sweet water at six months of age than babies not given this experience (Beauchamp & Moran, 1982). The desire for salt in a specific food may also be established early in infancy (Beauchamp & Cowart, 1990; Harris & Booth, 1985; Sullivan & Birch, 1990). Infants can detect flavors from their mothers' milk as well—for example, garlic, alcohol, and vanilla—an ability that might familiarize them to the foods common to their families and cultures (Mennella & Beauchamp, 1996). Although learning appears to be important in the emergence of odor and taste preferences, we should emphasize that until about two years of age, children will put just about anything into their mouths. Thus, among the most important things they must learn is what *not* to taste (Rozin, 1990).

KEY THEME
Nature/Nurture

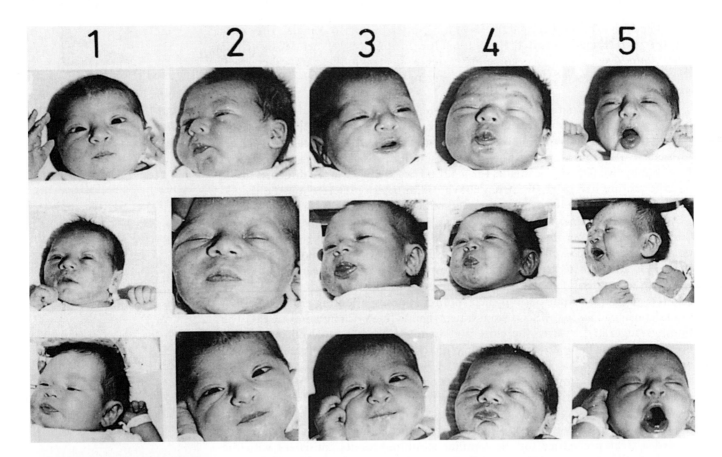

FIGURE 6.9

Discriminating Tastes

Babies produce different facial expressions depending on what they taste. The first column shows the resting faces of three newborns. Column 2 shows the same babies after they received distilled water—their expressions show very little change. After sweet stimulation, the babies' facial expressions are more positive and relaxed, resembling a smile or licking of the upper lip as shown in column 3. However, their mouths become more pursed after sour stimulation (column 4) and more arch-shaped after bitter stimulation (column 5).

Touch, Temperature, and Pain   Skin contains more than one hundred types of receptors sensitive to touch, pressure, temperature, and pain (Reisman, 1987). As we saw in Chapter 4, even the fetus responds to touch. In the newborn, stimulation can also elicit a variety of reflexes (see Chapter 5). And just as caregivers recognize their babies by odor shortly after birth, so can they recognize them by touch. After only a couple of hours of contact, mothers and fathers identified their infants on the basis of stroking only the backs of the babies' hands (Kaitz et al., 1992, 1994). This ability, which may be adaptive in encouraging caregivers to be responsive to their offspring, is another illustration of the sensory communication that can facilitate social interactions between infant and caregiver.

A difficult problem for newborns, particularly premature infants, is regulation of body temperature (Moffat & Hackel, 1985). Cooling awakens babies, makes them more restless, and increases their oxygen consumption, responses that facilitate heat production. Because many newborns are unable to sweat or pant, exposure to high temperatures produces reddening skin, less activity, and more sleep, events that decrease heat production and assist heat loss (Harpin, Chellappah, & Rutter, 1983). When warm, babies also assume a sunbathing position, extending their extremities, perhaps a good clue for a caregiver who is trying to decide whether a baby is too warm (Reisman, 1987).

Although work on pain sensitivity is limited due to ethical concerns, heel pricks, circumcision, and other medical procedures involving newborns have come under increasing scrutiny in recent years. In practice, newborns experiencing

CONTROVERSY: THINKING IT OVER

How Should We Confront Potential Pain in Infants?

such invasive procedures have rarely been given pain reduction medication (Ramenghi et al., 1996a). And in the past, minor and even major operations on very young infants were carried out with no efforts to diminish pain.

Why has pain control in infants generated so little concern? For many years, newborns were believed to have neither the neurological capacity to experience pain nor the memory capacity for pain to produce any long-term adverse consequences. Furthermore, pain-reducing medications may produce negative side effects, particularly on an immature respiratory system, or, if used repeatedly, increase the risk of addiction. Their use may also mask physiological and behavioral signs of serious physical and medical problems in infants too young to convey other information to the physician. Finally, some believe that even if discomfort is experienced, the event causes no long-term harm to infants and young children (Walco, Cassidy, & Schechter, 1995).

More recent research indicates that brain centers involved in the detection of pain are well developed prenatally. Moreover, behavioral (crying, facial expressions, etc.) and physiological responses are consistent with the notion that very young infants experience discomfort. These findings have led to guidelines for use of pain control procedures on infants. Yet these guidelines are not followed often. For example, the findings from a major urban area of Canada with respect to one common medical procedure performed on male infants are probably typical: as few as one in twenty physicians used any kind of analgesia to reduce potential pain associated with circumcision (Ryan & Finer, 1994). This practice has been linked to increased sensitivity to pain during vaccinations in infants four to six months later (Taddio et al., 1995).

Few people likely condone inflicting pain. But should newborns be offered greater pain control given the uncertainties associated with anesthesias and analgesics? Should, for example, analgesics be routinely administered even for such common practices as heel sticks? What about the potential for addiction to certain kinds of painkillers if offered repeatedly? Might such efforts lead to an overdependence on drugs when alternative ways to reduce discomfort may be available? For example, many of the indicators of distress that accompany heel pricks and other pain-inducing procedures can be diminished by giving an infant access to sucrose or other sweet-tasting solutions, presumably because these substances elicit release of the infant's own pain inhibitors (Blass & Shah, 1995; Ramenghi et al., 1996a, 1996b). Thus, less risky alternatives to pain reduction may go unexplored if we turn to drugs to reduce pain too quickly.

Though we now know the newborn really does feel pain, does the newborn remember it? How should we go about assessing this question? How much pain, if any, should infants be allowed to experience before steps are taken to reduce it?

Intermodal Perception

When we coordinate sensory information from several different modalities to perceive or make inferences about an object, we are demonstrating **intermodal perception**. The toddler who hears his mother's voice from another room expects to see her when he enters that room. The sight of a cup provides information about how to shape the mouth to drink from it. If we recognize that the cup holds milk, we also expect that the milk will taste a certain way and that we cannot pick the milk up with our fingers as we can pieces of popcorn. Sometimes, of course, we can be fooled. A luscious-looking dessert may taste like cardboard. A good ventriloquist really does make the dummy appear to be talking.

When does intermodal perception develop? This question has been debated for decades. In fact, the research on infant tongue protrusion discussed earlier suggests that intermodal perception exists early in infancy. If newborns imitate tongue protrusions, they must somehow understand that the sight of another's actions can be mimicked by their own mouth movements. Is intermodal perception innate, as some argue (Meltzoff & Moore, 1992)?

A kind of intermodal perception may indeed exist at birth, according to the Gibsons (E. J. Gibson, 1982; J. J. Gibson, 1979). They propose that perception is initially

KEY THEME
Nature/Nurture

intermodal perception Coordination of sensory information to perceive or make inferences about the characteristics of an object.

amodal, that is, undifferentiated; a newborn is unable to distinguish which sense is being stimulated. For example, if an object is visible and makes a noise, the baby perceives only something interesting and orients all receptors to it. Thus, intermodal perception does not depend on learning to coordinate the various senses (Spelke, 1987). Instead, with experience infants and children recognize which sense is being stimulated, part of a process the Gibsons call **perceptual differentiation**.

The Gibsons' position is a controversial one. Another explanation of intermodal perception emphasizes the initial separateness of the senses. Only after repeated experiences, this argument runs, are babies able to coordinate sensory information. Thus, intermodal perception involves, for example, learning that when objects are shaken, some rattle and make noise and others do not, material that feels soft can also look soft, and a peg that feels square will not fit into a hole that looks round. According to this viewpoint, intermodal perception is the outcome of *enrichment,* the association of sensations from two or more modalities, or, from a more Piagetian perspective, the outcome of constructing schemes involving multisensory experiences (Spelke, 1987). Note that learning is important in each of these views. The point of contention is whether intermodal perception comes about by breaking complex, undifferentiated stimulation into its specific constituents or by combining unique sensory experiences through association.

Sight and Sound   To determine whether infants link visual and auditory events, Elizabeth Spelke (1976) developed a simple procedure in which four-month-olds could look at either of two films shown side by side. At the same time, the infants could hear a soundtrack coming from a speaker located between the two viewing screens. The soundtrack matched events in one of the two films, for example, an unfamiliar woman engaged in a game of peek-a-boo or someone playing a percussion instrument. Would infants pay more attention to the film synchronized with the soundtrack? Spelke found this to be the case, at least when the percussion sounds could be heard.

Four-month-olds can match not only auditory and visual tempo and rhythm but other auditory-visual cues as well. In one study babies were shown two films, one depicting wet sponges being squeezed, the other two blocks being clapped together (Bahrick, 1983). When the babies heard a squishing sound, they attended more to the film showing the sponges; when they heard a banging sound, they attended more to the film of the rigid blocks. Five-month-olds could even link sounds such as an auto or a train coming or going with concordant visual progressions of approaching and retreating movement (Pickens, 1994; Walker-Andrews & Lennon, 1985).

Intermodal perception in infants extends to social relationships as well. For example, three-and-a-half-month-olds are likely to look at the parent, seated to one side, whose voice is coming from a speaker centered in front of the baby (Spelke & Owsley, 1979). By six months, babies who hear a strange male or female voice also look longer at a face of the same sex than a face of the opposite sex; three-month-olds do not show this ability (Francis & McCroy, 1983).

Intermodal cues can influence perception in some perhaps unexpected ways. Speech perception, for example, may be greatly affected by what a person sees. Harry McGurk and John MacDonald (1976) played videotapes of an adult uttering simple syllables such as *ba ba.* Sometimes, however, the video picture was synchronized with another sound, such as *ga ga.* Three-year-olds through adults often reported hearing something quite different, for example, *da da* or another utterance. By five months of age, babies also recognize auditory-visual correspondence, attending more to facial expressions articulating sounds that match than facial expressions that do not match what they hear (Meltzoff & Kuhl, 1994).

Sight and Touch   By six months of age, infants who explore an object with their hands alone can recognize it by sight alone (Pineau & Streri, 1990; Rose, Gottfried, & Bridger, 1981; Ruff & Kohler, 1978). But coordination of visual and tactile information exists much earlier when the mouth is used to explore objects. In one study, one-

perceptual differentiation
Process postulated by Eleanor and James Gibson in which experience contributes to the ability to make increasingly finer perceptual discriminations and to distinguish stimulation arising from each sensory modality.

month-olds were allowed to mouth either a smooth or a nubby sphere, neither of which was made visible to them. When permitted to view the objects, the infants preferred to look at the one they had not mouthed (Meltzoff & Borton, 1979). In another experiment, one-month-olds also recognized objects they had mouthed but, perhaps because of a difference in the procedure, preferred looking at the familiar object to looking at the unfamiliar one (Gibson & Walker, 1984).

Babies can even be surprised by a discrepancy between vision and touch. Emily Bushnell (1981) showed infants a solid object within a box. Its location was distorted by mirrors. When babies reached for it, they touched another object that differed in size, shape, and texture. Infants younger than nine months failed to investigate the novel object actively or search for the one they could see, but older infants did both. Thus, there is substantial evidence that intermodal perception also changes with experience. Much of the knowledge and skill involved in sensory coordination can be gained only through opportunities to look at, listen to, and smell, taste, and touch the surrounding world.

To summarize our discussion of sensory and perceptual development, it is fair to say that very young infants can boast of surprisingly sophisticated capacities that undergo rapid improvement and refinement. Babies come equipped to gain access to a rich variety of sensory stimulation and quickly come to make sense of it. Their perceptual development reveals an order and a purpose that are beautifully adapted to responding to and learning from experience. We must conclude that babies, as well as older children, are highly competent information processors, able to explore and learn through vision, hearing, touch, smell, and taste. Furthermore, they interpret and organize information in many ways that appear to be similar to the older child's and adult's. Of course, infants do not perceive and comprehend their surroundings in exactly the same way older children and adults do. However, they are equipped with sensory and perceptual tools that allow them to become responsive to family, community, and culture in an astonishingly short amount of time.

PERCEPTUAL DEVELOPMENT THROUGHOUT CHILDHOOD

Richard Aslin and Linda Smith (1988) have noted a predicament facing anyone interested in learning about perceptual development after infancy. As research has increasingly documented sophisticated abilities in newborns and infants, the importance of studying perceptual development at older ages appears to have faded.

Perception also becomes more difficult to investigate without considering at the same time the child's developing linguistic and cognitive skills. Nevertheless, several important features of perceptual development are evident throughout childhood. Perceptual skills become more focused, organized, and confined to the meaningful and important features of the environment; in other words, perception becomes increasingly efficient with development. Eleanor Gibson (1969, 1982, 1988) has outlined one major view of perceptual learning to account for such findings.

Perceptual Learning

Eleanor Gibson's theory of perceptual learning emphasizes three changes with age: increasing specificity in perception, improved attention, and more economical and efficient acquisition of perceptual information. Much of the infant's first year is spent learning the sensory properties of objects, the spatial layout of the infant's world, and the perceptual repercussions of his or her actions. But perceptual learning continues. For example, children acquire new kinds of visual discriminations when they learn to read. They must begin to pay attention to consistencies and variations in letters and text, aspects of their visual environment they may have largely ignored before.

This toddler very likely feels the soft, cold texture of snow while at the same time seeing its white, fluffy visual qualities. Both visual and tactual cues will change if she holds on to the snow long enough and, she may soon add another sensory input, taste, if she hasn't done so already, to define this experience. Stimulation often takes place through several sensory modalities.

KEY THEME
Interaction Among Domains

KEY THEME
Child's Active Role

Sensitivity to Perceptual Differences

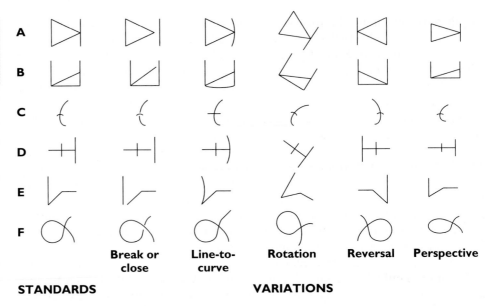

STANDARDS   VARIATIONS

Source: Adapted from Pick, 1965.

Column 1 gives different letter-like forms used as standards in a sorting task. Columns 2 through 6 display various transformations of each standard. Four-to-eight-year-olds, when shown a stack of the figures and asked to select only those identical to the standard, commit relatively few errors on variations that involve a break in the figure, presumably because the distinction is important for identifying many objects as well as alphabetic symbols. With increasing age, errors involving rotation, reversal, and line/curve variations decrease substantially because, according to Eleanor Gibson, children who are beginning to learn to read must pay attention to these features of the stimuli. Errors involving perspective remain high at all ages, perhaps because the transformation is not important for identifying either objects or letters of the alphabet.

Eleanor Gibson and her colleagues (E. J. Gibson et al., 1962) created different sets of letterlike figures such as those shown in Figure 6.10. One member of each set was designated a standard, but each set included variations of that standard. A straight line, for example, might be redrawn as a curved line, the standard rotated or reversed, a break introduced in a continuous line, or the line's perspective changed by tipping or elongating some aspect of the figure. Children four through eight years of age were shown a stack of each set of figures and asked to pick out only those identical to the standard.

Children made many more errors for some kinds of variations in the stimuli than for others. For example, children of all ages seldom confused the standard with versions that contained breaks, perhaps because these features are important for identifying common objects in the environment as well as letters of the alphabet. On the other hand, older children did substantially better than younger children in discriminating rotations and reversals and line/curve transformations, presumably because children who are learning to read must begin to distinguish such variations. Finally, children of all ages found it difficult to discriminate changes in perspective from the standard, a variation that can and normally should be ignored for identifying both physical objects and letters of the alphabet.

Eleanor Gibson believes the age-related improvements in performance on this activity do not come about by reinforcing children to make the discriminations. In fact, when asked to classify the letterlike forms in a series of trials, children showed steady improvement in sorting without any feedback about their accuracy. Gibson argues that through repeated exposure to and inspection of letters of the alphabet, children are afforded the opportunity to recognize certain critical features distinguishing such figures. Opportunities to experience the regularities and differences among similar stimuli, rather than the systematic reinforcements of parents or teachers, enable children to distinguish them. Perceptual learning, then, is indispensable not only for infants learning to distinguish objects but also throughout development for learning to read and accomplish many other technical skills that demand subtle and sophisticated perceptual discriminations.

Part-Whole Perception

As we have already learned, within a matter of weeks after birth babies can see patterns, forms, and objects—the wholes or configural cues, so to speak, not just their isolated features. In fact, the perception of preschoolers frequently is influenced by wholes, and young children occasionally have difficulty making precise and systematic judgments about the similarity of objects based on a single feature or attribute (Smith, 1989). For example, preschoolers might put a red rubber ball with a slightly smaller ball of pink yarn because the balls' overall appearances are similar, whereas older children might lump the red rubber ball with a white foam ball of exactly the same size, using the size dimension as the criterion for defining similarity. A preference for configural cues is also observed in preschoolers' sorting of objects by touch, a preference that gives way to specific local features in both sighted and blind older children (Morrongiello et al., 1994).

Whether children see the inner parts or features rather than the whole is probably greatly influenced by how complex and distinctive both levels are. However, a related question is whether children are able to see both the wholes and the parts. Consider the stimuli shown in Figure 6.11, a set of figures with identifiable pieces arranged to form meaningful wholes. David Elkind and his colleagues asked children ages four to nine to describe what they saw (Elkind, Koegler, & Go, 1964). Younger children generally reported only the parts. Only eight- and nine-year-olds were likely to mention both wholes and parts, leading the researchers to conclude that younger children have difficulty perceiving both features. But other studies reveal that when the parts and the wholes are relatively simple stimuli or the parts are arranged in configurations that can influence one another, children as young as three process both levels (Prather & Bacon, 1986; Stiles, Delis, & Tada, 1991).

Finally, one additional change appears with respect to the salience of different parts of perceptual arrays, at least when pictures of faces are involved. In a developmental progression somewhat analogous to what we observed with infants, younger children are more likely to recognize a human face on the basis of external cues rather than inner features. For example, Ruth Campbell and her colleagues found that when shown a photo depicting the hairline, chin, and mouth of a child, children less than about seven years of age were better able to identify a classmate than when shown a photo depicting the individual's inner features such as eyes, nose, and mouth (see Figure 6.12). However, older children and adults were better able to utilize the inner features of the face to make such judgments (Campbell & Tuck, 1995; Campbell, Walker, & Baron-Cohen, 1995).

Developmental trends in childhood concerning the perception of parts and wholes must be interpreted cautiously. On simple perceptual tasks, preschoolers can perform as well as older children do, and if older children or adults are given limited time or a difficult task, their perception is also likely to take on a less complicated

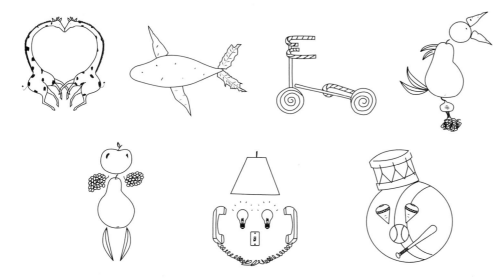

Source: Adapted from Elkind, Koegler, & Go, 1964.

FIGURE 6.11

Part-Whole Perception

Elkind and his colleagues created stimuli to test whether young children can perceive both the parts and the whole. Younger children reported seeing only the parts. When the wholes are made simpler than those shown here, however, even three-year-olds can see both the parts and the whole. Difficulty in reporting seeing both may stem from conceptual and verbal constraints rather than from perceptual limitations.

| FIGURE 6.12 | Identifying Classmates on the Basis of Perceptual Features |

Ruth Campbell and her colleagues asked children between three and eleven years of age to indicate which photos depicted children who were classmates in their school. Children at all ages were quite accurate when a photo of the complete face was shown. Children at the younger ages were also fairly good at recognizing their classmates when the outer features (hair, chin, ears) were visible. However, older children were much better than younger children at recognizing classmates based on inner features of their faces (eyes, nose, and mouth). Future research will help to determine whether this age-related change in the recognition of external and internal features is unique to faces or a more general aspect of perceptual development.

 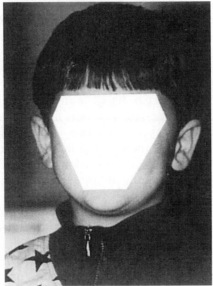 

Source: Campbell, Walker, & Baron-Cohen, 1995.

KEY THEME
Interaction Among Domains

KEY THEME
Nature/Nurture

KEY THEME
Individual Differences

quality, such as reporting only the whole (Smith & Kemler-Nelson, 1984). The findings suggest that cognitive as well as perceptual factors affect performance on many perceptual tasks (Smith & Evans, 1989).

Experience and Perceptual Development

How do experience and inborn sensory capacities interact to determine perception? Throughout the history of psychology this has been an important question, and it continues to be so as medical and technical advances provide opportunities to compensate for some kinds of sensory disabilities. For example, blind children can perceive the existence of distant objects, presumably from changes in auditory cues they receive while moving about (Ashmead, Hill, & Talor, 1989). As a consequence, blind infants are now being fitted with sonic devices to help them hear echoes to signal the direction, distance, and other qualities of objects.

The effects of these efforts with blind children are still to be demonstrated, but we can be sure of one thing from research on sensory deprivation: experience is extremely important for maintaining many perceptual capacities. For example, when monkeys are reared with light but no contours or patterns are visible, their ability to discriminate objects is gradually and permanently lost (Riesen, 1965). The same appears to be true in humans, as studies of infants born with cataracts have demonstrated (Walk, 1981). Research with kittens indicates that the ability to perceive contours of different orientations requires exposure to a variety of horizontal, vertical, and oblique patterns of stimulation (Blakemore & Mitchell, 1973). Moreover, if a person's eyes fail to function together during the first months and years of life, the individual's binocular vision may be permanently affected (Aslin & Dumais, 1980). Thus, there are sensitive periods early in perceptual development during which visual stimulation must occur to prevent the loss of perceptual capacities.

These children in the Sudan receive their education in front of a round schoolhouse. Does a child who grows up in a culture where linear perspective is uncommon, as in many parts of Africa and island regions in the Pacific Ocean, perceive things differently than a child who grows up in an environment filled with straight lines, right angles, and many opportunities to see distances based on orderly linear cues?

KEY THEME
Sociocultural Influence

Experience also helps to explain cross-cultural differences in perception. Environments around the world differ in their degree of "carpenteredness" (Segall, Campbell, & Herskovits, 1966). In most urban, technically advanced societies, houses are constructed on rectilinear principles, which involve perpendicular and right-angle dimensions. Even the layouts of roads and other artifacts of the environment often follow these principles. In other environments, such as in Oceanic and many African cultures, walls and roofs may be curved and straight lines and angular intersections may be few.

In one study, field workers administered several optical illusions to samples of children and adults in locations in Africa, the Philippines, and the United States (Segall, Campbell, & Herskovits, 1966). The two horizontal lines in the Müller-Lyer illusion (see Figure 6.13) are actually the same length, as are the horizontal and vertical segments of the horizontal-vertical illusion. The researchers theorized that individuals living in a carpentered environment, who often see rectangular intersecting contours, would have greater difficulty seeing the lines as equal in the Müller-Lyer illusion than people living in noncarpentered environments. They based this prediction on the fact that inward-pointing, finlike perspectives often accompany edges

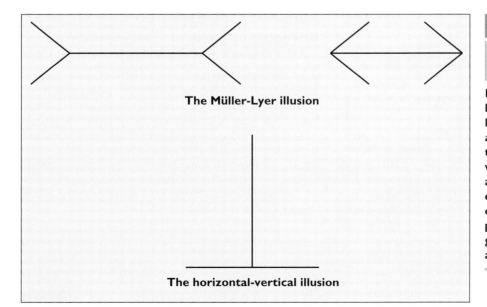

The Müller-Lyer illusion

The horizontal-vertical illusion

FIGURE 6.13

Cross-Cultural Differences in Perception

Is one of the two horizontal lines in the Müller-Lyer illusion longer than the other? What about the vertical and horizontal lines in the horizontal-vertical illusion? Children and adults who live in "carpentered" environments are more susceptible to these illusions than people who live in forested regions where cues to distance are less prevalent.

that are seen as being nearer and outward-pointing, finlike perspectives are frequently associated with edges seen as being farther away. Thus, in the Müller-Lyer illusion, an individual perceives greater depth when the fins point outward and judges the line to be longer. The researchers also predicted that because the vertical line in the horizontal-vertical illusion may signal depth—that is, a line receding in space—the illusion of the vertical line as being longer should be more prominent among people living in open plains or deserts, who regularly experience these cues to distance, than among people residing in heavily wooded tropical forests. In fact, their results conformed to the predictions.

Other research has challenged the carpentered-world hypothesis. Nevertheless, children and adults in cultures with minimal formal education, little experience with pictures, or artworks that incorporate few depth cues are unlikely to perceive pictures or photos in three dimensions (Pick, 1987). Thus, the ways in which children and adults interpret their sensory environment can be greatly affected by cultural opportunities, a finding that fits well with the conclusion that perception is influenced by experience.

CHAPTER RECAP

SUMMARY OF DEVELOPMENTAL THEMES

NATURE/NURTURE   What roles do nature and nurture play in learning and perceptual development?

We cannot help but be impressed by the remarkably adaptive resources immediately available to infants for gaining knowledge of their environment. The basic mechanisms of learning—habituation, classical and operant conditioning, and perhaps even imitation—are ready to influence behavior at or shortly after birth. A newborn's sense organs are sufficiently developed to provide rudimentary capacities to see, hear, feel, taste, and smell, and often function even before birth. We have also seen, however, that sensory and perceptual capacities improve substantially as a result of experiential fine-tuning. Thus, the environment plays an early and powerful role in determining which capacities are acquired and maintained.

SOCIOCULTURAL INFLUENCE   How does the sociocultural context influence learning and perceptual development?

Experiences the culture provides—the behaviors that are reinforced and punished and opportunities to observe others engaged in work, play, and social interactions—have substantial effects on what a child learns. Although formal instruction and education assist learning in some societies, in all cultures the actions of caregivers and other models provide plentiful opportunities for children to gain knowledge of what is socially accepted and expected. Specific cultural demands, such as discriminating the printed word, and culturally related physical layouts, such as carpentered environments, may have considerable bearing on perceptual development.

CHILD'S ACTIVE ROLE   How does the child play an active role in learning and perceptual development?

Mechanisms of learning typically do not emphasize an active role for the child. Yet what the child learns certainly affects the kinds of interactions she or he will experience and opportunities for further learning. In this sense, the knowledge and skills a child possesses actively contribute to further social interactions, learning, and development. With respect to perceptual development, Eleanor Gibson's theory highlights the important role the activity of the child, including visuomotor and other sensorimotor mechanisms, plays in perceptual development. Children construct perceptions of whole, multisensory arrays at an early age, and their perceptual learning increasingly reflects deliberate and organized exploration of the environment.

INDIVIDUAL DIFFERENCES   How prominent are individual differences in learning and perceptual develoment?

All normal children are equipped with the basic capacities to learn and perceive. But individual differences are built on those capacities as each child experiences various role models, educational practices, cultural conventions, and other phenomena unique to his or her circumstances. What the child learns establishes the knowledge base on which he or she displays a rich variety of accomplishments and skills. Accompanying these achievements may also be different ways of using the senses and perceiving the environment that contribute to the individual's unique view of the world.

INTERACTION AMONG DOMAINS   How do learning and perceptual development interact with development in other domains?

Learning plays a substantial role in almost every aspect of development. The child learns social skills, acceptable ways to express thoughts and feelings, techniques to achieve academic and occupational success, and numerous other behaviors. The child who learns about the alphabet, about having to sit quietly in the classroom, about when and when not to speak to an adult, or about behaviors effective in hunting, shepherding, domestic, or other activities of the culture can be expected to achieve social status, prestige, and other resources that will benefit development in many other domains. Furthermore, gains in perception are substantially influenced by physiological and neural advances. Rapidly improving intellectual and motor skills introduce demands for making new perceptual discriminations (such as reading) that, once mastered, lead to further progress in cognitive, social, and other domains.

SUMMARY OF TOPICS

■ BASIC LEARNING PROCESSES IN INFANCY AND CHILDHOOD

Learning includes mechanisms that permit adaptation to the environment. Infants are capable of *classical* and *operant conditioning, habituation* and *recovery from habituation,* and possibly imitation as well. Thus, babies are equipped to adapt to their environment and to learn from it. Observational learning plays a major role in socialization as well as in acquisition of knowledge. Caregivers and tutors often utilize these mechanisms to assist children in the acquisition of a wide range of skills in a social context.

■ SENSORY AND PERCEPTUAL CAPACITIES

Although it was once assumed that newborns' sensory receptors do not yet function, every sense is operative at birth and, in some cases, even before. Studies reveal preferential behaviors for certain kinds of stimuli, habituation to familiar and recovery to new stimuli, and learning to discriminate among various objects and events.

Newborns both look for and see visual events. Within a few months of birth the lens of the baby's eye readily *accommodates* to the varying distances of objects to permit seeing them in focus. Newborns also display *saccadic* eye movements, which in a matter of weeks become more rapid and accurate in the exploration and search for stimuli in the visual field. Ability to perform *smooth visual pursuit* is limited but improves during the first eight months as well. *Vergence,* the capacity to focus both eyes on an object, reaches a mature level even sooner.

Visual acuity is limited, but newborns can detect contour, and their ability to see edges and transitions in surfaces under varying intensities of light is nearly adultlike by six months of age. Color vision and *stereopsis* emerge within the first few months of life and in fact may be present even earlier. Other cues to depth, such as *kinetic cues* based on self-induced movement or movement in the environment, are available to young infants. Sensitivity to many two-dimensional cues in pictures begins to be evident at about five to seven months of age, at least among children in the United States.

Newborns do not examine patterns of stimuli systematically and are often attracted to larger external features showing high contrast or movement. By two to three months of age, infants perceive more detailed patterns and begin to prefer looking at such things as the human face, although they may display a bias to attend to it even earlier. Kinetic cues are important for the detection of the unity and coherence of objects and signal movement arising from another person.

The ability to detect sounds and their locations appears at birth, although the ability undergoes substantial improvement during the first few months. In fact, auditory sensitivities continue to improve throughout childhood. Auditory pattern perception is present by about three months of age, and infants prefer patterns that conform to acceptable phrasing in musical passages. Moreover, infants are able to discriminate most, if not all, sounds used in different languages, a capacity that becomes limited by the end of the first year as a result of exposure to only a subset of sounds in the language(s) the baby hears. This phenomenon, along with *categorical perception* of speech sounds, has given rise to theoretical debates about whether speech perception is achieved through special acoustic mechanisms or through more general auditory capacities.

Newborns can discriminate basic tastes and pleasant and unpleasant smells. They agree with adults' judgments of the pleasantness of odors and quickly recognize the smells of their caregivers. Babies also respond to tactile stimuli and demonstrate *intermodal perception.* Behavioral and other responses suggest that the newborn can feel pain. The ability to integrate sensory information from more than one modality may be present at birth, although differentiation and considerable learning resulting from intermodal perception also develop.

■ PERCEPTUAL DEVELOPMENT THROUGHOUT CHILDHOOD

Investigations of perceptual development in children have been infrequent. Research based on Eleanor Gibson's theory of perceptual learning has revealed that perception becomes more focused, organized, and confined to the meaningful and important features of the environment. Perception becomes increasingly efficient as children have opportunities to learn about the constant and critical features of their sensory environment. Children perceive both the parts and the wholes of stimuli, although there are likely developmental differences in which features are more easily detected. Opportunities early in development to observe patterns, depth, and sounds important in language help to maintain perceptual abilities. Perceptual learning may contribute to differences among children from various cultures in their perceptions of their environment.

7 LANGUAGE

THE COURSE OF LANGUAGE ACQUISITION

EXPLAINING LANGUAGE ACQUISITION

THE FUNCTIONS OF LANGUAGE

CHAPTER RECAP

NATURE/NURTURE
What roles do nature and nurture play in language development?

SOCIOCULTURAL INFLUENCE
How does the sociocultural context influence language development?

CHILD'S ACTIVE ROLE
How does the child play an active role in the process of language development?

CONTINUITY/DISCONTINUITY
Is language development continuous or discontinuous?

INDIVIDUAL DIFFERENCES
How prominent are individual differences in language development?

INTERACTION AMONG DOMAINS
How does language development interact with development in other domains?

Sue and Dan had been so diligent in recording the achievements of their young daughter, Sara. She was their first child and, like many proud new parents, they photographed and videotaped every new milestone, sending copies to doting grandparents living miles away. Today eleven-month-old Sara was sitting in her high chair having lunch, banging her bottle gleefully against her dish. All at once, the bottle escaped her grasp and fell to the floor with a loud thud. Sara, looking distressed, pointed to the bottle and uttered, "Baba." Sue's expression, one of irritation at having to retrieve the fallen bottle, instantly changed. This was the first time Sara had said something that Sue could distinguish as a word. As Sue picked up the bottle, she cheered, "YEESS, Sara, that's a bottle! Good girl! Bottle! Hooray!" Placing the bottle on the high chair, Sue hoped Sara would say "Baba" again, but not before she found the video camera!

The scene above—a parent jubilant at her child's first word—replays itself in thousands of households, not just in the United States but all over the world. At about one year of age, most children make their formal entrance into the world of human communication, and parents respond with equal delight and amazement. By age five, most children have moved from Sara's effective but rudimentary mix of verbal and nonverbal messages to more complex achievements. They have mastered the bewildering variety of sounds in their native language to produce thousands of recognizable words, and they understand the meanings of words reasonably well. They also become aware of the interactive and sociocultural rules of communication.

By age five, in fact, most children have become highly proficient listeners and speakers, a marvel indeed given the overwhelming abundance of sounds, vocabulary words, grammatical rules, and social conventions that go into producing mature, adult-sounding speech. You probably do not have a vivid memory of how you learned to speak; most of us have little specific recall of this extremely complex, yet entirely natural process. But if you have ever tried to learn a foreign language, you probably have some sense of how remarkable children's mastery of communication is. How do infants and children manage such a seemingly overwhelming task?

In this chapter, we will first examine the major milestones in the acquisition of communication and language skills from infancy through childhood, the sequence of events that unfolds as the child comes to comprehend and produce language. Next, we will look at the most important theories of language development and the factors that account for the observable commonalities in how children acquire language. Of all the themes of development, none has been more central to theories of language development than the nature-versus-nurture debate, the extent to which either biological predispositions or environmental influences dictate the child's developing linguistic competence. Finally, we will briefly examine the functions of language, particularly as they interact with children's growing cognitive skills and ability to regulate their own behavior.

THE COURSE OF LANGUAGE ACQUISITION

A baby's contact with language is—initially, at least—noticeably one-sided. Although she may gurgle or coo, most of her experience is as a listener. Among her first tasks is to learn to identify the myriad sounds that make up her native language. That is, she must distinguish specific sounds in the stream of spoken language, note the regularities in how they are combined, recognize which combinations constitute words, and eventually, when she makes the transition from listener to speaker, form the consonant-vowel combinations that are the building blocks of words and sentences. The fundamental sound units and the rules for combining them in a given language make up that language's **phonology**. If you have studied a foreign language, you will recognize that some sounds appear only in certain languages, such as the prolonged nasal *n* sound in Spanish and the French vowel that is spoken as though *e* and *u* are combined. Furthermore, each language has its own rules for combining sounds. In English, for example, the *sr* combination does not occur, whereas *sl* and *st* appear frequently. Even at this basic level of phonology, the child has to absorb an enormous amount of information about those sounds and combinations of sounds that are acceptable in her native language.

Another basic language skill the child must master is linking the combinations of sounds he hears to the objects, people, events, or relationships they label. **Semantics** is the meanings of words or combinations of words. For example, *cookie* is an arbitrary grouping of sounds, but speakers of English use it to refer to a specific class of objects. The child thus attaches words to conceptual groups, learning when it is appropriate to use them and when it is not (for example, *cookie* does not refer to all objects or edible goods found in the bakery). The child also learns that some words describe actions (*eat*), whereas others describe relationships (*under* or *over*) or modify objects (*chocolate cookie*). Mapping combinations of sounds to their referents (that is, the things to which words refer) is a major task in the acquisition of language.

As the child begins to combine words, she learns the principles of **syntax,** or the grammatical rules that dictate how words can be combined. The order in which words are spoken conveys meaning; for example, "Eat kitty" and "Kitty eat" do not mean the same thing, even in the simplified language of the young child. A word's position in a sentence can signify whether the word is an agent or the object of an action, for example. The rules of syntax vary widely from one language to another, but within a given language they operate with consistency and regularity. One of the most remarkable features of language acquisition is the child's ability to detect the regularity of syntax and use it to create meaningful utterances of his own with little direct instruction.

The process of acquiring language also includes learning **pragmatics,** the rules for using language effectively and appropriately according to social conventions. The effective use of language includes a host of nonverbal behaviors, rules of etiquette, and even changing the content of speech according to the identity of the listener and the context of the communication. How do you ask someone for a favor? Not, the child soon learns, by saying, "Hey, you, get me that ball!" The child also learns that if someone did not hear what she said, she can sometimes add a gesture to complete the communication. And the proper way to speak to an adult who has some authority will probably include more polite forms and fewer terms of familiarity than when speaking to a peer. As they acquire language, then, children also absorb the equally important sociocultural dimension of pragmatics.

phonology   Fundamental sound units and combinations of units in a given language.

semantics   Meanings of words or combinations of words.

syntax   Grammatical rules that dictate how words can be combined.

pragmatics   Rules for using language effectively within a social context.

Clearly, language is a multifaceted skill with many overlapping dimensions, from understanding and uttering sounds to appreciating the sometimes subtle rules of social communication. Despite the complexities, by the time they are four or five years old, most children speak much as adults do. Their progress in mastering vocabulary, syntax, and pragmatics continues during the school years and thereafter, but they acquire the essential elements of the language system in an impressively brief period.

From Sound to Meaning: Phonological and Other Prelinguistic Skills

What does it take to learn a language? The infant's first step consists of both attending to the sounds of speech as a special type of auditory stimulation and deciphering phonology, the units of sound that occur in a given language. Thus, during much of the infant's first year, the emphasis is on phonological development, both in receiving messages from others and in being able to produce them on his own.

Early Responses to Human Speech   Right from birth, the human infant has a special sensitivity to the sounds other human beings make. Newborns show a distinct preference for human voices over other sounds and like to hear their own mothers' voices more than a stranger's (DeCasper & Fifer, 1980; Gibson & Spelke, 1983). Most important, however, infants respond in specific ways to small acoustic variations in human speech that distinguish one word or part of a word from another.

As we discussed in Chapter 6, the basic building blocks of spoken language are called *phonemes,* the smallest units of sound that change the meanings of words. In the words *pat* and *bat,* for example, the phonemes /p/ and /b/ make a big difference in the meaning of the word. Recall from Chapter 6 that infants as young as one month can discriminate different phonemes and they do so categorically, ignoring small acoustic variations in a sound unless the sound pattern crosses a phonemic boundary (Aslin, Pisoni, & Jusczyk, 1983; Kuhl, 1987). At two months of age, infants add to their repertoires the ability to discriminate vowels (Marean, Werner, & Kuhl, 1992). Remarkably, young infants show an ability to detect phonemes and vowel sounds from a variety of languages. However, by six to ten months of age, infants show a decline in the ability to distinguish those basic sounds that do not appear in their native language (Kuhl et al., 1992; Polka & Werker, 1994; Werker & Tees, 1984). That is, their experiences with the language spoken around them quickly begin to constrain the small units of sound to which they are sensitive.

Even though very young infants are responsive to phonemes from many of the world's languages, as early as two days of age they show a clear preference for hearing a stream of speech from their native language as opposed to a foreign language (Moon, Cooper, & Fifer, 1993). Sometime between six and nine months of age, another interesting developmental change occurs: infants begin to show a preference to listen to unfamiliar isolated words from their native language. For example, American infants prefer unfamiliar English words over Dutch words. They also prefer words with a strong-weak stress pattern (e.g., *crossing* versus *across*) that are more common in English (Jusczyk, Cutler, & Redanz, 1993; Jusczyk, Friederici, et al., 1993). It seems, then, that as infants approach the end of their first year, they zero in on both the distinctive features and the more global patterns of speech that appear in the language they hear most often.

A final aspect of spoken speech to which infants show an early sensitivity is **prosody,** the patterns of intonation, stress, and rhythm that communicate meaning. One example of a prosodic feature is the pattern of intonation that distinguishes questions from declarative statements. When you raise your voice at the end of a question, you are signaling a different communicative intent than when you let your voice fall at the end of a declarative sentence. Researchers have found that infants prefer the prosodic features associated with the high-pitched, exaggerated, musical

prosody Patterns of intonation, stress, and rhythm that communicate meaning in speech.

speech, often called "baby talk," that mothers typically direct to their young children. Figure 7.1 illustrates some of the acoustical properties of mothers' speech to infants. In one study, Anne Fernald (1985) trained four-month-olds to turn their heads to activate a loudspeaker positioned on either side of them. The infants were more likely to make this response if their "reward" was a female stranger's voice speaking as the woman would speak to a baby than if she used normal adult speech. In a subsequent study, researchers found that it was the high pitch of the "baby talk" that infants preferred, not the loudness or rhythm of that speech (Fernald & Kuhl, 1987). In light of these preferences, it seems fitting that mothers from cultures as diverse as France, Italy, Germany, Britain, Japan, China, and the Xhosa tribe of southern Africa have been found to raise their pitch when they speak to their young infants (Fernald, 1991; Papousek, 1992).

In summary, infants show an amazing ability to respond to some important elements of human speech, an ability that prepares them for the even more sophisticated language achievements to come. Because these competencies appear so early in life, they suggest that human language has biological underpinnings. At the same time, the role of the environment in language acquisition is clear. Babies' preference for unfamiliar words in their native language and the increasing difficulty they have in making phoneme discriminations in nonnative languages demonstrate that the specific language a child hears exerts a steady influence on his or her linguistic skills, even in the first year of life.

KEY THEME
Nature/Nurture

FIGURE 7.1

The Acoustical Properties of Maternal Speech to Infants

These two samples of maternal speech show the special acoustical qualities that make speech to infants (bottom) distinct from speech to adults (top). The vertical axis represents fundamental frequency, a measure of auditory pitch. Note the frequent use of modulation of pitch and the predominance of high pitch in maternal speech to infants. Babies seem to be especially responsive to the qualities of this type of speech.

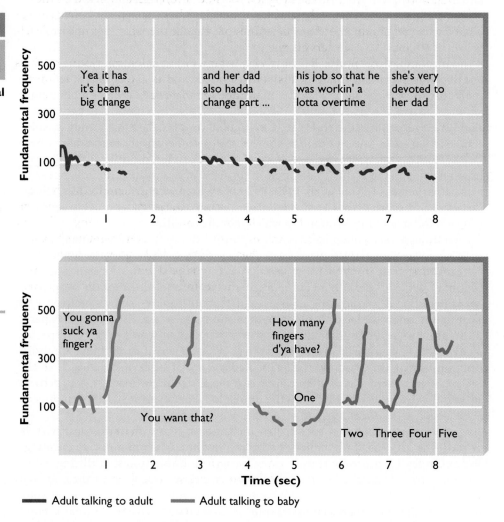

Source: Adapted from Fernald, 1985.

A substantial number of children, perhaps as many as 20 percent, fail to develop normal speech and language (Beitchman et al., 1986). They may have trouble pronouncing words, have a limited spoken vocabulary, and show poor language comprehension. For many of these children, delayed language skills can mean severe reading difficulties, called *dyslexia,* once they enter school. Many researchers now believe that this wide array of problems is due to phonological processing deficits (Catts, 1993; Olson, 1994; Siegel, 1993; Stanovich, 1993). These children have particular difficulty in discriminating phonemes, precisely the type of skill at which many infants are so adept. Compared to normal children, these children are slower and less accurate when asked to read nonsense words such as *calch* and *tegwop;* they also have difficulty when asked to make words into a familiar children's language called Pig Latin (e.g., making the word *pig* into *igpay*) (Connors & Olson, 1990). These processing deficits can persist well into adulthood (Bruck, 1993).

Paula Tallal and her colleagues (1996) have found that many of these children can be helped by being trained with taped exercises in which speech has been modified to help them identify auditory sounds that change quickly. In these exercises, the speech signal was slowed down by 50 percent, but its natural quality was preserved. In addition, the elements of speech that typically change rapidly were amplified in volume. The children had to act out commands they heard in the exercises or repeat syllables, words, and phrases. The program was intensive; children worked on the exercises three hours each weekday and were also given homework every night. At the end of only one month, the children's scores on several measures of language development improved by two years on average.

Just why language-impaired children lag behind in phonological processing skills is still not well understood. But this body of research makes very clear the importance of mastering phonology in the acquisition of language.

ATYPICAL DEVELOPMENT

Language-Impaired Children

Cooing and Babbling: Prelinguistic Speech   Well before the child utters her first word, she produces sounds that increasingly resemble the language spoken in her environment. At birth, the infant's vocal capabilities are limited to crying and a few other brief sounds such as grunts, sighs, or clicks. Between six and eight weeks, a new type of vocalization, **cooing,** emerges. These brief, vowel-like utterances are sometimes accompanied by consonants, usually those produced in the back of the mouth, such as /g/ or /k/. Infants coo when they are in a comfortable state or when a parent has made some attempt to communicate, either with speech or coos of his or her own. In the weeks that follow, the infant's vocalizations become longer and begin to include consonants formed at the front of the mouth, as in /m/ or /b/.

The next significant accomplishment is the emergence of **babbling,** the production of consonant-vowel combinations such as *da* or *ba.* Most children begin to babble at about three to six months and refine their skills in the succeeding months. To many listeners, the infant's babbling sounds like active experimentation with the production of different sounds. In the succeeding weeks, the infant will repeat syllables, such as *bababa* or *dadada.* The repetition of the same consonant-vowel pair is called **reduplicated babbling**. At nine or ten months, the child's babbling includes more numerous and complex consonant-vowel combinations, as well as variations in intonation. In fact, a casual listener might think the child is actually speaking, although he is not yet producing real words.

The changes in children's productive capabilities are linked to physiological changes in their vocal apparatus and central nervous systems that occur during the

cooing Vowel-like utterances that characterize the infant's first attempts to vocalize.

babbling Consonant-vowel utterances that characterize the infant's first attempts to vocalize.

reduplicated babbling Repetition of simple consonant-vowel combinations in the early stages of language development.

KEY THEME
Interaction Among Domains

KEY THEME
Nature/Nurture

first year. In the months after birth, the infant's larynx descends farther into the neck, the oral cavity grows, and the baby can place her tongue in different positions in her mouth (not just forward and backward as at birth). At the same time, the cortex of the brain replaces the brainstem in controlling many of the child's behaviors. In general, early reflexlike vocalizations, such as cries, fade as more controlled voluntary utterances, such as coos and babbles, enter the child's repertoire (Stark, 1986).

The fact that most infants, regardless of their culture, begin to coo and babble at similar ages adds further evidence that biological factors direct the onset of these behaviors. Even deaf children vocalize with coos and babbles in the first few months of life (Stoel-Gammon & Otomo, 1986), and those exposed to sign language make repetitive, rhythmic hand gestures akin to babbling at ten months of age (Petitto & Marentette, 1991). Nature thus plays a distinct role in the emergence of the child's utterances. But even at this early stage of language development, the form the child's vocalizations take is influenced by the language spoken around her. Studies have shown identifiable differences in babbling among infants from varying cultures. One group of researchers conducted a spectral analysis of the vowel sounds made by ten-month-olds in Paris, London, Algiers, and Hong Kong. The procedure involved translating the acoustic properties of speech into a visual representation of the intensity, onset, and pattern of vocalization. Infants from different countries varied in the average frequencies of the sounds they produced; the differences paralleled those of adult speakers from the same countries (Boysson-Bardies et al., 1989). Thus, the child's linguistic environment has a distinct effect on his own speech before he can speak true words.

Gesture as a Communication Tool   Late in the first year, before or as they speak their first words, many children begin to use such gestures as pointing, showing, or giving as a means to communicate with other people (Bates, Camaioni, & Volterra, 1975). Carlotta, a ten-month-old infant Elizabeth Bates and her colleagues observed, was able to display several kinds of nonverbal communication. In one episode, Carlotta held up her toy and extended her arm in a showing motion to an adult. Here she was using a **protodeclarative communication** that, much as a declarative sentence does, called the adult's attention to the object. Another time, Carlotta pointed to the kitchen sink and said, "Ha!", a **protoimperative communication** intended to get the adult to do something (Bates, 1979). Often (such as when Carlotta wanted her drink of water) children's gestures are accompanied by direct eye contact with the communication's recipient. Children may also repeat their communications if the messages are not understood. This constellation of behaviors and the context in which they occur suggest that children use gestures as a purposeful means to an end (Scoville, 1983).

Linda Acredolo and Susan Goodwyn (1988) found that a child between eleven and twenty-four months of age uses gestures not just to show or request but also to symbolize objects or events. The child may signify a flower, for example, by making a sniffing gesture or the desire to go outside with a knob-turning motion. A significant number of children's gestures recreate the functions of objects rather than their forms or shapes. For example, participants in the study would put their fist to one ear to signify a telephone or wave their hands to represent a butterfly.

Acredolo and Goodwyn believe a strong relationship exists between the development of gestures and verbal abilities because both appear at approximately the same point in development, with gestures usually preceding words by a few weeks (Acredolo & Goodwyn, 1988; Goodwin & Acredolo, 1993). Recognizing that one thing can symbolize another represents a major cognitive advance, one that is essential for the use of both gestures and spoken language. Gestures drop out of the child's repertoire by the middle of the second year, however, because they are less useful when the "listener" is out of view and they are usually correctly understood by only a limited number of adults. Parents also probably tend to encourage the child's verbalizations more than they do the use of gestures (Acredolo & Goodwyn, 1990a).

protodeclarative communication   Use of a gesture to call attention to an object or event.

protoimperative communication   Use of a gesture to issue a command or request.

Beginning about one year of age, many young children use gestures to communicate, a sign that they are putting into practice important facets of language. In particular, children show that they are able to use symbols, such that a gesture may stand for an object or request. The ability to use symbols is a prerequisite for spoken speech, as well.

Content: The Acquisition of Semantics

As we saw at the beginning of the chapter, few moments in life rival the excitement parents feel when they hear their children say their first words, typically at about one year of age. "Cookie," "Mama," and "Dada" are joyfully entered into the baby book alongside other momentous events, such as the infant's first steps. Certainly the uttering of first words is a major accomplishment, marking the visible entry of the child into the world of spoken, shared communication. The child's comprehension and production of words also signal a new focus in the mastery of language: semantic development. Although the child continues to refine his or her understanding of phonology, the major task confronting the child now is unraveling the meanings of words.

The One-Word Stage   From about twelve to twenty months of age, most children speak only one word at a time. Children's first words are most frequently **nominals,** labels for objects, people, or events, although action words (*give*), modifiers (*dirty*), and personal-social words (*please*) also occur (Bates et al., 1994; Nelson, 1973). Children's early words usually refer to people or objects important in their lives, such as parents and other relatives, pets, or familiar objects. Children are also more likely to acquire labels for dynamic objects (*clock, car, ball*) or those they can use (*cup, cookie*) than for items that are stationary (*wall, window*). Figure 7.2 shows how the proportion of word types changes in the vocabularies of children between one and two-and-a-half years of age.

Children acquire their first ten words slowly; the typical child adds about one to three words to his or her repertoire each month (Barrett, 1989). From about age eighteen months onward, however, many children show a virtual explosion in the acquisition of new words. This remarkable period in language development is called the **vocabulary spurt** (Barrett, 1985; Bloom, 1973). In one longitudinal study of vocabulary growth in one-to-two-year-olds, some learned to say as many as twenty new words, mostly nouns, during each week of the vocabulary spurt (Goldfield & Reznick, 1990). Figure 7.3 shows the rapid rate of vocabulary growth for three children in the middle of their spurt. Within the same two-month period, children also

nominals   Words that label objects, people, or events; the first type of words most children produce.

vocabulary spurt   Period of rapid word acquisition that typically occurs early in language development.

FIGURE 7.2

Changes in the Proportion of Word Types in Children's Vocabularies

As children's vocabularies grow from only a few words to several hundred (the horizontal axis on the graph), the proportion of nouns rises and remains high. The proportion of other types of words children learn, such as predicates (verbs and adjectives) and closed class words (prepositions, conjunctions, and other relational words), remains lower. The children in this study ranged in age from sixteen to thirty months.

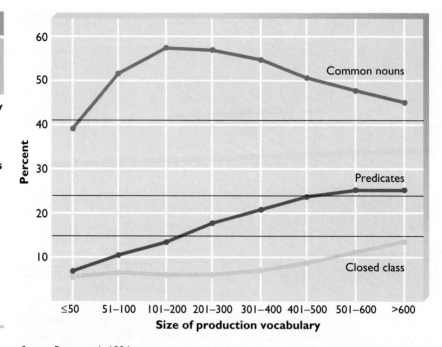

Source: Bates et al., 1994.

typically show a spurt in the number of words they understand (Reznick & Goldfield, 1992). In addition to learning new labels for objects and actions, children begin to use words to express internal states (*yay!*) and to direct the actions of others (*go*) (Nelson, 1973).

Some of the child's first words are bound to a specific context: that is, the child uses the word to label objects in limited situations. Lois Bloom (1973) observed that one nine-month-old used the word *car* only when she was looking out the living room window at cars moving on the street. She did not say "car" to refer to parked

FIGURE 7.3

The Vocabulary Spurt in Three Young Children

Many children show a vocabulary spurt, a sharp rise in the number of new words they learn, as they approach two years of age. However, children may begin their spurts at different ages, as the graph clearly shows. Child A showed an early spurt, beginning at fifteen months. Child B's spurt began at the more typical age of eighteen months. Child C showed a late spurt at twenty-one months.

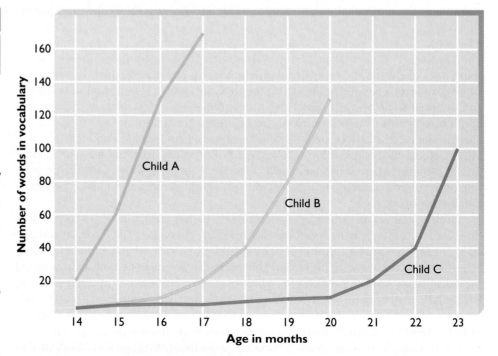

Source: Adapted from Goldfield & Reznick, 1990.

cars, pictures of cars, or cars she was sitting in. This type of utterance, used when the child applies a label to a narrower class of objects than the term signifies, is called an **underextension**. Over time, the child begins to use single words more flexibly in a wider variety of contexts (Barrett, 1986).

Children may also show **overextension,** applying a label to a broader category than the term signifies. For example, a toddler may call a horse or a cow "doggie." The child often applies the same word to objects that look alike perceptually (Clark, 1973). At other times, the child may misuse a word when objects share functions, such as calling a rolling quarter a "ball" (Bowerman, 1978). As with underextensions, the child's use of overextensions declines after the second year.

Comprehension Versus Production   If you have ever tried to learn a new language, you undoubtedly found it easier to understand what another speaker was saying than to produce a sentence in the new language yourself. An important point to remember about children's early language is that their **receptive language,** what they comprehend, far exceeds their **productive language,** their ability to say and use the words. In one study, parents reported an average of 5.7 words produced by their ten-month-olds but a comprehension average about three times greater, 17.9 words (Bates, Bretherton, & Snyder, 1988).

That young children understand so much of what is said to them means they have acquired some important information about language before they actually speak. They know that people, objects, and events have names. They know that specific patterns of sounds represent objects and events in their environment. Most important, they begin to appreciate the usefulness of language as a means of expressing ideas, needs, and feelings.

Individual and Cultural Differences in Language Development   Although children show many common trends in the way they acquire language, they also show significant individual differences in rates and types of language production. You may have heard a family member or friend report that her child said virtually nothing for two or three years and then began speaking in complete sentences. Although such dramatic variations in language milestones are not frequent, children sometimes show unique patterns in their linguistic accomplishments, patterns that still lead to the attainment of normal language by later childhood.

One example of wide individual variation is the age at which children say their first word. Some children produce their first distinguishable word as early as nine months, whereas others may not do so until sixteen months (Barrett, 1989). Similarly, some children show good pronunciation, whereas others have difficulty making certain sounds, consistently substituting *t* for *k* or *b* for *v,* for example (Smith, 1988). In addition, not all children display the vocabulary spurt (Acredolo & Goodwyn, 1990b), or they may start their spurts at different ages, as Figure 7.3 indicates. The results of one recent study of more than eighteen hundred children underscore just how variable the size of children's vocabularies can be: at sixteen months of age, some children spoke 10 or fewer words whereas others spoke as many as 180 words (Fenson et al., 1994).

Children may also differ in the content of their one-word speech. Most one-year-olds tend to use nominals predominantly, displaying what Katherine Nelson (1973) termed a **referential style**. Other children show a different pattern: rather than naming objects, they frequently use words that have social functions, such as *hello* or *please,* thus displaying an **expressive style**. Expressive children use words to direct or comment on the behavior of other people. According to some research, referential children tend to have larger vocabularies and show more rapid advances in language development, at least in the early stages (Bates, Bretherton, & Snyder, 1988; Nelson, 1973).

How do we explain these individual differences in the rates and styles with which children acquire language? There are several hypotheses. Perhaps individual differences result from differences in the neurological structures that control language or

KEY THEME
Individual Differences

underextension Application of a label to a narrower class of objects than the term signifies.

overextension Tendency to apply a label to a broader category than the term actually signifies.

receptive language Ability to comprehend spoken speech.

productive language Meaningful language spoken or otherwise produced by an individual.

referential style Type of early language production in which the child uses mostly nominals.

expressive style Type of early language production in which the child uses many social words.

Chinese mothers use more verbs and action sequences in their speech to children than American mothers. It is interesting to note that Chinese-speaking toddlers use more verbs than nouns in their early speech. Thus, the form of early speech is influenced by the sociocultural context in which the child lives.

KEY THEME
Sociocultural Influence

from inborn differences in temperament. For example, expressive children may be more sociable by nature and thereby use language for interpersonal purposes. Another possibility is that parents influence the rate and form of children's vocabulary development. Some parents, for example, may spend a great deal of time encouraging their infants to speak, focusing especially on labeling objects. Others may be more relaxed about letting the infant proceed at his or her own pace. Researchers have confirmed that the overall amount of speech parents produce when their infants are sixteen months old is related to the acceleration of vocabulary growth (Huttenlocher et al., 1991). In another study, the amount of time parents spent reading stories to their twenty-four-month-olds predicted the child's language ability up to two years later (Crain-Thoreson & Dale, 1992).

Cultural differences in how children speak in the one-word stage bolster the idea that what children hear others say influences what they themselves say. Unlike American children, Korean toddlers show a "verb spurt" before a "noun spurt" (Choi & Gopnik, 1995); similarly, Mandarin-speaking toddlers utter more verbs than nouns in their early speech (Tardif, 1996). Mothers from both Asian groups pepper their speech with many more verbs and action sequences, saying things such as "What are you doing?" and "You put the car in the garage"; American mothers, in contrast, use far more nouns (e.g., "That's a ball") and ask questions that require a nominal as an answer (e.g. "What is it?").

Deriving the Meanings of Words   The number of new words the child learns grows rapidly from age eighteen months through the preschool years. By the time they enter school, children know more than fourteen thousand words (Carey, 1978); by age ten, they comprehend almost forty thousand words. These numbers translate into an astonishing rate of learning of between six and twelve new words per day among school-age children (Anglin, 1993)! Researchers have put forth several hypotheses about how children learn the meanings of words.

One suggestion is that certain elements in early parent-child interactions provide children with clues to the meanings of words. For example, parents of infants tend to label many objects, often in the context of joint book reading or the child's manifest interest in a particular object or person in her surroundings (Ninio & Bruner, 1978). A typical scenario goes like this: The infant turns his head, points, and maybe even coos as the family dog enters the room. The mother also turns and looks, and says "Doggie." Such interactions, in which the parent follows the child's attention and labels the target of her interest, are common between nine and eighteen months of age. Researchers have noted that these are precisely the conditions under which infants seem to remember the words that name objects. For example, one researcher found that children's vocabulary development is strongly related to the tendency of parents to label objects at which the child points (Masur, 1982). In other studies, researchers report that when an adult supplies a label after rather than before the child has looked at an object, the child comprehends the label more accurately (Dunham, Dunham, & Curwin, 1993; Tomasello, 1988, 1992). Thus, children seem to learn words best when they already have the object in mind.

KEY THEME
Child's Active Role

Young language learners, however, are also able to use more subtle cues than labels for explicitly pointed-to objects. Suppose an adult says, "Let's find the *gazzer*" and looks at an object, rejects it, and excitedly picks up another object without naming it. The infant assumes the second object is the *gazzer* (Tomasello, Strosberg, & Akhtar, 1996). Or suppose an adult and an infant are playing with several unfamiliar, unnamed objects; then the adult introduces a new object, saying, "Look, I see a *modi!*" without pointing to any object. Again, the infant assumes the newest object is the *modi* (Akhtar, Carpenter, & Tomasello, 1996). These studies demonstrate that infants have an impressive ability to interpret social cues in deciding how labels and objects match up.

As children begin to speak, parents continue to supply them with information about word meanings, often in the form of corrections when the children make a mistake. "That's not a glass; that's a cup," or "Your soup is not hot; it's cool" are examples of parental verbalizations that not only point out the child's error but also provide the correct words. Children profit from these forms of *linguistic contrast* to learn new terms and labels (Au & Laframboise, 1990).

KEY THEME
Nature/Nurture

A second group of hypotheses places less emphasis on environmental cues and more on the belief that young children actively construct ideas about the meanings of words. Some researchers, for example, suggest that the child acquires word meanings by a process called **fast-mapping,** in which the context in which the child hears words spoken provides the key to their meanings. Often the child's initial comprehension of a word is an incomplete guess, but a fuller understanding of its meaning follows from successive encounters with it in other contexts (Carey, 1978). Suppose the child hears his mother say, "This room looks messy!" as she walks into his toy-strewn bedroom. He might surmise that the word *messy* refers to some characteristic of the room that has to do with the toys being out of the toybox. Another time, he might hear his father say, "You look messy" as the child climbs out of the sandbox. Noticing his dirty T-shirt and sneakers and drawing on his previous interpretation of the word, the child concludes that *messy* refers to a state of disarray. Children are often able to derive the meanings of words quickly, even when the exposure is brief, if the context in which they hear those words is meaningful (Rice & Woodsmall, 1988).

KEY THEME
Child's Active Role

Certain biases operate in the child's literal "search for meaning." Consider the toddler who hears a new word such as *eggbeater*. What does that word mean? Logically, it could refer to a host of objects or perhaps an action instead of an object. Testing the numerous hypotheses could take an inordinate amount of time. Several researchers argue that children are biased to form more restricted hypotheses about the meanings of words; if they were not, they would not learn language so rapidly and with so few errors. *Constraints* on word learning, presumed by many theorists to be innate, give young children an edge in figuring out the meanings of words from the vast array of possibilities.

KEY THEME
Nature/Nurture

One hypothesized bias in word learning is called the **mutual exclusivity bias,** the idea that young children tend to assume that new words label unfamiliar objects

fast-mapping Deriving meanings of words from the contexts in which they are spoken.

mutual exclusivity bias Tendency for children to assume that unfamiliar words label new objects.

There may be constraints on how children learn new words. Children will assume, for example, that a new word such as "eggbeater" labels an unfamiliar object. This tendency is called the *mutual exclusivity bias*.

(Littschwager & Markman, 1994; Markman, 1987, 1990). Researchers have been able to demonstrate experimentally that children tend to treat new words as labels for new objects rather than as synonyms for words they already know. For example, Ellen Markman and Gwyn Wachtel (1988) showed three-year-olds pairs of objects; in each set, one object was familiar and the other was unfamiliar (for example, a banana and a pair of tongs). When children were told, "Show me the *x*" where *x* was a nonsense syllable, they tended to select the unfamiliar objects. The mutual exclusivity bias emerges at about age three and continues to play a role in the ways older children and adults attach meaning to new words (Merriman & Bowman, 1989).

Other biases in word learning include the child's assumption that a new word labels an entire object rather than a part or feature of the object and that the same new word can be extended to include other objects that come from the same conceptual category. Consider a study conducted by Ellen Markman and Jean Hutchinson (1984). Four- and five-year-olds looked at a picture as the experimenter labeled it with a nonsense syllable. For example, a cow was called a *dax*. Then two other pictures were presented, in this case a pig and milk. When asked, "Can you find another *dax*?" most children pointed to the pig, not the milk. In contrast, when children heard no label for the cow and were simply instructed to "find another one," they tended to associate the cow with milk.

Not all researchers agree that constraints on word learning are critical in the earliest stages of language acquisition. For example, Katherine Nelson (1988, 1991) has pointed out that most studies such as those just described involved preschoolers who already had a good deal of experience with language. Thus, it is difficult to argue for innately given constraints on word learning; perhaps word learning biases arise from prior experiences with language. They may also arise from growth in general knowledge about objects and their relationships to one another (Smith, 1995). Other researchers have recently suggested that some word learning biases, such as the "whole object bias," are more important in the early stages of semantic development, whereas others, such as the "category bias," play a larger role in later stages (Golinkoff, Mervis, & Hirsh-Pasek, 1994). Nonetheless, the idea that children are predisposed to learn certain aspects of language continues to be popular for explaining not only semantic development but the emergence of syntax as well.

no bed	boot off	more car	airplane all gone
no down	light off	more cereal	Calico all gone
no fix	pants off	more cookie	Calico all done
no home	shirt off	more fish	all done milk
no mama	shoe off	more high	all done now
no more	water off	more hot	all gone juice
no pee	off bib	more juice	all gone outside
no plug		more read	all gone pacifier
no water		more sing	salt all shut
no wet		more toast	
		more walk	
		outside more	

TABLE 7.1

One Child's Pivot Grammar

This table shows several examples of one two-year-old's two-word speech. Frequently one word—the pivot word—is repeated while several other words—open words—fill the other slot. The pivot word can occupy either the first or second position in the child's utterances.

Source: Adapted from Braine, 1976.

Form: The Acquisition of Syntax

Around the child's second birthday, another significant achievement in language production appears: the child becomes able to produce more than one word at a time to express ideas, needs, and desires. At first, two-word utterances such as "Doggie go" and "More juice" prevail, but the child soon combines greater numbers of words in forms that loosely resemble the grammatical structure of his or her native language. In combining words, the child displays an awareness of the different syntactic categories into which words fall. "Doggie go" illustrates the child's understanding of nouns and verbs as distinct classes of words. Moreover, when children combine words, they are stating more than just labels for familiar items; they are expressing relationships among objects and events in the world. All of this represents no small feat for a two-year-old.

Early Grammars: The Two-Word Stage   At first, children's two-word utterances consist of combinations of nouns, verbs, and adjectives and omit the conjunctions, prepositions, and other modifiers that give speech its familiar flow. Because speech at this stage usually contains only the elements essential to getting the message across, it is often described as **telegraphic speech**.

In his systematic observations of the language of three children, Martin Braine (1976) noted that speech at this stage contained a unique syntactic structure that he dubbed **pivot grammar**. The speech of the children he observed contained noticeable regularities: one word often functioned in a fixed position, while other words filled in the empty slot. For example, one child said, "More car, more cookie, more juice, more read." In this string of utterances, *more* functions as a *pivot word*, an anchor for a variety of *open words*. The child's grammar could consist of [pivot word + open word], as in the example, or [open word + pivot word], as in "Boots off, pants off, water off." Table 7.1 contains several other examples of a two-year-old's early word combinations.

Linguists have described other regularities in children's grammars that reflect the incorporation of semantic knowledge into the use of syntax. Table 7.2 summarizes the regularities of child speech in the two-word stage that one researcher found in ten different cultures (Brown, 1973). In children's verbalizations, agents consistently precede actions, as in "Mommy come" or "Daddy sit." At the same time, inanimate objects are usually not named as agents. The child rarely says, "Wall go." To avoid

telegraphic speech   Early two-word speech that contains few modifiers, prepositions, or other connective words.

pivot grammar   Early two-word grammar in which one word is repeated and a series of other words fills the second slot.

	Semantic Relation	Examples
TABLE 7.2	agent + action	Mommy come; Adam write
Examples of Semantic Relations in Child Syntax	action + object	eat cookie; wash hand
	agent + object	Mommy sock; Eve lunch
	action + location	sit chair; go park
	entity + location	lady home; baby highchair
	possessor + possession	my teddy; Daddy chair
	entity + attribute	block yellow; box shiny
	demonstrative + entity	dat book; dis doggie

Children's word orders often reflect knowledge of semantic relationships, such as the idea that agents precede actions or that actions are followed by locations. Roger Brown believes the semantic relations shown in this table are incorporated into the syntactic constructions of children in many different cultures.

Source: Adapted from Brown, 1973.

KEY THEME
Individual Differences

making this utterance, the child must know the meaning of *wall* and that walls do not move. The child's semantic knowledge is thus related to the production of highly ordered two-word utterances.

Many experts currently believe that no one syntactic system defines the structure of early language for all children (Maratsos, 1983; Tager-Flusberg, 1985). Some children speak with nouns, verbs, adjectives, and sometimes adverbs in the pivot grammar described by Braine, whereas others pepper their speech with pronouns and other words such as *I, it,* and *here* (Bloom, Lightbown, & Hood, 1975). Most researchers agree, however, that individual children frequently use consistent word orders and that their understanding of at least a small set of semantic relationships is related to that word order. Moreover, numerous detailed observations of children's language indicate that they never construct "wild grammars"; some utterances, such as "Big he" or "Hot it," are simply never heard (Bloom, 1990). Such observations have distinct implications for explanations of syntactic development.

Later Syntactic Development   At age two-and-a-half, children's speech often exceeds two words in length and includes many more of the modifiers and connective words that enrich the quality of speech. Adjectives, pronouns, and prepositions are added to the child's repertoire (Valian, 1986). Between ages two and five, the child's speech also includes increasingly sophisticated grammatical structures. **Inflections,** endings to words (such as *-s, -ed,* and *-ing*) that signal plurals or verb tense, become incorporated into routine utterances, as do more articles and conjunctions. Also, the child comes to use negatives, questions, and passives correctly.

In her examination of language acquisition in four children, Lois Bloom (1991) found a predictable sequence in the use of negatives. Initially, children use the negative to express the nonexistence of objects, as in "no pocket," said as the child searches for a pocket in her mother's skirt. In the second stage, children use the negative as they reject objects or events. For example, one of Bloom's subjects said "no sock" as she pulled her sock off her foot. Finally, negatives are used to express denial, such as when the child states "No dirty" in response to his mother's comment about his dirty sock. Young children form negatives not just by putting the negative marker at the beginning of an utterance but also by embedding it deep within a statement, as in "My sweetie's no gone" (de Villiers & de Villiers, 1979).

Questions too are formed in a fairly consistent developmental sequence, although not all children display the pattern we are about to describe (Maratsos, 1983). Children's earliest questions do not contain inverted word order but consist instead of an affirmative sentence or a declarative preceded by a *wh-* word (*who, what, why, when, where*), with a rising intonation at the end of the statement ("Mommy is tired?"). Subsequently, children form questions by inverting word order for affirmative ques-

inflection Alteration to a word, such as tense or plural form, that indicates its syntactical function.

tions ("Where will you go?") but not negative ones ("Why you can't do it?"). Finally, by age four, children form questions for both positive and negative instances as adults do (Klima & Bellugi, 1966).

One of the more difficult linguistic constructions for children to understand is the passive voice, as in "The car was hit by the truck." Children typically begin to comprehend the meaning of a passive construction by the later preschool years, but they may not use this grammatical form spontaneously and correctly until several years later. Generally, children understand passive constructions that convey some action, such as "The boy was kissed by the girl," before they understand those without action, such as "John was liked by Mary" (Maratsos et al., 1979). This finding suggests that action is a salient feature not only as children learn their first words but also as they acquire the rules of syntax.

One interesting phenomenon of the preschool and early school years is the child's tendency to use **overregularizations,** the application of grammatical rules to words that require exceptions to those rules. From time to time, for example, young children use words such as *goed* or *runned* to express past tense even if they previously used the correct forms, *went* and *ran*. Perhaps children make these mistakes because they forget the exception to the general rule for forming a tense (Marcus, 1996). Whatever the reason, these constructions plainly indicate that the child is learning the general rules for forming past tense, plurals, and other grammatical forms (Marcus et al., 1992).

What are the common patterns in children's acquisition of the complexities of syntax? We have seen that children comprehend negatives, questions, and passives well before they can correctly produce them. In addition, children's own uses of these sophisticated grammatical forms begin as imperfect versions that gradually approach the more adult versions. Thus, the child's progression to mature speech shows a distinct orderliness. Accounting for the consistencies in children's acquisition of syntax remains a major challenge for psychologists concerned with language development.

Context: The Acquisition of Pragmatics

Just as important as semantic and syntactic rules are cultural requirements or customs pertaining to the proper use of speech in a social context. Is the child speaking with an elder or a peer? Is the context formal or informal? How does the speaker express politeness? Each situation suggests some unique characteristics of speech, a tone of voice, a formal or more casual syntactic structure, and the choice of specific words. In the context of playing with a best friend, saying "Gimme that" might be perfectly appropriate; when speaking with the first-grade teacher, saying "Could I please have that toy?" will probably produce a more favorable reaction. These examples demonstrate the child's grasp of pragmatics.

Acquiring Social Conventions in Speech   When do children first understand that different situations call for different forms of speech? When Jean Gleason and Rivka Perlmann (1985) asked two-to-five-year-olds and their parents to play "store," they observed that at age three some children modified their speech depending on the role they were playing. For example, one three-and-a-half-year-old boy who was the "customer" pointed to a fake milk bottle and said, "I want . . . I would like milk." His revision showed an understanding that an element of politeness is required of a customer. Preschoolers also have some limited understanding that different listeners are typically spoken to in different ways. In a study in which four- and five-year-olds were asked to speak to dolls portraying adults, peers, or younger children, the participants used more imperatives with dolls representing children and fewer with dolls representing adults and peers (James, 1978).

The child's facility with social forms of politeness increases with age. Researchers in one study instructed two-to-six-year-olds to *ask* or *tell* another person to give them a puzzle piece. Older children were rated by adults as being more polite than

overregularization   Inappropriate application of syntactic rules to words and grammatical forms that show exceptions.

When speaking to children younger than themselves, four- and five-year-olds often repeat their utterances and use attention-getting devices. These behaviors indicate that young children are sensitive to the requirements of the listener, an important aspect of *referential communication*. Thus, during the preschool years, children show progress in understanding the pragmatic aspects of language.

KEY THEME
Nature/Nurture

the younger children, particularly when they were asking for the puzzle piece. Usually, older children included such words as *please* in their requests of another person (Bock & Hornsby, 1981).

Parents undoubtedly play a significant role in at least some aspects of the acquisition of pragmatics, especially because they deliberately train their children to speak politely. Esther Greif and Jean Gleason (1980) observed the reactions of parents and children after children had received a gift from a laboratory assistant. If the child did not say "thank you" spontaneously (and most of the preschoolers in the sample did not), the parent typically prompted the child with "What do you say?" or "Say thank you." Parents also serve as models for politeness routines; most parents in the study greeted the laboratory assistant upon entry and said goodbye when the assistant departed.

Incorporating social conventions into language often involves learning subtle nuances in behaviors, the correct words, vocal intonations, gestures, or facial expressions that accompany speech in different contexts. Children may get direct instruction on the use of forms of politeness, but it is not yet clear exactly how they acquire the other behaviors that accompany socially skilled communication.

Referential Communication   A group of experiments that has been especially useful in providing information on children's awareness of themselves and others as effective communicators centers on **referential communication,** situations that require the child to either talk about a topic specified by the experimenter or evaluate the effectiveness of a message describing some sequence of events. Researchers note whether the child's message is sufficient to communicate his or her intent or, alternatively, whether the child is able to detect ambiguous or uninformative components in the messages heard.

In a classic study of referential communication, Robert Krauss and Sam Glucksberg (1969) asked four- and five-year-olds to describe a series of unfamiliar geometric forms to another child who could not see them (see Figure 7.4). The speaker had to provide the listener with enough information to duplicate an array the speaker was constructing. The results showed that children this age often rely on personal descriptions of the stimuli (e.g., "It looks like Daddy's shirt"), messages that are not at all helpful to the listener. Thus, young children's ability to understand the requirements of the listener and to adjust their speech accordingly is limited when they are describing unfamiliar items and when the interaction is not face to face.

referential communication
Communication in situations that require the speaker to describe an object to a listener or to evaluate the effectiveness of a message.

Source: Adapted from Krauss & Glucksberg, 1969.

FIGURE 7.4

An Experiment in Referential Communication

In Krauss and Gluckberg's (1969) study of referential communication, four- and five-year-olds had to describe a series of unfamiliar geometric forms (pasted on blocks) to other children who could not see them. In this illustration, for example, the speaker on the left must explain to the listener on the right which forms to place on the stacking peg. The results showed that children this age are generally ineffective in transmitting this type of information. Research in more naturalistic settings, however, demonstrates that preschoolers can engage in effective referential communication.

On the other hand, observations of children in more natural interactions with one another suggest that well before they enter school, children appreciate at least some of the requirements of the listener and can modify their speech to make their communication effective. In a study of the communication skills of preschool-age children, Marilyn Shatz and Rochel Gelman (1973) asked four-year-olds to describe a toy to either an adult or a two-year-old listener. When the children spoke to the younger child, they shortened their utterances, used simple constructions, repeated utterances, and employed more attention-getting devices than when they spoke to the adult. Other researchers have also observed that even two-year-olds use techniques to make sure their messages get across during the normal interactions that occur in a nursery school. Children point, seek eye contact with listeners, and use verbal attention getters such as "hey" to ensure that listeners hear what they have to say (Wellman & Lempers, 1977).

Developmental advances occur in referential communication skills. By the time they enter elementary school, children show the ability to detect problems in other people's messages and can even suggest revisions. The ability to evaluate the adequacy of a communication is called **comprehension monitoring**. Carole Beal (1987) asked children to trace a route on a road map according to a set of instructions that was read to them. While most children were able to identify uninformative instructions as such and to suggest revisions that would make the message clearer, second graders showed greater skill in doing so than first-graders.

Children ages seven to thirteen show wide individual differences in the ability to interact effectively with others (Anderson, Clark, & Mullen, 1994). The mature use of language involves the ability to understand the demands of the situation, be sensitive to the needs of the listener, and employ subtle nuances in speech that are compatible with the situation. The child's failure to acquire the social skills that are a part of effective communication can have broad consequences for the qualities of relationships she or he establishes with parents, teachers, and peers, among others.

KEY THEME
Individual Differences

KEY THEME
Interaction Among Domains

Abstraction: The Acquisition of Metalinguistic Awareness

During the period of most rapid language learning, from about eighteen months through age five, children may lack a full understanding of what it means for a sentence to be grammatical or how to gauge their linguistic competencies, even when their speech is syntactically correct and effective in delivering a communication. The ability to reflect abstractly on the properties of language and to conceptualize the self

comprehension monitoring
Ability to evaluate the adequacy of a communication.

as a more or less proficient user of this communication tool is called **metalinguistic awareness**. By most accounts, the child does not begin to think about language in this way until at least the early school years. However, there are some indicators that a rudimentary ability begins sometime before that.

Reflecting on Properties of Language   One of the first studies to explore children's ideas about the function of grammar was conducted by Lila Gleitman and her colleagues (Gleitman, Gleitman, & Shipley, 1972). The investigators had mothers read grammatically correct and incorrect passages to their two-, five-, and eight-year-old children. After each sentence, an experimenter said "Good" at the end of an acceptable passage, such as "Bring me the ball," or "Silly" at the end of an unacceptable one, such as "Box the open." When the children were given the opportunity to judge sentences themselves, even the youngest children were generally able to discriminate between correct and incorrect versions. They were not able, however, to correct improper constructions or to explain the nature of the syntactic problem until age five.

Not until age six or seven do most children appreciate that words are different from the concepts to which they are linked. For example, four-year-olds frequently believe *train* is a long word because its referent is long (Berthoud-Papandropoulou, 1978). Some changes in metalinguistic understanding are undoubtedly linked to advances in cognition, particularly the development of more flexible and abstract thought.

Humor and Metaphor   One visible way in which children demonstrate their metalinguistic awareness is through language play: creating funny words, telling jokes or riddles, or using words in a figurative sense. The ways in which children comprehend and produce humorous verbalizations undergo clear developmental changes from the preschool to later school years. Three-to-five-year-olds frequently experiment with the sounds of words, altering phonemes to create humorous facsimiles (for example, *watermelon* becomes *fatermelon*) (McGhee, 1979). By the early school years, the basis of children's humor expands to include riddles or jokes based on semantic ambiguities, as in the following:

> *Question:* How can hunters in the woods find their lost dogs?
> *Answer:*   By putting their ears to a tree and listening to the bark.

Still later—as every parent who has ever had to listen to a seemingly endless string of riddles and jokes from a school-age child can testify—children begin to understand and be fascinated by jokes and riddles that require them to discern syntactic ambiguities (Hirsch-Pasek, Gleitman, & Gleitman, 1978), as in the following:

> *Question:* Where would you go to see a man-eating shark?
> *Answer:*   A seafood restaurant.

Thus, children's appreciation of humor mirrors their increasingly sophisticated knowledge of the various features of language, beginning with its fundamental sounds and culminating with the complexities of syntactic and semantic rules. It appears that each change in the orientation of children's humor comes after children have conquered a particular facet of language.

Similarly, children's understanding of **metaphor,** figurative language in which a term that typically describes one object or event is applied to another context (for example, calling a shadow a "piece of the night" or skywriting a "scar in the sky"), undergoes developmental change. Even preschoolers show a rudimentary comprehension of figurative language, especially when it refers to perceptual similarities between two objects. A four-year-old understands expressions such as "A string is like a snake," for example (Winner, 1979). In later childhood and adolescence, children understand and even prefer metaphors grounded in conceptual relationships, such as "The volcano is a very angry man" (Silberstein et al., 1982).

The development of metalinguistic skills necessarily follows the acquisition of phonological, semantic, and syntactic knowledge. After all, the ability to reflect on and even play with the properties of language demands that a person first possess a basic

KEY THEME
Interaction Among Domains

metalinguistic awareness
Ability to reflect on language as a communication tool and on the self as a user of language.

metaphor   Figurative language in which a term is transferred from the object it customarily designates to describe a comparable object or event.

understanding of those properties. In addition, metalinguistic skill is probably tied to advances in thinking skills in general. Just how children move from concrete to abstract thinking and come to reflect on their thought processes are topics to which we will return in the next chapter, when we discuss the development of cognition.

The Sequence of Language Acquisition: An Overview

The Chronology on page 236 summarizes the child's progression in attaining language. Three points about the sequence are especially noteworthy. First, language development proceeds in an orderly fashion. Although individuals may vary in the ages at which they attain language milestones or in the precise form of those achievements, children do not acquire language in a haphazard fashion. Second, children learn language rapidly and with seemingly little effort. With the exception of those with some serious physical or psychological problem, all children learn to speak within only a few years, despite the diverse range of skills required. Third, children produce *generative* language; that is, they do not merely duplicate what others say but create novel and unique expressions of their own. How can we account for these remarkable achievements? Although we have already alluded to some possibilities in describing language development, it is time to more closely examine several major theoretical positions.

EXPLAINING LANGUAGE ACQUISITION

Psychologists, linguists, and others intrigued by the process of language development have proposed a number of theories to account for the sequence of acquisition. The theories range from biological and linguistic accounts that underscore the importance of innate language predispositions to theories that emphasize children's experiences in the environment. This section examines five major perspectives on the development of language.

The Biological Perspective

The human brain contains several areas associated with the understanding and production of language. As we saw in Chapter 5, the right and left hemispheres of the brain have specialized functions, a phenomenon called *lateralization*. The primary regions that control language processing in most people are found in the left hemisphere. A major question arising from knowledge of the brain's involvement in language is the extent to which the milestones of language acquisition are controlled by physiological maturation of brain structures and, more specifically, by lateralization.

The Brain and Language   Studies of individuals who have suffered brain damage due to stroke, traumatic injury, or illness have pinpointed two specific regions in the left hemisphere that play a vital role in the ability to use language. The first is **Broca's area,** located in the left frontal region near the motor cortex (see Figure 7.5). Patients who have damage in this region evidence **expressive aphasia,** or the inability to speak fluently, although their comprehension abilities remain intact. The second region, **Wernicke's area,** is in the temporal region of the left hemisphere, close to the areas of the brain responsible for auditory processing. Damage to Wernicke's area results in **receptive aphasia,** in which speech seems fluent—at least on the surface—but contains nonsense or incomprehensible words; the ability to understand the speech of others is also impaired. An important finding is that children are more likely than adults to recover language functions following injury to the left hemisphere (Annett, 1973; Basser, 1962); their brains are said to have greater *plasticity*.

Recent technological advances in the ability to record electrical activity in the brain have yielded further information on the brain's involvement in language. When adults are asked to engage in a semantic task, brain wave activity is greatest in the top central regions; when the task involves syntax, brain wave activity is greatest in the

KEY THEME
Nature/Nurture

Broca's area   Portion of the cerebral cortex that controls expressive language.

expressive aphasia   Loss of the ability to speak fluently.

Wernicke's area   Portion of the cerebral cortex that controls language comprehension.

receptive aphasia   Loss of the ability to comprehend speech.

CHRONOLOGY
Language Development

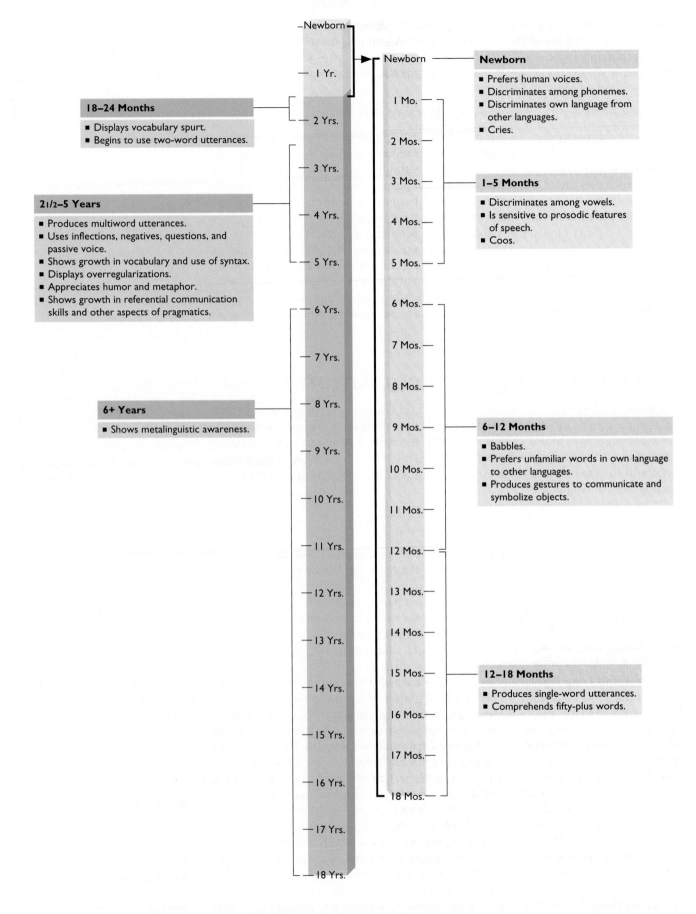

Newborn

- Prefers human voices.
- Discriminates among phonemes.
- Discriminates own language from other languages.
- Cries.

1–5 Months

- Discriminates among vowels.
- Is sensitive to prosodic features of speech.
- Coos.

6–12 Months

- Babbles.
- Prefers unfamiliar words in own language to other languages.
- Produces gestures to communicate and symbolize objects.

12–18 Months

- Produces single-word utterances.
- Comprehends fifty-plus words.

18–24 Months

- Displays vocabulary spurt.
- Begins to use two-word utterances.

2 1/2–5 Years

- Produces multiword utterances.
- Uses inflections, negatives, questions, and passive voice.
- Shows growth in vocabulary and use of syntax.
- Displays overregularizations.
- Appreciates humor and metaphor.
- Shows growth in referential communication skills and other aspects of pragmatics.

6+ Years

- Shows metalinguistic awareness.

This chart describes the sequence of language development based on the findings of research. Children often show individual differences in the exact ages at which they display the various developmental achievements outlined here.

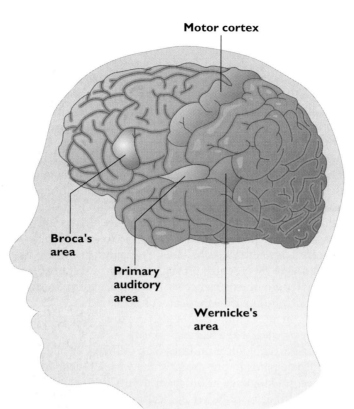

Motor cortex

Broca's area

Primary auditory area

Wernicke's area

FIGURE 7.5

The Two Portions of the Left Cortex of the Brain Responsible for Language Processing

Broca's area governs the production of speech, and Wernicke's area is responsible for the comprehension of speech. Damage to the former produces expressive aphasia, whereas damage to the latter leads to receptive aphasia.

side portion of the left hemisphere (Munte, Heinze, & Mangun, 1993). Recordings of brain wave activity also indicate that before young children begin speaking, brain wave activity as they listen to words they comprehend is distributed across many regions of the brain. Once they start speaking, brain waves become more focused in the left hemisphere (Mills, Coffey-Corina, & Neville, 1993, 1994). *Neuropsychological studies* such as these suggest that some (but perhaps not all) language processing is localized in the left hemisphere and that localization occurs after the first year.

Several other features of language acquisition suggest a strong biological component. Like motor milestones, language milestones are attained in a predictable sequence, regardless of the environment in which the child grows up (except for a few rare cases of extreme environmental deprivation). In addition, all languages share such features as phonology, semantics, and syntax, elements that Lenneberg (1967) and others believed derive from the biologically determined capabilities of human beings. Indeed, children do seem to be driven to learn language, even in the absence of linguistic stimulation. One group of researchers studied a group of congenitally deaf preschool-age children who had not been taught sign language because parents were led to believe it would impede their ability to learn oral communication. None of them had learned to speak yet. Even so, the children had developed a unique gestural system of communication that followed the same sequence used by hearing children, that is, a one-symbol stage, followed by a two-symbol stage, and so forth (Feldman, Goldin-Meadow, & Gleitman, 1978). For these children, language literally "dripped" out of their fingers.

Critical Periods and Language Learning Lenneberg (1967) claimed that to speak and comprehend normally, children must acquire all language basics by adolescence, when physiological changes in the brain make language learning more difficult. He thus proposed a *critical period* for the acquisition of language. A few rare case studies of children who have been isolated from social contact for protracted periods support his position. One girl, Genie, had minimal human contact from age twenty months until thirteen years due to isolation imposed by her parents. She did not

KEY THEME
Continuity/Discontinuity

speak at all. After she was found and received extensive therapy, Genie made some progress in learning words but never learned to speak normally, showing special difficulty in completely mastering the rules of syntax (Curtiss, 1977). Other evidence comes from studies of deaf people who learned American Sign Language (ASL) at different times in life. Elissa Newport (1990) found that participants who learned ASL after age twelve showed consistent errors in the use of grammar, whereas participants who were exposed to ASL from birth displayed a normal course in the development of the language.

Another implication of Lenneberg's hypothesis is that children will also find it difficult to learn a second language if they begin during or after adolescence. Here too there is evidence to support his ideas. Jacqueline Johnson and Elissa Newport (1989) assessed the ability of Chinese and Korean immigrants who learned English as a second language to judge the grammatical correctness of more than two hundred English sentences. Some participants started to learn English as early as age three, others not until age seventeen or later. The older they were before learning English, the poorer were their scores on the grammar test. Other analyses showed that factors such as length of experience with English, amount of formal instruction in English, or identification with American culture could not account for the findings. Newport (1990) concludes that "in language . . . the child, and not the adult, appears to be especially privileged as a learner" (p. 12).

Neuropsychological findings with bilingual speakers complement the above findings. Participants in one recent study were Chinese adults who had acquired English as a second language at different points in their lifetimes. While participants read sentences that were either correct or violated semantic or syntactic rules, the researchers monitored their brain wave activity. Brain wave patterns suggested that the age of second-language acquisition made a special difference for syntactic tasks; if English had been acquired after age four, electrical activity in the left hemisphere showed a different pattern than if English had been acquired earlier in childhood (Weber-Fox & Neville, 1996).

Critics point to problems in interpreting some of the research cited in support of the critical-period hypothesis. Genie, for example, may have suffered serious cognitive, physiological, and emotional deficits because of her prolonged isolation from other humans, deficits that could well account for her lack of mature language. Deaf people who learn ASL later in life still learn a good deal about the syntactic system and are able to communicate. And some individuals who learn a second language in adulthood acquire the phonology, vocabulary, and syntax of that language with na-

Acquiring a second language in early childhood typically leads to greater facility with that language compared with learning the second language later in childhood or adulthood. It is not uncommon, for example, for children of immigrants to help their parents in communicating in the nonnative language. Observations such as these provide support for the idea that there is a critical period for language learning.

tivelike proficiency (Snow, 1987b). In fact, in the early stages of acquisition, adults typically learn a second language more rapidly than children do (McLaughlin, 1984). Nonetheless, children may have a distinct advantage over adults in language learning, which makes early childhood an ideal time to acquire a second language.

To summarize, ample and convincing evidence exists for a biological explanation for language development. An explanation based solely on biology, however, cannot account for all aspects of language development. Languages vary enormously in the ways they express relations and concepts. Let us take one example: how specificity versus generality is expressed. In English, we say "I want *the* car" or "I want *a* car" to represent the respective ideas. In some African languages, however, different intonation patterns rather than different words convey the distinction (Maratsos, 1989). Clearly, biology alone cannot explain the vast differences in the ways languages express ideas or the fact that children end up speaking different languages depending on their culture. It is obvious that a place must be found for the role of nurture, or experience.

KEY THEME
Nature/Nurture

KEY THEME
Sociocultural Influence

The Learning Perspective

One of the earliest attempts to explain language acquisition came from learning theorists. B. F. Skinner (1957) and other behaviorists regarded language as a behavior like any other, whose appearance and development could be accounted for by the basic principles of learning. Reinforcement and imitation were the mechanisms that explained the child's acquisition of phonology, semantics, syntax, and pragmatic rules.

KEY THEME
Nature/Nurture

Learning theorists believe productive language is initially shaped through the selective reinforcement of the child's earliest vocalizations. At first, utterances that even remotely resemble the child's native language are rewarded by caregivers with smiles, hugs, or an enthusiastic "Good!", whereas other, random sounds are ignored or discouraged. Gradually, parents and others expect the child's verbalizations to conform more closely to the phonological and syntactic structure of their language before they will reward her. Later in infancy, the verbalization "Baba" may not receive the reinforcements it once did when the child signals for her bottle; only a more accurate pronunciation will do.

Imitation also plays a significant role, according to the learning theorists. As parents and other more experienced users of language label objects for children and speak in syntactically correct sentences, they provide models of competent and mature language use for young language learners. Children do, after all, learn the phonology, syntax, and conversational rules of the culture into which they are born; they must be influenced by the linguistic models in their environment.

Do parents differentially reinforce grammatically correct and incorrect sentences with any consistency? Some evidence suggests that parents tend to respond to the truth value of children's utterances rather than their grammatical correctness. Thus, a grammatically flawed statement, such as "I no like spinach," might be followed by "Yes, I know" from the parent, whereas a perfectly constructed statement, such as "I'm sleeping" would probably be met with "No, you're not" (Brown & Hanlon, 1970).

Parents, however, do sometimes provide indirect feedback about the correctness of child speech. A mother (the parent whose verbalizations to children have been studied most) often follows the child's grammatically incorrect utterances with **recasts,** repetitions of the child's verbalization with some elaboration: when the child says, "Ball fall," his mother might reply, "Yes, the ball fell." Recasts provide children with cues that their verbalization needs improvement and a model for how to improve. Children often imitate the parent's recasts (Farrar, 1992). On the other hand, parents frequently follow the child's grammatically correct utterances with extensions of the topic rather than expansion of the child's syntactic form. Extensions of the topic suggest to the child that his message was understood and therefore correctly expressed (Penner, 1987). Other researchers have noted that parents are more likely to ask for clarification after a poorly formed sentence than after a well-formed one

recast Repetition of a child's utterance along with some new elements.

(Bohannon & Stanowicz, 1988; Demetras, Post, & Snow, 1986). Thus, although parents do not always directly reinforce the grammatical correctness of child speech, they do sometimes provide subtle feedback regarding the child's use of syntactic rules.

While learning theory may help us understand some facets of language acquisition, it has some significant limitations. One is its inability to account for the occurrence of *overregularizations,* for example, when a preschooler uses a word such as *goed* or *runned.* The child is not likely to encounter models for these grammatical mistakes in her language environment. It is also unlikely that parents encourage children to generate these erroneous constructions. The phenomenon of overregularization suggests instead that children actively abstract the general rules for forming tenses, plurals, and other grammatical forms from the language they hear spoken around them and then overuse the rules.

Another important limitation of the learning perspective is the assumption that the child plays a passive role in acquiring language. We have already seen that even in the earliest stages of learning language, children actively experiment with the production of sounds regardless of the reactions of caregivers. They point to objects that their parents subsequently label for them and create two- or three-word utterances that others have never spoken to them. Indeed, the fact that so much of language acquisition is "child driven" lies behind the emergence of alternative theories of language development.

The Linguistic Perspective

Noam Chomsky (1980, 1986) and other linguists emphasize the structures that all languages share, those syntactic regularities that the young language learner quickly identifies in the course of everyday exposure to speech, such as when the child learning English notices that nouns representing agents precede verbs and nouns representing the objects of actions follow verbs. According to Chomsky, children possess an innate system of language learning, called *universal grammar,* that predisposes them to notice the general linguistic properties of any language. As children are exposed to a specific language, a process called *parameter setting* takes place; that is, "switches" for the grammatical rules that distinguish English from Japanese or Arabic from French are set. After abstracting the general rules of language, children apply them to form their own novel and creative utterances. Language learning, say most linguists, is different from other forms of learning; there are constraints on what the child will be predisposed to learn, and language learning is governed by distinct principles, separate from those that guide cognition and other domains. Furthermore, many linguists believe language is a uniquely human enterprise, one that is not part of the behavioral repertoire of other species.

Research evidence supports many of the tenets linguists hold regarding how language is acquired. Children learn syntactic rules for forming plurals, past tense, and other grammatical forms rapidly in their first five years and can even apply them to words they have never heard before. In a famous experiment, Jean Berko (1958) demonstrated this phenomenon by presenting children with several nonsense words such as *wug.* Children were able to state correctly that the plural form of *wug* is *wugs,* although they had never heard made-up words such as these. Moreover, linguistic theories fare better than learning theories in explaining the occurrence of overregularizations; these can be seen as the product of a language learner who has done too good a job, implementing rules even in cases where exceptions exist.

What kinds of cues does spoken language provide to children for deducing the rules of syntax? Some clues may come from the phonology or sounds of language. Is the word *record* a noun or a verb, for example? The answer depends on which syllable is stressed; if the first, the word is a noun; if the second, it is a verb. Children may pick up cues from stress, the number of syllables in a word, or other tips from the sounds of language to help them classify words as nouns, verbs, or other grammatical categories (Kelly, 1992).

KEY THEME
Child's Active Role

KEY THEME
Nature/Nurture

KEY THEME
Child's Active Role

Other cues about syntax may come from the meanings of words. According to the **semantic bootstrapping hypothesis,** for example, when children learn that a certain animal is called a *dog,* they also notice that it is a thing (noun) and, later in development, that it is an agent (subject) or a recipient (object) of action (Pinker, 1984, 1987). The tendency to make such assumptions is hypothesized to be innate.

Linguistic approaches help to explain just how children can master the complex, abstract rules that characterize all languages, given what some have called the "impoverished input" provided by the environment (Lightfoot, 1982). That is, the stream of speech most children hear is fraught with incomplete or ungrammatical utterances. Nor do children learn language from explicit teaching of the rules of grammar or lists of vocabulary words. However, critics point out that linguistic approaches may reflect more closely the biases of adult theoreticians who attempt to describe the logical necessities of language achievements than the actual processes children use. In addition, it is not clear that language abilities are limited to the human species, as many linguists claim. In the past several decades, numerous attempts have been made to train members of the ape family to use language, all with some apparent success (Gardner & Gardner, 1971; Premack, 1971; Rumbaugh, Gill, & von Glasersfield, 1973). Many early studies were criticized on methodological grounds (Terrace et al., 1979). Nevertheless, in one recent, well-controlled study, an ape named Kanzi was raised from infancy with exposure to human speech similar to that provided to a young girl named Alia. When Kanzi was eight years old and Alia was two, they were tested on their ability to comprehend an assortment of novel sentences, such as "Take the potato outdoors." On many of the sentences, ape and child performed equally well (Savage-Rumbaugh et al., 1993). Therefore, language may have an evolutionary heritage in species that predate humans. Whatever its shortcomings, though, the linguistic approach has helped to capture some of the complexities of language development overlooked by other theoretical perspectives.

The Cognitive Perspective

According to the cognitive perspective, language follows from the path set by advances in the child's thinking processes. Theorists vary, however, in the precise way they link cognition with language.

In Piaget's framework, children must have certain knowledge about the concepts to which given labels apply before they can use names for objects, events, or people. In particular, infants must have grasped fully the notion of *object permanence,* the fact that an object continues to exist even when it is no longer in view. In addition, Piaget believed that during most of their first two years, children do not yet use symbolic schemes; hence, their language abilities are quite limited before this age. Once the **semiotic function,** or the cognitive ability to symbolize, emerges, however, language becomes possible. Piaget's ideas—that changes in underlying cognitive structures precede language—explain why children's first words usually name objects rather than other semantic categories and also account for the rapid expansion of vocabulary at age eighteen months.

Other theorists argue that children's language attainments reflect different emerging cognitive skills. For example, it may be no accident that children's first words tend to be nouns such as *dog* and not *animal* or *collie.* Learning to organize objects at this intermediate level seems to be easier for young children than using either broader or more specific categories (Mervis, 1984; Mervis & Crisafi, 1982; Rosch et al., 1976), and the child's language reflects this cognitive preference. Growth in memory, the ability to analyze and dissect complex stimuli, as well as the ability to classify objects in the first place, are other candidates for cognitive precursors of language (Bates, Thal, & Marchman, 1991).

Do cognitive achievements precede linguistic milestones, as Piaget and others suggest? In studies in which researchers have explored the relationship between attainment of object permanence and language, the correlations have been only moderate or weak (Corrigan, 1979). On the other hand, Elizabeth Bates and her colleagues

KEY THEME
Nature/Nurture

KEY THEME
Interaction Among Domains

semantic bootstrapping hypothesis Idea that children derive information about syntax from the meanings of words.

semiotic function Ability to symbolize objects.

found that skills such as imitation, tool use, and the complex manipulation of objects do predict language attainments (Bates et al., 1979). Alison Gopnik and Andrew Meltzoff (1986) have identified still other cognitive skills that seem to emerge just before certain language accomplishments. For example, children who can find a hidden object after it has been moved from one location to another begin within a few weeks to use words such as *gone* to signify disappearance. Similarly, they begin to use words representing success and failure (for example, *there* and *uh-oh*) after learning to solve a complex means-ends task, such as using a stick to obtain an object. Gopnik and Meltzoff (1987, 1992) also noted that children who are able to sort groups of toys into two distinct categories, such as dolls and cars or boxes and balls, have more words in their vocabulary. According to these researchers, children develop linguistic labels consistent with cognitive problems that interest them at a given stage of development.

Does cognitive development lay the groundwork for language, or does language development follow a unique and independent path, as the linguists maintain? The answer is not yet clear. If anything, perhaps the two domains develop independently but concurrently and overlap at certain points in development, especially at the early stages of language learning (Rice, 1989).

The Social Interaction Perspective

KEY THEME
Interaction Among Domains

KEY THEME
Nature/Nurture

Many researchers of child language hold as a central tenet that language is a social activity, one that arises from the desire to communicate with others and is nurtured in social interactive contexts. Though these researchers acknowledge the biological and innate predispositions of the young human organism to learn language, they emphasize the role experiences with more mature, expert speakers play in fostering linguistic skill. Like learning theorists, they maintain that children need support and feedback as they make their first attempts at communication. However, social interaction researchers claim that children need models whose speech does not exceed children's processing abilities. Many qualities of parental speech directed at children are well suited to the child's emerging receptive and productive skills, providing a *scaffolding* or framework from which the child can learn.

When caregivers talk to infants and young children, they employ simple sentences, exaggerate their intonation, and speak with a high pitch. Infants are especially responsive to these qualities of "motherese," which seem to provide a helpful framework for learning language.

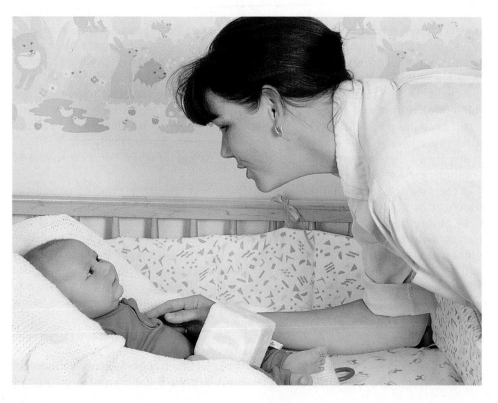

Parents have a unique way of talking to their young children. Most parents present a scaled-down version of spoken language as they interact with their young offspring, a version that contains simple, well-formed sentences and is punctuated by exaggerated intonation, high pitch, and clear pauses between segments of speech (Newport, 1977). Caregivers describe concrete events taking place in the present and often refer to objects with diminutives such as *kitty* or *doggie*. **Motherese,** as this form of communication is called, also includes repetitions of what the child has said, as well as many questions. Questions in particular serve to facilitate the occurrence of **turn taking,** the alternating vocalization by parent and child. Some questions are also used as **turnabouts,** elements of conversation that explicitly request a response from the child, as in "You like that, don't you?" or "What did you say?" Finally, as noted earlier in this chapter, *recasts* are an especially important component of motherese because they highlight for the child the discrepancies between the child's simple utterance and a more advanced form (Nelson, 1989).

Consider the following exchange between one seven-month-old, Ann, and her mother, observed by Catherine Snow (1977):

MOTHER	ANN
Ghhhhh ghhhhh ghhhhh ghhhhh *Grrrrr grrrrr grrrrr grrrrr*	
	(protest cry)
Oh, you don't feel like it, do you?	
	aaaaa aaaaa aaaaa
No, I wasn't making that noise	
I wasn't going *aaaaa aaaaa*.	
	aaaaa aaaaa
Yes, that's right.	

Notable in the exchange is the mother's pattern of waiting for her child's vocalization to end before she begins her response, an example of turn taking. If the child had spoken actual words, a real conversation would have taken place. The mother also repeated the child's vowel-like sound but embedded it in more elaborate speech. By the time the infant reaches eighteen months, the mother's tendency to expand or explain her utterances becomes even more pronounced, as in the following brief episode (Snow, 1977):

MOTHER	ANN
	(blowing noises)
That's a bit rude.	
	Mouth.
Mouth, that's right.	
	Face.
Face, yes, mouth is in your face.	
What else have you got in your face?	
	Face. (closing eyes)
You're making a face, aren't you?	

According to Snow (1984), two general principles operate during caregiver-child interactions. First, parents generally interpret their infants' behaviors as attempts to communicate, even when that interpretation may not seem warranted to an objective observer. Second, children actively seek relationships among objects, events, and people in their world and the vocal behaviors of their caregivers. The result of these two tendencies is that parents are motivated to converse with their children and children have a mechanism for learning language.

Motherese may serve a number of functions in the child's growing competence with language. First, this form of speech may assist the child's acquisition of word

motherese Simple, repetitive, high-pitched speech of caregivers to young children; includes many questions.

turn taking Alternating vocalization by parent and child.

turnabout Element of conversation that requests a response from the child.

meaning. Mothers tend to say the names for objects more loudly than other words in their speech to infants, and often they place the object label in the last position in their sentence, as in "Do you see the *rattle*?" (Messer, 1981). Mothers also tend to highlight new words by raising their pitch as they say them (Fernald & Mazzie, 1991). Second, the intonations of motherese may facilitate the child's acquisition of syntax. One study demonstrated that seven-to-ten-month-olds oriented more frequently to motherese that contained pauses at clausal boundaries than to motherese that was interrupted within clauses. Infants did not show these differential preferences in response to regular adult speech (Kemler Nelson et al., 1989). Infants show a similar sensitivity to even smaller grammatical units, the phrases and even the words within a sentence, but only when sentences are spoken in motherese (Jusczyk et al., 1992; Myers et al., 1996). The prosodic features of motherese may thus assist the infant in identifying syntactically relevant elements of language. Finally, exposure to motherese may provide lessons in conversational turn taking, one aspect of pragmatics that governs speech in interactions with others.

Are there any other effects of interactions with caregivers on child language development? Researchers have observed that the more mothers talk with their children, the more words their children acquire (Huttenlocher et al., 1991; Olson, Bayles, & Bates, 1986; Tomasello & Todd, 1983). It is not just how much mothers talk to their children that makes a difference, however; *how* they talk also matters. When mothers use many directives to control their children's behaviors and are generally intrusive, language development is slowed. When mothers (or teachers) use questions and conversational turn taking to elicit language from children or follow the children's vocalizations with a response, language development proceeds more rapidly (Hoff-Ginsberg, 1986; McDonald & Pien, 1982; Nelson, 1973; Valdez-Menchaca & Whitehurst, 1992). By engaging their young children in conversations, mothers increase children's attention to the properties of language and at the same time provide them with a rich set of information about those characteristics (Hoff-Ginsberg, 1990).

As important as motherese may seem, however, it is not a universal phenomenon. Although features of motherese have been observed in many languages and even among deaf mothers signing to their deaf infants (Gleason & Weintraub, 1978; Masataka, 1996), mothers in some cultures adopt a distinctly different style in talking with their infants. Consider the following two examples of maternal speech, one American and the other Japanese, as observed by Anne Fernald and Hiromi Morikawa (1993):

> *American mother:* That's a car. See the car? You like it? It's got nice wheels.
> *Japanese mother:* Here! It's a vroom vroom. I give it to you. Now you give it to me. Give me. Yes! Thank you.

KEY THEME
Sociocultural Influence

Whereas American mothers tend to name objects and focus on the exchange of information, Japanese mothers rarely name objects, using them instead to engage their infants in social routines. Perhaps it is not surprising, then, that American infants use substantially more nouns in their speech at nineteen months of age. Similarly, other researchers have noted that Japanese mothers ask fewer questions but use more nonsense sounds and songs than American mothers (Bornstein et al., 1992; Toda, Fogel, & Kawai, 1990). Thus, mothers may have different agendas as they speak with their children, and their style of speech may subtly shape the children's utterances.

Another example of variation in the use of motherese can be found in the Kaluli society of Papua New Guinea. In this culture, talking with others is a highly valued social skill, yet few adult verbalizations are directed to infants. Infants may be called by their names, but until they pass their first year, little else is said to them. When mothers do begin to talk to their babies, their speech contains few of the elements of motherese. Turn taking, repetitions, and elaborations are absent; usually mothers simply make directive statements that require no response from the child. Nevertheless, Kaluli children become proficient users of their language within developmental norms (Schieffelin & Ochs, 1983). Joint linguistic interactions between caregiver and child thus may not be essential to the emergence of language.

Linguistic exchanges with other interaction partners—fathers, siblings, peers, and others—may uniquely influence the child's eventual level of linguistic skill. For example, when fifteen-month-olds "converse" with their fathers, they experience more communication breakdowns than when they talk with their mothers: fathers more often request clarification, change the topic, or do not acknowledge the child's utterance after they fail to understand what she or he said (Tomasello, Conti-Ramsden, & Ewert, 1990). Thus, in communicating with fathers, children are challenged to make adjustments to maintain the interaction. Children also learn language by overhearing conversations between mothers and older siblings (Ashima-Takane, Goodz, & Derevensky, 1996). Children are normally exposed to a rich and varied range of linguistic stimuli from different communication partners; many theorists believe this fact ensures that children will learn the details of linguistic structures that may not be present in the verbalizations of a single conversation partner, such as the mother (Gleitman, Newport, & Gleitman, 1984; Wexler, 1982).

RESEARCH APPLIED TO PARENTING

Reading to Children

It was several months after Sue had captured Sara's first word on videotape for posterity. As the weeks had passed, Sara's vocabulary expanded rapidly and she started stringing words together. Sue marveled at the progress Sara was making as she prepared her daughter's bed and eavesdropped on Sara and her father in their evening ritual. This was Dan's favorite time of day. Every night, just before Sara was put to bed, Dan would pull her up in his lap and take a picture book from the shelf. At first, he just pointed to and named things in the book, often encouraging Sara to participate by asking, "What's that?" As her vocabulary increased, Dan elaborated on her answers and asked other questions: "What does the doggie say?" "Woof-woof!" squealed Sara, enjoying the ritual perhaps every bit as much, maybe even more, than her father. Sue had learned to have the camera handy for records of some of these exchanges, too.

The research findings discussed earlier show that how and how often mothers speak to children can influence language development. One context in which mothers' speech tends to be particularly lavish is during book reading. Erika Hoff-Ginsberg (1991) found that when mothers and two-year-olds were reading books, mothers showed the greatest diversity in the vocabulary they used, the greatest complexity of syntax, and the highest rate of replies to their children compared to other contexts, such as mealtime or toy play. As a result of such findings, many child development experts encourage parents to read to their young children.

Grover Whitehurst and his colleagues have developed a program called *dialogic reading* to stimulate language development in preschool children at risk for academic failure, but the general principles can be applied by any parent interested in promoting his or her child's language development. Here is some advice the researchers have developed for parents of two- and three-year-olds:

1. *Ask what questions (such as "What is this?") to stimulate the child to speak.* Avoid yes/no questions that require only brief answers.

2. *Follow the child's answer with a question.* Ask for example, what shape or color an object has or what it is used for.

3. *Repeat the child's utterance in the form of a recast.* For example, follow "Cow" with "Yes, that's right, it's a cow." This gives the child feedback that she is correct.

4. *If the child doesn't have an answer, provide a model and ask him to repeat.* For example, say "That's a bottle. Can you say *bottle?*"

5. *Be generous with praise and encouragement.* Make comments such as "Good talking" or "Nice job."

6. *Be responsive to the child's interests.* When the child expresses an interest in a picture or part of the story, follow her interest with encouragement to talk.

7. *Have fun.* Do not pressure the child; take turns with the child, and even make the activity a game.

Researchers have identified
several techniques that parents
can use to promote language
development in the context of
reading to their children.
Among them are asking
"what" questions, following the
child's answer with another
question, and using recasts.
Making the experience positive and fun for the child is
also important.

Dialogic reading has been shown to increase language skills in children from different social classes when used by day care teachers as well as parents (Arnold &
Whitehurst, 1994). Of course, children learn language skills in many other contexts,
such as mealtime conversations (Snow, 1993) and even while watching educational
television (Mason, 1980). Thus, children whose parents do not read to them often
are not necessarily fated to have poor language skills (Scarborough & Dobrich, 1993).
Nonetheless, reading to children, perhaps especially when they are infants, leads to
desirable outcomes in language development (DeBaryshe, 1993).

In summary, each of the five theoretical positions makes an important contribution
to the understanding of language development. Specialized biological structures are
responsible for human language processing, and biology evidently also sets the
child's early predispositions to respond to the unique features of language. The
child's cognitive growth assists in the acquisition process. As linguistic theorists suggest, part of the child's task, and one that the child does well, is to filter out the regularities that occur in spoken language so that he or she can use the general rules to
create unique utterances. Learning and social interaction theories also help our understanding of language development. Caregivers provide models of correct speech;
deliver indirect feedback as to the correctness of the child's utterances; and, by using
motherese, provide linguistic models compatible with the child's level of language
skill. Given the complexities involved in language development, it is no wonder that
explanations of the phenomenon are multifaceted.

THE FUNCTIONS OF LANGUAGE

Aside from its obvious usefulness as a social communication tool, what functions
does language serve? Does the human propensity to learn and employ language
affect other aspects of functioning, specifically, mental processes, the regulation of
behavior, and socialization? At the very least, language enriches the human experience by providing a useful vehicle for enhancing cognition and behavior; it also

exerts powerful influences on other areas of human activity. In this section, we will examine briefly some broad effects of language on the domains of cognition, behavior, and socialization.

How Language Influences Cognition

The relationship between language and cognition has been a controversial subject for many years, especially with respect to which activity precedes the other. Some psychologists and anthropologists have argued that language shapes thinking, whereas others contend that cognition paves the way for language. Most now acknowledge that the link between language and cognition is bidirectional and that each domain influences the other. We have already pointed out some ways cognition might influence language. How might language have a powerful influence on the child's cognitive attainments?

KEY THEME
Interaction Among Domains

Language, Memory, and Classification   If you ask a child to perform a cognitive task, such as remembering a list of words or grouping a set of similar objects, you will notice that he will often spontaneously use language to aid his performance. The best examples of this behavior come from research findings on developmental changes in children's memory. There are distinct differences in the way preschool and school-age children approach the task of remembering. Older children are far more likely than younger children to employ deliberate strategies for remembering, strategies that typically involve the use of verbal skills. In one study, John Flavell and his colleagues (Flavell, Beach, & Chinsky, 1966) asked kindergarten, second-, and fifth-graders to watch as the experimenter pointed to three pictures in an array of seven. The children's job was to point to the same three pictures either immediately or after a delay of fifteen seconds. During the delay, the experimenters noticed that most children in the oldest group made spontaneous lip movements, suggesting that they were verbally repeating the items to be recalled. Moreover, the superior performance of the oldest group on the memory test was attributed to their spontaneous repetition of the names of the items. The use of verbal labels seemed to bridge the gap between the time the items were first seen and the time they were to be recalled.

Language can also influence how children categorize related groups of objects. Stan Kuczaj and his colleagues showed children twelve unfamiliar objects that could be grouped into three sets (Kuczaj, Borys, & Jones, 1989). Children who were taught the names of one category member from each group were more successful in sorting the objects than children who were not given labels. Language provides children with cues that classes of stimuli differ from one another, and these cues can influence how children form conceptual groups. If some four-legged animals are called *dogs* and others are called *cats,* the different linguistic labels will highlight for the child that the features of these two groups differ.

Bilingualism and Cognition   One of the more interesting ways in which the influence of language on thought has been studied has been to compare, on a variety of tasks, the performances of bilingual children equally fluent in two languages with monolinguals fluent in only one. Bilingual children have been characterized as more analytic and flexible in their approach to different types of thought problems. Sandra Ben-Zeev (1977) compared monolingual children with children who spoke both Hebrew and English and found that bilinguals performed better on a symbol substitution task. The task required that subjects substitute certain words for others in a series of sentences, such as *spaghetti* for *I* in the sentence "I am cold." Bilingual children also perform better than monolinguals on nonverbal problems, such as the Raven Progressive Matrices (see Figure 7.6) (Hakuta & Diaz, 1985). Finally, bilingual children have been found to display greater metalinguistic awareness than monolingual children, even those who are chronologically older. When given sentences such as "Why is the cat barking so loudly?" bilingual children were more likely than monolingual children to ignore conflicting semantic information and state that the sentences were grammatically correct (Bialystok, 1986).

FIGURE 7.6

Cognitive Achievements of Bilingual and Monolingual Children

Bilingual children outperform monolingual children on non-verbal tests such as the Raven Progressive Matrices, which requires subjects to select the segment that correctly fits into the larger pattern. Bilingual children generally seem to be more analytical than monolingual children in their approach to various problem-solving tasks.

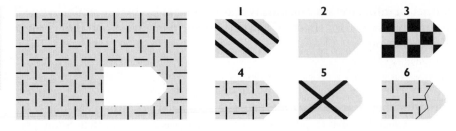

Source: Raven, 1962.

One hypothesis to explain their superior performance is that bilingual children are forced to think more abstractly and analytically because they have had experience with analyzing the structure and detail of not just one language but two. A second possibility is that they are generally more verbally oriented in their thinking and have a greater tendency to produce verbalizations that enhance their performance even in nonverbal tasks. Finally, they may have an increased objective awareness of language and hence more control over cognitive processing in general (Bialystok, 1991; Diaz & Klingler, 1991). Whatever the mechanism, these studies demonstrate that speaking a second language affects cognitive processes.

The term *bilingual education* can be confusing. It can refer to teaching all children two languages, or it can refer to teaching language-minority children to speak the majority language. In Canada, where both French and English are official languages, the first goal has been paramount in many bilingual education programs. In the United States and many other countries that have a large number of immigrants, the second goal has been more prominent. Estimates are that about 22 percent of school-age children in the United States currently have limited English proficiency (Waggoner, 1994), a characteristic that could hinder success in school.

CONTROVERSY: THINKING IT OVER

How Should Bilingual Education Programs Be Structured?

Philosophies of teaching language-minority children have varied. Some believe children should receive most of their education in their primary language, whether it be Spanish, Cambodian, or French, and make the transition to English only when they are ready. This approach, according to advocates, promotes basic language development, which in turn creates the foundation for acquiring the second language. In addition, children will develop a sense of belonging in the school and their self-esteem will be high (Wong, Fillmore & Meyer, 1992). Some research findings suggest that this approach assists in learning both core academic subjects and English (Meyer & Fienberg, 1992). At the other extreme are advocates of immersion, the idea that children should be totally surrounded by the second language, learning it in the same way the young child learns the first language. These models have been successful in Canada, Spain, and other countries (Artigal, 1991; Tucker & d'Anglejan, 1972) but have usually been used in classrooms in which all children started out as monolinguals.

Many bilingual education programs fall between these two extremes. For example, a popular approach is to include the teaching of English as an extra "subject" by a bilingual teacher while children take their core academic subjects in English. Another tactic has been to teach language-majority and minority children in two languages, initially presenting the bulk of instruction in the non-English language. Elementary school students in such programs have been found to make gains in both languages (Lindholm & Fairchild, 1990). Unfortunately, evaluations of the effectiveness of most bilingual education programs have yielded ambiguous results and have been fraught with methodological difficulties (Willig & Ramirez, 1993).

What does research on the process of language development suggest about the best way to structure bilingual education programs? Does the idea of a critical period for language acquisition have any bearing on the approach one might recommend? Do the apparent benefits of being bilingual have relevance? How do social and motivational factors enter into this discussion?

How Language Influences Self-regulation

Language takes on an increasingly important role in regulating behavior as the child develops, according to two prominent Russian psychologists, Lev Vygotsky and Alexander Luria. Vygotsky (1962) believed the child's initial utterances serve an interpersonal function, signaling others about the child's affective state. In the preschool years, however, speech takes on a different function. Specifically, the child's **private speech,** or overt, audible "speech-for-self," comes to guide his or her observable activities. If you have ever observed a toddler coloring and simultaneously saying something like "Now, I'll use the blue crayon. I'll make the sky blue," you have seen an example of private speech. Eventually, speech-for-self becomes interiorized; **inner speech** dictates the direction of the child's thoughts.

KEY THEME
Interaction Among Domains

Luria (1961) expanded these ideas by proposing three stages in the verbal regulation of behavior (see Table 7.3). In the first stage, from about eighteen months to three years, the verbalizations of others can prompt motor activity, but they rarely inhibit behavior. In an experiment in which children were to squeeze a rubber ball according to the commands of an adult, they would start pressing after the command "Go!" but did not stop when given negative commands such as "Don't squeeze." In the second stage, lasting from about three to five years of age, children's external speech (either from others or vocalized overtly by the children) can increasingly initiate and inhibit behavior, but only if the physical qualities of the speech match the requirements of the task. If children in the above experiment said, "Go, go," they squeezed the rubber ball twice; if they said, "I shall press twice," however, they squeezed the ball only once. Finally, at about age five, children's speech becomes internalized to control thoughts and actions. In addition, the content of speech, and not just its superficial qualities, becomes effective in regulating behavior.

KEY THEME
Continuity/Discontinuity

Attempts to find empirical support for the ideas of Vygotsky and Luria have met with mixed success. One problem has been the failure to observe much overt speech-for-self among preschoolers, although that may be a function of the particular settings and tasks psychologists have used (Fuson, 1979). On the other hand, in one study, when children younger than four-and-a-half were given negative commands in a loud voice, such as "Don't touch your toes!", they were more likely to perform

Age	Characteristics	Example	TABLE 7.3
18 Months–3 Years	Verbalizations of others initiate child's motor behavior but do not inhibit it.	Child squeezes ball when adult says, "Go," but does not stop squeezing when adult says, "Don't press."	Luria's Stages of the Verbal Regulation of Behavior
3–5 Years	Adult's or child's own speech initiates and inhibits behavior but only if physical qualities of speech match task requirements.	If child says, "Go, go," child squeezes ball twice; if child says, "I shall press twice," child will only squeeze once.	
5+ Years	Content of child's internalized speech controls thoughts and actions.	Child says, "I shall press twice" and squeezes rubber ball two times.	

private speech Children's vocalized speech to themselves that directs behavior.

inner speech Interiorized form of private speech.

Young children often use private speech when they are engaged in new or challenging tasks. This overt "speech-for-self" guides children's actions and eventually becomes interiorized into a form called *inner speech*. Language thus helps children to regulate their own behavior.

the prohibited act than when the instruction was issued softly. That is, the loudness of the command was more powerful in initiating a behavior than the content was in stopping it. In contrast, older children attended more to the content of the message than to its physical qualities (Saltz, Campbell, & Skotko, 1983). Moreover, Laura Berk (1986) noted that when first-graders were solving math problems in school, they engaged in high levels of externalized private speech to guide their problem solving. Third-graders also showed evidence of private speech, but a more internalized form—through mutterings and lip movements—as they attempted to solve math problems. Thus, children do use private speech in some contexts, and they progress from overt private speech to a more interiorized form.

How important is private speech in directing behavior? You may have noticed that you tend to talk to yourself when you are under stress or when you have a lot to do. Research has confirmed that children, like adults, use private speech when they find tasks difficult or when they make errors, and that when they use task-relevant private speech, their performance on a variety of tasks improves (Berk, 1992). In addition, a longitudinal study demonstrated that as children progress from overt to more internal private speech, they also show fewer distracting body movements and greater sustained attention in school (Bivens & Berk, 1990). Such studies suggest that language becomes an increasingly powerful regulator of children's behavior as they develop.

How Language Influences Cultural Socialization

KEY THEME
Sociocultural Influence

Still another way in which language can have a broad influence on development is by helping children discern the social roles, relationships, and values of their culture. Many languages have specific grammatical forms that are used to convey gender, age, or social power. In acquiring language, children are sensitized to the specific ways their own culture creates social order. For example, in Japanese, the word particle *zo* signifies affective intensity and a male speaker, and the particle *wa* conveys hesitancy and a female speaker. Children learning Japanese are therefore likely to associate hesitancy with females and forcefulness with males (Ochs, 1990). In many other languages, specific words have formal and informal versions, with the formal used when speaking with individuals who have more authority or power and the informal with individuals who share equal status or are related. Again, such linguistic distinctions highlight important social relationships within the cultural group.

A good example of how language can influence socialization comes from traditional Samoan culture, which emphasizes community and group accomplishments over the attainments of individuals. In Samoan speech, few verbalizations include praise or blame for individuals. Most statements concern the success or failure of the group and emphasize the life of the community. When Samoan children are exposed to verbalizations of this type, they are being socialized into the collective orientation of their culture (Ochs, 1990).

Researchers are just beginning to explore the ways in which the words and social conventions within a specific language are related to cultural values and beliefs. However, it is apparent that through language, children learn far more than simply how to communicate; they also learn about the broader belief systems of their society.

CHAPTER RECAP

SUMMARY OF DEVELOPMENTAL THEMES

NATURE/NURTURE   What roles do nature and nurture play in language development?

There are several indicators that for humans, nature sets early predispositions to develop language: the infant's sensitivity to phonemes and prosody, the child's tendency to progress through language milestones in a predictable sequence, and the devotion to language functions of certain portions of the brain are just some examples. Nurture, in the form of the child's experiences with more mature language users, interacts with these biological tendencies to lead the child to acquire the phonology, semantics, and syntax of a particular language and learn the social conventions that accompany spoken language in his or her culture.

SOCIOCULTURAL INFLUENCE   How does the sociocultural context influence language development?

Cultures vary in the extent to which caregivers use motherese with their growing children, a factor that may influence the rate of language acquisition. The specific elements of phonology, semantics, syntax, and pragmatics also vary widely across languages. Often the content and structure of a specific language provide cues to the culture's social order and values.

CHILD'S ACTIVE ROLE   How does the child play an active role in the process of language development?

Even in the earliest stages of language acquisition, children often influence which objects or people caregivers will label when they look at or point to specific items. Although children do benefit by merely listening to language use in the environment, they also actively use context and other word-learning biases to derive the meanings of words. In addition, their rapid acquisition of the rules of syntax and their production of overregularizations suggest that children abstract the regularities in language to generate their own verbalizations.

CONTINUITY/DISCONTINUITY   Is language development continuous or discontinuous?

Descriptions of early language production often seem stagelike because children appear to spend distinct periods of time in a babbling stage, a one-word stage, and so on. However, there are continuities among different events in language acquisition. For example, the sounds in infant babbling are related to the language the child will eventually speak. Luria posits that the verbal regulation of behavior develops in stages. However, rather than disappearing at a particular age, private speech often resurfaces, even among older children and adults, when tasks become difficult or stressful.

INDIVIDUAL DIFFERENCES   How prominent are individual differences in language development?

Children frequently show striking differences in the rate at which they achieve language milestones. They may differ, for example, in the age at which they say their first words or when (even if) they show a vocabulary spurt. Some may develop a referential style of speech, whereas others may speak expressively. Nonetheless, there is a pronounced regularity in the sequence of language attainments among children, regardless of the culture in which they grow up.

INTERACTION AMONG DOMAINS   How does language development interact with development in other domains?

In early childhood, the ability to produce spoken language parallels the physiological maturation of the vocal apparatus and the central nervous system. The emergence of language also coincides with the onset of certain cognitive skills, such as conceptual understanding. Language is nurtured largely within the context of social interactions with caregivers. Thus, physical, cognitive, and social factors affect the process of language acquisition. By the same token, language has a clear effect on other domains. Children's use of language enhances their ability to remember, form concepts, and, as studies of bilingual individuals suggest, may even promote analytic thinking and mental flexibility. In addition, children's ability to be successful communicators can have important repercussions for social relationships with parents, peers, and others.

SUMMARY OF TOPICS

■ THE COURSE OF LANGUAGE ACQUISITION

Acquiring language is a developmental task with four main components: phonology, semantics, syntax, and pragmatics. In the early stages of acquisition, children focus on *phonology*; they learn to segment and produce the basic sounds of language and show a predisposition to respond to language as a unique auditory stimulus. During the first year, they vocalize by *cooing* and *babbling,* but they also communicate and symbolize objects by producing gestures.

By one year of age, most children are speaking in one-word utterances, usually *nominals,* or nouns. A general characteristic of *semantic* development, the learning of word meanings, is that children comprehend far more language than they are able to produce. Children learn the meanings of words through *fast-mapping,* parental labeling of objects to which children point, linguistic contrast, and their tendency to have biases in learning labels for objects. Their growing conceptual knowledge is also thought to be part of learning word meanings. Although most children achieve language milestones at specific ages, individual differences occur in patterns of acquisition.

Once children begin combining two or more words, they show evidence of *syntactic* awareness, awareness of the grammatical rules that state how words are combined. Although it is difficult to describe their grammar, children use *inflections* and other systematic relationships among words to convey meaning. Later in childhood, children learn to form negatives, construct questions, and use the passive voice. Two other later developments are the acquisition of *pragmatics,* the social conventions regarding effective communication, and *metalinguistic* *awareness,* the ability to reflect abstractly on language as a communication tool and the self as a language user.

■ EXPLAINING LANGUAGE ACQUISITION

Theories of language development have centered primarily on the nature-nurture debate. Those leaning toward a biological explanation have pointed to the regularities in language attainments across cultures and the brain structures specifically devoted to language processing. A major question stemming from the biological position is whether a critical period exists for the acquisition of language. Learning theorists have emphasized the roles of shaping, reinforcement, and imitation in language acquisition. Linguistic theorists emphasize the child's abstraction of general grammatical principles from the stream of speech. Cognitive theorists point out that certain advances in thinking, such as classification skills, precede language attainments. Finally, social interaction theorists highlight the characteristics of caregiver-child speech that facilitate development, such as the use of *recasts, turn taking,* and simple, clear verbalizations.

■ THE FUNCTIONS OF LANGUAGE

Language serves numerous functions in the child's life in addition to simple communication. It can influence specific cognitive processes, such as memory or classification. It can serve to direct children's behavior in the form of *private speech* and, later, *inner speech,* particularly when tasks are new or difficult. Finally, it can play a role in the socialization of children by introducing them directly to specific values and expectations of their native culture.

8 COGNITION: PIAGET AND VYGOTSKY

NATURE/NURTURE
What roles do nature and nurture play in cognitive development?

CONTINUITY/DISCONTINUITY
Is cognitive development continuous or discontinuous?

SOCIOCULTURAL INFLUENCE
How does the sociocultural context influence cognitive development?

INDIVIDUAL DIFFERENCES
How prominent are individual differences in cognitive development?

CHILD'S ACTIVE ROLE
How does the child play an active role in the process of cognitive development?

INTERACTION AMONG DOMAINS
How does cognitive development interact with development in other domains?

raig could hear the bantering in the dining room as he finished preparing dinner. Nine-year-old James and five-year-old Melissa were arguing over who had gotten the bigger glass of chocolate milk. "They're the same!" James said forcefully. "No, they're not," retorted Melissa. "You have more than me!" This spat between the siblings reminded Craig of countless similar scenes from his own childhood, growing up with two brothers. They had always compared the sizes of their slices of cake, portions of candy bars, and scoops of ice cream. Craig was impressed, though, as he continued to eavesdrop. James had collected himself and was trying to explain the logic of the situation to his younger sister. "Look, Melissa, your glass is shorter than mine, but it's also a lot fatter. Mine is tall and skinny. That means we end up having the same amount of chocolate milk, see?" Craig thought, "I couldn't have done better myself."

Melissa sat silently for a moment and then blurted out, "No, we don't!" The logic of James's argument apparently had escaped her. Craig could see there was only one way to preserve the peace for dinner. He grabbed another glass identical to Melissa's for James to use for his chocolate milk.

One of the most active research areas of child development focuses on **cognition**—those thought processes and mental activities, including attention, memory, concept formation, and problem solving, that are evident from early infancy onward. As the scene above suggests, older children do seem to think differently than younger children, and not just about quantities of chocolate milk. But exactly how do they think differently? Do young children remember as well as older children do? Does the way in which children form concepts change as they grow? Do older children solve problems the same way younger children do? Are they, in fact, more logical? These are the types of questions that psychologists interested in cognitive development ask.

Virtually every aspect of a child's development has some connection to emerging cognitive capabilities. We saw in Chapter 7 that a child's use of language is linked to his or her growing conceptual development. Similarly, as we will discuss in later chapters, the child's increasing knowledge of effective social interaction can influence the quality of relations with peers. These are just a few of the numerous examples of how changes in thinking influence and interact with other areas of the child's development.

In this chapter, we focus our discussion of cognitive development on two of the most important theoretical positions framing research on children's thought: those of Jean Piaget and Lev Vygotsky. We begin by summarizing Piaget's major ideas and evaluating his contributions to our understanding of cognitive development. We also

cognition Processes involved in thinking and mental activity, such as attention, memory, and problem solving.

254

discuss several topics explored by contemporary researchers influenced or provoked by Piaget's writings, including the development of children's understanding of physical objects, their ability to classify objects, and their understanding of concepts such as number, space, and psychological states. Finally, we review the major features of Vygotsky's sociocultural theory of development, along with research that his work has stimulated.

PIAGET'S THEORY OF COGNITIVE DEVELOPMENT

As we saw in Chapter 1, one of the most important beliefs espoused by Piaget is that children actively construct their knowledge of the world, incorporating new information into existing knowledge structures, or *schemes,* through *assimilation.* As a result, schemes are modified or expanded through the process of *accommodation.* For example, the young infant may attempt to grasp a new, round squeeze toy into a pre-existing scheme for grasping objects. As a consequence, that scheme becomes altered to include information about grasping round objects. The outcome is greater *equilibrium* or balance among the pieces of knowledge that make up the child's understanding. Thus, what a child can understand or mentally grasp at any given point in time is heavily influenced by what the child already knows or understands. At the same time, the child's schemes are constantly transformed, as equilibrium is continually disrupted by the never-ending flow of information from the surrounding world.

KEY THEME
Child's Active Role

Piaget maintained that thought processes become reorganized into distinct stages at several points in development. Though the schemes in early stages lay the foundation for later knowledge structures, their reorganization is so thorough that schemes in one stage bear little resemblance to those in other stages. According to Piaget, the child progresses through the *sensorimotor, preoperational, concrete operational,* and *formal operational* stages, reflecting major transitions in thought in which early, action-based schemes evolve into symbolic, then logical, and finally abstract mental structures.

KEY THEME
Continuity/Discontinuity

Stages of Development

Piaget maintained that all children progress through the stages of cognitive development in an invariable sequence in which no stage is skipped. In addition, each stage contains a period of formation and a period of attainment. When the child begins a new stage, his schemes are somewhat unstable and loosely organized. By the end of the stage, his schemes are well formed and well organized. Even though Piaget provided age norms for the acquisition of each stage, he believed that because cognitive development is the result of maturational factors working in concert with environmental experiences, some children may reach a stage more quickly or more slowly, depending on the opportunities for learning their environment provided. Ultimately, though, the evolution of thought shows a universal regularity, according to Piaget.

KEY THEME
Nature/Nurture

The Sensorimotor Stage (Birth to Two Years)   The most striking characteristic of human thinking during the **sensorimotor stage** is its solid basis in action. Each time the child reaches for an object, sucks on a nipple, or crawls along the floor, she is obtaining varied feedback about her body and its relationship to the environment that becomes part of her internal schemes. At first, the infant's movements are reflexive, not deliberate or planned. As the child passes through each of the six substages of the sensorimotor period, outlined in Table 8.1, her actions become increasingly goal directed and aimed at solving problems. Moreover, she is able to distinguish self from environment and learns about the properties of objects and how they are related to one another.

sensorimotor stage In Piagetian theory, the first stage of cognitive development, from birth to approximately two years of age, in which thought is based primarily on action.

TABLE 8.1	The Six Substages of Piaget's Sensorimotor Stage	
Substage	**Major Features**	**Object Concept**
Reflexive Activity (Birth–1 month)	Formation and modification of early schemes based on reflexes such as sucking, looking, and grasping	No attempt to locate objects that have disappeared
Primary Circular Reactions (1–4 months)	Repetition of behaviors that produce interesting results centered on own body (e.g., Lucienne accidentally, then repeatedly touches her quilt)	No attempt to locate objects that have disappeared
Secondary Circular Reactions (4–8 months)	Repetition of behaviors that produce interesting results in the external world (e.g., Lucienne accidentally, then repeatedly kicks the dolls in her bassinet)	Search for objects that have dropped from view or are partially hidden
Coordination of Secondary Schemes (8–12 months)	Combination of actions to achieve a goal (e.g., Lucienne pulls a doll to make her bassinet hood sway)	Search for completely hidden objects
Tertiary Circular Reactions (12–18 months)	Experimentation with different actions to achieve the same goal or observe the outcomes (e.g., Laurent drops a case of soap, then a piece of bread)	Ability to follow visible displacements of an object
Invention of New Means Through Mental Combinations (18–24 months)	Thinking through of potential solutions to problems and imitation of absent models (e.g., Jacqueline imitates her playmate's tantrum)	Ability to follow invisible displacements of an object

A significant accomplishment of the sensorimotor stage is the infant's progression toward **means-ends behavior,** the deliberate use of an action to accomplish some goal. During the early substages of sensorimotor development, the infant often initiates actions accidentally rather than purposefully. When Piaget's daughter Lucienne was almost four months old, she was observed to shake her bassinet

> *by moving her legs violently (bending and unbending them, etc.), which makes the cloth dolls swing from the hood. Lucienne looks at them, smiling, and recommences at once. (Piaget, 1952b, pp. 157–158)*

Lucienne repeated her kicking to make the dolls shake in what Piaget calls a **circular reaction,** the repetition of a motor act to experience the pleasure it brings. Her first kick, however, was totally accidental. Several months afterward, when Lucienne was eight months old, Piaget placed a new doll over the hood of her bassinet. This time her behavior revealed a greater degree of intentionality:

> *She looks at it for a long time, touches it, then feels it by touching its feet, clothes, head, etc. She then ventures to grasp it, which makes the hood sway. She then pulls the doll while watching the effects of this movement. (Piaget, 1952b, p. 256)*

Throughout the first two years, the child increasingly uses actions as a means to obtain some end or goal. He also experiments with new means to reach the same goal, as Piaget's son Laurent did when he successively dropped a soap case and then a piece of bread to investigate how objects fall.

A second aspect of sensorimotor development is the child's gradual separation of self from the external environment. Initially, the child derives pleasure from actions that center on her own body. At three months of age, Lucienne "strikes her quilt with

means-ends behavior
Deliberate behavior employed to attain a goal.

circular reaction   In Piagetian theory, repetition of some action or behavior to experience the pleasure it brings.

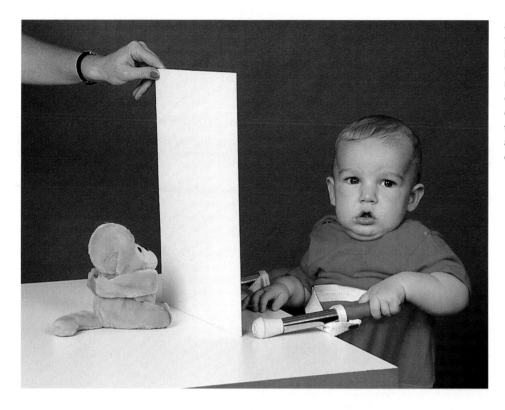

A significant attainment in infancy is the child's understanding of object permanence. Children under three to four months of age act as if a hidden or obstructed object no longer exists. By age eight months, though, children will remove a barrier to look for a hidden object.

her right hand; she scratches it while carefully watching what she is doing, then lets it go, grasps it again, etc." (Piaget, 1952b, p. 92). The circular reaction, in this case, was repeated because of the satisfying sensations it brought to Lucienne's hand. Weeks later, in the episode of the swinging dolls, Lucienne's kicking in the bassinet produced a gratifying result in the external environment. In general, the child becomes less centered on the self and more oriented to the external world.

A third important accomplishment of this stage is the attainment of the **object concept,** or *object permanence*. Infants who possess the object concept realize that objects continue to exist even though they are not within immediate sight or within reach to be acted on. Up to three months of age, the saying "out of sight, out of mind" characterizes the child's understanding of objects. At about four months of age, he will lift a cloth from a partially covered object or show some reaction, such as surprise or puzzlement, when an object disappears. At about eight months of age, he will search for an object that has completely disappeared, for example, when it has been covered entirely by a cloth. In the last two phases of the attainment of the object concept, he will be able to follow visible and then invisible displacements of the object. In the first instance, the twelve-month-old will follow and find a toy that has been moved from under one cloth to another, as long as the movement is performed while he is watching. In the second instance, the eighteen-month-old can find an object moved from location A to location B, even if the displacement from A to B is done while he is not looking.

The completion of the sensorimotor stage and the beginning of the next stage is signaled by the child's display of *deferred imitation,* the ability to imitate a model who is no longer present. At age sixteen months, Piaget's daughter Jacqueline was playing with a boy who suddenly had a dramatic temper tantrum. The next day, the normally well-behaved Jacqueline mimicked the little boy's behaviors with remarkable accuracy. To do so, she must have had the ability to represent the boy's overt behaviors in internal form and to draw on that representation hours later. This ability to represent events and objects internally marks the beginning of a major transition in thought.

The Preoperational Stage (About Two to Seven Years) The key feature of the young child's thought in the **preoperational stage** is the *semiotic function,* the child's

object concept Realization that objects exist even when they are not within view. Also called *object permanence*.

preoperational stage In Piagetian theory, the second stage of development, from approximately two to seven years of age, in which thought becomes symbolic in form.

Children in Piaget's preoperational stage are able to use symbols to stand for real objects or events. Drawings, like this one made by a five-year-old, are a good example of the application of this cognitive attainment. Fantasy play and imitation are additional manifestations of the child's ability to symbolize.

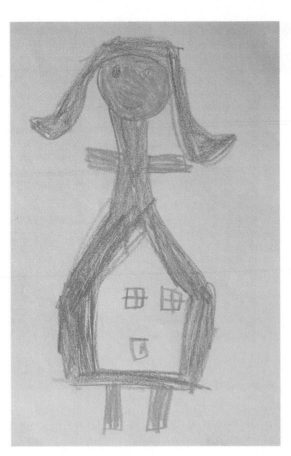

ability to use a symbol, an object, or a word to stand for something. The child can play with a cardboard tube as though it were a car or draw a picture to represent the balloons from her third birthday party. The semiotic function is a powerful cognitive ability because it permits the child to think about past and future events and to employ language. In fact, Piaget asserted that language would not be possible without this significant characteristic of thought; the child must possess the general cognitive ability to let one thing stand for another before she can use words to represent objects, events, and relationships. The semiotic function is also a prerequisite for imitation, imagery, fantasy play, and drawing, all of which the preschool child begins to manifest.

Despite this tremendous advance in thinking, preoperational thought has distinct limitations. One is that children in this stage are said to be **egocentric,** a term that describes the child's inability to separate his own perspective from that of others. Put into words, his guiding principle might be "You see what I see, you think what I think." An example is the three-year-old who thinks he is hiding from an older sibling or a parent by crouching behind a chair. Even though his legs and feet might be sticking out for all present to see, the youngster believes he is well concealed because he himself is unable to see anyone. According to Piaget, the preschooler's egocentrism has ramifications for both his social communicative behavior and his perceptual skills. Piagetian theory predicts poor referential communication skills in children under age seven years and, as we will see later in this chapter, the inability to appreciate the perspectives of others in perceptual tasks.

The second limitation of preoperational thought lies in the child's inability to solve problems flexibly and logically. The major tasks Piaget used to assess the status of the child's cognitive development are called the **conservation tasks.** These "thinking problems" generally require the child to observe some transformation in physical quantities that are initially equivalent and to reason about the impact of the transformation. Figure 8.1 shows several conservation tasks.

KEY THEME
Interaction Among Domains

egocentrism Preoperational child's inability to separate his or her own perspective from that of others.

conservation tasks Problems that require the child to make judgments about the equivalence of two displays; used to assess stage of cognitive development.

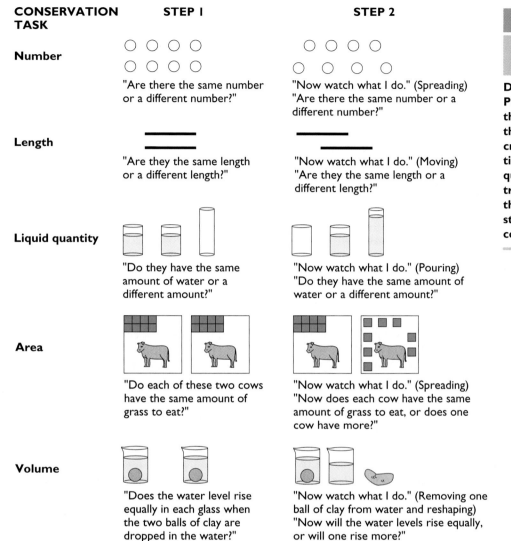

CONSERVATION TASK

FIGURE 8.1

Examples of Conservation Tasks

Depicted here are several Piagetian conservation tasks that children can solve once they reach the stage of concrete operations. Preoperational children usually say the quantities change after the transformation. Piaget believed they lack the logical thought structures necessary to reason correctly.

Suppose we use the conservation of liquid quantity task to illustrate how the preoperational child thinks. The four- or five-year-old will usually quickly agree that two equal-size glasses of water contain the same amount of liquid. If the liquid from one glass is poured into a tall cylinder, however, the child, like Melissa in this chapter's opening scene, will state that the cylinder now contains more than the glass does. According to Piaget, this error is the result of several limitations in preoperational thinking. One is **centration,** that is, focusing on one aspect of the problem—in this case, the height of the cylinder—to the exclusion of all other information, such as its narrower width, that could help to produce a correct solution. A second cognitive trait at work here is lack of **reversibility**. The preoperational child cannot mentally reverse the action of pouring from the tall cylinder to the shorter glass; if she could, she would realize that the two containers still hold the same amount of liquid that they did at the start of the problem. Third, the preoperational child tends to **focus on states** rather than on the events that occur between states. It is as though he has stored two static photographs of the two equal-size glasses, followed by static photographs of the shorter glass and the tall cylinder, rather than a video of the sequence of events. He fails to realize the connection between the two components of the conservation problem and, as a result, fails the conservation task.

The Concrete Operational Stage (About Seven to Eleven Years)   Children enter the **concrete operational stage** when they begin to be able to solve the conservation

centration   In Piagetian theory, tendency of the child to focus on only one aspect of a problem.

reversibility   In Piagetian theory, the ability to mentally reverse or negate an action or a transformation.

focus on states   Preoperational child's tendency to treat two or more connected events as unrelated.

concrete operational stage   In Piagetian theory, the third stage of development, from approximately seven to eleven years of age, in which thought is logical when stimuli are physically present.

tasks correctly. At first, the six- or seven-year-old may solve only a few of the simpler problems, such as conservation of length, number, or liquid quantity. Later, she will succeed on tasks that involve area or volume. Piaget called this extension of the same cognitive structures to solve increasingly difficult problems within a given stage *horizontal décalage.*

The reason for this shift is that the child is now capable of performing **operations,** mental actions such as *reversibility,* that allow him to reason about the events that have transpired. He can pour the liquid back from the cylinder to the glass "in his head" or think about the narrow width of the tall cylinder as compensating for its height. In other words, the child now thinks logically, although the physical components of the problem must still be present (if not externally in the world, then as images in the mind). The child's thought is also less egocentric, allowing him to understand that other individuals' perceptions, beliefs, and feelings may differ from his own. The concrete operational child is becoming a true "thinker," as long as there are specific objects or events to which he can apply his logic.

The Formal Operational Stage (About Eleven Years and Beyond)   By the time the child reaches adolescence, she will most likely have moved to the final stage in Piaget's theory, the **formal operational stage.** Thinking in this stage is both logical and abstract. Problems such as "Bill is shorter than Sam but taller than Jim. Who is tallest?" can now be solved without seeing the individuals or conjuring up concrete images of them. The adolescent can also reason **hypothetically;** that is, she can generate potential solutions to problems in a thoroughly systematic fashion, much as a scientist approaches an experiment.

Piaget's pendulum problem allows us to examine the thinking of the formal operational adolescent. In this task, the person is shown an object hanging from a string and asked to determine the factor that influences the frequency of oscillation, or the rate at which the pendulum swings. The length of the string, the weight of the object, the force of the push on the object, and the height from which the object is released can all be varied. How do children in earlier Piagetian stages approach this problem? Children in the preoperational and concrete operational stages typically try various manipulations in a haphazard fashion. They might compare the effect of a long string attached to a heavy weight and a short string tied to a light weight. Or they might vary the weight of the object and force of the push but leave out the length of the string. In contrast, formal operational children are both systematic and complete in testing the potential influences on oscillation. For example, while keeping weight constant, they observe the effects of varying length, push, and height; while keeping length the same, they investigate the effects of varying weight, push, and height; and so forth. Most adolescents, Piaget observed, could correctly determine that the length of the string was the critical factor in how fast the pendulum swings (Inhelder & Piaget, 1958).

In the social realm, achieving abstract thought means the adolescent can think about the nature of society and his own future role in it. Idealism is common at this developmental stage because he understands more fully concepts such as justice, love, and liberty and thinks about possibilities rather than just realities. In some ways, the adolescent may be more of a "dreamer" or utopian than the adult because he has not yet had to confront the practical facts of living and working in the world (Inhelder & Piaget, 1958).

The contemplative nature of adolescent thought may manifest itself in two other ways, according to David Elkind (1976, 1981a). First, adolescents may believe others scrutinize and evaluate them as much as they think about themselves. This belief, called the **imaginary audience,** may cause a young girl to avoid going out because she just got braces on her teeth ("Everybody will see me!") or make a teenage boy avoid answering a question in class because he is certain all his classmates will think he is "dumb." Second, adolescents may show signs of holding a **personal fable,** the belief that they are unique, that no one can fully understand them, and even that they are invulnerable. A teenage boy prohibited from going to a late-night rock concert by his parents might say, "You just don't understand how important this is to me!"

operation   In Piagetian theory, a mental action such as reversibility.

formal operational stage   In Piagetian theory, the last stage of development, from approximately eleven to fifteen years of age, in which thought is abstract and hypothetical.

hypothetical reasoning   Ability to systematically generate and evaluate potential solutions to a problem.

imaginary audience   Individual's belief that others are examining and evaluating him or her.

personal fable   Belief that one is unique and perhaps even invulnerable.

The development of formal operational thought represents the culmination of the reorganizations in thought that have taken place throughout each stage in childhood. By adolescence thought has become logical, flexible, and abstract, and its internal guiding structures are now highly organized.

Implications for Education

Piaget's theory carries some clear implications for teaching children. The first is that the individual child's current stage of development must be carefully taken into account as teachers plan lessons. For example, a seven-year-old who is in the stage of concrete operations should be given problems involving actual physical objects to observe or manipulate rather than abstract word problems or diagrams (Flavell, 1963). Similarly, a four-year-old preoperational child may have difficulty with tasks requiring the use of logic; a more fruitful strategy might be to foster the imagination and creativity that result from the recently acquired semiotic function. By encouraging drawing, pretend play, and vocal expression, teachers can capitalize on the preschooler's cognitive strengths.

A second, related implication is that what the child knows already will determine what new information she is able to absorb. Because her current cognitive structures limit what she will be able to assimilate, it is important that the teacher be aware of the child's current state of knowledge. In addition, cognitive advances are most optimally made when new material is only slightly different from what the child already knows (Ginsburg & Opper, 1988). Thus, the teacher's task is to plan lessons that are tailored to the needs of the individual child rather than to the class as a whole and to be flexible in devising instructional materials that stretch the child one step beyond what she already knows.

One of Piaget's most important statements about cognitive development is that it is the result of the *active engagement of the child*. Early sensorimotor schemes and later mental operations are all founded first on the child's physical activity and later on mental actions. Thus, education too must be structured in such a way that it will promote the child's active participation. Instead of emphasizing rote learning, teachers following a Piagetian model provide children with experiments that allow them to discover scientific principles on their own. Children do not memorize numerical relationships, such as the multiplication tables, but discover them by manipulating

KEY THEME
Child's Active Role

One implication of Piaget's assumption that children are active learners is that education should present children with "hands-on" opportunities to discover principles of science or math. In Piaget's view, active learning promotes deeper and more enduring understanding than rote memorization.

sets of objects under the close guidance of the teacher. According to Piagetian thinking, active learning of this sort promotes deeper and more enduring understanding.

Educational programs based on a Piagetian model have varied in their instructional goals. Some have emphasized the teaching of specific skills such as conservation; others have focused on more general principles, such as fostering children's active participation in the educational process (Crain, 1992). Many of these programs have been specifically targeted for preschool-age children, probably for good reasons. One difficulty in implementing Piagetian-based education in higher grades is that individualized instruction is not always possible when there are twenty or more students in a classroom; in preschool classrooms, which tend to have fewer students, individualized instruction is more feasible. Nevertheless, many teachers have found inspiration in the rich theoretical framework Jean Piaget devised for thinking about how and what to teach children.

Evaluating Piaget's Theory

Piaget is widely acknowledged as being one of the most influential of all thinkers in the history of psychology and a founder of the study of cognitive development as we know it (Brainerd, 1996; Flavell, 1996). By introducing questions about *what* develops as well as *how* development occurs, Piaget went well beyond the descriptions of norms of behavior that had been the staple of the early years of research in developmental psychology. Moreover, once American psychologists learned of his ideas in the 1960s and early 1970s, they could no longer conceptualize development solely in terms of learning theory, which was a dominant psychological view at that time. Finally, Piaget's method of closely watching the nuances of children's behaviors and listening as they explained their reasoning provided an important and inspiring lesson for developmental psychologists: that "grand questions can actually be answered by paying attention to the small details of the daily lives of our children" (Gopnik, 1996, p. 225).

The fact that Piaget's theory has stimulated so much research in developmental psychology is not surprising, given its wide-ranging scope. In sheer numbers of empirical studies generated by the writings of one person, Jean Piaget has no rival in developmental psychology. Like all good theories, Piaget's has spawned a host of debates about the fundamental nature of cognitive change. These debates are a tribute to the power of his ideas and his contribution to the scientific process.

Contemporary evaluations of Piaget's theory have raised several key points. First, did Piaget provide an accurate portrayal of the ages at which individuals acquire different cognitive skills? Second, does cognitive development proceed in a stagelike fashion? Third, might there be alternative explanations for the behaviors Piaget observed in children of different ages?

What Are the Ages of Acquisition?   One criticism of Piaget's theory is that Piaget underestimated the abilities of infants and young children. Many researchers have found that when cognitive tasks are simplified or restructured, or when children are observed in more naturalistic settings, they display cognitive skills at much earlier ages than Piaget believed possible.

Take the object concept, for example. Piaget maintained that the first real notions about the permanence of objects do not emerge until about eight or nine months of age, when infants will search for objects that are completely covered. Renée Baillargeon (1987a), however, was able to demonstrate that infants as young as four months have a rudimentary understanding of the continuing existence of objects. Figure 8.2 shows the phases of this experiment. At first, the infants observed a screen that rotated 180 degrees over repeated trials. As you might expect, they showed habituation of visual fixation to this display after it was repeated for several trials. Next, a box was placed behind the screen. While the screen was still flat against the table, the box was visible, but as the screen rotated away from the child, it hid the box from view. In the possible-event condition, the screen stopped moving at the point where it hit the box. In the impossible-event condition, the box was surreptitiously

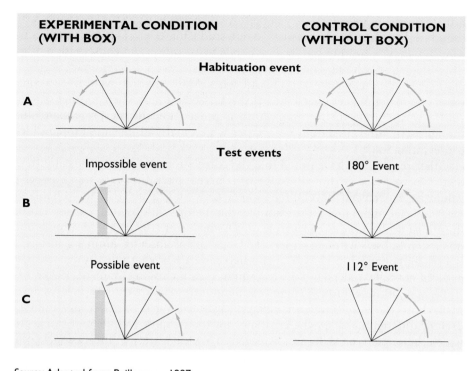

EXPERIMENTAL CONDITION (WITH BOX)	CONTROL CONDITION (WITHOUT BOX)

Habituation event

A

Test events

Impossible event   180° Event

B

Possible event   112° Event

C

Source: Adapted from Baillargeon, 1987a.

FIGURE 8.2

Do Infants Have an Object Concept?

In Baillargeon's experiment, infants were habituated to a screen rotating 180 degrees (A). Next, infants in the *impossible-event* condition saw the screen appearing to pass through the location of a box (B, on left), while infants in the *possible-event* condition saw the screen stop at the location of the box (C, on left). Infants in the *impossible-event* condition looked significantly longer at this event, suggesting that they were puzzled by what they saw and therefore had an object concept. The control conditions (shown at right) were included to make sure the infants were not responding to the arc of the screen's movement.

removed and the screen passed through the space the box would have occupied. In two control conditions, the screen either moved or stopped, as in the two experimental conditions, but no box was present. Infants looked significantly longer at the impossible event than the possible event, apparently noticing that the screen was moving through the space that the box should have occupied. Looking time did not differ in the two control conditions, indicating that the type of movement did not determine the infants' responses. Thus, infants seemed to be aware that the box in the impossible-event condition should have had an effect on the movement of the screen, even though they could not see it. This awareness, argues Baillargeon, is an indicator of the object concept.

Similarly, Rochel Gelman (1969) noted that conservation of number could be demonstrated in five-year-old children, who, in Piaget's view, are still in the preoperational stage of development and lack the logical thought structures to perform this task correctly. Gelman first determined that all the children in her sample were unable to conserve number. Then she provided training on the "oddity problem." On each trial, children saw three stimuli and were directed to indicate which one was different from the other two. On some trials, the "odd" stimulus differed in number from the other two; on others, the "odd" stimulus differed in length. After the training period, the children were tested on the conservation of length and number. The majority performed correctly even when they were tested several weeks after the training period. In fact, in later work, Gelman has shown that under some circumstances, even three- and four-year-olds are able to conserve number after training (Gelman, 1972). These results show that the ability to think logically is present well before children reach age seven.

Piaget himself was less concerned with the specific ages at which children acquire cognitive skills than with the sequence of development. For others, however, the fact that many cognitive attainments occur earlier than he suggested is problematic. As researchers sought explanations for the presence of cognitive skills at earlier ages, they raised other questions about the nature of cognitive development.

KEY THEME
Continuity/Discontinuity

Is Cognitive Development Stagelike?   If cognitive development proceeds in stages, children should show common features in how they think within a stage and distinctive differences in how they think across stages. One problem with Piagetian theory is that it posits more consistency in performance within a given stage than is actually found in the behavior of children. In one study, Ina Uzgiris (1968) tested children who should have been in the stage of concrete operations on conservation of quantity, weight, and volume. The same tasks were tested with different materials, such as plasticine balls, metal cubes, and plastic wires. Many children were able to conserve when one material (say, plasticine balls) was used but not when another (say, metal cubes) was employed. If conservation is indeed tied to the presence of logical thought structures, it should not matter which materials are used to conduct the conservation tests.

Other researchers have noted that the correlations among various abilities predicted to co-occur within the stage of concrete operations are much lower than would be expected if development were truly stagelike (Gelman & Baillargeon, 1983). Piaget maintained, for example, that before children can conserve number they must understand the principle of class inclusion, the idea that some groups of objects are subsets within a larger set. "Dogs" are a subset of "animals," just as "five" is a set contained within "six." Yet children can conserve number by age six or seven and still not fully understand the concept of class inclusion (Brainerd, 1978a).

Because of these findings, many contemporary researchers now believe development shows more continuity than Piaget suggested. What seems to vary among children of different ages, say the critics, is not their cognitive skills but the degree to which the same basic skills are displayed in a wide variety of increasingly complex situations (for example, Brainerd, 1978b). Another position retains an emphasis on stagelike development but suggests that when new levels of thinking are reached, they are less broadly and generally applied than Piaget initially proposed. Cognitive development, these theorists say, proceeds as Piaget outlined, but in some domains—say, number or spatial relationships—growth is more rapid than in other domains (for example, Fischer, 1980). We will consider these perspectives more fully in our discussion of neo-Piagetian approaches to cognitive development later in this chapter.

Are There Alternative Explanations for Development? Many studies have confirmed Piaget's general claims about the patterns of behavior children display at different ages. Without special training, for example, most children under age six or seven years fail conservation tasks, whereas older children perform them successfully. Adolescents are indeed capable of solving problems more systematically and abstractly than their younger counterparts. Yet many psychologists disagree with Piaget about the precise mechanisms that account for such patterns in the development of thinking processes.

The basic challenge to Piaget's theory centers on whether cognitive development is best understood in terms of emerging symbolic, logical, and hypothetical thought structures or whether some other explanation is more tenable. A case in point is the successful training of conservation by Rochel Gelman (1969) as previously described. Gelman suggests that young children normally fail conservation tasks because they fail to attend to the correct portions of the problem, not because they lack mental operations such as reversibility. If children's attention is directed to the salient cues, Gelman and others argue, they will be successful in conserving. Younger children may also be less skilled at remembering than older children, forgetting elements of problems that are essential to reaching the correct solutions. Thus, cognitive development may result from a change in how information is gathered, manipulated, and stored rather than from the alteration of cognitive structures themselves.

Another central Piagetian tenet is that maturation, in conjunction with experience, is responsible for the unfolding of more sophisticated thought structures. The heavy emphasis Piaget places on maturation implies that the sequence of development is universal. Yet not all children reach the stage of formal operations, and some do not even attain the highest levels of concrete operations. Many American adults, in fact, fail to display formal operational thought (Neimark, 1979). Moreover, members of many non-Western cultures do not display formal operational thinking, especially when they have little experience with formal schooling (Dasen, 1972; Rogoff, 1981).

KEY THEME
Nature/Nurture

KEY THEME
Individual Differences

KEY THEME
Sociocultural Influence

At the same time, specific kinds of cultural experiences may accelerate the emergence of conservation and formal operational thought. Douglass Price-Williams and his colleagues examined two groups of rural Mexican children six to nine years old on standard conservation problems (Price-Williams, Gordon, & Ramirez, 1969). Half of the children came from pottery-making families, the other half from families that practiced other trades. Children who had experience in manipulating clay for pottery making were far more likely to conserve than the other children. Studies such as these imply that the child's experiences in the sociocultural context may shape the nature of thought to a greater degree than Piaget acknowledged. They also challenge the notion that Western scientific thinking represents the highest form of thought and the endpoint of development (Greenfield, 1976). The ability to solve problems like a miniature scientist may be highly valued in our own culture but less so in cultures in which other skills such as hunting, farming, or even social facility are more essential to successful living.

Despite these criticisms, several important strands of Piaget's work run through contemporary ideas about cognitive development. First and foremost is the idea that children are active participants in their own growth: few researchers believe children merely absorb information like sponges. Moreover, many modern accounts of cognition assume that what the individual knows at a given time determines the knowledge he or she can acquire, a distinctly Piagetian idea. Finally, Piaget opened the doors to the exploration of important topics in cognitive development. How do infants understand the properties of objects? How do children classify objects that have potential relationships to one another? What do children understand about the properties of numbers? What do children understand about different mental states, their own and those of others? These questions, suggested by Piaget's pioneering work, are being actively explored by contemporary developmental psychologists, and it is to these questions that we now turn our attention.

CONCEPT DEVELOPMENT

When and how does the child begin to understand that horses, dogs, and cats all belong to a common category called "animals"? When does she realize that numbers such as "2" or "4" represent specific quantities, no matter what objects are being counted? And how does she mentally organize her spatial environment, such as the layout of her house or the path from home to school? In each case, we are concerned with the ways the child organizes a set of information about the world, using some general or abstract principle as the basis for that organization. In other words, we are describing the child's use of **concepts**.

As one psychologist put it, "Concepts and categories serve as the building blocks for human thought and behavior" (Medin, 1989). Concepts allow us to group isolated pieces of information on the basis of common themes or properties. The result is greater efficiency in cognitive processing. Suppose someone tells you, "A quarf is an animal." Without even seeing one, you already know many of the quarf's properties: it breathes, eats, locomotes, and so on. Because concepts are linked to one of the most powerful human capabilities—language—and other aspects of cognition, understanding how concepts develop is an important concern of developmental psychologists. Many modern-day accounts of concept development arose out of attempts to test or expand the ground-breaking ideas Piaget set forth concerning children's understanding of objects, classes of objects, number, and space.

Properties of Objects

The most fundamental early concepts, of course, have to do with the objects infants and young children encounter. What exactly do they understand about the properties of objects, for example, the fact of their continual existence or how one object might cause another to launch forward or zigzag across the room?

concept Definition of a set of information on the basis of some general or abstract principle.

The Object Concept   We already discussed how Piaget believed that significant accomplishments such as the object concept emerge late in the first year of life and do not become fully elaborated until the second year. We have also seen that experiments such as those of Renée Baillargeon suggest that by three to four months of age, infants understand far more about the properties of physical objects, like the object concept, than Piaget surmised (Baillargeon, 1987a; Baillargeon & DeVos, 1991).

According to Baillargeon, such young infants not only understand that objects exist when out of sight but also understand that the objects' size continues to be preserved as well (Baillargeon, 1987b). In a series of experiments involving the rotation of a screen similar to that shown in Figure 8.2, the rectangular box was either upright (as shown in the figure) or lying flat. Three- and four-month-olds seemed to understand that the screen could not rotate as far when the box was in the upright position as it could when lying down. Moreover, if the object was something that could be squeezed, such as a ball of gauze the infants had previously played with, they were not surprised by the continued rotation of the screen in front of it. They did show surprise when the screen seemed to rotate past the position of a hard and rigid box. Apparently, young infants quickly move beyond simply understanding that an object exists under a cover or behind a barrier; they also develop ideas about physical properties of objects such as their height and rigidity (Baillargeon, 1995).

A series of studies by Adele Diamond and her colleagues further demonstrates the extent of young infants' knowledge about objects. A common error that occurs when the child is about seven to nine months of age is the A$\overline{\text{B}}$ (or "A, not B") error. In this task, an object is hidden in location A, found by the infant, and then, in full view of the infant, moved to location B. Piaget observed that the child would mistakenly but persistently search for the object in location A. He hypothesized that the infant's incomplete knowledge of the object concept leads to this error, in large part because the sensorimotor scheme for searching in location A still controls the child's thought. Diamond, however, proposes that other factors account for the A$\overline{\text{B}}$ error.

When watching infants make the A$\overline{\text{B}}$ error, Diamond noticed that even though some infants mistakenly *reached* for A, they actually *looked* at B, the correct location of the hidden toy (see Figure 8.3) (Diamond, 1985). They behaved as though they knew the correct location of the toy but could not stop themselves from reaching to

FIGURE 8.3

Alternative Explanations for the A$\overline{\text{B}}$ Error

In the first photograph, a toy has been hidden first in the right well (location A), then in the well on the left (location B) as the infant looks on. The next three photographs show that even though the infant reaches for location A, he looks persistently at location B, suggesting that he has the object concept when there are visible displacements of the object. Diamond (1991) believes infants reach for the incorrect location because of failure to inhibit motor responses.

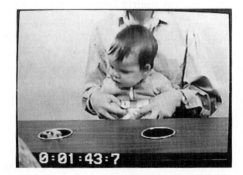

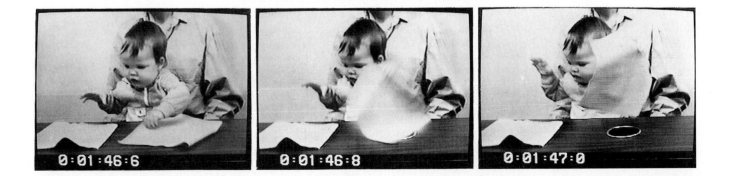

Direct launching

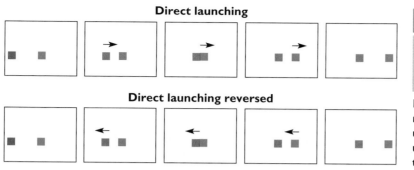

Direct launching reversed

Source: Leslie & Keeble, 1987.

FIGURE 8.4

A Demonstration of Infant Discrimination of Physical Causality

In Leslie's experiment, six-month-old infants viewed stimulus sequences that occurred under different conditions. The top row shows a red brick moving and touching a green brick, after which the green brick moves. Infants habituated to this sequence showed dishabituation when the reverse sequence, the green brick moving and striking the red brick, was shown; that is, they noticed when the object causing the physical movement switched. In another condition, the red brick moved and touched the green brick, but the green brick moved only after a delay; that is, the cues did not suggest the red brick was causing the green brick to move. Infants habituated to this latter sequence showed less dishabituation to the reversal.

A. In other studies, adult monkeys, which normally perform successfully on the $A\overline{B}$ task, make mistakes identical to those of seven-to-nine-month-old human infants when lesions are made in very specific areas of their frontal cortex; these are the brain areas that control the inhibition of responses (Diamond & Goldman-Rakic, 1989). Diamond (1991) proposes that infants have the object concept well before age seven months but, due to the physical immaturity of this special cortical area, they cannot suppress their tendency to reach for location A. Lending support to this hypothesis is recent data showing that infants who are successful in the $A\overline{B}$ task display more powerful brain electrical activity from the same frontal region of the cortex (Bell & Fox, 1992). Thus, the behaviors Piaget originally observed in the $A\overline{B}$ task may be due to infants' inability to inhibit reaching, not the lack of object concept (Diamond, Cruttenden, & Neiderman, 1994).

Physical Causality   Imagine the following scene: a red brick moves halfway across a screen, hits a green brick, and the green brick moves across the rest of the screen. Most adults would conclude that the red brick caused the green brick to glide across the screen. They would not reach that conclusion, however, if they saw the bricks did not touch each other or if there was a pause between the time the two bricks made contact and the time the green brick started to move (Michotte, 1963).

In a series of experiments, Alan Leslie showed that infants as young as six months exhibit similar reactions (Leslie, 1982, 1984; Leslie & Keeble, 1987). In one condition, infants observed one object collide with another object and propel it forward for a series of trials. After they showed habituation to this scene, they viewed the reverse situation, in which the second object hit and launched the first. Infants showed dishabituation; that is, they treated the two event sequences (depicted in Figure 8.4) as though they were different. In a control condition, infants were habituated to the same events, but the second object moved only after a delay. Now, though, when the event was reversed, little dishabituation was observed. These experiments showed that infants notice something unique about causal events. Other research has demonstrated that for infants to react to physical causality, the same objects must be used repeatedly during habituation trials. Reactions to physical causality diminish when the objects themselves change from trial to trial or when the objects are more complex (Cohen & Oakes, 1993; Oakes, 1994; Oakes & Cohen, 1990). Thus, it seems that the infant's conceptual understanding of physical causality appears early in life and develops as a result of repeated experiences with specific, simple objects.

Of course, the infant studies just described do not suggest a full-blown appreciation of the concept of causality; they simply imply that before age one year, infants notice something unique about contiguous event sequences in which one object seems to "cause" another to do something. How do slightly older children—preschoolers—understand concepts of causality?

Piaget (1930, 1974) believed that up until the early school years, ages seven or eight years, children lack an awareness of physical causality. Once they are verbal and can discuss causality, they make some interesting errors. One type of error is **animism,** attributing lifelike properties to inanimate objects. In one of Piaget's examples of animism, a six-year-old boy named Vern was asked why a boat floats on water but a little stone sinks. Vern answered, "The boat is more intelligent than the stone" (Piaget, 1929, p. 223). Another child, age seven, is asked if the sun can do whatever it likes. The child responds affirmatively; asked why the sun doesn't stop giving light, the child says, "It wants it to be fine weather" (Piaget, 1929, p. 227). Animism is often accompanied by **artificialism,** the belief that people cause naturally occurring events. Piaget provides the example of a six-year-old named Hub:

Piaget: Has the sun always been there?
Hub: No, it began.
Piaget: How?
Hub: With fire. . . .
Piaget: How did that start?
Hub: With a match. . . .
Piaget: Who struck it?
Hub: A man. (Piaget, 1929, p. 266)

In Piaget's view, children are slow to shed their animistic and artificial beliefs; the latter may persist until age ten years or so (Piaget, 1929).

Susan Gelman and Kathleen Kremer (1991) attempted to replicate some of Piaget's studies by asking preschoolers, "Do you think people made (or make)_____?" where the blank was filled in by an object such as the sun, the moon, dogs, flowers, dolls, and shoes. Few of the children showed evidence of artificialism; most recognized that objects such as dolls are made by humans, but the sun and moon are not. Moreover, these young children often cited natural causes for the behaviors of living things (for example, birds fly because they have wings) and human causes for the things artificial objects do (for example, cars go uphill because people make them do so). Why the discrepancy from Piaget's observations? Gelman and Kremer (1991) postulate that direct questions, such as the ones they used, were more likely to tap children's underlying knowledge of causality than the free-ranging interview questions Piaget employed.

Classification

Aside from learning about the properties of single objects, as in the object concept, children also quickly learn about relationships that can exist among sets of objects. Sometimes objects resemble one another perceptually and seem to "go together" because they are the same color or shape. At other times, the relationships among objects can be more complex; the perceptual similarities may be less obvious and, moreover, some sets can be embedded within others. Cocker spaniels and Great Danes, two different-looking dogs, can be classified together in the group "dogs," and both breeds fit into a larger category of "animals." As with many other cognitive skills, Piaget believed that before age seven years, children's ability to classify objects, particularly in the hierarchical manner of the latter example, is limited. Ask a young child who sees six brown beads and three white beads, all of which are wooden, "Do I have more brown beads or wooden beads?" Chances are the four- or five-year-old will respond, "More brown beads." According to Piaget, preoperational children lack the logical thought structures to permit understanding that some classes can be subsets of others (Piaget, 1952a). Piaget was right in claiming that classification skills undergo changes with development, but the research that followed his work has revealed a far more complex portrait of this cognitive skill.

Early Classification   One of the earliest signs of classification skills in young children occurs toward the end of the first year, when children begin to group *perceptually similar* objects together. Susan Sugarman (1982, 1983) carefully watched the behaviors of

animism   Attribution of lifelike qualities to inanimate objects.

artificialism   Belief that naturally occurring events are caused by people.

one-to-three-year-olds as they played with successive sets of stimuli that could be grouped into two classes, such as plates and square blocks or dolls and boats. Even the youngest children displayed a spontaneous tendency to group similar-looking objects together by pointing consecutively to items that were alike. At age two, children went one step further and began to move objects resembling one another into two distinct groups, that is, plates with plates and blocks with blocks. Thus, the tendency to group objects together on the basis of shared perceptual characteristics emerges early in development.

Between ages one and three years, children experience a rapid growth in classification skills. Infants as young as fourteen months successively touch objects that appear in common contexts, such as "kitchen things" and "bathroom things" (Mandler, Fivush, & Reznick, 1987). Two-year-olds will match items on the basis of *thematic relations,* clustering items that function together or complement one another, such as a baby bottle and a baby. They will also occasionally classify items *taxonomically,* grouping objects that may not look alike on the basis of some abstract principle, such as a banana with an apple. They are more likely to group items taxonomically, though, when items show at least some perceptual similarities. For example, linking a shoe with a boot is easier for the two-year-old than linking a shoe with a shirt (Fenson, Vella, & Kennedy, 1989). Taxonomic classification is also easier for young children when they hear that objects from the same category share the same label even though they may not look very much alike (e.g., a panther and a tabby house cat are both called "cats") or their similarities are pointed out in some other way (Deák & Bauer, 1996).

Not until age seven years or so do children spontaneously use the different kinds of relationships possible within taxonomic classes. In one recent study, four- and seven-year-olds were asked to say "the first word you think of" as they were given different stimulus words. The stimulus list included words such as *shirt, pants, socks, dog, cat, guinea pig,* and so on. Whereas seven-year- olds typically gave responses such as "animal" or "collie" when they heard the word *dog,* four-year-olds were more apt to say "cat" or, even more commonly, a word such as "bark" (Lucariello, Kyratzis, & Nelson, 1992). In other words, only school-age children showed a tendency to use the vertical relations within a taxonomic category, whereas preschoolers employed horizontal or thematic relations. Thus, as children grow older, they become capable of using a wider range of relations to classify objects, their exclusive reliance on shared perceptual features lessens, and they display spontaneous hierarchical knowledge of categories.

Basic-Level Categories   Eleanor Rosch and her colleagues have proposed another way to frame our understanding of the way concepts develop in children (Rosch et al., 1976). These researchers believe that some groupings of objects can be described as *basic level;* that is, objects go together when they look alike and can be used in similar ways, and when we can think of "average" members of the class. "Chair" is an example of a basic-level concept because virtually all chairs have seats, legs, and backs; all are used for sitting; and we can think of such a thing as a "typical" chair. In contrast, other concepts are *superordinate level.* Members of superordinate-level groups, such as "furniture," do not necessarily share many perceptual attributes, and they are broader and more general than basic-level concepts. Rosch and her colleagues believe that because basic-level groups carry more information, especially perceptual information, than superordinate-level groups, they are easier for children to process. Figure 8.5 illustrates this example of a basic-level and a superordinate-level grouping.

Rosch and her colleagues found that children under age five years readily put together four pictures of different shoes or four pictures of different cars; that is, they could sort according to basic-level groupings (Rosch et al., 1976). In fact, a more recent study shows that the ability to sort basic-level stimuli is evident as early as eighteen months of age (Gopnik & Meltzoff, 1992). We also saw in Chapter 7 how many of the child's first words are basic-level terms. Children in Rosch's study could not, however, proficiently sort on the basis of superordinate category by putting a

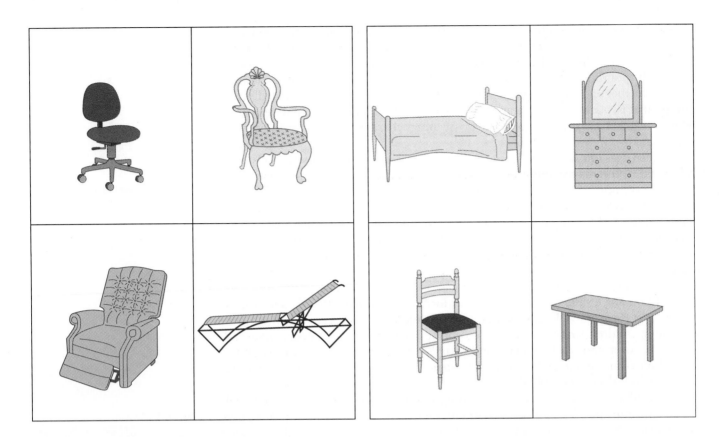

FIGURE 8.5

Basic- and Superordinate-Level Categories

The left panel gives an example of objects that are considered a basic-level grouping. These stimuli share perceptual features, and an "average" member of the class can be conceptualized. The right panel gives an example of superordinate-level grouping. Members of such classes do not necessarily share many perceptual features, and it is more difficult to think of an "average" class member. Basic-level categories are easier for young children to employ than superordinate-level groupings.

natural domains Concepts or categories that children acquire especially rapidly and effortlessly.

shoe, shirt, sock, and pants together until they reached age eight or nine years. These results reaffirm that children's classification skills undergo significant development in the years from three to nine.

Natural Domains   Recently several developmental psychologists have asserted that some concepts or categories of objects are easier to acquire than others. Just as children seem to be biologically "programmed" to learn language rapidly and easily (see Chapter 7), so do they seem to learn about certain conceptual domains quickly and effortlessly. In other words, some objects and events in the environment offer "privileged relationships" for the child to learn about (Gallistel et al., 1991). Among these so-called **natural domains** is knowledge about biological entities.

Children show a dramatically early ability to classify animate versus inanimate objects. For example, a twenty-four-month-old will show obvious surprise when a chair seems to move forward on its own (Golinkoff et al., 1984), and a twelve-month-old will fuss and cry more when a robot starts to move as opposed to a human stranger (Poulin-Dubois, Lepage, & Ferland, 1996). Three-year-olds know that living things can feel emotions but inanimate objects cannot; they say a person can feel sad, but a doll or a rock cannot (Gelman, Spelke, & Meck, 1983). Even subtle distinctions between animate and inanimate objects are made. When shown a mechanical monkey, young children in Susan Carey's (1985) studies said the monkey physically resembles a person but cannot eat or sleep as a human being can.

Similarly, preschool children view the qualities of biological offspring, such as the color of a flower, as deriving from a parent—a biological source. In contrast, they recognize the qualities of nonbiological artifacts, such as the color of a can, as mechanically derived. Thus, preschoolers already form a distinction between reproduction involving biological entities and production involving the manufacture of inanimate objects (Springer & Keil, 1991). Preschoolers also begin to recognize that other processes, such as growth, illness, healing, and death, are unique to biological organisms (Backscheider, Shatz, & Gelman, 1993; Rosengren et al., 1991; Siegal, 1988).

Part of the usefulness of concepts, of course, is that they permit us to make assumptions about other category members, as in our earlier example of the "quarf." That is, we go beyond the information given, perhaps even beyond the similarities of perceptual features of objects, to make conceptually based judgments or inductions about them. According to Susan Carey (1985) and Frank Keil (1989), children's inductions are largely guided by "theories" they construct about the nature of specific concepts. For the domain of biological entities, Carey found that children's theories undergo revision with development to allow more and more accurate judgments. For example, a four-year-old who is told that humans have "omenta" will say that only other animals that are very similar to humans also have "omenta." His theory about biology centers around what he knows about humans. In contrast, an older child would state that even animals physically dissimilar from humans have "omenta." Her theory of biology extends beyond resemblances to human beings to the broader properties that characterize living things. According to Carey, then, concept development in the biological domain is actually the development of a systematic and coherent theory of biology.

Individual and Cultural Variations in Classification   Implicit in Piagetian ideas about classification is the notion that there should be many similarities in concept development among children, even those from different cultures. However, research suggests that this is not the case. For example, some three-year-olds show a clear propensity to use thematic classification, whereas others prefer taxonomic classification. Interestingly, these individual differences in classification preferences are linked to earlier unique profiles in play and language use. As one-year-olds, "thematic" children have been noted to play with objects in spatial, functional ways and, at age two, use words such as *in* and *down* more than "taxonomic" children do; that is, they have seemingly stable preferences to focus on how objects work in relation to one another (Dunham & Dunham, 1995).

KEY THEME
Individual Differences

Cultural variations in classification occur too. One group of researchers found that residents of rural Mexico with little formal schooling tended to group objects on the basis of their functional relations. "Chicken" and "egg" were frequently classified together because "the chicken lays eggs." On the other hand, subjects with more education relied on taxonomic classification, grouping "chicken" with "horse" because "they are animals" (Sharp, Cole, & Lave, 1979). It may be that taxonomic classification strategies are taught explicitly in schools or that education fosters the development of more abstract thought, a basic requirement for taxonomic grouping.

KEY THEME
Sociocultural Influence

Other cultural differences may also be important in concept development, specifically by influencing the types of theories children and adults construct about groupings of objects and events. Sheila Walker (1992) studied understanding of biological concepts among rural, urban poor, and highly educated adults in western Nigeria, where familiarity with supernatural beliefs is more widespread than in the United States. Subjects were asked questions about the identities of animals that underwent transformations in religious ritualistic contexts and in nonritualistic contexts. Adults from all backgrounds were more likely to accept a change in the biological identity of an organism—say, a cat changing to a dog—in the ritualistic context than in the nonritualistic context. This finding sheds further light on the view that classifications are theory based by pointing out the substantial role that cultural contexts—in this case, a context in which the supernatural is familiar—can play in those theories. Any full explanation of the development of classification skills will have to take into account the experiences of children within their specific sociocultural contexts.

Numerical Concepts

Children as young as two years of age frequently use number terms, either to count toys, snacks, or other items or in playful ways, such as shouting, "One, two, three, jump!" as they bounce off their beds (Saxe, Guberman, & Gearhart, 1987). But do

By the age of four years, many children are able to count and appreciate at least some of the principles of numerical relationships, including *cardinality*. Thus, by claiming that children do not have a conceptual understanding of number, Piaget may have underestimated children's numerical skills.

young children really understand the full significance of numbers as a tool for establishing quantitative relationships? Or are they merely repeating a series of words they have heard someone else say without fully appreciating the conceptual underpinnings of those words?

Early Concepts of Number   Piaget's (1952a) position was that children under age seven years or so, before they enter the concrete operational stage, lack a full grasp of the meaning of numbers. One indication is the failure of preoperational children to succeed in the conservation of number task. In this problem, you will recall, children see two equal rows of objects—say, red and white poker chips—as shown in Figure 8.1. Initially the rows are aligned identically, and most children will agree that they have equal numbers of chips. But when the chips in one row are spread out, the majority of children state that this row now has more chips even though no chips have been added or subtracted.

Preoperational children, Piaget maintained, fail to comprehend the **one-to-one correspondence** that still exists among items in the two rows; that is, each element in a row can be mapped onto an element in the second row, with none left over. Moreover, he believed young children have not yet attained an understanding of two important aspects of number. The first is **cardinality,** or the total number of elements in a class, as in *six* red poker chips. The second is **ordinality,** the order in which an item appears in the set, as in the *second* poker chip. According to Piaget, the child must grasp both these concepts to judge two sets of items as being equivalent.

Many contemporary researchers believe Piaget underestimated preschool children's understanding of number concepts. For example, two-year-olds will correctly point to a picture with three items, and not a picture with one item, when asked, "Can you show me the three fish?" (Wynn, 1992). By age four years, many children say number words in sequence and, in so doing, appreciate at least some basic principles of numerical relationships. Rochel Gelman and her associates have argued that even young children have a knowledge of certain important fundamental principles

one-to-one correspondence Understanding that two sets are equivalent in number if each element in one set can be mapped onto a unique element in the second set with none left over.

cardinality   Principle that the last number in a set of counted numbers refers to the number of items in that set.

ordinality   Principle that a number refers to an item's order within a set.

of counting (Gelman & Gallistel, 1978; Gelman & Meck, 1983). Among these principles are (1) using the same sequence of counting words when counting different sets, (2) employing only one counting word per object, (3) using the last counting word in the set to represent the total number, (4) understanding that any set of objects can be counted, and (5) appreciating that objects can be counted in any order.

When young children count, their words are not devoid of numerical meaning. In one experiment, three- and four-year-olds saw six dolls and five rings and were asked, "There are six dolls. Is there a ring for every doll?" Most of the four-year-olds used number words to answer questions about one-to-one correspondence. For example, many said, "No, because there are six dolls and five rings" (Becker, 1989). Similarly, many preschoolers spontaneously resort to counting when they encounter the following type of problem. Six dolls are arranged in a row. Two dolls are given two teddy bears each. If the rest of the dolls get two teddy bears each, how many teddy bears are needed? (Becker, 1993). In addition, four-year-olds are able to compare quantities, answering correctly such questions as "Which is bigger, five or two?" (Siegler & Robinson, 1982). Thus, their understanding of number terms includes relations such as "larger" and "smaller." One interesting pattern, though, is that young children have more difficulty in making such comparisons when the numbers themselves are large (ten versus fourteen) or when the difference between two numbers is small (eight versus nine). The same is true when children have to add, subtract, and perform other calculations with numbers (Levine, Jordan, & Huttenlocher, 1992).

Children's sensitivity to basic aspects of numerical relationships is evident even well before the preschool years, according to some recent dramatic findings. In one experiment, five-month-old infants watched as a toy was placed in a case and then was hidden by a screen. The infants watched as a second, identical toy was placed behind the screen. When the screen was removed and only one toy remained—an impossible outcome if the infants appreciated there should still be two toys—they showed surprise and looked longer than they did when two toys were visible (Wynn, 1992). Other researchers have confirmed that even before the second half of their first year, babies show numerical competencies that likely serve as the foundation for more complex reasoning about quantities (Canfield & Smith, 1996; Simon, Hespos, & Rochat, 1995).

Learning Mathematics   Once children enter school, of course, they are expected to master the formal properties of numbers through mathematics. Lauren Resnick (1986) believes that before children learn the systematic rules for addition, subtraction, algebra, and other mathematical systems, they develop intuitive concepts about how numbers can be manipulated. How would Pitt, one of her seven-year-old participants, add 152 and 149?

> I would have the two 100's, which equals 200. Then I would have 50 and the 40, which equals 90. So I have 290. Then plus the 9 from 49, and the 2 from the 52 equals 11. And then I add the 90 plus the 11 . . . equals 102. 102? 101. So I put the 200 and the 101, which equals 301. (p. 164)

All of this came from a young boy who had mastered only first-grade arithmetic!

Other researchers have observed the remarkable computational skills of child street vendors in Brazil, skills that contrast with their poor performance on more school-like arithmetic problems (Nunes, Schliemann, & Carraker, 1993). Resnick suggests that it is puzzling that many children experience difficulties with mathematics in school given their early competencies with numbers. Perhaps, she suggests, teachers should frame more complex mathematical operations, such as ratios and algebraic expressions, in terms of simple additive properties or other intuitions children have about numbers, at least when they are first being learned (Resnick, 1995; Resnick & Singer, 1993).

Children use a wide variety of strategies when they solve mathematics problems. We will say more about these strategies when we discuss the development of problem-solving skills in Chapter 9.

Regardless of whether the participants in studies are kindergartners or college students, the findings are consistent: Asian students score significantly higher than students from the United States on tests of mathematics (Fuligni & Stevenson, 1995; Geary et al., 1993; Stevenson, Chen, & Lee, 1993). Why do children from Asia so consistently outperform their American counterparts?

One hypothesis is that there are cross-national differences in intelligence (Lynn, 1982). However, a number of research results are inconsistent with this hypothesis. For one thing, when Chinese, Japanese, and American children and adults have been administered a series of tasks to assess basic cognitive abilities such as processing speed or memory, no systematic differences favoring Asian individuals were found (Geary et al., 1996; Stevenson et al., 1985). Moreover, when the mathematics abilities of Chinese college students were compared to those of sixty-to-seventy-year-old Chinese adults, the younger Chinese participants fared better. However, younger and older Americans show similar patterns of mathematics scores, so aging is not a likely explanation for the decline in performance of Chinese elders (Geary et al., 1996). These results suggest that the superiority of Asian children may be a relatively recent phenomenon rather than a trait biologically linked to an ethnic group.

Another possibility is that Asian children use more sophisticated strategies than American children to solve mathematics problems. Korean children, for example, add the numbers 8 + 6 by first trying to reach 10; that is, they add 8 + 2 to make 10 and then add the difference between 6 and 2 to reach the answer, 14. It is interesting to note that in the Korean language, names for numbers in the teens are "ten one" (eleven), "ten two" (twelve), and so on. Thus, Korean children may be used to thinking in terms of tens. Addition and subtraction strategies based on a system of tens are also explicitly taught in Korea (Fuson & Kwon, 1992). Perhaps these strategies translate into a deeper understanding of mathematical principles. Likewise, Chinese children use different strategies than their American counterparts do; instead of counting on their fingers to solve addition problems as American children do, they use retrieval of math facts from memory (Geary, Fan, & Bow-Thomas, 1992).

Finally, some researchers have reported interesting differences in how children from different nationalities spend their time, both in school and at home. Harold Stevenson and his colleagues report that Chinese and Japanese children spend proportionately more time learning mathematics in school than American children (Stevenson, Lee, & Stigler, 1986). Perhaps not surprisingly, first-through-third-grade Chinese children show greater gains in arithmetic scores over the academic year than their American counterparts (Geary et al., 1996). Furthermore, Chinese adolescents spend more time studying than Americans, a factor that is positively correlated with mathematics scores, while American adolescents spend more time working and socializing with friends, which is negatively correlated with mathematics performance (Fuligni & Stevenson, 1995).

Why might it be important to identify the factors related to cross-cultural differences in mathematics performance? Does the research on the development of numerical concepts have relevance in this debate? Some of the research on this issue is correlational; what types of studies would make a stronger case for one hypothesis over the others? Are these hypotheses necessarily mutually exclusive? What are the implications of this debate for how we teach children mathematics?

Spatial Relationships

From early infancy onward, children organize the objects in their world in still another way: according to relationships in space. Where does the toddler find his shoes or an enticing snack? Usually the infant and the young child have developed a mental picture of their homes and other familiar physical spaces to guide their search for missing objects or to reach a desired location. For the older child, spatial understanding extends to finding her way to school, grandparents' homes, or other, more remote locations. As he did for many other areas of cognitive development, Piaget set forth some of the first hypotheses about the child's concepts of space, ideas that later researchers have modified or enriched.

During infancy, Piaget (1954) stated, the child's knowledge of space is based on her sensorimotor activities within that space. For example, the child searches for objects by using *egocentric* frames of reference. That is, if a ball disappears under a couch or chair, the infant represents its location in relation to her own body ("to the left of my arm") rather than in relation to some other external object ("to the left of the door"). Only with the advent of symbolic ability at the end of the sensorimotor stage are children able to use frames of reference external to the self.

Many researchers have confirmed that children, in the absence of environmental cues, indeed rely on the positions of their own bodies in space to locate objects. For example, experimenters in one study hid an object under one of two covers situated to the left and right of their nine-month-old subjects. The infants readily learned to locate the item in one of the two positions, either to the right or to the left, depending on which training condition they were in. After the training trials, the children were shifted to the opposite side of the table, a 180-degree change in position. Now infants were unable to locate the hidden objects, a finding that suggests they were relying on the position of the object relative to their own bodies to find it (Bremner & Bryant, 1977). In an interesting modification, however, the investigator made the covers of the two hiding locations of distinctively different colors. Under these conditions, infants were able to locate the hidden toy even when they were moved to a different position around the table (Bremner, 1978). Thus, infants are not egocentric when other information is available to assist them in finding objects.

After infancy, children quite literally reach out into the world for cues denoting spatial relationships. The ability to use **landmarks** denoting the physical locations of objects helps preschool-age children find objects in larger spatial environments. Linda Acredolo and her colleagues demonstrated this skill in an experiment in which three-through-eight-year-olds were taken on a walk through an unfamiliar building in one of two conditions (Acredolo, Pick, & Olsen, 1975). In the first condition, the hallway through which the experimenter led each child contained two chairs; in the second, there were no chairs. The children saw the experimenter drop a set of keys during the walk, and in the "landmark" condition this event occurred near one of the chairs. Later, when children were asked to retrieve the keys, performance was best in the "landmark" condition for the preschoolers; older children did well regardless of the experimental condition. Thus, prominent landmarks help younger children encode specific locations within their spatial environment. In fact, by age four, children begin to use landmarks in their speech as they describe the locations of objects to others, making statements such as "The soda is in the bag by the stove" (Plumert, Ewert, & Spear, 1995).

Preschoolers are also able to use distance cues without the benefit of landmarks to search for objects. Janellen Huttenlocher and her colleagues asked children ages sixteen to twenty-four months to find a toy buried in a five-foot-long sandbox that had no distinguishing landmarks. The success rate for these young children was impressively high. This research team gave a different spatial memory task to four-to-six-year-olds: to remember the location of a dot drawn in the outline of a rectangle. Children at this age gave evidence of using a strategy of dividing the rectangle into mental quadrants and recalling the location of the dot based on this mental "tool" (Huttenlocher, Newcombe, & Sandberg, 1994).

Alexander Siegel and his associates believe knowledge about large-scale spaces proceeds from landmark knowledge to a new level: route mapping (Siegel, Kirasic, & Kail, 1978). **Route mapping** consists of knowledge about sequential directional changes that must take place as one negotiates a path through space, such as "Take a left at the store, then a right at the traffic light." Children rely on this form of spatial

landmark Distinctive location or cue that the child uses to negotiate or represent a spatial environment.

route mapping Child's use of sequential directional changes to negotiate or represent a spatial environment.

representation during their early school years. At age ten years or so, children display even more sophisticated spatial understanding, called **configurational knowledge,** the ability to represent landmarks and routes as integrated, holistic entities. They can draw reasonably accurate maps of their neighborhood or the spatial layout of their school (Anooshian & Young, 1981; Curtis, Siegel, & Furlong, 1981).

Developmental improvements in spatial knowledge are associated with the child's improving memory (Allen & Ondracek, 1995) and with increasing familiarity with a given physical space. In the study conducted by Siegel and his associates, when kindergartners were walked through a model town several times, they were able to produce maps of the town as accurate as those of fifth-graders. Their ability to produce a mature spatial layout, one that required configurational representation, was enhanced simply by having had experience with that physical space (Siegel, Kirasic, & Kail, 1978). Instructions to "look back" as the child is traversing a path can help, too. Twelve-year-olds (but not six-year-olds) who took a walk on an unfamiliar university campus were better able to find their way back to their starting point if they were periodically reminded to "turn around and look where we came from" (Cornell, Heth, & Rowat, 1992).

In summary, young children initially locate objects in space by using simple cues, especially the positions of objects relative to their own bodies. Gradually their spatial representations include more discrete elements—especially cues that are external to the self, such as landmarks—and their representations become better integrated. Why does spatial knowledge develop in this way? A likely explanation is that the child's growing attentional and memory skills contribute to the ability to process, retain, and integrate more numerous physical cues.

UNDERSTANDING PSYCHOLOGICAL STATES

KEY THEME
Interaction Among Domains

Our knowledge extends beyond understanding of physical objects, classes, number, and space. It also includes an awareness of our minds and how they and the minds of others work. How do children understand and judge the motives, feelings, needs, interests, capacities, and thoughts of playmates, siblings, parents, and others? And how and when do children come to understand and reflect on the psychological states of the self? This type of cognition, thinking about the self and its relationship to the social world, is called *social cognition.* In comparison to the world of physical objects and events, thinking about the social world presents unique challenges to the developing child. People may act unpredictably; their feelings and moods, and even their appearances, may shift unexpectedly. Just how children piece together their understanding of social experiences has been the focus of several lines of research. Here too contemporary researchers owe Piaget recognition for his initial efforts to study how children think about thinking.

Perspective Taking: Taking the Views of Others

configurational knowledge
Child's use of landmarks and routes in integrated, holistic ways to represent physical space.

perspective taking Ability to take the role of another person and understand what that person is thinking, is feeling, or knows, often with the purpose of solving some problem in communicating or interacting with that individual.

Perspective taking is the ability to put oneself in another person's place, to consider that person's thoughts, feelings, or knowledge in order to interact with the individual more effectively. To successfully explain something to another person, the child must have knowledge of the other's background and abilities. By "putting oneself in another's shoes," a child can also more effectively assist or support that person. When and how does this ability develop in young children?

One basic element of perspective taking is understanding what others see. For example, does the child realize that his sister, who is standing across the room, cannot see the brightly colored pictures in the book he is eagerly examining? In 1956, Jean Piaget and Barbel Inhelder published a classic experiment illustrating children's limited knowledge of the visual perspectives of others. Children seated in front of three

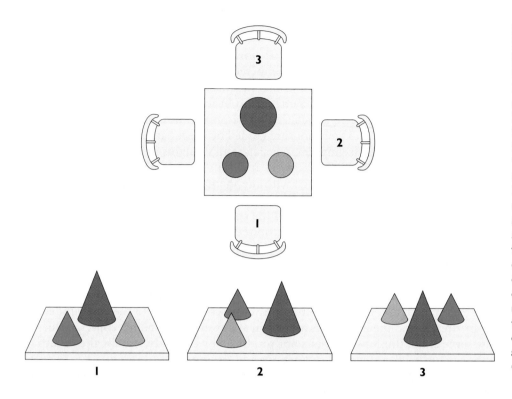

FIGURE 8.6

Visual Perspective Taking

How well can children adopt another person's perspective? Piaget asked this question by seating a child at a table (location 1) containing three "mountains" of different size and color, then asking the child how the scene would look to a doll (or another person) seated at other locations (locations 2 and 3) around the table. Piaget found that preschoolers often chose a view similar to their own. More recent research indicates that preschoolers can more successfully accomplish this task when familiar and easily distinguishable scenes are used.

different papier-mâché mountains (see Figure 8.6) were asked to indicate what a doll would see in viewing the array from various locations. Four-to-six-year-olds showed considerable *egocentrism* in their responses; they typically indicated that the doll's view would be identical to their own. By six to nine years of age, children began to realize the doll's perspective would differ, although they still had difficulty figuring out what the doll would actually see. Nine- and ten-year-olds were able to determine the doll's perspective accurately. More recent research has shown that the difficulty of the doll and mountain task may have led Piaget and Inhelder to underestimate children's role-taking competence. When simpler visual arrays or familiar everyday scenes are used, or when the method of interviewing children is simplified, three- and four-year-olds can answer some of these kinds of questions reasonably well (Borke, 1975; Newcombe & Huttenlocher, 1992).

John Flavell and his colleagues have identified two levels of visual perspective-taking skill in children (Flavell, 1978; Lempers, Flavell, & Flavell, 1977). At the first level, from late infancy until about three years, children come to realize that their own and another's view are not identical. Thirty-month-olds, for example, acknowledge that an object that they can see but is screened from another person's view will be visible only to themselves. Toddlers may even adjust pictures or objects to help others see them more easily (Flavell, Shipstead, & Croft, 1978). Thus, very young children recognize a different visual perspective for others.

A second, more advanced level of visual perspective taking appears in three- and four-year-olds and continues to be refined for several years thereafter. Now children begin to successfully determine the specific limitations of another's view. Four-year-olds, for example, can say whether an object another person sees will look right side up (Masangkay et al., 1974). They also realize that a view of one portion of an animal may not provide enough cues to allow someone else to determine what the animal is doing but, until age six, believe others will have little difficulty identifying the animal even if only a few ambiguous details are visible (Taylor, 1988). Throughout the early school years, children become increasingly proficient at determining how the relationships among specific features of a complex array will change when viewed from several perspectives (Rosser, 1983). These advances reflect cognitive gains both in differentiating oneself from another and in knowledge of space and spatial relationships (Shantz, 1983).

The Child's Theory of Mind

Children's understanding of their social world extends beyond visual perspective-taking skills. Emerging among their competencies is an expanding and increasingly coherent appreciation of the kinds of mental qualities that contribute to the behavior of self and others. Did the playmate who broke a favorite toy *intend* to do the damage? Would a close friend *believe* that Mom will not let them go to the park alone? Many of our social behaviors are guided by the judgments and inferences we make about the desires, feeling states, beliefs, and thoughts of other people (Aston-ton, Harris, & Olson, 1988; Slomkowski & Dunn, 1996; Wellman, 1990). In fact, it would be rare *not* to be concerned with the mental states of others in the normal course of interactions with them.

When do children become aware of the concept of mental states, their own and those of others? How are these ideas acquired, and how do they change with development? Once again, Piaget has provided much of the impetus for research on this topic. His position was quite clear. As Piaget put it, "The child knows nothing about the nature of thought . . ." (Piaget, 1929, p. 37). Dubbing this characteristic of children **realism,** Piaget maintained that children are not capable of distinguishing between mental and physical entities until the school years. To the child under age eight, dreams and mental images are as real as any event in waking, conscious life. To the same child, thinking is a behavior produced by the body, usually the mouth or the head; physical and mental acts are one and the same.

Despite Piaget's strong claims, developmental researchers have uncovered considerable evidence to the contrary. By age three, children readily distinguish between mental and physical entities and, after that age, show further developments in their understanding of their own mental states and those of others (Flavell, 1993). Children apparently have a well-articulated "theory of mind" by the time they are ready to enter school.

In one experiment, three-year-olds were told stories such as the following: "Judy doesn't have a kitty, but right now she is thinking about a kitty." Could they see or touch the kitty? Could the kitty be seen by someone else or touched at some time in the future? Children had no problem identifying this as a mental event, one in which the kitty could not be seen or touched. In contrast, when they heard other stories, as in "Judy had a kitty," they correctly stated that these real events could be seen and touched (Wellman & Estes, 1986). Other research indicates that by twenty-eight months of age, children realize when others are engaged in pretend or "make-believe" activity (Harris et al., 1991; Harris & Kavanaugh, 1993).

Young children also understand the meanings of specific mental states. Eighteen-month-olds show a beginning appreciation for what it means to "desire" (Repacholi & Gopnik, 1997). While three-year-olds understand the concept of "pretend," they still have difficulty with the concept of "belief" (Lillard & Flavell, 1992). Between ages six and ten, children begin to understand "the mind" as an active entity discrete from the self as they interpret metaphors such as "My mind was racing" or "My mind was hungry" (Wellman & Hickling, 1994).

A particularly useful scenario to assess aspects of children's theory of mind has been the "false belief" task. Children are shown a doll named Maxi who puts some chocolate in a cupboard and leaves the scene. Maxi's mother moves the chocolate to a new location. When Maxi returns, children are asked, "Where will he look for the chocolate?" Most three-year-olds say in the new location. Four-year-olds, though, recognize that Maxi holds a "false belief" and will look for the chocolate in the cupboard (Wimmer & Perner, 1983). Similarly, three-year-olds have some difficulty understanding that their own past beliefs may not be the same as their current beliefs; four-year-olds no longer have this difficulty (Gopnik & Slaughter, 1991; Wellman, 1990).

Why do younger children have difficulty with the "false belief" task? Perhaps they fail to understand that beliefs, which are mental states, need not match external reality. But over the next year, that realization quickly becomes part of the child's cogni-

realism   Inability to distinguish between mental and physical entities.

tive repertoire. In fact, this may be a very significant cognitive transition for all children (Flavell, 1988). Children from several cultures, including China, Japan, and the preliterate Baka society of Cameroon, show similar developmental changes in their understanding of "beliefs" (Avis & Harris, 1991; Flavell et al., 1983; Gardner et al., 1988). The ability to understand false beliefs has been linked to increasing language skills and larger family size (Jenkins & Astington, 1996; Lewis et al., 1996). Perhaps as children have more opportunities to see the relationships and conflicts between beliefs and behaviors (including the nature of misrepresentation) and derive fuller concepts of words such as *belief* and *know,* their theories of mind become more fully articulated.

KEY THEME
Interaction Among Domains

ATYPICAL DEVELOPMENT

Childhood Autism

Childhood autism is a puzzling disorder affecting about one or two of every one thousand children born. The disorder, more common among boys than girls, is characterized by the child's preference to be alone, poor eye contact and general lack of social skills, often the absence of meaningful language, and a preference for sameness and elaborate routines. Some autistic children show unusual skills, such as being able to recite lengthy passages from memory, put together complex jigsaw puzzles, or create intricate drawings. Often these children show a fascination with spinning objects or repeating the speech patterns of someone else. The hallmark trait, though, is the lack of contact these children have with the social world, starting at an early age. Kanner's (1943) description of one autistic boy captures the syndrome well: "He seems almost to draw into his shell and live within himself" (p. 218).

Since Leo Kanner first identified this psychopathology, numerous causes of autism have been proposed, ranging from deprived early emotional relationships with parents to defective neurological wiring in the brain (Waterhouse, Fein, & Modahl, 1996). An intriguing suggestion recently put forth by a team of researchers is that autistic children, for biological reasons, lack the ability to think about mental states; that is, they lack a "theory of mind" that most children begin to develop during the preschool years. Consider how autistic children behave in one standard task testing the child's theory of mind. As in the "false belief" task described earlier, children are told a story about Sally and Anne, represented by puppets, who are playing together. Sally puts a marble in a basket and leaves the room. Anne moves the marble to a box. Sally returns. Where will Sally look for her marble? Normal children, at age four, typically state that Sally will look in the basket, realizing that Sally does not have the same information they have. In contrast, most nine-year-old autistic children tested with this problem still think Sally would look in the box (Baron-Cohen, Tager-Flusberg, & Cohen, 1993; Frith, 1993). These results suggest that autistic children cannot conceptualize the mental state of another individual. Autistic children, the argument proceeds, have severe deficits in communication and social interaction precisely because they cannot appreciate what the contents of another person's mind might be.

Not all researchers believe the absence of a "theory of mind" explains childhood autism. Some maintain that autistic children cannot disengage their attention from a stimulus on which they are focusing, such as the box in the "false belief" task (Hughes & Russell, 1993). Others suggest that problems with memory, executive control processes, or the ability to process social meaning are responsible (Bennetto, Pennington, & Rogers, 1996; Boucher, 1981; Rutter, 1983). Whatever the ultimate basis for autism, however, it seems likely that understanding basic cognitive processes will be helpful in deciphering the mechanisms underlying this perplexing childhood disorder.

NEO-PIAGETIAN APPROACHES

We have seen throughout this chapter how Piaget's theory and observations of children have sparked a wealth of research on cognitive development. The major achievements described in this chapter are outlined in the Chronology on the next page. We have noted that some of Piaget's ideas, such as the active participation of the child in the construction of his or her own knowledge, have been widely and enthusiastically embraced. Other central tenets of his theory have met with more skepticism. For example, just how broad and general are the features of a child's thinking within a given stage of development? Or does cognitive development proceed in a more "modular" fashion, unfolding rapidly in some domains and more slowly in others? Put another way, does cognitive development proceed in a *domain-general* or a *domain-specific* way?

Several developmental psychologists have modified and expanded Piaget's theory to address some of these criticisms. Because their ideas build on those Piaget initially proposed, these theorists are often called *neo-Piagetians*. Like Piaget, neo-Piagetians believe children show distinct, even stagelike advances in general thinking skills, probably because of maturation. They also agree that what children know at a given time heavily influences what they will be able to learn and think about. Neo-Piagetians, though, are much more willing than Piaget was to acknowledge the role specific experiences play in shaping the child's knowledge in a given area (Flavell, 1992).

Fischer's Skill Theory

KEY THEME
Continuity/Discontinuity

KEY THEME
Nature/Nurture

Kurt Fischer, like Piaget, believes the emergence of general, broad thinking skills contributes to cognitive development (Fischer, 1980; Fischer & Farrar, 1988; Fischer & Pipp, 1984). These skills, he proposes, are organized into four stages or "tiers": reflex, sensorimotor, representational, and abstract. Unlike Piaget, though, Fischer adds that within the same individual, skills may develop more rapidly in some domains—say, numerical understanding or classifying familiar objects—than others, depending on the child's experiences. The child who is given ample access to art materials but not to math problems, for example, may show greater skill in the first area than the second.

KEY THEME
Individual Differences

In Fischer's theory, skills are similar to Piaget's schemes: mental structures that stem from action. In contrast to schemes, however, which are highly generalized structures, skills are more specific to particular objects and tasks. If the environment supports a variety of skills, development in all skills will proceed relatively evenly. Fischer suggests, however, that uniform access to skill development is unlikely. At any one time in development, most children show different levels of skill depending on the domain, be it numerical reasoning, spatial understanding, classification of objects, or some other. Specific skills used in limited contexts eventually become more powerful and are used in more generalized contexts (Fischer & Bidell, 1991). By emphasizing the emergence of separate skills that are heavily dependent on the specific experiences available to the child, Fischer offers a picture of development that is more continuous and gradual than that proposed by Piaget.

Case's Theory

KEY THEME
Continuity/Discontinuity

KEY THEME
Nature/Nurture

Robbie Case (1985, 1992) has also built on many Piagetian ideas. For example, Case proposes four stages of development similar to those outlined by Piaget. Case's theory differs notably from Piaget's, however, in terms of its explanation of transitions from one stage to the next. Whereas Piaget emphasized maturational constraints on the process of cognitive development, Case allows a greater role for experience in pushing the child's abilities forward. Case proposes that infants begin life with certain innate but limited capacities and attentional resources. Through both maturation and sensorimotor practice, the infant's actions gradually become more efficient and automatic, eventually permitting the child to think about as well as act

CHRONOLOGY
Cognitive Development I

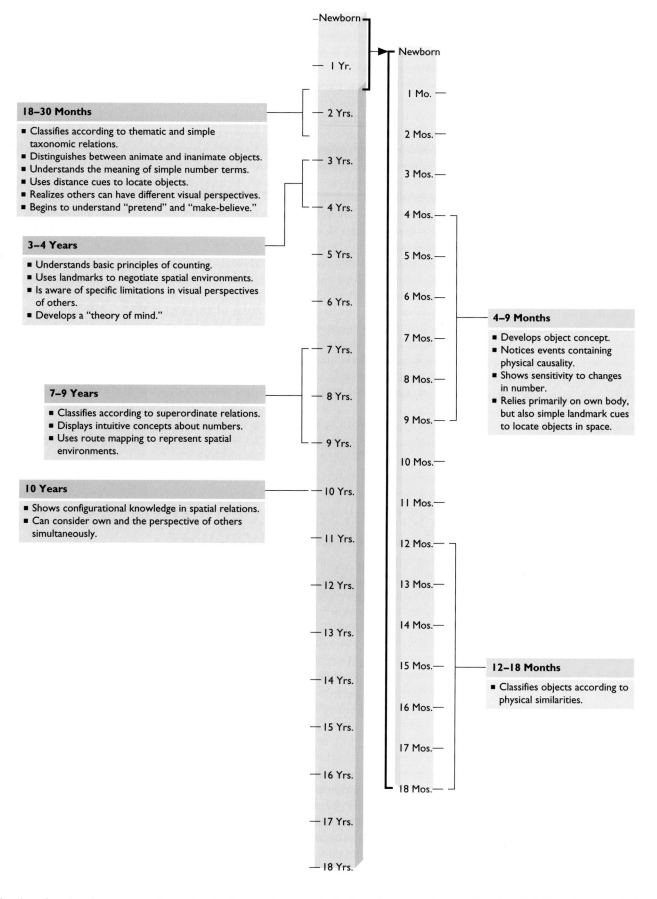

Newborn

Newborn

— 1 Yr.

1 Mo.

18–30 Months

- Classifies according to thematic and simple taxonomic relations.
- Distinguishes between animate and inanimate objects.
- Understands the meaning of simple number terms.
- Uses distance cues to locate objects.
- Realizes others can have different visual perspectives.
- Begins to understand "pretend" and "make-believe."

— 2 Yrs.

2 Mos.

— 3 Yrs.

3 Mos.

— 4 Yrs.

4 Mos.

3–4 Years

- Understands basic principles of counting.
- Uses landmarks to negotiate spatial environments.
- Is aware of specific limitations in visual perspectives of others.
- Develops a "theory of mind."

— 5 Yrs.

5 Mos.

— 6 Yrs.

6 Mos.

4–9 Months

- Develops object concept.
- Notices events containing physical causality.
- Shows sensitivity to changes in number.
- Relies primarily on own body, but also simple landmark cues to locate objects in space.

— 7 Yrs.

7 Mos.

8 Mos.

7–9 Years

- Classifies according to superordinate relations.
- Displays intuitive concepts about numbers.
- Uses route mapping to represent spatial environments.

— 8 Yrs.

9 Mos.

— 9 Yrs.

10 Mos.

10 Years

- Shows configurational knowledge in spatial relations.
- Can consider own and the perspective of others simultaneously.

— 10 Yrs.

11 Mos.

— 11 Yrs.

12 Mos.

— 12 Yrs.

13 Mos.

— 13 Yrs.

14 Mos.

15 Mos.

12–18 Months

- Classifies objects according to physical similarities.

— 14 Yrs.

16 Mos.

— 15 Yrs.

17 Mos.

— 16 Yrs.

18 Mos.

— 17 Yrs.

— 18 Yrs.

This chart describes the sequence of cognitive development based on the findings of research. Children often show individual differences in the exact ages at which they display the various developmental achievements outlined here.

on these objects and entities and, still later, integrate information about their dimensions, features, and qualities to solve problems.

Beyond infancy, the increasing efficiency of cognitive *operations,* processes such as identifying stimuli and recognizing relationships among them, paves the way for greater memory capacity. If children expend a substantial amount of mental effort on identifying or recognizing stimuli, fewer resources will be available for storage and retention of information. Conversely, as children become more proficient at identifying letters, colors, and other features of stimuli, they will have more resources available for remembering. A simple experiment illustrates how these principles work. Three- and six-year-olds were asked to perform two tasks: repeat a list of words one at a time as rapidly as possible and then recall that same list of words. Children who were quick to repeat the words had better memory scores than children who were slower at repetition (Case, Kurland, & Goldberg, 1982). As operational efficiency increased with development, more cognitive resources were available for remembering.

According to Case, increases in children's ability to process information quickly are tied to maturational changes in the nervous system as well as to practice with various cognitive activities. One important physiological change that occurs through adolescence is the *myelinization* of areas of the cortex that control alertness and higher-order thinking processes; portions of some neurons develop a fatty coating that speeds neural transmission (Yakovlev & Lecours, 1967). It is plausible that this process is related to the increasing speed of cognitive processing. Practice also helps. The more times the child identifies numbers, words, or other stimuli, the more facile she or he will become in this activity. As a result of practice and experience, children develop *central conceptual structures* that guide their performance in specific domains, such as numerical or spatial reasoning. As you will see in Chapter 9, many of the ideas Case proposed draw from another theoretical school of cognitive development: the information-processing perspective.

VYGOTSKY'S SOCIOCULTURAL THEORY OF COGNITIVE DEVELOPMENT

Piaget assumed that cognitive processes function in similar ways across cultures, that the nature and development of thinking have universal qualities. Standing in sharp contrast to these claims are the theoretical ideas of the prominent Russian psychologist Lev Vygotsky (1978). As we saw in Chapter 1, Vygotsky wrote that the child's cognitive growth must be understood in the context of the culture in which he or she lives. Vygotsky believed that in formal and informal exchanges with children, caregivers, peers, and tutors cultivate in them the particular skills and abilities their cultural group values. Gradually, regulation and guidance of the child's behavior by others is replaced by internalized self-regulation. Lev Vygotsky made such *social activity* the cornerstone of his theory of development.

Scaffolding

The concept of **scaffolding** is a way of thinking about the social relationship involved in learning from another person (Wood, Bruner, & Ross, 1976). A scaffold is a temporary structure that gives the support necessary to accomplish a task. An effective caregiver or teacher provides such a structure in problem-solving situations, perhaps by defining the activity to be accomplished, demonstrating supporting skills and techniques in which the learner is still deficient, and motivating the beginner to complete the task. The collaboration advances the knowledge and abilities of the apprentice, as illustrated by the following study of a toddler learning to label objects. Anat Ninio and Jerome Bruner (1978) visited the child in his home every two weeks from

KEY THEME
Interaction Among Domains

KEY THEME
Sociocultural Influence

KEY THEME
Nature/Nurture

scaffolding   Temporary aid provided by one person to encourage, support, and assist a lesser-skilled person in carrying out a task or completing a problem. The model provides knowledge and skills that are learned and gradually transferred to the learner.

age eight months to two years. One commonly shared activity they observed was reading from a picture book, with the boy's mother providing the scaffold for the child to learn more about his language.

> The mother's (often quite unconscious) approach is exquisitely tuned. When the child responds to her "Look!" by looking, she follows immediately with a query. When the child responds to the query with a gesture or a smile, she supplies a label. But as soon as the child shows the ability to vocalize in a way that might indicate a label, she raises the ante. She withholds the label and repeats the query until the child vocalizes, and then she gives the label if the child does not have it fully or correctly.
>
> Later, when the child has learned to respond with shorter vocalizations that correspond to words, she no longer accepts an indifferent vocalization. When the child begins producing a recognizable, constant label for an object, she holds out for it. Finally, the child produces appropriate words at the appropriate place in the dialogue. Even then the mother remains tuned to the developing pattern, helping her child recognize labels and make them increasingly accurate. For example, she develops two ways of asking, "What's that?" One, with a falling intonation, inquires about those words for which she believes her child already knows the label; the other, with a rising intonation, marks words that are new. (Bruner, 1981, pp. 49–50)

Scaffolding involves a teaching/learning relationship that uses the expert or tutor who intervenes as required and gradually withdraws as assistance becomes unnecessary. Patricia Greenfield (1984) observed this phenomenon among girls learning to weave in Zinacantan, Mexico. Beginners, in the presence of at least one expert weaver (usually the mother), started by weaving small items and performed only the simpler parts of the task. The more experienced the learner, the less likely the teacher was to intervene to complete the more technically difficult steps. Novices were more likely to receive direct commands from the teachers, whereas experienced weavers were more likely to receive statements or comments. Both verbal and nonverbal assistance declined as the girls became increasingly proficient weavers, although the expert continued to be a role model for both specific techniques and more general principles of weaving. Remarkably, the scaffolding the tutor provided yielded a woven product from beginners indistinguishable from those completed by expert weavers. These examples illustrate what Vygotsky (1978) called the **zone of proximal development,** the span or disparity between what children are able to do without the assistance of others and what they are often able to accomplish by having someone more expert assist them at key points. Vygotsky claimed the most effective assistance from the expert is that just slightly beyond or ahead of the child's current capacities.

The Role of Skilled Collaborators

As the phenomena of scaffolding and the zone of proximal development suggest, a role model who is sensitive to the learner's level of knowledge contributes greatly to the effective transmission of skills. The effect can be demonstrated in tasks as diverse as the three-year-old's learning to distinguish the colors and shapes of pictures (Diaz, Neal, & Vachio, 1991) to fifth-graders learning how to carry out long division in mathematics assignments (Pratt et al., 1992). Of course, some tutors may be better at these activities than others. Barbara Radziszewska and Barbara Rogoff (1988) examined how nine- and ten-year-olds learned to plan errands. One group of children worked with their parents to organize a shopping trip through an imaginary town, while a second group of children worked with a peer to plan the expedition. Children who worked with adults were exposed to more sophisticated planning strategies; they explored a map of the town more frequently, planned longer sequences of activities, and verbalized more of their plans. Instead of using a step-by-step strategy ("Let's go from this store to the next closest store") as the peer pairs did, children working with adults formulated an integrated sequence of actions ("Let's mark all the stores we have to go to in blue and see what is the best way between them"). In the second part

zone of proximal development Range of various kinds of support and assistance provided by an expert (usually an adult) who helps children to carry out activities they currently cannot complete but will later be able to accomplish independently.

By watching skilled collaborators and participating in guided learning, this Guatemalan girl is learning how to weave, an ability that is highly valued in her culture. Vygotsky emphasized the importance of sociocultural context in influencing which skills and abilities will be nurtured among children. Caregivers transmit knowledge by providing children with the *scaffolding* necessary to complete a task, gradually withdrawing as the child gains competence.

KEY THEME
Child's Active Role

of the experiment, all of the children were observed as they planned a new errand in the same town, this time by themselves. Children who had initially worked with their parents employed more efficient planning strategies than children who had worked with peers.

Why does collaboration with adults work so well? In a follow-up study, Radziszewska and Rogoff (1991) observed that when children worked with adults, they participated in more discussion of the best planning strategy—more "thinking out loud"—than when they worked with peers who had expertise in planning. When working with adults, children were generally more actively involved in the cognitive task, whereas they tended to be more passive observers when their tutor was another child.

Recently Barbara Rogoff and her colleagues (1993) have suggested that the extent to which children and adults take an active role in learning the skills, values, and knowledge of their community differs across cultures. In general, in all communities adults provide a scaffolding for children to begin engaging in mature activities, a process the researchers label *guided participation*. However, children take on a greater burden of responsibility for managing their attention, desire, and interest in mature activities in communities in which they are routinely in the company of adults. The guidance caregivers provide in this context is likely to be in the form of supporting children's observations and efforts rather than in the form of instruction. In contrast, when much of a child's day is spent separate from adults, the child will need more directed lessons and training to acquire mature skills. In this context, the caregivers assume comparatively greater responsibility in helping children to observe and understand the world.

Rogoff and her colleagues (1993) found that in communities in India and Guatemala, where young children could watch and enter into adult social and work activities, caregivers were likely to assist and support children in carrying out the more mature responsibilities, such as learning to dress themselves or play with a new toy. On the other hand, in middle-income communities in Turkey and the United States, where children were more likely to be segregated (and parents could not be as consistently attentive and supportive), caregivers were likely to promote play and conversation or provide lessons or learning opportunities in interacting with children to teach them new skills. These interactions, in other words, looked more like the kind typically found with older children in formal school settings. Thus, although all caregivers provided guidance for more mature behavior in each community, its specific form differed, a confirmation of the diverse ways learning may be encouraged in various cultural contexts.

In general, research has confirmed Vygotsky's proposition that skilled collaborators—parents and teachers in particular—can and do provide children with direct instruction in how to succeed in different cognitive tasks. But several ingredients are necessary for the child to fully grasp that skill and be able to use it independently in other contexts. First, both adult and child must be motivated, the adult to find occasions to push the child forward and the child to engage in the activity in the first place. Second, the adult must be facile at modifying the skill in question so that it suits the needs of the child. Finally, the adult must be adept at assessing the child's current level of competence and judging the level of difficulty the child is able to master; that is, the adult must be able to locate and work within the zone of proximal development (Belmont, 1989). The result is a constantly modulated interaction leading to the child's cognitive development.

Developmental psychologists have recently shown widespread interest in Vygotsky's theory. Many have accepted his claims for the social basis of cognitive development and the importance of understanding the sociocultural context in which the child grows up. Despite the fundamental differences between the ideas of Piaget and Vygotsky, both "theoretical giants" have attempted to capture the dynamism and complexity of how children *develop* in their thinking.

RESEARCH APPLIED TO EDUCATION

Reciprocal Teaching

While Craig had always been impressed with James's logical and mathematical skills, he and Marta, his wife, were more concerned with how James was doing in reading in school. Although he could read aloud fairly well, he seemed to have consistent problems in understanding what he read. This was beginning to affect his performance in social studies, science, and other subjects where students were expected to do quite a bit of independent fact-finding. James seemed to stumble through these assignments and was beginning to feel embarrassed by the grades he was getting. At the last parent-teacher conference, though, Craig and Marta were reassured. The third-grade teacher was trying a new approach to reading called "reciprocal teaching," and she was very encouraged by the visible changes she saw in students' performance and attitudes toward their schoolwork.

Several facets of Vygotsky's theory can be seen in action in a special program developed to foster the emergence of reading comprehension strategies in junior high school students (Brown et al., 1991; Palincsar & Brown, 1984, 1986). The students received instruction in several important reading skills with an instructional method called *reciprocal teaching*. According to this method, teachers should do the following:

1. *Introduce students to four key reading comprehension strategies.* These strategies are summarizing, clarifying word meanings and confusing passages, generating questions about the passage, and predicting what might happen next.

2. *Provide the scaffolding for how to use comprehension strategies.* For one paragraph, the teacher models how to summarize the theme, isolate material that needs to be clarified, anticipate questions, and predict what will happen next.

Reciprocal Teaching	
Student 1:	*(Question)* My question is, what does the aquanaut need when he goes under water?
Student 2:	A watch.
Student 3:	Flippers.
Student 4:	A belt.
Student 1:	Those are all good answers.
Teacher:	*(Question)* Nice job! I have a question too. Why does the aquanaut wear a belt? What is so special about it?
Student 3:	It's a heavy belt and keeps him from floating up to the top again.
Teacher:	Good for you.
Student 1:	*(Summary)* For my summary now: This paragraph was about what aquanauts need to take when they go under the water.
Student 5:	*(Summary)* And also about why they need those things.
Student 3:	*(Clarify)* I think we need to clarify gear.
Student 6:	That's the special things they need.
Teacher:	Another word for gear in this story might be equipment, the equipment that makes it easier for the aquanauts to do their job.
Student 1:	I don't think I have a prediction to make.
Teacher:	*(Prediction)* Well, in the story they tell us that there are "many strange and wonderful creatures" that the aquanauts see as they do their work. My prediction is that they'll describe some of these creatures. What are some of the strange creatures you already know about that live in the ocean?
Student 6:	Octopuses.
Student 3:	Whales?
Student 5:	Sharks!

Source: Palincsar & Brown, 1986.

TABLE 8.2

An Example of Reciprocal Teaching

This conversation illustrates the types of exchanges that typify reciprocal teaching. The teacher and, eventually, the students model question asking, summarizing, clarifying, and predicting. In this particular excerpt, students have begun to assume control over their own learning. Students who participated in this program showed significant gains in reading comprehension.

3. *Ask students to engage in the same four activities for the next paragraph.* The teacher adjusts instructions according to the needs of the individual students, working within what Vygotsky would call each student's *zone of proximal development.* The teacher also provides feedback, praise, hints, and explanations. The teacher invites other students to react to a student's statements, adding other questions, making predictions, or requesting clarification. Teacher and students alternate paragraphs in the early stages of this process.

4. *Become less directive as the students become more skilled in each component of reading.* The students gradually take charge of the process, and the teacher becomes more of an observer, adding suggestions and support when necessary.

Table 8.2 gives an example of the teacher-student exchanges that typically occur with this method.

The results of training were impressive. Whereas during the pretests students averaged 20 percent correct in answering ten questions from reading a paragraph of material, after twenty sessions of reciprocal teaching they averaged 80 percent correct on similar tests. Six months later, students trained in this method moved up from the twentieth percentile in reading ability in their school to the fifty-sixth percentile. Several other studies have documented similar success of reciprocal teaching from as early as first grade (Rosenshine & Meister, 1994). In addition, students appear to adopt many positive features associated with reciprocal teaching on their own, as the following exchange between a researcher and a student in the program illustrates:

Researcher: Do you use reciprocal teaching on your own?
Student: Oh, yes, I use it all the time.
Researcher: (skeptically) How do you do that?
Student: When I read hard things, I use the strategies. I try to remember what has happened so far and ask myself what the major questions are. I try to think about what is not clear—clarifying is where my team helps me the most. A lot of time, I wish my teammates were with me because they always help me understand what we're reading. Sometimes I try to think about the questions they might ask me because they often look at things in different ways than me. (Campione, Shapiro, & Brown, 1995, p. 65)

The key to the success of reciprocal teaching, many experts believe, is the carefully modulated interaction between teacher and students, a point Vygotsky consistently emphasized.

CHAPTER RECAP

SUMMARY OF DEVELOPMENTAL THEMES

NATURE/NURTURE What roles do nature and nurture play in cognitive development?

A central tenet of Piaget's theory is that maturation, in conjunction with experience, is responsible for the child's cognitive growth. Neo-Piagetian theorists echo the same theme. Thus, the interaction between nature and nurture is central in these theories. When we examine the child's concept development, we may find that certain natural domains offer the child "privileged relationships" to learn about. The role of nature is implicated here. At the same time, studies of concept formation in different cultures suggest that experiences, like formal schooling, also play a role in determining whether children will display specific kinds of classification skills. The role of experts in guiding the child's development—that is, nurture—is emphasized in Vygotsky's theory.

SOCIOCULTURAL INFLUENCE How does the sociocultural context influence cognitive development?

Piaget's theory emphasizes the universal cognitive attainments of all children, regardless of their cultural background. However, research has shown that the sociocultural context, the cornerstone of Vygotsky's theory, cannot be ignored. For example, not all children in all cultures attain formal operational thought. We have also seen that children with formal schooling employ taxonomic classification more frequently than unschooled children and that theories about biological kinds may be influenced by cultural beliefs. Cultural beliefs are often transmitted to children through the scaffolding provided by experts.

CHILD'S ACTIVE ROLE How does the child play an active role in the process of cognitive development?

A central assumption in Piaget's theory of cognitive development is that the child actively organizes cognitive schemes and knowledge to more effectively adapt to the demands of the environment. In fact, this idea, a hallmark of Piaget's work, is widely accepted by developmental psychologists of different theoretical persuasions. Vygotsky, too, emphasized the active role of the child, in the sense that what the child has learned contributes to the kinds of interactions she or he will be exposed to.

CONTINUITY/DISCONTINUITY Is cognitive development continuous or discontinuous?

The extent to which cognitive advances are stage determined is an issue that remains to be resolved. Piaget, of course, stressed stagelike attainments in thinking. Others who have empirically reevaluated his work make claims for more continuous changes in cognition in their focus on the underlying basic processes that contribute to development. Unlike Piaget, Vygotsky did not emphasize discontinuities in development.

INDIVIDUAL DIFFERENCES How prominent are individual differences in cognitive development?

Piaget emphasized the common features of thought displayed by all children. His explicit goal was to explain the general characteristics of cognition as children move from the sensorimotor through the formal operational stage of development. Although Piaget acknowledged that some children may reach a given stage earlier or later than others, his main concern was not with individual differences among children. Others, including the neo-Piagetians, argue that children may show greater or lesser abilities within particular domains, depending on the specific experiences they are exposed to. Thus, substantial individual differences in cognitive development may occur among children of similar ages. Finally, Vygotsky argued that children will show differences in development depending on the values of the larger culture and the sensitivity of skilled collaborators to the child's needs in the learning situation.

INTERACTION AMONG DOMAINS   How does cognitive development interact with development in other domains?

The child's emergent cognitive skills interact with almost every other aspect of development. For example, children's decreasing cognitive egocentrism will affect their ability to make judgments in perspective-taking tasks, which have important social ramifications. By the same token, development in other domains can influence cognitive growth. For example, cognition may be affected by maturation of the central nervous system, which is hypothesized to contribute to progress in the speed and efficiency of cognitive processing. The child's thinking is thus both the product of and a contributor to development in many other domains.

SUMMARY OF TOPICS

■ PIAGET'S THEORY OF COGNITIVE DEVELOPMENT

One of the most comprehensive theories of cognitive development was proposed by Jean Piaget. Piaget championed the active role of the child in the construction of knowledge and the transformation of cognitive schemes as a result of maturation combined with experience. Piaget believed that development proceeds from *sensorimotor* through *preoperational, concrete operational,* and *formal operational* stages. The child's thought in each stage has unique characteristics, beginning with the action-based schemes of the sensorimotor stage and progressing to the symbolic, then logical, and finally abstract thought of succeeding stages. Challenges to Piaget's theory have focused on whether his description of the ages of acquisition of cognitive skills is accurate, whether development is indeed stagelike, and whether there are alternative explanations for the behaviors he observed among children.

■ CONCEPT DEVELOPMENT

An important area of cognitive development is the emergence of *concepts.* Infants have a good grasp of the *object concept* and preliminary notions of the concept of physical causality. One-year-olds begin to group items together on the basis of perceptual similarities, and slightly older children rely on thematic and taxonomic relations. By age seven, children are able to employ more complex hierarchical relations as they sort objects. Similarly, children show an awareness of the concept of numbers before starting school and later develop an intuitive understanding of mathematical operations such as addition. The development of spatial concepts begins with the child's use of *landmarks* and proceeds to *route mapping* and *configurational knowledge.* Spatial knowledge is related to the child's ability to select useful landmarks and familiarity with a given physical space.

■ UNDERSTANDING PSYCHOLOGICAL STATES

Children begin to show *perspective taking* during the preschool years, and this ability improves in successive years. A related achievement is the child's acquisition of a "theory of mind," an understanding of the difference between mental and physical states as well as what is meant by mental concepts such as "belief" and "desire." This understanding is fairly well formed before children start school.

■ NEO-PIAGETIAN APPROACHES

Fischer and Case have expanded and modified Piaget's original ideas to include the possibility that achievements within specific domains are an integral part of cognitive development. Fischer emphasizes the development of skills in specific domains, whereas Case describes the impact of greater cognitive efficiency on thinking as a whole.

■ VYGOTSKY'S SOCIOCULTURAL THEORY OF COGNITIVE DEVELOPMENT

The culture in which the child lives is an important influence on cognitive development. According to Vygotsky, adults play a critical role in the transmission of skills, particularly as they teach children within the *zone of proximal development.* The availability of formal schooling is another key variable. In describing and explaining cognitive development, we must take into consideration the valued and frequently used skills within a given cultural context.

9 COGNITION: INFORMATION PROCESSING

"Tomorrow's geography test is going to be really tough," Nate lamented to his friend on the way home from school. "I should have paid more attention in class and kept up with my assignments. Now I have to study so much!" Normally a good student, Nate had been preoccupied with the success of his baseball team. Now there was a price to be paid as he prepared for the next day's test, and he was decidedly anxious about it. Nate had made up one "trick" for remembering the states in the Southeast: he strung their first letters to make the phrase "True aces forget no states" for Tennessee, Alabama, Florida, Georgia, North Carolina, and South Carolina, respectively. And it helped him to identify some of the states by tying their shapes to things he knew; for example, Florida really did look as though it had a "panhandle." But there was so much more to remember! Maybe he could just repeat the capitals of the states over and over to himself. One thing he knew for sure: next time he would not save all of his studying for the night before the test.

Nate, as it turns out, had a pretty good understanding of his mental capabilities. He knew that paying attention in class was helpful and that certain techniques, such as rehearsal, mental imagery, and other "tricks," could help him remember information. He also knew there were limits to what he could accomplish in the few hours he had to prepare for his exam. In fact, many aspects of Nate's own thinking—attention, memory, and even the fact that he could evaluate his thought capabilities—have been topics of great interest to developmental psychologists. As Nate rightly surmised, attention is important in the attainment of knowledge, and although one's memory capabilities have limits, several techniques can be marshaled to improve memory performance.

In this chapter, we continue our examination of cognitive development, this time from an important alternative to the perspectives described in Chapter 8: the information-processing perspective. First, we will summarize the major features of this theoretical model. Then we will survey several topics that have been studied extensively from the viewpoint of information-processing theory, including attention, memory, and problem solving.

THE INFORMATION-PROCESSING APPROACH

As we saw in Chapter 1, information-processing theorists believe human cognition is best understood as the management of information through a system with limited space or resources. In the information-processing approach, mental processing is usually broken down into several components or levels of activity. For example, memory processes are often partitioned into *encoding, storage,* and *retrieval* phases. Moreover, information is assumed to move forward through the system in time and each stage of processing is of some duration (Massaro & Cowan, 1993; Palmer & Kimchi, 1986).

Many traditional information-processing models are called **multistore models** because they posit several mental structures through which information flows sequentially, much as data pass through a computer. Most multistore models distinguish between psychological structures and control processes. Psychological *structures,* as we saw in Chapter 1, are analogous to the hardware of a computer. The *control processes* are mental activities that move information from one structure to another, much as software functions for the computer.

Suppose someone asks you to repeat a list of words, such as *shoe, car, truck, hat, coat, bus.* If you have paid attention to all of the words and, like an efficient computer, "input" them into your cognitive system, processing will begin in the **sensory store.** Information is held here for a fraction of a second in a form very close to the original stimuli, in this case the audible sounds you experienced. Next, the words may move to the *memory stores,* of which there are two. **Working memory** (often called *short-term store*) holds information for no more than a couple of minutes. If you were to repeat the words over and over to yourself—that is, rehearse them—you would be employing a *control process* to retain information in working memory. You might also use the second memory store, **long-term memory,** the repository of more enduring information, and notice that the items belong to two categories, clothing and vehicles. The *central processor,* which functions like an executive decision maker, oversees this communication among the structures of the information-processing system. Finally, when you are asked to say the words aloud, your *response system* functions to help you reproduce the sounds you heard moments earlier.

Other theorists in this field have advanced a **limited-resource model** of the cognitive system that emphasizes a finite amount of available cognitive energy that can be deployed in numerous ways, but only with certain tradeoffs. Unlike multistore models, limited-resource models emphasize the allocation of energy for various cognitive activities rather than the mental structures themselves. The basic assumption is that the pool of resources available for processing, retaining, and reporting information is finite (Bjorklund & Harnishfeger, 1990). In one such model, introduced in Chapter 8, Robbie Case proposes an inverse relationship between the amount of space available for operating on information and that available for storage (Case, 1985; Case, Kurland, & Goldberg, 1982). *Operations,* as we have seen, include processes such as identifying the stimuli and recognizing relationships among them; *storage* refers to the retention of information for use at a later time. If a substantial amount of mental effort is expended on operations, less space is available for storage or retention.

In the simple memory experiment we just examined, the effort used to identify the words and notice the categorical relationships among them will determine the space left over for storing those words. If we are proficient at recognizing words and their relationships, storage space will be available. If these tasks cost us substantial effort, however, our resources will be taxed and little will be left for the task of remembering. Robert Kail's research (1986, 1991a, 1991b) supports the idea that a central component of cognitive development is an increase in processing speed with age. As children grow older, they can mentally rotate images, name objects, or add numbers more rapidly. More resources then become available for other cognitive tasks.

How do these two general information-processing frameworks, the multistore model and the limited-resource model, account for cognitive development? Multistore models allow for two possibilities. Changes in cognition can stem from either an increase in the size of the structures—the "hardware"—or increasing proficiency in employing the "software" or control processes. For example, the capacity of the mental structure working memory may increase with age, or, as children grow older,

multistore model Information-processing model that describes a sequence of mental structures through which information flows.

sensory store Memory store that holds information for very brief periods of time in a form that closely resembles the initial input.

working memory Short-term memory store in which mental operations such as rehearsal and categorization take place.

long-term memory Memory that holds information for extended periods of time.

limited-resource model Information-processing model that emphasizes the allocation of finite energy within the cognitive system.

they may increase their tendency to rehearse items to keep information in working memory or even push it into long-term memory. Limited-resource models suggest that what changes during development is processing efficiency. As children become more proficient in manipulating information, more internal space is freed up for storage.

THE DEVELOPMENT OF ATTENTION

Have you ever noticed that sometimes a seven- or eight-year-old can spend hours absorbed in a single activity, such as doing a jigsaw puzzle or playing Nintendo, whereas a toddler seems to bound from activity to activity? Most of us have a sense that older children are better able than younger ones to "pay attention" to a given task. Parents read brief stories to their two-year-olds but expect their adolescents to read lengthy passages from novels. Preschool teachers present their charges with only occasional brief, structured tasks, such as painting or coloring; high school teachers expect their students to follow their lessons for a half-hour or more at a time. Clearly, children's attentional processes undergo recognizable changes with development.

Attention has been conceptualized as a state of alertness or arousal that allows the individual to focus on a selected aspect of the environment, often in preparation for learning or problem solving (Kahneman, 1973). Attention represents the first step in cognitive processing and, as such, is a critical phase. Unless information enters the system in the first place, there will be few opportunities to develop memory, concepts, or other cognitive skills. Children with a poor capacity to attend will have difficulties in learning, the ramifications of which can be enormous, especially as they enter school. Research evidence corroborates that children who have greater attention spans and persistence in tasks at ages four to five years have higher intelligence scores and school achievement by the time they get to second grade (Palisin, 1986).

Sustaining Attention

One of the most obvious developmental trends is the dramatic increase in the child's ability to *sustain* attention on some activity or set of stimuli. Holly Ruff and Katharine Lawson (1990) observed one-, two-, and three-and-a-half-year-olds while the children played with an array of six toys. They observed a steady increase with age in the amount of attention directed to individual toys. On average, one-year-olds showed focused attention for 3.33 seconds, two-year-olds for 5.36 seconds, and three-and-a-half-year-olds for 8.17 seconds. The attention span continues to increase throughout the early school years and adolescence, and shows a particularly marked improvement around age ten years (Milich, 1984; Yendovitskaya, 1971).

Why does sustained attention increase with age? Perhaps maturation of the central nervous system is partly responsible. The reticular activating system, the portion of the lower brainstem that regulates levels of arousal, is not fully mature until adolescence. Another factor may be the increasing complexity of the child's interests. Young children seem to be intrigued by the physical properties of objects, but since these are often not too complex, simply looking at or touching objects quickly leads to habituation. On the other hand, older children are more concerned with creative and varied ways of playing with objects (Ruff & Lawson, 1990). As children actively generate more possible uses for stimuli, their active engagement with stimuli captivates and feeds back to influence attention.

One other aspect of sustained attention has been revealed in studies examining how children watch television. Daniel Anderson and his colleagues have noted that when children watch programs such as "Sesame Street," the longer they look at the screen, the longer they keep looking (Anderson, Choi, & Lorch, 1987). If preschool children attended to the TV program for fifteen seconds, it was highly unlikely that they would be distracted by other environmental events. This greater likelihood of continued looking after longer initial looks is called **attentional inertia**. Research has

KEY THEME
Interaction Among Domains

KEY THEME
Child's Active Role

attention State of alertness or arousal that allows the individual to focus on a selected aspect of the environment.

attentional inertia Continued sustained attention after an initial period of focused attention.

yet to reveal how attentional inertia might change with age. However, it may serve a valuable function in cognitive growth by maintaining the flow of information passing through the system.

Deploying Attention

A second developmental change in attentional processes involves the ability of older children to control their attention in a systematic manner; that is, they *deploy* their attention effectively, such as when they are comparing two complex stimuli. The work of Eliane Vurpillot (Vurpillot, 1968; Vurpillot & Ball, 1979) illustrates these developmental changes in how children attend to their environment. Children were shown a picture of two houses, each having six windows, and were asked to judge whether the houses were identical (see Figure 9.1). As they inspected the houses, their eye movements were filmed by a camera. Preschoolers scanned the windows less thoroughly and systematically than older children. For example, when the houses were identical, four- and five-year-olds looked at only about half of the windows before making a decision, but older children looked at nearly all of them. When the windows differed, older children were more likely than younger children to stop scanning as soon as they detected a discrepancy. Finally, older children were more likely to look back and forth at windows in the same locations of the two houses; younger children displayed more haphazard fixations, looking at a window in one house, then a different window in the other house.

In another experiment, Patricia Miller and Yvette Harris (1988) found that children not only become more systematic but also use more *efficient* attentional strategies as they grow older. Preschoolers were asked to determine whether one row of six drawings of toys contained the same elements in sequence as a second row of six drawings. To accomplish this task, they had to open doors that covered the pictures. Three-year-olds tended to be systematic but not very efficient: they opened one entire row first, then opened the next row. In contrast, four-year-olds adopted a systematic and more efficient strategy for comparing: they opened each vertically aligned pair from one end of the array to the next. Perhaps as a consequence, the older participants were more accurate in their judgments about whether or not the rows were identical.

Selective Attention

Still another aspect of attention that changes with development is the ability to be *selective*. Older children are much more likely than younger children to ignore information that is irrelevant or distracts from some central activity or problem (Lane & Pearson, 1982). An experiment conducted by George Strutt and his colleagues illustrates this effect (Strutt, Anderson, & Well, 1975). Children ages six, nine, and twelve

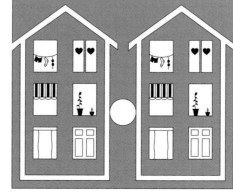

Source: Adapted from Vurpillot, 1968.

FIGURE 9.1

Comparing Houses

Children were asked to explore houses to make judgments about whether they were the same or different while a camera photographed their eye movements. Preschoolers explored the windows less thoroughly, efficiently, and systematically than older children.

years participated in a *speeded classification task*. They were given decks of cards that varied on one or more stimulus dimensions: form (circle or square), orientation of a line (horizontal or vertical), and location of a star (above or below the center). The objective was to sort the cards on the basis of one predetermined dimension as quickly as they could. But what happened when an irrelevant dimension was added to the cards in the deck? This manipulation interfered with the ability of six-year-olds to sort the cards but had little effect on the performance of older children. What about the effect of adding a second irrelevant dimension? Again, the six-year-olds were the most dramatically affected by the addition of distracting information.

KEY THEME
Child's Active Role

The ability to attend to some parts of an event or activity to the exclusion of others signals the child's increasing skill at controlling his own cognitive processing. Contributing to this change may be the child's growing understanding that his attentional capacity is limited and that cognitive tasks are best accomplished with focused attention. In other words, the child shows gains in **metacognition,** the knowledge and awareness of his own cognitive processes. Growth in this knowledge occurs during the preschool and early school years. In one study, three- and four-year-olds were asked if they would rather listen to pairs of stories simultaneously or one at a time. The three-year-olds were willing to listen to two tape recordings at once, but the four-year-olds preferred to listen to one at a time (Pillow, 1988). In another study, six-year-olds stated that a person who is concentrating on one task would not pay much attention to other things, whereas four-year-olds did not exhibit this understanding (Flavell, Green, & Flavell, 1995).

Experiences in multiple sensory modalities may also play a role. In one recent study, deaf children fitted with cochlear implants to improve their hearing were compared to deaf children who did not have implants on a test of visual attention. The children with implants performed significantly better than the children without them. Moreover, the researchers observed that selective attention developed very rapidly once children obtained the implants (Quittner et al., 1994). Why should experience with sounds make a difference in visual attention? The answer is not clear, but perhaps auditory cues (especially noticeable ones such as a shout, a loud whistle, or a sudden popping sound) are powerful stimuli in drawing one's visual attention to events in the environment. It seems that a full account of the development of attention will have to involve processes beyond those connected to any single sensory system.

Between 5 and 10 percent of children in the United States, usually boys, show a pattern of impulsivity, high levels of motor activity, and attention problems called *attention deficit hyperactivity disorder* or *ADHD* (American Psychiatric

ATYPICAL DEVELOPMENT

Attention Deficit Hyperactivity Disorder

Association, 1987; Ross & Ross, 1982). The disorder is puzzling because its cause is unclear and an unambiguous diagnosis is often difficult to obtain. At the same time, for parents, teachers, and the children themselves, the consequences of the disorder—poor school achievement, behavior management problems, poor peer relationships, and low self-esteem among them—can be serious (Erhardt & Hinshaw, 1994; Rapport, 1995). While hyperactivity and impulsivity may decline in adolescence, problems with attention often persist for years (Hart et al., 1995).

As the diagnostic label implies, a major assumption about the nature of ADHD is that these children have some type of deficit in attention. But what precisely is the nature of that deficit? A number of hypotheses abound, but one that seems tenable is that ADHD children are highly distractible; they have difficulty in being selective when confronted with numerous stimuli that compete for their attention. An experiment comparing six-to-twelve-year-old ADHD boys with non-ADHD boys as they watched television demonstrates this effect (Landau, Lorch, & Milich, 1992). Each boy

metacognition Awareness and knowledge of cognitive processes.

watched four segments of a show called "3-2-1 Contact" for fourteen minutes, half the time with several distracting toys in the room and half the time without toys. All participants were told they would have to answer some questions about the televised segments at the end of the viewing period. When distracting toys were present, ADHD boys paid about half as much attention to the shows as the non-ADHD boys. However, the two groups did not differ in their attention in the absence of distracting toys. These results suggest that ADHD children do not have a pervasive problem in sustaining attention; rather, they have difficulty filtering out extraneous stimulation.

What is the source of the difficulties these children display? Several studies implicate biological factors. Individuals with ADHD show abnormal brain wave activity, slower blood flow, and lower glucose metabolism in the prefrontal regions of the brain that are associated with regulating attention and motor activity (Rapport, 1995). There is also some evidence that ADHD may have an inherited component. In one investigation, 65 percent of the ADHD children in the sample had at least one relative with the disorder (Biederman et al., 1990). Other risk factors for attention problems include prenatal exposure to alcohol (Streissguth et al., 1995) and possibly nicotine, cocaine, or other drugs that may affect the developing brain of the fetus (NIMH, 1996). However, it is premature to discount the role of early caregiving practices. A recent study by Elizabeth Carlson and her colleagues found that the most powerful predictor of distractibility in early childhood was the extent to which caregivers provided an overstimulating, intrusive environment. Children of mothers who tended to disrupt their children's ongoing activity were more distractible in early childhood, which in turn predicted hyperactivity in middle childhood (Carlson, Jacobvitz, & Sroufe, 1995).

ADHD children are frequently treated with medications, such as Ritalin, that are classified as stimulants but actually serve to "slow them down." This treatment helps many children, but some experts worry that too many children are placed on this medication simply because they exhibit behavior problems rather than genuine ADHD. Clearly, a better understanding of ADHD is needed to sharpen its clinical diagnosis and develop treatment strategies for these children.

THE DEVELOPMENT OF MEMORY

Few cognitive skills are as basic as the ability to store information encountered at a given time for potential retrieval seconds, minutes, days, or even years later. It is hard to imagine how any other cognitive activity, such as problem solving or concept formation, could take place without the ability to draw on previously experienced information. How could we classify dogs, horses, and giraffes into the category "animals" without remembering the shared features of each? How could we solve a problem such as Piaget's pendulum task, described in Chapter 8, without remembering the results of each of our mini-experiments with the length of the string, weight of the object, and so on? In one way or another, memory is a crucial element in most of our thinking.

However, memory is far from a simple or unitary construct. One distinction is drawn between episodic and semantic memory. **Episodic memory** is memory for events that occurred at a specific time and place in the past ("What did you do on your first day of school?"). **Semantic memory,** on the other hand, consists of general concepts or facts that are stored without reference to a specific previous event ("How many inches are there in a foot?"). We can make another distinction, one between recognition and recall memory. Tasks that measure **recognition memory** require participants to indicate whether they have encountered a picture, word, or other stimulus before ("Have you seen this picture on previous trials of this experiment?"). Participants are required merely to give a *yes* or *no* answer or some other simple response that signals they have previously encountered an item. In **recall memory**

episodic memory Memory for events that took place at a specific time and place.

semantic memory Memory for general concepts or facts.

recognition memory Ability to identify whether a stimulus has been previously encountered.

recall memory Ability to reproduce stimuli that one has previously encountered.

tasks, participants must reproduce previously presented stimuli ("Tell me the twelve words you heard me say a few minutes ago."). The fact that memory can be conceptualized in such different ways has complicated the task of describing developmental processes. Nevertheless, three decades of research on this multifaceted area of cognition have begun to suggest some clear and predictable trends in the development of memory.

Recognition Memory

How early can we demonstrate the presence of memory? How long do those memories last? How much information can be retained through recognition memory? Two techniques useful in documenting young infants' perceptual abilities and discussed in Chapter 6, *habituation* and *operant conditioning,* have also been fruitful in yielding answers to these questions about infants' and young children's abilities to recognize previously experienced stimuli.

Much of the earliest research on infant recognition memory was conducted by Joseph Fagan, who used the habituation procedure. First, a visual stimulus such as a photograph of a human face or a geometric figure (some examples are shown in Figure 9.2) is presented to the infant for a predetermined period of time. On a subsequent trial, the same stimulus is paired with a completely new item, and the time the infant spends looking at each picture is recorded. In this *paired-comparison procedure,* infants typically look longer at the novel stimulus than at the familiar one, suggesting that they remember the familiar item. Using this basic approach, Fagan (1974) demonstrated that five-to-six-month-olds familiarized with black-and-white photos of human faces for only a few minutes retain information about them for surprisingly long periods of time. When the recognition test occurred three hours or up to fourteen days after the initial familiarization, infants showed consistently longer visual fixations to the novel stimulus. This is an impressive level of performance for infants only a few months old!

Carolyn Rovee-Collier and her colleagues have used a different technique relying on operant conditioning to demonstrate infants' early memory capabilities (Rovee-Collier & Hayne, 1987; Rovee-Collier & Shyi, 1992). As shown in Figure 9.3, an infant lies in a crib with a ribbon running from his ankle to an overhead mobile. Within a few minutes, the infant recognizes the contingency between his foot kicks and the movement of the mobile; his rate of kicking increases dramatically. Suppose, however, that the mobile is removed from the crib for two weeks. When the mobile is

---

FIGURE 9.2

Infant Recognition Memory

Fagan tested infant recognition memory by using visual stimuli in a paired-comparison procedure. For each row, one of the stimuli was presented repeatedly until habituation occurred. Then one of the other stimuli in the row was paired with the familiar stimulus to see if infants preferred the novel item. Infants only a few months old looked longer at novel items up to fourteen days after the initial familiarization.

Source: Adapted from Fagan, 1974.

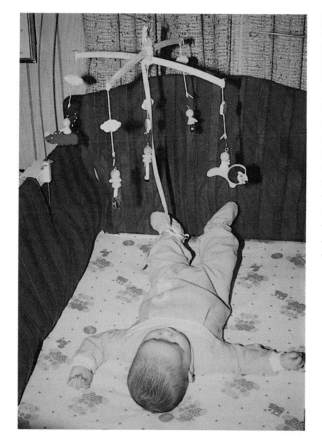

FIGURE 9.3

Using Operant Conditioning to Study Early Memory

Infants in Rovee-Collier's studies had a ribbon attached between their foot and an interesting mobile overhead. Infants quickly learned that kicking made the mobile move. When the mobile was removed and then reintroduced after a delay interval, infants showed that they "remembered" it by vigorously kicking again.

Source: Rovee-Collier & Hayne, 1987.

reintroduced, does the infant remember that this is the object that he can move with a foot kick? The answer is yes: three-month-olds vigorously kicked when the familiar mobile was replaced over the crib but did not kick as much when a brand-new mobile was put in the same position (Enright et al., 1983).

These early memories are easily disrupted, however, by changes in the context of the task. Suppose an infant learns the original contingency between a foot kick and the movement of the mobile when she is in a playpen lined with a yellow cloth with green squares. Twenty-four hours later, the mobile is reintroduced, but this time the cloth liner is blue with red stripes. Now the infant does not show a memory for the previous day's events; she does not kick nearly as much as she did at the end of training the previous day (Rovee-Collier et al., 1992). Thus, infants six months of age and under encode very detailed and specific information about an event, even when that information is not the central focus of attention. Put another way, infants will show evidence of memory only when the conditions during training and memory testing are as similar as possible (Hayne & Rovee-Collier, 1995).

At just how young an age do infants display recognition memory, and precisely how long do early infant memories last? Two important studies address these questions. One experiment shows that even newborns can retain information for at least a twenty-four-hour period (Swain, Zelazo, & Clifton, 1993). On the first day of the study, newborns heard a tape of a word, either *beagle* or *tinder,* that was repeated during the experimental session while an observer recorded the number of head turns the infants made toward the sound. As you would expect with the habituation procedure, the number of head turns declined over the session. One day later, one group of infants heard the same word again, while a second, experimental group heard a new word. Infants in the first group made fewer head turns toward the stimulus word and more head turns away from it than infants in the second group. Evidently, they remembered some very specific properties of the auditory stimulus for a duration of many hours.

The second study demonstrates perhaps even more dramatically the long duration of early memories. A number of children had participated in a study of infant auditory localization when they were six months of age. The experimental task had required them to reach in the dark for a shaking rattle. Now, almost two years later, these same children revisited the laboratory and experienced the same experimental conditions without any instructions or description of the task. In comparison to the control group, children who had prior experience with the experiment during infancy were much more likely to reach out in the dark for the shaking rattle (Perris, Myers, & Clifton, 1990). Evidently, an event that was experienced only briefly at six months of age was accessible in memory two years later!

Levels of recognition accuracy among older infants and preschool-age children are no less impressive. Typically, researchers present children with a large number of pictures, sometimes as many as one hundred. On test trials, the "old" pictures are interspersed with "new" ones, and children state whether they had seen the picture before. Alternatively, researchers note whether children look longer at the novel pictures. In general, children correctly recognize an impressive percentage—75 percent or more—of stimulus items even when they are tested several weeks later (Brown & Scott, 1971; Daehler & Bukatko, 1977).

In summary, the ability to recognize previously viewed stimuli appears to be rudimentary, present right from birth. Recognition memory is enduring and, at least among slightly older children, encompasses the retention of a good deal of information. The ability to distinguish the familiar from the novel probably has a biological basis because it appears so early in human infants and is evident in other species as well. Considering how important memory is to other cognitive activities, it is not surprising that this early form of retention is so robust and appears so early in the developmental process.

Developmental Changes in Recall

Suppose someone asks you to repeat a string of digits, such as a phone number. Like most adults, you should be able to repeat between seven and nine digits with relatively little difficulty as long as no more than approximately thirty seconds elapse after you first hear the digits. Tasks such as these measure **memory span,** the number of stimulus items that can be *recalled* after a brief interval. Children under age ten years remember fewer items than do adults. As Figure 9.4 shows, two-year-olds typically remember only about two items, four-year-olds about three or four, and seven-year-olds about five (Dempster, 1981).

Do these changes in memory span occur because the storage capacity of memory increases? That is, does the "hardware" of the information-processing system hold increasingly greater amounts of information as the child grows? Numerous memory experiments suggest that this is not necessarily the case. Instead, children's ability to employ **memory strategies,** activities to enhance the encoding and retrieval of information, increases with age. Children seven years and older are more likely than younger children to rehearse items or reorganize them into more meaningful, and hence more memorable, units. For instance, noting that the numbers 1, 3, 5, and 7 form the sequence of odd numbers makes the list easier to recall. So does simply repeating them over and over. Alternatively, as we saw in Chapter 8, Robbie Case and his colleagues have proposed that increases in memory span can be understood as a result of the increasing operational efficiency children display as they mature (Case, Kurland, & Goldberg, 1982). As operational efficiency increases, more cognitive resources are available for storage.

The memory span task is usually believed to tap working memory, or short-term memory, because the interval between presentation of the stimuli and the memory test is relatively brief. Other recall studies have examined the ability of children to remember lists of words, sentences, or other items for longer than a few seconds. Nearly all of these experiments demonstrate that older children remember more information than younger children.

KEY THEME
Nature/Nurture

KEY THEME
Child's Active Role

memory span Number of stimulus items that can be recalled after a brief interval of time.

memory strategy Mental activity, such as rehearsal, that enhances memory performance.

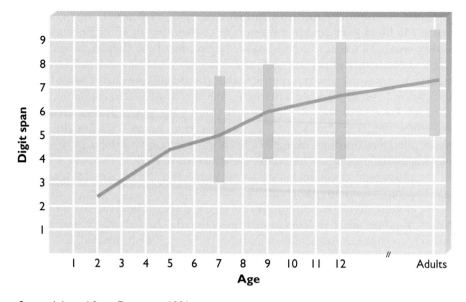

Source: Adapted from Dempster, 1981.

FIGURE 9.4

Developmental Changes in Memory Span

In the memory span task, participants are asked to repeat a string of digits after an interval of a few seconds. The points on the curve represent the average number of digits participants are able to recall. The bars represent the ranges of typical performance at each age. Memory span increases throughout childhood and approaches the adult level between ages ten and twelve years.

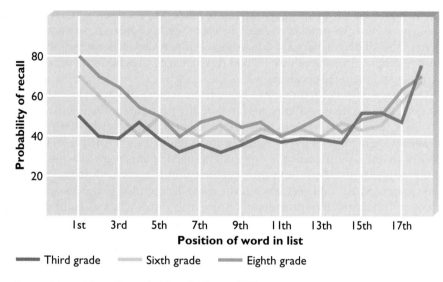

Source: Adapted from Ornstein, Naus, & Liberty, 1975.

FIGURE 9.5

Developmental Differences in Free Recall

This graph shows the probability that a word will be recalled by third-, sixth-, and eighth-graders in a free-recall task. Few developmental differences appear in memory for the last few items in the list, but older children show elevated levels of recall for the first few items. This pattern suggests that older children are more likely than younger children to employ memory strategies such as rehearsal to remember the early items.

In *free-recall* tasks, children are given a list of words or objects that they are to repeat, after a specified delay period, in any order they wish. As Figure 9.5 shows, few developmental differences in recall are usually noted for items later in the list (Ornstein & Naus, 1978; Ornstein, Naus, & Liberty, 1975). Children of all ages recall these items well, at least by the time they are of elementary school age. This elevated recall for later items, called the **recency effect,** is viewed as the extraction of information from more immediate memory, a task that is usually not too demanding for children age four years and older. Older children, however, show a clear advantage for recalling items that appeared in the early or middle positions in the list. The fact that older children show good memory for early items is called the **primacy effect.** Developmental differences in the primacy effect can be explained as the result of the tendency of older children, those age seven years or older, to engage in deliberate strategies to improve recall. They repeat items aloud, make up sentences connecting the items, or think of mental images that connect the items. In fact, much of the research on memory development has centered on detailing the types of strategies children of different ages display. We now turn to these investigations.

recency effect   Tendency for individuals to show good recall for the last few items in a list.

primacy effect   Tendency for individuals to display good recall for early items in a list.

Memory Strategies How do you make sure you remember your grocery list or where you hung your coat in a restaurant coatroom? Or, as in the case of Nate, the underprepared student described at the beginning of the chapter, how do you make sure you remember important facts and concepts for a test in school? Ordinarily, you must perform some activity to ensure that the stimuli are correctly and enduringly encoded in the first place. As a mature rememberer, you often capitalize on cues that may later "trigger" retrieval. Thus, you might say the words in your grocery list over and over to yourself ("milk, eggs, bread; milk, eggs, bread") or note the characteristics of the location of an object ("I hung my coat next to the bright red one"). In general, as children grow older, they become more likely to employ self-generated strategies for both encoding and retrieval and to take advantage of external information that can potentially aid recall.

We already identified one useful memory tactic, **rehearsal**—simply repeating, either aloud or silently, items to be remembered. The fact that young children are unlikely to engage spontaneously in rehearsal is well documented. In a study mentioned in Chapter 7, investigators asked kindergartners, second-graders, and fifth-graders to observe as an experimenter pointed to three specific pictures in an array of seven (Flavell, Beach, & Chinsky, 1966). When asked to point to the same sequence after a fifteen-second delay, fifth-graders showed significantly greater accuracy than the other two age groups. More important, during the delay period the researchers recorded any signs that the children may have been rehearsing the items to be remembered, such as moving their lips or vocalizing to themselves. They found that 85 percent of the fifth-graders engaged in spontaneous rehearsal, whereas only 10 percent of the kindergartners did. Moreover, children who rehearsed showed the best recall. In other words, there was a direct link between the children's production of this strategy and memory performance.

Not only does the tendency to rehearse increase with age; the nature of the **rehearsal set,** the items actually repeated by the participant during the delay period, changes too. Peter Ornstein and his colleagues asked third-, sixth-, and eighth-graders to remember a list of eighteen unrelated words (Ornstein, Naus, & Liberty, 1975). In one condition of the experiment, participants were instructed to rehearse aloud whatever list items went through their minds as each additional stimulus word was presented. As Table 9.1 reveals, third-graders tended to repeat only the current item and perhaps one immediately preceding word, whereas eighth-graders constructed a more cumulative rehearsal set. Thus, older children tend to engage in active, purposive behaviors designed to ensure that they remember as many stimulus items as possible.

Older children also exhibit another important memory strategy called **organization,** the tendency to reorder items to fit some category or higher-order scheme. If the items to be recalled can be grouped conceptually, older children do so, and the amount they recall increases accordingly. For example, if the stimulus list contains words from the categories *animals, furniture, vehicles,* and *clothing* (for example, *sofa, dog, chair,* etc.), ten- and eleven-year-olds spontaneously cluster conceptually related items together as they recall them, whereas five- and six-year-olds do not (Moely et al., 1969). Furthermore, instructing children to group the words or objects they are to remember into categories significantly enhances recall (Bjorklund, Ornstein, & Haig, 1977; Black & Rollins, 1982). Even if young children do not cluster stimulus lists categorically on their own and are not shown how to do so, they are often still able to profit from organizational structure. For example, Marion Perlmutter and Nancy Myers (1979) presented two- to four-year-olds with objects from related categories (animals, transportation, utensils) or unrelated categories (bell, clock, drum, flag, horse, leaf, pen, star, truck). Children from both age groups remembered significantly more objects from the related list. The fact that older, school-age children tend to order items spontaneously within some meaningful framework means they have a powerful tool in the service of memory.

Still another helpful memory technique is the use of **elaboration,** thinking of a sentence or an image that links together items to be remembered. If you have to remember the list *cat, shoe, piano,* you might construct the sentence "The cat wearing

rehearsal Memory strategy that involves repetition of items to be remembered.

rehearsal set The specific group of items participants repeat during the delay period in a memory test.

organization Memory strategy in which individuals reorder items to be remembered on the basis of category or some other higher-order relationship.

elaboration Memory strategy in which individuals link items to be remembered in the form of an image or a sentence.

	Rehearsal Sets	
Word Presented	**Eighth-Grade Subject**	**Third-Grade Subject**
Yard	Yard, yard, yard	Yard, yard, yard, yard, yard
Cat	Cat, yard, yard, cat	Cat, cat, cat, cat, yard
Man	Man, cat, yard, man, yard, cat	Man, man, man, man, man
Desk	Desk, man, yard, cat, man, desk, cat, yard	Desk, desk, desk, desk

Source: Adapted from Ornstein, Naus, & Liberty, 1975.

TABLE 9.1

Rehearsal Sets of a Third- and an Eighth-Grader

As children grow older, they are more likely to employ a rehearsal set that includes more items from the list to be remembered. In this example, with one exception, the third-grader repeats only the word the experimenter has just presented. In contrast, the eighth-grader incorporates previous items from the stimulus list into the rehearsal set.

shoes played the piano" or think of a visual image portraying this scene. Elaboration is one of the latest memory strategies to appear; usually children do not spontaneously use images or elaborative verbalizations until adolescence or later (Pressley & Levin, 1977).

One last facet of the strategic behavior of older children is their tendency to use **retrieval cues,** aids that help them extract information already stored in memory. One of the best illustrations of this phenomenon comes from a study conducted by Akira Kobasigawa (1974). Children ranging from six through eleven years of age were shown twenty-four pictures of objects that belonged to eight categories. For each stimulus item, a cue card that served to categorize it was provided. For example, pictures of a monkey, a camel, and a bear were accompanied by a picture of a zoo with three cages and pictures of a seesaw, a slide, and a swing were presented with a picture of a park. There were three experimental conditions: (1) a control condition, in which children were given standard free-recall instructions; (2) a cue condition, in which, at the time of recall, children were told they could consult the cue cards if they wanted to; and (3) a directive-cue condition, in which children were specifically asked to name the items that went with each cue card. Figure 9.6 shows the results. In the directive-cue condition, few developmental differences in recall emerged; children of all ages performed at high levels compared to the control condition. When left to their own devices in the cue condition, however, only the older children chose to use the cue cards as retrieval aids. As a result, their memory was clearly superior to that of the younger participants in the same condition.

Throughout this discussion, the recurring theme has been the tendency of children over seven years of age to initiate some activity that will improve their recall. In contrast, younger children do not generate memory strategies on their own, a phenomenon termed **production deficiency** (Flavell, 1970). It is important to note that when younger, nonstrategic children are instructed to employ strategies such as rehearsal, organization, or the use of retrieval cues, their recall markedly improves (Bjorklund, Ornstein, & Haig, 1977; Keeney, Cannizzo, & Flavell, 1967; Moely et al., 1969; Ornstein & Naus, 1978). The only exception appears to occur when children are first learning a strategy; there seems to be a transition time during which younger children's recall does not improve substantially when they first employ a memory strategy, a phenomenon called **utilization deficiency** (Miller, Woody-Ramsey, & Aloise, 1991). With development, though, strategy use becomes less effortful and more likely to produce gains in memory (Miller & Seier, 1994).

At the same time, preschool-age children are not completely deficient in the use of strategies. For example, when preschoolers are instructed to "remember" a set of objects, they are more likely to name and look at them than children who are instructed to "play with" the objects (Baker-Ward, Ornstein, & Holden, 1984). Thus, strategy use does not suddenly appear among seven-year-olds. A developmental progression occurs that leads to a greater degree and more varied forms of strategy use.

Sources of Memory Strategies How can we explain children's tendency to become more strategic and planful with age? Perhaps parents play a role. Hilary Ratner (1984) found a positive relationship between three-year-olds' memory performance

retrieval cue Aid or cue to extract information that has already been stored in memory.

production deficiency Failure of children under age seven years to spontaneously generate memory strategies.

utilization deficiency Phenomenon by which a memory strategy, when first applied, may fail to improve memory in a noticeable way.

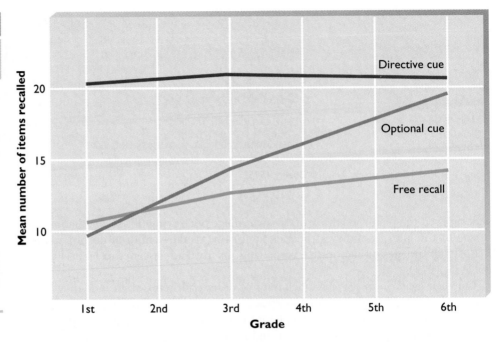

Source: Adapted from Kobasigawa, 1974.

and the frequency with which their mothers asked them questions about past events. Such memory demands may help children learn about encoding and retrieval processes that aid memory.

Another possibility is that children are taught memory strategies directly or indirectly by teachers. Barbara Moely and her colleagues (Moely et al., 1989) noted that 83 percent of the elementary school teachers they interviewed *believed* they encouraged their pupils to employ repetition to learn vocabulary words, science concepts, and other material. However, when these researchers directly observed classroom activities in grades kindergarten through six, they found that teachers gave little direct instruction about strategies (Moely et al., 1992).

Direct instruction in using memory strategies may be less important than the exposure children have to environments that provide information in an organized, structured way (Ornstein, Baker-Ward, & Naus, 1988). For example, teachers usually present lessons in a cohesive, integrated manner. Pupils who have this repeated experience may discover on their own memory strategies they can apply to other situations. Support for this idea comes from a study in which third-graders were given the chance to spontaneously sort a group of highly related pictures. They were given no explicit instructions on how to sort the stimuli. Later, when they had a group of items that were only loosely associated, they grouped them categorically and showed high levels of recall for those items. Indirect experience of this type was actually more effective in producing improved memory than explicitly telling children how to sort the groups of stimuli (Best, 1993). Thus, children may deduce techniques for improving memory from experiences with manipulating information.

Another explanation for the emergence of strategies is that children become more conscious of their own thinking capabilities with age and realize the need to implement strategies. **Metamemory,** an aspect of metacognition, refers to the understanding of memory as a process. It includes the ability to assess one's own memory characteristics and limitations, the demands made by different memory tasks, and the strategies likely to benefit memory (Flavell & Wellman, 1977; Guttentag, 1987). It also includes the ability to monitor the contents of one's own memory and to make decisions about how to allocate cognitive resources ("Have I memorized everything thoroughly? Do I still need to study some items?") (Kail, 1990). Advances in each of these aspects of metamemory may be responsible for improvements in memory as

metamemory Understanding
of memory as a cognitive process.

children get older. For example, unlike older children, younger children often manifest unrealistic ideas about the extent of their memories. When John Flavell and his colleagues asked nursery school through fourth-grade children to predict the number of pictures they could recall in a set of ten, many of the youngest participants stated they could remember them all (Flavell, Friedrichs, & Hoyt, 1970). In fact, they could actually recall only three or four. In contrast, older children were much more accurate in estimating their memory span. Similarly, older children have a better understanding that shorter lists are easier to remember than longer ones and that events from the distant past are more difficult to remember than more recent events (Kreutzer, Leonard, & Flavell, 1975; Lyon & Flavell, 1993; Wellman, 1977). Thus, children's general knowledge about the characteristics of memory increases with age.

Finally, it may be that the child's general knowledge about the world must develop. For example, to use the strategy of organization, a child must appreciate the conceptual categories to which objects can belong. Before she can categorically cluster *couch, chair,* and *table* in a list of words to be recalled, she must understand that they all belong to the category *furniture*. In other words, the child's production of memory strategies arises, in part, from her expanding general knowledge base.

Memory and the Growth of General Knowledge   Do younger children ever remember more than older children or adults? In a unique experiment, Michelene Chi (1978) found that in certain situations they do. Adults and children averaging ten years of age were asked to remember lists of ten digits presented by the experimenter. Typically, the adults' performance surpassed the children's. However, when the memory task consisted of reproducing chess positions previously seen for only ten seconds on a chessboard, children significantly outperformed adults. How did they accomplish this remarkable feat? Chi (1978) explains that the children who participated were experts in the game of chess, whereas the adults (who were college educated) had only casual knowledge of the game. By having greater knowledge, these children probably could encode the familiar patterns of chess pieces more efficiently, whereas adults were probably seeing random arrangements of rooks, knights, and pawns. Thus, *domain-specific knowledge,* information about a specific content area, can influence the individual's ability to remember.

Memory researchers now recognize that the knowledge the child has already acquired can influence subsequent memory. Thus, many psychologists have begun to explore the nature and development of semantic memory, knowledge about the meanings of words, concepts, and other general knowledge. An important question here is: How is knowledge stored internally? One popular hypothesis is that information about the world is stored in the form of **networks,** groups of associations in which closely related items are represented in close proximity. Thus, for example, the concepts "sunset," "sunrise," and "clouds" are stored in close proximity to one another, whereas "apples" and "ambulance" are more distant.

David Bjorklund (1987) suggests that if a network representation of semantic memory is accurate, what changes with development is the number of items stored in semantic memory, the number of features or links associated with each item, and the strength of the relationships among items. As children become more familiar with new and different objects and concepts, they establish more and stronger links with other concepts and can more easily activate relations among items. Thus, Bjorklund maintains that as children mature, they become better able to retrieve information automatically. Memory development, according to Bjorklund, is more than just the emergence of effortful strategy use; it also includes the greater use of *effortless processing*. This, in turn, leaves more space available for storage. These ideas are consistent with the limited-resources concept of cognition.

The effect of a growing knowledge base on memory has been described in another way: in terms of scripts. **Scripts** are the organized schemes of knowledge individuals possess about commonly encountered events. For example, by the time they are three or four years old, most children have a general schematic representation for the events that occur at dinner time—cooking the food, setting the table, sitting down to

network   Model of semantic memory that consists of associations among closely related items.

script   Organized scheme or framework for commonly experienced events.

By the time they reach age three or four, many children display organized general knowledge of familiar routines and events, such as birthday parties. These *scripts* can serve as frameworks within which specific memories are stored.

eat—as well as for other routine events such as going to school or attending a birthday party (Fivush, 1984; Nelson & Gruendel, 1981). When asked to remember stories based on such familiar scripts, children typically recall script-based activities such as "eating dinner" better than other details less closely related to scripts (McCartney & Nelson, 1981). Thus, scripts serve as general frameworks within which specific memories can be stored and may be one of the earliest building blocks for memory.

Other Factors That Influence Memory   Researchers studying early memory abilities have identified a number of additional factors that influence the durability of memories. One is whether the events a child has experienced are linked by logical or causal relations. When preschoolers witness a logically ordered event such as making "fundough," they remember more details about the event than when the event consists of arbitrary segments, such as different activities in sand play (Fivush, Kuebli, & Clubb, 1992). Likewise, eleven-month-olds show an excellent ability to imitate the following sequence of causally connected actions: push a button through a slot in a transparent box, then shake it. Imitation will occur even if children are presented with the objects three months after they first saw them; however, arbitrary sequences of actions are not remembered as well (Bauer & Mandler, 1992; Mandler & McDonough, 1995).

Reminders of the event to be remembered also make a difference, but when they occur is apparently crucial. Recall the infant memory studies conducted by Carolyn Rovee-Collier and her colleagues. If infants who had learned to make a foot-kick in the presence of a mobile were given a "memory boost" by seeing the mobile again within three days, they showed memory for the mobile by kicking in its presence eight days later. Reminders given more than three days later did not have this effect; infants seemed to have forgotten the mobile at the eight-day test (Rovee-Collier, Evancio, & Earley, 1995). Figure 9.7 summarizes the results of this experiment. Rovee-Collier (1995) proposes that there are *time windows* within which a reminder can provide an "inoculation" against forgetting. Reminders toward the end of the time window rather than at its beginning may be especially effective, according to some preliminary research findings (Rovee-Collier, Greco-Vigorito, & Hayne, 1993).

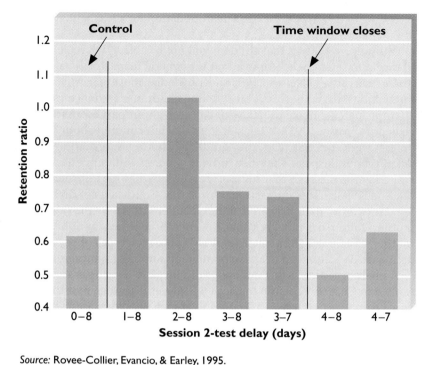

Source: Rovee-Collier, Evancio, & Earley, 1995.

Note: The retention ratio on the vertical axis is a mathematical measure of how much infants remembered. It is the proportion of training kicking rate that infants displayed during the long-term memory test.

FIGURE 9.7

Time Windows in Remembering

In an experiment conducted by Carolyn Rovee-Collier and her colleagues, three-month-old infants were trained to kick in the presence of a mobile. The numbers along the horizontal axis give the days on which the various components of the study occurred. Day 0 is the day of original training. Days 1–8 refers to the fact that the reminder occurred one day after the initial training and the long-term memory test occurred on day 8 and so on. The graph shows that infants who had received a "reminder" of the event up to three days after the initial training had improved memories.

Autobiographical Memory

Think back to your childhood and try to identify your earliest memory. How old were you? It is unlikely that you will report that you were an infant or perhaps even a toddler. Most people are not able to recount memories for experiences prior to age three years (Pillemer & White, 1989), a phenomenon called **infantile amnesia.** The question of why infantile amnesia occurs has intrigued psychologists for decades, especially in light of the ample evidence that infants and young children can display impressive memory capabilities. Many find that understanding the general nature of **autobiographical memories,** that is, memory for events that have occurred in one's own life, can provide some important clues to this mystery. Between ages three and four, children begin to give fairly lengthy and cohesive descriptions of events in their past (Fivush, Haden, & Adam, 1995). What factors are responsible for this developmental turning point?

Perhaps the explanation goes back to some ideas raised by Piaget, namely that children under age two years represent events in a qualitatively different form than older children. According to this line of thought, the verbal abilities that blossom in the two-year-old allow events to be coded in a form radically different from the action-based codes of the infant. Verbal abilities of one-year-olds are, in fact, related to their memories for events one year later. When Patricia Bauer had one-year-olds imitate an action sequence one year after they first saw it, there was a correlation between the children's verbal skills at the time they first saw the event and their success on the later memory task. However, even children with low verbal skills showed evidence of remembering the event; thus, memories may be *facilitated* by but are not *dependent* on those verbal skills (Bauer & Wewerka, 1995).

Another suggestion is that before children can talk about past events in their lives, they need to have a reasonable understanding of the self as a psychological entity (Howe & Courage, 1993). As we will see in Chapter 12, the development of the self becomes evident between the first and second years of life and shows rapid elaboration in subsequent years. The realization that the physical self has continuity in time,

KEY THEME
Continuity/Discontinuity

infantile amnesia Failure to remember events from the first two to three years of one's life.

autobiographical memory Memory for specific events in one's own life.

according to this hypothesis, lays the foundation for the emergence of autobiographical memory.

A third possibility is that children will not be able to tell their own "life story" until they understand something about the general form stories take, that is, the structure of narratives (Nelson, 1993a). Knowledge about narratives arises from social interactions, particularly the storytelling children experience from parents and the attempts parents make to talk with children about past events in their lives (Reese, Haden, & Fivush, 1993). When parents talk with children about "what we did today" or "last week" or "last year," they guide the children's formation of a framework for talking about the past. They also provide children with reminders about the memory and relay the message that memories are valued as part of the cultural experience (Nelson, 1993b). It is interesting to note that Caucasian children have earlier childhood memories than Korean children (Mullen, 1994). By the same token, Caucasian mother-child pairs talk about past events three times more often than do Korean mother-child pairs (Mullen & Yi, 1995). Thus, the types of social experiences children have do factor into the development of autobiographical memories.

A final suggestion is that children must begin to develop a "theory of mind," as described in Chapter 8, before they can talk about their own past memories. Once children begin to accurately answer questions such as "What does it mean to *remember*?" and "What does it mean to *know* something?" improvements in memory seem to occur (Perner & Ruffman, 1995).

It may be that the developments just described are intertwined with and influence one another. Talking with parents about the past may enhance the development of the self-concept, for example, as well as help the child understand what it means to "remember" (Welch-Ross, 1995). No doubt the ability to talk about one's past represents memory of a different level of complexity than simple recognition or recall.

Most individuals do not remember events that occurred in their lives prior to age three or four, a phenomenon called *infantile amnesia*. One explanation for the emergence of autobiographical memory (or memory for the events in one's own life) is that children learn the framework for telling their "story" from parents who remind them of their past experiences. This framework is like a script within which personal events can be stored.

The research on children's memory, particularly recognition memory, suggests that their ability to remember events from the past is very impressive. But as children are increasingly called on to testify in courts after they have witnessed or

Should Children Provide Eyewitness Testimony?

been victims of abuse, neglect, or other crimes, their capability to render an accurate account of past events has been called into question. At the heart of the matter is whether children's memories of past events are susceptible to suggestive or leading questions by attorneys, clinicians, and other interrogators (Ceci & Bruck, 1993). Can children be misled by certain kinds of information or questions? Are they able to report events accurately in the highly charged setting that often accompanies this kind of testimony?

Some researchers report that children, especially preschoolers, are likely to misreport a past event under certain conditions. Stephen Ceci and his colleagues tested children ages three through twelve years on their ability to remember the details of a story (Ceci, Ross, & Toglia, 1987). A day later, children in one of the experimental conditions were asked leading questions that distorted the original information, such as "Do you remember the story about Loren, who had a headache because she ate her cereal too fast?" In the original story, Loren had a stomachache from eating her eggs too fast. Compared to children who did not hear misleading questions, children who heard biased questions made more errors on a subsequent test that required them to select pictures depicting the original story: they chose the pictures showing a girl eating cereal and having a headache. This tendency to err was especially pronounced in children ages four and under.

On the other hand, other researchers believe younger children are no more suggestible than older children or adults. In one study, children witnessed a live staged event of an argument between two adults. The researchers found no age differences in susceptibility to misinformation (Marin et al., 1979). Although college students in this study were able to recall more details of the event two weeks later, children ages five, eight, and twelve years were no more likely to "fall for" misleading information than young adults.

Many factors may influence how suggestible children really are. One is exactly who is doing the questioning. For example, in Ceci's study described above, misinformation provided by an adult tended to distort memory more than misinformation provided by another child; the perceived power of the questioner may make a difference. Moreover, questioning by strangers leads to greater susceptibility to suggestions than questioning by mothers (Goodman et al., 1995). Second, when children are asked questions repeatedly, particularly *yes-no* questions, they are likely to change their answers or speculate inappropriately (Poole & White, 1991, 1993). Preschoolers especially may perceive the repeated question as a signal that their first answer was incorrect. In addition, when children are exposed to misinformation repeatedly or to stereotypes about the character of a story, their false memories increase (Leichtman & Ceci, 1995). Finally, children may be particularly vulnerable to giving false reports in the emotionally charged atmosphere of the courtroom, especially when they are the victims of abuse or assault and are in the presence of the person they are accusing (Goodman et al., 1991; Goodman et al., 1992).

Should children be called on to give eyewitness testimony? If so, what is the best way for professionals in the criminal justice system to encourage children to give reliable eyewitness accounts based on what we know from research? What kinds of ethical issues apply in conducting research on this topic? Finally, how do we protect children as well as the rights of defendants in such confrontational settings?

Brain Development and Memory

Ultimately, any account of cognitive development will have to be connected to changes in the structures or processes that occur in the brain. Neuroscientists have been actively exploring brain functioning in both animals and humans to try to establish the underlying substrates of different cognitive processes, including memory. Fruitful approaches have included studying the memory performance of animals that have had different portions of the brain lesioned (or damaged), "scanning" the brain to measure metabolism and blood flow, and recording the electrical activity of the brain while individuals perform memory tasks.

We noted earlier that even very young infants show a robust preference for novel stimuli, indicating their recognition memory for "old" items they have seen before. Infant monkeys show similar patterns of behavior; however, when their hippocampus is removed at fifteen days of age, preferences for novelty disappear (Bachevalier, Brickson, & Hagger, 1993). As Figure 9.8 shows, the hippocampus is a brain structure located below the cerebral cortex and has long been known to be involved in memory functioning. Apparently, the hippocampus, which is a part of the *limbic system,* is an early developing structure that is necessary for the display of fundamental memory processes (Nelson, 1995).

Toward the latter part of the first year, portions of the temporal and prefrontal lobes of the brain (see Figure 9.8) begin to mature, as is revealed by *positron emission tomography,* or PET scans. PET scans allow neuroscientists to measure, among other things, the glucose activity in different portions of the brain. Interestingly, the levels of glucose metabolism in the temporal lobes of monkeys begin to look adultlike at four months of age, the age at which they begin to reach for a novel object after a short delay (Bachevalier, Hagger, & Mishkin, 1991). Similarly, glucose metabolism in the prefrontal lobes begins to appear mature in one-year-old human infants (Chugani, 1994). This is also the age at which infants correctly search for objects in the "A not B" task (see Chapter 8) and at which they can locate objects after a delay (Nelson, 1995). Thus, as the cortex develops, so does the ability to perform more demanding memory tasks.

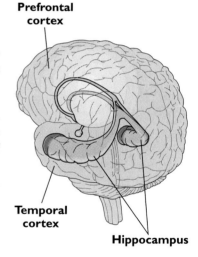

Prefrontal cortex

Temporal cortex

Hippocampus

FIGURE 9.8

The Brain and Memory Development

Several regions of the brain are implicated in memory development. The hippocampus matures early, and part of its function may be to direct recognition memory. Portions of the temporal and prefrontal cortex mature later in the first year and apparently are involved in more demanding memory tasks.

Researchers have also begun to record the electrical activity of the brain while infants participate in recognition memory tasks. In one recent study, five-month-old infants heard a succession of one hundred identical stimuli, either a click or a tone. The next day, fifty of the "old" stimuli were presented with fifty "new" ones (for example, a tone if a click had originally been heard). Electrical firing patterns of the brain were more pronounced for familiar than for unfamiliar stimuli. Brain waves also had less variable onset times for familiar stimuli on the second day compared to the first day (Thomas & Lykins, 1995). Put another way, physiological responses were more consistent and more pronounced for the stimuli that had been put into memory.

Neuropsychological studies hold great promise in unlocking some of the mysteries of brain-behavior relationships. No doubt, they will also provide important information about the factors that influence cognitive development.

THE DEVELOPMENT OF PROBLEM-SOLVING SKILLS

One of the most powerful and uniquely human cognitive skills is the ability to solve problems. Whether you are completing an analogy, computing an arithmetic solution, or testing a scientific hypothesis, problem solving typically involves several steps or phases. Often you start with planning the steps to the solution of the problem, considering both the information you have at the start and the final goal. Clearly, you must attend to the portions of the problem that are relevant to its solution. You will probably select from a number of strategies to help you achieve your goal (for example, count on your fingers or use a calculator). In many cases, you must rely on your understanding of what different symbols in the problem (for example, "+" or "=") represent. Frequently you must draw on a body of information from memory and examine relationships among several pieces of that information. Once you have the solution, you will often apply this new knowledge to similar contexts. Given the number of steps involved and the complex, intertwined relationships among them, you can see why problem solving is considered to be an example of what is called "higher-order thinking."

What are the earliest instances of problem-solving activity in humans? Piaget's descriptions of the development of means-ends behavior during the sensorimotor stage of development, discussed in Chapter 8, suggest that infants show the beginnings of problem solving. Other researchers have confirmed that infants are capable of solving problems, combining several subgoals to reach an interesting toy. In an experiment conducted by Peter Willatts (1990), twelve-month-olds saw a barrier in front of a cloth on which was placed a string attached to a toy (Figure 9.9). To get the toy, infants had to remove the barrier, pull the cloth, and then pull the string. In a control condition, the toy was not attached to the string. Infants in the first group tended to remove the barrier without playing with it, quickly pulled the cloth, and grasped the string to reach the toy. Their behavior suggested that reaching the attractive toy was of utmost interest. In contrast, infants in the control group played with the barrier, were slower to reach for the cloth, and frequently did not grasp the string, probably because they recognized that the barrier, cloth, and string could not help to bring the toy closer. Willatts (1990) concluded that infants are capable of putting together several subgoals with the deliberate intent of reaching a goal.

Problem-solving skills become more elaborate and complex as children pass through the preschool and school years. A major question has been whether the child's increasing proficiency in solving complex and abstract problems results from an abrupt, qualitative shift in the ability to think logically or whether improvements in problem solving result from gradual gains in memory, attention, and other component cognitive skills. As we saw in Chapter 8, Piaget believed in abrupt, qualitative shifts; he posited that the cognitive structures that permit completely logical and abstract thought do not evolve until adolescence, when children reach the stage of formal operations. In contrast, many information-processing theorists have emphasized

KEY THEME
Continuity/Discontinuity

the continuous growth and refinement of component skills involved in problem solving. According to them, children of all ages possess the fundamental ability to manipulate information in a logical fashion but may forget some of those elements during the process of problem solution or fail to attend to them sufficiently in the first place. With age, however, improvements in children's attention, memory, or other cognitive skills result in corresponding improvements in problem solving. Let us take a closer look at the components of problem solving that are considered essential in information-processing views of cognitive development.

Components of Problem Solving

Just think about the typical day of the average school-age child and you will undoubtedly discern many problem-solving situations the child encounters: a set of arithmetic problems to complete on a worksheet at school, a computer maze or jigsaw puzzle to solve for fun, or several bus routes to choose from to get to an after-school job. More mature and efficient problem solvers deploy several "executive" cognitive skills, much as the central processor directs the various functions of a computer. For instance, can I add these numbers in my head or should I get a calculator? What is the best strategy to use—should the puzzle be started with the edge pieces or the entire top left corner? Will learning how to do a simple computer maze provide any clues about how to do a more complex one? As researchers have explored children's problem solving, they have discovered a number of developmental changes in important components that characterize higher-order thinking.

FIGURE 9.9

Simple Problem Solving by Infants

This one-year-old knocks down the barrier and pulls the cloth to obtain the string to which an attractive toy is attached. Such behavior suggests that young infants can deliberately put together several subgoals to reach a goal.

An important cognitive skill that emerges about age three is the understanding that a symbol or model may *represent* a real-life event. Representation is a fundamental skill necessary for problem-solving.

Representation   One of the most basic capacities required for problem solving, most information-processing theorists agree, is the ability to use symbols—images, words, numbers, pictures, maps, or other configurations that represent real objects in the world. As we noted in Chapter 8, Piaget argued that children are unable to think with symbols, that is, use representations, until near the end of the sensorimotor stage of development at about eighteen months of age. Others, however, have challenged this position and argue that representational capacities are evident much earlier in infancy. Jean Mandler (1988) has pointed out a number of early abilities infants display that support this thesis. For example, we noted in Chapter 7 that infants begin to use gestures to stand for objects or events prior to age one year. Similarly, Baillargeon's experiments on object concept in infancy, described in Chapter 8, suggest that infants must hold some internal representation of objects in order to show surprise when the objects seem to disappear.

Although infants may have basic representational capacities, toddlers and older children far more readily recognize that external symbols of real objects in the world can be used to further their problem-solving efforts. For example, Judy DeLoache (1987) asked two- and three-year-olds to search for a small toy hidden in a scale model of a room. Next, the children were brought into a life-size room that corresponded to the scale model they had just seen. Could they find the real-life toy that corresponded to the smaller replica in the previous segment of the experiment? If they saw a small Snoopy toy under a miniature couch, would they look for a large Snoopy under the couch in the life-size room? The three-year-olds could find the hidden object on more than 70 percent of the trials. But the two-year-olds could do so on only 20 percent of the trials. Later, when both age groups were asked to locate the toy back in the scale model, they did so with few errors. Thus, the search failures of two-year-olds in the life-size room were not due to memory problems. DeLoache concluded that two-year-olds have difficulty understanding that a scale model *represents* a life-size room. By age three, however, children understand that a symbol or a model can "stand for" a real-life event.

Another way to understand the role of representations in children's problem solving is to observe their use of maps. Children show developmental gains here as well. In one study, kindergartners through sixth-graders were shown a map of their classrooms and were asked to place stickers denoting their seats, the location of the teacher, the location of the experimenter, and so forth. Even kindergartners were successful with this task, showing a basic understanding that maps represent a given physical space and that a correspondence exists between the physical location and the

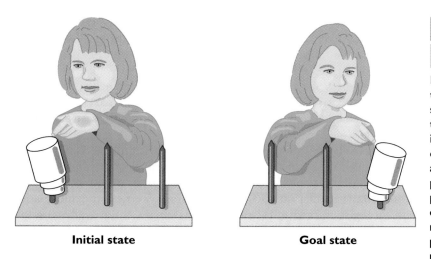

Initial state   **Goal state**

FIGURE 9.10

The Tower of Hanoi

In the Tower of Hanoi problem, the child must move three cans stacked on the first peg to the third peg so that they end up in the same order. Only one can may be moved at a time, and a smaller can may not be placed on a larger one. This problem gives researchers the opportunity to study developmental changes in children's planning activities as they solve problems.

space on a map. But performance declined for all children, especially the younger groups, when the map was rotated 180 degrees relative to the actual classroom scene. Only the fifth- and sixth-graders showed evidence of beginning to understand correspondences when map and classroom did not match in alignment (Liben & Downs, 1993). Thus, after children attain a general understanding that symbols on maps represent real-life locations, they must still refine their understanding to include the precise geometric relationships depicted on maps, even when the map and the actual location are not aligned with each other.

Planning   One of the hallmarks of a mature problem solver is the ability to plan an approach to obtaining a goal. Planning, of course, depends on representational capacities, since symbols may be employed or manipulated as part of the plan. It also depends on having general knowledge about the events being planned for—what is involved in going grocery shopping versus taking a trip to the beach, for example (Hudson, Shapiro, & Sosa, 1995). Moreover, planning has at least two aspects: (1) deciding on the steps one needs to take ahead of time and (2) knowing when to be flexible and perhaps modify or discard advance plans if the situation calls for it (Baker-Sennett, Matusov, & Rogoff, 1993).

KEY THEME
Child's Active Role

David Klahr's classic research using the Tower of Hanoi problem, illustrated in Figure 9.10, shows that there are clear developmental differences in planning (Klahr, 1978; Klahr & Robinson, 1981). In this problem, one of three pegs has three cans of different sizes stacked on it. The goal is to move the cans to the third peg so they end up in the same order they were on the first peg. Two rules apply: only one can may be moved at a time, and a smaller can cannot be placed on a larger one.

Klahr found that six-year-olds were better planners than three-year-olds in two respects: they were more likely to pursue long-term goals, and they could keep more subgoals in mind as they attempted to solve the problem. For example, three-year-olds single-mindedly moved the cans to the third peg without thinking of the intermediate steps that might be necessary; their plan encompassed only the short-term goal to get the cans to the final peg. They could think of only one or two steps to attain the goal and broke the rules of the game. In contrast, six-year-olds used five or six steps to solve the problem, looking ahead a step or more as they planned their moves and anticipating potential traps in or obstacles to their placement of the cans.

With development, children also show changes in the flexibility of their planning. This phenomenon is illustrated by another study in which children were asked to plan a route through a maze (Gardner & Rogoff, 1990). When the task involved no time pressure, seven-to-ten-year-olds planned the entire route through the maze before they drew in the path. However, when the experimenter told children to work as fast as they could, these older children used a more efficient approach under the circumstances: they planned less. Younger children, ages four to seven years, were less likely to adapt their planning strategies to the particular demands of the task.

Strategy Choice   When a child encounters a problem—say, an addition problem—he will most likely choose from among several strategies. Robert Siegler has closely examined children's strategies as they solve simple addition problems and has found that children often rely on more than one approach (Siegler & Crowley, 1991; Siegler & Jenkins, 1989; Siegler & Shrager, 1984). Most children, he noted, first turned to one strategy, but also usually had a back-up strategy or two. Having multiple strategies affords the child useful flexibility as she encounters new situations and gains new knowledge (Siegler, 1989).

Suppose the child's assignment is to add the numbers 3 and 1. Several strategies are possible. The child can represent each number on his fingers and then count to the total. Alternatively, he can represent the larger number on his fingers and then count off the smaller number. Or he can simply retrieve the information from memory. Siegler found that if the problem was simple, children drew on memory for the answer since that approach is the fastest (Siegler & Shrager, 1984). If the problem was more difficult, however, children used other strategies that ensured greater accuracy, such as counting on their fingers.

With development, as children have more successes with solving problems and become more confident about their approach, they are more likely to use memory as opposed to finger counting to solve addition problems. They also learn new strategies, often when they fail to solve a problem and need to search for alternative solutions. But children can learn from their successes, too. Siegler and Jenkins (1989) noticed that children often came up with new strategies for problems they had solved correctly earlier in the experiment.

However, children do not merely substitute one strategy for another as they become more mature problem solvers. Rather, they incorporate new blends of strategies as they learn new ones and discard older ones. Children are constantly selecting from a pool of multiple strategies, depending on whether the task demands that they be fast or accurate and on what they remember about the success of the particular strategy in the past (Siegler, 1989). In their use of strategies, children frequently show much variability from one problem-solving session to another and from one child to the next (Kuhn et al., 1995; Siegler, 1994).

Transferring Skills   One final essential element in higher-order thinking is the ability to use what you have learned in one situation and apply it to other, similar problems. How well do children extend their existing problem-solving skills to new circumstances? This has been a long-standing question in psychology, particularly among researchers who have studied the role of generalization in learning. It has also been a question of paramount importance to educators, who assume children will find some application in their everyday lives for what they have learned in the classroom.

The ability to transfer knowledge requires that children have learned the original problem well, note the resemblance between the old and new problems, and apply the appropriate activities to the new problem. This process is called **analogical transfer** in that the child must notice the one-to-one correspondence that exists between the elements of one problem and those of another and then apply the familiar skills to the novel context.

An experiment by Ann Brown and her coresearchers illustrates how this process can occur (Brown, Kane, & Echols, 1986). Three-to-five-year-olds were read a story in which a magical genie had to move his jewels from one bottle across a high wall to another bottle. Several items were available to help the genie: glue, paper clips, sheets of paper, and so on. The experimenter and each child enacted the solution, rolling up the paper into a tube and using it to transport the jewels from one bottle to the other. The children were then presented with a different problem having the same general solution (a rabbit that needs to get its Easter eggs across a river can roll paper into a tube to transport them). Whether the children were able to transfer the solution to a new problem depended on whether they recalled the goal structure of the previous problem. If they remembered the major actor, his goal, and the solution to his problem, even three-year-olds could solve the new problem. In fact, based on children's performance on a variety of problem-solving tasks employed by Ann Brown and other researchers (Baillargeon & DeVos, 1991; Brown, 1990), Usha Goswami (1996) has concluded that certainly toddlers, and possibly even infants, demonstrate analogical transfer.

Brown hypothesizes that for transfer of problem solving to take place, the child must represent the problem in general mental terms, that is, abstract out the goal, problem, and solution dissociated from the specific fact that it was a genie who had to transfer jewels. Children can be encouraged to discern such common goal structures in consecutive problems. Zhe Chen and Marvin Daehler (1989) found that when six-year-olds were explicitly prompted to formulate an answer to the question of how problems were alike, they then performed significantly better on a transfer problem than control participants who did not receive this training. Thus, parents and teachers may play a crucial role in facilitating the transfer of learning by pointing out commonalities across the solutions to several problems. Similarities in the problems themselves may also help, either when the characters and story themes across problems share resemblances or when the goal sequences in problems are the same (Chen, 1996).

KEY THEME
Nature/Nurture

RESEARCH APPLIED TO EDUCATION

Facilitating Transfer in the Classroom

As the teacher collected each student's paper, Nate was thinking how glad he was to have the geography test over with. Science was next, and science was without doubt his favorite subject in school. The class was studying electricity and had learned about how to make a circuit, the properties of conductors and insulators, and the role of a battery. Now the teacher was asking pairs of students to make a series of three light bulbs work by putting together wires and batteries in the correct order. Nate and his partner, Eliza, looked at the equipment before them and were stumped. How would they even begin? As they experimented, though, the principles they discussed in the previous day's lesson began to creep into their thinking. By the end of only a few minutes, their bulbs were assembled and shining as brightly as their proud faces.

If you stop and think about it, probably the greatest overarching goal of education is to ensure that students transfer what they learn in one lesson, problem, or assignment to new situations both in and outside of the classroom. We expect students to go beyond the specific content of one particular mathematics problem, scientific experiment, or writing assignment and apply what they have learned in new situations. Is there anything teachers can do to promote this important process?

Robert Sternberg and Peter Frensch (1993) offer the following suggestions based on their review of numerous studies of both memory and transfer:

1. *"Teach for transfer" by providing multiple settings in which information is encoded.* This tactic, according to numerous studies of memory, should make retrieval of information more likely because there are more cues associated with it. Teachers should demonstrate to students how information they learn can be applied in different contexts and even ask students to think of applications themselves. That is, knowledge should not be "encapsulated" or taught as a "stand-alone" topic. As an example, principles of algebra could be taught in the context of a science class as well as a math class. The results should be that those principles are remembered well and their usefulness in different subject areas is apparent to students.

2. *Organize information so that transfer is more likely to occur.* Classroom presentations should have an obvious organizational structure and should be connected to information students already have. Such an approach would provide students with a framework, much like a *script,* that would enhance understanding and learning.

Teachers can use several techniques to encourage students to transfer knowledge from one situation to another. One of these techniques is to explain to students why the material they are learning is important in their lives so that they can develop a scheme or script for that information.

Sternberg and Frensch (1993) add that teachers rarely begin lessons with a discussion of why the information is important in students' lives (that is, where it fits in their personal scheme of things), but to enhance learning, they should.

3. *Help students see the general features that are common across different content areas to be learned and which are specific to a given lesson.* Sternberg and Frensch (1993) describe a personal experience in learning Spanish in which the general features of the language were explicitly pointed out. At the same time, pronunciations and vocabulary that were unique to a given region or country were also highlighted for students. Learning should proceed more efficiently under circumstances where common themes and exceptions to those themes are deliberately highlighted.

4. *Test students on their ability to apply what they have learned to new situations rather than on their ability to recall specific pieces of information.* This approach would establish in students a "mental set" for the idea that they will have to engage in transfer—that this is an important expectation of them.

All of these pointers have a common aim: to make students aware of transfer as an explicit goal of learning. In a sense, the preceding suggestions ask teachers and students to be more "metacognitive" about the learning process, to overtly and frequently discuss and reflect on how transfer might be promoted. The more teachers incorporate this goal into their daily classroom instruction, according to these researchers, the more likely students will learn in the truest sense of the word.

Formal Reasoning

Many of us associate problem solving with the types of formal reasoning tasks we have encountered in science or mathematics classes in school or on the occasional aptitude tests given in different grades. Among the typical formal reasoning tasks studied by developmental psychologists are class inclusion problems ("If there are six roses and three daisies, are there more flowers or more roses?"), analogies (*boat:rudder* as *bicycle:handlebars*), and transitive inference problems ("If Sue is taller than Becky and Becky is taller than Allison, who is taller, Sue or Allison?"). These tasks share the requirement that the child consider relations among objects to draw a logical conclusion and, as such, allow us to understand more about the child's awareness of logical relationships.

Class Inclusion   In one of Piaget's classic tasks, the class inclusion problem, children are asked questions such as "If there are seven horses and three cows, are there more horses or animals?" (Inhelder & Piaget, 1964). Preoperational and sometimes even concrete operational children often mistakenly say, "There are more horses." Piaget attributed young children's errors on this problem to their failure to understand that one class of objects, in this case horses, can simultaneously also be a part of another class, such as animals. In other words, Piaget said, there are fundamental differences in the logical reasoning abilities of younger versus older children.

However, alternative explanations exist for children's difficulties with class inclusion problems. For example, when children's attention is drawn to the part-whole relations within the problem, they answer correctly more frequently. In one study, five- and six-year-olds were shown pictures of frogs labeled as "mother," "father," and "four babies." In some instances, children were asked, "Who would have more pets, someone who owned the baby frogs or someone who owned the family?" In this case, the word *family* draws the child's attention to the qualities of the group far more than when the question is phrased "Who would have more pets, someone who owned the baby frogs or someone who owned the frogs?" The latter is the form of the standard class inclusion question. Children who were asked questions of the first type were more likely to answer correctly than when they were asked the standard class inclusion question (Markman & Siebert, 1976). Thus, the logic class inclusion tasks demand may be available to preschool children, although their reasoning may be easily disrupted by difficulties in processing the specific content or wording of the problem (Markman, 1989).

Analogies   A common type of formal reasoning task is the analogy, wherein the individual is required to detect a similarity between one set of relations and another; that is, if A:B, then C:? Intuitively, we might judge this type of problem to be difficult for children; but evidence suggests, to the contrary, that three- and four-year-olds can solve analogies if they understand the underlying relations among the stimulus items. For example, Usha Goswami and Ann Brown (1989) showed three-, four-, and six-year-olds pictures laid out in a series depicting analogical relations. One set showed playdough, cut playdough, and an apple. Children were to supply the next item in the series, choosing from a pool of pictures that included a cut apple. A surprising number of children were successful in this task, probably because of their sufficient experiences with objects that have been cut.

An alternative framework for understanding analogical reasoning is provided by Robert Sternberg and his associates (Sternberg & Nigro, 1980; Sternberg & Rifkin, 1979). Sternberg believes analogical reasoning can be partitioned into a number of component processes. One is *encoding*, inputting the relevant features of the related objects. Another is *mapping*, comparing the features of A and C in the analogy. *Inference* refers to noting the relationship between A and B. Sternberg's research reveals that eight-, ten-, and twelve-year-olds all showed evidence of using these subprocesses in solving analogies. The major developmental difference was that older participants carried out these component processes much more rapidly.

Mapping, in fact, may be one of the most rudimentary and early appearing skills in analogical reasoning. In one recent study, three- and four-year-olds had three different sizes of cups lined up in front of them. The experimenter also had three cups of the same relative sizes, but they differed in absolute size from the cups each child had. When the experimenter selected a cup from her array, the children were to select the corresponding cup from theirs. The results showed that children were correct 80 to 90 percent of the time. As just noted, though, familiarity with the items that were used in each mapping problem made a difference; children were more successful when the items were known to them (Goswami, 1995). Thus, the cognitive ability to map relations from one set of items to another may not change developmentally. Rather, the child's growing knowledge base concerning the specific objects themselves and how they might be related may be the key to understanding the growth of analogical reasoning.

Transitive Inferences   If stick A is longer than stick B and B is longer than stick C, what is the relationship between A and C? To solve this problem, the child must perform a *transitive inference;* that is, she must decide on the relationship between two objects based on their relationships to other objects. All the information necessary to solve the problem is available; the child must simply put it together correctly. Piaget (1970) observed that preoperational children have difficulty with problems such as these and suggested that they lack the logical thought structures to make the required inferences.

However, other researchers have noted that children as young as four years show the ability to make transitive inferences when the problem is modified slightly. For example, Peter Bryant and Tom Trabasso (1971) asked preschoolers to learn the relationships among a series of sticks of different sizes, although the children could not see the actual lengths of the sticks. Thus, they learned that A is greater than B, B is greater than C, C is greater than D, and D is greater than E. The critical part of this experiment was that Bryant and Trabasso made sure their participants thoroughly learned the initial premise information. Next, children were asked to compare the lengths of B and D, even though they had not directly learned about the relationship between these two specific sticks. Approximately 78 percent of the four-year-olds correctly stated that B was longer than D. Why were these young children so successful? Bryant and Trabasso maintained that young children are capable of making transitive inferences when their memory for each component of the problem is ensured. When they fail the task, it is not so much because they are illogical as because they have forgotten the initial premises.

Still another explanation has been proposed for young children's failures on transitive inference problems. Charles Brainerd and Valerie Reyna (1990, 1992, 1993) suggest that children's failures on transitive inference problems are less the result of a failure of memory than of their use of a different approach to problem solution. According to these researchers, children use the "gist" of the premise information rather than the precise and accurate details a verbatim memory provides. Thus, they might encode that "things are getting smaller to the right" as they receive information about the relationships among sticks. Sometimes, though, other, irrelevant "gists" interfere or the child's "gist" does not include the full amount of information necessary to solve the problem logically. Under such circumstances, children (and occasionally adults as well) will make errors.

Research on children's formal reasoning thus demonstrates that while preschoolers demonstrate certain basic logical abilities, they improve as their attention, memory, speed of processing, and general knowledge grow. Perhaps the key to children's improvement, though, lies in still another aspect of cognitive development. Some researchers maintain that adolescents are indeed better formal reasoners than younger children because they begin to understand more about the nature and requirements of logical reasoning; that is, they can *think* about what is necessary for thinking. For example, around age ten years, children begin to appreciate the concept of *logical necessity.* In one study, researchers presented fourth- and seventh-graders, as well as college students, with premises and conclusions, some of which did not describe truthful relations (Moshman & Franks, 1986). One set was "If dogs are bigger than elephants and elephants are bigger than mice, then dogs are bigger than mice." Could participants recognize that the conclusion "Dogs are bigger than mice," was logically necessary even though the premise information was not true? Not until about ten or twelve years of age, according to the findings. Fourth-graders unflinchingly attended to the truth value of the premise information; they could not grasp the concept of logical necessity of a problem's solution as the seventh-graders and adults could. Thus, noticeable improvements in the ability to engage in formal reasoning seem to be strongly related to this growth in understanding about the nature of logic (Byrnes & Overton, 1988; Goswami, 1991; Moshman, 1990).

The Development of Scientific Thinking

Most of us have received at least some formal training in the complex type of reasoning called *scientific thinking.* Scientific reasoning involves formulating a hypothesis, designing experiments in which one factor varies while others are held constant, and deciding on the validity of the hypothesis based on the observable evidence. Many of the formal reasoning skills described earlier, such as drawing inferences and analogies, can be seen as components of scientific thinking. According to Piaget, you will recall, this form of logical thought is not observed prior to the start of the formal operational stage, usually at preadolescence. Contemporary research confirms that there are indeed observable developmental accomplishments in scientific reasoning; however, children who are just starting school show impressive knowledge about some of the basic tenets of scientific thinking.

One element of scientific thinking is the ability to see the relationship between a hypothesis and some observable outcome. Let us consider one example used in a study of children's scientific reasoning. The child is presented with a series of pictures depicting the phases of the moon along with two theories about why they occur: (1) clouds cover different portions of the moon at different times, or (2) the moon has a dark and a light side. Then the child hears the evidence: an astronaut reports that the moon is dry and has no water, that he landed on some white rock, and that he later walked on black gravel. Which theory about the moon could possibly be correct? Most first-, third-, and fifth-graders in this study chose the second theory, the one that was consistent with the evidence (Samarapungavan, 1992). Other researchers have confirmed that first-graders can correctly identify whether a specific piece of empirical evidence provides conclusive or inconclusive support for a hypothesis (Sodian, Zaitchik, & Carey, 1991).

Yet scientific thinking involves greater complexities. For example, hypotheses must be formed in the first place and usually several hypotheses are concurrently in the mind of the scientist. Often several variables operate at the same time. Experiments must be designed and conducted and their outcomes coordinated with the hypotheses to determine which variable causes the observed outcomes (Klahr & Dunbar, 1988). It is here that developmental changes are most apparent. When third-graders are asked to generate and evaluate hypotheses by running a series of experiments, they usually are not systematic in designing experiments that isolate the key variable and do not write down the outcomes of their experiments. Sixth-graders show improvements but still design a limited number of experiments, and their experiments are often difficult to interpret. Adults do the best, but not because their reasoning about the relationship between theory and evidence is stronger. Rather, adults can coordinate the generation of hypotheses with the design of the set of experiments necessary to test them (Klahr, Fay, & Dunbar, 1993).

When children are encouraged to engage repeatedly in scientific problem solving, their skills improve noticeably. Deanna Kuhn and her colleagues (Kuhn, Schauble, &

KEY THEME
Nature/Nurture

Research shows that when children have the opportunity to engage in repeated scientific problem-solving, they become more proficient in designing experiments and drawing valid conclusions from them. For example, several variables can potentially determine the speed of a moving car. With experience, children become better able to propose experiments where only one variable changes while the others are held constant so that the cause of greater speed can be determined.

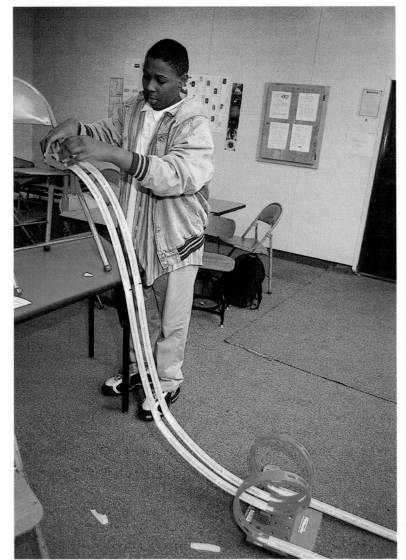

Garcia-Mila, 1992) asked preadolescents to identify which variables affected the speed of a model boat being towed in a tank of water: the water depth, boat size, boat weight, sail color, or sail size. A similar problem involved determining the variables that affect the speed of a racing car. The instructor gave minimal feedback to the students, but they were encouraged to make a plan about what they wished to find out, state what they found out after each experiment, and record their findings in a notebook. The results showed that over only a few weeks of repeated exposure to these problems, students became markedly more proficient at designing valid and focused experiments and at drawing valid inferences from the data they collected. Follow-up studies show that this knowledge is subsequently applied to new problems (Kuhn et al., 1995; Schauble, 1996).

In this chapter, we have chronicled numerous developmental changes in children's attention, memory, and problem solving. The Chronology on the next page outlines the most notable accomplishments. As you can see, the changes involve the ability to input information, manipulate and store it, and direct the flow of information through the system. Whether the information-processing approach will continue to dominate the field of cognitive development as it does now remains to be seen. Undoubtedly, though, this model has been extremely useful in uncovering some of the mysteries of the child's mind.

─Newborn─

─ 1 Yr.

→ Newborn ──────── **Newborn**

■ Shows recognition memory for simple stimuli.

1 Mo. ─

2 Years ──────── 2 Yrs.

2 Mos. ─

■ Has memory span of about two items.
■ Uses naming and looking as simple memory strategies.

─ 3 Yrs.

3 Mos. ─

3 Years

■ Shows recognition memory for fifty-plus items.
■ Has memory span of about three items.
■ Knows scripts for familiar routines.
■ Displays autobiographical memory.
■ Understands that scale models represent real objects.
■ Shows analogical transfer following training and the ability to map relations between sets of stimuli.
■ Can solve simple analogies.

─ 4 Yrs. ──── 4 Mos. ─

─ 5 Yrs. ──── 5 Mos. ─

─ 6 Yrs. ──── 6 Mos. ─

4–6 Years

■ Uses systematic and efficient attention strategies.
■ Has memory span of about four to five items.
■ Can think of several steps in planning solutions to problems.
■ Can solve class inclusion problems.
■ Can solve transitive inference problems.

7 Mos. ─

─ 7 Yrs. ──── 8 Mos. ─

─ 8 Yrs. ──── 9 Mos. ─

7–8 Years

■ Produces rehearsal as a memory strategy.
■ Has memory span of about five to six items.
■ Shows flexibility in planning solutions to problems.

─ 9 Yrs. ──── 10 Mos. ─

─ 10 Yrs. ──── 11 Mos. ─

9–10 Years

■ Shows improvement in focused and selective attention.
■ Produces accurate estimates of memory span.
■ Produces organizational strategies for memory.
■ Can use symbols on maps that are not aligned with the physical space they represent.
■ Appreciates the concept of logical necessity.
■ Develops scientific reasoning skills.

─ 11 Yrs. ──── 12 Mos. ──── **1 Year**

■ Performs simple problem solving by combining subgoals.

13 Mos. ─

─ 12 Yrs.

14 Mos. ─

─ 13 Yrs.

11 Years

15 Mos. ─

■ Produces elaboration strategies for memory.
■ Uses retrieval strategies for memory.

─ 14 Yrs.

16 Mos. ─

13 Years ──────── 15 Yrs.

■ Uses cumulative rehearsal sets.

17 Mos. ─

─ 16 Yrs. ──── 18 Mos. ─

─ 17 Yrs.

─ 18 Yrs.

This chart describes the sequence of cognitive development based on the findings of research. Children often show individual differences in the exact ages at which they display the various developmental achievements outlined here.

CHAPTER RECAP

SUMMARY OF DEVELOPMENTAL THEMES

NATURE/NURTURE   What roles do nature and nurture play in cognitive development?

Some of the changes in cognition documented by information-processing theorists have links to underlying alterations in the structure of the brain. For example, changes in attention and, perhaps, the speed of information processing may be associated with maturation of parts of the central nervous system. Likewise, changes in memory have been observed to accompany the maturation of certain portions of the brain. These connections between cognition and biology point to the role of nature. On the other hand, the child's exposure to specific experiences that nurture the emergence of cognitive skills is also important. As an example, parents and teachers serve as important guides for how to approach cognitive tasks such as planning and transfer of learning.

SOCIOCULTURAL INFLUENCE   How does the sociocultural context influence cognitive development?

The culture in which the child grows up plays a vital role in cognitive development. Cognitive skills such as memory strategies or the notion of autobiographical memory may be transmitted directly by parents, teachers, or other experts in the environment. They may also be transmitted more indirectly through the types of problems and tasks children confront.

CHILD'S ACTIVE ROLE   How does the child play an active role in the process of cognitive development?

Many of the child's cognitive achievements reflect active rather than passive processing. From the child's increasing control of his or her attention to the deployment of memory strategies, from the use of planning in problem solving to the selection of strategies in problems, the portrait of the child that emerges from studies of cognition is of an engaged, dynamic processor of information.

CONTINUITY/DISCONTINUITY   Is cognitive development continuous or discontinuous?

Most information-processing researchers reject the notion that there are qualitative, stagelike changes in cognition with development. Their studies have confirmed that many cognitive achievements in the childhood years, such as improvement in formal reasoning, are related to small, successive increments in component cognitive skills, such as attention and memory.

INDIVIDUAL DIFFERENCES   How prominent are individual differences in cognitive development?

Information-processing theorists have focused on documenting general changes in cognition with age and, until recently, have been relatively unconcerned with individual differences. Nonetheless, the general features of information-processing skill may vary from child to child. A case in point is ADHD, which appears to involve significant disruptions in attention skills. Individual differences may also be observed in the extent and effectiveness with which strategies are implemented in memory and problem solving.

INTERACTION AMONG DOMAINS   How does cognitive development interact with development in other domains?

There are many examples of how cognition is influenced by development in other domains. For example, cognition may be affected by maturation of the central nervous system, which is hypothesized to contribute to the development of sustained attention; the speed of information processing; and memory. Cognition can also be influenced by the child's emotional state, as illustrated by research on eyewitness testimony. Social interactions with parents, teachers, and others form the basis for cognitive development within a given cultural context. At the same time, cognitive development affects how the child functions in other arenas, such as language, emotion, and social interactions.

SUMMARY OF TOPICS

■ THE INFORMATION-PROCESSING APPROACH

Information-processing theories emphasize the flow of information through the cognitive system. *Multistore models* include such structures as the *sensory store, working memory,* and *long-term memory,* along with control processes such as *rehearsal*. *Limited-resource models* describe tradeoffs made between energy used to operate on stimuli and the capacity left over for storage.

■ THE DEVELOPMENT OF ATTENTION

Several important developmental changes in attention occur. These include the child's increasing ability to sustain attention for longer durations, control attention systematically and efficiently, and select certain aspects of the environment to attend to while ignoring others. These changes appear to be tied to maturation of the central nervous system and to advances in other aspects of cognition, such as the ability to think about the potential uses of objects and *metacognition*. A developmental disorder thought to be linked to problems in attention is attention deficit hyperactivity disorder. Neuropsychological studies suggest that advances in memory are associated with changes in the functioning of some portions of the brain.

■ THE DEVELOPMENT OF MEMORY

Although even infants display good *recognition memory,* the ability to *recall* previously seen stimuli increases with age. Improvements in memory result in part from the tendency of older children to spontaneously produce strategies that enhance memory. Among these are *rehearsal, organization, elaboration,* and *retrieval strategies.* Children develop these strategies as their *metamemory,* or awareness of memory, develops. They may also learn strategies indirectly from experiences with structured, organized information. The growth of general knowledge in the form of *semantic memory* and *scripts* is also related to improvements in memory. Another important developmental achievement is the emergence of *autobiographical memory.*

■ THE DEVELOPMENT OF PROBLEM-SOLVING SKILLS

Although infants show the ability to solve simple problems, significant advances in problem solving continue through adolescence. Children show advances in several components of problem solving, including the ability to use representations, to plan, to choose strategies, and to transfer skills from one problem to another. Although preschoolers show basic logical reasoning capabilities, children's ability to engage in formal reasoning improves with age as attention, memory, and general knowledge improve. Another important developmental change is the ability to appreciate the principle of logical necessity. The emergence of scientific reasoning in preadolescence includes the ability to consider how hypotheses and observable data are coordinated.

10 INTELLIGENCE

WHAT IS INTELLIGENCE?

Psychometric Approaches
Information-Processing Approaches
Approaches to Intelligence: An Overview

MEASURING INTELLIGENCE

Atypical Development: Exceptional Intelligence
Standardized Tests of Intelligence
Stability and Prediction
Research Applied to Education: Interpreting IQ Test Scores

FACTORS RELATED TO INTELLIGENCE

Group Differences in IQ Scores
Experiences in the Child's Home
The Child's Sociocultural Environment
Controversy: Can Early Intervention Programs Boost IQ?

CHAPTER RECAP

Summary of Developmental Themes
Summary of Topics

NATURE/NURTURE
What roles do nature and nurture play in the development of intelligence?

SOCIOCULTURAL INFLUENCE
How does the sociocultural context influence the development of intelligence?

CHILD'S ACTIVE ROLE
How does the child play an active role in the development of intelligence?

CONTINUITY/DISCONTINUITY
Is the development of intelligence continuous or discontinuous?

INDIVIDUAL DIFFERENCES
How prominent are individual differences in the development of intelligence?

INTERACTION AMONG DOMAINS
How does the development of intelligence interact with development in other domains?

on Van Nguyen stared intently at the school psychologist's desk. Son was embarrassed to be stuck, and especially embarrassed about the nature of the questions he was having trouble with. After three years in America, this ten-year-old was proud of the English he had learned. But he had been having serious problems with his reading and just couldn't stay focused on his work. The teacher had recommended to his parents that he be tested, but he really didn't understand what the test was for. He was relieved when the school psychologist announced that the test was done.

At lunchtime he approached Manuela Gomez, whom he considered to be an "expert" on American life because her family had lived in the States four years longer than his family had. "What does inscription *mean?" he asked her.*

"Oh, that's easy. It's words you write or carve on something, like a tombstone."

Son was impressed but suspicious. "How did you know that?"

"It's the same as in Spanish: inscripción.*"*

Manuela was acting so superior that he almost didn't want to confess his ignorance. When he asked her another question from the test, she hooted with laughter. "Are you ever dumb! Don't you know anything? Everybody knows Christopher Columbus discovered America. We all knew that back in Chihuahua before we even moved here."

Son's worst fears about himself had just been confirmed. Although the teacher and the school psychologist had tried to explain to him about the test he was to take, he had not really understood. Now he did. And at that moment the truth seemed all too plain to Son: compared to Manuela, he was not intelligent.

Psychologists who have tested large numbers of children and adults on intelligence tests have found noticeable differences in individual performance, such as those that presumably existed between Son and his classmate. What do these differences mean? In contrast to cognitive psychologists, who are interested in identifying *common processes* in children's and adults' thinking, some researchers focus on identifying and explaining *individual differences* in mental capabilities. Researchers look for these differences in subjects' responses on tests of word meanings, general knowledge, and visual-spatial performance and describe the results as a measure of intelligence.

But what *is* intelligence? To the layperson, the term usually includes the abilities to reason logically, speak fluently, solve problems, learn efficiently, and display an interest in the world at large (Siegler & Richards, 1982; Sternberg et al., 1981). Most of us

323

6-Month-Olds	2-Year-Olds	10-Year-Olds	Adults
Recognition of people and objects	Verbal ability	Verbal ability	Reasoning
Motor coordination	Learning ability	Learning ability; problem solving; reasoning (all three tied)	Verbal ability
Alertness	Awareness of people and environment		Problem solving
Awareness of environment	Motor coordination		Learning ability
Verbalization	Curiosity	Creativity	Creativity

Source: Adapted from Siegler & Richards, 1982.

TABLE 10.1

Popular Notions of Age-Specific Intelligence

This table shows the five most important traits that characterize intelligence at different ages according to one survey of college students. The students identified perceptual and motor abilities as most important for infants. They saw problem solving and reasoning as abilities that become increasingly important later in development.

probably have a sense that the abilities to profit from experience and adapt to the environment are also part of intelligent human functioning. We might even postulate that intelligent behavior is defined by different kinds of skills at different ages, as did the college-age participants in one study of popular notions of intelligence (see Table 10.1). Yet despite the average person's ability to give what sounds like a reasonable description of intelligent behavior, in the field of psychology the formal definition of *intelligence* has proven surprisingly elusive. Although the concept has been the subject of research and theorizing for more than a century, no single definition has been commonly agreed on, and no one measurement tool assesses intelligence to everyone's satisfaction.

Despite the lack of consensus on how to define and measure intelligence, we now have many tests designed to measure it in children as well as adults. Most of the commonly used tests assess the kinds of thinking people do in academic settings as opposed to common sense or "practical intelligence" (Sternberg, 1995). These tests are routinely used in schools as well as in medical, mental health, and employment settings to make decisions about educational strategies, therapeutic interventions, or job placements. Given this use of intelligence tests in many different contexts, it is vital that we closely examine the concept of intelligence and how it is measured.

Our objective in this chapter is to present both historical and contemporary ideas about intelligence—what it is, how we measure it, and the factors that influence it—while keeping in mind that many of the long-standing controversies surrounding this topic are still unresolved. For the most part, we will discuss intelligence in terms of the kinds of perceptual, verbal, spatial, and reasoning skills traditionally associated with successful performance in school. We will see, however, that because psychologists have taken a renewed interest in intelligence in recent years, some newer definitions incorporate broader skills such as social adaptability or artistic talent.

WHAT IS INTELLIGENCE?

Among the many attempts to define intelligence, one prominent issue has been and continues to be whether intelligence is a unitary phenomenon or consists of various separate skills and abilities. In the first view, an intelligent person has a global ability to reason and acquire knowledge that manifests itself in all sorts of ways, such as memorizing a long poem or solving a maze. Intelligence by this definition is a general characteristic that shows up in the multiple and varied observable behaviors and activities of any one person. In the second view, an intelligent person may possess specific talents in some areas but not others and so, for instance, may be able to compose a sonata but unable to solve a verbal reasoning problem. The various component skills of intelligence are seen as essentially independent, and each individual may have areas of strength and weakness.

A second major issue has been the best way to conceptualize intelligence. Should it be defined in terms of the *products* individuals generate, such as test scores? Or should it be defined in terms of the *processes* people use to solve problems? The earliest theories about intelligence came from the *psychometric tradition,* which emphasized a product approach, quantifying individual differences in test scores to establish a rank order of capabilities among the subjects tested. More recently, psychologists have put forth alternative ideas about the nature of intelligence based on theories about the processes people employ to acquire knowledge.

Psychometric Approaches

The notion that human beings may differ from one another in certain skills originated in the late nineteenth century with the work of Sir Francis Galton. Galton (1883) believed people differ in their ability to discriminate among varying physical stimuli, such as auditory tones of different pitch, and in their speed of reaction to sensory stimuli. Such differences, according to Galton, are largely innate. Expanding on these ideas, James McKean Cattell (1890) devised a series of psychophysical tests that assessed a person's ability to sense physical stimuli or perform different motor actions. It was Cattell who coined the term *mental test.* Based on subsequent empirical studies, the idea that intelligence is functionally equivalent to psychophysical skill was temporarily shelved, but the notion of testing individuals to compare their levels of performance remained alive.

The first formal intelligence test was created in 1905 by Alfred Binet and Théophilius Simon. Commissioned by the minister of public instruction in Paris to devise an instrument that would identify children who could not profit from the regular curriculum in the public schools due to lower mental abilities, Binet and Simon (1905) designed a test that assessed children's ability to reason verbally, solve simple problems, and think logically. With the Binet-Simon test, the mental testing movement was born, and psychometrics became firmly entrenched as a model for understanding intelligence.

Psychometric models of intelligence are based on the testing of large groups of individuals to quantify differences in abilities. The basic assumption is that some people will perform better than others and that those who perform below some average or normative level are less intelligent, whereas those who perform above that level are more intelligent. Within the general psychometric framework, however, theorists have taken contrasting positions on the exact nature of intelligence.

Spearman's Two-Factor Theory Charles Spearman (1904) believed that intelligence consists of two parts: *g,* a general intelligence factor that he equated with "mental energy," and *s*'s, specific knowledge and abilities such as verbal reasoning or spatial problem solving that are evident only in specific tasks. According to Spearman, the role of *g* is central in the concept of intelligence; *g* is involved in any task requiring cognitive activity and accounts for commonalities in levels of performance that people typically demonstrate in various kinds of intellectual tasks. Thus, the influence of *g* might enable a person to obtain a high score on a verbal test as well as on a test of visual-spatial skill.

Spearman (1923, 1927) claimed to find high correlations among tests of various mental abilities, concluding they were caused by the presence of the single factor *g.* Not all statisticians agreed with Spearman that the data on relatedness of test scores fit his conceptual model. The idea that intelligence is a unitary phenomenon, however, took hold in some theoretical camps, and it continues to be a part of contemporary thinking about intelligence (Thorndike, 1994).

Thurstone's Primary Mental Abilities In contrast to Spearman, Louis Thurstone (1938) believed intelligence is composed of several distinct fundamental capabilities that are completely independent of one another. After analyzing the intelligence test scores of many college students, Thurstone concluded that there was little evidence

KEY THEME

Individual Differences

psychometric model Theoretical perspective that quantifies individual differences in test scores to establish a rank order of abilities.

for *g*. Instead, he proposed that the following seven mental abilities are components of intelligence: *visual comprehension,* as measured by vocabulary and reading comprehension tests; *word fluency,* the ability to generate a number of words (for example, those beginning with *b*) in a short period of time; *number facility,* the ability to solve arithmetic problems; *spatial visualization,* the mental manipulation of geometric forms or symbols; *memory,* the ability to recall lists of words, sentences, or pictures; *reasoning,* the ability to solve analogies or other problems involving formal relations; and *perceptual speed,* the ability to recognize symbols rapidly.

Subsequent studies found that the correlations among Thurstone's seven skill areas were higher than he initially thought, but Thurstone continued to maintain that any underlying general skill is secondary in importance to the separate skill areas themselves (Thurstone, 1947). In Thurstone's conception of intelligence, individuals possess areas of strength and weakness rather than the global entity of intelligence.

Guilford's Structure-of-Intellect Approach   J. P. Guilford (1967, 1985, 1988) extended Thurstone's ideas about discrete mental abilities in a model that proposes 180 factors in intelligence. These factors are generated by three elements: operations, contents, and products. According to Guilford, there are six *operations,* mental processes such as memory and divergent production (the ability to produce several different answers to a question). There are also five *contents,* modalities to which intelligence can be applied. For example, some tasks require visual processing, whereas others are auditory in nature. Finally, there are six *products* that an individual may master; these include units, classes, or relations involving a series of objects. Operations, contents, and products can be combined in a multiplicative fashion to create a 5 × 6 × 6 matrix, resulting in 180 different aspects of intelligence as shown in Figure 10.1.

By giving individuals tests designed to assess specific combinations of contents, operations, and products, Guilford (1985) claimed to find empirical evidence for a substantial number of the factors represented by the small cubes in Figure 10.1. Not all researchers agree, however, that human intellectual abilities can be broken down into all of these separate categories.

Fluid and Crystallized Intelligence   According to Raymond Cattell and John Horn, a distinction can be made between two types of intelligence, each with a unique de-

---

FIGURE 10.1

The Intelligence Cube

Guilford's model of intelligence consists of 180 factors, the products of 5 types of content × 6 products × 6 operations. Each factor (the small cubes) represents a unique feature of intelligence as a whole (the larger cube).

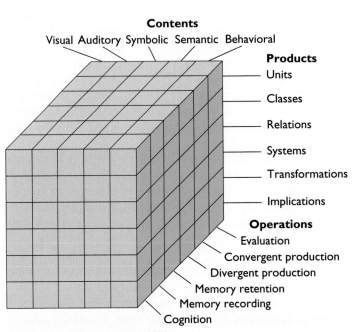

Source: Adapted from Guilford, 1988.

According to Cattell and Horn, crystallized intelligence consists of skills that are acquired as the result of living in a specific culture. For example, these Sri Lankan children have learned how to stilt-fish, a skill which is not likely to be acquired by children living in urban settings or highly industrialized countries.

velopmental course (Cattell, 1971; Horn, 1968; Horn & Cattell, 1967). **Fluid intelligence** consists of biologically based mental abilities that are relatively free of cultural influence, such as the ability to remember a list of words or to group abstract figures together. **Crystallized intelligence** consists of skills one acquires as a result of living in a specific culture, such as knowledge of vocabulary, reading comprehension, or general information about the world. Cattell and Horn believed that fluid intelligence is tied to physiological maturation and that it increases until adolescence, when it levels off, and then declines in later adulthood. On the other hand, they hypothesized that crystallized intelligence increases over much of the life span because individuals continually acquire knowledge from the cultural groups in which they live.

Contemporary researchers have found that fluid intelligence does eventually decline with age, especially after ages seventy to eighty. Crystallized intelligence increases through the middle adult years but also declines with aging, although on a somewhat slower trajectory than fluid intelligence. These decreases are probably linked to physiological changes in the ability of the brain and other portions of the nervous system to process information. It is important to note, however, that wide individual differences occur in age-related changes in intelligence (Brody, 1992; Hertzog, 1989).

In summary, psychometric models of intelligence have been valuable in demonstrating individual differences in performance on questions about general information, vocabulary, nonverbal reasoning, and a variety of other mental tasks. Moreover, although psychometric models have not definitively resolved the debate over whether intelligence is a unitary trait or a cluster of separate abilities, the patterns of correlations among tests for different skills suggest the presence of some underlying general factor as well as several specific skills (Kail & Pellegrino, 1985). Some researchers, however, have challenged the idea that asking people questions about knowledge they have *already* acquired is a good indicator of intelligence. Many have chosen an alternative path to understanding intelligence, studying the processes by which people learn and acquire information.

Information-Processing Approaches

Newer theoretical ideas about intelligence are directly derived from the information-processing model of cognition discussed in Chapter 9. The analysis of each step involved in the chain of cognitive processes, from encoding to retrieval, has generated

KEY THEME
Nature/Nurture

KEY THEME
Sociocultural Influence

KEY THEME
Interaction Among Domains

KEY THEME
Individual Differences

fluid intelligence Biologically based mental abilities that are relatively uninfluenced by cultural experiences.

crystallized intelligence Mental skills derived from cultural experience.

definitions of intelligence based on concepts such as speed of processing, a growing knowledge base, or metacognitive skill. Rather than identifying the structures of mental ability, as the psychometricians did, information-processing theorists have focused on describing the mental processes necessary to accomplish different types of tasks. In this section, we will briefly consider three formulations of intelligence that are based on the general principles of information-processing theory.

Intelligence as Speed of Processing   Individuals vary in the speed with which they conduct certain cognitive activities. For example, studies with infants show that some babies habituate more quickly than others to visual stimuli and show a more pronounced reaction when a novel stimulus appears. Michael Lewis and Jeanne Brooks-Gunn (1981) showed a group of three-month-old infants a picture of twenty straight colored lines repeated over six trials. On the seventh trial, twenty curved colored lines appeared. Some infants in this study were more likely than others to habituate quickly to the repeated straight lines and to show rapid recovery of attention to the novel stimulus. Data from this and other studies suggest that individual differences in visual attention exist from early childhood and reflect variations in the speed of processing visual information (Bornstein & Benasich, 1986; Colombo, 1993).

People also vary in the time it takes them to react in simple psychophysical tasks, an idea that goes back to the work of Galton and Cattell. Consider a typical *choice reaction-time* task. A participant sits in front of an apparatus that contains eight lights, her finger resting on a "home" button. As soon as one of the eight lights comes on, the participant must move her finger to a button below that light to turn it off. People show notable differences in the speed with which they carry out this task. Several researchers have proposed that such individual differences in speed of processing information may be related to intelligence, particularly *g*, the general intelligence originally described by Spearman (Jensen, 1982; Jensen & Munroe, 1979; Vernon, 1983).

Is there evidence that speed of information processing is a component of intelligence? As we will soon see, infants who are rapid habituators perform more effectively than infants who habituate less rapidly on a variety of intelligence and other cognitive tasks when they are several years older. Similarly, researchers have observed at least moderate relationships between reaction-time measures and scores on standardized tests of intelligence among adults (Jensen, 1982; Vernon, 1983); these relationships are weaker among young children (Miller & Vernon, 1996).

At the same time, individuals may differ in their processing speed because of variations in motivation and attention to the task rather than differences in intellectual ability. Some participants in the choice reaction-time task may be distracted by the equipment in the experimental room or may become anxious, and hence slower, in their attempts to do their best. Because reaction times are measured in fractions of a second, they are particularly vulnerable to these types of disruptions. In addition, different cultures and ethnic groups place varying emphases on the value of speed in mental processes. In our own Western culture, we place high priority on getting things done quickly, but the same may not be true for cultures in which time is not a major factor in daily routines. A person who does not have a heightened consciousness of time and speed may not choose to perform mental tasks rapidly, even when he or she has the capability to do so (Marr & Sternberg, 1987). Finally, not all intelligent problem solving is done in a speedy way. Consider the problem of deciding on a career or whom to marry. Rushing to a solution can hardly be considered "smart" in these situations (Sternberg, 1982). Thus, we must be cautious about interpreting the results of tasks that assess speed of processing as an element of intelligence.

Sternberg's Triarchic Theory of Intelligence   Robert Sternberg (1985) has proposed a broad contemporary theory of intelligence based on the principles of information processing. The **triarchic theory** of intelligence (see Figure 10.2) consists of three major subtheories that describe mental functioning in terms of what cognitive psychologists have learned in the past two decades about how people think.

triarchic theory   Theory developed by Robert Sternberg that intelligence consists of three major components: (1) the ability to adapt to the environment, (2) the ability to employ fundamental information-processing skills, and (3) the ability to deal with novelty and automatize processing.

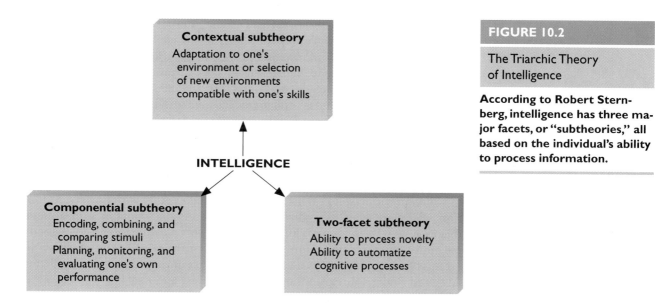

FIGURE 10.2

The Triarchic Theory of Intelligence

According to Robert Sternberg, intelligence has three major facets, or "subtheories," all based on the individual's ability to process information.

The first of these subtheories, called the *contextual subtheory,* asserts that intelligence must be considered as an adaptation to the unique environment in which the individual lives. This means, for example, that we would not administer an intelligence test designed for children in the United States to children from a completely different culture, such as that of the Australian aborigines. In Sternberg's words, intelligence consists of "purposive adaptation to, and selection and shaping of, real-world environments relevant to one's life" (1985, p. 45). Intelligent people are thus able to meet the specific demands their environment places on them—by learning to hunt if their culture requires that skill or by perfecting reading or mathematical skills in societies that stress formal education. By the same token, intelligent people will change their environment to utilize their unique skills and abilities most effectively. For instance, changing jobs or moving to a different locale may demonstrate intelligent adaptive behavior, according to Sternberg.

KEY THEME
Sociocultural Influence

An important aspect of Sternberg's triarchic theory of intelligence is the individual's ability to adapt to the demands of the environment. In our culture, for example, there is heavy emphasis on verbal skills and literacy. Adapting to the environment is part of the contextual subtheory.

The *componential subtheory* focuses on the internal mental processes involved in intelligent functioning, including the ability to encode, combine, and compare stimuli—the basic aspects of information processing described in Chapter 9. Other components of intelligence are higher-order mental processes, such as relating new information to what one already knows. Finally, the ability to plan, monitor, and evaluate one's performance—the metacognitive activities we described in Chapter 9—is also part of intelligent functioning. Thus, Sternberg stresses *how* individuals acquire knowledge rather than *what* they know as indicators of intelligence.

The *two-facet subtheory* describes intelligent individuals in terms of (1) their ability to deal with novelty and (2) their tendency to automatize cognitive processes. Devising a creative solution to an unfamiliar problem or figuring out how to get around in a foreign country are examples of coping successfully with novelty. Automatization takes place when the individual has learned initially unfamiliar routines so well that executing them requires little conscious effort. Learning to read is a good example of this process. The beginning reader concentrates on the sounds symbolized by groups of letters and is very aware of the process of decoding a string of letters. The advanced reader scans groups of words effortlessly and may not even be aware of his mental activities while in the act of reading.

The triarchic theory captures the enormous breadth and complexity of what it means to be intelligent. Sternberg believes it is difficult to assess this human quality with one measure or test score because such a number would mask the extremely different patterns of abilities that individuals show. One child may have exceptional componential skills but behave maladaptively in her environment. Another may be highly creative in tackling novel problems but show poor componential skills. A new test of intelligence based on the tenets of the triarchic theory is in the development phase (Okagaki & Sternberg, 1993).

Gardner's Theory of Multiple Intelligences   Howard Gardner defines intelligence as "an ability (or skill) to solve problems or to fashion products which are valued within one or more cultural settings" (1986, p. 74). Like Sternberg, Gardner believes information-processing abilities are at the core of intelligence. Gardner's (1983) emphasis, though, is on the idea that people often show marked individual differences in their ability to process specific kinds of information. Accordingly, he identified the following seven distinct intelligences:

Linguistic: A sensitivity to the meanings and order of words, as well as the functions of language
Musical: A sensitivity to pitch, tone, and timbre, as well as musical patterns
Logico-mathematical: The ability to handle chains of reasoning, numerical relations, and hierarchical relations
Spatial: The capacity to perceive the world accurately and to transform and recreate perceptions
Bodily-kinesthetic: The ability to use one's body or to work with objects in highly differentiated and skillful ways
Intrapersonal: The capacity to understand one's own feelings and use them to guide behavior
Interpersonal: The ability to notice and make distinctions among the moods, temperaments, motivations, and intentions of others

Gardner finds support for the existence of these discrete areas of intelligence on several fronts. For each skill, he says, it is possible to find people who excel or show genius, such as Mozart, T. S. Eliot, and Einstein. It is also possible, in many instances, to show a loss of or a deficit in a specific ability due to damage to particular areas of the brain. Lesions to the parts of the left cortex specifically dedicated to language function, for example, produce a loss of linguistic intelligence. Yet the other intelligences usually remain intact. Finally, it is possible to identify a core of information-processing operations uniquely relevant to each area. For musical intelligence, one core process is sensitivity to pitch. For bodily-kinesthetic intelligence, it is the ability to imitate the movement made by another person.

KEY THEME
Individual Differences

One of the distinct abilities identified by Gardner in his theory of multiple intelligences is musical intelligence, a sensitivity to pitch, tone, timbre, and musical patterns. According to Gardner, exceptional talent in specific domains such as music may be inborn, but many children can profit from exposure to music.

How do each of the intelligences develop? Gardner believes propensities or talents in certain areas may be inborn, but the child's experiences are also of paramount importance. Some children, for example, may show a unique ability to remember melodies, but all children would profit from exposure to musical sequences. Moreover, Gardner reminds us that it is important to remember the cultural values to which the child is exposed. In our culture, linguistic and logico-mathematical skills are highly valued and are emphasized as measures of school success. Among the Puluwat islanders of the South Pacific, the navigational skills required for successful sailing are critical, and hence spatial intelligence receives great recognition in that culture.

KEY THEME
Nature/Nurture

KEY THEME
Sociocultural Influence

Although no formal test is yet available to assess individuals on the various intelligences, Gardner's theory has refueled the debate over intelligence as a unitary construct versus a set of distinct skills. The theory of multiple intelligences clearly falls into the latter category.

Approaches to Intelligence: An Overview

What is intelligence? The psychometric and information-processing views emphasize reasoning and problem-solving skills as key components of intelligence. Newer approaches have broadened our understanding of intelligence to include adaptability to one's environment, social skill, and even control of one's own body and self-understanding. In addition, psychometric models help to identify patterns of individual differences in performance, and information-processing models have begun to identify and describe the precise mental activities involved in intelligent behavior. Yet few theories explicitly describe the *development* of intelligence. Most models of intelligence are derived from data gathered from young adults and provide few suggestions about the way intelligence changes from early childhood through adulthood.

MEASURING INTELLIGENCE

Over the years, we have come to use the term *IQ* as a synonym for *intelligence*. In fact, the abbreviation IQ means "intelligence quotient" and refers only to the score a person obtains on the standardized intelligence tests now widely used in Western societies. The results of these tests have become so closely associated with intelligence as

How Intelligence Is
Distributed in the
General Population

**Intelligence scores are assumed
to be normally distributed in
the population, with a mean
score of 100. Most people's
scores fall within 15 points (or
one standard deviation) above
or below the mean, and almost
the entire population falls
within three standard deviation
units of the mean. In reality,
a slightly greater number of
individuals than we would theoretically expect fall at the
lower end of the distribution,
probably due to genetic, prenatal, or early postnatal risks that
can affect intelligence.**

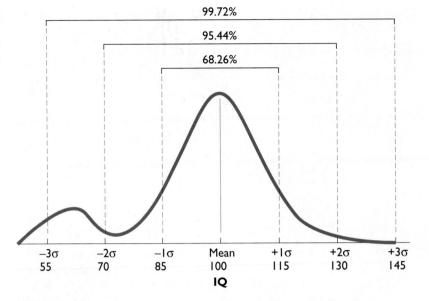

an attribute of human functioning that we have virtually ceased to make a distinction between them. Yet, as we saw in the opening scene about Son, the IQ score may
or may not be a good indicator of intelligent functioning.

Standardized tests of intelligence are based on many shared assumptions about
how this characteristic is distributed among individuals. As Figure 10.3 shows, IQ
scores are assumed to be normally distributed in the population, with the majority
falling in the middle of the distribution and fewer at the upper and lower extremes.
The average or *mean* IQ score on most tests is 100. Usually a statistical measure of
the average variability of scores around the mean, or *standard deviation,* is also calculated. The standard deviation gives a picture of how clustered or spread out the
scores are around the mean. On many tests, the standard deviation has a value of 15.

The normal distribution of scores can also be partitioned into "standard deviation units." As Figure 10.3 shows, the majority of IQ scores (about 68 percent) fall
within one standard deviation on either side of the mean, and almost all scores in the
population (about 99 percent) fall within three standard deviations above or below
the mean. In reality, the percentage of scores below the mean is slightly greater than
the theoretical normal distribution would predict. This fact is probably the result of
genetic, prenatal, or early postnatal factors that can put young infants at risk for
lower intellectual development (Vandenberg & Vogler, 1985; Zigler, 1967).

L ess than 3 percent of the population
falls outside the typical range of intelligence, that is, beyond two standard
deviation units of the mean for IQ scores. A
child who obtains an IQ score greater than
130 is generally regarded as gifted, whereas a child who obtains a score below 70 is
often classified as mentally retarded.

ATYPICAL DEVELOPMENT

Exceptional Intelligence

Giftedness

The U.S. Office of Education has defined giftedness as a capability or potential ability in any of the following areas: (1) intellectual ability, (2) academic aptitude,
(3) creativity, (4) leadership, and (5) visual or performing arts (Marland, 1972).
Gifted children are identified as having exceptional general intellectual skill and may

have unique special talents as well, such as unusual musical ability or facility with mathematics.

Probably the most extensive study of gifted children was conducted by Lewis Terman beginning in 1921 (Terman, 1954; Terman & Oden, 1959). More than a thousand children with IQ scores of 140 or greater were studied longitudinally from early adolescence into their adult years. What were these children like? Contrary to popular stereotypes, they were not frail, sickly, antisocial, "bookish" types. They tended to be taller than average, were physically healthy, and often assumed positions of leadership among their peers. By the time they were young adults, about 70 percent of those in the sample completed college (a very high proportion for that generation), and many obtained advanced degrees. The majority entered professional occupations where they became very productive as adults—authoring books, plays, and scientific articles, for example. Unfortunately, however, because the children in Terman's sample were nominated by their teachers, gifted children who were quieter or did not fit a teacher's conception of a "good student" were probably overlooked. Thus, while the findings of Terman's large-scale study show that gifted children generally enjoyed many successes in life, the results must be viewed with caution.

Does giftedness simply reveal itself naturally during the childhood years? Not according to other researchers examining the underpinnings of exceptional talent. In one study, two children who were expert chess players and one who was an accomplished musician were found to spend many hours practicing their skills under the tutelage of special teachers (Feldman, 1979). In another study, world-class musicians, mathematicians, and athletes reported that their childhood years were marked by strong encouragement of their early natural abilities. Parents, coaches, and teachers were important sources of motivation, and typically these talented individuals spent years in intensive training of their skills (Bloom, 1982).

Drawing on his triarchic theory of intelligence, Robert Sternberg has extended our understanding of giftedness beyond the psychometric criterion of high IQ score. According to Sternberg (1981, 1986), gifted children show several unique information-processing skills. First, when solving problems, they tend to spend much of their time in planning—selecting and organizing strategies and information, for example—and less time in encoding the details stated in the problem. That is, their approach tends to be more "global" than "local," reflecting greater metacognitive skills, an idea that has received support in several studies of gifted children (Alexander, Carr, & Schwanenflugel, 1995). Second, Sternberg hypothesizes that gifted children are better able to deal with novelty and to automatize their information processing. Given novel, unusual insight problems, for example, gifted children are better able than children of average ability to recognize useful strategies for solutions (Sternberg, 1986).

Finally, gifted children are apparently more efficient and speedier in processing stimuli that match their particular talents. Veronica Dark and Camilla Benbow (1993) asked extremely gifted seventh- and eighth-graders to judge, as quickly as they could, whether two stimuli were the same or different. When the stimuli were digits, the response patterns of students most gifted in mathematics showed faster access to numerical representations than other children. The response patterns of students most gifted in verbal skills showed faster access to verbal representations when the stimuli were words. Based on their analyses of many studies of giftedness, Dark and Benbow (1993) concluded that the difference between gifted and other children is not qualitative; rather, it is simply a matter of degree, in this case, the degree to which basic cognitive skills are used quickly and efficiently.

Mental Retardation

The American Association on Mental Retardation defines mental retardation as subaverage intelligence combined with limitations in two or more adaptive behaviors that first become evident during childhood (Luckasson et al., 1992). *Adaptive behavior* refers to a range of social skills typically required to function in the everyday world, such as self-care skills, the ability to get to school or home on one's own, or, eventually, the capacity to find a job and handle personal finances. Within this broad definition, four levels of retardation have been identified: mild, moderate, severe, and profound. Whereas a child with mild retardation can usually be expected to profit from school instruction and eventually hold a job and live independently as an adult, a child with profound retardation will require special assistance throughout life with almost every aspect of daily functioning.

As we saw in Chapters 3 and 4, some instances of mental impairment are linked to genetic factors, as in the case of Down syndrome or PKU, or to experiences in the prenatal or perinatal environment that interfere with brain and central nervous system development and functioning, such as exposure to rubella or oxygen deprivation during birth. When a clear biological cause exists, the retardation is called *organic*. Generally, the most severe forms of retardation fall into this category. In other cases, the retardation has no obvious organic roots but is suspected to have resulted from an impoverished, unstimulating environment, the inheritance of the potential for a low range of intelligence, or a combination of both factors. About 70 to 75 percent of cases of mental retardation fall into this category, called *nonorganic* or *familial retardation* (Zigler & Hodapp, 1986). Usually the level of retardation among children in this second class is mild or moderate.

Do children with mental retardation differ qualitatively from children with at least average intelligence, or do their mental capacities differ only in degree? Psychologists who have studied the cognitive processing of children with familial retardation have noted that they show deficits on a number of fronts. First, they have difficulty focusing attention on the task at hand and become distracted easily. Second, they show notable deficits in working memory and an impoverished general knowledge base. One reason may be that they rarely produce the strategies for remembering typically displayed by children of average or above-average intelligence, strategies such as rehearsal and organization described in Chapter 9. Thus, their ability to retain information in both short- and long-term memory is hampered. Finally, children who have nonorganic retardation often fail to transfer knowledge from one learning situation to another. If the child was trained, for example, to repeat a string of digits to improve recall, he would fail to employ that strategy when given a new but similar task such as recalling a set of letters (Campione, Brown, & Ferrara, 1982). All of these findings suggest that children with mental retardation develop just as children of average intelligence do, only slower. On the other hand, say some experts, we do not know whether children with organic retardation have the same structure of intelligence that others possess. Their developmental progression in attaining cognitive skills may be unique (Zigler & Hodapp, 1986).

Negative stereotypes are often associated with the label "mental retardation," and over the years there has been much debate about what term best capsulizes intellectual impairment. Specialists have offered various alternative labels, such as "slow learners," "exceptional children," or "special-needs children," but these terms are not universally accepted. Other controversies concern the effective care and education of children with mental retardation. The trend in recent years has been to "deinstitutionalize" all but those with the most profound retardation. Likewise, the placement of children with mental retardation in special education schools and classrooms has given way to the practice of *mainstreaming* these children within normal classrooms, where they are encouraged to participate in and benefit from as many regular classroom activities as their abilities permit.

Standardized Tests of Intelligence

Educators, clinicians, and others who must assess and diagnose children have a number of standardized tests to choose from. Usually intelligence tests are administered in special situations, such as when parents or teachers suspect that a child is unusually gifted. Alternatively, there may be a need to assess a child whose schoolwork falls below the level of other children in the class, as in the case of Son described at the beginning of this chapter. Does the child have a learning disability (which is usually accompanied by normal intellectual functioning), or is the child's general ability to learn impaired? Are there other reasons (for example, emotional factors) the child is not performing well? A special educational plan designed to meet the needs of the student is then implemented. Intelligence tests may also be employed to assess the developmental progress of children who are at risk for any one of a number of reasons; perhaps they were premature at birth or suffered some trauma that could affect the ability to learn. Although many children will not have the experience of taking an IQ test, a variety of special circumstances may dictate administering such a test.

How are IQ tests designed? **Psychometricians,** psychologists who specialize in the construction and interpretation of tests, typically administer a new test to a large sample of individuals during the test construction phase, both to assess the test's *reliability* and *validity* (see Chapter 2) and to establish the norms of performance against which to compare other individuals. A central concern is to ensure that each item included in the test is related to the overall concept being measured, in this case, intelligence. Moreover, if the test is valid, the scores obtained should be related to scores on other, similar tests. Needless to say, the business of designing intelligence tests requires careful thought and skill. Some intelligence tests are designed to be administered to individual children; others can be given to large groups. Ethical standards dictate that psychologists be carefully trained in both the administration and scoring of IQ tests before being permitted to administer them.

Infant Intelligence Tests   Most tests of infant intelligence are based on norms for behaviors that are expected to occur in the first year or two of life. Because most of the infant's accomplishments are in the domains of motor, language, and socioemotional development, these areas appear most frequently on the various tests. Almost without exception, the tests are administered individually to infants.

Perhaps the most widely used infant test is the *Bayley Scales of Infant Development,* designed by Nancy Bayley (1993) to predict later childhood competence. The test consists of two scales. The Mental Scale assesses the young child's sensory and perceptual skills, memory, learning, acquisition of the object concept, and linguistic skill. The Motor Scale measures the child's ability to control and coordinate the body, from large motor skills to finer manipulation of the hands and fingers. Table 10.2 shows some sample items from each scale. Designed for infants from one through forty-two months of age, the test yields a *developmental index* for both the mental and the motor scale. That is, the infant's scores are compared to the scores for the standardization sample (the large sample of normal infants whose performance was assessed at the time the test was developed) and are expressed in terms of how much they deviate from the average scores of that sample. The Bayley scales also contain a Behavior Rating Scale to assess the infant's interests, emotions, and general level of activity compared to the standardization sample.

One of the most recently developed measures of infant intelligence is the *Fagan Test of Infant Intelligence,* designed for infants between six and twelve months old and based on infants' recognition memory capabilities. During the test, the child sits on the parent's lap and views a picture for a predetermined period of time. The familiar picture is then presented alongside a novel one, and the infant's looking time to the novel stimulus is recorded. As you saw in Chapter 9, infants show their "memory" for the familiar stimulus by looking longer at the new item. Several of these "novelty problems" are presented in succession. The test is designed to screen for children at risk for intellectual deficits based on the premise that their response to novelty is depressed. In one study, scores infants obtained on the Fagan Test of Infant Intelligence correlated +.49 with their scores on several standard tests of intelligence at age three years. Furthermore, a series of studies found that if infants directed fewer than 53 percent of their visual fixations to the novel stimuli, they were especially likely to fall into the category of "intellectually delayed" (Fagan & Montie, 1988).

psychometrician Psychologist who specializes in the construction and interpretation of standardized tests.

TABLE 10.2	Sample Items from the Bayley Scales of Infant Development	
Age	**Mental Scale**	**Motor Scale**
2 months	Turns head to sound Plays with rattle Reacts to disappearance of face	Holds head erect and steady for 15 seconds Turns from side to back Sits with support
6 months	Lifts cup by handle Looks for fallen spoon Looks at pictures in book	Sits alone for 30 seconds Turns from back to stomach Grasps foot with hands
12 months	Builds tower of 2 cubes Turns pages of book	Walks with help Throws ball Grasps pencil in middle
17–19 months	Imitates crayon stroke Identifies objects in photograph	Stands alone on right foot Walks up stairs with help
23–25 months	Matches pictures Uses pronoun(s) Imitates a 2-word sentence	Laces 3 beads Jumps distance of 4 inches Walks on tiptoe for 4 steps
38–42 months	Names 4 colors Uses past tense Identifies gender	Copies circle Hops twice on 1 foot Walks down stairs, alternating feet

Source: Bayley Scales of Infant Development—Copyright © 1969 by the Psychological Corporation. Reproduced by permission. All rights reserved. "Bayley Scales of Infant Development" is a registered trademark of the Psychological Corporation.

Individual IQ Tests for Older Children   The two most widely used individually administered intelligence tests for school-age children are the Stanford-Binet Intelligence Scale and the Wechsler Intelligence Scale for Children–III (or WISC-III). Both are based on the psychometric model and measure similar mental skills.

The *Stanford-Binet Intelligence Scale,* adapted from the original Binet scales by Lewis Terman of Stanford University, was most recently revised in 1986 (Terman, 1916; Terman & Merrill, 1937; Terman & Merrill, 1973; Thorndike, Hagen, & Sattler, 1986). When Binet originally designed the test, he chose mental tasks the average child at each age could perform. He also assumed that children of a specific age—say, eight years—who performed as their older counterparts—say, ten years—did had a higher *mental age.* By the same token, an eight-year-old who passed only the items the average six-year-old could answer had a lower mental age. Thus, intelligence was thought to be the extent to which children resemble their agemates in performance.

Terman translated, modified, and standardized the Binet scales for use in the United States. He also borrowed from William Stern, a German psychologist, an equation for expressing the results of the test. The child's **intelligence quotient,** or **IQ,** was computed as follows:

$$IQ = \text{mental age/chronological age} \times 100$$

Thus, a ten-year-old who obtained a mental age score of 12 would have an IQ of 120. The Stanford-Binet Intelligence Scale rapidly came into use among educators and clinicians eager to find a useful diagnostic tool for children.

The Stanford-Binet test assesses four broad areas of mental functioning: verbal reasoning, abstract/visual reasoning, quantitative reasoning, and short-term memory. The test is scaled for use with individuals from two years of age through adulthood. During the administration of the test, children are given tasks according to year level. Once they fail all or most of the tasks for two consecutive year levels, the test session is terminated. In the newest edition of the Stanford-Binet, the concept of mental age has been replaced by a **deviation IQ.** The child's score in each of the four test areas is compared to those of similar-age children in the standardization sample, and an IQ score is obtained for each. An overall IQ score can also be computed. Thus, this test permits psychologists to not only assess the child's overall abilities but also isolate specific areas of strength and weakness.

intelligence quotient (IQ)
Numerical score received on an intelligence test.

deviation IQ   IQ score computed by comparing the child's performance with that of a standardization sample.

The *Wechsler Intelligence Scale for Children,* the major alternative to the Stanford-Binet, is scaled for use with children ages six through sixteen years. The original version was constructed in 1949 by David Wechsler and most recently revised in 1991 (Wechsler, 1991). The revised version, called the WISC-III, contains three scales: (1) the Verbal Scale, which includes items assessing vocabulary, arithmetic skills, digit span performance, and knowledge of general information; (2) the Performance Scale, which includes tests of visual spatial skill, puzzle assembly, and arranging pictures to form a story; and (3) a Full Scale IQ, which represents a composite of the two scales. Thus, like the Stanford-Binet, this test allows the examiner to assess patterns of strength and weakness in the child's mental abilities. In addition, like the Stanford-Binet, the child's score on the WISC-III is computed on the basis of the deviation IQ. Figure 10.4 shows some items resembling those from the Verbal and Performance scales of the WISC-III.

VERBAL SCALE

General Information
  1. How many nickels make a dime?
  2. Who wrote *Tom Sawyer?*

General Comprehension
  1. What is the advantage of keeping money in a bank?
  2. Why is copper often used in electrical wires?

Arithmetic
  1. Sam had three pieces of candy and Joe gave him four more. How many pieces of candy did Sam have all together?
  2. If two buttons cost fifteen cents, what will be the cost of a dozen buttons?

Similarities
  1. In what way are a saw and a hammer alike?
  2. In what way are an hour and a week alike?

Vocabulary
  This test consists simply of asking, "What is a _____?" or "What does _____mean?" The words cover a wide range of difficulty.

PERFORMANCE SCALE

Picture Arrangement

I want you to arrange these pictures in the right order so they tell a story that makes sense. Work as quickly as you can. Tell me when you have finished.

Object Assembly

Put this one together as quickly as you can.

Source: Simulated items similar to those in the Wechsler Intelligence Scale for Children–Revised. Copyright © 1974 by The Psychological Corporation. Reproduced by permission. All rights reserved. "Wechsler Intelligence Scale for Children" and "WISC" are registered trademarks of the Psychological Corporation.

FIGURE 10.4

Sample Items from the Wechsler Intelligence Scale for Children–III

The WISC-III contains two scales, the Verbal Scale and the Performance Scale. Shown here are examples that resemble items from the several subtests that contribute to each scale.

A relatively new intelligence test for two-through-twelve-year-olds is the *Kaufman Assessment Battery for Children* or *K-ABC* (Kaufman & Kaufman, 1983). This test is based on the assumption that intelligence is related to the quality of mental processing; the focus is on how children produce correct solutions to problems rather than on the content of their knowledge. The test includes three scales: (1) the Sequential Processing Scale, which assesses the ability to solve problems in a step-by-step fashion; (2) the Simultaneous Processing Scale, which tests the ability to solve problems through integration and organization of many pieces of information; and (3) the Mental Processing Composite, a combination of the first two scales. The K-ABC also includes an Achievement Scale to assess knowledge the child has acquired in the home and school. Figure 10.5 illustrates some of the items found on the K-ABC.

Most of the items on the K-ABC were specifically designed to be neutral in content so that processing differences among children could be validly assessed; that is, the intent was to minimize the influence of the child's previous learning history on performance. In addition, the emphasis in test administration is on obtaining the child's best performance. Whereas administration of the Stanford-Binet and the

FIGURE 10.5

Sample Items from the Kaufman Assessment Battery for Children

The K-ABC contains a Sequential and a Simultaneous Processing Scale. One goal of this test is to assess intelligence apart from the specific content children already have learned.

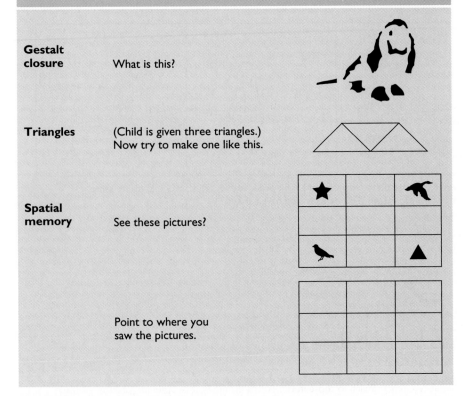

SEQUENTIAL PROCESSING

Hand movements	Watch my hand. Now you try it.	
Number recall	Say these numbers just as I do.	5 – 4 – 8 – 1 – 10
Word order	Cat–hand–shoe–ball. Now touch the pictures that I named.	

SIMULTANEOUS PROCESSING

Gestalt closure	What is this?
Triangles	(Child is given three triangles.) Now try to make one like this.
Spatial memory	See these pictures?
	Point to where you saw the pictures.

Source: Kaufman & Kaufman, 1983.

WISC-III requires strict adherence to test protocol, examiners giving the K-ABC are encouraged to use alternative wording, gestures, or even languages other than English to make sure the child understands what is expected. Thus, in terms of content and mode of administration, the K-ABC represents a departure from many traditional tests of intelligence.

Group Tests of Intelligence   Not all intelligence tests are administered to individual children. Many of us remember having our normal school routine altered so the class could take a special test, one that we were told would assess our special talents and abilities. Group tests are obviously less time consuming and more efficient to administer and score than individual tests. However, because children must work relatively independently on the group test, they may be at a disadvantage if they have poor reading skills or language difficulties. Moreover, individual tests often yield clinical insights apart from the responses to the test items themselves; a school psychologist, for example, might note during the test session that a child is overly anxious or has a poor attention span. Such insights are lost in group testing situations. Despite these drawbacks, however, group tests have been shown to be as reliable and valid as individual tests (Lennon, 1985). Some examples of group tests include the *Otis-Lennon School Ability Test,* the *Differential Aptitude Tests,* and the *Test of Cognitive Skills.*

Intelligence Tests: An Overview   In summary, the most widely used intelligence tests are based on the idea that levels of performance on academic types of tasks reveal something about an individual's general mental abilities. They often assume intelligent persons have acquired a specific body of knowledge that many other members of our Western industrialized culture have also obtained. Newer tests, such as the *Fagan Test of Infant Intelligence* and the *Kaufman Assessment Battery,* assess intelligence from alternative perspectives that emphasize differences in mental processing activities such as recognition memory capacity. So far, however, no test captures the breadth of human intelligent functioning as it displays itself in adaptive behavior overall or in specific dimensions such as social competence, artistic talent, or other nonacademic skills.

Stability and Prediction

Intelligence tests were first developed with the goal of predicting children's future functioning. Binet, you recall, was asked to design a tool that would anticipate children's achievement in school. Those who followed with other theories and assessment tools for measuring intelligence likewise assumed, either explicitly or implicitly, that scores on the tests would forecast the individual's successes or failures in some areas of life. Moreover, many (although not all) psychologists assumed "intelligence" is a quality people carry with them over the whole life span. They believed, in other words, that IQ scores would show continuity and stability.

The Stability of IQ   If intelligence is a reasonably invariant characteristic, a child tested repeatedly at various ages should obtain approximately the same IQ scores. In one major longitudinal research project, the Berkeley Growth Study, a group of children was given intelligence tests every year from infancy through adulthood. The correlations between the scores obtained during the early school years and scores at ages seventeen and eighteen years were generally high; the correlation between IQ scores at ages seven and eighteen years, for example, was .80 (Jones & Bayley, 1941; Pinneau, 1961). Even though the results point to a moderate degree of stability, however, about half of the sample showed differences of 10 points or more when IQ in the early school years was compared to IQ in adolescence.

In another extensive project, the Fels Longitudinal Study, the stability of intelligence was assessed from the preschool years to early adulthood. Although correlations for scores were high when the ages were adjacent, they were much lower as the years between testing increased; the correlation between IQ score at ages three and four years, for example, was .83, but dropped to .46 between ages three and twelve years. Furthermore, as in the Berkeley data, individual children frequently showed dramatic changes in scores—sometimes as much as 40 points—between ages two and seventeen years (McCall, Appelbaum, & Hogarty, 1973; Sontag, Baker, & Nelson, 1958). Taken together, the results of these two major longitudinal studies suggest that for many children, IQ scores can be stable, especially if the two test times are close together, but large fluctuations in individual scores are also possible.

Why do the scores of some children shift so dramatically? The presence or absence of family stress can be a factor. Children in the Berkeley study who showed significant declines in IQ often experienced a dramatic alteration in life experience, such as loss of a parent or a serious illness (Honzik, Macfarlane, & Allen, 1948). Similarly, a recent longitudinal study found a relationship between IQ scores and the number of environmental risk factors to which a child is exposed (Sameroff et al., 1993). As children matured from ages four to thirteen years, those with lower IQ scores also experienced a greater number of risks, factors such as unemployment of a parent, physical illness of a family member, or absence of the father from the household. The child's personality attributes or parental interaction styles can also play a role. In the Fels study, children who showed gains in IQ were described as independent, competitive in academics, and self-initiating. In addition, the parents of these children encouraged intellectual achievement and used a discipline style that emphasized moderation and explanation. In contrast, children whose IQ scores decreased with age had parents who were overly restrictive or permissive in discipline style (McCall, Appelbaum, & Hogarty, 1973). Qualities of a parent's personality, a parent's style of interaction with the child, and the type of home environment provided can also contribute to instability in IQ scores (Pianta & Egeland, 1994). This body of studies suggests that IQ scores can be vulnerable to environmental influences that can affect the child's performance on a test at a given point in time or, more broadly, his or her motivation to achieve in the intellectual domain.

KEY THEME
Nature/Nurture

The Stability of Infant Intelligence   The correlations between scores on infant intelligence tests and IQ scores in later childhood have been particularly low, at least according to research conducted before the start of this decade (Kopp & McCall, 1980; McCall, Hogarty, & Hurlburt, 1972). One review of studies measuring IQ at age one year and again at ages three through six years found that the average correlation was only .14 (Fagan & Singer, 1983). In another review, Nancy Bayley (1949) reported essentially no relationships between scores obtained in the first four years of life and those obtained in young adulthood. Only when children reached age five years were correlations of .60 seen with adult scores (see Figure 10.6).

Several hypotheses have been advanced to explain why infant IQ scores do not correlate closely with scores later in childhood. One possibility, of course, is that there is no such thing as a general intelligence factor (or *g*) or, if it exists, it is not a stable trait. Another possibility is that intelligence in infancy differs qualitatively from intelligence in later years, implying that intellectual development is discontinuous. One problem in drawing any conclusions is that the types of skills measured by infant intelligence tests are very different from those measured by tests such as the Stanford-Binet and WISC-III. Recall, for example, some of the items from the Bayley Scales of Infant Development, many of which center on the child's sensory and motor accomplishments: the ability to roll over, reach, or jump on one foot. We have little reason to believe the infant's skill in these areas should be related to the verbal, memory, and problem-solving skills measured by traditional IQ tests for older children.

On the other hand, recent tests that assess the infant's response to familiar and novel stimulus items hold more promise in identifying those features of mental functioning that might remain constant over a span of years. Recall that the Fagan Test of Infant Intelligence, based on the infant's tendency to respond to novelty, correlates closely with IQ scores three years later. Several other researchers have reported strong relationships among recognition memory, speed of habituation, and visual reaction time during infancy, and IQ up to age eleven years (Bornstein & Sigman, 1986;

KEY THEME
Continuity/Discontinuity

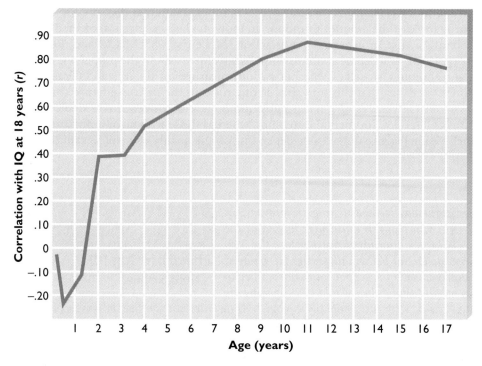

FIGURE 10.6

Is Intelligence Stable over Time?

The graph shows the correlations between IQ scores obtained in infancy and childhood and IQ scores at age eighteen years. Note that IQ scores obtained before age four years are poor predictors of subsequent IQ.

Source: Adapted from Bayley, 1949.

Dougherty & Haith, 1997; McCall & Carriger, 1993; Rose & Feldman, 1995). When the characteristics of visual attention are used as measures, mental development seems to be more continuous than developmental psychologists previously thought. Moreover, these data suggest that the ability to discern the familiar from the novel may represent a fundamental cognitive skill that plays a role in other higher-order mental processes.

The Predictive Utility of IQ Tests   What do IQ tests predict? IQ tests do a good job of telling us which children will be successful in school and which will have difficulties. Most studies have found that the correlations between intelligence tests and measures of educational achievement average about .50, with the correlations slightly higher for elementary school children than for high school or college students (Brody & Brody, 1976; Jensen, 1980). In addition, the correlations are strongest with academic subjects that emphasize verbal skills, such as reading (Horn & Packard, 1985). One reason IQ scores predict school achievement so successfully is that many of the skills assessed in intelligence tests overlap with the skills essential to educational success. Verbal fluency, the ability to solve arithmetic problems, and rote memory, some of the abilities IQ tests measure, are part of most children's school routines. Thus, IQ tests predict best exactly what Binet originally designed them to foretell.

Do IQ tests predict any developmental outcomes other than school success? IQ scores are related to job status during adulthood, according to one research program. In his longitudinal study of children with IQs of 140 or higher, Lewis Terman (Terman, 1925; Terman & Oden, 1959) found that many of these exceptionally bright individuals eventually became scientists, executives, and college faculty members. As usual, however, we must be cautious about how we interpret correlational data. If, as we saw earlier, IQ scores are strongly related to educational achievement, it may be that occupational success is the result of education and not a direct outcome of IQ (Fulker & Eysenck, 1979; Jencks, 1972).

Aside from these relationships, do IQ scores predict other measures of success in life? Social scientists disagree. According to some, IQ scores predict economic status in adulthood (Herrnstein & Murray, 1994); others claim that IQ scores do not necessarily forecast the amount of money an individual earns, physical or mental health, job satisfaction, or general life satisfaction (M. Lewis, 1983; McClelland, 1973; Sternberg, 1995). The debate abounds with disagreements about the proper use of statistical techniques as well as whether various measures of IQ are valid (Fraser, 1995). Suffice it to say that this topic has strong roots in the nature-nurture controversy; generally, advocates of a nature position believe intelligence is a stable trait that affects later developmental outcomes, whereas those who favor a nurture position believe intelligence is malleable depending on the quality of a child's experiences.

A number of factors can affect a child's performance on an IQ test, including unfamiliarity with the adult administering the test and language and cultural barriers that may interfere with the child's performance. Therefore, IQ scores must be interpreted with caution.

T*he day seemed to drag on forever. Son Van Nguyen must have looked at the clock a hundred times before the 3:00* P.M. *dismissal bell finally rang. He trudged slowly toward the school counselor's office to meet his family; they would be discussing his test results with the school psychologist. As he entered the office, he saw his parents already seated, silent and looking as apprehensive as he felt.*

RESEARCH APPLIED TO EDUCATION

Interpreting IQ Test Scores

After a brief greeting, the school psychologist launched into a description of the test Son had taken. Then she suddenly stopped.

"Do your parents understand English?" she asked.

"No," he replied softly.

"I should have realized that. Can you translate my comments for them?"

"I can try," responded Son as his confidence slowly resurfaced. "I often have to do that for my parents."

"The main thing you should tell them is that you did very well on many parts of the test." Son was visibly relieved. Maybe he had at least some intelligence, he thought.

The psychologist continued, "You just need to continue to work on your English and . . ."

"I borrowed some books from the library," interrupted Son as he pulled one from his backpack. "See? This one is all about Christopher Columbus." He stopped, looking up sheepishly as he realized he had not waited for the psychologist to finish.

"That's terrific!" she laughed. "Now can you please tell your parents what I said?"

Because of the controversy surrounding IQ tests—which (if any) tests are most valid, for example—and because scores on IQ tests can fluctuate markedly for any individual child, many psychologists advocate that educators and parents use caution when interpreting test scores. Here are several important aspects of testing to keep in mind:

1. *Recognize that a child may obtain a low score on a given test because of poor motivation, anxiety about taking a test, unfamiliarity with the English language, or vastly different cultural experiences.* Psychologists who administer tests are trained to try to make the child feel comfortable, but it may be impossible to make him or her feel completely free of stress under the usual test-taking conditions: a separate, perhaps strange room, an unfamiliar adult, lots of questions with little feedback about the answers. Moreover, barriers created by language and cultural differences may be difficult to remove. These issues are addressed later in this chapter when we discuss cultural differences in IQ scores.

2. *Avoid labeling a child on the basis of an IQ score as an "underachiever" or a "slow learner," because this practice creates its own set of risks.* For example, teachers and parents may lower expectations of that child, a phenomenon that can, in turn, further lower her achievement. This is an example of a "self-fulfilling prophecy."

3. *Be aware that IQ test scores usually do not have direct implications for specific remedial education practices or instructional techniques.* The assignment of a child to a particular reading group or math skill level has less to do with the number the child

received on an IQ test than with his successes or failures on various class assignments and observations of his behavior and problem-solving strategies in the classroom *(Boehm, 1985; Bruer, 1994).* In other words, optimizing performance in and out of the classroom, regardless of the scores on intelligence tests, should remain the primary goal of teachers and parents.

These caveats do not necessarily mean IQ tests are useless. They may give a clinician a good sense of the child's pattern of strengths and weaknesses, can assist in the diagnosis of learning problems, and give other clinical insights. However, care must be taken not to focus on the single number—the IQ score—to the exclusion of other information about the child (Weinberg, 1989).

FACTORS RELATED TO INTELLIGENCE

KEY THEME
Nature/Nurture

In Chapter 3, we saw that genetics can influence intelligence. Chromosomal abnormalities and single-gene effects such as fragile X syndrome, Down syndrome, and PKU can have profound consequences for the child's intellectual growth. The higher correlations among IQ scores of identical twins reared apart compared to fraternal twins or nontwin siblings reared in the same environment and the strong correlations between IQs of adopted children and their biological parents also suggest a role for heredity.

Yet even if we agree that genetic differences contribute, perhaps even substantially, to the child's intellectual competence, it would be a mistake to conclude that IQ scores are not influenced by environmental experiences (Angoff, 1988; Scarr, 1981). Consider two traits very strongly influenced by heredity: physical height and the presence of the trait for PKU. In each instance, the presence of the genotype bears a great resemblance to the phenotype. Yet it is also true that environmental factors can influence the eventual outcome for the child. Recall from the discussion of secular trends in physical height in Chapter 5, and also from Chapter 3, that dietary modifications for infants born with PKU can result in essentially normal mental development. In each case, a highly canalized human characteristic is modified by the environment. The ever-present role of the environment is an important factor to keep in mind as we discuss the roots of intelligence.

What factors are especially important in shaping the child's intellectual attainments? We begin by examining group differences in IQ scores, findings that have provided much of the backdrop for the nature-nurture debate. Next, we examine those elements of the child's home experience that may be crucial to mental growth as well as the role of the sociocultural environment in shaping specific mental skills. Finally, we consider the impact of early intervention programs on the intellectual attainment of children from culturally different backgrounds. In each case we will see that there are many conditions, even given the contributions of heredity, under which intelligence is not fixed but modified by the timing, extent, and range of environmental experiences.

Group Differences in IQ Scores

Children from different socioeconomic and ethnic backgrounds do not perform equally well on traditional IQ tests. One well-established finding is that African American children in the United States typically score 15 points lower than Caucasian children on tests such as the Stanford-Binet and the WISC (Jensen, 1980; Loehlin, Lindzey, & Spuhler, 1975). Another finding is that children from lower socioeconomic classes obtain lower IQ scores than those from middle and upper classes (Deutsch, Katz, & Jensen, 1968; Lesser, Fifer, & Clark, 1965). Of the many hypotheses put forward about the sources of these differences, some have rekindled the nature-nurture debate and others focus on the validity of IQ tests for children who are members of minority and lower socioeconomic groups.

Racial Differences in IQ and Nature Versus Nurture   In 1969, Arthur Jensen published a paper suggesting that racial differences in IQ scores could, in large part, be accounted for by heredity. According to Jensen, there is a high degree of *heritability* in IQ; that is, about 80 percent of the variation in IQ scores in the population could be explained by genetic variation. He argued that because racial and ethnic subgroups within the population tend not to marry outside their groups, African American–Caucasian differences in IQ scores have a strong genetic component.

Jensen's propositions created a storm of controversy, one that has reemerged as a result of similar claims made more recently by Richard Herrnstein and Charles Murray (1994). One of the most immediate criticisms of Jensen's argument (which has also been applied to its modern-day counterpart) was that *within-group* estimates of heritability cannot be used to explain *between-group* differences in performance. Even if the heritability of IQ were .80 for both Caucasian and African American populations (actually the heritability estimates for IQ were derived solely from samples of Caucasian children and their families), other factors, such as differences in the environmental experiences of each group, could not be ruled out in explaining racial differences in IQ scores (Loehlin, Lindzey, & Spuhler, 1975). For example, a 15-point difference in IQ could still arise if most Caucasian children grew up in enriched environments and most African American children experienced environments that did not promote optimal intellectual development.

A **cross-fostering study** by Sandra Scarr and Richard Weinberg (1976, 1978, 1983) in which children were raised in environments markedly different from those of their biological families demonstrated just how this effect might take place. In their transracial adoption study, Scarr and Weinberg selected 101 Caucasian middle-class families that had adopted African American children, most of whom were under one year of age at the time of adoption. Many of these families also had biological children of their own. The adoptive families were highly educated, were above average in occupational status and income, and had high IQ scores. The biological families of the adopted children had lower educational levels and lower-status occupations.

Scarr and Weinberg found that the average IQ among the African American adopted children was 106, higher than the average score of both African American children and those in the general population. The researchers argued that because the adopted children were raised in environments that exposed them to Caucasian culture and the verbal and cognitive skills customarily assessed in IQ tests, they performed better than African American children with similar genetic backgrounds who did not have that experience. At the same time, however, the IQs of the adopted children were more strongly correlated with the educational levels of their biological parents ($r = 0.36$) than with the IQs of their adoptive parents ($r = 0.19$). Thus, the role of heredity cannot be ruled out either.

Many researchers reject a genetic explanation of racial differences in IQ as too simplistic. We saw in Chapter 3 that heredity and environment interact in complex ways to produce varied developmental outcomes; neither by itself is sufficient to explain most human behaviors. Furthermore, in the United States race is a variable confounded by the other variables of social class, educational achievement, educational opportunities, and income. All of these factors can contribute to the types of learning experiences young children undergo. Parents with greater financial resources can provide the books, toys, and other materials that stimulate intellectual growth. Moreover, families with economic stability are likely to experience less stress than economically unstable families, a factor that can be related to intellectual performance, as we saw earlier in this chapter. Rather than settling the nature-nurture question, then, racial differences in IQ have served to highlight the complexity of interactions among variables associated with intelligence.

cross-fostering study   Research study in which children are reared in environments that differ from those of their biological parents.

Test Bias Another hypothesis put forth to account for group differences in IQ scores is based on the notion of **test bias**. According to this view, the content of traditional tests is unfamiliar to children from some social or cultural backgrounds. In other words, traditional psychometric tests are not *culturally fair*. Recall the dilemma Son Van Nguyen faced at the beginning of this chapter and the erroneous conclusion he drew about his own intelligence based on his failure to define *inscription* and to answer the question "Who discovered America?" Unfortunately, his IQ test score may reflect the same conclusion. Children who have not encountered such specific information in their own cultural experiences will fail those items and score lower on many intelligence tests.

KEY THEME
Sociocultural Influence

What happens when tests that are more culturally fair are administered to children from varied sociocultural backgrounds? The research findings are mixed. In Chapter 7, you were introduced to the Raven Progressive Matrices, a nonverbal test of reasoning ability that is assumed to contain minimal cultural bias. Caucasian children still score significantly higher on this test than African American children do (Jensen, 1980). Yet when another culturally fair test, the Kaufman Assessment Battery, was administered to children of different cultural backgrounds, the difference in test scores between Caucasian and African American children was smaller than when tests such as the WISC were given (Kaufman, Kamphaus, & Kaufman, 1985).

Finally, there are questions about whether minority children have the same experiences with, and attitudes toward, taking tests that majority children do. Some of the skills required to perform well on standardized tests include understanding directions, considering all response alternatives before selecting one, and attending to one item at a time (Oakland, 1982). Minority children may lack this basic "savvy" regarding how to take tests. Since most tests do not permit examiners to be flexible in administering them, they may underestimate minority children's skills (Miller-Jones, 1989). Moreover, minority children may score lower simply because they do not see the point of performing well or have not acquired the same drive to achieve in academic settings that is part of the majority culture (Gruen, Ottinger, & Zigler, 1970; Zigler & Butterfield, 1968). For some, IQ tests may even represent a part of the majority culture that is to be rejected outright (Ogbu, 1994).

Not all researchers are convinced that test bias and motivational factors play a large part in explaining the lower IQ scores of certain groups of children (Jensen, 1980). Even for the skeptics, however, these ideas have highlighted the importance of structuring test situations so that *all* children are given the opportunity to display their best performance.

Experiences in the Child's Home

The generally lower performance of children from minority groups and lower socioeconomic classes on IQ tests has prompted many researchers to take a closer look at how interactions in the home as well as the values of the larger culture might affect intellectual development. Not surprisingly, some elements in caregiver-child interactions are related to higher scores on IQ tests.

KEY THEME
Nature/Nurture

The HOME Inventory In 1970, an ambitious project got under way in Little Rock, Arkansas. Initiated by Bettye Caldwell and her associates (Caldwell & Bradley, 1978), the goal of the project was to identify characteristics of the young child's environment that might be related to later competence, including intellectual achievement. A sample of infants and their parents was recruited for a longitudinal study that would last eleven years.

The *Home Observation for Measurement of the Environment (HOME)* inventory was designed to measure a number of characteristics of the child's home surroundings, including the quality of caregiver-child interactions, the availability of objects and activities to stimulate the child, and the types of experiences family members provide to nurture the child's development (see Table 10.3 for the subscales and

test bias Idea that the content of traditional standardized tests does not adequately measure the competencies of children from diverse cultural backgrounds.

(1) Emotional and verbal responsivity of mother
Sample item: Mother caresses or kisses child at least once during visit.

(2) Avoidance of restriction and punishment
Sample item: Mother does not interfere with child's actions or restrict child's movements more than three times during visit

(3) Organization of physical and temporal environment
Sample item: Child's play environment appears safe and free of hazards.

(4) Provision of appropriate play materials
Sample item: Mother provides toys or interesting activities for child during interview.

(5) Maternal involvement with child
Sample item: Mother tends to keep child within visual range and to look at the child often.

(6) Opportunities for variety in daily stimulation
Sample item: Child eats at least one meal per day with mother and father.

Source: Adapted from Elardo & Bradley, 1981.

KEY THEME
Interaction Among Domains

some sample items). Researchers collected data for the inventory through interviews and direct observations in the children's homes and gave children in the sample standard intelligence and school achievement tests. The results identified several key features of the home environment as being related to subsequent IQ (Bradley, 1989).

First, significant correlations were found among several measures of the home environment taken at age twelve months and children's IQ scores at ages three and four-and-a-half years. Particularly important were scales that measured parental emotional and verbal responsivity to the child, the availability of appropriate play materials, and parental involvement with the child (Bradley & Caldwell, 1976; Elardo, Bradley, & Caldwell, 1975). The correlations among these factors and the children's later IQ ranged from .39 to .56. Second, HOME scores at age two years were significantly related to language competencies at age three years (Elardo, Bradley, & Caldwell, 1977). The same three scales on the HOME inventory were especially related to the children's linguistic competence. A follow-up of these children showed that parental involvement and availability of toys at age two years were significantly related to school achievement at age eleven years (Bradley, 1989).

This series of studies shows that important processes occur between children and their parents early in life that can have long-lasting implications for future intellectual achievement. For one thing, children who have responsive parents may develop a sense of control over their environments, and their resulting general socioemotional health may facilitate intellectual growth. In addition, the opportunity to play with toys may provide contexts for children to learn problem-solving skills from their parents as well as the chance to develop knowledge from direct manipulation of the play materials. Language development is also enhanced because verbal interactions with parents during play and at other times teach children the properties of spoken speech (Bradley & Caldwell, 1984). A recent project demonstrated that when mothers provided an environment rich in learning experiences such as those described in the HOME studies, the difference in IQ scores between African American and Caucasian children dropped by 28 percent (Brooks-Gunn, Klebanov, & Duncan, 1996).

Parenting Practices The HOME studies must be interpreted with caution because, as with any correlational research that uncovers relationships, we do not necessarily know the direction of influence. Parental responsiveness may have been responsible for children's IQ scores. But it is also possible that intelligent infants may have engendered more parental responsiveness and involvement simply because of their greater exploration of the environment or advanced verbal skills.

Some of these difficulties are addressed in a study by Luis Laosa (1982), who used sophisticated statistical techniques to extract information about the directions of influence in correlational relationships. To see how certain parental characteristics and behaviors might directly influence children's intellectual development at age three years, Laosa studied fifty families through interviews, observations of mother-child interactions, and standardized tests of children's intellectual levels. From this rich set of data, a number of strong causal relationships emerged.

Several aspects of parenting practices predicted children's IQ scores. Among them were how much time family members spent reading to the child and the extent to which mothers used physical demonstration, or modeling, as a teaching strategy with their children. Another extremely important factor was the mothers' socioeducational values. This variable was expressed through the mothers' educational and occupational status as well as the amount of reading they did with their children. It is significant that reading to children and modeling problem-solving tasks proved to be substantial influences. Reading and the verbal exchanges that accompany it provide an excellent context for the development of verbal skills, which are a primary component of intelligence tests. Furthermore, three-year-old children are cognitively capable of profiting from modeling as a teaching style, whereas more complex forms of teaching may be beyond the preschooler's cognitive reach.

Of course, many questions remain about the specific ways in which the child's home environment influences intellectual attainment. For example, are there teaching strategies, aside from modeling, that more effectively promote intellectual advances in older children? Are there other important parental behaviors that remain to be identified? And, in keeping with the position that caregiver-child effects are often reciprocal, what is the child's role in the caregiver-child interactions that foster intellectual development? One of the principal aims of current research is to identify more of the specific family characteristics that lead to intellectual advances across the span of childhood.

The Child's Sociocultural Environment

Children from different cultural backgrounds often display unique patterns of intellectual abilities. For example, the Inuit people of the Arctic region show exceptional visual-spatial skills compared to those of United States residents (Berry, 1966; Vernon, 1966). How does the larger culture within which the child lives influence his or her pattern of mental abilities?

KEY THEME
Sociocultural Influence

The child's sociocultural environment can influence specific patterns of intellectual skills. For example, among the Inuits, superior visual-spatial skills may be tied to that culture's emphasis on hunting in large, expansive terrains.

The role of culture in intellectual development may be examined in terms of activities and behaviors essential for adaptation and survival. The Inuits depend on hunting and gathering in their native terrain, activities that require the ability to perceive small changes in large, expansive fields of vision; in this context, the prominence of their visual-spatial skills is understandable. Similarly, as we saw in Chapter 8, Mexican children with extensive experience in making clay pottery were found to be more advanced on a Piagetian measure of intelligence, the conservation of quantity task, than children without experience in pottery making (Price-Williams, Gordon, & Ramirez, 1969). Intensive practice in specialized skills that are an integral part of one's cultural experience can heighten "intelligence" in those domains.

Another way to understand the role of culture is in terms of parental beliefs about children that affect their interaction styles. When Shirley Brice Heath (1983) examined the communication patterns of middle- and lower-class parents as they interacted with their children, she found some striking differences. Middle-class parents tended to ask their children frequent questions and expected them to provide explanations. They tended to give their children lots of reasons for events and behaviors even when their children were only one month of age. Lower-class parents, in contrast, delivered frequent commands without providing a rationale and expected children to *show* what they knew rather than *tell* what they knew. Moreover, children in these families were discouraged from asking questions, which were viewed as a sign of disrespect. Although this study focused on social class differences more than cultural differences, we can see how a culture's views regarding the proper place of children and the behaviors appropriate for parents and their offspring may translate into specific interaction styles that influence intellectual styles.

One additional way in which the culture into which the child is born can influence patterns of intellectual activity is the degree to which that culture emphasizes formal schooling. Cross-cultural studies have shown that children with formal education are more likely to use mnemonic strategies to learn lists of words and to classify objects according to a consistent rule (Sharp, Cole, & Lave, 1979; Wagner, 1978). Although memory and classification performance, the dependent measures in these studies, are not explicit indices of intelligence, they are cognitive skills that are frequently embedded in psychometric tests. Moreover, if intelligence is assumed to be reflected in IQ scores, children may learn specific skills in school that enable them to do well on intelligence tests (Ceci, 1991). Performing on a time-limited test, understanding and following directions, and being able to consider a number of response alternatives are all general test-taking skills that children are likely to absorb in school. Furthermore, the answers to specific questions found on intelligence tests, such as "Who discovered America?" or "What is the distance from New York to Los Angeles?", are usually learned in school.

CONTROVERSY: THINKING IT OVER

Can Early Intervention Programs Boost IQ?

During the 1960s, the idea of compensatory education became popular in the United States. Researchers wanted to see whether the poor performance of children from lower socioeconomic classes on IQ and achievement tests could improve if the children received the kinds of cognitive stimulation presumably available to middle-class children. If compensatory education programs worked, the idea that IQ is malleable or modifiable by experience would receive strong support, and a genetic explanation of class and race differences in IQ would be less tenable.

The first federally funded program for compensatory education was Project Head Start, begun in the 1960s as a preschool enrichment program for "underprivileged children." The program includes nutritional and medical assistance as well as a structured educational program designed to provide cognitive stimulation. The first evaluations of Head Start were disappointing. In 1969, the Westinghouse Learning

Project Head Start is a federally funded program designed to provide nutritional and medical assistance, as well as to strengthen school readiness skills of children growing up in poverty. Children who attend Head Start show gains in some measures of educational achievement and social competence, and at least short-term increases in IQ scores.

Corporation/Ohio University report compared the intellectual development of about four thousand children from similar backgrounds, half of whom had participated in the first Head Start programs around the country and half of whom did not participate. Essentially no differences were found in the intellectual performance of the two groups; both remained below the norms for their age groups. This evaluation, however, has been criticized on a number of grounds, including the fact that the evaluation was done prematurely, just barely after the program got off the ground.

More recent evaluations of Head Start have yielded more optimistic results. The Head Start Evaluation, Synthesis, and Utilization Project was an attempt to summarize all research on the impact of Head Start (McKey et al., 1985). This review concluded that Head Start produced significant effects on the intellectual performance of program participants, at least for the short term. Head Start children performed well in the first year or two after they started elementary school, showing average gains of 10 points in IQ score, but the effects of the program faded in subsequent years.

Another important early intervention project, the Carolina Abecedarian Project, begun in 1972, aimed to prevent the lower intellectual functioning of children at risk (Ramey & Campbell, 1981; Ramey, Lee, & Burchinal, 1989). A sample of 121 low-income, pregnant women with low educational achievement and low IQ scores (an average of 84) was selected. Once the infants were born, roughly half were assigned to the experimental group and half to the control group. Infants in the experimental group received medical care, nutritional supplements, and a structured program of day care that emphasized the development of cognitive, language, social, and motor skills. In addition, the researchers provided a toy-lending library and a home visiting program as well as parent support groups. During the first year, few differences on Bayley scores were found between infants in the experimental and control groups. From age eighteen months onward, however, the IQs of the experimental group consistently exceeded those of the control group, even when the children reached twelve years of age (Campbell & Ramey, 1994). Yet some researchers remain pessimistic about the significance of these findings. For example, Herman Spitz (1986) pointed out that by age five years, the differences between the experimental and control groups diminished to an average of only 7 points. Therefore, say the critics, the effects of this intensive intervention were not substantial.

Is Head Start "America's most successful educational experiment," as some have claimed (Zigler & Muenchow, 1992)? Or are early intervention programs examples of social experiments that failed? Why might the initial gains of Head Start and Abecedarian children have "washed out" in successive years? Are IQ scores the best indicators of the impact of Head Start and other early intervention programs? One collaborative study of the effects of eleven early intervention programs showed that children who had participated were less likely than nonparticipants to be assigned to special education classes, less likely to be "held back" in grade, and more likely to cite their school achievements as a source of pride (Lazar & Darlington, 1982). Edward Zigler, a key figure in the formulation of Project Head Start, and his colleagues have also suggested that Head Start children show gains in social competence (Zigler & Berman, 1983; Zigler & Trickett, 1978). Are these outcomes just as important as gains in IQ scores?

CHAPTER RECAP

SUMMARY OF DEVELOPMENTAL THEMES

NATURE/NURTURE **What roles do nature and nurture play in the development of intelligence?**

The nature-nurture debate becomes an especially thorny issue in the matter of intelligence. Few psychologists would dispute that heredity plays a role in the child's intellectual development. For example, early individual differences in the speed of infant habituation and recognition memory may signal differences in some aspects of later intellectual functioning. In addition, genetic effects such as Down syndrome and the high correlations between IQ scores of identical twins reared apart suggest a role for "nature." Yet research also shows that children's early experiences within the home, together with the intellectual skills touted by the larger culture, modulate how their genetic blueprints unfold.

SOCIOCULTURAL INFLUENCE **How does the sociocultural context influence the development of intelligence?**

Culture broadly influences the kinds of skills that its members value and nurture and that are believed to constitute "intelligence." Is speed of executing tasks important? Are good visual-spatial or verbal skills essential for successful adaptation to the environment? A culture's demands and expectations frame the way intelligent behavior will be defined in the first place. From the narrower perspective of performance on standardized IQ tests, children who have experiences consistent with the knowledge tapped by test items will perform well, whereas those with more impoverished backgrounds will be at a disadvantage. Other sociocultural factors often associated with social class, such as parental emphasis on intellectual achievement or the amount of emotional stress within the family system, can also impinge on IQ test performance.

CHILD'S ACTIVE ROLE **How does the child play an active role in the development of intelligence?**

Traditional psychometric theories have rarely assumed that the child plays an active role in affecting her intelligence. However, the information-processing perspective has focused on executive control skills, the child's ability to monitor his own cognitive processes, and other cognitive activities as significant contributors to intellectual development.

CONTINUITY/DISCONTINUITY **Is the development of intelligence continuous or discontinuous?**

Some would argue that intelligence does not really develop at all, that it is a stable, relatively unchanging, inborn human characteristic. Information-processing theorists, in contrast, see intelligence as largely the by-product of normal, continuous developmental processes wherein the child learns more complex relations among stimuli in the surrounding world and becomes capable of more sophisticated cognitive processing with age.

INDIVIDUAL DIFFERENCES **How prominent are individual differences in the development of intelligence?**

From the psychometric perspective, the concept of intelligence is rooted in the assumption that individual differences exist in performance on certain mental tasks. Other theories, particularly Gardner's theory of multiple intelligences, stress the patterns of strength and weakness a given individual shows across a spectrum of domains. Studies of how the environment influences intelligence also suggest that an individual's score on an IQ test can be a function of the specific parenting practices she or he has experienced or other elements of the childhood environment.

INTERACTION AMONG DOMAINS   How does the development of intelligence interact with development in other domains?

Children who obtain high scores on intelligence tests are more likely to be successful in school and, as adults, to hold high-status jobs and be productive in those jobs. Thus, to some extent, IQ scores can predict certain aspects of success in life. According to more recent theoretical perspectives, the child's experiences in various domains can also influence intelligence. For example, in Gardner's theory of multiple intelligences, bodily-kinesthetic intelligence can be fostered through athletic experiences and interpersonal intelligence can grow through extensive social experience.

SUMMARY OF TOPICS

■ WHAT IS INTELLIGENCE?

Definitions of intelligence vary in two major ways: (1) whether intelligence is seen as a global characteristic or a set of separate abilities and (2) whether the emphasis is on the products or processes of intelligent behavior. The *psychometric* model emphasizes individual differences in test scores, whereas information-processing models underscore the mental activities in which individuals engage as they solve problems.

■ MEASURING INTELLIGENCE

Intelligence is usually expressed in terms of the *intelligence quotient (IQ),* the individual's score derived from an intelligence test. Most intelligence tests, those administered both individually and to groups, are based on the psychometric model and assess a range of verbal, visual-spatial, and problem-solving skills. Common intelligence tests for infants are the Bayley Scales of Infant Mental and Motor Development and the Fagan Test of Infant Intelligence. School-age children are most frequently tested with either the Stanford-Binet Intelligence Scale or the Wechsler Intelligence Scale for Children–III (WISC-III). More recently, tests based on alternative conceptions of intelligence have grown in popularity.

Although most children fall within the normal range of IQ scores, some score at the upper and lower boundaries of exceptionality. For many children, the scores obtained on IQ tests are stable over time, especially after age five years, although individual children can show dramatic fluctuations. Studies of infant attention and memory suggest that there may be some continuities in mental abilities. IQ scores generally predict academic success but are not necessarily related to other measures of life satisfaction.

■ FACTORS RELATED TO INTELLIGENCE

Intelligence is the result of the complex interactions between heredity and environment. Racial and social class differences in IQ scores illustrate the difficulty of drawing simple conclusions about the sources of intelligence. One problem is that estimates of the heritability of IQ do not necessarily explain between-group differences in scores. *Test bias* can be a factor in the performance of children from some social or cultural backgrounds on tests designed for the cultural mainstream. The child's experiences in the home and the skills valued by the larger culture can have an impact on the child's level and pattern of intellectual performance.

11 EMOTION

NATURE/NURTURE
What roles do nature and nurture play in emotional development?

SOCIOCULTURAL INFLUENCE
How does the sociocultural context influence emotional development?

CHILD'S ACTIVE ROLE
How does the child play an active role in the process of emotional development?

CONTINUITY/DISCONTINUITY
Is emotional development continuous or discontinuous?

INDIVIDUAL DIFFERENCES
How prominent are individual differences in emotional development?

INTERACTION AMONG DOMAINS
How does emotional development interact with development in other domains?

t's a quiet time on Sunday morning, just after a big breakfast, and Cindy admires her eight-month-old son Michael as he sits in his infant seat. He is looking at her so intently, raising his eyebrows a bit and scanning her face, gurgling contentedly. Suddenly the phone rings. Michael falls silent and opens his eyes wide. Cindy raises her eyebrows into two big arches and opens her mouth, making an exaggerated "Oohh" sound suggesting surprise. Her baby eyes her with fascination, chortles, then smiles. Cindy smiles back broadly, chuckles, and says, "Must be Grandma calling to see how you are. Let me answer the phone, OK, honey?" She touches Michael affectionately under the chin as she gets up to reach for the phone. The baby lets out a shriek of delight and smiles again. Cindy can't help but laugh at the antics of her young son.

The scene above, in all its simplicity, is a typical one in many families. Babies and caregivers revel in each other's company, and although the infant cannot yet speak, he participates fully in the interaction in nonverbal ways. The communication vehicle relies less on language than on both overt and subtle nuances in facial expressions and sounds that communicate emotional state. Some have characterized the back-and-forth nature of this exchange as a well-choreographed "waltz" wherein each partner looks to the other for cues about what to do next so the interaction proceeds smoothly and enjoyably. The episode also suggests some fundamental questions about the nature of human emotions and the forces that guide emotional development. Are our emotions innately determined, the result of a biological "prewiring"? Or are our displays and conceptions of emotions derived from learning the rules and conventions of our culture?

On the surface, the interaction between Cindy and her infant may suggest that nurture rather than nature is the determining factor, especially when the exchange is contrasted with interactions typical among the Gusii of Kenya. The Gusii culture places great emphasis on suppressing intense emotions, probably to maintain harmony in the small, tribal living units characteristic of that group. Consequently, mothers maintain a bland, neutral expression when interacting with their infants and try to inhibit strong shows of emotion from their children (Dixon et al., 1981). These differing cultural norms are reflected in the parenting styles of each culture and the behaviors children eventually display. At the same time, however, as we will see in this chapter, recent research with young infants suggests that emotions possess biological underpinnings as well.

In this chapter, we will see how children's expression and understanding of emotions change with age. Many of these accomplishments are tied to advances in cognition that permit children to think about complex feeling states within themselves as

353

well as in others. In addition, even though emotions are the personal expressions of the individual's moods or feeling states, they also function as a mode of communicating with others. Given the social dimension of emotions, we will investigate the role they play in the child's relationships with others, specifically in the special "attachments" that emerge between child and caregivers. What is the psychological significance of these emotional bonds, and how do they influence the child's later development?

WHAT ARE EMOTIONS?

Although many of us have an intuitive understanding of what an emotion is, the formal psychological definition of this term has been surprisingly elusive. Many theorists agree, however, that **emotions** are a complex set of behaviors produced in response to some external or internal event, or elicitor, and include several components. First, emotions have a *physiological* component, involving changes in autonomic nervous system activities such as respiration and heart rate. Fear or anxiety, for example, may be accompanied by more rapid breathing, increased heart rate and blood pressure, and perspiration. Second, emotions include an *expressive* component, usually a facial display that signals the emotion. Smiles, grimaces, cries, and laughter overtly express a person's emotional state. Third, emotions have an *experiential* component, the subjective feeling or cognitive judgment of having an emotion (Izard, Kagan, & Zajonc, 1984; Sroufe, 1996). Just how a person interprets and evaluates an emotional state depends on his level of cognitive development and the experiences he has had. For a child to be able to state, "I feel happy," he must recognize the internal cues and external contexts associated with "happiness," which are derived from experience. In addition, he must have a relatively mature concept of the self as a feeling, responding being, a sign of cognitive maturity.

The Functions of Emotions

What role do emotions play in the psychological development of the child? On one level, they serve to organize and regulate the child's own behavior. If a child is learning to ride a two-wheel bicycle and succeeds in tottering down the sidewalk without keeling over, she undoubtedly will feel elated and probably more motivated to practice this new skill for a few more minutes or even hours. If, on the other hand, she falls repeatedly or even injures herself, she may feel angry and discouraged and quit riding for a few days. Thus, the child's emotional states regulate what she will decide to do (Campos et al., 1983).

Emotions also have important links to cognition. Children often smile, show surprise, or even display fear as they engage in cognitive activities. For example, an infant who perceives depth while perched over the rail of his crib expresses wariness. A ten-month-old who observes an object disappear behind a screen acts surprised; she has the concept of object permanence and understands the object still exists, but is perplexed over its whereabouts. The school-age child beams proudly after mastering an intellectual challenge such as completing a difficult puzzle or school assignment. In each case, the child's cognitive activity leads to the display of an emotion.

Not only do many cognitive processes produce emotional expressions; the child's emotional state can also influence cognitive processes. One example concerns the relationship between emotion and learning. Research indicates that children who show an interest in certain objects or topics—a strong feeling of attraction or pleasure—pay more attention to those stimuli and remember them better in a subsequent memory test compared to objects that do not interest them (Renninger, 1992).

Of special importance is the fact that emotions serve to initiate, maintain, or terminate interactions with others. The baby's cry or smile almost invariably prompts contact with the caregiver. A toddler's frustration and anger over an unshared toy may lead him to abandon a playmate temporarily. In fact, a social dialogue com-

---

KEY THEME
Interaction Among Domains

KEY THEME
Interaction Among Domains

emotions Complex behaviors involving physiological, expressive, and experiential components produced in response to some external or internal event.

Emotion and cognition are frequently interrelated. For example, children often show emotions such as pride or shame following performance of a cognitive task. This girl's face clearly communicates how she feels after obtaining an "A" on her paper.

pletely devoid of emotional content is unusual. "Moods," more enduring emotional states, may help us understand the child's personality attributes, such as the tendency to be shy, dependent, or aggressive. Personality traits too can influence the frequency and form of the child's social contacts. Thus, understanding emotional development can increase our appreciation of a broad range of children's accomplishments in other domains.

Measuring Emotions

Given the complex nature of emotions, how to measure them becomes an important issue for researchers because all three dimensions—physiological, expressive, and cognitive—must be considered. One approach is to record changes in physiological functions such as heart rate (acceleration or deceleration), heart rate variability (the individual's basic heart rate pattern), or EEG patterns showing brain activity as affective stimuli are presented (Fox, 1991; Fox & Davidson, 1986). Another strategy is to conduct fine-grained analyses of the child's facial expressions or vocalizations. Tiny movements of the muscles in the brow, eye, and mouth regions produce the facial configurations associated with joy, sadness, anger, and other emotions (Izard & Dougherty, 1982). Similarly, the frequency, loudness, duration, and sound patterns of the child's vocalizations indicate emotion (Papousek, Papousek, & Koester, 1986). Often facial expressions, body movements, and vocalizations function as an ensemble of emotion indicators; for example, a facial expression of anger, raising arms upward, and crying combine to signal "pick me up" (Weinberg & Tronick, 1994). Finally, the child's interpretations of her own and others' emotions can be assessed through the use of self-report measures (for example, "Tell me how often you felt cheerful in the last week") and tasks requiring the child to label, match, or produce emotional expressions ("Tell me how the person in this picture feels" or "Show me the person who feels sad").

Although each methodological approach has helped to illuminate aspects of the child's emotional life, researchers must be cautious when interpreting their data. When physiological changes such as decelerated heart rate occur as the infant watches a lively segment of "Sesame Street," is he experiencing interest or surprise? The emotion that corresponds to a specific reaction of the nervous system is not always clear. Likewise, an overt emotional expression such as crying might represent a number of possible internal emotional states, such as sadness, joy, or fear. Self-reports of the child's emotional states present their own difficulties. As we saw in Chapter 2, some children may answer researchers' questions based on the way they think they should reply rather than on how they really feel. Others may be reluctant to discuss their inner feelings at all. Despite these methodological difficulties, researchers have learned a good deal about emotional development in the last two decades.

THEORIES OF EMOTIONAL DEVELOPMENT

Are human emotions biologically based, preprogrammed responses to specific environmental stimuli, or are they the products of the myriad learning experiences that accumulate over the course of infancy and childhood? The familiar nature-nurture debate has an historically rich tradition when we examine the varying explanations for the emergence of human emotions.

The Foundations of Modern Theory: Darwin and Watson

KEY THEME
Nature/Nurture

The biological underpinnings of emotion were emphasized by Charles Darwin, the nineteenth-century scientist best known for his theory of evolution. According to Darwin (1872, 1877), emotions and their expressions in humans and animals serve a survival function; they prepare the organism for action and signal to others the action to be taken. On encountering a predator, for example, some apes will express fear with a bared-teeth grimace before fleeing. Other members of the troop will read this expression and take flight as well.

As we saw in Chapter 2, Darwin made extensive observations of his own child in his investigation of human emotions, keeping a diary of his son's emotional expressions and states. He identified seven basic emotions, each with its own accompanying facial expression: anger, fear, affection, pleasure, amusement, discomfort, and jealousy. He argued that humans from many different cultures show similar expressions for the basic emotions and that human expressions are similar to those of other primates. Darwin concluded that emotions and their expression are innate and biologically determined.

With the emergence of behaviorism in the first part of the twentieth century, this prevailing view shifted. Emotions, like most other responses in the child's repertoire, were now seen as products of the child's learning experiences. In his book *Behaviorism* (1930), John Watson stated that three emotional reactions—fear, rage, and love—are innate but are emitted to only a limited range of stimuli. Loud noises, for example, automatically result in a display of fear in very young infants. Through learning, however, these primitive emotions develop into the more complex array of affective responses that children and adults produce to various stimuli.

To illustrate his theory, in his famous case study of little Albert, Watson demonstrated that fear of a specific stimulus can be learned through the process of classical conditioning. Albert, an eleven-month-old infant, initially showed no fear responses to a white rat but did display a marked reaction to loud sounds. Watson systematically paired the sound of a steel bar being struck by a hammer, producing a startle or fear reaction, with every attempt Albert made to touch the white rat. Eventually the sight of the rat alone made Albert begin to whimper and cry, a reaction Watson called a **conditioned emotional response**. Moreover, Albert showed a generalization of the fear response to other objects that were similar in appearance, such as a rabbit and a piece of fluffy cotton. Although researchers today would raise ethical questions about conducting such an experiment because of the potential psychological harm to the child, this early study does point out how basic learning processes can account for the display of emotions to initially neutral stimuli.

conditioned emotional response Emergence of an emotional reaction to an originally neutral stimulus through classical conditioning.

Contemporary Perspectives on Emotional Development

Modern-day theorists are more likely than either Darwin or Watson were to acknowledge the interaction of biological and environmental factors in explaining the complexity and range of the child's emotional behaviors and experiences. Nevertheless, some investigators continue to stress the biological foundations of emotions, whereas others believe the child's socialization history and the cognitions underlying emotions play a more significant role.

KEY THEME
Nature/Nurture

Biologically Based Explanations   Today the main champions of a strong biological view of emotions are Paul Ekman and Carroll Izard. After studying people in various cultures, Ekman (1972, 1973) concluded that there are universal facial expressions for certain basic emotions that are interpreted in similar ways across cultures. Ekman showed photographs of six faces, each depicting a particular emotion—happiness, sadness, anger, fear, surprise, or disgust—to participants in the United States, Japan, Chile, Brazil, and Argentina. As they looked at each photograph, participants were asked to identify the emotion displayed. Ekman found a high degree of agreement across cultures as to which emotions were represented (Ekman, 1972).

Similarly, Izard believes that because certain emotional expressions are displayed by very young infants, they are necessarily innate and have distinct adaptive value (Izard, 1978; Izard & Malatesta, 1987). When the newborn infant tastes a bitter substance such as quinine, for example, she will pull up her upper lip, wrinkle her nose, and squint her eyes, indicating she has detected the unpleasant stimulus. No learning is necessary to produce this reaction of disgust. The caregiver observing this type of signal might respond by removing a potentially harmful substance from the baby's mouth, thereby ensuring her well-being. The experience of emotion, Izard states, is the automatic product of the internal sensory feedback the individual elicits from making the facial expression; wrinkling the face produces the feeling of disgust. Izard also maintains that once an emotion is activated, it in turn motivates the individual

There are many cross-cultural commonalities in the expression and interpretation of emotions. Most people, regardless of their own cultural background, would identify this Mexican girl's expression as happiness or joy.

to act. The experience of disgust, in other words, may lead the baby to spit out the distasteful substance.

Both Ekman and Izard acknowledge that learning may play a role in emotional development, especially as children learn to control and regulate their emotions. They maintain, however, that the role of biological factors is paramount and that emotions originate in the genetic blueprints with which the child begins life.

A Cognitive-Socialization Explanation   Michael Lewis and Linda Michalson (1983) have provided an alternative account of the emotional life of the child, one that emphasizes both the cognitive activities involved in emotional experiences and the role of socialization. According to these theorists, an environmental event does not directly produce an emotional expression. Instead, the child relies on cognitive processes to assess the event, how it compares with past events, and the social rules surrounding the event. Suppose, for example, the child encounters a barking dog. Whether he cries with fear or smiles at the noisy animal depends on his past experiences with dogs (has he ever been bitten?) and on what parents and others have instructed him to believe about animals ("Barking dogs will bite—stay away!" or "Some dogs get excited when they want to play—it's okay"). Cognitive processes thus act as *mediators,* or mental events that bridge the gap between environmental stimuli and the response the individual ultimately expresses. According to Lewis and Michalson, this conceptualization accounts for individual differences in emotional reactions when the same event produces different responses from two people.

According to Lewis and Michalson, socialization plays an important role in shaping the time and the manner in which emotions are displayed. Children in our culture learn that it is appropriate to feel happy at birthday parties and sad when a friend's grandmother dies and that a smiling face and a sad face should be made at these events, respectively. Socialization also guides the way emotions are managed. Young children in many cultures, for example, learn to inhibit expressions of fear and anger. Finally, socialization directs the way children label and interpret emotions. When the young child cries due to a physical injury and the parent says, "That hurts, doesn't it?" the interpretation provides pain as the reason for the tears. When crying is the response to the collapse of a tower of toy blocks, the parent may provide a different interpretation for the child, such as "That's frustrating." These kinds of communications serve as an important vehicle by which children learn how to interpret their own emotional states.

KEY THEME
Interaction Among Domains

KEY THEME
Individual Differences

EXPRESSING, RECOGNIZING, AND UNDERSTANDING EMOTIONS

Researchers focus on emotional development from various angles. First, they examine whether children change in the way they *express* their own emotions. Do infants exhibit the full range of emotions that we see in adults, or does a developmental progression occur in the types of emotions children display? Second, do children change in their ability to *recognize* emotions in others, to read the facial expressions, vocalizations, and other body movements that carry messages about positive or negative affect? Finally, are children likely to change in how they *understand* emotions, such as the events that precipitate and follow an emotional display or the complexities of masking emotions?

Early Emotional Development

Much of the groundwork for emotional development occurs during the first year or so of life. Parents and young infants rely less on language to communicate with each other than on nonverbal signals that frequently are laden with emotional overtones. Just what behaviors are infants capable of showing and "reading"?

Emotional Expression in Infancy   Even infants only a few days or weeks old are capable of producing the facial expressions associated with several emotions, including interest, distress, disgust, joy, sadness, anger, and surprise (Field, Woodson et al., 1982; Izard, 1978; Izard et al., 1995). Observers who are asked to label emotions depicted in slides and videotapes of infant faces have identified each of these discrete emotions reliably. By seven months of age, the infant has added expressions of fear to his repertoire (Izard et al., 1980). The fact that these discrete facial expressions appear so early in infancy, before much learning can have taken place, provides strong support for the idea that emotional expressions are to some extent biologically determined. These emotions are often called **basic** (or *primary*) **emotions.**

Besides displaying a wide range of expressive signals, infants show a high rate of change in their facial displays, sometimes spontaneously and sometimes in response to the expressions of others. For example, in one study, as three-month-olds engaged in face-to-face play with their mothers, they changed their expression about once every seven seconds (Malatesta & Haviland, 1982). As we saw in this chapter's opening scene, the facial displays of infants, in turn, often produce a reaction from the caregiver—delight at the infant's smile and concern at an expression of distress, for example. Thus, caregivers' responses to infants' signals lead to interactions that play a crucial role in their developing relationship.

Although even the earliest displays of basic emotions usually are recognized readily by adults, their form and the conditions that elicit them may change over the first few months. The development of two important emotional expressions in infancy, smiling and crying, demonstrates these changes.

Smiling   One of the most captivating and irresistible infant behaviors is the smile. In the newborn this behavior occurs primarily during the state of REM sleep, when dreaming is thought to occur, in bursts of several smiles in succession (Emde & Koenig, 1969). The mouth stretches sideways and up, producing a simple version of the eagerly anticipated smile. Although many hypotheses attempt to explain why very young infants produce this facial gesture (including the popular but mistaken notion that "gas" is responsible), the most consistent finding is that neonates smile when they experience a shift in physiological arousal state, such as when they fall asleep or become drowsy (Wolff, 1987).

At approximately two weeks of age, the form of the smile changes. The corners of the lips retract even farther, the cheek muscles contract, and the skin around the eyes wrinkles. Now the infant smiles during states of wakefulness, sometimes in response to familiar voices and sounds, sweet tastes, and pleasant food odors (Fogel, 1982; Steiner, 1979). By three months of age, smiles increase in frequency and occur in the presence of visual stimuli, most notably the sight of the baby's primary caregiver, usually the mother (Adamson & Bakeman, 1985; Fogel, 1982). Because this "social smile" plays a substantial role in initiating and maintaining interactions between the infant and significant adults in her life, it is considered an important milestone in infant development.

At about four months of age, infants begin to laugh as well as smile, initially at the presence of tactile or auditory stimuli, such as tickling or interesting verbalizations, and later at amusing visual events, such as the game of peek-a-boo (Sroufe & Waters, 1976). Thus, what began as a spontaneous, reflexlike behavior that occurred during certain physiological states becomes a voluntary, controlled response that serves an important social-communicative function.

The developmental course of these positive emotional expressions is related to the child's increasing cognitive maturity. With age, the child smiles and laughs in response to increasingly complex stimuli, stimuli that are incongruent with his past experiences or that suggest events he remembers from the past. One-year-olds laugh at stimuli such as their mothers walking like a penguin or sucking on a baby bottle; they also laugh in anticipation of being kissed on the stomach (Sroufe & Wunsch, 1972). In each situation, children rely on their memory of familiar events to perceive novelty or incongruity. Second, children increasingly produce on their own the stimuli

KEY THEME
Nature/Nurture

KEY THEME
Child's Active Role

KEY THEME
Interaction Among Domains

basic emotion   Emotion such as joy, sadness, or surprise that appears early in infancy and seems to have a biological foundation. Also called *primary emotion.*

KEY THEME
Child's Active Role

KEY THEME
Interaction Among Domains

KEY THEME
Child's Active Role

KEY THEME
Individual Differences

that generate smiling and laughter. After age two years, for example, children will laugh more when they cover an observer's face with a cloth than when the observer covers her own face (Sroufe & Wunsch, 1972). Finally, the shift from smiling as a reflexlike behavior to a controlled, voluntary response parallels the increasing maturation of the cerebral cortex, which is responsible for higher-order mental processes and deliberate, goal-directed behaviors.

Crying   Crying is another common way in which infants express emotion. Newborn babies cry for a variety of reasons, but primarily because they are hungry, cold, wet, in pain, or disturbed from their sleep. The nature of the baby's distress is often reflected in the type of cry she emits. In an extensive study of eighteen infants observed in their homes, Peter Wolff (1969) identified three patterns of crying. The first is the *basic* (or hungry) *cry,* a rhythmical sequence consisting of a vocalization, a pause, an intake of air, and another pause. The second is the *angry cry,* in which extra air is forced through the vocal cords during the vocalization segment of the basic cry. Finally, in the *pain cry,* the infant produces a long vocalization followed by an even longer silence as he holds his breath and then gasps.

Like smiling, crying is a response that promotes contact between the infant and the caregiver. Mothers usually react to their young infants' cries promptly, especially an angry or a pain cry, and when they do, infants actually cry less in succeeding weeks and months (Bell & Ainsworth, 1972; Wolff, 1969). Usually the first order of business is to make sure the infant's physical needs are met. Other effective techniques for soothing the crying infant include providing a pacifier, swaddling with a blanket, and tapping some part of his body, that is, providing some form of rhythmic or continuous stimulation (Brackbill, 1975). Picking up the baby and holding her on one's shoulder also is soothing, probably because this act provides the infant with a broad range of stimulation that distracts her from crying (Korner, 1972).

By the time the infant is about two months of age, the causes of crying are no longer purely physiological. An infant might cry when the caregiver puts him down in his crib or when a favorite toy is removed from his grasp. At about this time, a new type of cry emerges: the *fussy* or *irregular cry,* which varies in intensity, is less rhythmical, and seems to function as a demand for particular objects or actions. At eight months of age, the infant will pause in crying to see if the mother or other adults are receiving the message (Bruner, 1983). As the infant gains more voluntary control over his vocalizations, crying patterns become even more varied and controlled and are displayed in a wider range of situations to signal an assortment of messages. Individual differences in the crying patterns of some infants also might be useful in diagnosing developmental abnormalities. Malnourished infants, for example, display more variability in the pitch of their cries, whereas children who have suffered oxygen deprivation produce shorter, higher-pitched cries (Michelsson, Sirvio, & Wasz-Hockert, 1977; Zeskind, 1981). Variations in individual patterns of crying may affect caregiver-infant relationships. In particular, the infant's *shrill* or *aversive cry,* typical of the preterm baby, may interfere with the normal interactions that pave the way for healthy parent-child relationships (Zeskind & Lester, 1981).

Recognizing and Imitating Others' Expressions   Besides producing expressions themselves, infants are capable of discriminating and responding to emotional displays in others. Several remarkable studies conducted by Tiffany Field and her colleagues suggest that three-day-old infants are capable of imitating the facial expressions for happiness, surprise, and sadness when an adult models these expressions (Field, Woodson et al., 1982, 1983). Infants widened their eyes and opened their mouths on "surprise" trials, drew back their lips on "happiness" trials, and tightened their mouths and furrowed their brows on "sadness" trials. Although some researchers offer alternative explanations for these findings (see Chapter 6), many believe infants have an early sensitivity to emotional expressions in others.

Other researchers use the *habituation paradigm* to examine the infant's ability to recognize facial expressions in photographs. Typically, a stimulus representing one

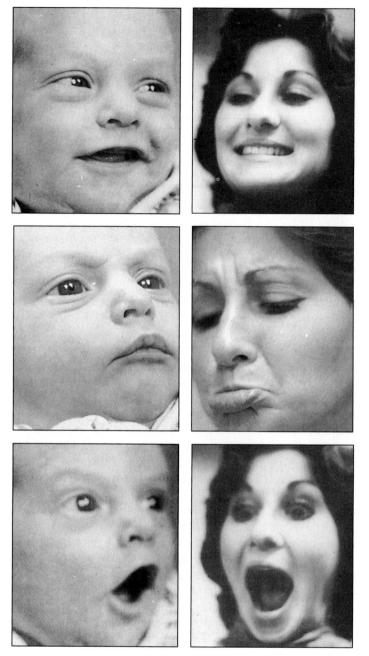

According to some research, three-day-old infants are capable of imitating expressions for happiness (top), sadness (middle), and surprise (bottom) when they are modeled by an adult. These emotions are categorized as *basic emotions.*

emotional expression is presented repeatedly while the duration of the infant's visual fixation is monitored. After looking time decreases to a certain predetermined level, a stimulus containing a new expression is presented. If the infant's looking time increases, there is good reason to believe she has detected the change in expression. Researchers have also examined whether infants show preferences for some expressions over others.

The use of these experimental procedures has shown that three- and four-month-olds are able to distinguish among several expressions, particularly happiness versus anger, surprise, and sadness, and that they prefer to see joy over anger (Barrera & Maurer, 1981a; LaBarbera et al., 1976; Young-Browne, Rosenfeld, & Horowitz, 1977). They can even identify variations in a single expression. Three-month-olds in one experiment consistently preferred looking at photographs of a woman exhibiting a smile over one displaying a neutral expression (see Figure 11.1) and looked longer at increasingly intense versions of the smile (Kuchuk, Vibbert, & Bornstein, 1986).

FIGURE 11.1

Showing Preferences for Adult Facial Expressions

When three-month-olds were shown a neutral face (far left) paired with one of the other photos of a smile, they consistently preferred to look at the smile and looked longer at the more intense smiles.

KEY THEME
Child's Active Role

KEY THEME
Interaction Among Domains

social referencing Looking to another individual for emotional cues in interpreting a strange or ambiguous event.

interactive synchrony
Reciprocal, mutually engaging cycles of caregiver-child behaviors.

Social Referencing Do infants derive meaning from the facial expressions they observe in others, or do they simply respond to changes in isolated facial features that contribute to these expressions (for example, the upward curve of the mouth in the smile)? Because, as noted in Chapter 6, some researchers report that infants under age two or three months do not systematically scan the entire human face, it seems unlikely that they respond to any expression as a totality. In fact, not until the latter half of the first year do infants show evidence that they understand the meanings of facial expressions.

At this age, a phenomenon called **social referencing** indicates an infant's ability to interpret facial expressions. If infants are placed in an unfamiliar situation or encounter a strange object and are uncertain how to respond, they often will look to their caregivers for cues. The facial expression the caregiver displays typically will influence the infant's own emotional response and subsequent actions. For example, in one study, twelve-month-olds were placed on the shallow side of the visual cliff apparatus, which, as we saw in Chapter 6, is used to assess the perception of depth. They were coaxed to move toward the place on the cliff where the surface appears to drop off. At this point, half of the participants' mothers posed a happy expression and the other half exhibited fear. Of the infants whose mothers smiled, 74 percent crossed the deep side of the cliff. In contrast, *none* of the infants whose mothers showed fear crossed the deep side. Moreover, these babies tended to produce fearful expressions on their own faces (Sorce et al., 1985). Thus, infants not only "read" the expression they saw on their mothers' faces but also correctly interpreted its message.

Social referencing provides a good example of the child's active involvement in the process of emotional development. When he encounters a puzzling or ambiguous event, he actively seeks information from the environment about how to react. He then uses the emotional expressions of others to derive meaning from that event and decide on a course of action (Tronick, 1989). Social referencing is linked to advances in cognition and is probably an early sign of the child's internalization of the views and values of parents, a process that will continue throughout the early years of childhood (Desrochers et al., 1994; Kochanska, 1994).

Emotions as Regulators of Social Interactions Observations of infants' ability to express and identify emotions in the context of interactions with others have suggested to developmental psychologists that emotions serve an important function in regulating and modulating early social exchanges. This dynamic process begins at about two or three months of age, when, as in the scene that opened this chapter, the infant looks into the adult's eyes and produces a "social smile" or a cry, to which the adult responds. The adult vocalization or facial expression, in turn, often precipitates another emotional response from the infant. Such episodes of reciprocal, mutually engaging cycles of caregiver-child behaviors are called **interactive synchrony**. During the child's first year, interactive synchrony characterizes about 30 percent of face-to-face interactions between infant and caregiver (Tronick & Cohn, 1989).

At about three months, primary caregivers typically assume the major responsibility for guiding interactions, producing repetitions of exaggerated faces and vocalizations to which the infant pays rapt attention (Stern, 1974). Infants, without doubt, notice and react to their mothers' expressive displays. When mothers do not return a smile but show a still face or a neutral pose, infants respond with a quizzical or sober look, avert their gaze, and touch themselves or some nearby object (Toda & Fogel, 1993; Tronick et al., 1978). When mothers show a positive expression, infants follow suit. If mothers look depressed, infants react by averting their gaze and, sometimes, crying (Cohn & Tronick, 1983). By about six to nine months of age, infants more clearly take the initiative; their displays of positive affect now more often precede their mothers' (Cohn & Tronick, 1987). Thus, throughout early infancy, the child becomes an increasingly active partner in an emotionally toned, interactive "duet" with the caregiver.

But what about the other 70 percent of the time, when infant-caregiver interactions are *asynchronous* or uncoordinated with each other? Edward Tronick and his colleagues believe these episodes, which constitute the majority of infant-caregiver relations, also play an important part in normal emotional development. A common occurrence after a sequence in which infant and caregiver are not coordinated is the infant's attempt to repair the "interactive error." When the mother looks sad, for example, the infant's subsequent gaze aversion or crying encourages the mother to modify her own behavior, and frequently she does (Cohn & Tronick, 1983). Thus, episodes of asynchrony give infants opportunities to learn about the rules of interaction and, in cases in which they are able to repair an interaction, give them a sense of mastery or control over their environment (Tronick & Cohn, 1989).

Affective exchanges between infant and caregiver lay the groundwork for social behavior and emotional dispositions at later ages. Researchers have observed that depressed mothers tend to be less positive in face-to-face interactions with their infants (Campbell, Cohn, & Meyers, 1995). Perhaps as a consequence, infants of clinically depressed mothers express a good deal of negative affect in face-to-face interactions (Cohn et al., 1986). They tend to express more sadness and anger, and their negative affect extends to other adults who are not depressed (Field, 1995; Field et al., 1988; Pickens & Field, 1993). These infants also show brain wave patterns similar to those of depressed adults (Dawson, 1994; Field et al., 1995). Thus, the dominance of negative emotions during early mother-child interactions culminates in a general mood or background emotional state that apparently pervades the child's own behaviors (Tronick, Ricks, & Cohn, 1982). The child may bring this general affective tone to new situations; for example, an anxious child is likely to interpret a new event as frightening, whereas a happy child may react with curiosity. Finally, the nature of the affective exchanges between mother and child influences the strength of the emotional bond, or *attachment*, between them. Infants who attempt to elicit responses from their mothers by smiling, vocalizing, or crying at six months of age are more likely to have healthy attachments at age one year than children who withdraw from such interactions (Tronick, Ricks, & Cohn, 1982); depressed mothers tend to have children with poorer-quality attachments (Teti et al., 1995). As we will see later in this chapter, healthy attachments, in turn, are correlated with many other positive developmental outcomes in social and cognitive functioning. Hence, the tone of these early interactions is a crucial facet of child development.

Later Emotional Development

By their second year, many children begin to show emotions that reflect a more complex understanding of the self and social relationships. Shame, guilt, and envy, for example, each require the child to understand the perspective of another person—that the person may be disappointed with the child, may be hurt, or may feel affection for a third party. Such emotions also require a consciousness about the self and one's relations to others, a facet of development described in Chapter 12 (Campos et al., 1983; Lewis, 1989). Accordingly, emotions such as envy and guilt are known as **complex emotions**.

The visible signs of complex emotions can be multifaceted: a child displaying shame lowers her head and eyes, collapses her body, and often has an odd smile on her face (Lewis, Alessandri, & Sullivan, 1992). At age two years, children also show discernible signs of jealousy. The child may wedge himself between his mother and

complex emotion Emotion such as guilt and envy that appears later in childhood and requires more complex cognitive and social skills.

father as they are hugging or hit a sibling whom his parent just kissed (Cummings, Zahn-Waxler, & Radke-Yarrow, 1981).

Another emotion, fear, also undergoes developmental changes, particularly in the types of stimuli that elicit it. Whereas early expressions of fear result from loud noises or strange people, later in childhood fear occurs as a response to more complex events, such as the possibility of failing in school or being rejected by peers (Morris & Kratchowill, 1983; Rutter & Garmezy, 1983). Thus, as the child's cognitive skills and social awareness grow, he expresses more complex emotions or more elaborate and controlled forms of the basic emotions.

Understanding Emotions   With the advent of language, children can communicate feelings by verbalizing instead of just furrowing their brow and crying or making some other facial display. Children begin to use language to describe feeling states between eighteen and thirty-six months of age, shortly after they begin to talk. Inge Bretherton and Marjorie Beeghly (1982) asked mothers of twenty-eight-month-olds to keep a diary of their children's verbalizations that referred to psychological states. Table 11.1 shows the percentage of children who used words for various emotions to describe either themselves or others. Besides being able to apply a wide range of terms to express both positive and negative feelings, these children were able to discuss the conditions that led to a specific emotion and the actions that followed as a consequence. Several children, for example, made statements similar to "Grandma mad. I wrote on wall," suggesting an understanding of the reasons for another's emotion. Another type of utterance made by several children—"I cry. Lady pick me up and hold me"—signifies an understanding that emotions may be related to subsequent actions.

From age three to four years and onward, children become more proficient in verbally describing the causes and consequences of emotions (Barden et al., 1980). They

KEY THEME
Interaction Among Domains

KEY THEME
Interaction Among Domains

TABLE 11.1	Emotion Terms	Percentage of Children Using Word for Self or Others
The Emotion Vocabulary of 28-Month-Olds	**Positive**	
	Good (moral)	93
Mothers of thirty 28-month-olds collected data on their children's verbalizations that referred to psychological states. This table shows the percentage of children who used emotion terms to describe themselves or others. The majority of children used at least some emotion terms.	Love	87
	Like	80
	Funny	77
	Have fun	67
	Happy	60
	(Feel) good	47
	To be all right	37
	Have a good time	30
	Proud	27
	(Feel) better	27
	Surprised	13
	Negative	
	Bad (moral)	87
	Scared	73
	Mad	73
	Sad	57
	Scary	40
	Yucky	33
	Messy	30
	Angry	17
	(Feel) bad	10

Source: Adapted from Bretherton & Beeghly, 1982.

tend to agree that certain events, such as receiving a compliment, lead to happy emotions, whereas others, such as being shoved, lead to negative feelings. Furthermore, they are able to suggest ways to ameliorate another's negative emotions, such as hugging a crying sibling or sharing toys to placate an angered playmate (Fabes et al., 1988).

Knowledge about emotions can have ramifications for the child's social development. For example, children who have substantial knowledge about the emotions that usually accompany given situations have higher scores on tests of moral development, are less likely to evidence behavior problems, and are better liked by their peers (Cook, Greenberg, & Kusche, 1994; Denham et al., 1990; Dunn, Brown, & Maguire, 1995). The reason may be that children who have greater knowledge about emotions are more likely to respond appropriately to the emotional expressions of their agemates.

Knowledge about emotions is probably gleaned, at least in part, from parents. Children who have greater knowledge about emotions—who can label emotional expressions on faces, describe the feelings of another person in an emotion-related situation, and discuss the causes of emotions—typically have mothers who discuss and explain emotions, often in the context of the child expressing a negative emotion himself. In addition, when parents display more negative affect, children's understanding of emotions is poorer (Denham, Zoller, & Couchoud, 1994; Dunn & Brown, 1994). Parents who are angry probably end up providing fewer informative explanations about the nature of emotions.

Emotional development in older children is closely affiliated with advances in cognition that allow them to think in more complex, abstract terms. By the time they enter school, children begin to understand that changes in thoughts may lead to changes in feelings—that thinking happier thoughts, for example, might make a sad mood go away (Weiner & Handel, 1985). In addition, they comprehend the possibility of experiencing two contrasting emotions at the same time, such as feeling happy at receiving a gift but disappointed that it cannot yet be opened (Brown & Dunn, 1996).

As children approach adolescence, their concepts of emotions center increasingly on internal psychological states. That is, whereas younger children identify their own emotional states based on the situations they are in ("I'm happy when it's my birthday"), preadolescents and adolescents refer more frequently to their mental states ("I'm happy when I feel good inside") (Harris, Olthof, & Meerum Terwogt, 1981). In explaining why emotions fade with time, younger children refer to the fact that situations change; for example, sadness over a lost dog gives way to happiness when the family adopts another dog. At age ten years, children's explanations center around notions of forgetting or not thinking about one's previous emotional state (Harris et al., 1985).

Regulating Emotions In addition to becoming more adept at understanding various emotions, during the early and middle school years children generally become better able to regulate their own emotional states. Being able to calm down after getting angry or trying to change one's feelings of sadness may have important repercussions for the child's social relationships and, perhaps, mental health. For example, Richard Fabes and his colleagues found that children who heard a baby cry but were able to quickly regulate their state of physiological arousal were also likely to try to behave prosocially by comforting the baby. In contrast, children who became aroused but could not regulate their emotional state tended to withdraw from the situation or react with irritation, seeming to focus on their own feelings rather than those of another (Fabes et al., 1994).

Another recent study echoes the same theme. Preschool-age children, some of whom were identified as being at risk for behavior problems, were invited to a laboratory to participate in several cognitive tasks. After each child finished the session, he or she was offered a prize that was undesirable and disappointing. The children's

KEY THEME
Interaction Among Domains

KEY THEME
Interaction Among Domains

Emotion Regulation in Children at Risk for Conduct Problems

What happens when children who are at risk for behavior problems experience disappointment? In a study assessing this question, children who had been identified as being at high, medium, or low risk for conduct problems were given a prize that was disappointing to them. The graph shows that boys who were at risk showed a high percentage of negative emotions whether or not the experimenter was in the room with them. Low-risk boys were better able to regulate their negative feelings when someone was present in the room with them. Girls, in general, expressed fewer negative emotions regardless of whether or not they were with someone. The exception was low-risk girls, who expressed more negative emotions when alone.

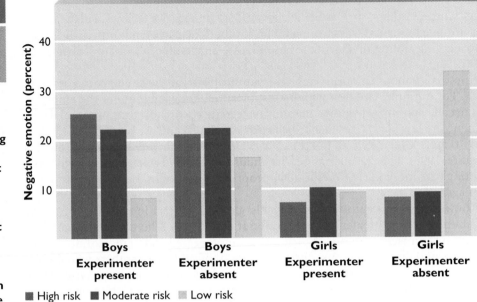

Source: Cole, Zahn-Waxler, & Smith, 1994.

KEY THEME
Interaction Among Domains

KEY THEME
Interaction Among Domains

display rules   Cultural guidelines concerning when, how, and to what degree to display emotions.

emotional expressions were observed in both the presence and absence of the experimenter. As Figure 11.2 indicates, boys who were at risk for conduct problems expressed more anger, speaking rudely and with obvious negative emotion, compared to low-risk boys; high-risk boys also maintained that anger for longer periods of time while in the presence of the experimenter. Low-risk boys showed anger too, but only when they were alone. The pattern for girls differed: girls from all risk categories expressed fewer negative emotions, with the exception of low-risk girls, who expressed more anger when alone. These results suggest that boys who are reported by parents and teachers to have fewer behavior problems are better able to manage their emotions when in a social setting. Boys with conduct problems, on the other hand, seem to have difficulty regulating their anger, a fact that could be a source of their disruptive behavior (Cole, Zahn-Waxler, & Smith, 1994). Thus, children's ability to control their emotions may have important consequences for the quality of social relationships with peers and the tendency to "get into trouble" later in childhood (Eisenberg et al., 1995).

Researchers have begun to chart the developmental course of emotion regulation, noting that infants often manage high arousal by looking away, as we saw earlier in this chapter. Two-year-olds use different strategies; when they are presented with a snack or a gift but must wait to obtain it, they typically shift their attention to other objects. Normally, this strategy alleviates their distress (Grolnick, Bridges, & Connell, 1996). By age three, many children show fewer tantrums and intense negative outbursts as they increasingly rely on language to communicate their intents and desires (Kopp, 1992). Researchers suspect that early childhood is a time when the frontal portions of the brain, which control excitation and inhibition of emotion-linked behavior, are maturing (Fox, 1994).

One skill that appears later in childhood is the ability to mask or "fake" an emotional state. By this time, children understand behaviors prescribed by cultural rules (for example, you are supposed to look happy when you receive a gift even if you don't like it) or behaviors necessary to obtain certain goals (you should smile even if you don't feel well if you want your mother to allow you to go to a friend's party). Paul Harris and his associates (Harris et al., 1986) examined this skill in using emotional **display rules,** the cultural guidelines governing when and how to express emotions, by asking six- and ten-year-olds to listen to stories in which the central

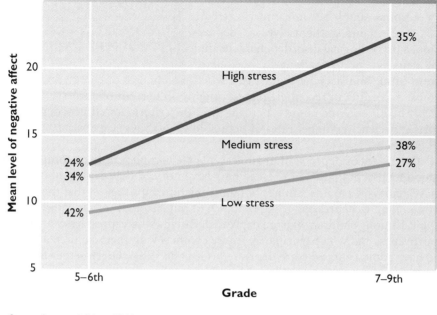

FIGURE 11.3

Frequency of Negative Affect Among Adolescents

To assess the types of emotions experienced by older children and adolescents, researchers "beeped" participants during their daily routines and asked them to report how they felt. The mean percentage of negative affect is shown along the vertical axis. The percentages indicated within the graph show the proportion of students in each grade reporting low, medium, or high stress associated with negative life events. Ninth-graders reported more negative affect than fifth-graders, and those who reported more stress in their lives were especially likely to experience negative emotions.

Source: Larson & Ham, 1993.

character felt either a positive or a negative emotion but had to hide it. After hearing the story, children were to describe verbally the facial expression of the protagonist along with how this person *really* felt. Even six-year-olds could state that the emotion displayed would not match the emotion felt, although ten-year-olds provided a fuller explanation. These results suggest that by the middle school years, children have developed a broad understanding of the social norms and expectations that surround the display of feelings.

The way children learn to manage their emotions probably depends on the kinds of experiences their parents provide (e.g., do parents provide opportunities for children to become aroused or to calm down?) as well as what children learn are the consequences of their own emotional displays (e.g., what happened when I had an angry tantrum versus when I "used my words"?). In addition, children may seek out experiences that are compatible with their emotional needs; some children may learn that sitting alone and playing is soothing, whereas others may seek the emotional release of a fast-paced basketball game (Thompson, 1994).

Emotions During Adolescence　By many popular accounts, adolescence is a unique phase in emotional development. Many laypeople, as well as professionals, believe adolescence is a time of "storm and stress," of emotional turmoil and extreme moodiness. Does research substantiate this belief? Although the evidence is somewhat mixed, several studies suggest that adolescents do experience more negative emotions than children of other ages and, in fact, may be at risk for psychological problems such as depression (Larson & Lampman-Petraitis, 1989; Petersen & Hamburg, 1986; Rutter, 1991).

In one recent study, for example, fifth-through-ninth-graders wore electronic pagers for one week as they went through their normal daily routines. At random times over the week, the researchers "beeped" the participants to indicate they should rate their mood just before the signal. In addition, the children and their parents filled out questionnaires assessing the number of positive and negative life events they experienced in the past six months. Figure 11.3 shows the results. Ninth-graders reported more negative affect than fifth-graders; moreover, for these young adolescents, negative emotions were associated with a greater number of negative life events, such as changing schools, breaking up with a boyfriend or girlfriend, or getting along poorly with parents (Larson & Ham, 1993).

For some adolescents, negative emotional states become more extreme and manifest themselves as depression, a psychological disorder characterized by dejected mood for lengthy periods of time, eating and sleeping problems, low self-esteem, loss of energy, and other symptoms. According to recent estimates, roughly 35 percent of adolescents experience depressed mood and about 7 percent meet the criteria for clinical depression, with girls experiencing higher rates of depression than boys (Ge et al., 1994; Petersen et al., 1993).

The causes of depression in adolescents are complex and not completely understood by psychologists, but researchers have noticed that depressed children often have depressed parents. Studies of family relationships suggest that there is a genetic component to depression (Pike et al., 1996) but also that certain family climates are typical among children who are depressed. Parents who express less warmth and supportiveness and who participate in more conflicts with their children are more likely to have adolescents who are depressed (Ge et al., 1996; Greenberger & Chen, 1996; Messer & Gross, 1995). Children who witness or are victims of domestic violence are also at risk for depression (Downey et al., 1994; Sternberg et al., 1993). Perhaps these parents, whose poor parenting skills may be due to their own depression, weaken their children's ability to regulate their own emotions or influence their children to form negative ideas about social relationships (Cummings, 1995). The result is the child, too, becomes depressed.

Why are adolescents especially vulnerable? Several explanations are possible. Changes in self-image may accompany the many biological changes in the body associated with puberty. Cognitive growth may mean the adolescent thinks more about the self and the future. For girls, confronting the conflicts presented by stereotypical gender roles—the desire to be competent in the face of societal roles for women that do not emphasize achievement—may play a significant part (Gjerde, 1995). In fact, it appears that depression in girls is linked to issues of self-concept, whereas in boys it is linked to acting-out behavior (Donnelly & Wilson, 1994). A switch from elementary to secondary school may mean adjustments in peer group relationships. Family relationships also may change; parents may have reached a stage in their relationship where they are considering divorce, for example (Petersen et al., 1993; Rutter, 1991). Clearly, understanding and preventing depression in adolescents requires a consideration of several domains of development.

ATYPICAL DEVELOPMENT

Adolescent Depression

Variations in Emotional Development

So far, our account of emotional development has emphasized commonalities across children in the expression and interpretation of emotions. Despite the generalities we have observed, however, there are noteworthy variations in emotional development among individuals and cultural groups.

KEY THEME
Individual Differences

Temperament Emotions are not just transitory states of feeling and expression; often we discern a child's more enduring emotional mood and describe her personality as "cheerful" or "hostile," "easygoing" or "irritable." Many researchers have found that infants and children vary in **temperament,** a style of behavioral functioning that encompasses the intensity of expression of moods, distractibility, adaptability, and persistence. Individual differences among infants in these qualities often remain relatively stable over time, even through middle childhood (Pedlow et al., 1993).

Stella Chess and Alexander Thomas (1982, 1990, 1991) have offered one conceptualization of temperament, identifying three basic patterns that many children display:

temperament Stable, early-appearing constellation of individual personality attributes believed to have a hereditary basis; includes sociability, emotionality, and activity level.

■ The *"easy"* child generally has positive moods, regular body functions, a low to moderate energy level in responses, and a positive approach to new situations. This child establishes regular feeding and sleeping schedules right from early infancy and adapts quickly to new routines, people, and places.

■ The *"difficult"* child is often in a negative mood, has irregular body functions, shows high-intensity reactions, withdraws from new stimuli, and is slow to adapt to new situations. The difficult child sleeps and eats on an unpredictable schedule, cries a good deal (and loudly), and has trouble adjusting to new routines.

■ The *"slow-to-warm-up"* child is somewhat negative in mood, has a low level of activity and intensity of reaction, and withdraws from new stimuli. However, with repeated exposure to new experiences, she or he begins to show interest and involvement.

Chess and Thomas (1991) note that children with different temperaments will evoke different patterns of reactions from their parents, teachers, and peers. "Easy" children usually elicit the most positive reactions from others, whereas children from the other two temperament categories typically draw more negative reactions. Later in life, children with "easy" temperaments may adjust more readily to important transitions, such as the start of school or making new friends. An important dimension of development, say Chess and Thomas, is the "goodness of fit" between the child's temperament and the demands placed on the child by the environment, specifically parents, teachers, peers, and others.

KEY THEME
Child's Active Role

In another set of studies, Jerome Kagan and his colleagues (Kagan et al., 1984; Kagan, Reznick, & Snidman, 1988) noted that some infants tend to show wariness and fearfulness when they encounter unfamiliar people, objects, or events, and others react with interest, spontaneity, and sociability. Both the first group, called *inhibited,* and the second, called *uninhibited,* tend to show their distinctive styles from infancy through middle childhood. Children in these two temperament categories also show different profiles of physiological responsiveness. Inhibited children, for example, show more pronounced cardiac reactions, a greater rise in blood pressure when changing from a sitting to a standing position, and more tension in skeletal muscles compared to uninhibited children. Kagan and his colleagues postulate that differential responsiveness in the limbic system, the portion of the brain below the cortex that controls emotions, may lie at the root of temperament differences (Kagan, Snidman, & Arcus, 1993). Studies comparing identical and fraternal twins, and parents and children, on these dimensions of temperament suggest that the tendency to be inhibited or uninhibited has a genetic component (Emde et al., 1992; Rickman & Davidson, 1994; Robinson et al., 1992). Other researchers have defined temperament similarly in terms of the tendency toward expressivity in manifesting basic emotions such as fear or pleasure (Goldsmith & Campos, 1982, 1990) or, more generally, in terms of excitability and the ability to regulate the self and one's level of arousal (Rothbart, 1986; Rothbart, Derryberry, & Posner, 1994).

While the temperament categories developed by different investigators have proven useful, recent research suggests that categorizing a child's temperament as fundamentally "positive" *or* "negative" is too simplistic. That is, children who tend to respond negatively may also be inclined to react positively; in fact, different combinations of these two emotional tendencies may exist across different children. A baby who is irritable may also tend to smile a lot. A child with this temperament pattern may be easier to interact with than a child who is irritable but doesn't smile (Belsky, Hsieh, & Crnic, 1996).

KEY THEME
Individual Differences

Another caution concerns the cross-cultural dimensions of temperament. Although the preceding categories may capture individual differences in the emotional styles of Western infants, they may not apply to children from other cultures. For example, when Japanese mothers were asked to describe the behavioral styles of their infants, the "easy/difficult" dimension appeared in their responses, but so did unique qualities such as "self-assertiveness" (for example, a tendency to like pleasant sounds, enjoy exercising the body, and feed quickly) (Shwalb, Shwalb, & Shoji, 1994). Cul-

KEY THEME
Sociocultural Influence

tural differences in parental expectations regarding children's temperament may, in turn, lead to differences in parenting styles.

Does early temperament predict any of the child's characteristics later in life? It appears so, according to the results of several recent studies. For example, the extent to which an infant tends to show negative emotions at three months of age predicts poorer cognitive abilities for that child at age four years, even when factors such as the mother's responsiveness are ruled out as influences on the child (Lewis, 1993). In the domain of social relationships, preschool boys who tend to exhibit negative affect often have poorer social skills and lower status among their peers (Eisenberg et al., 1993). Similarly, infants who tend to express anger and frustration score higher on measures of aggression at age six to seven years than children who express less anger as infants (Rothbart, Ahadi, & Hershey, 1994). Likewise, a relationship exists between a child's negativism, short attention span, and swings in emotions at age three and hyperactivity, attention problems, and antisocial behavior in adolescence (Caspi et al., 1995). It seems that the relatively stable emotional style a particular child displays early in life may have a far-reaching impact on both cognitive and social functioning later on.

Sex Differences in Emotions   According to the familiar stereotype, females are more emotionally expressive and more sensitive to the emotional states of others than are males. Do boys and girls actually differ in any facet of emotional development? Several recent studies suggest that the answer is yes. During the first six months of infancy, girls tend to show more positive emotions, including interest and joy, than boys (Matias & Cohn, 1993). In another study, when seven- and twelve-year-olds played a game with a peer, girls were more likely than boys to show a positive or negative emotion when the peer made a comment such as "she looks friendly" or "she doesn't look nice" (Casey, 1993). Later in adolescence, girls smile more than boys both on their own initiative and in response to the smile of another (Hall & Halberstadt, 1986). Girls also begin to show more anxieties than boys during the school years—fears about tests, family issues, health, and other concerns (Orton, 1982; Scarr et al., 1981). Finally, some researchers report that girls are better than boys at decoding the emotional expressions of others (Brown & Dunn, 1996; Hall, 1978, 1984).

Observations of parents' behaviors suggest that many of these sex differences may be taught or modeled directly. For example, mothers and fathers spend more time trying to get their infant daughters to smile than they do their infant sons (Moss, 1974). Mothers of preschoolers also mention feeling states more often and discuss a wider variety of emotions when they talk with their daughters than when conversing with their sons (Dunn, Bretherton, & Munn, 1987; Kuebli, Butler, & Fivush, 1995). Mothers are also more facially expressive when they play with their two-year-old girls compared to boys, thus exposing them to a greater range of emotions and displaying more social smiles (Malatesta et al., 1989). In general, parents encourage girls to maintain close emotional relationships and to show affection, whereas they instruct boys to control their emotions (Block, 1973). Thus, although biological explanations of sex differences cannot be ruled out completely, many of the emotional behaviors we see in males and females appear to be influenced by their learning histories.

Cross-Cultural Differences in Emotions   The tendency of children to express and detect emotions varies as a function of the culture in which they are raised. American children, for example, tend to smile more in response to the smile of a stranger than do Israeli children (Alexander & Babad, 1981). On the other end of the emotional spectrum, Chinese children are better able to identify fearful and sad situations than are American children (Borke, 1973). These differences may reflect the child's incorporation of particular cultural beliefs about emotions.

A study of crying among the Kipsigis of Kenya provides a good example of how parenting practices reflect cultural values and shape the child's emotional responses. In the Kipsigis culture, crying is regarded as a positive behavior among infants but a negative behavior among older children, particularly as they approach their passage to adulthood. To discourage crying in her growing child, the Kipsigi mother does not hurry to pick him up or hug him when he cries; instead, she waits for him to approach her. And, rather than focusing on the child's behavior and the reasons for it, she encourages him to talk about other things and to return to the activities in which he had been engaged prior to crying (Harkness & Super, 1985). We saw at the beginning of this chapter how, in a similar fashion, Gusii mothers prepare their children for a style of emotionally neutral interactions with others. Thus, the cultural norms governing emotions, mediated through parental behaviors, serve to elaborate and refine the child's earliest emotional tendencies.

ATTACHMENT: EMOTIONAL RELATIONSHIPS WITH OTHERS

One of the most widely discussed and actively researched aspects of emotional and social development is **attachment,** the strong emotional bond that emerges between infant and caregivers. The concept of attachment occupies a prominent place in developmental psychology because of its link with successful cognitive, social, and emotional development throughout childhood.

How does attachment emerge between infant and caregiver? In what ways is this emotional bond expressed? What roles do the caregiver and infant play in its formation? What is the significance of attachment in the later development of the child? Do we observe the same patterns of attachment among children across cultures? In this portion of the chapter, we will examine the course of attachment in infancy and early childhood and explore the answers to these questions.

The Origins of Attachment: Theoretical Perspectives

What forces govern the emergence of attachment? Psychological explanations have varied over the last several decades according to the dominant theoretical orientation. Learning theorists emphasize the importance of the feeding situation, ethologists identify biological predispositions, and cognitive theorists focus on the child's advances in thinking. Let us examine each of these perspectives in turn.

Learning Theory   Learning theorists believe certain basic drives, such as hunger, are satisfied by *primary reinforcers,* rewards that gratify biological needs. In the case of the young infant, an important primary reinforcer is food. Other rewards, called **secondary reinforcers,** acquire their reinforcing qualities from their association with primary reinforcers. Because they are connected repeatedly with the reduction of the hunger drive, mothers acquire secondary reinforcing properties. Eventually the mother's presence in contexts outside feeding is rewarding to the infant.

Is the activity of feeding related to the emergence of infant-mother attachments, as learning theorists predict? Evidently not, according to a series of classic experiments conducted by Harry Harlow and his associates (Harlow & Zimmerman, 1959). These investigators separated infant monkeys from their mothers and provided them instead with extended contact with two surrogate mothers, one a figure made of wire mesh and the other a figure covered with terry cloth. The wire surrogate was equipped for feeding half of the monkeys; the terry-cloth surrogate fed the other half. The infant monkeys lived with both their surrogates for at least 165 days, during which time several observations were made of the monkeys' behaviors. One measure was the number of hours per day spent with each surrogate. As Figure 11.4 shows, infant monkeys preferred the cloth "mother" regardless of which surrogate was providing nourishment. In a subsequent test of attachment, when a frightening stimulus such as a mechanical spider was introduced into the monkeys' cage, the monkeys chose the cloth mother to run and cling to, even if they had been fed by the wire mother.

KEY THEME
Nature/Nurture

attachment   Strong emotional bond that emerges between infant and caregiver.

secondary reinforcer   Object or person that attains rewarding value because of its association with a primary reinforcer.

Harlow's experiments showed that infant monkeys reared with surrogate mothers preferred the cloth mother even when the wire mother provided nourishment. Here, the infant monkey is actually nursing from the wire mother but still maintains contact with the cloth mother. These findings challenge the hypothesis that attachment arises from the caregiver's association with feeding the child.

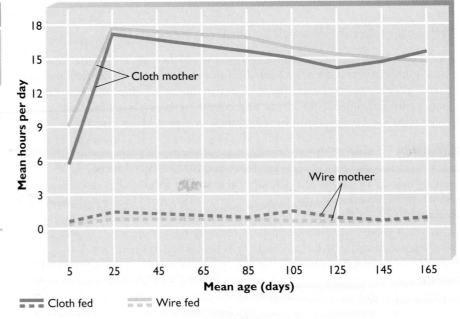

FIGURE 11.4

Forming Attachments: The "Cloth Mother" and "Wire Mother" Experiment

In Harlow's research, infant monkeys spent more time with a cloth surrogate mother than with a wire surrogate mother, regardless of which one fed them. This graph shows how much time infant monkeys spent with each surrogate as a function of feeding condition.

Source: Adapted from Harlow & Zimmerman, 1959.

Harlow's findings challenged the view that attachments are based on the mother's acquisition of secondary-drive characteristics. The fact that the infant monkeys did not seek out the surrogate that fed them under either normal or stressful conditions led Harlow to conclude that "contact comfort," the security provided by a physically soothing object, played a greater role in attachment than the simple act of feeding.

KEY THEME
Nature/Nurture

The Ethological View   Proponents of the ethological position state that attachments occur as the result of the infant's innate tendency to signal the caregiver and the caregiver's corresponding predisposition to react to these signals. As a result, infant and caregiver are brought together, a bond is forged between them, and the survival of the infant is ensured. In other words, attachment is an adaptive, biologically programmed response system that is activated early in the infant's development and follows many of the principles of *imprinting* described in Chapter 1.

The principal spokesperson for this perspective, John Bowlby (1958, 1969), initially was concerned with the detrimental effects of institutionalization on infants and young children. Scientists in the late 1940s had reported that children who spent extended periods of time in hospitals and orphanages during their early years often showed serious developmental problems, including profound withdrawal from social interactions, intellectual impairments, and, in some cases, physical delays (Skodak & Skeels, 1949; Spitz, 1946a). Bowlby proposed that the cause lay in the lack of a close emotional bond between child and primary caregiver.

Bowlby maintained that attachments develop in a fixed sequence, beginning with the infant's emission of **signaling behaviors,** such as crying and smiling. In the first two months, most infants emit these signals indiscriminately, but by six months of age, smiles and cries become increasingly restricted to the presence of the caregiver, usually the mother. From six to twelve months of age, clearer signs of the infant's strong attachment to the caregiver develop. At that point, most infants become visibly upset at the mother's departure, a phenomenon called **separation protest,** and also show signs of greeting her upon her return. Once they are able to move about, infants will ensure their nearness to their mothers by approaching and clinging to them. About the same time, they also display **stranger anxiety,** a wariness or fear at the approach of someone unfamiliar. The final phase of attachment occurs at about three years of age, when the relationship between mother and child becomes more of a partnership and the child comes to appreciate the mother's feelings, motives, and goals. The regularity with which infants show this sequence of behaviors, says Bowlby, suggests its biological basis.

According to Bowlby, infants become attached to those who respond consistently and appropriately to their signaling behaviors. Thus, Bowlby saw the maladaptive development of institutionalized infants as a consequence of the absence of the dynamic, contingent interaction between child and caregiver. Although institutional settings met children's basic physical needs, they often did so at the convenience of the caregiver's schedule rather than in response to the child's behaviors. Bowlby's general scheme concerning the origins and course of attachment has framed numerous modern-day investigations of the development of attachment.

Cognitive-Developmental Theory   Followers of Piaget assert that the development of attachment depends on the child's prior acquisition of certain cognitive capabilities, specifically the concept of *object permanence*. Before he can show stranger or separation anxiety, the infant must have an understanding of the continuing existence of objects and people. To be able to show stranger anxiety, for example, the child must have some internalized representation of the caregiver against which to compare the stranger's face. Similarly, separation protest depends on the infant's realization that the caregiver continues to exist in a location apart from him.

Is there evidence to suggest that recognition of object permanence either precedes or accompanies stranger and separation anxiety? Research shows that object permanence and strong indications of attachment are present in eight-month-olds almost simultaneously (Schaffer & Emerson, 1964). Moreover, infants who are in the more advanced stages of the development of object permanence display stronger, more forceful protests when their mothers depart (Lester et al., 1974). Evidently, advances in thinking do play at least some role in the development of attachments.

The Developmental Course of Attachment

For the most part, research has confirmed the sequence of behaviors outlined by Bowlby in the emergence of attachment. Infants can discriminate their mothers' faces

KEY THEME
Interaction Among Domains

signaling behavior   In ethological theory, a behavior such as crying or smiling that brings the caregiver physically close to the infant.

separation protest   Distress the infant shows when the caregiver leaves the immediate environment.

stranger anxiety   Fear or distress an infant shows at the approach of an unfamiliar person.

from that of a stranger at two days of age and their mothers' voices and odors a few days after that (DeCasper & Fifer, 1980; Field et al., 1984; MacFarlane, 1975). However, they emit their signals to anyone who is available. By about seven months of age, these indiscriminate behaviors give way to attachments to specific people, most notably the mother or primary caregiver. Stranger anxiety becomes full blown, and separation protest is usually manifested as well. In the months that follow, children show evidence of multiple attachments to fathers, substitute caregivers, and grandparents (Schaffer & Emerson, 1964).

At age two years most children continue to show strong attachments, but by age three years some of the manifestations of this bond begin to change. Separation distress diminishes for most children, probably due to advances in cognition. For example, children begin to appreciate the fact that even though the caregiver may depart for several hours, she always returns (Marvin, 1977). The impact of repeated experience with separation and reunion episodes may extend to a more general understanding that negative emotional experiences often yield to strong positive affect, that distress can be followed by stability (Schore, 1994). As children develop insights into the perspectives of others and as their communication skills improve, they can better understand the reasons for temporary separations and can express their emotions in ways other than crying or clinging. The Chronology on the next page summarizes the sequence of changes in emotional development and attachment.

Measuring Attachment   The **Strange Situation,** developed by Mary Ainsworth and her associates, is a standardized task frequently employed to measure the quality of the child's emotional ties to her mother (Ainsworth et al., 1978). Table 11.2 shows the eight episodes that comprise this measure, which is administered in a laboratory setting.

On the basis of her extensive observations of the patterns of behaviors shown by infants, Ainsworth (Ainsworth et al., 1978) distinguished three patterns of attachment, *secure attachment* and two categories of *insecure attachment*:

■ **Secure attachment**   Children in this group showed many clear signs of attachment by displaying stranger anxiety and separation protest, and greeting the mother enthusiastically upon her return. They also used the mother as a *secure base for exploration,* exploring their new surroundings but looking or moving back to the mother as though to "check in" with her. They obviously felt comfortable in the presence of the mother and distressed and apprehensive in her absence.

■ **Avoidant attachment**   Infants in this category were less distressed when the mother left and less enthusiastic in greeting her when she returned to the laboratory room. In fact, they tended to avoid or ignore her, playing in isolation even when she was present in the room.

■ **Ambivalent attachment**   Tension characterized the behaviors these children showed toward their mothers. Although they displayed noticeable proximity-seeking behaviors when the mother was in the room, sometimes clinging excessively to her, they also showed angry, rejecting behavior, even hitting or pushing her away. Some children in this category were extremely passive, showing limited exploratory play except for bouts of crying that were used as signals to be picked up and held.

In Ainsworth's original study, 63 percent of the infants were categorized as securely attached, 29 percent as avoidantly attached, and 8 percent as ambivalently attached. In our society, the behaviors of the securely attached group are generally seen as the healthiest, most desirable pattern against which other patterns are compared.

A newer way to measure attachment is the *Q-sort.* In this method, mother and infant are observed for a specified period of time, after which the observer sorts through a series of cards containing descriptions of the mother-infant relationship. Several piles are created from "least characteristic" to "most characteristic" of the child. The child's attachment score is based on the extent to which these ratings correlate with the characteristics of a securely attached child defined by a panel of experts on childhood attachment (Waters & Deane, 1985).

KEY THEME
Interaction Among Domains

Strange Situation   Standardized test that assesses the quality of infant-caregiver attachment.

secure attachment   Attachment category defined by the infant's distress at separation from the caregiver and enthusiastic greeting upon her return. The infant also displays stranger anxiety and uses the caregiver as a secure base for exploration.

avoidant attachment   Insecure attachment in which the infant shows little separation protest and does not pay much attention to the caregiver's return.

ambivalent attachment   Insecure attachment in which the infant shows separation protest but also distress upon the caregiver's return.

CHRONOLOGY
Emotional Development

—Newborn—

— 1 Yr.

Newborn —————— **Newborn**

- Discriminates mother's face, voice, and smell from others.
- Expresses interest, distress, disgust, joy, sadness, anger, and surprise.
- Imitates facial expressions for happiness, surprise, and sadness.
- Smiles during REM sleep.
- Cries when has physical needs.

— 2 Yrs.

1 Mo.

2 Mos.

18–24 Months

- Displays guilt, shame, and envy.
- Uses words to describe feeling states.
- Regulates emotions by shifting attention to objects that do not cause distress.

3 Mos.

1 Month

- Displays "fussy cry."

— 3 Yrs.

4 Mos.

— 4 Yrs.

3–4 Years

- Smiles more to same-sex peers.
- Describes the causes and consequences of emotions.
- Shows decline in tantrums and negative outbursts.
- Shows decline in separation distress and other attachment behaviors typical of infancy.

5 Mos.

3 Months

- Smiles at caregiver.
- Distinguishes among anger, surprise, and sadness.
- Participates in interactive synchrony.

— 5 Yrs.

6 Mos.

— 6 Yrs.

7 Mos.

4 Months

- Laughs in response to tactile and auditory stimuli.

6–7 Years

- Understands that emotions fade with time and that thoughts can control emotions.
- Understands the possibility of feeling two emotions at once.

— 7 Yrs.

8 Mos.

7 Months

- Expresses fear.
- Shows specific attachments, stranger anxiety, and separation protest.

— 8 Yrs.

9 Mos.

— 9 Yrs.

10 Mos.

11 Mos.

— 10 Yrs.

10–12 Years

- Can mask or "fake" emotions.
- Has concepts of emotions based on internal feeling states.

— 11 Yrs.

12 Mos.

12 Months

- Begins to display social referencing.

— 12 Yrs.

13 Mos.

— 13 Yrs.

14 Mos.

— 14 Yrs.

15 Mos.

— 15 Yrs.

16 Mos.

— 16 Yrs.

17 Mos.

— 17 Yrs.

18 Mos.

— 18 Yrs.

This chart describes the sequence of emotional development based on the findings of research. Children often show individual differences in the exact ages at which they display the various developmental achievements outlined here.

TABLE 11.2	The Episodes of the Strange Situation		
Number of Episode	**Persons Present**	**Duration**	**Brief Description of Action**
1	Mother, baby, and observer	30 seconds	Observer introduces mother and baby to experimental room, then leaves.
2	Mother and baby	3 minutes	Mother is nonparticipant while baby explores; if necessary, play is stimulated after 2 minutes.
3	Stranger, mother, and baby	3 minutes	Stranger enters. Minute 1: stranger silent. Minute 2: stranger converses with mother. Minute 3: stranger approaches baby. After 3 minutes mother leaves unobtrusively.
4	Stranger and baby	3 minutes or less[a]	First separation episode. Stranger's behavior is geared to that of baby.
5	Mother and baby	3 minutes or more[b]	First reunion episode. Mother greets and comforts baby, then tries to settle him again in play. Mother then leaves, saying bye-bye.
6	Baby alone	3 minutes or less[a]	Second separation episode.
7	Stranger and baby	3 minutes or less[a]	Continuation of second separation. Stranger enters and gears her behavior to that of baby.
8	Mother and baby	3 minutes	Second reunion episode. Mother enters, greets baby, then picks him up. Meanwhile stranger leaves unobtrusively.

[a]Episode is curtailed if the baby is unduly distressed. [b]Episode is prolonged if more time is required for the baby to become involved in play.
Source: Campos et al., 1983.

KEY THEME
Nature/Nurture

The Antedecents of Secure Attachment How do secure, high-quality attachments develop? Research by Mary Ainsworth and her colleagues suggests that the mother's style of interacting with her infant and her responsivity to the baby's signals may be key factors. The ability of caregiver and infant to achieve moments of interactive synchrony may also be important.

Ainsworth and her associates visited the homes of twenty-six infants and their mothers for about four hours every three weeks during the entire first year of the infants' lives (Ainsworth, Bell, & Stayton, 1971, 1972, 1974). When they were about a year old, the infants were brought to the laboratory to be tested in the Strange Situation and were classified according to the quality of attachment to their mothers. An attempt then was made to find relationships between the attachment classification and specific maternal behaviors observed earlier. The results of this study indicated that mothers of securely attached infants were *sensitive* to their children's signals, noticing their cues and interpreting them correctly. These mothers were *accepting* of their role as caregiver. They displayed *cooperation*; mothers of securely attached infants would wait until the child finished her activity or was in a good mood before imposing a request. Gentle persuasion rather than assertive control was used. Mothers in this group were also *accessible,* providing quick responses to the child's signals, particularly crying. They were not distracted by their own thoughts and activities. In contrast, mothers of the insecurely attached group were often rigid, unresponsive, and demanding in their parenting style and did not feel positively about their role as caregiver.

Other researchers have found that mothers of securely attached infants have higher self-esteem, feel more competent, and see themselves as being more accepted by their own parents and peers than do mothers of insecurely attached infants (Tronick, Ricks, & Cohn, 1982). Mothers of securely attached infants have also been found to be more affectionate, more positive, and less intrusive in their vocalizations than mothers of insecurely attached infants (Bates, Maslin, & Frankel, 1985; Isabella, 1993; Izard et al., 1991; Roggman, Langlois, & Hubbs-Tait, 1987). Similar patterns of mothering are associated with secure attachments in preschoolers (Stevenson-Hinde & Shouldice, 1995).

Interactive synchrony may also be important in the emergence of attachments. One group of researchers observed the interactions of mothers and their infants at one, three, and nine months of age, recording each instance in which the infants' and mothers' behaviors co-occurred and produced a mutually satisfying outcome. For example, if the infant gazed at the mother, the mother verbalized, or if the infant fussed and cried, the mother soothed him. The infants' attachments were then assessed at one year of age. According to the results, securely attached infants had experienced a greater number of synchronous interactions in the prior months, a finding other researchers have replicated (Isabella, Belsky, & von Eye, 1989; Scholmerich et al., 1995). Therefore, in accounting for the emergence of secure attachment, it is important to consider maternal behavior *as it is related to the child's behavior.*

Attachments to Fathers   Because mothers traditionally have fulfilled the role of primary caregiver, most of the emphasis in this chapter, and in the research in child psychology, has been on the emotional bond that develops between child and mother. With large numbers of women participating in the labor force, however, and challenges to the assumption that females have the exclusive role in child care, many caregiving responsibilities have been assumed by others either within or outside the family. Moreover, researchers in developmental psychology have begun to recognize the glaring absence of information on how another important family member, the father, interacts with his children. The result has been a growing literature on father-child interaction.

In general, fathers spend far less time interacting with and caring for their children than mothers do. Nevertheless, many infants clearly do form attachments to their fathers. In the Strange Situation, these infants show signs of separation protest when the father leaves the room and greet him upon his return. They also use him as a secure base for exploration (Kotelchuk, 1976). Mothers may still be preferred in certain circumstances, as in the presence of a stranger or when children seek to be comforted (Cohen & Campos, 1974). When fathers spend time in face-to-face interactions with their infants and display sensitivity and playfulness, however, their infants show clear signs of attachment to them (Chibucos & Kail, 1981; Cox et al., 1992). Securely attached infants also tend to have fathers who are sociable, are agreeable, and express positive emotions (Belsky, 1996). Given the opportunity to be nurturant and responsive, fathers certainly can become partners in strong, secure attachments.

Healthy relationships with fathers can buffer children who are at risk due to impaired interactions with their mothers. Recall how infants with depressed mothers often have poor-quality interactions with them. One group of researchers found that infants with depressed mothers often had more positive interactions with their fathers (Hossain et al., 1994). In adolescence, a positive relationship with the father seems to protect children from the behavior problems associated with having a depressed mother (Tannenbaum & Forehand, 1994). These studies suggest that *with*

Infants show clear signs of attachment to fathers, especially when fathers spend time in rewarding, mutually engaging interactions with them. Research shows that healthy attachments to fathers can buffer children who are at risk because of impaired interactions with their mothers.

whom children have positive interactions matters less than the fact that they have those interactions. They also suggest that fathers fulfill a role in the family that cannot be ignored.

Temperament and Attachment   Caregivers are not solely responsible for the emergence of attachment. Because attachments form in the context of interactions between caregiver and infant, it seems reasonable to postulate that the infant's own style as a communication partner contributes significantly to the growth of an affectional bond.

Several researchers have reported a link between infant characteristics such as irritability and proneness to distress and subsequent attachment behaviors in the Strange Situation (Bates, Maslin, & Frankel, 1985; Goldsmith & Alansky, 1987; Miyake, Chen, & Campos, 1985). For example, one recent study found that two-day-old infants' proneness to distress when a pacifier was removed from their mouths was related to insecure attachment at fourteen months of age (Calkins & Fox, 1992). Similarly, in a study of Dutch infants who were identified as very irritable newborns, 74 percent were classified as insecurely attached at eighteen months of age (van den Boom, 1994, 1995). Yet early irritability does not necessarily predispose children to become insecurely attached. In the same study of Dutch infants, a second group of irritable newborns and their mothers participated in an intervention program that resulted in only 28 percent being scored as insecurely attached later in infancy. The details of the intervention are discussed in the following feature.

KEY THEME
Child's Active Role

KEY THEME
Individual Differences

The phone call turned out to be from Gwen, Cindy's close friend. The two of them had shared many life experiences since their childhood days, but Cindy still found it remarkable that they had had their babies within three months of each other. Cindy knew, though, that motherhood was a challenge for Gwen. Gwen's son, unlike Michael, was hard to figure out and to keep happy. He didn't seem to like being held very much and was often cranky both before and

RESEARCH APPLIED TO PARENTING

Promoting Secure Attachment in Irritable Infants

after feeding. Gwen was a loving mother, but at times she was at her wits' end trying to think of ways to soothe her baby. When Cindy picked up the phone, she could tell from Gwen's voice that she was looking for advice on how to handle her difficult child.

What can parents do if their infant is born with a "difficult" temperamental style, showing more negative than positive emotions, fussing and crying, and smiling infrequently? Research carried out in the Netherlands in which mother-child interaction was observed in the home monthly up until the infants were six months of age shows that mothers of irritable infants displayed distinct patterns of reactions. They exhibited less visual and physical contact with their babies, were less involved with them, and responded less when their babies smiled or showed other positive social behaviors (van den Boom & Hoeksma, 1994). Although many of the differences between mothers of irritable and nonirritable infants disappeared by the time their children were six months old, such negative parent-child interactions may predispose children to develop insecure attachments.

In a second study (van den Boom, 1994, 1995), mothers of irritable newborns were randomly assigned to either an intervention group or a control group when their infants were six months of age. During three in-home training sessions conducted every three weeks, mothers in the intervention group were taught to be more responsive to the cues their infants provided. The infants and mothers were observed again when the children were twelve, eighteen, twenty-four, and forty-two months of age. The benefits of the intervention were clear: children in the experimental group were far more likely to be securely attached than children in the control group, even into toddlerhood. These children were also more cooperative, displayed fewer behavior problems, and engaged in more activities and verbal interactions with their mothers than the control group children. Even though mothers had received training up to several years earlier, they continued to show responsive, sensitive parenting.

What exactly were mothers in the intervention group taught? Following are the essential ingredients of the training package:

1. *Attend to the infant's signals, especially by imitating the baby's behaviors and repeating one's own verbalizations.* If the infant averts his gaze, remain silent, since gaze aversion often means the caregiver has not interpreted the child's signals correctly. These techniques aim to slow down the tempo of mother-infant interactions and to

One technique used in a program to promote secure attachments among irritable infants is to find the soothing technique that works for the infant and stick with that technique. For some infants, holding the baby on the shoulder is effective.

simplify them. The overall goal of these procedures is to help the mothers perceive and interpret infant signals accurately.

2. *Try to soothe the fussing or crying infant.* Since some infants seem to respond negatively to being cuddled or held in close physical contact, try to find a technique suitable for the particular child and her preferences, for example, feeding or vocalizing to her. Once an effective technique is identified, stick with it. Again, the idea is to avoid rapid changes in maternal behavior that might create further frustration and distress in the infant.

3. *Pay attention to the infant's positive signals instead of focusing on his negative behaviors.* Play with the infant using games and toys, paying attention to how he responds.

In general, the goal of the program was to help mothers correctly read and respond to their own infants' signals, characteristics of mothering that Ainsworth's early studies identified as precursors of secure attachment. As the results described earlier indicate, infants who participated in this intervention showed many desirable outcomes even years after the intervention itself was terminated.

The Modifiability of Attachments   How stable are attachments once they are formed? The attachment classification given to an infant at age twelve months typically remains the same when measured at eighteen months (Waters, 1978). Using a measure of attachment specifically developed for testing older children and based on behavior during a reunion with the mother, Mary Main and Jude Cassidy (1988) found that classifications made at six years of age could be predicted from classifications made at age twelve months for 84 percent of the sample. A similar rate of stability of attachment classification was observed among children growing up in southern Germany (Wartner et al., 1994). On the other hand, the most recent research on this issue suggests that the rate of stability of attachment is closer to 50 percent (Belsky et al., 1996). Perhaps procedural differences in these studies explain this discrepancy, or perhaps changes have occurred in the sociocultural environment in recent years that contribute to greater instability.

Psychologists have known for some time that stresses or changes in the family's circumstances can affect the quality of attachment. In a large-scale study conducted in Minneapolis, Brian Vaughn and his colleagues examined attachment classifications for infants at twelve months and again at eighteen months of age (Vaughn et al., 1979). The families of the majority of these infants were living at or below the poverty level. Most of the mothers were single parents, and many of the families experienced a significant change such as a shift in residence or the addition or loss of an adult in the living group during the six months between observations. In this study, 20 percent of the infants who had been securely attached at twelve months of age were insecurely attached at eighteen months. Furthermore, shifts from secure to insecure attachments were associated with maternal reports of a greater number of stressful events in their lives, such as loss of employment, financial problems, or illness. Another study showed, however, that when new mothers from low socioeconomic backgrounds are assisted by a volunteer coach who provides social support and information about child rearing, secure attachments among infants are more likely to result (Jacobson & Frye, 1991).

Attachment and Later Development   The importance of attachment has been underscored by research findings showing that secure attachments are related to positive developmental outcomes in both social and cognitive spheres when children become older. Leah Matas and her associates assessed the quality of attachments of forty-eight infants when they were eighteen months of age (Matas, Arend, & Sroufe, 1978). Six months later, these same children were observed for the quality of their play and their problem-solving styles. Children who had earlier been categorized as securely attached were more enthusiastic and compliant with their mothers' suggestions in the problem-solving tasks and showed more positive affect and persistence than their insecurely attached counterparts. They also engaged in more symbolic play and displayed less crying and whining. Other researchers have noted that securely attached children show advantages in cognitive reasoning well into the middle school years and adolescence. Perhaps the secure child's readiness to explore the environment provides the kind of intellectual stimulation that leads to better cognitive performance (Jacobsen, Edelstein, & Hofman, 1994).

KEY THEME
Interaction Among Domains

Securely attached children have also been found to be more socially competent with their peers at age three-and-a-half years, showing more leadership, greater sympathy, and less withdrawal from social interactions (Waters, Wippman, & Sroufe, 1979). They evidenced stronger signs of "ego resiliency" at age five years, meaning they responded to problems in a flexible, persistent, and resourceful manner (Arend, Gove, & Sroufe, 1979). In contrast, insecurely attached infants, particularly those who show avoidant patterns, do not fare so well in the preschool years, according to another study (Erickson, Sroufe, & Egeland, 1985). Children with this attachment classification were found to display many maladaptive and undesirable behaviors, such as high dependency, noncompliance, and poor social skills in peer interactions. They also were described by teachers as hostile, impulsive, and withdrawn. Moreover, avoidant children tend to have negative representations of peers and to interpret peers' behaviors as hostile (Cassidy et al., 1996).

The effects of early attachments may carry over well into adolescence and the adult years, perhaps because children construct *internal working models of relationships* that influence their future emotional ties to family, friends, and romantic partners (Bowlby, 1973; Main, Kaplan, & Cassidy, 1985). Adolescents who evidence secure attachments to their parents, in the sense of expressing affection for and trust in them, generally have high self-esteem, have a strong sense of personal identity, and display social competence (Rice, 1990). They also engage in more constructive problem solving when discussing controversial topics, such as dating and household rules, with their parents (Kobak et al., 1993). Furthermore, the quality of an individual's attachment during childhood may influence his or her parenting style as an adult. Margaret Ricks (1985) studied the intergenerational effects of attachment by assessing the self-esteem and childhood recollections of twenty-eight middle-class mothers. Mothers of securely attached infants had higher self-esteem scores and more positive recollections of their own childhood relationships with parents and peers. Researchers have also noted significant relationships between the attachment classifications given to parents through the Adult Attachment Interview (a measure based on parents' descriptions and evaluations of their own childhood attachment relations) and the attachment styles of their infants (Benoit & Parker, 1994; Steele, Steele, & Fonagy, 1996). Evidently, attachments have strong intergenerational links.

Three Special Cases: Prematurity, Adoption, and Abuse

In some contexts, the ideal pattern of caregiver-child interaction may be disrupted, for example, when mother and infant are physically separated during the early days of their partnership due to the infant's premature birth or when the child is placed for adoption and nonbiological parents assume the caregiving role. Other children are the victims of physical abuse or neglect. Is there any evidence that attachments suffer in such cases? A consideration of these issues will further illuminate the ways in which early caregiver-child relationships influence subsequent child development.

Prematurity   The preterm infant looks and behaves differently than the infant with the benefit of a full thirty-eight weeks in utero. In all likelihood, the premature infant will be very small and fragile looking, less alert and responsive to stimulation, and more difficult to comfort. Cries, but not smiles, are very frequent (Goldberg, 1979). In addition, mothers and their premature infants usually are separated physically, sometimes for several weeks, while the babies receive the medical care necessary to ensure their well-being and even survival. If attachments were based largely on mutually rewarding infant-caregiver interactions, we might expect premature infants to develop insecure attachments with their mothers.

In the hospital nursery, mothers of premature infants indeed behave in a markedly different manner than mothers of full-term infants. Mothers of premature babies touch, hold, and smile at their babies less often than do mothers of full-term infants (DiVitto & Goldberg, 1979). As their babies get older, however, mothers of premature infants actually become more active than mothers of full-term babies in stimulating them: they initiate and maintain more interactions, even to the point of being excessive. These behaviors may stem from the mother's desire to alter the premature's unresponsive pattern or to stimulate the child in an effort to spur slowed development. As Figure 11.5 shows, infants often react to these maternal behaviors by averting their gaze, as though to shut out the added stimulation (Field, 1977, 1982).

Given the differences in maternal styles with premature babies, is there a corresponding impact on the attachments of these infants? In a comparison of twenty full-term and twenty premature infants at eleven months of age, Ann Frodi and Ross Thompson (1985) observed no significant differences in the patterns of attachments. Most of the children in both groups were observed to be securely attached. By one year of age, many premature infants "rebound" from the negative effects of early birth, especially if they encounter a responsive, supportive environment. Mothers may also adapt their styles in later months to conform more closely with the rhythms and needs of the child. Thus, the early developmental risk posed by prematurity does not automatically lead to persistent problems in mother-child relations or other developmental patterns. On the other hand, very-low-birthweight infants—those under 1,250 grams—have been found to be at risk for insecure attachments at nineteen months of age (Mangelsdorf et al., 1996). These infants in particular may present greater stresses and challenges for their caregivers.

Adoption By the time they reach middle childhood and adolescence, adopted children show a noticeably higher incidence of psychological and academic problems compared to nonadopted children (Brodzinsky et al., 1984; Fergusson, Lynskey, & Horwood, 1995). Because most adoptions involve the separation of the infant from the biological mother at an early age, the disruption of the attachment process may play a role.

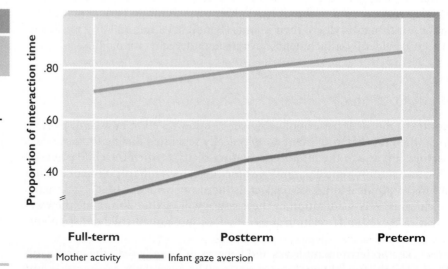

FIGURE 11.5

Maternal Interactions with Premature Babies

After an initial period of inactivity following the birth of their children, mothers of premature infants become more active in their exchanges with their infants than mothers of full- and postterm infants. At the same time, premature babies display more gaze aversion, as though they are seeking to terminate their mothers' overstimulation.

Source: Adapted from Field, 1982.

One of the few investigations of this issue showed that separation of the infant from the biological parents at six to seven months of age produces socioemotional difficulties even ten years later, particularly in the child's ability to form relationships with others (Yarrow et al., 1973). Separation at an earlier age, however, may have a lesser impact. When Leslie Singer and her colleagues assessed the attachments of adopted and nonadopted infants between thirteen and eighteen months of age, they found no difference in the classifications of attachments between these two groups (Singer et al., 1985). Most of the infants fell into the securely attached category. In this group, most of the adoptive placements had occurred at fairly early ages, the majority by three months of age. At this age children have not yet developed the concept of object permanence, and the early manifestations of attachment, such as stranger anxiety and separation protest, have not occurred. As in the case of premature infants, events that interfere with the establishment of stable relationships in the first part of infancy do not necessarily forecast poor attachment. These studies of adoption also suggest that disrupting stable relationships with caregivers later in infancy can be more harmful and that the first few months of life may represent a sensitive period for emotional development.

KEY THEME
Continuity/Discontinuity

Abuse   Physically or psychologically abused children are at risk for an assortment of cognitive and socioemotional difficulties. Because the trauma that accompanies within-family violence can be enduring, especially with repeated episodes of abuse, it is not surprising that attachments between abused children and their parents take on an aberrant character.

Infants and toddlers who have been maltreated by their caregivers are likely to fall into a category of insecure attachment, identified several years after Ainsworth's original research, called **disorganized/disoriented attachment.** Children in this attachment category show fear of their caregivers, confused facial expressions, and an assortment of avoidant and ambivalent attachment behaviors in the Strange Situation (Main & Solomon, 1986). These behaviors are accompanied by physiological signs of stress (Hertsgaard et al., 1996). Approximately 80 percent of maltreated infants fit this attachment profile (Carlson et al., 1989; Cicchetti, Toth, & Lynch, 1995). Like other attachment categories, the disorganized/disoriented pattern may predict later developmental outcomes. In one recent study, 71 percent of preschoolers who showed high levels of hostile behavior toward peers had been categorized as having disorganized attachments during infancy (Lyons-Ruth, Alpern, & Repacholi, 1993). In another study, researchers found that when children with disorganized/disoriented attachments were six years old, they tended to be depressed, disorganized in behavior, and even self-destructive in response to questions about their parents or family life (Main, Kaplan, & Cassidy, 1985).

Why do these maladaptive attachments form? Abusive parents tend to react negatively to many of their children's social signals, even positive ones. When Ann Frodi and Michael Lamb (1980) observed the reactions of abusive and nonabusive mothers to videotapes of smiling and crying infants, abusive mothers were more aroused physiologically by both cries and smiles than were nonabusive mothers and were less willing to interact with an infant, even a smiling one. These findings suggest, at the very least, that the abused infant has an unwilling and psychologically distant interaction partner.

In addition, abused children experience fear, an emotion that leads them to seek comfort from the caregiver but also makes them wary of further abuse. Thus, the tendency to seek proximity to the caregiver is counterbalanced by the tendency to avoid that same person. The resulting behaviors, such as freezing and appearing dazed, are characteristic of children in the disorganized/disoriented attachment category.

Taken together, studies of premature and adopted children reveal that secure attachment relationships can develop in circumstances that are less than optimal during the early part of infancy. At the same time, however, when interactions between caregivers and infants deviate too widely from the ideal, in terms of either the partnership's time of onset or the emotional tone of interactions, the consequences for the child can be serious and enduring.

disorganized/disoriented attachment   Infant-caregiver relations characterized by the infant's fear of the caregiver, confused facial expressions, and a combination of avoidant and ambivalent attachment behaviors.

Cross-Cultural Variations in Patterns of Attachment

Overall, children in most countries around the world show behaviors indicating secure attachment even if they have been reared in very different circumstances (Posada et al., 1995; Van IJzendoorn, 1995). Studies of children in Israel are a good example. Many Israeli infants are raised in the group setting of the kibbutz. While parents go to work, children are cared for by the *metapelet,* or caregiver, beginning sometime between six and twelve weeks of age and continuing after the first year. Children go to the group caregiving center (called the "children's house") in the morning and return home in the late afternoon, but most of their time is spent with the nonparental caregiver and peers. Do such arrangements interfere with the formation of attachments to mothers? One recent study showed that 80 percent of infants were securely attached to their mothers; interestingly, however, this finding held true only for infants who came home to sleep for the evening. Some infants sleep overnight at the "children's house," in keeping with more traditional practices of the kibbutz; among this group, only 48 percent were securely attached to their mothers (Sagi et al., 1994). Children raised on the kibbutz also showed notable attachments to their metapelet; 53 percent of infants were classified as securely attached to the caregiver (Sagi et al., 1985).

KEY THEME
Sociocultural Influence

Observations of infants in Germany, however, show a different pattern of results. In one study, about 49 percent of infants were scored as avoidantly attached (Grossmann et al., 1985). As in the Ainsworth studies, these researchers noted a relationship between maternal sensitivity and infant attachment: securely attached infants had mothers who interacted with them in a warm, responsive manner. However, although mothers varied in the sensitivity of responding when infants were two months of age, they did not vary by the time the infants were ten months old; most mothers had *low* sensitivity ratings by this time. Grossmann and her colleagues interpreted their findings in the context of the different attitudes toward child rearing held by parents in Germany and the United States. The emphasis in German culture is on fostering independence in one's offspring, encouraging the development of an obedient child who does not make demands on the parents. Responding to the infant's every cry is considered inappropriate. Thus, German mothers' tendency to pick up their children less frequently and for shorter periods of time and to display less affection reflects the goals of socialization in that culture.

Some researchers have suggested that the Strange Situation is not the optimal measure of the child's emotional feelings toward the caregiver (Lamb et al., 1985). Instead of assessing the qualities of children's affective bonds, it may gauge the influence of other social and cultural experiences. This idea is supported by studies showing that specific experiences in infancy may dampen the child's protests to the mother's departure. A child who has had frequent experiences in which the mother leaves and subsequently returns, for example, may show little or no separation protest even if he or she is securely attached (Kagan, 1976). The cross-cultural studies reviewed in this section underscore the point that variations in children's experiences and in cultural expectations for their behavior may influence responses to elements of the Strange Situation and may not reflect the actual intensity of emotional bonds between caregiver and child. As we begin to evaluate the impact of nonmaternal child care on children in our own society, we should be cautious about the measures we use to draw our conclusions.

One of the most difficult decisions many parents face concerns alternative child care arrangements when both mother and father work. As Table 11.3 shows, almost 70 percent of mothers with preschool-age children work and almost 60

CONTROVERSY: THINKING IT OVER

Does Day Care Affect Attachment?

percent of women with infants under one year of age are employed (U.S. Bureau of the Census, 1996). In fact, this latter group represents the fastest-growing category of

Age of Child	Percentage of Women in the Labor Force		
	1975	1985	1995
With children under 18	44.9	60.8	70.2
Under 6, total	36.7	53.4	63.5
Under 3	32.7	50.5	60.9
1 year or under	30.8	49.4	59.0
2 years	37.1	54.0	66.7
3 to 5 years	42.2	58.4	67.2
6 to 13 years	51.8	68.2	74.9
14 to 17 years	53.5	67.0	79.6

Source: Data from U.S. Bureau of the Census, 1996.

TABLE 11.3

Labor Force Participation Rates for Women with Children Under Age 18

This table shows the percentage of women with children under age eighteen who are employed outside the home (the table shows only the data for women whose husbands are present in the home). The participation rates for this group of women have grown rapidly since 1975, especially for those with children age one year and under.

women in the labor force. A substantial number of children are therefore receiving nonparental care, many beginning very early in life. Does this form of early experience influence the formation of attachments?

One problem in answering this question is that many variables operate when the child receives nonparental care. Is it the mother's absence or the quality of substitute care that produces any observable effects on child behavior? These two factors are difficult to separate. Does the age at which alternative care began make a difference? It may, but researchers have not always considered this variable when conducting their studies. Does it matter whether the child receives full-time or part-time care? Perhaps, but the tremendous variation in caregiving schedules has made this factor difficult to control in research studies. In addition, the kinds of alternative care children receive vary a great deal, ranging from a single caregiver coming to the home, to out-of-home family day care in which another parent provides care for several children, to center-based care. Given these complexities, it is understandable that simple and direct answers to parents' concerns have not been forthcoming.

When Alison Clarke-Stewart and Greta Fein (1983) reviewed a large number of studies on day care and attachment, they concluded that children in day care may behave differently than home-reared children, but only in some components of the Strange Situation. Day care children do not react differently than home-reared children to the mother's departure; children in both groups protest or ignore her to the same degree. Day care children, however, tend to spend less time in close proximity to their mothers, both in the presence and in the absence of a stranger. In addition, although the majority of studies show no difference, a sizable minority have found more avoidant responses among day care children than home-reared children when reunited with their mothers.

Jay Belsky and Michael Rovine (1988), for example, reported that infants who received more than twenty hours per week of nonmaternal care when under one year of age were more likely to be classified as insecurely attached and showed more avoidance of the mother at reunion compared to infants who received less nonmaternal care. Boys seemed to be more vulnerable than girls. Belsky and Rovine pointed out that 50 percent of the infants receiving full-time nonmaternal care did form secure attachments. Positive relationships were related to several child and mother characteristics: the child was more likely to be an "easy" baby, the mother was more sensitive and empathic, and the mother expressed greater satisfaction with her marriage. Also, secure attachments with mothers were more prevalent when the nonmaternal caregiver was the father. Overall, however, Belsky and Rovine conclude that "extensive nonmaternal (and nonpaternal) care in the first year is a risk factor in the development of insecure infant-parent attachment relationships" (p. 165).

Does this mean day care predisposes children toward impaired attachments? The answer is no, according to Clarke-Stewart and Fein (1983). The behaviors observed in day care children are subject to a number of other interpretations. Perhaps day care children show a precocious move toward independence, which most parents view as a desirable goal of socialization. They also may be used to interacting with unfamiliar people and to the comings and goings of their mothers, and their behavior may simply reflect these socialization experiences rather than insecure attachment.

Belsky and Braungart (1991) examined some of these hypotheses in a subsequent study of the specific behaviors of infants receiving either more or less than twenty hours per week of alternative care. Did the infants with extended day care experience show greater independence and less stress when reunited with their mothers in the Strange Situation than infants who had less nonparental care? The answer is no, according to the follow-up study: infants with extended day care experience whimpered and fussed more and played with objects less than infants with less day care experience.

As you can see, this controversy is far from resolved. One important factor to consider is the "file drawer" phenomenon. When researchers find no statistically significant differences between groups of children (in this case, between day care and home-reared children), their studies are not likely to be published (Roggman et al., 1994). How does one interpret the results of a few studies that report insecure attachments among day care children in the context of possibly many others that have found no differences? Do the results of the Belsky and Braungart (1991) study necessarily mean parents should limit the number of hours per week their infants spend in day care? Given the economic factors necessitating that both parents work, what can society do to ease their burden in seeking alternative caregiving arrangements? Drawing on the research on good "mothering" and good "fathering," what would be the qualities of good day care centers?

CHAPTER RECAP

SUMMARY OF DEVELOPMENTAL THEMES

NATURE/NURTURE   What roles do nature and nurture play in emotional development?

As we have stressed throughout this chapter, both nature and nurture contribute to the child's emotional development. Biology assumes a larger role in the child's early emotional capacities, for example, in the infant's ability to express and detect basic emotions such as joy and sadness. However, socialization and cognitive development become more prominent explanations for later emotional expression, particularly for complex emotions such as guilt and envy. Ethologists and child temperament researchers also maintain that nature guides the formation of attachments between children and caregivers, but other researchers suggest that qualities of parenting style are equally important.

SOCIOCULTURAL INFLUENCE   How does the sociocultural context influence emotional development?

Different cultures place varying emphasis on emotionality itself and on the specific emotions considered appropriate to display.

For example, among the Kipsigis, crying is actively discouraged almost as soon as children complete infancy. A culture's beliefs and values also can influence the child's responses in the Strange Situation. For example, German children often are classified as avoidantly attached, but their behavior may simply reflect parental stress on independence.

CHILD'S ACTIVE ROLE   How does the child play an active role in the process of emotional development?

The child is hardly passive in the construction of his or her emotional repertoire. There are numerous examples of how the child plays an active role in emotional development, including the phenomenon of social referencing, the infant's role in producing interactive synchrony with the caregiver, and the role of the child's temperament in the formation of attachments.

CONTINUITY/DISCONTINUITY   Is emotional development continuous or discontinuous?

Attachment patterns established during the first year of life endure for relatively long periods of time and forecast many desirable developmental outcomes. Thus, many researchers believe infancy is a sensitive period for the formation of attachments. Studies of adopted children in particular suggest that better socioemotional outcomes result when infants are placed with their adoptive parents prior to age six months.

INDIVIDUAL DIFFERENCES   How prominent are individual differences in emotional development?

Individual differences are especially evident in the enduring emotional moods infants and children display. For example, children may be "easy," "difficult," or "slow to warm up" in temperament, or may display inhibited or uninhibited styles. These relatively stable individual differences may affect how parents and others react to the child and, in turn, influence other developmental outcomes such as attachment.

SUMMARY OF TOPICS

■ WHAT ARE EMOTIONS?

Emotions are complex responses to internal or external events that include physiological, expressive, and experiential components. They are measured in a variety of ways, ranging from physiological measures and observer judgments of facial expressions to self-reports about moods and feelings. Emotions serve to organize and motivate the child's behavior, influence cognitive processes, and regulate social interactions. Thus, they play a comprehensive role in the child's development.

■ THEORIES OF EMOTIONAL DEVELOPMEMT

Some theorists, such as Izard, propose that certain *basic emotions* such as joy and disgust are innate and their expression has adaptive value. Environmental stimuli directly produce emotional responses that result in the experience of emotion. Cognitive-socialization theorists, such as Lewis, emphasize the role of experience in transmitting to the child the appropriate times and ways of expressing emotions. Thus, individuals may express different emotions in response to the same stimulus.

■ EXPRESSING, RECOGNIZING, AND UNDERSTANDING EMOTIONS

Research with infants reveals that many emotional expressions, including joy, sadness, surprise, and disgust, are observed from birth. However, the forms of emotional expressions such as smiling and crying change over the first year, as do the circumstances in which emotions are displayed. Advances in cognition are partly responsible, as is the maturation of portions of the brain that direct voluntary behaviors. Young infants also identify the emotional expressions of others and in many instances will imitate them. By the latter half of the first year, infants will use the emotional expressions of others to guide their behaviors, a phenomenon called *social referencing*. Infants' emotional expressions, in conjunction with those of caregivers, often co-occur in a synchronous manner, called *interactive synchrony*, laying the foundations for the formation of attachments.

Older children display more *complex emotions*, such as guilt and envy, as well as more controlled use of basic emotions.

INTERACTION AMONG DOMAINS   How does emotional development interact with development in other domains?

Emotions are closely intertwined with both cognition and social behavior. On the one hand, cognitive achievements, such as the attainment of object permanence or the ability to interpret social and personal experiences, lay the groundwork for advances in attachment and emotional expression. Similarly, children often learn about emotions through social experiences, such as interactions with their caregivers. On the other side of the equation, successful emotional development in the form of attachment is associated with positive social and cognitive achievements later in childhood. Children who are skilled at understanding, expressing, and regulating emotions also have better relations with their peers.

Preschoolers understand many of the situations that give rise to specific emotions and the consequences of displaying them. School-age children understand that they can control emotions with their own thoughts and that sometimes two emotions can be experienced simultaneously. The ability to disguise emotions appears later in childhood, as does an understanding of the nature of emotions based on internal feeling states. Many of these changes are related to cognitive development. Sex differences and cultural variations in the display of emotions also suggest a role for socialization.

■ ATTACHMENT: EMOTIONAL RELATIONSHIPS WITH OTHERS

The strong affectional bond between child and caregiver is known as *attachment*. Learning theorists explain attachment as the product of the mother's association with feeding and other activities the infant finds pleasurable. Ethologists say attachment is an innate, adaptive phenomenon that promotes proximity between infant and caregiver and thus ensures the infant's survival. Cognitive-developmental theorists link attachment to the infant's cognitive advances, specifically the emergence of object permanence.

Stranger anxiety and *separation protest*, two of the most pronounced indicators of attachment, typically emerge at about seven or eight months of age. Three basic patterns of attachment—*secure, avoidant,* and *ambivalent*—have been identified on the basis of the *Strange Situation* task. Secure attachments in particular are related to the most favorable developmental outcomes for the child. Several variables predict the formation of secure attachments, including the sensitivity and responsiveness of the caregiver, the *temperament* of the child, and the synchrony in caregiver-child interactional behaviors. Studies of premature infants, adoptees, and abused children indicate that attachments can form under less than optimal circumstances, but extreme deviations in caregiver-child interactional patterns can have serious negative consequences for the child. For example, many abused children show *disorganized/disoriented attachments*. Children in most cultures show secure attachments, but cultural variations in attachment patterns suggest that what seem to be insecure attachments may be the result of factors other than inadequate caregiver-child interactions.

12 SELF AND VALUES

NATURE/NURTURE
What roles do nature and nurture play in the development of the self and of values?

SOCIOCULTURAL INFLUENCE
How does the sociocultural context influence the development of the self and of values?

CHILD'S ACTIVE ROLE
How does the child play an active role in the development of the self and of values?

CONTINUITY/DISCONTINUITY
Is the development of the self and of values continuous or discontinuous?

INDIVIDUAL DIFFERENCES
How prominent are individual differences in the development of the self and of values?

INTERACTION AMONG DOMAINS
How does the development of the self and of values interact with development in other domains?

ichael had just finished his math assignment when he heard the door slam. Then he heard the loud, angry voice. "Kids today!" his grandfather fumed to no one in particular. "A couple of 'em almost ran me down on the sidewalk. Didn't bother to apologize. One even yelled, 'Get out of my way!' as she chased after her friends. Kids don't respect anybody, not even themselves—wearing those weird clothes, dying their hair every color you can think of, poking holes in their ears, even their noses! I suppose if I had stopped 'em, they'd have taken a swing at me or even worse. . . ." His voice trailed off to a mutter.

Michael had heard such tirades before: how the world has changed, how young people today do not know right from wrong, how they are just plain troublemakers. Michael also worried about reports on the news: the first-grader who punched his teacher, the large number of sixth-graders who felt cheating was okay, the junior high students suspended for bringing knives and guns to school.

Did his grandfather have a valid point? Just what values do young people have today?

To instill in children a sense of satisfaction with who they are and to recognize the standards of conduct considered acceptable and ethical within their community are among the most important goals of society. We expect children and adults to take pride in their accomplishments, learn to judge right from wrong, and refrain from actions that harm family, friends, or neighbors. Broadly speaking, survival in a social community depends on the ability to acquire behaviors, such as helping, cooperation, and sharing, that benefit others. Children display an awareness of self and the consequences of their conduct, both good and bad, early on, but these understandings undergo noticeable changes with development. This chapter describes age-related changes in the development of self, moral behavior, and values, areas of development that together undoubtedly contribute to mature, socially acceptable functioning.

Michael's grandfather believes his generation has witnessed a decline in a positive sense of self and in courtesy and concern for others. Although one might debate whether such a change has actually taken place, the concerns voiced by Michael's grandfather are not new. Philosophers, theologians, and scientists have debated for decades about whether human nature is good or evil and whether experience serves to channel children's inborn tendencies in either direction. In this sense, the nature-nurture debate remains embedded in contemporary discussions of the roots of self, moral behavior, and values. In this chapter, we will look first at the nature of "self" and how it relates to self-esteem and identity. We will consider too how self-regulation and self-control contribute to our development. We will then examine several formal theories of moral development. Finally, we will look at how and to what extent society promotes the development of self, moral behavior, and values.

THE CONCEPT OF SELF

"I know how."

"Look! See what I did!"

"I'm smart."

"I'm stronger than you!"

"I'm really good at this!"

These declarations express in no uncertain terms what children believe they can do, what they think they are like, and how they feel about their abilities. The statements reveal the child's awareness of self. How does this understanding of self—as someone who is an independent, unique person, able to reflect on his or her own beliefs and characteristics—develop?

To answer this question, it will be useful to adopt a distinction first offered by William James (1892) more than a century ago. For James, there were two components of self: the "me," or *objective self,* and the "I," or *subjective self.* James's objective, or the "me" aspect of self, is often called *self-concept.* An individual's self-concept includes an understanding of his or her physical qualities, possessions and status, skills, and psychological characteristics, including personality, beliefs, and value systems.

The "I," or the subjective component, is made up of several key realizations about the self: (1) I can be an agent of change and can control events in my life (sense of autonomy); (2) my experiences are unique and accessible to no one else in exactly the same way (sense of individuality); (3) my past, present, and future are continuous (sense of stability); and (4) I can reflect on, that is, think about, my self (sense of reflection, or self-consciousness). All contribute to the sense of the subjective "I."

Self as Object

Self as object, the **self-concept,** consists of the unique set of traits and characteristics an individual holds to be true about himself or herself. The seeds of such awareness already may be sown in the infant's recognition of how his own body movements take place. For example, the attentional preferences of babies as young as three months suggest that they recognize when left and right position and movements of their legs, viewed on videotape, are inverted (Rochat & Morgan, 1995). Awareness of self as object, however, is usually said to begin with the child's ability to recognize her own face and body.

Self-recognition　　When can young children, upon seeing their reflections in a mirror or pictures of themselves, declare, "That's me!"? The household mirror has become a helpful research tool in answering this question. A toddler younger than fifteen to eighteen months shows little evidence of recognizing herself in a mirror. How do we know? If a spot of rouge, for example, is placed surreptitiously on her nose, it is not until she is older than this age that, looking in the mirror, she will touch or rub her nose. She indicates by such behavior that she has formed a concept of the details that ordinarily make up her appearance (Amsterdam, 1972; Lewis & Brooks-Gunn, 1979). In just a few more months she will also say, "That's me" when asked, "Who's that?" as she stares at a picture or a reflection of herself.

The implications of becoming aware of physical appearance can be enormous. For one thing, it may signal the appearance of self-conscious emotions, such as embarrassment, shame, and pride, that emerge in toddlers, as we saw in the discussion of emotional development in Chapter 11 (Lewis, 1990; Lewis et al., 1989). For another, self-recognition seems to develop hand in hand with a growing awareness of others

self　Realization of being an independent, unique, stable, and self-reflective entity; the beliefs, knowledge, feelings, and characteristics the individual ascribes to himself or herself.

self-concept　Perceptions, conceptions, and values one holds about oneself.

This toddler, twenty months of age, seems to be studying her expression intently. By this age, most children recognize that it is a likeness of themselves being reflected in the mirror. Before about fifteen to eighteen months of age, children do not show evidence of self-recognition.

as distinct individuals. For example, a toddler who displays self-recognition on the mirror task also is likely to attend to a partner of a similar age and to encourage that child to play with matching toys, an indication of increased interest in sharing and enjoyment of the other child's activities (Asendorpf & Baudonnière, 1993). Thus, at a very young age, children have begun to unwrap a major piece of the total package of their self-concept, the first of many steps in the development of their identities.

Self-definition   A self-concept consists of much more than appearance. If asked to answer the question "Who are you?" a preschooler might say, "I'm a boy. I'm strong. I know the letters of the alphabet. I like pizza. I live with my mother and father. I go to nursery school." Thus, during the preschool years, knowledge of self extends beyond physical features to include activities the child likes and is good at, his possessions, and his relationships to others. In defining themselves, children at this age commonly establish a **categorical self,** that is, classify themselves in terms of membership in certain groups based on their sex, age, skills, what they own, where they live, and who their friends are.

Are preschoolers also aware of having psychological and social attributes? As we pointed out in Chapter 8, preschoolers know quite a bit about their own mental activities. They possess knowledge of themselves that goes beyond appearance and actions. Thus, responses such as "I have a friend" or "I'm a happy person" are among their self-descriptions. Preschoolers consistently select self-statements that reflect moods, feelings, achievements, and other psychological and social orientations. Self as object, as *me,* even for a young child, includes a sense of a psychological and social being (Damon & Hart, 1988; Eder, 1990).

When children reach about seven years of age, a new element enters their self-descriptions. Whereas younger children describe themselves in terms of typical categorical activities ("I run fast"), older children begin to make relational statements. For example, in response to the question "Who are you?" a fifth-grader might say, "I can run faster than anyone else in my class," "I'm not as pretty as my older sister," or "Other kids in my class are better than I am at math." Instead of itemizing their skills, actions, or social and psychological qualities, they compare their qualities with those of others (Livesley & Bromley, 1973; Ruble, 1983; Secord & Peevers, 1974).

As children become older, they view self in terms of more abstract and increasingly differentiated qualities (Harter & Monsour, 1992; Secord & Peevers, 1974). The emphasis further shifts to how attributes spur interactions with others and affect social relationships. The changes are evident in such responses from young adolescents

KEY THEME
Interaction Among Domains

categorical self   Conceptual process, starting in the early preschool years, in which the child begins to classify himself or herself according to easily observable categories such as sex, age, or physical capacities.

FIGURE 12.1

Concerns About Opposing Attributes

From early to middle adolescence, students increasingly report conflicting descriptions of self that depend on whether their evaluations are framed within the perspective of classroom, friends, close relationships, or parents. Concerns about these conflicting views increase at the same time. However, both the number of opposite attributes assigned to self and concerns about their effects on defining self begin to decline in later adolescence, as young people establish a more integrated identity and recognize that contradictions may be normal and even of some value.

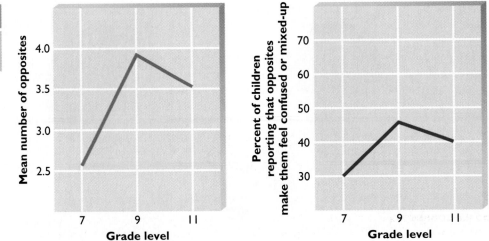

Source: Harter & Monsour, 1982.

KEY THEME
Sociocultural Influence

as "I play sports . . . because all the kids like athletes" and "I'm an honest person . . . people trust me because of it" (Damon & Hart, 1988).

By early adolescence, self can be viewed from multiple or even opposing perspectives. Susan Harter (1986) asked whether someone can have both positive and negative qualities. Can a person be both "smart" and "dumb" or "nice" and "nasty"? She found a substantial increase in the belief in this possibility between the seventh and ninth grades. The number of opposites, and concerns about feeling confused or bothered by qualities of self that conflict when, for example, interacting with parents, with friends, in a romantic relationship, or as a member of the classroom, becomes greatest during middle adolescence, as Figure 12.1 indicates (Harter & Monsour, 1992).

The impetus for conflicting selves may arise from a desire to impress or gain increased acceptance or simply as part of experimentation during the teenage years. Under these circumstances, "false" selves appear to be a normal and even healthy aspect of development. However, if, as may be the case for some adolescents, the inconsistencies arise from a belief that approval is contingent on "showing different faces" at the expense of one's true self, assuming a conflicting self may lead to more serious consequences, such as feeling depressed and confused about self (Harter et al., 1996). Fortunately, for most adolescents, concerns about conflicting selves typically lessen as they become older and establish an integrated and coherent picture of self based on principled ideas and comprehensive plans that include a more extended future and larger goals.

Can cultural, religious, and social class differences, which are highly laden with values in their own right, influence the development of self-concepts? William Damon and Daniel Hart (1988) believe such influence is likely. In some societies, for example, possessions or membership in the family or a social group may be far more important in determining perceptions of self than individual qualities, abilities, and achievements (Levine & White, 1986). To illustrate their point, Damon and Hart (1988) studied children living in a fishing village in Puerto Rico. The residents were relatively poor and had few educational and social services available to them. Children typically attended school for no more than three or four years, and obtaining a job often depended on a network of family and social relationships. Compared to middle-income youngsters from mainland regions of the United States, Puerto Rican children voiced far more apprehension about whether their *behavior* was good or bad than whether they were competent or talented. A twelve-year-old might say it is important to be nice and respect people because misbehavior would mean "everybody will hit me and hate me or not help me." Compared to their mainland counterparts, Puerto Rican children consistently expressed greater concern about whether others approved of their actions than about their relative competence with respect to some skill or capacity.

In cultures that reward individual superiority less than contributions to the collective community—for example, the Samoan culture—researchers may find that evaluations of self in terms of individual competencies are not seen as desirable. Many factors could contribute to these differences. The lives of children vary across cultures and communities in terms of styles of parenting, formal education, social structure, and the expectations of parents, peers, and community leaders. For example, in many Asian cultures, greater compliance to parental expectations, an emphasis on common academic tasks in school settings (Stevenson et al., 1986), and a high regard for modesty in interactions with others may contribute to a far different concept of the self than that found in many Western nations.

Social Comparison   During the early and middle school years, as we already indicated, children begin to reference others in describing themselves. Whether Jim feels he is nice or can run fast, or Ellen believes she is smart or throws a ball well, depends on how Jim or Ellen thinks he or she stacks up against agemates and friends. How important is this process, called **social comparison,** the tendency of people to use others as mirrors to evaluate their own abilities, interests, and values? The answer appears to be that it becomes increasingly important as children move through the elementary school years. For example, nine-year-olds who could not actually determine their success but were told they did better than, or not as well as, peers in a ball-throwing contest predicted future performance based on the feedback they received. If told they were successful, they expected to show continued superior ability; if told they were less successful, they expected to continue to perform more poorly than children who received no feedback. Five- and seven-year-olds, however, were unaffected by the information; they predicted they would do equally well, regardless of how they compared with others (Ruble et al., 1980).

Children, of course, observe things happening to others even in the preschool years. Two pieces of candy of unequal size shared between two four-year-olds can easily initiate conflict about who has the larger piece. At this age, however, observing others seems to be especially important for learning how to respond or gaining new skills for mastering a task (Butler, 1989; Ruble, 1983). Thus, the motivation of younger children to attend to others is often to find out how to do something (Veroff, 1969).

In fact, young children frequently are unrealistic about their skills; they claim they will do far better than they actually can (Butler, 1990). Moreover, kindergartners rate themselves more positively than older children do and tend to ignore feedback to adjust their evaluations, particularly when information about failure is indicated (Ruble, Eisenberg, & Higgins, 1994). However, by attending to the attributes and qualities of others, children may gain a more realistic means of predicting how well they can do. For example, Diane Ruble (1987) found that children in kindergarten and first grade who more frequently made social comparisons involving achievement tended to have greater knowledge of their relative standing in the classroom.

Older school-age children engage in increasingly subtle, indirect social comparisons to determine how well they are doing, perhaps because more conspicuous forms of information gathering are perceived as inappropriate behaviors. For example, nine- or ten-year-olds are more likely than younger children to ask classmates, "What question are you on?" to assess their progress among peers (Pomerantz et al., 1995). On the other hand, the kind of educational environment in which children participate also influences this behavior. In Israel, for example, children in kibbutz schools, which place greater emphasis on cooperative activity than more traditional urban schools in that country, continue to be more likely to interpret glances among one another as efforts to increase mastery rather than as social comparisons (Butler & Ruzany, 1993).

As children approach the adolescent years and become more competent, they are less likely to look to others to evaluate how well they are doing; instead, they begin to

KEY THEME
Child's Active Role

social comparison   Process in which individuals define themselves in relation to the skills, attributes, and qualities of others; an important contributor to self-concept during middle childhood.

A child's conception of self is often influenced by how others evaluate his activities and abilities. Athletic skill, for example, may be publicly recognized through the awarding of trophies. Moreover, at this age the child's definition of self is likely to include a comparison with others in terms of how well he is able to perform such activities.

use their own measures of performance on a task to judge success (Ruble & Flett, 1988). This may indicate an impending shift from social comparison to a more self-reliant and principled standard for evaluating self. This basis for a self-concept, rooted in internalized values and norms of mastery and competence, fits the criteria mature individuals use to evaluate their identity and often is observed in later adolescence and early adulthood.

In summary, the development of self as object reveals a fascinating progression, beginning with the toddler's recognition of his or her separateness from others in terms of physical appearance and features. Among preschoolers, self is usually organized around category membership, but children this young also have some understanding of psychological capacities. The self-concepts of older children increasingly reflect a consideration of others and involve active comparison. The process eventually gives way during the adolescent years to more formalized, autonomous standards for judging self, especially in areas in which the young person feels competent. Of course, social and cultural conditions may have an enormous effect on these progressions.

Self as Subject

Just as we can ask a child what she knows about her physical features or personal characteristics, so too can we ask whether she realizes that she influences and controls her surroundings, remains the same person over time, or is a unique individual. Such questions inquire about a child's understanding of her sense of agency or autonomy, individuality, and stability, and her capacity to reflect on these abilities. What do children know about such matters?

The Sense of Agency   The belief that a person can determine and influence his or her surroundings probably has its roots in infancy (Lewis & Brooks-Gunn, 1979). Robert White (1959) suggested that babies are born with a desire to master their environment, an ambition he termed **effectance motivation**. The active infant repeatedly stacks blocks, bangs pots, smiles at caregivers, and plays peek-a-boo, activities that often lead to consequences that he anticipates. If he cries, he typically is picked up, rocked, and comforted. The one-year-old who says "Mama" or another new word often becomes the center of attention. From the feedback associated with these actions, infants may learn to expect outcomes and how to make them happen again. Eventually, they begin to see themselves as being in control, capable of reaching desired goals and having the means to do so.

KEY THEME
Child's Active Role

KEY THEME
Nature/Nurture

effectance motivation Inborn desire theorized by Robert White to be the basis for the infant's and child's efforts to master and gain control of the environment.

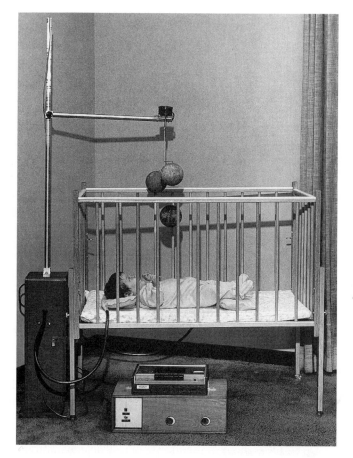

FIGURE 12.2

Learning Not to Learn

Babies who are provided with the ability to control a mobile's motion by moving their heads on a special pillow normally learn to master the mobile's movement quite rapidly. Infants who are initially not able to control the mobile but are then given the opportunity to do so have great difficulty learning to make the mobile move. Lack of opportunity to have an effect on the environment may sow the seeds for learned helplessness.

To illustrate how a responsive physical and social environment may be essential to acquiring a sense of mastery of the environment, researchers in one study placed mobiles above the heads of infants for ten minutes a day over a period of fourteen weeks (see Figure 12.2). When babies could make the mobile rotate rapidly by moving their heads on a pressure-sensitive pillow, they quickly learned to do so. But for other babies, their head movements on the pillow produced no results; the mobile rotated independently or simply remained stationary. When these infants subsequently had the opportunity to control the mobile by using the pillow, they did not learn to do so, even after extensive training (Watson, 1971; Watson & Ramey, 1972). In other words, once infants learned that their actions had no consequences, they seemed unable to recognize that the situation had changed and that they could control or gain mastery over the mobile's movements.

Many two-year-olds protest the attempts of others to help them in an activity such as dressing. Some researchers believe such protests further reveal an early desire to be an agent or to master an activity (Kagan, 1981; Lutkenhaus, Bullock, & Geppert, 1987). At about this same time, children also look to adults after completing a task as though to share their success (Stipek, Recchia, & McClintic, 1992). Thus, both social feedback and observations of the outcomes of activity may enter into a sense of competence at an early age.

From these kinds of consequences, many children very likely come to believe the world is increasingly responsive to their actions. For example, if asked, "How did you get to be the way you are?" a preschooler is likely to refer to uncontrollable factors ("I just grew. . . . My body just got bigger"), whereas a ten-year-old mentions her own efforts ("From getting good grades in school from studying"). By age thirteen, children also acknowledge the contributions of others to their sense of agency ("I learned from my parents, I even learned from friends, just listening to them and talking to them"). Older adolescents incorporate into their reasoning principled personal and moral qualities ("Well, I decided to be kind to people because I've seen lots of kids hurt other kids' feelings for no reason, and it's not right or fair.") (Damon &

This infant may have already gained a rudimentary sense of agency. His outstretched arms seem to shout, "Pick me up!" His behavior illustrates one of the many ways even babies actively influence the things that happen to them.

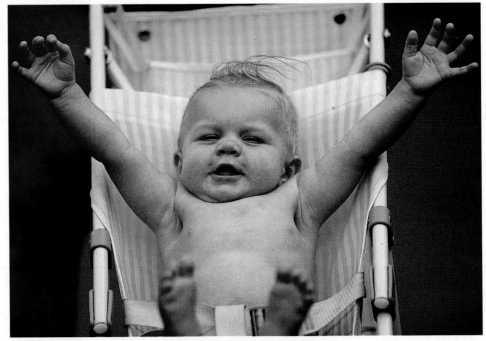

internal locus of control Individual's sense that his or her own efforts and activities influence success and failure and the events that happen to him or her.

mastery orientation Belief that achievements are based on one's own efforts rather than on luck or other factors beyond one's control.

external locus of control Individual's sense that outside factors such as luck, fate, and other people primarily influence success and failure and the events that happen to him or her.

learned helplessness Belief that one has little control over situations, perhaps because of lack of ability or inconsistent outcomes.

Hart, 1988). Even in societies that have emphasized a collective orientation, such as Russia, most children, at least with respect to school performance, believe individual effort is an important aspect of achieving success and avoiding failure, just as is the case in Western nations (Stetsenko et al., 1995).

Do children differ in their sense of self-determination and control? Indeed they do. Some children are convinced that what happens to them depends on their actions, that their choices, decisions, and abilities govern whether outcomes are good or bad, successful or unsuccessful. When asked how to find a friend, such a child might say, "Go up to someone you like and ask them to play with you." When asked how to do well on a test, the child might answer, "Study for it and you'll get smart!" Such children are said to have an **internal locus of control** (Rotter, 1966). Carol Dweck and Elaine Elliott (1983) note that such children have a strong **mastery orientation,** a belief that success stems from trying hard; failures, these children believe, are conditions to be overcome by working harder or with greater effort. A primary benefit of this orientation is a sense of having the *ability* to do well in a variety of situations.

Other children, in contrast, exhibit an **external locus of control**; they believe luck, fate, or other people have an inordinate influence on what happens to them (Rotter, 1966). When asked why he cannot catch a ball, such a child might say, "The others throw it too fast." When asked why he got a poor grade, he might say, "The teacher doesn't like me." Such children often express little confidence in their ability and feel powerless to influence the future. They perceive themselves as being unable to achieve, perhaps because their efforts have not led to regular success. In place of a sense of mastery, they have a sense of **learned helplessness,** the feeling of having little ability and therefore no reason to initiate efforts to do well (Dweck & Elliott, 1983).

Differing beliefs about competency have been shown to have a powerful bearing on academic achievement, participation in athletics and other physical activities, popularity, and self-esteem (Nowicki & Strickland, 1973). The child who thinks passing to the next grade depends on whether a teacher likes her rather than on how hard she works may have little reason to strive for success. Those who have an internal locus of control and recognize choices in pursuing a goal perform better in school and on standardized tests of achievement than children who have an external locus of control or are not aware of various ways to do well (Chapman, Skinner, & Baltes, 1990; Findley & Cooper, 1983).

The rule in *Michael's house was that once homework was finished, the remaining time before bedtime was his to do with as he wished. He often played chess with his grandfather. This evening, however, his grandfather had become busy on another project.* "Perhaps just as well," thought Michael as he reflected on the earlier exchange that had so angered his grandfather. Michael dialed his friend Jonathon. "Can you play some catch?" he queried when Jonathon answered the phone. "You must have finished your math already," Jonathon retorted. "I hate math, still have a lot more problems to do," he continued. But Michael quickly interjected, "You did really well on that last test." But before he could finish, Michael knew what Jonathon's reply would be: "I was lucky. The teacher asked the right questions. I wish I were good at math."

RESEARCH APPLIED TO PARENTING

Preventing Learned Helplessness

Children who believe they have some control, for example, over learning and mastery of coursework, are likely to be more successful in that effort. In contrast, children who believe their actions have few consequences may have little reason to persevere in a difficult situation or little motivation to generally work hard and are unlikely to deal with adversity in constructive ways (Bandura et al., 1996). These latter children, who are displaying evidence of learned helplessness, are caught in a vicious cycle of self-fulfilling anticipation of failure and rationalizing that they have little control over what happens. They are especially likely to expect failure on tasks found difficult in the past and may avoid them when given further opportunity to work on them (Dweck, 1991; Erdley et al., 1997). Deborah Phillips (1984) reports that nearly 20 percent of fifth-graders with high ability limit their goals and persistence in school activities. In the academic realm, this pattern occurs more frequently among girls than boys, perhaps because girls are more likely than boys to view their failures in terms of such uncontrollable factors as lack of ability (Crandall, 1969; Dweck, Goetz, & Strauss, 1980; Stipek & Hoffman, 1980).

Children who gain little mastery over their environment or face conflicting and inconsistent reactions, such as those they might receive from abusive parents, are among the most likely to display learned helplessness. But even well-intentioned parents and teachers may unwittingly help to foster a sense of helplessness. For example, when parents generally believe they can promote their children's intellectual development, their children seem to benefit (Bandura et al., 1996). Moreover, the seeds of a sense of helplessness, Karen Burhans and Carol Dweck (1995) believe, are sown in preschoolers who tend to judge their performance on tasks as "good" or "bad." When the value of self becomes contingent on feeling worthy or unworthy, young children become especially vulnerable to learned helplessness. Thus, this and other research suggests that parents can take several steps to reduce the likelihood that children will acquire a sense of learned helplessness:

1. *Avoid frequent criticism and punishment.* The child who is often criticized or punished for, say, being messy or failing to finish a task may start to believe he is "bad" and there is little reason to try to improve. Or he may shun similar challenges to avoid receiving further negative evaluations. Thus, it is important that parents help the child to avoid feelings of shame or limited self-worth when evaluating behavior.

2. *Motivate effort by identifying positive qualities.* As children become older and more knowledgeable about enduring traits and capacities, parents and teachers can promote a mastery orientation by rewarding stable inner qualities, such as the sense of ability, as they motivate children's efforts.

3. *Attribute poor performance to factors other than ability.* When a child does perform poorly, a parent's or teacher's evaluation should focus on nonintellectual and temporary factors that may have reduced the child's performance rather than on her intrinsic ability, thereby inspiring effort when the next opportunity arises.

Schoolwork should be viewed as an opportunity for learning rather than as a situation in which performance is being evaluated. A child who takes pride in his work and believes that he can accomplish the tasks he is assigned often gains confidence and the motivation to be more successful.

4. *View tasks as opportunities to learn rather than as tests of ability.* Parents and teachers can encourage children who are engaging in achievement tasks to view them as opportunities to learn rather than as situations in which their performance will be evaluated in terms of competence (or lack of competence) (Elliott & Dweck, 1988; Erdley et al., 1997).

Younger children must be convinced that their failures are not the outcome of being "bad" or "good." Older children should be assured that shortcomings in performance on, say, academic tasks stem less from lack of ability than from insufficient effort or some other factor that can be modified easily. To illustrate this point, Dweck (1975) identified twelve children who displayed learned helplessness on math tasks and asked them to complete a series of difficult math problems, which they were unable to solve. The children then participated in twenty-five training sessions. Six children were given problems on which they could consistently succeed and received tokens to emphasize their success, a procedure designed to build self-confidence. The other six children were assigned to *attribution retraining,* a procedure designed to change their beliefs about the cause of their failures. During each session, these children experienced a small number of "failures" and were explicitly told to work harder; lack of success thus was directly tied to their effort rather than their inability.

When the two groups of children attempted the initial set of problems again, those in the attribution retraining group improved in performance; the other children did not. The children whose training emphasized improved self-confidence continued to view themselves as unable to do well on mathematics problems, but children who received attribution retraining persisted longer and were more likely to credit any remaining failures to lack of effort. Thus, the attribution retraining led the latter group to recognize the means to change outcomes, which in turn encouraged them to be agents in charge of their behavior. Attribution retraining has become an effective method that parents and teachers may use to replace self-limiting styles and attitudes with positive approaches to success, a means of converting learned helplessness into a greater sense of mastery and agency (Dweck, 1986).

The Sense of Individuality   How does a child know that she cannot become someone else? In other words, what do children understand about individuality and uniqueness? In one study young people were asked, "What makes you different from everybody else in the world?" Preschoolers usually answered with their names ("'Cause there is only one person with my name"), their possessions, or specific features of their bodies. Eight-to-ten-year-olds added comparative statements involving abilities, activities, and personality ("Well, I think I'm friendlier than most kids I know"). Young adolescents were more likely to list unique psychological and other traits ("The way I act," "One thing else, I worry a lot," "Yeah, I worry too much and a lot of things that a lot of kids don't care about"). Older adolescents adopted even stronger views involving unique personal feelings and orientations ("Nobody else sees things or feels the same way about things as I do") (Damon & Hart, 1988).

The answer that emerges from this research is that the child gains his sense of individuality early and first links it to observable physical characteristics and features. As children grow, they begin to compare themselves with others, especially their private feelings and thoughts, and these qualities become the central criteria for their claim to uniqueness.

The Sense of Stability   Is an individual essentially the same person today that she was a year ago or will be a year from now? As with the sense of individuality, a child's understanding of continuity begins quite early, but the explanation for this stability changes with development. Preschoolers have more difficulty than older children recognizing that changes in mood, weight, and even age or height are possible while still retaining one's identity (Bales & Sera, 1995). When asked, "If you change from year to year, how do you know it's still always you?" preschoolers cite their names ("My name, and then I would know if it was me if someone called me"), physical features, possessions, or other categorical qualities as proof. An eight-to-ten-year-old is likely to refer to stable personal or internal qualities ("I know it's me because I still know the things I knew five years ago"). Young adolescents link the sense of continuity to others ("I'll still have my family. They always know I'm me and not someone else"). Older adolescents are likely to state their certainty more abstractly ("Well, nothing about me always stays the same, but I am always kind of like I was awhile ago") (Damon & Hart, 1988).

As in the case of individuality, children's sense of a stable self gradually expands from physical, highly observable attributes to include both inner psychological and broader contextual elements. Moreover, as children mature, they judge inner psychological qualities as increasingly important in decisions about their stability of self (Aboud & Skerry, 1983). Children and adolescents are also more likely to anticipate greater similarity between their present and future selves than between past and present selves (Hart, Fegly, & Brengelman, 1993). Still, anticipated changes in future selves are positive ones; children and adolescents expect to lose undesirable characteristics as they mature.

The Sense of Reflection   When does the ability to reflect on or contemplate the self emerge? Perhaps not until early adolescence, when its advent, along with new ways of thinking abstractly, helps to explain the preoccupations of young teenagers with appearance and worth, that is, a growing self-consciousness about who they are (Elkind, 1981a; Selman, 1980). Another consequence of the capacity to reflect on the self is a greater appreciation of how the mind contributes to experience. A fourteen-year-old may say, "I can fool myself into thinking I don't miss my lost puppy." Yet an older adolescent often realizes that completely controlling her feelings, even if she is unaware of them, may not be possible. Thus, the sense of reflection forms the basis for eventually distinguishing between the influence of conscious and unconscious psychological processes on behavior (Damon & Hart, 1988).

KEY THEME

Interaction Among Domains

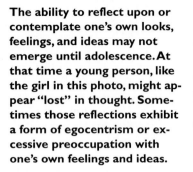

The ability to reflect upon or contemplate one's own looks, feelings, and ideas may not emerge until adolescence. At that time a young person, like the girl in this photo, might appear "lost" in thought. Sometimes those reflections exhibit a form of egocentrism or excessive preoccupation with one's own feelings and ideas.

Self-esteem: Evaluating Self

We turn now to another component of self: **self-esteem** or self-worth, the positive feelings of merit and the extent to which the child believes his attributes and actions are good, desired, and valued. This component of self appears to be related to social affiliations, success in school, and overall mental health. For example, later life satisfaction and happiness have been linked to high self-esteem (Bachman, 1970; Crandall, 1973); depression, anxiety, and poor adjustment in school and social relationships have been associated with low self-esteem (Damon, 1983).

Defining Self-esteem   How should we describe a child's self-esteem if the child takes pride in how smart she is, concludes that she is not very good at sports (but sports are unimportant anyway), and is unsure whether she is pretty enough to become a movie star? Work by Susan Harter and others (Harter, 1987; Eccles, Wigfield, et al., 1993) has revealed that children often give different evaluations of self when asked about academic competence, athletic skill, social acceptance, or physical appearance. Still, by about eight years of age, children can make global assessments to answer such questions as "Do you like yourself?" and "Are you happy the way you are?" The responses to these broad inquiries, however, are not simple summations of all the different evaluations made with respect to specific attributes and abilities. How, then, does the child arrive at a global sense of worth?

William James (1892) theorized that self-esteem depends on the success a person feels in areas in which she wants to succeed. Others emphasize that self-esteem originates in how a person thinks others see him; the *generalized other*—the combined evaluations of parents, peers, and teachers influential in a person's life—helps to determine sense of worth (Cooley, 1902; Mead, 1934).

Both success in a highly regarded domain and the perceived evaluations of others do appear to affect self-esteem. Harter (1987) obtained ratings of how children viewed themselves in scholastic competence, athletic competence, social acceptance, physical appearance, and behavioral conduct and in terms of global success. Children were also asked how critical it was for them to do well in each of these domains. Harter reasoned that greater discrepancies between perceived competence and the importance of a domain, especially one highly valued, would be linked to lower self-esteem. Children also rated how others (parents, peers) viewed them, felt they were important, liked them, and so on.

KEY THEME
Individual Differences

self-esteem   One's feelings of worth; extent to which one senses one's attributes and actions are good, desired, and valued.

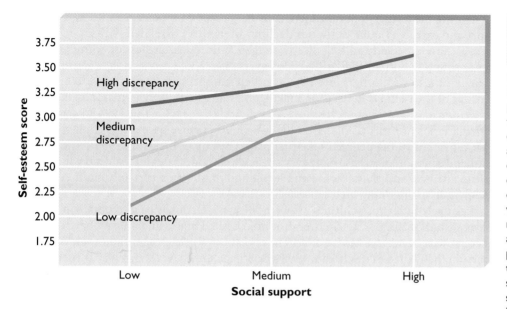

Source: Adapted from Harter, 1987.

FIGURE 12.3

How Self-esteem Develops

Self-esteem reflects the combined influence of social support and the discrepancy between the child's perceived and desired competence in some ability or attribute. Harter divided elementary school children into three groups based on these two measures. Those with the highest self-esteem reported high social support and a low discrepancy between perceived and desired competence. Those with the lowest self-esteem reported low social support and a high discrepancy between perceived and desired competence. The findings suggest that parents, teachers, and others concerned with increasing self-esteem need to consider both the kind of social encouragement and positive regard they provide and children's own beliefs about what is important.

For children in the third to eighth grades, the more an area rated as important outstripped a child's perception of her competence, the lower was the child's sense of her overall worth. In fact, children with low self-esteem seemed to have trouble disregarding the significance of domains in which they were not skilled (Harter, 1985). In contrast, children with high self-esteem minimized the value of those fields in which they were not especially competent and gained considerable satisfaction from areas in which they were relatively successful. But Harter found the perceived social support of others also correlated with the child's sense of self-worth. As Figure 12.3 shows, elementary school children with low discrepancy *and* high social support scores showed superior levels of self-worth. Children with high discrepancy and low social support displayed the lowest levels of self-esteem. Both factors contributed to overall sense of worth. Thus, efforts to improve self-esteem in children may require both a supportive social milieu and the formation and acceptance of realistic personal goals.

Are some domains more important than others for a child's overall sense of worth? The answer appears to be yes. Boys and girls of elementary and middle school age who were dissatisfied with and keenly concerned about their physical appearance tended to have especially low self-esteem. Although discrepancies were also important in other domains, they correlated less highly with judgments of overall self-worth. Harter (1987) speculates that in American culture, the relationship stems from the enormous emphasis on physical appearance in movies, television, and teen magazines as the key to success and acceptance. As children become older, discrepancy scores on social acceptance take on increasingly greater significance, whereas discrepancy scores on athletic competence show a decline in importance (Harter, 1987). Nevertheless, positive assessments of physical appearance continue to be an important predictor of higher self-esteem for girls as they enter the adolescent years (Lord, Eccles, & McCarthy, 1994). For boys, positive self-assessments, as well as positive judgments by peers, regarding academic ability correlate with sustained and even improved self-worth (Cole, 1991; Lord, Eccles, & McCarthy, 1994).

Developmental Changes in Self-esteem　In general, the self-esteem of children in early elementary school is high. Yet as they approach adolescence, self-esteem for a substantial portion, especially girls, declines (Block & Robins, 1993; Simmons & Blyth, 1987; Wigfield & Eccles, 1994). The change accompanies major transitions, such as the onset of puberty, entry into junior high school, and substantial realignments in friendship patterns. Often the decline accompanies a lowering of perceived competence in academic subjects such as math.

KEY THEME

Interaction Among Domains

KEY THEME
Sociocultural Influence

During the change to junior high, daily hassles tend to increase while teacher support and extracurricular activities decline, all factors correlated with a decrease in self-esteem, especially among disadvantaged children regardless of ethnic or racial background (Seidman et al., 1994). However, when adolescents retain a warm, strong orientation toward others and perceive their parents as being attuned to and supportive of their efforts in decision making, they are more likely to maintain high self-esteem throughout these transitions (Lord, Eccles, & McCarthy, 1994). Perhaps the association is not surprising, given that warm, responsive parenting is linked to high self-esteem in young people in the first place (Bishop & Ingersoll, 1989). And, as our earlier discussion of a sense of agency suggests, coping strategies that lead young people to attribute success to their competence and mastery are certainly another critical element in maintaining high self-esteem (Brooks, 1992).

Relatively little cross-cultural research on self-esteem has been reported, although several studies comparing children from the United States and Taiwan have revealed a consistent pattern: Chinese children report lower self-esteem than their counterparts in the United States (Chiu, 1992–93; Stigler, Smith, & Mao, 1985; Turner & Mo, 1984). The reasons may stem from cultural practices in Taiwan that emphasize humility rather than pride in one's accomplishments or qualities and provide less opportunity to receive social or public displays of success in academic and other settings. Also, Taiwanese family-rearing patterns emphasize obedience rather than individual achievement, and although children in Taiwan often do excel academically, other ways of gaining high self-esteem may be less available to them.

Identity

The burgeoning sense of self, along with the capacity to reflect on individual qualities, serves as the nucleus for the construction of an **identity,** a broad, coherent, internalized view of who a person is and what a person wants to be, believes, and values. A sense of identity solidifies and gives meaning to such fundamental questions about self as: Who am I? Why do I exist? What am I to become? A healthy identity, Erik Erikson pointed out (see Chapter 1), is fabricated during adolescence and young adulthood but builds on earlier progress in accepting and trusting others, being encouraged to explore interests and desires, and acquiring feelings of competence and skill. By formulating a unified sense of self as agent, separate from others and capable of reflecting on this agency, the adolescent creates a fully integrated identity and a healthy personality to accompany the transition to mature adulthood (Blasi & Glodis, 1995).

KEY THEME
Individual Differences

The Adolescent Identity Crisis   The period of adolescence has sometimes been viewed as filled with stress and uncertainty about self, riddled with sudden and frequent mood shifts, a time dubbed the **identity crisis.** Does such a crisis really take place? Erikson (1963) pointed out that in establishing an identity, adolescents enter a period of intense reflection on and dissatisfaction with who they are. During these years, thoughts and behavior often are devoted to exploring alternatives before committing to a course of action with respect to social relationships, vocation, and lifestyle (Marcia, 1980).

As they approach the teen years, children frequently engage in new ways of behaving and thinking that involve greater autonomy, independence, and expressions of intimacy with others. For example, teenagers increasingly view their actions and conduct as personal—their own business, so to speak (Smetana, 1988)—and believe such things as family chores, eating habits, curfews, and personal appearance are up to them, not their parents. Needless to say, this view can introduce conflict within the family, especially for parents who wish to maintain control.

For many adolescents, conflict is far less frequent and traumatic than the idea of a crisis would suggest (Hill, 1987; Powers, Hauser, & Kilner, 1989). The vast majority of adolescents are sociable, well-adjusted individuals on their way to adopting the

identity (personal)   Broad, coherent, internalized view of who a person is and what a person wants to be, believes, and values that emerges during adolescence.

identity crisis   Period, usually during adolescence, characterized by considerable uncertainty about the self and the role the individual is to fulfill in society.

mores and values of their culture and effectively coping with the pressures and demands society places on them (Offer, 1987). One key to successfully negotiating this period appears to be a family, educational environment, and social milieu that support the needs and interests of adolescents (Eccles, Midgley, et al., 1993a). For example, as children progress from elementary to junior high school, they find greater emphasis on control and discipline, less positive personal support from teachers, and more competitiveness and public evaluation of their work (Lord, Eccles, & McCarthy, 1994). Such changes may conflict with adolescents' need for fewer intellectual pressures and more opportunity to take charge in exploring and resolving uncertainties about their identity (Eccles et al., 1993a). From bargaining over their choices of friends and activities to use of the telephone or the family car, adolescents also test new ways of communicating with and relating to parents and others in authority (Powers, Hauser, & Kilner, 1989). Being able to establish a point of view seems to promote a strong sense of personal identity (Grotevant & Cooper, 1986; Hauser et al., 1987). Parents, teachers, and others play an important role in providing reassurance and support while permitting teenagers to weigh their ideas.

ATYPICAL DEVELOPMENT

Adolescent Suicide

Does an identity crisis occur during adolescence? Though the vast majority of young people may not experience an identity crisis during adolescence, 17 to 22 percent of youth are believed to have emotional or behavioral problems (Kazdin, 1993), and many of them receive little attention from professionals. One especially serious issue is suicide. Perhaps as many as five thousand young people ages fifteen to twenty-four commit suicide annually in the United States, and the number of attempted suicides is estimated to be one hundred times greater (Berman, 1987). In fact, most surveys suggest that 6 to 13 percent of adolescents have attempted suicide (Garland & Zigler, 1993). As Figure 12.4 suggests, adolescent suicides are far more frequent among males than females. This difference is a consequence of males typically choosing more lethal means of attempting suicide than females; in fact, the number of *attempted* suicides is greater in females than males. Suicide also increased substantially between 1980 and 1992, especially among young African American males. Yet the highest suicide rates are reported among some Native American groups (Berlin, 1987).

Nearly all adolescents who commit suicide suffer from some form of psychiatric illness (for example, depression or another emotional disorder, antisocial personality), although a small minority who suffer extreme anxiety may not have shown serious behavior or school problems (Shaffer, 1988). Studies in both the United States and Europe reveal a correlation between drug and alcohol consumption and marked increases in the frequency of suicide (Garland & Zigler, 1993). These factors, combined with stressful events and access to means to commit suicide (such as guns), create an especially lethal mix for the teenager contemplating this action.

The signs that a young person may be thinking about suicide are not always easy to read, since most teenagers who are considering suicide suffer from depression (see Chapter 11), a disorder that is difficult to discriminate from typical moodiness. However, grades that start to fall, drug use that begins or increases, withdrawal from family or friends (perhaps retreating to the bedroom more than usual), or avoidance of social events and sporting activities may be warning signs. When these behaviors are combined with becoming especially quiet or complaining about being unable to find interesting things to do, changes in eating and sleeping patterns, giving away valued possessions, or talking or writing about suicide, the adolescent may be signaling a need for help.

Programs designed to educate young people about suicide have been initiated in many schools, but so far have not been shown to be especially helpful in addressing

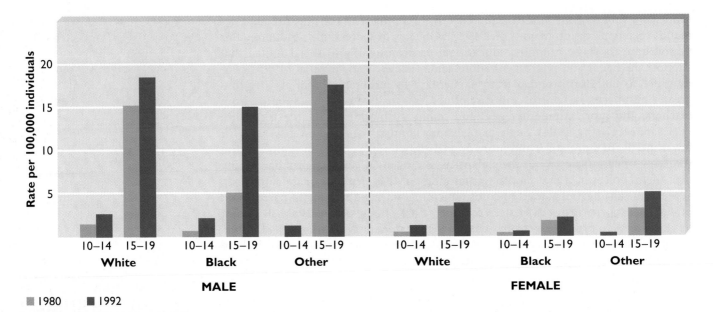

Source: Data from Suicide among children, adolescents, and young adults—United States, 1980–1992. (1995). *Morbidity and Mortality Weekly Report, 44*, 289–291.

FIGURE 12.4

Number of Suicides per 100,000 Individuals as a Function of Sex, Age, and Racial Group in the United States in 1980 and 1992

Although the frequency of suicide attempts is reported to be substantially greater among females, young males are far more likely than females to commit suicide, as this figure shows. Despite increased awareness of the problem, the number committing suicide grew substantially among both younger and older adolescents of both sexes in most racial groups in the United States between 1980 and 1992. Efforts to stem the increase need to take into account the role mental illness plays in suicide. Limiting access to highly lethal means of committing suicide and appropriate resources for identifying, treating, and preventing this action are needed to bring these numbers back down.

the problem. In fact, some professionals have been criticized for portraying suicide as a normative response to extreme stress rather than as unacceptable behavior accompanied by mental illness (Garland & Zigler, 1993). The Centers for Disease Control (1992) suggest that strategies to address the problem must include helping teachers and community leaders identify those most at risk, educating young people to become more knowledgeable about risk factors and intervention, developing screening, referral, and peer-support programs, support for crisis centers and hotlines, reducing access to lethal methods of suicide, and providing assistance to counter distress stemming from the extensive publicity that often accompanies suicide.

Ethnic Identity   Among the factors affecting a young person's identity is ethnic and racial background. **Ethnic identity** refers to the sense of belonging to a specific cultural group as opposed to simply adopting its social practices, known more generally as *acculturation* (Phinney, 1990). Research conducted in the United States suggests that preschool and younger children, even those who are members of a racial minority group, display a bias for choosing dolls or pictures depicting white individuals when asked whom they are most like, whom they want most to be like, or whom they prefer (Spencer & Markstrom-Adams, 1990). This bias has been found even in regions where white individuals are the minority, such as the West Indies, although these data may be flawed because the procedure used to measure such preferences may markedly influence their strength (Gopaul-McNicol, 1995).

As they become more capable of reflecting on and exploring their heritage, older children and adolescents do grapple with their racial and ethnic identities. Because the majority culture often views minority groups in a stereotypical and negative light, identifying with a minority ethnic or racial group can set the stage for personal conflict and confusion. Yet little evidence exists for this scenario. In fact, self-esteem among minority children can be as strong as self-esteem among others, especially when minority children have come to understand and value their ethnicity (Spencer & Markstrom-Adams, 1990; Verkuyten, 1995).

Valuing ethnicity seems to be fostered by responsive parents who are sensitive to ethnic issues (Phinney & Rosenthal, 1992). However, ethnic socialization for minor-

ethnic identity   The sense of belonging to a particular cultural group.

ity parents is carried out within, not at the expense of, broader child-rearing goals emphasized in most families: getting a good education, being a good human being, feeling satisfied about oneself, working hard, and so forth (Marshall, 1995). Nevertheless, our understanding of ethnic identity and its development remains quite limited, even though about 30 percent of youth in the United States alone are members of minority groups (Wetzel, 1987).

SELF-REGULATION AND SELF-CONTROL

Impulsive and easily upset, infants and young children have difficulty behaving in a patient or deliberate manner. Eventually, however, parents and others demand that children control their behavior and act in socially and morally acceptable ways. A three-year-old may be expected to stay away from the fireplace, use the toilet, say thank you, and share and put away toys. Older children and teenagers assume ever greater responsibility for their actions and are expected to conform to socially accepted rules and standards. But this transition from being dependent to becoming responsible and self-reliant can be a long and difficult one. A mother may have great difficulty persuading her daughter, who is eager to show off her tricycle-riding prowess, that it is a playmate's turn. And countless parents have wrestled with how best to convince their children that completing their homework is an important way to prepare themselves for future success.

Self-regulation refers to the capacity to monitor and direct one's activities to achieve certain goals or meet the demands imposed by others. **Self-control,** a related concept, is the ability to comply with expectations of caregivers or other adults, especially in their absence. Both of these concepts are especially important not only for instilling a sense of self but also for achieving ethical and moral behavior. We will first consider how self-regulation and self-control develop; then we will examine their broader ethical and moral implications.

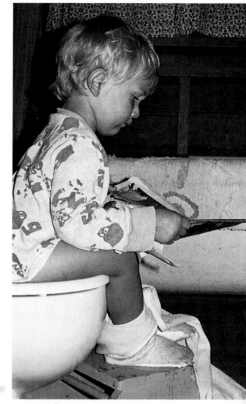

Toddlers are often asked to begin to regulate behaviors and activities so that they are displayed in socially acceptable ways. One such activity that most toddlers are expected to master is control of body functions.

Developmental Changes

For infants and young children, regulation of behavior might best be labeled *co-regulation* (Kopp, 1987) since children and their caregivers jointly manage behavior. In many families, efforts to limit activities begin when babies are about eight or nine months old. At this time, newly acquired motor skills increase risk of injury, heralding the need for restraining devices such as playpens and gates. Infants about one year of age may be warned to avoid dangerous or health-threatening objects and situations ("Don't touch the knife"; "Don't play with the cat litter"; "Hold on to my hand"). Efforts to preserve possessions ("Stay away from the VCR") and avoid harm to others ("Don't pinch") are also common concerns at about this time (Gralinski & Kopp, 1993).

As toddlers move beyond eighteen months of age, adults often supplement these *caregiving demands* with additional *demands for appropriate behavior,* such as keeping quiet and sitting up straight, and *demands for competent action,* such as helping to set the table or participating in social and family activities (Kuczynski & Kochanska, 1995). These efforts focus on encouraging acceptable social interactions, taking part in family routines and chores, and cultivating self-care and greater independence (for example, walking rather than being carried) (Gralinski & Kopp, 1993). By the time children reach twenty-four to thirty months of age, parental demands may decline in frequency as children become familiar with and respond to requests more routinely (Kopp, 1987). When caregivers emphasize "do" and behaving competently over "don't" and inhibiting social activities during this period, fewer compliance and behavior problems arise at age five (Kuczynski & Kochanska, 1995).

Children's self-initiated attempts to obey appear during the second year. A thirteen-month-old, for example, may look at, and perhaps even approach and touch, an electrical outlet while saying, "No, no!" Over the next few years, self-

self-regulation Process by which children come to control their own behaviors in accordance with the standards of their caregivers and community, especially in the absence of other adults.

self-control Ability to comply with sociocultural prescriptions concerning ethical or moral behavior.

restraint improves rapidly. For example, in a **delay-of-gratification** task, in which the child is asked to wait some period of time before performing an activity or attaining some highly desired outcome (such as playing with an attractive toy or eating a piece of candy), eighteen-month-olds have great difficulty complying. Between two and three years of age, children become increasingly more effective in delaying their behavior (Vaughn, Kopp, & Krakow, 1984). Thus, although self-control begins with attempts by others to govern the young child's actions, their efforts are transferred and gradually relinquished as warnings and guidance become less direct and as the child takes on more responsibility for regulating his behavior. How does this shift come about?

The Influence of Language and Attention

As we saw in Chapter 7, Lev Vygotsky (1962) and his students, particularly Alexander Luria (1961, 1969), theorized that language plays a pivotal role in the regulation of behavior. Consider what David, a preschooler, says while playing alone with Tinkertoys:

> *The wheels go here, the wheels go here. Oh we need to start it all over again. We need to close it up. See, it closes up. We're starting all over again. Do you know why we wanted to do that? Because I needed it to go a different way. Isn't it going to be pretty clever, don't you think? But we have to cover up the motor just like a real car.* (Kohlberg, Yaeger, & Hjertholm, 1968, p. 695)

According to Vygotsky, David's *private speech* is a form of self-regulation (Wertsch, 1985). Intended for no one else, the conversation appears to keep David on track by organizing and praising his own efforts. As we pointed out in Chapter 7, observations of the speech habits of preschoolers engaged in various activities do not always support Vygotsky's view that verbalization contributes to more competent performance (Kopp, 1987). One reason may be that expressions intended for self-regulation are most likely to occur in especially challenging circumstances (Frauenglass & Diaz, 1985). Thus, a child who talks to herself might be expected to do less well on a task than a child who proceeds without comment; after all, the silent child may no longer need verbalizations to assist problem solving.

Donald Meichenbaum and Joseph Goodman (1971) have explored this issue by training children to use language to control their behavior. Impulsive seven-to-nine-year-olds observed an adult engaged in a pencil-and-paper motor task. The adult verbalized the task requirements, described ways to direct and guide responses, and expressed positive feelings about performance. While performing the task, the adult uttered comments such as "I have to go slowly. . . . Draw the line down, good. Good, I'm doing fine so far." Simply having children observe this activity was not enough to help their performance. Successful training required a series of steps that mirrored Vygotsky's developmental model of self-regulation. Children had to perform the task first while being instructed by an adult, then while instructing themselves out loud, and finally by instructing themselves silently. Through this kind of training, the verbal communications provided by the adult and eventually adopted by children helped them meet the demands for self-reliant, systematic, and deliberate behavior.

Meichenbaum (1977) suggests that verbalizations help to regulate behavior because they direct attention to key dimensions and features of a task, assist in establishing and organizing ways to engage in activities, and preserve important task-related information in memory. Attentional factors do seem important. For example, the child directed not to eat a marshmallow who says, "The marshmallow is yummy"—words that focus attention on the forbidden treat—or who talks about sad things such as falling and hurting himself—ideas that provide little diversion—shows less ability to inhibit his behavior than someone who sings a pleasant but distracting nursery rhyme such as "Three Blind Mice" (Mischel, Ebbesen, & Zeiss, 1972). A fidgety third-grader eager for recess might be better advised to direct her attention to reading a book of her choice rather than staring at the classroom clock.

delay of gratification Capacity to wait before performing a tempting activity or attaining some highly desired outcome; a measure of ability to regulate one's own behavior.

Again, a developmental shift occurs in who assumes responsibility for regulating attention. At first, caregivers are more likely to initiate attempts to focus or distract the child. To illustrate this point, George Holden (1983) observed mothers and their two-and-a-half-year-olds as they completed grocery shopping, an activity that can test the limits of most caregivers because grocery displays are enticing. In this setting, mothers were frequently forced to respond to their children's requests and used a variety of tactics to do so: reasoning, not responding, physically or verbally intervening, acknowledging children's desires, and attempting to distract children. Mothers who tried to anticipate conflicts, either by diverting children's attention in advance or by engaging them in an interesting conversation, were most effective in preventing conflict while grocery shopping. Sensitive and consistent mothers who learned to use strategies to direct, maintain, and redirect their children's attention appeared to be most successful in regulating their behavior (Holden & West, 1989; Kopp, 1987).

During the later preschool and early school years, children display their own attentional strategies to keep on track and support their goals. For example, in a delay-of-gratification task, preschoolers often place a tempting reward in front of themselves rather than a picture of it or some other, irrelevant item. In doing so, they increase their exposure to the forbidden object, look at it more, and have greater difficulty delaying their response to it. By age five, children are less likely to create such self-defeating arrangements. They prefer to wait with the tempting reward covered rather than uncovered (Mischel & Mischel, 1983). Some will even shield their eyes, play games with their hands and feet, or try to go to sleep to help manage the delay (Cournoyer & Trudel, 1991; Mischel, Shoda, & Rodriguez, 1989).

> **KEY THEME**
> Child's Active Role

Older children show greater metacognitive understanding of helpful attentional and other tactics for regulating their activities (Mischel & Mischel, 1983; Holtz & Lehman, 1995). An eleven-year-old, for example, offered the following recommendation for distracting oneself: "You can take your mind off of it and think of Christmas or something like that. But the point is, think about something else." By this age, then, children have begun to reflect on ways they can most effectively control their behavior.

Individual Differences

Even ten years later, children who were better able to initiate delay-of-gratification strategies as preschoolers stand apart from children less able to delay gratification as preschoolers. Adolescents who had greater self-regulatory capacities as preschoolers are described by their parents as more academically and socially competent and better able to handle frustration and temptation. They also are reported to be more attentive, deliberate, and intelligent and seem better able to tolerate stress and cope with social and personal problems, even when their intellectual performance is similar to those of peers less able to delay gratification (Mischel, Shoda, & Rodriguez, 1989; Shoda, Mischel, & Peake, 1990).

> **KEY THEME**
> Individual Differences

Jeanne Block and Jack Block (1980) have identified yet another component of self-regulation, flexible and adaptive behavior in appropriate settings, that shows evidence of stable individual differences. Shouting, running, and responding impulsively, for example, may be unacceptable within the classroom but highly appropriate during recess. Some children display elasticity and are able to modify their behavior easily as the situation demands throughout childhood; others consistently show far less flexibility.

What accounts for these individual differences? Genetic factors may contribute, but researchers generally agree that socialization practices also play a significant role. Caregivers who encourage and use self-regulation provide opportunities for children to acquire skills, attitudes, and habits that promote persistence and effort and reduce frustration, yielding both social and academic benefits (Mischel, Shoda, & Rodriguez, 1989). Parents also need to strike a proper balance between dispensing control and encouraging self-regulation. Overcontrolling adults tend to have grown up

> **KEY THEME**
> Nature/Nurture

in families whose values emphasize considerable structure, order, and tradition (Block, 1971). Adults with relatively little control, on the other hand, tend to have grown up in families that placed little emphasis on achievement and responsible behavior and in which each parent had different caregiving values.

Self-regulation, in summary, begins as a joint venture between child and caregiver, but as children mature, most parents gradually relinquish and transfer the supervisory role to their offspring. By verbally directing children's activities and attention, caregivers provide role models and specific techniques children can adopt. Individual differences in these abilities emerge by the preschool years and are consistently maintained throughout adolescence. The Chronology on the next page summarizes some of the transitions in that ability, along with other major aspects of development of self.

MORAL DEVELOPMENT

As children gain increasing knowledge of the self and greater skill in regulating their own behavior, they are expected to increasingly conform to the rules and regulations considered socially acceptable for interacting with others in their community. Psychological theories of *moral development,* the process by which an individual comes to understand what society accepts as right and wrong, differ enormously in their explanations for how this change comes about. Perhaps this should not be surprising given the intense concern family members and others often express about what behaviors and relationships are acceptable. Theories arising from Freud's view of personality focus on *affective* dimensions of moral development. According to this perspective, the emotional relationships children have with their parents influence the degree to which they incorporate parental standards of conduct. Social learning theories emphasize the child's acquisition of moral *behaviors,* such as the tendency to behave acceptably and to resist temptation. Cognitive-developmental theories stress moral *reasoning,* or how the child thinks about moral problems and judges right and wrong. Each perspective makes a unique contribution to our understanding of moral development and values.

Freud's Theory

KEY THEME
Continuity/Discontinuity

Sigmund Freud's theory of moral development ([1925]1961) emphasized the *internalization* of standards as a by-product of the child's progression through the stages

Research on moral development and values has examined the roles of cognition and affect in an effort to fully understand the socialization of culturally permissible behavior. The effort to instill rules and regulations typically begins in the family, but other agencies, such as the school, play a significant role in this process as well.

CHRONOLOGY
Understanding Self and Self-regulation

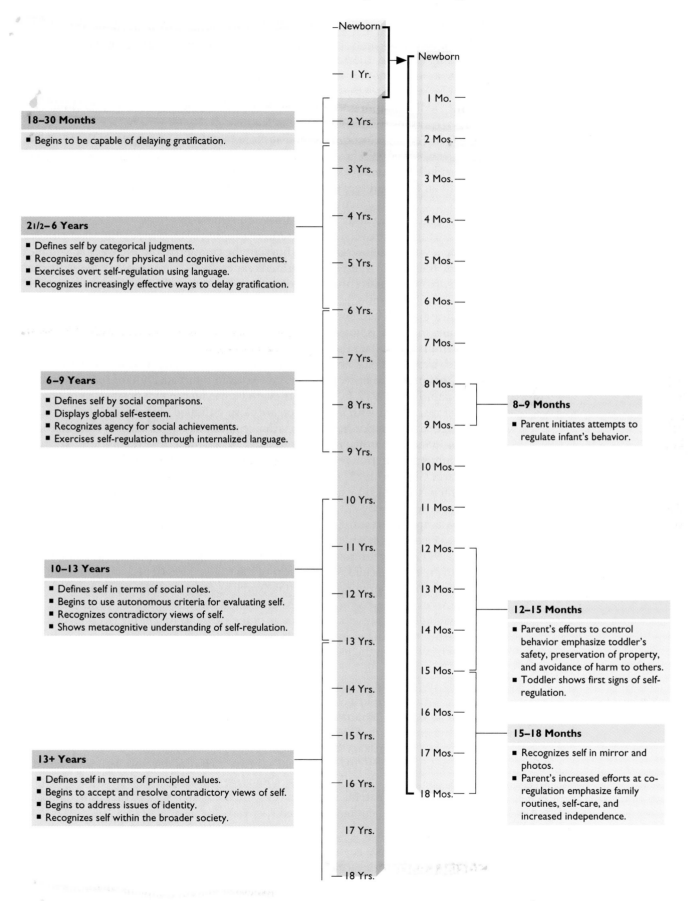

18–30 Months

- Begins to be capable of delaying gratification.

2 1/2– 6 Years

- Defines self by categorical judgments.
- Recognizes agency for physical and cognitive achievements.
- Exercises overt self-regulation using language.
- Recognizes increasingly effective ways to delay gratification.

6–9 Years

- Defines self by social comparisons.
- Displays global self-esteem.
- Recognizes agency for social achievements.
- Exercises self-regulation through internalized language.

10–13 Years

- Defines self in terms of social roles.
- Begins to use autonomous criteria for evaluating self.
- Recognizes contradictory views of self.
- Shows metacognitive understanding of self-regulation.

13+ Years

- Defines self in terms of principled values.
- Begins to accept and resolve contradictory views of self.
- Begins to address issues of identity.
- Recognizes self within the broader society.

Newborn

- 1 Yr.
- 2 Yrs.
- 3 Yrs.
- 4 Yrs.
- 5 Yrs.
- 6 Yrs.
- 7 Yrs.
- 8 Yrs.
- 9 Yrs.
- 10 Yrs.
- 11 Yrs.
- 12 Yrs.
- 13 Yrs.
- 14 Yrs.
- 15 Yrs.
- 16 Yrs.
- 17 Yrs.
- 18 Yrs.

Newborn

- 1 Mo.
- 2 Mos.
- 3 Mos.
- 4 Mos.
- 5 Mos.
- 6 Mos.
- 7 Mos.
- 8 Mos.
- 9 Mos.
- 10 Mos.
- 11 Mos.
- 12 Mos.
- 13 Mos.
- 14 Mos.
- 15 Mos.
- 16 Mos.
- 17 Mos.
- 18 Mos.

8–9 Months

- Parent initiates attempts to regulate infant's behavior.

12–15 Months

- Parent's efforts to control behavior emphasize toddler's safety, preservation of property, and avoidance of harm to others.
- Toddler shows first signs of self-regulation.

15–18 Months

- Recognizes self in mirror and photos.
- Parent's increased efforts at co-regulation emphasize family routines, self-care, and increased independence.

This chart describes the sequence in the development of understanding the self and self-regulation based on the findings of research. Children often show individual differences in the exact ages at which they display the various developmental achievements outlined here.

of psychosexual development. Freud believed a moral sense emerges near the end of the *phallic stage,* around age five or six years, when boys resolve the *Oedipal complex.* According to Freud, the boy experiences intense emotional conflict when his sexual attraction to his mother cannot be fulfilled and he comes to fear castration by his father (his competitor for his mother's affections).

The Oedipal conflict becomes resolved, Freud concluded, when the young boy suppresses his instinctual urges and allies himself with his powerful same-sex parent, his father. Through this process of *identification,* the child acquires his father's moral values and standards. The outcome is the formation of the **superego,** the component of the child's personality that functions both as a **conscience** (governing what not to do) and an **ego ideal** (governing appropriate and desirable behaviors). By acting in accordance with his parents' wishes, the child avoids feelings of guilt associated with violating these newly internalized values and standards.

Among the controversial aspects of Freud's theory is its prediction that girls will develop a weaker moral sense than boys. In the counterpart to the Oedipal complex, dubbed the *Electra complex,* daughters experience a strong attachment to their fathers. However, since they cannot fear castration, the resolution of this conflict involves far less emotional intensity for girls than it does for boys. As a result, a girl's identification with her mother occurs with less force, and the superego or conscience, according to Freud, is not as strong.

Attempts to validate the various claims made by Freud have not met with great success. Little evidence exists to show that the child's identification with the same-sex parent or fear of losing parental love leads to internalization of moral standards (Hoffman, 1970, 1971). In fact, there is growing evidence that positive emotional relationships, at least with the mother, are closely aligned with willing compliance to an assigned task and a healthy conscience for both boys and girls (Kochanska & Aksan, 1995; Kochanska, Aksan, & Koenig, 1995). Moreover, the notion that moral development is inferior or incomplete in girls has been highly criticized. For example, Carol Gilligan (1982) maintains that Freud's theory is a male's view of male development that fails to explore the unique dimensions of the female experience as they pertain to morality.

Contemporary research also shows that children begin to develop a conscience well before the age at which Freud claimed the superego emerges (Emde et al., 1991; Lamb, 1991). Early internalization of rules and an appreciation for right and wrong seem to arise in the child's second year of life (Kagan, 1984), perhaps as the ability to recognize positive emotional reactions as well as anger or displeasure in the communications of caregivers increases (Kochanska, 1993). By age three years, some children willingly comply with the requests of their parents to complete certain activities (for example, putting away toys) and avoid others (for example, touching prohibited objects), even when the parents are no longer present (Kochanska, Aksan, & Koenig, 1995). Three-year-olds also notice flawed objects (for example, a teddy bear with stuffing coming out or a broken cup), and, if led to believe the flaws are the consequence of their own behavior, they may voice apologies ("Sorry," "Didn't mean to."), offer reparations ("Put back in," "Clean up"), and exhibit distress ("Take this away," "I wanna go"), expressions of guilt and shame that are frequently manifestations of conscience (Kochanska, Casey, & Fukumoto, 1995).

Certainly the particulars of Freud's theory of moral development have failed to receive much support. Still, his ideas about the internalization of society's standards, the central role of parents in the process, and the importance of the child's emotions for moral development have endured.

Social Learning Theory

According to social learning theory, the rewards and punishments dispensed by parents and others shape the child's conduct, as do the actions and verbalizations a child

---

superego   In Freudian theory, a mental structure that monitors socially acceptable and unacceptable behavior.

conscience   In Freudian theory, the part of the superego that defines unacceptable behaviors and actions, usually as also defined by the parents.

ego ideal   In Freudian theory, the part of the superego that defines the positive standards for which an individual strives; acquired via parental rewarding of desired behaviors.

sees parents and others use (Aronfreed, 1976; Bandura, 1977b). In this sense, moral values are learned as any other behavior is. Social learning theorists see morality as a process of incremental growth in appropriate actions and increasing conformity with the rules of society. Thus, social learning theorists generally have not been concerned with how the child feels or thinks about moral problems. Moreover, the child plays a somewhat passive role in adopting the values and prescriptives of the parents and the culture more broadly.

How convincingly does the social learning model explain moral development? Studies investigating the child's ability to resist temptation—for example, learning not to play with a forbidden toy—suggest that reinforcement history is indeed a factor in moral behavior. Children quickly learn not to touch an attractive toy if an adult mildly reprimands them for initiating activities with it. In other words, they respond to the punishments the adult doles out.

Several factors influence children's tendency to transgress when left alone in the room with the forbidden toy after they have been punished. First, as social learning theory predicts, the timing of the punishment plays a role. When the punishment is administered as the child reaches for the forbidden toy but before she actually touches it, instead of after she has picked it up, she is less likely to violate the adult's commands during the "temptation period," when the adult is no longer present. Learning theory predicts that punishments will be most effective if they closely follow the undesired behavior—in this case, when the child first reaches for the forbidden toy. Second, providing a verbal explanation of why the toy is prohibited also has an effect. When children are told, for example, that the attractive toy might break if it is handled, they are much less likely to violate the adult's prohibition. According to social learning theorists, verbalizations facilitate the internalization of morally acceptable and unacceptable behaviors (Aronfreed, 1969, 1976).

Parents and others serving as models can also influence whether a child commits a transgression. Children who observe a model commit a prohibited act, such as touching a forbidden toy, are more likely to perform the act themselves, whereas children observing a model who resists temptation will commit fewer transgressions (Rosenkoetter, 1973). However, role models appear to be more powerful in *disinhibiting* than in inhibiting behavior that violates a rule or an expectation. Children are more likely to follow a role model's deviant behaviors than his or her compliant ones (Hoffman, 1970).

Many aspects of moral development can be explained by principles of reinforcement and observational learning. Some experts contend, however, that social learning theorists do not adequately consider the child's thinking and reasoning about moral issues. For example, early punishment in the forbidden-toy experiments may be effective because of extremely clear communication about what behaviors are acceptable and unacceptable: the toy should not be touched (Turiel, 1983). In contrast, when punishment is delivered late, the child may become confused, believing the behavior is acceptable in those first few moments of holding the toy before the adult expresses displeasure. Thus, the child's inability to sort out conflicting messages, rather than the late timing of reinforcement, leads to persistence of the "deviant" behavior. Other criticisms are that insufficient consideration is given to the intentions that inspire moral actions and that morality is viewed as nothing more than conforming to social norms (Walker, 1996).

Newer versions of social learning theory assign a larger role for cognitive processes in the emergence of moral values. In Albert Bandura's social cognitive theory (1986), children develop internalized standards of conduct, cognitive representations derived from observing role models and processing the explanations of moral behavior delivered by parents and others. Children, especially to the extent to which they accept and accurately perceive communications, attempt to behave in ways consistent with those representations (Grusec & Goodnow, 1994). Nevertheless, describing changes in the child's ability to reason about moral questions has been left largely to other theorists, such as Jean Piaget and Lawrence Kohlberg.

KEY THEME
Nature/Nurture

KEY THEME
Interaction Among Domains

Cognitive-Developmental Theories

Cognitive-developmental explanations of moral development highlight the ways children reason about moral problems. Should a person ever steal, even if the transgression would help another person? Are there any circumstances under which lying is acceptable? The child's capacity to think through the answers to such questions depends on his ability to reason and to consider the perspectives, needs, and feelings of others. In other words, moral development is intimately connected with advances in general thinking abilities. The two most prominent cognitive-developmental theorists concerned with moral development, Jean Piaget and Lawrence Kohlberg, have suggested stage theories in which children's reasoning about moral issues is qualitatively different depending on their level of development.

Piaget's Theory   Piaget ([1932]1965) derived his ideas about moral development from systematic and extensive observations of children in two contexts: as they played a formal game with a shared set of rules and as they encountered moral dilemmas created to assess thinking about ethical problems. Piaget began by observing and interviewing children playing marbles, a popular children's game. Children were asked several questions about this game: What are the rules? Can new rules be invented? Where do rules come from? Have they always been the same?

Piaget concluded that children's developing appreciation for the rules of the game occurred in several stages. Preschoolers, he stated, are not guided by rules. They engage in the activity for the pure pleasure it provides, and their play is largely solitary. Thus, young children may hide marbles or throw them randomly, ignoring the formal rules of the game. By about age six, however, children come to regard rules as sacred and inviolable. Rules, handed down by adults, must be respected and have always existed in the same form; people played marbles in exactly the same way over the years. By about ten years of age, children understand rules to be the result of cooperation and mutual consent among all the participants in the game. Thus, rules may be modified to suit the needs of the situation if all the players agree.

The second method Piaget used to study moral development consisted of noting responses of children to moral dilemmas, stories in which a central character committed a transgression. The intentions of that character and the consequences of his or her act varied, as the following stories illustrate:

> A. *A little boy who is called John is in his room. He is called to dinner. He goes into the dining room. But behind the door there was a chair, and on the chair there was a tray with fifteen cups on it. John couldn't have known that there was all this behind the door. He goes in, the door knocks against the tray, bang go the fifteen cups, and they all get broken!*

> B. *Once there was a little boy whose name was Henry. One day when his mother was out he tried to get some jam out of the cupboard. He climbed up onto a chair and stretched out his arm. But the jam was too high up and he couldn't reach it and have any. But while he was trying to get it he knocked over a cup. The cup fell down and broke. (Piaget,[1932] 1965, p. 122)*

Which boy is naughtier? Younger children typically choose John, the child who broke more cups. According to Piaget, children younger than about ten are in the stage of moral development called **moral realism,** or *heteronomy*. They judge the rightness or wrongness of an act by the objective visible consequences—in this case, how many cups were broken. They do not consider the boys' intentions to behave well or improperly.

In the stage of moral realism, rules are viewed as unbreakable; if the rules are violated, the child sees punishment as the inevitable consequence. The belief in **immanent justice** is reflected in such statements as "That's God punishing me," made when the child accidentally falls off a bike after lying to her mother, for example. Although the fall is unrelated to the child's transgression, she believes the causal link

KEY THEME
Interaction Among Domains

KEY THEME
Continuity/Discontinuity

KEY THEME
Continuity/Discontinuity

moral realism   In Piaget's theory of moral development, the first stage of moral reasoning, in which moral judgments are made on the basis of the consequences of an act. Also called *heteronomy*.

immanent justice   Young child's belief that punishment will inevitably follow a transgression.

exists. Children in this stage also believe in **expiatory punishment,** the notion that a punishment need not be related to the wrongful act if it is severe enough to teach a lesson. Thus, stealing a friend's toy can be punished by any means, not necessarily by returning the toy or making reparations, so long as the retribution is harsh.

From a limited ability to reason about moral issues, children progress to **moral relativism,** or *autonomy*. Now the transgressor's motives are taken into account. Henry is named as the naughtier boy; he intended to misbehave, even though he broke only one cup. The child no longer believes every violation will be punished. Still, punishments should relate to the misdemeanor so that the individual appreciates the consequences of his act. Piaget calls this concept **punishment by reciprocity**.

What precipitates the shift from moral realism to moral relativism? Piaget points to changes in the child's cognitive capabilities, especially decreasing egocentrism (see Chapter 8), as one important element. To understand another's intentions, for example, the child must be able to appreciate the point of view of that person as distinct from her own. Another important factor is the opportunity to interact with peers. Peer interactions force the child to consider the thoughts and feelings of others and eventually lead to an understanding of their intentions and motives. Parents can further encourage the transition from realism to relativism, notes Piaget, by encouraging mutual respect and understanding, pointing out the consequences of the child's actions for others and articulating their needs and feelings as parents.

Evaluating Piaget   How well does Piaget's theory stand up? Research confirms that reasoning about moral problems shifts as children grow older. With development children from many diverse cultures, from different social classes, and of varying intellectual abilities more fully consider intentions in judging the actions of another person. Beliefs in immanent justice, expiatory punishment, and obedience to authority decline with age (Hoffman, 1970; Lickona, 1976). Piaget's assertion that cognitive growth underlies changes in moral reasoning has also received support. As children reach the stage of concrete operations, become less egocentric, and demonstrate improved ability to take the perspective of another, they rely less on adult authority and are more likely to base their moral responses on the principle of reciprocity (Lee, 1971).

As for Piaget's contention that peer interaction promotes advances in moral thought, the evidence is mixed. Children reared on the Israeli kibbutz, or collective farm, where they have extensive experience with peers right from early infancy, display levels of moral reasoning similar to those of peers who grew up in nuclear family settings (Kugelmass & Breznitz, 1967). At the same time, other researchers have noted a positive relationship between sophisticated moral thought and opportunities to interact with peers in clubs, activities, and other settings (Harris, Mussen, & Rutherford, 1976; Keasey, 1971; Kruger, 1992).

Although many general aspects of Piaget's theory have been confirmed, some particulars have been challenged. For one thing, Piaget maintains that a child at a given stage should display all the characteristics associated with moral reasoning at that level; that is, his thought should show internal consistency. But children who believe in immanent justice sometimes fail to respond to moral dilemmas solely on the basis of objective consequences or adult authority (Lickona, 1976).

Young children also can be sensitive to the intentions behind a given act (Zelazo, Helwig, & Law, 1996). One set of researchers asked kindergarten, second-grade, and fifth-grade children to listen to stories about a girl who was being aggressive with another. In the "hostile" condition, the aggressive act was intended to make the victim feel bad. In the "prosocial" condition, the aggressive act protected someone else (for example, "Betty grabs the ball from Andrea so no one gets hit by it"). Even the youngest children indicated that aggression in the hostile condition was worse than in the prosocial condition, demonstrating their awareness of the intentions behind the aggressor's behavior (Rule, Nesdale, & McAra, 1974). Furthermore, even children as young as seven seem to realize that whether another person has authority does not

KEY THEME
Sociocultural Influence

expiatory punishment   Notion that punishment need not be related to a transgression as long as the punishment is severe enough.

moral relativism   In Piaget's theory of moral development, the second stage of moral reasoning, in which moral judgments are made on the basis of the actor's intentions. Also called *autonomy*.

punishment by reciprocity   Belief that punishment should be related to the transgression.

TABLE 12.1	Kohlberg's Six Substages of Moral Development	
Stage	**Motivation**	**Typical Moral Reasoning**

		Preconventional Level
1 Punishment and obedience orientation	The primary motive for action is the avoidance of punishment:	*Pro:* If you let your wife die, you will get in trouble. You'll be blamed for not spending the money to save her and there'll be an investigation of you and the druggist for your wife's death.
		Con: You shouldn't steal the drug because you'll be caught and sent to jail if you do. If you do get away, your conscience would bother you thinking how the police would catch up to you any minute. (Kohlberg, 1984, p. 52)
2 Naive instrumental hedonism	Actions are motivated by the desire for rewards:	*Pro:* If you do happen to get caught you could give the drug back and you wouldn't get much of a sentence. It wouldn't bother you much to serve a little jail term, if you have your wife when you get out.
		Con: He may not get much of a jail term if he steals the drug, but his wife will probably die before he gets out, so it wouldn't do him much good. If his wife dies, he shouldn't blame himself; it isn't his fault she has cancer. (Kohlberg, 1984, p. 52)

		Conventional Level
3 Good-boy morality	The child strives to avoid the disapproval of others (as distinct from avoidance of punishment):	*Pro:* No one will think you're bad if you steal the drug but your family will think you're an inhuman husband if you don't. If you let your wife die, you'll never be able to look anyone in the face again.
		Con: It isn't just the druggist who will think you're a criminal, everyone else will, too. After you steal it, you'll feel bad thinking how you've brought dishonor on your family and yourself; you won't be able to face anyone again. (Kohlberg, 1984, p. 52)

depend simply on being an adult but also depends on the social position that gives an adult, or even a peer, the status to make demands on another (Laupa, 1991).

It is clear from Piaget's work that the child's conceptualization of what is moral becomes more elaborate and complex with age and that any attempt to understand moral development must include an explanation of the child's thought as well as behavior. Subsequent theorists, Kohlberg in particular, have found Piaget's writings a useful springboard for their own theoretical formulations.

Kohlberg's Theory   Like Piaget, Lawrence Kohlberg (1969, 1976) proposed a stage theory of moral development in which progress through each stage proceeds in a universal order and regression to earlier modes of thinking is rare. Kohlberg based his theory on children's responses to a set of dilemmas that put obedience to authority or the law in direct conflict with helping a person in need (for example, "Should a man steal an overpriced drug that he cannot obtain legally in order to save his wife?")

Using an analysis of the reasoning of boys, ranging in age from ten to sixteen, for nine of these dilemmas, Kohlberg identified three general levels of moral orientation, each with two substages, to explain the varying responses of his participants (see Table 12.1). At the first level, called the **preconventional level,** the child's behavior is motivated by external pressures: avoidance of punishment, attainment of rewards, and preservation of his own self-interests. Norms of behavior are not yet derived from internalized principles, and the child's needs and desires are primary.

At the next level, the **conventional level,** conforming to the norms of the majority and maintaining the social order have become central to the child's reasoning. The child now considers the points of view of others, along with their intentions and mo-

KEY THEME
Continuity/Discontinuity

preconventional level In Kohlberg's theory, the first level of moral reasoning, in which morality is motivated by the avoidance of punishments and attainment of rewards.

conventional level In Kohlberg's theory, the second level of moral reasoning, in which the child conforms to the norms of the majority and wishes to preserve the social order.

TABLE 12.1 (Cont.)	Kohlberg's Six Substages of Moral Development	
Stage	**Motivation**	**Typical Moral Reasoning**
Conventional Level (Continued)		
4 Authority-maintaining morality	An act is always wrong if it violates a rule or does harm to others:	*Pro:* You should steal it. If you did nothing you'd be letting your wife die, it's your responsibility if she dies. You have to take it with the idea of paying the druggist. *Con:* It is a natural thing . . . to want to save his wife but it's always wrong to steal. He still knows he's stealing and taking a valuable drug from the man who made it. (Kohlberg, 1984, p. 50)
Postconventional Level		
5 Morality of contract and democracy	The individual is concerned with self-respect and maintaining the respect of others. Laws must be obeyed, because they represent a social contract, but they may sometimes conflict with moral values:	*Pro:* The law wasn't set up for these circumstances. Taking the drug in this situation isn't really right, but it's justified to do it. *Con:* You can't completely blame someone for stealing, but extreme circumstances don't really justify taking the law in your own hands. You can't have everyone stealing when they get desperate. The end may be good, but the ends don't justify the means. (Kohlberg, 1984, p. 50)
6 Morality of individual principles of conscience	Individuals are concerned with upholding their personal principles and may sometimes feel it necessary to deviate from rules when the rules conflict with moral principles:	*Pro:* This is a situation which forces him to choose between stealing and letting his wife die. In a situation where the choice must be made, it is morally right to steal. He has to act in terms of the principle of preserving and respecting life. *Con:* [The man] is faced with the decision of whether to consider other people who need the drug just as badly as his wife. [He] ought to act not according to his particular feelings toward his wife, but considering the value of all the lives involved. (Kohlberg, 1984, p. 51)

tives. The child also feels a sense of responsibility to contribute to society and to uphold the laws and institutions that serve its members by keeping the system going.

Finally, at the **postconventional level,** the individual has developed a fuller understanding of the basis for laws and rules. They are now seen as a social contract that all individuals must uphold because of shared responsibilities and duties. The individual recognizes the relative and sometimes arbitrary nature of rules, which may vary from group to group. Certain principles and values, however, such as justice and human dignity, must be preserved at all costs.

Kohlberg emphasized that changes in the child's perspective-taking ability are the basis for shifts in moral reasoning. The younger child focuses on the self and personal needs, but children increasingly appreciate the perspectives of others by the end of the preconventional level and throughout the conventional level. By the postconventional level, children consider the self and others within the context of the larger society. According to Kohlberg, changes in perspective-taking ability are promoted by opportunities for children to discuss others' points of view. Exposure to higher levels of moral reasoning displayed by older peers and adults, which can precipitate cognitive advances in children, also is critical.

Evaluating Kohlberg Numerous investigations of Kohlberg's theory have confirmed stagelike transitions in moral reasoning. For example, Anne Colby and her colleagues (1983) followed Kohlberg's original sample of adolescent boys during a twenty-year period and noted that their responses to moral dilemmas fit within the developmental stages delineated by Kohlberg (see Figure 12.5). With few exceptions,

postconventional level In Kohlberg's theory, the third level of moral reasoning, in which laws are seen as the result of a social contract and individual principles of conscience may emerge.

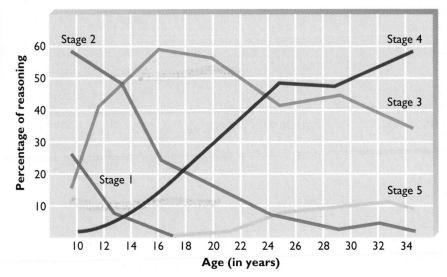

The Development of
Moral Reasoning

In a longitudinal follow-up
study of Kohlberg's original
sample, Anne Colby and her
colleagues confirmed that participants showed consistent upward advances in moral reasoning with age. The graph
shows the extent to which participants gave responses characteristic of each of Kohlberg's
six stages from age ten through
adulthood. With development,
responses associated with the
preconventional level (stages 1
and 2) declined, and responses
associated with the conventional level (stages 3 and 4)
increased. Few young adults
moved to the postconventional
level of moral reasoning.

Source: Adapted from Colby et al., 1983.

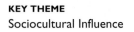

KEY THEME
Sociocultural Influence

participants progressed upward, although as adults most individuals still reasoned at
the conventional level. In fact, so few participants responded at the highest stage of
the postconventional level that Kohlberg came to question whether it was justified
(Kohlberg, 1984; Kohlberg, Levine, & Hewer, 1983). Moral development also was
found to correlate positively with IQ and educational level, consistent with
Kohlberg's emphasis on the cognitive basis of moral judgment. More recently,
Lawrence Walker (1989) reported that six-through-fifteen-year-olds tested during a
two-year period gained in moral reasoning and few children skipped stages or re-
gressed to earlier forms of reasoning.

Cross-cultural studies in countries as diverse as India, Turkey, Japan, Nigeria, and
Finland also have found that children show development of moral reasoning, from
preconventional to conventional levels, without skipping stages and without regress-
ing to previous stages. Postconventional reasoning, observed infrequently, is reported
more commonly in urban cultures and is virtually absent in tribal and village folk
societies (Snarey, 1985).

As with Piaget's theory, however, researchers have been unable to confirm some
specific propositions in Kohlberg's outline of moral development. Is perspective-
taking skill important in spurring advances in moral reasoning? Researchers report
no relationship between the two variables about as often as they report a significant
one (Kurdek, 1978). Do individuals within a stage respond consistently to different
moral dilemmas, as Kohlberg maintains they should? In one study of seventy-five
college students who responded to five moral dilemmas, not one person received the
same stage score for all stories (Fishkin, Keniston, & MacKinnon, 1973). Thus, while
individuals may exhibit a particular stage, they also display considerable variation in
their reasoning about moral issues. Finally, investigators have reported that when
adults do not continue their education, some tend to remain at one stage of moral
reasoning or a small percentage move down instead of up through the stages (Rest,
1983).

Another criticism of Kohlberg's theory is that it fails to capture the many modes
of moral reasoning evident in individuals and different cultural groups. In responding to moral dilemmas, people growing up on the Israeli kibbutz often address the
importance of the principle of happiness for everyone (Snarey, 1985). Asian cultures
too emphasize the idea of the collective good and a harmonious social order. The desirable way to resolve disputes is to reconcile people who are in conflict rather than
rely on laws to control their behavior. Thus, families often preserve harmony by
holding conferences to settle disputes. Kohlberg's moral dilemmas, which require a
choice between rules and the needs of individuals, do not permit the expression of
this cultural principle (Dien, 1982). Likewise, Indian cultures emphasize the value of

all life, not just human life; thus, a most serious transgression, as expressed by orthodox Hindu children and adults, is eating beef, chicken, or fish (Shweder, Mahapatra, & Miller, 1987). Such a concept does not appear in Kohlberg's outline of moral development. Buddhist beliefs about limits to self and to the value of intervention in preventing suffering are also difficult to reconcile within Kohlberg's framework (Huebner & Garrod, 1991). Thus, the movement of the individual toward the fullest understanding of the principle of justice, at least as conceptualized by Kohlberg, may be a singularly Western phenomenon.

The failure to consider alternative modes of moral reasoning has been an especially sensitive issue with respect to possible sex differences in moral development. In one early study, Kohlberg reported that most males function at the higher stage, whereas most females reason at the lower stage, within the conventional level of moral reasoning (Kohlberg & Kramer, 1969). The report provoked a strong reaction from some members of the psychological community and led Carol Gilligan to propose that moral development takes a different, not an inferior course in females (Gilligan, 1982, 1988; Gilligan & Attanucci, 1988). Gilligan states that because females tend to be concerned with relationships, caregiving, and intimacy, they typically develop a **morality of care and responsibility** in contrast to the **morality of justice** described by Kohlberg. The morality of care and responsibility concerns self-sacrifice and relationships with others rather than the tension between rules and the needs and rights of the individual.

An eleven-year-old girl's response to the story about whether or not to steal a drug illustrates the ethic of care that Gilligan holds to be typical of females:

> *If he stole the drug, he might save his wife then, but if he did, he might have to go to jail, and then his wife might get sicker again, and he couldn't get more of the drug, and it might not be good. So, they should really just talk it out and find some other way to make the money. (Gilligan, 1982, p. 28)*

Compare this response, which emphasizes an effort to come to mutual agreement and sacrifice, with the responses more typically obtained from boys (summarized in Table 12.1), which focus on the issue of justice and individual rights. Although this girl's response might receive a low score in Kohlberg's system because of its seemingly wavering noncommittal nature, Gilligan believes it reflects a mature understanding of the crisis a relationship might undergo when a law is broken.

morality of care and responsibility Tendency to make moral judgments on the basis of concern for others.

morality of justice Tendency to make moral judgments on the basis of reason and abstract principles of equity.

Are there sex differences in moral development? Of the large number of investigations based on Kohlberg's tasks, very few report substantial differences between males and females in level of moral reasoning (Walker, 1984; Wark & Krebs, 1996). But it has been found that both males and females tend to interpret moral decisions about impersonal situations (such as whether a man should steal a drug for his wife) in terms of justice and rights and decisions about dilemmas that they have personally confronted in terms of the ethic of care (Walker, 1996). Whether sex differences in moral development exist continues to be a controversial question. Whatever the conclusion, however, Gilligan's work has shown that researchers need to expand their understanding of what constitutes moral values.

KEY THEME
Sociocultural Influence

Morality as Domain-specific Knowledge   As we have just seen, definitions of morality can vary enormously, and the aspects of behavior judged acceptable or unacceptable often are embedded within the broad fabric of social knowledge and values represented in culture (Turiel & Wainryb, 1994). But perhaps a distinction needs to be made between moral and societal values (Turiel 1983; Turiel, Hildebrandt, & Wainryb, 1991). The *moral domain* consists of rules that regulate a person's own or another's rights or welfare; examples are the concepts of justice and responsibility toward others. The *societal domain* pertains to knowledge of **social conventions,** the rules that regulate social conventions such as how to dress appropriately for a given occasion and what degree of formality to use in speaking to someone, factors that can vary dramatically from one culture to another.

Turiel hypothesizes that the moral and societal domains develop along separate paths and that most theories of moral development have confused the two. Children begin distinguishing moral and social-conventional rules by age three (Smetana & Braeges, 1990). To illustrate, preschoolers will respond differently to transgressions of their playmates depending on whether the actions violate a social or a moral rule. When a child violates a moral rule, for example, by intentionally inflicting harm or taking another's possessions, other children typically react by physically intervening or making statements about the pain the victim experienced. On the other hand, when children observe another person violating a social convention such as eating while standing instead of sitting, they either do not react or simply comment on the rules surrounding proper social behavior (Nucci & Turiel, 1978). In addition, when questioned about social-conventional transgressions, most children say such an act would be acceptable if no rule existed about it in school, whereas moral transgressions are wrong, are more serious, and should receive greater punishment, even if the school has no rule pertaining to them (Smetana, Schlagman, & Adams, 1993).

How do children come to appreciate the distinction between moral and social conventions? Perhaps through the greater emotional affect associated with moral transgressions than with social infractions. When a child observes a peer hitting someone or is a victim of retaliation himself, the abuse may arouse a high degree of emotion in him. For example, when first- and third-graders are asked to rate how they would feel if they were hit without provocation or if another child stole their toys, they are more likely to indicate a negative emotion than when they line up outside the wrong classroom. Furthermore, children frequently justify intervening in a moral transgression by referring to their own or the victim's emotional state (Arsenio & Ford, 1985). In addition, adults may react differently to transgressions associated with moral issues compared to social conventions; as a result, the child learns to discriminate between these two domains (Glassman & Zan, 1995).

Evaluating Cognitive-Developmental Theories   Cognitive-developmental approaches fill a void left by Freudian and social learning theories by acknowledging that how the child thinks about moral situations and social conflict is every bit as important as how she feels or behaves. However, the approach also has shortcomings. A most important concern is whether moral reasoning is related to moral behavior. Scores on reasoning tests do not always correlate with tendencies to avoid cheating, to help others, or to abide by rules (Richards et al., 1992). The closest relationships are found between moral reasoning and specific negative social behaviors, such as

social conventions   Behavioral rules that regulate social interactions, such as dress codes and degrees of formality in speech.

TABLE 12.2	The Major Theories of Moral Development		
Theory	**Emphasis**	**Path of Development**	**Process of Moral Development**
Freudian	Affective dimensions	Stagelike	Resolution of Oedipal/Electra conflict followed by identification with same-sex parent
Social Learning	Moral behavior	Continuous	Reinforcement and modeling of standards of behavior followed by internalization of those standards
Cognitive-Developmental			
Piaget	Moral reasoning	Stagelike	Growth in cognitive and perspective-taking skills that lead to more abstract, other-oriented principles of morality
Kohlberg	Moral reasoning	Stagelike	
Turiel	Moral reasoning	Continuous	Growth in knowledge of moral rules as distinct from social conventions

aggression and delinquency in adolescents (Blasi, 1980; Gregg, Gibbs, & Basinger, 1994). Another limitation is that current formulations do not capture the full range of moral principles individuals use in making ethical judgments. Thus, contemporary researchers continue to explore moral reasoning across different cultures and between the sexes (Gilligan, Lyons, & Hanmer, 1989; Turiel & Wainryb, 1994).

Although they highlight different facets of moral progress, Freudian, social learning, and cognitive-developmental theories (summarized in Table 12.2) all portray the child as moving from a self-orientation to an other-orientation. They also share the view of a child motivated initially by external events, such as rewards and punishments, or the need to affiliate with his parents. With development, the standards of morality become internalized. Ultimately, however, a complete theory of moral development should describe the ways the affective, cognitive, and behavioral dimensions interact with one another. Perhaps research on more positive aspects of moral development can shed additional light on these complex interrelationships. It is to these more positive aspects that we now turn.

PROSOCIAL BEHAVIOR AND VALUES

A young child consoles a friend in distress, helps her pick up the pieces of a broken toy, or shares a snack. These **prosocial behaviors,** social actions performed to benefit others and perhaps the self, have come under increasing investigation in recent years as another way to understand the development of values and moral behavior in children. Among prosocial behaviors is **altruism,** behavior carried out to help others without expectation of rewards for oneself.

In contrast to research that focuses on justice and rights, prosocial and altruistic responses have a less obligatory, legalistic quality about them (Kahn, 1992). Acts of kindness or assistance are often discretionary but highly valued in many communities. Grade school children who tend to help others have better social skills (Eisenberg & Mussen, 1989), are more popular with peers (Gottman, Gonso, & Rasmussen, 1975; McGuire & Weisz, 1982), and are more self-confident, self-assured, and better adjusted (Mussen et al., 1970) than those who do not. Thus, altruism is associated with many desirable outcomes, particularly in children's social relationships. For many, the ability to assist others and to improve their well-being is also a central component of defining one's self. Thus, it is important to understand what influences the emergence of these qualities.

KEY THEME
Interaction Among Domains

prosocial behavior Positive social action performed to benefit others.

altruism Behavior carried out to help another without expectation of reward.

The Development of Prosocial Behaviors and Altruism

Several contemporary theorists believe an essential element underlying prosocial or altruistic behavior is **empathy,** a vicarious, shared emotional response involving the feelings of others that includes sympathetic concern for the person in need of assistance (Batson & Oleson, 1991; Eisenberg et al., 1996; Roberts & Strayer, 1996). Even infants show signs of sensitivity to the distress of others. Two- and three-day-olds may cry when other infants cry, but not in response to other, equally loud noises (Simner, 1971). In addition to crying, ten-to-fourteen-month-olds may whimper or silently attend to expressions of distress from another person. Often they respond by soothing themselves, sucking their thumbs, or seeking a parent for comfort (Radke-Yarrow & Zahn-Waxler, 1984). Perhaps because the boundary between self and another individual is not yet clear at this age, consoling the self is a form of coping with another's distress.

Between one and two years of age, new behaviors emerge: touching or patting the distressed person as though to provide solace, seeking assistance for the person, or even giving the person something to provide comfort, such as a cookie, blanket, or teddy bear. The person's emotional state may also be labeled with expressions such as "Cry," "Oh-oh!", or "Hurting" (Radke-Yarrow & Zahn-Waxler, 1984). Preschool children display more varied and complex responses to the needs of others. In a classic study of sympathy, Lois Murphy (1937) observed that children show a host of reactions to a peer's distress in a nursery school setting. Among them are comforting and helping the troubled child, asking questions of her, punishing the agent of the child's distress, protecting the child, and asking an adult for help. When asked why they share with or help someone else, nursery school children often state they simply want to or the other person needs help (Eisenberg-Berg & Neal, 1979).

Although many researchers report that helping and sharing increase with age, others note that older children actually help or share less (Radke-Yarrow, Zahn-Waxler, & Chapman, 1983). Between ages six and sixteen, increasing concerns about self-interests and the expectations of others may enter into decisions about assisting a person in need or performing another prosocial activity (Krebs & Van Hesteren, 1994). In addition, adolescents and young adults may begin to more fully consider the longer-term consequences of their activities (Eisenberg et al., 1995).

Are girls, often believed to be more nurturing, caring, and empathic than boys, also more altruistic? On the whole, children display few sex differences in the amount of helping and sharing (Radke-Yarrow, Zahn-Waxler, & Chapman, 1983). For example, when in the presence of a crying baby, girls are no more likely to assist than boys (Zahn-Waxler, Friedman, & Cummings, 1983). But sex differences do exist in how prosocial behaviors are expressed. For one thing, girls who hear a recording of an infant crying display more verbal sympathy than boys. The tendency for girls to be more expressive about prosocial activities is consistent with at least some research indicating that girls are more frequently rewarded by parents for helping than are boys (Fagot, 1978a). Girls may be trying to live up to societal expectations for females. Yet despite cultural stereotypes and differential patterns of parental reinforcement, evidence for sex differences in altruism is not strong.

The Relationship Between Empathy and Helping   Behaving prosocially, such as attempting to alleviate distress in others, may be a way to relieve a child's own empathic distress (Hoffman, 1976, 1982). Thus, if a boy sees that a friend who has just fallen down on the playground is crying, he feels uncomfortable. He knows how painful a skinned knee feels and shares his friend's anguish. To feel better himself, the boy rushes to help his playmate to the school nurse's office.

How strong is the connection between empathy and prosocial behavior? When children are asked to report their feelings, a consistent link between empathy and assisting others has not always been shown. However, empathy assessed by using nonverbal measures, such as facial expressions (for example, sadness) or behavioral gestures that connote empathy or lack of it (for example, looking away from the dis-

KEY THEME
Sociocultural Influence

empathy   Vicarious response to the feelings of others.

tressed person), is related to helping and sharing. Moreover, as children grow older, the relationship grows distinctly stronger (Eisenberg, 1986; Eisenberg & Miller, 1987; Roberts & Strayer, 1996).

A younger child may show signs of empathic distress but not know what form, if any, the assistance should take (Hoffman, 1976). If a playmate is crying as the result of a fall, should she be helped to stand up or left alone? Should the child say something comforting or reassuring or simply keep silent? As children mature, they are better able to interpret the emotions they are feeling, may feel them more strongly, and learn about the range of prosocial behaviors they can express. The distinction between self and other also matures and with it the realization that the other person's distress can be relieved by taking some action. However, individual differences in helpfulness do exist, and if the emotional arousal becomes too great, children may focus on their own uncomfortable feelings at the expense of helping (Fabes et al., 1994; Miller et al., 1996).

Do children help others only to reduce their own empathic distress? The answer seems to be no. When Randy Lennon and Nancy Eisenberg (1987) observed preschoolers in semistructured play, virtually every time a child shared a toy with another, both the child and the recipient displayed positive emotions before and after the sharing. Such findings are not easily explained by the concept of empathic distress and indicate that empathy needs to be more broadly construed as a response to both positive and negative emotions. Moreover, C. Daniel Batson (1990) has argued that care and concern for others is truly altruistic, that is, often expressed independently of personal needs.

Prosocial Reasoning Just as moral reasoning associated with justice changes with development, so does reasoning associated with prosocial behavior. Nancy Eisenberg (1986) formulated prosocial dilemmas in which the interests of one person are in conflict with those of another individual or group. The following story is an example:

> One day a girl (boy) named Mary (Eric) was going to a friend's birthday party. On her (his) way she (he) saw a girl (boy) who had fallen down and hurt her (his) leg. The girl asked Mary to go to her house and get her parents so the parents could come and take her to the doctor. But if Mary did run and get the child's parents, she would be late for the birthday party and miss the ice cream, cake, and all the games. What should Mary do? Why? (Eisenberg, 1986, p. 135)

Many preschool and some young school-age children in the United States use a **hedonistic orientation** in their reasoning, saying they would help to gain affection or material rewards such as candy or cake. A **needs-of-others orientation** prevails in the reasoning of early elementary school children, who typically express a concern for the physical or psychological needs of others ("He needs help"; "She's hurt"). An **approval and interpersonal orientation** is prevalent in the middle childhood years as the child's responses increasingly take into consideration the reactions of others ("Mary should help because the other girl would like Mary"). During the later elementary years and into high school, a more **self-reflective, empathic orientation** emerges ("I'm trying to put myself in his shoes"). Older adolescents develop an **internalized orientation,** focusing on the importance of such emotions as happiness and pride to match internalized abstract principles of behavior concerned with fulfilling societal obligations, avoiding guilt, and maintaining self-respect.

Table 12.3 outlines the stages of prosocial reasoning. As with other views of moral development, reasoning progresses from concern for external consequences to a more internalized, principled foundation. However, hedonistic responses do show some increase during the adolescent years, especially in boys (Eisenberg et al., 1995). As expected, level of orientation relates to behavior and how children are perceived by others. For example, children who reason hedonistically tend to donate toys, stickers, or other valued objects to other children less frequently and are evaluated less positively by peers than children of a similar age who reason at higher levels (Carlo et al., 1996; Eisenberg & Shell, 1986).

hedonistic orientation Form of prosocial reasoning in which children say they will help in order to obtain material rewards.

needs-of-others orientation Form of prosocial reasoning in which children express a concern for the physical or psychological needs of others.

approval and interpersonal orientation Form of prosocial reasoning in which children's reasons for assisting someone in need are based on the social approval or disapproval of others.

self-reflective, empathic orientation Form of prosocial reasoning in which children put themselves in another's place to understand that person's feelings.

internalized orientation Form of prosocial reasoning in which internalized beliefs and principles are followed to fulfill societal obligations and maintain self-respect.

Level	Age	Characteristics
Hedonistic orientation	Preschoolers and young elementary school children	Preoccupation with gain for the self as a result of being or not being altruistic
Needs-of-others orientation	Early and middle elementary school children	Concern for the physical and psychological needs of others although they may conflict with own
Approval and interpersonal orientation	Middle elementary and high school students	Reliance on stereotypes of good and bad and seeking approval from others for helping or not helping
Self-reflective, orientation	Late elementary and high school students	Concern for feelings of others and use of norms for prosocial behavior
Internalized orientation	High school students	Maintenance of self-respect for living up to internalized values and beliefs; belief in rights of all individuals and importance of fulfilling societal obligations

Source: Adapted from Eisenberg, 1986.

TABLE 12.3

Levels of Prosocial Reasoning

Nancy Eisenberg has outlined the accompanying progression in prosocial reasoning. Children move from a concern with the self to a concern for others and show more internal, abstract bases for helping as they grow older.

Cross-Cultural Investigations When asked to reason about prosocial dilemmas, children in other Western industrialized societies display similar patterns of development. German, Italian, and Polish children, for example, show the same progression from hedonistic to needs-of-others orientation that children in the United States do (Boehnke et al., 1989; Eisenberg et al., 1985). In other cultures, however, variations have been found. For example, elementary school children reared on the Israeli kibbutz reflect a more mature level of prosocial reasoning, voicing concern about the humaneness of the central character (Mary in the story about helping or going to the birthday party) and the importance of internalized norms ("She has a duty to help others") (Eisenberg, Hertz-Lazarowitz, & Fuchs, 1990). A somewhat different picture emerges for children from the Maisin tribe, a coastal village society of Papua New Guinea. Here children maintain a needs-of-others orientation well into adolescence and even adulthood (Tietjen, 1986). These developmental patterns mirror the values emphasized by each culture. On the Israeli kibbutz, the goal of contributing to the good of the entire community is stressed, whereas among the Maisin, children are taught explicitly to be aware of and respond to the needs of specific others rather than to those of the larger social group.

Might children also show cross-cultural differences in their tendency to behave prosocially related to their prosocial reasoning? Nancy Graves and Theodore Graves (1983) studied the inhabitants of Aitutaki Island, one of the Cook Islands in the South Pacific. A tremendous economic shift, from a subsistence to an industrialized market economy, took place on parts of this island and produced corresponding changes in family structure and the roles of family members. Children living in the unaffected rural villages grow up in extended families in which they make substantial contributions to family and community goals. They participate in most community affairs, are sent by elders to share food and goods with other village members, and bring the family contribution to church each week. In contrast, children growing up in urban, more modernized settings are reared in nuclear families and participate less in both family and community functions.

Graves and Graves (1983) observed that children five and six years of age in the urban communities were less likely to assist others in their homes and surrounding environs than were children in rural settings. The researchers conclude that prosocial behavior is more likely in societies in which the predominant ethic is one of interdependence and group orientation and in which the child participates in cooperative work experiences than it is in cultures that emphasize individualism and self-reliance.

Some children grow up in cultures in which they contribute to the needs of the entire community. For example, even children among the Klung Kung people in Bali, Indonesia, are expected to help with harvesting. Children reared in group-oriented societies tend to behave more prosocially than children reared in settings that emphasize individualism.

The Role of Socialization   What role do child-rearing techniques play in the emergence of prosocial behavior? As social learning theory would predict, reinforcement can be influential. Both material rewards (for example, money, candy, tokens) and social rewards ("You're a good boy!") increase the likelihood that children will share with or help others, although social rewards and acknowledgments seem to motivate greater care and concern for others (Grusec, 1991; Smith et al., 1979). Opportunities for observational learning are another potent factor. When a child sees someone make a donation to a needy person or group, he is likely to be charitable as well (Grusec & Skubiski, 1970).

What role models do appears to be more important than what they say (Rushton, 1975); yet the nature of caregivers' verbal communications also has a bearing on prosocial behavior. When parents use **induction,** that is, explain why transgressions are wrong, provide a rationale for rules and regulations, and present a reason for prosocial activity, their children are more likely to practice prosocial behaviors (Hoffman, 1975; Zahn-Waxler, Radke-Yarrow, & King, 1979). For example, a parent might say, "Don't pull Sam's hair! That hurts him. You don't like to have your hair pulled, do you?" Such messages emphasize clear communication about standards for behavior, arouse empathic feelings, and stimulate perspective taking (Eisenberg & Mussen, 1989). In contrast, a far less effective means of fostering prosocial behavior involves **power assertion,** forceful commands, physical punishment, or removal of material objects or privileges to influence behavior. For example, the parent might yell, "Stop that! You're not watching TV tonight!" as her son pulls his brother's hair.

Another socialization technique that may be as effective as induction is to emphasize the child's prosocial characteristics. When a child is told, "I guess you're the kind of person who helps others whenever you can," her tendency to behave prosocially greatly increases (Mills & Grusec, 1989). Perhaps attributing to the child a sense of concern for others changes her self-concept and she strives to behave in a manner consistent with that image (Grusec, 1982). Parents do not make prosocial attributions about their children often, but it is precisely the rarity of these comments that may make them so powerful in the eyes of the child (Grusec, 1991).

In summary, prosocial behaviors begin in early empathic responses to the emotional states of others. The child's reasoning about prosocial conflicts increasingly takes into account the feelings and needs of others. When altruistic acts are praised and children are encouraged to think about their own prosocial traits, they show an increase in positive moral behaviors. Moreover, parents serve as extremely potent

KEY THEME
Nature/Nurture

induction   Parental control technique that relies on the extensive use of reasoning and explanation as well as the arousal of empathic feelings.

power assertion   Parental control technique that relies on the use of forceful commands, physical punishment, and removal of material objects or privileges.

This boy and his father are having a serious discussion about some unacceptable behavior. Parents who frequently explain why behaviors are inappropriate and provide a rationale for rules tend to have children who act more altruistically compared with parents who attempt to manage their children's behavior through the use of power assertive techniques.

role models for concern for others. Research on prosocial behavior and altruism has demonstrated how the development of values involves the complex interplay of affect, cognition, and behavior. The Chronology on the next page summarizes many of the aspects of moral and prosocial development described in this chapter.

At the beginning of this chapter, we noted Michael's concern, and his grandfather's belief, that today's young people do not exhibit many of the positive values considered essential in a desirable, caring community. Increasingly frequent reports of lack of respect for others, dishonesty, theft, and a litany of other antisocial behaviors in schools and other contexts have led many to conclude that society is rapidly deteriorating. Table 12.4 provides the kind of evidence often used to justify this increased concern.

CONTROVERSY: THINKING IT OVER

Should Schools Play a Greater Role in Promoting Values?

Since the mid-1970s, public officials and citizens have expressed renewed interest in providing children with formal training in character education and values. Indeed, such training, sometimes including a strong religious orientation, is routinely incorporated into many school curricula, especially in Asia but in some Western nations as well (Cummings, 1988). For example, a heated controversy has erupted in the state of Brandenburg in former East Germany over having regular classroom teachers educate students about religion, moral values, and ethics instead of religious leaders, those who normally instruct German students in the public schools on such matters (Downey, 1996). In the United States and some other countries, of course, separation of church and state is a long-cherished tradition. Nevertheless, in the United States, public schools historically included a curriculum rich in efforts to strengthen character and values (Glazer, 1996). That emphasis declined substantially in recent decades and, where still found, is typically limited to lessens in civics (Glazer, 1996). Alarmed by the climbing rates of teenage pregnancy, crime, and substance abuse, as well as the breakdown of family, religious, and other socializing agencies, some believe children need more exposure to and training in character education and values in the public schools.

CHRONOLOGY
Understanding Moral and Prosocial Development

Newborn

Newborn

Newborn
- Reacts to cries of other infants in primitive empathic way.

1–2 Years
- Assists another in distress by patting, touching, or offering material objects.

2–3 Years
- Begins to show signs of guilt and remorse for misdeeds.

3–6 Years
- Discriminates moral and social-conventional rules.
- Judges moral dilemmas according to objective consequences and believes in immanent justice and expiatory punishment.
- Hedonistic and needs-oriented judgments dominate prosocial decisions.

7–10 Years
- Reasons according to rewards and punishments expected from authority figures.
- Approval and concerns about the reactions of others guide judgments about assisting others.

10–16 Years
- Judges moral dilemmas according to intentions of actor and believes in punishment by reciprocity.
- Reasons on the basis of rules and laws with a belief in maintaining social order.
- Empathic reasoning appears in prosocial judgments.

10–14 Months
- Shows various signs of empathy to distress of another but often soothes the self.

16+ Years
- Reasons according to internal principles of justice and care.
- Internalized principles guide prosocial behavior.

Timeline markers: 1 Yr., 2 Yrs., 3 Yrs., 4 Yrs., 5 Yrs., 6 Yrs., 7 Yrs., 8 Yrs., 9 Yrs., 10 Yrs., 11 Yrs., 12 Yrs., 13 Yrs., 14 Yrs., 15 Yrs., 16 Yrs., 17 Yrs., 18 Yrs.

Timeline markers: 1 Mo., 2 Mos., 3 Mos., 4 Mos., 5 Mos., 6 Mos., 7 Mos., 8 Mos., 9 Mos., 10 Mos., 11 Mos., 12 Mos., 13 Mos., 14 Mos., 15 Mos., 16 Mos., 17 Mos., 18 Mos.

This chart describes the sequence in the development of moral and prosocial behavior based on the findings of research. Children often show individual differences in the exact ages at which they display the various developmental achievements outlined here.

TABLE 12.4

Do We Have Reason to Be Concerned About Ethics Among Today's Youth?

Many claim that young people in the United States today no longer demonstrate the positive moral values and ethical behaviors they once displayed. This criticism is often echoed by adults around the world concerning the behavior of young people in their own countries. The Josephson Institute of Ethics recently carried out a survey of nearly twelve thousand Americans over age twelve to more fully understand the ethics of young people. A few of the findings are shown here. Are you surprised by the number who report having engaged in stealing or shoplifting or who indicate a willingness to lie? Should parents, schools, and other community programs take a more active role in helping to educate children and youth about what is acceptable behavior?

	At Least Once	More Than Once
Did you cheat on an exam or quiz during the previous 12 months?		
High school	65%	47%
College	33%	21%
Have you stolen something from a parent or relative in the previous 12 months?		
High school	29%	17%
College	13%	6%
Did you take something from a store without paying for it in the previous 12 months?		
High school	39%	26%
College	17%	9%

	Agreed	Disagreed
Do you agree that "If necessary to get or keep a job, I would lie"?		
High school	41%	59%
College	24%	76%

Source: Data from Josephson Institute of Ethics, 1996.

In the 1970s, "values clarification" was heralded as a new approach to character education. Its goal was to help children understand their values. Teachers were to be neutral, but from discussions of moral issues children were expected to eventually appreciate and engage in more socially acceptable and appropriate behaviors. Another approach, based on Kohlberg's theory, introduced children to moral conflicts and to moral reasoning one stage above the child's own as a way to foster values (Blatt & Kohlberg, 1975).

Should educational programs go well beyond *reasoning* about moral justice to strengthen values such as respect, caring, kindness, honesty, and responsibility (Noddings, 1992)? For example, in **cooperative learning** situations, peer groups work on joint projects to promote prosocial development. In one two-year project conducted in Tel Aviv, children worked in a collaborative fashion in small groups, investigating a topic, preparing a report, and presenting the findings to the class (Hertz-Lazarowitz & Sharan, 1984). This experience was designed to encourage mutual help and support, the exchange of ideas and resources, and common acceptance. Compared to those in traditional schools, children who participated in the project showed an increase in higher-level thinking skills (for example, evaluation, comparison, and analysis) and creativity. They also reported a more positive social climate in the classroom. The most important finding from the perspective of moral development, however, was an increase in the frequency of prosocial behaviors displayed by program participants.

Other programs, beginning in kindergarten, have encouraged children to be more socially responsible by creating a collaborative approach to learning and a "caring community" involving interactions among children of different ages. For example, in one of the few studies that followed students over a long period of time, middle school children in one California school district who were part of such a program displayed more self-esteem and were better at resolving conflicts than other children not associated with this approach (Glazer, 1996).

Are the schools doing enough in these areas? Many school programs have limited goals and often fail to address "hot button" topics such as sexual orientation and di-

cooperative learning Peer-centered learning experience in which students work together in small groups to solve academic problems.

versity, abortion, and sex education. But even if these topics are not the focus, a first question often raised about such efforts is "Whose values?" For example, does teaching civility mean encouraging the acceptance of alternative lifestyles? That would be problematic for some individuals and groups. Or are such efforts a thinly disguised façade for inserting narrow religious or ethical positions into the school curriculum? Further, if the curriculum avoids controversial issues, are schools simply left with a focus on good manners, which has always been a part of education?

Can a program that emphasizes trustworthiness, respect, responsibility, fairness, caring, citizenship, and similar qualities provide the cornerstone for positive character development? Is a mandate to teach character ten minutes of every school day (adopted in Alabama) the way to address this issue? Or would a requirement for community service be more effective? Will these programs infringe on what many believe are parental rights and responsibilities for teaching such concepts and behaviors? Should the school play a greater role in promoting values and, if so, what should those values be?

Additional Factors in Prosocial Behavior and Values

Surprisingly, developmental researchers have seldom investigated the many potential influences exposure to religious education and other social organizations such as scouting, boys' and girls' clubs, and other community programs may have on the development of values. Yet many parents would claim that such activities also play a vital role in the development of socially acceptable behaviors. For example, in one study of children given training in their Jewish or Christian faith, participants as young as ten years were found to distinguish between moral issues they considered to be unalterable (stealing, hitting, damaging another's property) and conventional religious practices that might change in certain circumstances or not apply to other individuals (dress customs, dietary laws, worship activities). Thus, they can distinguish moral issues involving justice and human welfare associated with their religion from social conventions that arise from exposure to their particular faith (Nucci & Turiel, 1993). In other words, recognizing what is moral and what is socially determined very likely is influenced not only by parental teachings and school practices but also by the myriad other activities and examples to which children are exposed in their particular social contexts. Issues of fairness and rights, caring and cooperation, and duties and personal responsibility are among those that individuals in most cultures believe are too important to be left to just one component of the child's experiences.

KEY THEME

Sociocultural Influence

CHAPTER RECAP

SUMMARY OF DEVELOPMENTAL THEMES

NATURE/NURTURE   What roles do nature and nurture play in the development of the self and of values?

Although early, biologically based tendencies for children to display a mastery orientation and empathy may exist, most researchers have described how the child's cognitions and social experiences shape self and values. For example, feedback from others certainly plays an enormous role in the child's characterization of self and prosocial behavior. Theorists such as Piaget

and Kohlberg suggest that maturation contributes in part to changes in moral reasoning. But even they believe children's experiences with peers and other socializing agents play a large role in spurring moral reasoning.

SOCIOCULTURAL INFLUENCE   How does the sociocultural context influence the development of the self and of values?

Children's evaluations of self are greatly determined by the extent to which they display autonomy, loyalty, cooperation, perseverance, and other qualities stressed by the culture. Self-esteem is affected by how well children live up to the society's expectations concerning beauty, athletic skill, academic ability, and other attributes the culture values. Moral reasoning and behavior further reflect the values of a culture. When responsibilities to the larger social group are emphasized, children tend to be more caring and display more prosocial reasoning than when the culture emphasizes the role of the individual. In addition, groups place different weights on law and justice versus other values, such as harmonious interactions with others. Children's responses to moral dilemmas often reflect their culture's unique beliefs.

CHILD'S ACTIVE ROLE   How does the child play an active role in the development of the self and of values?

Caregivers take on initial responsibility for instituting standards for the behavior of young children. As children gain cognitive and social skills, they initiate efforts to control their own activities and are assumed to internalize the values of the larger society. Children also begin to recognize that they are competent individuals, capable of influencing and controlling their environment in realistic ways. Their judgments about the appropriateness of moral and prosocial actions are assumed to influence their behavior as well.

CONTINUITY/DISCONTINUITY   Is the development of the self and of values continuous or discontinuous?

Although the child's understanding of self undergoes many developmental changes, evidence that these changes are stagelike remains limited. Even the identity crisis, often considered a hallmark of adolescence, may not be experienced by all young people and reflects a culmination of many earlier, gradual changes. Several influential theories of moral development are stage theories, specifically those of Piaget and Kohlberg. The empirical evidence, however, suggests that reasoning about moral, prosocial, and other values may occur at several levels within the same individual. Although stage theories are popular, domain-specific approaches emphasizing continuous growth are prominent as well.

INDIVIDUAL DIFFERENCES   How prominent are individual differences in the development of the self and of values?

Because the reactions of others play an important role in the development of self, children may differ enormously in how they view themselves and in how they interact with their world. Some may develop confidence and a sense of control; others may express considerable uncertainty and a sense of helplessness. As a result of their socialization experiences and opportunities to interact with peers, children also display considerable differences in their moral and prosocial values.

INTERACTION AMONG DOMAINS   How does the development of the self and of values interact with development in other domains?

Cognitive skills, such as the ability to reason abstractly about the feelings and intentions of others, play a role in evaluations of self and moral judgments. Emotions such as empathy contribute to prosocial behaviors and altruism. Physical changes and capacities, as well as the social environment, can dramatically affect self-esteem and the emergence of identity. At the same time, development of the self and of values has an effect on other domains. For example, high self-esteem and prosocial activity are associated with healthy peer interactions. Development of the self and of values represents an important interaction among affect, cognition, and social experience.

SUMMARY OF TOPICS

■ THE CONCEPT OF SELF

Researchers concerned with the development of *self*—the beliefs, knowledge, and feelings an individual uses to describe his personal characteristics—make the distinction between self as object and self as subject. Self as object consists of *self-concept,* the perceptions, ideas, and beliefs a person holds to be true of herself. Self as subject consists of how a person initiates, organizes, and interprets experience.

Children's sense of themselves as objects is first evident in their self-recognition at about fifteen to eighteen months of age. During the preschool years, they begin to define themselves in terms of a *categorical self,* that is, by referring to various categories that provide membership in one group or another. By the early school years, *social comparisons* involving others become important. By adolescence, children's effects on others and their relationships to broader sociocultural ideals become a central part of their definitions of self.

Among the elements of self as subject are a sense of agency, individuality, stability, and reflection. Infants seem to be born with an intrinsic desire to gain control of their world, but to the extent that an environment provides consistent feedback, children acquire an increasing sense of agency. Children with an *internal locus of control* or a *mastery orientation* believe they have considerable influence over what happens to them. Children who have an *external locus of control* or who experience *learned helplessness* believe they have little influence over what happens to them.

Self-esteem consists of the positive or negative feelings a person has about himself. Preschoolers are able to make this evaluation for specific domains. By the early school years, self-esteem takes the form of an overall sense of worth. Self-esteem is affected by feedback from others as well as how successful the child believes she is in areas thought to be important. Although self-esteem in adolescents may decline somewhat, many teenagers successfully establish an *identity* with relatively minimal disruption to their lives and those around them. However, some adolescents demonstrate emotional or behavioral problems associated with identity. Of special concern is suicide, which continues to increase among this population of individuals.

■ SELF-REGULATION AND SELF-CONTROL

In most societies, efforts to control behavior begin in the second half of the first year of life and continue throughout childhood. At first these efforts are initiated primarily by caregivers, then take the form of co-regulation. Self-initiated attempts to control behavior become more evident as children demonstrate increasing capacities for *delay of gratification* and other forms of compliance, planning, and orderly behavior. Verbal, attentional, and cognitive mechanisms are the means by which behavior comes under self-control.

■ MORAL DEVELOPMENT

Moral development is the child's acquisition of the standards of conduct considered ethical within the culture. Freudian theory focuses on the affective relationship between child and parents. Social learning theory centers on the emergence of moral behavior. Cognitive-developmental theories emphasize moral reasoning. All of the perspectives concur in describing moral development as a movement from a self-orientation to an other-orientation in which the child internalizes societal standards. Guilt and other responses indicating internalization of parental and cultural standards begin to be evident in the second year and are already displayed in a wide variety of ways among preschoolers.

Among the factors contributing to moral development are reinforcements children receive from parents and other agents of socialization. Observational learning is especially potent in the development of moral behaviors. Cognitive-developmental theorists, such as Piaget and Kohlberg, have outlined stages in the development of moral thought. In Piaget's theory, children progress from *moral realism* to *moral relativism* as their cognitive capabilities mature. In Kohlberg's outline, most children advance through *preconventional, conventional,* and *postconventional* levels of moral reasoning. Kohlberg maintains that the child's increasing perspective-taking skills are largely responsible for these shifts. Newer, domain-specific approaches describe how children acquire moral knowledge that is distinct from social-conventional knowledge.

■ PROSOCIAL BEHAVIOR AND VALUES

Researchers have demonstrated that *prosocial* and *altruistic* behaviors occur early in childhood, beginning with the *empathy* young infants display for the distress of others, followed by distinct efforts of preschool children to help others. Children who are empathetic and show high levels of prosocial behavior tend to help others. In addition, children who are rewarded for prosocial behaviors and observe parents and others acting similarly tend to help others more frequently. Children whose parents use *induction* as a disciplinary technique and apply prosocial attributions to their children, and who grow up in cultures that emphasize group values, are especially likely to demonstrate care and concern for others. The fostering of prosocial skills and values can be further assisted by schools and other cultural institutions.

13 GENDER

NATURE/NURTURE
What roles do nature and nurture play in gender development?

SOCIOCULTURAL INFLUENCE
How does the sociocultural context influence gender development?

CHILD'S ACTIVE ROLE
How does the child play an active role in the process of gender development?

CONTINUITY/DISCONTINUITY
Is gender development continuous or discontinuous?

INDIVIDUAL DIFFERENCES
How prominent are individual differences in gender development?

INTERACTION AMONG DOMAINS
How does gender development interact with development in other domains?

"Nicky," one of the authors said to her then five-year-old son, "what do you think should be on the cover of this book? It's about children, you know."

"Well," he thought for a moment, "how about a picture of a child?"

"A boy or a girl?" asked the mother.

"How about one of each?" he suggested. The mother was pleased that her son chose a girl as well as a boy. She had tried hard to teach him to think about gender in nonstereotypical ways, and his willingness to include girls seemed to indicate that her efforts were successful.

"What should they be doing?" the mother continued.

"Well, how about having the boy play with a computer?" he quickly responded.

"And the girl?" she asked.

"I think she should have a tea party or something."

This five-year-old's response is consistent with many **gender stereotypes** that exist in our society, that is, our beliefs and expectations about the characteristics of females and males. Boys, according to these stereotypes, are active, aggressive, independent, and interested in technology and science. Girls, on the other hand, are passive, nonaggressive, and socially oriented. At what ages and to what extent do children have knowledge of these stereotypes? Furthermore, are such common beliefs actually manifested in the everyday behaviors of children? Are any differences we might observe due to the biological makeup of males and females? What part does socialization play in this process? We will address these central questions in this chapter.

Before we proceed, however, we need to consider terminology. Each of us is classified at birth as either a boy or a girl; that is, we are assigned a *biological sex*. In general, the word *sex* is used when statements or comparisons are being made about males or females as biological entities. Thus, we speak of whether children display "sex differences" in behaviors or traits. The word *gender*, on the other hand, refers to *inferences* we make about the qualities of males and females (Deaux, 1993). *Gender*, in other words, is a distinctly psychological concept. Thus, for example, we might speak of **gender-role development,** the process by which children acquire the characteristics and behaviors prescribed for males and females in their culture.

Before the mid-1960s, most psychologists regarded the socialization of children into traditional masculine and feminine roles as both a natural and a desirable outcome of development. Behavioral sex differences were viewed as inevitable and were linked to comparable sex differences among nonhumans (Kohlberg, 1966; Mischel,

gender stereotypes Expectations or beliefs that individuals within a given culture hold about the behaviors characteristic of males and females.

gender-role development Process by which individuals acquire the characteristics and behaviors prescribed by their culture for their sex. Also called *sex typing*.

1966; Shaw & Darling, 1985). But changes in social values in the mid-1960s, especially those accompanying the women's movement, shifted the ways in which psychologists approached sex differences and gender-role socialization. Many of the questions that interest developmental psychologists today represent both a challenge to traditional assumptions about the nature and origins of gender roles and sex differences and a concerted effort to determine the developmental processes that underlie children's acquisition and enactment of gender roles.

GENDER STEREOTYPES VERSUS ACTUAL SEX DIFFERENCES

Throughout the recorded history of Western civilization, females and males have been assumed to differ in temperament, interests, educability, and susceptibility to mental illness, among other characteristics. Many of these beliefs persist unchanged in contemporary gender stereotypes.

The Stereotypes: What Are They?

Suppose a group of college students is asked to rate the "typical" man or woman, or boy or girl, on a number of psychological attributes. Will they rate certain traits as more typical of males than of females, and vice versa? Studies in which college students were asked to do precisely this task reveal that characteristics such as independence, aggression, and self-confidence are associated with masculinity. In general, attributes such as these, which are associated with acting on the world, are classified as **instrumental.** In contrast, emotional expressiveness, kindness, and gentleness are linked with femininity (T. Ruble, 1983). These perceived feminine characteristics are often classified as **expressive,** or associated with emotions and interactions with other people. Table 13.1 shows other traits associated with masculinity and femininity when college students are asked to describe a typical boy or girl (Martin, 1995).

These gender stereotypes are not limited to our own society. Researchers asked children and adults from thirty nations in North and South America, Europe, Africa, and Asia to indicate whether certain traits are more frequently associated with men or women in their culture. The results showed many cross-cultural similarities in the stereotypes adults attributed to males and females (Williams & Best, 1982).

Despite the many similarities in gender stereotypes across cultures, some differences occurred among nations in the specific characteristics attributed to males and females. For example, Italian adults stereotypically associated "endurance" with women, although most adults in other countries believed this is a masculine trait. Nigerian adults believed "affiliation" is neutral, whereas adults in other countries said it is a feminine characteristic. Thus, we cannot say that specific characteristics are always attributed to males or to females. We can say, however, that the tendency to stereotype on the basis of sex is found in a variety of cultural settings.

Children's Knowledge of Gender Stereotypes

Children begin to acquire gender-role stereotypes and employ them as guides for their behavior at a surprisingly early age—from two years onward. Spencer Thompson (1975) examined the levels of gender-stereotype knowledge exhibited among a group of twenty-four-, thirty-, and thirty-six-month-old children. Stereotype knowledge was assessed by asking children to sort photos of common sex-typed objects into boxes called things "for boys and men" and "for girls and women." Although older children showed more knowledge of gender stereotypes than younger children, even the youngest children were surprisingly knowledgeable. Twenty-four-month-olds identified 61 percent of the items consistently with the stereotypes; thirty-month-olds identified 78 percent; and thirty-six-month-olds identified 86 percent.

KEY THEME
Sociocultural Influence

instrumental characteristics
Characteristics associated with acting on the world; usually considered masculine.

expressive characteristics
Characteristics associated with emotions or relationships with people; usually considered feminine.

Mean Typicality Ratings by Sex of Child Target[a]			TABLE 13.1
Item Type	**Boys**	**Girls**	Stereotypic Characteristics Attributed to Males and Females
Sex-typed masculine[b]			
Self-reliant	5.05	3.69	When college students were asked to rate a typical boy or girl on a number of personality traits, strong patterns emerged among traits that were seen as being associated with each sex. Male traits generally fall into a cluster called *instrumentality* and female traits into a cluster labeled *expressiveness*.
Does dangerous things	4.96	2.57	
Enjoys mechanical objects	5.57	2.68	
Dominant	5.36	3.54	
Enjoys rough play	6.09	3.07	
Independent	4.95	3.59	
Competitive	5.70	4.16	
Noisy	5.78	3.93	
Physically active	6.23	4.80	
Aggressive	5.60	3.41	
Conceited	4.38	3.46	
Sex-typed feminine[c]			
Gentle	3.21	5.36	
Neat and clean	3.05	5.42	
Sympathetic	3.42	5.33	
Eager to soothe hurt feelings	3.35	5.33	
Well-mannered	4.01	5.44	
Cries and gets upset easily	3.20	4.95	
Easily frightened	3.27	4.89	
Soft-spoken	3.00	4.64	
Helpful around the house	3.27	5.31	
Gullible	3.74	4.33	
Reliable	4.33	4.74	
Truthful	4.31	4.91	
Likable	4.99	5.68	
Nonsex-typed			
Adaptable	4.90	4.72	

[a]Maximum scores = 7.0.
[b]Indicates that ratings for boys were significantly higher than for girls.
[c]Indicates that ratings for girls were significantly higher than for boys.
Source: Martin, 1995.

By two to three years of age, children show a fairly extensive understanding of gender stereotypes, the beliefs about the characteristics of males and females. Through the early and middle school years, this knowledge becomes even more fully elaborated.

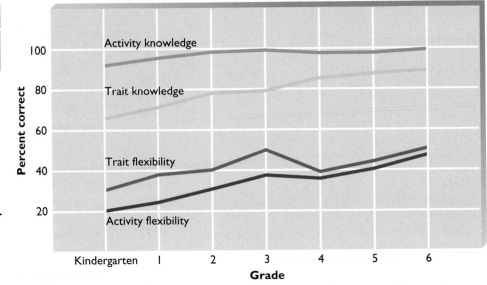

FIGURE 13.1

Developmental Trends in Gender-Role Knowledge

When kindergartners through sixth-graders were asked to identify which of twenty stereotyped objects were masculine and which were feminine, all children gave at least 90 percent correct answers (see the line for "activity knowledge"). However, if they were asked to indicate whether objects could be used by both sexes, a developmental increase in flexibility was observed (see the line for "activity flexibility"). Knowledge of stereotyped traits and flexibility with regard to those traits both increased over the age span studied.

Source: Serbin, Powlishta, & Gulko, 1993.

Other research has shown that children as young as two to three years begin to associate specific behaviors and future roles with each sex with startling consistency. Deanna Kuhn's data indicate that young preschoolers believe girls are nonaggressive, talk a lot, play with dolls, and will grow up to be nurses or teachers. In contrast, they say that boys are aggressive, play with trucks and cars, and will grow up to be the boss (Kuhn, Nash, & Brucken, 1978).

By age six or seven, children's knowledge of gender stereotypes is well established. Lisa Serbin and her colleagues (Serbin, Powlishta, & Gulko, 1993) asked five-through-twelve-year-olds to state whether twenty stereotyped objects (for example, *hammer, rifle, stove, broom*) belonged to male or female categories. As Figure 13.1 indicates, all children, regardless of age, showed extensive knowledge of the stereotypes. The figure also shows that children's knowledge of stereotyped personality traits (for example, *gentle, emotional, adventurous, messy*) expands through the middle school years. As children grow older, however, their knowledge of stereotypes also becomes more flexible in that they are more likely to say that both males and females can possess certain traits (Katz & Ksansnak, 1994; Levy, Taylor, & Gelman, 1995; Serbin, Powlishta, & Gulko, 1993). Other researchers have found that flexibility concerning gender stereotypes is especially high right when young adolescents experience a life transition that may involve reevaluation of past beliefs: entering junior high school. Later in adolescence, when individuals are more likely to be thinking about their future roles and responsibilities, flexibility regarding gender stereotypes declines (Alfieri, Ruble, & Higgins, 1996). Some researchers have described this return to traditional beliefs about gender during adolescence as *gender intensification* (Galambos, Almeida, & Petersen, 1990).

What Sex Differences Actually Exist?

In light of such durable and pervasive stereotypes about "femaleness" and "maleness," it is logical to ask whether researchers have documented actual differences in the characteristics or behaviors of females and males. For many human traits, the data show that average differences *between* the sexes are smaller than the variability in performance *within* each sex. Nonetheless, in some domains the characteristics of females and males have been found to differ.

Physical Attributes   Females and males physically differ in a number of ways, including the makeup of their chromosomes, their genitalia, and levels of certain hormones. Females are physically more mature at birth, whereas males show a special physical vulnerability during infancy. Compared to females, males are more likely to be miscarried, die in infancy, or develop hereditary diseases (Jacklin, 1989). Later in infancy and childhood, females walk, talk, and reach other developmental milestones earlier than males. By later childhood and adolescence, females reach puberty earlier and males develop greater height, weight, and muscle mass than females (Maccoby & Jacklin, 1974).

Cognition   One aspect of cognition for which males and females have been thought to differ is in verbal abilities. The popular belief has been that girls are more skilled than boys at verbal tasks, a belief that was modestly substantiated by an early review of the relevant research (Maccoby & Jacklin, 1974). More recent meta-analyses of cognitive sex differences, however, indicate minimal sex differences in verbal skills (Feingold, 1988; Hyde & Linn, 1988). Females have a slight advantage on tests that measure reading comprehension, spelling, or grammar (Feingold, 1993), but most researchers agree that even here the differences are so small that they warrant little notice.

In another meta-analysis of more than a hundred studies of sex differences in mathematics skills, the investigators concluded that boys and girls showed no overall differences in performance (Hyde, Fennema, & Lamon, 1990). When the scores of participants of different ages and from specific groups were examined more closely, however, sex differences in certain aspects of mathematics performance did emerge. During elementary school, for example, girls showed a slight superiority over boys in the area of computation; in the high school and college years, on the other hand, males did moderately better than females on tests of mathematical problem solving. Among groups selected for exceptional performance (such as students in gifted and talented programs), males performed better than females in tests of mathematics. The scores of males on mathematics tests are more variable than the scores of females, at least for children in the United States (Feingold, 1992). In other cultures, though, sex differences in the variability of scores have not been observed (Feingold, 1994b). Interestingly, sex differences in mathematics skills seem to be diminishing: studies published before 1973 are more likely to show a sex difference in this area than studies published after 1973. When differences across all the studies are averaged, males show only a very slight advantage. Figure 13.2 illustrates the overall magnitude of this sex difference.

In fact, the only notable sex difference in cognitive skills currently supported by empirical evidence involves visual-spatial abilities. Visual-spatial skills include a

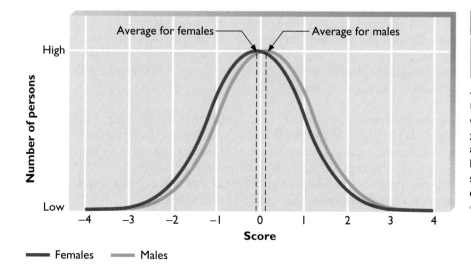

Females   Males

Source: Adapted from Hyde, Fennema, & Lamon, 1990.

FIGURE 13.2

Sex Differences in Mathematics Skills

Although sex differences in mathematics skills do exist, the differences are quite small. This graph illustrates the size of the average sex differences. The horizontal axis represents scores converted to a standardized form.

FIGURE 13.3

Sex Differences in Visual-
Spatial Skills

**Tests of visual-spatial skills
typically assess spatial perception (top), mental rotation
ability (middle), or spatial visualization (bottom). In the top
panel, participants are asked
to indicate which bottle has a
horizontal water line. In the
middle panel, participants must
identify the two responses that
depict rotated versions of the
standard. In the bottom panel,
participants are asked to identify the simple geometric figure on the top within the more
complex figure underneath.
Generally, males perform better than females on spatial
perception and mental rotation tasks.**

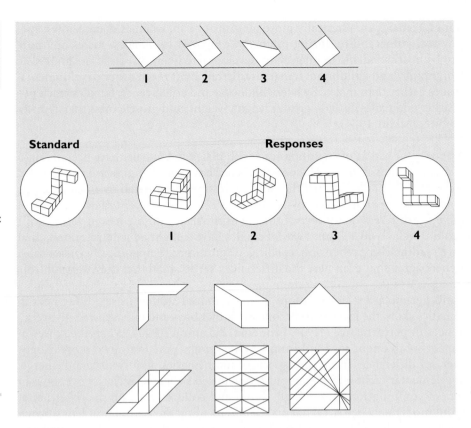

Source: Adapted from Linn & Petersen, 1985.

number of processes, all of which require the ability to visualize and transform
figures or objects in the mind. Figure 13.3 illustrates three tests of visual-spatial skills:
spatial perception, mental rotation, and spatial visualization. As you can see, spatial
perception tasks require participants to ignore distracting information to locate horizontal and vertical orientation. Mental rotation tasks demand that participants
transform two- and three-dimensional figures "in their heads." Spatial visualization
tasks require them to analyze relationships among different spatial representations.

Marcia Linn and Anne Petersen (1985, 1986) conducted a meta-analysis of thirty-
eight studies of visual-spatial skills in boys and girls that had been published between
1974 and 1982. The results indicated no sex differences on spatial visualization tasks.
Males do, however, show superior performance on mental rotation and, to a lesser
extent, spatial perception (the tasks depicted in the middle and top portions of Figure 13.3, respectively). Sex differences in mental rotation ability emerge at about age
ten years, usually the youngest age at which such tests can be used. Sex differences in
spatial perception are noticeably larger after age eighteen years. Furthermore, as with
mathematical skills, boys show greater variability in their visual-spatial scores than
do girls in our society (Feingold, 1992).

Social Behaviors   Researchers who have examined the results of hundreds of studies of social behaviors and personality characteristics have concluded that few actual
sex differences exist in the area of social behaviors (Feingold, 1994a; Maccoby & Jacklin, 1974). Although average scores of boys and girls consistently differ in some areas,
the performance of children of each sex shows considerable variability. The single
most notable exception to this pattern is aggression.

One of the most consistent findings in the research on sex differences is that, beginning in the preschool years, males are more aggressive than females. They engage
in more rough-and-tumble play, display more physical aggression, try to dominate
peers, and subsequently display more antisocial behaviors than girls (Block, 1983;
Huston, 1985). Meta-analyses substantiate that sex differences in aggression are
greatest among preschoolers and decrease through the college years (Eagly & Steffen,

One of the most consistent sex differences is the tendency for boys to display more physical aggression than girls, especially during the preschool years. Sex differences in aggression are more likely to be found in naturalistic settings such as playgrounds. Girls, on the other hand, are more likely to show relational aggression than boys.

1986; Hyde, 1984, 1986). Even though males generally are more aggressive than females, however, the magnitude of the sex difference varies as a function of where the aggression occurs and the type of aggression being measured. The largest sex differences are found in naturalistic settings, such as playgrounds, and when physical aggression, as opposed to verbal aggression, is being measured. Conclusions about sex differences in aggression must be tempered by how this construct is defined, however. When aggression is described as an attempt to harm another person through manipulation, gossip, or excluding peers from a social group (called *indirect* or *relational aggression*), girls are found to be more aggressive than boys (Bjorkqvist, 1994; Crick & Grotpeter, 1995).

Meta-analyses confirm that sex differences in other social behaviors, when they occur at all, tend to be fairly small. For example, studies show few consistent differences between the sexes in empathic behavior (Eisenberg & Lennon, 1983). Females report that they are more empathetic and cry more than males do, but no sex differences emerge when physiological or unobtrusive measures are used to assess empathy. Some researchers report that girls display more social smiles and gazing than boys do, especially in late adolescence (Eisenberg & Lennon, 1983; Hall & Halberstadt, 1986). Other evidence suggests that females may be more vulnerable to anxiety and worrying and less confident in problem-solving situations than males (Block, 1983; Silverman, LaGreca, & Wasserstein, 1995). Surveys of middle-class girls also indicate that when they reach adolescence, they report a dramatic decline in self-esteem (American Association of University Women, 1992). Many of these findings must be interpreted with caution, however, since they may reflect the fact that females are more likely than males to report their feelings and emotional states.

One last area in which moderate sex differences have been noted is in the domain of emotional expression. Judith Hall's (1984) review of research on this issue shows that female children and adults from widely varying cultures are better than males at identifying the positive versus negative emotions signified by nonverbal cues, particularly those transmitted through facial expressions. Moreover, girls tend to display more positive and negative facial expressions and are more accurate in labeling the emotions expressed on their own faces compared to boys (Casey, 1993).

Sex Differences in Perspective

Perhaps because of our tendency to think in terms of gender stereotypes, we tend to assume sex differences will be numerous. In fact, research on actual sex differences indicates that the behavior of people in general shows great variability and that males and females often are more alike than different. Psychologically, male and female children reliably differ on very few dimensions, most notably visual-spatial skills, aggression, and, to some extent, the ability to decode social messages from nonverbal cues. In fact, many sex differences that we think are "real" actually exist only in the form of gender stereotypes.

If the research indicates more similarities than differences between males and females, why do stereotypical beliefs persist? One explanation may be that we notice, and therefore retain our beliefs, when boys and girls display behaviors consistent with stereotypes. In contrast, when a girl or a boy behaves in a manner inconsistent with a stereotype, we ascribe this pattern to an individual difference. Thus, when Billy fights (a stereotypically masculine activity), we say that "boys will be boys." But when he cooks and helps around the house in stereotypically feminine tasks, we comment on how "helpful" (not how "feminine") he is compared to other boys his age. Perhaps, too, stereotypes result from the tendency of children (and adults) to form cognitive categories of social groups (Martin, 1991). Upon seeing one similarity among people in a group (for example, in terms of physical characteristics), we may be tempted to conclude that they resemble one another in other ways, too.

THEORIES OF GENDER-ROLE DEVELOPMENT

What are the origins of sex differences in behavior? This question was explored by many researchers in the 1960s and 1970s, when it was assumed actual sex differences are more numerous among children than contemporary research indicates. Biological, social learning, and cognitive theorists all contributed ideas about the origins of male and female characteristics.

Even though contemporary research shows that actual sex differences in behavior are relatively few, they are still differences that must be explained. In other words, children still show some behaviors that are sex-typed, or aligned with the definitions of masculinity and femininity in their culture. Most researchers today, however, are less interested in choosing one particular theoretical position to account for gender-role development than they are in identifying the complex interplay of biology, socialization, and the child's understanding that underlies this process.

Biological Theories

Biologically based explanations for sex differences focus largely on the influence of chromosomes, hormones, and the structure of the brain on behavior. These factors often work in ways that illustrate the complex interactions of biological systems to produce sex-differentiated behaviors.

As we saw in Chapter 3, the presence of an X or a Y sex chromosome begins a complex process that leads to sexual differentiation. Between six and twelve weeks after conception, the XY chromosomal configuration leads to the development of testes and the secretion of a class of male hormones called **androgens,** a process that results in further sexual differentiation. The penis and scrotum develop in response to the metabolism of *testosterone,* an androgen that is actually present in both sexes but in greater amounts in males (Whalen, 1984). In the absence of an XY configuration and the associated greater amounts of androgens, the female structures develop (Breedlove, 1994; Hood et al., 1987). These differences in biological structures form the bases by which a child is labeled "boy" or "girl," the categorization of biological sex.

Hormones and Behavior   Prenatal exposure to hormones, particularly androgens, influences the developing fetus in ways that may have an impact on biology and, perhaps, postnatal behavior. Most important for our discussion, androgens influence the developing organization of the central nervous system and the brain (Gorski, 1980; MacLusky & Naftolin, 1981). Hormone-related sex differences in the central nervous system may, in turn, have important influences on behavior and abilities.

Take the example of aggression. Explanations of sex differences in aggression from

androgen Class of male or masculinizing hormones.

a biological perspective have relied largely on experiments in which androgens were administered systematically to female animals during prenatal development. The animal studies show that these hormonally treated females subsequently display increased aggressive behaviors, such as threats and rough-and-tumble play, compared to normally developing females. These findings have been replicated in rats, monkeys, and a number of other species (Goy, 1970; Parsons, 1980).

Although this type of evidence implies a causal link between male hormones and aggression, some controversy concerning the relationship exists (Tieger, 1980). First, although hormones have been shown to precede and presumably influence certain behaviors, such as aggression, those behaviors may themselves have an impact on hormone levels. That is, levels of hormones, including testosterone, can also change *in response to* changes in the environment (Hood et al., 1987). Among nonhuman males, for example, increases in androgen levels frequently follow, rather than precede, an aggressive encounter (Hood et al., 1987). Thus, the link between aggression and levels of androgens is not unidirectional, and it is difficult to make causal statements. Second, because human beings have a nervous system that differs in important ways from those of other species—particularly in the size of the cortex, which directs voluntary behavior—it is not clear that findings from animal studies can be generalized to humans (Fausto-Sterling, 1992).

ATYPICAL DEVELOPMENT

Hormonal Disorders in Children

Among humans, there are several conditions in which genetic males or females may be exposed to a hormonal environment that is not typical for their sex. One such disorder is *congenital adrenal hyperplasia (CAH),* a condition that occurs in about one in five thousand to one in fifteen thousand births (Miller & Levine, 1987). This genetic disorder causes a deficiency in the production of adrenal steroids, with the result that high levels of androgens begin to be produced during the prenatal period. If the child is a genetic female, for example, she will be born with masculinized genitalia. Usually her physical appearance is surgically corrected, hormone therapy is begun to regulate the levels of androgens circulating in her body, and the child is raised as a girl. Even following treatment, however, CAH girls have been found to show many behavioral patterns that are "typical" of boys. They prefer toys geared for boys, like rough-and-tumble play, and show enhanced visual-spatial skills (Collaer & Hines, 1995).

Among boys, a failure of androgen to bind with its receptors can result in *androgen insensitivity syndrome (AI).* Because the boy is born with female-looking genitalia, he is usually raised as a girl; the disorder is typically discovered at puberty, when menstruation fails to begin (Breedlove, 1994). These children commonly show "female" play interests and visual-spatial skills that are poorer than those of normal females who served as controls (Collaer & Hines, 1995).

It is tempting to conclude from these unusual hormonal disorders that biological factors are responsible for sex differences in patterns of social behaviors and cognitive skills. CAH girls do, in fact, have masculine-typed behaviors and were exposed to unusually high levels of androgens even though they were later socialized as girls. AI boys have lower levels of androgens and, even though they are socialized as girls, their performance on some cognitive tasks is actually lower than that of the average female. Thus, it is difficult to argue simply for the effect of socialization on their behavior. On the other hand, studies of androgenized girls are difficult to interpret because parents were aware of their daughters' masculinized appearance at birth and may have tolerated or even encouraged more "boylike" behaviors. Although these studies suggest a role for biology in the emergence of some sex-linked behaviors, it would be premature to rule out the effects of socialization.

Brain Lateralization A second way in which biology can influence sex differences in behavior is through the organization and functions of the brain. A prominent biological explanation for sex differences in visual-spatial skills involves the process known as *lateralization of the brain*. During the course of development, as we saw in Chapter 5, the two halves of the brain become increasingly specialized to handle different types of information, such as speech perception and speech production. According to one version of the lateralization hypothesis, girls' brains mature more quickly and lateralize earlier than boys'. Since verbal skills are thought to develop sooner than visual-spatial skills, and since rapid maturation of the brain is assumed to produce less eventual lateralization, the verbal skills of girls are presumed to be more evenly distributed across the hemispheres. Verbal processing in the right and left hemispheres, in turn, interferes with the visual-spatial processing that usually takes place predominantly in the right hemisphere. Because lateralization takes longer in boys, their cerebral hemispheres are thought to become more specialized than girls'. The net result is that their visual-spatial skills are stronger. Some research evidence confirms that children (regardless of sex) who mature early score better on verbal tasks than on spatial tasks, whereas the reverse pattern holds for late maturers (Waber, 1976).

Before we accept the lateralization hypothesis, however, we should note that there are also nonbiological explanations of sex differences in visual-spatial skills. One such explanation relies on the contrasting play experiences of boys and girls. According to this formulation, masculine play activities, such as using building blocks or video games, facilitate the development of visual-spatial skills in boys (Block, 1983; Greenfield, 1994). Evidence for this explanation was found in a study in which ten-to-eleven-year-old boys and girls were given practice in playing either a visual-spatial or verbal video game. The results showed that both boys and girls who played the visual-spatial game improved in their visual spatial skills, whereas those who played the word game did not improve (Subrahmanyam & Greenfield, 1994). Thus, sex-typed play activities may account, at least in part, for sex differences in visual-spatial skills.

Social Learning Theory

KEY THEME
Nature/Nurture

One of the primary mechanisms accounting for sex differences in behavior, social learning theorists maintain, is sex-differentiated treatment of boys and girls. According to this position, boys and girls are reinforced and punished differentially for specific behaviors, which leads them to behave in sex-typed ways. Girls, for example, may be rewarded for playing with dolls and punished for climbing trees, whereas boys may receive the opposite treatment. Thus, because children are motivated to seek reinforcement and avoid punishment, they will behave in a sex-typed fashion.

Children attend both to the consequences of their own behavior and to the consequences others face for their behavior. In fact, imitation, or modeling, may be an even more powerful means by which children learn gender roles. By observing the experiences of other people, children develop expectations for reinforcement and punishment of their own behavior. These expectations may influence their behavior as strongly as the actual experiences of reward or punishment do (Bandura, 1969, 1977a). Children have numerous opportunities to observe models behaving in gender-stereotypic ways in the home, in the outside world, and in the media. Each time a child sees that Dad fixes things around the house and Mom does most of the cooking and cleaning, or that most little boys play baseball while little girls play house, she is adding to her storehouse of sex-typed behaviors.

Imitation of Sex-Typed Behaviors Several factors influence whether children will imitate the sex-typed behaviors of others. Albert Bandura and other researchers have proposed that children's *attention* to models in the first place is influenced by both the sex of the model and the **sex typicality** of the model's behavior, that is, how characteristic it is of the model's own sex (Bandura, 1977a; Perry & Bussey, 1979). According to this hypothesis, boys would, in general, be more likely than girls to attend

sex typicality Extent to which a behavior is usually associated with one sex as opposed to the other.

to the behavior of male models, although they would be less likely to attend to a male model who was exhibiting "feminine" behavior. The prediction that individuals will pay greater attention to same-sex models is based on the notion that observation of same-sex models should provide children with greater information about potential consequences for their own behavior. In addition, Bandura suggests, children *recognize* that certain behaviors are sex-typed, especially as they observe the frequency with which males and females, as a group, perform certain behaviors. Finally, Bandura (1977a) proposes that *motivational* factors, such as reward seeking and attempts to retain a sense of mastery, will influence behavior in a variety of realms. As children grow older, they rely less on others to regulate their behavior and more on *self-regulation,* based on personal standards of gender-appropriate behavior (Bandura, 1986).

Several studies have supported the idea that children are more likely to imitate same-sex than other-sex models (Bussey & Bandura, 1984; Bussey & Perry, 1982). Thus, same-sex parents, peers, and characters in the media can be powerful influences on the child. In addition, other studies have found that children are more likely to imitate models who behave in sex-typical ways than models who behave in sex-atypical ways (Perry & Bussey, 1979).

Moreover, self-regulation of sex-typed behavior does seem to increase with development, as a study by Kay Bussey and Albert Bandura (1992) shows. Two-to-four-year-olds privately rated how they would feel if they played with a series of toys, some of which were masculine (for example, a dump truck), some feminine (for example, a baby doll), and some neutral (for example, a xylophone). As Figure 13.4 shows, younger children expressed relatively neutral self-evaluations regarding playing with masculine and feminine toys. Older children, in contrast, indicated more positive self-evaluations when visualizing themselves playing with toys geared for their own sex.

Cross-Cultural Patterns of Sex Differences   The contexts in which gender-role development occurs are many and varied. Do children who grow up in urban versus rural areas or in industrialized versus nonindustrialized societies all acquire similar gender roles? Or do gender roles vary according to the beliefs and demands of a specific culture? Cross-cultural studies can shed some light on biological versus social learning explanations for sex typing. If sex typing results solely from biological influences, we would expect to see great unanimity in gender roles across periods of history and among different cultures. If, on the other hand, gender roles reflect values that are peculiar to a given era or culture, we would expect to see variability in the

According to social learning theory, a powerful vehicle for the transmission of gender roles is imitation. Parents can be especially potent models for gender-typed behaviors. Thus, the roles they take on in the household, as well as their attitudes and beliefs, can have an impact on the gender-role development of their children.

KEY THEME
Sociocultural Influence

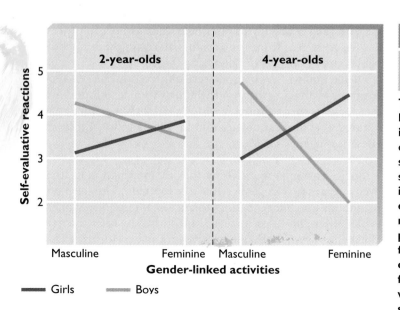

Source: Bussey & Bandura, 1992.

FIGURE 13.4

Self-Evaluations During Same-Sex Activities

Two- and four-year-olds rated how they would feel while playing with masculine, feminine, or neutral toys. The higher the score, the more favorable the self-evaluation. As the graph indicates, younger children, especially girls, gave relatively neutral self-evaluations for playing with masculine and feminine toys. In contrast, older children said they would feel better about themselves when they played with same-sex toys.

Similar gender-typed behaviors have been observed in several different cultures, including Mexico, this girl's home. Women and girls are expected to participate in household tasks and the care of children. Variations in gender roles across cultures have also been observed, however, suggesting that biology alone cannot account for their occurrence.

characteristics defined as masculine and feminine by different cultures or at different points in time. For example, the meta-analyses showing that the superiority of boys on mathematical tasks has disappeared in the last two decades suggest that these sociocultural forces do play a role.

Perhaps the most comprehensive cross-cultural comparison of children and the factors that influence their development was conducted by Beatrice Whiting and Carolyn Pope Edwards. In their Six-Culture study, these researchers examined aggression, nurturance, help seeking, sociability, and other social behaviors in children ages three to eleven living in Kenya, Okinawa, India, the Phillippines, Mexico, and the United States (Whiting & Edwards, 1988; Whiting & Whiting, 1975). The results showed that differences between boys and girls were more exaggerated in some cultures than in others; in fact, they were least pronounced for the American children in the sample. Furthermore, sex differences between males and females diminished when both boys and girls were involved in household tasks, particularly the care of younger siblings. For example, Nyansango boys in East Africa scored higher than girls on their tendency to offer help and support to others; they were also as likely as girls to retreat from aggression. Interestingly, many boys in this culture tend to babies and perform other domestic chores.

While many resemblances were observed in the sex-typed behaviors of children from these diverse cultures, variations were also found among cultures. The latter fact suggests that although biological factors in gender-role development cannot be ignored, they also cannot account for the diversity of roles that occurs across cultures (Best & Williams, 1993).

KEY THEME
Nature/Nurture

Social learning theories offer the best explanation for the roles parents, peers, and even cultures play in gender-role development. They also provide a credible set of explanations for children's imitation of sex-typical behavior. Traditional social learning explanations, however, appear to be limited by their theoretical emphasis on observable behavior rather than cognitive processes. More recent versions of social learning theories include cognitive and emotional phenomena such as attention, recognition, and motivation; this broader conceptualization enhances the ability of a social learning perspective to explain gender-role development. Other researchers, though, have placed even greater emphasis on how children *think* about gender.

Cognitive-Developmental Theories

Cognitive-developmental theories focus on the ways children understand gender roles in general and themselves as males or females in particular. In cognitive-developmental theories, *gender* is emphasized as a conceptual category, a way of classifying people on the basis of their overt appearance or behaviors.

Kohlberg's Cognitive-Developmental Theory   Lawrence Kohlberg (1966) proposed that gender roles emerge as a consequence of stagelike developments in cognition. The most basic of these cognitive milestones is acquisition of **gender identity**, the knowledge that self and others are female or male. This concept, which is acquired between ages two and three years, is crucial to later gender-role development because it provides a basic categorizing principle with which children begin to divide the world. After acquiring gender identity, around their fourth birthday children develop **gender stability**, a sense that gender does not change over time. Children who have acquired gender stability recognize that they were born one sex and will grow up to be a member of that same sex. Despite this knowledge, however, they may not yet be aware of the fact that genitalia determine biological sex. Rather, children assume external factors (such as clothing or hair length) are the determinants of sex. Thus, a young boy may believe he was a baby boy and will grow up to be a "daddy" (gender stability), but only if his behavior and physical characteristics (such as hair length) remain masculine. Children's lack of awareness of the genital basis of gender indicates their lack of **gender constancy**, the child's awareness that changes in external characteristics, behaviors, or desires do not lead to a change in biological sex. Thus, a boy may wear a dress and a girl may play with toy soldiers without altering their respective biological sexes. Kohlberg proposes that gender constancy, like other forms of Piagetian cognitive skills (such as conservation skills), is acquired at about age seven years.

For Kohlberg, the acquisition of gender constancy marks the child's mature awareness of the concept of gender differentiation. Moreover, because children value both their own sex and themselves, they are motivated to behave in a gender-typical fashion. From Kohlberg's perspective, cognitive development facilitates *self-socialization* among children. Kohlberg believes children are internally motivated by their positive self- and same-sex evaluations to behave in a manner consonant with their conceptions of what is sex appropriate. External motivators (such as reinforcements and punishments) are of minimal importance in the process of self-socialization.

Research has confirmed that children progress from attaining gender identity to gender stability and, finally, gender constancy from about two to nine years of age (Fagot, 1985; Slaby & Frey, 1975). This trend appears among children from several cultures, including Argentina, Belize, Kenya, Nepal, and American Samoa (DeLisi & Gallagher, 1991; Munroe, Shimmin, & Munroe, 1984). Most children learn to label themselves correctly as female or male between ages two and three years (Huston, 1985). Precisely when children develop this distinction can forecast subsequent patterns of behavior. Beverly Fagot and Mary Leinbach (1989) found that some children developed gender identity early (before age twenty-eight months) and others not until later. Boys and girls who were early identifiers engaged in significantly more gender-typical play, such as play with building toys for boys and doll play for girls, than did late identifiers. At two to three years of age, children who are able to apply gender labels correctly to others also have greater knowledge of gender stereotypes (Fagot, Leinbach, & O'Boyle, 1992).

How does gender identity develop? Perhaps parents and others provide this information directly by saying things to their young children such as "There's another little boy just like you" or "Be a good girl now, won't you?" Beverly Fagot's research also shows that children who are adept at using gender labels tend to have mothers who engage in sex-typed play with their children and espouse traditional beliefs about gender roles themselves (Fagot, Leinbach, & O'Boyle, 1992). Many researchers contend, however, that the messages about gender roles are so clear and pervasive in

gender identity   Knowledge, usually gained by age three years, that one is male or female.

gender stability   Knowledge, usually gained by age four years, that one's gender does not change over time.

gender constancy   Knowledge, usually gained around age six or seven years, that one's gender does not change as a result of alterations in appearance, behaviors, or desires.

our society that, even aside from the role parents may play, children cannot help but notice them and categorize themselves as males or females.

Gender Schema Theory   Another cognitive-developmental theory is *gender schema theory* (Bem, 1981; Martin & Halverson, 1981, 1987). Like Kohlberg's theory, gender schema theory stresses the importance of the acquisition of gender identity and children's intrinsic motivations to behave in a gender-typical manner. Unlike Kohlberg's theory, however, gender schema theory does not stress the attainment of gender constancy; rather, it focuses on the influence of children's active construction of gender knowledge on their behavior (Bem, 1981; Martin & Halverson, 1987; Signorella, 1987).

Carol Martin and Charles Halverson (1981) have proposed that children first acquire gender identity and then, in their attempts to create order in their social worlds, begin to construct two **gender schemas**, or cognitive organizing structures for information relevant to gender. The first one, the *same-sex/opposite-sex schema*, refers to the child's knowledge of one sex or the other. This is a fairly primitive cognitive structure composed largely of gender stereotypes, such as "boys fix cars" and "girls sew." Children also develop a second, more elaborate gender schema about behaviors relevant to their own sex. This *own-sex schema* provides a basis for guiding children's behavior. Thus, even though both boys and girls know that girls sew, girls are more likely to be motivated to learn to sew, whereas they may not want to learn how to fix a car. Researchers have confirmed that children explore and prefer neutral objects labeled as intended for their own sex more than they do for objects labeled for the other sex. Moreover, up to one week later, children remember more details about the "same-sex" objects than they do about the "other-sex" objects, even when they are offered a reward for remembering details (Bradbard et al., 1986; Martin, Eisenbud, & Rose, 1995).

According to Martin and Halverson (1981), children's gender schemas serve as a potent means of organizing information about their social worlds. Some children tend to be *gender schematic*; that is, they possess a strong gender schema, exhibit more consistent sex typing in their behavior, and process information along gender lines. In contrast, children who are *gender aschematic* possess a weaker gender schema, are less sex typed behaviorally, and focus their attention on aspects of information that are not related to gender. Gender-schematic children often distort information according to their beliefs about gender and are unlikely to remember events that are inconsistent with those beliefs. For example, gender-schematic children find it difficult to remember information about pictures of people engaged in sex-atypical activities, such as a boy playing with a doll, whereas they can easily remember information about people engaged in sex-typical activities, such as a girl playing with a tea set (Signorella, 1987; Welch-Ross & Schmidt, 1996). These effects are apparent as early as age twenty-five months, at least among boys (Bauer, 1993). Similarly, children distort stereotype-inconsistent information by actually changing the sex of the person engaged in the sex-atypical behavior. Gender-schematic children who see a picture of a boy playing with a doll are more likely to remember seeing a picture of a girl playing with a doll than a picture of a boy playing with a gender-typical toy (Carter & Levy, 1988).

In other studies, children are asked to imitate or remember sequences of events that are associated with one or the other sex, such as building with tools or doing laundry. Just as we saw in Chapter 9 that children develop scripts for events that have repeatedly occurred in their lives, children seem to develop *gender scripts,* generalized representations for activities associated with a given sex. Children remember more information associated with their own gender scripts than for scripts associated with the opposite sex (Levy & Fivush, 1993).

Why do many children become gender schematic? According to Bem (1983), children become gender schematic to the extent that they experience gender as a relevant social category. Thus, for example, when differences between males and females are

KEY THEME
Child's Active Role

KEY THEME
Individual Differences

gender schema   Cognitive organizing structure for information relevant to sex typing.

frequently pointed out to them by parents, teachers, or peers, children themselves will use gender as a way to classify social information. Furthermore, both peers and adults stress conformity to gender-typical roles, a fact that makes it difficult for most children in our society to become truly gender aschematic (Bem, 1983).

Cognitive-developmental theories are an effective way to explain how children's own knowledge contributes to their gender-role development. Concepts such as gender identity and self-socialization have proven to be useful ways to explain gender-role development. In addition, we have seen how children employ their prior conceptions of the sex typicality of models in deciding whether to imitate modeled behavior, a phenomenon predicted by cognitive-developmental theories. In short, how children think about gender seems to have far-reaching consequences.

To sum up, each of the preceding theories has some value for explaining the source of sex differences, many of which are outlined in the Chronology on page 446. The biological theories provide a basis for understanding the physiological underpinnings of male and female behavior. Social learning theory provides a mechanism for explaining how children learn discrete aspects of sex-typical behavior. Cognitive-developmental approaches explain how children's concepts of gender become integrated in their minds. Although each theory explains a specific feature of gender-role development better than the other theories do, none of them taken alone is adequate to explain the multifaceted nature of this aspect of development.

THE SOCIALIZATION OF GENDER ROLES

Whatever biological tendencies are associated with being a male and a female, it is worth exploring further the influences of the social environment on gender-role development and how it intermingles with the child's developing cognitions about gender. Particularly if we are concerned about the gender-associated problems children face, whether it be aggression among boys or the anxieties experienced by girls, we need to understand how social experiences can promote optimal development for both sexes.

KEY THEME
Nature/Nurture

The earliest messages about the social world, of course, come from the child's parents. From the moment of birth, when parents in our culture ask, "Is it a boy or a girl?", the sex of their child is a very prominent characteristic, one that elicits specific behaviors and reactions from mother and father. As children branch out to social relationships with peers, gender-role socialization continues in very powerful ways—in the games children play, the relationships they form, and how they react to one another's behaviors. Finally, another significant influence on gender-role development is the child's experiences in schools, in which teachers and the instructional materials they use can confirm (or disconfirm) early gender-role beliefs and behaviors.

The Influence of Parents

Traditionally, developmental psychologists have believed one of the most important sources of information about gender for children is the behavior of their parents and the environment parents create (Katz, 1987). Sometimes the messages are subtle. Parents commonly provide their children with sex-differentiated toys and room furnishings (Rheingold & Cook, 1975). They buy sports equipment, tools, and vehicles for their sons and dolls and doll furniture for their daughters. Boys' rooms typically are decorated in blue, girls' in yellow (Pomerleau et al., 1990). When parents provide boys and girls with different physical environments, they send messages that boys are indeed different from girls and set sex-related limits on the types of behavior that are acceptable and appropriate.

Other times the messages are more direct. Research shows that parents treat children differently on the basis of sex in early infancy, beginning at ages younger than

CHRONOLOGY
Gender Development

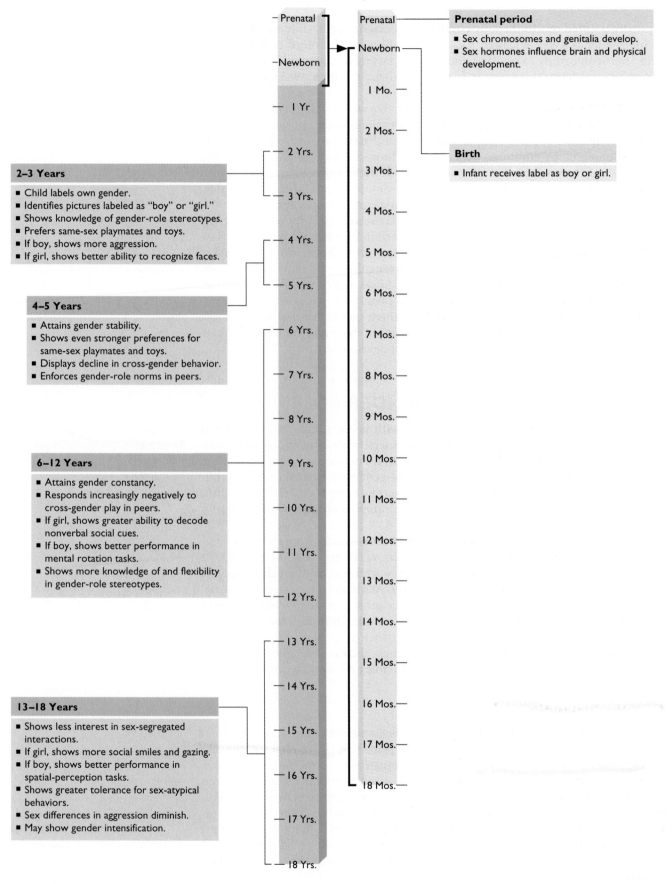

Prenatal period
- Sex chromosomes and genitalia develop.
- Sex hormones influence brain and physical development.

Birth
- Infant receives label as boy or girl.

2–3 Years
- Child labels own gender.
- Identifies pictures labeled as "boy" or "girl."
- Shows knowledge of gender-role stereotypes.
- Prefers same-sex playmates and toys.
- If boy, shows more aggression.
- If girl, shows better ability to recognize faces.

4–5 Years
- Attains gender stability.
- Shows even stronger preferences for same-sex playmates and toys.
- Displays decline in cross-gender behavior.
- Enforces gender-role norms in peers.

6–12 Years
- Attains gender constancy.
- Responds increasingly negatively to cross-gender play in peers.
- If girl, shows greater ability to decode nonverbal social cues.
- If boy, shows better performance in mental rotation tasks.
- Shows more knowledge of and flexibility in gender-role stereotypes.

13–18 Years
- Shows less interest in sex-segregated interactions.
- If girl, shows more social smiles and gazing.
- If boy, shows better performance in spatial-perception tasks.
- Shows greater tolerance for sex-atypical behaviors.
- Sex differences in aggression diminish.
- May show gender intensification.

This chart describes the sequence of gender-role development based on the findings of research. Children often show individual differences in the exact ages at which they display the various developmental achievement outlined here.

those at which actual behavioral sex differences emerge (Fagot & Leinbach, 1987). Right in the first week following the birth of their child, parents of daughters describe their infants as more delicate, less strong, and as having finer features than parents of boys (Karraker, Vogel, & Lake, 1995). Adults play more roughly with a male infant, tossing him in the air and tickling him vigorously, than they do with a female infant (Huston, 1983). During infancy and childhood, girls are more likely than boys to be protected and sheltered by adults, whereas boys are given greater opportunities than girls to explore their environments (Block, 1983; Burns, Mitchell, & Obradovich, 1989). Adult females respond more quickly to crying babies who they think are little girls, and parents encourage more nurturance and domestic themes in the play of their daughters than in the play of their sons (Condry, Condry, & Pogatshynik, 1978; Farver & Wimbarti, 1995; Huston, 1983). Similarly, both mothers and fathers use more emotion words when speaking with their preschool-age daughters than with their sons (Adams et al., 1995; Kuebli, Butler, & Fivush, 1995).

Direct Reinforcement   Parents take an active role in teaching and encouraging gender-typical behavior in their children, at least according to some research findings. For example, when their children are as young as three years, parents react more negatively when their daughters assert themselves than when their sons do. Fathers in particular tend to react positively when their daughters display compliant behavior and reward their sons for assertiveness (Kerig, Cowan, & Cowan, 1993). Similarly, parents give boys more positive evaluations and girls more negative evaluations when children are working on solving problems (Alessandri & Lewis, 1993). Parents also respond positively to boys who play with blocks and manipulate objects and reinforce girls' play with dolls and requests for help (Fagot & Leinbach, 1987). Fathers appear to be especially concerned about what they perceive as masculinity in their sons, at least during the preschool years (Jacklin, DiPietro, & Maccoby, 1984). Such concern is often expressed in parental interviews as well as in the consistently negative manner in which fathers respond to sex-atypical behavior in their sons.

However, a meta-analysis of 172 studies of parents' differential socialization of girls and boys suggests that we must be cautious about how much weight we give to the role of direct parental reinforcement in accounting for the various facets of gender-role development. In general, the overall impact of parental socialization was judged to be small in most areas of socialization, including achievement expectations, dependency, and aggression. The only socialization area that showed a significant effect was parental encouragement of sex-typed activities, such as doll play for girls and tool play for boys (Lytton & Romney, 1991). Particularly in these contexts, then, children may acquire well-defined ideas about maleness and femaleness.

Parental Attitudes   Another way in which parents influence their children's gender-role development is through their own general beliefs about masculine and feminine roles. Many parents believe children as young as two years differ along gender-stereotypic lines (McGuire, 1988). They report, for example, that their own sons like sports, enjoy using tools, and are energetic. On the other hand, parents of girls say their daughters like to be admired, enjoy playing with dolls, and like clothes. Such beliefs are frequently translated into sex-differentiated patterns in the types of chores boys and girls are assigned to do around the house: boys take out the garbage and mow the lawn; girls do more chores within the house, such as cleaning and cooking (Goodnow, 1988; Lackey, 1989). The tendency of children to participate in household tasks associated with their gender increases in early adolescence, especially if their own parents assume traditional roles in household tasks or parents openly encourage traditional chores (Antill et al., 1996; Crouter, Manke, & McHale, 1995).

Parents, especially fathers, are likely to stress academic and nonacademic achievement more for their sons than for their daughters (Eccles, 1983). When their children are in elementary school, parents have higher academic achievement expectations for their daughters than for their sons (Maccoby & Jacklin, 1974). Beginning in adolescence, however, parents expect their sons to perform better in academics than their

When fathers assume a greater role in parenting, children show less knowledge of gender stereotypes and are slower to acquire gender labels. Girls, especially, seem to profit from the greater involvement of the father in child-care activities. They show greater independence and feelings of control over events in their lives compared to girls whose fathers are less involved.

daughters, especially in areas such as mathematics (Eccles, 1983). Parents may convey such expectations directly (for example, through statements such as "Girls are never very good at math") or indirectly (for example, through encouraging boys and girls to pursue different occupational goals). Parents' encouragement of children's play with traditionally sex-typed toys may also have an impact on their children's academic endeavors. For example, parents may discourage girls from male-typed play, such as with blocks or construction toys, a pattern that may have the unintended consequence of inhibiting the development of their daughters' visual-spatial skills.

Gender Role in Nontraditional Families   A series of profound changes in the traditional American family over the last several decades may have an impact on gender-role development. First, an increasing number of children spend a large part of their lives in families headed by a single parent, usually the mother (Huston, 1983). According to social learning theorists, the absence of significant male models from the home should have an effect on the process of imitation, especially among boys. Second, as we described in Chapter 11, mothers increasingly are employed outside the home while their children are still young. Thus, these women may be providing their children with alternative models for feminine behavior.

Although few studies have addressed the development of gender roles in single-parent families, a large number have been conducted on gender-role development in children from families in which mothers are employed outside the home. In general, maternal employment facilitates the development of flexibility in children's conceptions of gender roles. Children with employed mothers are more likely to believe both males and females can exhibit a wide variety of behaviors and personality characteristics than children whose mothers are not employed outside the home. The effects on daughters of employed mothers are particularly dramatic. Daughters of mothers who work outside the home show higher levels of achievement motivation and are more likely to have personality styles that blend male-typed and female-typed traits than are the daughters of nonworking mothers (Hoffman, 1979; Huston, 1983). The effects of maternal employment on sons are mixed. Boys whose mothers work outside the home are more likely to have flexible views of women's roles than are the sons of nonworking mothers, but sons in both groups have equally masculine personalities and display equally masculine types of behavior (Hoffman, 1979).

Psychologists are also interested in the effects of nontraditional fathers—those who take on at least equal responsibility for child care—on children's gender-role development. Children whose mothers and fathers make a deliberate effort to share parenting are slower to adopt gender labels and show less knowledge of gender stereotypes during the children's preschool years (Fagot & Leinbach, 1995). Research shows that girls in particular profit from the involvement of fathers in child-oriented activities. Elementary school–age girls whose parents were less stereotyped in their marital and child-rearing roles also showed more independence and feelings of being in control over events in their lives (Hoffman & Kloska, 1995). In another research project that included traditional parents as well as parents who shared equally in child-related responsibilities, adolescent girls from egalitarian families maintained high levels of school achievement, whereas girls from traditional families showed declines in science and mathematics achievement as they made the transition to seventh grade. Boys showed no differences in achievement associated with parenting styles (Updegraff, McHale, & Crouter, 1996).

The Influence of Peers

Another major influence on children's gender-role development is the peer group. Peer groups not only provide children with opportunities for particular kinds of play but also offer a forum in which children can learn about social behavior and social interactions by watching models and obtaining feedback about their own behaviors. When children begin to interact with their peers, they enter an arena in which adult input is indirect and the opinions and behaviors of agemates become increasingly important. And although peers influence children in a variety of social dimensions, nowhere is their influence more marked than in the area of gender-role socialization (Carter, 1987).

Early Play Patterns   The influence of peers on gender-role development can be observed even among very young children. Carol Jacklin and Eleanor Maccoby (1978) observed same-sex and mixed-sex pairs of unacquainted two-year-olds to determine the influence of peers on toddlers' behavior. Children were dressed in a sex-neutral fashion (in yellow jumpsuits) and allowed to play in a room with their mothers present but nondirective. As Figure 13.5 shows, the toddlers' behavior varied as a function of the sex of their play partner even though the children were unaware of the true sex of the other child. In other words, the behaviors of the neutrally dressed children seemed to precipitate different reactions in their play partners. In general, children displayed more social behaviors, both positive overtures and negative acts, when they played with a peer of the same sex. Girls were more likely to be passive when they played with a boy peer than when they played with a girl peer. In addition, girls in girl-girl pairs exhibited greater sharing of toys and were less likely to become upset and cry than when they were in mixed-sex pairs. Finally, boys were less likely to obey a verbal prohibition from a girl than from a boy. Already at this young age, the dynamics of peer interactions were markedly influenced by the sex of the partners.

Peer Enforcement of Gender Roles   Peers continue to exert a strong influence on children's adoption of sex-typical behaviors as they begin preschool. A number of studies have shown, for example, that children respond differentially to sex-typical and sex-atypical behavior in their peers. Children may reward behavior they like by complimenting a child or by engaging in mutual play, and they may punish a behavior they do not approve of by name calling. Preschoolers and kindergartners reliably punish boys who engage in sex-atypical behavior, such as playing with dolls, while rewarding them for engaging in sex-typical behavior, such as playing with trucks (Fagot, 1977; Lamb, Easterbrooks, & Holden, 1980; Lamb & Roopnarine, 1979). In contrast, girls are rewarded for engaging in sex-typical behavior, such as playing house, but apparently they experience no consequences when they engage in sex-atypical behavior (Fagot, 1977). The differential responses of peers toward boys and girls who engage in sex-atypical behavior persist through at least the sixth grade (Carter & McCloskey, 1984).

The pressures the peer group exerts apparently work. Children are responsive to the positive and negative feedback they receive from their peers. They are likely to continue to engage in a sex-typical behavior in response to reinforcement and to terminate behaviors their peers punish (Lamb, Easterbrooks, & Holden, 1980). Furthermore, feedback from same-sex peers may be especially important. Beverly Fagot (1978a) found that both girls and boys age two years were more likely to continue a behavior if a same-sex peer responded positively and to discontinue a behavior if a same-sex peer reacted negatively. If the peer was of the other sex, however, the peer's feedback was largely ineffective. Interestingly, data indicate at the same time that among these young children, sex-atypical play is likely to be inhibited even in the presence of a peer of the other sex (Serbin, Connor, Burchardt, & Citron, 1979).

Cross-Gender Behavior   Some children (between 20 and 40 percent), more often girls than boys, fail to respond to their peers' disapproval of sex-atypical behavior (Sandberg et al., 1993). These children exhibit **cross-gender behavior**; that is, they adopt, in whole or in part, a variety of characteristics typical of the other sex (Fagot, 1977). Cross-gender boys, for example, exhibit a strong interest in feminine games and activities and play "dress-up" in girls' clothes. Cross-gender boys are likely to become social isolates over time because their male peers refuse to interact with them even when they play in a masculine fashion, and their female peers seem to merely tolerate their presence. Cross-gender girls, in contrast, appear to suffer very little for

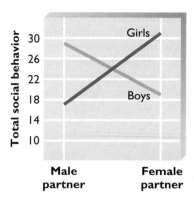

Source: Adapted from Jacklin & Maccoby, 1978.

FIGURE 13.5

Social Behavior as a Function of the Child's Play Partner

In a study by Jacklin and Maccoby, unacquainted two-year-olds were observed as they interacted with either a same-sex or an opposite-sex partner. The amount of social behavior (both positive overtures and negative acts such as aggression) was greater when children played with a peer of the same sex.

cross-gender behavior   Behavior usually seen in a member of the opposite sex. Term generally is reserved for behavior that is persistently sex atypical.

Both boys and girls may engage in cross-gender activities. However, it is usually easier for girls to cross gender boundaries than for boys; peers usually react more negatively in the latter case.

their sex-atypical behavior. At least in the preschool years, cross-gender girls cross play groups easily, playing with boys at "boy games" and with girls at "girl games" (Fagot, 1977). Thus, the consequences of cross-gender behavior are much more severe and long lasting for boys than for girls.

The tendency of children to disapprove of cross-gender behavior increases with age. When researchers interviewed kindergartners through sixth-graders to determine how these children would respond to hypothetical cases of cross-gender behavior in their peers, older children reported they would respond more negatively to cross-gender behavior than did younger children. Moreover, children stated they would respond more negatively to cross-gender behavior in their male peers than in their female peers. The degree of negativity children exhibited was particularly surprising. Only one child reported she would respond positively toward a cross-gender child, and children were virtually unanimous in their assertion that they would not want to play with a cross-gender child. Children's reports of how they would respond ranged from fairly innocuous comments (such as "I'd stay away") to statements indicating they would physically abuse cross-gender children (Carter & McCloskey, 1984).

Similar results were obtained when researchers asked preadolescents to describe the personal qualities of an actor who played a gender-inappropriate game with children of the opposite sex. If a boy actor played jumprope with a group of girls, he was viewed as significantly less popular than a female actor or a male actor playing a masculine game (Lobel et al., 1993). In another study of preadolescents attending summer day camps, researchers found that children who violated gender boundaries by associating with members of the opposite sex were rated as substantially less popular with peers (Sroufe et al., 1993). As we will see in Chapter 15, popularity with peers is, in turn, associated with other significant developmental outcomes. Children who are unpopular often have low self-esteem and poor academic achievement, and may be prone to aggression. Thus, cross-gender behavior can be stigmatizing and potentially far-reaching in its effects.

Sex Segregation   The influence of peers on sex typing in children's behavior is undoubtedly enhanced by the fact that boys and girls tend to interact in separate groups: starting at age three or four, boys play with boys and girls play with girls (Maccoby, 1988, 1990). This phenomenon is called **sex segregation**. In one observation of one hundred children on their preschool playgrounds, four-year-olds spent

KEY THEME
Interaction Among Domains

sex segregation   Clustering of individuals into same-sex groups.

three times as much time with same-sex partners as with opposite-sex partners. By age six, they spent eleven times more time with peers of the same sex (Maccoby & Jacklin, 1987). This tendency to prefer same-sex peers persists at least until early adolescence (Maccoby, 1990). As a result, the range of behaviors open to children and acceptable to their peers is limited by their choice of playmates of the same sex.

Maccoby (1990) believes children's experiences in same-sex groups foster different styles of social interaction in boys and girls. As boys play in their characteristic rough-and-tumble fashion or in team sports and games, they develop assertive, dominance-seeking styles of interaction. In contrast, girls' groups, which are oriented toward relationships and shared intimacy, promote cooperation and mutual support as well as a tendency to preserve the cohesiveness of the group. According to Maccoby, the same-sex peer group is an extremely powerful socialization environment throughout childhood.

Sex segregation begins to break down as children enter adolescence and begin to think about dating. The pressures of heterosexual interactions, however, may enhance rather than diminish the push toward conformity with gender-role norms (Eccles, 1987; Petersen, 1980). This pattern is particularly obvious among teenage girls, many of whom abandon "tomboyish" behaviors that were acceptable during an earlier period of development (Huston & Alvarez, 1990).

Adolescent Peer Influences   Peer acceptance and rejection become increasingly important during adolescence. Although sex-typing pressures remain high, popularity among adolescents of both sexes relies more on positive personality characteristics, such as leadership abilities and politeness, rather than merely the presence of sex-typed behavior (Sigelman, Carr, & Begley, 1986). Thus, the presence of cross-gender personality characteristics or behaviors may not lead to isolation from peers among older adolescents to the extent that it does for younger children (Huston & Alvarez, 1990; Katz & Ksansnak, 1994). Adolescents' greater tolerance for sex-atypical personality characteristics may reflect their increasing cognitive abilities, specifically their ability to consider multiple dimensions as they make judgments about individuals, including abstract qualities such as trustworthiness or loyalty (Eccles, 1987).

KEY THEME
Interaction Among Domains

The Influence of Teachers and Schools

Teachers, like peers and parents, treat children differentially according to sex, reinforce and punish sex-typed behaviors, and model sex-typical behavior for their students. Moreover, schools may foster sex typing through the teaching materials and curriculum to which children are exposed. For example, one survey of children's readers found that although boys and girls were portrayed with almost equal frequency, girls were more often the characters in stories in need of rescue and boys were rarely shown doing housework or displaying emotions (Purcell & Stewart, 1990).

Teacher Attitudes and Behaviors   Teachers, like other adults, often express stereotypical, gender-based views about the capacities of their students. They believe female students are feminine and male students are masculine, although more experienced teachers are less likely to hold stereotyped beliefs and more likely to treat students in an egalitarian fashion than are less experienced teachers (Fagot, 1978a; Huston, 1983). When teachers are asked to nominate their best students or those with the most potential, they are more likely to nominate boys than girls. They are especially likely to name boys as most skilled in mathematics. When asked to think of students who excel in language or social skill, teachers are more likely to name girls (BenTsvi-Mayer, Hertz-Lazarowitz, & Safir, 1989). These patterns in teacher responses occur despite the fact that actual sex differences in many of these domains are minimal.

In addition, teachers respond differently to students on the basis of sex as opposed to behavior. Boys, for example, receive more disapproval from teachers than girls do during preschool and elementary school, even when boys and girls engage in similar amounts of disruptive behavior (Huston, 1983; Serbin et al., 1973). Teachers' behavior may reflect a belief that boys are more likely than girls to cause trouble in the classroom unless rules are strictly enforced (Huston, 1983). On the other hand, teachers pay more attention to a girl when she sits quietly in the front of the classroom, whereas the amount of attention paid to a boy is high regardless of where he sits (Serbin et al., 1973). Moreover, within elementary school classrooms, teachers tend to call on boys more often than girls and give them more explicit feedback regarding their answers. When girls answer, they are more likely to receive a simple acceptance from the teacher ("okay"), whereas boys tend to receive more praise, constructive criticism, or encouragement to discover the correct answer (Sadker & Sadker, 1994). Thus, boys receive more explicit academic instruction and tend to dominate classroom interactions.

RESEARCH APPLIED TO EDUCATION

Promoting Gender Equity in the Classroom

Now eight years old, Nicky is sitting in a circle with the other third-graders in his class, listening to Brittany read the story she wrote during Writing Workshop. The children seem captivated by her story; even the most restless among them sits quietly, eyes glued on the storyteller. When Brittany is done, Ms. Klein says, "Okay, does anyone have any questions or comments about Brittany's story? Go ahead, Brittany. You can call on someone." Hands fly up eagerly.

"Stephen," says Brittany.

"Why did you make the character live by a pond?" asks Stephen.

"Because he has a lot of animal friends that live there," she responds.

More hands churn in the air. "Nicky," she calls out next. "Wait a minute," says Ms. Klein. "Remember our rule. You have to call on a girl next."

"Reesha," Brittany calls out.

"I like how the words you picked make me think of beautiful pictures in my head," comments Reesha. "Thank you," responds Brittany, a little shyly.

Nicky's mother, observing all of this, thinks maybe her son feels slighted for being passed over. Later, when she asks him about this, he firmly proclaims, "All Ms. Klein is trying to do is to be fair to the boys and girls in the class. I didn't feel bad at all. I think it's the right thing to do."

Just as teacher behavior can perpetuate stereotypes, it can change sex-typing patterns among children in classroom settings. A collection of studies suggests some specific techniques teachers can use to reduce sex segregation, modify children's beliefs about gender, and promote the participation of girls in the classroom.

1. *Use reinforcement to facilitate cooperative cross-sex play.* In one study involving preschoolers and kindergartners, teachers praised children who played in mixed-sex groups by pointing out their cooperative play to the class and complimenting the children. Cross-sex play subsequently increased (Serbin, Connor, & Iler, 1979; Serbin, Tonick, & Sternglanz, 1977).

2. *Prepare lessons that explicitly allow children to question gender stereotypes about personal qualities, occupations, and activities.* Researchers in Dublin, Ireland, had student teachers present a series of lessons to children in the first through sixth grades. The lessons encouraged children to think of counterexamples to common stereotypes, for example, instances where women show an interest in football or where men have been observed to be warm and gentle. Discussions were supplemented by opportunities to meet people who worked in nontraditional roles, such as a male nurse and a female veterinary surgeon. In addition, children read poetry, read fairy

Research has shown that boys receive more attention from teachers than girls. Teachers can promote sex equity in the classroom by deliberately calling on girls to answer questions, even when they do not volunteer. Waiting a few moments to give girls a chance to participate can also help.

tales, and had worksheets that brought up themes counter to traditional stereotypes. At the end of four months, children who had experienced the lessons had significantly lower stereotype scores than those in a control group (Gash & Morgan, 1993).

3. *Be conscious of the need to give girls a chance to participate.* One way to do this is to wait three to five seconds before calling on a student to answer a question. Girls, especially those who are shy or less confident, may need time to formulate their answers and decide they are willing to share them with the class. Also, do not just call on students who volunteer, since these are more likely to be boys. Teachers can even have an observer record the number of times they call on boys versus girls. Myra and David Sadker (1994) found that when teachers saw the results of such observations, and, further, when they received training on how to be more gender equitable, girls in their elementary and secondary school classrooms became more equal partners with boys in class participation.

Student Attitudes Toward Coursework   Research indicates that students, teachers, and parents alike view some academic subjects as masculine and others as feminine (Huston, 1983). As we noted earlier, mathematics is generally seen as a masculine activity and reading is viewed as feminine (Eccles, 1983; Eccles et al., 1993; Huston, 1983; Yee & Eccles, 1988). Such sex typing is not limited to American schoolchildren. In a study of first-through-fifth-grade Chinese, Japanese, and American boys and girls, the investigators found that most children believed boys are better in mathematics and girls are better at reading (Lummis & Stevenson, 1990). Moreover, boys in these three societies predicted they would do better in mathematics in high school than girls predicted they would do, although no sex differences were found in children's predictions of their future reading skills.

Students' attitudes toward academic subjects can influence whether they will in fact be exposed to these subjects and acquire their specific skills. Jacquelynne Eccles asked fifth-through-twelfth-graders to complete questionnaires about their perceptions of their mathematics skills, their attributions for success and failure in mathematics, the value of mathematics for them, and their plans to take mathematics courses in the future (Eccles, 1983; Yee & Eccles, 1988). In addition, she gathered scores on both classroom and standardized mathematics tests. Eccles and her colleagues collected data over a two-year period, allowing them to examine how attitudes toward mathematics at one point were related to later attitudes and experiences.

Although no sex differences were found in children's classroom or standardized mathematics test scores, girls perceived themselves as less competent at mathematics, were less willing to take mathematics courses in the future, and saw mathematics as less valuable than did boys. Moreover, girls and boys differed in their explanations for success and failure in mathematics. Girls explained success in terms of *external attributions* ("I was just lucky" or "The teacher likes me") and failure in terms of *internal attributions* ("I'm just no good at math"). Boys, in contrast, explained failure through external attributions ("The teacher hates me") and success in terms of internal attributions ("I'm smart"). Children's attitudes were predictive of later enrollment in mathematics classes. Girls were more likely to drop out of mathematics courses or to take lower-level mathematics courses than boys of the same ability levels. Moreover, girls developed higher levels of anxiety about mathematics than boys did. Clearly, children's gender-stereotyped views of courses can have an enormous impact on the direction their studies take.

Sex Differences in Achievement Expectations   A variety of factors may contribute to sex differences in children's interest in academic subjects and their expectations for academic success. One factor may be sex typing in the content of the curriculum. In one study, a group of investigators used two computer-based mathematics tutorials differing in sex typing to assess children's skills (Cooper, Hall, & Huff, 1990). The "masculine" tutorial was a typical arcade-type game designed to teach division in a war game format in which guns fired at tanks in response to children's answers to the problems. Tanks exploded when children answered correctly; incorrect responses produced misses. The "feminine" tutorial taught division of fractions using a word-oriented, nonaggressive format. Besides measuring children's liking for the two programs, the investigators collected children's perceptions of stress and their competence on the war game program. Overall, children preferred the tutorial program designed for their own sex and reported feeling less stress when working on the same-sex tutorial than on the other-sex one. In addition, boys' performance was superior to the performance of girls on the masculine tutorial. (No comparisons of performance were made on the feminine task.) Thus, sex typing of curricular content may affect children's preferences and performance in academic areas.

Another factor that appears to influence children's academic expectations is the nature of evaluative feedback they receive for their academic work and nonacademic behavior. Carol Dweck and her colleagues have proposed that evaluative criticism is more likely to result in both feelings of incompetence and lowered expectations of success if it is *discriminate*—in this case, directed primarily at academic work—than if it is *indiscriminate*—that is, directed at both academic and social behavior (Dweck et al., 1978). Dweck and her colleagues found that boys received greater indiscriminate criticism from teachers (more than two-thirds was for nonacademic behavior), whereas more than two-thirds of the criticism girls received concerned their academic efforts. Thus, girls' lower academic expectations may reflect the greater tendency for their academic work to be criticized. In contrast, since teachers are generally more critical of them, boys may attribute negative feedback to the attitudes of teachers rather than to the quality of their intellectual performance.

Girls do, in fact, show greater self-criticism of their academic work than boys do. Karin Frey and Diane Ruble (1987) have studied instances of self- and peer criticism for academic work in classroom settings. Children between ages five and ten years were observed at work in academic tasks in their classrooms, and their spontaneous critical and complimentary comments about themselves and their peers were tallied. Several sex differences emerged in the nature of comments children made. Overall, both girls and boys made more self-compliments than self-criticisms, but boys made a greater number of self-congratulatory statements relative to self-criticisms than girls did (see Figure 13.6). Boys complimented themselves and criticized their peers

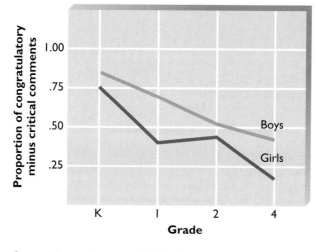

Source: Adapted from Frey & Ruble, 1987.

FIGURE 13.6

Self-Evaluation in Boys and Girls

In a study of elementary school children, Frey and Ruble found that both boys and girls made more self-congratulatory comments than self-critical ones, but girls showed a greater proportion of self-critical comments relative to self-congratulatory statements about their classroom performance. The data here represent the proportion of self-congratulatory comments minus self-critical comments.

more than girls did, whereas girls criticized themselves and complimented their peers more than boys did. Girls also were more likely to attribute their failures to a lack of ability ("I'm so stupid") than boys were. Thus, the patterns of girls' self-criticism match the discriminate criticism they hear from their teachers.

ALTERNATIVE CONCEPTUALIZATIONS OF GENDER

Changes in society's conceptions of the desirability of traditional sex typing have been reflected in changes in psychological theories. Although earlier theorists and researchers (Kohlberg, 1966; Mischel, 1966) assumed sex-atypical behavior is undesirable and perhaps indicative of psychopathology, more recent conceptions of gender-role development have taken two new directions. Rather than assuming traditional masculine and feminine roles are the most desirable, some psychologists have suggested that blending both sets of traits may expand our ability to respond adaptively to the demands of our environments. Others maintain that male and female development differ, but in ways that can be valued and embraced.

Androgyny

Traditionally, psychologists treated masculinity and femininity as opposite ends of a bipolar dimension: the more masculine one was, the less feminine, by definition, one could be. Sandra Bem (1974, 1975) challenged this view by proposing that masculinity and femininity are not mutually exclusive, as the bipolar formulation would suggest, but are separate, measurable dimensions of personality. Thus, a person of either sex could be assertive in situations in which that behavior was necessary and nurturant when nurturance was required. From Bem's perspective, **androgyny**, the coexistence of both masculine and feminine characteristics, allows the individual to be maximally adaptive.

Psychological androgyny should not be confused with the ways the popular media present androgyny. From a psychological perspective, people whose physical appearance is ambiguous, neither distinctively male nor distinctively female, are not necessarily androgynous. In Bem's formulation, *androgynous* people are those who exhibit high levels of both masculine and feminine personality characteristics. People who are highly masculine and possess fewer feminine characteristics are designated as *masculine,* whereas those who are highly feminine and possess fewer masculine characteristics are designated as *feminine.* People who have few masculine and feminine

androgyny Gender-role orientation in which a person possesses high levels of personality characteristics associated with both sexes.

TABLE 13.2

Classification of Sex Typing

In Sandra Bem's (1974, 1975) classification scheme, individuals who score high on traits associated with both masculinity and femininity are classified as "androgynous"; those scoring low on both dimensions are classified as "undifferentiated." "Feminine" and "masculine" individuals are those who score high on one sex-typing dimension and low on the other.

		Masculinity Score	
		High	**Low**
Femininity Score	**High**	Androgynous	Feminine
	Low	Masculine	Undifferentiated

KEY THEME
Interaction Among Domains

KEY THEME
Interaction Among Domains

characteristics are classified as *undifferentiated*. Table 13.2 presents this classification scheme.

Psychological health and popularity with peers have been found to be associated with androgyny. For example, androgynous adolescents are better adjusted psychologically than are sex-typed or undifferentiated people (Ziegler, Dusek, & Carter, 1984). Similarly, androgynous adolescents are liked better by their peers and report feeling less lonely than other groups of adolescents (Avery, 1982; Massad, 1981). Androgynous adolescents also are more likely to have resolved identity crises than are nonandrogynous adolescents (Dusek, 1987). Finally, androgynous girls are more likely to attribute success to internal factors, such as their own efforts or hard work, than to external factors, such as chance or the influences of others (Huston, 1983).

How does an individual become androgynous? A variety of theories have been proposed. It has been suggested, for example, that parental characteristics such as nurturance or maternal employment are likely to lead to the development of androgyny. The data on relationships between parental characteristics and androgyny in children are sparse, however. Another possibility involves the child's growing ability to conceptualize the self and social roles in complex, abstract terms. Eccles (1987) has proposed that children cannot become androgynous before adolescence because they are still in the process of acquiring a gender role. During adolescence, however, children's abilities to conceptualize sex roles in a more abstract manner lead them to view gender-role stereotypes as descriptive statements about regularities in behavior rather than as prescriptions for acceptable behavior. Simultaneously, as adolescents strive to define their identities, they may consider factors other than gender as a means of characterizing themselves. Though androgynous role models are likely to foster gender-role transcendence, according to Eccles (1987), the convergence of cognitive developmental changes and the emergence of self-definition, rather than external factors such as models, allow children to transcend traditional roles and emerge as androgynous.

The Relational Approach

Instead of emphasizing the blending of male and female traits, some theorists maintain that the development of females is unique and different from the development of males. For example, in Chapter 12, we saw how Carol Gilligan (1982) defined a "morality of care and responsibility" for females, a distinctive orientation toward relationships that characterizes responses of females to moral dilemmas, in contrast to the "morality of justice" that typifies male responses. Similarly, Jean Baker Miller (1986) maintains that a central feature of female development, largely ignored by mainstream developmental psychology, is the tendency to seek out and maintain relationships with others. This tendency represents a marked departure from the widely held notion that child development is, in large part, the process of becoming independent, autonomous, and self-reliant. For females, development may mean more, not less, connection with others. Further, instead of characterizing these tendencies of females as "dependency," a term that has negative connotations, theorists

According to the relational approach, girls' development is distinct from that of boys, revolving around the need to establish and maintain relationships with others. Rather than breaking away from parents during adolescence, for example, girls may desire to keep their connections with them.

of the relational school believe they are an important source of gratification and self-fulfillment (Miller, 1991; Surrey, 1991).

This framework opens up new interpretations for certain important developmental time periods. For example, adolescence has traditionally been seen as a phase in which children desire to separate from their parents, to realize their own potentials and strike out on their own. For females, however, breaking away from parents may not be the goal. Instead, the adolescent girl may wish to change the form of her relationships but still maintain them (Surrey, 1991). The dilemma of reconciling her inclinations toward relationship with her knowledge that the larger society expects her to "break away" may lead to intense conflicts for the adolescent female (Gilligan, Lyons, & Hanmer, 1990). Young girls who were at one time outspoken may become reluctant to verbalize their feelings; they may lose confidence in themselves, and their relationships with other females may suffer (Brown & Gilligan, 1992).

Researchers have begun to find other support for the idea that female development is distinct from male development in that it revolves around establishing and maintaining relationships with others. For example, in one recent study, high self-esteem in female adolescents was positively correlated with a strong desire to help female friends, that is, to feel connected with them. In contrast, high self-esteem in male adolescents was related to assertiveness with male friends, that is, wanting to stand apart and get ahead of them (Thorne & Michaelieu, 1996). In another study, girls in the eighth and tenth grades were more likely than boys to agree with questionnaire items such as "When making a decision, I take other people's needs and feelings into account." That is, they endorsed items that contained an orientation toward relationships (Jones & Costin, 1995). Parental socialization of girls may lead them to an orientation toward relationships. When mothers of preschoolers were observed conversing with their daughters, they spent more time than mothers of boys discussing their children's shared activities with others; mothers of boys tended to discuss comparisons of their children with peers more than mothers of girls did (Flannagan & Hardee, 1994). This perspective promises to shed new light on the nature of female development and represents a significant departure from more traditional views of gender development.

KEY THEME
Nature/Nurture

W e are currently witnessing a dilemma concerning gender-role socialization in our society. Feminist scholars in the 1970s and 1980s questioned the desirability of socializing children into differing roles on the basis of sex alone; that is, they advocated raising children in a nonsexist fashion (Bem, 1983; Pogrebin, 1980). Based on relational theories and research pointing out distinctive styles of male and female development, however, we might not be so quick to advocate gender-neutral socialization of our children (Jacklin & Reynolds, 1995).

CONTROVERSY: THINKING IT OVER

Is It Possible or Desirable to Raise Children in a Nonsexist Fashion?

Advocates of nonsexist child rearing point out that traditional sex typing encourages children to learn specific skills and roles that may be inconsistent with their interests or abilities. Sex typing, they argue, narrows the field of choices children can make, forcing them to choose among alternatives that limit the myriad possible behaviors available to human beings. How might parents raise their children in a nonsexist way? Sandra Bem (1983) suggests, first, that parents provide their children with information about the biological bases of gender at about the time children form their gender identities. Children should be apprised of the fact that genitals, not clothing, appearance, or behavior, determine gender. Second, parents should screen reading materials, television, and movies so that children have opportunities to view both sexes engaged in sex-typical and sex-atypical activities. Finally, Bem suggests that parents provide their children with a "sexism schema." According to Bem, just as we may teach our children to recognize that other families have social values (with regard to religion or politics, for example) that differ from those our families hold, we can teach children that other people may hold beliefs about the sexes that differ from our own.

Because gender is strongly emphasized in contemporary culture, however, raising children to be nonsexist may be an arduous, if not impossible, task. Children are exposed to powerful gender-stereotypical messages in their interactions with peers and teachers as well as from the media. Is it possible for parents to surmount such influential societal forces? Is imparting parental philosophies to children enough?

But even if we can successfully raise children in a nonsexist way, is it desirable to do so? As we just saw, many children who behave nontraditionally, especially boys who act in "feminine" ways, suffer significant negative consequences from their peers. What other societal changes must accompany shifts in parental child-rearing tactics so that children can feel comfortable about crossing gender boundaries? In particular, what can be done about the strong pressures peers and other social forces exert, especially on boys, to behave in sex-typed ways? In addition, if girls and boys truly do have different orientations during the process of development, each of which can be seen to have distinctive strengths, should parents work against those tendencies?

CHAPTER RECAP

SUMMARY OF DEVELOPMENTAL THEMES

NATURE/NURTURE   What roles do nature and nurture play in gender development?

According to some theorists, biological influences such as hormones and brain lateralization underlie sex differences in aggression and visual-spatial skill, and some experimental evidence is indeed consistent with such hypotheses. However, just as hormones, for example, can influence behavior, so can behavior influence levels of hormones. According to social learning theorists, the child's socialization experiences with parents and peers and in school contribute substantially to observed sex differences, as does the child's knowledge of gender-role stereotypes. Children learn about gender roles very early in life, well before actual sex differences in most behaviors are observed. Research also shows that parents, peers, and teachers treat boys and girls differently, providing support for the nurture position.

SOCIOCULTURAL INFLUENCE   How does the sociocultural context influence gender development?

Most cultures hold stereotypical beliefs about gender roles, although the specific characteristics associated with each sex can vary. The particular behaviors exhibited by males and females can also vary according to culture. Such findings demonstrate that although the tendency to stereotype is widespread, the characteristics associated with each sex are not necessarily fixed. Changes within American society, such as the increased proportion of women employed outside the home, underscore the idea that children's gender-role development can be affected by shifting sociocultural trends.

CHILD'S ACTIVE ROLE   How does the child play an active role in the process of gender development?

The child's active role in the construction of gender-based knowledge is emphasized in cognitive-developmental theories of gender development. For example, many children construct gender schemas based on their socialization experiences, schemas that in turn influence how they process gender-related information and how they themselves behave.

CONTINUITY/DISCONTINUITY   Is gender development continuous or discontinuous?

Theorists such as Lawrence Kohlberg describe gender development as a stagelike process. Kohlberg hypothesized that children progress through a sequence of attaining gender identity, gender stability, and gender constancy. In contrast, social learning theorists describe the cumulative and incremental effects of reinforcement and modeling on gender-role development. Research evaluating stage theories has confirmed that children pass through the general sequence of gender awareness outlined by Kohlberg.

INDIVIDUAL DIFFERENCES   How prominent are individual differences in gender development?

Some children acquire gender identity earlier than others; these children tend to behave in more sex-typed ways and have greater knowledge of gender stereotypes than children who acquire gender identity later in life. Later in childhood, some children tend to be gender schematic; that is, they tend to organize their world along sex-divided lines. These children may even distort information to make it consistent with their strong gender schemas. Finally, some children exhibit patterns of cross-gender behavior. These tendencies are usually met with negative feedback from peers, especially if the cross-gender child is a boy.

INTERACTION AMONG DOMAINS   How does gender development interact with development in other domains?

Attainments in cognition are thought to be related to many aspects of gender-role development. Bandura describes cognitive processes, such as attention, that influence which models, male or female, children will imitate. Kohlberg suggests that general cognitive advances pave the way for gender knowledge, such as gender constancy. By the same token, the child's state of gender-role development can influence cognitive processing. Gender-schematic children, for example, may show memory distortions consistent with their gender-role beliefs. Finally, a particular classification of gender role, androgyny, is associated with psychological health and popularity with peers.

SUMMARY OF TOPICS

■ GENDER STEREOTYPES VERSUS ACTUAL SEX DIFFERENCES

Gender stereotypes, beliefs about the behaviors and characteristics typical of females and males, exist in numerous cultures. Often identified male characteristics are *instrumental,* including traits such as independence and assertiveness, whereas identified female characteristics are *expressive,* emphasizing emotionality and sociability. In reality, however, male and female characteristics show more similarities than differences. Children become aware of gender stereotypes for many activities and traits during the preschool years, but their ideas become more flexible as they approach adolescence. That flexibility seems to decline later in adolescence.

In terms of quantifiable differences between the sexes, males are physically stronger but more vulnerable in infancy than females. Though past research showed that females had superior verbal skills and males excelled in mathematics and visual-spatial skills, recent studies suggest that verbal and mathematical skill differences have disappeared for the most part. Regarding social behavior, the most consistent finding is that males are more aggressive than females, particularly during early childhood. In addition, some evidence suggests that females are more skilled than males at decoding nonverbal social-emotional messages, such as the meanings of facial expressions.

■ THEORIES OF GENDER-ROLE DEVELOPMENT

Different theories of gender-role development have made unique contributions to our understanding of this phenomenon. Biological theories suggest that hormones, such as *androgens,* and brain lateralization help to explain sex differences in aggression and visual-spatial skill. Social learning theories claim that reinforcement and imitation of same-sex models who behave in sex-typical ways explain many sex differences. Cognitive-developmental theories stress how the child's growing awareness of and identification with his or her own sex—the successive notions of *gender identity, gender stability,* and *gender constancy*—influence sex typing. Alternatively, *gender schemas,* or cognitive constructs, are thought to influence gender-role development. Gender identity is usually formed by age three, an accomplishment that appears to be linked to sex-typed preferences in play activities and knowledge of stereotypes. Some children also tend to rely on gender schemas more than others as they process social information, a tendency that often makes them distort perceptions about sex-atypical behavior.

■ THE SOCIALIZATION OF GENDER ROLES

From birth onward, parents treat children differently on the basis of biological sex. Boys and girls are provided with sex-differentiated toys, and their parents tend to stress adherence to traditional gender-role norms. Fathers in particular appear concerned about their children's sex typing and exert an important influence on the development of sex-typed behavior in children. Parents are particularly upset when sons engage in sex-atypical behavior.

Children are perhaps the most ardent enforcers of gender-role norms. They develop a firm grasp on behaviors that are expected of their sex and enforce compliance with gender-role norms in their peers. Same-sex play and preferences for sex-typical toys and activities become the norm during the preschool and early elementary school years. These patterns of preferences persist at least through adolescence. Children who consistently behave in a *cross-gender* fashion are likely to become socially isolated from their peer groups.

Schools also exert an important influence on the development of sex typing in children. Teachers treat children differently in the classroom, focusing more attention on boys than girls. Boys and girls also acquire differing expectations about their academic skills. These separate expectations can influence the child's choice of academic courses and, ultimately, of occupation.

■ ALTERNATIVE CONCEPTUALIZATIONS OF GENDER

Androgyny is a gender-role orientation in which the individual possesses high levels of both feminine and masculine traits. Studies indicate that androgyny is associated with healthy psychological adjustment and may be linked to cognitive growth and the emergence of self-definition. The relational approach attempts to define the elements of female development that may be unique compared to male development. According to these theorists, females are more oriented toward seeking and maintaining relationships than are males; this quality has significance for other dimensions of psychological development.

14 THE FAMILY

Seven-year-old Joey looked at his loaded dinner plate and announced, "I'm not hungry. Can I just have dessert?" "No, you may not!" his embarrassed mother replied as she turned toward her house guest. "I can't think why he gets like this. He's stubborn as a mule." The guest wondered why no one mentioned that Joey, in full view of his mother, had eaten most of a gift box of cookies before dinner.

"I don't want this! It stinks! You stink!" Joey shouted. He pushed away his plate, got up from the table, and ran to the television, which he turned up to full volume.

"Turn that down this minute or go to your room!" his mother ordered. Joey ignored her. "He's been like this since his father and I split up," she told her guest in a lowered voice. "Everything's so different now. I feel like I have to be two parents instead of one. He used to be such a good boy." Spying Joey reaching for the cookie box, she warned, "Don't take that cookie!" Joey removed his hand from the box and gave his mother a mournful, pleading look. "All right, but just one!" she conceded. Joey took two and returned to the TV.

This episode represents but one brief experience in Joey's life, but the accumulation of experiences such as this within the context of the family can have a distinct effect on the developing child. Families are central to the process of **socialization,** the process by which children acquire the social knowledge, behaviors, and attitudes valued by the larger society. Parents, siblings, and others within the family unit are the people with whom the child usually spends the most time and forms the strongest emotional bonds, and they thus exert the most influence in the child's life.

The study of the impact of the family is no simple matter. For one thing, the child's experiences within the family can be affected by other factors, such as divorce or parental employment status, that can change the nature of interpersonal dynamics within the family. Joey's family experiences both before and after his parents' separation, for example, can have potentially long-lasting effects on his development. Moreover, the direction of influence within families runs along several paths. Just as parents and siblings affect the child's behavior, the child affects the reactions of other family members. Because the family experience includes fluid, constantly changing effects and outcomes for its various members, studying the influence of the family presents a special research challenge to developmental psychologists.

In a sense, virtually every domain of development is deeply influenced by the family environment. Cognition, moral awareness, gender identity, and emotional growth are all nurtured largely within the family. In this chapter we focus on the roles specific family members play in the child's social development, with special attention to adaptive and maladaptive patterns of interaction. We will also see how the family itself is a structure in flux, shaped by cultural values and shifting demographic trends such as divorce and maternal employment. The effects of these changes in family structure on the individual child's development are a major concern for developmental psychologists.

socialization Process by which children acquire the social knowledge, skills, and attitudes valued by the larger society.

UNDERSTANDING THE FAMILY

Historians, sociologists, and anthropologists who study the family as a social unit point to the changes in its structure and functions over the last two centuries. With the industrialization of nineteenth-century America, for example, the extended family, in which secondary relatives such as grandparents, aunts and uncles, or cousins lived in the same household as the primary family, gave way to the nuclear family, consisting solely of parents and their offspring living in a single household. Similarly, as we saw in Chapter 2, the modern notion that families are havens for nurturing the child's growth and development was not always prevalent. As we look back in history, we see that the family has been a changing social structure, and all signs indicate it will continue to take different shapes in the future to reflect larger social, economic, and historical trends.

The Demographics of the American Family

No one family structure typifies contemporary American society. The 1950s model of a two-parent family with two children and a nonworking mother no longer applies in today's circumstances. For example, as Figure 14.1 shows, only 69 percent of children younger than eighteen years lived with two parents in 1995, compared to 85 percent in 1970. Today 27 percent of American children live with only one parent (U.S. Bureau of the Census, 1996). A climbing divorce rate and the rise in single-parent births have contributed to this trend. Presently more than 50 percent of all marriages end in divorce (compared to about 15 percent in 1960), and more than 25 percent of all births are to single women (Bumpass, 1990; U.S. Bureau of the Census, 1996). Moreover, because adults now marry at later ages and more couples decide to have fewer children, many children today grow up with older parents and fewer siblings (Rossi, 1987). Finally, more than 70 percent of married women with children younger than eighteen years work outside the home, compared to about 45 percent in 1975. All of these changes in family structure have distinct implications for the child's experiences within the family.

KEY THEME
Sociocultural Influence

A Systems Approach

Many child development researchers have found it fruitful to focus on family dynamics, the interactions among all members of the group, rather than on the structure of the family per se as they study the impact of the family. An important influence on

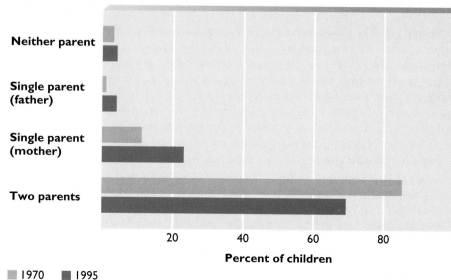

1970   1995

Source: Adapted from U.S. Bureau of the Census, 1996.

FIGURE 14.1

Demographic Changes in Family Structure

The percentage of children living with two parents has declined since 1970, and the percentage living with a single parent (most frequently the mother) has increased dramatically. About one-fourth of American children live with a single parent. The higher rates of divorce and single-parent births have contributed to this trend.

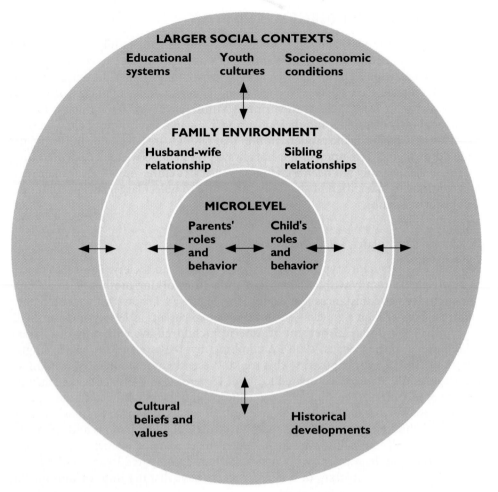

FIGURE 14.2

The Systems Model of the Family

According to systems theorists, reciprocal influences among family members occur at three levels: the individual or micro-level, the family environment, and the larger social context. At the micro-level, parent and child influence each other directly. Within the family, relationships among particular individuals, such as husband and wife, can affect interactions with children. Finally, larger social factors, such as the presence of economic stress, can affect parent-child relations. The individual child's development is thus embedded in this network of multidirectional interactions.

Source: Adapted from Peterson & Rollins, 1987.

contemporary thinking about the family is **systems theory**. The premise is that all members influence one another simultaneously and the interactions flow in a circular, reciprocal manner. In systems theory (see Figure 14.2), the individual child's development is understood as being embedded in the complex network of multidirectional interactions among all family members (Belsky, 1981; Bronfenbrenner, 1979, 1986).

Systems theory assumes families undergo periods of stability and change. The family tends to adapt to maintain a state of *homeostasis,* or equilibrium. Thus, as children attain milestones such as going to school or entering adolescence, the family system must readjust to absorb the child's new routines or demands for independence. At other times families may experience crises, such as financial hardship, moving, or divorce. In these instances, changing external circumstances require the child and all other family members to adapt to the new situation. Systems theory, then, regards families as dynamic, self-regulating social groups (Minuchin, 1988).

Families usually contain several subsystems, such as the relations maintained between spouses, among siblings, and between parent and child. A single family member is usually a member of more than one subsystem at the same time. The child has a relationship with each parent as well as with one or more siblings; mothers and fathers are spouses as well as parents. The quality of each of these separate relationships can have an impact on other relationships. Thus, for example, mothers who feel their marriages are close and confiding tend to be warmer and more sensitive with their infants; fathers who express similar feelings are more positive about their paternal role (Cox et al., 1989). Similarly, when parents have high-quality marital relationships, their relationships with their adolescent children are warmer and their children show more favorable psychological adjustment (Harold et al., 1997; Miller

systems theory Model for understanding the family that emphasizes the reciprocal interactions among various members.

et al., 1993). Siblings have more positive interactions with one another, too (MacKinnon, 1988). Within the systems model, family members have reciprocal influences on one another, and there are several layers of such interactions.

The family system itself is embedded in larger social networks, including the economic, political, legal, and educational forces that are part of the larger culture. Events in the workplace, school, and other extrafamilial settings can affect individual family members and hence the interactions that occur within the family unit. When one or both parents becomes unemployed, for example, the family experiences stress that often is expressed in increased conflict between parents and children (Flanagan, 1990). In other instances, both parents may work outside the home, which requires children to function independently, cooking their own meals or performing other household tasks. The *social ecology* of child development—that is, the impact of broad sociocultural factors on the child's social, cognitive, and emotional growth—has been given increasing emphasis by developmental psychologists.

KEY THEME
Sociocultural Influence

PARENTS AND SOCIALIZATION

In most cultures, the primary agents of the child's socialization are parents. As we will see in the next two chapters, teachers, peers, and the media also play a significant role; but perhaps no other individuals in the child's life have the powerful influence on future behaviors, attitudes, and personality that parents do.

Parents affect children's socialization in three primary ways. First, they socialize their children through direct training, providing information or reinforcement for the behaviors they find acceptable or desirable. Parents may, for example, encourage their children to share with playmates or instruct them on how to become acquainted with an unfamiliar peer. Second, as they interact with their children, parents serve as important models for the children's attitudes, beliefs, and actions. For example, parents who are warm, engaging, and verbally stimulating tend to have children who are popular in school. Finally, parents manage other aspects of their children's lives that in turn can influence children's social development. Parents choose the neighborhood in which the family lives; they also may enroll children in sports programs, arrange birthday parties, and invite children's friends to spend the night, all of which influence children's peer networks (Parke et al., 1988).

Of course, parents' major concerns and activities shift as the child develops. Parents of infants focus on caregiving activities and helping the child to learn such skills as self-feeding, dressing, and toileting. By the time their child is two years old, parents begin more deliberate attempts at socialization. Parents of preschoolers help their children to regulate their emotions—to control angry outbursts, for example—and start to instill social skills, such as polite forms of speech and sharing during play with peers. Parents of elementary school children are likely to be concerned with their children's academic achievement. When their children approach adolescence, most parents encourage independent, rational, and value-based decision making as their youngsters prepare to enter their own adult lives.

Parental roles also shift with development. Throughout early childhood, parents closely monitor much of their children's activity. Once children enter school, parents play less of a supervisory role. They begin to expect their children to be cooperative members of the family by avoiding conflicts and sharing in household tasks. Parents and children begin to negotiate as they make decisions and solve family problems. Finally, during adolescence, parents observe children's participation in the larger social world, in school and community activities and close personal relationships with peers. While parents are encouraging independence in some domains, such as school achievement, they may also be exerting more control in other domains, such as their children's social activities (Maccoby, 1984b; Maccoby & Martin, 1983; McNally, Eisenberg, & Harris, 1991).

As this quick sketch suggests, the child's own development often precipitates shifts in parental roles. As the child's language and cognitive skills mature, parents place greater expectations on her social communication behaviors. As she enters school,

Research has shown that parents who expect mature behavior from their children, provide explanations for their requests, and are supportive and warm in their interactions have children who display instrumental competence. These parents display what is called an *authoritative style.*

authoritarian parent   Parent who relies on coercive techniques to discipline the child and displays a low level of nurturance.

permissive parent   Parent who sets few limits on the child's behavior.

authoritative parent   Parent who sets limits on a child's behavior using reasoning and explanation and displays a high degree of nurturance.

instrumental competence   Child's display of independence, self-control, achievement orientation, and cooperation.

parents nurture greater independence. The physical changes associated with puberty often signal to parents that more mature child-adult interactions, such as deferring at times to the child's wishes rather than rigidly restricting his activities, are warranted (Steinberg, 1981). As systems theory suggests, the individual child's development within the family represents an ongoing give-and-take between child and parent, necessitating continual readjustment by all members to reinstate family equilibrium.

Styles of Parenting

Even the casual observer of parents interacting with their children in public places such as parks, shopping malls, and supermarkets will notice markedly different styles of parental behavior. Some parents are extremely controlling, using crisp, firm commands devoid of explanations to restrict their children's behavior. Others seem not to notice as their charges create chaos and pandemonium. Researchers have established that the pattern of interactions a parent adopts is an important variable in influencing the child's later development.

In a landmark series of observational studies, Diana Baumrind (1971, 1973) recorded the interpersonal and behavioral styles of nursery school children as they engaged in normal school activities. She also watched as they worked on a series of standardized problem-solving tasks, such as completing a set of puzzles. In addition, Baumrind gathered information on parenting styles by observing how mothers interacted with their children in both play and structured teaching settings, watching parents and their children in the home, and interviewing parents about their child-rearing practices. The children and parents were observed again when children were eight or nine years old. Based on these extensive observations, Baumrind identified several distinct patterns of parenting.

Some parents, Baumrind found, were extremely restrictive and controlling. They valued respect for authority and strict obedience to their commands and relied on coercive techniques, such as threats or physical punishment, rather than on reasoning or explanation, to regulate their children's actions. They were also less nurturant toward their children than other parents in the study. Baumrind identified this group as **authoritarian parents**. The second parenting style belonged to the group she called **permissive parents**. These parents set few limits and made few demands for mature behavior from their children. Children were permitted to make their own decisions about many routine activities such as TV viewing, bedtime, and mealtimes, for example. Permissive parents tended to be either moderately nurturant or cool and uninvolved. The third group of parents was high on both control and nurturance. These **authoritative parents** expected their children to behave in a mature fashion but tended to use rewards more than punishments to achieve their ends. They communicated their expectations clearly and provided explanations to help their children understand the reasons for their requests. They also listened to what their children had to say and encouraged a dialogue with them. Authoritative parents were distinctly supportive and warm in their interactions with their children. Figure 14.3 summarizes the characteristics of these three parental styles as well as a fourth style, *uninvolved parents,* which has been described in later research and will be discussed shortly.

Baumrind found a cluster of behavioral characteristics in children linked with each parental style. The offspring of authoritative parents were friendly with peers, cooperative with adults, independent, energetic, and achievement oriented. They also displayed a high degree of self-control. This set of characteristics often is termed **instrumental competence**. In marked contrast, children of authoritarian and permissive parents did not exhibit the social responsibility and independence associated with instrumental competence. Children who had authoritarian parents appeared unhappy; also, boys tended to be aggressive, whereas girls were likely to be dependent. Children of permissive parents, on the other hand, were low on self-control and self-reliance.

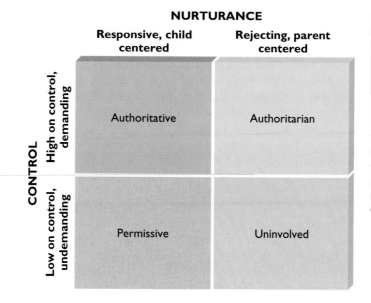

NURTURANCE

	Responsive, child centered	Rejecting, parent centered
High on control, demanding	Authoritative	Authoritarian
Low on control, undemanding	Permissive	Uninvolved

CONTROL

Source: Adapted from Maccoby & Martin, 1983.

FIGURE 14.3

Patterns of Parenting as a Function of Control and Nurturance

Four parenting styles can be identified in terms of the extent to which parents set limits on the child's behavior (control) and the level of nurturance and responsiveness they provide.

KEY THEME
Interaction Among Domains

The effects of parenting style extend to other dimensions of child development and reach into the adolescent years. Authoritarian parenting, especially with its use of coercive techniques for controlling behavior, is associated with less advanced moral reasoning and less prosocial behavior (Boyes & Allen, 1993; Hoffman, 1970; Krevans & Gibbs, 1996), lower self-esteem (Loeb, Horst, & Horton, 1980), and poorer adjustment to starting school (Barth, 1989). Extremely controlling parenting and the use of coercive techniques are also associated with higher levels of aggression in children (Maccoby & Martin, 1983), poor peer relations (Pettit et al., 1996; Putallaz, 1987), and lower school achievement in adolescence (Dornbusch et al., 1987). In contrast, by the time children reach adolescence, those with authoritative parents show more prosocial behaviors, fewer problem behaviors such as substance abuse, greater academic achievement, and higher self-confidence than adolescents whose parents use other parenting styles (Baumrind, 1991; Lamborn et al., 1991; Radziszewska et al., 1996).

Researchers have also identified a fourth parenting style: the **uninvolved,** or *neglectful,* **parent** (Maccoby & Martin, 1983). Like some parents in Baumrind's permissive group, these parents seem to be uncommitted to their parental role and emotionally detached from their children. Often these parents give greater priority to their own needs and preferences than to the child's. These parents may be uninterested in events at the child's school, unfamiliar with his playmates, and have only infrequent conversations with him (Pulkkinen, 1982). Uninvolved parenting is related to children's lower self-esteem (Loeb, Horst, & Horton, 1980), heightened aggression (Hatfield, Ferguson, & Alpert, 1967), and lower control over impulsive behavior (Block, 1971). As older adolescents, children with uninvolved parents show more maladjustment, lack of creativity, and greater alcohol consumption than adolescents who experienced other parenting styles (Weiss & Schwarz, 1996). Researchers are beginning to conclude that uninvolved parenting may present the greatest risks of all to healthy long-term development (Steinberg et al., 1994).

The most desirable developmental outcomes are associated with authoritative parenting, which has two key characteristics: setting limits on the child's behavior and responding to the child's needs and actions with warmth and nurturance. These themes echo the discussion of sensitive parenting and attachment presented in Chapter 11. Why does authoritative parenting work so well? Several explanations are possible. First, when parents make demands for mature behavior from their children, they make explicit the responsibilities individuals have toward one another when

uninvolved parent Parent who is emotionally detached from the child and focuses on his or her own needs as opposed to the child's.

they live in social groups. When parents set forth clear, consistent guidelines for behavior, they make the child's job of sorting out the social world much easier. Second, when parental demands are accompanied by reasonable explanations, the child is more likely to accept the limitations on her actions. Third, when parents take into account the child's responses and show affection, he is likely to acquire a sense of control over his actions and derive the sense that he has worth. One study confirms, for example, that adolescents who have authoritative parents have a healthy sense of autonomy and self-reliance and feel a sense of control over their lives (Steinberg, Elmen, & Mounts, 1989). Thus, the net outcome of authoritative parenting is a competent child who shows successful psychological adjustment.

Strategies of Parental Control

Parents control their children's behavior for a variety of reasons, ranging from protecting their safety to regulating socially unacceptable behaviors such as temper tantrums and aggression against others. Furthermore, we have seen that successful parenting includes warmth and responsiveness, but setting limits on the child's behavior as well. In this section, we take a closer look at the specific techniques parents use to manage their children's actions.

KEY THEME
Child's Active Role

How and When Do Parents Discipline?   As their children progress from age one to three years, parents decrease their reliance on physical means of control, such as pulling the child away from a forbidden object (for example, a stove) or forcibly holding his hand, and more frequently use verbal commands, reprimands, and persuasion. These changes in parental control parallel children's expressions of noncompliance. Initially, children display passive or defiant behaviors, such as whining and temper tantrums, to protest parental control. Older preschoolers attempt to negotiate with parents ("I'll do it later, OK?" or "I have a better idea!"). Some researchers believe the parental shift to discipline based on reasoning is derived from the child's active bargaining and parents' recognition of the child's growing autonomy (Kuczynski et al., 1987). Interestingly, even among two-year-olds, compliance on the part of the child is associated with maternal use of persuasion and suggestion, whereas defiance is associated with maternal use of power assertion (Crockenberg & Litman, 1990). Perhaps as their own experience in child rearing grows, parents come to recognize that control techniques based on reasoning often get the best results. Those suspicions turn out to be correct; when mothers emphasize the "do's" rather than the "don'ts" of behaviors they expect of their toddlers, their children show greater compliance and fewer behavior problems at age five (Kuczynski & Kochanska, 1995).

A survey of middle-class mothers and fathers of seventh- and ninth-graders yielded information on parenting strategies with older children (Smith, 1988). Parents were asked to recall any efforts to influence their children in the past year in such areas as choosing subjects in school, the amount of time spent doing homework, choice of peer associates, and several other common situations in which parents and children often disagree. The two most prevalent techniques on which parents relied were commands—that is, making imperative statements without threats ("Go clean your room, please!")—and self-oriented induction. *Self-oriented induction* consists of parental suggestions about the costs and rewards to the child of his behavior ("Spending more time on your homework will boost your grades"). When parents were concerned with producing an immediate result, such as when household chores were to be done or a curfew was being set, they issued commands. When long-term consequences of the child's actions were involved, such as in decisions relating to school, parents opted for self-oriented induction. Thus, at least for this middle-class sample of parents and children living in intact families, many parents usually relied on their legitimate power and on reasoning, rather than on physical coercion or threats, to direct their children's behavior.

How often do parents exercise their authority over children? Obviously, the extent of parental control varies as a function of the age of the child, parental child-rearing philosophy, and the specific behaviors the child displays. Observations of family interactions in the home, however, tell us that mothers of preschool children issue commands or disapprove of their behaviors about once every three to four minutes and these children disobey about 25 percent of the time (Wahler & Dumas, 1989). As children grow older and become more attuned to parental expectations and more capable of regulating their own behaviors, the need for parental control diminishes or changes.

Punishment In recent decades, the most widely discussed parental control technique has been *punishment,* the administration of an aversive stimulus or withdrawal of rewards to decrease the frequency of undesirable behaviors. A form of power assertion, punishment can include spanking, sharp verbal threats, or the loss of such privileges as TV viewing time or playtime with friends.

Laboratory studies carried out in the tradition of learning theory show that certain ways of administering punishment are more effective than others. One important factor is making sure the punishment closely follows the child's transgression so that the child makes the connection between her behavior and the consequences. Another powerful factor is providing an explanation for why the behavior is not desirable (Parke, 1969). The effectiveness of punishment also depends on the consistency with which it is applied. As we saw in the case of Joey and the cookies at the beginning of the chapter, children become particularly disobedient and aggressive when parents prohibit a behavior on one occasion and permit it on another. Consistency among caregivers (**interagent consistency**) and consistency of one caregiver from one occasion to the next (**intra-agent consistency**) are both important in giving children clear, unambiguous messages about acceptable and unacceptable behaviors (Deur & Parke, 1970; Sawin & Parke, 1979).

Although punishment can inhibit a child's misbehavior, many psychologists believe physical tactics such as spanking or hitting should not be used at all. In a 1985 survey of three thousand parents, Murray Straus and Richard Gelles found that 90 percent of parents of three- and four-year-olds reported striking their children in the previous year, as did 75 percent of parents of nine- and ten-year-olds. Infants and adolescents were spanked less often (Straus & Gelles, 1986). However, even half of the adolescents reported being hit by their parents, with an average of six to eight times in a year (Straus & Donnelly, 1993). Thus, in the United States many parents resort to physical punishment, at least on occasion, to control their children's behavior.

Physical punishment does modify the child's behavior in the short run, but its use is also associated with many negative outcomes, at least among European American groups (Deater-Deckard et al., 1996). The most serious is aggression, especially among boys (Martin, 1975; Rollins & Thomas, 1979; Weiss et al., 1992). For example, Dan Olweus (1980) found that aggression in a sample of adolescent Swedish boys was related to maternal reports of having been hostile and rejecting during their sons' childhood. In addition, parents who reported using physical punishment, threats, and violent outbursts had more aggressive sons than those who did not use such techniques. Many experts believe parents who use punishment serve as models of aggression for their children (Parke & Slaby, 1983). Children may learn that hitting, kicking, or pinching is an acceptable method for resolving conflicts. Moreover, especially when children receive insufficient attention from their parents, the spotlight placed on them when they are being punished actually may be a positive reinforcement. As a consequence, children maintain the behavior parents were trying to eliminate. Another undesirable outcome is that children who are punished frequently eventually avoid the punishing agents (Redd, Morris, & Martin, 1975). Parents are likely to be more effective as socializing agents if their children maintain good relations with them than if the children become physically and emotionally removed. Finally, under some circumstances, an overreliance on physical punishment can set the stage for child abuse. Parental acts of abuse often start out as attempts to discipline the child, and abusive parents rely more on power assertion, including physical punishment, than do nonabusive parents (Oldershaw, Walters, & Hall, 1986; Parke & Collmer, 1975). Among abusive families, a light slap can escalate into a physical assault on the child more quickly than it would in nonabusive families.

interagent consistency Consistency in application of disciplinary strategies among different caregivers.

intra-agent consistency Consistency in a single caregiver's application of discipline from one situation to the next.

After her dinner guest left and Joey was put to bed (with yet another struggle), his mother sat exhausted on the couch and thought about the difficulties she was having in controlling her child's behavior. Her embarrassment in front of her guest was just a small problem compared to the negative cycle in which she and Joey always seemed to end up. She loved her child beyond words, but things were just too far out of control and she needed help. A friend had suggested that she see a clinical psychologist for advice. She went to her dresser drawer and pulled out the psychologist's card; she would call Dr. Nagle in the morning.

At the visit with Dr. Nagle two weeks later, Joey's mother described some examples of her son's noncompliant behavior. Dr. Nagle nodded knowingly and then spoke of the need for parents to maintain reasonable control over their child's behavior. "Just how can I do that?" asked Joey's mother. "I don't believe in spanking. What else can I do to get him to listen to me?" Dr. Nagle then proceeded to outline the elements of a parent behavior management program.

RESEARCH APPLIED TO PARENTING

Managing Noncompliant Children

One of the most common problems parents face is the oppositional behavior their children show, often beginning at age two or three. A parent makes a request (e.g., "Time to go to bed"), and the child simply refuses to comply, adding a loud "No!" for emphasis. The child's response may reflect a healthy, growing desire for independence and self-assertion. But this pattern, if repeated for a length of time, can quickly lead to conflicts with parents and frustration on their part. For the child, persistent noncompliance has the potential to lead to major behavior problems, including aggression.

Rex Forehand and his colleagues (Forehand & McMahon, 1981; Wierson & Forehand, 1994) have described some basic behavior management techniques that can help parents control children's negative behaviors without resorting to spanking or physical punishment. They are based on having parents avoid two kinds of traps: a negative reinforcement trap and a positive reinforcement trap. In the first case, a parent issues a command, but the child whines, protests, and does not listen. If the parent gives in, the child has received a negative reinforcement, learning that whining will remove an aversive stimulus (the parent's commands). In the second case, the child's noncompliance receives a positive consequence—that is, extra attention—if parents spend a lot of time and effort talking with her about why she should obey. Therefore, parents should try to adhere to the following principles:

1. *Attend to the child's appropriate behavior each day.* Children will learn that attention and rewards follow when they behave as parents expect them to. When attending to the child's desirable behavior, avoid using commands, questions, and criticisms, all of which are associated with the child's noncompliance.

2. *Ignore inappropriate behaviors that are minor, such as crankiness and whining.* The lack of attention should cause the behavior to decrease.

3. *Give clear, succinct commands and reward the child with verbal praise for following them.* Do not engage in a long discussion with the child (which amounts to too much attention), but make sure the child understands what is expected.

4. *Use a technique called time-out if the child does not comply with a command.* Remove the child from all possible sources of reward, even subtle or accidental ones. Take him immediately to a quiet, neutral place and leave him alone there until a short period of time, usually two to five minutes, has elapsed. Time-out has been found to be effective in reducing or eliminating a variety of troublesome behaviors in children, including temper tantrums, fighting, and self-injurious behaviors (Varni, 1983). Time-out also gives both children and parents the opportunity to "cool down" after all parties have become aroused.

One effective technique for managing a child's behavior is the use of "time-out," sending the child to a neutral area for a specific amount of time after she or he misbehaves. Time-out has been found to reduce or eliminate a variety of behavior problems among children.

The techniques just described have been found to significantly reduce noncompliance in children who were referred to a clinic for their behavior problems. Not only did their behavior improve relative to their pretreatment baseline; it also compared favorably with that of a group of control children who had not been referred to the clinic. In addition, parents were found to use the techniques they learned with other siblings (Forehand & Long, 1988). Although the focus of this intervention was on families experiencing serious difficulties with child behavior management, many parents can undoubtedly benefit from using the techniques just outlined.

The Role of Attributions   *Attribution theory* suggests that an individual's behavior depends on the inferences the person makes about other people's actions: why they behave as they do, what traits they possess, and so on. Theodore Dix and Joan Grusec (1985) hypothesize that the kinds of attributions parents make about their children, particularly the causes of their children's behaviors, will influence the parenting strategies they adopt. If, for example, a parent believes his three-year-old is throwing a tantrum at the dinner table because she wants her dessert immediately, he will probably insist that she first eat all her vegetables. If, on the other hand, the parent suspects the child is ill, he will probably remove the child from the dinner table and nurture and console her.

Figure 14.4 presents a schematic diagram of Dix and Grusec's (1985) attribution model of socialization. The flow of events proceeds as follows. First, the parent observes the child's behavior and judges whether it is typical for the child or normative for her age group. The parent assesses whether the child has the skills, knowledge, and motive to behave intentionally in a certain way. Do most three-year-olds throw tantrums to get dessert? Is throwing a tantrum a typical behavior for that child? Parents make a causal attribution about the child's intentions. Next, parents' attributions affect their emotional and behavioral responses to the child. Parents become more upset and act more forcefully if they believe the child intends to misbehave—in this case, screaming for the explicit purpose of getting dessert. Finally, if parents have made the correct attribution, they will be effective in controlling the child. But if they

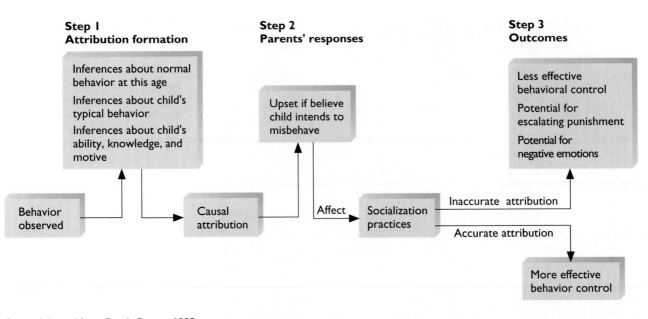

Step 1
Attribution formation

Step 2
Parents' responses

Step 3
Outcomes

Source: Adapted from Dix & Grusec, 1985.

FIGURE 14.4

The Attribution Model of Socialization

Dix and Grusec hypothesize that parents' judgments about the child's intentionality in misbehaving are critical in determining their response. Parents become more upset if they believe the child intended to transgress and select more forceful control strategies than they do if they believe the transgression was unintentional. If their attributions are correct, they will effectively control behavior. If they make an incorrect attribution, however, they will be less effective, may escalate the level of punishment, and may produce negative emotions in themselves and the child.

KEY THEME
Child's Active Role

---

control theory Hypothesis about parent-child interactions suggesting that the intensity of one partner's behavior affects the intensity of the other's response.

---

are wrong, the child may continue to misbehave, and both parents and child may feel negative emotions rising.

To examine the influence of attributions, Dix and his colleagues asked mothers and fathers of four-, eight-, and twelve-year-olds to react to several vignettes of child misconduct. In one story, for example, the actor fails to obey his mother's request to clean up the living room, an explicit violation of a norm. In another, the central character fails to act altruistically and eats candy while a boy without money to buy a snack looks on. All characters were represented as the same age and sex as the parent's own child. The results showed that parents of older children (who also heard stories about older children) made more attributions of the child's intentionality than parents of younger children (Dix et al., 1986). In a second, similar study, parents were more upset when they believed a child's transgressions were intentional or controllable. Furthermore, the more upset they were, the more important they thought it was to respond forcefully to the child's actions (Dix, Ruble, & Zambarano, 1989).

Parents' cognitions about the reasons for their children's behaviors may stem from their own experiences as children. If they were raised by authoritarian parents, they may have developed a tendency to blame others' personality types for observed behaviors and, eventually, their own children for the misdeeds the children perform. Parents' attachments to *their* parents and how they interpret those relationships may also play a role. For example, in one study, parents who recalled their attachment relationships as being ambivalent were found to be more likely to attribute misdeeds to the personalities of their children (Grusec & Mammone, 1995). Thus, how parents think about their children—which is rooted, in part, in their own childhood experiences—can influence how they act toward them.

Children's Influence on Parenting Strategies   The attribution model described here suggests that a child's behaviors may set in motion a series of parental judgments about the child's intentions and how the parent should respond. Another perspective on how the child influences the parent's choice of control strategies is provided by Richard Bell (Bell, 1971; Bell & Harper, 1977). In his **control theory,** Bell suggests that parents and children have upper and lower limits of tolerance for the types of behavior each shows the other. When the behavior of one approaches the other's upper limit, the recipient tries to reduce the excessive behavior with increasing levels of intensity. Thus, for example, a parent whose son is having a temper tantrum might first try to talk to him, then remove him to his room, and finally resort to physical punishment. Likewise, if the child's behavior approaches the parent's lower limits—in the child's shyness or withdrawal at the doctor's office, for example—the parent may try to stimulate the child by coaching her to speak and then promising her a reward if she vocalizes.

Control theory implies that when children's misbehavior pushes parents to their upper limits, parents will respond with more forceful and firmer control techniques. Furthermore, some children may transgress to this extent more frequently than others. Support for this idea comes from a study of six-to-eleven-year-old boys, sixteen normal and sixteen classified as conduct disordered due to their persistent aggression, fire setting, truancy, or temper tantrums. Mothers of conduct-disordered children were observed as they interacted with their own child, another conduct-disordered child, and a normal child. Similarly, mothers of normal children interacted with their own child, another normal child, and a conduct-disordered child. Mothers were unaware of the classification of children who were not their own. The researchers coded the frequency of the mothers' positive and negative behaviors as well as the number of requests they made for a change in the child's behavior. Both groups of mothers made more negative responses and requests to the conduct-disordered children than to the normal children. Thus, it was the type of child, not the type of mother, that determined the tone of the interaction (Anderson, Lytton, & Romney, 1986). It very well could be that children who evidence a persistent behavioral style of pushing parents to their "upper limits" precipitate a pattern of authoritarian, power-assertive parenting.

Problems in Parenting

There is no doubt that being a parent presents special rewards but also distinct challenges. In some instances, such extreme maladaptive styles of interaction develop between parent and child that physical and psychological harm can occur to both. Understanding the dynamics of these families is essential to any attempt at intervention and also provides an even greater understanding of how all families, both healthy and dysfunctional, work as systems.

Attentional Deficits and Problems in Parenting   Instead of assuming that parents in dysfunctional families use poor child management strategies, Robert Wahler and Jean Dumas (1984, 1989) suggest that troubled families experience stresses from the larger social system that make parents inattentive to the dynamics of child care. For example, a mother who is concerned about marital or financial problems will be hard pressed to attend closely to her child's behavior or to the effects on the child of her own parenting behaviors. In an evaluation of the long-term effects of a skills-based parent training program, Dumas and Wahler (1983) found that the program's success or failure was closely tied to measures of socioeconomic status and social isolation. Parents who were removed from contacts outside the family and were subject to the greatest financial strain were least likely to succeed with the training program.

According to the *attentional deficit model,* parents may know about good parenting practices or may learn them readily, but they often fail to apply them. Because they are distracted by other family problems, such parents typically overlook the child's positive behaviors or make hasty judgments that their child is misbehaving. Stressed parents also develop a limited repertoire of responses to their children. Instead of experimenting with various child management techniques to determine the most effective one, they fall back on stereotypical, repetitive methods that are often coercive. Parental depression may add to the problem. Several researchers have found that depressed mothers are especially likely to mislabel their child's behavior (Brody & Forehand, 1986; Greist, Wells, & Forehand, 1979).

Wahler and Dumas (1989) believe any long-term parent intervention program should include the following elements: (1) training parents to modify their habits so that they focus on the child's prosocial as well as aversive behaviors; (2) providing parents with coping strategies for external stressors, such as loss of employment or financial hardship; and (3) offering social support networks that assist parents with the day-to-day problems of living. In other words, by providing parents with ways to cope with external stress, clinicians and counselors can help them refocus on more positive ways to interact with their children.

Antisocial Behavior

Some children show abnormally high levels of aggression, especially as they enter the teenage years. They may lie, steal, engage in physical fights, and get into trouble with the law. The magnitude of this social problem is reflected in some disturbing statistics. In the past decade, the number of juveniles arrested for violent crime in the United States has increased by 75 percent, and juvenile violent crime has risen at a more rapid rate than for adults (Children's Defense Fund, 1996). The causes of antisocial behavior are, of course, complex. However, one place to begin exploring this problem lies within the dynamics of the family. Gerald Patterson and his colleagues (Patterson, 1982, 1986; Patterson, Reid, & Dishion, 1992) conducted extensive longitudinal studies of boys who exhibited pathological aggression and concluded that they acquired their behavior from routine family interactions in which both parents and children engaged in coercive behavior.

In Patterson's studies, preadolescent boys labeled as highly aggressive by schools, courts, or the families themselves were compared to nonaggressive boys from "normal" families over a period of several months. Detailed observations were made of family interactions in the home, including the sequences of behaviors displayed by parents, the target children, and their siblings. Patterson learned that the families of antisocial boys were characterized by high levels of aggressive interaction that rewarded coercive behaviors. When younger, the antisocial boys exhibited minor negative behaviors, such as whining, teasing, or yelling, in response to the aggression of another family member. About 70 percent of these behaviors were reinforced by the acquiescence of the child's interaction partner; in other words, the parent or sibling backed down, and the submission negatively reinforced the child's aggression. At other times, parental attention to the child's aggression was positively reinforcing. In addition, although parents were observed to nag, scold, or threaten their children, they seldom followed through on their threats. Such sequences between the target child and other family members occurred as often as hundreds of times each day in the aggressive families. Over time, the target boys' aggression escalated in frequency and progressed to physical assaults.

At this point, many parents attempted to control their sons' aggressive behaviors, but in doing so they too became highly aggressive. The chains of coercion increased in duration to form long bursts of negative interactions and often resulted in hitting between parent and child. After extended experience in these maladaptive familial exchanges, boys became out of control and acted violently in settings outside the home, such as the school. Aggression in school was related, in turn, to poor peer relations and academic failure, adding to the chain of negative events in the boys' lives.

Can such extreme patterns of aggression be controlled? Patterson and his colleagues have intervened in the maladaptive interactions of aggressive families by training parents in basic child management skills (Patterson et al., 1975). They focused on teaching parents to use discipline more effectively by dispensing more positive reinforcements for prosocial behaviors, using reasoning, disciplining consistently, and setting clear limits on even minor acts of aggression. Children significantly decreased their rates of deviant behavior after only a few weeks, and the results were maintained for as long as twelve months after the initial training period (Patterson & Fleischman, 1979). As an added benefit, parents' perceptions of their children became more positive (Patterson & Reid, 1973).

It would be too simplistic to conclude that maladaptive patterns of interactions with parents are the sole causes of antisocial behavior in children. As we will see in the next two chapters, antisocial behavior may be influenced by the peers with whom a child associates and even by the extent to which he or she watches violent television programs. Nonetheless, since children's primary contact with socialization agents is within the family, it is important to consider the role family dynamics plays in this developmental problem.

Child Abuse In 1994, more than 3 million children in the United States were reported to be abused or neglected (Children's Defense Fund, 1996). In fact, these statistics may represent an underestimate, because many cases of abuse are not reported (Emery, 1989). Aside from the immediate physical and psychological consequences of abuse, children who are the victims of family violence are predisposed to a number of developmental problems. Maltreated infants and toddlers are more likely to be anxiously attached to their mothers than are children who are not maltreated (Egeland & Sroufe, 1981a; Schneider-Rosen et al., 1985). These children are thus vulnerable to the social, emotional, and cognitive impairments associated with insecure attachment. Preschool and school-age children with a history of abuse score lower on tests of cognitive maturity and manifest low self-esteem and school learning problems (Aber & Allen, 1987; Barahal, Waterman, & Martin, 1981; Eckenrode, Laird, & Doris, 1993; Hoffman-Plotkin & Twentyman, 1984). Emotionally, they may display withdrawal and passivity or, on the other hand, aggressive, oppositional patterns of behavior, patterns that may be linked to their generally poor relationships with peers (Martin & Beezley, 1976; Salzinger et al., 1993). They also frequently display symptoms of clinical depression (Sternberg et al., 1993). Finally, abused and neglected children are at risk for delinquency and violent criminal behavior in adulthood (Widom, 1989) and may be prone to become abusive parents. In one study, women who had been abused as children were followed for a period of three years. Seventy percent were observed to maltreat their children or provide borderline care. Among women who were not abused, only one did not provide adequate care (Egeland, Jacobvitz, & Papatola, 1987).

The causes of abuse are neither simple nor easily ameliorated. Research on the interaction patterns in abusive families suggests that they differ in several respects from those in nonabusive families. Perhaps most significantly, parents in abusive families tend to rely on coercive or negative strategies to modify their children's behavior, even for routine or mild discipline problems. In general, members of abusive families interact infrequently with one another, and when they do, the tone of the interaction is negative. In one study, mothers in abusive families displayed 40 percent fewer positive interactions and 67 percent more negative interactions with their children than nonabusive mothers (Burgess & Conger, 1978). In another study, abusive and nonabusive mothers were observed as they engaged in a sequence of preparing a meal, playing, and cleaning up with their preschool-age children. Abusive mothers relied heavily on power-assertive techniques, such as threats, humiliation, or physical contact, to alter their children's behavior, whereas nonabusive mothers used predominantly positive strategies, including reasoning, bargaining, or modeling. Abusive mothers issued more than twice as many commands to their children as nonabusive mothers and also were inconsistent in reinforcing their children's compliance. Whereas the nonabusive mothers positively reinforced every instance of their children's obedience to a request, abusive mothers dispensed positive and negative reinforcements with equal frequency (Oldershaw, Walters, & Hall, 1986). As we saw earlier, inconsistent punishment usually leads to the persistence of undesirable behaviors in children.

Certain characteristics of children are also more commonly observed in abusive families. Parents often describe the abused child as irritable, difficult to put to sleep,

KEY THEME
Interaction Among Domains

KEY THEME
Child's Active Role

and prone to excessive crying (Ounsted, Oppenheimer, & Lindsay, 1974). A group at special risk for abuse is premature infants, who tend to have high-pitched, aversive cries and a less attractive appearance (Parke & Collmer, 1975). Abusive parents become especially sensitized to some of the child's objectionable behaviors and show heightened emotional reactivity to the child's cries or noncompliance (Frodi & Lamb, 1980; Wolfe et al., 1983). Older children in abusive families tend to be more aggressive and less compliant than children of similar ages from control families (Bousha & Twentyman, 1984; Egeland & Sroufe, 1981a; Parke & Collmer, 1975). Thus, both parental and child factors may contribute to a pattern of physically and psychologically harmful interactions.

Finally, abusive families tend to be isolated from the outside world and have fewer sources of social support than nonabusive families. In one study, abusive parents reported they were less involved with the community than nonabusive parents were; they tended not to join sports teams, go to the library, or take classes (Trickett & Susman, 1988). In another study, some mothers who were at risk for becoming abusive because of their own family history had normal, positive relationships with their children. These mothers also had extensive emotional support from other adults, a therapist, or a mate. In contrast, high-risk mothers who subsequently became abusive experienced greater life stress and had fewer sources of psychological support (Egeland, Jacobvitz, & Sroufe, 1988).

How can the spiral of abuse be broken? The guidelines offered by Wahler and Dumas (1989) provide a good start. Specifically, interventions should teach basic parenting skills, provide parents with mechanisms to cope with their emotional tension, and offer social support such as child care or counseling services (Belsky, 1993; Wolfe, 1985). Moreover, observers have noted our society's general acceptance of violence as a means of solving problems. This tendency is evident in the widespread endorsement of physical punishment as a technique for disciplining children, as well as in the pervasive displays of violence in the media (Belsky, 1980, 1993; Hart & Brassard, 1987). Altering broader societal attitudes about violence may be an additional and necessary step in breaking the cycle of child abuse. Finally, a national study of more than six thousand households showed that violence toward children was more prevalent in families experiencing unemployment, substance abuse, and financial difficulties (Wolfner & Gelles, 1993). As daunting as the task may seem, a broad attack on more general social problems may thus ameliorate the problem of child abuse.

Cultural and Social Class Variations in Parenting

KEY THEME
Sociocultural Influence

Do broader sociocultural beliefs and values play a role in parental socialization practices? If so, do children show specific patterns of behavior as a result of their different cultural experiences? Recent research suggests that the answer to both questions is yes.

Cross-Cultural Differences Beatrice Whiting and Carolyn Edwards (1988) have provided an extended analysis of variations in parenting by comparing societies as diverse as rural Kenya, Liberia, and the Philippines with urban America. Despite vast differences in economic, social, and political conditions, many similar, overarching patterns are apparent in the ways parents (specifically, mothers) socialize their children. With infants and toddlers, the universal emphasis is on nurturance, that is, providing routine care along with attention and support. By the time the child reaches age four or five years, most parents shift their focus to control, correcting or reprimanding misbehavior. Finally, when children reach school age, parents become concerned with training their children in the skills and social behavior their cultural group values.

At the same time, though, Whiting and Edwards (1988) observed notable differences. For example, mothers from rural villages in Kenya and Liberia emphasized training children to do chores responsibly and placed a high premium on obedience.

From an early age, children were taught how to care for the family's fields and animals, and they assumed a major role in caring for younger siblings. Children were punished for performing tasks irresponsibly and were rarely praised. Consistent with this orientation to child rearing was the family's dependence on women and children for producing food. Because women in these cultures typically had an enormous workload, they delegated some tasks to children as soon as children were physically capable of managing them; because accidents and injury to infants and the family's resources must be prevented, deviant behaviors were not tolerated in children. Children growing up in these communities were highly compliant to mothers' commands and suggestions.

An even more controlling style characterized the Tarong community in the Philippines, where subsistence farming was the mainstay but responsibilities for producing food were more evenly distributed among the group's members. When the mother did not rely so heavily on her children to work for the family's survival and when the goals of training were thus less clear, arbitrary commands and even punishing became more common. Children were scolded frequently for being in the way of adults or playing in inappropriate places. By middle childhood, Tarong children showed a marked decline in their tendency to seek attention from or be close to their parents.

These patterns provided a striking contrast to the "sociability" that characterized the middle-income American mothers in the sample. Interactions between mothers and children consisted of significant information exchange and warm, friendly dialogues. Mothers emphasized verbalization, educational tasks, and play, and they were liberal in their use of praise and encouragement. Because children in American society normally do not work to ensure the economic survival of the family unit, firm training and punishing were not part of these parents' styles. The emphasis on verbalization and educational activities was consistent with the high value Americans place on social interactions and schooling.

Other researchers examining parent-child relationships in Asian cultures have reaffirmed the idea that culture affects parenting styles. Japanese mothers use less physical punishment and more verbal reasoning to control their children than American mothers (Kobayashi-Winata & Power, 1989). Japanese culture emphasizes responsibilities and commitments to others, a socialization goal that is achieved more effectively through reasoning than through power-assertive techniques. Japanese children, in fact, comply with rules at home and in school more than their American counterparts do. Similarly, when Chinese parents are asked to describe their child-rearing practices, they report a greater emphasis on control and achievement in children than American parents (Chao, 1994; Lin & Fu, 1990). In Chinese society, character development and educational attainment are highly valued, and parental practices follow directly from these larger societal goals.

As Whiting and Edwards (1988) point out, parents around the world resemble one another in numerous ways because of the universal needs children have as they grow and develop. But it is also true that the specific ecology of each culture, its socialization goals, and the demands it places on the family unit can dramatically shape parenting practices and the course of the individual child's socialization.

Social Class and Ethnic Differences   Reliable social class differences exist in parenting practices. Middle-class mothers more frequently use induction, or reasoning, as they discipline their children than do lower-class mothers, who tend to use power-assertive techniques. Middle-class mothers also praise their children liberally and generally verbalize more than lower-class mothers, who in turn more frequently utter such commands as "Do it because I say so!" and dispense less positive reinforcement (Hoffman, 1984).

Social class (typically defined by the father's occupation) by itself, however, is not a variable that provides neat or meaningful explanations, because it is usually associated with other variables, such as access to health care, nutrition, physical environment, and educational experiences. Moreover, even within low-income families, significant variations in parenting styles can occur; a single characteristic style may

FIGURE 14.5

Effective Parenting and Peer Influences

The style of parenting that best predicts successful developmental outcomes may depend on other influences in the child's life. For example, researchers have found that for lower- and working-class adolescents, a more controlling style of parenting may lead to fewer problem behaviors if peers exert a negative influence. In this study, adolescents were divided into two groups: those who were above and below average in their exposure to negative peer influences. The amount of control parents exhibited was divided into four categories from least to most control (where 1 was equal to least control). As the graph shows, for adolescents exposed to higher-than-average negative peer influences, greater parental control was associated with fewer behavior problems. Levels of parental control mattered less for adolescents exposed to lower-than-average negative peer influences.

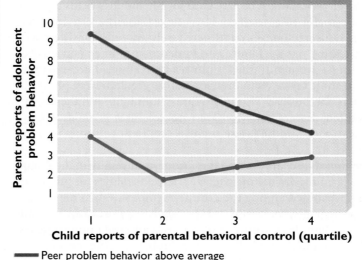

Peer problem behavior above average
Peer problem behavior below average

Source: Adapted from Mason et al., 1996.

not exist. For example, younger low-income mothers and mothers who are less religious tend to use more power-assertive parenting styles than older mothers or those who have strong religious beliefs (Kelley, Power, & Wimbush, 1992). Another factor to consider is how parenting practices might be related to the type of peer influence to which children are exposed. In one recent study, African American adolescents from lower- and working-class families were divided into two groups, those who were above and below average in their exposure to peer problem behaviors. As Figure 14.5 shows, for adolescents exposed to negative peer influences, fewer behavior problems occurred when parents exerted more control over their children. When exposure to negative peer influences was lower, the type of parental control made less of a difference (Mason et al., 1996). Although we have seen in much of this chapter that high parental control is associated with negative child outcomes, under some circumstances this type of parenting may actually be advantageous. Thus, we must be cautious in making sweeping generalizations about the role of social class in parenting.

Vonnie McLoyd (McLoyd, 1990; McLoyd et al., 1994) has provided an extended analysis of the growing literature on families under economic stress that illuminates the effects of social class. Because African American children experience a disproportionate share of the problems of poverty (a rate of 41 percent for African American children at the time of her analysis compared to 13 percent for Caucasian children), McLoyd focused on the social and family dynamics that can affect this racial minority.

In McLoyd's analysis, economic hardship has a serious negative impact on children's socioemotional development because of the psychological distress it causes parents. Parents under stress have a diminished ability to provide nurturant, consistent, involved care for their children. Children growing up with poverty are thus at risk for depression, poor peer relations, lower self-esteem, and conduct disorders. In one study of African American mothers, mothers' job loss was related to the tendency to report symptoms of depression. This fact was, in turn, related to their use of punishment and less parental nurturance (McLoyd et al., 1994). Similar findings have been reported for Caucasian middle-class families from the midwestern United States during a time of economic downturn. Rand Conger and his colleagues (Conger et al., 1992) found that parents who experienced economic hardship reported greater emotional distress; this factor, in turn, was related to less skillful parenting. The disruptions in parenting were associated with adjustment problems among the adolescent boys in the sample. These seventh-graders reported more feelings of hostility and depression than those whose families were not experiencing economic hardship.

At the same time, the demands poverty makes on many African American families may be related to unique family structures and socialization goals that are adaptive for their situation and help them to cope. For example, a significant number of African American children grow up in an extended family. About 10 percent of African American children younger than eighteen years—three times as many as Caucasian children—grow up with a live-in grandparent (Beck & Beck, 1989). Extended family members often bring additional income, child care assistance, and emotional support and counseling to families under stress, especially when the parent is single (M. Wilson, 1986). Extensive networks of social support have, in turn, been associated with responsive and involved parenting styles among low-income African American mothers (Burchinal, Follmer, & Bryant, 1996). Among African American adolescents, those who perceived their families as having extensive social support from relatives also perceived their homes as being organized and their parents as being involved in their schooling; these beliefs were linked to fewer problem behaviors, greater self-reliance, and higher grades in school than for adolescents whose perceptions differed (Taylor, 1996).

In addition, African American children often are socialized to have a positive orientation to their racial group and to develop interdependence and cooperation as opposed to independence and competition. These characteristics fit with the needs of a group of children who often encounter barriers to individual achievement (Harrison et al., 1990). The higher levels of involvement of African American families in religion also have a positive impact on children. Children of religious parents show less aggression and depression than those whose parents are less involved in religion (Brody, Stoneman, & Flor, 1996). Thus, although economic stress can have a negative effect on family dynamics, it can also foster alternative family structures and socialization goals that help to meet the needs of children.

RELATIONSHIPS WITH MOTHERS, FATHERS, AND SIBLINGS

Because women traditionally have been seen as the primary caregivers for children, most studies of parenting practices in the psychological literature have focused on mothering. Two decades of research on fathers, however, as well as even more recent studies of sibling relationships, have provided a much broader understanding of how each distinct relationship within the family influences the individual child's development.

Mothering Versus Fathering: Are There Differences?

For the most part, mothers still bear most of the responsibility for child rearing in American society, whether or not they are employed outside the home. However, the number of fathers participating in child care is increasing. For example, the number of single fathers who have custody of their children rose to more than 1.5 million in 1995. In addition, fathers assume primary child care responsibilities in 20 percent of the families in which both parents are employed (U.S. Bureau of the Census, 1996). Research resoundingly reveals that fathers are significant figures in their children's lives and are clearly competent in their parental role.

In this chapter, as well as in Chapter 11, we have underscored maternal sensitivity and responsiveness as key factors in fostering optimal child development. Studies have shown that fathers are just as responsive as mothers to the signals of their infants, and, when given the opportunity, they interact with their babies in ways similar to mothers. One team of researchers measured the physiological responsiveness of mothers and fathers as they observed quiet, smiling, or crying babies on a video monitor (Frodi et al., 1978). Mothers and fathers showed similar changes in heart

When given the opportunity, fathers respond to their children in much the same way that mothers do. They hold, touch, and vocalize to their infants, although they are more physical in their play than are mothers. When fathers participate in child care, their children show favorable developmental outcomes.

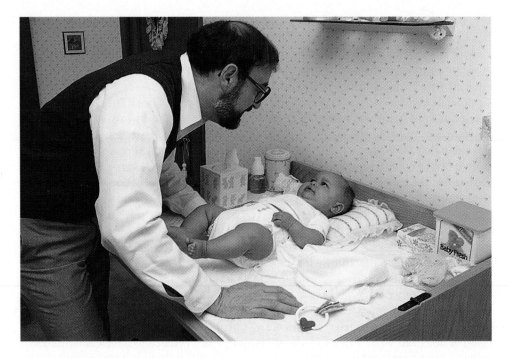

rate, blood pressure, and skin conductance when the babies smiled or cried. In another study of maternal and paternal behaviors toward infants in the newborn nursery, Ross Parke and Sandra O'Leary (1976) found that fathers were just as likely as mothers to hold, touch, and vocalize to their babies.

After the newborn period, fathers and mothers begin to manifest somewhat different styles of interacting with their infants. When they play face to face with their babies, fathers tend to provide physical and social stimulation in staccato bursts, whereas mothers tend to be more rhythmic and soothing (Yogman et al., 1977). Fathers engage in physical and unpredictable "idiosyncratic" play with their infants—throwing them up in the air, moving their limbs, and tickling them—whereas mothers spend more time in caregiving activities or calm games such as "pat-a-cake" (Lamb, 1976; Yogman, 1982). As a consequence, infants prefer fathers when they wish to play and seek out mothers when they desire care and comfort. This dichotomy in parental styles of interaction continues at least until middle childhood (Russell & Russell, 1987).

Despite their responsiveness and competence as parents, most fathers spend less time with their children than mothers do. Using a national sample, Joseph Pleck (1982) found that employed fathers whose children were younger than five spent an average of twenty-six minutes per day in caregiving or other interactions with their children. With children ages six to seventeen, that figure dropped to sixteen minutes per day. In general, fathers spend about one-third the time mothers do in direct contact with their children, even when the mother works outside the home (Ishii-Kuntz & Coltrane, 1992; Lamb et al., 1987). Some exceptions do exist, most notably in families in which fathers even serve as the primary caregiver. Furthermore, the extent of paternal involvement with children increased in the 1970s and 1980s (Juster, 1987). The bulk of the evidence suggests, however, that although fathers are capable and responsive parents, they still have fewer interactions with their children than mothers do, especially in direct caregiving activities. This pattern has been found in diverse ethnic groups and cultures, including African Americans, Chinese, and Japanese (Hossain & Roopnarine, 1994; Ishii-Kuntz, 1994; Sun & Roopnarine, 1996).

Why are fathers relatively uninvolved? Some may hold traditional beliefs about which family member should be responsible for child care. Another reason may be that fathers are not confident in their caregiving skills. Because males typically are not exposed to child care through such experiences as baby-sitting and home economics courses, they may feel insecure about feeding, bathing, or diapering a child (Lamb et al., 1987). Still another obstacle may be the resistance of mothers. Survey data with a national sample showed that only 23 percent of employed mothers and 31 percent of unemployed mothers stated they wanted more help from their husbands in child care (Pleck, 1982). It may be that women are socialized so strongly to excel in the caregiving role that they are reluctant to relinquish it, even if it places extraordinary demands on their time. On the other hand, some circumstances predict greater father involvement in child care: the fact that the mother works (in some cases, the mother has a job and the father is unemployed) and the father's memories of his own relationship with his father (Gottfried, Bathurst, & Gottfried, 1994; Radin, 1994). In some cases, the father may have learned to extend his caregiving role from observing the participation of his father; in other cases, he may be trying to have a better relationship with his own children than he had with his uninvolved father.

The Father's Influence on Child Development Do fathers have a different influence than mothers on the process of child development? During the 1960s and 1970s psychologists believed they do, based on studies of the effects of father absence, especially on boys. Boys growing up without fathers were more likely to have problems in academic achievement, gender-role development, and control of aggression (Biller, 1974; Lamb, 1981). An important theoretical construct driving much of the research was *identification:* the idea that boys assimilate the characteristics, attitudes, and behaviors of their fathers as they form an intense emotional bond with them. Presumably, boys without fathers did not have an identity figure or model for appropriate masculine, instrumentally competent behavior and thus suffered deficits in cognitive, social, and emotional domains.

Identification with the father may be less important than other variables, however. Michael Lamb (1987) points out that the effects of father absence may result not from the loss of a masculine identity figure for the son but from the loss of a source of emotional and financial support for the entire family. The tension and stress that result may produce maladaptive patterns of parenting, which in turn generate undesirable developmental outcomes for boys. Boys may be particularly vulnerable because they seem to be more generally susceptible than girls to the effects of deviant environments (Rutter, 1986).

A more contemporary view is that fathers make recognizable contributions to family life in general and child development in particular, but those contributions simply reflect aspects of good parenting. In other words, good fathering resembles good mothering, and the child will thrive by having two parents who fill those roles instead of just one. For example, the father's warmth emerges as a more powerful variable than his masculinity in predicting competence, achievement, and gender-role identity in sons (Radin, 1981; Radin & Sagi, 1982). In fact, the father's warmth is more powerful than the mother's warmth in predicting children's feelings of academic competence (Wagner & Phillips, 1992). When fathers express positive affection toward their first-born children, siblings also seem to act more prosocially toward one another than when fathers do not (Volling & Belsky, 1992).

In addition, there are some noteworthy effects when fathers are more highly involved than the norm in child care activities, that is, when they assume an equal or almost equal share of the responsibilities for feeding, bathing, and caring for children or when they are the primary caregivers. In one study, fathers and mothers of preschoolers were interviewed about their participation in child care tasks, and their children were given a number of standardized tests of achievement and psychosocial adjustment. Children of fathers who were highly involved in caregiving activities believed they controlled the events in their lives, scored higher on tests of cognitive competence, and held fewer stereotyped gender-role beliefs than children whose fathers were less involved. One reason for some of these gains might be that fathers of the better-adjusted children spent more time providing cognitively stimulating activities for their children, especially their daughters. In addition, when mothers and fathers share roles, they may feel greater life satisfaction and therefore engage in warmer, more positive interactions with their children (Radin, 1982, 1994). Thus, when fathers participate in child care, they provide an added source of enrichment for both their sons and their daughters.

Cross-Cultural Studies of Fathering   As in the United States, fathers in many cultures are becoming increasingly involved in the care of their children, especially during the newborn and infancy periods. In Britain, Sweden, Germany, and Australia, fathers are beginning to participate more fully as parents (Hwang, 1987; Jackson, 1987; Nickel & Kocher, 1987; Russell, 1987). The Swedish government in particular has established social policies designed to encourage paternal participation. Among the benefits available to fathers are a job-protected parental leave during the child's first two years (most of which is compensated), and the option to reduce the workday by as much as two hours until the child is eight years old. About 85 percent of Swedish fathers take advantage of the parental leave policy (Hwang, 1987; Kamerman, 1996).

In contrast, in other societies, particularly those with strong cultural beliefs about the proper roles for fathers and mothers, fathers' participation is comparably low. When investigators examined fathers' involvement in child care in a small town north of Rome, they found that few fathers were present at the births of their children, and once their infants were home, they did virtually no physical caregiving. Most of their infant-directed behaviors emanated from a distance; they looked at, talked to, or whistled at their babies but were unlikely to pick them up to play. As the children grew older, the fathers became even more passive and distant (New & Benigni, 1987).

A closer look at this culture's beliefs about parenting provides some insights into these fathers' lack of involvement. First, both women and men held the strong general belief that only a woman can properly care for a child, that is, respond to physical needs and provide affection and nurturance. The father's role is to provide financial support for the family. Second, these parents held rigid ideas about specific aspects of infant care; cleanliness and proper nutrition, for example, were great concerns. Most parents interviewed in this study believed only mothers have the specialized skills to care for the child "properly." Finally, the father had few opportunities to be alone with the child, because members of the extended family, usually women, were frequently present. Fathers probably felt reluctant to have their interactions with infants scrutinized by so many "experts."

In summary, fathers are capable of engaging in responsive parenting right from their children's infancy, and their children seem to benefit. Fathers may not always have the opportunity to participate in caregiving, however, due to cultural beliefs about the proper role of fathers or to their unfamiliarity with child care routines. As fathers in some societies come to participate more fully in child care, they are likely to greatly enrich the lives of both sons and daughters.

Siblings

Like parents, siblings serve as important sources of the child's social attitudes, beliefs, and behaviors. Although they may not wield as much power as parents, siblings certainly do attempt to control one another's behaviors (ask anyone who is not an only child!) and may be models for both desirable and undesirable actions. An emerging body of research on sibling relationships has provided yet another perspective on how families influence development.

The Only Child   One way to assess the impact of siblings on development is to examine children who have none. Are there notable differences between only children and children with one or more sisters or brothers? Popular opinion depicts the only child as spoiled, demanding, self-centered, and dependent (Thompson, 1974). But research evidence suggests the contrary, that only children may enjoy the benefits of having their parents' exclusive attention. Toni Falbo and Denise Polit (1986) summarized the results of 115 studies of only children and concluded that overall, only chil-

Only children often achieve more than children with two or more siblings, probably because parents have more time for high quality interactions with an only child. They have more verbal exchanges with their children, and are more vigilant and responsive to their children's behaviors.

dren showed higher achievement and intelligence scores than children with siblings. In addition, only-borns ranked higher on measures of character—that is, tendencies toward leadership, personal control, and maturity—than children with siblings. No overall differences emerged between only children and children with siblings on assessments of sociability and personal adjustment.

In explaining these findings, Falbo and Polit (1986) found support for the hypothesis that features of the parent-child relationship account for the advantages only children enjoy in certain domains. Only children were found to have more positive relationships with their parents than children having siblings. This effect probably occurs because parents of one child have more time to spend with their son or daughter and generally have high-quality interactions with their child (Falbo & Cooper, 1980). Parents and children in one study, for example, exchanged more information in mealtime conversations in one-child families than in families having two or three children (Lewis & Feiring, 1982). First-time parents are also more anxious about their child-rearing techniques and may thus be more vigilant and responsive to their child's behaviors (Falbo & Polit, 1986).

Falbo and Polit's (1986) meta-analysis showed that parent-child relations in one- and two-child families are actually more similar than different. Only when a third child is born does the quality of parent-child relations diminish significantly. Parents of more than two children probably become more relaxed about their child-rearing strategies and also have significantly more demands placed on their time. The result is less responsiveness and fewer deliberate attempts to instruct their children, aspects of parenting found to be related to cognitive achievements.

Family Size and Birth Order   Children growing up in contemporary American society have fewer siblings than children in earlier eras. In 1995, the typical American family with children had one or two children (U.S. Bureau of the Census, 1996). Many children thus grow up with only one other sibling. Does the size of the family make any difference in child development?

KEY THEME
Interaction Among Domains

In general, children from smaller families have higher intelligence test scores, achieve higher levels of education, and display greater self-esteem (Blake, 1989; Wagner, Schubert, & Schubert, 1985). As we have just seen, one reason for these effects may be that parents in larger families have less time to spend with their children and may not provide the kind of cognitive stimulation children in smaller families receive. Another important factor is financial circumstances: parents with a larger number of children often experience greater economic stress, which in turn may diminish the quality of their parenting (Rutter & Madge, 1976).

Regardless of family size, the child's birth order, whether first born or later born, can also be a factor in development. Like only children, first-borns tend to score higher on IQ tests and have higher achievement motivation than other children (Glass, Neulinger, & Brim, 1974; Zajonc, Markus, & Markus, 1979). They also tend to be more obedient and socially responsible (Sutton-Smith & Rosenberg, 1970). All these effects probably stem from the greater attention parents give to their first children. Later-borns seem to have an advantage in the social sphere, however. Youngest siblings tend to have better peer relationships than first-borns and are more confident in social situations (Lahey et al., 1980; Miller & Maruyama, 1976).

The Impact of a Sibling's Arrival   The birth of a sibling can have a dramatic effect on the life of a first-born child. Research on the consequences of a second child's arrival generally confirms that "sibling rivalry" is no myth. Judy Dunn and Carol Kendrick (1982) followed the progress of family relationships among forty first-born children who experienced the arrival of a sibling sometime between their first and fourth birthdays. Dunn and Kendrick observed normal home routines during the mother's last month of pregnancy and again when the baby sibling was one, eight, and fourteen months old. They also interviewed the mother at each stage about the older child's eating and sleeping habits, moods, and other routine behaviors.

For the majority of children, the arrival of a sister or brother led to marked changes in behavior; they became more demanding, clingy, unhappy, or withdrawn. Accompanying these changes in their behavior were significant decreases in maternal attention toward them; mothers engaged in less joint play, cuddling, and verbalization with their first-borns and in general initiated fewer interactions with them. At the same time, restrictive and punitive maternal behaviors increased. Over time, Dunn and Kendrick (1982) noted, two distinct patterns of sibling relationships emerged. Among some sibling pairs, almost all interactions eventually became friendly and positive; for others, a persistent pattern of hostility and aggression became the norm. The first pattern was more likely if mothers had previously prepared the older child for the newborn's arrival by referring to the infant as a person with needs and desires. Engaging the older child in caring for the infant also seemed to have positive consequences. In contrast, negative relationships between siblings resulted if the older child experienced a sharp drop in maternal contact. The discrepancy in pre- and postsibling maternal contact made the most difference: children who had less contact with their mothers before the sibling's birth were less profoundly affected by her attention to the new infant.

The timing of a sibling's arrival may also be important. Researchers have noted a drop in the security of a child's attachment to the mother following the birth of a second child. However, the decrease in attachment security was less noticeable if the older child was twenty-four months of age or younger (Teti et al., 1996). Younger children may not yet have the social cognitive capacities to see the new arrival as a threat or cause of change in family routines.

The arrival of a sibling demands a big adjustment for the older child, especially because another individual begins to compete for the parents' attention and affection. Siblings are highly aware of the differential treatment parents may knowingly or unwittingly bestow on them, at least prior to adolescence (when that awareness diminishes or when differential treatment matters less to them) (Kowal & Kramer, 1997; McHale et al., 1995). The greater the perceived discrepancy is, the greater the sibling conflict will be (Dunn, 1988). But not all aspects of sibling relationships are negative. Dunn and Kendrick (1982) noted that in certain circumstances, siblings fill

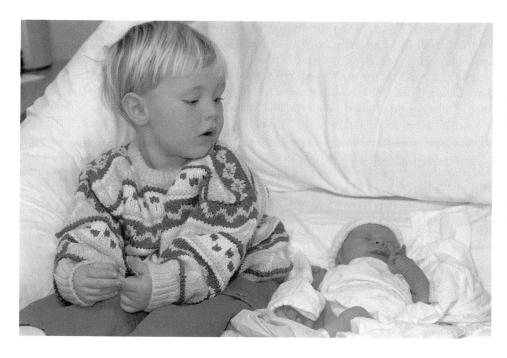

This young boy's reaction to a new sibling is typical. Although many children become clingy, withdrawn, or demanding when a new sibling first arrives, these reactions can be diminished if parents prepare the older child for the infant's arrival and involve him in the infant's care. Adjustment is also more difficult if the older child perceives that he must compete for the parents' affection and attention.

a void in parent-child relationships. When the mother and her older child have difficulties in their interactions, siblings may provide the attention and affection missing from the maternal relationship, thus helping to keep the family system in equilibrium. When parents display a high degree of marital conflict or even undergo divorce, siblings show an increase in emotional closeness and positive, friendly behavior toward one another (Dunn, 1996).

Sibling Interactions Among Older Children   How do older children interact as siblings? For one thing, children tend to fight more with their siblings than with their friends. When fifth-through-eighth-graders were asked to describe conflicts with their siblings, they reported that they allowed quarrels with siblings to escalate, often to the point where parents had to intervene, whereas they tried to resolve conflicts with friends. Most of the time, siblings fight about privacy and interpersonal boundaries (Raffaelli, 1989). In addition, interactions between siblings tend to be more negative when the older sibling is a male (MacKinnon, 1989a). Researchers have noted that the degree of conflict in sibling relationships is related to the amount of aggression a child shows in school, whereas the amount of warmth in sibling relationships is linked to emotional control and social competence in school (Stormshak et al., 1996).

Whether positive or negative in character, sibling relationships in early childhood tend to remain stable through middle childhood (Dunn, Slombowski, & Beardsall, 1994) and then typically change from middle childhood through adolescence. Duane Buhrmester and Wyndol Furman (1990) administered the Sibling Relationship Questionnaire to third-, sixth-, ninth-, and twelfth-graders to assess several dimensions of sibling interactions. Older siblings reported being more dominant and nurturant toward their younger siblings, and younger siblings confirmed that they received more often than dispensed dominance and nurturance. These differences between older and younger siblings apparently disappear over time, however. The older children in the sample reported having more egalitarian relationships with their siblings as well as less intense feelings of both warmth and conflict. Initial differences in power and nurturance usually disappeared when the younger sibling was twelve years old, by which time she or he had become more competent and needed less guidance and emotional support.

The style of parenting mothers and fathers employ also can affect the quality of sibling interactions. In one study, children of mothers who used nonpunitive control techniques and encouraged curiosity and openness to experience were found to be

KEY THEME
Interaction Among Domains

more prosocial toward one another than children of mothers who were punitive and restrictive (Brody, Stoneman, & MacKinnon, 1986). Fathers may have an even greater influence on sibling relationships. Fathers who express more positive behavior toward their children through hugging them or praising them and who attempt to be fair to each sibling have children who likewise express more positive behavior and display less conflict toward one another. The relationship of father-child behavior is noticeably stronger than that of mother-child behavior (Brody, Stoneman, & McCoy, 1992; Brody et al., 1992).

In summary, although the presence of siblings may mean the child has fewer opportunities to interact with parents, it also provides the context for developing other unique skills. Older siblings have opportunities to become nurturant and assertive, and younger siblings have more models for a range of behaviors than only children. Although many children grow up with siblings, we are just beginning to understand the role brothers and sisters play in child development.

FAMILIES IN TRANSITION

As we saw at the start of this chapter, the traditional nuclear family has been slowly disappearing from mainstream American society. Single-parent families, dual wage-earner families, and reconstituted families (in which adults who remarry bring their respective children into new families) are becoming more and more prevalent and offer new circumstances to which children must adapt. What are the effects of these emerging family structures on child development? Research shows that child development is influenced not so much by changes in family structure per se as by the ways in which structural changes affect interpersonal relations within the family.

Maternal Employment

In the last two decades, the percentage of married women with children in the labor force has increased dramatically. The working mother is now the norm. What is the effect of maternal employment on child development?

When psychologists compare children of employed mothers with children of women who remain at home, few differences emerge on measures of cognitive achievement and socioemotional development, at least among middle-class participants (Gottfried, Bathurst, & Gottfried, 1994; Hoffman, 1989). If anything, daughters of employed mothers derive some benefit; they are likely to show greater independence, greater achievement, and higher self-esteem than daughters of non-working mothers. Apparently these girls profit from having a successful, competent role model, at least as the larger society recognizes these qualities. (Women who remain at home "work" too, but traditionally have not been afforded recognition or status for that role.) One variable that may make a difference, though, is *when* mothers return to work. A study of more than 1,000 three- and four-year-olds indicated that when their mothers returned to work during their first year, scores on a cognitive test tended to be lower and the number of behavior problems tended to be higher than those of children whose mothers waited until the second year to return to work (Baydar & Brooks-Gunn, 1991). Another variable that may be important is the number of hours mothers work. A recent study of mostly Caucasian middle-class women found that the more hours mothers worked, the lower was the academic achievement of their kindergarten and first-grade children (Goldberg, Greenberger, & Nagel, 1996). On the other hand, a comprehensive longitudinal study of children from infancy through age twelve found that although academic achievement was negatively related to the number of hours the mothers worked when children were ages five and six, this relationship was not apparent as children grew older (Gottfried, Bathurst, & Gottfried, 1994).

For low-income families, maternal employment is related to some clear benefits for children. A recent longitudinal study examined 189 second-graders; most were

KEY THEME
Interaction Among Domains

born to adolescent mothers, and 41 percent lived in households with incomes below the poverty level. For this sample, maternal employment during the child's first three years was associated with greater household income, a higher-quality home environment as assessed by the HOME inventory (see Chapter 10), and higher mathematics achievement in school for the child compared to the effects when mothers did not work (Vandell & Ramanan, 1992).

In general, the clearest effect of maternal employment involves the gender-role attitudes of both sons and daughters. As we saw in Chapter 13, when mothers work outside the home, their children are less likely than children of at-home mothers to hold stereotypical beliefs about males and females and more likely to see both sexes as competent (Hoffman, 1984, 1989). When both mother and father work, sons and daughters have the opportunity to see both parents in multiple roles—as powerful, competent wage earners and nurturant, warm caregivers—a factor that may contribute to more egalitarian beliefs.

Overall, maternal employment is not a simple, "neat" variable in studying child development. Some mothers work out of sheer economic necessity, whereas others are more concerned with realizing personal or career goals, for example. As researchers point out, the impact of maternal employment is better understood through its effects on family dynamics, parental attitudes, and the alternative child care arrangements the family chooses (Beyer, 1995; Hoffman, 1989). It is to these factors that we now turn our attention.

Maternal Employment and Parent-Child Interaction   Mothers who work full time outside the home spend less time caring for their children, whether infants or high school age, than mothers who stay at home (Hill & Stafford, 1980). In terms of direct, one-to-one mother-child interaction, however, no significant differences have been found between employed and nonemployed mothers (Goldberg, 1977; Richards & Duckett, 1994). Employed mothers often compensate for the time they miss with their children during the workweek by allocating more time for them on weekends and evenings (Easterbooks & Goldberg, 1985). Thus, working mothers try to establish "quality time" with their children to make up for the hours they are separated from them. The picture for fathers is less clear. Although some studies show that fathers assume more responsibilities for child care when the mother works, others indicate they do not (Baruch & Barnett, 1981; Pederson et al., 1982; Pleck, 1983).

Does the quality of parent-child interaction differ between working and nonworking mothers? Employed mothers as a group tend to stress training in independence (Hoffman, 1989), a characteristic in children that will help the family function more smoothly given the more limited time mothers and fathers have to perform routine activities. Some researchers also report that employed mothers are more responsive and verbalize more to their children and engage in more social play than mothers who are not employed (Crockenberg & Litman, 1991; Pederson et al., 1982; Schubert, Bradley-Johnson, & Nuttal, 1980).

Overall, what matters more than whether or not the mother works is her attitude toward mothering and work and why she is working or staying home. In one study of mothers of infants, women who remained at home contrary to their preference had higher scores on tests of depression and stress than mothers who preferred to be at home and were not in the labor force and employed mothers who valued their positions in the work world (Hock & DeMeis, 1990). We saw earlier in this chapter that parental stress has been implicated as a factor in less consistent and less nurturant parenting. On the other hand, when maternal employment produces tension, parenting practices also may suffer. Researchers have found that mothers who worked more than forty hours per week, for example, were more anxious and unhappy and had less sensitive and less animated interactions with their infants than mothers who worked less than forty hours per week (Owen & Cox, 1988).

The Effects of Day Care   It is nearly impossible to extract the influence of maternal employment as a variable from the effect of alternative caregiving arrangements made for the child. The two factors almost invariably occur together.

Age of Child	Child's Home		Another Home		Organized Child-Care Facility	Other[a]
	Relative	Nonrelative	Relative	Nonrelative		
Under 1 year	28.2	7.5	20.0	20.5	11.5	7.6
1 to 2 years	33.2	5.5	13.4	20.4	17.5	10.0
3 to 4 years	26.8	4.3	10.1	14.4	32.9	12.5

[a]Includes mother caring for child at work, child caring for self, and child attending kindergarten or grade school.
Source: Adapted from U.S. Bureau of the Census, 1995.

TABLE 14.1

Child Care Arrangements for Children Whose Mothers Work

This table shows the percentage of children who receive different forms of child care. Most infants, toddlers, and preschoolers whose mothers work receive child care provided by a relative or nonrelative, either in the child's home or the caregiver's.

Child care arrangements take various forms, from in-home care provided by a relative or paid caregiver to group care in a formal, organized center. As Table 14.1 shows, up until age two most children are cared for in another home by a relative or someone else, and only a small percentage attend an organized day care center. This finding raises an interesting issue concerning the effect of day care on development. With rare exceptions, researchers have compared children who have spent varying amounts of time in center-based day care with children who have been reared by their parents at home. We must interpret the findings of this research cautiously, because the more common home-based care of young children whose mothers work—care in another person's home—has yet to be studied extensively.

Chapter 11 discussed the effects of day care on a specific aspect of development: the child's attachment to the mother. Here we consider the broader effects of alternative caregiving on child development. One area in which some (but not all) researchers have noted an effect of day care is in intellectual performance. Day care children tend to outperform children reared at home by parents on standardized tests of IQ as well as measures of problem-solving ability, creativity, language development, and arithmetic skills (Clarke-Stewart & Fein, 1983). Day care programs that stress cognitive activities have a greater effect on IQ scores than those that simply provide caregiving (McCartney et al., 1985). Moreover, the effect of day care on intellectual achievements shows up years later, when children are in elementary school. In one study that examined the academic achievements of sixth-graders, the amount of time children had spent in high-quality day care centers during infancy was positively related to their mathematics grades and their tendency to be enrolled in programs for gifted children (Field, 1991). In two other studies, conducted in Sweden, children who had day care experience performed better on measures of verbal and mathematics abilities and obtained better grades in school seven years later and beyond than children who had no experience with out-of-home care (Andersson, 1992; Broberg et al., 1997).

Day care also produces effects in the realm of social development. Specifically, children with experience in day care are more socially competent. They show greater self-confidence, assertiveness, independence, and prosocial behavior with peers than home-reared comparison groups. In addition to showing more positive behaviors, however, day care children also more frequently display aggression toward peers and noncompliance with adults, at least according to some (but not all) studies of this behavior (Clarke-Stewart & Fein, 1983). Two factors have been proposed as explanations for day care children's advanced social behaviors: the extensive peer contacts they have and the prosocial instruction many caregivers explicitly provide (Hamilton & Gordon, 1978; Rubenstein & Howes, 1979). Concerning their greater aggressive and noncompliant behavior, Alison Clarke-Stewart (1989) suggests that day care children are simply more likely to think independently but have not yet mastered the social skills to negotiate for the attainment of their goals.

To summarize, day care has few negative effects on children and may even facilitate cognitive and social development. It is important to remember, however, that most studies of day care have been conducted in high-quality centers, often associated with universities and populated by children from middle-to-upper- class families. But many parents lack the opportunity or financial resources to send their children to such high-caliber programs. In a disturbing report on the quality of child care centers in the United States, only 14 percent of centers were judged to offer care that promotes children's development; most provided only custodial-level care, and 12 percent were found to jeopardize children's development (Children's Defense Fund, 1996). What are the effects of less than excellent programs on children? Research suggests that when children are enrolled in low-quality centers before age one, they have more difficulty with peers and are distractible and less task oriented in kindergarten than children who are enrolled at later ages and those who attend high-quality centers (Howes, 1990). Thus, it is essential that parents be aware of the elements of high-quality day care.

Choosing a Day Care Center   Both the federal government and many states have set minimum requirements for day care services that regulate the qualifications of teachers, staff-child ratios, the size and safety of the physical facility, and the provision of nourishing meals. Although the guidelines and laws provide for minimum standards, most parents are concerned with providing their children with the best possible care during the hours they are at work. Alison Clarke-Stewart (1993) has drawn on the expanding body of research findings on day care to compile the following suggestions for parents:

■ Center-based care is more likely to include educational opportunities for children than home-based care, such as that provided by baby sitters and family day care. On the other hand, children are more likely to receive one-to-one supervision and authoritative discipline in home-based care.

■ Children are most likely to thrive intellectually and emotionally in programs that offer a balance between structured educational activities and an open, free environment.

■ The caregiving environment should provide ample physical space (at least twenty-five square feet per child) and a variety of materials and activities to foster sensorimotor, social, and cognitive development.

■ Class size should be small (fewer than ten children) and should include children within a two-year age range. Small centers (fewer than thirty children) usually have better staff-child ratios than centers with more children.

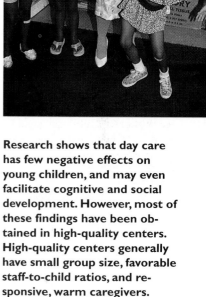

Research shows that day care has few negative effects on young children, and may even facilitate cognitive and social development. However, most of these findings have been obtained in high-quality centers. High-quality centers generally have small group size, favorable staff-to-child ratios, and responsive, warm caregivers.

■ The interaction style of the caregiver is a key aspect of quality care. The caregiver should be actively involved but not restrictive with the children. The caregiver should also be responsive and offer positive encouragement.

■ Caregivers who have training in child development and continuing opportunities for education are most likely to provide high-quality care.

■ The individual characteristics of the child should be taken into account. Some children will probably do well in a program that balances structure and openness; others may profit from either more structure or a more flexible and relaxed program.

Other important factors include a high staff-child ratio and low staff turnover. Research shows, for example, that when the staff-child ratio is at least one to three for infants, one to four for toddlers, and one to nine for preschoolers, the quality of caregiving and of children's activities within the center are both good. Likewise, when the overall class size is six or fewer for infants, twelve or fewer for toddlers, and eighteen or fewer for preschoolers, children have better-quality experiences than those in larger groups (Howes, Phillips, & Whitebook, 1992).

In essence, the qualities of good day care mirror the qualities of good parenting. In other words, parents should seek a warm, responsive environment that provides the child, at least some of the time, with opportunities for structured play and prosocial learning.

The Effects of Divorce

KEY THEME
Sociocultural Influence

As we pointed out at the start of this chapter, the statistics are dramatic: the divorce rate among couples in the United States has tripled since 1960, and estimates suggest that 40 to 50 percent of children born in the late 1970s and early 1980s will live through the divorce of their parents (Glick & Lin, 1986). Far from being an atypical event, divorce affects a significant proportion of American children. Unfortunately, the effects of divorce on children are rarely positive; the absence of one parent, the emotional and financial tension, and sometimes continuing conflicts between parents that accompany divorce frequently lead to a range of psychological problems for both boys and girls, at least in the period immediately following the breakup of the family. The ability of children to cope with the stresses of divorce, particularly in the long run, depends on a number of variables. Most important is the way parents manage the transition in family structure.

A major longitudinal study of the effects of divorce on parents and children conducted by E. Mavis Hetherington and her associates illuminated how parental separation affects children and how the nature of parent-child interactions changes (Hetherington, Cox, & Cox, 1982). The researchers compared two groups over a period of two years, a sample of forty-eight preschool-age, middle-class children whose parents divorced and another group of forty-eight middle-class children matched on several variables, such as age and sex, whose families were intact. In all the divorced families, mothers had custody of their children. During the course of the study, the researchers made several assessments of both parents and children, including parental interviews, observations of parent-child interactions in the laboratory and at home, observations and ratings of children's behavior in the home and at school, and personality tests.

KEY THEME
Interaction Among Domains

The results of the study indicated that the worst period for most children was the first year after the divorce, when they exhibited many negative characteristics such as aggression, distractability, and noncompliance. The extent of their undesirable behaviors even surpassed those of children from intact families with a high level of conflict, and it was particularly noticeable in boys. Two years after the divorce, many of the effects on children had diminished, especially for girls. In a six-year follow-up, however, many boys continued to show patterns of aggression and noncompliance, academic difficulties, poor relations with peers, and extremely low self-esteem (Hetherington, 1989).

A look at family interaction styles after divorce helps to account for the poor initial adjustment of children. Hetherington and her colleagues noted that soon after they separated from their husbands, mothers tended to adopt a more authoritarian style of parenting (Hetherington, Cox, & Cox, 1982). They gave out numerous commands and prohibitions and displayed little affection or responsiveness to their children. These mothers were undoubtedly having problems coping with their new status as single parents in both emotional and practical terms. At the same time, the fathers withdrew, participating little in the management of their children's behavior. Children, particularly boys, became less compliant, and mothers in turn responded with increased restrictiveness and punitiveness. Caught up in a spiral of frustration, helplessness, and feelings of incompetence, these mothers responded negatively to many of their children's behaviors, even those that were neutral or positive, and, despite their harsh threats, followed up on few of the directives they gave. The result was a coercive cycle of parent-child interaction such as that described earlier in this chapter and typified by this chapter's opening scene between Joey and his mother.

Other researchers have confirmed that many children show heightened aggression, lower academic achievement, disruptions in peer relationships, and depression after their parents' divorce than they had previously (Camara & Resnick, 1988; Stolberg & Anker, 1984; Wallerstein, Corbin, & Lewis, 1988). Sibling interactions also suffer. Carol MacKinnon (1989b) observed elementary school–age children as they played games with their siblings in the laboratory. Siblings whose parents had been divorced for one year or longer showed more teasing, quarreling, physical attacks, and other negative behaviors toward one another than children from intact families.

Children ages six to eight years seem to have the most difficulty adjusting to divorce; they are old enough to recognize the seriousness of the family's situation but do not yet have the coping skills to deal with feelings of sadness and guilt that often accompany the change in family structure (Wallerstein & Kelly, 1980). Older children often have a better understanding of divorce and the notion that conflicts between parents must somehow be resolved (Kurdek, 1989). However, even adolescents often suffer negative psychological consequences after their parents divorce. Adolescent boys in particular were found to be more likely to use alcohol or illicit drugs after their parents separated than boys in a control group whose parents remained married (Doherty & Needle, 1991). For some individuals, the aftermath of divorce may last well into young adulthood. According to data collected as part of a major longitudinal study in Great Britain, young adults whose parents had previously divorced reported more depression, anxiety, and other emotional problems than adults from intact families (Chase-Lansdale, Cherlin, & Kiervan, 1995).

Given these deleterious consequences and the prevalence of divorce, can anything be done to ease the adjustment of children? Research findings suggest some potentially useful strategies.

Adjusting to Divorce　　The consequences of divorce are not always so grim for all children. Hetherington (1989) observed that after six years, some of the children in her original study recovered from the family crisis and showed a healthy adaptation to their new family lifestyle whether or not their mothers remarried. These children displayed few behavior problems, high self-esteem, successful academic performance, and positive relations with peers.

What factors were associated with this favorable pattern of adjustment? For one thing, mothers of children in this group had become less authoritarian and more authoritative in their parental style, encouraging independence but also providing a warm, supportive climate for their sons and daughters. If the mother was not available, many of these children had contact with some other caring adult, such as a relative, teacher, or neighbor. In addition, several children in this category had responsibility for the care of another individual: a younger sibling, an aging grandparent, or someone with a physical or emotional problem. These relationships may have offered children an opportunity to feel needed and provided an alternative source of emotional gratification and support. In contrast, mothers of children with long-lasting adjustment problems continued to manifest coercive styles of interaction. Mothers and sons were especially likely to fall into this pattern. Finally, children are more likely to show successful adjustment to divorce when conflict between divorced parents is low and when the child does not feel "caught" between the two parents (Amato & Rezac, 1994; Buchanan, Maccoby, & Dornbusch, 1991; Guidubaldi, Perry, & Cleminshaw, 1984).

Divorce represents a difficult transition for all members of the family. A key variable to understanding its effect is the quality of relationships among all family members: the more conflict and negative emotion associated with the process and the more prolonged the maladaptive patterns of interaction, the worse the outcomes for the child.

After divorce, most children reside with their mothers, in large part because of long-standing societal beliefs about the privileged nature of mother-child relationships. Yet when children live with their mothers after a divorce, they are more likely to experience economic hardship than if they live with their fathers. Studies have found that income for divorced women with children declines an average of 30 percent, whereas income for

**CONTROVERSY:
THINKING IT OVER**

What Type of Custody Arrangement Is Best for Children of Divorce?

fathers declines much less or even increases (Burkhauser et al., 1991; Weitzman, 1985). Children living with their mothers also typically show a dramatic impairment in relationships with their fathers. For example, according to one national study, more than a third of the children in the sample did not see their fathers *at all* or saw them only a few times a year (Selzer, 1991).

Many states now have laws that favor joint custody of children following divorce. In most cases, this means both parents have equal responsibility for making decisions about the child's medical care and education; that is, they have *joint legal custody*. In other cases, children reside for substantial periods of time with each parent; this arrangement refers to *joint physical custody*.

Some experts believe joint custody results in negative outcomes for children because it increases the likelihood that children will be exposed to their parents' hostility and will feel caught in the conflict between them (Johnston & Campbell, 1987; Reppucci, 1984; Stahl, 1984; Wallerstein & Kelly, 1980). If joint custody means the child must change residence during the year, relationships with friends and experiences in school may also be disrupted.

Others note no differences in the adjustment of children in joint-custody versus sole-custody families (Kline et al., 1989; Maccoby et al., 1993). Still other evidence suggests that children may adapt better when they are in the custody of the same-sex parent (Camara & Resnick, 1988; Warshak & Santrock, 1983). For example, an analysis of data from several hundred high school sophomores whose parents divorced shows that adolescents who lived with the same-sex parent were less likely to drop out of high school than those who lived with the parent of the opposite sex (Zimiles & Lee, 1991).

On what basis should child custody decisions be made—the incomes of the parents, the child's preferred parent, or the same-sex parent? Or should the mother or the father usually obtain custody? Does the research on adjusting to divorce have any implications for whether sole- or joint-custody arrangements might be better for the child? Even if joint-custody arrangements have been made, can the child's relationships with each parent be truly equal? Does quality of contact with each parent matter more than the frequency of contact with him or her? Researchers have reported that parental participation in a wide range of activities, even everyday ones such as shopping and watching TV together, predicted children's successful adjustment better than the frequency of special trips or activities (Clarke-Stewart & Hayward, 1996). Might the effects of custody arrangements vary by ethnic group or by whether a crisis such as family violence or substance abuse is involved (Depner, 1994)? What types of research should developmental psychologists conduct to obtain clearer answers to these vexing but important questions?

KEY THEME
Interaction Among Domains

Relationships with Stepparents   Approximately 75 to 80 percent of divorced individuals remarry, the majority within five years after their divorce (Cherlin, 1992). As a consequence, about 35 percent of children born in the early 1980s will live with a stepparent (Glick, 1989). For children who have just experienced the separation of their parents, the introduction of a new "parent" can represent yet another difficult transition even though parental remarriage holds the promise of greater financial security and emotional support for both parents and children (Zill, Morrison, & Coiro, 1993).

Like divorce, a parent's remarriage often leads to aggression, noncompliance, poor peer relations, and academic difficulties among children (Bray, 1988; Zill, 1988). As Figure 14.6 shows, a survey of more than ten thousand children in grades six through twelve showed that children in stepfamilies look similar to children from single-parent families in the number of school-related problems experienced; both groups have more problems than children from two-parent families (Zill, 1994). The child usually has more difficulty adjusting when stepparents have larger numbers of their own children, when children from two previous marriages are assimilated into one

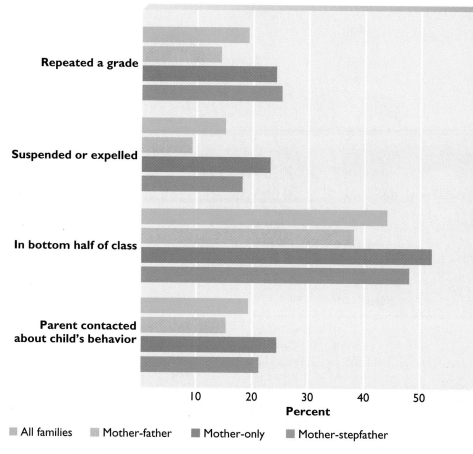

FIGURE 14.6

Family Type and Percentage of Children Experiencing Problems in School

According to a national study involving more than ten thousand children in grades six through twelve, children living in stepfamilies resemble those living in single-parent homes (with their mothers) in the patterns of difficulties they show in school. Both groups have more problems than children living in two-parent families, probably due to differences in parenting styles among the groups.

Repeated a grade

Suspended or expelled

In bottom half of class

Parent contacted about child's behavior

10   20   30   40   50
Percent

■ All families   ■ Mother-father   ■ Mother-only   ■ Mother-stepfather

Source: Adapted from Zill, 1994.

family, and when the custodial parent and stepparent have a new biological child of their own (Santrock & Sitterle, 1987; Zill, 1988). Adolescents have more problems adjusting to their new families than younger children, perhaps because their growing autonomy leads them to be more confrontational with parents (Brand, Clingempeel, & Bowen-Woodward, 1988; Hetherington & Jodl, 1994). In addition, girls in the middle school and adolescent years do not adjust as well as boys to parental remarriage; girls especially withdraw from their stepfathers (Brand, Clingempeel, & Bowen-Woodward, 1988; Vuchinich et al., 1991). Adjustment to a parent's remarriage can take time; in one study, adolescents showed little evidence of adjustment during the twenty-six months they were studied (Hetherington & Clingempeel, 1992).

Drawing from data collected in a national survey of parent-adolescent relations, Frank Furstenberg (1987) found that stepparents had reservations about their ability to discipline and provide affection to stepchildren. At the same time, stepchildren corroborated that stepparents were less involved than their biological parents in care and supervision. Other researchers examining stepparent-stepchild relationships over time confirm that stepparents typically do not fit the profile of authoritative parenting described earlier in this chapter (Hetherington & Jodl, 1994), and thus the benefits of that parenting style for children are not realized. If anything, stepparents often look like the disengaged parents described at the beginning of this chapter; they provide less support for and control over the behavior of their stepchildren compared to their biological children (Mekos, Hetherington, & Reiss, 1996).

Some difficulties in stepfamilies may stem from the uncertain social roles of stepparents. Should they be as strict as the biological parents, or will the child see too much control as intrusive? Stepparents who are trying to win the affections of their "new" children may be reluctant to use strong discipline. Parental remarriage thus presents special challenges that researchers are really just beginning to explore.

Children often have a difficult time adjusting to the presence of stepparents, generally because stepparents do not take an active role in disciplining and showing affection to their "new" children. Problems are more likely to occur when children from each parent's prior marriage become part of the new "blended" family.

Families in Transition: An Overview

We have seen that changes in the structure of the American family affect child development to the extent that they influence the interactions among members of the family system. Maternal employment, divorce, and remarriage can alter the emotional tone of parent-child interactions as well as the types of control strategies parents select, and it is the control strategies that can have a profound effect on the child's intellectual and socioemotional development. Considering how prevalent changes in family structures have become and how many children are affected by them, it is imperative that ways be established to support families undergoing these transitions. Assistance with child care, parent training programs for dysfunctional families, and counseling support for families experiencing stress are some of the programs that can be helpful.

CHAPTER RECAP

SUMMARY OF DEVELOPMENTAL THEMES

SOCIOCULTURAL INFLUENCE   How does the sociocultural context influence family processes?

Many goals parents have for their children's socialization are governed by attitudes the larger society holds, values and beliefs that change over time. Parents will emphasize cooperation, achievement, and sociability, for example, to the extent that the larger social group values these characteristics. Culture also influences who participates in child care and to what extent; in some cultures, for example, fathers and siblings take part in many routine child care tasks. Finally, economic and social trends, such as family size, single parenthood, maternal employment, alternative child care, divorce, and remarriage, can alter family structures. The changes in family dynamics these

factors introduce can have far-reaching consequences for child development.

CHILD'S ACTIVE ROLE   How does the child play an active role in family processes?

As integral members of the family system, children can have significant effects on interactions with parents, siblings, and others. The dramatic physical and cognitive changes associated with development require parents and siblings to adapt to the rapidly altering capabilities and needs of the child. In general, parents and siblings react to the child's growing independence and competence by displaying less dominance and regulation. In addition, the child's behaviors may influence the parents' choice of discipline style; for example, aggressive, difficult children may elicit more authoritarian parenting and premature children may be at risk for abuse.

The child's experiences within the family, particularly the type of parenting style to which the child is exposed, can have broad consequences for development. For example, children who experience authoritarian parenting show less advanced moral reasoning, lower self-esteem, poorer relations with peers, poorer school adjustment, and higher levels of aggression than children who experience authoritative parenting. Similarly, interactions with siblings often provide children with opportunities to develop such social skills as nurturance and assertiveness. Finally, transitions in families can introduce both new opportunities and new stresses that can affect children's emotional, social, and cognitive development.

SUMMARY OF TOPICS

■ UNDERSTANDING THE FAMILY

Many social scientists conceptualize the family as a *system* in which each relationship influences other relationships. In addition, the family is vulnerable to larger social influences such as cultural values and economic trends. Most psychologists recognize that the key to understanding the child's development lies in family dynamics.

■ PARENTS AND SOCIALIZATION

Parents serve as the child's primary *socialization* agents by teaching their children directly, serving as powerful models, and controlling other aspects of their children's social lives. One important element of parenting is the general style with which parents relate to their children. *Authoritative parenting,* characterized by moderate control and high nurturance, is associated with cooperation, independence, achievement orientation, and healthy peer relations among children. *Authoritarian parents* rely excessively on power-assertive techniques and display less nurturance and affection. Their children frequently are aggressive, have lower levels of moral reasoning, poor self-esteem, poor peer relations, and lower school achievement. *Permissive* and *uninvolved parents* also tend to have children with developmental problems.

Punishment can favorably alter the child's behavior in the short run, particularly if it is accompanied by an explanation and is used consistently. Physical punishment can, however, result in more aggression in children as well as avoidance of the punishing agent. The extent to which parents act forcefully to control their children depends on the attributions they make about the children's behavior.

Parents may know good parenting techniques but fail to apply them because they are distracted by financial or other stresses. Problems in parenting, such as child abuse, illustrate how power assertion can lead to escalating levels of violence within the family.

Cross-cultural and social class variations in parenting reflect the pressures exerted by larger social forces. In some rural societies in which children contribute to the family's subsistence, for example, children are expected to care for siblings and strictly obey their parents. Families affected by economic hardship provide another example of how an external factor can place stress on parents and influence their parenting style.

■ RELATIONSHIPS WITH MOTHERS, FATHERS, AND SIBLINGS

Although mothers have traditionally assumed the caregiver role, fathers and siblings also play an important part in the child's socialization. Fathers typically spend less time with their children than mothers do but behave similarly when given the opportunity. One difference is that fathers tend to engage in more physical interactions with their infants and young children. Sensitive, responsive fathering is associated with many desirable outcomes in children.

Siblings also affect development. The presence of siblings usually means parents have less time to spend with later-born children; this fact may explain the generally higher achievement of only and first-born children. Preschool-age siblings have both aggressive and prosocial exchanges, and older siblings are more dominant and nurturant than younger siblings. These differences among siblings diminish as they get older.

■ FAMILIES IN TRANSITION

In today's society, more families include mothers who work and more families experience divorce. Maternal employment is associated with higher levels of achievement, independence, and self-esteem in girls and less stereotyped gender-role attitudes in both boys and girls. More important than the fact of maternal employment is the mother's interaction style and the quality of substitute care the child receives. Mothers who are satisfied with their life circumstances and who display adaptive parenting techniques tend to have well-adjusted children. Studies of day care generally show that children who attend high-quality day care are more cognitively and socially competent than children reared solely at home by their parents.

Children whose parents divorce evidence socioemotional and academic difficulties, especially boys. Many effects disappear after the first year following the divorce, particularly among girls. Parental separation typically means increased stress on the family, a factor that can lead to ineffective parenting. Successful adjustment to divorce among children is associated with shifts from power assertive to authoritative parenting as well as low parental conflict in the period after separation. Children, especially adolescents, also have difficulty adjusting to the remarriage of their parents. These difficulties may stem in part from the reluctance of stepparents to exhibit nurturance or control in their interactions with their stepchildren.

PEERS

SOCIOCULTURAL INFLUENCE
How does the sociocultural context influence peer relations?

CHILD'S ACTIVE ROLE
How does the child play an active role in peer relations?

CONTINUITY/DISCONTINUITY
Are developmental changes in peer relations continuous or discontinuous?

INDIVIDUAL DIFFERENCES
How prominent are individual differences in peer relations?

INTERACTION AMONG DOMAINS
How do peer relations interact with other domains of development?

t was the start of the first day of school. Jan Nakamura, the third-grade teacher, surveyed her new charges as they played in the schoolyard before the bell rang. It was a familiar scene: the boys played a raucous game of kickball, cheering their teammates and urging victory. The girls gathered in small groups, talking with great animation about their summer experiences and their excitement about school. As always, certain children in both groups were the center of activity; they seemed to attract their agemates as a pot of honey draws bees. Other children seemed to fall into the background; few of their peers approached or spoke to them. Already Jan had a sense that third grade would be easier on some of these fresh new faces than others.

In many ways, Jan's intuitions were correct. She would find, as she learned to match names to faces in this year's class, that many of the playground stars made the transition to a new grade more easily than some of the less popular children. Research evidence suggests that the ability to have successful and rewarding interactions with peers during childhood can be the harbinger of successful later adjustment and that poor peer relations are often associated with a range of developmental problems. Boys and girls who have good peer relationships enjoy school more and are less likely to experience academic difficulties, drop out of school, or commit delinquent acts in later years than agemates who relate poorly with their peers (Ladd, 1990; Morison & Masten, 1991; Parker & Asher, 1987). Children who are accepted by their peers are also less likely to report feeling lonely, depressed, and socially anxious than children who are rejected (Boivin & Hymel, 1997; Cassidy & Asher, 1992; Crick & Ladd, 1993; Hymel & Franke, 1985; Vosk et al., 1982). Of course, the quality of peer relations is not the only factor that predicts later developmental outcomes. Nevertheless, experiences with peers play a substantial role in the lives of most children and thus have become an important focus of developmental research.

What do child development theorists say about the role of peers? Social learning theorists believe peers exert a powerful influence on the child's socialization by means of modeling and reinforcement. Piaget (1965/1932) and Vygotsky (1978) have discussed the ways in which peer contacts alter the child's cognitions, which can, in turn, direct social behavior. Piaget contends that peer interactions prompt, or even coerce, the child to consider the viewpoints of others, thus broadening her social perspective-taking ability and diminishing her egocentrism. The result is a greater capacity for social exchange. Vygotsky maintains that contact with peers, especially those who are more skilled in a given domain, stretches the child's intellectual and social capacities. As a result of experiences with peers, the child internalizes new modes of thinking and social interaction and then produces them independently.

The number of studies examining peer relations in childhood and adolescence has skyrocketed in the last decade, due in part to a recognition of the prevalence of peer experiences in children's lives and the undoubted power of peers as socializing agents. Researchers have especially focused on changes in peer relations with age, the dynamics of peer groups, and the factors related to social competence with peers. Because we humans are "social" beings, it is not surprising that our childhood experiences in social groups play such a large part in making us what we are.

DEVELOPMENTAL CHANGES IN PEER RELATIONS

Compared to any other human relationship, the special feature of peer relations is their egalitarian nature. In fact, strictly speaking, the term **peer** refers to a companion who is approximately the same age and developmental level. Parent-child interactions are characterized by a distinct dominant-subordinate hierarchy that facilitates the child's socialization as parents use their authority to transmit information about social rules and behaviors. Peers, however, usually function as equals, and it is primarily among equals that children can forge such social skills as compromising, competing, and cooperating. Thus, experiences with peers afford the child unique opportunities to construct social understanding and to develop social skills (Hartup, 1977, 1989; Youniss & Smollar, 1985).

Relationships with peers also contribute to the child's developing sense of self. Peers provide the child with direct feedback (verbal and sometimes nonverbal) about how well he is doing in the academic, social, and emotional realms, information that can significantly influence his self-esteem. Peers provide a natural comparison against which the child can gauge his own accomplishments (Furman & Robbins, 1985): "Am I really a good athlete?" "How am I doing as a student?" A child can answer questions such as these by comparing his own abilities to those of his peers.

The way in which children relate to their peers undergoes significant developmental changes. At first, peers are simply interesting (or, at times, annoying) companions in play, but eventually they assume a larger and more crucial part in the child's social and emotional life. Children's peer networks start out small. But as children enter day care and school, and as their cognitive, language, and social skills develop, their peer networks expand, and their relationships with a subset of those peers grow in intensity.

Early Peer Exchanges and Play

Infants show distinct reactions to peers even in the first few months of life. The sight of another baby often prompts a three-month-old to become generally aroused and active, a reaction that is very different from the ritualized greeting she usually reserves for her mother (Fogel, 1979) or the rapt and quiet attention she displays to her reflected image (Field, 1979). At six months, diffuse responses to peers give way to more specific signals, such as smiles, squeals, touching, and leaning in their direction (Hay, Nash, & Pedersen, 1983; Maudry & Nekula, 1939; Vandell, Wilson, & Buchanan, 1980). Older babies crawl toward one another and explore one another's facial features (Vandell & Mueller, 1980). Thus, from early on, infants recognize something special and interesting about strangers who resemble them in size and features. At the same time, most peer interactions during infancy are brief, lasting only a few seconds, and usually do not involve mutual exchanges of behaviors (Eckerman, Whatley, & Kutz, 1975; Vandell & Wilson, 1982).

In the second year, social exchanges with peers become longer and more coordinated. Two children will jointly manipulate toys and other objects, each child taking a turn playing and then offering the object to the playmate. Children also begin to play simple games together, such as hide-and-seek or tag, activities that require taking turns and switching roles (Howes, 1987a, 1987b). Later in toddlerhood, between ages two and three years, children engage in peer interactions more frequently. In-

KEY THEME
Interaction Among Domains

peer   Companion of approximately the same age and developmental level.

In *parallel play,* children play independently while they are beside or close to other children. This pattern of play is typical of preschoolers, but children this age may also show patterns of solitary and cooperative play.

stead of revolving around objects such as toys, these interactions contain many positive social and affiliative behaviors, such as giving attention, smiling, sharing, and cooperating (Bronson, 1981).

Mildred Parten (1932) found that the peer relations of young children are characterized by three forms of play. In **solitary play,** children play alone with toys, apart from other children and without regard for what they are doing. One child might be stacking rings while another does a puzzle; neither notices or cares about the other's activities. In **parallel play,** children play independently while alongside or close to other children. Several children might be gathered at a sandbox, one digging with a shovel, another making "pies," and still another dragging a truck through the sand. Even though they are in close proximity, one child's activities do not influence the play of the others. In **cooperative play,** children interact. They share toys, follow one another, and make mutual suggestions about what to do next. Although Parten believed that a stagelike developmental progression takes place from solitary to parallel and then cooperative play, other research suggests that all three types of play occur among preschoolers (Barnes, 1971; Rubin, Maioni, & Hornung, 1976). Moreover, the type of play in which preschoolers engage may depend on the socialization goals of parents and teachers. For example, in Korean American preschools, teachers encourage individual academic achievement and task persistence rather than social interaction with other children. Korean American preschoolers engage in significantly less cooperative play and more parallel play than Anglo American preschoolers do (Farver, Kim, & Lee, 1995).

Preschoolers also begin to display **social pretend play** (also called *sociodramatic play*), in which they invoke "make-believe" to change the functions of objects, create imaginary situations, and enact pretend roles, often with the cooperation of one or two peers (Rubin, Fein, & Vandenberg, 1983; Smilansky, 1968). Children use sticks and pots as band instruments, ride "magic carpets" together, and play "Mommy and Daddy." Growth in the child's cognitive, perspective-taking, and communication skills helps to explain these changes (Hartup, 1983; Howes, 1987a). To conceive of a stick as representing a flute, for example, the child must develop symbolic capabilities that allow him to let one object represent another. To play "Mommy," a young girl must relinquish her own perspective and appreciate another person's social role: what "mommies" do and how they speak to children. Finally, for complex and coordinated exchanges of pretend play to occur, such as when one child sets the table and prepares the food while the other cries like a baby, children must understand the

KEY THEME
Continuity/Discontinuity

KEY THEME
Sociocultural Influence

solitary play   Individual play, performed without regard for what others are doing.

parallel play   Side-by-side, independent play that is not interactive.

cooperative play   Interactive play in which children's actions are reciprocal.

social pretend play   Play that makes use of imaginary and symbolic objects and social roles, often enacted among several children. Also called *sociodramatic play.*

FIGURE 15.1

Changes in Time Spent with Same-Sex Friends During Early Childhood

The amount of time children spend with same-sex peers increases dramatically during early childhood, as this study of children's behavior during free play at school shows. At the same time, the proportion of time spent playing with opposite-sex peers decreases noticeably.

KEY THEME
Interaction Among Domains

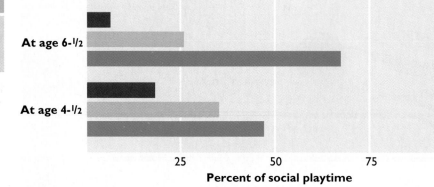

Percent of social playtime

■ With other sex ■ In mixed group ■ With same sex

Source: Adapted from Maccoby & Jacklin, 1987.

rules of social dialogue and communication. When we watch three-year-olds engage in pretend play with one another, we are witnessing an intersection of their growing competence in several arenas: social, language, and cognitive skills (Howes, Unger, & Seidner, 1989).

The School Years and Adolescence

Elementary school–age children begin to participate more in group activities than in the dyads (two-person groups) that characterize earlier peer relations. As noted in Chapter 13, they show a clear preference for same-sex peers and, to a lesser extent, for children who are racially similar. In fact, as Figure 15.1 shows, the tendency to play with other children of the same sex begins in the preschool years and grows stronger throughout the elementary school years (Maccoby & Jacklin, 1987). It's not that children dislike others of the opposite sex; they simply prefer to play with same-sex peers (Bukowski et al., 1993). They also prefer to associate with peers who have similar behavior styles; for example, aggressive children tend to "hang out" with other aggressive children (Cairns & Cairns, 1994). In general, quarrels and physical aggression with peers eventually wane, although older children do use abusive language such as threats and insults when they have conflicts with peers. Concurrently, prosocial behaviors such as sharing and helping others increase (Hartup, 1983).

A special form of play, called **rough-and-tumble play,** emerges around age two years and becomes more visible during the elementary school years, especially among boys. Children chase one another, pretend to fight, or sneak up and pounce on one another. Rough-and-tumble play differs from aggression in that children do not intend to hurt other players and it often occurs among children who like one another. Smiling and laughing often accompany rough-and-tumble play, and children will often continue to play together after a bout, all signs that these interactions are friendly. In one naturalistic observation of seven-, nine-, and eleven-year-olds, rough-and-tumble play took up about 10 percent of the children's playground time (Humphreys & Smith, 1987). In another study, kindergartners, second-, and fourth-graders were observed on their school playgrounds during recess. For some children, notably popular children, episodes of rough-and-tumble play were often followed by organized games with rules rather than aggression. A playful chase, for example, often led to a game of tag. In addition, popular children who engaged in rough-and-tumble play had higher scores on a test of social problem solving. These results suggest that for some children, rough-and-tumble play provides a context for learning role exchange (for example, "Now you chase *me*") and prosocial behaviors such as cooperation. On the other hand, when unpopular children played roughly, they were more likely to end up in a real physical fight. Their rough-and-tumble play escalated into aggression 28 percent of the time and was positively correlated with a measure of general antisocial behavior (Pellegrini, 1988).

rough-and-tumble play
Active, physical play that carries no intent of imposing harm on another child.

Activity	Time Spent
Conversing	6.76
Hanging out	6.57
Walking at school	5.65
Telephone	5.63
Travel to/from school	5.57
TV/records	5.39
Physical games	5.26
Noncontact sports	5.17
Academic	5.15
Acting silly	5.12

Source: Adapted from Zarbatany, Hartmann, & Rankin, 1990.

TABLE 15.1

Peer Activities in Later Childhood

Fifth- and sixth-graders were asked to indicate those peer activities at which they spent the most time. They rated a series of activities on a scale in which 0 indicated the activity was never performed and 7 indicated the activity was performed more than once a day. The results (average ratings) showed that preadolescents participated in a wide range of activities with one another, from conversing to simply watching TV.

What kinds of activities do school-age children most frequently engage in with their peers? A survey of eighty-one fifth- and sixth-graders in Canada showed that peer activities are diverse (Zarbatany, Hartmann, & Rankin, 1990). Participants were asked to scan a list of twenty-nine activities and rate how often they engaged in each activity with their peers. As Table 15.1 shows, preadolescents spend a lot of time talking with one another, participating in sports, and listening to music or watching television together. These activities are likely to serve a number of functions, including promoting relationships, providing opportunities for learning, and allowing children to validate their own interests and self-worth.

Peer relations during adolescence become more intense on one level and involve larger networks on another level. Adolescents form close, intimate friendships with a subset of their peers, relationships they greatly value. Many children also form **cliques,** groups of five to ten children, usually in the same class at school, who frequently interact together (Brown, 1989). Clique membership is often supplemented by identification with a **crowd,** a larger group of peers with a specific reputation, such as "jocks" or "brains." Members of crowds do not necessarily spend time together but share a label based on a stereotype. Interestingly, even though youngsters may see themselves as members of particular cliques, their membership in crowds is often identified or labeled by others (Brown, 1989). That is, a girl may not see herself as a "brain" but receive that label from peers who observe her academic achievements and studious behaviors. Membership in cliques and crowds in the middle and later school years reflects the child's growing need for group belonging at a time when he is orienting away from parents and other adults. At the same time, the values parents encourage can influence the crowds with which their adolescent children affiliate themselves. If a parent encourages achievement, for example, the child's academic success may place her in the group of "brains" (Brown et al., 1993). The norms of cliques and crowds can be powerful shapers of behavior; they often provide the adolescent with prescriptions on how to dress, act, and even what ambitions to have for the future.

As adolescents approach young adulthood and feel more secure about their self-identities, they are less interested in cliques and crowds and become oriented once again toward relationships with individuals. In one study, third-through-twelfth-graders were asked to list their closest friends in the entire school as well as the people they spent time with (Shrum & Cheek, 1987). Analysis of the patterns of relationships among children showed a sharp decline toward later adolescence in the percentage of students who were members of cliques.

One other significant change in adolescence is that some peer relations begin to include elements of sexuality. Dating becomes one of the major social activities of

clique Peer group of five to ten children who frequently interact together.

crowd Large group of peers characterized by specific traits or reputation.

During adolescence, peer groups form on the basis of shared interests or engaging in common activities. Mixed-sex interactions are more likely to occur than in the earlier years of childhood.

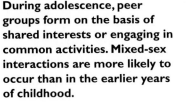

adolescence, and interest in peers of the opposite sex generally heightens (Damon, 1983). During this time, adolescents develop new social skills, such as the ability to have mutually engaging conversations with members of the opposite sex, that reinforce this shift toward romantic relationships. Again, interest in members of the opposite sex reflects the adolescent's concerns with entering the adult world. The Chronology on the next page summarizes these major developmental changes in peer relations.

PEER GROUP DYNAMICS

When we observe preschoolers or elementary school children, we see that they often associate in groups. Peer groups, however, become especially visible and significant during the middle school and early secondary school years (Crockett, Losoff, & Petersen, 1984). Adolescents frequently "hang out" in groups, desire to be members of the most popular groups, and look to the peer group for standards of appearance, conduct, and attitudes. Parents may find that their son or daughter *must* have a certain haircut or *must* buy a particular video game, only to discover that everyone else in the child's circle of friends has the same "look" or library of games. The social dynamics of large groups often differ from the dynamics of two-person groups, or dyads; the power exerted by the group in shaping how the child acts and thinks can be enormous.

Peer Group Formation

How do peer groups form in the first place? Undoubtedly, they coalesce on the basis of children's shared interests, backgrounds, or activities. Children associate with other members of their classroom, soccer team, or school band, for example. Other variables, such as socioeconomic status or ethnic and racial group membership, can also contribute. Youngsters often join with others of similar social class or ethnic/racial background (Clasen & Brown, 1985; Larkin, 1979). As we have seen in Chapter 13 and in this chapter, gender is another powerful variable; groups, for the most part, tend to be of the same sex throughout childhood and early adolescence.

A particularly enlightening description of how peer groups form and operate can be found in a classic experiment called the Robber's Cave Study, named after the state park in Oklahoma where it took place. Muzafer Sherif and his colleagues invited

CHRONOLOGY
Peer Relations

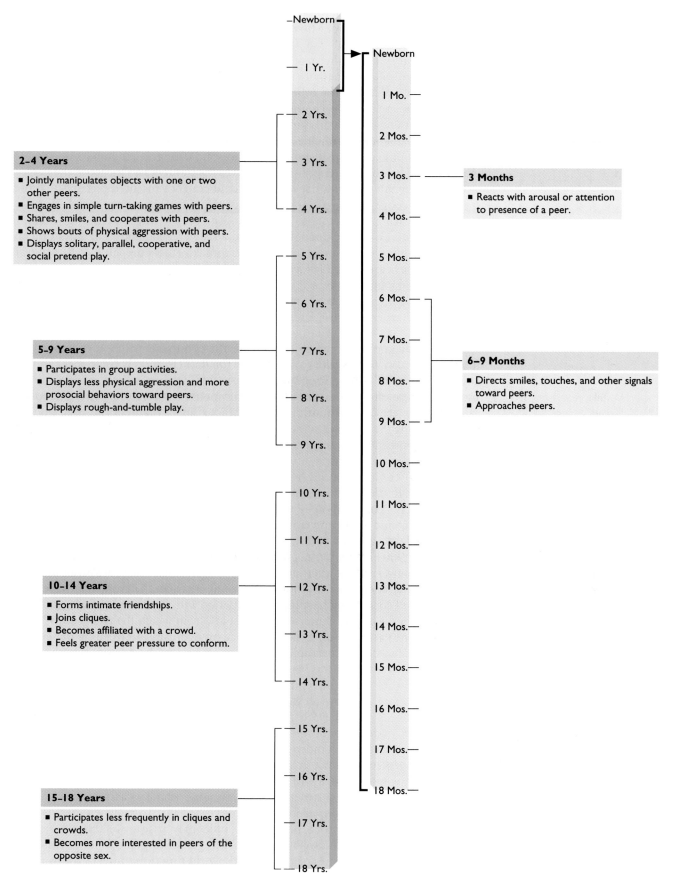

2–4 Years

- Jointly manipulates objects with one or two other peers.
- Engages in simple turn-taking games with peers.
- Shares, smiles, and cooperates with peers.
- Shows bouts of physical aggression with peers.
- Displays solitary, parallel, cooperative, and social pretend play.

5–9 Years

- Participates in group activities.
- Displays less physical aggression and more prosocial behaviors toward peers.
- Displays rough-and-tumble play.

10–14 Years

- Forms intimate friendships.
- Joins cliques.
- Becomes affiliated with a crowd.
- Feels greater peer pressure to conform.

15–18 Years

- Participates less frequently in cliques and crowds.
- Becomes more interested in peers of the opposite sex.

3 Months

- Reacts with arousal or attention to presence of a peer.

6–9 Months

- Directs smiles, touches, and other signals toward peers.
- Approaches peers.

Newborn — 1 Yr. — 2 Yrs. — 3 Yrs. — 4 Yrs. — 5 Yrs. — 6 Yrs. — 7 Yrs. — 8 Yrs. — 9 Yrs. — 10 Yrs. — 11 Yrs. — 12 Yrs. — 13 Yrs. — 14 Yrs. — 15 Yrs. — 16 Yrs. — 17 Yrs. — 18 Yrs.

Newborn — 1 Mo. — 2 Mos. — 3 Mos. — 4 Mos. — 5 Mos. — 6 Mos. — 7 Mos. — 8 Mos. — 9 Mos. — 10 Mos. — 11 Mos. — 12 Mos. — 13 Mos. — 14 Mos. — 15 Mos. — 16 Mos. — 17 Mos. — 18 Mos.

This chart describes the sequence of peer relations based on the findings of research. Children often show individual differences in the exact ages at which they display the various developmental achievements outlined here.

twenty-two fifth-grade boys who did not know one another to participate in a summer camp program (Sherif et al., 1961). The boys were divided into two groups that lived in separate parts of the state park. Initially, each group participated in its own program of typical camp activities—hiking, crafts, structured games—and was unaware of the existence of the other group. In this initial period of the experiment, each group began to develop a unique identity, and individual members performed distinct roles in relation to this group identity. One group became "tough"; the boys swore, acted rough, and ridiculed those who were "sissies." Members of the other group were polite and considerate. As group solidarity grew, members decided to name themselves, the former calling themselves the Rattlers and the latter the Eagles.

The experimenters found that when they deliberately structured certain situations to encourage cooperation, group identities could be further strengthened. One day, for example, each group returned to the campsite only to find that the staff had not prepared dinner; only the uncooked ingredients were available. The boys quickly took over, dividing up the tasks so that some cooked, others prepared drinks, and so forth. Some boys assumed a leadership role, directing the suppertime activities, and others followed their directives. It was quite apparent that the boys had a strong sense of identity with the group and that the group had a clear structure. In other words, for both the Rattlers and the Eagles, there was strong intragroup cooperation and identity.

Another change in circumstances made the group identities even more pronounced. The camp counselors arranged for the Rattlers and Eagles to meet and organized a series of competitions for them, including games such as baseball and tug-of-war. The effects of losing in these competitions were dramatic. The losing group became very disharmonious and conflict ridden. Members accused one another of causing the loss, and some boys who had previously enjoyed status and prestige were demoted in standing if they had contributed to the group's humiliation.

After these initial conflicts, however, group identity became stronger than ever. The effects of competition on behavior *between* the groups were even more pronounced. The Rattlers and Eagles verbally antagonized each other and retaliated for a loss in the day's competition by raiding each other's campsites and stealing possessions such as comic books and clothing. Each episode forged intragroup identity but also increased intergroup hostility.

In the last phase of this social experiment, the counselors attempted to lessen the bad feelings between the Rattlers and the Eagles by having them share meals or watch movies together. Instead of promoting harmony between the groups, however, this tactic produced continuing hostilities, punctuated with fights and verbal assaults. In contrast, when the experimenters created situations in which the two groups had to work together to achieve some common goal, antagonisms between them began to crumble. One hot day, for example, when the counselors "discovered" that the water pipeline for the campsites was broken, boys from both Rattlers and Eagles began to search together for the broken pipes. On another occasion, the food delivery truck broke down; again, the boys all worked together to restart the engine. The acrimonious behavior between the two groups diminished, and boys from the two groups actually began to form friendships with one another.

Thus, groups form when individuals share activities and have some common goal or purpose. Identity with the group becomes stronger as children have more and more rewarding interactions within them and as the group accomplishes its goals. Groups also quickly develop structures wherein some members assume a more dominant role than others. Group identity becomes especially strong when there is competition with other groups, but intergroup conflict may arise as well. Barriers among groups break down when they actively work together to achieve some common, overarching goal. Few studies of the formation and function of peer groups match the scope of the Robber's Cave Study, which revealed many of the intricacies of peer group dynamics and, in doing so, suggests strategies for breaking down animosities among children's peer groups.

Peer-group identity becomes stronger when children participate in cooperative activities that involve some common goal or purpose. Here, fifth graders participate in a camp activity intended to build group solidarity.

Dominance Hierarchies

The scene: a standard laboratory playroom on a university campus. Six elementary school boys, strangers to one another, are brought together to play for forty-five minutes, five days in a row. Beginning the first day, researchers discover, the boys establish dominance hierarchies, distinct levels of social power in the relationships among group members. Some boys initiate more activity, verbally persuade the other group members to act a certain way, or use aggression to get their way. Others play a more submissive role, giving in to the actions of the dominant boys. Based on the frequencies with which they display these behaviors, each boy can be rated as most or least dominant or somewhere in between (Pettit et al., 1990).

KEY THEME
Individual Differences

As laboratory studies and field experiments such as the Robber's Cave Study show, the dominance relations among members of the peer group form quickly and remain stable over a period of months or even longer (Strayer & Strayer, 1976). Especially among younger children, dominance is established through physical power and aggression; the most powerful children are those who physically coerce or threaten the other members of the group into compliance. The basis of dominance changes, however, as group members get to know one another. When preschoolers are observed over the period of a school year, for example, their aggression is highly correlated with dominance in the beginning of the year but is unrelated to dominance by the end of the year (LaFreniere & Charlesworth, 1983). As children approach adolescence, the basis for dominance shifts from physical power to characteristics such as intelligence, creativity, and interpersonal skill (Pettit et al., 1990; Savin-Williams, 1980).

KEY THEME
Child's Active Role

What function do dominance hierarchies serve in the social behavior of children? First, groups can more easily meet their objectives when certain individuals within the group assume a leadership role. Ethologists have long observed that many species of animals, especially primates, have clear lines of power that probably enhance the obtaining of food, protection against natural enemies, and control of reproduction. Among children, dominance hierarchies can serve to get games going on the playground or accomplish school projects that require group efforts. Second, dominance hierarchies make social relationships more predictable for members of the group. Each individual has a specific role, whether as leader or follower, and the behaviors associated with those roles are often clearly defined (Savin-Williams, 1979). Finally, dominance hierarchies are thought to control aggression among members of the group. Usually, once the most dominant members of the group have emerged, few other members resort to aggression. In one naturalistic observation of preschool children's free play, only 20 percent of the interactions among children were classified as counterattacks to aggression (Strayer & Strayer, 1976).

Peer Pressure and Conformity

One of the most widely accepted beliefs about peer groups is that they control the behavior of children, sometimes more than parents and other adults would like. And in fact, peer pressure *is* a very real phenomenon. When seventh-through-twelfth-graders were asked to rate how much pressure they felt from agemates in several domains, they did report pressure, and the greatest pressure was to simply be involved with peers: spend time with them, go to parties, and otherwise associate with them (Brown, Clasen, & Eicher, 1986; Clasen & Brown, 1985). They also felt pressure to excel and to complete their education. Contrary to popular opinion, however, they reported the least peer pressure to engage in misconduct, such as smoking, drinking, or having sexual relations. Older adolescents, however, felt more pressure to engage in misconduct than younger adolescents.

How willing are children to conform to these peer pressures? Again, when researchers ask them, children give different answers depending on their age (Berndt, 1979; Brown, Clasen, & Eicher, 1986; Gavin & Furman, 1989). Vulnerability to peer pressure peaks in early adolescence, usually between the sixth and ninth grades (see Figure 15.2), and may lead to conflicts with parents. In fact, adolescents report the greatest number of disagreements with their parents right around the ninth-grade mark. By late adolescence, however, the influence of peers on conformity declines. Thus, the relationship between age and peer conformity is a curvilinear one.

These developmental changes can be explained, in part, by the adjustments young people must make at different points in adolescence. Most young adolescents move from elementary school to a middle school or junior high school, where many students are strangers to one another and new relationships must be established. For many children, this is an anxiety-ridden task; they fear they "won't know anybody," a phrase many a preadolescent's parent has heard. In addition, adolescents in junior high typically move from one class to another over the course of the day; the peer group does not remain constant as it did in elementary school, and relationships may be more difficult to establish in this context. As they are adjusting to the new school setting, young adolescents also become more independent from their parents and increasingly search for their "selfhood." By conforming to the norms of the peer group and thereby becoming accepted, young adolescents meet many of their socioemo-

KEY THEME
Interaction Among Domains

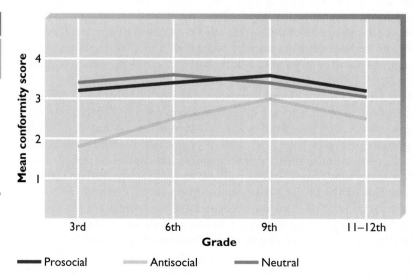

FIGURE 15.2

Developmental Changes in Conformity to Peer Pressure

Conformity to peer pressure, whether it involves prosocial, antisocial, or neutral behavior, peaks in early adolescence, then declines. The higher numbers in this graph represent greater willingness to conform.

Source: Adapted from Berndt, 1979.

tional needs, especially the need for affiliation. By virtue of their style of parenting, parents may also be responsible for adolescents' tendencies to seek out the peer group. When parents of young adolescents maintain their power and restrictiveness, limiting their children's opportunities for decision making, their children tend to turn to their peer group for advice (Fuligni & Eccles, 1993).

In contrast, older adolescents are approaching a new phase in their lives, a time when they must seek jobs, further their education, or make other major decisions. These are individual choices of great importance that require less input from peers. The older adolescent has also developed a stronger sense of self and feels less need to rely on the advice or norms of the peer group (Brown, 1989). Thus, the role of the peer group varies with the developmental tasks of different age groups.

Exactly how do peer groups exert their pressure? Most likely by rewarding individuals who conform to the group's norms and reacting negatively to those who resist. Children who conform to the norms of the group get invited to the "right" parties or receive compliments on their attire. Those who don't conform may get "the silent treatment" or, worse yet, become the objects of teasing and ridicule. Few researchers have actually observed the dynamics of peer groups as they try to enforce norms, but participants in some studies report that negative interactions within peer groups increase during early adolescence and decrease in late adolescence. The same developmental trend shows up when participants are asked how much they are bothered by these negative interactions; children are increasingly bothered in early adolescence and less bothered toward the end of the adolescent years (Gavin & Furman, 1989).

Finally, how much do the pressures peers exert conflict with those placed by parents? As we saw earlier, peers, like parents, expect the growing child to be competent and to achieve in school. In that sense, peers and parents pressure children toward some of the same goals. We also saw, however, that as adolescents approach young adulthood, the pressures to engage in behaviors frowned on by adults increase. Moreover, the results of one study show that when young adolescents strongly value conforming to adult norms (for example, by saying that getting drunk and skipping school are negative), they are less popular with their peers. Conversely, adolescents who place less value on conforming to adult norms are more popular (Allen, Weissberg, & Hawkins, 1989). Thus, adults and peers provide overlapping support in encouraging general competence but conflicting pressures when it comes to certain behaviors, such as drinking or smoking, with which some older adolescents are likely to experiment.

PEERS AS AGENTS OF SOCIALIZATION

Like parents, teachers, and the media, peers are the child's source of information about the "do's and don'ts" of the social world. Because children have such extensive social relations with their peers, there are few better sources of feedback on acceptable and unacceptable behaviors. Peers socialize their agemates in two main ways: as models and as reinforcers. In their behaviors, peers also reflect the values of the larger society.

Peers as Models

According to social learning theory, the greater the similarity between a model and an observer, the more likely it is that the observer will imitate the model's behavior (Bandura, 1969). Peers therefore are prime candidates for prompting imitation in children. Although peer imitation declines by middle childhood, it occurs quite frequently in the early years. In one study, the number of imitative acts occurring in the free play of preschoolers averaged 14.82 per hour (Abramovitch & Grusec, 1978).

There is ample evidence that a host of social behaviors can be transmitted through peer modeling. Display of aggression is a prime example. When children observe a peer acting aggressively with toys, they spontaneously perform similar aggressive acts (Hicks, 1965). On the opposite end of the spectrum, models can promote sharing and other altruistic acts in child observers (Elliott & Vasta, 1970; Hartup & Coates, 1967). Peer models can also influence gender-role behaviors. Most children are reluctant to play with toys meant for the opposite sex. Yet if a peer model displays cross-sex play, children's tendency to follow suit increases (Kobasigawa, 1968; Wolf, 1973).

A powerful variable influencing imitation is the model's competence as perceived by the child observer, especially when new skills or behaviors are involved. Children prefer older, friendly models who are similar to themselves in background and interests (Brody & Stoneman, 1981; Hartup & Coates, 1967; Rosekrans, 1967). Especially in the realm of social behaviors, children may imitate competent peer models over adult models because they see the behaviors selected by peers as more appropriate for themselves.

Peers as Reinforcers

Peers not only model certain behaviors but also actively reinforce their friends' behaviors. Peers communicate clear signals about the social behaviors they prefer and those they won't tolerate, messages that may either maintain or inhibit the child's behaviors. Consider the case of sex-typed behaviors. Researchers observed the reactions of peers as preschool-age children engaged in sex-appropriate or inappropriate play in their nursery schools (Lamb & Roopnarine, 1979). They found that boys who engaged in male-typed activities such as playing ball or chase received more praise and approval (mostly from other boys) than girls did when they attempted these same behaviors. Similarly, peers more frequently reinforced girls than boys who played with dolls or kitchen items or assumed female character roles. Peers controlled behavior through punishment, too, although it was reserved largely for cross-sex activities. This study demonstrates how forcefully peers can enforce stereotypical codes of behavior for boys and girls by directly rewarding activities consistent with those codes.

In the same way, peer reactions can regulate the frequency of other social behaviors, such as aggression. In their observations of aggression among preschoolers, Gerald Patterson and his colleagues noted that about three-fourths of the aggressive behaviors that took place were reinforced by victims' compliance or submission (Patterson, Littman, & Bricker, 1967). The consequence was that aggressors maintained their combative styles of interaction. If a peer responded with counteraggression, however, the perpetrator was less likely to repeat the action with that child, choosing either another victim or another behavior. Thus, peers powerfully affect one another by means of their positive and negative reactions.

PEER POPULARITY AND SOCIAL COMPETENCE

Parents, teachers such as Jan Nakamura in this chapter's opening scene, and others who have the opportunity to observe children over time usually notice the two extreme ends of the sociability spectrum: some children seem to be at the center of many activities, from school projects to playground games, whereas others are ridiculed or ignored. Frequently the patterns of peer acceptance that become established in the early school years persist for years afterward, along with the psychological rewards or disappointments that accompany them. Psychologists have uncovered several factors related to peer acceptance and popularity and have applied this knowledge to helping children at the unpopular extreme of the spectrum.

Measuring Peer Acceptance

Given the relationship between peer acceptance and later development described at the start of this chapter, the task of identifying children with problems in this domain

Name _____

EXAMPLES:

HOW MUCH DO YOU LIKE TO PLAY WITH THIS PERSON AT SCHOOL?

	I don't like to				I like to a lot
Louise Blue	1	2	3	4	5
Russell Grey	1	2	3	4	5
John Armon	1	2	3	4	5
Andrea Brandt	1	2	3	4	5
Sue Curtis	1	2	3	4	5
Sandra Drexel	1	2	3	4	5
Jeff Ellis	1	2	3	4	5
Bill Fox	1	2	3	4	5
Diane Higgins	1	2	3	4	5
Harry Jones	1	2	3	4	5
Jill Lamb	1	2	3	4	5
Steve Murray	1	2	3	4	5
Jo Anne Norman	1	2	3	4	5
Pam Riley	1	2	3	4	5
Jim Stevens	1	2	3	4	5

HOW MUCH DO YOU LIKE TO PLAY WITH THIS PERSON AT SCHOOL?

1	2	3	4	5
I don't like to				I like to a lot

Source: Asher, 1985.

FIGURE 15.3

A Sociometric Rating Scale

In this peer assessment tool, the child is asked to rate each peer on a series of items, such as "How much do you like to play with this person at school?" The average rating each target child receives from peers is an index of that child's peer acceptance.

is all the more important. Psychologists have relied on teachers or their own observations of children's behaviors to assess the quality of peer relations, but they especially rely on the assessments provided by children's agemates.

Peer assessments frequently consist of a **sociometric nomination** measure in which children are asked to name a specified number of peers (usually between three and five) who fit a certain criterion. For example, children might be asked to "name three classmates you especially like (or dislike)" or "list three peers you would like to walk home from school with." The number of positive or negative nominations the child receives from other children serves as a measure of his popularity. Alternatively, children are sometimes asked to rate each peer in the class or group on a **sociometric rating scale,** a series of items such as "How much do you like to be with this person at school?" (see Figure 15.3). The target child's average rating by the other children is the index of peer acceptance.

Peer nomination measures, in turn, are used to classify children's *peer status. Popular* children receive many more positive ("like") than negative ("dislike") nominations. *Rejected* children, in contrast, receive few positive but many negative nominations; they are overtly disliked by their peers. *Neglected* children receive low numbers of nominations in either category; although they lack friends, they are not actively disliked (Asher & Dodge, 1986). *Controversial* children receive high numbers of both positive and negative nominations. They have a high degree of "social impact" because they are active and visible, but they are generally not preferred as social partners (Coie, Dodge, & Coppotelli, 1982). Finally, *average* children do not receive extreme scores on peer nomination measures. Table 15.2 summarizes these categories of peer status.

What exactly is it about unpopular children that makes them so unappealing to their agemates and places them so consistently in an undesirable status? This is a particularly important question for those attempting to intervene in these children's "at-risk" circumstances.

KEY THEME
Individual Differences

sociometric nomination
Peer assessment measure in which children are asked to name a specified number of peers who fit a certain criterion, such as "peers you would like to walk home with."

sociometric rating scale Peer assessment measure in which children rate peers on a number of social dimensions.

TABLE 15.2

Classifications of Peer Status

The number of positive and negative peer nominations received determines whether a child's peer status is classified as controversial, rejected, neglected, or popular. Average children receive less extreme scores on peer nomination measures.

		Positive Peer Nominations	
		Many	Few
Negative peer nominations	Many	Controversial	Rejected
	Few	Popular	Neglected

KEY THEME
Individual Differences

KEY THEME
Sociocultural Influence

KEY THEME
Child's Active Role

KEY THEME
Child's Active Role

Characteristics of Popular and Unpopular Children

Peer popularity is related to a number of variables, some of which lie within the child's control and some of which, unfortunately, do not. The child's physical attractiveness and, perhaps, motor skills fall into the latter category, whereas social skills belong to the former.

Physical Attractiveness   When asked to rate photographs of unfamiliar children, both preschool- and elementary school–age children believe children with attractive faces are more friendly, intelligent, and socially competent than unattractive children (Dion & Berscheid, 1974; Langlois & Stephan, 1981). Correlations between children's ratings of peers' attractiveness and sociometric measures of peer acceptance typically range between +0.35 and +0.50, indicating a moderately strong relationship between these two variables (Cavior & Dokecki, 1973; Lerner & Lerner, 1977). Body type makes a difference too. For example, boys with broad shoulders and large muscles are the most popular, and short, chubby boys are the least popular (Staffieri, 1967). The reasons for these stereotypic beliefs are unknown, but they can lead to self-fulfilling behaviors in children who have been labeled (Hartup, 1983). For example, a child who receives peer attention because of attractiveness may have numerous opportunities to develop the social skills that lead to even greater peer acceptance. Finally, as we saw in Chapter 5, boys who mature early and girls who mature later during adolescence are more likely to be accepted by peers.

Motor Skills   Another factor related to peer acceptance is the child's proficiency in motor activities. Both boys and girls who are coordinated, strong, and skilled in activities such as throwing a ball are rated as more popular by peers and as more socially competent by their teachers and parents (Hops & Finch, 1985). It may be that the value our society places on athletic prowess is reflected in children's preferences in playmates. Alternatively, motor skill may facilitate the manipulation of objects and game playing that constitute the majority of children's shared activities. Those who are talented in this arena will naturally have more peer contacts and eventually be better liked.

Social Skills   One of the most important factors in peer acceptance is the constellation of social behaviors displayed by popular and unpopular children. Researchers who have observed the overt activities of accepted and unaccepted peers have learned that each presents a distinct behavioral profile. In general, popular children engage in prosocial, cooperative, and normative behaviors and show a high degree of social skill. In contrast, rejected and neglected children behave in aggressive, withdrawn, or other socially inappropriate ways for which they receive little social reinforcement (Parkhurst & Asher, 1992; Pettit et al., 1996).

For example, when Gary Ladd (1983) observed third- and fourth-grade students during recess, he noted several differences in the behavioral styles of popular and rejected children. Popular children spent more time in cooperative play, social conversation, and other positive social interactions with peers than their rejected counterparts. Rejected children, on the other hand, spent more time engaging in antagonistic behaviors such as arguing and playing in a rough-and-tumble fashion, or playing or standing alone at a distance from peers.

Children who lack social skills may be rejected or neglected by their peers. In contrast, popular children display prosocial behaviors and a wide range of social knowledge.

According to the results of another study that examined the peer-directed behaviors of first- and third-grade boys, neglected and controversial children display still other clusters of behaviors (Coie & Dodge, 1988). Neglected boys were the least aggressive of any group observed. They tended to engage in isolated activities and had low visibility with peers. Controversial boys were intellectually, athletically, or socially talented and very active, but they were sometimes prone to anger and rule violations. The mixture of their positive and negative social behaviors thus elicited a concomitantly mixed reaction from their classmates. Thus, children may be unpopular with their peers for a number of reasons, ranging from social withdrawal to outright aggression.

The social competence of popular children becomes markedly apparent when they are asked to enter a group of unfamiliar children who are already at play. Kenneth Dodge and his colleagues observed as individual kindergartners entered a room where two other children they did not know were already playing with blocks (Dodge et al., 1983). Popular, rejected, and neglected children used different tactics to gain entry into the group, with popular children generally the most successful. Rejected children tended to disrupt the group's ongoing activity by pushing the blocks off the table or making intrusive statements, usually about themselves (for example, "I have a baby brother"). In return, their peer hosts responded negatively to them. Neglected children were not disruptive but employed another ineffective strategy. Instead of making some verbal or nonverbal attempt to join the group, these children passively watched as their peers played—and they were ignored. Popular children seemed to know exactly what to do. Rather than calling attention to themselves or disrupting the group's activities, they made statements about their peers or what they were doing, such as "That looks like a fun game you are playing." These diplomatic verbalizations paved the way for their smooth integration into the group.

In the second part of the same research project, Dodge and his associates organized play groups for seven- and eight-year-old boys during the summer when school was out of session. None of the boys knew one another at the outset, so it was possible to observe how they initiated entry into a play group under natural circumstances. Boys who were successful in entering a group that was already playing followed a three-step sequence that consisted of (1) waiting and watching the group, (2) mimicking the group's activity (for example, playing basketball or singing), and (3) making a group-oriented statement, such as describing what the group was doing. In general, successful children began with low-risk tactics and, as they received positive feedback, moved toward higher-risk strategies. They also kept the focus of attention on the peer group rather than on themselves.

Popular children are particularly effective at maintaining cohesive social interactions with their peers. When Betty Black and Nancy Hazen (1990) observed the social entry behaviors of preschool-age children, they found that disliked children made significantly more irrelevant comments when they spoke with peers. The following segment illustrates how such a conversation might go:

Mary: We're being witches here, and I am the mean witch.
Sandy: My mom is taking me to get shoes today. (p. 387)

In contrast, children who were liked tended to maintain organized, thematically coherent conversations with their peers.

Thus, observations of popular children show that they display a range of social skills their more unpopular agemates often lack. But does their social skill actually cause their popularity, or do children develop reputations that precipitate subsequent successful or maladaptive patterns of social interaction? A child who is initially rejected because of his appearance, for example, may develop an aggressive style in retaliation. Gary Ladd and his associates examined this question more closely by observing preschool children in the playground during three 6-week intervals at the beginning, middle, and end of the academic year (Ladd, Price, & Hart, 1988). Episodes of cooperative play, arguments, and other positive and negative forms of interaction were recorded. In addition, children's sociometric status was assessed at each of these three points in time. The results showed that children who engaged in more cooperative play at the beginning of the school year made gains in peer acceptance by the end of the school year, whereas children who frequently argued showed a decline in acceptance by the middle of the school year. These results are consistent with the idea that children's behaviors precede their social status.

Some children are "loners." They have few or no friends, and they end up playing or doing their schoolwork on their own, even if surrounded by other children. Along with aggression, social withdrawal is considered by many child development experts to be one of the two most important indicators of a behavior problem (Rubin & Asendorpf, 1993). Withdrawn children are prone to express anxiety, negative conceptions of themselves, and depression (Rubin, Hymel, & Mills, 1989), and lack of social contact is a feature of several clinical categories of psychopathology (Rubin & Asendorpf, 1993).

ATYPICAL DEVELOPMENT

Social Withdrawal

Children may have limited interactions with their peers for a number of reasons. Some children may simply prefer to play by themselves, curling up with a book or becoming involved with an interesting toy. This pattern is usually noted in the preschool and early school years and is not necessarily an indication that the child is at risk for abnormal development. If this pattern persists, however, peers may react negatively and outrightly reject the child (Rubin, 1993). A second pattern is that of the shy child, who is nervous about being in new environments or with strangers but generally desires social interactions. This characteristic may stem from a biologically based temperament that results in the child's wariness and inhibition (Kagan, Snidman, & Arcus, 1993). Early negative experiences due to a shy temperament can escalate into more severe social withdrawal as the childhood years progress. A third category is children who desire social interactions but, because of their inept social skills, are avoided by their peers. These children may react with aggression, which further contributes to their isolation (Rubin & Asendorpf, 1993).

Researchers are just beginning to understand some of the factors, aside from biological temperament, that may contribute to social withdrawal in children. For example, Rosemary Mills and Kenneth Rubin (1993) found that mothers of four-year-olds who were withdrawn were highly controlling and directive when attempting to teach their children how to interact with peers. They also expressed more anger, disappointment, and guilt about their children's behaviors than mothers of aggressive and "average" children. The reactions of peers may make a difference too. First-grade children do not seem to think about social withdrawal as a liability when asked to rate the likability of children described in vignettes. By age ten, though, social withdrawal was viewed as an abnormal behavior (Younger, Gentile, & Burgess, 1993). Interestingly, even in China, where adults value shyness as a personality trait, children shift from positive to negative evaluations of shy children at around age twelve (Chen, Rubin, & Li, 1995). These studies, along with the different patterns of social withdrawal described above, suggest the complex nature of this style of social functioning.

Despite these complexities, it is important that researchers continue to examine the nature of social withdrawal in childhood because of its potential lingering impact even well into adulthood. Kenneth Rubin gives one example in a letter he received from a 51-year-old individual who had read about his research:

> *I recall one instance in my third year of grade school and my teacher approached me after recess with the enquiry "have you no one to play with—I have noticed you standing by yourself at recess for several days now." I recalled replying and LYING— "yes I've friends." The teacher was observant and I give her credit for this, however, I wish, oh how I wish, something had been done about my isolation at the tender age of 7 or 8. It has been a long, lonely road. (Rubin & Asendorpf, 1993, p. 4)*

The Origins of Social Competence

What factors are responsible for the skilled social behaviors of some children and the seeming social ineptness of others? Researchers draw their answers from a number of perspectives, from the early attachment relationships children form with their caregivers to capabilities in processing the subtle cues that form such an integral part of social interactions.

Attachment Relationships   As we saw in Chapter 11, infants who are securely attached to their caregivers are predisposed to have positive peer relations in toddlerhood (Waters, Wippman, & Sroufe, 1979). A plausible hypothesis is that in their relationships with caregivers, children have the opportunity to learn and practice a variety of social skills, such as turn taking, compromise, and effective communication. Once honed and refined, these abilities can later be employed with peers and other individuals in the child's life. Attachment also teaches children about emotional ties: how to recognize affection and how to show it. This knowledge about the central ingredients of relationships and the "internal working models" they construct regarding relationships may assist children as they expand their social worlds (Hay, 1985; Sroufe, 1983). Longitudinal studies confirm that school-age children who have more positive relationships with peers tended to have secure attachments with their parents during infancy and toddlerhood (Booth et al., 1995; Youngblade & Belsky, 1992). Other researchers have noted that seven-to-twelve-year-olds who reported positive relationships with their mothers also had positive cognitions about relationships with peers. For example, those who characterized their mothers as being indifferent made similar judgments about interactions with peers (Rudolph, Hammen, & Burge, 1995).

KEY THEME
Interaction Among Domains

Parental Influences   Parents play an influential role in the relationships their children form with peers. Broadly speaking, parents who exhibit an authoritative style (see Chapter 14)—that is, are responsive, are nurturant, and provide verbal explanations—tend to have children who are popular and who display prosocial behaviors with peers. In contrast, children of authoritarian, power-assertive parents are more likely to be classified as rejected (Dekovic & Janssens, 1992; Hart et al., 1992; Pettit et al., 1996).

Parents serve as important models of social competence for their children; they may also provide explicit instruction on appropriate ways to behave in social situations. In one study, mothers of popular and unpopular preschoolers were observed as they introduced their children to a pair of peers busily playing with blocks. Mothers of unpopular children tended to disrupt the ongoing play and use their authority to incorporate their own child into the group. In many ways, their behaviors resembled those of the unpopular children we discussed earlier. In contrast, mothers of popular children encouraged them to become involved in play without intervening in the activity of the host peers. Moreover, in a subsequent interview, these mothers displayed greater knowledge of how to encourage their children to make friends, resolve conflicts, and display other positive social behaviors (Finnie & Russell, 1988). Others have noted that compared to mothers of less popular children, mothers of popular children are generally less disagreeable and demanding when they play with their children and are more likely to focus on feelings when talking with both their own and other children (Putallaz, 1987). In addition, both mothers and fathers of unpopular children have been found to shift conversations to irrelevant topics, speak while someone else is talking, and ignore their children's requests. Perhaps not surprisingly, their children showed similar ineffective communication styles (Black & Logan, 1995).

Finally, parents can influence children's social competence on another level: by managing their children's social activities. Parents vary in the extent to which they create opportunities for their children to interact with peers, experiences that provide the context for the emergence of social skills. Some parents seek out play groups for their preschoolers, enroll them in nursery school, or periodically get together with friends who have children. When parents deliberately arrange peer contacts for their preschoolers, their children have a greater variety of playmates and a larger number of consistent play partners, display more prosocial behaviors at preschool, and have higher sociometric status (at least among boys) than when parents do not make such efforts (Ladd & Golter, 1988; Ladd & Hart, 1992). Opportunities to interact with peers provide the child with a natural arena to discover those behaviors that generate positive responses from peers and those that do not.

Parents influence children's peer-group relations by structuring the kinds of opportunities children have to socialize with age-mates. They also serve as models of social competence and may provide instruction on how to behave in social situations.

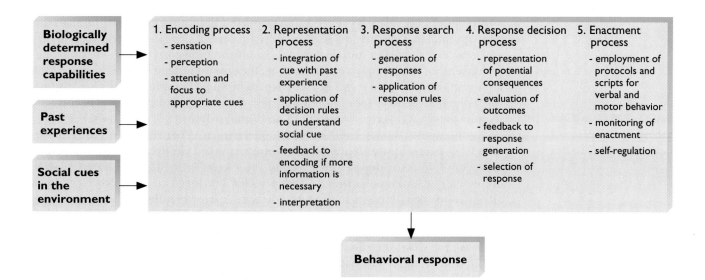

| Biologically determined response capabilities | 1. Encoding process
- sensation
- perception
- attention and focus to appropriate cues | 2. Representation process
- integration of cue with past experience
- application of decision rules to understand social cue
- feedback to encoding if more information is necessary
- interpretation | 3. Response search process
- generation of responses
- application of response rules | 4. Response decision process
- representation of potential consequences
- evaluation of outcomes
- feedback to response generation
- selection of response | 5. Enactment process
- employment of protocols and scripts for verbal and motor behavior
- monitoring of enactment
- self-regulation |

Behavioral response

Source: Adapted from Dodge, 1986.

FIGURE 15.4

Social Competence: An Information-Processing Model

Kenneth Dodge has proposed a five-step model of social competence based on the child's growing social information-processing skills. The process begins when the child is able to correctly encode and then interpret a social cue. Next, the child generates a set of possible responses and evaluates the potential outcomes of each. Finally, the child enacts the behavior he or she internally selected. The origins of these five steps lie in the child's biological makeup, past experiences, and social cues surrounding the event. Children low in social competence may have difficulties at any step in this model.

Day Care When children have more experiences with peers because they are enrolled in day care (as many children do in today's society), they show greater social competence than children reared solely at home by their parents. Carollee Howes (1987a) conducted an extensive longitudinal study of the peer relationships of one-to-six-year-olds who were enrolled in child care programs. Among her findings was the discovery that popular or average-status children had entered child care at earlier ages (about ten to nineteen months on average) than rejected children (about thirty to thirty-three months). Early experience was not the sole important factor, however. Howes found the stability of the peer group was significant as well. Toddlers who had spent a year or more *with the same peers* were more socially competent in that they showed more cooperative forms of play. These children were also rated by teachers as having fewer difficulties than children who had moved to a different group. Evidently, experiences with peers indeed provide an excellent context for mastering social skills, especially if there is sustained contact with familiar agemates.

Social-Cognitive Development The studies of peer group entry strategies described earlier vividly illustrate that the social competence of children includes an array of intertwined cognitive and behavioral skills. A five-step information-processing model of social competence formulated by Kenneth Dodge (see Figure 15.4) suggests more precisely how cognitions and behaviors are related and where problems in social functioning might occur (Dodge, 1986; Dodge et al., 1986).

According to Dodge, the first step in processing social information is to focus on the correct cues. For example, suppose a boy initiates a conversation with a peer. It is more important for the child to encode the peer's facial expression ("Is that a smile or a sneer?") than the color of her clothing. Second, the child must meaningfully interpret the social cues based on his past experiences. Most children would interpret a scowl on a peer's face as a sign of hostility and a smile as a mark of friendliness. In the third step of processing, the child generates one or more potential behavioral responses. If he perceives the peer as hostile, he may contemplate avoiding her or matching her hostility. If he reads her signals as friendly, he may consider smiling back or beginning to talk. Fourth, the child learns to evaluate the potential consequences of each possible behavior. Hostility and aggression could lead to physical harm whereas avoidance might not, and hence avoidance might be preferable. Finally, the child enacts the chosen response verbally or physically, monitors the outcome of his behavior, and, if necessary, modifies it, engaging in the five-step cycle over again. This model thus includes a number of steps at which things can go wrong to disrupt a smooth, mutually rewarding social interaction.

KEY THEME
Interaction Among Domains

Studies of peer relations suggest that popular children are more skillful than un-popular (and, in particular, rejected) children at several steps in the model. First, they are better able to encode and decipher social information correctly. In one study, elementary school children were asked to label the emotions depicted in sets of pictures. For example, one was a series of faces depicting anger, happiness, sadness, disgust, surprise, and fear. Rejected children were less able than popular children to correctly identify the emotions represented in these stimuli (Monfries & Kafer, 1987).

Second, some rejected children tend to make incorrect attributions about the behaviors of peers. In one experiment, researchers asked children to view videotaped episodes of an actor destroying a second actor's toy with either hostile, prosocial, accidental, or ambiguous intent. Both rejected and neglected children tended to attribute hostile intentions to the actor's actions, even when the acts were accidental or prosocial. Popular children were more often correct in their judgments (Dodge, Murphy, & Buchsbaum, 1984). In fact, rejected children maintain their hostile attributions even when they are told the victim in a story feels happy (Keane & Parrish, 1992). Numerous studies have confirmed that aggressive children in particular tend to make more hostile attributions about the intentions of others than nonaggressive children. This finding holds true for children from the middle school years through adolescence and for children from different ethnic backgrounds (Dodge & Somberg, 1987; Graham, Hudley, & Williams, 1992; Slaby & Guerra, 1988). As a result of these mistaken attributions, aggressive children often retaliate with further negative behavior. Children who exhibit this style of overattributing hostile intent are called *reactive-aggressive* (Crick & Dodge, 1996).

Third, some rejected children tend to suggest inappropriate strategies to resolve social problems and have difficulty devising alternative paths to attain their social goals (Rubin & Krasnor, 1986). Researchers typically assess social problem-solving skills by presenting children with hypothetical social dilemmas and examining their proposed solutions. Researchers in one study asked kindergartners to react to a series of dilemmas in which, for example, one child takes away another's toy. Unpopular children were much more likely than popular children to recommend an aggressive solution, such as "Punch him" or "She could beat her up." A preference for aggressive solutions to problems is typical of children who are *proactive aggressive* (Crick & Dodge, 1996). In addition, when Kenneth Rubin and Linda Krasnor observed children's strategies for handling social problems in naturalistic settings, they noted that rejected children were rigid in their attempts (Rubin & Krasnor, 1986). If, for example, a rejected child failed to convince another child to give him an object, he simply repeated the same unsuccessful behavior. Popular children often tried a different approach to attaining their goal, indicating a broader and more flexible repertoire of social problem-solving skills.

Popular children thus possess social knowledge that leads to successful interactions with their peers and also behave in ways that manifest this expertise. They know what strategies are needed to make friends (for example, ask others their names, invite them to do things) and can describe prosocial behaviors that tend to foster peer relationships (for example, be generous, keep promises) (Wentzel & Erdley, 1993). They also recognize that the achievement of their social goals may require time and work and adjust their behaviors according to the sometimes subtle demands of the situation (Asher, 1983). Rejected children, on the other hand, have a more limited awareness of how to solve social problems, believing particularly in the effectiveness of aggression. Unfortunately, their antagonistic actions frequently lead to a spiral of continuing rejection. As they become disassociated from more socially skilled, popular peers, they have fewer opportunities to learn the basics of successful social interaction from them. Moreover, the child who receives consistently negative feedback from peers would probably be hard pressed to be positive, cooperative, and friendly. Neglected children have their own special problems. Rubin and Krasnor (1986) believe children in this special category do not display social cognitive deficits but insecurities and anxieties about the consequences of their social actions. What they need is more self-confidence in their abilities to interact with and be accepted by their peers.

*J*an's attention was drawn to the loud shouts of a circle of boys at the back of the playground. As she approached, she saw two boys in the middle of the circle, one waving clenched fists and yelling at the other. Quickly she stepped in and broke up the fight, fortunately before anyone got hurt. She recognized the older of the two boys; he was a fourth-grader who had a reputation for being a "bully." The other child was a small, frightened-looking second-grader who was on the verge of tears. Jan knew she would have some talking to do to both of them, and probably to their parents as well.

RESEARCH APPLIED TO PARENTING

Helping the Victims of Aggression

Researchers have documented many of the characteristics of children who are rejected, particularly those who are aggressive with their peers. But what about children who are the victims of aggression? About 9 percent of children are chronic targets of peer aggression, a pattern that can begin as early as kindergarten age. Being a victim is associated with poorer school adjustment, anxiety, low self-esteem, loneliness, and depression (Boulton & Underwood, 1992; Kochenderfer & Ladd, 1996; Olweus, 1993a). Given these characteristics of victims, is there anything parents (and perhaps teachers) can do to stop this negative cycle?

Dan Olweus has studied the problem of bullies and victims among children in grades one through nine in Norway and Sweden. He has found that victims are often anxious, sensitive, and quiet children who react to bullying by crying and giving in. Often they are physically weaker than most children their age and generally have few friends. Olweus believes this pattern of passive characteristics signals to other children that they are unlikely to retaliate against aggression (Olweus, 1993a). Other researchers have confirmed that chronic victims tend to be unassertive and submissive when they are with their peers (Schwartz, Dodge, & Coie, 1993). A major intervention program to deal with the problems of bullying was launched in Norway over a three-year period. The program involved about twenty-five hundred students from forty-two elementary and junior high schools, as well as their parents and teachers. Advice to the parents of chronic victims included the following:

1. *Help the child to develop self-confidence by encouraging special talents or abilities he displays.* Children who gain confidence are more likely to be assertive and refuse to tolerate the behaviors of bullies.

2. *Encourage the child to undertake some form of physical training or participate in sports.* By doing so he will feel less anxiety about his body and send out "signals" of strength rather than weakness to potential aggressors.

One way to help children who are the victims of bullies is to encourage their physical development so that they do not send cues suggesting "weakness" to potential aggressors. Building the victim's confidence by encouraging special abilities and talents can also be beneficial.

3. *Help the child get to know a friendly student in the class who has similar interests or is also looking for a friend.* A relationship with another peer can help with feelings of loneliness and depression.

4. *Encourage the child's attempts to become involved with people or activities outside the family.* This suggestion is especially helpful if the family tends to attempt to protect the child every time he is attacked.

This advice was combined with several other programmatic changes involving the school, including teachers' institution of class rules against bullying, better supervision of lunch and recess, talks with the parents of bullies, and promotion of more positive classroom experiences and cooperative learning (Olweus, 1993b). The results showed a 50 percent reduction in the number of children being bullied (and in those acting as bullies as well). In addition, the incidence of other antisocial behavior such as thefts and vandalism was reduced, and the social climate of the classroom became more positive. A key to the program's success was the involvement of *all* children in the program (not just bullies and victims), greater supervision of children during the school day, and good communication between teachers and parents (Olweus, 1994). It seems that many children, not just victims and bullies, can profit from these multifacted intervention techniques.

Training Social Skills

Can children be taught the elements of socially skilled behavior and thereby gain greater acceptance from their peers? Answering this question is important in light of findings that the longer children experience rejection from peers, the more likely they are to have academic, social, and psychological problems (DeRosier, Kupersmidt, & Patterson, 1994). Several forms of intervention, usually employed in schools and clinical settings, have produced improvements in children's interpersonal strategies.

Modeling   One effective training technique is *modeling*, that is, exposing children to live or recorded models displaying desirable behaviors. For example, one research team presented a group of socially withdrawn preschoolers with short videotapes depicting young children engaging in social behaviors accompanied by a narration of their thoughts (Jakibchuk & Smeriglio, 1976). The soundtrack included the following self-directed statements as the model approached a group of peers: "Those children over there are playing together. . . . I would like to play with them. But I'm afraid. I don't know what to do or say. . . . This is hard. But I'll try. . . . I'm close to them. I did it. Good for me. . . ." Compared with their baseline behaviors, withdrawn children who watched these videotapes for four days increased the number of their social interactions and in turn were the objects of more positive social behaviors from others. The results were dramatic when children who received this treatment were compared to children who received no intervention at all or who saw a film on another subject (see Figure 15.5). From the perspective of social learning theory, by identifying with the model, observing how the model acted, and noting the positive consequences of the model's behavior, children were able to expand their repertoire of social behaviors and increase their likelihood of performing those behaviors.

Reinforcement   A second type of intervention uses social or material *reinforcement* to shape socially skilled behaviors and increase their frequency, a technique of operant conditioning (see Chapter 6). Suppose a withdrawn child merely looks at a group of peers playing on the opposite side of the room. The teacher or parent immediately reacts with a "Good!" or a pat on the head. Next, the young child might take a few steps in the direction of the group. Again, the adult promptly delivers a reinforcer. The teacher or parent rewards each successive approximation to the target behavior—in this case, joining the group—until the child has actually entered the group.

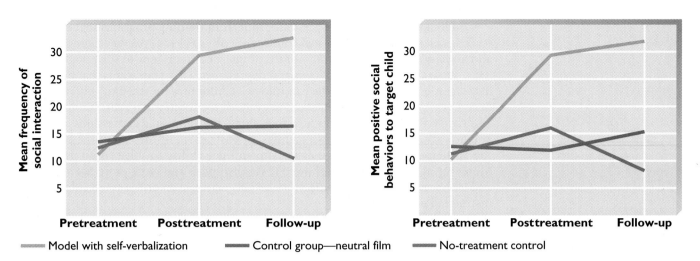

Source: Adapted from Jakibchuk & Smeriglio, 1976.

FIGURE 15.5

Training Social Skills

In an experiment that evaluated the effects of several treatment strategies with socially withdrawn preschoolers, researchers found that children who observed a model approach a group of peers while verbalizing his thoughts later increased in their number of social interactions compared to the pretreatment (or baseline) period. These children also experienced more positive social behaviors from others. The graphs show both measures for this treatment group compared to a group that saw a neutral film and to a no-treatment control group. These last two groups were included to ensure that any gains in social behavior were not the result of simple contact with the experimenters or exposure to a film per se.

In general, direct reinforcement of social behaviors is a very effective technique, especially for increasing their frequency (Schneider & Byrne, 1985).

Sometimes the operant approach is combined with other techniques, such as modeling. In one investigation, withdrawn nursery school children received social reinforcement whenever they interacted with their peers. Those who also saw a model demonstrating social interactions showed the greatest gains in the amount of time spent with peers (O'Connor, 1972).

Coaching   The most popular training technique has been *coaching,* or direct instruction in displaying an assortment of social behaviors. In this approach, a verbal presentation of the "right" and "wrong" ways to act is frequently accompanied by discussion about why certain techniques work and by opportunities for children to *roleplay,* or act out the desirable behaviors. The goal is to expand children's knowledge of socially desirable behaviors and develop social problem-solving skills. For example, in one social skills training program, elementary school children learn how to join a conversation:

> *Teacher:*   Chances are that if you don't know how to start talking with another person or join in when others are talking, you won't be a part of many conversations. . . . For example, pretend that some of your classmates are talking about a TV show that you happened to see last night and you want to get in on the conversation. . . . What you might do is walk over to the group and, when there is a slight pause in the talking, say something like, "Are you talking about 'Star Trek'? I saw that and really liked it a lot too." At this point you have joined the conversation.
>
> Next, you want to make sure that you participate in what's going on. You should listen and add comments to what is being said. . . . Can you give me different examples of how you can now add to or take part in a conversation or what else you would say? (Michelson et al., 1983, pp. 116–117)

Karen Bierman (1986) has added still another component to a social skills training program based on coaching: conducting the intervention as a cooperative activity among both popular and unpopular peers. Each target child in her group of preadolescents met with two socially accepted classmates for ten half-hour sessions to produce a film together but also to receive coaching on expressing feelings, asking questions, and displaying leadership. This two-pronged approach led to greater improvements in conversational skills than social skills training alone, possibly because peers could observe firsthand the positive changes occurring in initially unskilled children and could reinforce them immediately.

Children as young as four years can profit from training programs that explicitly teach social skills. George Spivack and Myrna Shure (1974) provided preschoolers and kindergartners with several months of instruction on how to solve social problems. Situations such as the following were presented: "This girl wants that boy to get his wagon out of the way so she can ride by." Children were asked to generate solutions to the problems and then asked to evaluate the solutions' merits. Children were also taught other skills, such as how to evaluate the emotional expressions of others and how to cope with their own feelings of frustration. At the end of the program, the participants showed significant gains in their ability to solve social problems. Moreover, aggressive children showed fewer disruptive and more prosocial behaviors and withdrawn children became more socially active, even one year after the formal instruction ended.

M odeling, reinforcement, and coaching have all been effective in treating both aggression and social withdrawal in children (Bierman & Montminy, 1993; Schneider & Byrne, 1985). Moreover, some studies have found that children show gains in their sociometric

CONTROVERSY: THINKING IT OVER

Can Social Skills Training Programs Change a Child's Peer Status?

status following their participation in a social skills training program (Asher, Parker, & Walker, 1996). This finding is consistent with the large body of evidence showing that popular children are socially skilled. Shouldn't unpopular children gain status when they acquire similarly adept social behaviors?

Social acceptance does not always follow social skills training, however. For example, in one study, third-through-fifth-graders who were low on peer acceptance were given four weeks of training in skills such as greeting others, extending invitations, and carrying on conversations. Even though these children showed greater knowledge and use of social skills than the control groups that didn't receive explicit training, there were no significant changes in their acceptance by peers (La Greca & Santogrossi, 1980). Perhaps unpopular children have reputations that outlast the positive changes in their interpersonal behaviors (Hymel, Wagner, & Butler, 1990). Under such circumstances, should children who have learned new social skills be transferred to another school to "start fresh" with a new group of peers, as some have suggested (Perry, Williard, & Perry, 1990)?

Another factor to consider is the types of attributions peers make about the unpopular child. If children see the target child as *responsible* for his own problems—his obesity, for example—they like him less than when he is viewed as not responsible (Juvonen, 1992). Indeed, aggressive children more than socially withdrawn children are seen as being responsible for their behavior and deserving of less sympathy (Graham & Hoehn, 1995). Should social skills training programs therefore be extended to popular children to convince them that their unpopular peers are *not responsible* for their traits? Could there be repercussions for the target children themselves when they hear they are not responsible for their own behaviors?

Finally, while social skills training programs typically focus on an individual child, group dynamics may play an important role in the type of social behavior that child displays. In one recent study, groups of children who were unfamiliar with one another participated in five play sessions (DeRosier et al., 1994). The tendency for children to behave aggressively was influenced by a complex set of factors, including the level of physical activity within the group, the degree of competition in their play, and the extent of aversive behavior, such as teasing, criticism, and verbal disagreement. Given this finding, what is the best way to design social skills training programs so that unpopular children gain in social status?

CHILDREN'S FRIENDSHIPS

Certain peer relations are special. They are marked by shared thoughts and experiences, trust, intimacy, and joy in the other's company. Children's relationships with friends differ from those with other peers. Friends express more emotion and loyalty toward each other, see each other more frequently, and both cooperate and disagree more than mere acquaintances do (Bigelow, Tesson, & Lewko, 1992; Hartup & Sancilio, 1986; Newcomb & Bagwell, 1995). In fact, when researchers observe the face-to-face interactions of sixth-graders with friends versus acquaintances, they note more positive affect, more playfulness, more involvement, and fewer physiological signs of stress in the child-friend pairs (Field et al., 1992). Even though childhood friendships may not endure, their impact on social and emotional development can rival that of the family and may provide a needed buffer when children feel psychological strains. Friendships are also an important source of cognitive and social support (Hartup, 1996).

Children's Patterns and Conceptions of Friendship

About 80 percent of three-to-four-year-olds spend a substantial amount of time with at least one peer who is a "strong associate" or friend. Most preschoolers observed in their nursery school classrooms spend at least 30 percent of their time with one other peer, usually someone of the same sex (Hinde et al., 1985). For the three-year-old, however, the concept of *friend* does not encompass the full range of psychological complexities that it does for the older child. At this age, the term is virtually synonymous with *playmate*.

Preschoolers' activities with friends usually consist of games, object sharing, and pretend sequences (for example, "You be the baby and I'll be the Mommy"). Conversations between friends often contain a good deal of social comparison, a search for differences as well as similarities. Preschool children are fascinated not so much by the specific *things* they have in common as by the fact that they *have* things in common. Hence the following typical conversation recorded by Jeffrey Parker and John Gottman (1989):

Child A: We both have chalk in our hands.
Child B: Right!

Preschoolers try to avoid disagreements and negative affect in their interactions with friends more so than older children do (Gottman & Parkhurst, 1980). Preschoolers especially value friends who give them positive feedback, prefer to play with them over other children, and engage in low levels of conflict with them (Ladd, Kochenderfer, & Coleman, 1996).

In the middle school years (roughly ages eight through twelve), children are very concerned with being accepted by their peers and avoiding the insecurity peer rejection brings; both factors motivate friendship formation. Most friends are of the same age and sex, although relationships with younger and older children occasionally occur as well. Cross-sex friendships are rare, however, constituting only about 5 percent of the mutual friendships reported in one study of more than seven hundred third- and fourth-graders (Kovacs, Parker, & Hoffman, 1996). Researchers in another study even found their fifth-grade participants to be openly resistant to the idea that they might have a friend of the opposite sex (Buhrmester & Furman, 1987). By the time children approach preadolescence, the time they spend with same-sex friends surpasses the time they spend with either parent.

Friendship partners may change, though, over the childhood years. As part of a comprehensive longitudinal study of the social development of children beginning in fourth grade, Robert and Beverly Cairns (1994) asked children to name their best friends each year through eleventh grade. Figure 15.6 shows that the friend named in fourth grade was unlikely to be named again in successive years. Friendships can even shift within a time span of a few weeks. When Robert Cairns and his colleagues

FIGURE 15.6

Changes in Best Friends

In a longitudinal study of best friends, Cairns and Cairns (1994) found that children named as best friends in fourth grade were seldom renamed as best friends in successive years. Friendships may therefore be less stable than generally thought. On the other hand, other research suggests that the stability of friendships over time may depend on the specific personality characteristics of individual children.

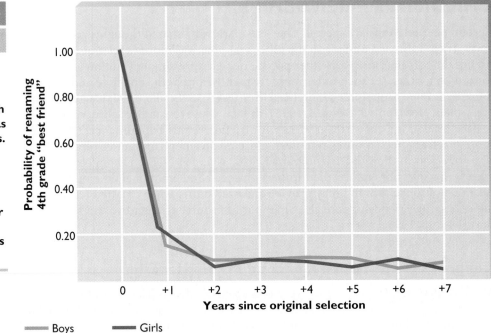

Source: Cairns & Cairns, 1994.

KEY THEME
Individual Differences

observed the nature of fourth- and seventh-graders' friendships, they found that children who mutually nominated each other as friends the first time they were interviewed usually did not name each other as close friends three weeks later (Cairns et al., 1995). However, the tendency for children to have new mutual friends at different points in time may depend on the characteristics of the child. In another project, children who switched friends more frequently over the four weeks of a summer camp session tended to be perceived by other children as playful, humorous, and "gossipy," but also as aggressive, unreliable, and untrustworthy; that is, they had qualities that probably both attracted and disappointed friends (Parker & Seal, 1996).

In middle childhood, friendship interactions typically include conflicts as well as cooperation (Hartup et al., 1993), and gossip becomes a predominant format for communication, as the following episode between two girls illustrates:

E: Oh, see, um, you know that tub she gave us for the spider?
M: Yeah.
E: She acts like she owns the whole thing.
M: The whole spider.
E: I know.   (Parker & Gottman, 1989, p. 114)

Parker and Gottman (1989) believe gossip allows children to sample the attitudes and beliefs of their agemates without taking the risk of revealing their own views. Because gossip involves the sharing of "privileged" information, it also solidifies the child's membership in the friendship circle.

During this age period, the internal psychological aspects of friendship grow in importance. When sixth-graders are asked, "How do you know that someone is your best friend?", they respond with statements such as "I can talk to her about my problems" or "He'll keep a secret if you tell him." In other words, intimacy and trust as well as loyalty, generosity, and helpfulness become integrated into the child's understanding of friendship (Berndt, 1981). Girls in particular speak of the value they place on intimacy in friendship relations. Girls cite the importance of sharing confidences and private feelings with friends far more frequently than boys do and find their same-sex friendships provide more support than boys find in their friendships (Buhrmester & Furman, 1987; Furman & Buhrmester, 1992; Jones & Dembo, 1989). This tendency, however, may stem in part from their stereotyped knowledge that female relationships are *supposed* to be close (Bukowski & Kramer, 1986).

Boys and girls differ in the patterns of their friendships. Boys tend to have a larger circle of friends with whom they tend to play group games and team sports. Girls' friendships, in contrast, tend to involve smaller networks and center on affective communication and self-disclosure.

Sex differences in concepts of friendship are accompanied by heightened differences in the structure of boys' and girls' friendship networks during the middle school years. Boys' friendships are usually *extensive;* their circle of friends is larger, and play is frequently enacted in groups. For boys, friendship is oriented around shared activities, especially sports (Erwin, 1985). In contrast, girls' friendships tend to be *intensive.* Girls have smaller networks of friends, but they engage in more intensive affective communication and self-disclosure. Girls usually play with only one other girl and may even be reluctant to include a third girl in the relationship. Girls also become more distressed over the breakup of a friendship (Eder & Hallinan, 1978; Maccoby & Jacklin, 1987; Waldrop & Halverson, 1975). It may be that these sex differences in friendship patterns are derived from the games children play. Boys are encouraged to play group games and team sports, such as baseball, which involve a number of children and do not promote intimacy and close interaction. Girls' games, such as "house" and "dolls," involve smaller groups and provide an ideal environment for the exchange of thoughts and emotions. Another possibility is that sex differences in friendships are due to larger socialization forces that foster sensitivity to others and affective sharing in girls and autonomy and emotional reserve in boys (Winstead, 1986).

By adolescence, the importance of intimacy in friendship is firmly solidified. Adolescents say they value the ability to share thoughts and feelings with friends and expect mutual understanding and self-disclosure in friendships (Bigelow & LaGaipa, 1975; Furman & Bierman, 1984). They share problems, solutions to those problems, and private feelings with friends. These qualities fit the needs of individuals who are struggling to define who they are and who they will become. A sample exchange between two adolescent friends drawn from Parker and Gottman's (1989) research illustrates these themes:

> A: I don't know. Gosh, I have no idea what I want to do. And it really doesn't bother me that much that I don't have my future planned. [laughs]
> B: [laughs]
> A: [laughs] Like it bothers my Dad a lot, but it doesn't bother me.
> B: Just tell your dad what I always tell my Dad: "Dad, I *am.*"
> A: [laughs] Exactly!
> B: "And whatever happens tomorrow, I *still* will be!"

Adolescents continue to prefer same-sex friends, although the frequency of boy-girl interactions increases. At this age, similarities in attitudes about academics, dating, drinking, smoking, and drug use influence whether children become friends (Dishion,

Andrews, & Crosby, 1995; Epstein, 1983; Tolson & Urberg, 1993). Adolescent friendships become more selective with age; teenagers have fewer mutual friends than younger children do, but mutual friends comprise a greater proportion of their total network of friends. The tendency for girls to have smaller friendship networks than boys, observed earlier in childhood, disappears (Urgerg et al., 1995). Adolescents also say that the time they spend with their friends is the most enjoyable part of their day (Csikszentmihalyi & Larson, 1984). Friendship is thus a key element in the social and emotional life of the older child.

Friendship and Social Cognition

Robert Selman (1981) believes developmental changes in children's conceptions of friendship are grounded in their social perspective-taking ability, that is, their capacity to understand the viewpoints, thoughts, and feelings of another person (see Chapter 8). Put another way, conceptions of friendship are linked to advances in social cognition. Selman has proposed a five-stage model of the development of friendship concepts that reflects the growing perspective-taking abilities of children:

Stage 0 (about 3–7 years): Momentary Physicalistic Interaction   Friendship is defined strictly in terms of physical proximity. A friend is someone who lives nearby or is a playmate.

Stage 1 (about 4–9 years): One-Way Assistance   Friends are conceptualized as helpers. The child who helps pick up a spilled lunch, for example, is a friend.

Stage 2 (about 6–12 years): Fair-Weather Cooperation   The roles of reciprocity and mutual adjustment in friendship are recognized, but definitions of friendship still center around self-interest rather than mutual concerns. Arguments can terminate the relationship.

Stage 3 (about 9–15 years): Intimate and Mutually Shared Relationships   The affective and durable qualities of friendship are recognized. However, friendships can contain an element of possessiveness.

Stage 4 (12 years–adult): Autonomous and Independent Friendships   Friendship is seen as an avenue for mutual support and a means by which both partners may derive psychological strength from each other. The importance of relationships with others is now recognized.

In Selman's model, young children's egocentricity limits their conception of friendship to concrete, self-oriented situations. Once they have gained the ability to reflect on the legitimacy of another's perspective—and, later, on how individuals relate to larger social groups—children's notions of friendship expand to include reciprocity and respect for the internal needs and desires of the other.

In addition, say other psychologists, as children gain an increasingly sophisticated understanding of the concept of *reciprocity,* their ideas of friendship change. Young children conceptualize reciprocity concretely; they match a peer's helping or sharing, for example, with a similar behavior of their own. Adolescents view reciprocity in a more abstract way; they see friendships as entailing mutual cooperation and a sharing of identities rather than just sharing objects (Youniss, 1980). Thus, the older child's more elaborate reasoning capabilities are assumed to pave the way for abstract, psychological concepts of friendship.

Research on children's understanding of friendship relies almost exclusively on children's ability to verbalize their ideas about what friends do and why they are valuable. Other studies on how children behave with friends, however, show that children's friendships are far more complex than they themselves are able to describe. One clue to that complexity comes from investigations of how children form friendships in the first place.

How Children Become Friends

How do two previously unacquainted children form a friendship? What behaviors must occur to produce an affiliative bond between these two peers? A time-intensive investigation by John Gottman (1983) provides a fascinating glimpse into the process of friendship formation among children who initially met as strangers. Gottman's method involved tape-recording the conversations of eighteen unfamiliar dyads ages three to nine years as they played in their homes for three sessions. Even in this short time, friendships among some of the pairs began to emerge. In all cases, each member of the pair was within one year of the age of the other. Some were same-sex pairs, others opposite-sex. The behaviors of the child whose home it was (the host child) and the visiting child (the guest) were coded separately; the sequences of behaviors these children displayed—that is, how one child's behavior influenced the other's—were also analyzed.

Children who "hit it off" in the first play session showed several distinct patterns of interaction. First, they were successful in exchanging information, as in the following conversation one pair had:

A: Hey, you know what?
B: No, what?
A: Sometime you can come to my house.

Children who became friends made efforts to establish a common ground by finding activities they could share or by identifying similarities and differences between them.

In addition, any conflicts that occurred as they played were successfully resolved, either by one member of the dyad explaining the reason for the disagreement or by one child complying with the other child's demands, as long as they were not excessive or unreasonable. Alternatively, as activities escalated from simply coloring side by side ("I'm coloring mine green") to one child issuing a command ("Use blue. That'd be nice"), children who became friends tempered potential conflict by de-escalating the intensity of play (in this case, going back to side-by-side coloring) or using another element of play that was "safe"—namely, information exchange (for example, "I don't have a blue crayon. Do you?"). In contrast, children who did not become friends often persisted in escalating their play until the situation was no longer amicable. Children who became friends thus modulated their interactions to preserve a positive atmosphere.

Over time, other social processes also came into play. One influential variable was the clarity of communication, as evidenced by a child giving clear answers to requests for information from the other. The following sequence is an example of a clear communication:

A: Hand me the truck.
B: Which truck?
A: The red one.

Also significant was the amount of self-disclosure in children's interactions, that is, one child's revelation of feelings in response to a question about them from the other. Other researchers point out that children seem to be drawn to agemates who resemble themselves in the maturity of their play styles. Children who engage in exploratory play become friends with others who prefer that play style, for example (Rubin et al., 1994).

Friendship formation, like other aspects of peer interaction, requires a sensitivity to social cues and knowledge of how to manage interactions that have positive and negative moments. And indeed socially skilled children have more friends than socially unskilled children do.

The Functions of Friendship

By virtue of their special qualities, friendships contribute to the child's development in ways that differ from other, more transient peer interactions. Friendships involve extended contact between peers and a significant affective investment from each child. Thus, they provide a fertile ground for the child's social and emotional development.

Because friendships include the sharing of affection and emotional support, especially among older children, they may play a vital role in protecting children from anxiety and stress. For example, boys seem to adjust better to the practical and psychological consequences of divorce when they have friends (Wallerstein & Kelly, 1980). Likewise, the relationship between friendship quality and feelings of self-worth is stronger among children who come from rigid, less emotionally involved families (Gauze et al., 1996). In addition, children who have close and intimate friendships have higher levels of self-esteem, experience less anxiety and depression, and are more sociable in general than those with few close friends (Buhrmester, 1990; Mannarino, 1978). Because many studies of friendship are correlational, the direction of influence is not always clear. That is, less anxious children may be more capable of forming intimate friendships, or the reverse may be true: friendships may make them less anxious. Nonetheless, it is reasonable to hypothesize that friends provide an important source of social support for and feedback about one's competence and self-worth. In fact, as Figure 15.7 shows, having even just one "best friend" can mean less loneliness for the child (Parker & Asher, 1993; Renshaw & Brown, 1993).

Interactions with friends also provide a context for the development of certain social skills, such as cooperation, competition, and conflict resolution. In one study, researchers observed teams of four- and five-year-olds playing a game in which cooperation led to both partners winning, whereas competition led to losses for both (Matsumoto et al., 1986). Teachers independently rated the degree of friendship for each pair of children. The results showed that the greater the degree of friendship, the more the children cooperated to win the game. In another longitudinal study of three-year-olds in day care, Carollee Howes (1983) observed that children showed the greatest increases in the complexity of their social interactions—their ability to initiate an interaction or participate in an elaborate exchange, for example—when they played with one or two stable friends. Such gains were not observed when children played with peers who were not friends.

Similarly, because of their investment in friendships, when children have conflicts with friends they frequently seek to negotiate and resolve those conflicts rather than letting the argument escalate or terminate the friendship (Laursen, Hartup, & Koplas, 1996). In observing four-year-olds in nursery school over a period of several weeks, William Hartup and his colleagues noted instances of spontaneous conflict in which one child attempted to influence another but met with resistance (Hartup et al., 1988). They found that when conflicts occurred between friends, children were more likely to either negotiate and bargain or physically turn away from the situation. When conflicts occurred between nonfriends, children were more likely to stand firm and insist on their original goal.

Finally, the intimacy required in friendships may also promote healthier relations with others later in life. Harry Stack Sullivan (1953) believed the capacity for intimacy nurtured by same-sex friendships in childhood provides the foundation for intimacy in more mature adult relationships. The failure to acquire this capacity in the formative years of childhood may impair a person's later functioning as a romantic partner, spouse, or parent. Although little research has been conducted to evaluate the validity of this claim, the idea of continuity between the capacity for intimacy in childhood and later life continues to have broad appeal.

While friends can have exceedingly positive benefits for development, research has revealed that friends can also be a factor in deviant behavior, especially among antisocial children. Adolescents who were close friends with other adolescents who used drugs increased their own drug use over the year they were studied. This trend was especially true for teenagers whose parents were less authoritative, the parenting style described in Chapter 14 (Mounts & Steinberg, 1995). Thomas Dishion and his colleagues (Dishion, Patterson, & Griesler, 1994) observed that ten-year-old aggressive boys who had been rejected by most of their peers often became friends with other aggressive boys. Over time, they talked more about deviant behavior such as substance abuse and delinquency. By age fourteen, association with antisocial friends was found to contribute statistically to the tendency to engage in deviant behaviors.

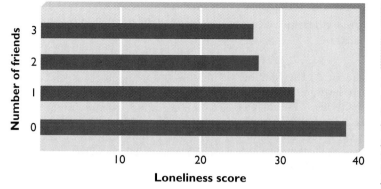

Source: Renshaw & Brown, 1993.

FIGURE 15.7

Friendship as a Buffer Against Loneliness

Having even one "best friend" can significantly lower children's reports of loneliness. In this study, third-through-sixth-graders filled out a questionnaire assessing their feelings of loneliness and social dissatisfaction partway through the school year. A high score indicated greater feelings of loneliness. Children who had a reciprocal relationship with at least one friend had significantly lower loneliness scores than children who had no such relationship.

These findings suggest that breaking the cycle of antisocial behavior may require more than intervening in an individual child's pattern of behaviors; monitoring his or her friendship networks may be just as important.

Our knowledge of the impact of friendships on child development is relatively incomplete compared to other influences. However, this area of research is likely to grow considering the accumulating evidence that "the company they keep" has important repercussions for the pathways of development (Hartup, 1996).

CHAPTER RECAP

SUMMARY OF DEVELOPMENTAL THEMES

SOCIOCULTURAL INFLUENCE How does the sociocultural context influence peer relations?

As more children in our society enter day care, they also have more extensive experiences with peers than previous generations. In general, children who spend more time with peers show advances in social development and often tend to prefer cooperation to competition. Culture can also influence the standards that shape peer acceptance. For example, our society highly values athletic capabilities and social skill, and consequently children who are proficient in these domains typically enjoy more peer popularity.

CHILD'S ACTIVE ROLE How does the child play an active role in peer relations?

On one level, many of the physical qualities the child possesses influence the reactions of peers. Physical attractiveness, body build, motor skill, and rate of maturation all engender different responses from other children. On another level, the child's social skill clearly affects how peers react. Children who can accurately read the emotions of others, gauge the consequences of their own behaviors on others, and employ the strategies that facilitate effective social interactions are more popular with their peers. Similarly, children who are aggressive and display physical power often rise to the top of peer group dominance

hierarchies, but may become unpopular with peers, as evidenced when those peers are asked to name children they like or prefer to associate with.

CONTINUITY/DISCONTINUITY Are developmental changes in peer relations continuous or discontinuous?

According to Mildred Parten, the development of play with peers progresses in a stagelike fashion. Similarly, Robert Selman has proposed a stage theory of children's understanding of friendship. However, research now shows that preschoolers often concurrently display several types of play. In addition, young children's interactions with friends suggest more complexity than Selman's social cognitive model hypothesizes. Thus, the development of peer relations may be more continuous than discontinuous.

INDIVIDUAL DIFFERENCES How prominent are individual differences in peer relations?

Children vary in the extent to which they are accepted by their peers. Some children are popular, whereas others are rejected, neglected, or controversial. A child's popularity may be linked to aspects of physical appearance, motor skills, and social skills. Children may also show individual differences in their tendency to keep the same friends over time.

INTERACTION AMONG DOMAINS How do peer relations interact with other domains of development?

First, healthy relations with peers are associated with a number of successful developmental outcomes in other arenas. Popular children do well in school, have high levels of self-esteem, and suffer fewer emotional difficulties, such as depression, than unpopular children. Second, the ability to interact successfully with peers is related to attainments in several other developmental domains. Children who are reared in a positive emotional environment and are skillful in deciphering emotional cues tend to be more socially competent with peers. The formation of early emotional attachments and growth in social knowledge may also play a role. The child's emerging cognitive capabilities, especially perspective-taking skills, allow the child to think about the reactions and expectations of others and to anticipate the consequences of his or her own behaviors. Clear communication skills add to the child's effectiveness in establishing successful relationships with peers. Successful peer interaction is thus both a product of and a contributor to the child's emotional, cognitive, and social achievements.

SUMMARY OF TOPICS

■ DEVELOPMENTAL CHANGES IN PEER RELATIONS

Children show a direct interest in their peers from infancy, although coordinated social interchanges, such as turn taking, do not emerge until age two years or so. Preschool children typically engage in three kinds of play: *solitary play, parallel play,* and *cooperative play.* They also engage in *social pretend play.* Children's relationships with peers display their growing linguistic, cognitive, and social competencies.

During the school years and adolescence, peer groups assume greater importance for children. Children associate in same-sex groups and groups based on other similarities, such as shared interests. *Rough-and-tumble play* is frequently observed. Adolescents form larger groups called *cliques* and *crowds;* toward the end of adolescence, they develop an interest in peers of the opposite sex.

■ PEER GROUP DYNAMICS

Children typically show strong identity with the peer groups they join. At the same time, conflicts between peer groups can occur. One way to break down such intergroup hostilities is to have groups work together on some common goal. Peer groups quickly form dominance hierarchies, organized structures in which some children become leaders and others followers. Dominance hierarchies seem to serve a number of adaptive social functions.

Susceptibility to peer pressure heightens during early adolescence but declines as young adulthood approaches. Peers pressure one another to spend time together and, less frequently, to misbehave. Peers enforce their norms by reacting positively to individuals who conform and negatively to those who resist. At times, peer pressures directly conflict with pressures from adults.

■ PEERS AS AGENTS OF SOCIALIZATION

Peers are important agents of socialization who model and reinforce both desirable and undesirable behaviors for others. Aggression and sex-typed play are two examples of behaviors modeled and regulated by peers.

■ PEER POPULARITY AND SOCIAL COMPETENCE

Peer acceptance is measured through such peer assessment devices as *sociometric nominations* or *sociometric rating scales.* The child's peer status is related to his or her physical attractiveness, name, motor skills, and social skills. In general, popular children engage in prosocial behaviors, know how to enter peer groups smoothly, and effectively maintain cohesive social interactions.

Social competence may have its roots in the child's earliest attachment relationships, but it is also influenced by parental styles of social interaction. Socially competent children are also more skilled at perceiving and interpreting social cues and have good social problem-solving ability. Modeling, reinforcement, and coaching are some of the techniques used to enhance social skills in children who have social problems such as aggression and withdrawal.

■ CHILDREN'S FRIENDSHIPS

Friendships are an important part of children's peer relations. Preschoolers view friends as peers to play with, but with development they come to value friends for their psychological benefits. Children approaching adolescence increasingly see their friends as providers of intimacy and trust. These changes in children's concepts of friendship parallel changes in social cognition. Children form friendships by keeping social interactions positive in tone, exchanging information, and, at later ages, through clear communication and self-disclosure. Friendships provide a context for developing skills such as cooperation and conflict resolution and may help the child learn the benefits of intimacy in relationships. Friendships can also provide a context for the development of problem behaviors.

16 SCHOOL AND MEDIA

SOCIOCULTURAL INFLUENCE
How does the sociocultural context influence the child's experiences with school and media?

CHILD'S ACTIVE ROLE
How does the child play an active role in experiences with school and media?

INTERACTION AMONG DOMAINS
How do the child's experiences with school and media interact with development in other domains?

"Double click on the icon for your web browser," Allison instructed Jamie, a new student in Allison's seventh-grade class who was seated at the computer next to her. "Then type in the name of the location you want to go to." She was patiently trying to help Jamie pick up the basics of surfing the Net and accessing information through the World Wide Web. Jamie struggled, forgetting to insert the colon and typing a backslash instead of the necessary forward slash. After finally typing the address correctly, he beamed as the screen began to fill with pictures and phrases that indicated he was at the site he was searching for. In a few minutes, he was scrolling away. Locating the right pointer, he clicked on it to bring up the information he was seeking.

Such exchanges between thirteen-year-olds in a junior high school computer laboratory are becoming increasingly commonplace; the words may sound strange to some adults, but to many children they have clear and practical meaning. Childhood in the 1990s is an enterprise vastly different from growing up even two decades ago. Would a seventh-grader in the 1970s have had the vaguest idea what Allison and Jamie were talking about?

Historically, of course, parents and peers have played a major role in socializing children and helping them build their cognitive skills, and they continue to serve this function in contemporary society. Nevertheless, formal education in the schools and, in more recent decades, computers and access to the information highway, along with television and videocassette recorders, have come to play a significant part in these processes as well.

We begin this chapter by taking a closer look at schools and their effects, both pedagogical and social, on development. For example, questions about academic and social success and its relationship to the physical structure of schools, the programs schools offer, and teachers' roles in the educational process continue to be of concern to parents and educators. We then consider a host of questions that have sprung up around the influence of more recent technological marvels on child development. For example, can children learn more effectively, both at school and at home, using electronic tools? Will their social development be impaired if they get "hooked" on a computer or television screen? What other aspects of their cognitive or social development might these more recent cultural innovations be affecting?

SCHOOL

In many nations today, children are legally required to attend school. By the time children graduate from high school, they have logged nearly fifteen thousand hours in school. Thus, it is important to understand the nature of that experience and how variations produce specific effects in the child.

The main aim of education is to provide children with the skills necessary to function as independent, responsible, and contributing members of society. Academic accomplishment is the chief point of emphasis. However, the child's experiences in school can also have a profound effect on other aspects of development, most notably self-concept and psychological well-being. Several factors in the school experience influence learning and socialization, including the school's physical environment, the educational philosophies of school personnel, transition points in schooling, and, most important, the attitudes and behaviors of teachers.

What Are the Effects of School on the Developing Child?

As we discussed in Chapter 8, societies vary in the extent to which they stress the experience of formal schooling. Rural agrarian subcultures in some countries, for example, do not have compulsory schooling. School experience in turn cultivates such cognitive skills as rote memory, taxonomic classification, and logical reasoning (Morrison, Smith, & Dow-Ehrensberger, 1995; Rogoff, 1981; Rogoff & Morelli, 1989). One especially powerful outcome of schooling is the development of literacy, the ability to read and write using the symbol system of the culture's language. Literacy is virtually a prerequisite for survival in most societies, and it is linked to other specific cognitive and linguistic attainments (Scribner & Cole, 1981).

The ability to read and write will assume even more importance in the decades to come. As adolescents approach adulthood in the twenty-first century, they will find that more and more jobs are in the professional and technical sectors, areas that require not only reading and writing skills but also the ability to communicate, reason, and apply mathematical and scientific concepts (Jackson & Hornbeck, 1989). The responsibility for fostering these skills will lie mainly with the schools.

Academic Achievement   In some measure, most children in the United States and many other countries attain the basic goals educators and parents have set for academic achievement in school. For example, in the United States, nearly 90 percent of young people who have yet to receive their high school degree remained in school in the period from 1990 through 1994, although the dropout rates were higher for students from low-income families and racial and ethnic minorities (U.S. Department of Education, 1996).

How well are children learning in schools? Several recent major national surveys conclude that academic achievement among American students is not high or does not compare favorably with that of students from other industrialized countries. Here are some representative data:

■ Only 11 percent of all thirteen-year-olds in the United States are adept readers, meaning they can understand relatively complicated written information (Mullis & Jenkins, 1990).

■ Only 13 percent of eighth-graders write essays that are adequate or better when the task requires them to "compare and contrast" (Applebee et al., 1990).

■ The United States ranks below many other countries in student performance on tests in science and mathematics, as Table 16.1 indicates (U.S. Department of Education, 1996). Recent data from The Third International Mathematics and Science Study (TIMSS), a project in which more than half a million children from forty-five countries have participated, reveals that seventh- and eight-graders from countries in East Asia and Eastern Europe typically perform the best (Vogel, 1996).

These results are both alarming and perplexing. Have American schools shirked their commitment to academic excellence? Have the characteristics of the student population changed in some way? There are no simple explanations for the national survey data, nor are there quick, obvious ways to remedy the problems. What these results plainly call for is a better understanding of how parents, peers, *and* schools contribute to students' academic attainments.

TABLE 16.1

Mathematics and Science Scores for Thirteen-Year-Olds

This table presents the rank order of performance by thirteen-year-old children from fourteen countries on international tests designed to assess knowledge of mathematics and science in 1991. The rank of 1 represents the highest score (some of the data indicate tied ranks). Children in the United States do not perform as well on these tests as children from many other countries.

	Mathematics	Science
Canada	8	8
France	6	8
Hungary	5	4
Ireland	10	13
Israel	7	6
Jordan	14	14
Korea	1	1
Scotland	9	10
Slovenia	11	6
Soviet Union	4	5
Switzerland	3	3
Taiwan	1	2
Spain	12	10
United States	13	12

Source: Data from U.S. Department of Education, 1996.

KEY THEME

Interaction Among Domains

Factors Predicting Academic Success   Before we consider the specific influences of schools, let us examine the roles of several other factors associated with academic success. Not surprisingly, parents are of paramount importance. Several recent studies demonstrate that the climate parents create in the home and the feelings of competence and control they instill in children are related to children's academic performance.

Consider, for example, a model proposed by Wendy Grolnick and her colleagues (Grolnick, Ryan, & Deci, 1991) and illustrated in Figure 16.1. According to these researchers, parental support for their children's autonomy (for example, encouraging independent decision making) and their involvement with their children (such as spending time talking with them about the children's problems) are related to the strength of children's "inner resources." That is, children develop feelings of competence, autonomy, and control, which in turn influence academic performance. To test these ideas, the researchers measured both parental and child qualities that were components of the model, as well as children's academic success. Using sophisticated statistical techniques, they were able to show the relationships they had predicted. Other researchers have confirmed that authoritative parenting (characterized by warmth and extensive verbal explanation) and the social support parents provide predict, at least indirectly, exactly how well children will do in school during middle childhood and adolescence (DeBaryshe, Patterson, & Capaldi, 1993; Dubow et al., 1991; Steinberg et al., 1992). Frequent transitions in parenting (for example, divorce and remarriage followed by another divorce) and a more discordant family climate are also related to less positive outcomes in school (Kurdek, Fine, & Sinclair, 1995).

Peers make a difference too. As early as fourth grade, children tend to sort themselves into groups that have different levels of school motivation, and children who are members of a particular group at the start of the school year become even more aligned with the group's motivation level by the end of this period (Kindermann, 1993). Given these findings, it should not be surprising to learn that the behavior of an adolescent's friends can affect that adolescent's behavior in school. For example, when a student at the beginning of the school year has friends who consider them-

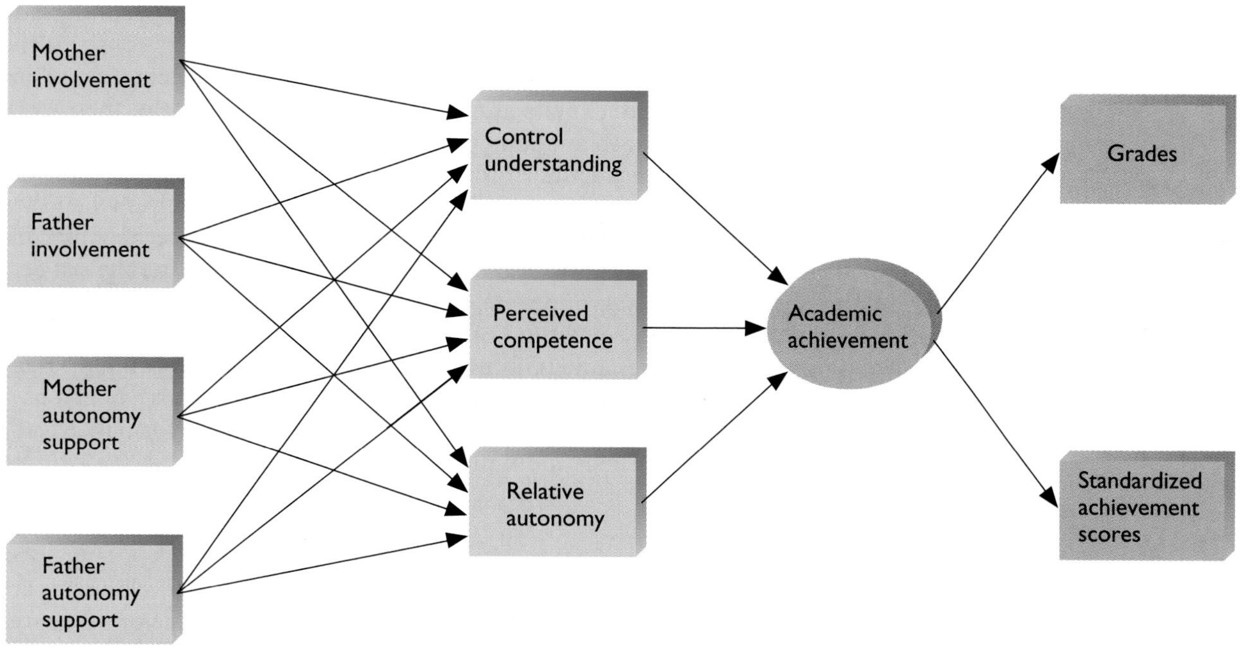

Source: Grolnick, Ryan, & Deci, 1991.

FIGURE 16.1

A Model of Parental Influences on Children's Academic Achievement

One model of children's academic achievement suggests that parental involvement and support of children's autonomy predict children's "inner resources." These resources include children's feelings of control, competence, and autonomy. These characteristics, in turn, predict academic achievement. Research has found support for the major elements of this model.

selves disruptive in school, that student will begin to demonstrate more disruptive behavior as the school year progresses (Berndt & Keefe, 1995).

Peers may also enhance or offset the effects of different parenting styles on children's academic achievement. Laurence Steinberg and his associates found that among Asian American adolescents, for example, peer support for academic excellence lessened the negative effects of authoritarian parenting (characterized by a low level of nurturance and use of coercive disciplinary techniques) on academic achievement. For Caucasian adolescents, peer support for achievement complemented parents' tendency to be authoritative (Steinberg, Dornbusch, & Brown, 1992). A supportive family context may be an important factor in encouraging children to gain the interpersonal and cognitive skills that will lead to interactions with peers who promote academic success in the first place (Kurdek, Fine, & Sinclair, 1995; Steinberg, 1995).

Still another factor that can affect academic performance of older children is whether they hold jobs before or after school. In general, adolescents who work more than fifteen to twenty hours per week attain poorer grades and show less commitment to school than adolescents who work fewer hours or not at all (Steinberg et al., 1982; Steinberg, Fegley, & Dornbusch, 1993).

Taken together, the research described here suggests that children's academic achievement is best understood from the ecological perspective described in Chapter 1.

Self-esteem   In addition to building academic skills, children's experience in school can have a major effect on their feelings of competence and self-worth, both in a general sense and in terms of academic self-esteem. Schoolmates and teachers provide constant feedback to children about how they are doing, from casual comments friends make at recess ("You did great on that poem this morning!") to the formal academic grades determined by the teacher.

In general, self-esteem correlates positively with academic achievement, usually measured by grades. Students who obtain good grades have more favorable attitudes about themselves (Byrne, 1984). But does high self-esteem lead students to perform better in school, or does academic competence nurture the development of high self-esteem? Most experts agree that both processes are at work. For example, self-esteem

KEY THEME
Interaction Among Domains

in kindergarten can be a good predictor of reading achievement in second grade (Wattenberg & Clifford, 1964). A study of sixth- and seventh-graders confirms the other direction of influence: students who showed gains in self-esteem started out with a more favorable school climate and higher teacher evaluations of their work habits than those who did not show gains (Hoge, Smit, & Hanson, 1990).

By the same token, experimental studies have demonstrated that academically competent children can be made to feel more negative about themselves when they experience failure. In an illustrative experiment, two groups of high-achieving children were given a test of self-esteem and then three academic tests. After the last test, children in the experimental group were given a slip of paper stating that they had failed. Their scores on a subsequent test of self-esteem declined, but the scores of the control group remained the same (Gibby & Gibby, 1967). Although contemporary researchers might question the ethics of subjecting students to such stress in a psychological experiment, the results clearly point to the power of performance feedback in shaping students' feelings about themselves.

The Physical Environment of the School

Among the characteristics of schools that play a role in the child's development are school size, class size, and the physical layout of the classroom. Each factor influences the frequency and range of opportunities for students to interact with teachers and peers in the school setting.

School Size   Although some controversy surrounds the importance of school size, any significant effects researchers have found usually favor students from smaller schools (Moore & Lackney, 1993; Rutter, 1983). In a major study of thirteen high schools ranging in size from thirteen to more than two thousand students, researchers noted that students from smaller schools were less alienated, participated more in school activities, felt more competent, and found themselves more challenged (Barker & Gump, 1964). One probable reason is the greater availability of roles for students to fill in smaller schools, particularly leadership roles. Students who have the opportunity to edit the school newspaper or be captain of the band typically receive positive feedback from parents, teachers, and peers for fulfilling these roles. They are also likely to identify strongly with the school and develop a greater sense of personal control and responsibility. Furthermore, participating in school-based extracurricular programs seems to reduce the likelihood that young people will drop out of school, especially among those who are less academically competitive (Mahoney & Cairns, 1997).

KEY THEME
Child's Active Role

Class Size   Class size is another important aspect of school structure. In general, children in small classes show academic advances over children in large classes (Moore & Lackney, 1993). Few investigations have randomly assigned children to classes of different sizes to explore the effects on achievement, although this procedure would allow us to draw the strongest conclusions about the causal influence of class size. However, a study of seventy-six schools across one state, Tennessee, followed precisely this procedure. Kindergarten children and teachers were randomly assigned to one of three conditions: small classes of thirteen to seventeen students; classes of twenty-two to twenty-five students, the "regular" size; or regular-size classes with a teacher's aide. By the end of first grade, children in the small classes showed markedly greater improvements in performance on standardized tests of reading and mathematics than children from regular-size classes, although the presence of an aide did improve scores somewhat. The benefits of small classes were especially pronounced for minority children (Finn & Achilles, 1990).

The long-term consequences of smaller class size have also been investigated. Children who were assigned to small classes in kindergarten through third grade in the Tennessee study continued to do better than their classmates assigned to larger classes in kindergarten through third grade, even after entering regular-size classrooms beginning in fourth grade (Mosteller, 1995). The benefits of the smaller-class experience continued to be exhibited by children in later grades as well. Moreover, when small class sizes were introduced to the poorest districts in the state, children in these districts moved from displaying reading and mathematics scores that were well below average to scores above average for the state.

Why do smaller classes work? For one thing, teachers probably have greater enthusiasm and higher morale when they are not burdened with large numbers of students. Teachers also have more time to spend with individual students, and students are more likely to be attentive and engaged in classroom activities and show fewer behavioral problems in small classes (Finn & Achilles, 1990; Mosteller, 1995).

The Physical Arrangement of the Classroom   In the traditional classroom, precisely aligned rows of desks face the teacher to enhance communication between teacher and individual pupils. This arrangement discourages interactions among students. Also, it creates clear zones that foster greater student-teacher exchange for only select groups of students: students seated across the front row and down the center aisle (see Figure 16.2) are most likely to interact with the teacher (Gump, 1978). Even gregarious and actively involved students become less engaged with the teacher when they are seated outside the "action zone" of the traditional classroom (Koneya, 1976).

The best way to encourage the attention and active participation of more students in the class is to place the desks in a circle so that all students have equal access to the teacher. Researchers have noted that when desks are arranged this way, children raise their hands more frequently and make more spontaneous comments about the lesson than when desks are positioned in rows and columns (Rosenfield, Lambert, & Black, 1985).

Philosophies of Education

The traditional model of education emphasizes the role of the teacher as a transmitter of information to students and channels the major interactions in the classroom so that they flow from teacher to student. Students are required to work on problems and assignments individually; their work is evaluated according to widely shared standards; and a climate of competition is the norm. Teachers assume an authority

FIGURE 16.2

The "Action Zones" of the Traditional Classroom

Students who sit in the front row and center aisle of the classroom are likely to have the largest number of interactions with the teacher. The best way to encourage the participation of more students is to arrange the desks in a circle.

Source: Adapted from Adams & Biddle, 1970.

Results (percentage of studies)			
Variable (number of studies)	**Open Better**	**Traditional Better**	**Mixed Results**	**No Significant Differences**
---	---	---	---	---
Academic achievement (102)	14	12	28	46
Self-concept (61)	25	3	25	47
Attitude toward school (57)	40	4	25	32
Creativity (33)	36	0	30	33
Independence and conformity (23)	78	4	9	9
Curiosity (14)	43	0	36	21
Anxiety and adjustment (39)	26	13	31	31
Locus of control (24)	25	4	17	54
Cooperation (9)	67	0	11	22
(Overall average)	(39)	(4)	(24)	(33)

Source: Adapted from Horwitz, 1979.

TABLE 16.2

The Effects of Open Versus Traditional Classrooms

The results of 102 studies show that although open classrooms have few effects on academic achievement, they are likely to promote creativity, curiosity, independence, and a number of other desirable social characteristics.

role, and their goal is to convey primarily academic information as opposed to personal, emotional, or social knowledge. Alternative models of education, however, deemphasize the teacher as authority, the student as individual learner, and the academic environment as competitive.

The Open Classroom   In the **open classroom,** students are encouraged to collaborate and the teacher's primary role is to structure lessons so that they offer opportunities for intellectual sharing and problem solving. Movable furniture, large, open spaces, and activity centers replace the fixed, regular rows of student desks to encourage pupil interaction. The teacher is often considered a joint partner in learning and a collaborator in the process of discovery; team teaching is also common. Goals other than strictly academic ones—fostering the child's creativity, inquisitiveness, and socialization—are equally valued. Rarely are one child's accomplishments compared to those of others; instead, achievement is measured by the degree of progress the individual child shows.

Contemporary open classrooms provide children with structured opportunities to "discover" principles of science, mathematics, and other academic subjects. Instead of reading a chapter on photosynthesis, for example, children may have access to a science table at which they can manipulate the amount of sunlight and water different plants receive during a period of days to determine those elements necessary for green leaves; another activity center might be devoted to mathematical problems; and so forth. Children are free to explore different areas of the room under the careful guidance of the teacher.

Do children in open classrooms display academic and social profiles different from those who learn in traditional classrooms? As Table 16.2 shows, in the realm of academics, more than one hundred studies point to no consistent differences in the average performance of children in one classroom type versus the other (Horwitz, 1979). In the domain of social development, however, children from open classrooms show clear gains. Open-classroom students are generally more cooperative, have a wider variety of interactions with peers in both schoolwork and socially related

open classroom Nontraditional educational approach that emphasizes peer interaction, free-flowing movement of students around different activity centers in the classroom, and structured opportunities for students to "discover" knowledge.

Open classrooms, like the one shown in this picture contain large open spaces, movable furniture, and activity centers designed to help children learn by "discovery." Here, one child is pouring materials into a container, another is drawing, and other students in the classroom are engaged in individual or small-group projects.

matters, and develop broad networks of relationships with peers (Hallinan, 1976; Horwitz, 1979; Minuchin & Shapiro, 1983). Thus, open classrooms represent an interesting and important alternative in educational practice.

Magnet Schools   In many larger, urban school districts, educators have begun to create "magnet" schools, schools designed to carry out a distinctive mission. Although initially established to assist desegregation in the United States, these schools often include a focus, such as on the sciences or the arts, as a way to encourage students and teachers to join together as a community of scholars with similar interests (Steel & Levine, 1994). The schools thus provide an alternative educational environment to comprehensive schools whose goals and purposes are often criticized for being unfocused and diffuse.

The benefits of these schools are difficult to assess, especially since students who elect to attend them (and their parents) may have particular interests or other characteristics that set them apart from students who attend the typical neighborhood or comprehensive school. However, one recent evaluation of achievement in math, science, reading, and social studies points to distinct benefits of magnet schools for high school students (Gamoran, 1996). When prior achievement, gender, race, ethnicity, and family structure were statistically controlled, students in the magnet schools achieved at higher levels than students in the comprehensive public schools and even students in the parochial and private schools. Why students in magnet schools did so well remains unclear. These benefits did not seem to stem from higher teacher morale, greater teacher interest in students, or a higher priority on learning in the magnet schools, although additional measures are needed to see what role such factors play in the student outcomes (Gamoran, 1996). Perhaps other elements, such as the additional resources school districts are often willing to allocate to magnet schools, are the basis for the academic improvement their students show (Steel & Levine, 1994).

Peer Learning   Several unique, peer-centered learning experiences demonstrate that there are benefits to educational models that deemphasize teacher-to-student transmission of information. One such model, introduced in Chapter 1 and described more fully in Chapter 12, is *cooperative learning,* in which students work in groups rather than individually to solve academic problems or complete assignments.

A prime example is the *Student Teams-Achievement Divisions (STAD)* method developed by Robert Slavin (1990b). Students are assigned to four- or five-person learning teams composed of children with a range of abilities. Each group is deliberately structured to contain both boys and girls and children from a variety of racial or ethnic backgrounds. After the teacher introduces a new topic or set of materials, team members in each group work on related problems, quiz one another, and study together until they decide collectively that they understand the unit. Then each individual is quizzed to assess the knowledge gained.

Cooperative learning works. Students who participate in STAD classrooms show greater achievement in language arts, social studies, and mathematics than control participants who learn the same material from more traditional methods. Using specific group rewards—that is, overt public recognition of the teams' accomplishments—has proven to be an especially important factor in producing gains. In addition, the STAD program increases the number of cross-racial friendships, improves self-esteem, and produces more favorable attitudes toward academic achievement (Slavin, 1990b). As with the children in the Robber's Cave Study described in Chapter 15, when students work in groups toward common objectives, barriers to interpersonal relationships dissolve and commitments to the goals of the group strengthen.

A more recent study provides further confirmation that cooperative learning works. Hanna Shachar and Shlomo Sharan (1994) compared the communication and achievement skills of 197 eighth-graders assigned to cooperative learning classrooms in history and geography to those of 154 students in classrooms taught by traditional teacher-led methods. The study, carried out in Israel, included Jewish students from Western and Middle Eastern backgrounds. The classes were taught for six months. The cooperative learning groups were reconstituted several times throughout the year to give students the opportunity to work with a number of different peers. At the end of the year, a videotaped discussion of a topic in history and geography involving six-person groups revealed that those who participated in cooperative learning expressed themselves more frequently, were more likely to take a personal position and expand on the ideas expressed by another student, and were less likely to interrupt their peers than students who participated in traditional classrooms. The gains in communication skills were especially great for Middle Eastern students; those who came from the traditional classroom were far less likely to express themselves than their peers from Western backgrounds. Gains in scores on achievement tests in history were also much higher among students who participated in the cooperative groups than among students in the traditional classroom.

Another form of peer learning is called **peer collaboration**. Here pairs of students work jointly on the same problems without competing with other groups. For example, in one study, fourth-graders worked in pairs on mathematics and spatial reasoning problems, some requiring rote learning and copying and others formal reasoning (Phelps & Damon, 1989). After six sessions of peer collaboration, children showed significant gains in performance on math and spatial problems compared to a control group of children who did not participate in peer collaboration. This effect occurred for tasks that required formal reasoning but not for those that required rote learning or copying. Another interesting outcome was that the superiority of boys over girls on spatial problems at the start of the study significantly diminished.

Both Piaget (1926) and Vygotsky (1978) have proposed that peer interactions encourage the advancement of cognitive skills. In Piagetian theory, the cognitive conflicts and disequilibrium created in peer exchanges lead to reorganizations in the child's thinking. For Vygotsky, peers facilitate cognitive growth not only because they often operate within similar *zones of proximal development* but also because they display enough differences that one student's advanced knowledge in a given area can provide the *scaffolding* for another student's learning. Perhaps these processes also benefit from the more open and elaborated communication patterns that accompany peer interactions and help to explain why the effectiveness of cooperative learning seems to be greatest for tasks involving less structured problems (Cohen, 1994). Peer

---

KEY THEME
Interaction Among Domains

KEY THEME
Interaction Among Domains

peer collaboration Peer-centered learning experience in which pairs of students work together on academic problems, usually without competing against other students.

One form of learning is called *peer collaboration*, where pairs of students work together on science or mathematics problems. Compared with students who receive more traditional methods of instruction, peer collaborators show significant increases in performance in these academic subjects.

learning may also heighten children's motivation to learn. In team learning, an individual's goals can be met only if the group is successful and group members pressure individual students to display their best efforts. Consistent with the tenets of behavior theory, peer praise or criticism serves to regulate the individual accomplishments of group members (Slavin, 1987b).

Should Students Be Grouped According to Academic Ability?

Separating children into groups according to ability is standard practice in most North American schools. Sometimes students are simply given colorful group names, such as the Jets and the Falcons. Other times the names are less likely to obscure the differences between groups; some children are the Advanced Readers, others are the Slow Readers. Regardless of the names, most students and their parents realize they are being grouped (or "tracked") according to their academic abilities. One of the longest-running controversies in American education centers on the pros and cons of just this practice.

The arguments for tracking are numerous. Proponents of this procedure maintain that ability grouping helps teachers adapt their instructional styles to the specific needs of students. Bright students are more likely to be challenged and motivated when grouped with other bright students and can advance at a more rapid pace than if they are placed in slower classrooms. Slower learners, in turn, are spared the embarrassment of continual failure and have more opportunities to participate when they do not have to compete with bright students. They can learn more when they receive more individual attention from the teacher and when the pace of learning is adjusted to their level of ability.

Many educators have found these arguments convincing. As a consequence, grouping students according to academic ability is common in most elementary and secondary schools, whether done for reading groups within an elementary class or curriculum tracks (for example, college preparatory versus vocational) in the higher grades.

Critics point out, however, that ability grouping can have several damaging consequences. Chief among these are the low expectations and diminished morale slow learners often develop (Gamoran, 1992; Rosenbaum, 1980; Useem, 1990). When students find they are in a lower track, they often feel demoralized and begin to live out the expectations of others. One student's comments during a research interview poignantly illustrate this point:

> I felt good when I was with my [elementary] class, but when they went and separated us—that changed us. That changed our ideas, our thinking, the way we thought about each other, and turned us to enemies toward each other—because they said I was dumb and they were smart. . . . The devil with the whole thing—you lose—something in you—like it goes out of you. (Schafer & Olexa, 1971, pp. 62–63)

There are other problems, too. Because many teachers prefer not to teach students in the lower tracks, some educational researchers maintain that those students actually get poorer-quality instruction (Gamoran, 1989; Oakes, 1985; Page, 1991). In addition, students from lower socioeconomic levels and racial and ethnic minorities are more likely to be grouped in lower tracks because they are low achievers (but not necessarily because they are low in ability) (Persell, 1977; Rosenbaum, 1980). Once students are placed in a given academic track, they can find it exceedingly difficult to switch to another, especially because the grouping is often presumed to reflect innate ability rather than achievement level. Thus, tracking may serve to perpetuate the degree of access students from various economic and ethnic backgrounds have to educational resources.

In two major reviews of the research on academic ability grouping in elementary and secondary schools, Robert Slavin (1987a, 1990a) concluded that this educational strategy has no overall effect on the academic achievements of students. The only exception is that elementary school children who are grouped across grades according to reading ability (such as when higher-level first-graders are grouped with lower-level second-graders) or within grades for mathematics instruction achieve at slightly higher levels. Given the potential negative effects of tracking, Slavin argues that this popular educational practice has no good reason to continue. On the other hand, Slavin's analysis included studies that relied almost exclusively on standardized tests as measures of achievement, measures that may not capture the benefits of tracking because they do not necessarily measure what students are actually taught in school (Hallinan, 1990).

Which arguments about academic tracking seem most compelling? What research should psychologists conduct to further evaluate the pros and cons of academic tracking? Are there alternative ways to structure classroom experiences to provide more comprehensive benefits for students than academic ability grouping?

School Transitions

In addition to the physical ecology of school and philosophies of education, the school transitions children are expected to make at specific ages may influence development. Most children begin kindergarten at age five or six, and the way in which they adjust to this first experience of school frequently determines how much they will like later grades. For most children, a second important transition occurs in adolescence, when entering junior or senior high school makes new academic and social demands on them.

Starting School   Few times in a child's life are as momentous as the first day of school. Parents typically find this a time of mixed emotions, of eager anticipation of the child's future accomplishments coupled with anxieties about whether school will provide positive and rewarding experiences for their child. Children have many major adjustments to handle, including accommodating to a teacher and a new physical environment, making new friends, and mastering new academic challenges. Success in making the initial transition to school can set the tone for later academic and socioemotional development. Because these early behavior patterns and impressions of school tend to persist, we need to identify and understand the factors that make adjustment to school smooth and successful.

Gary Ladd and Joseph Price (1987) followed a sample of fifty-eight children as they moved from preschool to kindergarten. They assessed children on a number of social measures at three different times: before entering kindergarten, at the beginning of the school year, and at the end of the school year. Ladd and Price found that both the social behaviors of the children and the familiarity of the groups they entered contributed to healthy school adjustment. Children who as preschoolers displayed high levels of cooperative play and had extensive positive social contacts were well liked by the other kindergartners and were rated as involved with peers by teachers. Children who had been aggressive as preschoolers tended to be disliked by their kindergarten peers and were rated as hostile by teachers.

The presence of familiar peers in the kindergarten classroom also facilitated peer acceptance. Perhaps a nucleus of familiar others provides a secure base from which to develop other social relationships. Moreover, the presence of familiar peers was related to more positive attitudes toward school and fewer anxieties at the start of the school year. In general, factors promoting continuity between the preschool and kindergarten experiences were most beneficial to the child's adjustment, suggesting that parents should consider ways to foster their children's friendships with peers who will be future classmates. These results underscore the fact that the transition to school can be a particularly crucial time and that successes in one domain, peer relations, are related to successes in another, competence in school.

Another major controversy that surrounds this first school transition is the age of the child upon school entry. Some researchers claim the younger members of the classroom do not perform as well academically as the older members and continue to have difficulty in the later school years (Breznitz & Teltsch, 1989; Davis, Trimble, & Vincent, 1980; May, Kundert, & Brent, 1995). Others, however, have pointed out methodological and other problems in this research and have failed to find evidence that younger and older children in the classroom differ in any meaningful way (Alexander & Entwisle, 1988; Shepard & Smith, 1986). Frederick Morrison and his colleagues have carried out further work on this issue with Canadian schoolchildren (Morrison, Griffith, & Alberts, 1997). They found that younger children do tend to score below older children on reading and mathematics achievement tests at the end of the school year. However, the same is true even at the beginning of the school year. In fact, when measures of progress in reading and mathematics were used as the criteria, younger first-graders gained just as much as older first-graders did. Furthermore, the first-graders, whether younger or older, gained more than children who remained in kindergarten but could have been enrolled in first grade. Although additional research needs to be carried out examining factors influencing academic success in the classroom, these findings suggest entrance age by itself may not be an important factor in academic progress and children should not be delayed in entering school on that basis alone.

A Second Transition: Junior High   Another important transition occurs later in many children's schooling careers when they move from elementary school to a middle or junior high school. In the United States, this transition is usually the visible signal of childhood's end and the beginning of adolescence. Once again children must adapt to a new physical environment, new teachers, and, often, new peers; and now, rather than staying with the same classmates in the same room for most of the school day, they move from class to class, each usually with its own set of students. Frequently the difference in student body size is dramatic. In one study, the mean school size from grade six to grade seven increased from 466 to 1,307, and the mean number of children in each grade went from 59 to 403 (Simmons et al., 1987). It is

KEY THEME
Interaction Among Domains

Entry into junior high or middle school is a source of new opportunities for learning, as well as new challenges and difficulties. In making the change, students such as these in the school cafeteria often find themselves in a much larger school and as a result may need to build new friendships.

KEY THEME
Interaction Among Domains

no wonder that many researchers report a decline in school satisfaction and academic motivation in pre- and early adolescence, as well as a drop in grades and participation in extracurricular activities (Eccles, Midgley, et al., 1993; Hirsch & Rapkin, 1987; Schulenberg, Asp, & Petersen, 1984; Simmons & Blyth, 1987).

Some researchers have also observed a decline in self-esteem at this time, particularly among preadolescent girls, and an increase in physical complaints (Hirsch & Rapkin, 1987; Simmons et al., 1979). Early-maturing sixth-grade girls have been found to have better images of themselves when they attend schools with kindergarten through eighth-grade classes, presumably because they feel less pressured to adopt dating and other activities that become prevalent among seventh- and eighth-graders. On the other hand, those girls entering puberty at more typical ages and at about the same time they enter a new school program or undergo other significant transitions tend to have lower self-images and more difficulties in school, possibly because multiple changes in life are difficult to handle (Simmons et al., 1987).

For some adolescents, the difficulties encountered in junior high school may set in motion a pattern of academic decline that leads them to drop out of school (Eccles & Midgley, 1988). According to some researchers, this is because the junior high school experience does not fit the specific developmental needs of preadolescents. At a time when youngsters seek stronger peer associations and a supportive climate for resolving identity issues, they confront an educational environment that is more impersonal than elementary school and fragments peer relationships. Junior high school classrooms, compared to elementary school classrooms, also tend to emphasize greater teacher control and discipline, offer fewer personal and positive teacher-student interactions, use a higher standard of evaluating student competence while focusing on more public evaluation of the quality of work, and can often be less cognitively challenging as classrooms become more teacher directed and provide fewer opportunities for student-initiated learning (Eccles, Midgley, et al., 1993). In addition, the transition to junior high school frequently happens to coincide with several other life changes, such as the onset of puberty and dating. Entry into a new educational setting compounds the stresses already confronting many preadolescents (Simmons et al., 1987).

What happens when alternatives to the traditional junior high school and high school structures are instituted? In one study, students about to begin high school were assigned to special homerooms in which the teacher played an expanded role in providing academic and personal counseling, contacted parents when students were absent, and encouraged other communication with parents. Thus, the homeroom teachers in this setting provided more social support than usual throughout the entire first year of high school. Students were also assigned to classes with many of the same students, a strategy that presumably would enhance peer support and provide a stable environment for students. At the end of the school year, students from this program showed higher levels of academic success and less psychological dysfunction than a control group; after four years, they showed a substantially lower school dropout rate (21 percent) than the control group students (43 percent) (Felner & Adan, 1988; Felner, Ginter, & Primavera, 1982).

We see from these studies that whenever children face a school transition, whether it be the start of kindergarten or of secondary school, they adjust best if they have social and emotional supports adequate to help them cope with the demands of the new environment. When children are buttressed by strong relationships with peers and teachers, they show higher academic performance, less anxiety, and more favorable attitudes toward school than when they lack these supports.

Teachers: Key Agents of Influence

No single factor in the school experience plays a more critical role in student achievement and self-esteem than teachers. The expectations teachers have of students, their classroom management strategies, and the climate they create in the classroom are all major elements in student success or failure.

The Role of Expectations   A highly publicized study by Robert Rosenthal and Lenore Jacobson (1968) documented how teachers' expectations of students' performance can affect students' actual attainments. The researchers told teachers that certain elementary school children could be expected to show sudden gains in intellectual skills during the course of the school year based on their scores on an IQ test administered at the beginning of the term. In reality, the students they designated as "rapid bloomers" were chosen randomly. When Rosenthal and Jacobson administered the IQ test again at the end of the school year, the targeted children indeed showed significantly greater improvement than other students in the class, an outcome they called the *Pygmalion effect*. The investigators explained the findings by suggesting that teachers somehow treated the targeted children differently based on their beliefs about the children's intellectual potential, thereby creating a self-fulfilling prophecy.

One of the most important factors in a child's school experience is teacher encouragement. Effective teachers are involved in all phases of instruction, provide clear feedback, and create a positive emotional climate in the classroom.

Subsequent studies have confirmed that high achievers *are* treated differently in the classroom; they are given more opportunities to participate, given more time to answer questions, receive more praise for being correct, and receive less criticism than lower achievers (Minuchin & Shapiro, 1983). In other words, the classroom climate is most supportive for those who have already demonstrated success, whereas those who most need the teacher's attention and encouragement may actually get it least. Many teachers are undoubtedly unaware of the ways their expectations influence their own behaviors toward students. Yet the forms of the interactions that ensue can have important repercussions for students' academic accomplishments and feelings of self-worth.

Classroom Management Strategies   Students achieve most in school when their teachers maximize the time spent in actual learning. This statement may seem obvious, but not all school time is spent in direct instruction. Effective teachers plan their lessons well, monitor the entire classroom continuously, minimize the time spent in disciplining children who misbehave, and keep transitions between activities brief and smooth (Brophy, 1986). They make sure there is little "dead time" in the classroom when students are unoccupied, and they keep the focus on instruction.

Another key ingredient in a teacher's success is active involvement in the learning process. This means teachers remain personally involved in every phase of instruction, from the initial presentation of a new lesson to supervising the individual work of students. *Involvement* also refers to the teacher's enjoyment and knowledge of students. Even when students are working in groups, teachers who guide the discussion or progress of the group will foster higher levels of mastery and greater feelings of competence than those who leave students completely on their own (Brophy, 1986; Skinner & Belmont, 1993). Effective teachers also provide students with clear feedback on the quality of their performance and on what is expected of them (Rutter, 1983).

The Classroom Climate   Students achieve less when they are the targets of frequent criticism or ridicule from the teacher. On the other hand, when the classroom provides a warm, friendly environment, student achievement is high (Linney & Seidman, 1989). Teachers who set limits on students' behaviors make the classroom run more smoothly (Rutter, 1983). In a large-scale investigation of the effectiveness of secondary schools, Michael Rutter and his colleagues found that schools in which students received frequent praise and experienced a pleasant, comfortable environment had children who were more likely to complete school and achieved more than children in less supportive school environments (Rutter et al., 1979). Positive feedback encourages both acceptable behavior and achievement as well as fostering high student morale (Rutter, 1983). Like the authoritative parents discussed in Chapter 14, teachers who control students but use reasoning and positive emotions are likely to foster the greatest academic and personal gains among their students (Baumrind, 1972).

Not surprisingly, when teachers assign grades frequently, make public announcements about grades, and openly emphasize the poor accomplishments of some students, they create situations that may lower self-esteem and lead some students to see themselves as less competent (Rosenholtz & Simpson, 1984). A particularly important dimension is the extent to which the teacher promotes *autonomy,* or student initiative within the classroom. Children who perceive that teachers give them responsibility within the classroom have higher self-esteem scores than those who perceive teachers as controlling and directive (Ryan & Grolnick, 1986).

Cultural Differences in School Achievement

The school experience is not the same for children of different racial and ethnic backgrounds. Children who attend school bring with them attitudes about school that are first nurtured within their families, as well as cultural beliefs that may be in synchrony or in conflict with the predominant belief system of the school (Gibson & Ogbu, 1991). For example, are schools a vehicle for economic and personal advancement? Cultural and ethnic groups may vary in their responses to this question. Is verbal, rational expression (which schools emphasize) the optimal means of human communication as opposed to emotional or spiritual sharing? Again, cultures may vary in the extent to which they value some skills over others. One of the major challenges facing educators is how to ensure the academic success of children who come from a range of cultural-ethnic backgrounds.

School Achievement Among Minority Children A persistent finding in past research on school achievement in the United States is that children from some minority groups—for example, African American children—score significantly lower than Caucasian children on many measures of academic performance. In the 1960s, the prevailing explanation for the school difficulties of minority children centered on the *cultural deficit hypothesis,* the notion that some deficiency in the backgrounds of minority children hindered children's preparation for the academic demands of school. However, Herbert Ginsberg (1972) pointed out that rather than being culturally deficient, minority children are culturally different; that is, the behaviors minority children display help them to adapt to their specific life circumstances. For example, rather than having poor language skills, African American children who speak Black English display rich images and poetic forms when speaking to one another. Other psychologists and educators have come to believe that we must consider the cultural backgrounds of the members of any minority group to understand their school failure or success. According to the **cultural compatibility hypothesis,** school instruction produces greater improvements in learning if it is consistent with the practices of the child's own culture (Tharp, 1989).

An example of an educational intervention specifically designed to be compatible with the child's cultural background is the Kamehameha Early Education Program (KEEP), developed by Roland Tharp and his collaborators in Hawaii (Tharp et al., 1984). Like many minority children in other parts of the United States, youngsters of native Hawaiian ancestry have been the lowest achieving in the state. In one administration of a standardized test of reading achievement, more than half of native Hawaiian children scored below the fortieth percentile. School achievement deteriorated from the first grade on. Native Hawaiian children were also found to be overrepresented among juvenile offenders arrested for serious crimes such as larceny, rape, and homicide.

The KEEP program was instituted as an early education program in language arts for kindergartners through third-graders. Several unique features of the program were tied to the practices and beliefs of traditional Hawaiian culture. First, because collaboration and cooperation are highly valued in that society, classrooms were organized into small groups of four to five children working on independent projects under the close supervision of a teacher. Teachers made a deliberate attempt to establish warm, nurturant relationships with their charges through the frequent use of praise and the avoidance of authoritarian methods of control. Second, the program attempted to improve responsiveness to teachers by capitalizing on the tendency of native Hawaiian children to engage their peers in rich and animated verbal interactions. Each day teachers conducted small-group discussions of some academic topic and did not discourage children's interruptions, overlapping speech, and rapidly paced discussions. Third, reading was taught with the aim of developing comprehension as opposed to mechanics, and children were encouraged to relate personal experiences that were triggered by reading a given text.

What were the results of this broad-based intervention? Participants in KEEP scored at approximately the national norms on several tests of reading achievement, whereas control participants from similar low-income backgrounds continued to place below national averages (Tharp et al., 1984). The KEEP program is an excellent example of how modifying classroom practices to incorporate cultural patterns of language, communication, and social organization can enhance the school performance of children.

KEY THEME
Interaction Among Domains

cultural compatibility hypothesis Theory that school instruction is most effective if it is consistent with the practices of the child's background culture.

African American Culture and Education   In a study of achievement patterns of African American and Caucasian children in the first two years of school, Karl Alexander and Doris Entwisle (1988) found that African American and Caucasian first-graders did not differ significantly on a standardized test of verbal and quantitative achievement when they were assessed at the beginning of the school year. But by the end of the year and during the second year, the scores of African American and Caucasian students began to diverge noticeably. The authors hypothesize that African American parents may be less attentive to the performance levels of their children or may be less involved in providing academic supports because of external pressures they face, such as economic hardship.

Alexander and Entwisle's (1988) data, however, are also consistent with another possibility: parental influences may diminish in the face of other, more powerful factors that in turn may influence the achievement of African American children. In keeping with the cultural compatibility hypothesis, some have argued that for many African American students, a conflict exists between their background culture and the social and cognitive structure of traditional schools. For example, the spiritualism, expressiveness, and rich oral tradition characteristic of the African American heritage frequently clash with the materialism, emotional control, and emphasis on printed materials characteristic of European Americans and their schools (Boykin, 1986; Heath, 1989; Slaughter-DeFoe et al., 1990). These children may perceive that academic success does not necessarily lead to occupational or economic success, or they may believe that "acting white" is the only way to achieve success. John Ogbu (1974) found that inner-city African American children do poorly on academic tests because they do not take them seriously, do not persevere, and do not see their performance as being linked to later success. Furthermore, many African American children persist in believing they will do well in school even though past performance indicates they are likely to do otherwise. These children may need not only to overcome the hurdles imposed by racism but also to more fully understand what behaviors will be necessary to achieve their expectations, that is, to become motivated to master the academic materials and skills necessary to achieve their goals (Alexander, Entwisle, & Bedinger, 1994; Steinberg, 1995).

In focusing on cultural differences, however, researchers need to recognize that they may be unwittingly contributing to stereotypes about African American children and their development. After all, many African American children, and indeed many children in all cultural and ethnic groups in the United States, are doing well in school. What factors are contributing to their success? Tom Luster and Harriette McAdoo (1994) have provided some answers for African American children between ages six and nine years, and the answers should not be too surprising. African American children who are high achieving, just as other children who are high achieving, experience relatively supportive home environments in which mothers display self-esteem and are members of smaller families whose incomes are above the poverty line. Other factors, such as absence of a father figure or the mother's age at the birth of the first child, are not directly linked to differences in high-achieving and low-achieving children. However, this does not mean these factors have little consequence, since they can influence important variables such as family income.

In a more recent study, Luster and McAdoo (1996) followed African American children from preschool age until young adulthood. All the children lived in families with low socioeconomic status during the preschool period. Previous research had demonstrated that the preschool experience benefited these children compared to others who had not participated in preschool (Berrueta-Clement et al., 1984). But these children showed substantial individual differences in accomplishments throughout the school years. Consistent with our earlier discussion emphasizing the importance of parents in promoting school success, the cognitive competence and academic motivation these children brought to the public school setting, as well as their degree of social adjustment, predicted performance on achievement tests during the elementary school years. Children of mothers who were more involved with their children's schooling also tended to do better in the lower grades, although this relationship did not hold up during adolescence. However, parents' expectations for

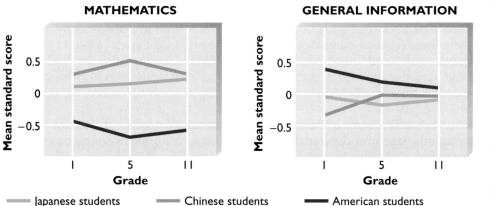

Source: Stevenson, Chen, & Lee, 1993.

FIGURE 16.3

Mathematics Achievement and General Information Scores as a Function of Sociocultural Context

Chinese and Japanese students score higher than American students on tests of mathematics achievement beginning in first grade, and their superiority in this area continues throughout high school. However, on tests of general information, children from all three cultures perform at similar levels, especially in the higher grades. The better performance on mathematics tests by East Asian children may reflect both school- and family-related cultural influences.

success in the school was correlated with achievement throughout the school years. These findings further confirm the important role families play in the education of African American children just as in the education of all children (Steinberg, 1995).

Achievement Among Asian Children   Since the mid-1980s, Harold Stevenson and his associates have been conducting comparative research in three countries on the academic abilities of Taiwanese Chinese, Japanese, and American students. This research has been guided by an effort to understand why Asian students seem to do particularly well in the areas of mathematics and science. For example, first- and fifth-grade students from middle-to-upper-class backgrounds in all three countries were tested on a battery of specially designed cognitive tasks that assessed, among other things, spatial relations, perceptual speed, auditory and verbal memory, and vocabulary along with reading and mathematics achievement (Stevenson, Lee, & Stigler, 1986).

Most noteworthy about the findings was that American children scored noticeably lower in mathematics than the other two groups (see Figure 16.3). The distinctive patterns of achievement could not be explained by superior cognitive skills in any one group. The researchers found no predictive relationships between scores on the various cognitive assessments and scores on achievement tests. In fact, what was striking was the similarity across cultural groups in the children's cognitive profiles by the time they reached fifth grade (Stevenson et al., 1985). When these children were again tested in eleventh grade, American children continued to lag well behind the Chinese and Japanese, although, as Figure 16.3 shows, on age-appropriate tests of general information (for example, "What are two things a plant needs in order to grow?" or "Why has it been possible to make smaller computers in recent years?"), the Asian children were not superior to the American children (Stevenson, Chen, & Lee, 1993).

In a more recent study, Chuansheng Chen and Harold Stevenson included comparisons between Caucasian American and Asian American high school students on mathematics achievement (Chen & Stevenson, 1995). Asian Americans scored higher than Caucasian Americans but somewhat lower than Taiwan Chinese or Japanese students on mathematics tests. What accounts for this pattern of findings? Stevenson's research group reported significant differences in children's school routines and parents' attitudes and beliefs among the Chinese, Japanese, and American groups, as well as differences between Asian American and Caucasian American families. For example, during the year Chinese and Japanese children attend school about fifty more days than American children do. Furthermore, Chinese and Japanese high school students spend close to fifty hours a week in school and students in the United States about thirty-six hours a week (Fuligni & Stevenson, 1995).

The percentage of classroom time actually spent in academic activities also differs. For fifth-grade students, the figures were 64.5 percent of the time for American children, 91.5 percent for Chinese children, and 87.4 for Japanese children. Furthermore, American children studied language arts more than twice as long as mathematics, whereas Chinese and Japanese children spent equal amounts of time on each subject. Thus, the American children received far less instruction in mathematics than their Chinese and Japanese counterparts did (Stevenson, Lee, & Stigler, 1986). In addition, Japanese and Chinese teachers were far more likely to use their time in mathematics classes directly teaching the entire class, whereas American children spent more than half their time in mathematics classes working alone (Stigler, Lee, & Stevenson, 1987).

Stevenson's research group also examined attitudes and behaviors related to homework. American children devoted substantially less time to doing homework— an average of 46 minutes per day among fifth-graders, according to mothers' estimates—compared to 114 and 57 minutes for Chinese and Japanese children, respectively. American mothers were not dissatisfied with the small amount of homework their children received, nor were Chinese and Japanese mothers dissatisfied with the large amounts their children were assigned (Stevenson, Lee, & Stigler, 1986). In addition, compared to American students, high school students, their peers, and their parents in the two Asian cultures seemed to expect higher standards and voiced greater concern about education, with Asian Americans surpassing their Caucasian American counterparts on these measures (Chen & Stevenson, 1995). American high school students were also far more likely to work, date, and engage in other leisure time activities than East Asian students. Finally, East Asian students were also more likely than American students to believe their own effort was the best route to accomplishments; Asian Americans outscored Caucasian Americans on this measure as well (Chen & Stevenson, 1995).

These data confirm that a number of factors other than pure cognitive ability determine the child's level of achievement in school. As we have seen throughout this section, the characteristics of the given school (especially the events that transpire in the classroom), parental attitudes, and larger cultural influences are all related to patterns of academic success or failure. As we also saw at the outset of this chapter, academic performance can have important repercussions for the child's self-esteem and personal adjustment. If we are concerned about the educational attainments of students and their overall psychological development, research on the influence of schools reveals that there are many ways to more fully engage children of all ability levels and diverse sociocultural backgrounds (Steinberg, 1995).

The goal of public education in the United States is to help all children achieve to the level of their potential. As a consequence, schools are responsible for educating all children regardless of their background or ability. Children enter the public schools with various strengths and

ATYPICAL DEVELOPMENT

Education and Youths with Serious Emotional Disturbances

sometimes with disabilities. In fact, approximately 11 percent of students in the United States are identified as having one or more disabilities (Wagner, 1995). How well do such students do? There is no simple story to tell about the success of children with disabilities in the schools, since enormous variability occurs among this population of children. Some children—for example, those with sensory impairments—are just as likely to further their education beyond high school as youngsters in the general population, but may not do as well in the labor market. Others, such as those with learning disabilities, often obtain jobs quickly after high school, although they are less likely to pursue further education.

One group of youth, those with serious emotional disturbances—children who display problems over a long period of time such as unexplained difficulty in learning, inability to establish satisfying interpersonal relationships with peers or adults, pervasive depression or fears, or other inappropriate behaviors or emotions in normal circumstances—seem to have an especially difficult time both in school and afterward. These children often become disengaged from school as evidenced by frequent absenteeism and failure to make friends among schoolmates. The consequence is often poor school performance and dropping out. Only a relatively small proportion continue their education (Wagner, 1995).

Are there ways the schools can improve on these outcomes? One concern is that these students do not always receive the kind of support they need to achieve their goals. For example, the few special services they are likely to receive are academic (tutoring, slower-paced instructions, and so forth) rather than directed at their emotional or behavioral problems. Moreover, the vast majority of youth with serious emotional disturbances attend large, comprehensive high schools, and the classes in which they enroll are the same as those populated by students without disabilities. Thus, they are expected to compete just as other students do despite their additional needs and different career goals. Under these sink-or-swim conditions, perhaps it is little wonder that youngsters with serious emotional disorders often find school frustrating and difficult; even those who do graduate still have difficulty obtaining jobs.

What interventions might help these children? As repeatedly observed in our discussion of the impact of school on children, the involvement of parents in promoting learning, holding high expectations for their children's efforts, and becoming involved in the school seems to contribute to success for youngsters with serious emotional disorders as well (Henderson, 1994). However, schools also may need to assist by offering these students more, and perhaps earlier, vocational and technical courses that maintain their interest in education and provide the job skills they need to be successful (Wagner, Blackorby, & Hebbeler, 1993). When student interest is maintained, participation in regular courses in the later school years is likely to be more positive. Finally, fostering integration with other students, through sports, hobbies, or other social activities, along with greater collaboration with mental health and social service agencies to address the specific needs of individual children, can also yield positive outcomes for youngsters with serious emotional disturbances (Wagner, 1995).

Computers

Perhaps there is no more visible symbol of the technological age than the computer. Just as most adults in many countries are now likely to encounter computers in their daily experiences, so are children, particularly in school but also in the home. Moreover, computer games are staples in many children's play routines. So ubiquitous are computers in contemporary American society that many now speak of computer literacy as a skill akin to reading.

What is the effect of computers on children's development? Can computer-presented instructional materials enhance children's mastery of academic subjects? Does experience with computers influence the ways children tackle problem solving and other cognitive tasks? Are young computer "hackers" who spend long hours glued to the video screen missing other critical experiences, particularly the social interactions crucial to their socioemotional development? The pervasive presence of computers in today's world makes these questions well worth exploring. The emerging answer is clear: there is no such thing as an "effect of computers" per se on child development. What matters, rather, is the way children use them (Salomon & Gardner, 1986).

Academic Mastery   The first relatively widespread use of computers in education began in the 1960s, when **computer-assisted instruction (CAI)** was touted as a valuable, efficient educational tool. CAI programs serve primarily to supplement classroom instruction, providing highly structured tutorial information along with drill-and-practice exercises in content areas such as mathematics and reading. Several

computer-assisted instruction (CAI) Use of computers to provide tutorial information and drill-and-practice routines.

principles are presumed to make CAI programs effective teaching tools. First, the child can work through a lesson at her own pace, reviewing topics if necessary. CAI thus provides an individually paced learning experience in which the content can be tailored to the specific needs of the student. Second, the child receives immediate feedback about the correctness of his responses to questions and exercises and may even receive periodic summaries of performance. These features usually enhance learning and heighten motivation. Finally, CAI programs often employ sound effects and graphics designed to promote the child's attention to and interest in the material being presented.

How effective are CAI approaches to instruction? Meta-analyses of the hundreds of studies evaluating CAI have shown that on average, students with CAI experience improve in achievement test scores and that this effect is moderately strong (Lepper & Gurtner, 1989). CAI is especially effective with elementary school and special-needs children, who seem to profit most from individualized approaches to learning (Kulik, Kulik, & Bangert-Drowns, 1985; Niemiec & Walberg, 1987). Children given CAI experience also have more positive attitudes toward computers and the subject area they are studying (Kulik, Bangert, & Williams, 1983).

Newer educational software places less emphasis on rote memorization and more on providing children with opportunities to use higher-order thinking skills as they master academic subjects. Consider fourth- and fifth-graders who are learning about the laws of physics, such as the principle that once an object is set in motion, an equal force in the opposite direction is necessary to stop it. In a study of how computers can help children learn the laws of motion, one group of children received tutorial material followed by questions and feedback, along the lines of the traditional CAI approach (Rieber, 1990). Another group was given a different type of computer experience, a simulation that allowed them to experiment with a free-floating starship whose speed they could increase or decrease. As the children interacted with the starship, they could observe the effects of their physical manipulations on its course and "discover" the laws of motion. Still a third group, serving as a control, was given the lesson material with no questions or simulation experiences. Students who participated in the simulations later obtained higher scores on a test of the laws of motion than those in the other two groups. One reason may be that the simulation encouraged students to make a more active mental engagement with the scientific principles underlying the motion of the starship. Software such as the starship simulation allows students to conduct experiments they may not be able to try in the typical elementary school science laboratory and is a prime example of how computer instruction can extend beyond simple drill-and-practice routines to enhance academic learning.

Cognition   More than simply vehicles of direct instruction, computers may also be a means of enriching analytic thinking skills and creativity, particularly when children learn to do their own programming. Seymour Papert (1980), a creator of the computer language Logo, believes programming experiences represent an ideal setting for learning because children can test their own theories and models of physical laws, mathematical relationships, and other forms of knowledge. Under such conditions, claims Papert, children can master abstract concepts and ideas much earlier than they normally would.

Because it is specifically designed for children, the Logo program has been the focus of most studies investigating the influence of programming on children's cognition. Logo is an interactive program that allows children to create graphic displays by instructing a "turtle," a triangular pointer, to move around on the computer screen. To draw a square, the child might write this program:

```
TO SQUARE
FORWARD 100
RIGHT 90
FORWARD 100
```

KEY THEME
Child's Active Role

```
RIGHT 90
FORWARD 100
RIGHT 90
FORWARD 100
RIGHT 90
END
```

After using the Logo program, many children begin to have spontaneous insights into how to make their programming more efficient—by, for example, modifying the sequence of commands just given to read:

```
TO SQUARE
REPEAT 4
FORWARD 100
RIGHT 90
END
```

Here the child realizes that the goal can be achieved by "factoring" two commands, an example of more abstract, higher-order thinking.

Papert (1980) maintains that by using Logo to direct the pointer's path, children become familiar with notions of planning and debugging (fixing errors and learning from that process) as well as heuristic strategies for solving problems. **Heuristic strategies** are those mental reflections that focus on accomplishing a goal, such as in dividing a problem into smaller parts or connecting it to other, successfully solved problems. Furthermore, because computer programming requires the precise articulation of the steps necessary to reach a solution, children should also become aware of the logical and hierarchical nature of problem solving.

Researchers evaluating these claims have reported conflicting results. Some researchers have reported that children with Logo experience show significant cognitive gains—for example, increased ability in classification, sorting, and seriation of shapes and objects—and increased creativity (Clements, 1986). Experience with Logo has also been linked to greater spatial and analytic skill, enhanced rule learning, and a reflective cognitive style, in which children solve problems slowly and accurately rather than quickly and with many errors (Clements & Gullo, 1984; Mayer & Fay, 1987; Nastasi, Clements, & Battista, 1990). However, others have found little transfer of skills from programming to problem-solving tasks (Pea, Kurland, & Hawkins, 1985; Salomon & Perkins, 1987).

One hypothesized reason positive outcomes are reported for the emergence of some higher-order skills is that Logo is often used in group settings in which pairs or small groups of children help one another to solve programming problems. As we have already seen, cooperative learning seems to promote academic achievement. In these contexts, children often disagree on ways to conceptualize a given problem (for example, how to make a house with the turtle) and share several potential solutions. As children attempt to resolve their cognitive conflicts, they are pushed to more advanced modes of thinking (Nastasi, Clements, & Battista, 1990).

The studies show that the computer itself, as well as the interactions with peers it often precipitates, may function within the child's zone of proximal development (Salomon, Globerson, & Guterman, 1989). Children who are capable of learning cognitive skills such as spatial relations or mathematical concepts may be pushed to acquire these skills in their interactions with sophisticated software programs or as they work on joint problem-solving tasks with peers. Although some researchers believe Papert's initial claims about the power of the computer to shape cognition were overstated, others hold that "intelligent" computer programs and experiences with programming languages have vast potential to enhance children's thinking skills (Khayrallah & Van Den Meiraker, 1987; Salomon, Globerson, & Guterman, 1989).

Social Development Contrary to popular opinion, the interactions a child has with the computer do not necessarily displace other activities of a more social

heuristic strategies Methods of problem solving that involve higher-order analyses, such as subdividing the problem into smaller parts or comparing it to previously solved problems.

The introduction of computers into the classroom may have some surprising benefits. For example, when children use computers in school, they often do so in small groups. Thus, computers can provide opportunities for collaborative learning and may also promote socialization skills.

KEY THEME
Interaction Among Domains

nature, nor is computer use itself necessarily a solitary activity (Crook, 1992). In one survey of more than five hundred children, those with microcomputers at home resembled nonowners in the frequency with which they visited friends, participated in club meetings, and engaged in sports (Lieberman, 1985). In fact, the computer may actually stimulate the formation of social relationships; children who play computer games say they visit their friends more often than those who do not (Lieberman, 1985). Furthermore, children who work on computer projects in school tend to collaborate and share ideas more in these settings than they do in other school activities (Hawkins et al., 1982). In one observation of four-year-olds who had a computer in their child care center, 63 percent of the time they spent at the computer was in joint participation with a peer and 70 percent of the interactions consisted of active sharing of the computer (Muller & Perlmutter, 1985). Thus, rather than inhibiting social interactions, computer activities may actually promote them, especially when teachers encourage group problem solving as opposed to individual projects (Bergin, Ford, & Hess, 1993). As they work on shared projects or spontaneously exchange ideas at the computer, children have opportunities to develop skills in cooperation and social problem solving.

Sex Differences   Ask children ranging from kindergarten age to twelfth grade to rate the word *computer* on a scale labeled M (for "male") at one end and F (for "female") at the other. Ask them also to rate how much they like the item. Researchers who have followed this procedure have found that children place computers toward the "male" side of the rating scale and that boys like computers more than girls do (Wilder, Mackie, & Cooper, 1985). Other researchers have reported that boys are far more likely than girls to enroll in computer camps (by a ratio of three to one) and that males outnumber females in computer courses in school (Hess & Miura, 1985; Linn, 1985). Yet these gender differences are apparent primarily at the elementary and high school level and are not present at younger ages; preschoolers and kindergartners are much less likely to display these stereotypes, at least with respect to interest in the computer (Bergin, Ford, & Hess, 1993; Collis & Ollila, 1990; Krendl & Broihier, 1992). Nor do girls shy away from all computer activities. For example, although girls spend less time than boys doing programming or playing computer games, they are just about equally disposed to use word-processing programs (Lockheed, 1985). Why, then, do we see sex differences among older children in the tendency to use computers?

Several explanations are possible. First, teachers and parents may encourage boys to use computers because of their own stereotypic beliefs about appropriate activities for each sex. Parents especially may see computer skills as being linked to promising careers for their sons and may be more willing to invest in computers, software, and camp programs for them than for their daughters. Second, girls may be less attracted to the aggressive and competitive themes that frequently characterize computer games and educational software, many with titles such as "Submarine Attack" or "Alien Intruder" (Hess & Miura, 1985). Furthermore, when a limited number of computers are available, boys tend to be more aggressive in gaining control of them (Silvern, Williamson, & Countermine, 1988). Finally, both boys and girls are socialized to link computers with science and mathematics, academic subjects that are frequently perceived as more appropriate for boys (Lockheed, 1985). Unfortunately, the persistence of the stereotypes creates for girls unnecessary barriers to experiences with computers that may promote abstract, analytical thinking.

In summary, computers add a unique dimension to children's experiences by encouraging them to engage in active and analytical reflection on the nature of problem solving and by promoting exchanges with peers, interactions that may further enhance both cognitive and social development. Early signs are that computers enhance rather than detract from the process of development.

TELEVISION

Almost all American homes (nearly 99 percent) have at least one television set, and according to most estimates, American children watch a great deal of television. Babies as young as six months of age attend to television and on average are exposed to more than one hour per day (Hollenbeck & Slaby, 1979). As Figure 16.4 shows, the time children spend attending to television increases dramatically during the preschool years, especially after age two-and-a-half, peaks between ages ten to twelve, and declines during adolescence (Anderson & Levin, 1976; Anderson et al., 1986; Calvert et al., 1982). Children, at least in the United States, spend more time watching television than at any other activity except sleep (Huston, Watkins, & Kunkel, 1989). Moreover, with the advent of cable television and videocassette recorders (VCR), children have more opportunities than ever to spend time in front of a television screen.

KEY THEME
Sociocultural Influence

Television viewing among children shows large individual differences. One research team investigating the viewing habits of three-to-five-year-olds found that some children did not watch television at all during a one-week span, whereas others watched as much as seventy-five hours. Moreover, individual patterns of TV viewing were found to remain stable during a period of two years. Thus, the television-viewing habits children acquire in early childhood can be relatively long lasting (Huston et al., 1990).

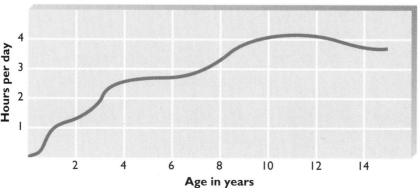

FIGURE 16.4

Hours of TV Watching as a Function of Children's Age

The amount of time children spend watching television increases throughout early childhood, peaks at about age ten or twelve years, and then declines in adolescence.

Source: Adapted from Liebert & Sprafkin, 1988.

As they grow older, children also show changes in the types of programs they prefer to watch. Preschoolers prefer nonanimated, informative programs specifically designed for children, such as "Sesame Street" or "Mister Rogers' Neighborhood." These programs feature language that children can comprehend easily and characters that are repeated across segments, and they do not require the child to integrate complex elements of a plot or story. Interest in these programs peaks at ages three-and-a-half to four and then declines. From ages three to five, children watch more cartoons; by ages five to seven, they watch comedies and entertainment shows aimed at general audiences. With age, then, children watch shows that make increasing demands on their ability to comprehend plots and themes (Huston et al., 1990).

Choices regarding television watching may also be influenced by parents; although children tend to watch children's programs alone, they often view general audience programs selected by their parents (St. Peters et al., 1991). Boys and girls watch television for equally long periods of time, but children from lower socioeconomic levels tend to be more frequent viewers than children from higher-income backgrounds (Greenberg, 1986).

Children's TV Viewing: Active or Passive?

Contrary to popular belief, television viewing is not always a passive process in which a mesmerized child sits gazing at the screen. The fact that preferences for shows change with age is just one example of the ways children actively control their TV viewing. Daniel Anderson and his colleagues have conducted numerous studies further demonstrating that children's selection of television programs is influenced by their ability to comprehend content. Certain formal, or structural, features of television serve to draw the viewer in, particularly such sound effects as laughter, music, and children's and women's voices. Other features, such as visual cuts, motion, and special sound effects, hold the child's attention (Alwitt et al., 1980). But the formal features of television programs are not the sole determinants of what children watch.

Anderson and his coresearchers recorded the visual attention of two- and five-year-olds as they watched a one-hour, specially edited version of "Sesame Street" in a laboratory room (Anderson et al., 1981). The videotape contained a regular program segment along with other portions that were altered to reduce the show's comprehensibility while keeping its formal features constant. In one version, the dialogue was presented backward; in another, the auditory portion was dubbed in Greek; and so on. The results indicated that children's visual attention was greater during the normal portions than in any of the altered segments. In other words, children ac-

Television is a powerful influence on child development. According to some estimates, as much as one-third of a child's waking life will have been spent watching television.

tively direct their attention to those portions of the show that they most readily understand; they are not influenced by sound effects or visual cuts alone.

Children do not always have control of the programs they watch. Families frequently view television together, and parents often pick the shows everyone will see. Furthermore, children's program selections are limited by those shows the broadcasters choose to air on a given day and at a specified time. Thus, children are frequently exposed to programming that falls outside their range of comprehension (Huston et al., 1990). Nevertheless, much of children's television viewing is guided by their active selection of programming they understand.

Children's Comprehension of Television Programs

What exactly do young children understand about the various behaviors, roles, and stories that unfold during the programs they watch? Do developmental changes occur in children's comprehension of TV programs? Many television shows have complex plots and use subtle cues that require inferences about characters' motives, intentions, and feelings. In addition, most programs contain changes of scene that require viewers to integrate information from several scenes. Research indicates that clear developmental differences exist in children's ability to understand information from television shows, differences that accompany changes in cognitive processing.

Preschoolers can understand short story segments in programs specifically targeted for children. When five-year-olds in one study saw four segments from "Sesame Street," each a few minutes long, they were later able to remember the most central elements of each story (Lorch, Bellack, & Augsbach, 1987). When the plots and themes of television shows become more complex, however, young children have difficulties.

More specifically, when they watch programs designed for general audiences, younger children are less likely than older children to remember the *explicit* content of programs, that is, the discrete scenes that are essential to understanding the plot. Second- and third-graders in one study remembered only 65 percent of the central content compared to 90 percent and more for eighth-graders. Even when they do remember explicit information, younger children frequently fail to grasp the *implicit* content communicated by relationships among scenes (Collins et al., 1978). For example, young children may fail to understand a character's motive for aggression if the message is communicated in two scenes separated by several other sequences (Collins, 1983).

W. Andrew Collins (1983) believes children's comprehension of implicit content is specifically tied to their emerging ability to integrate two pieces of information separated by time or other events. He further suggests that children's general knowledge and previous experiences can affect their comprehension of the programs they watch. Suppose, for example, that children are asked to retell the content of a show about a murder and the suspect's eventual capture. Children frequently mention *script-based* knowledge (see Chapter 9), drawing from their general storehouse of information on the events that surround the relationships between police and criminals. Older children are more likely than younger children, however, to describe content specific to the program they watched, such as the fact that some police officers in the show did not wear uniforms (Collins, 1983). As children's general knowledge about the world grows, their comprehension of more detailed, specific information in television programs expands as well.

Other research has shown that still another skill, children's growing verbal competency, underlies their ability to understand TV programs. When five-year-olds were given standardized IQ tests and tested on their memory of the central and incidental events on a thirty-five-minute television program, their scores on the verbal subscales of the tests correlated significantly with their ability to comprehend the show's central events (Jacobvitz, Wood, & Albin, 1989).

One other important developmental change is in children's ability to recognize that most television programming is fictional. Children under four years of age often have difficulty distinguishing the boundaries between events that occur on television and those that take place in the real world (Flavell et al., 1990; Jaglom & Gardner, 1981). Many five- and six-year-olds do not fully understand that television characters are actually actors playing roles, and not until age eight and older do the majority of children completely grasp this concept. There is, however, a burgeoning awareness of the distinction between television and the real world early in development. For example, even kindergartners realize that cartoons are fantasy. They are also quite accurate about deciding whether their favorite programs occur as part of real life or just on television. In fact, they tend to be biased in assuming that most television programming does not occur in real life (Wright et al., 1994). Thus, the developmental course seems to progress from failing to make a distinction between events on television and events in the real world to a belief that few events depicted on television occur in the real world to, finally, a more complete understanding of which events occurring on television are fictional and which are not (Wright et al., 1994).

Children are increasingly able to distinguish between fantasy and reality on television by the contextual cues provided in the programs themselves, such as the genre of the show or the use of animation. If a child labels a program as a cartoon or an entertainment show, he will see it as pretend; if he labels it as a news or a sports show, he will conclude that it is real. With age, children are more likely to consider the specific events and actions carried out by characters, rather than simply the type of show, in determining whether a program is about real life or fantasy (Dorr, 1983; Wright et al., 1994).

KEY THEME
Interaction Among Domains

Television's Influence on Cognitive and Language Development

Today most preschoolers in the United States readily recognize Big Bird and the Cookie Monster as characters from "Sesame Street," the popular educational program specifically designed to teach cognitive skills to preschool children. But they also learn a lot more, according to research on educational television. Evaluations of the effects of such shows as "Sesame Street" demonstrate that television can teach children a range of problem-solving, mathematical, reading, and language skills.

Cognition   "Sesame Street" was specifically designed to provide entertaining ways to teach children, especially those who might be underprepared for school, the letters of the alphabet, counting, vocabulary, and similar school-readiness skills. The programs also deliberately include both male and female characters from many racial and ethnic backgrounds. Preschoolers, many from disadvantaged backgrounds, who watched the show most frequently were found to show the greatest gains on several skills, including writing their names and knowing letters, numbers, and forms (see Figure 16.5). Frequent viewers also obtained higher scores on a standardized vocabulary test, adapted better to school, and had more positive attitudes toward school and people of other races than nonwatchers (Bogatz & Ball, 1970, 1972; Rice et al., 1990). Thus, the show had effects not only on children's cognitive skills but also on their prosocial attitudes.

Not all aspects of "Sesame Street" have met with enthusiasm, however. "Sesame Street" and other television programs have been criticized for their short, unrelated segments and fast-paced format that some developmental psychologists believe may actually impede learning. Jerome and Dorothy Singer (Singer & Singer, 1983) caution that repeated exposure to fast-paced programs may cause children to become overly aroused and inattentive. Children may also come to expect equally high-tempo learning experiences in school and, not finding them, may fail to develop reflective, sustained strategies for learning.

In fact, it is not uncommon to read criticisms in the popular press arguing that television viewing contributes to an inability to maintain a long attention span, difficulty in concentrating, lower task perseverance, and a lowered capacity to think (Mielke, 1994). How sound are these criticisms? Although many gaps continue to

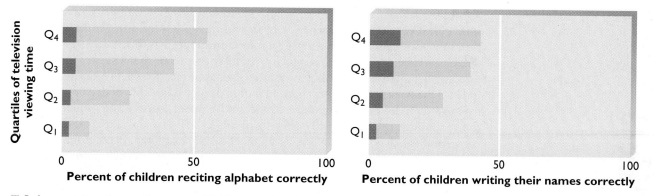

Before watching *Sesame Street*　　**After watching** *Sesame Street*

Source: Adapted from Liebert & Sprafkin, 1988.

exist in our knowledge about this matter, meta-analyses and major reviews of the research suggest that television viewing is unrelated to cognitive development and academic achievement or, at least when done in moderation, may not be such an undesirable activity (Anderson & Collins, 1988; Neuman, 1991; Williams et al., 1982) and may even have positive benefits (Collins et al., 1997). For example, children who watched television no more than about ten hours a week were found to score higher on academic achievement tests than children who watched no television (Williams et al., 1982). On the other hand, those who watched television a great deal of time—say, thirty-five to forty hours or more per week—did poorest on academic achievement tests. Thus, there may be a curvilinear relationship between television viewing and academic achievement. Such a finding raises many other questions. For example, might other factors be correlated with, and therefore help to explain, why some children are watching so much television as well as scoring poorly on achievement tests (Mielke, 1994)? Does what children are watching on television make a difference (Anderson & Collins, 1988)?

Language　Mabel Rice and her colleagues (1990) suggest that television can promote children's language development. Many programs targeted for children, such as "Mister Rogers' Neighborhood," include simplified language, repetitions, recasts, and elaboration on the meanings of words. As we saw in Chapter 7, these devices can enhance the child's acquisition of vocabulary and syntax (Rice, 1983). Parents also sometimes use television as a "video picture book" in which events portrayed on the show stimulate verbal exchanges and language learning. For example, when mothers watch television with their preschoolers, they frequently identify objects, repeat new words, ask questions, or relate the content of the show to the child's own experiences (Lemish & Rice, 1986). Such verbal interactions are especially likely when parent and child watch age-appropriate shows such as "Sesame Street."

Is there direct evidence that television can function as a vehicle for vocabulary acquisition? Investigators exposed three- and five-year-olds to twenty new words in a fifteen-minute animated television story and found that both age groups showed gains in comprehension after only two viewings. Three-year-olds learned an average of one to two new words, and five-year-olds learned four to five words (Rice & Woodsmall, 1988). These findings are all the more impressive considering the brevity of the children's exposure to new vocabulary items and the limited efforts of the experimenters to highlight or exaggerate the new words.

Television's Influence on Social Development

Whipping a towel over his shoulders, a seven-year-old jumps off the couch after watching the movie *Superman* on television. A brother and sister brandish toy swords, the brother mimicking the low voice of Shredder in *Teenage Mutant Ninja*

FIGURE 16.5

Television and Enhancement of Language Skills

Preschoolers who watched "Sesame Street" showed gains in a number of prereading skills, including the ability to recite the alphabet and write their names. The graph indicates that children who watched the show the most displayed the greatest gains in performance. (Children in quartile 1 rarely watched the show; those in quartile 2 watched two to three times per week; those in quartile 3 watched four to five times per week; and those in quartile 4 watched more than five times per week.)

Turtles. These common scenes in American households illustrate the power of television to influence children's behavior by providing models for direct imitation. Sometimes the messages are more subtle: a male announcer's authoritative voice decrees that a new detergent is twice as effective as other brands or that a sugary cereal is fortified with vitamins. When mostly men's voices appear in television commercials, the indirect message is that males more than females have the knowledge and authority to make such definitive statements. Whether by directly providing models for children to imitate or by indirectly offering messages about social categories, television can promote behaviors as diverse as aggression and sex typing. Psychologists and social policymakers have been particularly concerned about how television affects the child's social behavior and understanding, for better or for worse.

Aggression   Any child who turns on the television has an extraordinarily good chance of encountering a portrayal of violence. On average, five to six acts of physical aggression per hour occur on prime-time television. The rate is even higher on weekends, when children's programming predominates (Gerbner et al., 1986). Does viewing televised violence produce aggression in children? Hundreds of research studies have examined this issue, and government agencies and professional organizations have issued several reports on the topic. The report of the Surgeon General's Scientific Advisory Committee on Television and Social Behavior in 1972, the report of the National Institutes of Mental Health in 1982, and the American Psychological Association in 1985 agree that a small but consistent causal relationship exists between viewing aggression on TV and aggressive behavior in children (Huston, Watkins, & Kunkel, 1989).

Many researchers believe televised violence provides children with frequent and potent models for aggression, models that, in keeping with the principles of social learning theory, suggest to the child that physical attacks are acceptable in a person's repertoire of behaviors. According to social learning theory, two processes operate: first, children may learn new acts of aggression; second, aggressive behaviors already in their response repertoires are disinhibited (Bandura, 1969).

Albert Bandura and his colleagues (Bandura, Ross, & Ross, 1963a, 1963b) designed a number of laboratory studies to explore the effects of viewing aggression.

These photos, taken from Bandura's classic experiments, illustrate with stark clarity the power of imitation in influencing children's aggression. In the top row, an adult model displays various aggressive actions against a "Bobo doll." The middle and bottom rows depict the sequence of imitative aggression shown by a male and female subject in the experiment. Their behaviors closely mimic the specific actions they had previously seen the adult perform.

For example, nursery school children in one experiment were randomly assigned to one of five experimental conditions. The first group watched from behind a one-way mirror as a model in the next room performed a series of unusual acts of physical and verbal aggression on a plastic, inflated Bobo doll. For example, the model hit the doll with a hammer, kicked it, and said, "Hit the Bobo doll!" and "Kick the Bobo doll!" A second group of children watched a model perform the same actions, but the presentation was on film. A third group watched an adult disguised as a cartoon figure behave like the models in the previous two conditions. A fourth group observed an adult model behaving in a nonaggressive manner, sitting quietly and ignoring the Bobo doll and the toys associated with aggressive behavior. The last group of children saw no model at all.

Figure 16.6 shows the mean number of aggressive responses displayed by children in each condition. Children who had seen an aggressive model performed a large number of imitative aggressive acts, copying even the subtle details of the model's behaviors. In addition, they frequently added their own forms of physical and verbal aggression. Most important, from the standpoint of this discussion, the performance of children in the film-model group was no different from that of children who saw the real-life model. Models on film were just as powerful as "live" models in eliciting aggression.

Some researchers have questioned whether the act of punching a Bobo doll should be considered aggressive rather than "playful" behavior and whether the film segment Bandura used resembles the kinds of scenes depicted in actual television programs (Freedman, 1984). Another criticism is that when a child sees a violent program in the laboratory, her attention becomes focused on the experiment's theme. The child may think the experimenter condones or even expects aggression and therefore behaves more aggressively then she normally would. Finally, laboratory studies of aggression may have limited generalizability to real-life situations. Most studies have not used real TV shows as stimuli, and observations are typically conducted in settings unlike those most children experience in their daily routines.

Field experiments in which children are exposed to actual television programs and are observed in more natural contexts have responded to many of these criticisms. Lynette Friedrich and Aletha Stein (1973) found that preschool children who viewed violent cartoons declined on several measures of self-control, including the ability to tolerate delays, obedience to school rules, and task perseverance. At the same time, children who saw prosocial programs displayed higher tolerance for delays, more rule obedience, and greater task perseverance than control children.

Large-scale correlational studies add to the evidence connecting violence on television with aggression. One study of almost one thousand children showed that aggression and televised violence are actually linked in a reciprocal way (Huesmann,

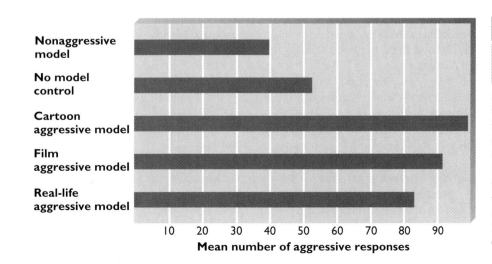

FIGURE 16.6

The Effect of Watching Modeled Aggression

After children saw a live, filmed, or live dressed-up "cartoon" model behave aggressively in the laboratory (bottom three bars), they were much more likely to imitate the model's aggression than were children who had seen no model at all or viewed a model behaving nonaggressively.

Mean number of aggressive responses

Source: Adapted from Bandura & Walters, 1963.

Lagerspetz, & Eron, 1984). The investigators asked each child's peers to rate how aggressive the child was, and they also noted how much television violence each child watched. The number of violent TV shows children watched at the start of the study predicted how aggressive they were three years later. In turn, aggression also influenced TV viewing. Children who were aggressive at the start of the study watched more violent shows three years later than they did initially. The findings are consistent with a bidirectional model of influence: children become more aggressive after a diet of violent television, and their aggression seems to stimulate even more viewing of violent shows.

Can parents do anything to mitigate the potentially harmful consequences of certain television shows on their children's behavior? One obvious tactic is to limit the amount of time children are permitted to watch violent programs. Another is to watch television with their children and discuss the negative consequences of violence. By suggesting prosocial methods of conflict resolution, parents can help youngsters develop a more critical attitude toward the programs they watch (Dorr, 1986). In a school-based intervention program, 170 children who frequently watched violent programs were divided into an experimental and a control group. During a period of six to eight weeks, children in the experimental group participated in regular training sessions in which they were taught, after watching high-action, "super-hero" shows, that (1) the behaviors of aggressive TV characters are not representative of the way most people act, (2) aggressive scenes on TV are not real but are staged by means of special effects and camera techniques, and (3) the average person uses more positive strategies to resolve interpersonal problems than those shown on violent TV programs. During the same time period, control participants saw nonviolent shows and engaged in neutral discussions. By the end of the study, children in the experimental group were significantly less aggressive than the control children, demonstrating that the real-life behaviors of children can be modified by effecting changes in their attitudes about television (Huesmann et al., 1983).

Prosocial Behavior   Just as television can encourage negative social behaviors, it can foster prosocial development. Friedrich and Stein (1973) found that children who watched "Mister Rogers' Neighborhood" for a four-week period showed increases in prosocial interpersonal behaviors. Other researchers have also found that programs that contain messages about cooperation, altruism, and sharing promote these behaviors in children.

Consider what happens when children view two segments from "Lassie," one that shows the main character, Jeff, risking his life to save a puppy and one that does not show an example of helping. Children were randomly assigned to one of the two conditions or, alternatively, watched an episode from the "Brady Bunch" series. After children saw one of the shows, they were invited to play a game in which they could earn points to win desirable toys. While the children played, they could hear the sounds of a dog's barking that became increasingly frantic. Children who saw the prosocial episode of "Lassie" were much more likely to show helping behaviors than children in the other two conditions (Sprafkin, Liebert, & Poulos, 1975).

A meta-analysis of 190 studies of prosocial television indicates that such programs can have powerful effects on children's behavior. In fact, the statistical findings indicated that the effects of prosocial programming are even greater than the effects of antisocial programming on children's behavior (Hearold, 1986). Unfortunately, the power of television to influence children in these positive ways has yet to be used fully.

Gender Stereotypes   Television does occasionally portray males and females in nontraditional roles: fathers cook and care for their children, and women are employed outside the home. These programs, however, are not standard fare on commercial television. Women appear in only one-third or fewer of the roles in television programs and commercials, and when they do they typically play romantic or family roles. Working women, when they are shown, are likely to be employed in gender-typical roles (for example, as secretaries and nurses); if they occupy positions of authority, they are often cast as villains (Huston & Alvarez, 1990). Consistent with stereotypes of female behavior, girls and women on television act nurturantly, passively, or emotionally. In contrast, males are more frequently the central characters of television shows, and they act forcefully, have more power and authority than women, and display reason rather than emotion (Lovdal, 1989; Signorielli, 1989). Portrayal of these gender stereotypes may be declining, but they continue to exist in much of television programming.

Children's attention to these stereotypes, so prevalent in much of television programming, very likely depends on other developmental changes children undergo. For example, five-year-old boys who demonstrate gender constancy (see Chapter 13) are more likely to watch male characters on television and prefer programs that contain a greater proportion of males than five-year-old boys who do not display gender constancy (Luecke-Aleksa et al., 1995). In addition, gender-constant boys are more likely to watch programs created for adult entertainment, particularly sports and action shows, than their counterparts who still do not exhibit gender constancy. This difference in viewing preferences does not seem to be linked to earlier maturity in other cognitive abilities.

In contrast, gender constancy in five-year-old girls has relatively little effect on their television preferences or viewing habits. Perhaps this sex difference reflects the greater attractiveness of male roles in much of television programming and, therefore, accounts for such programs' increased interest value for boys who have gained gender constancy. Alternatively, perhaps this sex difference reflects a lessened need on the part of girls to exploit television as a basis for gender-role differentiation.

The televised stereotypes of male and female behaviors apparently do affect children. Correlational studies show that the more television children watch, the more closely they identify with stereotyped roles of their own sex (Frueh & McGhee, 1975; McGhee & Frueh, 1980). Longitudinal studies point out that the correlations do not arise simply because gender-typed children watch more television. In Michael Morgan's work (1982, 1987), the viewing habits of adolescents during the initial phases of his studies correlated slightly with their gender-role attitudes, but the relationships became stronger six months and one year later, suggesting that beliefs about male and female roles change after a heavy diet of television viewing.

In the same way television is able to reinforce traditional gender-role standards, it has the power to make these standards less stereotyped. In 1975, a television series called "Freestyle" was developed to counteract children's stereotypical beliefs about sex-typed characteristics and behaviors. Each episode presented stories of people in gender-atypical activities. In one episode, for example, a mother returns to work outside the home after teaching the other members of her family how to take care of themselves by performing household chores. The story revolves around the father's recognition that his wife's job increases her self-esteem and the happiness of the family and depicts his gradually increasing pleasure in performing "feminine" household chores. Studies of children who watched this series indicate they were more accepting of nontraditional roles, activities, and occupations than children who did not watch the series, and the differences persisted for as long as nine months after viewing the series (Johnston, Ettema, & Davidson, 1980).

Consumer Behavior   Because of their tremendous spending power, either directly or through their parents, children are the targets of a significant number of television commercials. Of special concern to many child advocates is the proliferation of television shows linked to specific toys (for example, cartoon shows that portray the same characters as toys) and product endorsements for expensive items, such as athletic shoes, by popular sports figures and other celebrities, all of which put pressure on children to spend money.

Children do respond to the messages of commercials. For one thing, they frequently request the cereals and other foods they see advertised (Taras et al., 1989). By age three, children distinguish commercials from other programming, but they do not always recognize commercials as messages specifically intended to influence their behavior; four- and five-year-olds, for example, believe "commercials are to help and entertain you." It is usually not until children are eight years of age or older that they understand that commercials are intended to influence viewers' buying habits (Ward, Reale, & Levinson, 1972). Because young children are not able to critically evaluate the information presented to them in commercials, they may pressure their parents to purchase expensive toys and clothes, heavily sugared foods, and other products (Kunkel & Roberts, 1991).

Fortunately, children respond to materials designed to educate them about commercials. When children in one study saw one-minute segments describing the intent of commercials and pointing out that commercials are not always truthful, they were more skeptical about the product claims than children who had not seen these educational messages (Christenson, 1982).

"**N**eat!" *Jamie exclaimed as he continued his search with the web browser. "Alison, look at this. . . . Hey, did you see that movie on TV last night? That FBI agent was awesome! I didn't think he would get loose, but he sure took care of the crooks. I don't think there was one alive after he blew them away. Did you see him drive that truck off the cliff? I hope I can be an FBI agent someday."*

RESEARCH APPLIED TO PARENTING

Encouraging Critical Skills in Television Viewing

As we have seen, television holds enormous promise to enhance children's intellectual and social functioning. However, there is also clear evidence of potential dangers, especially when television viewing takes up much of a child's time or is directed at programs that are age inappropriate. Apart from the option to not have a television set available in the home (an alternative that relatively few parents defend), what steps might parents take to promote positive benefits from this medium? Any recommendations, will, of course, depend on the maturity of the child as well as the values caregivers wish to promote. However, developmental psychologists and others concerned about the influence of television on children will generally agree with the following guidelines:

1. *Be aware of how much time is being spent watching television and what is being watched.* Parents may not always realize how much of the day their children spend in front of the television set, what they are watching, or how the program is affecting them. Continuous supervision may not be possible while parents are busy with other household duties or away at work. However, knowing what children are watching, and for how long, is the first step in understanding what they might be learning from television.

2. *Decide what is acceptable to watch.* Even very young children may be attracted to programming that is frightening or inappropriate, not because they necessarily enjoy it but because the rapid pace of events or some other convention of the programming is attracting their attention. Parents have the responsibility to determine which programs are permissible and ensure that children limit their television viewing to those programs.

3. *Establish acceptable times for watching television.* Family members need to know when they can watch television. For example, can the television be on during the dinner hour? Is watching television permitted if homework, chores, or other obligations are not yet finished? How late in the evening is television viewing allowed?

4. *Watch television with children whenever possible.* When jointly watching programs with their children, parents have the opportunity to discuss such things as what is real and what is fantasy, how conflict might be resolved other than through

The effects of television viewing on children's development probably depend on the types of programs watched as well as how much time is spent in front of the television set. When parents view television programs along with their children, opportunities become available for parents to promote a variety of critical skills in their children's thinking.

violence, the stereotypes being portrayed, the goals of advertising, and many other issues presented through this medium that are valued or not approved within the household. In addition, by commenting on the material, parents can stimulate vocabulary development and provide different perspectives that may promote cognitive and social skills.

Given the amount of time children watch television, helping them to be critical and discerning about the messages they receive from it may promote an important skill that will continue to serve them throughout their developmental years. Only when television's potential to promote desirable outcomes is realized will its many critics be reassured. Parents have an important role to play in reaching that goal.

CHAPTER RECAP

SUMMARY OF DEVELOPMENTAL THEMES

SOCIOCULTURAL INFLUENCE How does the sociocultural context influence the child's experiences with school and media?

The society in which the child grows up determines what kind of exposure she will have to school, computers, or television in the first place. Not all cultures emphasize formal schooling, and not all children have access to television or computers. In terms of school, the child's cultural background may either harmonize or conflict with the predominant values of the educational system. In the latter case, the child may experience academic failure as well as lower self-esteem. The KEEP model suggests that the child's academic performance climbs when educational practices are compatible with his culture.

CHILD'S ACTIVE ROLE   How does the child play an active role in experiences with school and media?

In their school experiences, children show greater academic achievement and higher self-esteem when school structures facilitate their greater participation in the educational process. In addition, educational techniques such as peer collaboration, classroom autonomy, and computer activities in group contexts all seem to foster development by promoting the child's active involvement. In their television viewing, children actively direct their attention to programs they understand.

INTERACTION AMONG DOMAINS   How do the child's experiences with school and media interact with development in other domains?

Children's developmental accomplishments affect their school experience, and vice versa. Children who have good peer rela-

tions are more likely to adjust well to school in the first place. Once in school, children typically have experiences that can promote their intellectual advancement, peer relations, and self-concept. For example, open classrooms can enhance peer interaction skills, and the academic feedback students receive can influence self-esteem. Peer learning techniques especially foster developmental accomplishments in many domains. Experiences with computers also can facilitate cognitive and social development. As children's cognitive skills grow, so does their ability to comprehend information portrayed on television. At the same time, television programs can enhance cognitive growth in such areas as prereading skills. Moreover, television can influence social behavior through the strong messages it portrays about violence, prosocial acts, and gender-role stereotypes.

SUMMARY OF TOPICS

■ SCHOOL

The major influence school exerts on children lies in fostering academic achievement and shaping self-esteem. Several aspects of the school's physical environment, including school size, class size, and the physical arrangement of the classroom, bear on development. Philosophies of education, which are translated into specific teaching models, also play a role. Some alternative educational practices, such as the *open classroom, peer collaboration,* and *cooperative learning,* have been found to produce especially positive effects on students' social and personal development.

The ways in which children adjust to school transitions, such as the start of school or junior high school, can influence their subsequent attitudes toward and accomplishments in school. The most important element of the school experience, however, is the teacher. Teachers' expectations, the classroom management techniques teachers employ, and the classroom climate all make a difference in students' academic achievement and self-esteem.

Children's school achievement can vary according to their cultural background. Research demonstrates that children's academic performance rises when educational tactics incorporate elements of their background culture. Children in Asian societies show higher levels of achievement than American children, especially in mathematics and science, patterns that are

associated with elements of the students' classroom experiences and family expectations.

Computers can influence both cognitive and social development. Children with *computer-assisted instruction (CAI)* experience show modest gains in academic achievement, and children who are exposed to tutoring software or programming may gain in higher-order cognitive skills, such as *heuristic strategies* for problem solving. Computers can enhance social development by stimulating peer exchanges as students attempt to solve problems. Boys are more likely than girls to learn computer skills, which may be the result of gender-role stereotypes among parents, teachers, and students themselves.

■ TELEVISION

One of childhood's most frequent activities is watching television. Children tend to watch increased amounts of television until adolescence, at which point TV viewing declines. Although the formal features of television often guide young children's attention, children also actively attend to the portions of programs they comprehend. As children's cognitive and verbal skills expand, so does their ability to comprehend both the explicit and implicit elements of programs. Television can promote certain prereading skills, such as knowledge of the alphabet and numbers, as well as increase children's vocabulary. Television can also influence social behavior, specifically in the display of aggression, prosocial behavior, gender-role stereotypes, and consumer behavior.

Accommodation   In Piagetian theory, a component of adaptation; process of modification in thinking (schemes) that takes place when old ways of understanding something no longer fit.

Adaptation   In Piagetian theory, the inborn tendency to adjust or become more attuned to conditions imposed by the environment; takes place through assimilation and accommodation.

Age-history confound   In longitudinal studies, the co-occurrence of historical factors with changes in age; affects the ability to interpret results.

Allele   Alternate form of a specific gene; provides a genetic basis for many individual differences.

Altruism   Behavior carried out to help another without expectation of reward.

Ambivalent attachment   Insecure attachment in which the infant shows separation protest but also distress upon the caregiver's return.

Amniocentesis   Method of sampling the fluid surrounding the developing fetus by insertion of a needle. Used to diagnose fetal genetic and developmental disorders.

Amniotic sac   Fluid-filled, transparent protective membrane surrounding the fetus.

Anal stage   In Freudian theory, the second psychosexual stage, between about one and three years of age, during which libidinal energy is focused on control of defecation.

Analogical transfer   Ability to employ the solution to one problem in other, similar problems.

Androgen   Class of male or masculinizing hormones.

Androgyny   Gender-role orientation in which a person possesses high levels of personality characteristics associated with both sexes.

Animism   Attribution of lifelike qualities to inanimate objects.

Approval and interpersonal orientation   Form of prosocial reasoning in which children's reasons for assisting someone in need are based on the social approval or disapproval of others.

Artificialism   Belief that naturally occurring events are caused by people.

Assimilation   In Piagetian theory, a component of adaptation; process of interpreting an experience in terms of current ways (schemes) of understanding things.

Attachment   Strong emotional bond that emerges between infant and caregiver.

Attention   State of alertness or arousal that allows the individual to focus on a selected aspect of the environment.

Attentional inertia   Continued sustained attention after an initial period of focused attention.

Authoritarian parent   Parent who relies on coercive techniques to discipline the child and displays a low level of nurturance.

Authoritative parent   Parent who sets limits on a child's behavior using reasoning and explanation and displays a high degree of nurturance.

Autobiographical memory   Memory for specific events in one's own life.

Autosomes   Twenty-two pairs of homologous chromosomes. The two members of each pair are similar in size, shape, and genetic function. The two sex chromosomes are excluded from this class.

Avoidant attachment   Insecure attachment in which the infant shows little separation protest and does not pay much attention to the caregiver's return.

Babbling   Consonant-vowel utterances that characterize the infant's first attempts to vocalize.

Basic emotion   Emotion such as joy, sadness, or surprise that appears early in infancy and seems to have a biological foundation. Also called *primary emotion.*

Behavior analysis   Learning theory perspective that explains the development of behavior according to the principles of classical and operant conditioning.

Behavior genetics   Study of how characteristics and behaviors of individuals, such as intelligence and personality, are influenced by the interaction between genotype and experience.

Broca's area   Portion of the cerebral cortex that controls expressive language.

Canalization   Concept that the development of some attributes is governed primarily by the genotype and only extreme environmental conditions will alter the phenotypic pattern for these attributes.

Cardinality   Principle that the last number in a set of counted numbers refers to the number of items in that set.

Case study   In-depth description of psychological characteristics and behaviors of an individual.

Catch-up growth   Increase in growth rate after some factor, such as illness or poor nutrition, has disrupted the expected, normal growth rate.

Categorical perception   Inability to distinguish among sounds that vary on some basic physical dimension except when those sounds lie at opposite sides of a critical juncture point on that dimension.

Categorical self   Conceptual process, starting in the early preschool years, in which the child begins to classify himself or herself according to easily observable categories such as sex, age, or physical capacities.

Centration   In Piagetian theory, tendency of the child to focus on only one aspect of a problem.

Cephalocaudal development   Pattern in which organs, systems, and motor movements near the head tend to develop earlier than those near the feet.

Chorionic villus sampling   Method of sampling fetal chorionic cells. Used to diagnose embryonic genetic and developmental disorders.

Chromosomes   Threadlike structures of DNA, located in the nucleus of cells, that form a collection of genes. A human body cell normally contains forty-six chromosomes.

Circular reaction   In Piagetian theory, repetition of some action or behavior to experience the pleasure it brings.

Classical conditioning   Type of learning in which a neutral stimulus repeatedly paired with another stimulus that elicits a reflexive response eventually begins to elicit the reflexlike response by itself.

Clinical method   Flexible, open-ended interview method in which questions are modified in reaction to the child's responses.

Clique   Peer group of five to ten children who frequently interact together.

Codominance   Condition in which individual, unblended characteristics of two alleles are reflected in the phenotype.

Cognition   Processes involved in thinking and mental activity, such as attention, memory, and problem solving.

Cognitive-developmental theory   Theoretical orientation, most frequently associated with Piaget, emphasizing the active construction of psychological structures to interpret experience.

Cohort effects   Characteristics shared by individuals growing up in a given sociohistorical context that can influence developmental outcomes.

Complex emotion   Emotion such as guilt and envy that appears later in childhood and requires more complex cognitive and social skills.

Comprehension monitoring   Ability to evaluate the adequacy of a communication.

Computer-assisted instruction (CAI)   Use of computers to provide tutorial information and drill-and-practice routines.

Concept   Definition of a set of information on the basis of some general or abstract principle.

Concordance rate   Percentage of pairs of twins in which both members have a specific trait identified in one twin.

Concrete operational stage   In Piagetian theory, the third stage of development, from approximately seven to eleven years of age, in which thought is logical when stimuli are physically present.

Conditioned emotional response   Emergence of an emotional reaction to an originally neutral stimulus through classical conditioning.

Conditioned response (CR)   Learned response that is exhibited to a previously neutral stimulus (CS) as a result of pairing the CS with an unconditioned stimulus (UCS).

Conditioned stimulus (CS)   Neutral stimulus that begins to elicit a response similar to the unconditioned stimulus (UCS) with which it has been paired.

Configurational knowledge   Child's use of landmarks and routes in integrated, holistic ways to represent physical space.

Conscience   In Freudian theory, the part of the superego that defines unacceptable behaviors and actions, usually as also defined by the parents.

Conservation tasks   Problems that require the child to make judgments about the equivalence of two displays; used to assess stage of cognitive development.

Control theory   Hypothesis about parent-child interactions suggesting that the intensity of one partner's behavior affects the intensity of the other's response.

Conventional level   In Kohlberg's theory, the second level of moral reasoning, in which the child conforms to the norms of the majority and wishes to preserve the social order.

Cooing   Vowel-like utterances that characterize the infant's first attempts to vocalize.

Cooperative learning   Peer-centered learning experience in which students work together in small groups to solve academic problems.

Cooperative play   Interactive play in which children's actions are reciprocal.

Correlation coefficient (*r*)   Statistical measure, ranging from +1.00 to −1.00, that summarizes the strength and direction of the relationship between two variables; does not provide information about causation.

Correlational study   Study that assesses whether changes in one variable are accompanied by systematic changes in another variable.

Cross-cultural study   Study that compares subjects in different cultural contexts.

Cross-fostering study   Research study in which children are reared in environments that differ from those of their biological parents.

Cross-gender behavior   Behavior usually seen in a member of the opposite sex. Term generally is reserved for behavior that is persistently sex atypical.

Crossing over   Process during the first stage of meiosis when genetic material is exchanged between autosomes.

Cross-sectional study   A study in which children of different ages are examined at the same point in time.

Crowd   Large group of peers characterized by specific traits or reputation.

Crystallized intelligence   Mental skills derived from cultural experience.

Cultural compatibility hypothesis   Theory that school instruction is most effective if it is consistent with the practices of the child's background culture.

Debriefing   Providing research participants with a statement of the true goals of a study after initially deceiving them about its purposes.

Deferred imitation   Ability to imitate a model's behavior hours, days, and even weeks after observation.

Delay of gratification   Capacity to wait before performing a tempting activity or attaining some highly desired outcome; a measure of ability to regulate one's own behavior.

Deoxyribonucleic acid (DNA)   Long, spiral staircase–like sequence of molecules created by nucleotides identified with the blueprint for genetic inheritance.

Dependent variable   Behavior that is measured; suspected effect of an experimental manipulation.

Development   Physical and psychological changes in the individual over a lifetime.

Developmental psychology   The systematic and scientific study of changes in human behaviors and mental activities over time.

Deviation IQ   IQ score computed by comparing the child's performance with that of a standardization sample.

Dishabituation   See *recovery from habituation*.

Disorganized/disoriented attachment   Infant-caregiver relations characterized by the infant's fear of the caregiver, confused facial expressions, and a combination of avoidant and ambivalent attachment behaviors.

Display rules   Cultural guidelines concerning when, how, and to what degree to display emotions.

Dominant allele   Allele whose characteristics are reflected in the phenotype even when part of a heterozygous genotype. Its genetic characteristics tend to mask the characteristics of other alleles.

Ecological systems theory   Bronfenbrenner's theory that development is influenced by experiences arising from broader social and cultural systems as well as a child's immediate surroundings.

Effectance motivation   Inborn desire theorized by Robert White to be the basis for the infant's and child's efforts to master and gain control of the environment.

Egocentrism   Preoperational child's inability to separate his or her own perspective from those of others.

Ego ideal In Freudian theory, the part of the superego that defines the positive standards for which an individual strives; acquired via parental rewarding of desired behaviors.

Elaboration Memory strategy in which subjects link items to be remembered in the form of an image or a sentence.

Embryonic period Period of prenatal development during which major biological organs and systems form. Begins about the tenth to fourteenth day after conception and ends about the eighth week after conception.

Emotions Complex behaviors involving physiological, expressive, and experiential components produced in response to some external or internal event.

Empathy Vicarious response to the feelings of others.

Empiricism Theory that environmental experiences shape the individual; more specifically, that all knowledge is derived from sensory experiences.

Episodic memory Memory for events that took place at a specific time and place.

Equilibration In Piagetian theory, an innate self-regulatory process that, through accommodation and assimilation, results in more organized and powerful schemes for adapting to the environment.

Ethnic identity The sense of belonging to a particular cultural group.

Ethology Theoretical orientation and discipline concerned with the evolutionary origins of behavior and its adaptive and survival value in animals, including humans.

Exosystem In Bronfenbrenner's ecological systems theory, environmental settings that indirectly affect the child by influencing the various microsystems forming the child's immediate environment.

Experimental design Research method in which one or more independent variables are manipulated to determine the effect on other, dependent variables.

Expiatory punishment Notion that punishment need not be related to a transgression as long as the punishment is severe enough.

Expressive aphasia Loss of the ability to speak fluently.

Expressive characteristics Characteristics associated with emotions or relationships with people; usually considered feminine.

Expressive style Type of early language production in which the child uses many social words.

External locus of control Individual's sense that outside factors such as luck, fate, and other people primarily influence success and failure and the events that happen to him or her. Contrast with *internal locus of control*.

Externality effect Tendency for infants younger than two months to focus on the external features of a complex stimulus and explore the internal features less systematically.

Failure to thrive Label applied to any child whose growth in height or weight is below the third percentile for children of the same age.

Fast-mapping Deriving meanings of words from the contexts in which they are spoken.

Fetal alcohol syndrome (FAS) Cluster of fetal abnormalities stemming from mother's consumption of alcohol; includes growth retardation, defects in facial features, and intellectual retardation.

Fetal monitoring device Medical device used to monitor fetal heartbeat during delivery.

Fetal period Period of prenatal development, from about the eighth week after conception to birth, marked by rapid growth and preparation of body systems for functioning in the postnatal environment.

Field experiment Experiment conducted in a "natural," real-world setting such as the child's home or school.

Fluid intelligence Biologically based mental abilities that are relatively uninfluenced by cultural experiences.

Focus on states Preoperational child's tendency to treat two or more connected events as unrelated.

Formal operational stage In Piagetian theory, the last stage of development, from approximately eleven to fifteen years of age, in which thought is abstract and hypothetical.

Fragile X syndrome Disorder associated with a pinched region of the X chromosome; a leading genetic cause of mental retardation in males.

Fraternal twins Siblings who share the same womb at the same time but originate from two different eggs fertilized by two different sperm cells. Also called *dizygotic twins*.

Gametes Sperm cells in males, egg cells in females, normally containing only twenty-three chromosomes.

Gender constancy Knowledge, usually gained around age six or seven years, that one's gender does not change as a result of alterations in appearance, behaviors, or desires.

Gender identity Knowledge, usually gained by age three years, that one is male or female.

Gender schema Cognitive organizing structure for information relevant to sex typing.

Gender stability Knowledge, usually gained by age four years, that one's gender does not change over time.

Gender stereotypes Expectations or beliefs that individuals within a given culture hold about the behaviors characteristic of males and females.

Gender-role development Process by which individuals acquire the characteristics and behaviors prescribed by their culture for their sex. Also called *sex typing*.

Gene Large segment of nucleotides within a chromosome that codes for the production of proteins and enzymes. These proteins and enzymes underlie traits and characteristics inherited from one generation to the next.

Genetic counseling Medical and counseling specialty concerned with determining and communicating the likelihood that prospective parents will give birth to a baby with a genetic disorder.

Genetic screening Systematic search using a variety of tests to detect individuals at developmental risk due to genetic anomalies.

Genital stage In Freudian theory, the final psychosexual stage, beginning with adolescence, in which sexual energy is directed toward peers of the opposite sex.

Genotype Total genetic endowment inherited by an individual.

Germinal period Period lasting about ten to fourteen days following conception before the fertilized egg becomes implanted in the uterine wall. Also called *period of the zygote*.

Gestational age Age of fetus derived from onset of mother's last menstrual period.

Glial cells Brain cells that provide the material from which myelin is created, nourish neurons, and provide a scaffolding for neuron migration.

Habituation Gradual decline in intensity, frequency, or duration of a response over repeated or lengthy occurrences of the same stimulus.

Hedonistic orientation Form of prosocial reasoning in which children say they will help in order to obtain material rewards.

Heritability Proportion of variability in the phenotype that is estimated to be accounted for by genetic influences.

Heterozygous Genotype in which two alleles of a gene are different. The effects on a trait will depend on how the two alleles interact.

Heuristic strategies   Methods of problem solving that involve higher-order analyses, such as subdividing the problem into smaller parts or comparing it to previously solved problems.

Homozygous   Genotype in which two alleles of a gene are identical, thus having the same effects on a trait.

Hormones   Chemicals produced by various glands that are secreted directly into the bloodstream and can therefore circulate to influence cells in other locations of the body.

Human genome   Entire inventory of nucleotide base pairs comprising the genes and chromosomes of humans.

Huntington's disease   Dominant genetic disorder characterized by involuntary movements of the limbs, mental deterioration, and premature death. Symptoms appear between thirty and fifty years of age.

Hypothetical reasoning   Ability to systematically generate and evaluate potential solutions to a problem.

Identical twins   Two individuals who originate from a single zygote (one egg fertilized by one sperm), which early in cell division separates to form two separate cell masses. Also called *monozygotic twins*.

Identity (personal)   Broad, coherent, internalized view of who a person is and what a person wants to be, believes, and values that emerges during adolescence.

Identity   In Eriksonian psychosocial theory, the acceptance of both self and society, a concept that must be achieved at every stage but is especially important during adolescence.

Identity crisis   Period, usually during adolescence, characterized by considerable uncertainty about the self and the role the individual is to fulfill in society.

Imaginary audience   Individual's belief that others are examining and evaluating him or her.

Immanent justice   Young child's belief that punishment will inevitably follow a transgression.

Imprinting   Form of learning, difficult to reverse, during a sensitive period in development in which an organism tends to stay near a particular stimulus.

Independent variable   Variable manipulated by the experimenter; the suspected cause.

Individual differences   Unique characteristics that distinguish a person from other members of a larger group.

Induction   Parental control technique that relies on the extensive use of reasoning and explanation as well as the arousal of empathic feelings.

Infantile amnesia   Failure to remember events from the first two to three years of one's life.

Inflection   Alteration to a word, such as tense or plural form, that indicates its syntactical function.

Information processing   Theoretical approach that views humans as having a limited ability to process information, much like computers.

Informed consent   Participant's formal acknowledgment that he or she understands the purposes, procedures, and risks of a study and agrees to participate in it.

Inner speech   Interiorized form of private speech.

Instrumental characteristics   Characteristics associated with acting on the world; usually considered masculine.

Instrumental competence   Child's display of independence, self-control, achievement orientation, and cooperation.

Intelligence quotient (IQ)   Numerical score received on an intelligence test.

Interactive synchrony   Reciprocal, mutually engaging cycles of caregiver-child behaviors.

Interagent consistency   Consistency in application of disciplinary strategies among different caregivers.

Intermodal perception   Coordination of sensory information to perceive or make inferences about the characteristics of an object.

Internal locus of control   Individual's sense that his or her own efforts and activities influence success and failure and the events that happen to him or her. Contrast with *external locus of control*.

Internalized orientation   Form of prosocial reasoning in which internalized beliefs and principles are followed to fulfill societal obligations and maintain self-respect.

Intra-agent consistency   Consistency in a single caregiver's application of discipline from one situation to the next.

Karyotype   Pictorial representation of an individual's chromosomes.

Kinetic cue   Perceptual information provided by movement of eyes, head, or body or of objects in the environment; important source of information for depth perception, even for infants.

Lagging-down growth   Decrease in growth rate after some factor, such as a congenital or hormonal disorder, has accelerated the expected, normal growth rate.

Landmark   Distinctive location or cue that the child uses to negotiate or represent a spatial environment.

Latency   In Freudian theory, a period from about six to eleven years of age when libidinal energy is suppressed and energies are focused on intellectual, athletic, and social achievements appropriate to the adult years.

Lateralization   Process by which one hemisphere of the brain comes to dominate the other, for example, processing of language in the left hemisphere or of spatial information in the right hemisphere.

Learned helplessness   Belief that one has little control over situations, perhaps because of lack of ability or inconsistent outcomes.

Learning   Relatively permanent change in behavior as a result of such experiences as exploration, observation, and practice.

Limited-resource model   Information-processing model that emphasizes the allocation of finite energy within the cognitive system.

Long-term memory   Memory that holds information for extended periods of time.

Longitudinal study   Research in which the same subjects are repeatedly tested over a period of time, usually years.

Macrosystem   In Bronfenbrenner's ecological systems theory, major historical events and the broad values, practices, and customs promoted by a culture.

Mastery orientation   Belief that achievements are based on one's own efforts rather than on luck or other factors beyond one's control.

Means-ends behavior   Deliberate behavior employed to attain a goal.

Meiosis   Process of cell division that forms the gametes; normally results in twenty-three chromosomes in each human egg and sperm cell rather than the full complement of forty-six chromosomes.

Memory span   Number of stimulus items that can be recalled after a brief interval of time.

Memory strategy   Mental activity, such as rehearsal, that enhances memory performance.

Menarche   First occurrence of menstruation.

Mesosystem   In Bronfenbrenner's ecological systems theory, the environment provided by the interrelationships among the various settings of the microsystem.

Meta-analysis   Statistical examination of a body of research studies to assess the effect of the common central variable.

Metacognition   Awareness and knowledge of cognitive processes.

Metalinguistic awareness   Ability to reflect on language as a communication tool and on the self as a user of language.

Metamemory   Understanding of memory as a cognitive process.

Metaphor   Figurative language in which a term is transferred from the object it customarily designates to describe a comparable object or event.

Microsystem   In Bronfenbrenner's ecological systems theory, the immediate environment provided in such settings as the home, school, workplace, and neighborhood.

Mitosis   Process of cell division that takes place in most cells of the human body and results in a full complement of identical material in the forty-six chromosomes in each cell.

Moral realism   In Piaget's theory of moral development, the first stage of moral reasoning, in which moral judgments are made on the basis of the consequences of an act. Also called *heteronomy*.

Moral relativism   In Piaget's theory of moral development, the second stage of moral reasoning, in which moral judgments are made on the basis of the actor's intentions. Also called *autonomy*.

Morality of care and responsibility   Tendency to make moral judgments on the basis of concern for others.

Morality of justice   Tendency to make moral judgments on the basis of reason and abstract principles of equity.

Motherese   Simple, repetitive, high-pitched speech of caregivers to young children; includes many questions.

Multistore model   Information-processing model that describes a sequence of mental structures through which information flows.

Mutation   Sudden change in molecular structure of a gene; may occur spontaneously or be caused by an environmental event such as radiation.

Mutual exclusivity bias   Tendency for children to assume that unfamiliar words label new objects.

Myelin   Sheath of fatty cells that insulates and speeds neural impulses by about tenfold.

Natural domains   Concepts or categories that children acquire especially rapidly and effortlessly.

Naturalistic observation   Study in which observations of naturally occurring behavior are made in real-life settings.

Nature-nurture debate   Ongoing theoretical controversy over whether development is the result of the child's genetic endowment or the kinds of experiences the child has had.

Needs-of-others orientation   Form of prosocial reasoning in which children express a concern for the physical or psychological needs of others.

Negative correlation   Relationship in which changes in one variable are accompanied by systematic changes in another variable in the opposite direction.

Negative punishment   Withdrawal or loss of a desired stimulus or reward that, upon its removal, weakens or decreases the frequency of a behavior.

Negative reinforcement   Withdrawal of an aversive stimulus that, upon its removal, serves to strengthen a preceding response.

Network   Model of semantic memory that consists of associations among closely related items.

Neuron   Nerve cell within the central nervous system that is electrochemically designed to transmit messages between cells.

Niche picking   Tendency to actively select an environment compatible with a genotype.

Nominals   Words that label objects, people, or events; the first type of words most children produce.

Norms   Measures of average values and variations in some aspect of development, such as physical size and motor skill development, in relation to age.

Nucleotide   Repeating basic building block of DNA consisting of nitrogen-based molecules of adenine, thymine, cytosine, and guanine.

Object concept   Realization that objects exist even when they are not within view. Also called *object permanence*.

Observational learning   Learning that takes place by simply observing another person's behavior.

Observer bias   Tendency of researchers to interpret ongoing events as being consistent with their research hypotheses.

One-to-one correspondence   Understanding that two sets are equivalent in number if each element in one set can be mapped onto a unique element in the second set with none left over.

Open classroom   Nontraditional educational approach that emphasizes peer interaction, free-flowing movement of students around different activity centers in the classroom, and structured opportunities for students to "discover" knowledge.

Operant conditioning   Type of learning in which the pattern and frequency of behaviors that are learned depend on whether the behaviors produce rewarding or desired outcomes. Also called *instrumental conditioning*.

Operation   In Piagetian theory, a mental action such as reversibility.

Operational definition   Specification of variables in terms of measurable properties.

Oral stage   In Freudian theory, the first psychosexual stage, between birth and about one year of age, during which libidinal energy is focused on the mouth.

Ordinality   Principle that a number refers to an item's order within a set, as in the third finisher in a race.

Organization   In Piagetian theory, the inborn tendency for structures and processes to become more systematic and coherent. Also memory strategy in which subjects reorder items to be remembered on the basis of category or some other higher-order relationship.

Overextension   Tendency to apply a label to a broader category than the term actually signifies.

Overregularization   Inappropriate application of syntactic rules to words and grammatical forms that show exceptions.

Parallel play   Side-by-side, independent play that is not interactive.

Participant reactivity   Tendency of individuals who know they are under observation to alter natural behavior.

Peer   Companion of approximately the same age and developmental level.

Peer collaboration   Peer-centered learning experience in which pairs of students work together on academic problems, usually without competing against other students.

Perception   Process of organizing and interpreting sensory information.

Perceptual differentiation   Process postulated by Eleanor and James Gibson in which experience contributes to the ability to make increasingly finer perceptual discriminations and to distinguish stimulation arising from each sensory modality.

Perinatal period   Period beginning about the seventh month of pregnancy and continuing until about four weeks after birth.

Period of the zygote   See *germinal period*.

Permissive parent   Parent who sets few limits on the child's behavior.

Personal fable   Belief that one is unique and perhaps even invulnerable.

Perspective taking   Ability to take the role of another person and understand what that person is thinking, feeling, or knows, often with the purpose of solving some problem in communicating or interacting with that individual.

Phallic stage   In Freudian theory, the third psychosexual stage, between about three and five years of age, when libidinal energy focuses on the genitals and resolution of unconscious conflict leads to the formation of the superego.

Phenotype Observable and measurable characteristics and traits of an individual; a product of the interaction of the genotype with the environment.

Phenylketonuria (PKU) Recessive genetic disorder in which phenylalanine, an amino acid, fails to be metabolized. Unless dietary changes are made to reduce intake of phenylalanine, severe mental retardation occurs.

Phoneme Smallest unit of sound that changes the meanings of words.

Phonology Fundamental sound units and combinations of units in a given language.

Pivot grammar Early two-word grammar in which one word is repeated and a series of other words fills the second slot.

Placenta Support organ formed by cells from both blastocyst and uterine lining; serves as exchange site for oxygen, nutrients, and waste products.

Plasticity Capacity of immature systems, including regions of the brain and the individual neurons within those regions, to take on different functions as a result of experience.

Polygenic Phenotypic characteristic influenced by two or more genes.

Positive correlation Relationship in which changes in one variable are accompanied by systematic changes in another variable in the same direction.

Positive punishment An aversive stimulus that, when occurring following a response, serves to decrease the frequency of the response.

Positive reinforcement Occurrence of a stimulus that strengthens a response when it follows that response. Also known as a reward.

Postconventional level In Kohlberg's theory, the third level of moral reasoning, in which laws are seen as the result of a social contract and individual principles of conscience may emerge.

Postnatal development Period in development following birth.

Power assertion Parental control technique that relies on the use of forceful commands, physical punishment, and removal of material objects or privileges.

Pragmatics Rules for using language effectively within a social context.

Preconventional level In Kohlberg's theory, the first level of moral reasoning, in which morality is motivated by the avoidance of punishments and attainment of rewards.

Prenatal development Period in development from conception to the onset of labor.

Preoperational stage In Piagetian theory, the second stage of development, from approximately two to seven years of age, in which thought becomes symbolic in form.

Prepared childbirth Procedures practiced during pregnancy and childbirth designed to minimize pain and reduce the need for medication during delivery. Also called *natural childbirth.*

Primacy effect Tendency for subjects to display good recall for early items in a list.

Private speech Children's vocalized speech to themselves that directs behavior.

Production deficiency Failure of children under age seven years to spontaneously generate memory strategies.

Productive language Meaningful language spoken or otherwise produced by an individual.

Prosocial behavior Positive social action performed to benefit others.

Prosody Patterns of intonation, stress, and rhythm that communicate meaning in speech.

Protodeclarative communication Use of a gesture to call attention to an object or event.

Protoimperative communication Use of a gesture to issue a command or request.

Proximodistal development Pattern in which organs and systems of the body near the middle tend to develop earlier than those near the periphery.

Psychometric model Theoretical perspective that quantifies individual differences in test scores to establish a rank order of abilities.

Psychometrician Psychologist who specializes in the construction and interpretation of standardized tests.

Psychosexual theory of development Freud's theory that an individual's personality originates in early forms of childhood sexuality and that gratification of this sexuality changes throughout various stages of development.

Psychosocial theory of development Erikson's theory that personality develops through eight stages of adaptive functioning to meet the demands framed by society.

Puberty Developmental period during which a sequence of physical changes takes place that transforms the person from an immature individual to one capable of reproduction.

Punishment by reciprocity Belief that punishment should be related to the transgression.

Quasi-experiment Study in which the assignment of subjects to experimental groups is determined by their natural experiences.

Questionnaire Set of standardized questions administered to subjects in written form.

Random assignment Use of principles of chance to assign participants to treatment and control groups; avoids systematic bias.

Range of reaction Range of phenotypic differences possible as a result of different environments interacting with a specific genotype.

Realism Inability to distinguish between mental and physical entities.

Recall memory Ability to reproduce stimuli that one has previously encountered.

Recast Repetition of a child's utterance along with some new elements.

Recency effect Tendency for individuals to show good recall for the last few items in a list.

Receptive aphasia Loss of the ability to comprehend speech.

Receptive language Ability to comprehend spoken speech.

Recessive allele Allele whose characteristics do not tend to be expressed when part of a heterozygous genotype. Its genetic characteristics tend to be masked by other alleles.

Recognition memory Ability to identify whether a stimulus has been previously encountered.

Recovery from habituation Reinstatement of the intensity, frequency, or duration of a response to a stimulus that has changed. Also called *dishabituation.*

Reduplicated babbling Repetition of simple consonant-vowel combinations in the early stages of language development.

Referential communication Communication in situations that require the speaker to describe an object to a listener or to evaluate the effectiveness of a message.

Referential style Type of early language production in which the child uses mostly nominals.

Reflex Involuntary movement in response to touch, light, sound, or other form of stimulation; controlled by subcortical neural mechanisms.

Rehearsal Memory strategy that involves repetition of items to be remembered.

Rehearsal set The specific group of items participants repeat during the delay period in a memory test.

Reliability   Degree to which a measure will yield the same results if administered repeatedly.

Retrieval cue   Aid or cue to extract information that has already been stored in memory.

Reversibility   In Piagetian theory, the ability to mentally reverse or negate an action or a transformation.

Rhythmical stereotypies   Repeated sequences of movements, such as leg kicking, hand waving, or head banging, that have no apparent goal.

Rough-and-tumble play   Active, physical play that carries no intent of imposing harm on another child.

Route mapping   Child's use of sequential directional changes to negotiate or represent a spatial environment.

Saccade   Rapid eye movement to inspect an object or view a stimulus in the periphery of the visual field.

Scaffolding   Temporary aid provided by one person to encourage, support, and assist a lesser-skilled person in carrying out a task or completing a problem. The model provides knowledge and skills that are learned and gradually transferred to the learner.

Scheme   In Piagetian theory, the mental structure underlying a coordinated and systematic pattern of behaviors or thinking applied across similar objects or situations.

Scientific method   Use of objective, measurable, and repeatable techniques to gather information.

Script   Organized scheme or framework for commonly experienced events.

Secondary reinforcer   Object or person that attains rewarding value because of its association with a primary reinforcer.

Secular trend   Consistent pattern of change over generations.

Secure attachment   Attachment category defined by the infant's distress at separation from the caregiver and enthusiastic greeting upon his or her return. The infant also displays stranger anxiety and uses the caregiver as a secure base for exploration.

Self   Realization of being an independent, unique, stable, and self-reflective entity; the beliefs, knowledge, feelings, and characteristics the individual ascribes to himself or herself.

Self-concept   Perceptions, conceptions, and values one holds about oneself.

Self-control   Ability to comply with sociocultural prescriptions concerning ethical or moral behavior.

Self-esteem   One's feelings of worth; extent to which one senses one's attributes and actions are good, desired, and valued.

Self-reflective, empathic orientation   Form of prosocial reasoning in which children put themselves in another's place to understand that person's feelings.

Self-regulation   Process by which children come to control their own behaviors in accordance with the standards of their caregivers and community, especially in the absence of other adults.

Semantic bootstrapping hypothesis   Idea that children derive information about syntax from the meanings of words.

Semantic memory   Memory for general concepts or facts.

Semantics   Meanings of words or combinations of words.

Semiotic function   Ability to symbolize objects.

Sensation   Basic information in the external world that is processed by the sensory receptors.

Sensitive period   Brief period during which specific kinds of experiences have significant positive or negative consequences for development and behavior. Also called *critical period*.

Sensorimotor stage   In Piagetian theory, the first stage of cognitive development, from birth to approximately two years of age, in which thought is based primarily on action.

Sensory store   Memory store that holds information for very brief periods of time in a form that closely resembles the initial input.

Separation protest   Distress the infant shows when the caregiver leaves the immediate environment.

Sequential study   Study that examines groups of children of different ages over a period of time; usually shorter than a longitudinal study.

Sex segregation   Clustering of individuals into same-sex groups.

Sex typicality   Extent to which a behavior is usually associated with one sex as opposed to the other.

Sickle cell anemia   Genetic blood disorder common in regions of Africa and other areas where malaria is found and among descendants of these regions. Abnormal blood cells carry insufficient oxygen.

Sickle cell trait   Symptoms shown by those possessing a heterozygous genotype for sickle cell anemia.

Signaling behavior   In ethological theory, a behavior such as crying or smiling that brings the caregiver physically close to the infant.

Single-case design   Study that follows only one or a few individuals over a period of time.

Skeletal maturity   Extent to which cartilage has ossified to form bone; provides the most accurate estimate of how much additional growth will take place in the individual.

Smooth visual pursuit   Consistent, unbroken tracking by the eyes that serves to maintain focus on a moving visual target.

Social comparison   Process in which individuals define themselves in relation to the skills, attributes, and qualities of others; an important contributor to self-concept during middle childhood.

Social conventions   Behavioral rules that regulate social interactions, such as dress codes and degrees of formality in speech.

Social learning theory   A theoretical approach emphasizing the importance of learning through observation and imitation of behaviors modeled by others.

Social pretend play   Play that makes use of imaginary and symbolic objects and social roles, often enacted among several children. Also called *sociodramatic play*.

Social referencing   Looking to another individual for emotional cues in interpreting a strange or ambiguous event.

Socialization   Process by which children acquire the social knowledge, skills, and attitudes valued by the larger society.

Sociohistorical theory   Vygotsky's developmental theory emphasizing the importance of cultural tools, symbols, and ways of thinking that the child acquires from more knowledgeable members of the community.

Sociometric nomination   Peer assessment measure in which children are asked to name a specified number of peers who fit a certain criterion, such as "peers you would like to walk home with."

Sociometric rating scale   Peer assessment measure in which children rate peers on a number of social dimensions.

Solitary play   Individual play, performed without regard for what others are doing.

Sound localization   Ability to determine a sound's point of origin.

Stage   Developmental period during which the organization of thought and behavior is qualitatively different from that of an earlier or later period.

Stereopsis   Ability to perceive a single image of an object even though perceptual input is binocular and differs slightly for each eye; significant source of cues for depth perception.

Strange Situation   Standardized test that assesses the quality of infant-caregiver attachment.

Stranger anxiety   Fear or distress an infant shows at the approach of an unfamiliar person.

Structured interview   Standardized set of questions administered orally to individuals.

Structured observation   Study in which behaviors are recorded as they occur within a situation constructed by the experimenter, usually in the laboratory.

Sudden infant death syndrome (SIDS)   Sudden, unexplained death of an infant or a toddler as a result of cessation of breathing during sleep.

Superego   In Freudian theory, a mental structure that monitors socially acceptable and unacceptable behavior.

Syntax   Grammatical rules that dictate how words can be combined.

Systems theory   Model for understanding the family that emphasizes the reciprocal interactions among various members.

Telegraphic speech   Early two-word speech that contains few modifiers, prepositions, or other connective words.

Temperament   Stable, early-appearing constellation of individual personality attributes believed to have a hereditary basis; includes sociability, emotionality, and activity level.

Teratogen   Any environmental agent that can cause deviations in prenatal development. Consequences may range from behavioral problems to death.

Test bias   Idea that the content of traditional standardized tests does not adequately measure the competencies of children from diverse cultural backgrounds.

Theory   Set of ideas or propositions that helps to organize or explain observable phenomena.

Triarchic theory   Theory developed by Robert Sternberg that intelligence consists of three major components: (1) the ability to adapt to the environment, (2) the ability to employ fundamental information-processing skills, and (3) the ability to deal with novelty and automatize processing.

Trisomy   Condition in which an extra chromosome is present.

Turn taking   Alternating vocalization by parent and child.

Turnabout   Element of conversation that requests a response from the child.

Ultrasonography   Method of using sound wave reflections to obtain a representation of the developing fetus. Used to estimate gestational age and detect fetal physical abnormalities.

Umbilical cord   Conduit of blood vessels through which oxygen, nutrients, and waste products are transported between placenta and embryo.

Unconditioned response (UCR)   Response that is automatically elicited by the unconditioned stimulus (UCS).

Unconditioned stimulus (UCS)   Stimulus that, without prior training, elicits a reflexlike response (unconditioned response).

Underextension   Application of a label to a narrower class of objects than the term signifies.

Uninvolved parent   Parent who is emotionally detached from the child and focuses on his or her own needs as opposed to the child's.

Utilization deficiency   Phenomenon by which a memory strategy, when first applied, may fail to improve memory in a noticeable way.

Validity   Degree to which an assessment procedure actually measures the variable under consideration.

Variable   Factor having no fixed or constant value in a given situation.

Vergence   Ability of the eyes to rotate in opposite directions to fixate on objects at different distances; improves rapidly during first few months after birth.

Viability   Ability of the baby to survive outside the mother's womb.

Visual accommodation   Visuomotor process by which small involuntary muscles change the shape of the lens of the eye so that images of objects seen at different distances are brought into focus on the retina.

Visual acuity   Ability to make fine discriminations among elements in a visual array by detecting contours, transitions in light patterns that signal borders and edges.

Visual cliff   Experimental apparatus used to test depth perception in which the surface on one side of a glass-covered table is made to appear far below the surface on the other side.

Vocabulary spurt   Period of rapid word acquisition that typically occurs early in language development.

Wernicke's area   Portion of the cerebral cortex that controls language comprehension.

Working memory   Short-term memory store in which mental operations such as rehearsal and categorization take place.

X chromosome   Larger of the two sex chromosomes associated with genetic determination of sex. Normally females have two X chromosomes and males only one.

Y chromosome   Smaller of the two sex chromosomes associated with genetic determination of sex. Normally males have one Y chromosome and females none.

Zone of proximal development   Range of various kinds of support and assistance provided by an expert (usually an adult) who helps children to carry out activities they currently cannot complete but will later be able to accomplish independently.

Zygote   Fertilized egg cell.

Abel, E. L. (1981). Behavioral teratology of alcohol. *Psychological Bulletin, 90,* 564–581.

Abel, E. L. (1982). Consumption of alcohol during pregnancy: A review of effects on growth and development of offspring. *Human Biology, 54,* 421–453.

Abel, E. L. (1989). *Behavioral teratogenesis and behavioral mutagenesis: A primer in abnormal development.* New York: Plenum Press.

Aber, J. L., & Allen, J. P. (1987). Effects of maltreatment on young children's socioemotional development: An attachment theory perspective. *Developmental Psychology, 23,* 406–414.

Aboud, F. E., & Skerry, S. (1983). Self and ethnic concepts in relation to ethnic constancy. *Canadian Journal of Behavioral Science, 15,* 14–26.

Abramovitch, R., & Grusec, J. E. (1978). Peer imitation in a natural setting. *Child Development, 49,* 60–65.

Abrams, B. (1996). Weight gain and energy intake during pregnancy. *Clinical Obstetrics and Gynecology, 37,* 515–527.

Abramson, L. (1991). Facial expressivity in failure to thrive and normal infants: Implications for their capacity to engage in the world. *Merrill-Palmer Quarterly, 37,* 159–182.

Achenbach, T. M., Howell, C. T., Aoki, M. F., & Rauh, V. A. (1993). Nine-year outcome of the Vermont Intervention Program for Low Birth Weight Infants. *Pediatrics, 91,* 45–55.

Acredolo, L. P., & Goodwyn, S. W. (1988). Symbolic gesturing in normal infants. *Child Development, 59,* 450–466.

Acredolo, L. P., & Goodwyn, S. W. (1990a). Sign language among hearing infants: The spontaneous development of symbolic gestures. In V. Volterra & C. J. Erting (Eds.), *From gesture to language in hearing and deaf children.* New York: Springer-Verlag.

Acredolo, L. P., & Goodwyn, S. W. (1990b). Sign language in babies: The significance of symbolic gesturing for understanding language development. In R. Vasta (Ed.), *Annals of child development* (Vol. 7). Greenwich, CT: JAI Press.

Acredolo, L. P., Pick, H. L., & Olsen, M. G. (1975). Environmental differentiation and familiarity as determinants of children's memory for spatial location. *Developmental Psychology, 11,* 495–501.

Adair, R., Zuckerman, B., Bauchner, H., Philipp, B., & Levenson, S. (1992). Reducing night waking in infancy: A primary care intervention. *Pediatrics, 89,* 585–588.

Adams, R. J., Courage, M. L., & Mercer, M. E. (1994). Systematic measurement of human neonatal color vision. *Vision Research, 34,* 1691–701.

Adams, R. S., & Biddle, B. J. (1970). *Realities of teaching.* New York: Holt, Rinehart & Winston.

Adams, S., Kuebli, J., Boyle, P. A., & Fivush, R. (1995). Gender differences in parent-child conversations about past emotions: A longitudinal investigation. *Sex Roles, 33,* 309–323.

Adamson, L. B., & Bakeman, R. (1985). Affect and attention: Infants observed with mothers and peers. *Child Development, 56,* 582–593.

Adler, S. P. (1992). Cytomegalovirus and pregnancy. *Current Opinions in Obstetrics and Gynecology, 4,* 670–675.

Adoh, T. O., & Woodhouse, J. M. (1994). The Cardiff Acuity Test used for measuring visual acuity development in toddlers. *Vision Research, 34,* 555–560.

Ainsworth, M. D. S., Bell, S. M., & Stayton, D. J. (1971). Individual differences in Strange Situation behavior of one-year-olds. In H. R. Schaffer (Ed.), *The Origins of human social relations.* London: Academic Press.

Ainsworth, M. D. S., Bell, S. M., & Stayton, D. J. (1972). Individual differences in the development of some attachment behaviors. *Merrill-Palmer Quarterly, 18,* 123–143.

Ainsworth, M. D. S., Bell, S. M., & Stayton, D. J. (1974). Infant-mother attachment and social development: "Socialization" as a product of reciprocal responsiveness to signals. In M. R. Richards (Ed.), *The integration of the child into a social world.* London: Cambridge University Press.

Ainsworth, M. D. S., Blehar, M. C., Waters, E., & Wall, S. (1978). *Patterns of attachment: A psychological study of the strange situation.* Hillsdale, NJ: Erlbaum.

Akhtar, N., Carpenter, M., & Tomasello, M. (1996). The role of discourse novelty in early word learning. *Child Development, 67,* 635–645.

Alan Guttmacher Institute. (1993). *Facts in Brief, March* (pp. 1–2). Chicago: Alan Guttmacher Innstitute.

Alberto, P. A., & Troutman, A. C. (1995). *Applied behavior analysis for teachers* (4th ed.). Englewood Cliffs, NJ: Prentice-Hall.

Alessandri, S. M., & Lewis, M. (1993). Parental evaluation and its relation to shame and pride in young children. *Sex Roles, 29,* 335–343.

Alessandri, S. M., Sullivan, M. W., Imaizumi, S., & Lewis, M. (1993). Learning and emotional responsivity in cocaine-exposed infants. *Developmental Psychology, 29,* 989–997.

Alexander, I. E., & Babad, E. Y. (1981). Returning the smile of a stranger: Within-culture and cross-cultural comparisons of Israeli and American children. *Genetic Psychology Monographs, 103,* 31–77.

Alexander, J. M., Carr, M., & Schwanenflugel, P. J. (1995). Development of metacognition in gifted children: Directions for future research. *Developmental Review, 15,* 1–37.

Alexander, K. L., & Entwisle, D. R. (1988). Achievement in the first 2 years of school: Patterns and processes. *Monographs of the Society for Research in Child Development, 53*(2, Serial No. 218).

Alexander, K. L., Entwisle, D. R., & Bedinger, S. D. (1994). When expectations work: Race and socioeconomic differences in school performance. *Social Psychology Quarterly, 57,* 283–299.

Alfieri, T., Ruble, D. N., & Higgins, E. T. (1996). Gender stereotypes during adolescence: Developmental changes and the transition to junior high school. *Developmental Psychology, 32,* 1129–1137.

Allen, D. B. (1996). Safety of human growth hormone therapy: Current topics. *Journal of Pediatrics, 128,* S8–S13.

Allen, G. L., & Ondracek, P. J. (1995). Age-sensitive cognitive abilities related to children's acquisition of spatial knowledge. *Developmental Psychology, 31,* 934–945.

Allen, J. P., Weissberg, R. P., & Hawkins, J. A. (1989). The relation between values and social competence in early adolescence. *Developmental Psychology, 25,* 458–464.

Alsaker, F. D. (1992). Pubertal timing, overweight, and psychological adjustment. *Journal of Early Adolescence, 12,* 396–419.

Alwitt, L. F., Anderson, D. R., Lorch, E. P., & Levin, S. R. (1980). Preschool children's visual attention to attributes of television. *Human Communication Research, 7,* 52–67.

Amato, P. R., & Rezac, S. J. (1994). Contact with nonresident parents, interparental conflict, and children's behavior. *Journal of Family Issues, 15,* 191–207.

American Academy of Pediatrics. Committee on Substance Abuse and Committee on Children with Disabilities. (1993). Fetal alcohol syndrome and fetal alcohol effects. *Pediatrics, 91,* 1004–1006.

American Association of University Women. (1992). *How schools shortchange girls.* Washington, DC: AAUW Educational Foundation.

American College of Obstetricians and Gynecologists. (1994). Substance abuse in pregnancy. *ACOG Technical Bulletin No. 195.*

American Psychiatric Association. (1987). *Diagnostic and statistical manual of mental disorders* (3rd ed., rev.). Washington, DC.

Amsterdam, B. K. (1972). Mirror self-image reactions before age two. *Developmental Psychobiology, 5,* 297–305.

Anderson, A. H., Clark, A., & Mullen, J. (1994). Interactive communication between children: Learning how to make language work in dialogue. *Journal of Child Language, 21,* 439–463.

Anderson, D. R., Choi, H. P., & Lorch, E. P. (1987). Attentional inertia reduces distractibility during young children's TV viewing. *Child Development, 58,* 798–806.

Anderson, D. R., & Collins, P. A. (1988). *The impact of children's education: Television's influence on cognitive development* (Working Paper No. 2). Washington, DC: Office of Educational Research and Improvement.

Anderson, D. R., & Levin, S. R. (1976). Young children's attention to "Sesame Street." *Child Development, 47,* 806–811.

Anderson, D. R., Lorch, E. P., Field, D. E., Collins, P. A., & Nathan, J. G. (1986). Television viewing at home: Age trends in visual attention and time with TV. *Child Development, 57,* 1024–1033.

Anderson, D. R., Lorch, E. P., Field, D. E., & Sanders, J. (1981). The effects of TV program comprehensibility on preschool children's television viewing behavior. *Child Development, 52,* 151–157.

Anderson, K. E., Lytton, H., & Romney, D. M. (1986). Mothers' interactions with normal and conduct-disordered boys: Who affects whom? *Developmental Psychology, 22,* 604–609.

Andersson, B. (1992). Effects of day-care on cognitive and socioemotional competence of thirteen-year-old Swedish schoolchildren. *Child Development, 63,* 20–36.

Andiman, W. A., & Horstmann, D. M. (1984). Congenital and perinatal viral infections. In M. B. Bracken (Ed.), *Perinatal epidemiology.* New York: Oxford University Press.

Anglin, J. M. (1993). Vocabulary development: A morphological analysis. *Monographs of the Society for Research in Child Development, 59* (5, Serial No. 242).

Angoff, W. H. (1988). The nature-nurture debate: Aptitudes and group differences. *American Psychologist, 43,* 713–720.

Anisfeld, M. (1996). Only tongue protrusion modeling is matched by neonates. *Developmental Review, 16,* 149–161.

Annett, M. (1973). Laterality of childhood hemiplegia and the growth of speech and intelligence. *Cortex, 9,* 4–33.

Anooshian, L. J., & Young, D. (1981). Developmental changes in cognitive maps of a familiar neighborhood. *Child Development, 52,* 341–348.

Antill, J. K., Goodnow, J. J., Russell, G., & Cotton, S. (1996). The influence of parents and family context on children's involvement in household tasks. *Sex Roles, 34,* 215–236.

Antonov, A. N. (1947). Children born during the siege of Leningrad in 1942. *Journal of Pediatrics, 30,* 250–259.

Apgar, V. (1953). A proposal for a new method of evaluation of the newborn infant. *Anesthesia and Analgesia: Current Researches, 32,* 260–267.

Applebee, A. N., Langer, J. A., Mullis, I. V. S., & Jenkins, L. B. (1990). *The writing report card, 1984–1988.* Princeton, NJ: Educational Testing Service.

Arend, R., Gove, F. L., & Sroufe, L. A. (1979). Continuity of individual adaptation from infancy to kindergarten: A predictive study of ego-resiliency and curiosity in preschoolers. *Child Development, 50,* 950–959.

Ariès, P. (1962). *Centuries of childhood: A social history of family life* (R. Baldick, Trans.). New York: Vintage.

Arnold, D. S., & Whitehurst, G. J. (1994). Accelerating language development through picture book reading: A summary of dialogic reading and its effects. In D. K. Dickinson (Ed.), *Bridges to literacy: Children, families, and schools.* Cambridge, MA: Blackwell.

Aronfreed, J. (1969). The concept of internalization. In D. A. Goslin (Ed.), *Handbook of socialization theory and research.* Chicago: Rand McNally.

Aronfreed, J. (1976). Moral development from the standpoint of a general psychological theory. In T. Lickona (Ed.), *Moral development and moral behavior.* New York: Holt, Rinehart & Winston.

Arsenio, W. F., & Ford, M. E. (1985). The role of affective information in social-cognitive development: Children's differentiation of moral and conventional events. *Merrill-Palmer Quarterly, 31,* 1–17.

Artigal, J. M. (1991). *The Catalan immersion program: A European point of view.* Norwood, NJ: Ablex.

Asendorpf, J. B., & Baudonnière, P-M. (1993). Self-awareness and other-awareness: Mirror self-recognition and synchronic imitation among unfamiliar peers. *Developmental Psychology, 29,* 88–95.

Asher, S. R. (1983). Social competence and peer status: Recent advances and future directions. *Child Development, 54,* 1427–1434.

Asher, S. R. (1985). An evolving paradigm in social skill training research with children. In B. H. Schneider, K. H. Rubin, & J. E. Ledingham (Eds.), *Children's peer relations: Issues in assessment and intervention.* New York: Springer-Verlag.

Asher, S. R., & Dodge, K. A. (1986). The identification of socially rejected children. *Developmental Psychology, 22,* 444–449.

Asher, S. R., Parker, J. G., & Walker, D. L. (1996). Distinguishing friendship from acceptance: Implications for intervention and assessment. In W. M. Bukowski, A. F. Newcomb, & W. W. Hartup (Eds.), *The company they keep: Friendship in childhood and adolescence.* New York: Cambridge University Press.

Ashima-Takane, Y., Goodz, E., & Derevensky, J. L. (1996). Birth order effects on early language development: Do secondborn children learn from overheard speech? *Child Development, 67,* 621–634.

Ashmead, D. H., Clifton, R. K., & Perris, E. E. (1987). Precision of auditory localization in human infants. *Developmental Psychology, 23,* 641–647.

Ashmead, D. H., Hill, E. W., & Talor, C. R. (1989). Obstacle perception by congenitally blind children. *Perception & Psychophysics, 46,* 425–433.

Ashmead, D., McCarty, M. E., Lucas, L. S., & Belvedere, M. C. (1993). Visual guidance in infants' reaching toward suddenly displaced targets. *Child Development, 64,* 1111–1127.

Aslin, R. N. (1987a). Motor aspects of visual development in infancy. In P. Salapatek & L. Cohen (Eds.), *Handbook of infant perception: From sensation to perception* (Vol. 1). Orlando, FL: Academic Press.

Aslin, R. N. (1987b). Visual and auditory development in infancy. In J. D. Osofsky (Ed.), *Handbook of infant development* (2nd ed.). New York: Wiley.

Aslin, R. N. (1993). Perception of visual direction in human infants. In C. Granrud (Ed.), *Visual perception and cognition in infancy.* Hillsdale, NJ: Erlbaum.

Aslin, R. N., & Dumais, S. T. (1980). Binocular vision in infants: A review and a theoretical framework. In H. W. Reese & L. P. Lipsitt (Eds.), *Advances in child development and behavior* (Vol. 15). New York: Academic Press.

Aslin, R. N., Pisoni, D. B., & Jusczyk, P. W. (1983). Auditory development and speech perception in infancy. In M. M. Haith & J. J. Campos (Eds.), *Handbook of child psychology: Vol. II. Infancy and developmental psychobiology.* New York: Wiley.

Aslin, R. N., & Smith, L. B. (1988). Perceptual development. *Annual Review of Psychology, 39,* 435–473.

Astington, J. W., Harris, P. L., & Olson, D. R. (1988). *Developing theories of mind.* New York: Cambridge University Press.

Atkinson, R. C., & Shiffrin, R. M. (1968). Human memory: A proposed system and its control processes. In K. W. Spence & J. T. Spence (Eds.), *The psychology of learning and motivation: Advances in research and theory* (Vol. 2). New York: Academic Press.

Au, T. K., & Laframboise, D. E. (1990). Acquiring color names via linguistic contrast: The influence of contrasting terms. *Child Development, 61,* 1808–1823.

Autti-Rämö, I., Korkman, M., Hilakivi-Clarke, L., Lehtonen, M., Halmesmäki, E., & Granström, M. (1992). Mental development of 2-year-old children exposed to alcohol in utero. *Journal of Pediatrics, 120,* 740–746.

Avery, A. W. (1982). Escaping loneliness in adolescence: The case for androgyny. *Journal of Youth and Adolescence, 11,* 451–459.

Avis, J., & Harris, P. L. (1991). Belief-desire reasoning among Baka children: Evidence for a universal conception of mind. *Child Development, 62,* 460–467.

Aylward, G. P., Pfeiffer, S. I., Wright, A., & Verhulst, S. J. (1989). Outcome studies of low birth weight infants published in the last decade: A meta-analysis. *Journal of Pediatrics, 115,* 515–520.

Azuma, S. D., & Chasnoff, I. J. (1993). Outcome of children prenatally exposed to cocaine and other drugs: A path analysis of three-year data. *Pediatrics, 92,* 396–402.

Bachevalier, J., Brickson, M., & Hagger, C. (1993). Limbic-dependent recognition memory in monkeys develops early in infancy. *Neuro Report, 4,* 77–80.

Bachevalier, J., Hagger, C., & Mishkin, M. (1991). Functional maturation of the occipitotemporal pathway in infant rhesus monkeys. In N. A. Lassen, D. H. Ingvar, M. E. Raichle, & L. Friberg (Eds.), *Brain work and mental activity* (pp. 231–240). Copenhagen: Munksgaard.

Bachman, J. G. (1970). *The impact of family background and intelligence on tenth grade boys: Vol. 2. Youth in transition.* Ann Arbor: Survey Research Center, Institute for Social Research.

Backscheider, A. G., Shatz, M., & Gelman, S. A. (1993). Preschoolers' ability to distinguish living kinds as a function of regrowth. *Child Development, 64,* 1242–1257.

Baillargeon, R. (1987a). Object permanence in 3½- and 4½-month-old infants. *Developmental Psychology, 23,* 655–664.

Baillargeon, R. (1987b). Young children's reasoning about the physical and spatial characteristics of a hidden object. *Cognitive Development, 2,* 179–200.

Baillargeon, R. (1995). Physical reasoning in infancy. In M. S. Gazzaniga (Ed.), *The cognitive neurosciences* (pp. 181–204). Cambridge, MA: MIT Press.

Baillargeon, R., & DeVos, J. (1991). Object permanence in young infants: Further evidence. *Child Development, 62,* 1227–1246.

Baird, P. A., Anderson, T. W., Newcombe, H. B., & Lowry, R. B. (1988). Genetic disorders in children and young adults: A population study. *American Journal of Human Genetics, 42,* 677–693.

Baker-Sennett, J., Matusov, E., & Rogoff, B. (1993). Planning as a developmental process. In H. W. Reese (Ed.), *Advances in child development and behavior.* Vol. 24. San Diego, CA: Academic Press.

Baker-Ward, L., Ornstein, P. A., & Holden, D. J. (1984). The expression of memorization in early childhood. *Journal of Experimental Child Psychology, 37,* 555–575.

Baldwin, J. M. (1930). [Autobiography]. In C. Murchison (Ed.), *A history of psychology in autobiography* (Vol. 1). Worcester, MA: Clark University Press.

Bales, D. W., & Sera, M. D. (1995). Preschoolers' understanding of stable and changeable characteristics. *Cognitive Development, 10,* 69–107.

Ball, W., & Tronick, E. (1971). Infant responses to impending collision: Optical and real. *Science, 171,* 818–820.

Ballard, B. D., Gipson, M. T., Guttenberg, W., & Ramsey, K. (1980). Palatability of food as a factor influencing obese and normal-weight children's eating habits. *Behavior Research and Therapy, 18,* 598–600.

Balogh, R. D., & Porter, R. H. (1986). Olfactory preferences resulting from mere exposure in human neonates. *Infant Behavior and Development, 9,* 395–402.

Bandura, A. (1965). Vicarious processes: A case of no-trial learning. In L. Berkowitz (Ed.), *Advances in experimental social psychology* (Vol. 2). New York: Academic Press.

Bandura, A. (1969). *Principles of behavior modification.* New York: Holt, Rinehart & Winston.

Bandura, A. (1977a). Self-efficacy: Toward a unifying theory of behavioral change. *Psychological Review, 84,* 191–215.

Bandura, A. (1977b). *Social learning theory.* Englewood Cliffs, NJ: Prentice-Hall.

Bandura, A. (1986). *Social foundations of thought and action: A social cognitive theory.* Englewood Cliffs, NJ: Prentice-Hall.

Bandura, A. (1989). Social cognitive theory. In R. Vasta (Ed.), *Annals of child development: Vol. 6. Six theories of child development: Revised formulations and current issues.* Greenwich, CT: JAI Press.

Bandura, A., Barbaranelli, C., Caprara, G. V., & Pastorelli, C. (1996). Multifaceted impact of self-efficacy beliefs on academic functioning. *Child Development, 67,* 1206–1222.

Bandura, A., Ross, D., & Ross, S. A. (1963a). Imitation of film-mediated aggressive models. *Journal of Abnormal and Social Psychology, 66,* 3–11.

Bandura, A., Ross, D., & Ross, S. A. (1963b). Vicarious reinforcement and imitative learning. *Journal of Abnormal and Social Psychology, 67,* 601–607.

Bandura, A., & Walters, R. H. (1959). *Adolescent aggression.* New York: Ronald Press.

Bandura, A., & Walters, R. H. (1963). *Social learning and personality development.* New York: Holt, Rinehart & Winston.

Banks, M. S. (1980). The development of visual accommodation during early infancy. *Child Development, 51,* 646–666.

Banks, M. S., Aslin, R. N., & Letson, R. D. (1975). Sensitive period for the development of human binocular vision. *Science, 190,* 675–677.

Banks, M. S., & Shannon, E. (1993). Spatial and chromatic visual efficiency in human neonates. In C. Granrud (Ed.), *Visual perception and cognition in infancy* (pp. 1–46). Hillsdale, NJ: Erlbaum.

Barahal, R. M., Waterman, J., & Martin, H. P. (1981). The social cognitive development of abused children. *Journal of Consulting and Clinical Psychology, 49,* 508–516.

Barden, R. C., Zelko, F., Duncan, S. W., & Masters, J. C. (1980). Children's consensual knowledge about the experiential components of emotion. *Journal of Personality and Social Psychology, 39,* 968–976.

Barinaga, M. (1994). Looking to development's future. *Science, 266,* 561–564.

Barker, R., & Gump, P. (1964). *Big school, small school: High school size and student behavior.* Stanford, CA: Standard University Press.

Barnard, K. E. (1987). Paradigms for intervention: Infant state modulation. In N. Gunzenhauser (Ed.), *Infant stimulation: For whom, what kind, when, and how much?* (Johnson & Johnson Baby Products Company Pediatric Round Table Series No. 13). Skilman, NJ: Johnson & Johnson.

Barnes, K. (1971). Preschool play norms: A replication. *Developmental Psychology, 5,* 99–103.

Barnhart, H. X., Caldwell, M. B., Thomas, P., Mascola, L., Ortiz, I., Hus, H. W., Schulte, J., Parrott, R., Maldonado, Y., Byers, R., and the Pediatric Spectrum of Disease Clinical Consortium. (1996). Natural history of human immunodeficiency virus disease in perinatally infected children: An analysis from the Pediatric Spectrum of Disease Project. *Pediatrics, 97,* 710–716.

Baron-Cohen, S., Tager-Flusberg, H., & Cohen, D. J. (1993). *Understanding other minds: Perspectives from autism.* New York: Oxford University Press.

Barr, R., Dowden, A., & Hayne, H. (1996). Developmental changes in deferred imitation by 6- to 24-month-old infants. *Infant Behavior and Development, 19,* 159–170.

Barrera, M. E., & Maurer, D. (1981a). The perception of facial expressions by the three-month-old. *Child Development, 52,* 203–206.

Barrera, M. E., & Maurer, D. (1981b). Recognition of mother's photographed face by the three-month-old infant. *Child Development, 52,* 714–716.

Barrett, M. D. (1985). Issues in the study of children's single-word speech. In M. D. Barrett (Ed.), *Children's single-word speech.* Chichester, England: Wiley.

Barrett, M. D. (1986). Early semantic representations and early word usage. In S. A. Kuczaj & M. D. Barrett (Eds.), *The development of word meaning.* New York: Springer-Verlag.

Barrett, M. D. (1989). Early language development. In A. Slater & G. Bremner (Eds.), *Infant development.* London: Erlbaum.

Barth, J. M. (1989, April). *Parent-child relationships and children's transition to school.* Paper presented at the biennial meeting of the Society for Research in Child Development, Kansas City, MO.

Baruch, G. K., & Barnett, R. C. (1981). Fathers' participation in the care of their preschool children. *Sex Roles, 7,* 1043–1055.

Basser, L. S. (1962). Hemiplegia of early onset and the faculty of speech with special reference to the effects of hemispherectomy. *Brain, 85,* 427–460.

Bates, E., Benigni, L., Bretherton, I., Camaioni, L., & Volterra, V. (1979). *The emergence of symbols: Cognition and communication in infancy.* New York: Academic Press.

Bates, E., Bretherton, I., & Snyder, L. (1988). *From first words to grammar.* Cambridge, UK: Cambridge University Press.

Bates, E., Camaioni, L., & Volterra, V. (1975). The acquisition of performatives prior to speech. *Merrill-Palmer Quarterly, 21,* 205–224.

Bates, E., Marchman, V., Thal, D., Fenson, L., Dale, P., Reznick, J. S., Reilly, J., & Hartung, J. (1994). Developmental and stylistic variation in the composition of early vocabulary. *Journal of Child Language, 21,* 85–123.

Bates, E., Thal, D., & Marchman, V. (1991). Symbols and syntax: A Darwinian approach to language development. In N. A. Krasnegor, D. M. Rumbaugh, R. L. Schiefelbusch, & M. Studdert-Kennedy (Eds.), *Biological and behavioral determinants of language.* Hillsdale, NJ: Erlbaum.

Bates, J. E., Maslin, C. A., & Frankel, K. A. (1985). Attachment security, mother-child interaction, and temperament as predictors of behavior-problem ratings at age three years. In I. Bretherton & E. Waters (Eds.), *Growing points of attachment theory and research. Monographs of the Society for Research in Child Development, 50*(1–2, Serial No. 209).

Batson, C. D. (1990). How social an animal? The human capacity for caring. *American Psychologist, 45,* 336–346.

Batson, C. D., & Oleson, K. C. (1991). Current status of the empathy-altruism hypothesis. In M. S. Clark (Ed.), *Review of personality and social psychology: Prosocial behavior* (Vol. 12). Newbury Park, CA: Sage.

Bauer, P. J. (1993). Memory for gender-consistent and gender-inconsistent event sequences by twenty-five-month-old children. *Child Development, 64,* 285–297.

Bauer, P. J., & Mandler, J. M. (1992). Putting the horse before the cart: The use of temporal order in recall of events by one-year-old children. *Developmental Psychology, 28,* 441–452.

Bauer, P. J., & Wewerka, S. S. (1995). One- to two-year-olds' recall of events: The more expressed, the more impressed. *Journal of Experimental Child Psychology, 59,* 475–496.

Baum, C. G., & Foreham, R. (1984). Social factors associated with adolescent obesity. *Journal of Pediatric Psychology, 9,* 293– 302.

Baumrind, D. (1971). Current patterns of parental authority. *Developmental Psychology Monographs, 4*(1, Pt. 2).

Baumrind, D. (1972). From each according to her ability. *School Review, 80,* 161–197.

Baumrind, D. (1973). The development of instrumental competence through socialization. In A. D. Pick (Ed.), *The Minnesota symposia on child psychology* (Vol. 7). Minneapolis: University of Minnesota Press.

Baumrind, D. (1991). The influence of parenting style on adolescent competence and substance abuse. *Journal of Early Adolescence, 11,* 56–94.

Baumrind, D. (1993). The average expectable environment is not good enough: A response to Scarr. *Child Development, 64,* 1299–1317.

Baydar, N., & Brooks-Gunn, J. (1991). Effects of maternal employment and child-care arrangements on preschoolers' cognitive and behavioral outcomes: Evidence from the Children of the National Longitudinal Survey of Youth. *Developmental Psychology, 27,* 932–945.

Bayley, N. (1949). Consistency and variability in the growth of intelligence from birth to eighteen years. *Journal of Genetic Psychology, 75,* 165–196.

Bayley, N. (1993). *Bayley Scales of Infant Development* (2nd ed.). San Antonio: The Psychological Corporation.

Beal, C. R. (1987). Repairing the message: Children's monitoring and repair skills. *Child Development, 58,* 401–408.

Beauchamp, G. K., & Cowart, B. J. (1990). Preference for high salt concentrations among children. *Developmental Psychology, 26,* 539–545.

Beauchamp, G. K., & Moran, M. (1982). Dietary experience and sweet taste preferences in human infants. *Appetite, 3,* 139–152.

Beaudet, A. L., Scriver, C. R., Sly, W. S., & Valle, D. (1995). Genetics, biochemistry, and molecular basis of variant human phenotypes. In C. R. Scriver, A. L. Beaudet, W. S. Sly, & D. Valle (Eds.), *The metabolic and molecular bases of inherited disease,* Vol. I (7th ed., pp. 53–118). New York: McGraw-Hill.

Beck, R. W., & Beck, S. H. (1989). The incidence of extended households among middle-aged black and white women. *Journal of Family Issues, 10,* 147–168.

Becker, J. (1989). Preschoolers' use of number words to denote one-to-one correspondence. *Child Development, 60,* 1147–1157.

Becker, J. (1993). Young children's numerical use of number words: Counting in many-to-one situations. *Developmental Psychology, 29,* 458–465.

Beckett, K. (1995). Fetal rights and "crack moms": Pregnant women in the war on drugs. *Contemporary Drug Problems, 22,* 587–612.

Beilin, H. (1989). Piagetian theory. In R. Vasta (Ed.), *Annals of child development: Vol. 6. Six theories of child development: Revised formulations and current issues.* Greenwich, CT: JAI Press.

Beilin, H. (1992). Piaget's enduring contribution to developmental psychology. *Developmental Psychology, 28,* 191–204.

Beilin, H., & Pufall, P. B. (1992). *Piaget's theory: Prospects and possibilities.* Hillsdale, NJ: Erlbaum.

Beitchman, J. H., Nair, R., Clegg, M., & Patel, P. G. (1986). Prevalence of speech and language disorders in 5-year-old kindergarten children in the Ottawa-Carleton region. *Journal of Speech and Hearing Disorders, 51,* 98–110.

Bell, M. A., & Fox, N. A. (1992). The relations between frontal brain electrical activity and cognitive development during infancy. *Child Development, 63,* 1142–1163.

Bell, R. Q.(1968). A reinterpretation of the direction of effects in studies of socialization. *Psychological Review, 75,* 81–95.

Bell, R. Q. (1971). Stimulus control of parent or caretaker behavior by offspring. *Developmental Psychology, 4,* 63–72.

Bell, R. Q., & Harper, L. V. (1977). *Child effects on adults.* Hillsdale, NJ: Erlbaum.

Bell, S. M., & Ainsworth, M. D. S. (1972). Infant crying and maternal responsiveness. *Child Development, 43,* 1171–1190.

Belmont, J. M. (1989). Cognitive strategies and strategic learning: The socio-instructional approach. *American Psychologist, 44,* 142–148.

Belsky, J. (1980). Child maltreatment: An ecological integration. *American Psychologist, 35,* 320–335.

Belsky, J. (1981). Early human experience: A family perspective. *Developmental Psychology, 17,* 3–23.

Belsky, J. (1993). Etiology of child maltreatment: A developmental-ecological analysis. *Psychological Bulletin, 114,* 413–434.

Belsky, J. (1996). Parent, infant, and social-contextual antecedents of father-son attachment security. *Developmental Psychology, 32,* 905–913.

Belsky, J., & Braungart, J. M. (1991). Are insecure-avoidant infants with extensive day-care experience less stressed by and more independent in the Strange Situation? *Child Development, 62,* 567–571.

Belsky, J., Campbell, S. B., Cohn, J. F., & Moore, G. (1996). Instability of infant-parent attachment security. *Developmental Psychology, 32,* 921–924.

Belsky, J., Hsieh, K., & Crnic, K. (1996). Infant positive and negative emotionality: One dimension or two? *Developmental Psychology, 32,* 289–298.

Belsky, J., & Rovine, M. J. (1988). Nonmaternal care in the first year of life and the security of infant-parent attachment. *Child Development, 59,* 157–167.

Bem, S. L. (1974). The measurement of psychological androgyny. *Journal of Consulting and Clinical Psychology, 42,* 155–162.

Bem, S. L. (1975). Sex role adaptability: One consequence of psychological androgyny. *Journal of Personality and Social Psychology, 31,* 634–643.

Bem, S. L. (1981). Gender schema theory: A cognitive account of sex-typing. *Psychological Review, 88,* 354–364.

Bem, S. L. (1983). Gender schema theory and its implications for child development: Raising gender aschematic children in a gender schematic society. *Signs, 8,* 598–616.

Ben-Zeev, S. (1977). The influence of bilingualism on cognitive strategy and cognitive development. *Child Development, 48,* 1009–1018.

Bender, B. G., Harmon, R. J., Linden, M. G., & Robinson, A. (1995). Psychosocial adaptation of 39 adolescents with sex chromosome abnormalities. *Pediatrics, 96,* 302–308.

Bender, B. G., Linden, M. G., & Robinson, A. (1987). Environment and developmental risk in children with sex chromosome abnormalities. *Journal of the Academy of Child and Adolescent Psychiatry, 26,* 499–503.

Bennetto, L., Pennington, B. F., & Rogers, S. J. (1996). Intact and impaired memory functions in autism. *Child Development, 67,* 1816–1835.

Benoit, D., & Parker, K. (1994). Stability and transmission of attachment across three generations. *Child Development, 65,* 1444–1456.

Benson, J. B. (1988). The significance and development of crawling in human infancy. In J. E. Clark & J. H. Humphrey (Eds.), *Advances in motor development* (Vol. 3). New York: AMS Press.

BenTsvi-Mayer, S., Hertz-Lazarowitz, R., & Safir, M. P. (1989). Teachers' selections of boys and girls as prominent pupils. *Sex Roles, 21,* 231–245.

Bentur, Y., & Koren, G. (1991). The three most common occupation exposures reported by pregnant women: An update. *American Journal of Obstetrics and Gynecology, 165,* 429–437.

Bergin, D. A., Ford, M. E., & Hess, R. D. (1993). Patterns of motivation and social behavior associated with microcomputer use of young children. *Journal of Educational Psychology, 85,* 437–445.

Bergman, R. (1994, December 5). The birthplace boom. *Hospitals & Health Networks, 68,* pp. 47–48.

Berk, L. E. (1986). Relationship of elementary school children's private speech to behavioral accompaniment to task, attention, and task performance. *Developmental Psychology, 22,* 671–680.

Berk, L. E. (1992). Children's private speech: An overview of theory and the status of research. In R. M. Diaz & L. E. Berk (Eds.), *Private speech: From social interaction to self-regulations.* Hillsdale, NJ: Erlbaum.

Berko, J. (1958). The child's learning of English morphology. *Word, 14,* 150–177.

Berlin, I. N. (1987). Suicide among American Indian adolescents: An overview. *Suicide and Life-Threatening Behavior, 17,* 218–232.

Berman, A. L. (1987, Spring). The problem of adolescent suicide. *Division of Child, Youth, and Family Services Newsletter, 10*(2), American Psychological Association Division 37. pp. 1, 14.

Berndt, T. J. (1979). Developmental changes in conformity to peers and parents. *Developmental Psychology, 15,* 608–616.

Berndt, T. J. (1981). Relations between social cognition, nonsocial cognition, and social behavior: The case of friendship. In J. H. Flavell & L. D. Ross (Eds.), *Social cognitive development: Frontiers and possible futures.* Cambridge, UK: Cambridge University Press.

Berndt, T. J., & Keefe, K. (1995). Friends' influence on adolescents' adjustment to school. *Child Development, 66,* 1312–1329.

Berne, L. A., & Huberman, B. K. (1995). Sexuality education: Sorting fact from fiction. *Phi Delta Kappan, 77,* 229–232.

Berrueta-Clement, J. R., Schweinhart, L., Barnett, W., Epstein, A., & Weikart, D. (1984). *Changed lives: The effects of the Perry Preschool Program on youths through age 19.* Ypsilanti, MI: High/Scope Educational Research Foundation.

Berry, J. W. (1966). Temne and Eskimo perceptual skills. *International Journal of Psychology, 1,* 207–229.

Bertenthal, B. I. (1993). Infants' perception of biomechanical motions: Intrinsic image and knowledge-based constraints. In C. Granrud (Ed.), *Visual perception and cognition in infancy* (pp. 175–214). Hillsdale, NJ: Erlbaum.

Berthier, N. E. (1996). Learning to reach: A mathematical model. *Developmental Psychology, 32,* 811–823.

Berthoud-Papandropoulou, I. (1978). An experimental study of children's ideas about language. In A. Sinclair, R. J. Jarvella, & W. J. M. Levelt (Eds.), *The child's conception of language.* Heidelberg: Springer-Verlag.

Best, C. T., McRoberts, G. W., LaFleur, R., & Silver-Isenstadt, J. (1995). Divergent developmental patterns for infants' perception of two nonnative consonant contrasts. *Infant Behavior and Development, 18,* 339–350.

Best, D. L. (1993). Inducing children to generate mnemonic organizational strategies: An examination of long-term retention and materials. *Developmental Psychology, 29,* 324–336.

Best, D. L., & Williams, J. E. (1993). A cross-cultural viewpoint. In A. E. Beall & R. J. Sternberg (Eds.), *The psychology of gender.* New York: Guilford Press.

Beyer, S. (1995). Maternal employment and children's academic achievement: Parenting styles as mediating variable. *Developmental Review, 15,* 212–253.

Bialystok, E. (1986). Factors in the growth of linguistic awareness. *Child Development, 57,* 498–510.

Bialystok, E. (1991). Metalinguistic dimensions of bilingual language proficiency. In E. Bialystok (Ed.), *Language processing in bilingual children.* Cambridge, UK: Cambridge University Press.

Biederman, J., Faraone, S. V., Keenan, K., Knee, D., & Tsuang, M. T. (1990). Family-genetic and psychosocial risk factors in DSM-III attention deficit disorder. *Journal of the American Academy of Child and Adolescent Psychiatry, 29,* 526–533.

Bierman, K. L. (1986). Process of change during social skills training with preadolescents and its relation to treatment outcome. *Child Development, 57,* 230–240.

Bierman, K. L., & Montminy, H. P. (1993). Developmental issues in social-skills assessment and intervention with children and adolescents. *Behavior Modification, 17,* 229–254.

Bigelow, B. J., & LaGaipa, J. J. (1975). Children's written descriptions of friendship: A multidimensional analysis. *Developmental Psychology, 11,* 857–858.

Bigelow, B. J., Tesson, G., & Lewko, J. H. (1992). The social rules that children use: close friends, other friends, and "other kids" compared to parents, teachers, and siblings. *International Journal of Behavioral Development, 15,* 315–335.

Bijou, S. W. (1989). Behavior analysis. In R. Vasta (Ed.), *Annals of child development: Vol 6. Six theories of child development: Revised formulations and current issues.* Greenwich, CT: JAI Press.

Biller, H. B. (1974). *Paternal deprivation: Family, school, sexuality and society.* Lexington, MA: Heath.

Billing, L., Eriksson, M., Jonsson, B., Steneroth, G., & Zetterström, R. (1994). The influence of environmental factors on behavioral problems in 8-year-old children exposed to amphetamine during fetal life. *Child Abuse & Neglect, 18,* 3–9.

Binet, A., & Simon, T. (1905). Méthodes nouvelles pour le diagnostic du niveau intellectuel des anormaux. *L'Anée Psychologique, 11,* 191–244.

Bingham, C. R., & Crockett, L. J. (1996). Longitudinal adjustment patterns of boys and girls experiencing early, middle, and late sexual intercourse. *Developmental Psychology, 32,* 647–658.

Bishop, S. M., & Ingersoll, G. M. (1989). Effects of marital conflict and family structure on the self-concepts of pre- and early adolescents. *Journal of Youth and Adolescence, 18,* 25–38.

Bithoney, W. G., Van Sciver, M. M., Foster, S., Corson, S., & Tentindo, C. (1995). Parental stress and growth outcome in growth-deficient children. *Pediatrics, 96,* 707–711.

Bivens, J. A., & Berk, L. E. (1990). A longitudinal study of the development of elementary school children's private speech. *Merrill-Palmer Quarterly, 36,* 443–463.

Bjorkland, D. F. (1987). How age changes in knowledge base contribute to the development of children's memory: An interpretive review. *Developmental Review, 7,* 93–130.

Bjorkland, D. F., & Harnishfeger, K. K. (1990). The resources construct in cognitive development: Diverse sources of evidence and a theory of inefficient inhibition. *Developmental Review, 10,* 48–71.

Bjorkland, D. F., Ornstein, P. A., & Haig, J. R. (1977). Development of organization and recall: Training in the use of organizational techniques. *Developmental Psychology, 13,* 175–183.

Bjorkqvist, K. (1994). Sex differences in physical, verbal, and indirect aggression: A review of recent research. *Sex Roles, 30,* 177–188.

Black, B., & Hazen, N. L. (1990). Social status and patterns of communication in acquainted and unacquainted preschool children. *Developmental Psychology, 26,* 379–387.

Black, B., & Logan, A. (1995). Links between communication patterns in mother-child, father-child, and child-peer interactions and children's social status. *Child Development, 66,* 255–271.

Black, M. M., & Rollins, H. A., Jr. (1982). The effects of instructional variables on young children's organization and recall. *Journal of Experimental Child Psychology, 33,* 1–19.

Blackman, J. A. (1991). Neonatal intensive care: Is it worth it? *Pediatric Clinics of North America, 38,* 1497–1511.

Blake, J. (1989). Number of siblings and educational attainment. *Science, 245,* 32–36.

Blakemore, C., & Mitchell, D. E. (1973). Environmental modification of the visual cortex and the neural basis of learning and memory. *Nature* (London), *241,* 467–468.

Blampied, N. M., & France, K. G. (1993). A behavioral model of infant sleep disturbance. *Journal of Applied Behavior Analysis, 26,* 477–492.

Blasco, P. A. (1994). Primitive reflexes: Their contribution to the early detection of cerebral palsy. *Clinical Pediatrics, 33,* 388–397.

Blasi, A. (1980). Bridging moral cognition and moral action: A critical review of the literature. *Psychological Bulletin, 88,* 1–45.

Blasi, A., & Glodis, K. (1995). The development of identity: A critical analysis from the perspective of the self as subject. *Developmental Review, 15,* 404–433.

Blass, E. M., Ganchrow, J. R., & Steiner, J. E. (1984). Classical conditioning in newborn humans 2–48 hours of age. *Infant Behavior and Development, 7,* 223–235.

Blass, E. M., & Shah, A. (1995). Pain-reducing properties of sucrose in human newborns. *Chemical Senses, 20,* 29–35.

Blass, E. M., & Smith, B. A. (1992). Differential effects of sucrose, fructose, glucose, and lactose on crying in 1- to 3-day-old human infants: Qualitative and quantitative considerations. *Developmental Psychology, 28,* 804–810.

Blatt, M. M., & Kohlberg, L. (1975). The effects of classroom moral discussion upon children's level of moral judgment. *Journal of Moral Education, 4,* 129–161.

Blinkov, S. M., & Glezer, I. I. (1968). *The human brain in figures and tables: A quantitative handbook.* New York: Basic Books.

Block, J. H. (1971). *Lives through time.* Berkeley, CA: Bancroft Books.

Block, J. H. (1973). Conceptions of sex role: Some cross-cultural and longitudinal perspectives. *American Psychologist, 28,* 512–526.

Block, J. H. (1983). Differential premises arising from differential socialization of the sexes: Some conjectures. *Child Development, 54,* 1335–1354.

Block, J. H., & Block, J. (1980). The role of ego-control and ego-resiliency in the organization of behavior. In W. A. Collins (Ed.), *The Minnesota symposia on child psychology: Vol. 13. Development of cognition, affect, and social relations.* Hillsdale, NJ: Erlbaum.

Block, J. H., & Robins, R. W. (1993). A longitudinal study of consistency and change in self-esteem from early adolescence to early adulthood. *Child Development, 64,* 909–923.

Bloom, B. S. (1982). The role of gifts and markers in the development of talent. *Exceptional Children, 48,* 510–522.

Bloom, L. (1973). *One word at a time.* The Hague: Mouton.

Bloom, L. (1991). *Language development from two to three.* Cambridge, UK: Cambridge University Press.

Bloom, L., Lightbown, P., & Hood, L. (1975). Structure and variation in child language and the acquisition of grammatical morphemes. *Monographs of the Society for Research in Child Development, 40* (2, Serial No. 160).

Bloom, P. (1990). Syntactic distinctions in child language. *Journal of Child Language, 17,* 343–355.

Bock, J. K., & Hornsby, M. E. (1981). The development of directives: How children ask and tell. *Journal of Child Language, 8,* 151–163.

Boddy, J. M., & Skuse, D. H. (1994). Annotation: The process of parenting in failure to thrive. *Journal of Child Psychology and Psychiatry, 35,* 401–424.

Boehm, A. (1985). Educational applications of intelligence testing. In B. B. Wolman (Ed.), *Handbook of intelligence.* New York: Wiley.

Boehnke, K., Silbereisen, R. K., Eisenberg, N., Reykowski, J., & Palmonari, A. (1989). Developmental pattern of prosocial motivation: A cross-national study. *Journal of Cross-Cultural Psychology, 20,* 219–243.

Bogatz, G., & Ball, S. (1972). *The second year of Sesame Street: A continuing evaluation.* Princeton, NJ: Educational Testing Service.

Bohannon, J. N., & Stanowicz, L. (1988). The issue of negative evidence: Adult responses to children's language errors. *Developmental Psychology, 24,* 684–689.

Boivin, M., & Hymel, S. (1997). Peer experiences and social self-perceptions: A sequential model. *Developmental Psychology, 33,* 135–145.

Bonds, R. (1969). Growth, maturation, and performance of Philadelphia Negro and White elementary school children. Unpublished doctoral dissertation, University of Pennsylvania, Philadelphia.

Bookstein, F. L., Sampson, P. D., Streissguth, A. P., & Barr, H. M. (1996). Exploiting redundant measure of dose and developmental outcome: New methods from the behavioral teratology of alcohol. *Developmental Psychology, 32,* 404–415.

Booth, C. L., Rose-Krasnor, L., McKinnon, J., & Rubin, K. H. (1995). Predicting social adjustment in middle childhood: The role of preschool attachment security and maternal style. *Social Development, 3,* 189–204.

Borke, H. (1973). The development of empathy in Chinese and American children between three and six years of age: A cross-culture study. *Developmental Psychology, 9,* 102–108.

Borke, H. (1975). Piaget's mountains revisited: Changes in the egocentric landscape. *Developmental Psychology, 11,* 240–243.

Bornstein, M. H., & Benasich, A. A. (1986). Infant habituation: Assessments of individual differences and short-term reliability at five months. *Child Development, 57,* 87–99.

Bornstein, M. H., & Sigman, M. D. (1986). Continuity in mental development from infancy. *Child Development, 57,* 251–274.

Bornstein, M. H., Tal, J., Rahn, C., Galperín, G. Z., Pêcheux, M., Lamour, M., Toda, S., Azuma, H., Ogino, M., & Tamis-LeMonda, C. S. (1992). Functional analysis of the contents of maternal speech to infants of 5 and 13 months in four cultures: Argentina, France, Japan, and the United States. *Developmental Psychology, 28,* 593–603.

Borstelmann, L. J. (1983). Children before psychology: Ideas about children from antiquity to the late 1800s. In W. Kessen (Ed.), *Handbook of child psychology: Vol. I. History, theory, and methods.* New York: Wiley.

Bouchard, T. J., Jr. (1984). Twins reared together and apart: What they tell us about human diversity. In S. W. Fox (Ed.), *Individuality and determinism: Chemical and biological bases.* New York: Plenum Press.

Bouchard, T. J., Jr. (1994). Genes, environment, and personality. *Science, 264,* 1700–1701.

Bouchard, T. J., Jr., Lykken, D. T., McGue, M., Segal, N. L., & Tellegen, A. (1990). Sources of human psychological differences: The Minnesota Study of Twins Reared Apart. *Science, 250,* 223–228.

Boucher, J. (1981). Immediate free recall in early childhood autism: Another point of behavioral similarity with the amnesic syndrome. *British Journal of Psychology, 72,* 211–215.

Boulton, M. J., & Underwood, K. (1992). Bully/victim problems among middle school children. *British Journal of Educational Psychology, 62,* 73–87.

Bousha, D. M., & Twentyman, C. Y. (1984). Mother-child interactional style and abuse, neglect, and control groups: Naturalistic observations in the home. *Journal of Abnormal Psychology, 93,* 106–114.

Bowerman, M. (1978). The acquisition of word meaning: An investigation of some current conflicts. In N. Waterson & C. Snow (Eds.), *The development of communication.* New York: Wiley.

Bowlby, J. (1958). The nature of the child's tie to his mother. *International Journal of Psychoanalysis, 39,* 350–373.

Bowlby, J. (1969). *Attachment and loss: Vol. 1. Attachment.* New York: Basic Books.

Bowlby, J. (1973). *Attachment and loss. Vol. 2. Separation: Anxiety and anger.* New York: Basic Books.

Boyes, M. C., & Allen, S. G. (1993). Styles of parent-child interaction and moral reasoning in adolescence. *Merrill-Palmer Quarterly, 39,* 551–570.

Boykin, A. W. (1986). The triple quandary and the schooling of Afro-American children. In U. Neisser (Ed.), *The school achievement of minority children: New perspectives.* Hillsdale, NJ: Erlbaum.

Boysson-Bardies, B. de, Halle, P., Sagart, L., & Durand, C. (1989). A cross-linguistic investigation of vowel formants in babbling. *Journal of Child Language, 16,* 1–17.

Brackbill, Y. (1975). Continuous stimulation and arousal level in infancy: Effects of stimulus intensity and stress. *Child Development, 46,* 364–369.

Brackbill, Y., McManus, K., & Woodward, L. (1985). *Medication in maternity: Infant exposure and maternal information.* Ann Arbor: University of Michigan Press.

Bradbard, M. R., Martin, C. L., Endsley, R. C., & Halverson, C. F. (1986). Influence of sex stereotypes on children's exploration and memory: A competence versus performance distinction. *Developmental Psychology, 22,* 481–486

Bradley, R. H. (1989). The use of the HOME inventory in longitudinal studies of child development. In M. H. Bornstein & N. A. Krasnegor (Eds.), *Stability and continuity in mental development: Behavioral and biological perspectives.* Hillsdale, NJ: Erlbaum.

Bradley, R. H., & Caldwell, B. M. (1976). The relation of infants' home environments to mental test performance at fifty-four months: A follow-up study. *Child Development, 47,* 1172–1174.

Bradley, R. H., & Caldwell, B. M. (1984). The relation of infants' home environments to achievement test performance in first grade: A follow-up study. *Child Development, 55,* 803–809.

Braine, M. D. S. (1976). Children's first word combinations. *Monographs of the Society for Research in Child Development, 41*(1, Serial No. 164).

Brainerd, C. J. (1978a). *Piaget's theory of intelligence.* Englewood Cliffs, NJ: Prentice-Hall.

Brainerd, C. J. (1978b). The stage question in cognitive-developmental theory. *Brain and Behavioral Science, 2,* 173–213.

Brainerd, C. J. (1996). Piaget: A centennial celebration. *Psychological Science, 7,* 191–195.

Brainerd, C. J., & Reyna, V. F. (1990). Gist is the grist: Fuzzy-trace theory and the new intuitionism. *Developmental Review, 10,* 3–47.

Brainerd, C. J., & Reyna, V. F. (1992). Explaining "memory free" reasoning. *Psychological Science, 3,* 332–339.

Brainerd, C. J., & Reyna, V. F. (1993). Memory independence and memory interference in cognitive development. *Psychological Review, 100,* 42–67.

Brand, E., Clingempeel, W. E., & Bowen-Woodward, K. (1988). Family relationships and children's psychological adjustment in stepmother and stepfather families: Findings and conclusions from the Philadelphia Stepfamily Research Project. In E. M. Hetherington & J. D. Arasteh (Eds.), *Impact of divorce, single-parenting, and stepparenting on children.* Hillsdale, NJ: Erlbaum.

Bray, J. H. (1988). Children's development during early remarriage. In E. M. Hetherington & J. D. Arasteh (Eds.), *Impact of divorce, single parenting, and stepparenting on children.* Hillsdale, NJ: Erlbaum.

Brazelton, T. B. (1973). *Neonatal Behavioral Assessment Scale.* Philadelphia: J. B. Lippincott.

Brazelton, T. B., Nugent, K. J., & Lester, B. M. (1987). Neonatal Behavioral Assessment Scale. In J. D. Osofsky (Ed.), *Handbook of infant development* (2nd ed.). New York: Wiley.

Breedlove, S. M. (1994). Sexual differentiation of the human nervous system. *Annual Review of Psychology, 45,* 389–418.

Bremner, J. G. (1978). Egocentric versus allocentric spatial coding in nine-month-old infants: Factors influencing the choice of code. *Developmental Psychology, 14,* 346–355.

Bremner, J. G., & Bryant, P. E. (1977). Place versus response as the basis for spatial errors made by young infants. *Journal of Experimental Child Psychology, 23,* 162–171.

Bresnitz, Z., & Teltsch, T. (1989). The effect of school entrance age on academic achievement and social-emotional adjustment of children: Follow-up study of fourth graders. *Psychology in the Schools, 26,* 62–68.

Bretherton, I., & Beeghly, M. (1982). Talking about internal states: The acquisition of an explicit theory of mind. *Developmental Psychology, 18,* 906–921.

Broberg, A. G., Wessels, H., Lamb, M. E., & Hwang, C. P. (1997). Effects of day care on the development of cognitive abilities in 8-year-olds: A longitudinal study. *Developmental Psychology, 33,* 62–69.

Brody, E. B., & Brody, N. (1976). *Intelligence: Nature, determinants, and consequences.* New York: Academic Press.

Brody, G. H., & Forehand, R. (1986). Maternal perceptions of child maladjustment as a function of the combined influence of child behavior and maternal depression. *Journal of Consulting and Clinical Psychology, 54,* 237–240.

Brody, G. H., & Stoneman, Z. (1981). Selective imitation of same-age, older, and younger peer models. *Child Development, 52,* 717–720.

Brody, G. H., & Stoneman, Z. (1994). Sibling relationships and their association with parental differential treatment. In E. M. Hetherington, D. Reiss, & R. Plomin (Eds.), *Separate social worlds of siblings* (pp. 129–142). Hillsdale, NJ: Erlbaum.

Brody, G. H., Stoneman, Z., & Flor, D. (1996). Parental religiosity, family processes, and youth competence in rural, two-parent African American families. *Developmental Psychology, 32,* 696–706.

Brody, G. H., Stoneman, Z., & MacKinnon, C. E. (1986). Contributions of maternal child-rearing practices and play contexts to sibling interactions. *Journal of Applied Developmental Psychology, 7,* 225–236.

Brody, G. H., Stoneman, Z., & McCoy, J. K. (1992). Associations of maternal and paternal direct and differential behavior with sibling relationships: Contemporaneous and longitudinal analyses. *Child Development, 63,* 82–92.

Brody, G. H., Stoneman, Z., McCoy, J. K., & Forehand, R. (1992). Contemporaneous and longitudinal associations of sibling conflict with family relationship assessments and family discussion about sibling problems. *Child Development, 63,* 391–400.

Brody, N. (1992). *Intelligence* (2nd ed.). San Diego: Academic Press.

Brodzinsky, D. M., Schecter, D. E., Braff, A. M., & Singer, L. M. (1984). Psychological and academic adjustment in adopted children. *Journal of Consulting and Clinical Psychology, 52,* 582–590.

Bronfenbrenner, U. (1977). Toward an experimental ecology of human development. *American Psychologist, 32,* 513–531.

Bronfenbrenner, U. (1979). *The ecology of human development.* Cambridge: Harvard University Press.

Bronfenbrenner, U. (1986). Ecology of the family as a context for human development: Research perspectives. *Developmental Psychology, 22,* 723–742.

Bronfenbrenner, U. (1989). Ecological systems theory. In R. Vasta (Ed.), *Annals of child development: Vol 6. Six theories of child development: Revised formulations and current issues.* Greenwich, CT: JAI Press.

Bronfenbrenner, U. (1993). The ecology of cognitive development: Research models and fugitive findings. In R. H. Wozniak & K. W. Fischer (Eds.), *Development in context: Acting and thinking in specific environments* (pp. 3–44). Hillsdale, NJ: Erlbaum.

Bronfenbrenner, U., & Ceci, S. J. (1994). Nature-nurture reconceptualized in developmental perspective: A bioecological model. *Psychological Review, 101,* 568–586.

Bronson, G. W. (1994). Infants' transitions toward adult-like scanning. *Child Development, 65,* 1243–1261.

Bronson, W. (1981). Toddlers' behavior with age-mates: Issues of interaction, cognition, and affect. In L. Lipsitt (Ed.), *Monographs on infancy* (Vol. 1). Norwood, NJ: Ablex.

Brooks, R. B. (1992). Self-esteem during the school years: Its normal development and hazardous decline. *Pediatric Clinics of North America, 39,* 537–550.

Brooks-Gunn, J. (1984). The psychological significance of different pubertal events to young girls. *Journal of Early Adolescence, 4,* 315–327.

Brooks-Gunn, J. (1989). Pubertal processes and the early adolescent transition. In W. Damon (Ed.), *Child development today and tomorrow.* San Francisco: Jossey-Bass.

Brooks-Gunn, J., & Furstenberg, F. F. (1986). The children of adolescent mothers: Physical, academic, and psychological outcomes. *Developmental Review, 6,* 224–251.

Brooks-Gunn, J., Klebanov, P. K., & Duncan, G. J. (1996). Ethnic differences in children's intelligence test scores: Role of economic deprivation, home environment, and maternal characteristics. *Child Development, 67,* 396–408.

Brooks-Gunn, J., Klebanov, P. K., Liaw, F., & Spiker, D. (1993). Enhancing the development of low-birthweight, premature infants: Changes in cognition and behavior over the first three years. *Child Development, 64,* 736–754.

Brooks-Gunn, J., & Reiter, E. O. (1990). The role of pubertal processes. In S. S. Feldman & G. R. Elliott (Eds.), *At the threshold.* Cambridge, MA: Harvard University Press.

Brooks-Gunn, J., & Ruble, D. (1980). Menarche: The interaction of physiology, cultural, and social factors. In A. J. Dan, E. A. Graham, & C. P. Beecher (Eds.), *The menstrual cycle: A synthesis of interdisciplinary research.* New York: Springer-Verlag.

Brooks-Gunn, J., Warren, M. P., Samelson, M., & Fox, R. (1986). Physical similarity of and disclosure of menarcheal status to friends: Effects of grade and pubertal status. *Journal of Early Adolescence, 6,* 3–14.

Brophy, J. (1986). Teacher influences on student achievement. *American Psychologist, 41,* 1069–1077.

Brown, A. L. (1990). Domain-specific principles affect learning and transfer in children. *Cognitive Science, 14,* 107–133.

Brown, A. L., Campione, J. C., Ferrara, R. A., Reeve, R. A., & Palincsar, A. S. (1991). Interactive learning and individual understanding: The case of

reading and mathematics. In L. T. Landsmann (Ed.), *Culture, schooling, and psychological development.* Norwood, NJ: Ablex.

Brown, A. L., Kane, M. J., & Echols, C. H. (1986). Young children's mental models determine analogical transfer across problems with a common goal structure. *Cognitive Development, 1,* 103–121.

Brown, A. L., & Scott, M. S. (1971). Recognition memory for pictures in preschool children. *Journal of Experimental Child Psychology, 11,* 401–412.

Brown, B. B. (1989). The role of peer groups in adolescents' adjustment to secondary school. In T. J. Berndt & G. W. Ladd (Eds.), *Peer relationships in child development.* New York: Wiley.

Brown, B. B., Clasen, D. R., & Eicher, S. A. (1986). Perceptions of peer pressure, peer conformity dispositions, and self-reported behavior among adolescents. *Developmental Psychology, 22,* 521–530.

Brown, B. B., Mounts, N., Lamborn, S. D., & Steinberg, L. (1993). Parenting practices and peer group affiliation in adolescence. *Child Development, 64,* 467–482.

Brown, J. L., & Pollitt, E. (1996, February). Malnutrition, poverty and intellectual development. *Scientific American, 274,* 38–43.

Brown, J. R., & Dunn, J. (1996). Continuities in emotion understanding from three to six years. *Child Development, 67,* 789–802.

Brown, L. M., & Gilligan, C. (1992). *Meeting at the crossroads: Women's psychology and girls' development.* Cambridge, MA: Harvard University Press.

Brown, P. J., & Konner, M. (1987). An anthropological perspective on obesity. *Annals of the New York Academy of Sciences, 499,* 29–46.

Brown, R. (1973). *A first language: The early stages.* Cambridge, MA: Harvard University Press.

Brown, R., & Hanlon, C. (1970). Derivational complexity and order of acquisition in child speech. In J. R. Hayes (Ed.), *Cognition and the development of language.* New York: Wiley.

Brown, R. M., & Fishman, R. H. B. (1984). An overview and summary of the behavioral and neural consequences of perinatal exposure to psychotropic drugs. In J. Yanai (Ed.), *Neurobehavioral teratology.* New York: Elsevier.

Bruck, K. (1962). Temperature regulation in the newborn infant. *Biological Neonatorum, 3,* 65–119.

Bruck, M. (1993). Word recognition and component phonological processing skills of adults with childhood diagnosis of dyslexia. *Developmental Review, 13,* 258–268.

Bruer, J. T. (1994). Classroom problems, school culture, and cognitive research. In K. McGilly (Ed.), *Classroom lessons: Integrating cognitive theory and classroom practice.* Cambridge, MA: MIT Press.

Bruner, J. S. (1981). Intention in the structure of action and interaction. In L. P. Lipsitt (Ed.), *Advances in infancy research* (Vol. 1). Norwood, NJ: Ablex.

Bruner, J. S. (1983). *Child's talk: Learning to use language.* New York: W. W. Norton.

Bryant-Waugh, R., & Lask, B. (1995). Annotation: Eating disorders in children. *Journal of Child Psychology and Psychiatry, 36,* 191–202.

Buchanan, G. R. (1993). Sickle cell disease: Recent advances. *Current Problems in Pediatrics, 23,* 219–229.

Buhrmester, D. (1990). Intimacy of friendship, interpersonal competence, and adjustment during preadolescence and adolescence. *Child Development, 61,* 1101–1111.

Buhrmester, D., & Furman, W. (1987). The development of companionship and intimacy. *Child Development, 58,* 1101–1113.

Buhrmester, D., & Furman, W. (1990). Perceptions of sibling relationships during middle childhood and adolescence. *Child Development, 61,* 1387–1398.

Buitendijk, S., & Bracken, M. B. (1991). Medication in early pregnancy: Prevalence of use and relationship to maternal characteristics. *American Journal of Obstetrics and Gynecology, 165,* 33–40.

Bukowski, W. M., Gauze, C., Hoza, B., & Newcomb, A. F. (1993). Differences and consistency between same-sex and other-sex peer relationships during early adolescence. *Developmental Psychology, 29,* 255–263.

Bukowski, W. M., & Kramer, T. L. (1986). Judgments of the features of friendship among early adolescent boys and girls. *Journal of Early Adolescence, 6,* 331–338.

Bumpass, L. L. (1990). What's happening to the American family? Interactions between demographic and institutional change. *Demography, 27,* 483–498.

Burchinal, M. R., Follmer, A., & Bryant, D. M. (1996). The relations of maternal social support and family structure with maternal responsiveness and child outcomes among African American families. *Developmental Psychology, 32,* 1073–1083.

Burgess, R. L., & Conger, R. D. (1978). Family interaction in abusive, neglectful, and normal families. *Child Development, 49,* 1163–1173.

Burkhauser, R. V., Duncan, G. J., Hauser, R., & Bernsten, R. (1991). Wife or frau, women do worse: A comparison of men and women in the United States and Germany after marital dissolution. *Demography, 28,* 353–360.

Burnhans, K. K., & Dweck, C. S. (1995). Helplessness in early childhood: The role of contingent worth. *Child Development, 66,* 1719–1738.

Burns, A. L., Mitchell, G., & Obradovich, S. (1989). Of sex role and strollers: Female and male attention to toddlers at the zoo. *Sex Roles, 20,* 309–315.

Bushnell, E. W. (1981). The ontogeny of intermodal relations: Vision and touch in infancy. In R. D. Walk & H. L. Pick, Jr. (Eds.), *Intersensory perception and sensory integration.* New York: Plenum Press.

Bushnell, E. W. (1985). The decline of visually guided reaching during infancy. *Infant Behavior and Development, 8,* 139–155.

Bushnell, E. W., & Boudreau, J. P. (1993). Motor development and the mind: The potential role of motor abilities as a determinant of aspects of perceptual development. *Child Development, 64,* 1005–1021.

Bushnell, I. W. R., Gerry, G., & Burt, K. (1983). The externality effect in neonates. *Infant Behavior and Development, 6,* 151–156.

Bushnell, I. W. R., Sai, F., & Mullin, J. T. (1989). Neonatal recognition of the mother's face. *British Journal of Developmental Psychology, 7,* 3–15.

Buss, A. H., & Plomin, R. (1984). *Temperament: Early developing personality traits.* Hillsdale, NJ: Erlbaum.

Bussey, K., & Bandura, A. (1984). Influence of gender constancy and social power on sex-linked modeling. *Journal of Personality and Social Psychology, 47,* 1292–1302.

Bussey, K., & Bandura, A. (1992). Self-regulatory mechanisms governing gender development. *Child Development, 63,* 1236–1250.

Bussey, K., & Perry, D. G. (1982). Same-sex imitation: The avoidance of cross-sex models or the acceptance of same-sex models. *Sex Roles, 8,* 773–784.

Butler, J., Abrams, B., Parker, J., Roberts, J. M., & Laros, R. K., Jr. (1993). Supportive nurse-midwife care is associated with a reduced incidence of cesarean section. *American Journal of Obstetrics and Gynecology, 168,* 1407–1413.

Butler, N. R., & Goldstein, H. (1973). Smoking in pregnancy and subsequent child development. *British Medical Journal, 4,* 573–575.

Butler, R. (1989). Mastery versus ability appraisal: A developmental study of children's observations of peers' work. *Child Development, 60,* 1350–1361.

Butler, R. (1990). The effects of mastery and competitive conditions on self-assessment at different ages. *Child Development, 61,* 201–210.

Butler, R., & Ruzany, N. (1993). Age and socialization effects on the development of social comparison motives and normative ability assessment in kibbutz and urban children. *Child Development, 64,* 532–543.

Byers, T. (1992). The epidemic of obesity in American Indians. *American Journal of Diseases of Children, 146,* 285–286.

Byrne, B. M. (1984). The general/academic self-concept nomological network: A review of construct validation research. *Review of Educational Research, 54,* 427–456.

Byrnes, J. P., & Overton, W. F. (1988). Reasoning about logical connections: A developmental analysis. *Journal of Experimental Child Psychology, 46,* 194–218.

Caccia, N., Johnson, J. M., Robinson, G. E., & Barna, T. (1991). Impact of prenatal testing on maternal-fetal bonding: Chorionic villus sampling versus amniocentesis. *American Journal of Obstetrics and Gynecology, 165,* 1122–1125.

Cairns, R. B. (1992). The making of developmental science: The contributions and intellectual heritage of James Mark Baldwin. *Developmental Psychology, 28,* 17–24.

Cairns, R. B., & Cairns, B. D. (1994). *Lifelines and risks: Pathways of youth in our time.* Cambridge, UK: Cambridge University Press.

Cairns, R. B., Leung, M., Buchanan, L., & Cairns, B. D. (1995). Friendships and social networks in childhood and adolescence: Fluidity, reliability, and interrelations. *Child Development, 66,* 1330–1345.

Cairns, R. B., & Ornstein, P. A. (1979). Developmental psychology. In E. Hearst (Ed.), *The first century of experimental psychology.* Hillsdale, NJ: Erlbaum.

Caldwell, B. M., & Bradley, R. H. (1978). *Home Observation for Measurement of the Environment.* Little Rock: University of Arkansas.

Calkins, S. D., & Fox, N. A. (1992). The relations among infant temperament, security of attachment, and behavioral inhibition at twenty-four months. *Child Development, 63,* 1456–1472.

Calvert, S. L., Huston, A. C., Watkins, B. A., & Wright, J. C. (1982). The relationship between selective attention to televised forms and children's comprehension of content. *Child Development, 53,* 601–610.

Camara, K. A., & Resnick, G. (1988). Interparental conflict and cooperation: Factors moderating children's post-divorce adjustment. In E. M. Hetherington & J. Arasteh (Eds.), *Impact of divorce, single-parenting, and stepparenting on children.* Hillsdale, NJ: Erlbaum.

Campbell, F. A., & Ramey, C. T. (1994). Effects of early intervention on intellectual and academic achievement: A follow-up study of children from low-income families. *Child Development, 65,* 684–698.

Campbell, R., & Tuck, M. (1995). Recognition of parts of famous-face photographs by children: An experimental note. *Perception, 24,* 451–456.

Campbell, R., Walker, J., & Baron-Cohen, S. (1995). The development of differential use of inner and outer face features in familiar face identification. *Journal of Experimental Child Psychology, 59,* 196–210.

Campbell, S. B., Cohn, J. F., & Meyers, T. (1995). Depression in first-time mothers: Mother-infant interaction and depression chronicity. *Developmental Psychology, 31,* 349–357.

Campione, J. C., Brown, A. L., & Ferrara, R. A. (1982). Mental retardation and intelligence. In R. J. Sternberg (Ed.), *Handbook of human intelligence.* Cambridge, UK: Cambridge University Press.

Campione, J. C., Shapiro, A. M., & Brown, A. L. (1995). Forms of transfer in a community of learners: Flexible learning and understanding. In A. McKeough, J. Lupert, & A. Marini (Eds.), *Teaching for transfer: Fostering generalization in learning.* Hillsdale, NJ: Erlbaum.

Campos, J. J., Barrett, K. C., Lamb, M. E., Goldsmith, H. H., & Stenberg, C. (1983). Socioemotional development. In M. M. Haith & J. J. Campos (Eds.), *Handbook of child psychology: Vol. II. Infancy and developmental psychobiology.* New York: Wiley

Campos, J. J., Langer, A., & Krowitz, A. (1970). Cardiac responses on the visual cliff in prelocomotor human infants. *Science, 170,* 196–197.

Canfield, R. L., & Smith, E. G. (1996). Number-based expectations and sequential enumeration by 5-month-olds. *Developmental Psychology, 32,* 269–279.

Carey, S. (1978). The child as word learner. In M. Halle, J. Bresnan, & G. A. Miller (Eds.), *Linguistic theory and psychological reality.* Cambridge, MA: MIT Press.

Carey, S. (1985a). Are children fundamentally different thinkers and learners than adults? In S.F. Chipman, J.W. Segal, & R. Glaser (Eds.), *Thinking and learning skills* (Vol. 2). Hillsdale, NJ: Erlbaum.

Carey, S. (1985b). *Conceptual changes in childhood.* Cambridge, MA: MIT Press.

Carlo, G., Koller, S. H., Eisenberg, N., Da Silva, M. S., & Frohlich, C. B. (1996). A cross-national study on the relations among prosocial moral reasoning, gender role orientations, and prosocial behaviors. *Developmental Psychology, 32,* 231–240.

Carlson, E. A., Jacobvitz, D., & Sroufe, L. A. (1995). A developmental investigation of inattentiveness and hyperactivity. *Child Development, 66,* 37–54.

Carlson, V., Cicchetti, D., Barnett, D., & Braunwald, K. (1989). Contributions of the study of maltreated infants to the development of the disorganized ("D") type of attachment relationship. In D. Cicchetti & V. Carlson (Eds.), *Child maltreatment: Theory and research on the causes and consequences of child abuse and neglect.* Cambridge, UK: Cambridge University Press.

Carter, D. B. (1987). The roles of peers in sex role socialization. In D. B. Carter (Ed.), *Current conceptions of sex roles and sex-typing: Theory and research.* New York: Praeger.

Carter, D. B., & Levy, G. D. (1988). Cognitive aspects of early sex-role development: The influence of gender schemas on preschoolers' memories and preferences for sex-typed toys and activities. *Child Development, 59,* 782–792.

Carter, D. B., & McCloskey, L. A. (1984). Peers and the maintenance of sex-typed behavior: The development of children's understanding of cross-gender behavior in their peers. *Social Cognition, 2,* 294–314.

Casaer, P. (1993). Old and new facts about perinatal brain development. *Journal of Child Psychology and Psychiatry, 34,* 101–109.

Case, R. (1985). *Intellectual development: A systematic reinterpretation.* New York: Academic Press.

Case, R. (1992). *The mind's staircase: Exploring the conceptual underpinnings of children's thought and knowledge.* Hillsdale, NJ: Erlbaum.

Case, R., Kurland, D. M., & Goldberg, J. (1982). Operational efficiency and the growth of short term memory span. *Journal of Experimental Child Psychology, 33,* 386–404.

Casey, R. J. (1993). Children's emotional experience: Relations among expression, self-report, and understanding. *Developmental Psychology, 29,* 119–129.

Caspi, A., Henry, B., McGee, R. O., Moffitt, T. E., & Silva, P. A. (1995). Temperamental origins of child and adolescent behavior problems: From age three to age fifteen. *Child Development, 66,* 55–68.

Cassel, W. S., Roebers, C. E. M., & Bjorkland, D. F. (1996). Developmental patterns of eyewitness responses to repeated and increasingly suggestive questions. *Journal of Experimental Child Psychology, 61,* 116–133.

Cassidy, J., & Asher, S. R. (1992). Loneliness and peer relations in young children. *Child Development, 63,* 350–365.

Cassidy, J., Kirsh, S. J., Scolton, K. L., & Parke, R. D. (1996). Attachment and representations of peer relationships. *Developmental Psychology, 32,* 892–904.

Cattell, J. M. (1890). Mental tests and measurements. *Mind, 15,* 373–381.

Cattell, R. B. (1971). *Abilities: Their structure, growth, and action.* Boston: Houghton Mifflin.

Catts, H. W. (1993). The relationship between speech-language impairments and reading disabilities. *Journal of Speech and Hearing Research, 36,* 948–958.

Cauffman, E., & Steinberg, L. (1996). Interactive effects of menarcheal status and dating on dieting and disordered eating among adolescent girls. *Developmental Psychology, 32,* 631–635.

Cavior, N., & Dokecki, P. R. (1973). Physical attractiveness, perceived attitude similarity, and academic achievement as contributors to interpersonal attraction among adolescents. *Developmental Psychology, 9,* 44–54.

Ceci, S. J. (1990). *On intelligence . . . more or less: A bio-ecological treatise on intellectual development.* Englewood Cliffs, NJ: Prentice Hall.

Ceci, S. J. (1991). How much does schooling influence general intelligence and its cognitive components? A reassessment of the evidence. *Developmental Psychology, 27,* 703–722.

Ceci, S. J., & Bruck, M. (1993). Suggestability of the child witness: A historical review and synthesis. *Psychological Bulletin, 113,* 403–439.

Ceci, S. J., Ross, D. F., & Toglia, M. P. (1987). Suggestibility of children's memory: Psychological implications. *Journal of Experimental Psychology: General, 116,* 38–49.

Centers for Disease Control. (1991). Premarital sexual experience among adolescent women—United States, 1970–1988. *Morbidity and Mortality Weekly Report, 39,* 929–932.

Centers for Disease Control (1992). Youth suicide prevention programs: A resource guide. Atlanta: U.S. Department of Health and Human Services, Public Health Service.

Centers for Disease Control (1993). Rates of Cesarean delivery—United States 1991. *Morbidity and Mortality Weekly Report, 42,* 285–289.

Centers for Disease Control (1995a). Trends in sexual risk behavior among high school students—United States, 1990, 1991, and 1993. *Morbidity and Mortality Weekly Report, 44,* 124–125, 131–132.

Centers for Disease Control (1995b). Update: Trends in fetal alcohol syndrome—United States, 1979–1993. *Morbidity and Mortality Weekly Report, 44,* 249–251.

Cernoch, J. M., & Porter, R. H. (1985). Recognition of maternal axillary odors by infants. *Child Development, 56,* 1593–1598.

Chao, R. K. (1994). Beyond parental control and authoritarian parenting style: Understanding Chinese parenting through the cultural notion of training. *Child Development, 65,* 1111–1119.

Chapman, M., Skinner, E. A., & Baltes, P. B. (1990). Interpreting correlations between children's perceived control and cognitive performance: Control, agency, or means-ends beliefs? *Developmental Psychology, 26,* 246–253.

Chapman, M., & Zahn-Waxler, C. (1981). *Young children's compliance and noncompliance to parental discipline in a natural setting.* Unpublished manuscript.

Chase-Lansdale, P. L., Cherlin, A. J., & Kiernan, K. E. (1995). The long-term effects of parental divorce on the mental health of young adults: A developmental perspective. *Child Development, 66,* 1614–1634.

Chasnoff, I. J. (1986). Perinatal addiction: Consequences of intrauterine exposure to opiate and nonopiate drugs. In I. J. Chasnoff (Ed.), *Drug use in pregnancy: Mother and child.* Lancaster, England: MTP Press.

Chasnoff, I. J. (1992). Cocaine, pregnancy, and the growing child. *Current Problems in Pediatrics, 22,* 302–321.

Chen, C., & Stevenson, H. W. (1995). Motivation and mathematics achievement: A comparative study of Asian-American, Caucasian-American, and East Asian high school students. *Child Development, 66,* 1215–1234.

Chen, X., Rubin, K. H., & Li, Z. (1995). Social functioning and adjustment in Chinese children: A longitudinal study. *Developmental Psychology, 31,* 531–539.

Chen, Z. (1996). Children's analogical problem solving: The effects of superficial, structural, and procedural similarity. *Journal of Experimental Child Psychology, 62,* 410–431.

Chen, Z., & Daehler, M. W. (1989). Positive and negative transfer in analogical problem-solving by 6-year-olds. *Cognitive Development, 4,* 327–344.

Cherlin, A. J. (1992). *Marriage, divorce, remarriage* (Rev. ed.). Cambridge, MA: Harvard University Press.

Chess, S., & Thomas, A. (1982). Infant bonding: Mystique and reality. *American Journal of Orthopsychiatry, 52,* 213–222.

Chess, S., & Thomas, A. (1986). Developmental issues. In S. Chess & A. Thomas (Eds.), *Annual progress in child psychiatry and child development.* New York: Brunner/Mazel.

Chess, S., & Thomas, A. (1990). Continuities and discontinuities in temperament. In L. N. Robins & M. Rutter (Eds.). *Straight and devious pathways from childhood to adolescence.* Cambridge, UK: Cambridge University Press.

Chess, S., & Thomas, A. (1991). Temperament and the concept of goodness of fit. In J. Strelau & A. Angleitner (Eds.), *Explorations in temperament: International perspectives on theory and measurement.* New York: Plenum.

Chi, M. T. H. (1978). Knowledge structure and memory development. In R. Siegler (Ed.), *Children's thinking: What develops?* Hillsdale, NJ: Erlbaum.

Chibucos, T., & Kail, P. R. (1981). Longitudinal examination of father-infant interaction and infant-father interaction. *Merrill-Palmer Quarterly, 27,* 81–96.

Children's Defense Fund. (1996). *The state of America's children: Yearbook.* Washington, DC: Author.

Chiu, L. H. (1992–93). Self-esteem in American and Chinese (Taiwanese) children. *Current Psychology: Research & Reviews, 11,* 309–313.

Choi, S., & Gopnik, A. (1995). Early acquisition of verbs in Korean: A cross-linguistic study. *Journal of Child Language, 22,* 497–529.

Chomsky, N. (1980). *Rules and representations.* New York: Columbia University Press.

Chomsky, N. (1986). *Knowledge of language: Its nature, origin, and use.* New York: Praeger.

Christenson, P. G. (1982). Children's perceptions of TV commercials and products: The effects of PSAs. *Communication Research, 9,* 491–524.

Chugani, H. T. (1994). Development of regional brain glucose metabolism in relation to behavior and plasticity. In G. Dawson & K. Fischer (Eds.), *Human behavior and the developing brain* (pp. 153–175). New York: Guilford.

Cicchetti, D., Toth, S. L., & Lynch, M. (1995). Bowlby's dream comes full circle: The application of attachment theory to risk and psychopathology. *Advances in Clinical Child Psychology, 17,* 1–75.

Clark, E. V. (1973). What's in a word? On the child's acquisition of semantics in his first language. In T. E. Moore (Ed.), *Cognitive development and the acquisition of language.* New York: Academic Press.

Clark, J. E. (1988). Development of voluntary motor skill. In E. Meisami & P. S. Timiras (Eds.), *Handbook of human growth and developmental biology* (Vol. 1, part B). Boca Raton, FL: CRC Press.

Clarke-Stewart, K. A. (1989). Infant day care: Maligned or malignant? *American Psychologist, 44,* 266–273.

Clarke-Stewart, K. A. (1993). *Daycare* (Rev. ed.). Cambridge, MA: Harvard University Press.

Clarke-Stewart, K. A., & Fein, G. G. (1983). Early childhood programs. In M. M. Haith & J. J. Campos (Eds.), *Handbook of child psychology: Vol. II. Infancy and developmental psychobiology.* New York: Wiley.

Clarke-Stewart, K. A., & Hayward, C. (1996). Advantages of father custody and contact for the psychological well-being of school-age children. *Journal of Applied Developmental Psychology, 17,* 239–270.

Clarkson, M. G. (1996). Infants' intensity discrimination: Spectral profiles. *Infant Behavior and Development, 19,* 181–190.

Clarren, S. K., Alvord, E. C., Suni, S. M., & Streissguth, A. P. (1978). Brain malformations related to prenatal exposure to ethanol. *Journal of Pediatrics, 92,* 64–67.

Clasen, D. R., & Brown, B. B. (1985). The multidimensionality of peer pressure in adolescence. *Journal of Youth and Adolescence, 14,* 451–468.

Clements, D. H. (1986). Effects of Logo and CAI environments on cognition and creativity. *Journal of Educational Psychology, 78,* 309–318.

Clements, D. H., & Gullo, D. F. (1984). Effects of computer programming on young children's cognition. *Journal of Educational Psychology, 76,* 1051–1058.

Clifton, R., Muir, D. W., Ashmead, D. H., & Clarkson, M. G. (1993). Is visually guided reaching in early infancy a myth? *Child Development, 64,* 1099–1110.

Clifton, R., Perris, E., & Bullinger, A. (1991). Infants' perception of auditory space. *Developmental Psychology, 27,* 187–197.

Cliver, S. P., Goldenberg, R. L., Cutter, G. R., Hoffman, H. J., Davis, R. O., & Nelson, K. G. (1995). The effect of cigarette smoking on neonatal anthropometric measurements. *Obstetrics & Gynecology, 85,* 625–630.

Cobb, H. V. (1954). Role wishes and general wishes of children and adolescents. *Child Development, 25,* 161–171.

Cohen, E. G. (1994). Restructuring the classroom: Conditions for productive small groups. *Review of Education Research, 64,* 1–35.

Cohen, L., & Campos, J. (1974). Father, mother and stranger as elicitors of attachment behaviors in infancy. *Developmental Psychology, 10,* 146–154.

Cohen, L. B., & Oakes, L. M. (1993). How infants perceive a simple causal event. *Developmental Psychology, 29,* 421–433.

Cohen, R. L. (1966). Experimental and clinical chemateratogenesis. *Advances in Pharmacology, 4,* 263–349.

Cohn, J. F., Matias, R., Tronick, E. Z., Connell, D., & Lyons-Ruth, D. (1986). Face-to-face interactions of depressed mothers and their infants. In E. Z. Tronick & T. M. Field (Eds.), *New directions for child development: No. 34. Maternal depression and infant disturbance.* San Francisco: Jossey-Bass.

Cohn, J. F., & Tronick, E. Z. (1983). Three-month-old infants' reaction to simulated maternal depression. *Child Development, 54,* 185–193.

Cohn, J. F., & Tronick, E. Z. (1987). Mother-infant face-to-face interaction: The sequence of dyadic states at 3, 6, and 9 months. *Developmental Psychology, 23,* 68–77.

Coie, J. D., & Dodge, K. A. (1988). Multiple sources of data on social behavior and social status in the school: A cross-age comparison. *Child Development, 59,* 815–829.

Coie, J. D., Dodge, K. A., & Coppotelli, H. (1982). Dimensions and types of social status: A cross-age perspective. *Developmental Psychology, 18,* 557–570.

Colby, A., Kohlberg, L., Gibbs, J., & Lieberman, M. (1983). A longitudinal study of moral judgment. *Monographs of the Society for Research in Child Development, 48*(1–2, Serial No. 200).

Cole, P. M., Zahn-Waxler, C., & Smith, K. D. (1994). Expressive control during a disappointment: Variations related to preschoolers' behavior problems. *Developmental Psychology, 30,* 835–846.

Collaer, M. L., & Hines, M. (1995). Human behavioral sex differences: A role for gonadal hormones during early development? *Psychological Bulletin, 118,* 55–107.

Collins, J. A. (1995). A couple with infertility. *Journal of the American Medical Association, 274,* 1159–1164.

Collins, P. A., Wright, J. C., Anderson, D. R., Huston, A. C., Schmitt, K., & McElroy, E. S. (1997). Effects of early childhood media use on adolescent achievement. Paper presented at Biennial Meetings of the Society for Research in Child Development. Washington, DC.

Collins, W. A. (1983). Social antecedents, cognitive processing, and comprehension of social portrayals on television. In E. T. Higgins, D. N. Ruble, & W. W. Hartup (Eds.), *Social cognition and social development.* Cambridge, UK: Cambridge University Press.

Collins, W. A., Wellman, H., Keniston, A. H., & Westby, S. D. (1978). Age-related aspects of comprehension and inference from a televised dramatic narrative. *Child Development, 49,* 389–399.

Collis, B., & Ollila, L. (1990). The effects of computer use on grade 1 children's gender stereotypes about reading, writing, and computer use. *Journal of Research and Development in Education, 24,* 14–20.

Colombo, J. (1993). *Infant cognition: Predicting later intellectual functioning.* Thousand Oaks, CA: Sage.

Colombo, J., Mitchell, D. W., Coldren, J. T., & Freeseman, L. J. (1991). Individual differences in infant visual attention: Are short lookers faster processors or feature processors? *Child Development, 62,* 1247–1257.

Committee on Genetics. (1994). American Academy of Pediatrics: Prenatal genetic diagnosis for pediatricians. *Pediatrics, 93,* 1010–1014.

Committee on Genetics. (1996). Newborn screening fact sheet. *Pediatrics, 98,* 473–501.

Condry, S. M., Condry, J. C., & Pogatshynik, L. W. (1978, August). *Sex differences: A study of the ear of the beholder.* Paper presented at the annual meeting of the American Psychological Association, Toronto.

Conger, R. D., Conger, K. J., Elder, G. H., Jr., Lorenz, F. O., Simons, R. L., & Whitbeck, L. B. (1992). A family process model of economic hardship and adjustment of early adolescent boys. *Child Development, 63,* 526–541.

Connolly, K., & Elliott, J. (1972). The evolution and ontogeny of hand function. In N. B. Jones (Ed.), *The growth of competence.* Cambridge, UK: Cambridge University Press.

Connors, F., & Olson, R. K. (1990). Reading comprehension in dyslexic and normal readers: A component-skills analysis. In D. A. Balota, G. B. Flores d'Arcais, & K. Rayner (Eds.), *Comprehension processes in reading.* Hillsdale, NJ: Erlbaum.

Cook, E. T., Greenberg, M. T., & Kusche, C. (1994). The relations between emotional understanding, intellectual functioning, and disruptive behavior problems in elementary-school-aged children. *Journal of Abnormal Child Psychology, 22,* 205–219.

Cooley, C. H. (1902). *Human nature and the social order.* New York: Scribner's.

Cooper, J., Hall, J., & Huff, C. (1990). Situational stress as a consequence of sex-stereotyped software. *Personality and Social Psychology Bulletin, 16,* 419–429.

Copper, R. L., Goldenberg, R. L., Cliver, S. P., DuBard, M. B., Hoffman, H. J., & Davis, R. O. (1993). Anthropometric assessment of body size differences of full-term male and female infants. *Obstetrics and Gynecology, 81,* 161–164.

Cornell, E. H. (1975). Infants' visual attention to pattern arrangement and orientation. *Child Development, 46,* 229–232.

Cornell, E. H., Heth, C. D., & Rowat, W. L. (1992). Wayfinding by children and adults: Response to instructions to use look-back and retrace strategies. *Developmental Psychology, 28,* 328–336.

Corrigan, R. (1979). Cognitive correlates of language: Differential criteria yield differential results. *Child Development, 50,* 617–631.

Costanzo, P. R., & Woody, E. Z. (1979). Externality as a function of obesity in children: Pervasive style or eating-specific attribute? *Journal of Personality and Social Psychology, 37,* 2286–2296.

Cournoyer, M., & Trudel, M. (1991). Behavioral correlates of self-control at 33 months. *Infant Behavior and Development, 14,* 497–503.

Coustan, D. R., & Felig, P. (1988). Diabetes mellitus. In G. N. Burrow & T. F. Ferris (Eds.), *Medical complications during pregnancy* (3rd ed.). Philadelphia: W. B. Saunders.

Cowan, W. M. (1979, September). The development of the brain. *Scientific American, 241,* 113–133.

Cox, M. J., Owen, T. J., Henderson, V. K., & Margand, N. A. (1992). Prediction of infant-father and infant-mother interaction. *Developmental Psychology, 28,* 474–483.

Cox, M. J., Owen, M. T., Lewis, J. M., & Henderson, V. K. (1989). Marriage, adult adjustment, and early parenting. *Child Development, 60,* 1015–1024.

Crain, W. C. (1992). *Theories of development: Concepts and applications* (3rd ed.). Englewood Cliffs, NJ: Prentice-Hall.

Crain-Thoreson, C., & Dale, P. S. (1992). Do early talkers become early readers? Linguistic precocity, preschool language, and emergent literacy. *Developmental Psychology, 28,* 421–429.

Crandall, R. (1973). The measurement of self-esteem and related concepts. In J. P. Robinson & P. R. Shaver (Eds.), *Measures of social psychological attitudes* (rev. ed.). Ann Arbor: Institute for Social Research.

Crandall, V. C. (1969). Sex differences in expectancy of intellectual and academic reinforcement. In C. P. Smith (Ed.), *Achievement-related motives in children.* New York: Russell Sage.

Cratty, B. J. (1986). *Perceptual and motor development in infants and children* (3rd ed.). Englewood Cliffs, NJ: Prentice-Hall.

Crick, N. R., & Dodge, K. A. (1996). Social information-processing mechanisms in reactive and proactive aggression. *Child Development, 67,* 993–1002.

Crick, N. R., & Grotpeter, J. K. (1995). Relational aggression, gender, and social-psychological adjustment. *Child Development, 66,* 710–722.

Crick, N. R., & Ladd, G. W. (1993). Children's perceptions of their peer experiences: Attributions, loneliness, social anxiety, and social avoidance. *Developmental Psychology, 29,* 244–254.

Crockenberg, S., & Litman, C. (1990). Autonomy as competence in 2-year-olds: Maternal correlates of child defiance, compliance, and self-assertion. *Developmental Psychology, 26,* 961–971.

Crockenberg, S., & Litman, C. (1991). Effects of maternal employment on maternal and two-year-old child behavior. *Child Development, 62,* 930–953.

Crockett, L., Losoff, M., & Petersen, A. C. (1984). Perceptions of the peer group and friendship in early adolescence. *Journal of Early Adolescence, 4,* 155–181.

Crook, C. (1992). Cultural artifacts in social development: The case of computers. In H. McGurk, (Ed.), *Childhood social development: Contemporary perspectives.* Hove, UK: Erlbaum.

Cross, J. C., Werb, Z., & Fisher, S. J. (1994). Implantation and the placenta: Key pieces of the development puzzle. *Science, 266,* 1508–1518.

Crouter, A. C., Manke, B. A., & McHale, S. M. (1995). The family context of gender intensification in early adolescence. *Child Development, 66,* 317–329.

Csikszentmihalyi, M., & Larson, R. (1984). *Being adolescent.* New York: Basic Books.

Cummings, E. M. (1995). Security, emotionality, and parental depression: A commentary. *Developmental Psychology, 31,* 425–427.

Cummings, E. M., Iannotti, R. J., & Zahn-Waxler, C. (1985). Influence of conflict between adults on the emotions and aggression of young children. *Developmental Psychology, 21,* 495–507.

Cummings, E. M., Zahn-Waxler, C., & Radke-Yarrow, C. (1981). Young children's responses to expressions of anger and affection by others in the family. *Child Development, 52,* 1274–1282.

Cummings, W. K. (1988). Policy options for values education. In W. K. Cummings, S. Gopinathan, & Y. Tomodu (Eds.), *The revival of values education in Asia and the West.* New York: Pergamon.

Cunningham, J. D. (1993). Experiences of Australian mothers who gave birth either at home, at a birth centre, or in hospital labour wards. *Social Science and Medicine, 36,* 475–483.

Curtis, L. E., Siegel, A. W., & Furlong, N. E. (1981). Developmental differences in cognitive mapping: Configurational knowledge of familiar large-scale environments. *Journal of Experimental Child Psychology, 31,* 456–469.

Curtiss, S. (1977). *Genie: A psycholinguistic study of a modern-day "wild child."* New York: Academic Press.

Daehler, M. W., & Bukatko, D. (1977). Recognition memory for pictures in very young children: Evidence from attentional preferences using a continuous presentation procedure. *Child Development, 48,* 693–696.

Dahl, R. E., Scher, M. S., Williamson, D. E., Robles, N., & Day, N. (1995). A longitudinal study of prenatal marijuana use: Effects on sleep and arousal at age 3 years. *Archives of Pediatric and Adolescent Medicine, 149,* 145–150.

Dalterio, S., & Bartke, A. (1979). Perinatal exposure to cannabinoids alters male reproductive function in mice. *Science, 205,* 1420–1422.

Damon, W. (1983). *Social and personality development: Infancy through adolescence.* New York: W. W. Norton.

Damon, W., & Hart, D. (1988). *Self-understanding in childhood and adolescence.* New York: Cambridge University Press.

Daniels, K. (1989). Waterbirth: The newest form of safe, gentle and joyous birth. *Journal of Nurse-Midwifery, 34,* 198–205.

Dark, V. J., & Benbow, C. P. (1993). Cognitive differences among the gifted: A review and new data. In D. K. Detterman (Ed.), *Current topics in human intelligence. Vol. 3. Individual differences and cognition.* Norwood, NJ: Ablex.

Darwin, C. (1872). *The expression of emotions in man and animals.* London: John Murray.

Darwin, C. (1877). A biographical sketch of an infant. *Mind, 2,* 285–294.

Dasen, P. R. (1972). Cross-cultural Piagetian research: A summary. *Journal of Cross-Cultural Psychology, 3,* 23–39.

Davis, B. G., Trimble, C. S., & Vincent, D. R. (1980). Does age of entrance affect school achievement? *The Elementary School Journal, 80,* 133–143.

Dawson, G. (1994). Development of emotion expression and emotion regulation in infancy. In G. Dawson & K. W. Fischer (Eds.), *Human behavior and the developing brain.* New York: Guilford.

de Gaston, J. F., Jensen, L., & Weed, S. (1995). A closer look at adolescent sexual activity. *Journal of Youth and Adolescence, 24,* 465–479.

de Villiers, P. A., & de Villiers, J. G. (1979). Form and function in the development of sentence negation. *Papers and Reports in Child Language, 17,* 57–64.

Deák, G. O., & Bauer, P. J. (1996). The dynamics of preschoolers' categorization choices. *Child Development, 67,* 740–767.

Deater-Deckard, K., Dodge, K. A., Bates, J. E., & Pettit, G. S. (1996). Physical discipline among African American and European American mothers: Links to children's externalizing behaviors. *Developmental Psychology, 32,* 1065–1072.

Deaux, K. (1993). Commentary: Sorry, wrong number—a reply to Gentile's call. *Psychological Science, 4,* 125–126.

DeBaryshe, B. D. (1993). Joint picture-book reading correlates of early oral language skill. *Journal of Child Language, 20,* 455–461.

DeBaryshe, B. D., Patterson, G. R., & Capaldi, D. M. (1993). A performance model for academic achievement in early adolescent boys. *Developmental Psychology, 29,* 795–804.

DeCasper, A. J., & Fifer, W. P. (1980). Of human bonding: Newborns prefer their mothers' voices. *Science, 208,* 1174–1176.

DeCasper, A. J., Lecanuet, J.-P., Busnel, M.-C., Granier-Deferre, C., & Maugeais, R. (1994). Fetal reactions to recurrent maternal speech. *Infant Behavior and Development, 17,* 159–164.

DeCasper, A. J., & Spence, M. J. (1986). Prenatal maternal speech influences newborns' perception of speech sounds. *Infant Behavior and Development, 9,* 133–150.

Declercq, E. R. (1993). Where babies are born and who attends their births: Findings from the revised 1989 United States Standard Certificate of Live Birth. *Obstetrics and Gynecology, 81,* 997–1004.

DeFries, J. C., Gervais, M. C., & Thomas, E. A. (1978). Response to 30 generations of selection for open-field activity in laboratory mice. *Behavior Genetics, 8,* 3–13.

Dekovic, M., & Janssens, J. (1992). Parents' child-rearing style and child's sociometric status. *Developmental Psychology, 28,* 925–932.

DeLisi, R., & Gallagher, A. M. (1991). Understanding of gender stability and constancy in Argentinian children. *Merrill-Palmer Quarterly, 37,* 483–502.

DeLoache, J. (1987). Rapid change in the symbolic functioning of young children. *Science, 238,* 1556–1557.

Demany, L., McKenzie, B., & Vurpillot, E. (1977). Rhythm perception in early infancy. *Nature, 266,* 718–719.

Demetras, M., Post, K., & Snow, C. (1986). Feedback to first language learners: The role of repetitions and clarification questions. *Journal of Child Language, 13,* 275–292.

Demmler, G. J. (1991). Summary of a workshop on surveillance for congenital cytomegalovirus disease. *Review of Infectious Diseases, 13,* 315–329.

Dempster, F. N. (1981). Memory span: Sources of individual and developmental differences. *Psychological Bulletin, 89,* 63–100.

Denham, S. A., McKinley, M., Couchoud, E. A., & Holt, R. (1990). Emotional and behavioral predictors of preschool ratings. *Child Development, 61,* 1145–1152.

Denham, S. A., Zoller, D., & Couchoud, E. A. (1994). Socialization of preschoolers' emotion understanding. *Developmental Psychology, 30,* 928–936.

Dennis, W. (1960). Causes of retardation among institutional children: Iran. *Journal of Genetic Psychology, 96,* 47–59.

Dennis, W., & Dennis, M. G. (1940). The effect of cradling practices upon the onset of walking in Hopi children. *Journal of Genetic Psychology, 56,* 77–86.

Depner, C. E. (1994). Revolution and reassessment: Child custody in context. In A. E. Gottfried, & A. W. Gottfried (Eds.), *Redefining families: Implications for children's development.* New York: Plenum.

DeRosier, M. E., Cillessen, A. H. N., Coie, J. D., & Dodge, K. A. (1994). Group social context and children's aggressive behavior. *Child Development, 65,* 1068–1079.

DeRosier, M. E., Kupersmidt, J. B., & Patterson, C. J. (1994). Children's academic and behavioral adjustment as a function of the chronicity and proximity of peer rejection. *Child Development, 65,* 1799–1813.

Desmond, M. M., Rudolph, A. J., & Phitakspghraiwan, P. (1963). The clinical behavior of the newly born. *Journal of Pediatrics, 63,* 307–325.

Desrochers, S., Ricard, M., Decarie, T. G., & Allard, L. (1994). Developmental synchrony between social referencing and Piagetian sensorimotor causality. *Infant Behavior and Development, 17,* 303–309.

Deur, J. L., & Parke, R. D. (1970). Effects of inconsistent punishment on aggression in children. *Developmental Psychology, 2,* 403–411.

Deutsch, M., Katz, I., & Jensen, A. R. (1968). *Social class, race, and psychological development.* New York: Holt, Rinehart & Winston.

Devoe, L. D., Murray, C., Youssif, A., & Arnaud, M. (1993). Maternal caffeine consumption and fetal behavior in normal third-trimester pregnancy. *American Journal of Obstetrics and Gynecology, 168,* 1105–1112.

Diamond, A. (1985). The development of the ability to use recall to guide action as indicated by infants' performance on A$\overline{\text{B}}$. *Child Development, 56,* 868–883.

Diamond, A. (1991). Neuropsychological insights into the meaning of object concept development. In S. Carey & R. Gelman (Eds.), *The epigenesis of mind: Essays on biology and cognition.* Hillsdale, NJ: Erlbaum.

Diamond, A. (1993, March). *Nature and causes of cognitive deficits in phenylketonuria (PKU) even with dietary treatment: Longitudinal study and animal model.* Paper presented at the 60th semiannual meeting of the Society for Research in Child Development, New Orleans, LA.

Diamond, A., Cruttenden, L., & Neiderman, D. (1994). A$\overline{\text{B}}$ with multiple wells: 1. Why are multiple wells sometimes easier than two wells? 2. Memory or memory + inhibition? *Developmental Psychology, 30,* 192–205.

Diamond, A., & Goldman-Rakic, P. S. (1989). Comparison of human infants and rhesus monkeys on Piaget's AB̄ task: Evidence for dependence on dorsolateral prefrontal cortex. *Experimental Brain Research, 74,* 24–40.

Diaz, R. M., & Klingler, C. (1991). Towards an explanatory model of the interaction between bilingualism and cognitive development. In E. Bialystok (Ed.), *Language processing in bilingual children.* Cambridge, UK: Cambridge University Press.

Diaz, R. M., Neal, C. J., & Vachio, A. (1991). Maternal teaching in the zone of the proximal development: A comparison of low- and high-risk dyads. *Merrill-Palmer Quarterly, 37,* 83–108.

Dick-Read, G. (1959). *Childbirth without fear.* New York: Harper & Row.

Dien, D. S. (1982). A Chinese perspective on Kohlberg's theory of moral development. *Developmental Review, 2,* 331–341.

Dion, K. K., & Berscheid, E. (1974). Physical attractiveness and peer perception among children. *Sociometry, 37,* 1–12.

Dishion, T. J., Andrews, D. W., & Crosby, L. (1995). Anti-social boys and their friends in early adolescence: Relationship characteristics, quality, and interactional process. *Child Development, 66,* 139–151.

Dishion, T. J., Patterson, G. R., & Griesler, P. C. (1994). Peer adaptations in the development of antisocial behavior: A confluence model. In L. R. Huesmann (Ed.), *Aggressive behavior: Current perspectives.* New York: Plenum.

DiVitto, B., & Goldberg, S. (1979). The effect of newborn medical status on early parent-infant interactions. In T. M. Field, A. M. Sostek, S. Goldberg, & H. H. Shuman (Eds.), *Infants born at risk.* New York: S. P. Medical & Scientific Books.

Dix, T. H., & Grusec, J. E. (1985). Parent attribution processes in the socialization of children. In I. E. Sigel (Ed.), *Parental belief systems: The psychological consequences for children.* Hillsdale, NJ: Erlbaum.

Dix, T. H., Ruble, D. N., Grusec, J. E., & Nixon, S. (1986). Social cognition in parents: Inferential and affective reactions to children of three age levels. *Child Development, 57,* 879–894.

Dix, T. H., Ruble, D. N., & Zambarano, R. J. (1989). Mothers' implicit theories of discipline: Child effects, parent effects, and the attribution process. *Child Development, 60,* 1373–1391.

Dixon, S., Tronick, E., Keeler, C., & Brazelton, T. B. (1981). Mother-infant interaction among the Gusii of Kenya. In T. M. Field, A. M. Sosteck, P. Vietze, & P. H. Leiderman (Eds.), *Culture and early interactions.* Hillsdale, NJ: Erlbaum.

Dodge, K. A. (1986). A social information processing model of social competence in children. In M. Perlmutter (Ed.), *The Minnesota symposia on child psychology: Vol. 18. Cognitive perspectives on children's social and behavioral development.* Hillsdale, NJ: Erlbaum.

Dodge, K. A., Murphy, R. R., & Buchsbaum, K. (1984). The assessment of intention-cue detection skills in children: Implications for developmental psychopathology. *Child Development, 55,* 163–173.

Dodge, K. A., Pettit, G. S., & Bates, J. E. (1994). Socialization mediators of the relation between socioeconomic status and child conduct problems. *Child Development, 65,* 649–665.

Dodge, K. A., Pettit, G. S., McClaskey, C. L., & Brown, M. M. (1986). Social competence in children. *Monographs of the Society for Research in Child Development, 51*(2, Serial No. 213).

Dodge, K. A., Schlundt, D. C., Schocken, I., & Delugach, J. D. (1983). Social competence and children's sociometric status: The role of peer group entry strategies. *Merrill-Palmer Quarterly, 29,* 309–336.

Dodge, K. A., & Somberg, D. R. (1987). Hostile attributional biases among aggressive boys are exacerbated under conditions of threats to self. *Child Development, 58,* 213–224.

Dodwell, P. C., Humphrey, G. K., & Muir, D. W. (1987). Shape and pattern perception. In P. Salapatek & L. Cohen (Eds.), *Handbook of infant perception: From perception to cognition* (Vol. 2). Orlando, FL: Academic Press.

Doherty, W. J., & Needle, R. H. (1991). Psychological adjustment and substance use among adolescents before and after parental divorce. *Child Development, 62,* 328–337.

Donnelly, M., & Wilson, R. (1994). The dimensions of depression in early adolescence. *Personality and Individual Differences, 17,* 425–430.

Dornbusch, S. M., Ritter, P. L., Leiderman, P. H., Roberts, D. F., & Fraleigh, M. J. (1987). The relation of parenting style to adolescent school performance. *Child Development, 58,* 1244–1257.

Dorr, A. (1983). No shortcuts to judging reality. In J. Bryant & D. R. Anderson (Eds.), *Children's understanding of television: Research on attention and comprehension.* New York: Academic Press.

Dorr, A. (1986). *Television and children: A special medium for a special audience.* Beverly Hills: Sage.

Doty, R. L., Shaman, P., Applebaum, S. L., Giberson, R., Sikorski, L., & Rosenberg, L. (1984). Smell identification ability: Changes with age. *Science, 226,* 141–143.

Dougherty, T. M., & Haith, M. M. (1997). Infant expectations and reaction time as predictors of childhood speed of processing and IQ. *Developmental Psychology, 33,* 146–155.

Downey, G., Feldman, S., Khuri, J., & Friedman, S. (1994). Maltreatment and childhood depression. In W. M. Reynolds & H. F. Johnston (Eds.), *Handbook of depression in children and adolescents: Issues in clinical child psychology.* New York: Plenum.

Downey, W. E. (1996, August 28). Teaching values: A controversial plan in Germany. *Christian Century, 113,* p. 804–805.

Dreher, M. C., Nugent, K., & Hudgins, R. (1994). Prenatal marijuana exposure and neonatal outcomes in Jamaica: An ethnographic study. *Pediatrics, 93,* 254–260.

Drotar, D. (1991). The family context of nonorganic failure to thrive. *American Journal of Orthopsychiatry, 61,* 23–34.

Drug and Therapeutics Committee of the Lawson Wilkins Pediatric Endocrine Society. (1995). Guidelines for the use of growth hormone in children with short stature. *Journal of Pediatrics, 127,* 857–867.

Dubow, E. F., Tisak, J., Causey, D., Hryshko, A., & Reid, G. (1991). A two-year longitudinal study of stressful life events, social support, and social problem-solving skills: Contributions to children's behavioral and academic adjustment. *Child Development, 62,* 583–599.

Dugan, E., Kamps, D., Leonard, B., Watkins, N., Rheinberger, A., & Stackhaus, J. (1995). Effects of cooperative learning groups during social studies for students with autism and fourth-grade peers. *Journal of Applied Behavior Analysis, 28,* 175–188.

Dumas, J. E., & Wahler, R. G. (1983). Predictors of treatment outcome in parent training: Mother insularity and socioeconomic disadvantage. *Behavioral Assessment, 5,* 301–313.

Dunham, P., & Dunham, F. (1995). Developmental antecedents of taxonomic and thematic strategies at 3 years of age. *Developmental Psychology, 31,* 483–493.

Dunham, P., Dunham, F., & Curwin, A. (1993). Joint-attentional states and lexical acquisition at 18 months. *Developmental Psychology, 29,* 827–831.

Dunn, J. (1988). Connections between relationships: Implications of research on mothers and siblings. In R. A. Hinde & J. Stevenson-Hinde (Eds.), *Relationships within families: Mutual influences.* Oxford: Clarendon Press.

Dunn, J. (1996). Brothers and sisters in middle childhood and early adolescence: Continuity and change in individual differences. In G. H. Brody (Ed.), *Sibling relationships: Their causes and consequences.* Norwood, NJ: Ablex.

Dunn, J., Bretherton, I., & Munn, P. (1987). Conversations about feeling states between mothers and their young children. *Developmental Psychology, 23,* 132–139.

Dunn, J., & Brown, J. (1994). Affect expression in the family, children's understanding of emotions, and their interactions with others. *Merrill Palmer Quarterly, 40,* 120–137.

Dunn, J., Brown, J. R., & Maguire, M. (1995). The development of children's moral sensibility: Individual differences and emotion understanding. *Developmental Psychology, 31,* 649–659.

Dunn, J., & Kendrick, C. (1982). *Siblings: Love, envy, and understanding.* Cambridge, MA: Harvard University Press.

Dunn, J., & McGuire, S. (1994). Young children's nonshared experiences: A summary of studies in Cambridge and Colorado. In E. M. Hetherington, D. Reiss, & R. Plomin (Eds.), *Separate social worlds of siblings: The impact of nonshared environment on development.* Hillsdale, NJ: Erlbaum.

Dunn, J., Slombowski, C., & Beardsall, L. (1994). Sibling relationships from the preschool period through middle childhood and early adolescence. *Developmental Psychology, 30,* 315–324.

Dusek, J. B. (1987). Sex roles and adjustment. In D. B. Carter (Ed.), *Current conceptions of sex roles and sex typing: Theory and research.* New York: Praeger.

Dweck, C. S. (1975). The role of expectations and attributions in the alleviation of learned helplessness. *Journal of Personality and Social Psychology, 31,* 674–685.

Dweck, C. S. (1986). Motivational processes affecting learning. *American Psychologist, 41,* 1040–1048.

Dweck, C. S. (1991). Self-theories and goals: Their role in motivation, personality, and development. In R. Diestbier (Ed.), *Nebraska Symposium on Motivation, 1990* (Vol. 36). Lincoln: University of Nebraska Press.

Dweck, C. S., Davidson, W., Nelson, S., & Enna, B. (1978). Sex differences in learned helplessness: II. The contingencies of evaluative feedback in the classroom and III. An experimental analysis. *Developmental Psychology, 14,* 268–276

Dweck, C. S., & Elliott, E. S. (1983). Achievement motivation. In E. M. Hetherington (Ed.), *Handbook of child psychology: Vol. IV. Socialization, personality, and social development.* New York: Wiley.

Dweck, C. S., Goetz, T. E., & Strauss, N. L. (1980). Sex differences in learned helplessness: IV. An experimental and naturalistic study of failure generalization and its mediators. *Journal of Personality and Social Psychology, 38,* 441–452.

Dye, N. S. (1986). The medicalization of birth. In P. S. Eakins (Ed.), *The American way of birth.* Philadelphia: Temple University Press.

Eagly, A. H., & Steffen, V. J. (1986). Gender and aggressive behavior: A meta-analytic review of the social psychological literature. *Psychological Bulletin, 100,* 309–330.

Eakins, P. S. (1984). The rise of the free standing birth center: Principles and practice. *Women and Health, 9,* 49–64.

Easterbrooks, M. A., & Goldberg, W. A. (1985). Effects of early maternal employment on toddlers, mothers, and fathers. *Developmental Psychology, 4,* 774–783.

Eccles, J. (1983). Expectancies, values, and academic behaviors. In J. T. Spence (Ed.), *Achievement and achievement motives: Psychological and sociological approaches.* San Francisco: W. H. Freeman.

Eccles, J. S. (1987). Adolescence: Gateway to androgyny? In D. B. Carter (Ed.), *Current conceptions of sex roles and sex typing: Theory and research.* New York: Praeger.

Eccles, J. S., & Midgeley, C. (1989). Stage/environment fit: Developmentally appropriate classrooms for early adolescents. In R. E. Ames & C. Ames (Eds.), *Research on motivation in education* (Vol. 3, pp. 139–186). San Diego, CA: Academic Press.

Eccles, J. S., Midgley, C., Wigfield, A., Buchanan, C. M., Reuman, D., Flanagan, C., & Mac Iver, D. (1993). Development during adolescence: The impact of stage-environment fit on young adolescents' experiences in schools and families. *American Psychologist, 48,* 90–101.

Eccles, J., Wigfield, A., Harold, R. D., & Blumenfeld, P. (1993). Age and gender differences in children's self- and task perceptions during elementary school. *Child Development, 64,* 830–847.

Eckenrode, J., Laird, M., & Doris, J. (1993). School performance and disciplinary problems among abused and neglected children. *Developmental Psychology, 29,* 53–62.

Eckerman, C. O., & Stein, M. R. (1990). How imitation begets imitation and toddlers' generation of games. *Developmental Psychology, 26,* 370–378

Eckerman, C. O., Whatley, J. L., & Kutz, S. L. (1975). Growth of social play with peers during the second year of life. *Developmental Psychology, 11,* 42–49.

Eder, D., & Hallinan, M. T. (1978). Sex differences in children's friendships. *American Sociological Review, 43,* 237–250.

Eder, R. A. (1990). Uncovering young children's psychological selves: Individual and developmental differences. *Child Development, 61,* 849–863.

Editor. (1994). Sex education in schools: Peers to the rescue? *The Lancet, 344,* 899–900.

Egeland, B., Jacobvitz, D., & Papatola, K. (1987). Intergenerational continuity of abuse. In R. J. Gelles & J. B. Lancaster (Eds.), *Child abuse and neglect: Biosocial dimensions.* Hawthorne, NY: Aldine de Gruyter.

Egeland, B., Jacobvitz, D., & Sroufe, L. A. (1988). Breaking the cycle of abuse. *Child Development, 59,* 1080–1088.

Egeland, B., & Sroufe, L. A. (1981a). Attachment and early maltreatment. *Child Development, 52,* 44–52.

Egeland, B., & Sroufe, L. A. (1981b). Developmental sequelae of maltreatment in infancy. In R. Rizley & D. Cicchetti (Eds.), *New directions for child development: No. 11. Developmental perspectives on child maltreatment.* San Francisco: Jossey-Bass.

Eilers, R. E., & Berlin, C. (1995). Advances in early detection of hearing loss in infants. *Current Problems in Pediatrics, 25,* 60–66.

Eilers, R. E., & Oller, D. K. (1994). Infant vocalizations and the early diagnosis of severe hearing impairment. *Journal of Pediatrics, 124,* 199–203.

Eimas, P. D., Siqueland, E. R., Jusczyk, P., & Vigorito, J. (1971). Speech perception in infants. *Science, 171,* 303–306.

Eisenberg, N. (1986). *Altruistic emotion, cognition, and behavior.* Hillsdale, NJ: Erlbaum.

Eisenberg, N., Boehnke, K., Schuhler, P., & Silbereisen, R. K. (1985). The development of prosocial behavior and cognition in German children. *Journal of Cross-Cultural Psychology, 16,* 69–82.

Eisenberg, N., Carol, G., Murphy, B., & Van Court, P. (1995). Prosocial development in late adolescence: A longitudinal study. *Child Development, 66,* 1179–1197.

Eisenberg, N., Fabes, R. A., Bernzweig, J., Karbon, M., Poulin, R., & Hanish, L. (1993). The relations of emotionality and regulation to preschoolers' social skills and sociometric status. *Child Development, 64,* 1418–1438.

Eisenberg, N., Fabes, R. A., Murphy, B., Karbon, M., Smith, M., & Maszk, P. (1996). The relations of children's dispositional empathy-related responding to their emotionality, regulation, and social functioning. *Developmental Psychology, 32,* 195–209.

Eisenberg, N., Fabes, R. A., Murphy, B., Maszk, P., Smith, M., & Karbon, M. (1995). The role of emotionality and regulation in children's social functioning: A longitudinal study. *Child Development, 66,* 1360–1384.

Eisenberg, N., Hertz-Lazarowitz, R., & Fuchs, I. (1990). Prosocial moral judgment in Israeli kibbutz and city children: A longitudinal study. *Merrill-Palmer Quarterly, 36,* 273–285.

Eisenberg, N., & Lennon, R. (1983). Sex differences in empathy and related capacities. *Psychological Bulletin, 94,* 100–131.

Eisenberg, N., & Miller, P. A. (1987). The relation of empathy to prosocial and related behaviors. *Psychological Bulletin, 101,* 91–119.

Eisenberg, N., & Mussen, P. H. (1989). *The roots of prosocial behavior in children.* Cambridge, UK: Cambridge University Press.

Eisenberg, N., Roth, K., Bryniarski, K. A., & Murray, E. (1984). Sex differences in the relationship of height to children's actual and attributed social and cognitive competencies. *Sex Roles, 11,* 719–734.

Eisenberg, N., & Shell, R. (1986). Prosocial moral judgment and behavior in children: The mediating role of cost. *Personality and Social Psychology Bulletin, 12,* 426–433.

Eisenberg-Berg, N., & Neal, C. (1979). Children's moral reasoning about their own spontaneous prosocial behavior. *Developmental Psychology, 15,* 228–229.

Ekman, P. (1972). Universals and cultural differences in facial expressions of emotion. In J. K. Cole (Ed.), *Nebraska symposium on motivation, 1971.* Lincoln: University of Nebraska Press.

Ekman, P. (1973). Cross-cultural studies of facial expression. In P. Ekman (Ed.), *Darwin and facial expression.* New York: Academic Press.

Elardo, R., & Bradley, R. H. (1981). The Home Observation for Measurement of the Environment (HOME) scale: A review of research. *Developmental Review, 1,* 113–145.

Elardo, R., Bradley, R. H., & Caldwell, B. M. (1975). The relation of infants' home environments to mental test performance from six to thirty-six months: A longitudinal analysis. *Child Development, 46,* 71–76.

Elardo, R., Bradley, R., & Caldwell, B. M. (1977). A longitudinal study of the relation of infants' home environments to language development at age three. *Child Development, 48,* 595–603.

Elkind, D. (1976). *Child development and education.* New York: Oxford.

Elkind, D. (1981a). *Children and adolescents: Interpretive essays on Jean Piaget* (3rd ed.). New York: Oxford University Press.

Elkind, D., Koegler, R. R., & Go, E. (1964). Studies in perceptual development: 2. Part-whole perception. *Child Development, 35,* 81–90.

Elliott, E. S., & Dweck, C. S. (1988). Goals: An approach to motivation and achievement. *Journal of Personality and Social Psychology, 54,* 5–12.

Elliott, R., & Vasta, R. (1970). The modeling of sharing: Effects associated with vicarious reinforcement, symbolization, age, and generalization. *Journal of Experimental Child Psychology, 10,* 8–15.

Emde, R. N., Biringen, Z., Clyman, R. B., & Oppenheim, D. (1991). The moral self of infancy: Affective core and procedural knowledge. *Developmental Review, 11,* 251–270.

Emde, R. N., & Koenig, K. L. (1969). Neonatal smiling, frowning and rapid eye movement states. *Journal of the American Academy of Child Psychiatry, 8,* 57–67.

Emde, R. N., Plomin, R., Robinson, J., Corley, R., DeFries, J., Walker, D. W., Reznick, J. S., Campos, J., Kagan, J., & Zahn-Waxler, C. (1992). Temperament, emotion, and cognition at fourteen months: The MacArthur longitudinal twin study. *Child Development, 63,* 1427–1455.

Emery, R. E. (1989). Family violence. *American Psychologist, 44,* 321–328.

Emmons, L. (1996). The relationship of dieting to weight in adolescents. *Adolescence, 31,* 167–178.

Engen, T., Lipsitt, L. P., & Kaye, H. (1963). Olfactory responses and adaptation in the human neonate. *Journal of Comparative and Physiological Psychology, 56,* 73–77.

Enright, M. K., Rovee-Collier, C. K., Fagen, J. W., & Caniglia, K. (1983). The effects of distributed training on retention of operant conditioning in human infants. *Journal of Experimental Child Psychology, 36,* 512–524.

Epstein, C. J. (1989). Down syndrome (Trisomy 21). In C. R. Scriver, A. L. Beaudet, W. S. Sly, & D. Valle (Eds.), *The metabolic basis of inherited disease* (6th ed. Vol. I). New York: McGraw-Hill.

Epstein, C. J. (1995). Down syndrome (Trisomy 21). In C. R. Scriver, A. L. Beaudet, W. S. Sly, & D. Valle (Eds.), *The metabolic and molecular bases of inherited disease,* Vol. I (7th ed., pp. 749–794). New York: McGraw-Hill.

Epstein, J. L. (1983). Examining theories of adolescent friendship. In J. L. Epstein & N. L. Karweit (Eds.), *Friends in school.* San Diego: Academic Press.

Epstein, L. H., & Wing, R. R. (1987). Behavioral treatment of childhood obesity. *Psychological Bulletin, 101,* 331–342.

Epstein, L. H., Wing, R. R., & Valoski, A. (1985). Childhood obesity. In P. B. Penchanz (Ed.), *Pediatric clinics of North America, 32,* 363–380.

Erdley, C. A., Cain, K. M., Loomis, C. C., Dumas-Hines, F., & Dweck, C. S. (1997). Relations among children's social goals, implicit personality theories, and responses to social failure. *Developmental Psychology, 33,* 263–272.

Erhardt, D., & Hinshaw, S. P. (1994). Initial sociometric impressions of attention-deficit hyperactivity disorder and comparison boys: Predictions from social behaviors and from nonbehavioral variables. *Journal of Consulting and Clinical Psychology, 62,* 833–842.

Erickson, M. F., Sroufe, L. A., & Egeland, B. (1985). The relationship between quality of attachment and behavior problems in preschool in a high-risk sample. In I. Bretherton & E. Waters (Eds.), *Growing points of attachment theory and research. Monographs of the Society for Research in Child Development, 50*(1–2, Serial No. 209).

Erikson, E. H. (1950). *Childhood and society.* New York: W. W. Norton.

Erikson, E. H. (1963). *Childhood and society* (2nd ed.). New York: W. W. Norton.

Eron, L. D., Huesmann, L. R., & Zelli, A. (1991). The role of parental variables in the learning of aggression. In D. J. Pepler & K. H. Rubin (Eds.), *The development and treatment of childhood aggression* (pp. 169–188). Hillsdale, NJ: Erlbaum.

Erwin, P. (1985). Similarity of attitudes and constructs in children's friendships. *Journal of Experimental Child Psychology, 40,* 470–485.

Eskenazi, B. (1984). Neurobehavioral teratology. In M. B. Bracken (Ed.), *Perinatal epidemiology.* New York: Oxford University Press.

Eveleth, P. B., & Tanner, J. M. (1990). *Worldwide variation in human growth* (2nd ed.). Cambridge, UK: Cambridge University Press.

Eyer, D. E. (1993). *Mother-infant bonding: A scientific fiction.* New Haven: Yale University Press.

Eyer, D. E. (1994). Mother-infant bonding: A scientific fiction. Special Issue: Birth management. *Human Nature, 5,* 69–94.

Fabes, R. A., Eisenberg, N., Karbon, M., Troyer, D., & Switzer, G. (1994). The relations of children's emotion regulation to their vicarious emotional responses and comforting behaviors. *Child Development, 65,* 1678–1693.

Fabes, R. A., Eisenberg, N., McCormick, S. E., & Wilson, M. S. (1988). Preschoolers' attributions of the situational determinants of others' naturally occurring emotions. *Developmental Psychology, 24,* 376–385.

Fagan, J. F., & Montie, J. E. (1988). The behavioral assessment of cognitive well-being in the infant. In J. Kavanagh (Ed.), *Understanding mental retardation: Research accomplishments and new frontiers.* Baltimore: Paul H. Brookes.

Fagan, J. F., & Singer, L. T. (1983). Infant recognition memory as a measure of intelligence. In L. P. Lipsitt (Ed.), *Advances in infancy research* (Vol. 2). Norwood, NJ: Ablex.

Fagan, J. F., III. (1974). Infant recognition memory: The effects of length of familiarization and type of discrimination task. *Child Development, 45,* 351–356.

Fagot, B. I. (1977). Consequences of moderate cross-gender behavior in preschool children. *Child Development, 48,* 902–907.

Fagot, B. I. (1978a). The influence of sex of child on parental reactions to toddler children. *Child Development, 49,* 459–465.

Fagot, B. I. (1978b). Reinforcing contingencies for sex-role behaviors: Effect of experience with children. *Child Development, 49,* 30–36.

Fagot, B. I. (1985). Changes in thinking about early sex role development. *Developmental Review, 5,* 83–98.

Fagot, B. I., & Leinbach, M. D. (1987). Socialization of sex roles within the family. In D. B. Carter (Ed.), *Current conceptions of sex roles and sex typing: Theory and research.* New York: Praeger.

Fagot, B. I., & Leinbach, M. D. (1989). The young child's gender schema: Environmental input, internal organization. *Child Development, 60,* 663–672.

Fagot, B. I., & Leinbach, M. D. (1995). Gender knowledge in egalitarian and traditional families. *Sex Roles, 32,* 513–526.

Fagot, B. I., Leinbach, M. D., & O'Boyle, C. (1992). Gender labeling, gender stereotyping, and parenting behaviors. *Developmental Psychology, 28,* 225–230.

Falbo, T., & Cooper, C. R., (1980). Young children's time and intellectual ability. *Journal of Genetic Psychology, 173,* 299–300.

Falbo, T., & Polit, D. F. (1986). Quantitative review of the only child literature: Research evidence and theory development. *Psychological Bulletin, 100,* 176–189.

Fangman, J. J., Mark, P. M., Pratt, L., Conway, K. K., Healey, M. L., Oswald, J. W., & Uden, D. L. (1994). Prematurity prevention programs: An analysis of successes and failures. *American Journal of Obstetrics and Gynecology, 170,* 744–750.

Fantz, R. L. (1961, May). The origin of form perception. *Scientific American, 204,* pp. 66–72.

Farr, K. A. (1995). Fetal abuse and the criminalization of behavior during pregnancy. *Crime and Delinquency, 41,* 235–245.

Farrar, M. J. (1992). Negative evidence and grammatical morpheme acquisition. *Developmental Psychology, 28,* 90–98.

Farrington, D. P. (1991). Childhood aggression and adult violence: Early precursors and later-life outcomes. In D. J. Pepler & K. H. Rubin (Eds.), *The development and treatment of childhood aggression* (pp. 5–29). Hillsdale, NJ: Erlbaum.

Farver, J. M., Kim, Y. K., & Lee, Y. (1995). Cultural differences in Korean- and Anglo-American preschoolers' social interaction and play behaviors. *Child Development, 66,* 1088–1099.

Farver, J. M., & Wimbarti, S. (1995). Paternal participation in toddlers' pretend play. *Social Development, 4,* 17–31.

Faust, M. S. (1983). Alternative constructions of adolescent growth. In J. Brooks-Gunn & A. C. Petersen (Eds.), *Girls at puberty: Biological and psychosocial perspectives.* New York: Plenum Press.

Fausto-Sterling, A. (1992). *Myths of gender: Biological theories about women and men* (2nd ed.). New York: Basic Books.

Feingold, A. (1988). Cognitive gender differences are disappearing. *American Psychologist, 43,* 95–103.

Feingold, A. (1992). Sex differences in variability in intellectual abilities: A new look at an old controversy. *Review of Educational Research, 62,* 61–84.

Feingold, A. (1993). Cognitive gender differences: A developmental perspective. *Sex Roles, 29,* 91–112.

Feingold, A. (1994a). Gender differences in personality: A meta-analysis. *Psychological Bulletin, 116,* 429–456.

Feingold, A. (1994b). Gender differences in variability in intellectual abilities: A cross-cultural perspective. *Sex Roles, 30,* 81–92.

Feldman, D. (1979). The mysterious case of extreme giftedness. In H. Passow (Ed.), *The gifted and talented.* Chicago: University of Chicago Press.

Feldman, H. A. (1982). Epidemiology of toxoplasma infections. *Epidemiological Review, 4,* 204–213.

Feldman, H., Goldin-Meadow, S., & Gleitman, L. (1978). Beyond Herodotus: The creation of language by linguistically deprived children. In A. Locke (Ed.), *Action, gesture, and symbol: The emergence of language.* New York: Academic Press.

Felner, R. D., & Adan, A. M. (1988). The School Transitional Environment Project: An ecological intervention and evaluation. In R. H. Price, E. L. Cowan, R. P. Lorion, I. Serrano-Garcia, & J. Ramos-McKay (Eds.), *14 ounces of prevention: A casebook for practitioners.* Washington, DC: American Psychological Association.

Felner, R. D., Ginter, M., & Primavera, J. (1982). Primary prevention during school transitions: Social support and environmental structure. *American Journal of Community Psychology, 10,* 277–290.

Fenson, L., Dale, P. S., Reznick, J. S., Bates, E., Thal, D. J., & Pethick, S. J. (1994). Variability in early communicative development. *Monographs of the Society for Research in Child Development, 59* (5, Serial No. 242).

Fenson, L., Vella, D., & Kennedy, M. (1989). Children's knowledge of thematic and taxonomic relations at two years of age. *Child Development, 60,* 911–919.

Ferber, R. (1985). *Solve your child's sleep problems.* New York: Simon and Schuster.

Fergusson, D. M., Horwood, L. J., & Lynskey, M. T. (1993). Maternal smoking before and after pregnancy: Effects on behavioral outcomes in middle childhood. *Pediatrics, 92,* 815–822.

Fergusson, D. M., Lynskey, M., & Horwood, L. J. (1995). The adolescent outcomes of adoption: A 16-year longitudinal study. *Journal of Child Psychology and Psychiatry and Allied Disciplines, 36,* 597–615.

Fernald, A. (1985). Four-month-olds prefer to listen to motherese. *Infant Behavior and Development, 8,* 181–195.

Fernald, A. (1991). Prosody in speech to children: Prelinguistic and linguistic features. In R. Vasta (Ed.), *Annals of child development: Vol. 8.* London: Jessica Kingsley.

Fernald, A., & Kuhl, P. (1987). Acoustic determinants of infant preference for motherese speech. *Infant Behavior and Development, 10,* 279–293.

Fernald, A., & Mazzie, C. (1991). Prosody and focus in speech to infants and adults. *Developmental Psychology, 27,* 209–221.

Fernald, A., & Morikawa, H. (1993). Common themes and cultural variations in Japanese and American mothers' speech to infants. *Child Development, 64,* 637–656.

Fernald, A., Taeschner, T., Dunn, J., Papousek, M., DeBoysson-Bardies, B., & Fukui, I. (1989). A cross-language study of prosodic modifications in mothers' and fathers' speech to preverbal infants. *Journal of Child Language, 16,* 477–501.

Fernandez, M., & Bahrick, L. E. (1994). Infants' sensitivity to arbitrary object-odor pairings. *Infant Behavior and Development, 17,* 471–474.

Feuerstein, R., Rand, Y., & Rynders, J. (1988). *Don't accept me as I am: Helping "retarded" people to excel.* New York: Plenum.

Field, J., Muir, D., Pilon, R., Sinclair, M., & Dodwell, P. (1980). Infants' orientation to lateral sounds from birth to three months. *Child Development, 51,* 295–298.

Field, T. (1979). Differential behavior and cardiac responses of 3-month-olds to a mirror and a peer. *Infant Behavior and Development, 2,* 179–184.

Field, T. (1991). Quality infant day-care and grade school behavior and performance. *Child Development, 6,* 863–870.

Field, T. (1995). Infants of depressed mothers. *Infant Behavior and Development, 18,* 1–13.

Field, T., Fox, N. A., Pickens, J., & Nawrocki, T. (1995). Relative right frontal EEG activation in 3- to 6-month-old infants of "depressed" mothers. *Developmental Psychology, 31,* 358–363.

Field, T., Greenwald, P., Morrow, C., Healy, B., Foster, T., Guthertz, M., & Frost, P. (1992). Behavior state matching during interactions of preadolescent friends versus acquaintances. *Developmental Psychology, 28,* 242–250.

Field, T., Healy, B., Goldstein, S., Perry, S., Bendell, D., Schanberg, S., Zimmerman, E. A., & Kuhn, C. (1988). Infants of depressed mothers show "depressed" behavior even with nondepressed adults. *Child Development, 59,* 1569–1579.

Field, T. M. (1977). Effects of early separation, interactive deficits, and experimental manipulations on infant-mother face-to-face interactions. *Child Development, 48,* 763–771.

Field, T. M. (1982). Affective displays of high-risk infants during early interactions. In T. Field & A. Fogel (Eds.), *Emotion and early interaction.* Hillsdale, NJ: Erlbaum.

Field, T. M., Cohen, D., Garcia, R., & Greenberg, R. (1984). Mother-stranger face discrimination by the newborn. *Infant Behavior and Development, 7,* 19–25.

Field, T. M., Woodson, R., Cohen, D., Greenberg, R., Garcia, R., & Collins, K. (1983). Discrimination and imitation of facial expressions by term and preterm neonates. *Infant Behavior and Development, 6,* 485–489.

Field, T. M., Woodson, R., Greenberg, R., & Cohen, D. (1982). Discrimination and imitation of facial expressions by neonates. *Science, 218,* 179–181.

Finch, E. (1978). *Clinical assessment of short stature.* Unpublished medical school thesis, Yale University.

Findley, M. J., & Cooper, H. M. (1983). Locus of control and academic achievement. A literature review. *Journal of Personality and Social Psychology, 44,* 419–427.

Fine, M. (1988). Sexuality, schooling, and adolescent females: The missing discourse of desire. *Harvard Educational Review, 58,* 29–53.

Finn, J. D., & Achilles, C. M. (1990). Answers and questions about class size: A statewide experiment. *American Educational Research Journal, 27,* 557–577.

Finnie, V., & Russell, A. (1988). Preschool children's social status and their mothers' behavior and knowledge in the supervisory role. *Developmental Psychology, 24,* 789–801.

Fioravanti, F., Inchingolo, P., Pensiero, S., & Spanio, M. (1995). Saccadic eye movement conjugation in children. *Vision Research, 35,* 3217–3228.

Fischbein, S. (1981). Heredity-environment influences on growth and development during adolescence. In L. Gedda, P. Parisi, & W. E. Nance (Eds.), *Twin research 3: Pt. B. Program in clinical and biological research.* New York: Liss.

Fischer, K. W. (1980). A theory of cognitive development: The control and construction of hierarchies of skills. *Psychological Review, 87,* 477–531.

Fischer, K. W., & Bidell, T. (1991). Constraining nativist inferences about cognitive capacities. In S. Carey & R. Gelman (Eds.), *The epigenesis of mind: Essays on biology and cognition.* Hillsdale, NJ: Erlbaum.

Fischer, K. W., & Farrar, M. J. (1988). Generalizations about generalization: How a theory of skill development explains both generality and specificity. In A. Demetriou (Ed.), *The neo-Piagetian theories of cognitive development: Toward an integration.* North-Holland: Elsevier.

Fischer, K. W., & Pipp, S. L. (1984). Processes of cognitive development: Optimal level and skill acquisition. In R. J. Sternberg (Ed.), *Mechanisms of cognitive development.* New York: W. H. Freeman.

Fischman, J. (1994). Putting a new spin on the birth of human birth. *Science, 264,* 1082–1083.

Fisher, C. B. (1994). Reporting and referring research participants: Ethical challenges for investigators studying children and youth. *Ethics & Behavior, 4,* 87–95.

Fishkin, J., Keniston, K., & MacKinnon, C. (1973). Moral reasoning and political ideology. *Journal of Personality and Social Psychology, 27,* 109–119.

Fivush, R. (1984). Learning about school: The development of kindergartners' school scripts. *Child Development, 55,* 1697–1709.

Fivush, R., Haden, C., & Adam, S. (1995). Structure and coherence of preschoolers' personal narratives over time: Implications for childhood amnesia. *Journal of Experimental Child Psychology, 60,* 32–56.

Fivush, R., Kuebli, J., & Clubb, P. A. (1992). The structure of events and event representations: A developmental analysis. *Child Development, 63,* 188–201.

Flanagan, C. A. (1990). Change in family work status: Effects on parent-adolescent decision making. *Child Development, 61,* 163–177.

Flannagan, D., & Hardee, S. D. (1994). Talk about preschoolers' interpersonal relationships: Patterns related to culture, SES, and gender of child. *Merrill-Palmer Quarterly, 40,* 523–537.

Flavell, J. H. (1963). *The developmental psychology of Jean Piaget.* New York: Van Nostrand Reinhold.

Flavell, J. H. (1970). Developmental studies of mediated memory. In H. W. Reese & L. P. Lipsitt (Eds.), *Advances in child development and behavior* (Vol. 5). New York: Academic Press.

Flavell, J. H. (1978). The development of knowledge about visual perception. In C. B. Keasey (Ed.), *Nebraska symposium on motivation* (Vol. 25). Lincoln: University of Nebraska Press.

Flavell, J. H. (1988). The development of children's knowledge about the mind: From cognitive connections to mental representations. In J. W. Astington, P. L. Harris, & D. R. Olson (Eds.), *Developing theories of mind.* New York: Cambridge University Press.

Flavell, J. H. (1992). Cognitive development: Past, present, and future. *Developmental Psychology, 28,* 998–1005.

Flavell, J. H. (1993). Young children's understanding of thinking and consciousness. *Current Directions in Psychological Science, 2,* 40–43.

Flavell, J. H. (1996). Piaget's legacy. *Psychological Science, 7,* 200–203.

Flavell, J. H., Beach, D. H., & Chinsky, J. M. (1966). Spontaneous verbal rehearsal in a memory task as a function of age. *Child Development, 37,* 283–299.

Flavell, J. H., Flavell, E. R., Green, F. L., & Korfmacher, J. E. (1990). Do young children think of television images as pictures or real objects? *Journal of Broadcasting & Electronic Media, 34,* 399–419.

Flavell, J. H., Friedrichs, A. G., & Hoyt, J. D. (1970). Developmental changes in memorization processes. *Cognitive Psychology, 1,* 324–340.

Flavell, J. H., Green, F. L., & Flavell, E. R. (1995). The development of children's knowledge about attentional focus. *Developmental Psychology, 31,* 706–712.

Flavell, J. H., Miller, P. H., & Miller, S. A. (1993). *Cognitive development* (3rd ed.). Englewood Cliffs, NJ: Prentice-Hall.

Flavell, J. H., Shipstead, S. G., & Croft, K. (1978). Young children's knowledge about visual perception: Hiding objects from others. *Child Development, 49,* 1208–1211.

Flavell, J. H., & Wellman, H. M. (1977). Metamemory. In R. V. Kail & J. W. Hagen (Eds.), *Perspectives on the development of memory and cognition.* Hillsdale, NJ: Erlbaum.

Flavell, J. H., Zhang, X-D, Zou, H., Dong, Q., & Qi, S. (1983). A comparison of the appearance-reality distinction in the People's Republic of China and the United States. *Cognitive Psychology, 15,* 459–466.

Fodor, J. A. (1983). *The modularity of mind.* Cambridge, MA: MIT Press.

Fogel, A. (1979). Peer- vs. mother-directed behavior in 1- to 3-month-old infants. *Infant Behavior and Development, 2,* 215–226.

Fogel, A. (1982). Early adult-infant face-to-face interaction: Expectable sequences of behavior. *Journal of Pediatric Psychology, 7,* 1–22.

Forehand, R., & Long, N. (1988). Outpatient treatment of the acting out child: Procedures, long term follow-up data, and clinical problems. *Advances in Behavior Research and Therapy, 10,* 129–177.

Forehand, R., & McMahon, R. (1981). *Helping the noncompliant child.* New York: Guilford.

Fox, N. A. (1991). If it's not left, it's right: Electroencephalograph asymmetry and the development of emotion. *American Psychologist, 46,* 863–872.

Fox, N. A. (1994). Dynamic cerebral processes underlying emotion regulation. In N. A. Fox (Ed.), *The development of emotion regulation: Biological and behavioral considerations. Monographs of the Society for Research in Child Development, 59* (Nos. 2–3, Serial No. 240).

Fox, N. A., & Davidson, R. J. (1986). Psychophysiological measures of emotion: New directions in developmental research. In C. E. Izard & P. B. Read (Eds.), *Measuring emotions in infants and children* (Vol. 2). Cambridge, UK: Cambridge University Press.

Fox, R., Aslin, R. N., Shea, S. L., & Dumais, S. T. (1980). Stereopsis in human infants. *Science, 207,* 323–324.

Fraiberg, S. (1977). *Insights from the blind.* New York: Basic Books.

Francis, P. L., & McCroy, G. (1983, April). *Bimodal recognition of human stimulus configurations.* Paper presented at the biennial meeting of the Society for Research in Child Development, Detroit.

Frankenburg, W. K., Dodds, J., Archer, P., Shapiro, H., & Bresnick, B. (1992). The Denver II: A major revision and restandardization of the Denver Developmental Screening Test. *Pediatrics, 89,* 91–97.

Fraser, S. (1995). *The bell curve wars: Race, intelligence, and the future of America.* New York: Basic Books.

Frauenglass, M. H., & Diaz, R. M. (1985). Self-regulatory functions of children's private speech: A critical analysis of recent challenges to Vygotsky's theory. *Developmental Psychology, 21,* 357–364.

Freedland, R. L., & Bertenthal, B. I. (1994). Developmental changes in interlimb coordination: Transition to hands-and-knees crawling. *Psychological Science, 5,* 26–32.

Freedman, D. (1979). Ethnic differences in babies. *Human Nature, 2,* 26–43.

Freedman, J. L. (1984). Effect of television violence on aggressiveness. *Psychological Bulletin, 96,* 227–246.

Freud, S. (1961). Some psychical consequences of the anatomical distinction between the sexes. In J. Strachey (Ed. and Trans.), *Standard edition of the complete psychological works of Sigmund Freud* (Vol. 19). London: Hogarth Press. (Original work published 1925)

Frey, K. S., & Ruble, D. N. (1987). What children say about classroom performance: Sex and grade differences in perceived competence. *Child Development, 58,* 1066–1078.

Frick, J. E., & Colombo, J. (1996). Individual differences in infant visual attention: Recognition of degraded visual forms by four-month-olds. *Child Development, 67,* 188–204.

Fried, P. A. (1986). Marijuana and human pregnancy. In I. J. Chasnoff (Ed.), *Drug use in pregnancy: Mother and child.* Lancaster, England: MTP Press.

Fried, P. A., & Watkinson, B. (1990). 36- and 48-month-neurobehavioral follow-up of children prenatally exposed to marijuana, cigarettes and alcohol. *Journal of Developmental and Behavioral Pediatrics, 11,* 49–58.

Friedrich, L. K., & Stein, A. H. (1973). Aggressive and prosocial television programs and the natural behavior of preschool children. *Monographs of the Society for Research in Child Development, 38*(4, Serial No. 151).

Frisch, R. E. (1983). Fatness, puberty and fertility. In J. Brooks-Gunn & A. C. Petersen (Eds.), *Girls at puberty: Biological and psychosocial perspectives.* New York: Plenum Press.

Frith, U. (1993). Autism. *Scientific American, 268,* 108–114.

Frodi, A. M., & Lamb, M. E. (1980). Child abusers' responses to infant smiles and cries. *Child Development, 51,* 238–241.

Frodi, A. M., Lamb, M. E., Leavitt, L. A., & Donovan, W. L. (1978). Fathers' and mothers' responses to infant smiles and cries. *Infant Behavior and Development, 1,* 187–198.

Frodi, A. M., & Thompson, R. (1985). Infants' affective responses in the strange situation: Effects of prematurity and of quality of attachment. *Child Development, 56,* 1280–1290.

Frueh, T., & McGhee, P. (1975). Traditional sex-role development and amount of time spent watching television. *Developmental Psychology, 11,* 109.

Fuligni, A. J., & Eccles, J. S. (1993). Perceived parent-child relationships and early adolescents' orientation toward peers. *Developmental Psychology, 29,* 622–632.

Fuligni, A. J., & Stevenson, H. W. (1995). Time use and mathematics achievement among American, Chinese, and Japanese high school students. *Child Development, 66,* 830–842.

Fulker, O. W., & Eysenck, H. J. (1979). Nature, nurture and socio-economic status. In H. J. Eysenck (Ed.), *The structure and measurement of intelligence.* Berlin: Springer-Verlag.

Furman, W., & Bierman, K. L. (1984). Children's conceptions of friendship: A multimethod study of developmental changes. *Developmental Psychology, 20,* 925–931.

Furman, W., & Buhrmester, D. (1992). Age and sex differences in perceptions of networks of personal relationships. *Child Development, 63,* 103–115.

Furman, W., & Robbins, P. (1985). What's the point? Issues in the selection of treatment objectives. In B. H. Schneider, K. H. Rubin, & J. E. Ledingham (Eds.), *Children's peer relations: Issues in assessment and intervention.* New York: Springer-Verlag.

Furstenberg, F. F., Jr. (1987). The new extended family: The experience of parents and children after remarriage. In K. Paley & M. Ihinger-Tallman (Eds.), *Remarriage and stepparenting.* New York: Guilford Press.

Furstenberg, F. F., Jr., Brooks-Gunn, J., & Chase-Lansdale, L. (1989). Teenaged pregnancy and childbearing. *American Psychologist, 44,* 313–320.

Fuson, K. C. (1979). The development of self-regulating aspects of speech: A review. In G. Zivin (Ed.), *The development of self-regulation through private speech.* New York: Wiley.

Fuson, K. C., & Kwon, Y. (1992). Korean children's understanding of multidigit addition and subtraction. *Child Development, 63,* 491–506.

Gaddis, A., & Brooks-Gunn, J. (1985). The male experience of pubertal change. *Journal of Youth and Adolescence, 14,* 61–69.

Gagnon, M., & Ladouceur, R. (1992). Behavioral treatment of child stutterers: Replication and extension. *Behavior Therapy, 23,* 113–129.

Galambos, N. L., Almeida, D. M., & Petersen, A. C. (1990). Masculinity, femininity, and sex role attitudes in early adolescence. *Child Development, 61,* 1905–1914.

Gallahue, D. L. (1989). *Understanding motor development: Infants, children, adolescents.* Indianapolis, IN: Benchmark Press.

Galler, J. R., Ramsey, F. C., Morley, D. S., Archer, E., & Salt, P. (1990). The long-term effects of early kwashiorkor compared with marasmus. IV. Performance on the National High School Entrance Exam. *Pediatric Research, 28,* 235–239.

Gallistel, C. R., Brown, A. L., Carey, S., Gelman, R., & Keil, F. C. (1991). Lessons from animal learning for the study of cognitive development. In S. Carey & R. Gelman (Eds.), *The epigenesis of mind: Essays on biology and cognition.* Hillsdale, NJ: Erlbaum.

Galton, F. (1883). *Inquiries into human faculty and its development.* London: Macmillan.

Gamoran, A. (1989). Measuring curriculum differentiation. *American Journal of Education, 97,* 129–143.

Gamoran, A. (1992). Is ability grouping equitable? *Educational Leadership, 50,* 11–17.

Gamoran, A. (1996). Student achievement in public magnet, public comprehensive, and private city high schools. *Educational Evaluation and Policy Analysis, 18,* 1–18.

Garabino, J. (1982). Sociocultural risk: Dangers to competence. In C. Kopp & J. Krakow (Eds.), *Child development in a social context.* Reading, MA: Addison-Wesley.

Gardner, B. T., & Gardner, R. A. (1971). Two-way communication with an infant chimpanzee. In A. M. Schrier & F. Stollnitz (Eds.), *Behavior of non-human primates.* New York: Academic Press.

Gardner, D., Harris, P. L., Ohmoto, M., & Hamasaki, T. (1988). Japanese children's understanding of the distinction between real and apparent emotion. *International Journal of Behavioral Development, 11,* 203–218.

Gardner, H. (1983). *Frames of mind: The theory of multiple intelligences.* New York: Basic Books.

Gardner, W., & Rogoff, B. (1990). Children's deliberateness of planning according to task circumstances. *Developmental Psychology, 26,* 480–487.

Garland, A. F., & Zigler, E. (1993). Adolescent suicide prevention: Current research and social policy implications. *American Psychologist, 48,* 169–182.

Garmezy, N. (1993). Children in poverty: Resilience despite risk. *Psychiatry, 56,* 127–136.

Gash, H., & Morgan, M. (1993). School-based modifications of children's gender-related beliefs. *Journal of Applied Developmental Psychology, 14,* 277–287.

Gauze, C., Bukowski, W. M., Aquan-Assee, J., & Sippola, L. K. (1996). Interactions between family environment and friendship and associations with self-perceived well-being during early adolescence. *Child Development, 67,* 2201–2216.

Gavin, L. A., & Furman, W. (1989). Age differences in adolescent's perceptions of their peer groups. *Developmental Psychology, 25,* 827–834.

Ge, X., Best, K. M., Conger, R. D., & Simons, R. L. (1996). Parenting behaviors and the occurrence and co-occurrence of adolescent depressive symptoms and conduct problems. *Developmental Psychology, 32,* 717–731.

Ge, X., Lorenz, F. O., Conger, R. D., Elder, G. H., Jr., & Simons, R. L. (1994). Trajectories of stressful life events and depressive symptoms during adolescence. *Developmental Psychology, 30,* 467–483.

Geary, D. C., Bow-Thomas, C. C., Fan, L., & Siegler, R. S. (1993). Even before formal instruction, Chinese children outperform American children in mental addition. *Cognitive Development, 8,* 517–529.

Geary, D. C., Bow-Thomas, C. C., Liu, F., & Siegler, R. S. (1996). Development of arithmetical competencies in Chinese and American children: Influence of age, language, and schooling. *Child Development, 67,* 2022–2044.

Geary, D. C., Fan, L., & Bow-Thomas, C. C. (1992). Numerical cognition: Loci of ability differences comparing children from China and the United States. *Psychological Science, 3,* 180–185.

Geary, D. C., Salthouse, T. A., Chen, G., & Fan, L. (1996). Are East Asian versus American differences in arithmetic ability a recent phenomenon? *Developmental Psychology, 32,* 254–262.

Gelman, R. (1969). Conservation acquisition: A problem of learning to attend to relevant attributes. *Journal of Experimental Child Psychology, 7,* 167–187.

Gelman, R. (1972). Logical capacity of very young children: Number invariance rules. *Child Development, 43,* 75–90.

Gelman, R., & Baillargeon, R. (1983). A review of some Piagetian concepts. In J. H. Flavell & E. M. Markman (Eds.), *Handbook of child psychology. Vol. III. Cognitive development.* New York: Wiley.

Gelman, R., & Gallistel, C. R. (1978). *The child's understanding of number.* Cambridge, MA: Harvard University Press.

Gelman, R., & Meck, E. (1983). Preschoolers' counting: Principles before skill. *Cognition, 13,* 343–359.

Gelman, R., Spelke, E. S., & Meck, E. (1983). What preschoolers know about animate and inanimate objects. In D. Rogers & J. A. Sloboda (Eds.), *The acquisition of symbolic skills.* New York: Plenum.

Gelman, S. A., & Kremer, K. E. (1991). Understanding natural cause: Children's explanations of how objects and their properties originate. *Child Development, 62,* 396–414.

Gerbner, G., Gross, L., Morgan, M., & Signorielli, N. (1986). Living with television: The dynamics of the cultivation process. In J. Bryant & D. Zillman (Eds.), *Perspectives on media effects.* Hillsdale, NJ: Erlbaum.

Geschwind. M., & Galaburda, A. M. (1987). *Cerebral lateralization.* Cambridge, MA: MIT Press.

Gesell, A., & Thompson, H. (1934). *Infant behavior: Its genesis and growth.* New York: McGraw-Hill.

Gesell, A., & Thompson, H. (1938). *The psychology of early growth.* New York: Macmillan.

Gewirtz, J. L., & Peláez-Nogueras, M. (1992). B. F. Skinner's legacy to human infant behavior and development. *American Psychologist, 47,* 1411–1422.

Ghidini, A., Sepulveda, W., Lockwood, C. J., & Romero, R. (1993). Complications of fetal blood sampling. *American Journal of Obstetrics and Gynecology, 168,* 1339–1344.

Ghim, H-R. (1990). Evidence for perceptual organization in infants: Perception of subjective contours by young infants. *Infant Behavior and Development, 13,* 221–248.

Ghim, H-R., & Eimas, P. D. (1988). Global and local processing by 3- and 4-month-old infants. *Perception & Psychophysics, 43,* 165–171.

Gibby, R. G., Sr., & Gibby, R. G., Jr. (1967). The effects of stress resulting from academic failure. *Journal of Clinical Psychology, 23,* 35–37.

Gibson, E. J. (1969). *Principles of perceptual learning and development.* New York: Appleton.

Gibson, E. J. (1982). The concept of affordances in development: The renascence of functionalism. In W. A. Collins (Ed.), *The Minnesota symposia on child psychology: Vol. 15. The concept of development.* Hillsdale, NJ: Erlbaum.

Gibson, E. J. (1988). Exploratory behavior in the development of perceiving, acting, and the acquiring of knowledge. *Annual Review of Psychology, 39,* 1–41.

Gibson, E. J., Gibson, J. J., Pick, A. D., & Osser, H. (1962). A developmental study of the discrimination of letter-like forms. *Journal of Comparative and Physiological Psychology, 55,* 897– 906.

Gibson, E. J., & Spelke, E. S. (1983). The development of perception. In J. H. Flavell & E. M. Markman (Eds.), *Handbook of child psychology: Vol. III. Cognitive development.* New York: Wiley.

Gibson, E. J., & Walker, A. (1984). Development of knowledge of visual-tactual affordances of substance. *Child Development, 55,* 453–460.

Gibson, J. J. (1966). *The senses considered as perceptual systems.* Boston: Houghton Mifflin.

Gibson, J. J. (1979). *The ecological approach to visual perception.* Boston: Houghton Mifflin.

Gibson, M., & Ogbu, J. (Eds.). (1991). *Minority status and schooling: A comparative study of immigrant and involuntary minorities.* New York: Garland.

Gilligan, C. (1982). *In a different voice: Psychological theory and women's development.* Cambridge, MA: Harvard University Press.

Gilligan, C. (1988). Remapping the moral domain: New images of self in relationship. In C. Gilligan, J. V. Ward, J. M. Taylor, & B. Bardige (Eds.), *Mapping the moral domain.* Cambridge, MA: Harvard University Press.

Gilligan, C., & Attanucci, J. (1988). Two moral orientations: Gender differences and similarities. *Merrill-Palmer Quarterly, 34,* 223–237.

Gilligan, C., Lyons, N. P., & Hanmer, T. J. (Eds.). (1989). *Making connections: The relational worlds of adolescent girls at Emma Willard School.* Cambridge, MA: Harvard University Press.

Gilligan, C., Lyons, N. P., & Hanmer, T. J. (1990). *Making connections.* Cambridge, MA: Harvard University Press.

Gillis, J. S. (1982). *Too tall, too small.* Champaign, IL: Institute for Personality and Ability Testing.

Ginsberg, H. P. (1972). *The myth of the deprived child: Poor children's intellect and education.* Englewood Cliffs, NJ: Prentice-Hall.

Ginsburg, H. P. & Opper, S. (1988). *Piaget's theory of intellectual development* (3rd ed.). Englewood Cliffs, NJ: Prentice-Hall.

Gjerde, P. F. (1995). Alternative pathways to chronic depressive symptoms in young adults: Gender differences in developmental trajectories. *Child Development, 66,* 1277–1300.

Glass, D. C., Neulinger, J., & Brim, O. G. (1974). Birth order, verbal intelligence, and educational aspiration. *Child Development, 45,* 807–811.

Glassman, M., & Zan, B. (1995). Moral activity and domain theory: An alternative interpretation of research on young children. *Developmental Review, 15,* 434–457.

Glazer, S. (1993). Preventing teen pregnancy: Is better sex education the answer? *CQ Researcher, 3,* 409–418.

Glazer, S. (1996). Teaching values: Do school-based programs violate parents' beliefs? *CQ Researcher, 6,* 529–552.

Gleason, J. B., & Perlmann, R. Y. (1985). Acquiring social variation in speech. In H. Giles & R. N. St. Clair (Eds.), *Recent advances in language, communication, and social psychology.* London: Erlbaum.

Gleason, J. B., & Weintraub, S. (1978). Input language and the acquisition of communicative competence. In K. Nelson (Ed.), *Children's language* (Vol. 1). New York: Gardner Press.

Gleitman, L. R., Gleitman, H., & Shipley, E. F. (1972). The emergence of the child as grammarian. *Cognition, 1,* 137–164.

Gleitman, L. R., Newport, E. L., & Gleitman, H. (1984). The current status of the motherese hypothesis. *Journal of Child Language, 11,* 43–79.

Glick, P. C. (1989). Remarried families, stepfamilies, and stepchildren: A brief demographic analysis. *Family Relations, 38,* 24–27.

Glick, P. C., & Lin, S. (1986). Recent changes in divorce and remarriage. *Journal of Marriage and the Family, 48,* 737–747.

Goldberg, R. J. (1977, April). *Maternal time use and preschool performance.* Paper presented at the biennial meeting of the Society for Research in Child Development, New Orleans.

Goldberg, S. (1979). Premature birth: Consequences for the parent-infant relationship. *American Scientist, 67,* 582–590.

Goldberg, S. (1983). Parent-infant bonding: Another look. *Child Development, 54,* 1355–1382.

Goldberg, W. A., Greenberger, E., & Nagel, S. K. (1996). Employment and achievement: Mothers' work involvement in relation to children's achievement behaviors and mothers' parenting behaviors. *Child Development, 67,* 1512–1527.

Goldenberg, R. L., Clivar, S. P., Cutter, G. R., Hoffman, H. J., Cassady, G., Davis, R. O., & Nelson, K. G. (1991). Black-white differences in newborn anthropometric measurements. *Obstetrics and Gynecology, 78,* 782–788.

Goldfield, B. A., & Reznick, J. S. (1990). Early lexical acquisition: Rate, content, and the vocabulary spurt. *Journal of Child Language, 17,* 171–183.

Goldsmith, H. H., & Alansky, J. A. (1987). Maternal and infant temperamental predictors of attachment: A meta-analytic review. *Journal of Consulting and Clinical Psychology, 55,* 805–816.

Goldsmith, H. H., & Campos, J. J. (1982). Toward a theory of infant temperament. In R. N. Emde & R. J. Harmon (Eds.), *The development of attachment and affiliative systems.* New York: Plenum.

Goldsmith, H. H., & Campos, J. J. (1990). The structure of temperamental fear and pleasure in infants: A psychometric perspective. *Child Development, 61,* 1944–1964.

Golinkoff, R. M., Harding, C. G., Carlson, V., & Sexton, M. E. (1984). The infant's perception of causal events: The distinction between animate and inanimate objects. In L. L. Lipsitt & C. Rovee-Collier (Eds.), *Advances in infancy research. Vol. 3.* Norwood, NJ: Ablex.

Golinkoff, R. M., Mervis, C. B., & Hirsh-Pasek, K. (1994). Early object labels: The case for a developmental lexical principles framework. *Journal of Child Language, 21,* 125–155.

Golombok, S., Cook, R., Bish, A., & Murray, C. (1995). Families created by the new reproductive technologies: Quality of parenting and social and emotional development of the children. *Child Development, 66,* 285–298.

Gomby, D. S., & Shiono, P. H. (1991). Estimating the number of substance-exposed infants. *The Future of Children: Drug Exposed Infants, 1,* 17–25.

Goodman, G. S., Levine, M., Melton, G. B., & Ogden, D. W. (1991). Child witnesses and the confrontation clause. *Law and Human Behavior, 15,* 13–29.

Goodman, G. S., Sharma, A., Thomas, S. F., & Considine, M. G. (1995). Mother knows best: Effects of relationship status and interviewer bias on children's memory. *Journal of Experimental Child Psychology, 60,* 195–228.

Goodman, G. S., Taub, E. P., Jones, D. P. H., England, P., Port, L. K., Rudy, L., & Prado, L. (1992). Testifying in criminal court. *Monographs of the Society for Research in Child Development, 57* (5, Serial No. 229).

Goodnow, J. (1988). Children's household work: Its nature and functions. *Psychological Bulletin, 103,* 5–26.

Goodwin, S. W., & Acredolo, L. P. (1993). Symbolic gesture versus word: Is there a modality advantage for onset of symbol use? *Child Development, 64,* 688–701.

Gopaul-McNicol, S.-A. (1995). A cross-cultural examination of racial identity and racial preference of preschool children in the West Indies. *Journal of Cross-Cultural Psychology, 26,* 141–152.

Gopnik, A. (1996). The post-Piaget era. *Psychological Science, 7,* 221–225.

Gopnik, A., & Meltzoff, A. N. (1986). Relations between semantic and cognitive development in the one-word stage: The specificity hypothesis. *Child Development, 57,* 1040–1053.

Gopnik, A., & Meltzoff, A. N. (1987). The development of categorization in the second year and its relation to other cognitive and linguistic attainments. *Child Development, 58,* 1523–1531.

Gopnik, A., & Meltzoff, A. N. (1992). Categorization and naming: Basic-level sorting in eighteen-month-olds and its relation to language. *Child Development, 63,* 1091–1103.

Gopnik, A., & Slaughter, V. (1991). Young children's understanding of changes in their mental states. *Child Development, 62,* 98–110.

Gorski, P. A. (1991). Developmental intervention during neonatal hospitalization: Critiquing the state of the science. *Pediatric Clinics of North America, 38,* 1469–1479.

Gorski, R. A. (1980). Sexual differentiation of the brain. In D. T. Krieger & J. C. Hughes (Eds.), *Neuroendocrinology.* New York: Rockefeller University Press.

Gortmaker, S. L., Dietz, W. H., Jr., Sobol, A. M., & Wehler, C. A. (1987). Increasing pediatric obesity in the United States. *American Journal of Diseases of Children, 141,* 535–540.

Goswami, U. (1991). Analogical reasoning: What develops? A review of theory and research. *Child Development, 62,* 1–22.

Goswami, U. (1995). Transitive relational mappings in three- and four-year-olds: The analogy of Goldilocks and the Three Bears. *Child Development, 66,* 877–892.

Goswami, U. (1996). Analogical reasoning and cognitive development. In H. W. Reese (Ed.), *Advances in child development and behavior.* San Diego: Academic Press.

Goswami, U., & Brown, A. L. (1989). Melting chocolate and melting snowmen: Analogical reasoning and causal relations. *Cognition, 35,* 69–95.

Gottesman, I. I., & Shields, J. (1982). *Schizophrenia: The epigenetic puzzle.* Cambridge, UK: Cambridge University Press.

Gottfried, A. E., Bathurst, K., & Gottfried, A. W. (1994). Role of maternal and dual-earner employment status in children's development. In A. E. Gottfried, & A. W. Gottfried (Eds.), *Redefining families: Implications for children's development.* New York: Plenum.

Gottlieb, G. (1991). Experimental canalization of behavioral development: Theory. *Developmental Psychology, 27,* 4–13.

Gottlieb, G. (1995). Some conceptual deficiencies in "developmental" behavior genetics. *Human Development, 38,* 131–141.

Gottman, J. M. (1983). How children become friends. *Monographs of the Society for Research in Child Development, 48*(2, Serial No. 201).

Gottman, J. M., Gonso, J., & Rasmussen, B. (1975). Social interaction, social competence, and friendship in children. *Child Development, 46,* 709–718.

Gottman, J. M., & Parkhurst, J. T. (1980). A developmental theory of friendship and acquaintanceship processes. In W. A. Collins (Ed.), *The Minnesota symposia on child development: Vol. 13. Development of cognition, affect, and social relations.* Hillsdale, NJ: Erlbaum.

Gouin-Decarie, T. (1969). A study of the mental and emotional development of the thalidomide child. In B. M. Foss (Ed.), *Determinants of infant behavior IV.* London: Methuen.

Goy, R. (1970). Early hormonal influences on the development of sexual and sex-related behavior. In F. Schmitt, G. Quarton, T. Melnechuck, & G. Adelman (Eds.), *The neurosciences: Second study program.* New York: Rockefeller University Press.

Graber, J. A., Brooks-Gunn, J., & Warren, M. P. (1995). The antecedents of menarcheal age: Heredity, family environment, and stressful life events. *Child Development, 66,* 346–359.

Grady, D. (1987, June). The ticking of a time bomb in the genes. *Discover,* pp. 26–39.

Graham, S., & Hoehn, S. (1995). Children's understanding of aggression and withdrawal as social stigmas: An attributional analysis. *Child Development, 66,* 1143–1161.

Graham, S., Hudley, C., & Williams, E. (1992). Attributional and emotional determinants of aggression among African-American and Latino young adolescents. *Developmental Psychology, 28,* 731–740.

Gralinski, J. H., & Kopp, C. B. (1993). Everyday rules for behavior: Mothers' requests to young children. *Developmental Psychology, 29,* 573–584.

Granrud, C. E., Yonas, A., Smith, I. M. E., Arterberry, M. W., Glicksman, M. L., & Sorknes, A. C. (1984). Infants' sensitivity to accretion and deletion of texture as information for depth at an edge. *Child Development, 55,* 1630–1636.

Grantham-McGregor, S., Powell, C., Walker, S., Change, S., & Fletcher, P. (1994). The long-term follow-up of severely malnourished children who participated in an intervention program. *Child Development, 65,* 428–439.

Graves, N. B., & Graves, T. D. (1983). The cultural context of prosocial development: An ecological model. In D. L. Bridgeman (Ed.), *The nature of prosocial development: Interdisciplinary theories and strategies.* New York: Academic Press.

Green, E. D., Cox, D. R., & Myers, R. M. (1995). The Human Genome Project and its impact on the study of human disease. In C. R. Scriver, A. L. Beaudet, W. S. Sly, & D. Valle (Eds.), *The metabolic and molecular bases of inherited disease,* Vol. I (7th ed., pp. 401–436). New York: McGraw-Hill.

Greenberg, B. S. (1986). Minorities and the mass media. In J. Bryant & D. Zillman (Eds.), *Perspectives on mass media effects.* Hillsdale, NJ: Erlbaum.

Greenberger, E., & Chen, C. (1996). Perceived family relationships and depressed mood in early and late adolescence: A comparison of European and Asian Americans. *Developmental Psychology, 32,* 707–716.

Greenfield, P. M. (1976). Cross-cultural research and Piagetian theory: Paradox and progress. In K. Riegel & J. Meacham (Eds.), *The developing individual in a changing world* (Vol. 1). The Hague: Mouton.

Greenfield, P. M. (1984). A theory of the teacher in the learning activities of everyday life. In B. Rogoff & J. Lave (Eds.), *Everyday cognition: Its development in social context.* Cambridge, MA: Harvard University Press.

Greenfield, P. M. (1994). Video games as cultural artifacts. *Journal of Applied Developmental Psychology, 15,* 3–12.

Greenough, W. T., Black, J. E., & Wallace, C. S. (1987). Experience and brain development. *Child Development, 58,* 539–559.

Gregg, V., Gibbs, J. C., & Basinger, K. S. (1994). Patterns of developmental delay in moral judgment by male and female delinquents. *Merrill-Palmer Quarterly, 40,* 538–553.

Greif, E. B., & Gleason, J. B. (1980). Hi, thanks, and goodbye: More routine information. *Language in Society, 9,* 159–166.

Greif, E. B., & Ulman, K. J. (1982). The psychological impact of menarche on early adolescent females: A review of the literature. *Child Development, 53,* 1413–1430.

Greist, D., Wells, K. C., & Forehand, R. (1979). An examination of predictors of maternal perceptions of maladjustment in clinic-referred children. *Journal of Abnormal Psychology, 88,* 277–281.

Grolnick, W. S., Bridges, L. J., & Connell, J. P. (1996). Emotion regulation in two-year-olds: Strategies and emotional expression in four contexts. *Child Development, 67,* 928–941.

Grolnick, W. S., Ryan, R. M., & Deci, E. L. (1991). Inner resources for school achievement: Motivational mediators of children's perceptions of their parents. *Journal of Educational Psychology, 83,* 508–517.

Grossmann, K., Grossmann, K. E., Spangler, G., Suess, G., & Unzner, L. (1985). Maternal sensitivity and newborns' orientation responses as related to quality of attachment in northern Germany. In I. Bretherton & E. Waters (Eds.), *Growing points of attachment theory and research. Monographs of the Society for Research in Child Development, 50* (1–2, Serial No. 209).

Grotevant, H. D., & Cooper, C. R. (1986). Individuation in family relationships. *Human Development, 29,* 82–100.

Gruen, G., Ottinger, D., & Zigler, E. (1970). Level of aspiration and the probability learning of middle- and lower-class children. *Developmental Psychology, 3,* 133–142.

Grusec, J. E. (1982). The socialization of altruism. In N. Eisenberg (Ed.), *The development of prosocial behavior.* New York: Academic Press.

Grusec, J. E. (1991). Socializing concern for others in the home. *Developmental Psychology, 27,* 338–342.

Grusec, J. E. (1992). Social learning theory and developmental psychology: The legacies of Robert Sears and Albert Bandura. *Developmental Psychology, 28,* 776–786.

Grusec, J. E., & Goodnow, J. J. (1994). Impact of parental discipline methods on the child's internalization of values: A reconceptualization of current points of view. *Developmental Psychology, 30,* 4–19.

Grusec, J. E., & Mammone, N. (1995). Features and sources of parents' attributions about themselves and their children. In N. Eisenberg (Ed.), *Review of personality and social psychology: Social development* (Vol. 15). Thousand Oaks, CA: Sage.

Grusec, J. E., & Skubiski, L. (1970). Model nurturance, demand characteristics of the modeling experiment, and altruism. *Journal of Personality and Social Psychology, 14,* 352–359.

Guidubaldi, J., Perry, J. D., & Cleminshaw, H. K. (1984). The legacy of parental divorce: A nationwide study of family status and selected mediating variables on children's academic and social competencies. In B. B. Lahey & A. E. Kazdin (Eds.), *Advances in clinical child psychology* (Vol. 7). New York: Plenum Press.

Guilford, J. P. (1967). *The nature of human intelligence.* New York: McGraw-Hill.

Guilford, J. P. (1985). The structure-of-intellect model. In B. B. Wolman (Ed.), *Handbook of intelligence.* New York: Wiley.

Guilford, J. P. (1988). Some changes in the structure-of-intellect model. *Educational and Psychological Measurement, 48,* 1–4.

Guinan, M. E. (1995). Artificial insemination by donor: Safety and secrecy. *Journal of the American Medical Association, 273,* 890–891.

Gump, P. V. (1978). School environments. In I. Altman & J. F. Wohlwill (Eds.), *Children and the environment.* New York: Plenum Press.

Gundy, J. H. (1987). The pediatric physical examination. In R. A. Hoekelman, S. Blatman, S. B. Friedman, N. M. Nelson, & H. M. Seidel (Eds.), *Primary pediatric care.* Washington, DC: C. V. Mosby.

Gunston, G. D., Burkimsher, D., Malan, H, & Sive, A. A. (1992). Reversible cerebral shrinkage in kwashiorkor: An MRI study. *Archives of Disease in Childhood, 67,* 1030–1032.

Gusfield, J. (1981). *The culture of public problems: drinking, driving and the symbolic order.* Chicago: University of Chicago Press.

Guttentag, R. E. (1987). Memory and aging: Implications for theories of memory development during childhood. *Developmental Review, 5,* 56–82.

Guyer, B., Strobino, D. M., Ventura, S. J., & Singh, G. K. (1995). Annual summary of vital statistics–1994. *Pediatrics, 98,* 1029–1039.

Guyer, M. S., & Collins, F. S. (1993). The Human Genome Project and the future of medicine. *American Journal of Disease in Children, 147,* 1145–1152.

Gwinn, M. & Wortley, P. M. (1996). Epidemiology of HIV infection in women and newborns. *Clinical Obstetrics and Gynecology, 39,* 291–304.

Hafner-Eaton, C., & Pearce, L. K. (1994). Birth choices, the law, and medicine: Balancing individual freedoms and protection of the public's health. *Journal of Health Politics, Policy and Law, 19,* 813–835.

Hagay, Z. J., Biran, G., Ornoy, A., & Reece, E. A. (1996). Congenital cytomegalovirus infection: A long-standing problem still seeking a solution. *American Journal of Obstetrics and Gynecology, 174,* 241–245.

Hagerman, R. J. (1996). Biomedical advances in developmental psychology: The case of fragile X syndrome. *Developmental Psychology, 32,* 416–424.

Hainline, L., & Riddell, P. M. (1995). Binocular alignment and vergence in early infancy. *Vision Research, 35,* 3229–3236.

Haith, M. M. (1980). *Rules that babies look by: The organization of newborn visual activity.* Hillsdale, NJ: Erlbaum.

Haith, M. M. (1990). Progress in the understanding of sensory and perceptual processes in early infancy. *Merrill-Palmer Quarterly, 36,* 1–26.

Hakuta, K., & Diaz, R. M. (1985). The relationship between degree of bilingualism and cognitive ability: A critical discussion and some new longitudinal data. In K. E. Nelson (Ed.), *Children's language* (Vol. 5). Hillsdale, NJ: Erlbaum.

Hall, G. S. (1891). The contents of children's minds on entering school. *Pedagogical Seminary, 1,* 139–173.

Hall, J. A. (1978). Gender effects in decoding nonverbal cues. *Psychological Bulletin, 85,* 845–857.

Hall, J. A. (1984). *Nonverbal sex differences: Communication accuracy and expressive style.* Baltimore: Johns Hopkins University Press.

Hall, J. A., & Halberstadt, A. G. (1986). Smiling and gazing. In J. S. Hyde & M. C. Linn (Eds.), *The psychology of gender: Advances through meta-analysis.* Baltimore: Johns Hopkins University Press.

Hallinan, M. T. (1976). Friendship patterns in open and traditional classrooms. *Sociology of Education, 49,* 254–265.

Hallinan, M. T. (1990). The effects of ability grouping in secondary schools: A response to Slavin's best-evidence synthesis. *Review of Educational Research, 60,* 501–504.

Halpern, D. F. (1986). *Sex differences in cognitive abilities.* Hillsdale, NJ: Erlbaum.

Halpern, L. F., MacLean, W. E., Jr., & Baumeister, A. A. (1995). Infant sleep-wake characteristics: Relation to neurological status and the prediction of developmental outcome. *Developmental Review, 15,* 255–291.

Hamilton, V. J., & Gordon, D. A. (1978). Teacher-child interactions in preschool and task persistence. *American Educational Research Journal, 15,* 459–466.

Hanna, E., & Meltzoff, A. N. (1993). Peer imitation by toddlers in laboratory, home, and day-care contexts: Implications for social learning and memory. *Developmental Psychology, 29,* 701–710.

Hansen, J. D. L. (1990). Malnutrition review. *Pediatric Reviews and Communication, 4,* 201–212.

Harbison, R. D., & Mantilla-Plata, B. (1972). Prenatal toxicity, maternal distribution and placental transfer of tetrahydrocannabinol. *Journal of Pharmacology and Experimental Therapeutics, 180,* 446–453.

Hareven, T. (1985). Historical changes in the family and the life course: Implications for child development. In A. B. Smuts & J. W. Hagen (Eds.), *History and research in child development. Monographs of the Society for Research in Child Development, 50*(4–5, Serial No. 211).

Harkness, S., & Super, C. M. (1985). Child-environment interactions in the socialization of affect. In M. Lewis & C. Saarni (Eds.), *The socialization of emotions.* New York: Plenum Press.

Harlow, H. F., & Zimmerman, R. R. (1959). Affectional responses in the infant monkey. *Science, 130,* 421–432.

Harold, G. T., Fincham, F. D., Osborne, L. N., & Conger, R. D. (1997). Mom and Dad are at it again: Adolescent perceptions of marital conflict and adolescent psychological distress. *Developmental Psychology, 33,* 333–350.

Harpin, V., Chellappah, G., & Rutter, N. (1983). Responses of the newborn infant to overheating. *Biology of the Neonate, 44,* 65–75.

Harriman, A. E., & Lukosius, P. A. (1982). On why Wayne Dennis found Hopi children retarded in age at onset of walking. *Perceptual and Motor Skills, 55,* 79–86.

Harris, G., & Booth, D. (1985). Sodium preference in food and previous dietary experience in 6-month-old infants. *IRCS Medical Science, 13,* 1177–1178.

Harris, P. L., Brown, E., Marriott, C., Whittall, S., & Harmer, S. (1991). Monsters, ghosts and witches: Testing the limits of the fantasy-reality distinction. *British Journal of Developmental Psychology, 9,* 105–123.

Harris, P. L., Donnelly, K., Guz, G. R., & Pitt-Watson, R. (1986). Children's understanding of the distinction between real and apparent emotion. *Child Development, 57,* 895–909.

Harris, P. L., Guz, G. R., Lipian, M. S., & Man-Shu, Z. (1985). Insight into the time-course of emotion among Western and Chinese children. *Child Development, 56,* 972–988.

Harris, P. L., & Kavanaugh, R. D. (1993). Young children's understanding of pretense. *Monographs of the Society for Research in Child Development, 58* (1, Serial No. 231).

Harris, P. L., Olthof, T., & Meerum Terwogt, M. (1981). Children's knowledge of emotion. *Journal of Child Psychology and Psychiatry, 22,* 247–261.

Harris, R. T. (1991, March). Anorexia nervosa and bulimia nervosa in female adolescents. *Nutrition Today* pp. 30–34.

Harris, S., Mussen, P. H., & Rutherford, E. (1976). Some cognitive, behavioral, and personality correlates of maturity of moral judgment. *Journal of Genetic Psychology, 128,* 123–135.

Harrison, A. O., Wilson, M. N., Pine, C. J., Chan, S. Q., & Buriel, R. (1990). Family ecologies of ethnic minority children. *Child Development, 61,* 347–362.

Harrison, M. R. (1996). Fetal surgery. *American Journal of Obstetrics and Gynecology, 174,* 1255–1264.

Hart, C. H., De Wolf, D. M., Wozniak, P., & Burts, D. C. (1992). Maternal and paternal disciplinary styles: Relations with preschoolers' playground behavioral orientations and peer status. *Child Development, 63,* 879–892.

Hart, D., Fegley, S., & Brengelman, D. (1993). Perceptions of past, present and future selves among children and adolescents. *British Journal of Developmental Psychology, 11,* 265–282.

Hart, E. L., Lahey, B. B., Loeber, R., Applegate, B., & Frick, P. J. (1995). Developmental change in attention-deficit hyperactivity disorder in boys: A four-year longitudinal study. *Journal of Abnormal Child Psychology, 23,* 729–749.

Hart, S. N., & Brassard, M. R. (1987). A major threat to children's mental health. *American Psychologist, 42,* 160–165.

Harter, S. (1985). Processes underlying the construct, maintenance and enhancement of the self-concept in children. In J. Suls & A. Greenwald (Eds.), *Psychological perspectives on the self* (Vol. 3). Hillsdale, NJ: Erlbaum.

Harter, S. (1986). Cognitive-developmental processes in the integration of concepts about emotions and the self. *Social Cognition, 4,* 119–151.

Harter, S. (1987). The determinants and mediational role of global self-worth in children. In N. Eisenberg (Ed.), *Contemporary topics in developmental psychology.* New York: Wiley.

Harter, S., Marold, D. B., Whitesell, N. R., & Cobbs, G. (1996). A model of the effects of perceived parent and peer support on adolescent false self behavior. *Child Development, 67,* 360–374.

Harter, S., & Monsour, A. (1992). Developmental analysis of conflict caused by opposing attributes in the adolescent self-portrait. *Developmental Psychology, 28,* 251–260.

Hartup, W. W. (1977, Fall). Peers, play, and pathology: A new look at the social behavior of children. *Newsletter of the Society for Research in Child Development,* pp. 1–3.

Hartup, W. W. (1983). Peer relations. In E. M. Hetherington (Ed.), *Handbook of child psychology: Vol. IV. Socialization, personality, and social development.* New York: Wiley.

Hartup, W. W. (1989). Social relationships and their developmental significance. *American Psychologist, 44,* 120–126.

Hartup, W. W. (1996). The company they keep: Friendships and their developmental significance. *Child Development, 67,* 1–13.

Hartup, W. W., & Coates, B. (1967). Imitation of a peer as a function of reinforcement from the peer group and rewardingness of the model. *Child Development, 38,* 1003–1016.

Hartup, W. W., French, D. C., Laursen, B., Johnston, M. K., & Ogawa, J. R. (1993). Conflict and friendship relations in middle childhood: Behavior in a closed field situation. *Child Development, 64,* 445–454.

Hartup, W. W., Laursen, B., Stewart, M. I., & Eastenson, A. (1988). Conflict and the friendship relations of young children. *Child Development, 59,* 1590–1600.

Hartup, W. W., & Sancilio, M. F. (1986). Children's friendships. In E. Shopler & G. B. Mesibov (Eds.), *Social behavior in autism.* New York: Plenum Press.

Harvey, S. M., & Spigner, C. (1995). Factors associated with sexual behavior among adolescents: A multivariate analysis. *Adolescence, 30,* 253–264.

Hatfield, J. S., Ferguson, L. R., & Alpert, R. (1967). Mother-child interaction and the socialization process. *Child Development, 38,* 365–414.

Haubenstricker, J., & Seefeldt, V. (1986). Acquisition of motor skills during childhood. In V. Seefeldt (Ed.), *Physical activity and well-being.* Reston, VA: American Alliance for Health, Education, Recreation, and Dance.

Hauser, S. T., Powers, S. I., Noam, G. G., & Bowlds, M. K. (1987). Family interiors of adolescent ego development trajectories. *Family Perspectives, 21,* 263–282.

Hawkins, J., Sheingold, K., Gearhart, M., & Berger, C. (1982). Microcomputers in classrooms: Impact on the social life of elementary classrooms. *Journal of Applied Developmental Psychology, 3,* 361–373.

Hawley, T. L. (1994). The development of cocaine-exposed children. *Current Problems in Pediatrics, 24,* 259–266.

Hawn, P. R., & Harris, L. J. (1983). Hand differences in grasp duration and reaching in two- and five-month old infants. In G. Young, S. Segalowitz, C. M. Carter, & S. E. Trehub (Eds.), *Manual specialization and the developing brain.* New York: Academic Press.

Hay, D. F. (1985). Learning to form relationships in infancy: Parallel attainments with parents and peers. *Developmental Review, 5,* 122–161.

Hay, D. F., Nash, A., & Pedersen, J. (1983). Interaction between 6-month-old peers. *Child Development, 54,* 557–562.

Hayne, H., & Rovee-Collier, C. (1995). The organization of reactivated memory. *Child Development, 66,* 893–906.

Hearold, S. (1986). A synthesis of 1043 effects of television on social behavior. In G. A. Comstock (Ed.), *Public communications and behavior* (Vol. 1). New York: Academic Press.

Heath, S. B. (1983). *Ways with words.* Cambridge: Cambridge University Press.

Heath, S. B. (1989). Oral and literate traditions among black Americans living in poverty. *American Psychologist, 44,* 367– 373.

Hebb, D. O. (1980). *Essay on mind.* Hillsdale, NJ: Erlbaum.

Held, R., Birch, E., & Gwiazda, J. (1980). Stereoacuity in human infants. *Proceedings of the National Academy of Sciences of the U.S.A., 77,* 5572–5574.

Henderson, A. A. (1994). *A new generation of evidence: The family is critical to student achievement.* Washington, DC: National Committee for Citizens in Education.

Hendrickse, R. G. (1991). Kwashiorkor: The hypothesis that incriminates aflatoxins. *Pediatrics, 88,* 376–379.

Henifin, M. S. (1993). New reproductive technologies: Equity and access to reproductive health care. *Journal of Social Issues, 49,* 61–74.

Hepper, P. G., & Shahidullah, B. S. (1994). Development of fetal hearing. *Archives of Disease in Childhood, 71,* F81–F87.

Herrnstein, R. J., & Murray, C. (1994). *The bell curve: Intelligence and class structure in American life.* New York: Free Press.

Hertsgaard, L., Gunnar, M., Erickson, M. F., & Nachmias, M. (1996). Adrenocortical responses to the Strange Situation in infants with disorganized/disoriented attachment relationships. *Child Development, 66,* 1100–1106.

Hertz-Lazarowitz, R., & Sharan, S. (1984). Enhancing prosocial behavior through cooperative learning in the classroom. In E. Staub, D. Bar-Tel, J. Karylowski, & J. Reykowski (Eds.), *Development and maintenance of prosocial behavior.* New York: Plenum Press.

Hertzog, C. (1989). Influences of cognitive slowing on age differences in intelligence. *Developmental Psychology, 25,* 636–651.

Hess, R. D., & Miura, I. T. (1985). Gender differences in enrollment in computer camps and classes. *Sex Roles, 13,* 193– 203.

Hetherington, E. M. (1989). Coping with family transitions: Winners, losers, and survivors. *Child Development, 60,* 1–14.

Hetherington, E. M., & Clingempeel, W. G. (1992). Coping with marital transitions: A family systems perspective. *Monographs of the Society for Research in Child Development* (2–3, Serial No. 227).

Hetherington, E. M., Cox, M., & Cox, R. (1982). Effects of divorce on parents and children. In M. Lamb (Ed.), *Nontraditional families*. Hillsdale, NJ: Erlbaum.

Hetherington, E. M., & Jodl, K. M. (1994). Stepfamilies as settings for child development. In A. Booth & J. Dunn (Eds.), *Stepfamilies: Who benefits? Who does not?* Hillsdale, NJ: Erlbaum.

Hetherington, E. M., Reiss, D., & Plomin, R. (Eds.) (1994). *Separate social worlds of siblings: Importance of nonshared environment on development*. Hillsdale, NJ: Erlbaum.

Hicks, D. J. (1965). Imitation and retention of film-mediated aggressive peer and adult models. *Journal of Personality and Social Psychology, 2*, 97–100.

Hilgard, J. R. (1932). Learning and maturation in preschool children. *Journal of Genetic Psychology, 41*, 36–56.

Hill, C. R., & Stafford, F. P. (1980). Parental care of children: Time diary estimates of quantity, predictability, and variety. *Journal of Human Resources, 15*, 219–289.

Hill, J. P. (1987). Research on adolescents and their families: Past and prospect. In C. E. Irwin (Ed.), *Adolescent social behavior and health*. San Francisco: Jossey-Bass.

Hill, S. T., & Shronk, L. K. (1979). The effect of early parent-infant contact on newborn body temperature. *Journal of Obstetric and Gynecological Nursing, 8*, 287–290.

Hinde, R. A. (1965). Interaction of internal and external factors in integration of canary reproduction. In F. Beach (Ed.), *Sex and behavior*. New York: Wiley.

Hinde, R. A. (1989). Ethological and relationships approaches. In R. Vasta (Ed.), *Annals of child development: Vol 6. Six theories of child development: Revised formulations and current issues*. Greenwich, CT: JAI Press.

Hinde, R. A., Titmus, G., Easton, D., & Tamplin, A. (1985). Incidence of "friendship" and behavior to strong associates versus non-associates in preschoolers. *Child Development, 56*, 234–245.

Hirsch, B. J., & Rapkin, B. D. (1987). The transition to junior high school: A longitudinal study of self-esteem, psychological symptomatology, school life, and social support. *Child Development, 58*, 1235–1243.

Hirsch-Pasek, K., Gleitman, L. R., & Gleitman, H. (1978). What does the brain say to the mind? A study of the detection and report of ambiguity by young children. In A. Sinclair, R. J. Jarvella, & W. J. M. Levelt (Eds.), *The child's conception of language*. Berlin: Springer-Verlag.

Hock, E., & DeMeis, D. K. (1990). Depression in mothers of infants: The role of maternal employment. *Developmental Psychology, 26*, 285–291.

Hoff, T. L. (1992). Psychology in Canada one hundred years ago: James Mark Baldwin at the University of Toronto. *Canadian Psychology, 33*, 683–694.

Hoff-Ginsberg, E. (1986). Function and structure in maternal speech: Their relation to the child's development of syntax. *Developmental Psychology, 22*, 155–163.

Hoff-Ginsberg, E. (1990). Maternal speech and the child's development of syntax: A further look. *Journal of Child Language, 17*, 85–99.

Hoff-Ginsberg, E. (1991). Mother-child conversation in different social classes and communicative settings. *Child Development, 62*, 782–796.

Hoffman, L. W. (1979). Maternal employment: 1979. *American Psychologist, 34*, 859–865.

Hoffman, L. W. (1984). Maternal employment and the young child. In M. Perlmutter (Ed.), *The Minnesota symposia on child psychology: Vol. 17. Parent-child interaction and parent-child relations in child development*. Hillsdale, NJ: Erlbaum.

Hoffman, L. W. (1989). Effects of maternal employment in the two-parent family. *American Psychologist, 44*, 283–292.

Hoffman, L. W., & Kloska, D. D. (1995). Parents' gender-based attitudes toward marital roles and child rearing: Development and validation of new measures. *Sex Roles, 32*, 273–295.

Hoffman, M. L. (1970). Moral development. In P. H. Mussen (Ed.), *Carmichael's manual of child psychology* (Vol. 2). New York: Wiley.

Hoffman, M. L. (1971). Identification and conscience development. *Child Development, 42*, 1071–1082.

Hoffman, M. L. (1975). Altruistic behavior and the parent-child relationship. *Journal of Personality and Social Psychology, 31*, 937–943.

Hoffman, M. L. (1976). Empathy, role-taking, guilt, and the development of altruistic motives. In T. Lickona (Ed.), *Moral development and moral behavior: Theory, research, and social issues*. New York: Holt, Rinehart & Winston.

Hoffman, M. L. (1982). Development of prosocial motivation: Empathy and guilt. In N. Eisenberg (Ed.), *The development of prosocial behavior*. New York: Academic Press.

Hoffman-Plotkin, D., & Twentyman, C. (1984). A multimodal assessment of behavioral and cognitive deficits in abused and neglected preschoolers. *Child Development, 52*, 13–30.

Hofsten, C. von, & Rönnqvist, L. (1993). The structuring of neonatal arm movement. *Child Development, 64*, 1046–1057.

Hoge, D. R., Smit, E. K., & Hanson, S. L. (1990). School experiences predicting changes in self-esteem of sixth- and seventh-graders. *Journal of Educational Psychology, 82*, 117–127.

Holden, G. W. (1983). Avoiding conflict: Mothers as tacticians in the supermarket. *Child Development, 54*, 233–240.

Holden, G. W., & West, M. J. (1989). Proximate regulation by mothers: A demonstration of how differing styles affect young children's behavior. *Child Development, 60*, 64–69.

Hollenbeck, A. R., & Slaby, R. G. (1979). Infant visual and vocal responses to television. *Child Development, 50*, 41–45.

Holmbeck, G. N., & Hill, J. P. (1991). Conflictive engagement, positive affect, and menarche in families with seventh-grade girls. *Child Development, 62*, 1030–1048.

Holton, J. B. (1995). Long-term results of treatment of some inherited metabolic diseases. *Pediatric Reviews and Communications, 8*, 139–156.

Holtz, B. A., & Lehman, E. B. (1995). Development of children's knowledge and use of strategies for self-control in a resistance-to-distraction task. *Merrill-Palmer Quarterly, 41*, 361–380.

Honzik, M. P., Macfarlane, J. W., & Allen, L. (1948). The stability of mental test performance between two and eighteen years. *Journal of Experimental Education, 17*, 309–329.

Hood, K. E., Draper, P., Crockett, L. J., & Petersen, A. C. (1987). The ontogeny and phylogeny of sex differences in development: A biopsychosocial synthesis. In D. B. Carter (Ed.), *Current conceptions of sex roles and sex typing: Theory and research*. New York: Praeger.

Hopkins, B., & Westra, T. (1990). Motor development, maternal expectations, and the role of handling. *Infant Behavior and Development, 13*, 117–122.

Hops, H., & Finch, M. (1985). Social competence and skill: A reassessment. In B. H. Schneider, K. H. Rubin, & J. E. Ledingham (Eds.), *Children's peer relations: Issues in assessment and intervention*. New York: Springer-Verlag.

Horn, J. L. (1968). Organization of abilities and the development of intelligence. *Psychological Review, 75*, 242–259.

Horn, J. L., & Cattell, R. B. (1967). Refinement and test of the theory of fluid and crystallized ability intelligences. *Journal of Educational Psychology, 57*, 253–270.

Horn, J. M., & Packard, T. (1985). Early identification of learning problems: A meta-analysis. *Journal of Educational Psychology, 77*, 349–360.

Horowitz, F. D. (1987a). *Exploring developmental theories: Toward a structural/behavioral model of development*. Hillsdale, NJ: Erlbaum.

Horowitz, F. D. (1987b). Targeting infant stimulation efforts: Theoretical challenges for research and intervention. In N. Gunzenhauser (Ed.), *Infant stimulation: For whom, what kind, when, and how much?* (Johnson & Johnson Baby Products Company Pediatric Round Table Series No. 13). Skilman, NJ: Johnson & Johnson.

Horwitz, R. A. (1979). Psychological effects of the "open classroom." *Review of Educational Research, 49*, 71–86.

Hossain, Z., Field, T., Gonzalez, J., Malphurs, J., Del Valle, C., & Pickens, J. (1994). Infants of "depressed" mothers interact better with their non-depressed fathers. *Infant Mental Health Journal, 15*, 348–357.

Hossain, Z., & Roopnarine, J. L. (1994). African-American fathers' involvement with infants: Relationship to their functioning style, support, education, and income. *Infant Behavior and Development, 17*, 175–184.

Howe, M. L. & Courage, M. L. (1993). On resolving the enigma of infantile amnesia. *Psychological Bulletin, 113*, 305–326.

Howe, P. E., & Schiller, M. (1952). Growth responses of the school child to changes in diet and environmental factors. *Journal of Applied Physiology, 5*, 51–61.

Howes, C. (1983). Patterns of friendship. *Child Development, 54*, 1041–1053.

Howes, C. (1987a). Peer interaction of young children. *Monographs of the Society for Research in Child Development, 53* (1, Serial No. 217).

Howes, C. (1987b). Social competence with peers in young children. *Developmental Review, 7*, 252–272.

Howes, C. (1990). Can age of entry and the quality of childcare predict adjustment in kindergarten? *Developmental Psychology, 26*, 292–303.

Howes, C., Phillips, D. A., & Whitebook, M. (1992). Thresholds of quality: Implications for the social development of children in center-based child care. *Child Development, 63*, 449–460.

Howes, C., Unger, O., & Seidner, L. B. (1989). Social pretend play in toddlers: Parallels with social play and with solitary pretend. *Child Development, 60,* 77–84.

Hsieh, F.-J., Shyu, M.-K., Sheu, B.-C., Lin, S.-P., Chen, C.-P., & Huang, F.-Y. (1995). Limb defects after chorionic villus sampling. *Obstetrics and Gynecology, 85,* 84–88.

Hsu, L. K. G. (1990). *Eating disorders.* New York: Guilford Press.

Hsu, L. K. G. (1996). Outcome of early onset anorexia nervosa: What do we know? *Journal of Youth and Adolescence, 25,* 563–568.

Hubel, D. H., & Wiesel, T. N. (1979, September). Brain mechanisms of vision. *Scientific American, 241,* pp. 150–162.

Hudson, J. A., Shapiro, L. R., & Sosa, B. B. (1995). Planning in the real world: Preschool children's scripts and plans for familiar events. *Child Development, 66,* 984–998.

Huebner, A., & Garrod, A. (1991). Moral reasoning in a karmic world. *Human Development, 34,* 341–352.

Huesmann, L. R., Lagerspetz, K., & Eron, L. D. (1984). Intervening variables and the TV violence-aggression relation: Evidence from two countries. *Developmental Psychology, 20,* 746–775.

Hughes, C., & Russell, J. (1993). Autistic children's difficulty with mental disengagement from an object: Its implications for theories of autism. *Developmental Psychology, 29,* 498–510.

Humphreys, A. P., & Smith, P. K. (1987). Rough and tumble, friendship, and dominance in schoolchildren: Evidence for continuity and change with age. *Child Development, 58,* 201–212.

Huntsinger, P. W. (1959). Differences in speed between American Negro and white children in the performance of the 35-yard-dash. *Research Quarterly, 30,* 366–368.

Hur, Y.-M., & Bouchard, T. J., Jr. (1995). Genetic influences on perceptions of childhood family environment: A reared apart twin study. *Child Development, 1995,* 330–345.

Huston, A. C. (1983). Sex typing. In E. M. Hetherington (Ed.), *Handbook of child psychology: Vol. IV. Socialization, personality, and social development.* New York: Wiley.

Huston, A. C. (1985). The development of sex typing: Themes from recent research. *Developmental Review, 5,* 1–17.

Huston, A. C., & Alvarez, M. M. (1990). The socialization context of gender role development in early adolescence. In R. Montemayor, G. R. Adams, & T. P. Gullota (Eds.), *From childhood to adolescence: A transitional period?* Newbury Park, CA: Sage.

Huston, A. C., Watkins, B. A., & Kunkel, D. (1989). Public policy and children's television. *American Psychologist, 44,* 424–433.

Huston, A. C., Wright, J. C., Rice, M. L., Kerkman, D., & St. Peters, M. (1990). Development of television viewing patterns in early childhood: A longitudinal investigation. *Developmental Psychology, 26,* 409–420.

Huttenlocher, J., Haight, W., Bryk, A., Seltzer, M., & Lyons, T. (1991). Early vocabulary growth: Relation to language input and gender. *Developmental Psychology, 27,* 236–248.

Huttenlocher, J., Newcombe, N., & Sandberg, E. H. (1994). The coding of spatial location in young children. *Cognitive Psychology, 27,* 115–148.

Huttenlocher, P. R. (1994). Synaptogenesis in human cerebral cortex. In G. Dawson & K. W. Fischer (Eds.), *Human behavior and the developing brain* (pp. 137–152). New York: Guilford.

Hwang, P. (1987). The changing role of Swedish fathers. In M. E. Lamb (Ed.), *The father's role: Cross-cultural perspectives.* Hillsdale, NJ: Erlbaum.

Hyde, J. S. (1984). How large are gender differences in aggression? A developmental meta-analysis. *Developmental Psychology, 20,* 722–736.

Hyde, J. S. (1986). Gender differences in aggression. In J. S. Hyde & M. C. Linn (Eds.), *The psychology of gender: Advances through meta-analysis.* Baltimore: Johns Hopkins University Press.

Hyde, J. S., Fennema, E., & Lamon, S. J. (1990). Gender differences in mathematics performance: A meta-analysis. *Psychological Bulletin, 107,* 139–155.

Hyde, J. S., & Linn, M. C. (1988). Gender differences in verbal ability: A meta-analysis. *Psychological Bulletin, 104,* 53–69.

Hymel, S., & Franke, S. (1985). Children's peer relations: Assessing self-perceptions. In B. H. Schneider, K. H. Rubin, & J. E. Ledingham (Eds.), *Children's peer relations: Issues in assessment and intervention.* New York: Springer-Verlag.

Hymel, S., Wagner, E., & Butler, L. J. (1990). Reputational bias: Views from the peer group. In S. R. Asher & J. D. Coie (Eds.), *Peer rejection in childhood.* Cambridge, UK: Cambridge University Press.

Inhelder, B., & Piaget, J. (1958). *The growth of logical thinking from childhood to adolescence.* New York: Basic Books.

Inhelder, B., & Piaget, J. (1964). *The early growth of logic in the child: Classification and seriation.* London: Routledge.

Isabella, R. A. (1993). Origins of attachment: Maternal interactive behavior across the first year. *Child Development, 64,* 605–621.

Isabella, R. A., Belsky, J., & von Eye, A. (1989). Origins of infant-mother attachment: An examination of interactional synchrony during the infant's first year. *Developmental Psychology, 25,* 12–21.

Isensee, W. (1986, September 3). *The Chronicle of Higher Education, 33.*

Ishii-Kuntz, M. (1994). Paternal involvement and perception toward fathers' roles: A comparison between Japan and the United States. *Journal of Family Issues, 15,* 30–48.

Ishii-Kuntz, M., & Coltrane, S. (1992). Predicting the sharing of household labor: Are parenting and housework distinct? *Sociological Perspectives, 35,* 629–647.

Izard, C. E. (1978). On the ontogenesis of emotions and emotion-cognition relationships in infancy. In M. Lewis & L. A. Rosenblum (Eds.), *The development of affect.* New York: Plenum Press.

Izard, C. E., & Dougherty, L. M. (1982). Two complementary systems for measuring facial expressions in infants and children. In C. E. Izard (Ed.), *Measuring emotions in infants and children* (Vol. 1). Cambridge, UK: Cambridge University Press.

Izard, C. E., Fantauzzo, C. A., Castle, J. M., Haynes, O. M., Rayias, M. F., & Putnam, P. H. (1995). The ontogeny and significance of infants' facial expressions in the first 9 months of life. *Developmental Psychology, 31,* 997–1013.

Izard, C. E., Haynes, O. M., Chisolm, G., & Baak, K. (1991). Emotional determinants of infant-mother attachment. *Child Development, 62,* 906–917.

Izard, C. E., Huebner, R. R., Risser, D., McGinnes, G., & Dougherty, L. (1980). The young infant's ability to produce discrete emotion expressions. *Developmental Psychology, 16,* 132–140.

Izard, C. E., Kagan, J., & Zajonc, R. B. (1984). Introduction. In C. E. Izard, J. Kagan, & R. B. Zajonc (Eds.), *Emotions, cognition, and behavior.* Cambridge, UK: Cambridge University Press.

Izard, C. E., & Malatesta, C. Z. (1987). Perspectives on emotional development: I. Differential emotions theory of early emotional development. In J. D. Osofsky (Ed.), *Handbook of infant development* (2nd ed.). New York: Wiley.

Jacklin, C. N. (1989). Female and male: Issues of gender. *American Psychologist, 44,* 127–133.

Jacklin, C. N., DiPietro, J. A., & Maccoby, E. E. (1984). Sex-typing behavior and sex-typing pressure in child/parent interaction. *Archives of Sexual Behavior, 13,* 413–425.

Jacklin, C. N., & Maccoby, E. E. (1978). Social behavior at thirty-three months in same-sex and mixed-sex dyads. *Child Development, 49,* 557–569.

Jacklin, C. N., & Reynolds, C. (1995). Gender and childhood socialization. In A. E. Beall & R. J. Sternberg (Eds.), *The psychology of gender.* New York: Guilford Press.

Jackson, A. W., & Hornbeck, D. W. (1989). Educating young adolescents: Why we must restructure middle grade schools. *American Psychologist, 44,* 831–836.

Jackson, J. F. (1993). Human behavioral genetics, Scarr's theory, and her views on interventions: A critical review and commentary on their implications for African American children. *Child Development, 64,* 1318–1332.

Jackson, S. (1987). Great Britain. In M. E. Lamb (Ed.), *The father's role: Cross-cultural perspectives.* Hillsdale, NJ: Erlbaum.

Jacobs, P. A., & Hassold, T. J. (1995). The origin of numerical chromosome abnormalities. *Advances in Genetics, 33,* 101–133.

Jacobsen, T., Edelstein, W., & Hofman, V. (1994). A longitudinal study of the relation between representations of attachment in childhood and cognitive functioning in childhood and adolescence. *Developmental Psychology, 30,* 112–124.

Jacobson, J. L., & Jacobson, S. W. (1996). Methodological considerations in behavioral toxicology in infants and children. *Developmental Psychology, 32,* 390–403.

Jacobson, S. W., & Frye, K. F. (1991). Effect of maternal social support on attachment: Experimental evidence. *Child Development, 62,* 572–582.

Jacobvitz, R. S., Wood, M., & Albin, K. (1989, April). *Cognitive skills and young children's comprehension of television.* Paper presented at the biennial meeting of the Society for Research in Child Development, Kansas City, MO.

Jaglom, L. M., & Gardner, H. (1981). The preschool television viewer as anthropologist. In H. Kelly & H. Gardner (Eds.), *New directions in child development: Viewing children through television* (pp. 9–30). San Francisco: Jossey-Bass.

Jakibchuk, Z., & Smeriglio, V. L. (1976). The influence of symbolic modeling on the social behavior of preschool children with low levels of social responsiveness. *Child Development, 47,* 838–841.

James, S. (1978). Effect of listener age and situation on the politeness of children's directives. *Journal of Psycholinguistic Research, 7,* 307–317.

James, W. (1890). *The principles of psychology.* New York: Henry Holt.

James, W. (1892). *Psychology: The briefer course.* New York: Henry Holt.

Jellife, D. B., & Jelliffe, E. F. P. (1992). Causation of kwashiorkor: Toward a multifactorial consensus. *Pediatric, 90,* 110–113.

Jencks, C. (1972). *Inequality: A reassessment of the effect of family and schooling in America.* New York: Basic Books.

Jenkins, J. M., & Astington, J. W. (1996). Cognitive factors and family structure associated with theory of mind development in young children. *Developmental Psychology, 32,* 70–78.

Jensen, A. R. (1980). *Bias in mental testing.* New York: Free Press.

Jensen, A. R. (1982). The chronometry of intelligence. In R. J. Sternberg (Ed.), *Advances in the psychology of human intelligence* (Vol. 1). Hillsdale, NJ: Erlbaum.

Jensen, A. R., & Munroe, E. (1979). Reaction time, movement time, and intelligence. *Intelligence, 3,* 121–126.

Johnson, J., & Newport, E. (1989). Critical period effects in second language learning: The influence of maturational state on the acquisition of English as a second language. *Cognitive Psychology, 21,* 60–99.

Johnson, J. W. C., & Yancey, M. K. (1996). A critique of the new recommendations for weight gain in pregnancy. *American Journal of Obstetrics and Gynecology, 174,* 254–258.

Johnson, M. (1991). Infant and toddler sleep: A telephone survey of parents in one community. *Journal of Developmental and Behavioral Pediatrics, 12,* 108–114.

Johnson, M. H. (1992). Imprinting and the development of face recognition: From chick to man. *Current Directions in Psychological Science, 1,* 52–55.

Johnson, M. H., Dziurawiec, S., Ellis, H. D., & Morton, J. (1991). Newborns' preferential tracking of face-like stimuli and its subsequent decline. *Cognition, 40,* 1–21.

Johnson, S. L., & Birch, L. L. (1994). Parents' and children's adiposity and eating style. *Pediatrics, 94,* 653–661.

Johnston, J. R., & Campbell, L. E. G. (1987). Instability in family networks of divorced and disputing parents. In E. J. Lawler & B. Markovsky (Eds.), *Advanced in group processes* (Vol. 4). Greenwich, CT: JAI.

Johnston, J., Ettema, J., & Davidson, T. (1980). *An evaluaton of "Freestyle": A television series to reduce sex role stereotypes.* Ann Arbor: Institute for Social Research.

Jones, D. C., & Costin, S. E. (1995). Friendship quality during adolescence: The contributions of relationship orientations, instrumentality, and expressivity. *Merrill-Palmer Quarterly, 41,* 517–535.

Jones, G. P., & Dembo, M. H. (1989). Age and sex role differences in intimate friendships during childhood and adolescence. *Merrill-Palmer Quarterly, 35,* 445–462.

Jones, H. E., & Bayley, N. (1941). The Berkeley Growth Study. *Child Development, 12,* 167–173.

Jones, K. L., & Smith, D. W. (1973). Recognition of the fetal alcohol syndrome in early infancy. *Lancet, 2,* 999–1001.

Jones, M. C. (1965). Psychological correlates of somatic development. *Child Development, 36,* 899–911.

Josephson Institute of Ethics. (1996). *1996 report card on American integrity.* Marina de Rey, CA: Joseph & Edna Josephson Institute of Ethics.

Jusczyk, P. W., Cutler, A., & Redanz, L. (1993). Infants' sensitivity to predominant stress patterns in English. *Child Development, 64,* 675–687.

Jusczyk, P. W., Friederici, A. D., Wessels, J. M. I., Svenkerud, V. Y., & Jusczyk, A. M (1993). Infants' sensitivity to the sound patterns of native language words. *Journal of Memory and Language, 32,* 402–420.

Jusczyk, P. W., Hirsh-Pasek, K., Kemler Nelson, D. G., Kennedy, L. J., Woodward, A. & Piwoz, J. (1992). Perception of acoustic correlates of major phrasal units by young infants. *Cognitive Psychology, 24,* 252–293.

Juster, F. T. (1987). A note on recent changes in time use. In F. T. Juster & F. Stafford (Eds.), *Studies in the measurement of time allocation.* Ann Arbor: Institute for Social Research.

Juvonen, J. (1992). Negative peer reactions from the perspective of the reactor. *Journal of Educational Psychology, 84,* 314–321.

Kagan, J. (1976). Emergent themes in human development. *American Scientist, 64,* 186–196.

Kagan, J. (1981). *The second year: The emergence of self-awareness.* Cambridge, MA: Harvard University Press.

Kagan, J. (1984). *The nature of the child.* New York: Basic Books.

Kagan, J. (1994). *Galen's prophecy: Temperament in human nature.* New York: Basic Books.

Kagan, J., Arcus, D., Snidman, N., Feng, W. Y., Hendler, J., & Greene, S. (1994). Reactivity in infants: A cross-national comparison. *Developmental Psychology, 30,* 342–345.

Kagan, J., Kearsley, R. B., & Zelazo, P. R. (1978). *Infancy: Its place in human development.* Cambridge, UK: Cambridge University Press.

Kagan, J., Reznick, J. S., Clarke, C., Snidman, N., & Garcia-Coll, C. (1984). Behavioral inhibition to the unfamiliar. *Child Development, 55,* 2212–2225.

Kagan, J., Reznick, J. S., & Snidman, N. (1988). Biological basis of childhood shyness. *Science, 240,* 167–171.

Kagan, J., Snidman, N., & Arcus, D. M. (1992). Initial reactions to unfamiliarity. *Current Directions in Psychological Science, 1,* 171–174.

Kagan, J., Snidman, N., & Arcus, D. (1993). On the temperamental categories of inhibited and uninhibited children. In K. H. Rubin & J. B. Asendorpf (Eds.), *Social withdrawal, inhibition, and shyness in children.* Hillsdale, NJ: Erlbaum.

Kahn, P. H., Jr., (1992). Children's obligatory and discretionary moral judgments. *Child Development, 63,* 416–430.

Kahneman, D. (1973). *Attention and effort.* Englewood Cliffs, NJ: Prentice-Hall.

Kail, R. (1986). Sources of age differences in speed of processing. *Child Development, 57,* 969–987.

Kail, R. (1990). *The development of memory in children* (3rd ed.). New York: W. H. Freeman.

Kail, R. (1991a). Development of processing speed in childhood and adolescence. In H. W. Reese (Ed.), *Advances in child development and behavior* (Vol. 23). San Diego, CA: Academic Press.

Kail, R. (1991b). Processing time declines exponentially during childhood and adolescence. *Developmental Psychology, 27,* 259–266.

Kail, R., & Pellegrino, J. W. (1985). *Human intelligence: Perspectives and prospects.* New York: W. H. Freeman.

Kaitz, M., Lapidot, P., Bronner, R., & Eidelman, A. I. (1992). Parturient women can recognize their infants by touch. *Developmental Psychology, 28,* 35–39.

Kaitz, M., Shiri, S., Danziger, S., Hershko, Z., & Eidelman, A. I. (1994). Fathers can also recognize their newborns by touch. *Infant Behavior and Development, 17,* 205–207.

Kajii, T., Kida, M., & Takahashi, K. (1973). The effect of thalidomide intake during 113 human pregnancies. *Teratology, 8,* 163–166.

Kamerman, S. B. (1996). Child and family policies: An international overview. In E. F. Zigler, S. L. Kagan, & N. W. Hall (Eds.), *Children, families, and government.* New York: Cambridge University Press.

Kanner, L. (1943). Autistic disturbances of affective contact. *Nervous Children, 2,* 217–250.

Kaplan, H., & Dove, H. (1987). Infant development among the Ache of Eastern Paraguay. *Developmental Psychology, 23,* 190–196.

Karmel, B. Z., & Maisel, E. B. (1975). A neuronal activity model for infant visual attention. In L. B. Cohen & P. Salapatek (Eds.), *Infant perception: From sensation to cognition* (Vol. 1). New York: Academic Press.

Karmiloff-Smith, A. (1995). Annotation: The extraordinary cognitive journey from foetus through infancy. *Journal of Child Psychology and Psychiatry, 36,* 1293–1313.

Karniol, R. (1989). The role of manual manipulative stages in the infant's acquisition of perceived control over objects. *Developmental Review, 9,* 205–233.

Karraker, K. H., Vogel, D. A., & Lake, M. A. (1995). Parents' gender-stereotyped perceptions of newborns: The eye of the beholder revisited. *Sex Roles, 33,* 687–701.

Katz, P. A. (1987). Variations in family constellation: Effects on gender schemata. In L. S. Liben & M. L. Signorella (Eds.), *New directions for child development: No. 38. Children's gender schemata.* San Francisco: Jossey-Bass.

Katz, P. A. & Ksansnak, K. R. (1994). Developmental aspects of gender role flexibility and traditionality in middle childhood and adolescence. *Developmental Psychology, 30,* 272–282.

Kaufman, A. S., Kamphaus, R. W., & Kaufman, N. L. (1985). New directions in intelligence testing: The Kaufman Assessment Battery for Children (K-ABC). In B. B. Wolman (Ed.), *Handbook of intelligence.* New York: Wiley.

Kaufman, A. S., & Kaufman, N. L. (1983). *K-ABC administration and scoring manual.* Circle Pines, MN: American Guidance Service.

Kaye, K., & Marcus, J. (1981). Infant imitation: The sensorimotor agenda. *Developmental Psychology, 17,* 258–265.

Kazdin, A. E. (1993). Adolescent mental health: Prevention and treatment programs. *American Psychologist, 48,* 127–141.

Keane, S. P., & Parrish, A. E. (1992). The role of affective information in the determination of intent. *Developmental Psychology, 28,* 159–162.

Keasey, C. B. (1971). Social participation as a factor in the moral development of preadolescents. *Developmental Psychology, 5,* 216–220.

Keeney, T. J., Cannizzo, S. R., & Flavell, J. H. (1967). Spontaneous and induced rehearsal in a recall task. *Child Development, 38,* 953–966.

Keil, F. C. (1989). *Concepts, kinds, and cognitive development.* Cambridge, MA: MIT Press.

Kelley, M. L., Power, T. G., & Wimbush, D. D. (1992). Determinants of disciplinary practices in low-income black mothers. *Child Development, 63,* 573–582.

Kellman, P. J. (1993). Kinematic foundations of infant visual perception. In C. Granrud (Ed.), *Visual perception and cognition in infancy* (pp. 121–173). Hillsdale, NJ: Erlbaum.

Kellman, P. J. (1996). The origins of object perception. In R. Gelman & T. Au (eds.), *Perceptual and cognitive development* (pp. 3–48). New York: Academic Press.

Kellman, P. J., & Spelke, E. S. (1983). Perception of partly occluded objects in infancy. *Cognitive Psychology, 15,* 483–524.

Kelly, M. H. (1992). Using sound to solve syntactic problems: The role of phonology in grammatical category assignments. *Psychological Review, 99,* 349–364.

Kemler Nelson, D. G., Hirsh-Pasek, K., Jusczyk, P. W., & Cassidy, K. W. (1989). How the prosodic cues in motherese might assist language learning. *Journal of Child Language, 16,* 55–68.

Kemp, J. S., Nelson, V. E., & Thach, B. T. (1994). Physical properties of bedding that may increase risk of Sudden Infant Death Syndrome in prone-sleeping infants. *Pediatric Research, 36,* 7–11.

Kendrick, J. S., & Merritt, R. K. (1996). Women and smoking: An update for the 1990s. *American Journal of Obstetrics and Gynecology, 175,* 528–535.

Kennell, J., Klaus, M., McGrath, S., Robertson, S. & Hinkley, C. (1991). Continuous emotional support during labor in a U.S. hospital. *Journal of the American Medical Associaton, 265,* 2197–2201.

Keogh, J., & Sugden, D. (1985). *Movement skill development.* New York: Macmillan.

Kerig, P. K., Cowan, P. A., & Cowan, C. P. (1993). Marital quality and gender differences in parent-child interaction. *Developmental Psychology, 29,* 931–939.

Kerlinger, F. N. (1964). *Foundations of behavioral research: Educational and psychological inquiry.* New York: Holt, Rinehart & Winston.

Kerns, L. L., & Davis, G. P. (1986). Psychotropic drugs in pregnancy. In I. J. Chasnoff (Ed.), *Drug use in pregnancy: Mother and child.* Lancaster, England: MTP Press.

Kessler, S. (1992). Psychological aspects of genetic counseling, VII: Thoughts on directiveness. *Journal of Genetic Counseling, 1,* 9–18.

Khayrallah, M., & Van Den Meiraker, M. (1987). LOGO programming and the acquisition of cognitive skills. *Journal of Computer-Based Instruction, 14,* 133–137.

Kindermann, T. A. (1993). Natural peer groups as contexts for individual development: The case of children's motivation in school. *Developmental Psychology, 29,* 970–977.

Kinsbourne, M., & Hiscock, M. (1983). The normal and deviant development of functional lateralization of the brain. In M. M. Haith & J. C. Campos (Eds.), *Infancy and developmental psychobiology: Vol. II. Handbook of child psychology.* New York: Wiley.

Kirby, D., Short, L., Collins, J., Rugg, D., Kolbe, L., Howard, M., Miller, B., Sonenstein, F., & Zabin, L. S. (1994). School-based programs to reduce sexual risk behaviors: A review of effectiveness. *Public Health Reports, 109,* 339–360.

Kirkpatrick, S. W., & Sanders, D. M. (1978). Body image stereotypes: A developmental comparison. *Journal of Genetic Psychology, 132,* 87–95.

Kisilevsky, B. S., & Muir, D. W. (1991). Human fetal and subsequent newborn responses to sound and vibration. *Infant Behavior and Development, 14,* 1–26.

Klahr, D. (1978). Goal formation, planning, and learning by preschool problem solvers or: "My socks are in the dryer." In R. S. Siegler (Ed.), *Children's thinking: What develops?* Hillsdale, NJ: Erlbaum.

Klahr, D. (1989). Information-processing approaches. In R. Vasta (Ed.), *Annals of child development: Vol 6. Six theories of child development: Revised formulations and current issues.* Greenwich, CT: JAI Press.

Klahr, D., & Dunbar, K. (1988). Dual space search during scientific reasoning. *Cognitive Science, 12,* 1–55.

Klahr, D., Fay, A. L., & Dunbar, K. (1993). Heuristics for scientific experimentation: A developmental study. *Cognitive Psychology, 25,* 111–146.

Klahr, D., & Robinson, M. (1981). Formal assessment of problem solving and planning processes in preschool children. *Cognitive Psychology, 13,* 113–148.

Klaus, M., & Kennell, J. (1976). *Maternal infant bonding.* St. Louis: C. V. Mosby.

Klaus, M., & Kennell, J. (1982). *Parent-infant bonding.* St. Louis: C. V. Mosby.

Klebanov, P. K., Brooks-Gunn, J., & McCormick, M. C. (1994). Classroom behavior of very low birth weight elementary school children. *Pediatrics, 94,* 700–708.

Klima, E. S., & Bellugi, U. (1966). Syntactic regularities in the speech of children. In J. Lyons & R. J. Wales (Eds.), *Psycholinguistic papers: The proceedings of the 1966 Edinburgh conference.* Edinburgh: Edinburgh University Press.

Kline, M., Tschann, J. M., Johnston, J. R., & Wallerstein, J. S. (1989). Children's adjustment in joint and sole physical custody families. *Developmental Psychology, 25,* 430–438.

Klonoff-Cohen, S., Edelstein, S. L., Lefkowitz, E. S., Srinivasan, I. P., Kaegi, D., Chang, J. C., & Wiley, K. J. (1995). The effect of passive smoking and tobacco exposure through breast milk on sudden infant death syndrome. *Journal of the American Medical Association, 273,* 795–798.

Knowles, R. V. (1985). *Genetics, society and decisions.* Columbus, OH: Merrill.

Kobak, R. R., Cole, H. E., Ferenz-Gillies, R., & Fleming, W. S. (1993). Attachment and emotion regulation during mother-teen problem-solving: A control theory analysis. *Child Development, 64,* 231–245.

Kobasigawa, A. (1968). Inhibitory and disinhibitory effects of models on sex-inappropriate behavior in children. *Psychologia, 11,* 86–96.

Kobasigawa, A. (1974). Utilization of retrieval cues by children in recall. *Child Development, 45,* 127–134.

Kobayashi-Winata, H., & Power, T. G. (1989). Child rearing and compliance: Japanese and American families in Houston. *Journal of Cross-Cultural Psychology, 20,* 333–356.

Kochanska, G. (1993). Toward a synthesis of parental socialization and child temperament in early development of conscience. *Child Development, 64,* 325–347.

Kochanska, G. (1994). Beyond cognition: Expanding the search for the early roots of internalization and conscience. *Developmental Psychology, 30,* 20–22.

Kochanska, G., & Aksan, N. (1995). Mother-child mutually positive affect, the quality of child compliance to requests and prohibitions, and maternal control as correlates of early internalization. *Child Development, 66,* 236–254.

Kochanska, G., Aksan, N., & Koenig, A. L. (1995). A longitudinal study of the roots of preschoolers' conscience: Committed compliance and emerging internalizations. *Child Development, 66,* 1752–1769.

Kochanska, G., Casey, R. J., & Kukumoto, A. (1995). Toddlers' sensitivity to standard violation. *Child Development, 66,* 643–656.

Kochanska, G., DeVet, K., Goldman, M., Murray, K., & Putnam, S. P. (1994). Maternal reports of conscience development and temperament in young children. *Child Development, 65,* 852–868.

Kochenderfer, B. J., & Ladd, G. W. (1996). Peer victimization: Cause or consequence of school maladjustment? *Child Development, 67,* 1305–1317.

Koff, E., & Rierdan, J. (1991). Perceptions of weight and attitude toward eating in early adolescent girls. *Journal of Adolescent Health, 12,* 307–312.

Koff, E., & Rierdan, J. (1995). Preparing girls for menstruation: Recommendations from adolescent girls. *Adolescence, 30,* 795–811.

Kohlberg, L. (1966). A cognitive-developmental analysis of children's sex-role concepts and attitudes. In E. E. Maccoby (Ed.), *The development of sex differences.* Stanford, CA: Stanford University Press.

Kohlberg, L. (1969). Stage and sequence: The cognitive-developmental approach to socialization. In D. A. Goslin (Ed.), *The handbook of socialization theory and research.* Chicago: Rand McNally.

Kohlberg, L. (1976). Moral stages and moralization: The cognitive developmental approach. In T. Lickona (Ed.), *Moral development and moral behavior: Theory, research, and social issues.* New York: Holt, Rinehart & Winston.

Kohlberg, L. (1984). *Essays on moral development: Vol. 2. The psychology of moral development.* San Francisco: Harper & Row.

Kohlberg, L., & Kramer, R. (1969). Continuities and discontinuities in childhood moral development. *Human Development, 12,* 93–120.

Kohlberg, L., Levine, C., & Hewer, A. (1983). *Moral stages: A current formulation and a response to critics.* Basel: Karger.

Kohlberg, L., Yaeger, J., & Hjertholm, E. (1968). Private speech: Four studies and a review of theories. *Child Development, 45,* 127–134.

Kolb, B. (1989). Brain development, plasticity, and behavior. *American Psychologist, 44,* 1203–1212.

Koneya, M. (1976). Location and interaction in row-and-column seating arrangements. *Environment and Behavior, 8,* 265–282.

Kopp, C. B. (1979). Perspectives on infant motor system development. In M. Bornstein & W. Kessen (Eds.), *Psychological development from infancy.* Hillsdale, NJ: Erlbaum.

Kopp, C. B. (1987). The growth of self-regulation: Caregivers and children. In N. Eisenberg (Ed.), *Contemporary topics in developmental psychology.* New York: Wiley.

Kopp, C. B. (1992). Emotional distress and control in young children. In N. Eisenberg & R. A. Fabes (Eds.), *Emotion and its regulation in early development* (*New Directions in Child Development,* No. 55). San Francisco: Jossey-Bass.

Kopp, C. B., & McCall, R. B. (1980). Stability and instability in mental performance among normal, at-risk, and handicapped infants and children. In P. B. Baltes & O. G. Grim, Jr. (Eds.), *Life-span development and behavior* (Vol. 4). New York: Academic Press.

Korner, A. F. (1972). State as a variable, as obstacle, and mediator of stimulation in infant research. *Merrill-Palmer Quarterly, 18,* 77–94.

Korner, A. F. (1987). Preventive intervention with high-risk newborns: Theoretical, conceptual, and methodological perspectives. In J. D. Osofsky (Ed.), *Handbook of infant development* (2nd ed.). New York: Wiley.

Kotelchuk, M. (1976). The infant's relationship to the father: Experimental evidence. In M. E. Lamb (Ed.), *The role of the father in child development.* New York: Wiley.

Kovacs, D. M., Parker, J. G., & Hoffman, L. W. (1996). Behavioral, affective, and social correlates of involvement in cross-sex friendship in elementary school. *Child Development, 67,* 2269–2286.

Kowal, A., & Kramer, L. (1997). Children's understanding of potential differential treatment. *Child Development, 68,* 113–126.

Kraemer, H. C., Korner, A., Anders, T., Jacklin, C. N., & Dimiceli, S. (1985). Obstetric drugs and infant behavior: A re-evaluation. *Journal of Pediatric Psychology, 10,* 345–353.

Krafchuk, E. E., Tronick, E. Z., & Clifton, R. K. (1983). Behavioral and cardiac responses to sound in preterm infants varying in risk status: A hypothesis of their paradoxical reactivity. In T. Field & A. Sostek (Eds.), *Infants born at risk: Physiological, perceptual, and cognitive processes.* New York: Grune & Stratton.

Krauss, R. H., & Glucksberg, S. (1969). The development of communication. *Child Development, 40,* 255–266.

Krebs, D. L., & Van Hesteren, F. (1994). The development of altruism: Toward an integrative model. *Developmental Review, 14,* 103–158.

Kremenitzer, J. P., Vaughan, H. G., Kurtzberg, D., & Dowling, K. (1979). Smooth-pursuit eye movements in the newborn infant. *Child Development, 50,* 442–448.

Krendl, K. A., & Broihier, M. (1992). Student responses to computers: A longitudinal study. *Journal of Educational Computing Research, 8,* 215–227.

Kreutzer, M. A., Leonard, S. C., & Flavell, J. H. (1975). An interview study of children's knowledge about memory. *Monographs of the Society for Research in Child Development, 40*(1, Serial No. 159).

Krevans, J., & Gibbs, J. C. (1996). Parents' use of inductive discipline: Relations to children's empathy and prosocial behavior. *Child Development, 67,* 3263–3277.

Krogman, W. M. (1972). *Child growth.* Ann Arbor, MI: University of Michigan Press.

Kruger, A. C. (1992). The effects of peer and adult-child transactive discussions on moral reasoning. *Merrill-Palmer Quarterly, 38,* 191–211.

Krumhansl, C. L., & Jusczyk, P. W. (1990). Infants' perception of phrase structure in music. *Psychological Science, 1,* 70–73.

Kuchuk, A., Vibbert, M., & Bornstein, M. H. (1986). The perception of smiling and its experiential correlates in three-month-old infants. *Child Development, 57,* 1054–1061.

Kuczaj, S. A., Borys, R. H., & Jones, M. (1989). On the interaction of language and thought: Some thoughts and developmental data. In A. Gellatly, D. Rogers, & J. A. Sloboda (Eds.), *Cognition and social worlds.* Oxford: Clarendon Press.

Kuczynski, L., & Kochanska, G. (1995). Function and content of maternal demands: Developmental significance of early demands for competent action. *Child Development, 66,* 616–628.

Kuczynski, L., Kochanska, G., Radke-Yarrow, M., & Girnius-Brown, O. (1987). A developmental interpretation of young children's noncompliance. *Developmental Psychology, 23,* 799–806.

Kuczynski, L., Zahn-Waxler, C., & Radke-Yarrow, M. (1987). Development and content of imitation in the second and third year of life: A socialization perspective. *Developmental Psychology, 23,* 276–282.

Kuebli, J., Butler, S., & Fivush, R. (1995). Mother-child talk about past emotions: Relations of maternal language and child gender over time. *Cognition and Emotion, 9,* 265–283.

Kugelmass, S., & Breznitz, S. (1967). The development of intentionality in moral judgment in city and kibbutz adolescents. *Journal of Genetic Psychology, 111,* 103–111.

Kuhl, P. K. (1987). Perception of speech and sound in early infancy. In P. Salapatek & L. Cohen (Eds.), *Handbook of infant perception: From perception to cognition* (Vol. 2). Orlando, FL: Academic Press.

Kuhl, P. K., & Miller, J. D. (1978). Speech perception by the chinchilla: Identification functions for synthetic VOT stimuli. *Journal of the Acoustical Society of America, 63,* 905–917.

Kuhl, P. K., & Padden, D. M. (1983). Enhanced discriminability at the phonetic boundary for the place feature in macaques. *Journal of the Acoustical Society of America, 73,* 1003–1010.

Kuhl, P. K., Williams, K. A., Lacerda, F., Stevens, K. N., & Lindblom, B. (1992). Linguistic experience alters phonetic perception in infants by 6 months of age. *Science, 255,* 606– 608.

Kuhn, D., Garcia-Mila, M., Zohar, A., & Andersen, C. (1995). Strategies of knowledge acquisition. *Monographs of the Society for Research in Child Development, 60* (No. 4, Serial No. 245).

Kuhn, D., Nash, S. C., & Brucken, L. (1978). Sex role concepts of two- and three-year-olds. *Child Development, 49,* 445–451.

Kuhn, D., Schauble, L., & Garcia-Mila, M. (1992). Cross-domain development of scientific reasoning. *Cognition and Instruction, 9,* 285–327.

Kulik, J. A., Bangert, R. L., & Williams, G. W. (1983). Effects of computer-based teaching on secondary school students. *Journal of Educational Psychology, 75,* 19–26.

Kulik, J. A., Kulik, C. C., & Bangert-Drowns, R. L. (1985). Effectiveness of computer-based education in elementary schools. *Computers in Human Behavior, 1,* 59–74.

Kunkel, D., & Roberts, D. (1991). Young minds and marketplace values: Issues in children's television advertising. *Journal of Social Issues, 47,* 57–72.

Kuppermann, M., Gates, E., & Washington, A. E. (1996). Racial ethnic differences in prenatal diagnostic test use and outcomes: Preferences, socioeconomics, or patient knowledge? *Obstetrics and Gynecology, 87,* 675–682.

Kurdek, L. A. (1978). Perspective-taking as the cognitive basis of children's moral development: A review of the literature. *Merrill-Palmer Quarterly, 24,* 3–28.

Kurdek, L. A. (1989). Siblings' reactions to parental divorce. *Journal of Divorce, 12,* 203–219.

Kurdek, L. A., Fine, M. A., & Sinclair, R. J. (1995). School adjustment in sixth graders: Parenting transitions, family climate, and peer norm effects. *Child Development, 66,* 430–445.

La Greca, A. M., & Santogrossi, D. A. (1980). Social skills training with elementary school students: A behavioral group approach. *Journal of Consulting and Clinical Psychology, 48,* 220–227.

LaBarbera, J. D., Izard, C. E., Vietze, P., & Parisi, S. A. (1976). Four- and six-month-old infants' visual responses to joy, anger, and neutral expressions. *Child Development, 47,* 535–538.

Ladd, G. W. (1983). Social networks of popular, average, and rejected children in school settings. *Merrill-Palmer Quarterly, 29,* 283–307.

Ladd, G. W. (1990). Having friends, keeping friends, making friends, and being liked by peers in the classroom: Predictors of children's early school adjustment? *Child Development, 61,* 1081–1100.

Ladd, G. W., & Asher, S. R. (1985). Social skill training and children's peer relations. In L. L'Abate & M. Milan (Eds.), *Handbook of social skills training.* New York: Wiley.

Ladd, G. W., & Golter, B. S. (1988). Parents' management of preschooler's peer relations: Is it related to children's social competencies? *Developmental Psychology, 24,* 109–117.

Ladd, G. W., & Hart, C. H. (1992). Creating informal play opportunities: Are parents' and preschoolers' initiations related to children's competence with peers? *Developmental Psychology, 28,* 1179–1187.

Ladd, G. W., Kochenderfer, B. J., & Coleman, C. C. (1996). Friendship quality as a predictor of young children's early school adjustment. *Child Development, 67,* 1103–1118.

Ladd, G. W., & Price, J. M. (1987). Predicting children's social and school adjustment following the transition from preschool to kindergarten. *Child Development, 58,* 1168–1189.

Ladd, G. W., Price, J. M., & Hart, C. H. (1988). Predicting preschoolers' peer status from their playground behaviors. *Child Development, 59,* 986–992.

LaFreniere, P., & Charlesworth, W. R. (1983). Dominance, attention, and affiliation in a preschool group: A nine-month longitudinal study. *Ethology and Sociobiology, 4,* 55–67.

Lahey, B. B., Hammer, D., Crumrine, P. L., & Forehand, R. L. (1980). Birth order sex interactions in child behavior problems. *Developmental Psychology, 16,* 608–615.

Lalonde, C. E., & Werker, J. F. (1995). Cognitive influences on cross-language speech perception in infancy. *Infant Behavior and Development, 18,* 459–475.

Lamaze, F. (1970). *Painless childbirth: Psychoprophylactic method.* Chicago: Henry Regnery.

Lamb, M. E. (1981). *The role of the father in child development* (rev. ed.). New York: Wiley.

Lamb, M. E. (1987). Introduction: The emergent American father. In M. E. Lamb (Ed.), *The father's role: Cross-cultural perspectives.* Hillsdale, NJ: Erlbaum.

Lamb, M. E., Easterbrooks, M. A., & Holden, G. (1980). Reinforcement and punishment among preschoolers: Characteristics and correlates. *Child Development, 51,* 1230–1236.

Lamb, M. E., Pleck, J. H., Charnov, E. L., & Levine, J. A. (1987). A biosocial perspective on paternal behavior and involvement. In J. B. Lancaster, J. Altmann, A. S. Rossi, & L. R. Sherrod (Eds.), *Parenting across the life span: Biosocial dimensions.* New York: Aldine de Gruyter.

Lamb, M. E., & Roopnarine, J. L. (1979). Peer influences on sex-role development in preschoolers. *Child Development, 50,* 1219–1222.

Lamb, M. E., Thompson, R. A., Gardner, W., & Charnov, E. L. (1985). *Infant-mother attachment: The origins and developmental significance of individual differences in strange situation behavior.* Hillsdale, NJ: Erlbaum.

Lamb, S. (1991). First moral sense: Aspects of and contributors to a beginning morality in the second year of life. In W. M. Kurtines & J. L. Gewirtz (Eds.), *Handbook of moral behavior and development: Vol. 2. Research.* Hillsdale, NJ: Erlbaum.

Lamborn, S. D., Mounts, N. S., Steinberg, L., & Dornbusch, S. M. (1991). Patterns of competence and adjustment among adolescents from authoritative, authoritarian, indulgent, and neglectful families. *Child Development, 62,* 1049–1065.

Lampl, M., Veldhuis, J. D., & Johnson, M. L. (1992). Saltation and stasis: A model of human growth. *Science, 258,* 801–803.

Landau, S., Lorch, E. P., & Milich, R. (1992). Visual attention to and comprehension of television in attention-deficit hyperactivity disordered and normal boys. *Child Development, 63,* 928–937.

Landesman-Dwyer, S., Keller, L. S., & Streissguth, A. P. (1978). Naturalistic observations of newborns: Effects of maternal alcohol intake. *Alcoholism, 2,* 171–177.

Lane, D. M., & Pearson, D. A. (1982). The development of selective attention. *Merrill-Palmer Quarterly, 28,* 317–345.

Langlois, J. H., & Stephan, C. (1981). Beauty and the beast: The role of physical attractiveness in the development of peer relations and social behavior. In S. S. Brehm, S. H. Kassin, & F. X. Gibbons (Eds.), *Developmental social psychology.* New York: Oxford University Press.

Laosa, L. M. (1982). Families as facilitators of children's intellectual development at 3 years of age: A causal analysis. In L. M. Laosa & I. E. Sigel (Eds.), *Families as learning environments for children.* New York: Plenum Press.

Larkin, R. W. (1979). *Suburban youth in cultural crisis.* New York: Oxford University Press.

Larson, R. W., & Ham, M. (1993). Stress and "storm and stress" in early adolescence: The relationship of negative events with dysphoric affect. *Developmental Psychology, 29,* 130–140.

Larson, R. W., & Lampman-Petraitis, C. (1989). Daily emotional stress as reported by children and adolescents. *Child Development, 60,* 1250–1260.

Laupa, M. (1991). Children's reasoning about three authority attributes: Adult status, knowledge, and social position. *Developmental Psychology, 27,* 321–329.

Lawson, M. (1980). Development of body build stereotypes, peer ratings, and self-esteem in Australian children. *Journal of Psychology, 104,* 111–118.

Lazar, I., & Darlington, R. (1982). Lasting effects of early education: A report from the Consortium for Longitudinal Studies. *Monographs of the Society for Research in Child Development, 47*(2–3, Serial No. 195).

LeBoyer, F. (1975). *Birth without violoence.* New York: Knopf.

Lee, L. C. (1971). The concommitant development of cognitive and moral modes of thought: A test of selected deductions from Piaget's theory. *Genetic Psychology Monographs, 83,* 93–146.

Lee, R. V. (1988). Sexually transmitted infections. In G. N. Burrow & T. F. Ferris (Eds.), *Medical complications during pregnancy.* Philadelphia: W. B. Saunders.

Lefkowitz, M. M. (1981). Smoking during pregnancy: Long-term effects on offspring. *Developmental Psychology, 17,* 192–194.

Legido, A., Tonyes, L., Carter, D., Schoemaker, A., Di George, A., & Grover, W. D. (1993). Treatment variables and intellectual outcome in children with classic phenylketonuria: A single-center-based study. *Clinical Pediatrics, 32,* 417–425.

Leichtman, M. D., & Ceci, S. J. (1995). The effects of stereotypes and suggestions on preschoolers' reports. *Developmental Psychology, 31,* 568–578.

Lemish, D., & Rice, M. (1986). Television as a talking picture book: A prop for language acquisition. *Journal of Child Language, 13,* 251–274.

Lempers, J. D., Flavell, E. R., & Flavell, J. H. (1977). The development in very young children of tacit knowledge concerning visual perception. *Genetic Psychology Monographs, 95,* 3–53.

Lenneberg, E. (1967). *Biological foundations of language.* New York: Wiley.

Lennon, R. T. (1985). Group tests of intelligence. In B. B. Wolman (Ed.), *Handbook of intelligence.* New York: Wiley.

Lennon, R., & Eisenberg, N. (1987). Emotional displays associated with preschoolers' prosocial behavior. *Child Development, 58,* 992–1000.

Lepper, M. R., & Gurtner, J. (1989). Children and computers: Approaching the twenty-first century. *American Psychologist, 44,* 170–178.

Lerner, R. M., & Lerner, J. V. (1977). Effects of age, sex, and physical attractiveness on child-peer relations, academic performance, and elementary school adjustment. *Developmental Psychology, 13,* 585–590.

Leslie, A. M. (1982). The perception of causality in infants. *Perception, 11,* 15–30.

Leslie, A. M. (1984). Spatiotemporal continuity and the perception of causality in infants. *Perception, 13,* 287–305.

Leslie, A. M., & Keeble, S. (1987). Do six-month-olds perceive causality? *Cognition, 25,* 265–288.

Lesser, G. S., Fifer, F., & Clark, D. H. (1965). Mental abilities of children of different social-class and cultural groups. *Monographs of the Society for Research in Child Development, 30*(4, Serial No. 102).

Lester, B. M., & Brazelton, T. B. (1982). Cross-cultural assessment of neonatal behavior. In D. Wagner & H. W. Stevenson (Eds.), *Cultural perspectives on child development.* San Francisco: W. H. Freeman.

Lester, B. M., & Dreher, M. (1989). Effects of marijuana use during pregnancy on newborn cry. *Child Development, 60,* 765–771.

Lester, B. M., Kotelchuk, M., Spelke, E., Sellers, M. J., & Klein, R. E. (1974). Separation protest in Guatemalan infants: Cross-cultural and cognitive findings. *Developmental Psychology, 10,* 79–85.

Levay, S., & Hamer, D. H. (1994, May). Evidence for a biological influence in male homosexuality. *Scientific American, 270,* 43–57.

Levine, M. P., Smolak, L., & Hayden, H. (1994). The relation of sociocultural factors to eating attitudes and behaviors among middle school girls. *Journal of Adolescence, 14,* 471–490.

Levine, R., & White, M. (1986). *Human conditions: The cultural basis for educational development.* New York: Routledge & Kegan Paul.

Levine, S. C., Jordan, N. C., & Huttenlocher, J. (1992). Development of calculation abilities in young children. *Journal of Experimental Child Psychology, 53,* 72–103.

Levitt, M. J., Guacci-Franco, N., & Levitt, J. L. (1993). Convoys of social support in childhood and early adolescence: Structure and function. *Developmental Psychology, 29,* 811–818.

Levy, G. D., & Fivush, R. (1993). Scripts and gender: A new approach for examining gender-role development. *Developmental Review, 13,* 126–146.

Levy, G. D., Taylor, M. G., & Gelman, S. A. (1995). Traditional and evaluative aspects of flexibility in gender roles, social conventions, moral rules, and physical laws. *Child Development, 66,* 515–531.

Lewis, C., Freeman, N. H., Kyriakidou, C., Maridaki-Kassotaki, K., & Berridge, D. M. (1996). Social influences on false belief access: Specific sibling influences or general apprenticeship? *Child Development, 67,* 2930–2947.

Lewis, M. (1969). Infants' responses to facial stimuli during the first year of life. *Developmental Psychology, 1,* 75–86.

Lewis, M. (1983). On the nature of intelligence. In M. Lewis (Ed.), *Origins of intelligence.* New York: Plenum Press.

Lewis, M. (1989, April). *Self and self-conscious emotions.* Paper presented at the biennial meeting of the Society for Research in Child Development, Kansas City, MO.

Lewis, M. (1990). Social knowledge and social development. *Merrill-Palmer Quarterly, 36,* 93–116.

Lewis, M. (1993). Early socioemotional predictors of cognitive competency at 4 years. *Developmental Psychology, 29,* 1036–1045.

Lewis, M., Alessandri, S., & Sullivan, M. (1992). Differences in shame and pride as a function of children's gender and task difficulty. *Child Development, 63,* 630–638.

Lewis, M., & Brooks-Gunn, J. (1979). *Social cognition and the acquisition of self.* New York: Plenum Press.

Lewis, M., & Brooks-Gunn, J. (1981). Visual attention at three months as a predictor of cognitive functioning at two years of age. *Intelligence, 5,* 131–140.

Lewis, M., & Feiring, C. (1982). Some American families at dinner. In L. M. Laosa & I. E. Sigel (Eds.), *Families as learning environments for children.* New York: Plenum Press.

Lewis, M., & Freedle, R. O. (1973). Mother-infant dyad: The cradle of meaning. In P. Pilner, L. Krames, & T. Alloway (Eds.), *Communication and affect: Language and thought.* New York: Academic Press.

Lewis, M., & Michalson, L. (1983). *Children's emotions and moods: Developmental theory and measurement.* New York: Plenum Press.

Lewis, M., Sullivan, M. W., Stanger, C., & Weiss, M. (1989). Self development and self-conscious emotions. *Child Development, 60,* 146–156.

Lewis, T. L., Maurer, D., & Kay, D. (1978). Newborns' central vision: Whole or hole? *Journal of Experimental Child Psychology, 26,* 193–203.

Liben, L. S., & Downs, R. M. (1993). Understanding person-space-map relations: Cartographic and developmental perspectives. *Developmental Psychology, 29,* 739–752.

Lickona, T. (1976). Research on Piaget's theory of moral development. In T. Lickona (Ed.), *Moral development and behavior: Theory, research, and social issues.* New York: Holt, Rinehart & Winston.

Lieb, J. J., & Sterk-Elifson, C. (1995). Crack in the cradle: social policy and reproductive rights among crack-using females. *Contemporary Drug Problems, 22,* 687–705.

Lieberman, D. (1985). Research on children and microcomputers: A review of utilization and effect studies. In M. Chen & W. Paisley (Eds.), *Children and microcomputers: Research on the newest medium.* Beverly Hills: Sage.

Liebert, R. M., & Sprafkin, J. (1988). *The early window: Effects of television on children and youth* (3rd ed.). New York: Pergamon Press.

Liggon, C., Weston, J., Ambady, N., Colloton, M., Rosenthal, R., & Reite, M. (1992). Content-free voice analysis of mothers talking about their failure-to-thrive children. *Infant Behavior and Development, 15,* 507–511.

Lightfoot, D. (1982). *The language lottery: Toward a biology of grammars.* Cambridge, MA: MIT Press.

Lillard, A. S., & Flavell, J. H. (1992). Young children's understanding of different mental states. *Developmental Psychology, 28,* 626–634.

Limb, C. J., & Holmes, L. B. (1994). Anencephaly: Changes in prenatal detection and birth status, 1972 through 1990. *American Journal of Obstetrics and Gynecology, 170,* 1333–1338.

Lin, C. C., & Fu, V. R. (1990). A comparison of child-rearing practices among Chinese, immigrant Chinese, and Caucasian-American parents. *Child Development, 61,* 429–433.

Lindholm, K. J. (1990). Bilingual immersion education: Criteria for program development. In A. M. Padilla, H. H. Fairchild, & C. Valadez (Eds.), *Bilingual education: Issues and strategies.* Newbury Park, CA: Sage.

Lindholm, K. J., & Fairchild, H. H. (1990). Evaluation of an elementary school bilingual immersion program. In A. M. Padilla, H. H. Fairchild, & C. Valadez (Eds.), *Bilingual education: Issues and strategies.* Newbury Park, CA: Sage.

Linn, M. C. (1985). Fostering equitable consequences from computer learning environments. *Sex Roles, 13,* 229–240.

Linn, M. C., & Petersen, A. C. (1985). Emergence and characterization of sex differences in spatial ability: A meta-analysis. *Child Development, 56,* 1479–1498.

Linn, M. C., & Petersen, A. C. (1986). A meta-analysis of differences in spatial ability: Implications for mathematics and science achievement. In J. S. Hyde & M. C. Linn (Eds.), *The psychology of gender: Advances through meta-analysis.* Baltimore: Johns Hopkins University Press.

Linney, J. A., & Seidman, E. N. (1989). The future of schooling. *American Psychologist, 44,* 336–340.

Lipsitt, L. P. (1982). Infant learning. In T. M. Field, A. Huston, H. C. Quay, L. Troll, & G. E. Finley (Eds.), *Review of human development.* New York: Wiley.

Lipsitt, L. P., Engen, T., & Kaye, H. (1963). Developmental changes in the olfactory threshold of the neonate. *Child Development, 34,* 371–376.

Littleton, K., Light, P. H., Joiner, R., & Messer, R. (1992). Pairing and gender effects on children's computer-based learning. *European Journal of Psychology of Education, 7,* 311–324.

Littschwager, J. C., & Markman, E. M. (1994). Sixteen- and 24-month-olds' use of mutual exclusivity as a default assumption in second-label learning. *Developmental Psychology, 30,* 955–958.

Livesley, W. J., & Bromley, D. B. (1973). *Person perception in childhood and adolescence.* London: Wiley.

Loader, A., Hutton, E., & MacKay, D. Y. on behalf of the National Childbirth Trust. (1985). *Pregnancy and parenthood* (2nd ed.). New York: Oxford University Press.

Lobel, T. E., Bempechat, J., Gewirtz, J. C., Shoken-Tpaz, T., & Bashe, E. (1993). The role of gender-related information and self-endorsement of traits in preadolescents' inferences and judgments. *Child Development, 64,* 1285–1294.

Lockheed, M. E. (1985). Women, girls, and computers: A first look at the evidence. *Sex Roles, 13,* 115–122.

Lockman, J. J., & Thelen, E. (1993). Developmental biodynamics: Brain, body, behavior connections. *Child Development, 64,* 953–959.

Loeb, R. C., Horst, L., & Horton, P. J. (1980). Family interaction patterns associated with self-esteem in preadolescent girls and boys. *Merrill-Palmer Quarterly, 26,* 203–217.

Loehlin, J. C. (1992). *Genes and environment in personality development.* Newbury Park, CA: Sage.

Loehlin, J. C., Horn, J. M., & Willerman, L. (1990). Heredity, environment, and personality change: Evidence from the Texas Adoption Project. *Journal of Personality, 58,* 221–243.

Loehlin, J. C., Lindzey, G., & Spuhler, J. N. (1975). *Racial differences in intelligence.* San Francisco: W. H. Freeman.

Loehlin, J. C., Willerman, L., & Horn, J. M. (1988). Human behavior genetics. *Annual Review of Psychology, 39,* 101–133.

Lorch, E. P., Bellack, D. R., & Augsbach, L. H. (1987). Young children's memory for televised stories: Effects of importance. *Child Development, 58,* 453–463.

Lord, S. E., Eccles, J. S., & McCarthy, K. A. (1994). Surviving the junior high school transition: Family processes and self-perceptions as protective and risk factors. *Journal of Early Adolescence, 14,* 162–199.

Lorenz, K. Z. (1966). *On aggression* (M. K. Wilson, Trans.). New York: Harcourt, Brace, & World. (Original work published 1963)

Lovdal, L. T. (1989). Sex role messages in television commercials: An update. *Sex Roles, 21,* 715–724.

Lozoff, B. (1983). Birth and "bonding" in non-industrialized societies. *Developmental Medicine and Child Neurology, 25,* 595–600.

Lucariello, J., Kyratzis, A., & Nelson, K. (1992). Taxonomic knowledge: What kind and when? *Child Development, 63,* 978–998.

Luckasson, R., Caulter, D. L., Polloway, E. A., Reiss, S., Schalock, R. L., Snell, M. E., Spitalnik, D. M., & Stark, J. A. (1992). *Mental retardation: Definition, classification, and systems of supports.* Washington, DC: American Association on Mental Retardation.

Luecke-Aleksa, D. R., Anderson, D. R., Collins, P. A., & Schmitt, K. L. (1995). Gender constancy and television viewing. *Developmental Psychology, 31,* 773–780.

Luke, B., Mamelle, N., Keith, L., Munoz, F., Minogue, J., Papiernik, E., Johnson, T. R. B. in collaboration with the Research Committee of the Association of Women's Health, Obstetric, and Neonatal Nurses. (1995). The association between occupational factors and preterm birth: A United States nurses' study. *American Journal of Obstetrics and Gynecology, 173,* 849–862.

Lukeman, D., & Melvin, D. (1993). Annotation: The preterm infant: Psychological issues in childhood. *Journal of Child Psychology and Psychiatry, 54,* 837–849.

Lummis, M., & Stevenson, H. W. (1990). Gender differences in beliefs and achievement: A cross-cultural study. *Developmental Psychology, 26,* 254–263.

Luria, A. R. (1961). *The role of speech in the regulation of normal and abnormal behavior.* New York: Liveright.

Luria, A. R. (1969). Speech and formation of mental processes. In M. Cole & I. Maltzman (Eds.), *A handbook of contemporary Soviet psychology.* New York: Basic Books.

Luster, T., & McAdoo, H. P. (1994). Factors related to the achievement and adjustment of young African American children. *Child Development, 65,* 1080–1994.

Luster, T., & McAdoo, H. P. (1996). Family and child influences on educational attainment: A secondary analysis of the High/Scope Perry Preschool data. *Developmental Psychology, 32,* 26–39.

Lutkenhaus, P., Bullock, M., & Geppert, U. (1987). Toddlers' actions: Knowledge, control, and the self. In F. Halisch & J. Kuhl (Eds.), *Motivation, intention, and volition.* Berlin: Springer.

Lykken, D. T. , McGue, M. Tellegen, A., & Bouchard, T. J., Jr. (1992). Emergenesis: Genetic traits that may not run in families. *American Psychologist,* 47, 1565–1577.

Lynn, R. (1982). IQ in Japan and the United States shows a growing disparity. *Nature, 297,* 222–223.

Lyon, T. D., & Flavell, J. H. (1993). Young children's understanding of forgetting over time. *Child Development, 64,* 789–800.

Lyons-Ruth, K., Alpern, L., & Repacholi, B. (1993). Disorganized infant attachment classification and maternal psychosocial problems as predictors of hostile-aggressive behavior in preschool children. *Child Development, 64,* 572–585.

Lytton, H., & Romney, D. M. (1991). Parents' differential socialization of boys and girls: A meta-analysis. *Psychological Bulletin, 109,* 267–296.

MacFarlane, J. A. (1975). Olfaction in the development of social preferences in the human neonate. In M. A. Hofer (Ed.), *Parent-infant interaction.* Amsterdam: Elsevier.

MacKinnon, C. E. (1988). Influences on sibling relations in families with married and divorced parents. *Journal of Social Issues, 9,* 469–477.

MacKinnon, C. E. (1989a). An observational investigation of sibling interactions in married and divorced families. *Developmental Psychology, 25,* 36–44.

MacKinnon, C. E. (1989b). Sibling interactions in married and divorced families: Influence of ordinal position, socioeconomic status, and play context. *Journal of Divorce, 12,* 221–251.

MacKinnon-Lewis, C., Volling, B. L., Lamb, M. E., Dechman, K., Rabiner, D., & Curtner, M. E. (1994). A cross-contextual analysis of boys' social competence: From family to school. *Developmental Psychology, 30,* 325–333.

MacLeod, C. L., & Lee, R. V. (1988). Parasitic infections. In G. N. Burrow & T. F. Ferris (Eds.), *Medical complications during pregnancy.* Philadelphia: W. B. Saunders.

MacLusky, N. J., & Naftolin, F. (1981). Sexual differentiation of the nervous system. *Science, 211,* 1294–1303.

Maccoby, E. E. (1984a). Middle childhood in the context of the family. In W. A. Collins (Ed.), *Development during middle childhood: The years from six to twelve.* Washington, DC: National Academy Press.

Maccoby, E. E. (1984b). Socialization and developmental change. *Child Development, 55,* 317–328.

Maccoby, E. E. (1988). Gender as a social category. *Developmental Psychology, 24,* 755–765.

Maccoby, E. E. (1990). Gender and relationships: A developmental account. *American Psychologist, 45,* 513–520.

Maccoby, E. E., Buchanan, C. M., Mnookin, R. H., & Dornbusch, S. M. (1993). Postdivorce roles of mothers and fathers in the lives of their children. *Journal of Family Psychology, 7,* 24–38.

Maccoby, E. E., & Jacklin, C. N. (1974). *The psychology of sex differences.* Stanford, CA: Stanford University Press.

Maccoby, E. E., & Jacklin, C. N. (1987). Gender segregation in childhood. In H. W. Reese (Ed.), *Advances in child development and behavior* (Vol. 20). Orlando, FL: Academic Press.

Maccoby, E. E., & Martin, J. A. (1983). Socialization in the context of the family: Parent-child interaction. In E. M. Hetherington (Ed.), *Handbook of child psychology: Vol. IV. Socialization, personality, and social development.* New York: Wiley.

Maffeis, C., Schutz, Y., Zaffanello, M., Piccoli, R., & Pinelli, L. (1994). Elevated energy expenditure and reduced energy intake in obese prepubertal children: Paradox of poor dietary reliability in obesity? *Journal of Pediatrics, 124,* 348–354.

Maggioni, A., & Lifshitz, F. (1995). Nutritional management of failure to thrive. *Pediatric Nutrition, 42,* 791–810.

Magnusson, D., Stattin, H., & Allen, V. (1986). Differential maturation among girls and its relations to social adjustment: A longitudinal perspective. In P. B. Baltes, D. L. Featherman, & R. M. Lerner (Eds.), *Life-span development and behavior* (Vol. 7). Hillsdale, NJ: Erlbaum.

Mahoney, J. L., & Cairns, R. B. (1997). Do extracurricular activities protect against early school dropout? *Developmental Psychology, 33,* 241–253.

Main, M., & Cassidy, J. (1988). Categories of response to reunion with the parent at age 6: Predictable from attachment classifications and stable over a 1-month period. *Developmental Psychology, 24,* 415–426.

Main, M., Kaplan, N., & Cassidy, J. (1985). Security in infancy, childhood, and adulthood: A move to the level of representation. In I. Bretherton & E. Waters (Eds.), *Growing points of attachment theory and research. Monographs of the Society for Research in Child Development, 50*(1–2, Serial No. 209).

Main, M., & Solomon, J. (1986). Discovery of a disorganized/disoriented attachment pattern. In T. B. Brazelton & M. W. Yogman (Eds.), *Affective development in infancy.* Norwood, NJ: Ablex.

Makin, J. W., & Porter, R. H. (1989). Attractiveness of lactating females' breast odors to neonates. *Child Development, 60,* 803–810.

Malatesta, C. Z., Culver, C., Tesman, J. R., & Shepard, B. (1989). The development of emotion expression during the first two years of life. *Monographs of the Society for Research in Child Development, 54*(1–2, Serial No. 219).

Malatesta, C. Z., & Haviland, J. M. (1982). Learning display rules: The socialization of emotion expression in infancy. *Child Development, 53,* 991–1003.

Malina, R. M. (1980). Biosocial correlates of motor development during infancy and early childhood. In L. S. Greene & F. E. Johnstone (Eds.), *Social and biological predictors of nutritional status, physical growth, and neurological development.* New York: Academic Press.

Malinowski, B. (1927). *Sex and repression in savage society.* London: Routledge & Kegan Paul.

Mandler, J. (1992). How to build a baby: II. Conceptual primitives. *Psychological Review, 99,* 587–604.

Mandler, J. M. (1988). How to build a baby: On the development of an accessible representational system. *Cognitive Development, 3,* 113–136.

Mandler, J. M., Fivush, R., & Reznick, J. S. (1987). The development of contextual categories. *Cognitive Development, 2,* 339–354.

Mandler, J. M., & McDonough, L. (1995). Long-term recall of event sequences in infancy. *Journal of Experimental Child Psychology, 59,* 457–474.

Mangelsdorf, S. C., Plunkett, J. W., Dedrick, C. F., Berlin, M., Meisels, S. J., McHale, J. L., & Dichtellmiller, M. (1996). Attachment security in very low birth weight infants. *Developmental Psychology, 32,* 914–920.

Mannarino, A. P. (1978). Friendship patterns and self-concept development in preadolescent males. *Journal of Genetic Psychology, 133,* 105–110.

Maratsos, M. P. (1983). Some current issues in the study of the acquisition of grammar. In J. H. Flavell & E. M. Markman (Eds.), *Handbook of child psychology: Vol. III. Cognitive development.* New York: Wiley.

Maratsos, M. P. (1989). Innateness and plasticity in language acquisition. In M. L. Rice & R. L. Schiefelbusch (Eds.), *The teachability of language.* Baltimore: Paul H. Brookes.

Maratsos, M. P., Kuczaj, S. A., II, Fox, D. E. C., & Chalkley, M. A. (1979). Some empirical studies in the acquisition of transformational relations. In W. A. Collins (Ed.), *Minnesota symposia on child psychology* (Vol. 12). Hillsdale, NJ: Erlbaum.

Marcia, J. (1980). Identity in adolescence. In J. Adelson (Ed.), *Handbook of adolescent psychology.* New York: Wiley.

Marcus, G. F. (1996). Why do children say "breaked"? *Current Directions in Psychological Science, 5,* 81–85.

Marcus, G. F., Pinker, S., Ullman, M., Hollander, M., Rosen, T. J., & Xu, F. (1992). Overregularization in language acquisition. *Monographs of the Society for Research in Child Development, 57,* (4 Serial No. 228).

Marean, G. C., Werner, L. A., & Kuhl, P. K. (1992). Vowel categorization by very young infants. *Developmental Psychology, 28,* 395–405.

Marin, B. V., Holmes, D. L., Guth, M., & Kovac, P. (1979). The potential of children as eyewitnesses. *Law and Human Behavior, 3,* 295–305.

Markman, E. M. (1987). How children constrain the possible meanings of words. In U. Neisser (Ed.), *Concepts and conceptual development: Ecological and intellectual factors in categorization.* Cambridge, UK: Cambridge University Press.

Markman, E. M. (1989). *Categorization and naming in children: Problems of induction.* Cambridge, MA: MIT Press.

Markman, E. M. (1990). Constraints children place on word meanings. *Cognitive Science, 14,* 57–77.

Markman, E. M., & Hutchinson, J. E. (1984). Children's sensitivity to constraints on word meaning: Taxonomic versus thematic relations. *Cognitive Psychology, 16,* 1–27.

Markman, E. M., & Siebert, J. (1976). Classes and collections: Internal organization and resulting holistic properties. *Cognitive Psychology, 8,* 561–577.

Markman, E. M., & Wachtel G. F. (1988). Children's use of mutual exclusivity to constrain the meanings of words. *Cognitive Psychology, 20,* 121–157.

Marland, S. (1972). *Education of the gifted and talented.* Report to the Congress of the United States by the U.S. Commission on Education. Washington, DC: U.S. Government Printing Office.

Marr, D. B., & Sternberg, R. J. (1987). The role of mental speed in intelligence: A triarchic perspective. In P. A. Vernon (Ed.), *Speed of information-processing and intelligence.* Norwood, NJ: Ablex.

Marshall, S. (1995). Ethnic socialization of African American children: Implications for parenting, identity development, and academic achievement. *Journal of Youth and Adolescence, 24,* 377–396.

Marshall, W. A., & Tanner, J. M. (1970). Variations in the pattern of pubertal changes in boys. *Archives of Disease in Childhood, 45,* 13–23.

Marshall, W. A., & Tanner, J. M. (1986). Puberty. In F. Falkner & J. M. Tanner (Eds.), *Human Growth* (Vol. 2, 2nd ed.). New York: Plenum.

Martin, B. (1975). Parent-child relations. In F. D. Horowitz (Ed.), *Review of child development research* (Vol. 4). Chicago: University of Chicago Press.

Martin, C. L. (1991). The role of cognition in understanding gender effects. In H. W. Reese (Ed.), *Advances in child development and behavior* (Vol. 23). San Diego, CA: Academic Press.

Martin, C. L. (1995). Stereotypes about children with traditional and non-traditional gender roles. *Sex Roles, 33,* 727–751.

Martin, C. L., Eisenbud, L., & Rose, H. (1995). Children's gender-based reasoning about toys. *Child Development, 66,* 1453–1471.

Martin, C. L., & Halverson, C. F. (1981). A schematic processing model of sex typing and stereotyping in children. *Child Development, 52,* 1119–1134.

Martin, C. L., & Halverson, C. F. (1987). The roles of cognition in sex role acquisition. In D. B. Carter (Ed.), *Current conceptions of sex roles and sex typing: Theory and research.* New York: Praeger.

Martin, H. P., & Beezley, P. (1976). Personality of abused children. In H. P. Martin (Ed.), *The abused child.* Cambridge: Ballinger.

Martin, J., Martin, D. C., Lund, C. A., & Streissguth, A. P. (1977). Maternal alcohol ingestion and cigarette smoking and their effects on newborn conditioning. *Alcoholism: Clinical and Experimental Research, 1,* 243–247.

Marvin, R. S. (1977). An ethological-cognitive model for the attenuation of mother-child attachment behavior. In T. M. Alloway, L. Krames, & P. Pliner (Eds.), *Advances in the study of communication and affect: Vol. 3. The development of social attachments.* New York: Plenum Press.

Masangkay, Z. S., McCluskey, K. A., McIntyre, C. W., Sims-Knight, J., Vaughn, B. E., & Flavell, J. H. (1974). The early development of inferences about the visual percepts of others. *Child Development, 45,* 357–366.

Masataka, N. (1996). Perception of motherese in a signed language by 6-month-old infants. *Developmental Psychology, 32,* 874–879.

Mason, C. A., Cauce, A. M., Gonzales, N., & Hiraga, Y. (1996). Neither too sweet nor too sour: Problem peers, maternal control, and problem behavior in African American adolescents. *Child Development, 67,* 2115–2130.

Mason, J. (1980). When do children begin to read: An exploration of four year old children's letter and word naming competencies. *Reading Research Quarterly, 15,* 203–227.

Massad, C. M. (1981). Sex role identity and adjustment during adolescence. *Child Development, 52,* 1290–1298.

Massaro, D. W., & Cowan, N. (1993). Information processing models: Microscopes of mind. In L. W. Porter & M. R. Rosenzweig (Eds.), *Annual Review of Psychology, 34,* 383–425.

Masur, E. F. (1982). Mothers' responses to infants' object-related gestures: Influences on lexical development. *Journal of Child Language, 9,* 23–30.

Matas, L., Arend, R. A., & Sroufe, L. A. (1978). Continuity of adaptation in the second year: The relationship between quality of attachment and later competence. *Child Development, 49,* 547–556.

Matheny, A. P., Jr. (1989). Children's behavioral inhibition over age and across situations. *Journal of Personality, 57,* 215–235.

Mathews, J. J., & Zadak, K. (1991). The alternative birth movement in the United States: History and current status. *Women & Health, 17,* 39–56.

Matias, R., & Cohn, J. F. (1993). Are max-specified infant facial expressions during face-to-face interaction consistent with differential emotions theory? *Developmental Psychology, 29,* 524–531.

Matsumoto, D., Haan, N., Yabrove, G., Theodorou, P., & Carney, C. C. (1986). Preschoolers' moral actions and emotions in prisoner's dilemma. *Developmental Psychology, 22,* 663–670.

Maudry, M., & Nekula, M. (1939). Social relations between children of the same age during the first two years of life. *Journal of Genetic Psychology, 54,* 193–215.

Maurer, D. (1983). The scanning of compound figures by young infants. *Journal of Experimental Child Psychology, 35,* 437–448.

May, D. C., Kundert, D. K., & Brent, D. (1995). Does delayed school entry reduce later grade retentions and use of special education services? *Remedial and Special Education, 16,* 288–294.

Mayer, R. E., & Fay, A. L. (1987). A chain of cognitive changes with learning to program in Logo. *Journal of Educational Psychology, 79,* 269–279.

Mayes, L. C., Bornstein, M. H., Chawarska, K., & Granger, R. H. (1995). Information processing and developmental assessments in 3-month-old infants exposed prenatally to cocaine. *Pediatrics, 95,* 539–545.

McAnarney, E. R. (1987). Young maternal age and adverse neonatal outcome. *American Journal of Diseases of Children, 141,* 1053–1059.

McAnarney, E. R., & Stevens-Simon, C. (1990). Maternal psychological stress/depression and low birth weight. *American Journal of Diseases of Children, 144,* 789–792.

McBride, W. G. (1961). Thalidomide and congenital abnormalities. *Lancet, 2,* 1358.

McCall, R. B. (1979). *Infants.* Cambridge, MA: Harvard University Press.

McCall, R. B., Appelbaum, M. I., & Hogarty, P. S. (1973). Developmental changes in mental performance. *Monographs of the Society for Research in Child Development, 38*(3, Serial No. 150).

McCall, R. B., & Carriger, M. S. (1993). A meta-analysis of infant habituation and recognition memory performance as predictors of later IQ. *Child Development, 64,* 57–79.

McCall, R. B., Hogarty, P. S., & Hurlburt, N. (1972). Transitions in sensorimotor development and the prediction of childhood IQ. *American Psychologist, 27,* 728–748.

McCall, R. B., Parke, R. D., & Kavanaugh, R. D. (1977). Imitation of live and televised models in children one to three years of age. *Monographs of the Society for Research in Child Development, 42*(3, Serial No. 171).

McCann, J. B., Stein, A., Fairburn, C. G., & Dungr, D. B. (1994). Eating habits and attitudes of mothers of children with non-organic failure to thrive. *Archives of Disease in Childhood, 70,* 234–236.

McCartney, K., Harris, M. J., & Bernieri, F. (1990). Growing up and growing apart: A developmental meta-analysis of twin studies. *Psychological Bulletin, 107,* 226–237.

McCartney, K., & Nelson, K. (1981). Children's use of scripts in story recall. *Discourse Processes, 4,* 59–70.

McCartney, K., Scarr, S., Phillips, D., & Grajek, S. (1985). Day care as intervention: Comparisons of varying quality programs. *Journal of Applied Developmental Psychology, 6,* 247–260.

McClelland, D. C. (1973). Testing for competence rather than for "intelligence." *American Psychologist, 28,* 1–14.

McCord, J. (1977). A comparative study of two generations of native Americans. In R. F. Meier (Ed.), *Theory in criminology* (pp. 83–92). Beverly Hills, CA: Sage.

McCormick, M. C., McCarton, C., Tonascia, J., & Brooks-Gunn, J. (1993). Early educational intervention for very low birth weight infants: Results from the Infant Health and Development Program. *Journal of Pediatrics, 123,* 527–533.

McCormick, M. C., Workman-Daniels, K., & Brooks-Gunn, J. (1996). The behavioral and emotional well-being of school-age children with different birth weights. *Pediatrics, 97,* 18–25.

Mittendorf, R., Williams, M. A., Berkley, C. S., Lieberman, E., & Monson, R. R. (1993). Predictors of human gestational length. *American Journal of Obstetrics and Gynecology, 168,* 480–484.

McDonald, L., & Pien, D. (1982). Mother conversational behavior as a function of interactional intent. *Journal of Child Language, 9,* 337–358.

McDonald, M. A., Sigman, M., Espinosa, M. P., & Neumann, C. G. (1994). Impact of temporary food shortage on children and their mothers. *Child Development, 65,* 404–415.

McGhee, P. E. (1979). *Humor: Its origin and development.* San Francisco: W. H. Freeman.

McGhee, P. E., & Frueh, T. (1980). Television viewing and the learning of sex role stereotypes. *Sex Roles, 6,* 179–188.

McGraw, M. B. (1935). *Growth: A study of Johnny and Jimmy.* New York: Appleton-Century.

McGregor, J. A., & French, J. I. (1991). *Chlamydia trachomatis* infection during pregnancy. *American Journal of Obstetrics and Gynecology, 165,* 1782–1789.

McGuire, J. (1988). Gender stereotypes of parents with two-year-olds and beliefs about gender differences in behavior. *Sex Roles, 19,* 233–240.

McGuire, K. D., & Weisz, J. R. (1982). Social cognition and behavior correlates of preadolescent chumship. *Child Development, 53,* 1478–1484.

McGurk, H., & MacDonald, J. (1976). Hearing lips and seeing voices. *Nature* (London), *264,* 746–748.

McHale, S. M., Crouter, A. C., McGuire, S. A., & Updegraff, K. A. (1995). Congruence between mothers' and fathers' differential treatment of siblings: Links with family relations and children's well-being. *Child Development, 66,* 116–128.

McKenna, J. J., Mosko, S., Dungy, C., & McAninch, J. (1990). Sleep and arousal patterns of co-sleeping human mother/infant pairs: A preliminary physiological study with implications for the study of sudden infant death syndrome (SIDS). *American Journal of Physical Anthropology, 83,* 331–347.

McKey, R. H., Condelli, L., Granson, H., Barrett, B., McConkey, C., & Plantz, M. (1985). *The impact of Head Start on children, families and communities* (Final report of the Head Start Evaluation, Synthesis and Utilization Project). Washington, DC: U.S. Government Printing Office.

McKusick, V. A. (1994). *Mendelian inheritance in man: A catalog of human genes and genetic disorders* (11th ed.). Baltimore: Johns Hopkins University Press.

McLaughlin, B. (1984). *Second-language acquisition in childhood: Vol. 2. School-age children.* Hillsdale, NJ: Erlbaum.

McLoyd, V. C. (1990). The impact of economic hardship on black families and children: Psychological distress, parenting, and socioemotional development. *Child Development, 61,* 311–346.

McLoyd, V. C., Epstein Jayaratne, T., Ceballo, R., & Borquez, J. (1994). Unemployment and work interruption among African American single mothers: Effects on parenting and adolescent socioemotional functioning. *Child Development, 65,* 562–589.

McManus, I. C., & Bryden, M. P. (1991). Geschwind's theory of cerebral lateralization: Developing a formal, causal model. *Psychological Bulletin, 110,* 237–253.

McNally, S., Eisenberg, N., & Harris, J. D. (1991). Consistency and change in maternal child-rearing practices and values: A longitudinal study. *Child Development, 62,* 190–198.

Mead, G. H. (1934). *Mind, self, and society.* Chicago: University of Chicago Press.

Medin, D. L. (1989). Concepts and conceptual structure. *American Psychologist, 44,* 1469–1481.

Meichenbaum, D. (1977). *Cognitive-behavior modification: An integrative approach.* New York: Plenum Press.

Meichenbaum, D., & Goodman, J. (1971). Training impulsive children to talk to themselves: A means of developing self-control. *Journal of Abnormal Psychology, 77,* 115–126.

Mekos, D., Hetherington, E. M., & Reiss, D. (1996). Sibling differences in problem behavior and parental treatment in nondivorced and remarried families. *Child Development, 67,* 2148–2165.

Meltzoff, A., & Borton, R. (1979). Intermodal matching by human neonates. *Nature* (London), *282,* 403–404.

Meltzoff, A. N., & Kuhl, P. K. (1994). Faces and speech: Intermodal processing of biologically relevant signals in infants and adults. In D. J. Lewkowicz & R. Lickliter (Eds.), *The development of intersensory perception: Comparative perspectives* (pp. 335–370). Hillsdale, NJ: Erlbaum.

Meltzoff, A. N., & Moore, M. K. (1983). Newborn infants imitate adult facial gestures. *Child Development, 54,* 702–709.

Meltzoff, A. N., & Moore, M. K. (1989). Imitation in newborn infants: Exploring the range of gestures imitated and the underlying mechanisms. *Developmental Psychology, 25,* 954–962.

Meltzoff, A. N., & Moore, M. K. (1992). Early imitation within a functional framework: The importance of person identity, movement, and development. *Infant Behavior and Development, 15,* 479–505.

Meltzoff, A. N., & Moore, M. K. (1994). Imitation, memory, and the representation of persons. *Infant Behavior and Development, 17,* 83–99.

Mennella, J. A., & Beauchamp, G. K. (1996). The human infant's response to vanilla flavors in mother's milk and formula. *Infant Behavior and Development, 19,* 13–19.

Merimee, T. J., Zapf, J., & Froesch, E. R. (1981). Dwarfism in the Pygmy: An isolated deficiency of insulin-like Growth Factor I. *New England Journal of Medicine, 305,* 965–968.

Mervis, C. (1984). Early lexical development: The contributions of mother and child. In C. Sophian (Ed.), *Origins of cognitive skills.* Hillsdale, NJ: Erlbaum.

Mervis, C., & Crisafi, M. (1982). Order of acquisition of subordinate-, basic-, and superordinate-level categories. *Child Development, 53,* 267–273.

Messer, D. J. (1981). The identification of names in maternal speech to infants. *Journal of Psycholinguistic Research, 10,* 69–77.

Messer, S. C., & Gross, A. M. (1995) Childhood depression and family interaction: A naturalistic observation study. *Journal of Clinical Child Psychology, 24,* 77–88.

Meyer, M., & Fienberg, S. (1992). *Assessing evaluation studies: The case of bilingual education strategies.* Washington, DC: National Academy Press.

Meyer, M. B., & Tonascia, J. A. (1977). Maternal smoking, pregnancy complications, and perinatal mortality. *American Journal of Obstetrics and Gynecology, 128,* 494–502.

Michel, G. F. (1988). A neuropsychological perspective on infant sensorimotor development. In C. Rovee-Collier & L. P. Lipsitt (Eds.), *Advances in infancy research* (Vol. 5). Norwood, NJ: Ablex.

Michelson, L., Sugai, D. P., Wood, R. P., & Kazdin, A. E. (1983). *Social skills assessment and training with children.* New York: Plenum Press.

Michelsson, K., Sirvio, P., & Wasz-Hockert, D. (1977). Pain cry in fullterm asphyxiated newborn infants correlated with late findings. *Acta Paediatrica Scandinavica, 66,* 611–616.

Michotte, A. (1963). *The perception of causality.* New York: Basic Books.

Mielke, K. W. (1994). On the relationship between television viewing and academic achievement. *Journal of Broadcasting & Electronic Media, 38,* 361–366.

Milich, R. (1984). Cross-sectional and longitudinal observations of activity level and sustained attention in a normative sample. *Journal of Abnormal Child Psychology, 12,* 261–275.

Miller, B., McCoy, J., Olson, T., & Wallace, C. (1986). Parental discipline and control attempts in relation to adolescent sexual attitudes and behavior. *Journal of Marriage and the Family, 48,* 503–512.

Miller, J. B. (1986). *Toward a new psychology of women.* Boston: Beacon Press.

Miller, J. B. (1991). The development of women's sense of self. In J. V. Jordan, A. G. Kaplan, J. B. Miller, I. P. Stiver, & J. L. Surrey (Eds.), *Women's growth in connection.* New York: Guilford.

Miller, L. T., & Vernon, P. A. (1996). Intelligence, reaction time, and working memory in 4- to 6-year-old children. *Intelligence, 22,* 155–190.

Miller, N. B., Cowan, P. A., Cowan, C. P., Hetherington, E. M., & Clingempeel, W. G. (1993). Externalizing in preschoolers and early adolescents: A cross-study replication of a family model. *Developmental Psychology, 29,* 3–18.

Miller, N., & Maruyama, G. (1976). Ordinal position and peer popularity. *Journal of Personality and Social Psychology, 33,* 123–131.

Miller, P. A., Eisenberg, N., Fabes, R. A., & Shell, R. (1996). Relations of moral reasoning and vicarious emotion to young children's prosocial behavior toward peers and adults. *Developmental Psychology, 32,* 210–219.

Miller, P. H., & Harris, Y. R. (1988). Preschoolers' strategies of attention on a same-different task. *Developmental Psychology, 24,* 628–633.

Miller, P. H., & Seier, W. L. (1994). Strategy utilization deficiencies in children: When, where, and why. In H. W. Reese (Ed.), *Advances in child development and behavior* (Vol. 25, pp. 107–156). San Diego: Academic Press.

Miller, P. H., Woody-Ramsey, J., & Aloise, P. A. (1991). The role of strategy effortfulness in strategy effectiveness. *Developmental Psychology, 27,* 738–745.

Miller, W. L., & Levine, L. S. (1987). Molecular and clinical advances in congenital adrenal hyperplasia. *Journal of Pediatrics, 111,* 1–17.

Miller-Jones, D. (1989). Culture and testing. *American Psychologist, 44,* 360–366.

Mills, D. L., Coffey-Corina, S. A., & Neville, H. J. (1993). Language acquisition and cerebral specialization in 20-month-old infants. *Journal of Cognitive Neuroscience, 5,* 317–334.

Mills, D. L., Coffey-Corina, S. A., & Neville, H. J. (1994). Variability in cerebral organization during primary language acquisition. In G. Dawson & K. W. Fischer (Eds.), *Human behavior and the developing brain.* New York: Guilford.

Mills, J. L., Graubard, B. I., Harley, E. E., Rhoads, G. G., Berends, H. W. (1984). Maternal consumption and birth weight: How much drinking in pregnancy is safe? *Journal of the American Medical Association, 252,* 1875–1879.

Mills, R. S. L., & Grusec, J. E. (1989). Cognitive, affective, and behavioral consequences of praising altruism. *Merrill-Palmer Quarterly, 35,* 299–326.

Mills, R. S. L., & Rubin, K. H. (1993). Socialization factors in the development of social withdrawal. In K. H. Rubin & J. B. Asendorpf (Eds.), *Social withdrawal, inhibition, and shyness in childhood.* Hillsdale, NJ: Erlbaum.

Minuchin, P. P. (1988). Relationships within the family: A systems perspective on development. In R. A. Hinde & J. Stevenson-Hinde (Eds.), *Relationships within families: Mutual influences.* Oxford: Clarendon Press.

Minuchin, P. P., & Shapiro, E. K. (1983). The school as a context for social development. In E. M. Hetherington (Ed.), *Handbook of child psychology: Vol. IV. Socialization, personality, and social development.* New York: Wiley.

Mischel, H. N., & Mischel, W. (1983). The development of children's knowledge of self-control strategies. *Child Development, 54,* 603–619.

Mischel, W. (1966). A social learning view of sex differences in behavior. In E. E. Maccoby (Ed.), *The development of sex differences.* Stanford, CA: Stanford University Press.

Mischel, W., Ebbesen, E. B., & Zeiss, A. R. (1972). Cognitive and attentional mechanisms in delay of gratification. *Journal of Personality and Social Psychology, 21,* 204–218.

Mischel, W., Shoda, Y., & Rodriguez, M. L. (1989). Delay of gratification in children. *Science, 244,* 933–938.

Mittendorf, R., Williams, M. A., Berkey, C. S., & Cotter, P. F. (1990). The length of uncomplicated human gestation. *Obstetrics and Gynecology, 75,* 929–932.

Miyake, K., Chen, S., & Campos, J. J. (1985). Infant temperament, mother's mode of interaction, and attachment in Japan: An interim report. In I. Bretherton & E. Waters (Eds.), *Growing points of attachment theory and research. Monographs of the Society for Research in Child Development, 50*(1–2, Serial No. 209).

Moely, B. E., Hart, S. S., Leal, L., Santulli, K. A., Rao, N., Johnson, T., & Hamilton, L. B. (1992). The teacher's role in facilitating memory and study strategy development in the elementary school classroom. *Child Development, 63,* 653–672.

Moely, B. E., Hart, S. S., Santulli, K. A., Leal, L., Kogut, D. J., McLain, E., Zhou, Z., & Johnson, T. D. (1989, April). *Teachers' cognitions about the memory processes of elementary school children: A developmental perspective.* Paper presented at the biennial meeting of the Society for Research in Child Development, Kansas City, MO.

Moely, B. E., Olson, F. A., Halwes, T. G., & Flavell, J. H. (1969). Production deficiency in young children's clustered recall. *Developmental Psychology, 1,* 26–34.

Moffat, R., & Hackel, A. (1985). Thermal aspects of neonatal care. In A. Gottfried & J. Gaiter (Eds.), *Infant stress under intensive care.* Baltimore: University Park Press.

Moffitt, T. E., Caspi, A., Belsky, J., & Silva, P. A. (1992). Childhood experience and the onset of menarche: A test of a sociobiological model. *Child Development, 63,* 47–58.

Monfries, M. M., & Kafer, N. F. (1987). Neglected and rejected children: A social-skills model. *Journal of Psychology, 121,* 401–407.

Moore, G. T., & Lackney, J. A. (1993). School design: Crisis, educational performance, and design patterns. *Children's Environments, 10,* 99–112.

Moore, K. L. (1988). *The developing human: Clinically oriented embryology* (4th ed.). Philadelphia: W. B. Saunders.

Moore, K. L. (1989). *Before we are born* (3rd ed.). Philadelphia: W. B. Saunders.

Morgan, M. (1982). Television and adolescents' sex-role stereotypes: A longitudinal study. *Journal of Personality and Social Psychology, 43,* 947–955.

Morgan, M. (1987). Television, sex-role attitudes, and sex-role behavior. *Journal of Early Adolescence, 7,* 269–282.

Morison, P., & Masten, A. S. (1991). Peer reputation in middle childhood as a predictor of adaptation in adolescence: A seven-year follow-up. *Child Development, 62,* 991–1007.

Morrelli, G., Rogoff, B., Oppenheim, D., & Goldsmith, D. (1992). Cultural variation in infants' sleeping arrangements: Questions of independence. *Developmental Psychology, 28,* 604–613.

Morris, R., & Kratchowill, T. (1983). *Treating children's fears and phobias.* New York: Pergamon Press.

Morrison, F. J., Griffith, E. M., & Alberts, D. M. (1997). Nature-nurture in the classroom: Entrance age, school readiness, and learning in children. *Developmental Psychology, 33,* 254–262.

Morrison, F. J., Smith, L., & Dow-Ehrensberger, M. (1995). Education and cognitive development: A natural experiment. *Developmental Psychology, 31,* 789–799.

Morrison, J. A., Barton, B., Biro, F. M., Sprecher, D. L., Falkner, F., & Obarzanek, E. (1994). Sexual maturation and obesity in 9- and 10-year-old black and white girls: The National Heart, Lung, and Blood Institute Growth and Health Study. *Journal of Pediatrics, 124,* 889–895.

Morrongiello, B. A. (1984). Auditory temporal pattern perception in 6- and 12-month-old infants. *Developmental Psychology, 20,* 441–448.

Morrongiello, B. A. (1988). The development of auditory pattern perception skills. In C. Rovee-Collier & L. P. Lipsitt (Eds.), *Advances in infancy research* (Vol. 5). Norwood, NJ: Ablex.

Morrongiello, B. A., Fenwick, K. D., & Chance, G. (1990). Sound localization acuity in very young infants: An observer-based testing procedure. *Developmental Psychology, 26,* 75–84.

Morrongiello, B. A., Humphrey, G. K., Tinmey, B., Choi, J., & Rocca, P. T. (1994). Tactual object exploration and recognition in blind and sighted children. *Perception, 23,* 833–848.

Moshman, D. (1990). The development of metalogical understanding. In W. F. Overton (Ed.), *Reasoning, necessity and logic: Developmental perspectives.* Hillsdale, NJ: Erlbaum.

Moshman, D., & Franks, B. A. (1986). Development of the concept of inferential validity. *Child Development, 57,* 153–165.

Moss, H. A. (1974). Early sex differences and mother-infant interaction. In R. C. Friedman, R. M. Richart, & R. L. Vande Wiele (Eds.), *Sex differences in behavior.* New York: Wiley.

Mosteller, F. (1995, Summer/Fall). The Tennessee study of class size in the early school grades. *The Future of Children, 5*(2), pp. 113–127.

Mounts, N. S., & Steinberg, L. (1995). An ecological analysis of peer influence on adolescent grade point average and drug use. *Developmental Psychology, 31,* 915–922.

Movshon, J. A., & Van Sluyters, R. C. (1981). Visual neuronal development. *Annual Review of Psychology, 32,* 477–522.

Mullen, M. K. (1994). Earliest recollections of childhood: A demographic analysis. *Cognition, 52,* 55–79.

Mullen, M. K., & Yi, S. (1995). The cultural context of talk about the past: Implications for the development of autobiographical memory. *Cognitive Development, 10,* 407–419.

Muller, A. A., & Perlmutter, M. (1985). Preschool children's problem-solving interactions at computers and jigsaw puzzles. *Journal of Applied Developmental Psychology, 6,* 173–186.

Mullis, I. V. S., & Jenkins, L. B. (1990). *The reading report card, 1971–1988.* Princeton, NJ: Educational Testing Service.

Munroe, R. H., Shimmin, H. S., & Munroe, R. L. (1984). Gender understanding and sex role preference in four cultures. *Developmental Psychology, 20,* 673–682.

Munte, T. F., Heinze, H., & Mangun, G. R. (1993). Dissociation of brain activity related to syntactic and semantic aspects of language. *Journal of Cognitive Neuroscience, 5,* 335–344.

Murphy, L. B. (1937). *Social behavior and child personality.* New York: Columbia University Press.

Mussen, P. H., & Jones, M. C. (1957). Self-conceptions, motivations, and interpersonal attitudes of late and early maturing boys. *Child Development, 28,* 243–256.

Mussen, P. H., & Jones, M. C. (1958). The behavior inferred motivations of late and early maturing boys. *Child Development, 29,* 61–67.

Mussen, P. H., Rutherford, E., Harris, S., & Keasey, C. (1970). Honesty and altruism among preadolescents. *Developmental Psychology, 3,* 169–194.

Myers, J., Jusczyk, P. W., Kemler Nelson, D. G., Charles-Luce, J., Woodward, A. L., & Hirsh-Pasek, K. (1996). Infants' sensitivity to word boundaries in fluent speech. *Journal of Child Language, 23,* 1–30.

Nahmias, A. J., Keyserling, H. L., & Kernick, G. M. (1983). Herpes simplex. In J. S. Remington & J. O. Klein (Eds.), *Infectious diseases of the fetus and newborn infant.* Philadelphia: W. B. Saunders.

Náñez, J. E., Sr., & Yonas, A. (1994). Effects of luminance and texture motion on infant defensive reactions to optical collision. *Infant Behavior and Development, 17,* 165–174.

Narod, S. A., de Sanjos, S., & Victora, C. (1991). Coffee during pregnancy: A reproductive hazard? *American Journal of Obstetrics and Gynecology, 164,* 1109–1114.

Nastasi, B. K., Clements, D. H., & Battista, M. T. (1990). Social-cognitive interactions, motivation, and cognitive growth in Logo programming and CAI problem-solving environments. *Journal of Educational Psychology, 82,* 150–158.

National Association for Perinatal Addiction Research and Education. (1988, October). Innocent addicts: High rate of prenatal drug abuse found. *ADAMHA News.*

National Commission on Excellence in Education. (1983). *A nation at risk: The imperative for educational reform.* Washington, DC: U.S. Government Printing Office.

National Research Council, Committee on Mapping and Sequencing the Human Genome. (1988). *Mapping and sequencing the human genome.* Washington, DC: National Academy Press.

Needleman, H. L., & Bellinger, D. (Eds.) (1994). *Prenatal exposure to toxicants: Developmental consequences.* Baltimore: Johns Hopkins University Press.

Neimark, E. D. (1979). Current status of formal operations research. *Human Development, 22,* 60–67.

Neisser, U., Boodoo, G., Bouchard, T. J., Jr., Boykin, A. W., Brody, N., Ceci, S. J., Halpern, D. F., Loehlin, J. C., Perloff, R., Sternberg, R. J., & Urbina, S. (1996). Intelligence: Knowns and unknowns. *American Psychologist, 51,* 77–101.

Nelson, C. A. (1995). The ontogeny of human memory: A cognitive neuroscience perspective. *Developmental Psychology, 31,* 723–738.

Nelson, C. A., & Horowitz, F. D. (1987). Visual motion perception in infancy: A review and synthesis. In P. Salapatek & L. Cohen (Eds.), *Handbook of infant perception: From perception to cognition* (Vol. 2). Orlando, FL: Academic Press.

Nelson, K. (1973). Structure and strategy in learning to talk. *Monographs of the Society for Research in Child Development, 38*(1–2, Serial No. 149).

Nelson, K. (1988). Constraints on word learning? *Cognitive Development, 3,* 221–246.

Nelson, K. (1989). Strategies for first language teaching. In M. L. Rice & R. L. Schiefelbusch (Eds.), *The teachability of language.* Baltimore: Paul H. Brookes.

Nelson, K. (1991). Concepts and meaning in language development. In N. A. Krasnegor, D. M. Rumbaugh, R. L. Schiefelbusch, & M. Studdert-Kennedy (Eds.), *Biological and behavioral determinants of language development.* Hillsdale, NJ: Erlbaum.

Nelson, K. (1993a). Events, narratives, memory: What develops? In C. A. Nelson (Ed.), *Memory and affect in development. The Minnesota symposia on child psychology* (Vol. 26, pp. 1–24). Hillsdale, NJ: Erlbaum.

Nelson, K. (1993b). The psychological and social origins of autobiographical memory. *Psychological Science, 4,* 7–14.

NIMH.(1996). (Internet site)

Nelson, K., & Gruendel, J. (1981). Generalized event representations: Basic building blocks of cognitive development. In M. E. Lamb & A. L. Brown (Eds.), *Advances in developmental psychology* (Vol. 1). Hillsdale, NJ: Erlbaum.

Neuman, S. B. (1991). *Literacy in the television age.* Norwood, NJ: Ablex.

Neumann, P. J., Gharib, S. D., & Weinstein, M. C. (1994). The cost of a successful delivery with in vitro fertilization. *New England Journal of Medicine, 331,* 239–243.

New, R. S., & Benigni, L. (1987). Italian fathers and infants: Cultural constraints on paternal behavior. In M. E. Lamb (Ed.), *The father's role: Cross-cultural perspectives.* Hillsdale, NJ: Erlbaum.

Newborg, J., Stock, J. R., & Wnek, L. (1984). *Battelle Developmental Inventory.* Allen, TX: LINC Associates.

Newcomb, A. F., & Bagwell, C. L. (1995). Children's friendship relations: A meta-analytic review. *Psychological Bulletin, 117,* 306–347.

Newcombe, N., & Huttenlocher, J. (1992). Children's early ability to solve perspective-taking problems. *Developmental Psychology, 28,* 635–643.

Newcomer, S., & Baldwin, W. (1992). Demographics of adolescent sexual behavior, contraception, pregnancy, and STDs. *Journal of School Health, 62,* 265–270.

Newnham, J., Evans, S. F., Michael, C. A., Stanley, F. J., & Landau, L. I. (1993). Effects of frequent ultrasound during pregnancy: A randomised controlled trial. *Lancet, 342,* 887–891.

Newport, E. L. (1977). Motherese: The speech of mothers to young children. In N. J. Castellan, D. B. Pisoni, & G. Potts (Eds.), *Cognitive theory* (Vol. 2). Hillsdale, NJ: Erlbaum.

Newport, E. L. (1990). Maturational constraints on language learning. *Cognitive Science, 14,* 11–28.

Newton, N. (1955). *Maternal emotions.* New York: P. B. Hoeber.

Nickel, H., & Kocher, E. M. T. (1987). West Germany and the German-speaking countries. In M. E. Lamb (Ed.), *The father's role: Cross-cultural perspectives.* Hillsdale, NJ: Erlbaum.

Nielson, A. C. (1994). Nielson media research. New York: Nielson.

Niemiec, R., & Walberg, H. J. (1987). Comparative effects of computer-assisted instruction: A synthesis of reviews. *Journal of Educational Computing Research, 3,* 19–37.

Nilsson, L. (1990). *A child is born.* New York: Dell.

Ninio, A., & Bruner, J. S. (1978). The achievement and antecedents of labelling. *Journal of Child Language, 5,* 1–15.

Noddings, N. (1992). *The challenge to care in schools: An alternative approach to education.* New York: Teachers College Press.

Noll, R. B., Vannatta, K., Koontz, K., Kalinyak, K., Bukowski, W. M., & Davies, W. H. (1996). Peer relationships and emotional well-being of youngsters with sickle cell disease. *Child Development, 67,* 423–436.

Norbeck, J. S., & Tilden, V. P. (1983). Life stress, social support, and emotional disequilibrium in complications of pregnancy: A prospective, multivariate study. *Journal of Health and Social Behavior, 24,* 30–46.

Nordentoft, M., Lou, H. C., Hansen, D., Nim, J., Pryds, O., Rubin, P., & Hemmingsen, R. (1996). Intrauterine growth retardation and premature delivery: The influence of maternal smoking and psychosocial factors. *American Journal of Public Health, 86,* 347–354.

Nowakowski, R. S. (1987). Basic concepts of CNS development. *Child Development, 58,* 568–595.

Nowicki, S., & Strickland, B. (1973). A locus of control scale for children. *Journal of Consulting and Clinical Psychology, 40,* 148–154.

Nucci, L. P., & Turiel, E. (1978). Social interactions and the development of social concepts in preschool children. *Child Development, 49,* 400–407.

Nucci, L. P., & Turiel, E. (1993). God's word, religious rules, and their relation to Christian and Jewish children's concepts of morality. *Child Development, 64,* 1475–1491.

Nugent, J. K., Lester, B. M., Greene, S. M., Wieczorek-Doering, D., & O'Mahony, P. (1996). The effects of maternal alcohol consumption and cigarette smoking during pregnancy on acoustic cry analysis. *Child Development, 67,* 1806–1815.

Nunes, T., Schliemann, A. D., & Carraker, D. W. (1993). *Street mathematics and school mathematics.* New York: Cambridge University Press.

Nussbaum, R. L., & Ledbetter, D. H. (1995). The fragile X syndrome. In C. R. Scriver, A. L. Beaudet, W. S. Sly, & D. Valle (Eds.), *The metabolic and molecular bases of inherited disease,* Vol. I (7th ed., pp. 795–810). New York: McGraw-Hill.

Oakes, J. (1985). *Keeping track: How schools structure inequality.* New Haven, CT: Yale University Press.

Oakes, L. M. (1994). Development of infants' use of continuity cues in their perception of causality. *Developmental Psychology, 30,* 869–879.

Oakes, L. M., & Cohen, L. B. (1990). Infant perception of a causal event. *Cognitive Development, 5,* 193–207.

Oakland, T. D. (1982). Nonbiased assessment in counseling: Issues and guidelines. *Measurement and Evaluation in Guidance, 15,* 107–116.

Ochs, E. (1990). Indexicality and socialization. In J. W. Stigler, R. A. Shweder, & G. Herdt (Eds.), *Cultural psychology.* Cambridge, UK: Cambridge University Press.

Offer, D. (1987). In defense of adolescents. *Journal of the American Medical Association, 257,* 3407–3408.

Ogbu, J. U. (1974). *The next generation: An ethnography of education in an urban neighborhood.* New York: Academic Press.

Ogbu, J. U. (1994). From cultural differences to differences in cultural frame of reference. In P. M. Greenfield & R. R. Cocking (Eds.), *Cross-cultural roots of minority child development.* Hillsdale, NJ: Erlbaum.

Okagaki, L., & Sternberg, R. J. (1993). Parental beliefs and children's school performance. *Child Development, 64.* 36–56.

Oldershaw, L., Walters, G. C., & Hall, D. K. (1986). Control strategies and noncompliance in abusive mother-child dyads: An observational study. *Child Development, 57,* 722–732.

Olsho, L. W. (1984). Infant frequency discrimination. *Infant Behavior and Development, 7,* 27–35.

Olson, R. K. (1994). Language deficits in "specific" reading disability. In M. A. Gernsbacher (Ed.), *Handbook of psycholinguistics.* New York: Academic Press.

Olson, S. L., Bayles, K., & Bates, J. E. (1986). Mother-child interaction and children's speech progress: A longitudinal study of the first two years. *Merrill-Palmer Quarterly, 32,* 1–20.

Olweus, D. (1980). Familial and temperamental determinants of aggressive behavior in adolescent boys: A causal analysis. *Developmental Psychology, 16,* 644–660.

Olweus, D. (1993a). Bullies on the playground: The role of victimization. In C. H. Hart (Ed.), *Children on playgrounds.* Albany: State University of New York Press.

Olweus, D. (1993b). *Bullying at school: What we know and what we can do.* Oxford, UK: Blackwell.

Olweus, D. (1994). Bullying at school: Long-term outcomes for the victims and an effective school-based intervention program. In L. R. Huesmann (Ed.), *Aggressive behavior: Current perspectives.* New York: Plenum.

Oostra, B. A., & Halley, D. J. J. (1995). Complex behavior of simple repeats: The fragile X syndrome. *Pediatric Research, 38,* 629–637.

Orenstein, S. R. (1992). Throwing out the baby with the bedding. *Clinical Pediatrics, 31,* 546–548.

Ornoy, A., Michailevskay, V., Lukashov, I., Barttamburger, R., & Harel, S. (1996). The developmental outcome of children born to heroin-dependent mothers, raised at home or adopted. *Child Abuse & Neglect, 20,* 385–396.

Ornstein, P. A., Baker-Ward, L., & Naus, M. J. (1988). The development of mnemonic skill. In F. E. Weinert & M. Perlmutter (Eds.), *Memory development: Universal changes and individual differences.* Hillsdale, NJ: Erlbaum.

Ornstein, P. A., & Naus, M. J. (1978). Rehearsal processes in children's memory. In P. A. Ornstein (Ed.), *Memory development in children.* Hillsdale, NJ: Erlbaum.

Ornstein, P. A., Naus, M. J., & Liberty, C. (1975). Rehearsal and organizational processes in children's memory. *Child Development, 46,* 818–830.

Orton, G. L. (1982). A comparative study of children's worries. *Journal of Psychology, 110,* 153–162.

Ostrea, E. M., Brady, M., Gause, S., Raymundo, A. L., & Stevens, M. (1992). Drug screening of newborns by meconium analysis: A large-scale, prospective epidemiological study. *Pediatrics, 89,* 107–113.

Ounsted, C., Oppenheimer, R., & Lindsay, J. (1974). Aspects of bonding failure: The psychopathology and psychotherapeutic treatment of families of battered children. *Developmental Medicine and Child Neurology, 16,* 447–452.

Owen, M. T., & Cox, M. J. (1988). Maternal employment and the transition to parenthood. In A. E. Gottfried & A. W. Gottfried (Eds.), *Maternal employment and children's development: Longitudinal research.* New York: Plenum Press.

Page, R. N. (1991). *Lower track classrooms: A curricular and cultural perspective.* New York: Teachers College Press.

Paikoff, R. L., & Brooks-Gunn, J. (1991). Do parent-child relationships change during puberty? *Psychological Bulletin, 110,* 47–66.

Palincsar, A. S., & Brown, A. L. (1984). Reciprocal teaching of comprehension-fostering and comprehension-monitoring activities. *Cognition and Instruction, 1,* 117–175.

Palincsar, A. S., & Brown, A. L. (1986). Interactive teaching to promote independent learning from text. *The Reading Teacher, 39,* 771–777.

Palisin, H. (1986). Preschool temperament and performance on achievement tests. *Developmental Psychology, 22,* 766–770.

Palmer, S. E., & Kimchi, R. (1986). The information processing approach to cognition. In T. J. Knapp & L. C. Robertson (Eds.), *Approaches to cognition: Contrasts and controversies.* Hillsdale, NJ: Erlbaum.

Papert, S. (1980). *Mindstorms: Children, computers, and powerful ideas.* New York: Basic Books.

Papousek, H. (1967). Experimental studies of appetitional behavior in human newborns and infants. In H. W. Stevenson, E. H. Hess, & H. L. Rheingold (Eds.), *Early behavior.* New York: Wiley.

Papousek, H., Papousek, M., & Koester, L. S. (1986). Sharing emotionality and sharing knowledge: A microanalytic approach to parent-infant communication. In C. E. Izard & P. B. Read (Eds.), *Measuring emotions in infants and children* (Vol. 2). Cambridge, UK: Cambridge University Press.

Papousek, M. (1992). Early ontogeny of vocal communication in parent-infant interactions. In H. Papousek, U. Jürgens, & M. Papousek (Eds.), *Nonverbal vocal communication: Comparative and developmental approaches.* Cambridge, UK: Cambridge University Press.

Parke, R. D. (1969). Effectiveness of punishment as an interaction of intensity, timing, agent nurturance, and cognitive structuring. *Child Development, 40,* 213–235.

Parke, R. D., & Collmer, C. W. (1975). Child abuse: An interdisciplinary analysis. In E. M. Hetherington (Ed.), *Review of child development research* (Vol. 5). Chicago: University of Chicago Press.

Parke, R. D., MacDonald, K. B., Beitel, A., & Bhavnagri, N. (1988). The role of the family in the development of peer relationships. In R. D. Peters & R. J. McMahon (Eds.), *Social learning and systems approaches to marriage and the family.* New York: Brunner/Mazel.

Parke, R. D., & O'Leary, S. (1976). Father-mother-infant interaction in the newborn period: Some findings, some observations, and some unresolved issues. In K. F. Riegel & J. Meacham (Eds.), *The developing individual in a changing world: Vol. 2. Social and environmental issues.* The Hague: Mouton.

Parke, R. D., & Slaby, R. G. (1983). The development of aggression. In E. M. Hetherington (Ed.), *Handbook of child psychology: Vol. IV. Socialization, personality, and social development.* New York: Wiley.

Parker, J. G., & Asher, S. R. (1987). Peer relations and later personal adjustment: Are low-accepted children at risk? *Psychological Bulletin, 102,* 357–389.

Parker, J. G., & Asher, S. R. (1993). Friendship and friendship quality in middle childhood: Links with peer group acceptance and feelings of loneliness and social dissatisfaction. *Developmental Psychology, 29,* 611–621.

Parker, J. G., & Gottman, J. M. (1989). Social and emotional development in a relational context: Friendship interaction from early childhood to adolescence. In T. M. Berndt & G. W. Ladd (Eds.), *Peer relations in childhood.* New York: Wiley.

Parker, J. G., & Seal, J. (1996). Forming, losing, renewing, and replacing friendships: Applying temporal parameters to the assessment of children's friendship experiences. *Child Development, 67,* 2248–2268.

Parkhurst, J. T., & Asher, S. R. (1992). Peer rejection in middle school: subgroup differences in behavior, loneliness, and interpersonal concerns. *Developmental Psychology, 28,* 231–241.

Parten, M. B. (1932). Social participation among pre-school children. *Journal of Abnormal and Social Psychology, 32,* 243–269.

Parving, A. (1994). Childhood hearing disability: Epidemiology and aetiology. *Annales Nestlé, 52,* 57–61.

Pascalis, O., de Schonen, S., Morton, J., Deruelle, C., & Fabre-Grenet, M. (1995). Mother's face recognition by neonates: A replication and an extension. *Infant Behavior and Development, 18,* 79–85.

Pass, R. F. (1987). Congenital and perinatal infections due to viruses and toxoplasma. In N. Kretchmer, E. J. Quilligan, & J. D. Johnson (Eds.), *Prenatal and perinatal biology and medicine: Vol. 2. Disorder, diagnosis, and therapy.* New York: Harwood Academic Publishers.

Patterson, D. (1987, August). The causes of Down syndrome. *Scientific American, 257,* pp. 52–61.

Patterson, G. R. (1982). *A social learning approach: Vol. 3. Coercive family process.* Eugene, OR: Castalia.

Patterson, G. R. (1986). Performance models for antisocial boys. *American Psychologist, 41,* 432–444.

Patterson, G. R., & Fleischman, M. J. (1979). Maintenance of treatment effects: Some considerations concerning family systems and follow-up data. *Behavior Therapy, 10,* 168–185.

Patterson, G. R., Littman, R. A., & Bricker, W. (1967). Assertive behavior in children: A step toward a theory of aggression. *Monographs of the Society for Research in Child Development, 32*(5, Serial No. 113).

Patterson, G. R., & Reid, J. B. (1973). Intervention for families of aggressive boys: A replication study. *Behavior Research and Therapy, 11,* 383–394.

Patterson, G. R., Reid, J. B., & Dishion, T. J. (1992). *A social learning approach: IV. Antisocial boys.* Eugene, OR: Castalia.

Patterson, G. R., Reid, J. B., Jones, R. R., & Conger, R. E. (1975). *A social learning approach: Vol. 1. Families with aggressive children.* Eugene, OR: Castalia.

Paxton, S. J., Wertheim, E. H., Gibbons, K., Szmukler, G. I., Hillier, L., & Petrovich, J. L. (1991). Body image satisfaction, dieting beliefs, and weight loss behaviors in adolescent girls and boys. *Journal of Youth and Adolescence, 20,* 362–379.

Pea, R. D., Kurland, D. M., & Hawkins, J. (1985). LOGO and the development of thinking skills. In M. Chen & W. Paisley (Eds.), *Children and microcomputers: Research on the newest medium.* Beverly Hills: Sage.

Peak, K., & Del Papa, F. S. (1993). Criminal justice enters the womb: Enforcing the "right" to be born drug-free. *Journal of Criminal Justice, 21,* 245–263.

Peckham, C. S., & Logan, S. (1993). Screening for toxoplasmosis during pregnancy. *Archives of Disease in Childhood, 68,* 3–5.

Pederson, F. A., Cain, R., Zaslow, M., & Anderson, B. (1982). Variation in infant experience associated with alternative family organization. In L. Laosa & I. Sigel (Eds.), *Families as learning environments for children.* New York: Plenum Press.

Pedlow, R., Sanson, A., Prior, M., & Oberklaid, F. (1993). Stability of maternally reported temperament from infancy to 8 years. *Developmental Psychology, 29,* 998–1007.

Pellegrini, A. D. (1988). Elementary-school children's rough-and-tumble play and social competence. *Developmental Psychology, 24,* 802–806.

Penner, S. G. (1987). Parental responses to grammatical and ungrammatical child utterances. *Child Development, 58,* 376– 384.

Perlmutter, M., & Myers, N. A. (1979). Development of recall in 2- to 4-year-old children. *Developmental Psychology, 15,* 73–83.

Perner, J., & Ruffman, T. (1995). Episodic memory and autonoetic consciousness: Developmental evidence and a theory of childhood amnesia. *Journal of Experimental Child Psychology, 59,* 516–548.

Perris, E. E., Myers, N. A., & Clifton, R. K. (1990). Long-term memory for a single infancy experience. *Child Development, 61,* 1796–1807.

Perry, D. G., & Bussey, K. (1979). The social learning theory of sex differences: Imitation is alive and well. *Journal of Personality and Social Psychology, 37,* 1699–1712.

Perry, D. G., Williard, J. C., & Perry, L. C. (1990). Peers' perceptions of the consequences that victimized children provide aggressors. *Child Development, 61,* 1310–1325.

Persell, C. H. (1977). *Education and inequality: A theoretical and empirical synthesis.* New York: Free Press.

Petersen, A. C. (1980). Biopsychosocial processes in the development of sex-related differences. In J. Parsons (Ed.), *The psychobiology of sex differences and sex roles.* New York: Hemisphere.

Petersen, A. C., Compas, B. E., Brooks-Gunn, J., Stemmler, M., Ey, S., & Grant, K. E. (1993). Depression in adolescence. *American Psychologist, 48,* 155–168.

Petersen, A. C., & Hamburg, B. (1986). Adolescence: A developmental approach to problems and psychopathology. *Behavior Therapy, 13,* 480–499.

Petersen, A. C. (1988). Adolescent development. *Annual Review of Psychology, 39,* 583–607.

Peterson, G. W., & Rollins, B. C. (1987). Parent-child socialization. In M. B. Sussman & S. K. Steinmetz (Eds.), *Handbook of marriage and the family.* New York: Plenum Press.

Petitto, L. A., & Marentette, P. F. (1991). Babbling in the manual code: Evidence for the ontogeny of language. *Science, 251,* 1493–1496.

Pettit, G. S., Clawson, M. A., Dodge, K. A. & Bates, J. E. (1996). Stability and change in peer-rejected status: The role of child behavior, parenting, and family ecology. *Merrill-Palmer Quarterly, 42,* 267–294.

Pettit, G. S., Dodge, K. A., Bakshi, A., & Coie, J. D. (1990). The emergence of social dominance in young boys' play groups: Developmental differences and behavioral correlates. *Developmental Psychology, 26,* 1017–1025.

Pharoah, P. O. D., Stevenson, C. J., Cooke, R. W. I., & Stevenson, R. C. (1993). Clinical and subclinical deficits at 8 years in a geographically defined cohort of low birthweight infants. *Archives of Disease in Children, 70,* 264–270.

Phelps, E., & Damon, W. (1989). Problem solving with equals: Peer collaboration as a context for learning mathematics and spatial concepts. *Journal of Educational Psychology, 81,* 639–646.

Phelps, L., & Bajorek, E. (1991). Eating disorders of the adolescent: Current issues in etiology, assessment, and treatment. *School Psychology Review, 1991,* 9–22.

Phillips, D. (1984). The illusion of incompetence among academically competent children. *Child Development, 55,* 2000–2016.

Phinney, J. S. (1990). Ethnic identity in adolescents and adults: Review of research. *Psychological Bulletin, 108,* 499–514.

Phinney, J. S., & Rosenthal, D. A. (1992). Ethnic identity in adolescence: Process, context and outcome. In G. R. Adams, T. P. Gullotta, & R. Montemayor (Eds.), *Adolescent identity formation.* Newbury Park, CA: Sage.

Piaget, J. (1926). *The language and thought of the child.* New York: Harcourt Brace.

Piaget, J. (1929). *The child's conception of the world.* London: Routledge & Kegan Paul.

Piaget, J. (1930). *The child's conception of physical causality.* London: Routledge & Kegan Paul.

Piaget, J. (1952a). *The child's conception of number.* New York: W. W. Norton.

Piaget, J. (1952b). *The origins of intelligence in children.* New York: W. W. Norton.

Piaget, J. (1954). *The construction of reality in the child.* New York: Basic Books.

Piaget, J. (1962). *Play, dreams, and imitation in childhood.* New York: W. W. Norton.

Piaget, J. (1965). *The moral judgment of the child.* New York: Free Press. (Original work published 1932)

Piaget, J. (1971). *Biology and knowledge: An essay on the relationship between organic regulations and cognitive processes.* Chicago: University of Chicago Press.

Piaget, J. (1974). *Understanding causality.* New York: W.W. Norton.

Piaget, J., & Inhelder, B. (1956). *The child's conception of space.* London: Routledge & Kegan Paul.

Pianta, R. C., & Egeland, B. (1994). Predictors of instability in children's mental test performance at 24, 48, and 96 months. *Intelligence, 18,* 145–163.

Pick, A. D. (1965). Improvement of visual and tactual discrimination. *Journal of Experimental Psychology, 69,* 331–339.

Pick, H. L., Jr. (1987). Information and the effects of early perceptual experience. In N. Eisenberg (Ed.), *Contemporary topics in developmental psychology.* New York: Wiley.

Pick, H. L., Jr. (1992). Eleanor J. Gibson: Learning to perceive and perceiving to learn. *Developmental Psychology, 28,* 787–794.

Pickens, J. (1994). Perception of auditory-visual distance relations by 5-month-old infants. *Developmental Psychology, 30,* 537–544.

Pickens, J., & Field, T. (1993). Facial expressivity in infants of depressed mothers. *Developmental Psychology, 29,* 986–988.

Pike, A., McGuire, S., Hetherington, E. M., Reiss, D., & Plomin, R. (1996). Family environment and adolescent depressive symptoms and antisocial behavior: A multivariate genetic analysis. *Developmental Psychology, 32,* 590–603.

Pillemer, D. B., & White, S. H. (1989). Childhood events recalled by children and adults. In H. W. Reese (Ed.), *Advances in child development and behavior* (Vol. 21, pp. 297–340). San Diego: Academic Press.

Pillow, B. H. (1988). Young children's understanding of attentional limits. *Child Development, 59,* 38–46.

Pineau, A., & Streri, A. (1990). Intermodal transfer of spatial arrangement of the component parts of an object in infants aged 4–5 months. *Perception, 19,* 795–804.

Pinker, S. (1984). *Language learnability and language development.* Cambridge, MA: Harvard University Press.

Pinker, S. (1987). The bootstrapping problem in language acquisition. In B. MacWhinney (Ed.), *Mechanisms of language acquisition.* Hillsdale, NJ: Erlbaum.

Pinneau, S. R. (1961). *Changes in intelligence quotient: Infancy to maturity.* Boston: Houghton Mifflin.

Pinon, M. F., Huston, A. C., & Wright, J. C. (1989). Family ecology and child characteristics that predict young children's educational television viewing. *Child Development, 60,* 846–856.

Pinyerd, B. J. (1992). Assessment of infant growth. *Journal of Pediatric Health Care, 6,* 302–308.

Platt, L. D., Koch, R., Azen, C., Hanley, W. B., Levy, H. L., Matalon, R., Rouse, B., de la Cruz, F., & Walla, C. A. (1992). Maternal phenylketonuria collaborative study, obstetric aspects and outcome: The first 6 years. *American Journal of Obstetrics and Gynecology, 166,* 1150–1162.

Pleck, J. H. (1982). *Husbands' and wives' paid work, family work, and adjustment.* Working papers. Wellesley, MA: Wellesley College Center for Research on Women.

Pleck, J. H. (1983). Husbands' paid work and family roles: Current research issues. In H. Z. Lopata & J. H. Pleck (Eds.), *Research in the interweave of social roles: Families and jobs.* Greenwich, CT: JAI Press.

Plomin, R. (1986). *Development, genetics, and psychology.* Hillsdale, NJ: Erlbaum.

Plomin, R. (1987). Developmental behavioral genetics and infancy. In J. D. Osofsky (Ed.), *Handbook of infant development* (2nd ed.). New York: Wiley.

Plomin, R. (1994). The Emmanuel Miller Memorial Lecture 1993: Genetic research and identification of environmental influences. *Journal of Child Psychology and Psychiatry and Allied Disciplines, 35,* 817–834.

Plomin, R. (1995). Genetics and children's experiences in the family. *Journal of Child Psychology and Psychiatry and Allied Disciplines, 36,* 33–68.

Plomin, R. (1996). Nature and nurture. In M. R. Merriens & G. G. Branigan (Eds.), *The developmental psychologists* (pp. 3–20). New York: McGraw-Hill.

Plomin, R., Corley, R., DeFries, J. C., & Fulker, D. W. (1990). Individual differences in television viewing in early childhood: Nature as well as nurture. *Psychological Science, 1,* 371–377.

Plomin, R., & Daniels, D. (1987). Why are children in the same family so different from one another? *Behavioral and Brain Science, 10,* 1–16.

Plomin, R., & DeFries, J. C. (1980). Genetics and intelligence: Recent data. *Intelligence, 4,* 15–24.

Plomin, R., DeFries, J. C., & Loehlin, J. C. (1977). Genotype-environment interaction and correlation in the analysis of human behavior. *Psychological Bulletin, 84,* 309–322.

Plomin, R., DeFries, J. C., & McClearn, G. E. (1990). *Behavioral genetics: A primer* (2nd ed.). New York: W. H. Freeman.

Plomin, R., & McClearn, G. E. (Eds.). (1993). *Nature-nurture and psychology.* Washington, DC: American Psychological Association.

Plomin, R., Owen, M. J., & McGuffin, P. (1994). The genetic basis of complex human behaviors. *Science, 264,* 1733–1739.

Plomin, R., Reiss, D., Hetherington, E. M., & Howe, G. W. (1994). Nature and nurture: Genetic contributions to measures of the family environment. *Developmental Psychology, 30,* 32–43.

Plumert, J. M., Ewert, K., & Spear, S. J. (1995). The early development of children's communication about nested spatial relationships. *Child Development, 66,* 959–969.

Pogrebin, L. C. (1980). *Growing up free: Raising your kids in the 80's.* New York: McGraw-Hill.

Polka, L. M., & Werker, J. F. (1994). Developmental changes in perception of nonnative vowel contrasts. *Journal of Experimental Psychology: Human Perception and Performance, 20,* 421–435.

Pollitt, E. (1994). Poverty and child development: Relevance of research in developing countries to the United States. *Child Development, 65,* 283–295.

Pollitt, E. (1996). Timing and vulnerability in research on malnutrition and cognition. *Nutrition Reviews, 54,* S49-S55.

Pollitt, E., Gorman, K. S., Engle, P. L., Martorell, R., & Rivera, J. (1993). Early supplementary feeding and cognition. *Monographs of the Society for Research in Child Development, 58* (7, Serial No. 235).

Pollock, L. A. (1983). *Forgotten children: Parent-child relations from 1500–1900.* Cambridge, UK: Cambridge University Press.

Pomerantz, E. M., Ruble, D. N., Frey, K. S., & Greulich, F. (1995). Meeting goals and confronting conflict: Children's changing perceptions of social comparison. *Child Development, 66,* 723–738.

Pomerleau, A., Bolduc, D., Malcuit, G., & Cossette, L. (1990). Pink or blue: Environmental gender stereotypes in the first two years of life. *Sex Roles, 22,* 359–367.

Poole, D. A., & White, L. T. (1991). Effects of question repetition on the eyewitness testimony of children and adults. *Developmental Psychology, 27,* 975–986.

Poole, D. A., & White, L. T. (1993). Two years later: Effects of question repetition and retention interval on the eyewitness testimony of children and adults. *Developmental Psychology, 29,* 844–853.

Porter, R. H., Balogh, R. D., & Makin, J. W. (1988). Olfactory influences on mother-infant interaction. In C. Rovee-Collier & L. P. Lipsitt (Eds.), *Advances in infancy research* (Vol. 5). Norwood, NJ: Ablex.

Porter, R. H., Makin, J. W., Davis, L. B., & Christensen, K. M. (1992). Breast-fed infants respond to olfactory cues from their own mother and unfamiliar lactating females. *Infant Behavior and Development, 15,* 85–93.

Posada, G., Gao, Y., Wu, F., Posada, R., Tascon, M., Schoelmerich, A., Sagi, A., Kondo-Ikemura, K., Haaland, W., & Synnevaag, B. (1995). The secure-base phenomenon across cultures: Children's behaviors, mothers' preferences, and experts' concepts. In E. Waters, B. E. Vaughn, G. Posada, & K. Kondo-Ikemura (Eds.), *Caregiving, cultural, and cognitive perspectives on secure-base behavior and working models: New growing points of attachment theory and research. Monographs of the Society for Research in Child Development, 60* (Nos. 2–3, Serial No. 244).

Poulin-Dubois, D., Lepage, A., & Ferland, D. (1996). Infants' concept of animacy. *Cognitive Development, 11,* 19–36.

Powers, S. I., Hauser, S. T., & Kilner, L. A. (1989). Adolescent mental health. *American Psychologist, 44,* 200–208.

Prader, A. (1978). Catch-up growth. *Postgraduate Medical Journal, 54,* 133–146.

Prather, P. A., & Bacon, J. (1986). Developmental differences in part/whole identification. *Child Development, 57,* 549–558.

Pratt, M. W., Green, D., MacVicar, J., & Bountrogianni, M. (1992). The mathematical parent: Parental scaffolding, parenting style, and learning outcomes in long-division mathematics homework. *Journal of Applied Developmental Psychology, 13,* 17–34.

Pressley, M., & Levin, J. R. (1977). Task parameters affecting the efficacy of a visual imagery learning strategy in younger and older children. *Journal of Experimental Child Psychology, 24,* 53–59.

Price-Williams, D., Gordon, W., & Ramirez, M. (1969). Skill and conservation: A study of pottery-making children. *Developmental Psychology, 1,* 769.

Pride, P. G., Drugan, A., Johnson, M. P., Isada, N. B., & Evans, M. I. (1993). Prenatal diagnosis: Choices women make about pursuing testing and acting on abnormal results. *Clinical Obstetrics and Gynecology, 36,* 496–509.

Proffitt, D. R., & Bertenthal, B. I. (1990). Converging operations revisited: Assessing what infants perceive using discrimination measures. *Perception & Psychophysics, 47,* 1–11.

Pulkkinen, L. (1982). Self-control and continuity from childhood to adolescence. In P. B. Baltes & O. G. Brim (Eds.), *Life-span development and behavior* (Vol. 4). New York: Academic Press.

Purcell, P., & Stewart, L. (1990). Dick and Jane in 1989. *Sex Roles, 22,* 177–185.

Putallaz, M. (1987). Maternal behavior and children's sociometric status. *Child Development, 58,* 324–340.

Quittner, A. L., Smith, L. B., Osberger, M. J., Mitchell, T. V., & Katz, D. B. (1994). The impact of audition on the development of visual attention. *Psychological Science, 5,* 347–353.

Radin, N. (1981). The role of the father in cognitive, academic, and intellectual development. In M. E. Lamb (Ed.), *The role of the father in child development.* New York: Wiley.

Radin, N. (1982). Primary caregiving and role-sharing fathers. In M. E. Lamb (Ed.), *Nontraditional families: Parenting and child development.* Hillsdale, NJ: Erlbaum.

Radin, N. (1994). Primary-caregiving fathers in intact families. In A. E. Gottfried & A. W. Gottfried (Eds.), *Redefining families: Implications for children's development.* New York: Plenum.

Radin, N., & Sagi, A. (1982). Childrearing fathers in intact families in Israel and the U.S.A. *Merrill-Palmer Quarterly, 28,* 111–136.

Radke-Yarrow, M., & Zahn-Waxler, C. (1984). Roots, motives, and patterns of children's prosocial behavior. In E. Staub, D. Bar-Tel, J. Karylowski, & J. Reykowski (Eds.), *Development and maintenance of prosocial behavior.* New York: Plenum Press.

Radke-Yarrow, M., Zahn-Waxler, C., & Chapman, M. (1983). Children's prosocial dispositions and behavior. In E. M. Hetherington (Ed.), *Handbook of child psychology: Vol. IV. Socialization, personality, and social development.* New York: Wiley.

Radziszewska, B., Richardson, J. L., Dent, C. W., & Flay, B. R. (1996). Parenting style and adolescent depressive symptoms, smoking, and academic achievement: Ethnic, gender, and SES differences. *Journal of Behavioral Medicine, 19,* 289–305.

Radziszewska, B., & Rogoff, B. (1988). Influence of adult and peer collaborators on children's planning skills. *Developmental Psychology, 24,* 840–848.

Radziszewska, B., & Rogoff, R. (1991). Children's guided participation in planning imaginary errands with skilled adult or peer partners. *Developmental Psychology, 27,* 381–389.

Raffaelli, M. (1989, April). *Conflict with siblings and friends in late childhood and early adolescence.* Paper presented at the biennial meeting of the Society for Research in Child Development, Kansas City, MO.

Rakic, P. (1981). Developmental events leading to laminar and areal organization of the neocortex. In F. O. Schmitt, F. G. Worden, G. Adelman, & S. G. Dennis (Eds.), *The organization of the cerebral cortex: Proceedings of a neurosciences research program colloquium.* Cambridge, MA: MIT Press.

Rallison, M. L. (1986). *Growth disorders in infants, children, and adolescents.* New York: Wiley.

Ramenghi, L. A., Griffith, G. C., Wood, C. M., & Levene, M. I. (1996a). Effect of non-sucrose sweet tasting solution on neonatal heel prick responses. *Archives of Disease in Childhood, 74,* F129–F131.

Ramenghi, L. A., Griffith, G. C., Wood, C. M., & Levene, M. I. (1996b). Reduction in pain response in premature infants using intraoral sucrose. *Archives of Disease in Childhood, 74,* F126–F128.

Ramey, C. T., Bryant, D. M., & Suarez, T. M. (1987). Early intervention: Why, for whom, how, at what cost? In N. Gunzenhauser (Ed.), *Infant stimulation: For whom, what kind, when, and how much?* (Johnson & Johnson Baby Products Company Pediatric Round Table Series No. 13). Skilman, NJ: Johnson & Johnson.

Ramey, C. T., Bryant, D. M., Wasik, B. H., Sparling, J. J., Fendt, K. H., & LaVange, L. M. (1992). Infant Health and Development Program for low birth weight, premature infants: Program elements, family participation, and child intelligence. *Pediatrics, 89,* 454–465.

Ramey, C. T., & Campbell, F. A. (1981). Educational intervention for children at risk for mild retardation: A longitudinal analysis. In P. Mittler (Ed.), *Frontiers of knowledge in mental retardation: Vol. 1. Social, educational, and behavioral aspects.* Baltimore: University Park Press.

Ramey, C. T., Lee, M. W., & Burchinal, M. R. (1989). Developmental plasticity and predictability: Consequences of ecological change. In M. H. Bornstein & N. A. Krasnegor (Eds.), *Stability and continuity in mental development: Behavioral and biological perspectives.* Hillsdale, NJ: Erlbaum.

Rapport, M. D. (1995). Attention-deficit hyperactivity disorder. In M. Hersen & R. T. Ammerman (Eds.), *Advanced abnormal psychology.* Hillsdale, NJ: Erlbaum.

Ratner, H. H. (1984). Memory demands and the development of young children's memory. *Child Development, 55,* 2173–2191.

Raven, J. C. (1962). *Coloured progressive matrices.* London: H. K. Lewis and Co.

Redd, W. H., Morris, E. K., & Martin, J. A. (1975). Effects of positive and negative adult-child interaction on children's social preferences. *Journal of Experimental Child Psychology, 19,* 153–164.

Reece, E. A., Hobbins, J. C., Mahoney, M. J., & Petrie, R. H. (1995). *Handbook of medicine of the fetus & mother.* Philadelphia: J. B. Lippincott.

Reese, E., Haden, C. A., & Fivush, R. (1993). Mother-child conversations about the past: Relationships of style and memory over time. *Cognitive Development, 8,* 403–430.

Reisman, J. E. (1987). Touch, motion, and proprioception. In P. Salapatek & L. Cohen (Eds.), *Handbook of infant perception: From sensation to perception* (Vol. 1). Orlando, FL: Academic Press.

Reissland, N. (1988). Neonatal imitation in the first hour of life: Observations in rural Nepal. *Developmental Psychology, 24,* 464–469.

Renninger, K. A. (1992). Individual interest and development: Implications for theory and practice. In K. A. Renninger, S. Hidi, & A. Krapp (Eds.), *The role of interest in learning and development.* Hillsdale, NJ: Erlbaum.

Renshaw, P. D. & Brown, P. J. (1993). Loneliness in middle childhood: Concurrent and longitudinal predictors. *Child Development, 64,* 1271–1284.

Repacholi, B. M., & Gopnik, A. (1997). Early reasoning about desires: Evidence from 14- and 18-month-olds. *Developmental Psychology, 33,* 12–21.

Report of National Institute of Child Health and Human Development (1993). Workshop on Chorionic Villus Sampling and Limb and Other Defects, October 20, 1992. *American Journal of Obstetrics and Gynecology, 169,* 1–6.

Reppucci, N. D. (1984). The wisdom of Solomon: Issues in child custody determination. In N. D. Reppucci, L. A. Weithorn, E. P. Mulvey, & J. Monahan (Eds.), *Children, mental health, and the law.* Beverly Hills, CA: Sage.

Resnick, L. B. (1986). The development of mathematical intuition. In M. Perlmutter (Ed.), *Perspectives on intellectual development: The Minnesota symposia on child psychology* (Vol. 19). Hillsdale, NJ: Erlbaum.

Resnick, L. B. (1995). Inventing arithmetic: Making children's intuitions work at school. In C. A. Nelson (Ed.), *Basic and applied perspectives on learning, cognition, and development. Minnesota Symposia on Child Psychology* (Vol. 28, pp. 75–101). Mahwah, NJ: Erlbaum.

Resnick, L. B., & Singer, J. A. (1993). Protoquantitative origins of ratio reasoning. In T. P. Carpenter, E. Fennema, & T. A. Romberg (Eds.), *Rational numbers: An integration of research.* Hillsdale, NJ: Erlbaum.

Rest, J. R. (1983). Morality. In J. H. Flavell & E. Markman (Eds.), *Handbook of child psychology: Vol. III. Cognitive development.* New York: Wiley.

Reznick, J. S., & Goldfield, B. A. (1992). Rapid change in lexical development in comprehension and production. *Developmental Psychology, 28,* 406–413.

Rheingold, H. L., & Cook, K. V. (1975). The contents of boys' and girls' rooms as an index of parents' behavior. *Child Development, 46,* 459–463.

Ribble, M. (1943). *The rights of infants.* New York: Columbia University Press.

Ricciuti, H. N. (1993). Nutrition and mental development. *Current Directions in Psychological Science, 2,* 43–46.

Rice, K. G. (1990). Attachment in adolescence: A narrative and meta-analytic review. *Journal of Youth and Adolescence, 19,* 511–538.

Rice, M. L. (1983). The role of television in language acquisition. *Developmental Review, 3,* 211–224.

Rice, M. L. (1989). Children's language acquisition. *American Psychologist, 44,* 149–156.

Rice, M. L., Huston, A. C., Truglio, R., & Wright, J. (1990). Words from "Sesame Street": Learning vocabulary while viewing. *Developmental Psychology, 26,* 421–428.

Rice, M. L., & Woodsmall, L. (1988). Lessons from television: Children's word learning when viewing. *Child Development, 59,* 420–429.

Richards, H. G., Bear, G. G., Stewart, A. L., & Norman, A. D. (1992). Moral reasoning and classroom conduct: Evidence for a curvilinear relationship. *Merrill-Palmer Quarterly, 38,* 176–190.

Richards, M. H., & Duckett, E. (1994). The relationship of maternal employment to early adolescent daily experience with and without parents. *Child Development, 65,* 225–236.

Rickman, M. D., & Davidson, R. J. (1994). Personality and behavior in parents of temperamentally inhibited and uninhibited children. *Developmental Psychology, 30,* 346–354.

Ricks, M. H. (1985). The social transmission of parental behavior: Attachment across generations. In I. Bretherton & E. Waters (Eds.), *Growing points of attachment theory and research. Monographs of the Society for Research in Child Development, 50*(1–2, Serial No. 209).

Rieber, L. P. (1990). Using computer animated graphics in science instruction with children. *Journal of Educational Psychology, 82,* 135–140.

Riesen, A. H. (1965). Effects of visual deprivation on perceptual function and the neural substrate. In J. de Ajuriaguerra (Ed.), *Dessafferentation experimental et clinique.* Geneva: Georg.

Rieser, J., Yonas, A., & Wikner, K. (1976). Radial localization of odors by human newborns. *Child Development, 47,* 856–859.

Rieser, P. A. (1992). Educational, psychologic, and social aspects of short stature. *Journal of Pediatric Health Care, 6,* 325–332.

Ris, M. D., Williams, S. E., Hunt, M. M., Berry, H. K., & Leslie, N. (1994). Early-treated phenylketonuria: Adult neuropsychologic outcome. *Journal of Pediatrics, 124,* 388–392.

Robbins, W. J., Brody, S., Hogan, A. G., Jackson, C. M., & Green, C. W. (Eds.). (1928). *Growth.* New Haven: Yale University Press.

Roberts, L. (1991). Does the egg beckon sperm when the time is right? *Science, 252,* 214.

Roberts, W., & Strayer, J. (1996). Empathy, emotional expressiveness, and prosocial behavior. *Child Development, 67,* 449–470.

Robertson, M. A. (1984). Changing motor patterns during childhood. In J. R. Thomas (Ed.), *Motor development during childhood and adolescence.* Minneapolis, MN: Burgess.

Robin, D. J., Berthier, N. E., & Clifton, R. K. (1996). Infants' predictive reaching for moving objects in the dark. *Developmental Psychology, 32,* 824–835.

Robinson, J. L., Kagan, J., Reznick, J. S., & Corley, R. (1992). The heritability of inhibited and uninhibited behavior: A twin study. *Developmental Psychology, 28,* 1030–1037.

Rochat, P. (1992). Self-sitting and reaching in 5- to 8-month-old infants: The impact of posture and its development on early eye-hand coordination. *Journal of Motor Behavior, 24,* 210–220.

Rochat, P., & Goubet, N. (1995). Development of sitting and reaching in 5- to 6-month-old infants. *Infant Behavior and Development, 18,* 53–68.

Rochat, P., & Morgan, R. (1995). Spatial determinants in perception of self-produced leg movements by 3- to 5-month-old infants. *Developmental Psychology, 31,* 626–636.

Rodgers, B. D., & Lee, R. V. (1988). Drug abuse. In G. N. Burrow & T. F. Ferris (Eds.), *Medical complications during pregnancy.* Philadelphia: W. B. Saunders.

Roe, K. V., Drivas, A., Karagellis, A., & Roe, A. (1985). Sex differences in vocal interaction with mother and stranger in Greek infants: Some cognitive implications. *Developmental Psychology, 21,* 372–377.

Roesler, T. A., Barry, P. C., & Bock, S. A. (1994). Factitious food allergy and failure to thrive. *Archives of Pediatrics and Adolescent Medicine, 148,* 1150–1155.

Roffwarg, H. P., Muzio, J. N., & Dement, W. C. (1966). Ontogenetic development of the human sleep-dream cycle. *Science, 152,* 604–619.

Roggman, L. A., Langlois, J. H., & Hubbs-Tait, L. (1987). Mothers, infants, and toys: Social play correlates of attachment. *Infant Behavior and Development, 10,* 233–237.

Roggman, L. A., Langlois, J. H., Hubbs-Tait, L., & Rieser-Danner, L. A. (1994). Infant day-care, attachment, and the "file drawer" problem. *Child Development, 65,* 1429–1443.

Rogoff, B. (1981). Schooling and the development of cognitive skills. In H. C. Triandis & A. Heron (Eds.), *Handbook of cross-cultural psychology: Developmental psychology* (Vol. 4). Boston: Allyn & Bacon.

Rogoff, B., Mistry, J., Göncü, A., & Mosier, C. (1993). Guided participation in cultural activity by toddlers and caregivers. *Monographs of the Society for Research in Child Development, 58*(8, Serial No. 236).

Rogoff, B., & Morelli, G. (1989). Perspectives on children's development from cultural psychology. *American Psychologist, 44,* 343–348.

Rollins, B. C., & Thomas, D. L. (1979). Parental support, power, and control techniques in the socialization of children. In W. R. Burr, R. Hill, F. I. Nye, & I. L. Reiss (Eds.), *Contemporary theories about the family: Research-based theories* (Vol. 1). New York: Free Press.

Rosch, E., Mervis, C. B., Gray, W. D., Johnson, D. M., & Boyes-Braem, P. (1976). Basic objects in natural categories. *Cognitive Psychology, 8,* 382–439.

Rose, S. A., & Feldman, J. F. (1995). Prediction of IQ and specific cognitive abilities at 11 years from infancy measures. *Developmental Psychology, 31,* 685–696.

Rose, S. A., Gottfried, A. W., & Bridger, W. H. (1981). Cross-modal transfer in 6-month-old infants. *Developmental Psychology, 17,* 661–669.

Rosekrans, M. A. (1967). Imitation in children as a function of perceived similarity to a social model and vicarious reinforcement. *Journal of Personality and Social Psychology, 7,* 307–315.

Rosenbaum, J. E. (1980). Social implications of educational grouping. *Review of Educational Research, 8,* 361–401.

Rosenberg, K. R. (1992). The evolution of modern human childbirth. *Yearbook of Physical Anthropology, 35,* 89–124.

Rosenblith, J. F., & Sims-Knight, J. E. (1985). *In the beginning: Development in the first two years of life.* Monterey, CA: Brooks/Cole.

Rosenfield, P., Lambert, N. M., & Black, A. (1985). Desk arrangement effects on pupil classroom behavior. *Journal of Educational Psychology, 77,* 101–108.

Rosengren, K. S., Gelman, S. A., Kalish, C. W., & McCormick, M. (1991). As time goes by: Children's early understanding of growth in animals. *Child Development, 62,* 1302–1320.

Rosenholtz, S. J., & Simpson, C. (1984). The formation of ability conceptions: Developmental trend or social construction? *Review of Educational Research, 54,* 31–63.

Rosenkoetter, L. I. (1973). Resistance to temptation: Inhibitory and disinhibitory effects of models. *Developmental Psychology, 8,* 80–84.

Rosenthal, R., & Jacobson, L. (1968). *Pygmalion in the classroom: Teacher expectation and pupils' intellectual development.* New York: Holt, Rinehart & Winston.

Rosenshine, B., & Meister, C. (1994). Reciprocal teaching: A review of research. *Review of Educational Research, 64,* 479–530.

Ross, D. M., & Ross, S. A. (1982). *Hyperactivity: Current issues, research, and theory* (2nd ed.). New York: Wiley.

Rosser, R. A. (1983). The emergence of spatial perspective taking: An information-processing alternative to egocentrism. *Child Development, 54,* 660–668.

Rossi, A. S. (1987). Parenthood in transition: From lineage to child to self-orientation. In J. B. Lancaster, J. Altmann, A. S. Rossi, & L. R. Sherrod (Eds.), *Parenting across the life span: Biosocial dimensions.* New York: Aldine de Gruyter.

Rothbart, M. K. (1986). Longitudinal home observations of infant temperament. *Developmental Psychology, 22,* 356–365.

Rothbart, M. K., Ahadi, S. A., & Hershey, K. L. (1994). Temperament and social behavior in childhood. *Merrill-Palmer Quarterly, 40,* 21–39.

Rothbart, M. K., & Derryberry, D. (1981). Development of individual differences in temperament. In M. E. Lamb & A. L. Brown (Eds.), *Advances in developmental psychology* (Vol. 1). Hillsdale, NJ: Erlbaum.

Rothbart, M. K., Derryberry, D., & Posner, M. I. (1994). A psychobiological approach to the development of temperament. In J. Bates & T. D. Wachs (Eds.), *Temperament: Individual differences at the interface of biology and behavior.* Washington, DC: American Psychological Association.

Rothberg, A. D., & Lits, B. (1991). Psychosocial support for maternal stress during pregnancy: Effect on birth weight. *American Journal of Obstetrics and Gynecology, 165,* 403–407.

Rotnem, D. L. (1986). Size versus age: Ambiguities in parenting short-statured children. In B. Stabler & L. E. Underwood (Eds.), *Slow grows the child: Psychological aspects of growth delay.* Hillsdale, NJ: Erlbaum.

Rotter, J. B. (1966). Generalized expectancies for internal versus external locus of control of reinforcement. *Psychological Monographs: General and Applied, 80,* 1–28.

Rousseau, J. J. (1895). *Émile or treatise on education* (W. H. Payne, Trans.). New York: Appleton. (Original work published 1762)

Rovee-Collier, C. K. (1987). Learning and memory in infancy. In J. D. Osofsky (Ed.), *Handbook of infant development* (2nd ed.). New York: Wiley.

Rovee-Collier, C. K. (1995). Time windows in cognitive development. *Developmental Psychology, 31,* 147–169.

Rovee-Collier, C. K., Evancio, S., & Earley, L. A. (1995). The time window hypothesis: Spacing effects. *Infant Behavior and Development, 18,* 69–78.

Rovee-Collier, C. K., Greco-Vigorito, C., & Hayne, H. (1993). The time window hypothesis: Implications for categorization and memory modification. *Infant Behavior and Development, 16,* 149–176.

Rovee-Collier, C. K., & Hayne, H. (1987). Reactivation of infant memory: Implications for cognitive development. In H. W. Reese (Ed.), *Advances in child development and behavior* (Vol. 28). San Diego, CA: Academic Press.

Rovee-Collier, C., Schechter, A., Shyi, G. C. W., & Shields, P. (1992). Perceptual identification of contextual attributes and infant memory retrieval. *Developmental Psychology, 28,* 307–318.

Rovee-Collier, C. K., & Shyi, G. (1992). A functional and cognitive analysis of infant long-term retention. In M. L. Howe, C. J. Brainerd, & V. F. Reyna (Eds.), *Development of long-term retention.* New York: Springer-Verlag.

Rozin, P. (1990). Development in the food domain. *Developmental Psychology, 26,* 555–562.

Rubenstein, J., & Howes, C. (1979). Caregiving and infant behavior in day care and in homes. *Developmental Psychology, 15,* 1–24.

Rubin, K. H. (1993). The Waterloo Longitudinal Project: Correlates and consequences of social withdrawal from childhood to adolescence. In K. H. Rubin & J. B. Asendorpf (Eds.), *Social withdrawal, inhibition, and shyness in childhood.* Hillsdale, NJ: Erlbaum.

Rubin, K. H., & Asendorpf, J. B. (1993). Social withdrawal, inhibition, and shyness in childhood: Conceptual and definitional issues. In K. H. Rubin & J. B. Asendorpf (Eds.), *Social withdrawal, inhibition, and shyness in childhood.* Hillsdale, NJ: Erlbaum.

Rubin, K. H., Fein, G. G., & Vandenberg, B. (1983). Play. In E. M. Hetherington (Ed.), *Handbook of child psychology: Vol. IV. Socialization, personality, and social development.* New York: Wiley.

Rubin, K. H., Hymel, S., & Mills, R. S. L. (1989). Sociability and social withdrawal in childhood: Stability and outcomes. *Journal of Personality, 57,* 238–255.

Rubin, K. H., & Krasnor, L. R. (1986). Social-cognitive and social behavioral perspectives on problem-solving. In M. Perlmutter (Ed.), *The Minnesota symposia on child psychology: Vol. 18. Cognitive perspectives on children's social and behavioral development.* Hillsdale, NJ: Erlbaum.

Rubin, K. H., Lynch, D., Coplan, R., Rose-Krasnor, L., & Booth, C. L. (1994). "Birds of a feather . . .": Behavioral concordances and preferential personal attraction in children. *Child Development, 65,* 1778–1785.

Rubin, K. H., Maioni, T. L., & Hornung, M. (1976). Free play behaviors in middle- and lower-class preschoolers: Parten and Piaget revisited. *Child Development, 47,* 414–419.

Ruble, D. N. (1983). The development of social-comparison processes and their role in achievement-related self-socialization. In E. T. Higgins, D. Ruble, & W. W. Hartup (Eds.), *Social cognition and social development: A sociocultural perspective.* Cambridge, UK: Cambridge University Press.

Ruble, D. N. (1987). The acquisition of self-knowledge: A self-socialization perspective. In N. Eisenberg (Ed.), *Contemporary topics in developmental psychology.* New York: Wiley.

Ruble, D. N., & Brooks-Gunn, J. (1982). The experience of menarche. *Child Development, 53,* 1557–1566.

Ruble, D. N., Boggiano, A. K., Feldman, N. S., & Loebl, J. H. (1980). Developmental analysis of the role of social comparison in self-evaluation. *Developmental Psychology, 16,* 105–115.

Ruble, D. N., Eisenberg, R., & Higgins, E. T. (1994). Developmental changes in achievement evaluation: Motivational implications of self-other differences. *Child Development, 65,* 1095–1110.

Ruble, D. N., & Flett, G. L. (1988). Conflicting goals in self-evaluative information seeking: Developmental and ability level analyses. *Child Development, 59,* 97–106.

Ruble, T. L. (1983). Sex stereotypes: Issues of change in the 1970s. *Sex Roles, 9,* 397–402.

Rudolph, K. D., Hammen, C., & Burge, D. (1995). Cognitive representations of self, family, and peers in school-age children: Links with social competence and sociometric status. *Child Development, 66,* 1385–1402.

Ruff, H. A., & Kohler, C. J. (1978). Tactual visual transfer in 6-month-old infants. *Infant Behavior and Development, 1,* 259–264.

Ruff, H. A., & Lawson, K. R. (1990). Development of sustained, focused attention in young children during free play. *Developmental Psychology, 26,* 85–93.

Rule, B. G., Nesdale, A. R., & McAra, M. J. (1974). Children's reactions to information about the intentions underlying an aggressive act. *Child Development, 45,* 794–798.

Rumbaugh, D. M., Gill, T. V., & von Glasersfeld, E. C. (1973). Reading and sentence completion by a chimpanzee (*Pan*). *Science, 182,* 731–733.

Rushton, J. P. (1975). Generosity in children: Immediate and long-term effects of modeling, preaching, and moral judgment. *Journal of Personality and Social Psychology, 31,* 459–466.

Russell, G. (1987). Fatherhood in Australia. In M. E. Lamb (Ed.), *The father's role: Cross-cultural perspectives.* Hillsdale, NJ: Erlbaum.

Russell, G., & Russell, A. (1987). Mother-child and father-child relationships in middle childhood. *Child Development, 58,* 1573– 1585.

Rutter, M. (1983a). Cognitive deficits in the pathogenesis of autism. *Journal of Child Psychology and Psychiatry, 24,* 513– 532.

Rutter, M. (1983b). School effects on pupil progress: Research findings and policy implications. *Child Development, 54,* 1–29.

Rutter, M. (1986). Meyerian psychobiology, personality development, and the role of life experiences. *American Journal of Psychiatry, 143,* 1077–1087.

Rutter, M. (1990). Psychosocial resilience and protective mechanisms. In J. Rolf, A. S. Masten, D. Cicchetti, K. H. Neuchterlein, & S. Weintraub (Eds.), *Risk and protective factors in the development of psychopathology* (pp. 79– 101). New York: Cambridge University Press.

Rutter, M. (1991). Age changes in depressive disorders: Some developmental considerations. In J. Garber & K. A. Dodge (Eds.), *The development of emotion regulation and dysregulation.* Cambridge, UK: Cambridge University Press.

Rutter, M., Bailey, A., Bolton, P., & Le Couteur, A. (1993). Autism: Syndrome definition and possible genetic mechanisms. In R. Plomin & G. E. McClearn (Eds.), *Nature, nurture, and psychology* (pp. 269–284). Washington, DC: American Psychological Association.

Rutter, M., & Garmezy, N. (1983). Developmental psychopathology. In E. M. Hetherington (Ed.), *Handbook of child psychology: Vol. IV. Socialization, personality, and social development.* New York: Wiley.

Rutter, M., & Madge, N. (1976). *Cycles of disadvantage.* London: Heinemann.

Rutter, M., Maughan, B., Mortimore, P., Ouston, J., & Smith, A. (1979). *Fifteen thousand hours: Secondary schools and their effects on children.* Cambridge, MA: Harvard University Press.

Ryan, C. A., & Finer, N. N. (1994). Changing attitudes and practices regarding local analgesia for newborn circumcision. *Pediatrics, 94,* 230–233.

Ryan, R. M., & Grolnick, W. S. (1986). Origins and pawns in the classroom: Self-report and projective assessments of individual differences in children's perceptions. *Journal of Personality and Social Psychology, 50,* 550–558.

Sadker, M. & Sadker, D. (1994). *Failing at fairness: How America's schools cheat girls.* New York: Charles Scribner's Sons.

Sagi, A., Lamb, M. E., Lewkowicz, K. S., Shoham, R., Dvir, R., & Estes, D. (1985). Security of infant-mother, -father, and -metapelet attachments among kibbutz-reared Israeli children. In I. Bretherton & E. Waters (Eds.), *Growing points of attachment theory and research. Monographs of the Society for Research in Child Development, 50*(1–2, Serial No. 209).

Sagi, A., Van IJzendoorn, M. H., Aviezer, O., Donnell, F., & Mayseless, O. (1994). Sleeping out of home in a kibbutz communal arrangement: It makes a difference for mother-child attachment. *Child Development, 65,* 991–1004.

Sakala, C. (1993). Midwifery care and out-of-hospital birth settings: How do they reduce unnecessary cesarean section births? *Social Science and Medicine, 37,* 1233–1250.

Salapatek, P. (1975). Pattern perception in early infancy. In L. B. Cohen & P. Salapatek (Eds.), *Infant perception: From sensation to cognition* (Vol. 1). New York: Academic Press.

Salomon, G., & Gardner, H. (1986). The computer as educator: Lessons from television research. *Educational Researcher, 15,* 13–19.

Salomon, G., Globerson, T., & Guterman, E. (1989). The computer as a zone of proximal development: Internalizing reading-related metacognitions from a reading partner. *Journal of Educational Psychology, 89,* 620–627.

Salomon, G., & Perkins, D. N. (1987). Transfer of cognitive skills for programming: When and how? *Journal of Educational Computing Research, 3,* 149–169.

Saltz, E., Campbell, S., & Skotko, D. (1983). Verbal control of behavior: The effects of shouting. *Developmental Psychology, 19,* 461–464.

Saltzman, R. L., & Jordan, M. C. (1988). Viral infections. In G. N. Burrow & T. F. Ferris (Eds.), *Medical complications during pregnancy.* Philadelphia: W. B. Saunders.

Salzinger, S., Feldman, R. S., Hammer, M., & Rosario, M. (1993). The effects of physical abuse on children's social relationships. *Child Development, 64,* 169–187.

Samarapungavan, A. (1992). Children's judgments in theory choice tasks: Scientific rationality in childhood. *Cognition, 45,* 1–32.

Sameroff, A. J. (1972). Learning and adaptation in infancy: A comparison of models. In H. W. Reese (Ed.), *Advances in child development and behavior* (Vol. 7). New York: Academic Press.

Sameroff, A. J. (1987). The social context of development. In N. Eisenberg (Ed.), *Contemporary topics in developmental psychology.* New York: Wiley.

Sameroff, A. J., & Chandler, P. J. (1975). Reproductive risk and the continuum of caretaking casualty. In F. D. Horowitz (Ed.), *Review of child development research* (Vol. 4). Chicago: University of Chicago Press.

Sameroff, A. J., Seifer, R., Baldwin, A., & Baldwin, C. (1993). Stability of intelligence from preschool to adolescence: The influence of social and family risk factors. *Child Development, 64,* 80–97.

Samuels, M., & Bennett, H. Z. (1983). *Well body, well earth: The Sierra Club environmental health sourcebook.* San Francisco: Sierra Club Books.

Samuels, M., & Samuels, N. (1986). *The well pregnancy book.* New York: Summit Books.

Sandberg, D. E., Brook, A. E., & Campos, S. P. (1994). Short stature: A psychosocial burden requiring growth hormone therapy? *Pediatrics, 94,* 832–840.

Sandberg, D. E., Meyer-Bahlburg, H. F., Ehrhardt, A. A., & Yager, T. J. (1993). The prevalence of gender-atypical behavior in elementary school. *Journal of the American Academy of Child and Adolescent Psychiatry, 32,* 306–314.

Santelli, J. S., & Beilenson, P. (1992). Risk factors for adolescent sexual behavior, fertility, and sexually transmitted diseases. *Journal of School Health, 62,* 271–279.

Santrock, J. W., & Sitterle, K. A. (1987). Parent-child relationships in stepmother families. In K. Pasley & M. Ihinger-Tallman (Eds.), *Remarriage and stepparenting: Current research and theory.* New York: Guilford Press.

Savage-Rumbaugh, E. S., Murphy, J., Sevcik, R. A., Brakke, K. E., Williams, S. L., & Rumbaugh, D. M. (1993). Language comprehension in ape and child. *Monographs of the Society for Research in Child Development, 58,* (3–4, Serial No. 233).

Savin-Williams, R. C. (1979). Dominance hierarchies in groups of early adolescents. *Child Development, 50,* 923–935.

Savin-Williams, R. C. (1980). Dominance hierarchies in groups of middle to late adolescent males. *Journal of Youth and Adolescence, 9,* 75–85.

Sawin, D. B., & Parke, R. D. (1979). The effects of interagent inconsistent discipline on children's aggressive behavior. *Journal of Experimental Child Psychology, 28,* 525–538.

Saxby, L., & Bryden, M. P. (1985). Left visual field advantage in children for processing visual emotional stimuli. *Developmental Psychology, 20,* 253–261.

Saxe, G. B., Guberman, S. R., & Gearhart, M. (1987). Social processes in early number development. *Monographs of the Society for Research in Child Development, 52* (2, Serial No. 216).

Scarborough, H. S., & Dobrich, W. (1993). On the efficacy of reading to preschoolers. *Developmental Review, 14,* 245–302.

Scarr, S. (1981). Genetics and the development of intelligence. In S. Scarr (Ed.), *Race, social class, and individual differences in IQ.* Hillsdale, NJ: Erlbaum.

Scarr, S. (1987). Three cheers for behavior genetics: Winning the war and losing our identity. *Behavior Genetics, 17,* 219–228.

Scarr, S. (1992). Developmental theories for the 1990s: Development and individual differences. *Child Development, 63,* 1–19.

Scarr, S. (1993). Biological and cultural diversity: The legacy of Darwin for development. *Child Development, 64,* 1333–1353.

Scarr, S., & McCartney, K. (1983). How people make their own environments: A theory of genotype → environment effects. *Child Development, 54,* 424–435.

Scarr, S., Webber, P. L., Weinberg, R. A., & Wittig, M. A. (1981). Personality resemblance among adolescents and their parents in biologically related and adoptive families. *Journal of Personality and Social Psychology, 40,* 885–898.

Scarr, S., & Weinberg, R. A. (1976). IQ test performance of black children adopted by white families. *American Psychologist, 31,* 726–739.

Scarr, S., & Weinberg, R. A. (1977). Intellectual similarities within families of both adopted and biological children. *Intelligence, 1,* 170–191.

Scarr, S., & Weinberg, R. A. (1978). The influence of "family background" on intellectual attainment. *American Sociological Review, 43,* 674–692.

Scarr, S., & Weinberg, R. A. (1983). The Minnesota adoption studies: Genetic differences and malleability. *Child Development, 54,* 260–267.

Schachter, F. F. (1982). Sibling deidentification and split-parent identification: A family tetrad. In M. E. Lamb & B. Sutton-Smith (Eds.), *Sibling relationships: Their nature and significance across the life-span.* Hillsdale, NJ: Erlbaum.

Schafer, W. E., & Olexa, C. (1971). *Tracking and opportunity.* Scranton, PA: Chandler.

Schaffer, H. R., & Emerson, P. E. (1964). The development of social attachments in infancy. *Monographs of the Society for Research in Child Development, 29*(3, Serial No. 94).

Schieffelin, B. B., & Ochs, E. (1983). A cultural perspective on the transition from prelinguistic to linguistic communication. In R. M. Golinkoff (Ed.), *The transition from prelinguistic to linguistic communication.* Hillsdale, NJ: Erlbaum.

Schlegel, A., & Barry, H. III. (1991). *Adolescence: An anthropological inquiry.* New York: Free Press.

Schlinger, H.D., Jr. (1992). Theory in behavior analysis: An application to child development. *American Psychologist, 47,* 1396–1410.

Schneider, B. H., & Byrne, B. M. (1985). Children's social skills training: A meta-analysis. In B. H. Schneider, K. H. Rubin, & J. E. Ledingham (Eds.), *Children's peer relations: Issues in assessment and intervention.* New York: Springer-Verlag.

Schneider, B., Trehub, S. E., Morrongiello, B. A., & Thorpe, L. A. (1986). Auditory sensitivity in preschool children. *Journal of the Acoustical Society of America, 79,* 447–452.

Schneider-Rosen, K., Braunwald, K., Carlson, V., & Cicchetti, D. (1985). Current perspectives on attachment theory: Illustrations from the study of maltreated infants. In I. Bretherton & E. Waters, (Eds.), *Growing points of attachment theory and research. Monographs of the Society for Research in Child Development, 50*(1–2, Serial No. 209).

Schubert, J. B., Bradley-Johnson, S., & Nuttal, J. (1980). Mother-infant communication and maternal employment. *Child Development, 51,* 246–249.

Schulenberg, J., Asp, C. E., & Petersen, A. (1984). School from the young adolescent's perspective: A descriptive report. *Journal of Early Adolescence, 4,* 107–130.

Schwartz, D., Dodge, K. A., & Coie, J. D. (1993). The emergence of chronic peer victimization in boys' play groups. *Child Development, 64,* 1755–1772.

Schwartz, M., & Day, R. H. (1979). Visual shape perception in early infancy. *Monographs of the Society for Research in Child Development, 44*(7, Serial No. 182).

Scoville, R. (1983). Development of the intention to communicate: The eye of the beholder. In L. Feagans, C. Garvey, & R. Golinkoff (Eds.), *The origins and growth of communication.* Norwood, NJ: Ablex.

Scribner, S., & Cole, M. (1981). *The psychology of literacy.* Cambridge, MA: Harvard University Press.

Scriver, C. R., Beaudet, A. L., Sly, W. S., & Valle, D. (1995). *The metabolic and molecular bases of inherited disease,* Vol I. New York: McGraw-Hill.

Scriver, C. R., & Clow, C. L. (1988). Avoiding phenylketonuria: Why parents seek prenatal diagnosis. *Journal of Pediatrics, 113,* 495–496.

Secord, P., & Peevers, B. H. (1974). The development and attribution of person concepts. In T. Mischel (Ed.), *Understanding other persons.* Oxford: Blackwell.

Segall, M. H., Campbell, D. T., & Herskovits, M. J. (1966). *The influence of culture on perception.* New York: Bobbs-Merrill.

Seidman, E., Allen, L., Aber, J. L., Mitchell, C., & Feinman, J. (1994). The impact of school transitions in early adolescence on the self-system and perceived social context of poor urban youth. *Child Development, 65,* 507–522.

Seitz, V., & Apfel, N. H. (1994). Effects of a school for pregnant students on the incidence of low-birthweight deliveries. *Child Development, 65,* 666–676.

Self, P. A., Horowitz, F. D., & Paden, L. Y. (1972). Olfaction in newborn infants. *Developmental Psychology, 7,* 349–363.

Selman, R. L. (1980). *The growth of interpersonal understanding: Developmental and clinical analysis.* New York: Academic Press.

Selman, R. L. (1981). The child as a friendship philosopher. In S. R. Asher & J. M. Gottman (Eds.), *The development of children's friendships.* Cambridge, UK: Cambridge University Press.

Selzer, J. A. (1991). Relationships between fathers and children who live apart: The father's role after separation. *Journal of Marriage and the Family, 53,* 79–101.

Serbin, L. A., Connor, J. M., Burchardt, C. J., & Citron, C. C. (1979). Effects of peer presence on sex-typing of children's play behavior. *Journal of Experimental Child Psychology, 27,* 303–309.

Serbin, L. A., Connor, J. M., & Iler, I. (1979). Sex-stereotyped and nonstereotyped introductions of new toys in the preschool classroom: An observational study of teacher behavior and its effects. *Psychology of Women Quarterly, 4,* 261–265.

Serbin, L. A., O'Leary, K. D., Kent, R. N., & Tonick, I. J. (1973). A comparison of teacher response to the preacademic and problem behavior of boys and girls. *Child Development, 44,* 796–804.

Serbin, L. A., Powlishta, K. K., & Gulko, J. (1993). The development of sex typing in middle childhood. *Monographs of the Society for Research in Child Development, 58* (No. 2, Serial No. 232).

Serbin, L. A., Tonick, I. J., & Sternglanz, S. H. (1977). Shaping cooperative cross-sex play. *Child Development, 48,* 924–929.

Shachar, H., & Sharan, S. (1994). Talking, relating, and achieving: Effects of cooperative learning and whole-class instruction. *Cognition and Instruction, 12,* 313–353.

Shaffer, D. (1988). The epidemiology of teen suicide: An examination of risk factors. *Journal of Clinical Psychiatry, 49,* 36–41.

Shahar, S. (1990). *Childhood in the Middle Ages.* London: Routledge.

Shantz, C. (1983). Social cognition. In J. H. Flavell & E. M. Markman (Eds.), *Handbook of child psychology: Vol. III. Cognitive development.* New York: Wiley.

Shapira, A., & Madsen, M. C. (1969). Cooperative and competitive behavior of kibbutz and urban children in Israel. *Child Development, 4,* 609–617.

Sharp, D., Cole, M., & Lave, C. (1979). Education and cognitive development: The evidence from experimental research. *Monographs of the Society for Research in Child Development, 44*(1–2, Serial No. 178).

Shatz, C. J. (1992, September). The developing brain. *Scientific American,* pp. 60–67.

Shatz, M., & Gelman, R. (1973). The development of communication skills: Modification in the speech of young children as a function of listener. *Monographs of the Society for Research in Child Development, 38*(5, Serial No. 152).

Shaw, E., & Darling, J. (1985). *Strategies of being female.* Brighton, England: Harvester Press.

Shepard, L. A., & Smith, M. L. (1986). Synthesis of research on school readiness and kindergarten retention. *Educational Leadership, 44,* 78–86.

Sherif, M., Harvey, O. J., White, B. J., Hood, W. R., & Sherif, C. W. (1961). *Inter-group conflict and cooperation: The Robber's Cave experiment.* Norman: University of Oklahoma Press.

Shoda, Y., Mischel, W., & Peake, P. K. (1990). Predicting adolescent cognitive and self-regulatory competencies from preschool delay of gratification: Identifying diagnostic conditions. *Developmental Psychology, 26,* 978–986.

Shostak, M. (1981). *Nisa: The life and words of a !Kung woman.* Cambridge, MA: Harvard University Press.

Shrum, W., & Cheek, N. H. (1987). Social structure during the school years: Onset of the degrouping process. *American Sociological Review, 52,* 218–223.

Shulman, L. P., Elias, S., Phillips, O. P., Grevengood, C., Dungan, J. S., & Simpson, J. L. (1994). Amniocentesis performed at 14 weeks' gestation or earlier: Comparison with first-trimester transabdominal chorionic villus sampling. *Obstetrics and Gynecology, 83,* 543–548.

Shupert, C., & Fuchs, A. F. (1988). Development of conjugate human eye movements. *Vision Research, 28,* 585–596.

Shwalb, B. J., Shwalb, D. W., & Shoji, J. (1994). Structure and dimensions of maternal perceptions of Japanese infant temperament. *Developmental Psychology, 30,* 131–141.

Shweder, R. A., Mahapatra, M., & Miller, J. G. (1987). Culture and moral development. In J. Kagan & S. Lamb (Eds.), *The emergence of morality in young children.* Chicago: University of Chicago Press.

Shy, K. K., Luthy, A. A., Bennett, F. C., Whitfield, M., Larson, E. G., Van Belle, G., Hughes, J. P., Wilson, J. A., & Stenchever, M. A. (1990). Effects of electronic fetal-heart-rate monitoring, as compared with periodic auscultation, on the neurological development of premature infants. *New England Journal of Medicine, 322,* 588–593.

Siegal, M. (1988). Children's knowledge of contagion and contamination as causes of illness. *Child Development, 59,* 1353–1359.

Siegel, A. W., Kirasic, K. C., & Kail, R. V., Jr. (1978). Stalking the elusive cognitive map: The development of children's representations of geographical space. In I. Altman & J. F. Wohlwill (Eds.), *Children and the environment.* New York: Plenum Press.

Siegel, L. S. (1993). Phonological processing deficits as the basis of a reading disability. *Developmental Review, 13,* 246–257.

Siegler, R. S. (1989). Mechanisms of cognitive development. In M. R. Rosenzweig & L. W. Porter (Eds.), *Annual Review of Psychology, 40,* 353–379.

Siegler, R. S. (1994). Cognitive variability: A key to understanding cognitive development. *Current Directions in Psychological Science, 3,* 1–5.

Siegler, R. S., & Crowley, K. (1991). The microgenetic method: A direct means for studying cognitive development. *American Psychologist, 46,* 606–620.

Siegler, R. S., & Ellis, S. (1996). Piaget on childhood. *Psychological Science, 7,* 211–215.

Siegler, R. S., & Jenkins, E. (1989). *How children discover new strategies.* Hillsdale, NJ: Erlbaum.

Siegler, R. S., & Richards, D. D. (1982). The development of intelligence. In R. J. Sternberg (Ed.), *Handbook of human intelligence.* Cambridge, UK: Cambridge University Press.

Siegler, R. S., & Robinson, M. (1982). The development of numerical understandings. In H. W. Reese & L. P. Lipsitt (Eds.), *Advances in child development and behavior* (Vol. 16). New York: Academic Press.

Siegler, R. S., & Shrager, J. (1984). Strategy choices in addition and subtraction: How do children know what to do? In C. Sophian (Ed.), *Origins of cognitive skills.* Hillsdale, NJ: Erlbaum.

Sigelman, C. K., Carr, M. B., & Begley, N. L. (1986). Developmental changes in the influence of sex-role stereotypes on person perception. *Child Study Journal, 16,* 191–205.

Signorella, M. L. (1987). Gender schemata: Individual differences and context effects. In L. S. Liben & M. L. Signorella (Eds.), *New directions for child development: No. 38. Children's gender schemata.* San Francisco: Jossey-Bass.

Signorielli, N. (1989). Television and conceptions about sex roles: Maintaining conventionality and the status quo. *Sex Roles, 21,* 341–360.

Silberstein, L., Gardner, H., Phelps, E., & Winner, E. (1982). Autumn leaves and old photographs: The development of metaphor preferences. *Journal of Experimental Child Psychology, 34,* 135–150.

Silverman, W. K., LaGreca, A. M., & Wasserstein, S. (1995). What do children worry about? Worries and their relation to anxiety. *Child Development, 66,* 671–686.

Silvern, S. B., Williamson, P. A., & Countermine, T. M. (1988). Young children's interaction with a microcomputer. *Early Childhood Development and Care, 21,* 23–35.

Simmons, R. G., & Blyth, D. A. (1987). *Moving into adolescence: The impact of pubertal change and school context.* Hawthorne, NY: Aldine de Gruyter.

Simmons, R. G., Blyth, D. A., & McKinney, K. L. (1983). The social and psychological effects of puberty on white females. In J. Brooks-Gunn & A. C. Petersen (Eds.), *Girls at puberty.* New York: Plenum Press.

Simmons, R. G., Blyth, D. A., Van Cleave, E. F., & Bush, D. M. (1979). Entry into early adolescence: The impact of school structure, puberty, and early dating on self-esteem. *American Sociological Review, 44,* 948–967.

Simmons, R. G., Burgeson, R., Carlton-Ford, S., & Blyth, D. A. (1987). The impact of cumulative change in early adolescence. *Child Development, 58,* 1220–1234.

Simon, T. J., Hespose, S. J., & Rochat, P. (1995). Do infants understand simple arithmetic? A replication of Wynn (1992). *Cognitive Development, 10,* 253–269.

Simonoff, E., Bolton, P., & Rutter, M. (1996). Mental retardation: Genetic findings, clinical implications and research agenda. *Journal of Child Psychology and Psychiatry, 37,* 359–280.

Simner, M. L. (1971). Newborn's response to the cry of another infant. *Developmental Psychology, 5,* 136–150.

Sinai, L. N., Kim, S. C., Casey, R., & Pinto-Martin, J. A. (1995). Phenylketonuria screening: Effect of early newborn discharge. *Pediatrics, 96,* 605–608.

Sinclair, D. (1985). *Human growth after birth* (4th ed.). New York: Oxford University Press.

Singer, J. L., & Singer, D. G. (1983). Implications of childhood television viewing for cognition, imagination, and emotion. In J. Bryant & D. R. Anderson (Eds.), *Children's understanding of television: Research on attention and comprehension.* New York: Academic Press.

Singer, L. M., Brodzinsky, D. M., Ramsay, D., Steir, M., & Waters, E. (1985). Mother-infant attachment in adoptive families. *Child Development, 56,* 1543–1551.

Siqueland, E. R., & Lipsitt, L. P. (1966). Conditioned head turning in human newborns. *Journal of Experimental Child Psychology, 4,* 356–376.

Skinner, B. F. (1953). *Science and human behavior.* New York: Macmillan.

Skinner, B. F. (1957). *Verbal behavior.* New York: Appleton-Century-Crofts.

Skinner, B. F. (1971). *Beyond freedom and dignity.* New York: Knopf.

Skinner, B. F. (1974). *About behaviorism.* New York: Knopf.

Skinner, E. A., & Belmont, M. J. (1993). Motivation in the classroom: Reciprocal effects of teacher behavior and student engagement across the school year. *Journal of Educational Psychology, 85,* 571–581.

Skodak, M., & Skeels, H. M. (1949). A final follow-up study of one hundred adopted children. *Pedagogical Seminary and Journal of Genetic Psychology, 75,* 85–125.

Slaby, R. G., & Frey, K. S. (1975). Development of gender constancy and selective attention to same-sex models. *Child Development, 46,* 849–856.

Slaby, R. G., & Guerra, N. G. (1988). Cognitive mediators of aggression in adolescent offenders: 1. Assessment. *Developmental Psychology, 24,* 580–588.

Slater, A., Johnson, S. P., Brown, E., & Badenoch, M. (1996). Newborn infants' perception of partly occluded objects. *Infant Behavior and Development, 19,* 145–148.

Slater, A., Rose, D., & Morison, V. (1984). New-born infants' perception of similarities and differences between two- and three-dimensional stimuli. *British Journal of Developmental Psychology, 3,* 211–220.

Slaughter-Defoe, D. T., Nakagawa, K., Takanishi, R., & Johnson, D. J. (1990). Toward cultural/ecological perspectives on schooling and achievement in African- and Asian-American children. *Child Development, 61,* 363–383.

Slavin, R. E. (1987). Developmental and motivational perspectives on cooperative learning: A reconciliation. *Child Development, 58,* 1161–1167.

Slavin, R. E. (1990). *Cooperative learning: Theory, research, and practice.* Englewood Cliffs, NJ: Prentice-Hall.

Slomkowski, C., & Dunn, J. (1996). Young children's understanding of other people's beliefs and feelings and their connected communication with friends. *Developmental Psychology, 32,* 442–447.

Smetana, J. G. (1988). Concepts of self and social conventions: Adolescents' and parents' reasoning about hypothetical and actual family conflicts. In M. R. Gunnar & W. A. Collins (Eds.), *The Minnesota symposia on child psychology: Vol. 21. Development during the transition to adolescence.* Hillsdale, NJ: Erlbaum.

Smetana, J. G., & Braeges, J. L. (1990). The development of toddlers' moral and conventional judgments. *Merrill-Palmer Quarterly, 36,* 329–346.

Smetana, J. G., Schlagman, N., & Adams, P. W. (1993). Preschool judgments about hypothetical and actual transgressions. *Child Development, 64,* 202–214.

Smilansky, S. (1968). *The effects of sociodramatic play on disadvantaged preschool children.* New York: Wiley.

Smilkstein, G., Helsper-Lucas, A., Ashworth, C., Montano, D., & Pagel, M. (1984). Prediction of pregnancy complications: An application of the biopsychosocial model. *Social Sciences & Medicine, 18,* 315–321.

Smith, C. L., Gelfand, D. M., Hartmann, D. P., & Partlow, M. P. (1979). Children's causal attributions regarding help giving. *Child Development, 50,* 203–210.

Smith, J. D., & Kemler-Nelson, D. G. (1984). Overall similarity in adults' classification: The child in all of us. *Journal of Experimental Psychology: General, 113,* 137–159.

Smith, J. E., & Krejci, J. (1991). Minorities join the majority: Eating disturbances among Hispanic and native American youth. *International Journal of Eating Disorders, 10,* 179–186.

Smith, L. B. (1989). From global similarities to kinds of similarities: The construction of dimensions in development. In S. Vosniadou & A. Ortony (Eds.), *Similarity and analogical reasoning.* New York: Cambridge University Press.

Smith, L. B. (1995). Self-organizing processes in learning to learn words: Development is not induction. In C. A. Nelson (Ed.), *Basic and applied perspectives on learning, cognition, and development. The Minnesota symposia in child psychology* (Vol. 28). Mahwah, NJ: Erlbaum.

Smith, L. B., & Evans, P. M. (1989). Similarity, identity, and dimensions: Perceptual classification in children and adults. In B. E. Shepp & S. Ballesteros (Eds.), *Object perception: Structure and process.* Hillsdale, NJ: Erlbaum.

Smith, T. E. (1988). Parental control techniques: Relative frequencies and relationships with situational factors. *Journal of Family Issues, 9,* 155–176.

Snarey, J. R. (1985). Cross-cultural universality of social-moral development: A critical review of Kohlbergian research. *Psychological Bulletin, 97,* 202–232.

Snow, C. E. (1977). The development of conversation between babies and mothers. *Journal of Child Language, 4,* 1–22.

Snow, C. E. (1984). Parent-child interaction and the development of communicative ability. In R. L. Schiefelbusch & J. Pickar (Eds.), *The acquisition of communicative competence.* Baltimore: University Park Press.

Snow, C. E. (1987). Relevance of the notion of a critical period to language acquisition. In M. H. Bornstein (Ed.), *Sensitive periods in development.* Hillsdale, NJ: Erlbaum.

Sobal, J., & Stunkard, A. J. (1989). Socioeconomic status and obesity: A review of the literature. *Psychological Bulletin, 105,* 260–275.

Society for Research in Child Development. (1996). Ethical standards for research with children. In *Directory of members.* Ann Arbor, MI: Author.

Sodian, B., Zaitchik, D., & Carey, S. (1991). Young children's differentiation of hypothetical beliefs from evidence. *Child Development, 62,* 753–766.

Sontag, L. W., Baker, C. T., & Nelson, V. L. (1958). Mental growth and personality development: A longitudinal study. *Monographs of the Society for Research in Child Development, 23*(2, Serial No. 68).

Sorce, J. F., Emde, R. N., Campos, J., & Klinnert, M. D. (1985). Maternal emotional signaling: Its effect on the visual cliff behavior of 1-year-olds. *Developmental Psychology, 21,* 195–200.

Spearman, C. (1904). "General intelligence," objectively determined and measured. *American Journal of Psychology, 15,* 72–101.

Spearman, C. (1923). *The nature of "intelligence" and the principles of cognition.* London: Macmillan.

Spearman, C. (1927). *The abilities of man.* London: Macmillan.

Spears, W., & Hohle, R. (1967). Sensory and perceptual processes in infants. In Y. Brackbill (Ed.), *Infancy and early childhood.* New York: Free Press.

Spelke, E. S. (1976). Infants' intermodal perception of events. *Cognitive Psychology, 8,* 553–560.

Spelke, E. S. (1985). Perception of unity, persistence and identity: Thoughts on infants' conceptions of objects. In J. Mehler & R. Fox (Eds.), *Neonate cognition: Beyond the blooming, buzzing confusion.* Hillsdale, NJ: Erlbaum.

Spelke, E. S. (1987). The development of intermodal perception. In P. Salapatek & L. Cohen (Eds.), *Handbook of infant perception: From perception to cognition* (Vol. 2). Orlando, FL: Academic Press.

Spelke, E. S., & Owsley, C. J. (1979). Intermodal exploration and knowledge in infancy. *Infant Behavior and Development, 2,* 13–27.

Spence, M. J., & Freeman, M. S. (1996). Newborn infants prefer the maternal low-pass filtered voice, but not the maternal whispered voice. *Infant Behavior and Development, 19,* 199–212.

Spencer, M. B., & Markstrom-Adams, C. (1990). Identity processes among racial and ethnic minority children in America. *Child Development, 61,* 290–310.

Spitz, H. H. (1986). *The raising of intelligence.* Hillsdale, NJ: Erlbaum.

Spitz, R. (1946a). Anaclitic depression. *Psychoanalytic Study of the Child, 2,* 313–342.

Spitz, R. (1946b). Hospitalism: A follow-up report. *Psychoanalytic Study of the Child, 2,* 113–117.

Spivack, G., & Shure, M. B. (1974). *Social adjustment of young children.* San Francisco: Jossey-Bass.

Sprafkin, J. N., Liebert, R. M., & Poulos, R. W. (1975). Effects of a prosocial televised example on children's helping. *Journal of Experimental Child Psychology, 20,* 119–126.

Sprauve, M. E. (1996) Substance abuse and HIV in pregnancy. *Clinical Obstetrics and Gynecology, 39,* 316–332.

Spreen, O., Tupper, D., Risser, A., Tuokko, H., & Edgell, D. (1984). *Human developmental neuropsychology.* New York: Oxford University Press.

Springer, K., & Keil, F. C. (1991). Early differentiation of causal mechanisms appropriate to biological and nonbiological kinds. *Child Development, 62,* 767–781.

Sroufe, L. A. (1983). Infant-caregiver attachment and patterns of adaptation in preschool: The roots of maladaptation and competence. In M. Perlmutter (Ed.), *The Minnesota symposia on child psychology: Vol. 16. Development and policy concerning children with special needs.* Hillsdale, NJ: Erlbaum.

Sroufe, L. A. (1996). *Emotional development: The organization of life in the early years.* New York: Cambridge University Press.

Sroufe, L. A., Bennett, C., Englund, M., & Urban, J. (1993). The significance of gender boundaries in preadolescence: Contemporary correlates and antecedents of boundary violation and maintenance. *Child Development, 64,* 455–466.

Sroufe, L. A., & Waters, E. (1976). The ontogenesis of smiling and laughter: A perspective on the organization of development in infancy. *Psychological Review, 83,* 173–189.

Sroufe, L. A., & Wunsch, J. P. (1972). The development of laughter in the first year of life. *Child Development, 43,* 1326–1344.

St. Peters, M. Fitch, M. Huston, A. C., Wright, J. C., & Eakins, D. J. (1991). Television and families: What do young children watch with their families? *Child Development, 62,* 1409–1423.

Staffieri, J. R. (1967). A study of social stereotypes of body image in children. *Journal of Personality and Social Psychology, 7,* 101–104.

Stagno, S., & Cloud, G. A. (1994). Working parents: The impact of day care and breast-feeding on cytomegalovirus infections in offspring. *Proceedings of the National Academy of Science, USA, 91,* 2384–2389.

Stahl, P. M. (1984). A review of joint and shared parenting literature. In J. Folberg (Ed.), *Joint custody and shared parenting.* Washington, DC: Bureau of National Affairs.

Stanovich, K. E. (1993). A model for studies of reading disability. *Developmental Review, 13,* 225–245.

Starfield, B., Shapiro, S., McCormick, M. C., & Bross, D. (1982). Mortality and morbidity in infants with intrauterine growth retardation. *Journal of Pediatrics, 101,* 978–983.

Stark, R. E. (1986). Prespeech segmental feature detection. In P. Fletcher & M. Garman (Eds.), *Language acquisition: Studies in first language development.* Cambridge, UK: Cambridge University Press.

Steele, H., Steele, M., & Fonagy, P. (1996). Associations among attachment classifications of mothers, fathers, and their infants. *Child Development, 67,* 541–555.

Steel, L., & Levine, R. (1994). *Educational innovation in multiracial contexts: The growth of magnet schools in American education.* Palo Alto, CA: American Institutes for Research.

Stein, J. H., & Reiser, L. W. (1994). A study of white middle-class adolescent boys' responses to "semenarche" (the first ejaculation). *Journal of Youth and Adolescence, 23,* 373–384.

Steinberg, L. (1981). Transformations in family relations at puberty. *Developmental Psychology, 17,* 833–840.

Steinberg, L. (1988). Reciprocal relation between parent-child distance and pubertal maturation. *Developmental Psychology, 24,* 122–128.

Steinberg, L. (1995). *Beyond the classroom: Why school reform has failed and what parents need to do.* New York: Simon & Schuster.

Steinberg, L., Dornbusch, S. M., & Brown, B. B. (1992). Ethnic differences in adolescent achievement: An ecological perspective. *American Psychologist, 47,* 723–729.

Steinberg, L., Elmen, J. D., & Mounts, N. S. (1989). Authoritative parenting, psychosocial maturity, and academic success among adolescents. *Child Development, 60,* 1424–1436.

Steinberg, L., Fegley, S., & Dornbusch, S. M. (1993). Negative impact of part-time work on adolescent adjustment: Evidence from a longitudinal study. *Developmental Psychology, 29,* 171–180.

Steinberg, L., Greenberger, E., Garduque, L., & McAuliffe, S. (1982). High school students in the labor force: Some costs and benefits to schooling and learning. *Educational Evaluation and Policy Analysis, 4,* 363–372.

Steinberg, L., Lamborn, S. D., Darling, N., Mounts, N. S., & Dornbusch, S. (1994). Over-time changes in adjustment and competence among adolescents from authoritative, authoritarian, indulgent, and neglectful families. *Child Development, 65,* 754–770.

Steinberg, L., Lamborn, S. D., Dornbusch, S. M., & Darling, N. (1992). Impact of parenting practices on adolescent achievement: Authoritative parenting, school involvement, and encouragement to succeed. *Child Development, 63,* 1266–1281.

Steiner, J. E. (1979). Human facial expressions in response to taste and smell stimulation. In H. W. Reese & L. P. Lipsitt (Eds.), *Advances in child development and behavior* (Vol. 13). New York: Academic Press.

Stern, D. N. (1974). The goal and structure of mother-infant play. *Journal of the American Academy of Child Psychiatry, 13,* 402–421.

Sternberg, K. J., Lamb, M. E., Greenbaum, C., Cicchetti, D., Dawud, S., Cortes, R. M., Krispin, O., & Lorey, F. (1993). Effects of domestic violence on children's behavior problems and depression. *Developmental Psychology, 29,* 44–52.

Sternberg, R. J. (1981). A componential theory of intellectual giftedness. *Gifted Child Quarterly, 25,* 86–93.

Sternberg, R. J. (1982). *Intelligence applied.* New York: Harcourt.

Sternberg, R. J. (1985). *Beyond IQ: A triarchic theory of human intelligence.* Cambridge, UK: Cambridge University Press.

Sternberg, R. J. (1986). Triarchic theory of intellectual giftedness. In R. J. Sternberg & J. E. Davidson (Eds.), *Conceptions of giftedness.* Cambridge, UK: Cambridge University Press.

Sternberg, R. J. (1995). Testing common sense. *American Psychologist, 50,* 912–927.

Sternberg, R. J., Conway, B. E., Ketron, J. L., & Bernstein, M. (1981). People's conceptions of intelligence. *Journal of Personality and Social Psychology, 41,* 37–55.

Sternberg, R. J., & Frensch, P. A. (1993). Mechanisms of transfer. In D. K. Detterman & R. J. Sternberg (Eds.), *Transfer on trial: Intelligence, cognition, and instruction.* Norwood, NJ: Ablex.

Sternberg, R. J., & Nigro, G. (1980). Developmental patterns in the solution of verbal analogies. *Child Development, 51,* 27–38.

Sternberg, R. J., & Rifkin, B. (1979). The development of analogical reasoning processes. *Journal of Experimental Child Psychology, 27,* 195–232.

Stetsenko, A., Little, T. D., Oettingen, G., & Baltes, P. B. (1995). Agency, control, and means-ends beliefs about school performance in Moscow children: How similar are they to beliefs of western children? *Developmental Psychology, 31,* 285–299.

Stevenson, H. W., Chen, C., & Lee, S. (1993). Mathematics achievement of Chinese, Japanese, and American children: Ten years later. *Science, 259,* 53–58.

Stevenson, H. W., Lee, S., & Stigler, J. W. (1986). Mathematics achievement of Chinese, Japanese, and American children. *Science, 231,* 693–699.

Stevenson, H. W., Stigler, J. W., Lee, S., Lucker, G. W., Kitamura, S., & Hsu, C. (1985). Cognitive performance and academic achievement of Japanese, Chinese, and American children. *Child Development, 56,* 718–734.

Stevenson, H. W., Stigler, J. W., Lucker, G. W., & Lee, S. Y. (1986). Classroom behavior and achievement of Japanese, Chinese, and American children. In R. Glaser (Ed.), *Advances in instructional psychology.* Hillsdale, NJ: Erlbaum.

Stevenson-Hinde, J., & Shouldice, A. (1995). Maternal interactions and self-reports related to attachment classifications at 4.5 years. *Child Development, 66,* 583–596.

Stigler, J. W., Lee, S., & Stevenson, H. W. (1987). Mathematics classrooms in Japan, Taiwan, and the United States. *Child Development, 58,* 1272–1285.

Stigler, J. W., Smith, S., & Mao, L.-W. (1985). The self-perception of competence by Chinese children. *Child Development, 56,* 1259–1270.

Stiles, J., Delis, D. C., & Tada, W. L. (1991). Global-local processing in preschool children. *Child Development, 62,* 1258–1275.

Stipek, D., & Hoffman, J. M. (1980). Children's achievement related expectancies as a function of academic performance histories and sex. *Journal of Educational Psychology, 72,* 861–865.

Stipek, D., Recchia, S., & McClintic, S. (1992). Self-evaluation in young children. *Monographs of the Society for Research in Child Development, 57,* (1, Serial No. 226).

Stolberg, A. L., & Anker, J. M. (1984). Cognitive and behavioral changes in children resulting from parental divorce and consequent environmental changes. *Journal of Divorce, 8,* 184–197.

Stormshak, E. A., Bellanti, C. J., Bierman, K. L., & the Conduct Problems Prevention Group. (1996). The quality of sibling relationships and the development of social competence and behavioral control in aggressive children. *Developmental Psychology, 32,* 79–89.

Straus, M. A., & Donnelly, D. A. (1993). Corporal punishment of adolescents by American parents. *Youth and Society, 24,* 419–442.

Straus, M. A., & Gelles, R. J. (1986). Societal change and change in family violence from 1975 to 1985 as revealed in two national surveys. *Journal of Marriage and the Family, 48,* 465–479.

Strayer, F. F., & Strayer, J. (1976). An ethological analysis of social agonism and dominance relations among preschool children. *Child Development, 47,* 980–989.

Streissguth, A. P., Bookstein, F. L., Sampson, P. D., & Barr, H. M. (1995). Attention: Prenatal alcohol and continuities of vigilence and attentional problems from 4 through 14 years. *Development and Psychopathology, 7,* 419–446.

Streissguth, A. P., Sampson, P. D., Barr, H. M., Bookstein, F. L., & Olson, H. C. (1994). The effects of prenatal exposure to alcohol and tobacco: Contributions from the Seattle Longitudinal Prospective Study and implications for public policy. In H. L. Needleman & D. Bellinger (Eds.), *Prenatal exposure to toxicants: Developmental consequences* (pp. 148–183). Baltimore: Johns Hopkins University Press.

Streissguth, A. P., Treder, R., Barr, H. M., Shepard, T., Bleyer, A., & Martin, D. (1984). Prenatal aspirin and offspring IQ in a large group. *Teratology, 29,* 59A–60A.

Strutt, G. F., Anderson, D. R., & Well, A. D. (1975). A developmental study of the effects of irrelevant information on speeded classification. *Journal of Experimental Child Psychology, 20,* 127–135.

Stunkard, A. J., Harris, J. R., Pedersen, N. L., & McClearn, G. E. (1990). The body-mass index of twins who have been reared apart. *New England Journal of Medicine, 322,* 1483–1487.

Subrahmanyam, K., & Greenfield, P. M. (1994). Effect of video game practice on spatial skills in girls and boys. *Journal of Applied Developmental Psychology, 15,* 13–32.

Sugarman, S. (1982). Developmental change in early representational intelligence: Evidence from spatial classification strategies and related verbal expressions. *Cognitive Psychology, 14,* 410–449.

Sugarman, S. (1983). *Children's early thought: Developments in classification.* New York: Cambridge University Press.

Sullivan, H. S. (1953). *The interpersonal theory of psychiatry.* New York: W. W. Norton.

Sullivan, S. A., & Birch, L. L. (1990). Pass the sugar, pass the salt: Experience dictates preference. *Developmental Psychology, 26,* 546–551.

Sun, L. C., & Roopnarine, J. L. (1996). Mother-infant, father-infant interaction and involvement in childcare and household labor among Taiwanese families. *Infant Behavior and Development, 19,* 121–129.

Super, C. M. (1976). Environmental effects on motor development: The case of "African infant precocity." *Developmental Medicine and Child Neurology, 18,* 561–567.

Super, C. M., & Harkness, S. (1982). The infant's niche in rural Kenya and metropolitan America. In L. Adler (Ed.), *Issues in cross-cultural research.* New York: Academic Press.

Super, C. M., Herrera, M. G., & Mora, J. O. (1990). Long-term effects of food supplementation and psychosocial intervention on the physical growth of Colombian infants at risk of malnutrition. *Child Development, 61,* 29–49.

Surrey, J. L. (1991). The "self-in-relation": A theory of women's development. In J. V. Jordan, A. G. Kaplan, J. B. Miller, I. P. Stiver, & J. L. Surrey (Eds.), *Women's growth in connection.* New York: Guilford.

Sutton-Smith, B., & Rosenberg, B. G. (1970). *The sibling.* New York: Holt, Rinehart & Winston.

Svejda, M. J., Campos, J. J., & Emde, R. N. (1980). Mother-infant "bonding": Failure to generalize. *Child Development, 51,* 775–779.

Swain, I. U., Zelazo, P. R., & Clifton, R. K. (1993). Newborn infants' memory for speech sounds retained over 24 hours. *Developmental Psychology, 29,* 312–323.

Szajnberg, N., Ward, M. J., Krauss, A., & Kessler, D. B. (1987). Low birthweight prematures: Preventive intervention and maternal attitude. *Child Psychiatry and Human Development, 17,* 152–165.

Taddio, A., Goldbach, M., Ipp, M., Stevens, B., & Koren, G. (1995). Effect of neonatal circumcision on pain responses during vaccination in boys. *Lancet, 345,* 291–292.

Tager-Flusberg, H. (1985). Putting words together: Morphology and syntax in the preschool years. In J. B. Gleason (Ed.), *The development of language.* Columbus, OH: Charles E. Merrill.

Tallal, P., Miller, S. L., Bedi, G., Byma, G., Wang, X., Nagarajan, S. S., Schreiner, C., Jenkins, W. M., & Merzenich, M. N. (1996). Language comprehension in language-learning impaired children improved with acoustically modified speech. *Science, 271,* 81–84.

Tannenbaum, L., & Forehand, R. (1994). Maternal depressive mood: The role of the father in preventing adolescent behavior problems. *Behavior Research and Therapy, 32,* 321–326.

Tanner, J. M. (1962). *Growth at adolescence* (2nd ed.). Oxford: Blackwell.

Tanner, J. M. (1978). *Fetus into man: Physical growth from conception to maturity.* Cambridge, MA: Harvard University Press.

Tanner, J. M. (1990). *Foetus into man: Physical growth from conception to maturity* (Rev. ed.). Cambridge, MA: Harvard University Press.

Taras, H. L., Sallis, J. F., Patterson, T. L., Nader, P. R., & Nelson, J. A. (1989). Television's influence on children's diet and physical activity. *Journal of Developmental and Behavioral Pediatrics, 10,* 176–180.

Tardieu, M., Mayaux, M.-J., Seibel, N., Funck-Brentano, I., Straub, E., Teglas, J. P., & Blanche, S. (1995). Cognitive assessment of school-age children infected with maternally transmitted human immunodeficiency virus type 1. *Journal of Pediatrics, 126,* 375–379.

Tardif, T. (1996). Nouns are not always learned before verbs: Evidence from Mandarin speakers' early vocabularies. *Developmental Psychology, 32,* 492–504.

Taub, D. E., & Blinde, E. M. (1992). Eating disorders among adolescent female athletes: Influence of athletic participation and sport team membership. *Adolescence, 27,* 833–848.

Taylor, M. (1988). Conceptual perspective taking: Children's ability to distinguish what they know from what they see. *Child Development, 59,* 703–718.

Taylor, R. D. (1996). Adolescents' perceptions of kinship support and family management practices: Association with adolescent adjustment in African American families. *Developmental Psychology, 32,* 687–695.

Teasdale, T. & Owen, K. (1985). Heredity and familial environment in intelligence and educational level—a sibling study. *Nature, 309,* 620–622.

Terman, L. M. (1916). *The measurement of intelligence.* Boston: Houghton Mifflin.

Terman, L. M. (1925). *Genetic studies of genius: Vol. 1. Mental and physical traits of a thousand gifted children.* Stanford, CA: Stanford University Press.

Terman, L. M. (1954). The discovery and encouragement of exceptional talent. *American Psychologist, 9,* 221–238.

Terman, L. M., & Merrill, M. A. (1937). *Measuring intelligence.* Boston: Houghton Mifflin.

Terman, L. M., & Merrill, M. A. (1973). *Stanford-Binet Intelligence Scale: Manual for the third revision.* Boston: Houghton Mifflin.

Terman, L. M., & Oden, M. H. (1959). *Genetic studies of genius: Vol. 4. The gifted group at midlife.* Stanford, CA: Stanford University Press.

Terrace, H. S., Pettito, L. A., Sanders, R. J., & Bever, T. G. (1979). Can an ape create a sentence? *Science, 206,* 891–900.

Teti, D. M., Gelfand, D. M., Messinger, D. S., & Isabella, R. (1995). Maternal depression and the quality of early attachment: An examination of infants, preschoolers, and their mothers. *Developmental Psychology, 31,* 364–376.

Teti, D. M., Wolfe Sakin, J., Kucera, E., & Corns, K. M. (1996). And baby makes four: Predictors of attachment security among preschool-age firstborns during the transition to siblinghood. *Child Development, 67,* 579–596.

Tharp, R. G. (1989). Psychocultural variables and constants: Effects on teaching and learning in schools. *American Psychologist, 44,* 349–359.

Tharp, R. G., Jordan, C., Speidel, G. E., Au, K. H., Klein, T. W., Calkins, R. P., Sloat, K. C. M., & Gallimore, R. (1984). Product and process in applied developmental research: Education and the children of a minority. In M. E. Lamb, A. L. Brown, & B. Rogoff (Eds.), *Advances in developmental psychology* (Vol. 3). Hillsdale, NJ: Erlbaum.

Thelen, E. (1996). The improvising infant: Learning about learning to move. In M. R. Merrens & G. G. Brannigan (Eds.), *The developmental psychologists: Research adventures across the life span* (pp. 21–36). New York: McGraw-Hill.

Thelen, E., Corbetta, D., Kamm, K., Spencer, J. P., Schneider, K., & Zernicke, R. F. (1993). The transition to reaching: Mapping intention and intrinsic dynamics. *Child Development, 64,* 1058–1098.

Thelen, E., Skala, K. D., & Kelso, J. A. S. (1987). The dynamic nature of early coordination: Evidence from bilateral leg movements in young infants. *Developmental Psychology, 23,* 179–186.

Thelen, E., & Smith, L. B. (1994). *A dynamic systems approach to the development of cognition and action.* Cambridge, MA: MIT Press.

Thelen, E., & Ulrich, B. D. (1991). Hidden skills: A dynamic systems analysis of treadmill stepping during the first year. *Monographs of the Society for Research in Child Development, 56*(1, Serial No. 223).

Thoman, A. (1993). Obligation and option in the premature nursery. *Developmental Review, 13,* 1–30.

Thomas, A., & Chess, S. (1977). *Temperament and development.* New York: Brunner/Mazel.

Thomas, D. G., & Lykins, M. S. (1995). Event-related potential measures of 24-hour retention in 5-month-old infants. *Developmental Psychology, 31,* 946–957.

Thompson, C. (1982). Cortical activity in behavioural development. In J. W. T. Dickerson & H. McGurk (Eds.), *Brain and behavioural development.* London: Surrey University Press.

Thompson, R. A. (1990). Vulnerability in research: A developmental perspective on risk research. *Child Development, 61,* 1–16.

Thompson, R. A. (1994). Emotion regulation: A theme in search of definition. In N. A. Fox (Ed.), *The development of emotion regulation. Monographs of the Society for Research in Child Development, 59* (Nos. 2–3, Serial No. 240).

Thompson, S. K. (1975). Gender labels and early sex role development. *Child Development, 46,* 339–347.

Thompson, V. D. (1974). Family size: Implicit policies and assumed psychological outcomes. *Journal of Social Issues, 30,* 93–124.

Thorn, F., Gwaizda, J., Cruz, A. V., Bauer, J. A., & Held, R. (1994). The development of eye alignment, convergence and sensory binocularity in young infants. *Investigative Ophthalmology and Visual Science, 35,* 544–553.

Thorndike, R. L. (1994). g. *Intelligence, 19,* 145–155.

Thorndike, R. L., Hagen, E. P., & Sattler, J. M. (1986). *The Stanford-Binet Intelligence Scale: Guide for administering and scoring* (4th ed.). Chicago: Riverside.

Thorne, A., & Michaelieu, Q. (1996). Situating adolescent gender and self-esteem with personal memories. *Child Development, 67,* 1374–1390.

Thurstone, L. L. (1938). *Primary mental abilities.* Chicago: University of Chicago Press.

Thurstone, L. L. (1947). *Multiple factor analysis.* Chicago: University of Chicago Press.

Tieger, T. (1980). On the biological basis of sex differences in aggression. *Child Development, 51,* 943–963.

Tietjen, A. M. (1986). Prosocial moral reasoning among children and adults in a Papua New Guinea society. *Developmental Psychology, 22,* 861–868.

Tinbergen, N. (1951). *The study of instinct.* London: Oxford University Press.

Toda, S., & Fogel, A. (1993). Infant response to the still-face situation at 3 and 6 months. *Developmental Psychology, 29,* 532– 538.

Toda, S., Fogel, A., & Kawai, M. (1990). Maternal speech to three-month-old infants in the United States and Japan. *Journal of Child Language, 17,* 279–294.

Tolson, J. M., & Urberg, K. A. (1993). Similarity between adolescent best friends. *Journal of Adolescent Research, 8,* 274–288.

Tomasello, M. (1988). The role of joint attentional processes in early language development. *Language Sciences, 10,* 69–88.

Tomasello, M. (1992). The social bases of language acquisition. *Social Development, 1,* 68–87.

Tomasello, M., Conti-Ramsden, G., & Ewert, B. (1990). Young children's conversations with their mothers and fathers: Differences in breakdown and repair. *Journal of Child Language, 17,* 115–130.

Tomasello, M., Strosberg, R., & Akhtar, N. (1996). Eighteen-month-old children learn words in non-ostensive contexts. *Journal of Child Language, 23,* 157–176.

Tomasello, M., & Todd, J. (1983). Joint attention and lexical acquisition style. *First Language, 4,* 197–212.

Touwen, B. C. L. (1974). The neurological development of the infant. In J. A. Davis & J. Dobbing (Eds.), *Scientific foundations of paediatrics.* Philadelphia: W. B. Saunders.

Trehub, S. E. (1987). Infants' perception of musical patterns. *Perception & Psychophysics, 41,* 635–641.

Trehub, S. E., Bull, D., & Thorpe, L. A. (1984). Infants' perception of melodies: The role of melodic contour. *Child Development, 55,* 821–830.

Trehub, S. E., Schneider, B. A., Morrongiello, B. A., & Thorpe, L. A. (1988). Auditory sensitivity in school-age children. *Journal of Experimental Child Psychology, 46,* 273–285.

Trehub, S. E., Thorpe, L. A., & Morrongiello, B. A. (1985). Infants' perception of melodies: Changes in a single tone. *Infant Behavior and Development, 8,* 213–223.

Treiber, F., & Wilcox, S. (1980). Perception of a "subjective" contour by infants. *Child Development, 51,* 915–917.

Trevathan, W. R. (1987). *Human birth: An evolutionary perspective.* New York: Aldine de Gruyter.

Trevathan, W. R. (1988). Fetal emergence patterns in evolutionary perspective. *American Anthropologist, 90,* 674–681.

Trickett, P. K., & Susman, E. J. (1988). Parental perceptions of child-rearing practices in physically abusive and nonabusive families. *Developmental Psychology, 24,* 270–276.

Troiano, R. P., Glegal, K. M., Kuczmarski, R. J., Campbell, S. M., & Johnson, C. L. (1995). Overweight prevalence and trends for children and adolescence: The National Health and Nutrition Examination Surveys, 1963 to 1991. *Archives of Pediatric and Adolescent Medicine, 149,* 1085–1091.

Tronick, E. Z. (1987). The Neonatal Behavioral Assessment Scale as a biomarker of the effects of environmental agents on the newborn. *Environmental Health Perspectives, 74,* 185–189.

Tronick, E. Z. (1989). Emotions and emotional communication in infants. *American Psychologist, 44,* 112–119.

Tronick, E. Z., Als, H., Adamson, L., Wise, S., & Brazelton, T. E. (1978). The infant's response to entrapment between contradictory messages in face-to-face interaction. *Journal of the American Academy of Child Psychiatry, 17,* 1–13.

Tronick, E. Z., & Cohn, J. F. (1989). Infant-mother face-to-face interaction: Age and gender differences in coordination and the occurrence of miscoordination. *Child Development, 60,* 85–92.

Tronick, E. Z., Ricks, M., & Cohn, J. F., (1982). Maternal and infant affective exchange: Patterns of adaptation. In T. Field & A. Fogel (Eds.), *Emotion and early interaction.* Hillsdale, NJ: Erlbaum.

Tröster, H., & Brambring, M. (1993). Early motor development in blind infants. *Journal of Applied Developmental Psychology, 14,* 83–106.

Tucker, G. R., & d'Anglejan, A. (1972). An approach to bilingual education: The St. Lambert experiment. In M. Swain (Ed.), *Bilingual schooling: Some experiences in Canada and the United States.* Ontario: Ontario Institute for Studies in Education.

Turiel, E. (1983). *The development of social knowledge: Morality and convention.* Cambridge, UK: Cambridge University Press.

Turiel, E., Hildebrandt, C., & Wainryb, C. (1991). Judging social issues. *Monographs of the Society for Research in Child Development, 56* (2, Serial No. 224).

Turiel, E., & Wainryb, C. (1994). Social reasoning and the varieties of social experiences in cultural contexts. *Advances in Child Development and Behavior, 25,* 289–326.

Turk, J. (1995). Fragile X syndrome. *Archives of Disease in Childhood, 72,* 3–5.

Turkheimer, E. (1991). Individual and group differences in adoption studies of IQ. *Psychological Bulletin, 110,* 392–405.

Turkheimer, E., Goldsmith, H. H., & Gottesman, I. I. (1995). Commentary. *Human Development, 38,* 142–153.

Turner, S. M., & Mo, L. (1984). Chinese adolescents' self-concept as measured by the Offer Self-Image Questionnaire. *Journal of Youth and Adolescence, 13,* 131–142.

United Nations Statistical Office (1996, July). *Population and Vital Statistics Report.* New York: United Nations.

U.S. Bureau of the Census. (1995). Statistical abstract of the United States (115th ed.). Washington, DC: U.S. Government Printing Office.

U.S. Bureau of the Census. (1996). *Statistical abstract of the United States* (116th ed.). Washington, DC: U.S. Government Printing Office.

U.S. Department of Education, National Center for Education Statistics. (1996). *Youth Indicators 1996.* NCES 96–027. Washington, DC: U.S. Government Printing Office.

U.S. Department of Health, Education, and Welfare. (1978). *Alcohol and health.* Rockville, MD: National Institute of Alcohol Abuse and Alcoholism.

Underwood, L. E. (1991, March/April). Normal adolescent growth and development. *Nutrition Today,* pp. 11–16.

Updegraff, K. A., McHale, S. M., & Crouter, A. C. (1996). Gender roles in marriage: What do they mean for girls' and boys' school achievement? *Journal of Youth and Adolescence, 25,* 73–88.

Urgerg, K. A., Degirmencioglu, S. M., Tolson, J. M., & Halliday-Scher, K. (1995). The structure of adolescent peer networks. *Developmental Psychology, 31,* 540–547.

Useem, E. L. (1990). You're good, but you're not good enough: Tracking students out of advanced mathematics. *American Educator, 14,* 24–27, 43–46.

Uzgiris, I. (1968). Situational generality of conservation. In I. E. Sigel & F. H. Hooper (Eds.), *Logical thinking in children.* New York: Holt, Rinehart & Winston.

Valdez-Menchaca, M. C., & Whitehurst, G. J. (1992). Accelerating language development through picture book reading: A systematic extension to Mexican day care. *Developmental Psychology, 28,* 1106–1114.

Valian, V. (1986). Syntactic categories in the speech of young children. *Developmental Psychology, 22,* 562–579.

van den Boom, D. C. (1994). The influence of temperament and mothering on attachment and exploration: An experimental manipulation of sensitive responsiveness among lower-class mothers with irritable infants. *Child Development, 65,* 1457–1477.

van den Boom, D. C. (1995). Do first-year intervention effects endure? Follow-up during toddlerhood of a sample of Dutch irritable infants. *Child Development, 66,* 1798–1816.

van den Boom, D. C., & Hoeksma, J. B. (1994). The effects of infant irritability on mother-infant interaction: A growth-curve analysis. *Developmental Psychology, 30,* 581–590.

Van IJzendoorn, M. H. (1995). Adult attachment representations, parental responsiveness and infant attachment: A meta-analysis on the predictive validity of the Adult Attachment Interview. *Psychological Bulletin, 117,* 387–403.

Vandell, D. L., Henderson, V. K., & Wilson, K. S. (1988). A longitudinal study of children with day-care experiences of varying quality. *Child Development, 59,* 1286–1292.

Vandell, D. L., & Mueller, E. C. (1980). Peer play and friendships during the first two years. In H. C. Foot, A. J. Chapman, & J. R. Smith (Eds.), *Friendship and social relations in children.* New York: Wiley.

Vandell, D. L., & Ramanan, J. (1992). Effects of early and recent maternal employment on children from low-income families. *Child Development, 63,* 938–949.

Vandell, D. L., & Wilson, K. S. (1982). Social interaction in the first year of life: Infants' social skills with peers versus mother. In K. H. Rubin & H. S. Ross (Eds.), *Peer relationships and social skills in childhood.* New York: Springer-Verlag.

Vandell, D. L., Wilson, K. S., & Buchanan, N. R. (1980). Peer interaction in the first year of life: An examination of its structure, content, and sensitivity to toys. *Child Development, 51,* 481–488.

Vandenberg, S. G. (1971). What do we know about the inheritance of intelligence and how do we know it? In R. Cancro (Ed.), *Intelligence: Genetic and environmental influences.* New York: Grune and Stratton.

Vandenberg, S. G., & Vogler, G. P. (1985). Genetic determinants of intelligence. In B. B. Wolman (Ed.), *Handbook of intelligence.* New York: Wiley.

Varni, J. W., (1983). *Clinical behavioral pediatrics: An interdisciplinary biobehavioral approach.* New York: Pergamon Press.

Vaughn, B. E., Egeland, B., Sroufe, L. A., & Waters, E. (1979). Individual differences in infant-mother attachment at twelve and eighteen months: Stability and change in families under stress. *Child Development, 50,* 971–975.

Vaughn, B. E., Kopp, C. B., & Krakow, J. B. (1984). The emergence and consolidation of self-control from eighteen to thirty months of age: Normative trends and individual differences. *Child Development, 55,* 990–1004.

Vaughn, B. E., Taraldson, B., Crichton, L., & Egeland, B. (1980). Relationships between neonatal behavioral organization and infant behavior during the first year of life. *Infant Behavior and Development, 3,* 78–89.

Verkuyten, M. (1995). Self-esteem, self-concept stability, and aspects of ethnic identity among minority and majority youth in the Netherlands. *Journal of Youth and Adolescence, 24,* 155–175.

Vernon, P. E. (1966). Educational and intellectual development among Canadian Indians and Eskimos. *Educational Review, 18,* 79– 91.

Veroff, J. (1969). Social comparison and the development of achievement motivation. In C. P. Smith (Ed.), *Achievement-related motives in children.* New York: Russell Sage.

Vogel, G. (1996). Asia and Europe top in world, but reasons hard to find. *Science, 274,* 1296.

Volling, B. R., & Belsky, J. (1992). The contribution of mother-child and father-child relationships to the quality of sibling interaction: A longitudinal study. *Child Development, 63,* 1209–1222.

Vorhees, C. V. (1986). Principles of behavioral teratology. In E. P. Riley & C. V. Vorhees (Eds.), *Handbook of behavioral teratology.* New York: Plenum Press.

Vosk, B., Forehand, R., Parker, J., & Rickard, K. (1982). A multimethod comparison of popular and unpopular children. *Developmental Psychology, 18,* 571–575.

Vuchinich, S., Hetherington, E. M., Vuchinich, R. A., & Clingempeel, W. G. (1991). Parent-child interaction and gender differences in early adolescents' adaptation to stepfamilies. *Developmental Psychology, 27,* 618–626.

Vurpillot, E. (1968). The development of scanning strategies and their relation to visual differentiation. *Journal of Experimental Child Psychology, 6,* 632–650.

Vurpillot, E., & Ball, W. A. (1979). The concept of identity and children's selective attention. In G. A. Hale & M. Lewis (Eds.), *Attention and cognitive development.* New York: Plenum Press.

Vuyk, R. (1981). *Overview and critique of Piaget's genetic epistemology 1965–1980* (Vols. 1 & 2). New York: Academic Press.

Vygotsky, L. S. (1962). *Thought and language* (E. Hanfmann & G. Vakar, Trans.). Cambridge, MA: MIT Press.

Vygotsky, L. S. (1978). *Mind in society: The development of higher psychological processes.* Cambridge, MA: Harvard University Press.

Waber, D. P. (1976). Sex differences in cognition: A function of maturation rate? *Science, 192,* 572–574.

Wachs, T. D. (1992). *The nature of nurture.* Newbury Park: CA: Sage.

Wachs, T. D., Bishry, Z., Sobhy, A., McCabe, G., Galal, O., & Shaheen, F. (1993). Relation of rearing environment to adaptive behavior of Egyptian toddlers. *Child Development, 64,* 586–604.

Waddington, C. H. (1971). Concepts of development. In E. Tobach, L. R. Aronson, & E. Shaw (Eds.), *The biopsychology of development.* San Diego, CA: Academic Press.

Wadhwa, P. D., Sandman, C. A., Porto, M., Dunkel-Schetter, C., & Garite, T. J. (1993). The association between prenatal stress and infant birth weight and gestational age at birth: A prospective investigation. *American Journal of Obstetrics and Gynecology, 169,* 858–865.

Waggoner, D. (1994). Language minority school age population now totals 9.9 million. *NABE News, 18,* 1–24.

Wagner, B. M., & Phillips, D. A. (1992). Beyond beliefs: Parent and child behaviors and children's perceived academic competence. *Child Development, 63,* 1380–1391.

Wagner, D. A. (1978). Memories of Morocco: The influence of age, schooling, and environment on memory. *Cognitive Psychology, 10,* 1–28.

Wagner, M. E., Schubert, H. J. P., & Schubert, D. S. P. (1985). Family size effects: A review. *Journal of Genetic Psychology, 146,* 65–78.

Wagner, M. M. (1995, Summer/Fall). Outcomes for youths with serious emotional disturbance in secondary school and early adulthood. *The Future of Children, 5*(2), pp. 90–112.

Wagner, M. M., Blackorby, J., & Hebbeler, K. (1993). *Beyond the report card: The multiple dimensions of secondary school performance of students with disabilities: A report from the National Longitudinal Transition Study of Special Education Students.* Menlo Park, CA: SRI International.

Wahler, R. G., & Dumas, J. E. (1984). Changing the observational coding styles of insular and noninsular mothers: A step toward maintenance of parent training effects. In R. F. Dangel & R. A. Polster (Eds.), *Parent training: Foundations of research and practice.* New York: Guilford Press.

Wahler, R. G., & Dumas, J. E. (1989). Attentional problems in dysfunctional mother-child interactions: An interbehavioral model. *Psychological Bulletin, 105,* 116–130.

Walco, G. A., Cassidy, R. C., & Schechter, N. L. (1995). Pain, hurt, and harm: The ethics of pain control in infants and children. *New England Journal of Medicine, 331,* 541–544.

Waldrop, M. F., & Halverson, C. F. (1975). Intensive and extensive peer behavior: Longitudinal and cross-sectional analyses. *Child Development, 46,* 19–26.

Walk, R. D. (1968). Monocular compared to binocular depth perception in human infants. *Science, 162,* 473–475.

Walk, R. D. (1981). *Perceptual development.* Monterey, CA: Brooks/Cole.

Walker, L. J. (1984). Sex differences in the development of moral reasoning: A critical review. *Child Development, 55,* 677–691.

Walker, L. J. (1989). A longitudinal study of moral reasoning. *Child Development, 60,* 157–166.

Walker, L. J. (1996). Is one sex morally superior? In M. R. Merrens & G. G. Brannigan (Eds.), *The developmental psychologists: Research adventures across the life span.* New York: McGraw-Hill.

Walker, S. J. (1992). Supernatural beliefs, natural kinds, and conceptual structure. *Memory & Cognition, 20,* 655–662.

Walker-Andrews, A. S., & Lennon, E. M. (1985). Auditory-visual perception of changing distance by human infants. *Child Development, 56,* 544–548.

Wallerstein, J. S., Corbin, S. B., & Lewis, J. M. (1988). Children of divorce: A ten-year study. In E. M. Hetherington & J. Arasteh (Eds.), *Impact of divorce, single-parenting, and stepparenting on children.* Hillsdale, NJ: Erlbaum.

Wallerstein, J. S., & Kelly, J. B. (1980). *Surviving the breakup: How children and parents cope with divorce.* New York: Basic Books.

Walters, J. H. (1995). Late effects of phenylketonuria. *Archives of Disease in Childhood, 73,* 485–486.

Wang, P. P., & Bellugi, U. (1993). Williams syndrome, Down syndrome, and cognitive neuroscience. *American Journal of Disease in Children. 147,* 1246–1251.

Ward, S., Reale, G., & Levinson, D. (1972). Children's perceptions, explanations, and judgments of television advertising. In E. A. Rubenstein, G. A. Comstock, & J. P. Murray (Eds.), *Television and social behavior: Vol. 4. Television in day-to-day life: Patterns of use.* Washington, DC: U.S. Government Printing Office.

Wark, G. R., & Krebs, D. L. (1996). Gender and dilemma differences in real-life moral judgment. *Developmental Psychology, 32,* 220–230.

Warkany, J., & Schraffenberger, E. (1947). Congenital malformations induced in rats by roentgen rays. *American Journal of Roentgenology and Radium Therapy, 57,* 455–463.

Warshak, R. A., & Santrock, J. W. (1983). The impact of divorce on father-custody and mother-custody homes: The child's perspective. In L. Kurdek (Ed.), *New directions for child development: No. 19. Children and divorce.* San Francisco: Jossey-Bass.

Wartner, U. G., Grossmann, K., Fremmer-Bombik, E., & Suess, G. (1994). Attachment patterns at age six in south Germany: Predictability from infancy and implications for preschool behavior. *Child Development, 65,* 1014–1027.

Waterhouse, L., Fein, D., & Modahl, C. (1996). Neurofunctional mechanisms in autism. *Psychological Review, 103,* 457–489.

Waters, E. (1978). The reliability and stability of individual differences in infant-mother attachment. *Child Development, 49,* 483–494.

Waters, E., & Deane, K. E. (1985). Defining and assessing individual differences in attachment relationships: Q-methodology and the organization of behavior in infancy and early childhood. In I. Bretherton & E. Waters (Eds.), *Growing points of attachment theory and research. Monographs of the Society for Research in Child Development, 50* (1–2, Serial No. 209).

Waters, E., Wippman, J., & Sroufe, L. A. (1979). Attachment, positive affect, and competence in the peer group: Two studies in construct validation. *Child Development, 50,* 821–829.

Watson, J. B. (1930). *Behaviorism.* New York: W. W. Norton.

Watson, J. S. (1971). Cognitive-perceptual development in infancy: Settings for the seventies. *Merrill-Palmer Quarterly, 17,* 139–152.

Watson, J. S., & Ramey, C. T. (1972). Reactions to response-contingent stimulation in early infancy. *Merrill-Palmer Quarterly, 18,* 219–227.

Wattenberg, W. W., & Clifford, C. (1964). Relation of self-concept to beginning achievement in reading. *Child Development, 35,* 461–467.

Weber-Fox, C. M., & Neville, H. J. (1996). Maturational contraints on functional specializations for language processing: ERP and behavioral evidence in bilingual speakers. *Journal of Cognitive Neuroscience, 8,* 231–256.

Wechsler, D. (1991). *Wechsler intelligence scale for children—Third edition: Manual.* New York: The Psychological Corporation.

Weinberg, M. K., & Tronick, E. Z. (1994). Beyond the face: An empirical study of infant affective configurations of facial, vocal, gestural, and regulatory behaviors. *Child Development, 65,* 1503–1515.

Weinberg, R. (1989). Intelligence and IQ: Landmark issues and great debates. *American Psychologist, 44,* 98–104.

Weiner, B., & Handel, S. J. (1985). A cognition-emotion-action sequence: Anticipated emotional consequences of causal attributions and reported communication strategy. *Developmental Psychology, 21,* 102–107.

Weiner, L., & Morse, B. A. (1988). FAS: Clinical perspectives and prevention. In I. J. Chasnoff (Ed.), *Drugs, alcohol, pregnancy and parenting.* Boston: Kluwer Academic Publishers.

Weiss, B., Dodge, K. A., Bates, J. E., & Pettit, G. S. (1992). Some consequences of early harsh discipline: Child aggression and a maladaptive social information processing style. *Child Development, 63,* 1321–1335.

Weiss, L. H., & Schwarz, J. C. (1996). The relationship between parenting types and older adolescents' personality, academic achievement, adjustment, and substance abuse. *Child Development, 67,* 2101–2114.

Weitzman, L. J. (1985). *The divorce revolution: The unexpected social and economic consequences for women and children in America.* New York: Free Press.

Weitzman, M., Gortmaker, S., & Sobol, A. (1992). Maternal smoking and behavior problems of children. *Pediatrics, 90,* 342–349.

Welch-Ross, M. K. (1995). An integrative model of the development of autobiographical memory. *Developmental Review, 15,* 338–365.

Welch-Ross, M. K., & Schmidt, C. R. (1996). Gender-schema development and children's constructive story memory: Evidence for a developmental model. *Child Development, 67,* 820–835.

Wellman, H. M. (1977). The early development of intentional memory. *Human Development, 20,* 86–101.

Wellman, H. M. (1990). *The child's theory of mind.* Cambridge, MA: MIT Press.

Wellman, H. M., & Estes, D. (1986). Early understanding of mental entities: A reexamination of childhood realism. *Child Development, 57,* 910–923.

Wellman, H. M., & Hickling, A. K. (1994). The mind's "I": Children's conception of the mind as an active agent. *Child Development, 65,* 1564–1580.

Wellman, H. M., & Lempers, J. D. (1977). The naturalistic communicative abilities of two-year-olds. *Child Development, 48,* 1052–1057.

Welsh, M. J., & Smith, A. E. (1995, December). Cystic fibrosis. *Scientific American, 273*(6), 52–59.

Wentzel, K. R., & Erdley, C. A. (1993). Strategies for making friends: Relations to social behavior and peer acceptance in early adolescence. *Developmental Psychology, 29,* 819–826.

Werker, J. F. (1989). Becoming a native listener. *American Scientist, 77,* 54–59.

Werker, J. F., & Desjardins, R. N. (1995). Listening to speech in the 1st year of life: Experiential influences on phoneme perception. *Current Directions in Psychological Science, 4,* 76–81.

Werker, J. F., & Lalonde, C. E. (1988). Cross-language speech perception: Initial capabilities and developmental change. *Developmental Psychology, 24,* 672–683.

Werker, J. F., & Tees, R. C. (1984). Cross-language speech perception: Evidence for perceptual reorganization during the first year of life. *Infant Behavior and Development, 7,* 49–63.

Werner, E. E. (1972). Infants around the world: Cross-cultural studies of psychomotor development from birth to two years. *Journal of Cross-Cultural Psychology, 3,* 111–134.

Werner, E. E. (1995). Resilience in development. *Current Directions in Psychological Science, 4,* 81–85.

Wertsch, J. V. (1985). *Vygotsky and the social formation of mind.* Cambridge, MA: Harvard University Press.

Wertsch, J. V. (1989). A sociocultural approach to mind. In W. Damon (Ed.), *Child development today and tomorrow.* San Francisco: Jossey-Bass.

Wertsch, J. V., & Tulviste, P. (1992). L. S. Vygotsky and contemporary developmental psychology. *Developmental Psychology, 28,* 548–557.

Wertz, D. C., & Fletcher, J. C. (1993). Feminist criticism of prenatal diagnosis: A response. *Clinical Obstetrics and Gynecology, 36,* 541–567.

Wertz, R. W., & Wertz, D. C. (1977). *Lying-in: A history of childbirth in America.* New York: Free Press.

Wetzel, J. (1987). *American youth: A statistical snapshot.* Washington, DC: William T. Grant Foundation.

Whalen, R. E. (1984). Multiple actions of steroids and their antagonists. *Archives of Sexual Behavior, 13,* 497–502.

White, R. W. (1959). Motivation reconsidered: The concept of competence. *Psychological Review, 66,* 297–333.

Whitehurst, G. J., Arnold, D. S., Epstein, J. N., Angell, A. L., Smith, M., & Fischel, J. E. (1994). A picture book reading intervention in day care and home for children from low-income families. *Developmental Psychology, 30,* 679–689.

Whiting, B. B., & Edwards, C. P. (1988). *Children of different worlds.* Cambridge, MA: Harvard University Press.

Whiting, B. B., & Whiting, J. W. M. (1975). *Children of six cultures: A psychocultural analysis.* Cambridge, MA: Harvard University Press.

Widmayer, S. M., & Field, T. M. (1981). Effects of Brazelton demonstrations for mothers on the development of preterm infants. *Pediatrics, 67,* 711–714.

Widom, C. S. (1989). The cycle of violence. *Science, 244,* 160–166.

Wierson, M., & Forehand, R. (1994). Parent behavioral training for child noncompliance: Rationale, concepts, and effectiveness. *Current Directions in Psychological Science, 4,* 146–150.

Wigfield, A., & Eccles, J. S. (1994). Children's competence beliefs, achievement values, and general self-esteem: Changes across elementary and middle school. *Journal of Early Adolescence, 14,* 107–138.

Wilder, G., Mackie, D., & Cooper, J. (1985). Gender and computers: Two surveys of computer-related attitudes. *Sex Roles, 13,* 215–228.

Willats, P. (1990). Development of problem-solving strategies in infancy. In D. F. Bjorklund (Ed.), *Children's strategies: Contemporary views of cognitive development* (pp. 23–66). Hillsdale, NJ: Erlbaum.

Williams, J. E., & Best, D. L. (1982). *Measuring sex stereotypes: A thirty nation study.* Beverly Hills, CA: Sage.

Williams, P. A., Haertel, E. H., Haertel, G. D., & Walberg, H. J. (1982). The impact of leisure-time television on school learning: A research synthesis. *American Educational Research Journal, 19,* 19–50.

Willig, A. C., & Ramirez, J. D. (1993). The evaluation of bilingual education. In M. B. Arias & U. Casanova (Eds.), *Bilingual education: Politics, practice, research.* Chicago: National Society for the Study of Education.

Willinger, M., Hoffman, H. J., & Hartford, R. B. (1994). Infant sleep position and risk for Sudden Infant Death Syndrome: Report of meeting held January 13 and 14, 1994, National Institutes of Health, Bethesda, MD. *Pediatrics, 93,* 814–819.

Wills, K. E., (1993). Neuropsychological functioning in children with spina bifida and/or hydrocephalus. *Journal of Clinical Child Psychology, 22,* 247–265.

Wilson, J. G. (1977). Current status of teratology: General principles and mechanisms derived from animal studies. In J. G. Wilson & F. C. Fraser (Eds.), *Handbook of teratology: Vol. 1. General principles and etiology.* New York: Plenum Press.

Wilson, M. N. (1986). The black extended family: An analytical consideration. *Developmental Psychology, 22,* 246–258.

Wilson, R. S. (1978). Synchronies in mental development: An epigenetic perspective. *Science, 202,* 939–948.

Wilson, R. S. (1983). The Louisville Twin Study: Developmental synchronies in behavior. *Child Development, 54,* 298–316.

Wilson, R. S. (1986). Continuity and change in cognitive ability profile. *Behavior Genetics, 16,* 45–60.

Wimmer, H., & Perner, J. (1983). Beliefs about beliefs: Representation and constraining function of wrong beliefs in young children's understanding of deception. *Cognition, 13,* 103–128.

Winner, E. (1979). New names for old things: The emergence of metaphoric language. *Journal of Child Language, 6,* 469–491.

Winner, E. (1986, August). Where pelicans kiss seals. *Psychology Today,* pp. 25–35.

Winstead, B. A. (1986). Sex differences in same-sex friendships. In V. J. Derlaga & B. A. Winstead (Eds.), *Friendship and social interaction.* New York: Springer-Verlag.

Wolf, T. M. (1973). Effects of live modeled sex-inappropriate play behavior in a naturalistic setting. *Developmental Psychology, 9,* 120–123.

Wolfe, D. A. (1985). Child-abusive parents: An empirical review and analysis. *Psychological Bulletin, 97,* 462–482.

Wolfe, D. A., Fairbank, J., Kelly, J. A., & Bradlyn, A. S. (1983). Child abusive parents' physiological responses to stressful and non-stressful behavior in children. *Behavioral Assessment, 5,* 363–371.

Wolff, P. H. (1969). The natural history of crying and other vocalizations in early infancy. In B. Foss (Ed.), *Determinants of infant behavior* (Vol. 4). London: Methuen.

Wolff, P. H. (1987). *The development of behavioral states and the expression of emotions in early infancy.* Chicago: University of Chicago Press.

Wolfner, G. D., & Gelles, R. J. (1993). A profile of violence toward children: A national study. *Child Abuse and Neglect, 17,* 197–212.

Wong Fillmore, L., & Meyer, L. (1992). The curriculum and linguistic minorities. In P. Jackson (Ed.), *Handbook of research on curriculum.* New York: Macmillan.

Wood, D. J., Bruner, J. S., & Ross, G. (1976). The role of tutoring in problem solving. *Journal of Child Psychology and Psychiatry, 17,* 89–100.

Woods, N. S., Eyler, F. D., Behnke, M., & Conlon, M. (1993). Cocaine use during pregnancy: Maternal depressive symptoms and infant neurobehavior over the first month. *Infant Behavior and Development, 16,* 83–98.

Worobey, J. (1985). A review of Brazelton-based interventions to enhance parent-infant interaction. *Journal of Reproductive and Infant Psychology, 3,* 64–73.

Worobey, J., & Belsky, J. (1982). Employing the Brazelton scale to influence mothering: An experimental comparison of three strategies. *Developmental Psychology, 18,* 736–743.

Wright, J. C., Huston, A. C., Reitz, A. L., & Piemyat, S. (1994). Young children's perceptions of television reality: Determinants and developmental differences. *Developmental Psychology, 30,* 229–239.

Wynn, K. (1992). Addition and subtraction by human infants. *Nature, 358,* 749–750.

Wynn, K. (1992). Children's acquisition of the number words and the counting system. *Cognitive Psychology, 24,* 220–251.

Yakovlev, P. I., & Lecours, A. R. (1967). The myelogenetic cycles of regional maturation of the brain. In A. Minkowski (Ed.), *Regional development of the brain in early life.* Oxford: Blackwell.

Yarrow, L. J., Goodwin, M. S., Manheimer, H., & Milowe, I. D. (1973). Infancy experiences and cognitive and personality development at 10 years. In L. J. Stone, H. T. Smith, & L. B. Murphy (Eds.), *The competent infant: Research and commentary.* New York: Basic Books.

Yazigi, R. A., Odom, R. R., & Polakoski, K. L. (1991). Demonstration of specific binding of cocaine to human spermatozoa. *Journal of the American Medical Association, 266,* 1956–1959.

Yee, D. K., & Eccles, J. S. (1988). Parent perceptions and attributions for children's math achievement. *Sex Roles, 19,* 317–333.

Yen, I. H., Khoury, M. J., Erickson, J. D., James, L. M., Waters, G. D., & Berry, R. J. (1992). The changing epidemiology of neural tube defects, United States 1968–1989. *American Journal of Diseases of Children, 146,* 857–861.

Yendovitskaya, T. V. (1971). Development of attention. In A. V. Zaporozhets & D. B. Elkonin (Eds.), *The psychology of preschool children.* Cambridge, MA: MIT Press.

Yogman, M. W. (1982). Observations on the father-infant relationship. In S. H. Cath, A. R. Gurwitt, & J. M. Ross (Eds.), *Father and child: Developmental and clinical perspectives.* Boston: Little, Brown.

Yogman, M. W., Dixon, S., Tronick, E., Als, H., Adamson, L., Lester, B. M., & Brazelton, T. B. (1977, April). *The goals and structure of face-to-face interaction between infants and their fathers.* Paper presented at the biennial meeting of the Society for Research in Child Development, New Orleans.

Yonas, A., & Owsley, C. (1987). Development of visual space perception. In P. Salapatek & L. Cohen (Eds.), *Handbook of infant perception: From perception to cognition* (Vol. 2). Orlando, FL: Academic Press.

Youngblade, L. M., & Belsky, J. (1992). Parent-child antecedents of 5-year-olds' close friendships: A longitudinal analysis. *Developmental Psychology, 28,* 700–713.

Young-Browne, G., Rosenfeld, H. M., & Horowitz, F. D. (1977). Infant discrimination of facial expression. *Child Development, 48,* 555–562.

Younger, A., Gentile, C., & Burgess, K. (1993). Children's perceptions of social withdrawal: Changes across age. In K. H. Rubin & J. B. Asendorpf (Eds.), *Social withdrawal, inhibition, and shyness in childhood.* Hillsdale, NJ: Erlbaum.

Youniss, J. (1980). *Parents and peers in social development: A Sullivan-Piaget perspective.* Chicago: University of Chicago Press.

Youniss, J., & Smollar, J. (1985). *Adolescent relations with mothers, fathers, and friends.* Chicago: University of Chicago Press.

Zagon, I. S., & McLaughlin, P. J. (1984). An overview of the neurobehavioral sequelae of perinatal opiod exposure. In J. Yanai (Ed.), *Neurobehavioral teratology.* New York: Elsevier.

Zahn-Waxler, C., Friedman, S. L., & Cummings, E. M. (1983). Children's emotions and behaviors in response to infants' cries. *Child Development, 54,* 1522–1528.

Zahn-Waxler, C., Radke-Yarrow, M., & King, R. A. (1979). Child rearing and children's prosocial initiations toward victims of distress. *Child Development, 50,* 319–330.

Zahn-Waxler, C., Robinson, J. A., & Emde, R. N. (1991). The development of empathy in twins. *Developmental Psychology, 28,* 1038–1047.

Zajonc, R. B., Markus, H., & Markus, G. B. (1979). The birth order puzzle. *Journal of Personality and Social Psychology, 37,* 1325–1341.

Zarbatany, L., Hartmann, D. P., & Rankin, D. B. (1990). The psychological functions of preadolescent peer activities. *Child Development, 61,* 1067–1080.

Zausmer, E., & Shea, A. M. (1984). Motor development. In S. M. Pueschel (Ed.), *The young child with Down syndrome.* New York: Human Sciences Press.

Zebrowitz, L. A., Kendall-Tackett, K., & Fafel, J. (1991). The influence of children's facial maturity on parental expectations and punishments. *Journal of Experimental Child Psychology, 52,* 221–238.

Zelazo, N. A., Zelazo, P. R., Cohen, K. M., & Zelazo, P. D. (1993). Specificity of practice effects on elementary neuromotor patterns. *Developmental Psychology, 29,* 686–691.

Zelazo, P. D., Helwig, C. C. & Lau, A. (1996). Intention, act, and outcome in behavioral prediction and moral judgment. *Child Development, 67,* 2478–2492.

Zelazo, P. R. (1983). The development of walking: New findings and old assumptions. *Journal of Motor Behavior, 15,* 99–137.

Zeskind, P. S. (1981). Behavioral dimensions and cry sounds of infants of differential fetal growth. *Infant Behavior and Development, 4,* 297–306.

Zeskind, P. S., & Lester, B. M. (1981). Analysis of cry features in newborns with differential fetal growth. *Child Development, 52,* 207–212.

Zeskind, P. S., & Ramey, C. T. (1981). Preventing intellectual and interactional sequelae of fetal malnutrition: A longitudinal, transactional and synergistic approach to development. *Child Development, 52,* 213–218.

Ziegler, C. B., Dusek, J. B., & Carter, D. B. (1984). Self-concept and sex-role orientation: An investigation of multidimensional aspects of personality development on adolescence. *Journal of Early Adolescence, 4,* 25–39.

Zigler, E. (1967). Familial mental retardation: A continuing dilemma. *Science, 155,* 292–298.

Zigler, E., & Berman, W. (1983). Discerning the future of early childhood intervention. *American Psychologist, 38,* 894–906.

Zigler, E., & Butterfield, E. C. (1968). Motivational aspects of changes in IQ test performance of culturally deprived nursery school children. *Child Development, 39,* 1–14.

Zigler, E., & Hodapp, R. M. (1986). *Understanding mental retardation.* Cambridge, UK: Cambridge University Press.

Zigler, E., & Muenchow, S. (1992). *Head Start: The inside story of America's most successful educational experiment.* New York: Basic Books.

Zigler, E., & Trickett, P. K. (1978). IQ, social competence, and evaluation of early childhood intervention programs. *American Psychologist, 33,* 789–798.

Zill, N. (1988). Behavior, achievement, and health problems among children in stepfamilies: Findings from a national survey of child health. In E. M. Hetherington & J. D. Arasteh (Eds.), *Impact of divorce, single-parenting, and stepparenting on children.* Hillsdale, NJ: Erlbaum.

Zill, N. (1994). Understanding why children in stepfamilies have more learning and behavior problems than children in nuclear families. In A. Booth & J. Dunn (Eds.), *Stepfamilies: Who benefits? Who does not?* Hillsdale, NJ: Erlbaum.

Zill, N., Morrison, D. R., & Coiro, M. J. (1993). Long-term effects of parental divorce on parent-child relationships, adjustment, and achievement in young adulthood. *Journal of Family Psychology, 7,* 1–13.

Zimiles, H., & Lee, V. E. (1991). Adolescent family structure and educational progress. *Developmental Psychology, 27,* 314–320.

Zuckerman, B., & Bresnahan, K. (1991). Developmental and behavioral consequences of prenatal drug and alcohol exposure. *Pediatric Clinics of North America, 38,* 1387–1406.

Zuckerman, B., & Frank, D. A. (1994). Prenatal cocaine exposure: Nine years later. *Journal of Pediatrics, 124,* 731–733.

Text Credits

Chapter 1: *Figure 1.5* Figure adapted from Kopp/Krakow, *Child Development in the Social Context,* © 1982 by Addison-Wesley Publishing Company, Inc. Reprinted by permission of Addison Wesley Longman.

Chapter 2: *Figure 2.4* Gagnon, Mireille, and Robert Ladouceur, "Behavioral Treatment of Child Stutterers: Replication and Extension," *Behavior Therapy, Volume 23.* Copyright 1992 by the Association for Advancement of Behavior Therapy. Reprinted by permission of the publisher and the author.

Chapter 3: *Figure 3.1* Adapted from Isensee, W. (September 3, 1986). *The Chronicle of Higher Education.* Used with permission. *Figure 3.10* Turkheimer, Goldsmith, & Gottesman (1995) Commentary. *Human Development,* 38, pp. 142–153. Reproduced with permission of S. Karger AG, Basel.

Chapter 4: *Figure 4.3* Moore, K.L., *Before We Are Born,* 1989, 3rd Edition, W.B. Saunders Company. Reprinted by permission. *Figure 4.9* Source: Brooks-Gunn, Kiebanow, Liaw, & Spiker, Enhancing the Development of Low-Birthweight, Premature Infants: Changes in Cognition and Behavior Over the First Three Years. *Child Development,* 64, 736–754. © Society for Research in Child Development, Inc. Reprinted by permission. *Table 4.5* Source: Reece, E.A., Hobbins, J.C., Mahoney, M.J., and Petrie, R.H., (1995) *Handbook of Medicine of the Fetus and the Mother.* Philadelphia: Lippincott-Raven Publishers. Reprinted with permission. *Table 4.6* Apgar, V. (1953). A proposal for a new method of evaluation of the new-born infant. *Anesthesia and Analgesia: Current Researches,* 32, 260–267. Reprinted by permission of International Anesthesia Research Society.

Chapter 5: *Figure 5.5* From "Malnutrition, Poverty and Intellectual Development" by J. Larry Brown and Ernesto Pollitt. Copyright © 1996 by Scientific American, Inc. All rights reserved. *Figure 5.7* Reprinted from *Neuropsychologia,* 28, Huttenlocher, P.R. Morphometric Study of Human Cerebral Cortex Development, pp. 517–527., Copyright 1990 with kind permission from Elsevier Science, Ltd, The Boulevard, Langford Lane, Kidlington OX5 1GB, UK. *Figure 5.9* Reprinted by permission of the publisher from *Fetus Into Man: Physical Growth from Conception to Maturity* by J.M. Tanner, Cambridge, Mass: Harvard University Press, Copyright © 1978,1989 by J.M. Tanner. *Figure 5.10* Source: Marshall, W.A., & Tanner, J.M. (1986). *Puberty,* In Faulkner & J.M. Tanner (eds). *Human Growth* (vol. 2, 2nd ed). New York, Plenum. p. 196. Reprinted by permission of Plenum Publishing Corporation.

Chapter 6: *Figure 6.3* Adapted from "The Origins of Form Perception," by R.L. Fantz. Copyright © 1961 by Scientific American, Inc. All rights reserved. *Figure 6.4* Adapted from Salapatek, P. (1975). "Pattern Perception in Early Infancy." In L.B. Cohen and P. Salapatek (Eds.), *Infant Perception: From Sensation to Cognition.* (Vol. 1). New York: Academic Press. *Figure 6.5* Frick & Colombo (1996), Individual Differences in Infant Visual Attention: Recognition of Degraded Visual Forms by Four-Month-Olds. *Child Development,* 64, pp. 188–204. © Society for Research in Child Development, Inc. Reprinted by permission. *Figure 6.6* Treiber, F., and Wilcox, S., (1980). "Perception of a 'subjective' contour by infants." Child Development, Inc. *Figure 6.7* Spelke, E.S. (1985). Perception of unity, persistence and identity: Thoughts on infants' conceptions of objects. From J. Mehler and R. Fox (Eds.), *Neonate Cognition: Beyond the Blooming, Buzzing Confusion.* Copyright © 1985 Lawrence Erlbaum. Reprinted by permission of Lawrence Erlbaum Associates, Inc., Publishers and the author. *Figure 6.10* Pick, A.D.

(1965). Improvement of visual and tactual discrimination. *Journal of Experimental Psychology,* 69, 331–339. Copyright 1969 by the American Psychological Association. Adapted by permission. *Figure 6.11* Elkind, D., Koeglar, R.R. and Go, E. (1964). Studies in perceptual development II: Part-whole perception. *Child Development,* 35, 81–90. © The Society for Research in Child Development, Inc.

Chapter 7: *Figure 7.1* Fernald, A. (1985). Four-month-olds prefer to listen to motherese. *Infant Behavior and Development,* 8, 181–195. Reprinted with permission of Albex Publishing Corporation. *Figure 7.2* Bates, Thal, Fenson, Dale, Reznick, Reilley, & Hartung (1994), "Developmental and Stylistic Variation in the Composition of Early Vocabulary," *Journal of Child Language,* 21, pp. 85–123. Copyright Cambridge University Press. Reprinted with the permission of Cambridge University Press. *Figure 7.3* Goldfield, B.A., and Reznick, J.S. (1990). Early lexical acquisition: Rate, content and the vocabulary spurt. *Journal of Child Language,* 17, 171–183. Reprinted by permission of Cambridge University Press. *Figure 7.4* Krauss, R.H. and Gluksberg, S. (1969). The development of communication. *Child Development,* 40, 255–266. © The Society for Research in Child Development, Inc. *Figure 7.6* Figure A1 from the Raven Standard Progressive Matrices is reproduced by permission of J.C. Raven Ltd. *Table 7.1* Braine, M.D.S. (1976). Children's first word combinations. *Monographs of the Society for Research in Child Development,* 41 (1, serial No. 164) © The Society for Research in Child Development, Inc. *Table 7.2* Modified and reprinted by permission of the publishers from *A first language* by R. Brown, Cambridge, Mass: Harvard University Press, Copyright © 1973 by the President and Fellows of Harvard College. Reprinted by permission of Harvard University Press and International Thomson.

Chapter 8: *Figure 8.2* Baillargeon, R. (1987). Object permanence in 3½–4½-month-old infants. *Developmental Psychology,* 23, 655–664. Copyright 1987 by the American Psychological Association. Reprinted by permission. *Figure 8.4* Reprinted from *Cognition,* Vol. 25, "Do six-month-olds perceive causality?" by A.M. Leslie and S. Keeble. Copyright © 1987 Elsevier Science Publishers. Used with permission from the publisher and the author. *Table 8.2* Figure from Palincsar, Annemarie Sullivan, & Brown, Ann L. (1986, April). Interactive Teaching to Promote Independent Learning from Text. The Reading Teacher, 39(8), 771–777. Reprinted with permission of Annemarie S. Palincsar and the International Reading Association. All rights reserved.

Chapter 9: *Figure 9.1* From Vurpillot, E. (1968), "The development of scanning strategies and their relation to visual differentiation," *Journal of Experimental Child Psychology,* 6, pp. 632–650. Reprinted by permission of Academic Press and the author. *Figure 9.3* Fagan, J.F. (1979). Infant recognition memory: The effects of length of familiarization and type of discrimination task. *Child Development,* 45, pp. 351–356. © The Society for Research in Child Development, Inc. *Figure 9.4* Source: Dempster, F.N. (1981), "Memory Span: Sources of Individual and Developmental Differences," *Psychological Bulletin,* 89, 63–100. Copyright © 1981 by the American Psychological Association. Reprinted by permission. *Figure 9.5* Ornstein, P.A., Naus, M.J., and Liberty, C. (1975). Rehearsal and organization processes in children's memory. *Child Development,* 46, pp. 818–830. © The Society for Research in Child Development, Inc. *Figure 9.6* Kobasigwa, A. (1974). Utilization of retrieval cues by children in recall. *Child Development,* 45, 127–134. © The Society for Research in Child Development, Inc. *Figure 9.7* Rovee-Collier, Evancio, and Earley (1995). The Time-Window Hypothesis: Spacing Effects. *Infant Behavior and Development,* 18. pp. 69–78. Reprinted by permission of Ablex Publishing Corp. *Table 9.1* Ornstein, P.A., Naus,

M.J., and Liberty, C. (1975). Rehearsal and organization processes in children's memory. *Child Development*, 46, 818–830. © The Society for Research in Child Development, Inc.

Chapter 10:   *Figure 10.1* Guilford, J.P. (1985). The structure of intellect model. In B.B. Wolman (Ed.), Handbook of Human Intelligence, p. 230. Copyright © 1985 by John Wiley and Sons, Inc. Reprinted by permission of John Wiley and Sons, Inc. *Figure 10.4* Simulated items similar to those from the *Wechsler Intelligence Scale for Children—Revised*. Copyright © 1974 by The Psychological Corporation. Reproduced by permission. All rights reserved. "Wechsler Intelligence Scale for Children" and "WISC" are registered trademarks of The Psychological Corporation. *Figure 10.5* Kaufman, A.S., and Kaufman, A.S. (1983). Kaufman Assessment Battery for Children (K-ABC). Circle Pines, MN: American Guidance Service, Inc. *Figure 10.6* "Is Intelligence Stable Over Time?" adapted from Bayley, N. (1949). "Consistency and Variability in the Growth of Intelligence from Birth to Eighteen Years." *Journal of Genetic Psychology*, 75, pp. 165–196, 1949. Reprinted with permission of the Helen Dwight Reid Educational Foundation. Published by Heldref Publications, 1319 Eighteenth St., N.W., Washington, D.C. 20036-1802. Copyright © 1949. *Table 10.1* Siegler, R.S., and Richards, D.D. (1982). The development of intelligence. In R.J. Sternberg (Ed.), *Handbook of Human Intelligence*, Cambridge University Press, p. 889. Reprinted by permission. Table 10.2 Bayley Scales of Infant Development. Copyright © 1969 by the Psychological Corporation. Reproduced by permission. All rights reserved. "Bayley Scales of Infant Development" is a registered trademark of The Psychological Corporation. *Table 10.3* Elardo, R., and Bradley, R.H. (1981). "The Home Observation for Measurement of the Environment (HOME) Scale: A review of Research. *Developmental Review*, 1, 113–145. Reprinted by permission of Academic Press and the author.

Chapter 11:   *Figure 11.2* Cole, Zahn-Waxler, & Smith (1994). "Expressive Control During a Disappointment: Variations Related to Preschoolers' Behavior Problems," *Developmental Psychology*, 30. pp. 835–846. Copyright © 1994 by the American Psychological Association. Reprinted with permission. *Figure 11.3* Larson, R. & Ham, M. (1993). "Stress and 'Storm and Stress' in early Adolescence: The relationship of negative events with dysphoric affect," *Developmental Psychology*, 29, 136. Copyright © 1993 by the American Psychological Association. *Figure 11.4* Reprinted with permission from Harlow, H.F., and Zimmerman, R.R. (1959). "Affectional Responses in the Infant Monkey," *Science*, 130, pp. 421–432. Copyright 1959 by the American Association for the Advancement of Science. Reprinted by permission of the publisher and the author. *Figure 11.5* From T. Field and A. Fogel (Eds.), Emotion and Early Interaction, p. 109. Copyright © 1982 Lawrence Erlbaum. Reprinted by permission of Lawrence Erlbaum Associates, Inc., Publishers and the author. *Table 11.1* Bretherton, I., & Beeghly, M. (1982). "Talking About Internal States: The Acquisition of an Explicit Theory of Mind," *Developmental Psychology*, 18, 906–921. Copyright 1982 by the American Psychological Association. Adapted by permission from the publisher and the author. *Table 11.2* M.M. Haith and J.J. Campos (Eds.), *Handbook of child psychology*, Vol II: Infancy and developmental psychobiology, p. 861. Copyright © 1983 by John Wiley and Sons, Inc. Reprinted by permission of John Wiley.

Chapter 12:   *Figure 12.1* Harter, S., & Monsour, A. (1992), "Developmental analysis of conflict caused by opposing attributes in the adolescent self-portrait," *Developmental Psychology*, 28, 251–260. Copyright © 1992 by the American Psychological Society. *Figure 12.3* Harter, S. (1987). The determinants and mediational role of global self-worth in children. In N. Eisenberg (Ed.), *Contemporary Topics in Developmental Psychology*, p. 227. Copyright © 1987 by John Wiley and Sons, Inc. Reprinted by permission of John Wiley and Sons, Inc. *Figure 12.5* Colby, A., Kohlberg, L., Gibbs, J., and Lieberman, M. (1983). A longitudinal study of moral judgment. *Monographs of the Society for Research in Child Development*, 48 (No. 1-2, Serial No. 200). The Society for Research in Child Development, Inc. *Table 12.4* Reprinted from 1996 Report Card on American Integrity with permission of the Josephson Institute of Ethics.

Chapter 13:   *Figure 13.1* Serbin, L.A., Powlishta, K.K., & Gulko, J. "The development of sex typing in middle childhood" from *Monographs of the Society for Research in Child Development*, 58 (No. 2, Serial No. 232), p. 35. Copyright © 1993 The Society for Research in Child Development. Used with permission. *Figure 13.2* Hyde, J.S., Fennema, E., and Lamon, S.J.

(1990). "Gender Differences in Mathematics Performance: a Meta-Analysis," *Psychological Bulletin*, 107, 139–155. Copyright 1990 by the American Psychological Association. Adapted by permission from the publisher and the author. *Figure 13.3* Linn, M.C., and Peterson, A.C. (1988). Emergence and characterization of sex difference in spatial ability: A meta-analysis. *Child Development*, 56, 1479–1498. © The Society for Research in Child Development, Inc. *Figure 13.4* Adapted from Self-regulatory mechanisms governing gender development by K. Bussy and A. Bandura from *Child Development*, Vol. 63, p. 1243. Copyright © 1992 The Society for Research in Child Development, Inc. Used with permission. *Figure 13.5* "Social Behavior as a Function of the Child's Play Partner" adapted from Jacklin, C.N. et al., "Social Behavior at 33 Months," *Child Development*, 49, 557–569. © The Society for Research in Child Development, Inc. Used by permission. *Figure 13.6* Frey, K.S., and Ruble, D.N. (1987). What children say about classroom performance: Sex and grade differences in perceived competence. *Child Development*, 58, 1066–1078. © The Society for Research in Child Development, Inc. *Table 13.1* Source: Martin, C.L. (1995). "Stereotypes about Children with Traditional and Nontraditional Gender Roles," *Sex Roles*, 33, pp. 727–751. Reprinted by permission of Plenum Publishing Corporation.

Chapter 14:   *Figure 14.2* Peterson, G.W., and Rollins, B.C. (1987). Parent-child socialization. In M.B. Sussman and S.K. Steinmetz (Eds.) *Handbook of Marriage and the Family*. Reprinted by permission of Plenum Publishing Corporation. *Figure 14.3* Maccoby, E.E., and Martin, J.A. (1983). Socialization in the context of the Family: Parent-child interaction. In E.M. Hetherington (Ed.), *Handbook of child psychology*. Vol. 4. Socialization, personality, and social development. Copyright © 1983 by John Wiley and Sons, Inc. Reprinted by permission of John Wiley and Sons, Inc. *Figure 14.4* Adapted from Dix, T.H. & Grusec, J.E. (1985). "Parent Attribution in the Socialization of Children." In I.E. Sigel (ed.) *Parental Belief Systems: The Psychological Consequences for Children*. Reprinted by permission of Lawrence Erlbaum Associates, Inc. *Figure 14.5* Mason, C.A. Cauce, A.M., Gonzales, N., & Hiraga, Y. (1996). Neither Too Sweet Nor Too Sour: Problem Peers, Maternal Control, and Problem Behavior in African American Adolescents. *Child Development*, 67, 2115–2130. © Society for Research in Child Development, Inc. Reprinted by permission. *Figure 14.6* From Zill, N. (1994). "Understanding Why Children in Stepfamilies Have More Learning and Behavior Problems Than Children in Nuclear Families." In A. Booth and J. Dunn (Eds.), *Stepfamilies: Who Benefits? Who Does Not?* Hillsdale, NJ: Erlbaum. Copyright © 1994 by Lawrence Erlbaum Associates, Inc. Reprinted by permission.

Chapter 15:   *Figure 15.1* From Maccoby, E.E. and Jacklin, C.N. (1987). "Gender Segregation in Childhood." In H.W. Reese (Ed.), *Advances in Child Development and Behavior*, Vol. 20. Reprinted by permission of Academic Press and the author. *Figure 15.2* Berndt, T.J. (1979). "Developmental Changes in Conformity to Peers and Parents," *Developmental Psychology*, 15, 608–616. Copyright 1979 by the American Psychological Association. Reprinted by permission of the publisher and the author. *Figure 15.3* Asher, S.R. (1985). An evolving paradigm in social skill training research with children. In B.H. Schneider, K.H. Rubin, and J.E. Ledingham (Eds.). *Children's Peer Relations: Issues in Assessment and Intervention*. New York: Springer-Verlag. Reprinted with permission. *Figure 15.4* Dodge, K.A. (1986). A social information processing model of social competence in children. From M. Perlmutter (Ed.), The Minnesota Symposia on Child Psychology: Cognitive Perspectives on Children's Social and Behavioral Development, Vol. 18. Copyright © 1986 Lawrence Erlbaum. Reprinted by permission of Lawrence Erlbaum Associates, Inc., Publishers and the author. *Figure 15.5* Jakibchuck, Z., and Smeriglio, V.L. (1976). The influence of symbolic modeling on the social behavior of preschool children with low levels of social responsiveness. *Child Development*, 47, 838–841. © The Society for Research in Child Development, Inc. *Figure 15.6* Cairns, R.B., and Cairns (B.D.), (1994). *Lifelines and Risks: Pathways of Youth in Our Time*. Cambridge, UK: Cambridge University Press. Copyright ©1994 by Robert B. Cairns and Beverly D. Cairns. Reprinted with the permission of Cambridge University Press. *Figure 15.7* Renshaw, P.D. & Brown, P.J. (1993). "Loneliness in Middle Childhood: Concurrent and Longitudinal Predictors." Child Development, 64, 1271–1284. © Society for Research in Child Development, Inc. Reprinted by permission.

Chapter 16:   *Figure 16.1* From the *Journal of Educational Psychology*, 83, p. 515. "Inner resources for school achievement: motivational mediators of children's perceptions of their parents" by W.S. Grolnick, R.M Ryan, and E.L.

Deci, Copyright © 1991 APA. Reprinted by permission of the publisher and the author. *Figure 16.3* Reprinted with permission from Stevenson, H.W., Chen, C. & Lee, S.Y. (1993). "Mathematics Achievement of Chinese, Japanese, and American Children: Ten Years Later.: *Science*, 259, 53–58. Copyright © 1993 American Association for the Advancement of Science. *Figure 16.4* Reprinted with permission from Liebert, R.M., and Sprafkin, J. (1988). *The early window: Effects of television on children and youth*, 3/e, 1988, Pergamon Press PLC. *Figure 16.5* Reprinted with permission from Liebert, R.M., and Sprafkin, J. (1988) *The early window: Effects of television on children and youth*, 3/e, 1988, Pergamon Press PLC. *Table 16.2* Horowitz, R.A. (1979). Psychological effects of the 'open classroom.' Review of Educational Research, 49, 71–86. Copyright 1979 by the American Educational Research Association. Reprinted by permission of the publisher.

Photo Credits

Chapter 1: **p. 2** © J. Sohm/The Image Works. **p. 6** © Lawrence Migdale/Stock Boston. **p. 13** © Paul Conklin. **p. 15** © B. Anderson/Monkmeyer. **p. 24** © Erik Homburger/Stock Montage. **p. 25** © Anthony Ray/Photo Researchers. **p. 29** © Elizabeth Harris/Tony Stone Images. **p. 30** Thomas McAvoy/Life Magazine © Time Warner Inc.

Chapter 2: **p. 35** © Eastcott/The Image Works. **p. 37** © Erich Lessing/Art Resource. **p. 40** Archives of the History of American Psychology. **p. 42** © Paul Damien/Tony Stone Images. **p. 44** © Bob Daemmrich . **p. 55** (both) © Elizabeth Crews. **p. 59** © Charlotte Miller.

Chapter 3: **p. 63** © John Coletti/Stock Boston. **p. 68** © Custom Medical Stock Photo. **p. 77** © Rosenan/Custom Medical Stock Photo. **p. 79** Billie Carstens/Denver Children's Hospital. **p. 81** © Cindy Karp/Black Star. **p. 85** © Hank Morgan/Photo Researchers. **p. 87** © Rob Nelson/Black Star. **p. 91** © Sotres/Monkmeyer. **p. 95** © Robert Brenner/PhotoEdit.

Chapter 4: **p. 94** © Elizabeth Crews. **p. 102** © David Philips/SS/Photo Researchers. **pp. 104–109** Lennart Nilsson/A CHILD IS BORN, Dell Publishing Company. **p. 111** © Alexander Tsiaras/Stock Boston. **p. 116** © George Steinmetz. **p. 126** © David Young-Wolff/PhotoEdit. **p. 129** © Peter Essick/Aurora. **p. 131** © Bob Daemmrich/Stock Boston. **p. 134** © Goodman/Monkmeyer. **p. 137** © John Ficara/Woodfin Camp & Assoc. **p. 139** © Elizabeth Crews.

Chapter 5: **p. 143** © Bob Daemmrich. **p. 146** © Elizabeth Crews. **p. 151** © Debbi Morello/Black Star. **p. 157** © Oliver Meckes/Ottawa/Photo Researchers. **p. 162** © Weddle/Sipa/Leo de Wys, Inc. **p. 163** © Goodwin/Monkmeyer. **p. 166** © Laura Dwight. **p. 169** © Herbert Lanks/Superstock. **p. 175** © Willie L. Hill, Jr./Stock Boston.

Chapter 6: **p. 180** ©Ullmann/Monkmeyer. **p. 185** © Billy E. Barnes/PhotoEdit. **p. 187** Nadja Reissland. **p. 193** © DEK/TexaStock. **p. 198** © Enrico Ferorelli. **p. 206** Jacob E. Steiner. **p. 209** © Paul Damien/Tony Stone Images. **p. 212** Campbell, R., Walker, J., and Baron-Cohen, S. (1995). The development of differential use of inner and outer face features in familiar face identification. Journal of Experimental Child Psychology, 59, 196 210. Reprinted with permission from Academic Press. **p. 213** © Press/Monkmeyer

Chapter 7: **p. 216** © Myrleen Cate/PhotoEdit. **p. 223** © Judith Kramer/The Image Works. **p. 226** Bruce Dale/National Geographic Society Image Collection. **p. 228** © Cathlyn Melloan/Tony Stone Images. **p. 232** © Brady/Monkmeyer. **p. 238** © Tony Freeman/PhotoEdit. **p. 242** © Diana Rasche/Tony Stone Images. **p. 246** © Robert Brenner/PhotoEdit. **p. 250** © Elizabeth Crews.

Chapter 8: **p. 253** © Elizabeth Crews. **p. 257** © Goodman/Monkmeyer. **p. 258** © Pollak/Monkmeyer. **p. 261** © Paul Conklin. **p. 266** Adele Diamond. **p. 272** © Andy Caulfield/The Image Bank. **p. 284** © Bob Daemmrich/The Image Works.

Chapter 9: **p. 289** © Bob Daemmrich/Stock Boston. **p. 297** Courtesy of Carolyn Rovee-Collier. **p. 304** © Mark C. Burnett/Stock Boston. **p. 306** © Tony Freeman/PhotoEdit. **p. 309** Dr. Peter Willatts. **p. 310** © Sobel/Klonsky/The Image Bank. **p. 314** © Bob Daemmrich/The Image Works. **p. 318** © Elizabeth Crews.

Chapter 10: **p. 322** © Ellen Senisi/The Image Works. **p. 327** © Francois Dardelet/The Image Bank. **p. 329** © Alan Carey/The Image Works. **p. 331** © A. Ramey/Stock Boston. **p. 342** © Bob Daemmrich/The Image Works. **p. 347** © John Eastcott/YVA Momatiuk/Stock Boston. **p. 349** © Paul Conklin.

Chapter 11: **p. 352** © Scott Rutherford/Black Star. **p. 355** © Michael Newman/PhotoEdit. **p. 357** © Winter/The Image Works. **p. 361** Dr. Tiffany Field. **p. 362** Kuchuk, A., Vibbert, M., & Bornstein, M. H. (1986). **p. 372** Harlow Primate Laboratory, University of Wisconsin. **p. 378** © Lynne J. Weinstein/Woodfin Camp & Assoc. **p. 379** © Bob Daemmrich.

Chapter 12: **p. 388** © Tomas Spangler/The Image Works. **p. 391** © Laura Dwight/PhotoEdit. **p. 394** © L. Kolvoord/The Image Works. **p. 395** John S. Watson. **p. 396** © Superstock. **p. 398** © Jeffrey Dunn/The Picture Cube. **p. 400** © Peter M. Miller. **p. 405** © Susan Lapides. **p. 408** © Richard Pan/The Image Bank. **p. 417** © R. Lord/The Image Works. **p. 423** © David Austen/Stock Boston. **p. 424** © Peter L. Chapman/Stock Boston.

Chapter 13: **p. 430** © Bachmann/Stock Boston. **p. 433** © Hazel Hankin/Stock Boston. **p. 437** © Rieder/Monkmeyer. **p. 441** © Michael Newman/PhotoEdit. **p. 442** © Bob Daemmrich. **p. 448** © Bob Daemmrich. **p. 450** © Bob Daemmrich/The Image Works. **p. 453** © Elizabeth Crews. **p. 457** © Bob Daemmrich.

Chapter 14: **p. 461** © Erica Lansner/Black Star. **p. 466** © Annie Griffiths Belt/Material World Woman's Project. **p. 471** © Goodman/Monkmeyer. **p. 480** © Blair Seitz/Photo Researchers. **p. 483** © Didier Dorval/Explorer/Photo Researchers. **p. 485** © Philip & Karen Smith/Tony Stone Images. **p. 489** © Bob Daemmrich. **p. 494** © M. Bridwell/PhotoEdit.

Chapter 15: **p. 496** © Louise Gubb/The Image Works. **p. 499** ©Goodwin/Woodfin Camp & Assoc. **p. 502** © Michael A. Dwyer/Stock Boston. **p. 505** © Bob Daemmrich/Stock Boston. **p. 511** © Bob Daemmrich/Stock Boston. **p. 514** © Vic Bider/PhotoEdit. **p. 517** © Tony Freeman/PhotoEdit. **p. 523** © Wolf/Monkmeyer.

Chapter 16: **p. 529** © Bob Daemmrich/Stock Boston. **p. 537** © Elizabeth Crews. **p. 539** © Paul Conklin. **p. 542** © David R. Frazier. **p. 543** © Wiley/Monkmeyer. **p. 552** © PhotoEdit. **p. 554** © Tom Pollack/Monkmeyer. **p. 558** Albert Bandura. **p. 563** © Myrleen Ferguson/PhotoEdit.

SUBJECT INDEX